THE
AFRICAN-AMERICAN
ODYSSEY

COMBINED VOLUME

THE

AFRICAN-AMERICAN

ODYSSEY

DARLENE CLARK HINE
MICHIGAN STATE UNIVERSITY

WILLIAM C. HINE
SOUTH CAROLINA STATE UNIVERSITY

STANLEY HARROLD
SOUTH CAROLINA STATE UNIVERSITY

PRENTICE HALL
UPPER SADDLE RIVER, NEW JERSEY 07458

Library of Congress Cataloging-in-Publication Data

Hine, Darlene Clark.
    The African-American odessey / Darlene Clark Hine, William C.
Hine, Stanley Harrold.
        p.   cm.
    Includes bibliographical references and index.
    ISBN 0-13-571852-X
    1. Afro-Americans.   2. Afro-Americans—History.   I. Hine, William
C. II. Harrold, Stanley.   III. Title.
    E185.H533   2000
    973'.0496073—dc21   99-29872
                                                               CIP

Vice President/Editorial Director: Charlyce Jones Owen
Acquisitions Editor: Todd Armstrong
Editor-in-Chief of Development: Susanna Lesan
Development Editors: David Chodoff and Gerald Lombardi
Director of Production and Manufacturing: Barbara Kittle
Production Editor: Louise Rothman
Manufacturing Manager: Nick Sklitsis
Prepress and Manufacturing Buyer: Lynn Pearlman
Marketing Director: Gina Sluss
Marketing Manager: Sheryl Adams
Creative Design Director: Leslie Osher

Cover and Interior Design: Ximena Tamvakopoulos
Editorial Assistant: Holly Jo Brown
Cover Art: Aaron Douglas, *Aspects of Negro Life: From Slavery Through Reconstruction*, 1934. Schomburg Center for Research in Black Culture, Art & Artifacts Division, The New York Public Library, Astor, Lenox and Tilden Foundation (Detail).
Photo Research Supervisor: Beth Boyd
Photo Researcher: Barbara Salz
Assistant Manager Art Production: Guy Ruggiero
Electronic Art Creation: CartoGraphics

Credits and acknowledgments for materials borrowed from other sources and reproduced, with permission, in this textbook, appear on pages C-1 to C-5.

This book was set in 10/12 Janson Text by The Clarinda Company and was printed and bound by Courier Westford. The cover was printed by Phoenix Color Corp.

©2000 by Prentice-Hall Inc.
A Pearson Education Company
Upper Saddle River, New Jersey 07458

Printed in the United States of America

10   9   8   7   6   5   4   3   2

0-13-571852-X

Prentice-Hall International (UK) Limited, *London*
Prentice-Hall of Australia Pty. Limited, *Sydney*
Prentice-Hall Canada Inc., *Toronto*
Prentice-Hall Hispanoamericana, S.A., *Mexico*
Prentice-Hall of India Private Limited, *New Delhi*
Prentice-Hall of Japan, Inc., *Tokyo*
Pearson Education Asia Pte. Ltd., *Singapore*
Editora Prentice-Hall do Brasil, Ltda., *Rio de Janeiro*

To Carter G. Woodson and Benjamin Quarles

Darlene Clark Hine received her undergraduate education at Roosevelt University and her master's and Ph.D. degrees from Kent State University. She is John A. Hannah Professor of History at Michigan State University. Her most recent book, *A Shining Thread of Hope: The History of Black Women in America* (1998), was co-written with Kathleen Thompson. Her earlier books include *Speak Truth to Power: Black Professional Class in United States History* (1996); *Hine Sight: Black Women and the Re-Construction of American History* (1994); *Black Women in White: Racial Conflict and Cooperation in the Nursing Profession, 1890-1950* (1989); and *Black Victory: The Rise and Fall of the White Primary in Texas* (1979). She is editor of *The State of Afro-American History, Past, Present, and Future* (1986), co-editor (with Elsa Barkley Brown and Rosalyn Terborg-Penn) of a two-volume set, *Black Women in America: An Historical Encyclopedia* (1993); *More Than Chattel: Black Women and Slavery in the Americas*, co-edited with David Barry Gaspar (1996); and *Crossing Boundaries: Comparative History of Black People in Diaspora*, co-edited with Jacqueline McLeod (1999). Professor Hine is also co-editor of the *Blacks in the Diaspora* series published by Indiana University Press. She is president-elect of the Organization of American Historians (2000-2001).

William C. Hine received his undergraduate education at Bowling Green State University, his master's degree at the University of Wyoming, and his Ph.D. at Kent State University. He is a professor of history at South Carolina State University. He has had articles published in several journals, including *Agricultural History*, *Labor History*, and the *Journal of Southern History*. He is currently writing a history of South Carolina State University.

Stanley Harrold, Professor of History at South Carolina State University, received his bachelor's degree from Allegheny College and his master's and Ph.D. degrees from Kent State University. He is co-editor of *Southern Dissent*, a book series published by the University Press of Florida. A recipient of two National Endowment for the Humanities Fellowships during the past decade, Professor Harrold is a historian of nineteenth-century American reform. His books include: *Gamaliel Bailey and Antislavery Union* (1986), *The Abolitionists and the South* (1995), and *Antislavery Violence: Sectional, Racial, and Cultural Conflict in Antebellum America* (co-edited with John R. McKivigan, 1999). He has published articles in *Civil War History*, *Journal of Southern History*, *Radical History Review*, and other journals. His current projects include a short history of the American abolitionists and a study of biracial antislavery activism in antebellum Washington, D.C.

BRIEF CONTENTS

CONTENTS

PART II SLAVERY, ABOLITION, AND THE QUEST FOR FREEDOM: THE COMING OF THE CIVIL WAR, 1793 - 1861 117

CHAPTER 6
LIFE IN THE COTTON KINGDOM 118

CHAPTER 7
FREE BLACK PEOPLE IN ANTEBELLUM AMERICA 140

CHAPTER 8
OPPOSITION TO SLAVERY, 1800-1833 164

MAPS

FIGURES AND TABLES

PREFACE

"One feels his two-ness—an American, a Negro, two souls, two thoughts, two unreconciled strivings, two warring ideas in one dark body." So wrote W. E. B. Du Bois in 1897. African-American history, Du Bois maintained, was the history of this double-consciousness. Black people have always been part of the American nation that they helped to build. But they have also been a nation unto themselves, with their own experiences, culture, and aspirations. African-American history cannot be understood except in the broader context of American history. American history cannot be understood without African-American history.

Since Du Bois's time our understanding of both African-American and American history has been complicated and enriched by a growing appreciation of the role of class and gender in shaping human societies. We are also increasingly aware of the complexity of racial experiences in American history. Even in times of great racial polarity some white people have empathized with black people and some black people have identified with white interests.

It is in light of these insights that *The African-American Odyssey* tells the story of African Americans. That story begins in Africa, where the people who were to become African Americans began their long, turbulent, and difficult journey, a journey marked by sustained suffering as well as perseverance, bravery, and achievement. It includes the rich culture—at once splendidly distinctive and tightly intertwined with a broader American culture—that African Americans have nurtured throughout their history. And it includes the many-faceted quest for freedom in which African Americans have sought to counter white oppression and racism with the egalitarian spirit of the Declaration of Independence that American society professes to embody.

Nurtured by black historian Carter G. Woodson during the early decades of the twentieth century, African-American history has blossomed as a field of study since the 1950s. Books and articles have appeared on almost every facet of black life. Yet this textbook is the first comprehensive survey of the African-American experience. It draws on recent research to present black history in a clear and direct manner, within a broad social, cultural, and political framework. It also provides thorough coverage of African-American women as active builders of black culture.

The African-American Odyssey balances accounts of the actions of African-American leaders with investigations of the lives of the ordinary men and women in black communities. This community focus helps make this a history of a people rather than an account of a few extraordinary individuals. Yet the book does not neglect important political and religious leaders, entrepreneurs, and entertainers. And it gives extensive coverage to African-American art, literature, and music.

African-American history started in Africa, and this narrative begins with an account of life on that continent to the sixteenth century and the beginning of the forced migration of millions of Africans to the Americas. Succeeding chapters present the struggle of black people to maintain their humanity during the slave trade and as slaves in North America during the long colonial period.

The coming of the American Revolution during the 1770s initiated a pattern of black struggle for racial justice in which periods of optimism alternated with times of repression. Several chapters analyze the building of black community institutions, the antislavery movement, the efforts of black people to make the Civil War a war for emancipation, their struggle for equal rights as citizens during Reconstruction, and the strong opposition these efforts faced. There is also substantial coverage of African-American military service, from the War for Independence through American wars of the nineteenth and twentieth centuries.

During the late nineteenth century and much of the twentieth century, racial segregation and racially motivated violence that relegated African Americans to second-class citizenship provoked despair, but also inspired resistance and commitment to change. Chapters on the late nineteenth and early twentieth centuries cover the great migration from the cotton fields of the South to the North and West, black nationalism, and the Harlem Renaissance. Chapters on the 1930s and 1940s—the beginning of a period of revolutionary change for African Americans—tell of the economic devastation and political turmoil caused by the Great Depression, the growing influence of black culture in America, the racial tensions caused by black participation in World War II, and the dawning of the civil rights movement.

The final chapters tell the story of African Americans during the second half of the twentieth century. They relate the successes of the civil rights movement at its peak during the 1950s and 1960s and the efforts of African Americans to build on those successes during the more conservative 1970s and 1980s. Finally, there are portrayals of black life during the concluding decades of the twentieth century and of the continuing impact of African Americans on life in the United States.

In all, *The African-American Odyssey* tells a compelling story of survival, struggle, and triumph over adversity. It will leave students with an appreciation of the central place of black people and black culture in this country and a better understanding of both African-American and American history.

SPECIAL FEATURES

The many special features and pedagogical tools integrated within *The African-American Odyssey* are designed to make the text accessible to students. They include a variety of tools to reinforce the narrative and help students grasp key issues.

- **Outlines** provide students with a brief overview of the material they are about to read.
- **Introductory quotations** set the theme for each chapter.
- **"Voices"** boxes provide students with first-person perspectives on key events in African-American history. Brief introductions and study questions help students analyze these primary source documents and relate them to the text.
- The biographical sketches in the **"Profiles"** boxes highlight the contributions and personalities of both prominent individuals and ordinary people, illuminating common experiences among African Americans at various times and places.
- Brief **chronologies** provide students with a snapshot of the temporal relationship among significant events.
- End-of-chapter **Time Lines** establish a chronological context for events in African-American history by juxtaposing them with events in American history and in the rest of the world.
- **Review questions** encourage students to analyze the material they have read and to explore alternative perspectives on that material.
- The **recommended reading** and **additional bibliography** lists direct students to more information about the subject of each chapter.
- **Maps, charts, and graphs** help students visualize the geographical context of events and grasp significant trends.

- Abundant illustrations, tied to the text with informative captions, provide a visual link to the African-American past.
- **Color inserts** provide a sample of the richness of the folk and fine art African Americans have produced throughout their history.

SUPPLEMENTARY INSTRUCTIONAL MATERIALS

The extensive package of both traditional and electronic supplements that accompanies *The African-American Odyssey* provides instructors and students with an array of resources that combine sound scholarship, engaging content, and a variety of pedagogical tools to enrich the classroom experience and students' understanding of African-American history.

Instructor's Manual with Test. The *Instructor's Manual* provides summaries, outlines, learning objectives, lecture and discussion topics, and audio/visual resources for each chapter. Test materials include multiple choice, essay, identification and short-answer, chronology, and map questions.

Prentice Hall Custom Test. This commercial-quality computerized test management program, available for Windows and Macintosh environments, allows instructors to select from testing material in the *Instructor's Manual with Tests* and design their own exams.

Study Guide (Volumes I and II). This student study aid includes a summary for each chapter, reviews key points and concepts, and provides multiple choice, essay, chronology, and map questions.

Documents Set (Volumes I and II). The *Documents Set* supplements the text with additional primary and secondary source material covering the social, cultural, and political aspects of African-American history. Each reading includes a short historical summary and several review questions.

The African American Odyssey Companion Website. The *Companion Website (www.prenhall.com/hine)* works with the text to provide students with additional study materials—including questions and labeling exercises—and directs them to appropriate sources on African-American history available on the Internet. A *Faculty Module* provides instructors with downloadable material from both the Instructor's Manual and the text to aid in course organization.

Living Words: An Audio CD of African-American Oral Traditions. The text comes with an audio CD with examples of the rich oral traditions of African-American culture. In the speeches, songs, stories, and poetry on the CD, students can hear the African roots of those traditions and their links to other cultures. See the end of this volume for a full description.

Microsoft® Encarta® Africana CD-ROM. This remarkable interactive CD-ROM takes students on an unforgettable exploration of the history of African Americans, the great accomplishments of ancient civilizations, and the traditions that Africans brought to the Americas, the Caribbean, Europe, and Asia. Contact your local Prentice Hall representative for information on student discounts of *Encarta® Africana* packaged with *The African-American Odyssey.*

ACKNOWLEDGMENTS

In preparing *The African-American Odyssey* we have benefited from the work of many scholars and the help of colleagues, librarians, friends, and family.

Special thanks are due to the following scholars for their substantial contributions to the development of this textbook:

Peter Banner-Haley, *Colgate University*
Robert L. Harris Jr., *Cornell University*
Wanda Hendricks, *Arizona State University*
Rickey Hill, *South Carolina State University*
William B. Hixson, *Michigan State University*
Barbara Williams Jenkins, *South Carolina State University*
Earnestine Jenkins, *University of Memphis*
Wilma King, *University of Missouri, Columbia*
Frank C. Martin, *South Carolina State University*
Jacqueline A. McLeod, *Michigan State University*
Freddie Parker, *North Carolina Central University*
Christopher R. Reed, *Roosevelt University*
Linda Reed, *University of Houston*
Robert Stewart, *Trinity School, New York*
Andrew Workman, *Mills College*

We are grateful to the reviewers who devoted valuable time to reading and commenting on *The African-American Odyssey.* Their insightful suggestions greatly improved the quality of the text.
Abiodun Goke-Pariola, *Georgia Southern University*
Claude A. Clegg, *Indiana University*
Delia Cook, *University of Missouri at Kansas City*
Mary Ellen Curtin, *Southwest Texas State University*
Roy F. Finkenbine, *Hampton University*
John H. Haley, *University of North Carolina at Wilmington*
Ebeneazer Hunter, *De Anza College*
Joseph Kinner, *Gallaudet University*
Kenneth Mason, *Santa Monica College*
Andrew T. Miller, *Union College*
John David Smith, *North Carolina State University at Raleigh*
Marshall Stevenson, *Ohio State University*
Harry Williams, *Carleton College*
Andrew Workman, *Mills College*

Many librarians provided valuable help tracking down important material. They include Ruth Hodges, Doris Johnson, Minnie Johnson, Barbara Keitt, Andrew Penson, and Mary L. Smalls, all of Miller F. Whittaker Library, South Carolina State University; James Brooks and Jo Cottingham of the interlibrary loan department, Cooper Library, University of South Carolina; and Allan Stokes of the South Caroliniana Library at the University of South Carolina. Kathleen Thompson and Marshanda Smith provided important documents and other source material.

Seleta Simpson Byrd of South Carolina State University and Linda Werbish of Michigan State University provided valuable administrative assistance.

Each of us also enjoyed the support of family members, particularly Barbara A. Clark, Robbie D. Clark, Emily Harrold, Judy Harrold, Carol A. Hine, Peter J. Hine, Thomas D. Hine, and Alma J. McIntosh.

Finally we gratefully acknowledge the essential help of the superb editorial and production team at Prentice Hall: Charlyce Jones Owen, Vice President and Editorial Director for the Humanities, whose vision got this project started and whose unwavering support saw it through to completion; Todd Armstrong, Executive Editor for History, who kept us on track; Todd's Editorial Assistant, Holly Jo Brown; David Chodoff, Senior Development Editor, and Gerald Lombardi, who provided valuable organizational, substantive, and stylistic insights; Leslie Osher, Creative Design Director; Ximena Tamvakopoulos, Art Director, who created the book's handsome design; Louise Rothman, Production Editor, who saw it efficiently through production; Barbara Salz, our photo researcher, who skillfully tracked down the book's many illustrations, some of them from obscure sources; Sheryl Adams, Senior Marketing Manager, who provided valuable insight into the history textbook market; Emsal Hasan, Assistant Editor, who pulled together the book's supplementary material; and Nick Sklitsis, Manufacturing Manager, Lynn Pearlman, Manufacturing Buyer, and Jan Stephan, Managing Editor, who kept the whole team on schedule.

THE
AFRICAN-AMERICAN
ODYSSEY

PART I

BECOMING

AFRICAN

AMERICAN

CHAPTER 1

AFRICA

This bronze plaque portrays a ruler of the West African Kingdom of Benin on horseback with two attendants. Benin, which flourished during the fifteenth through the eighteenth centuries, was renowned for its fine bronze reliefs.

These [West African] nations think themselves the foremost men in the world, and nothing will persuade them to the contrary. They imagine that Africa is not only the greatest part of the world but also the happiest and most agreeable.

Father Cavazzi, 1687

The ancestral homeland of most black Americans is West Africa. Other regions—Angola and East Africa—were caught up in the great Atlantic slave trade that carried Africans to the New World during a period stretching from the sixteenth to the nineteenth century. But West Africa was the center of the trade in human beings. Knowing the history of West Africa, therefore, is most important in achieving an understanding of the people who became the first African Americans.

That history is best understood within the larger context of the history and geography of the whole African continent. This chapter begins with a survey of the larger context, emphasizing the aspects of the broader African experience that shaped life in West Africa before the arrival of Europeans to that region. It then explores West Africa's unique heritage and the facets of its culture that have influenced the lives of African Americans from the diaspora—the original forced dispersal of Africans from their homeland—to the present.

A HUGE AND DIVERSE LAND

Africa, the second largest continent in the world, is bounded by the Mediterranean Sea to the north, the Atlantic Ocean to the west, and the Indian Ocean and the Red Sea to the east. A narrow strip of land in its northeast corner connects it to the Arabian Peninsula and beyond that to Asia and Europe.

From north to south, Africa is divided into a succession of climatic zones (Map 1-1). With the exception of a fertile strip along the Mediterranean coast and the agriculturally rich Nile River valley, most of the northern third of the continent consists of the

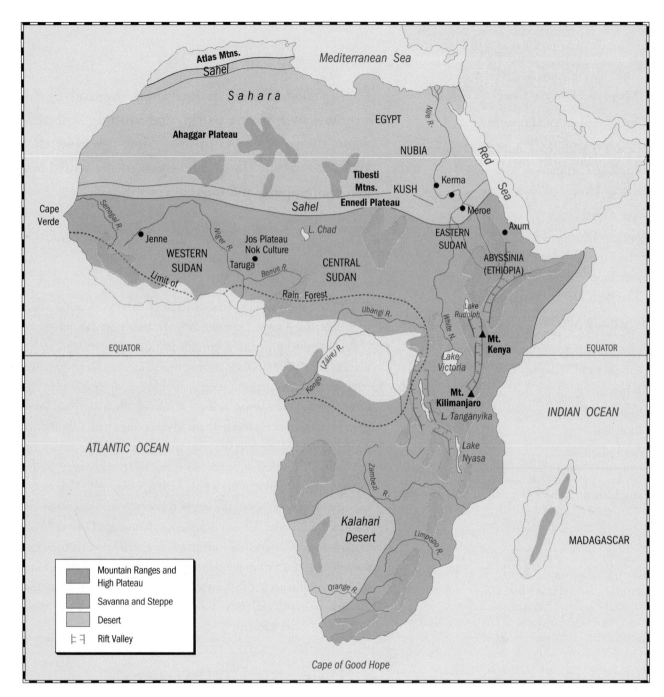

Map 1–1 Africa: Climatic Regions and Early Sites. Africa is a large continent with several climatic zones. It is also the home of several early civilizations.

Sahara Desert. For thousands of years, the Sahara has limited contact between the rest of Africa—known as sub-Saharan Africa—and the Mediterranean coast, Europe, and Asia. South of the Sahara is a semidesert region known as the Sahel, and south of it is a huge grassland or savannah stretching from Ethiopia westward to the Atlantic Ocean. Arab adventurers named this savannah *Bilad es Sudan*, meaning "land of the black people," and the term *Sudan* designates this entire region—rather than simply the modern nation of

Sudan. Much of the habitable part of West Africa falls within the savannah. The rest lies within the northern part of a rain forest that extends eastward from the Atlantic coast over most of the central part of the continent. Another region of savannah borders the rain forest to the south, followed by another desert—the Kalahari—and another coastal strip at the continent's southern extremity.

THE BIRTHPLACE OF HUMANITY

Paleoanthropologists—scientists who study the evolution and prehistory of humans—have concluded that the origins of humanity lie in the savannah regions of Africa. All people today, in other words, are very likely descendants of beings who lived in Africa millions of years ago.

Fossil and genetic evidence suggest that both humans and the forest-dwelling great apes (gorillas and chimpanzees) descended from a common apelike ancestor who lived in Africa about five to ten million years ago. The African climate was growing drier at that time, as it has continued to do into the present. Forests gave way to spreading savannahs dotted with isolated copses of trees.

The earliest known hominids (the term designates the biological family to which humans belong) were the australopithecines, who emerged about 4 million years ago. These creatures walked upright but otherwise retained many apelike characteristics and probably did not make stone tools. The first stone tools are associated with the emergence—about 2.4 million years ago—of Homo habilis, the earliest creature designated as within the homo (human) lineage. Individuals of the Homo habilis species had larger brains than the australopithecines. They butchered meat with stone cutting and chopping tools and built shelters with stone foundations. Like people in hunting and gathering societies today, they probably lived in small bands in which women foraged for plant food and men hunted and scavenged for meat.

Homo habilis fossils have been found only in Africa, but fossils of a more advanced human, Homo erectus, have been found in parts of Asia and Europe as well. Homo erectus, who emerged in Africa about 1.6 million years ago, is associated with the first evidence of human use of fire.

Paleoanthropologists agree that modern humans, Homo sapiens, evolved from Homo erectus, but they disagree how. According to a multiregional model,

Australopithecine hominids walking in the region of Laetoli, Tanzania, left these now fossilized footprints in falling ash from a nearby volcano some 3.6 million years ago.

modern humans evolved throughout Africa, Asia, and Europe from ancestral regional populations of Homo erectus and archaic Homo sapiens. According to the out-of-Africa model, modern humans emerged in Africa some 200,000 years ago and began migrating to the rest of the world about 100,000 years ago, eventually replacing all other existing human populations. Both of these models are consistent with recent genetic evidence and both indicate that all living peoples are very closely related. The "Eve" hypothesis, which supports the out-of-Africa model, suggests that all modern humans are descended from a single African woman who lived about 200,000 years ago. The multiregional model maintains that a continuous exchange of genetic material allowed archaic human populations in Africa, Asia, and Europe to evolve simultaneously into modern humans.

ANCIENT CIVILIZATIONS AND OLD ARGUMENTS

The earliest civilization in Africa and one of the two earliest civilizations in world history is that of ancient Egypt (see Map 1-1), which emerged in the Nile River valley in the fourth millennium BCE (before the common era). Mesopotamian civilization, the other of the two, emerged in the valleys of the Tigris and Euphrates rivers in southwest Asia with the rise of the city states of Sumer. In both regions, civilization appeared at the end of a long process in which hunting and gathering gave way to agriculture. The settled village life that resulted from this transformation permitted society to become increasingly hierarchical and specialized. Similar processes gave rise to civilization in the Indus valley in India around 2300 BCE, in China—with the founding of the Shang dynasty—around 1500 BCE, and in Mexico and Andean South America during the first millennium BCE.

The race of the ancient Egyptians and the nature and extent of their influence on later Western civilizations have long been a source of controversy that reflects more about racial politics of recent history than it reveals about the Egyptians themselves. It is not clear whether they were an offshoot of their Mesopotamian contemporaries, whether they were representatives of a group of peoples whose origins were in both Africa and Southeast Asia, or whether the ancestors of both the Egyptians and Mesopotamians were black Africans. What is clear is that the ancient Egyptians exhibited a mixture of racial features and spoke a language related to the languages spoken by others in the fertile regions of North Africa and Southeast Asia.

In this context the argument over whether the Egyptians were black or white is unlikely to be resolved. They were both or neither and certainly did not regard themselves in a way related to modern racial terminology. The argument began in the nineteenth century when African Americans and white liberals sought means to refute claims by racist pseudo-scientists that people of African descent were inherently inferior to whites. Unaware of the achievements of West African civilization, those who believed in human equality used evidence that the Egyptians were black to counter assertions that African Americans were incapable of civilization.

Recently there has been a more scholarly debate between Afrocentricists led by Martin Bernal and traditionalists led by Mary Lefkowitz. Bernal in his book *Black Athena* argues that black Egyptians colonized ancient Greece, which is usually regarded as the birthplace of the values associated with Western civilization. According to Bernal, the Egyptians supplied the Greeks with the basis of their scientific method and, therefore, Africans are the progenitors of Western civilization. Lefkowitz and her colleagues respond that the Egyptians were white, that there is no evidence that they colonized Greece, and that the Greeks were alone responsible for the origins of the Western empirical method of inquiry. While scholars question many of Bernal's claims, they have always recognized Egypt's contribution to the spread of civilization throughout the Mediterranean region. In religion, commerce, and art—if not in philosophy—Egypt helped shape the development of Greece and subsequent Western civilizations.

Egyptian Civilization

Egypt was, as Greek historian Herodotus observed 2,500 years ago, the "gift of the Nile." A gentle annual flooding regularly irrigates the banks of this great river, leaving behind a new deposit of fertile soil. It was the Nile that allowed Egyptians to cultivate wheat and barley and herd goats, sheep, pigs, and cattle in an otherwise desolate region. The Nile also provided the Egyptians with a transportation and communications artery, while its desert surroundings protected them from foreign invasion.

Egypt was unified into a single kingdom about 3150 BCE and was ruled by a succession of thirty-one dynasties until its incorporation into the Roman Empire in the first century BCE. Historians have divided this immensely long span into several epochs. During the early dynastic period (3100–2700 BCE) and Old Kingdom (2700–2200 BCE), Egypt's kings consolidated their authority and claimed the status of gods. After a period of instability following the end of the Old Kingdom, royal authority was reestablished during the Middle Kingdom (2050–1650). During the New Kingdom (1550–1100), Egypt expanded beyond the Nile valley to establish an empire over coastal regions of southwest Asia as well as Libya and Nubia in Africa. It was in this period that Egypt's kings began using the title *pharaoh*, which means "great house." During the Post-Empire period (1100–30 BCE) Egypt fell prey to a series of outside invaders. With the invasion of Alexander the Great's Macedonian army in 331 BCE, Egypt's ancient culture crumbled under the pressure of Greek ideas and institutions.

The way of life that took shape during the Old Kingdom, however, had resisted change for most of ancient Egypt's history. Kings presided over a strictly hierarchical society. Beneath them were classes of warriors, priests, merchants, artisans, and peasants. A class of scribes, who were masters of Egypt's complex hiero-glyphic writing, staffed a comprehensive bureaucracy.

Egyptian society was also strictly patrilineal and patriarchal. Royal incest was customary, with each king choosing a sister to be his queen. Kings maintained numerous concubines; other men could also take additional wives if the first failed to produce children. Egyptian women nonetheless held a relatively high status compared with women in much of the rest of the ancient world. They owned property independently of their husbands, oversaw household slaves, controlled the education of their children, held public office, served as priests, and operated businesses. There were several female rulers, one of whom, Hatshepsut, reigned for twenty years (1478–1458 BCE). She is depicted, however, in the regalia worn by male rulers, including the traditional false beard.

A complex polytheistic religion shaped every facet of Egyptian life. Although there were innumerable gods, two of the most important were the sun god Re (or Ra), who represented the immortality of the Egyptian state, and Osiris, the god of the Nile, who embodied each individual's personal immortality. In Egyptian myth Osiris was murdered by his evil brother Seth and resurrected by his sister/wife Isis. This myth, originally an allegory for the seasonal rebirth of vegetation brought by the Nile's annual flooding, came to symbolize the possibility of individual immortality. Egyptians came to regard Osiris as the judge of the worthiness of souls.

Personal immortality and the immortality of the state merged in the person of the king, as expressed in Egypt's elaborate royal funerary architecture. The most dramatic examples of that architecture, the Great Pyramids at Giza, were built more than 4,500 years ago to protect the bodies of three prominent kings of the Old Kingdom so that their souls might successfully enter the life to come. The pyramids also dramatically symbolized the power of the Egyptian state and have endured as embodiments of the grandeur of Egyptian civilization.

Kush, Meroe, and Axum

To the south of Egypt in the upper Nile River valley, in what is today the nation of Sudan, lay the ancient region known as Nubia. As early as the fourth millennium BCE, the indisputably black people who lived there interacted with the Egyptians. Recent archaeological evidence suggests that grain production and the concept of monarchy may have arisen in Nubia and subsequently spread northward to Egypt. But Egypt's population was always much larger than that of Nubia and during the second millennium BCE Egypt used its military power to make Nubia an Egyptian colony and control Nubian copper and gold mines. Egyptians also imported ivory, ebony, leopard pelts, and slaves from Nubia and required the sons of Nubian nobles to live in Egypt as hostages.

The hostages served as ambassadors of Egyptian culture when they returned home. As a result, Egyptian religion, art, hieroglyphics, and political structure became firmly established in Nubia. Then, with the decline of Egypt's New Kingdom at the end of the second millennium BCE, the Nubians established an independent kingdom known as Kush, which had its capital at Kerma on the upper Nile River. During the eighth century BCE the Kushites took control of upper Egypt, and in about 750 the Kushite king Piankhy added lower Egypt to his realm. Piankhy made himself pharaoh and founded Egypt's twenty-fifth dynasty, which ruled until the Assyrians, who invaded Egypt from southwest Asia, drove the Kushites out in 663 BCE.

Kush itself remained independent for another thousand years. Its kings continued for centuries to call themselves pharaohs and had themselves buried in pyramid tombs covered with Egyptian hieroglyphics. They and the Kushite nobility practiced the Egyptian religion and spoke the Egyptian language. But a resurgent Egyptian army destroyed Kerma in 540 BCE and the Kushites moved their capital southward to Meroe. The new capital was superbly located for trade with East Africa, with regions to the west across the Sudan, and with the Mediterranean world by way of the Nile River. Trade made Meroe extremely wealthy, and the development of an iron smelting technology capable of exploiting local deposits of iron transformed the city into Africa's first industrial center.

As Meroe's economic base expanded, the dependence of Kushite civilization on Egyptian culture declined. By the second century CE (Common Era), the Kushites had developed their own phonetic script to replace hieroglyphics. An architecture derived from that of Egypt gave way to an eclectic style that included Greek, Indian, and sub-Saharan African motifs as well as Egyptian.

Because of its commerce and wealth, Kush attracted powerful enemies. A Roman army, for example, invaded the kingdom in 23 BCE. But it was actually the decline of Rome and its Mediterranean economy that were the chief factors in Kush's destruction. As the Roman Empire grew weaker and poorer, its trade with Kush declined, and Kush too grew weaker. During the early fourth century CE, Kush fell to the neighboring Noba people and they in turn fell to the nearby kingdom of Axum, whose warriors destroyed Meroe.

The ruined pyramids of Meroe on the banks of the Upper Nile River are not as old as those at Giza in Egypt, and differ from them stylistically. But they nonetheless attest to the cultural connections between Meroe and Egypt.

Located in what is today Ethiopia, Axum emerged as a nation during the first century BCE as semitic people from the Arabian Peninsula, who were influenced by Hebrew culture, settled among a local black population. By the time it absorbed Kush during the fourth century CE, Axum had become the first Christian state in sub-Saharan Africa. By the eighth century, shifting trade patterns, environmental depletion, and Islamic invaders combined to reduce Axum's power. It nevertheless retained its unique culture and its independence.

WEST AFRICA

For centuries legend has held that the last kings of Kush retreated westward across the savannah to West Africa, bringing with them certain artistic motifs, the knowledge of iron making, and the concepts of divine kingship and centralized government. There is no archaeological evidence to support this belief, however. On the con-

trary, it now appears that ironworking arose earlier in West Africa than it did at Meroe. The immediate birthright of African Americans, then, is to be found not in the ancient civilizations of the Nile valley—although they are certainly part of the heritage of all Africans—but thousands of miles away among the civilizations that emerged in West Africa in the first millennium BCE.

Like Africa as a whole, West Africa is physically, ethnically, and culturally diverse. Much of West Africa south of the Sahara Desert falls within the great savannah that spans the continent from east to west. West and south of the savannah, however, in Senegambia (modern Senegal), stretching along the southwestern coast of West Africa and in the lands located along the coast of the Gulf of Guinea, there are extensive forests. These two environments—savannah and forest—were home to people of a great variety of cultures and languages. Patterns of settlement in the region ranged from isolated homesteads and hamlets through villages and towns to cities.

West Africans began cultivating crops and tending domesticated animals between 1000 BCE and 200 CE. Those who lived on the Savannah usually adopted settled village life well before those who lived in the forests. The early farmers produced millet, rice, and sorghum while tending herds of cattle and goats. By 500 BCE, beginning with the Nok people of the forest region, some of them were producing iron tools and weapons.

From early times the peoples of West Africa traded among themselves and with the peoples who lived across the Sahara Desert in North Africa. This extensive trade became an essential part of the region's economy and formed the basis for the three great western Sudanese empires that successively dominated the region from before 800 CE to the beginnings of the modern era.

Ancient Ghana

The first known kingdom in the western Sudan was Ghana (Map 1-2). Founded by the Soninke people in the area north of the modern republic of Ghana, its origins are unclear. It may have arisen as early as the fourth century CE or as late as the eighth century when Arab merchants began to praise its great wealth. Its name comes from the Soninke word for king, which Arab traders mistakenly applied to the entire kingdom.

The Soninke succeeded in dominating their neighbors and forging an empire through constant warfare and the possession of superior iron weapons. Ghana's boundaries reached into the Sahara desert to its north and modern Senegal to its south. But the empire's real power lay in commerce.

Ghana's kings were known in Europe and southwest Asia as the richest of monarchs, and the source of their wealth was trade. The key to this trade was the Asian camel, which was first introduced into Africa during the first century CE. With its ability to endure long journeys on small amounts of water, the camel dramatically increased trade across the Sahara between the Western Sudan and the coastal regions of North Africa.

Ghana traded in several commodities. From North Africa came silk, cotton, glass beads, horses, mirrors, dates, and especially salt, which was a scarce necessity in the torridly hot western Sudan. In return, Ghana

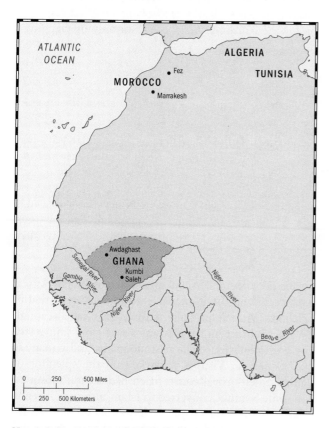

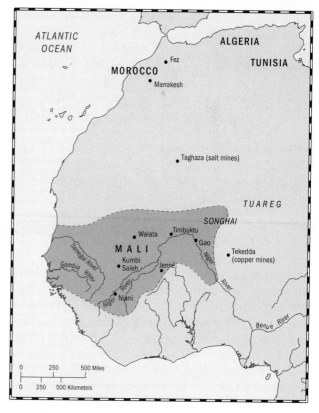

Map 1–2 The Empires of Ghana and Mali. The western Sudanese empires of Ghana and Mali helped shape West African culture. Ghana existed from as early as the fourth century CE to 1076. Mali dominated the western Sudan from 1230 to 1468.

V O I C E S

AL BAKRI DESCRIBES KUMBI SALEH AND GHANA'S ROYAL COURT

Nothing remains of the documents compiled by Ghana's Islamic bureaucracy. As a result, accounts of the civilization are all based on the testimony of Arab or Berber visitors. In the following passage, written in the eleventh century, Arab geographer Al Bakri describes the great wealth and power of the king of Ghana and suggests that there were tensions between Islam and the indigenous religion of the Soninke.

The city of Ghana [Kumbi Saleh] consists of two towns lying in a plain. One of these towns is inhabited by Muslims. It is large and possesses twelve mosques. . . . There are imams and muezzins, and assistants as well as jurists and learned men. Around the town are wells of sweet water from which they drink and near which they grow vegetables. The town in which the king lives is six miles from the Muslim one, and bears the name Al Ghaba [the forest]. The land between the two towns is covered with houses. The houses of the inhabitants are of stone and acacia wood. The king has a palace and a number of dome-shaped dwellings, the whole surrounded by an enclosure like the defensive wall of a city. In the town where the king lives, and not far from the hall where he holds his court of justice, is a mosque where pray the Muslims who come on diplomatic missions. Around the king's town are domed buildings, woods, and copses where live the sorcerers of these people, the men in charge of the religious cult. . . .

Of the people who follow the king's religion, only he and his heir presumptive, who is the son of his sister, may wear sewn clothes. All the other people wear clothes of cotton, silk, or brocade, according to their means. All men shave their beards and women shave their heads. The king adorns himself like a woman, wearing necklaces and bracelets, and when he sits before the people he puts on a high cap decorated with gold and wrapped in a turban of fine cotton. The court of appeal [for grievances against officials] is held in a domed pavilion around which stand ten horses with gold embroidered trappings. Behind the king stand ten pages holding shields and swords decorated with gold, and on his right are the sons of the subordinate kings of his country, all wearing splendid garments and their hair mixed with gold. . . . When the people professing the same religion as the king approach him, they fall on their knees and sprinkle their heads with dust, for this is their way of showing him their respect. As for the Muslims, they greet him only by clapping their hands.

QUESTIONS

1. What does this passage indicate about life in ancient Ghana?

2. According to Al Bakri, in what particular ways do customs in Kumbi Saleh differ from customs in Arab lands?

Source: Roland Oliver and Caroline Oliver, *Africa in the Days of Exploration* (Englewood Cliffs, NJ: Prentice Hall, 1965), 9–10.

exported pepper, slaves, and especially gold. The slaves were usually war captives and the gold came from mines in the Wangara region to the southwest of Ghana. The Soninke did not mine the gold themselves, but the kings of Ghana grew rich by taxing it as it passed through their lands.

Before the seventh century CE, when the Roman Empire dominated the Mediterranean region, Roman merchants and Berbers—the indigenous people of western North Africa—were West Africa's chief partners in the trans-Sahara trade. After the seventh century, as Roman power declined and Islam spread across North Africa, Arabs replaced the Romans. Arab merchants settled in Saleh, the Moslem part of Kumbi Saleh, Ghana's capital. By the twelfth century this was a large and impressive city, with stone houses, large stone tombs, and as many as 20,000 people. Visitors remarked on the splendor of Kumbi Saleh's royal court. Saleh had several mosques, and some Soninke converted to Islam, although it is unclear whether the royal family was among them. Moslems certainly dominated the royal bureaucracy and in the process introduced Arabic writing to the region.

A combination of commercial and religious interests finally destroyed Ghana during the twelfth century. The Almorvids, who were Islamic Berbers, had been Ghana's principal rivals for control of the trans-Sahara trade. In 992 Ghana's army captured Awdaghost, the Almorvid trade center northwest of Kumbi Saleh. Driven as much by religious fervor as by economic interest, the Almorvids retaliated decisively in 1076 by conquering Ghana. The Soninke regained their independence in 1087, but a little over a century later fell to the Sosso, a previously tributary people, who destroyed Kumbi Saleh.

The Empire of Mali, 1230–1468

Following the defeat of Ghana by the Almorvids many western Sudanese peoples competed for political and economic power. This contest ended in 1235 when the Mandinka, under their legendary leader Sundiata, defeated the Sosso at the Battle of Kirina. In the wake of this victory Sundiata went on to forge the Empire of Mali.

Mali (which means "where the emperor resides" in Mende, the language of the Mandinka) was socially, politically, and economically similar to Ghana. It was larger than Ghana, however—stretching 1,500 miles from the Atlantic coast to the region east of the Niger River—and was centered farther south, in a region of greater rainfall and more abundant crops. Its population grew as a result, reaching a total of eight million. Sundiata also gained direct control of the gold mines of Wangara, making his empire more wealthy than Ghana had been.

At some point in Mali's history, its emperors converted to Islam, but when that happened is not clear. According to legend, Sundiata was a skilled magician and was not likely to have been a Moslem. But it could not have been long after his time that Mali became at least superficially a Moslem state. West Africans had been converting to Islam since Arab traders began arriving in the region centuries before, although many converts continued to practice indigenous religions as well. By Sundiata's time most merchants and bureaucrats were Moslems and the empire's rulers gained stature among Arab states by converting to Islam as well.

To administer their vast empire at a time when communication was slow, Mali's rulers relied heavily on personal and family ties with local chiefs. Commerce, bureaucracy, and scholarship also played a role in holding the empire together. Mali's most important city was Timbuktu, which had been established during the eleventh century beside the Niger River near the southern edge of the Sahara Desert. Two other cities—Walata in the northwest and Gao in the east—also functioned as economic and cultural centers.

By the thirteenth century, Timbuktu was a major hub for trade in gold, slaves, and salt. It attracted merchants from throughout the Mediterranean world and became a center of Islamic learning. There were several mosques in the city, 150 islamic schools, a law school, and many book dealers. It supported a cosmopolitan community and impressed visitors with its absence of religious and ethnic intolerance. Even though Mali enslaved war captives and traded slaves, an Arab traveler noted in 1352–53, "the Negroes possess some admirable qualities. They are seldom unjust, and have a greater abhorrence of injustice than any other people."

The Mali empire reached its peak during the reign of Mansa Musa (1312–1337). One of the wealthiest rulers the world has known, Musa made himself and Mali famous when in 1324 he undertook a pilgrimage across Africa to the holy city of Mecca in Arabia. With an entourage of sixty thousand, a train of one hundred elephants, and a propensity for distributing huge amounts of gold to those who greeted him along the way, Musa amazed the Islamic world. After Musa's death, however, Mali declined. The empire's leading families vied with each other for wealth and power and its subject peoples began to rebel. In 1468, one of the most powerful of its formerly subject peoples, the Songhai, captured Timbuktu, and their leader, Sunni Ali, founded a new West African empire.

THE WESTERN SUDANESE EMPIRES	
c. 750	Ghana rises to prominence
1076	Almorvids conquer Ghana
1203	Sosso dislodge Almorvids from Kumbi Saleh
1235	Battle of Kirina leads to creation of the Empire of Mali
1312–1337	Mansa Musa reigns
1468	Sunni Ali captures Timbuktu and founds Empire of Songhai
1497	Askia Muhammad Toure makes pilgrimage to Mecca
1591	Moroccans crush the army of Songhai

The Sudanese city of Timbuktu, which began as a seasonal camp in the eleventh century, reached its peak as a center of trade and learning during the fourteenth through sixteenth centuries. By 1830, when this engraving was made, it had declined from its earlier splendor.

The Empire of Songhai, 1464–1591

Like the Mandinka and Soninke before them, the Songhai were great traders and warriors. The Songhai had seceded from Mali in 1375, and under Sunni Ali, who reigned from 1464 to 1492, they built the last and largest of the western Sudanese empires (Map 1-3). Sunni Ali required conquered peoples to pay tribute but otherwise let them run their own affairs. Nominally a Moslem, he—like Sundiata—was reputedly a great magician who derived power from the traditional spirits.

When Sunni Ali died by drowning, Askia Muhammad Toure led a successful revolt against Ali's son to make himself king of Songhai. The new king, who reigned from 1492 to 1528, extended the empire northward into the Sahara, westward into Mali, and eastward

to encompass the trading cities of Hausaland. He centralized the administration of the empire, replacing local chiefs with members of his family, substituting taxation for tribute, and establishing a bureaucracy to regulate trade.

A devout Moslem, Muhammad Toure used his power to spread the influence of Islam within the empire. During a pilgrimage to Mecca in 1497 he established diplomatic relations with Morocco and Egypt and recruited Moslem scholars to serve at the Sankore Mosque at Timbuktu. Subsequently the mosque became a widely known center for the study of theology, law, mathematics, and medicine. Despite these efforts, by the end of Muhammad Toure's reign (the aging ruler, senile and blind, was deposed by family members) Islamic culture was still weak in West Africa outside urban areas. Peasants, who

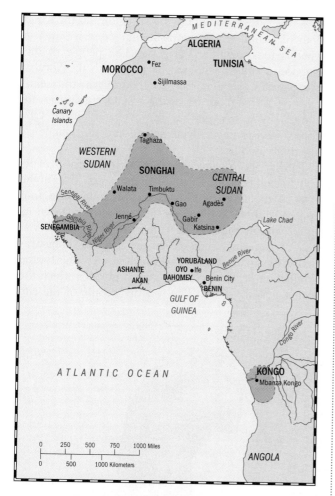

Map 1-3 West and Central Africa c. 1500. This map shows the Empire of Songhai (1464–1591), the Kongo kingdom (c. 1400–1700), and the major kingdoms of the West African forest region.

diers survived the grueling march to confront Songhai's elite cavalry at Tondibi on the approach to Gao. But the Songhai forces were armed only with bows and lances, which were no match for firearms, and the mercenaries routed them. Its army destroyed, the Songhai empire fell apart. The center of Islamic scholarship in West Africa shifted eastward from Timbuktu to Hausaland. The Moroccans soon left the region, and West Africa was without a government powerful enough to intervene when the Portuguese, other Europeans, and the African kingdoms of the Guinea Coast became more interested in trading for human beings than for gold.

The West African Forest Region

The area called the forest region of West Africa—which includes stretches of savannah—extends two thousand miles along the Atlantic coast from Senegambia (modern Senegal and Gambia) in the northwest to the former kingdom of Benin (modern Cameroon) in the east. Among the early settlers of the forest region were the Nok, who around 500 BCE, in what is today southern Nigeria, created a culture noted for its ironworking technology and its terra-cotta sculptures. But significant migration into the forests began only after 1000 CE as the western Sudanese climate became increasingly dry.

Because people migrated southward from the Sudan in small groups over an extended period of time, the process brought about considerable cultural diversification. A variety of languages, economies, political systems, and traditions came into existence. Some ancient customs survived, such as dividing types of agricultural labor by gender and living in villages composed of extended families. Nevertheless the forest region became a patchwork of diverse ethnic groups with related but sometimes quite different ways of life.

Colonizing a region covered with thick vegetation was hard work. In some portions of the forest, agriculture did not supplant hunting and gathering until the fifteenth and sixteenth centuries. In more open parts of the region, however, several small kingdoms emerged centuries earlier. Benin City, for example, dates to the thirteenth century and Ife in Nigeria to the eleventh. Although none of these kingdoms ever grew as large as the empires of the western Sudan, some were quite powerful. They were characteristically ruled by kings who claimed semidivine status but whose power was limited by local nobility and urban elites. Kings sought to extend their power by conquering and assimilating neighboring peoples. Secrecy and elaborate ritual marked royal courts, which were also centers of patronage for art and religion.

made up 95 percent of the population, spoke a variety of languages, continued to practice indigenous religions, and remained loyal to their local chiefs.

Songhai reached its peak of influence under Askia Daud between 1549 and 1582. But the political balance of power in West Africa was changing rapidly, and lacking new leaders as resourceful as Sunni Ali or Muhammad Toure, Songhai failed to adapt. Since the 1430s adventurers from the European country of Portugal had been establishing trading centers along the Guinea coast seeking gold and diverting it from the trans-Sahara trade. Their success threatened the Arab rulers of North Africa, Songhai's traditional partners in the trans-Sahara trade. In 1591, the king of Morocco, hoping to regain access to West African gold, sent an army of four thousand—mostly Spanish—mercenaries armed with muskets and cannons across the Sahara to attack Gao, Songhai's capital. Only one thousand of the sol-

The peoples of the forest region are of particular importance for African-American history because of the role they played in the Atlantic slave trade as both slave-traders and as victims of the trade. Space permits only a survey of the most important of these peoples, beginning with those of Senegambia in the northwest.

The inhabitants of Senegambia shared a common history and spoke closely related languages but were not politically united. Parts of the region had been incorporated within the empires of Ghana and Mali and had been exposed to Islamic influences. Senegambian society was strictly hierarchical, with royalty at the top and slaves at the bottom. Most people were farmers, growing such crops as millet, sorghum, plantains, beans, and bananas and supplementing their diet with fish, oysters, rabbits, and monkeys.

To the southeast of Senegambia were the Akan states. They emerged during the sixteenth century as the gold trade provided local rulers with the wealth they needed to clear forests and initiate agricultural economies. To accomplish this, the rulers traded gold from mines under their control for slaves, who did the difficult work of cutting trees and burning refuse. Then settlers received open fields from the rulers in return for a portion of their produce and services. When Europeans arrived, they traded guns for gold. The guns in turn allowed the Akan states to expand, and during the late seventeenth century, one of them, the Ashante, created a well-organized and densely populated kingdom, comparable in size to the modern country of Ghana. By the eighteenth century this kingdom not only dominated the central portion of the forest region but also used its army extensively to capture slaves for sale to European traders.

To the east of the Akan states (in modern Benin and western Nigeria) lived the people of the Yoruba culture, who gained ascendancy in the area as early as 1000 CE by trading kola nuts and cloth to the peoples of the western Sudan. The artisans of the Yoruba city of Ife were renowned for their fine bronze, brass, and terracotta sculptures. Ife was also notable for the prominent role of women in conducting its profitable commerce. During the seventeenth century, the Oyo people, employing a well-trained cavalry, imposed political unity on part of the Yoruba region. They, like the Ashanti, became extensively involved in the Atlantic slave trade.

Located to the west of the Oyo were the Fon people who formed the Kingdom of Dahomey, which rivaled Oyo as a center for the slave trade. The king of Dahomey was an absolute monarch who took thousands of wives for himself from leading Fon families as a way to assure the loyalty of potential rivals.

At the eastern end of the forest region was the Kingdom of Benin, which controlled an extensive area in what is today southern Nigeria. The people of this kingdom shared a common heritage with the Yoruba, who played a role in its formation during the thirteenth century. Throughout its history, Benin's politics were marked by a struggle for power between the Oba (king), who claimed divine status, and the kingdom's hereditary nobility.

During the fifteenth century, after a reform of its army, Benin began to expand—to the Niger River in the east, to the Gulf of Guinea to the south, and into Yoruba country to the west. The kingdom reached its apogee during the late sixteenth century. European visitors at that time remarked on the size and sophistication of its capital, Benin City, which was a center for the production of the fine bronze sculptures for which the region is still known. The wealthy people of the city

Figure of woman and children. Yoruba peoples, Nigeria. Wood, pigment. 38.5 cm (15¼″). Museum purchase, 85-1-11. Photograph by Franko Khoury. National Museum of African Art.

The Yoruba mother in this sculpture is engaged in a religious ritual. She carries an infant on her back and wears a distinctive headdress.

dined on beef, mutton, chicken, and yams. Its streets, unlike those of European cities of the time, were free of beggars.

Benin remained little influenced by Islam or Christianity, but like other coastal kingdoms, it became increasingly involved in the Atlantic slave trade. Beginning in the late fifteenth century, the Oba (king) of Benin allowed Europeans to enter the country to trade for gold, pepper, ivory, and slaves. Initially the Oba forbade the sale of his own subjects, but his large army—the first in the forest region to be provided with European firearms—captured others for the trade as it conquered neighboring regions. By the seventeenth century Benin's prosperity depended on the slave trade. As the kingdom declined during the eighteenth century,

it began to sell some of its own people to European slave traders.

KONGO AND ANGOLA

Although the forebears of most African Americans came from West Africa, many also came from Central Africa, in particular the region around the Congo River and its tributaries and the region to the south that the Portuguese called Angola. The people of these regions had much in common with those of the Guinea Coast. They divided labor by gender, lived in villages composed of extended families, and accorded semidivine status to their kings. And like the people of West Africa,

---

VOICES

A DUTCH VISITOR DESCRIBES BENIN CITY

Benin City was one of the few towns of the Guinea coast that were open to European travelers before the nineteenth century. As this account by a Dutch visitor in 1602 suggests, many of them compared it favorably to the cities of Europe during the same period.

The town seemeth to be very great; when you enter into it, you go into a great broad street, not paved, which seems to be seven or eight times broader than the Warmoes street in Amsterdam; which goeth right out and never crooks. . . . It is thought that street is a mile long [this is a Dutch mile, equal to about four English miles] besides the suburbs. At the gate where I entered on horseback, I saw a very high bulwark, very thick of earth, with a very deep broad ditch. . . . Without this gate there is a great suburb. When you are in the great street aforesaid, you see many great streets on the sides thereof, which also go right forth. . . . The houses in this street stand in good order, one close and even with the other, as the houses in Holland stand. . . . Their rooms within are four-square, over them having a roof that is not close[d] in the middle, at which place the rain, wind, and light come in, and therein they lie and eat their meat; they have other places besides, as kitchens and other rooms. . . .

The King's Court is very great, within it having many great four-square plains, which round about them have galleries, wherein there is always watch kept. I was so far within the Court that I passed over four such great plains, and wherever I looked, still I saw gates upon gates to go into other places. . . . I went as far as any Netherlander was, which was to the stable where his best horses stood, always passing a great long way. It seems that the King has many soldiers; he has also many gentlemen, who when they come to the court ride upon horses. . . . There are also many men slaves seen in the town, that carry water, yams, and palm-wine, which they say is for the King; and many carry grass, which is for their horses; and all of this is carried into the court.

QUESTIONS

1. According to the Dutch visitor, how does Benin City compare to Amsterdam?

2. What seems to impress the Dutch visitor most about Benin City?

Source: Quoted in Roland Oliver and J. D. Fage, *A Short History of Africa* (Baltimore: Penguin Books, 1973), 108–9.

"King mounted with attendants" Bronze, H. 19-½, W. 16-½ in. (49.5 cm.), The Metropolitan Museum of Art, The Michael C. Rockefeller Memorial Collection, Gift of Nelson A. Rockefeller, 1965. (1978.412.309)

This bronze plaque shows the King of Benin and two attendants. The heavy necklace symbolizes royal authority.

they were ensnared in the Atlantic slave trade as it grew to immense proportions after 1500.

In the fourteenth and fifteenth centuries, much of the Congo River system, with its fertile valleys and abundant fish, came under the control of the Kingdom of Kongo. The wealth of this kingdom also derived from its access to salt and iron and its extensive trade with the interior of the continent. Nzinga Knuwu, who was Mani Kongo (the Kongolese term for king) when Portuguese expeditions arrived in the region in the late fifteenth century, was more welcoming to the intruders than other African rulers. His son Nzinga Mbemba tried to convert the kingdom to Christianity and remodel it along European lines. The resulting unrest, combined with Portuguese greed and the effects of the slave trade, undermined royal authority and ultimately led to the breakup of the kingdom and the social disruption of the entire Kongo-Angola region.

WEST AFRICAN SOCIETY AND CULTURE

West Africa's great ethnic and cultural diversity makes it hazardous to generalize about the social and cultural

background of the first African Americans. The dearth of written records from the region south of the Sudan compounds the difficulties. But working with a variety of sources—including oral histories, traditions, and archaeological and anthropological studies—historians have nonetheless pieced together, and continue to flesh out, a broad understanding of the way the people of West Africa lived at the beginning of the Atlantic slave trade.

Families and Villages

By the early sixteenth century most West Africans were farmers. They usually lived in hamlets or villages composed of extended families and clans called lineages. Generally one lineage occupied each village, although some large lineages peopled several villages. The members of extended families were descended from a common ancestor, while the lineages claimed descent from a mythical personage. Depending on the ethnic group involved, extended families and lineages were either patrilineal or matrilineal. In patrilineal societies, social rank and property passed in the male line from fathers to sons. In matrilineal societies, rank and property, although controlled by men, passed from generation to generation in the female line. A village chief in a matrilineal society was succeeded by his sister's son, not his own. According to the Arab chronicler Al Bakri, the succession to the throne of the empire of Ghana followed this pattern. But many West Africans lived in stateless societies with no government other than that provided by extended families and lineages.

Nuclear families—husband, wife, and their children—or in some cases polygynous families—husband, *wives*, and children—acted as economic units in extended families. Both kinds of family units existed in the context of a broader family community composed of grandparents, aunts, uncles, and cousins. Elders in the extended family had great power over the economic and social lives of its members. Strictly enforced incest taboos prohibited people from marrying within their extended family.

Villages tended to be larger on the savannah than in the forest. In both regions villagers used forced earth or mud to construct small houses, which were round or rectangular in shape depending upon local tradition. The houses usually had thatched roofs, or sometimes, in the forest, palm roofs. In both savannah and forest, mud or mud-brick walls up to ten feet high surrounded villages. A nuclear or polygynous family unit might have several houses. In nuclear households the husband

NZINGA MBEMBA (AFFONSO I) OF KONGO

Nzinga Mbemba, baptised Dom Affonso, ruled as the Mani Kongo from about 1506 to 1543 CE. His life illustrates the complex and tragic relationships between African coastal kingdoms and Europeans in search of power, cultural hegemony, and wealth.

Mbemba was a son of Nzinga Knuwu who as Mani Kongo established diplomatic ties with Portugal. Portuguese vessels had reached Kongo in 1482 and in 1491 the Portuguese king sent a formal mission to Mbanza Kongo (the City of Kongo). Amid considerable ceremony, Knuwu converted to Christianity, not because of faith but because conversion gave him access to Portuguese musketeers he needed to put down a rebellion. Mbemba served as his father's general in the ensuing successful campaign.

By 1495 internal politics and Knuwu's inability to accept Christian monogamy had led him to renounce his baptism and to banish Christians—both Portuguese and Kongolese—from Mbanza Kongo. Mbemba, who was a sincere Christian, became their champion in opposition to a traditionalist faction headed by his half-brother Mpanza. Following Knuwu's death in 1506, the two princes fought over the succession. The victory of Mbemba's forces led to his coronation as Affonso and the execution of Mpanza.

By then Mbemba had learned to speak, read, and write Portuguese. He gained at least outward respect from the Portuguese monarchy as a ruler and devout Christian missionary. Soon there were hundreds of Portuguese advisers, priests, artisans, teachers, and settlers in Mbanza Kongo and its environs. In 1516 a Portuguese priest described Mbemba as "not . . . a man but an angel sent by the Lord to this kingdom to convert it." The priest went on to say of Mbemba, "Better than we, he knows the Prophets and the Gospel of Our Lord Jesus Christ." Mbemba destroyed fetishes and shrines associated with Kongo's traditional religion, replaced them with crucifixes and images of

Affonso I gives an audience to foreign ambassadors at his royal court.

saints, built several Christian churches in Mbanza Kongo, and had some of his opponents burned.

While seeking the spiritual salvation of his nation, Mbemba hoped also to modernize it on a European model. He dressed in Portuguese clothing, sent his sons and other young men to Portugal to be educated, and began schools to educate the children of Kongo's nobility. He corresponded with a series of Portuguese kings, and his son Dom Henrique, who became a Christian bishop, briefly represented Kongo at the Vatican, where he addressed the pope in Latin in 1513.

Mbemba put too much faith in his Portuguese patrons and too little in the traditions of his people. By 1508 Portuguese priests were trading in slaves and living with Kongolese mistresses. This disturbed Mbemba not because he opposed slavery, but because the priests undermined his authority. *He* was supposed to have a monopoly over the slave trade, and increasingly his own people were subjected to that trade.

Mbemba's complaints led to a formal agreement in 1512 called the *Regimento*, which actually worsened matters. It placed restrictions on the priests and pledged continued Portuguese military assistance. But it also recognized the right of Portuguese merchants to trade for copper, ivory, and slaves and exempted Portuguese from punishment under local law. Soon the trade and related corruption increased and so did unrest among Mbemba's increasingly unhappy subjects. In 1526 Mbemba created a commission designed to ensure that only war captives could be enslaved and, when that did not work, he begged the Portuguese king that "in these kingdoms there should not be any trade in slaves or market for slaves."

In response Portugal made alliances with Kongo's neighbors and withdrew much of its support from Mbemba, who died surrounded by scheming merchants, corruption, and dissension. In 1568—a quarter-century after his death—Kongo became a client state of Portugal and the slave trade expanded.

occupied the larger house and his wife the smaller. In polygynous households the husband had the largest house and his wives lived in smaller ones.

Villagers' few possessions included cots, rugs, stools, and wooden storage chests. Their tools and weapons included bows, spears, iron axes, hoes, and scythes. Households used grinding stones, woven baskets, and a variety of ceramic vessels to prepare and store food. Villagers in both the savannah and forest regions produced cotton for clothing, but their food crops were quite distinct. West Africans in the savannah cultivated millet, rice, and sorghum as their dietary staples, kept goats and cattle for milk and cheese, and supplemented their diets with peas, okra, watermelons, and a variety of nuts. Yams rather than grains were the dietary staple in the forest region. Other important forest region crops included bananas and coco yams, both ultimately derived from far-off Indonesia.

Farming in West Africa was not easy. Drought was common on the savannah. In the forest—where diseases carried by the tsetse fly sickened draft animals—plots were limited in size because they had to be cleared by hand. The fields surrounding forest villages averaged just two or three acres per family.

Although there was private ownership of land in West Africa, people generally worked land communally, dividing tasks by gender. Among the Akan of the Guinea coast, for example, men were responsible for clearing the land of trees and underbrush, while women tended the fields—planting, weeding, harvesting, and carrying in the harvested produce. Women also took care of children, prepared meals, and manufactured household pottery.

Women

In general men dominated women in West Africa. As previously noted, it was common for men to take two or more wives, and to a degree, custom held women to be the property of men. But West African women also enjoyed a relative amount of freedom that impressed Arab and European visitors. In ancient Ghana women sometimes served as government officials. Later, in the forest region, women sometimes inherited property and owned land—or at least controlled its income. Women—including enslaved women—in the royal court of Dahomey held high government posts. Ashante noblewomen could own property, although they themselves could be considered inheritable property. The Ashante queen held her own court to administer women's affairs.

Women retained far more sexual freedom in West Africa than was the case in Europe or southwest Asia. Ibn Battuta, a Moslem Berber from North Africa who visited Mali during the fourteenth century, was shocked to discover that in this Islamic country "women show no bashfulness before men and do not veil themselves, though they are assiduous in attending prayer." Battuta was even more dumbfounded to learn that in West Africa women could have male friends and companions other than their husbands or relatives.

Sexual freedom in West Africa was, however, more apparent than real. Throughout the region there existed secret societies that instilled in men and women ethical standards of personal behavior. The most important secret societies were the women's *Sande* and the men's *Poro*. They initiated boys and girls into adulthood and provided sex education. They also established standards for personal conduct especially in regard to issues of gender by emphasizing female virtue and male honor. Other secret societies influenced politics, trade, medical practice, recreation, and social gatherings.

Class and Slavery

Although many West Africans lived in stateless societies, most lived in hierarchically organized states headed by monarchs who claimed divine or semidivine status. These monarchs were far from absolute in the power they wielded, but they commanded armies, taxed commerce, and accumulated considerable wealth. Beneath the royalty were classes of landed nobles, warriors, peasants, and bureaucrats. Lower classes included blacksmiths, butchers, weavers, woodcarvers, tanners, and the oral historians called *griots*.

Slavery had been part of this hierarchical social structure since ancient times. Although it was very common throughout West Africa, slavery was less so in the forest region than on the savannah. It took a wide variety of forms and was not necessarily a permanent condition. Like people in other parts of the world, West Africans held war captives—including men, women, and children—to be without rights and suitable for enslavement. In Islamic regions, masters had obligations to their slaves similar to those of a guardian for a ward and were responsible for their slaves' religious well-being. In non-Islamic regions the children of slaves acquired legal protections such as the right not to be sold away from the land they occupied.

Slaves who served either in the royal courts of West African kingdoms or in the kingdoms' armies

often exercised power over free people and could acquire property. Also, the slaves of peasant farmers often had standards of living similar to those of their masters. Slaves who worked under overseers in gangs on large estates were far less fortunate. But, even for such enslaved agricultural workers, the work and privileges accorded to the second and third generations became little different from those of free people. Regardless of their generation, slaves retained a low social status, but in many respects slavery in West African societies functioned as a means of assimilation.

Religion

There were two religious traditions in fifteenth-century West Africa: Islamic and indigenous. Islam, which was introduced into West Africa by Arab traders and took root first in the Sudanese empires, was most prevalent in the more cosmopolitan savannah. Even there it was stronger in cities than in rural areas. Islam was the religion of merchants and bureaucrats. It fostered literacy in Arabic, the spread of Islamic learning, and the construction of mosques in the cities of West Africa. Islam is resolutely monotheistic, asserting that Allah is the only God. It recognizes its founder, Muhammad, as well as Abraham, Moses, and Jesus, as prophets, but regards none of them as divine.

West Africa's indigenous religions remained strongest in the forest region. They were polytheistic and animistic, recognizing a great number of divinities and spirits. Beneath an all-powerful but remote creator god were pantheons of lesser gods who represented the forces of nature. Other gods were associated with particular mountains, rivers, trees, and rocks. Indigenous West African religion, in other words, saw the force of God in all things.

In part because practitioners of West African indigenous religions perceived the creator god to be unapproachable, they invoked the spirits of their ancestors and turned to magicians and oracles for divine assistance. Like the Chinese, they believed that the spirits of their direct and remote ancestors could influence their lives. Therefore, ceremonies designed to sustain ancestral spirits and their power over the earth were a central part of traditional West African religions. These rituals were part of everyday life making organized churches and professional clergy rare. Instead, family members with an inclination to do so assumed religious duties. These individuals encouraged their relatives to participate actively in ceremonies that in-

This six-string wooden harp is a rare example of the type of instrument West African musicians and story tellers used to accompany themselves.

volved music, dancing, and animal sacrifices in honor of deceased ancestors. Funerals were especially important because they symbolized the linkage between living and dead.

Art and Music

As was the case in other parts of the world, West African art was intimately related to religious practice. West Africans excelled in woodcarving and sculpture in terra-cotta, bronze, and brass because they sought to preserve the images of their ancestors. Throughout the region artists produced wooden masks representing in highly stylized manners ancestral spirits as well as various divinities. Wooden and terra-cotta figurines, sometimes referred to as "fetishes," were also extremely common. West Africans used them in funerals, rituals related to ancestral spirits, in medical practice, and in coming-of-age ceremonies. In contrast to masks and "fetishes," the great bronze sculptures of Benin, which had political functions, were quite realistic in their approach to their subjects, which consisted

TIMELINE

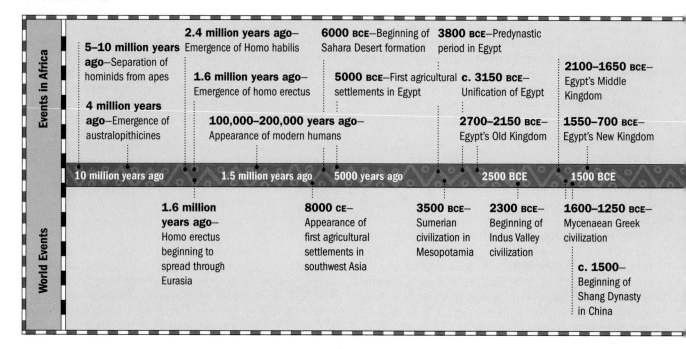

of kings, warriors, and nobles rather than deities and spirits.

West African music also served religion. Folk musicians employed such instruments as drums, xylophones, bells, flutes, and *mbanzas* (predecessor to the banjo) to produce a highly rhythmic accompaniment to the dancing that was an important part of religious rituals. A call and response style of singing also played an important role in ritual. Vocal music, produced in a full-throated but often raspy style, was characterized by polyphonic textures and sophisticated rhythm.

Literature: Oral Histories, Poetry, and Tales

West African literature was part of an oral tradition that passed from generation to generation. At its most formal this was a literature developed by specially trained poets and musicians who served kings and nobles. But West African literature was also a folk art that expressed the views of the common people.

At a king's court there could be several poet-musicians who had high status and specialized in poems glorifying rulers and their ancestors by linking fact and fiction. Often these poems were accompanied by drums and horns. Court poets also used their trained memories to recall historical events and precise genealogies. The self-employed poets, called *griots*, who traveled

from place to place were socially inferior to court poets but functioned in a similar manner. Both court poets and griots were male. It was in the genre of folk literature that women excelled. They joined men in the creation and performance of work songs and led in creating and singing dirges, lullabies, and satirical verses. Often these forms of literature used a call-and-response style similar to that of religious songs.

Just as significant for African-American history were the West African prose tales. Like similar stories told in other parts of Africa, these tales took two forms: those with human characters and those with animal characters who represented humans. The tales involving human characters dealt with such subjects as creation, the origins of death, paths to worldly success, and romantic love. Such tales often involved magic objects and potions.

The animal tales aimed both to entertain and to teach lessons. They focused on small creatures, often referred to as "trickster characters," who are pitted against two larger beasts. Among the heroes are the hare, the spider, and the mouse. Plots center on the ability of these weak animals to outsmart larger and meaner antagonists, such as the snake, leopard, and hyena. In all instances the animal characters have human emotions and goals. They are presented in human settings, although they retain animal characteristics. In West Africa these tales represented the ability of common people to counteract the power of kings and

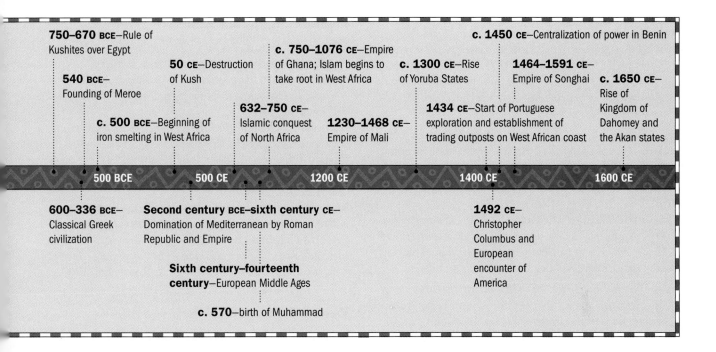

750–670 BCE–Rule of Kushites over Egypt

540 BCE– Founding of Meroe

c. 500 BCE–Beginning of iron smelting in West Africa

50 CE–Destruction of Kush

632–750 CE– Islamic conquest of North Africa

c. 750–1076 CE–Empire of Ghana; Islam begins to take root in West Africa

1230–1468 CE– Empire of Mali

c. 1300 CE–Rise of Yoruba States

1434 CE–Start of Portuguese exploration and establishment of trading outposts on West African coast

c. 1450 CE–Centralization of power in Benin

1464–1591 CE– Empire of Songhai

c. 1650 CE– Rise of Kingdom of Dahomey and the Akan states

500 BCE   500 CE   1200 CE   1400 CE   1600 CE

600–336 BCE– Classical Greek civilization

Second century BCE–sixth century CE– Domination of Mediterranean by Roman Republic and Empire

Sixth century–fourteenth century–European Middle Ages

c. 570–birth of Muhammad

1492 CE– Christopher Columbus and European encounter of America

nobles. When the tales reached America, they became allegories for the struggle between enslaved African Americans and their powerful white masters.

CONCLUSION

In recent years, paleoanthropologists, archaeologists, and historians have revealed much about Africa's history and prehistory, but much remains to be learned about the past of this vast and diverse continent. The evolution of humans, the role of ancient Egypt in world history, and Egypt's relationship to Nubia and Kush are all topics that continue to attract wide interest.

Yet the history of African Americans begins in West Africa, the region from which the ancestors of most of them were unwillingly wrested. Historians have discovered, as subsequent chapters will show, that West Africans taken to America and their descendants in America were able to preserve much more of their ancestral way of life than was previously believed possible. West African family organization, work habits, language structures and some words, religious beliefs, legends and stories, pottery styles, art, and music all made it to America. These African legacies, although often attenuated, influenced the way African Americans and other Americans lived in their new land and continue to shape American life down to the present.

REVIEW QUESTIONS

1. What was the role of Africa in the evolution of modern humanity?

2. Discuss the controversy concerning the racial identity of the ancient Egyptians. What is the significance of this controversy for the history of African Americans?

3. Compare and contrast the western Sudanese empires with the forest civilizations of the Guinea coast.

4. Discuss the role of religion in West Africa. What was the African religious heritage of black Americans?

5. Describe West African society on the eve of the expansion of the Atlantic slave trade. What were the society's strengths and weaknesses?

RECOMMENDED READING

J. F. Ade Ajayi and Michael Crowder, eds. *History of West Africa*. 3rd ed. 2 vols. Burnt Mill, England: Longman, 1984. A collection of essays on a variety of subjects by prominent scholars in the field of West African history.

Robert W. July. *A History of the African People*. 5th ed. Prospect Heights, IL: Waveland, 1998. A comprehensive and current social history with good coverage of West Africa and West African women.

Roland Oliver. *The African Experience: Major Themes in African History from Earliest Times to the Present.* New York: HarperCollins, 1991. Shorter and less encyclopedic than July's book but innovative in organization. It also provides insightful analysis of cultural relationships.

John Reader. *Africa: A Biography of the Continent.* New York: Knopf, 1998. The most up-to-date account of early African history, emphasizing the ways the continent's physical environment shaped human life there.

Christopher Stringer and Robin McKie. *African Exodus: The Origins of Modern Humanity.* New York: Henry Holt, 1997. A very clearly written account favoring the "out of Africa model."

John Thornton. *Africa and Africans in the Making of the Atlantic World, 1400–1689.* New York: Cambridge University Press, 1992. A thorough consideration of West African culture and its impact in the Americas.

ADDITIONAL BIBLIOGRAPHY

Prehistory, Egypt, and Kush

William Y. Adams. *Nubia—Corridor to Africa.* Princeton, NJ: Princeton University Press, 1984.

Martin Bernal. *Black Athena: The Afroasiatic Roots of Classical Civilization.* New Brunswick, NJ: Rutgers University, 1987.

Nicholas C. Grimal. *A History of Ancient Egypt.* Oxford, England: Blackwell, 1993.

Donald Johanson, Lenora Johanson, and Blake Edgar. *Ancestors: In Search of Human Origins.* New York: Villard Books, 1994.

Mary R. Lefkowitz and Guy MacLean Rogers, eds., *Black Athena Revisited.* Chapel Hill: University of North Carolina Press, 1996.

Michael Rice. *Egypt's Making: The Origins of Ancient Egypt, 5000–2000 B.C.* New York: Routledge, 1990.

Western Sudanese Empires

Nehemiah Levtzion. *Ancient Ghana and Mali.* London: Methuen, 1973.

Nehemiah Levtzion and J. F. Hopkins, eds. *Corpus of Early Arabic Sources for West African History*. New York: Cambridge University Press, 1981.

Roland Oliver and Brian M. Fagan. *Africa in the Iron Age*. New York: Cambridge University Press, 1975.

Roland Oliver and Caroline Oliver, eds. *Africa in the Days of Exploration*. Englewood Cliffs, NJ: Prentice Hall, 1965.

J. Spencer Trimington. *A History of Islam in West Africa*. New York: Oxford University Press, 1962.

The Forest Region of the Guinea Coast

I. A. Akinjogbin. *Dahomey and Its Neighbors, 1708–1818*. New York: Cambridge University Press, 1967.

Daryll Forde, ed. *African Worlds*. New York: Oxford University Press, 1954.

Samuel Johnson. *History of the Yorubas*. Lagos: C.M.S., 1921.

Robert W. July. *Precolonial Africa*. New York: Scribner's, 1975.

Robin Law. *The Oyo Empire, c. 1600–c.1836*. Oxford: Clarendon, 1977.

R. S. Rattray. *Ashanti*. Oxford: Clarendon, 1969.

Walter Rodney. *A History of the Upper Guinea Coast, 1545–1800*. Oxford: Clarendon, 1970.

Culture

Harold Courlander, ed. *A Treasury of African Folklore*. New York: Marlowe, 1996.

Susan Denyer. *African Traditional Architecture: An Historical and Geographical Perspective*. London: Heinemann, 1978.

Ruth Finnegan. *Oral Literature in Africa*. 1970; reprint, Nairobi: Oxford University Press, 1976.

Werner Gillon. *A Short History of African Art*. New York: Viking, 1984.

Paulin J. Hountondji. *African Philosophy: Myth and Reality*. Bloomington: University of Indiana Press, 1984.

John S. Mbiti. *An Introduction to African Religion*. London: Heinemann, 1975.

J. H. Kwabena Nketia. *The Music of Africa*. New York: Norton, 1974.

CHAPTER 2

MIDDLE PASSAGE

The slave quarters of the Spanish slaver *Albanoz*, painted shortly after it was captured by the British Navy in 1846

They felt the sea-wind tying them into one nation
of eyes and shadows and groans, in the one pain
that is inconsolable, the loss of one's shore.

They had wept, not for their wives only, their fading children, but for strange, ordinary things.
This one, who was a hunter

wept for a sapling lance whose absent heft sang in
his palm's hollow. One, a fisherman, for an ocher
river encircling his calves; one a weaver, for
the straw

fisherpot he had meant to repair, wilting in water.
They cried for the little thing after the big thing.
They cried for a broken gourd.

—Derek Walcott, *Omeros*

These words of a West Indian poet express the sorrow and loss the Atlantic slave trade inflicted on the enslaved Africans it tore from their homelands. This extensive enterprise, which lasted for more than three centuries, brought millions of Africans three thousand miles across the Atlantic Ocean to the Americas. It was the largest forced migration in history. By the eighteenth century, the voyage across the ocean in European ships called "slavers" had become known as the "middle passage." British sailors coined this innocuous phrase to describe the middle leg of a triangular journey first from England to Africa, then from Africa to the Americas, and finally from the Americas back to England. Yet today middle passage denotes an unbelievable descent into an earthly hell of cruelty and suffering. It was from the middle passage that the first African Americans emerged.

This chapter describes the Atlantic slave trade and the middle passage. It explores their origins both in European colonization in the Americas and in the slave trade that had existed in Africa itself for centuries. It focuses on the experience of the enslaved people whom the trade brought to America. For those who survived, the grueling journey was a prelude to servitude on huge agricultural factories called plantations. Many who became African Americans first experienced plantation life in the West Indies—the Caribbean islands—where they were prepared for lives as slaves in the Americas through a process called "seasoning."

THE EUROPEAN AGE OF EXPLORATION AND COLONIZATION

The origins of the Atlantic slave trade and its long duration were products of the expansion of the power of western Europe that began during the fifteenth century and continued into the twentieth century. For a variety of economic, technological, and demographic reasons, Portugal, Spain, the Netherlands, France, England, and other nations sought to explore, conquer, and colonize in Africa, Asia, and the Americas. Their efforts had important consequences for these areas.

Portugal took the lead during the early 1400s as ships from its ports reached Africa's western coast. Portuguese captains hoped to find Christian allies there against the Muslims of North Africa and to spread Christianity. But they were more interested in trade with African kingdoms, as were the Spanish, Dutch, English, and French who followed them.

Even more attractive than Africa to the Portuguese and their European successors as sources of trade and wealth were India, China, Japan, and the East Indian islands (modern Indonesia and Malaysia). In 1487, the Portuguese explorer Bartholomeau Dias discovered the Cape of Good Hope and thereby established that it was possible to sail around Africa to reach India and regions to its east. Ten years later Vasco da Gama initiated this route on behalf of Portuguese commerce. In between the voyages of Dias and Gama, a similar desire to reach these eastern regions motivated the Spanish monarchy to finance Christopher Columbus's westward voyages that began in 1492.

Columbus, who believed the earth to be much smaller than it actually is, hoped to reach Japan or India by sailing west, thereby opening a direct trade route between Spain and these eastern countries. Columbus's mistake led to his accidental landfall in the Americas. In turn, that encounter led to the European conquest, settlement, and exploitation of North and South America and the Caribbean islands, where Columbus first landed. Columbus and those who followed him quickly enslaved indigenous Americans as laborers in fields and mines. Almost as quickly, those indigenous peoples either died of European diseases and overwork or escaped beyond the reach of European power. Consequently European colonizers needed additional laborers. This demand for a workforce in the Americas caused the Atlantic slave trade.

THE SLAVE TRADE IN AFRICA

Yet slave labor was not peculiar to the European colonies in the Americas. Slavery and slave trading were ancient phenomena that existed in all cultures. As Chapter 1 indicates, slavery had existed in Africa for thousands of years, and slave labor was common in West Africa, although it was usually less oppressive than it became in the Americas.

When Portuguese voyagers first arrived at Senegambia, Benin, and Kongo, they found a thriving commerce in slaves. These kingdoms represented the southern extremity of an extensive trade conducted by Islamic nations that involved the capture and sale of Europeans and mixed-race North Africans called Berbers as well as black people from south of the Sahara Desert. Although Arabs nurtured antiblack prejudice, race was not the major factor in this Islamic slave trade. Arab merchants and West African kings, for example, imported white slaves from Europe.

Insofar as it affected West Africa, the Islamic slave trade was conducted by Sudanese horsemen. The horsemen invaded the forest region to capture people who could not effectively resist—often they came from stateless societies. The trade dealt mainly in women and children, who as slaves were destined for lives as concubines and domestic servants in North Africa and southwest Asia. This pattern contrasted with that of the later Atlantic slave trade, which primarily sought young men for agricultural labor in the Americas. The West African men who constituted a minority of those subjected to the trans-Sahara slave trade were more likely to become soldiers for such North African states as Morocco and Egypt than field workers.

The demand for slaves in Muslim countries remained high from the tenth through the fifteenth centuries

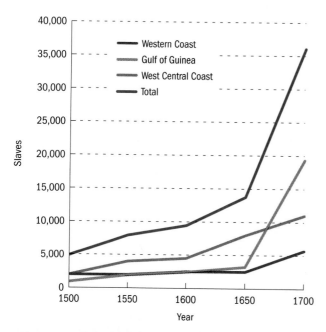

Figure 2-1 Estimated Annual Exports of Slaves from Africa, 1500-1700. Source: John Thornton, *Africa and Africans in the Making of the Atlantic World, 1400-1680* (New York: Cambridge University Press, 1992), 118.

because many died from disease or were freed and assimilated into Arab society. The trans-Sahara slave trade therefore rivaled the extensive trade in gold across the Sahara and helped make such West African cities as Timbuktu, Walata, Jenne, and Gao wealthy. According to historian Roland Oliver, it was not until 1600 that the Atlantic slave trade reached the proportions of the trans-Sahara slave trade (Figure 2-1).

THE ORIGINS OF THE ATLANTIC SLAVE TRADE

When Portuguese ships first arrived off the Guinea Coast, their captains traded chiefly for gold, ivory, and pepper. But they also wanted slaves. As early as 1441, Antam Goncalvez of Portugal enslaved a Berber and his West African servant and took them home as gifts for a Portuguese prince. During the following decades, Portuguese raiders captured hundreds of Africans for service as domestic servants in Portugal and Spain.

But usually the Portuguese and the other European and white Americans who succeeded them did not capture and enslave people themselves. Instead they purchased slaves from African traders. This arrangement began formally in 1472 when the Portuguese merchant Ruy do Siqueira gained permission from the Oba (king) of Benin to trade for slaves, as well as gold and ivory,

within the borders of the Oba's kingdom. Siqueira and other Portuguese found that a commercial infrastructure already existed in West Africa that could distribute European trade goods and procure slaves. The rulers of Benin, Dahomey, and other African kingdoms restricted the Europeans to a few points on the coast, while the kingdoms raided the interior to supply the Europeans with slaves.

Interethnic rivalries in West Africa led to the warfare that produced these slaves during the sixteenth century. Although Africans were initially reluctant to sell members of their own ethnic group to Europeans, they did not at first consider it wrong to sell members of their own race to foreigners. In fact, neither Africans nor Europeans had yet developed the concept of racial solidarity. By the eighteenth century, however, at least the victims of the trade had reached that conclusion. Ottobah Cugoano—who had been captured and sold during that century—wrote, "I must own to the shame of my countrymen that I was first kidnapped and betrayed by [those of] my own complexion."

Until the early sixteenth century, Portuguese seafarers conducted the Atlantic slave trade on a tiny scale to satisfy a limited market for domestic servants on the Iberian Peninsula (Portugal and Spain). Other European countries had no demand for slaves because their own workforces were already too large. But the impact of Columbus's voyages drastically changed the trade. The Spanish and the Portuguese—followed by the Dutch, English, and French—established colonies in the Caribbean, Mexico, and Central and South America. As the numbers of American Indians in these regions rapidly declined, Europeans relied on the Atlantic slave trade to replace them as a source of slave labor (Map 2-1). As early as 1502, there were African slaves on the island of Hispaniola—modern Haiti and the Dominican Republic (Map 2-2). Gold and silver mines in Spanish Mexico and Peru and especially sugar plantations in Portuguese Brazil produced an enormous demand for labor. The Atlantic slave trade grew to huge and tragic proportions to meet that demand (Table 2-1).

GROWTH OF THE ATLANTIC SLAVE TRADE

Because Europe provided an insatiable market for sugar, cultivation of this crop in the Americas became extremely profitable. Sugar plantations employing slave labor spread from Brazil to the Caribbean islands (West Indies). Later the cultivation of tobacco, rice, and indigo in British North America added to the demand for

The Granger Collection, New York

The city of Luanda, established by the Portuguese in 1575, became a center for the shipment of enslaved Africans to Brazil.

African slaves, although far more Africans went to Brazil than ever reached North America. By 1510 Spain had joined Portugal in the enlarged Atlantic slave trade, and a new, harsher form of slavery had become established in the Americas. Unlike slavery in Africa, Asia, and Europe, slavery in the Americas was based on race, most of the enslaved were males, and they were generally employed as agricultural laborers rather than soldiers or domestic servants. The enslaved also became *chattel*—meaning personal property—of their masters and lost their customary rights as human beings. Males predominated in part because Europeans believed they were stronger laborers than women. Another factor was that West Africans preferred to have women do agricultural work and therefore tended to withhold them from the Atlantic trade.

Portugal and Spain dominated the Atlantic slave trade during the sixteenth century. Both of these monarchies granted monopolies over the trade to private companies. In Spain this monopoly became known in 1518 as the *Asiento* (meaning contract). But the profits from the slave trade were so great that by 1550 the Dutch, French, and English were becoming involved.

Table 2-1 Estimated Slave Imports by Destination, 1451–1870	
Destination	**Total Slave Imports**
British North America	339,000
Spanish America	1,552,100
British Caribbean	1,665,000
French Caribbean	1,600,200
Dutch Caribbean	500,000
Danish Caribbean	28,000
Brazil	3,464,800
Old World	175,000

Source: Philip D. Curtin, *The Atlantic Slave Trade: A Census* (Madison: University of Wisconsin Press, 1969), 268.

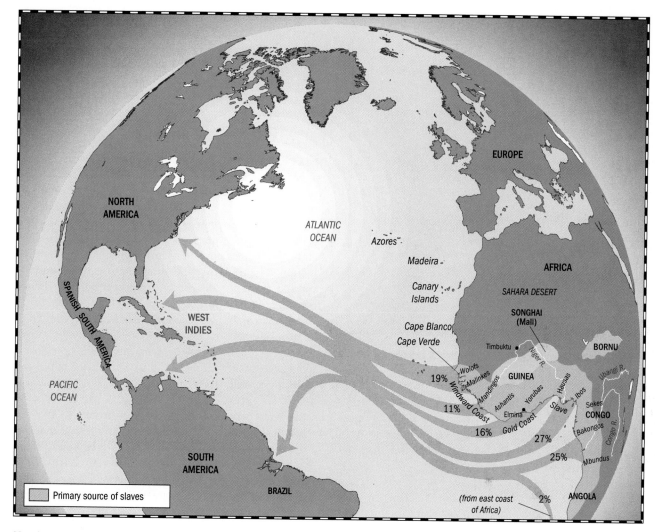

Map 2-1 The Atlantic Slave Trade.

During the early seventeenth century, the Dutch drove the Portuguese from the West African coast and became the principal European slave-trading nation. For the rest of that century, most Africans came to the Americas in Dutch ships—including the group of twenty in 1619 who are traditionally considered to have been the first of their race to reach British North America.

With the development of tobacco as a cash crop in Virginia and Maryland during the 1620s and with the continued expansion of sugar production in the West Indies, the demand for African slaves grew. The result was that England and France competed with the Dutch to control the Atlantic slave trade. After a series of wars, England emerged supreme. It had driven the Dutch out of the trade by 1674. Victories over France and Spain led in 1713 to English control of the *Asiento*, which allowed English traders the exclusive right to supply slaves to all of Spain's American colonies. After 1713, English ships dominated the slave trade, carrying about twenty thousand slaves per year from Africa to the Americas. At the peak of the trade during the 1790s, they transported fifty thousand per year.

The profits from the Atlantic slave trade, together with those from the sugar and tobacco produced in the Americas by slave labor, were invested in England and consequently helped fund the industrial revolution during the eighteenth century. In turn, Africa became a market for cheap English manufactured goods (Map 2-3). Eventually *two* triangular trade systems developed. In one, traders carried English goods to West Africa and exchanged the goods for slaves. Then the traders carried the slaves to the West Indies and exchanged them for sugar, which they took back to England on the third leg of the triangle. In the other triangular trade,

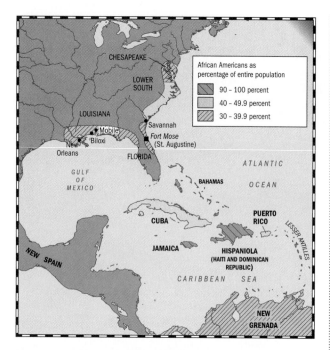

Map 2-2 Slave Colonies of the Seventeenth and Eighteenth Centuries.

white Americans from Britain's New England colonies carried rum to West Africa to trade for slaves. From Africa they took the slaves to the West Indies to exchange for sugar or molasses—sugar syrup—which they then took home to distill into rum.

THE AFRICAN-AMERICAN ORDEAL FROM CAPTURE TO DESTINATION

Recent scholarship indicates that the availability of large numbers of slaves in West Africa resulted from the warfare that accompanied the formation of states in that region. Captives suitable for enslavement were a by-product of these wars. Senegambia and nearby Sierra Leone, then Oyo, Dahomey, and Benin became in turn centers of the trade. Meanwhile on the west coast of Central Africa, slaves became available as a result of the conflict between the expanding kingdom of Kongo and its neighbors. The European traders provided the aggressors with firearms but did not instigate the wars. Instead they used the wars to enrich themselves.

Sometimes African armies enslaved the inhabitants of conquered towns and villages. At other times raiding parties captured isolated families or kidnapped individuals. As warfare spread to the interior, captives had to march for hundreds of miles to the coast where Euro-

pean traders awaited them. The raiders tied the captives together with rope or secured them with wooden yokes about their necks. It was a shocking experience, and many captives died from hunger, exhaustion, and exposure during the journey. Others killed themselves rather than submit to their fate, and the captors killed those who resisted.

Once the captives reached the coast, those destined for the Atlantic trade went to fortified structures called *factories*. Portuguese traders constructed the first factory at Elmina on the Guinea Coast in 1481—the Dutch captured it in 1637. Such factories contained the headquarters of the traders, warehouses for their trade goods and supplies, and dungeons or outdoor holding pens for the captives. In these pens, slave traders separated families and—as much as possible—ethnic groups to prevent rebellion. The traders stripped the captives naked and inspected them for disease and physical defects. Those considered fit for purchase were then branded like cattle with a hot iron bearing the symbol of a trading company.

In a rare account of such proceedings by a captive, Olaudah Equiano recalled during the 1780s how horrifying such treatment was. "Those white men with horrible looks, red faces, and long hair . . . looked and acted . . . in so savage a manner. I had never seen among my people such instances of brutal cruelty," he wrote. Like others before him, Equiano feared that the Europeans were cannibals who would take him to their country for food. According to historian Gary Nash, such fears were the product of deliberate European brutalization of the captives, part of the attempt to destroy the African's self-respect and self-identity.

The Crossing

After being held in a factory for weeks or months, captives faced the frightening prospect of leaving their native land for a voyage across an ocean that many of them had never before seen. Sailors rowed them out in large canoes to slave ships off shore. One English trader recalled that during the 1690s "the negroes were so wilful and loth to leave their own country, that they often leap'd out of the canoos, boat and ship, into the sea, and kept under water till they were drowned."

Once at sea, the slave ships followed the route established by Columbus during his voyages to the Americas: from the Canary Islands off West Africa to the Windward Islands in the Caribbean. Because ships taking this route enjoyed prevailing winds and westward currents, the passage normally lasted between two and three months. But the time required for the crossing varied widely. The larger ships were able to reach the

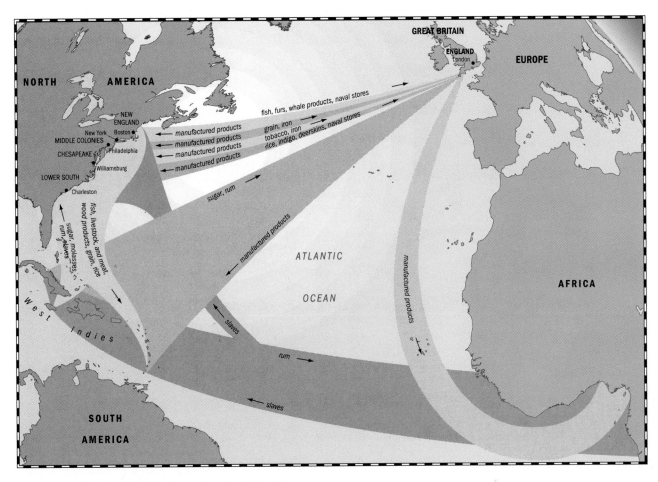

Map 2-3 The American, British, African Commercial Triangle.

Caribbean in forty days, but voyages could take as long as six months.

There were both human and natural causes for such delays. During the three centuries that the Atlantic slave trade endured, western European nations were often at war with each other, and slave ships became prized targets. As early as the 1580s, English "sea dogs," such as John Hawkins and Sir Francis Drake, attacked Spanish ships to steal their valuable human cargoes. Outright piracy peaked between 1650 and 1725 when demand for slaves in the West Indies greatly increased. There were also such potentially disastrous natural forces as doldrums—long windless spells at sea—and hurricanes, which could destroy ships, crews, and cargoes.

The Slavers

Slave ships were usually small and narrow. A ship's size, measured in tonnage, theoretically determined how many slaves it could carry, with the formula being two slaves per ton. A large ship of three hundred tons,

therefore, was expected to carry six hundred slaves. But captains often ignored the formula. Some kept their human cargo light, calculating that smaller loads lowered mortality and made revolt less likely. But most captains were "tight packers," who squeezed human beings together in hope that large numbers would offset increased deaths. For example, the 120-ton *Henrietta Marie*, a British ship that sailed from London on its final voyage in 1699, should have been fully loaded with 250 slaves. Yet it carried 350 from West Africa when it set out for Barbados and Jamaica. Another ship designed to carry 450 slaves usually carried 600.

The cargo space in slave ships was generally only five feet high. Ships' carpenters halved this vertical space by building shelves, so that slaves might be packed above and below on planks that measured only five and a half feet long and sixteen inches wide. Consequently slaves had only about twenty to twenty-five inches headroom. To add to the discomfort, the crews chained male slaves together in pairs to help prevent rebellion and lodged them away from women and children.

African slave traders conduct a group of bound captives from the interior of Africa toward European trading posts.

The most frequently reproduced illustration of a slaver's capacity for human cargo comes from the *Brookes*, which sailed from Liverpool, England, during the 1780s. At 300 tons, the *Brookes* was an exceptionally large ship for its time, and the diagrams show how tightly packed the slaves were who boarded it. While those who wished to abolish the Atlantic slave trade created the diagrams, their bias does not make the diagrams less accurate. In fact, as historian James Walvin points out in his study of the trade, the precise, unemotional renderings of the *Brookes*'s geometrically conceived design scarcely indicate the physical suffering it caused. The renderings do not show the constant shifting, crushing, and chafing among the tightly packed human cargo caused by the movement of the ship at sea. Also, during storms the crew often neglected to feed the slaves, empty the tubs used for excrement, take slaves on deck for exercise, tend to the sick, or remove the dead.

Not surprisingly, mortality rates were high because the crowded, unsanitary conditions encouraged seaboard epidemics. Between 1715 and 1775, slave deaths on French ships averaged 15 percent. The highest recorded mortality rate was 34 percent. By the nineteenth century, the death rate had declined to 5 percent. But overall, one-third of the Africans subjected to the trade perished between their capture and their embarkation on a slave ship. Another third died during the middle passage or during "seasoning" on a Caribbean Island. It would have been slight consolation to the enslaved to learn that because of the epidemics, the rate of death among slaver crews was proportionally higher than their own.

A Slave's Story

In his book *The Interesting Narrative of the Life of Olaudah Equiano or Gustavus Vassa*, published in 1789, former slave Olaudah Equiano provides a vivid account of his capture, sale, and voyage to America in 1755. Equiano was an Ibo, the dominant group in what is today southern Nigeria. When he was ten years old, African slave raiders captured him and forced him to march along with other captives to the Niger River or one of its tributaries where they traded him to other Africans. His new

OLAUDAH EQUIANO

Olaudah Equiano was probably born in 1745 in what is today eastern Nigeria. In his time the Kingdom of Benin exercised some influence over the region. As this chapter indicates, local slave raiders captured Equiano when he was ten years old. They sold him to African traders who sold him to Europeans on the coast. They in turn shipped him on a slaver to Barbados in the West Indies.

Portrait of Olaudah Equiano by an unknown artist, c. 1780.

After up to two weeks on Barbados, Equiano and those of his enslaved shipmates who could not be sold on the island were sent to Virginia on another slave ship. There Equiano spent "a few weeks weeding grass and gathering stones in a plantation." He was miserable because he had been separated from his shipmates and had no one to talk with. Equiano's luck improved when a visiting sea captain named Michael Henry Pascal purchased him. Pascal was the commander of a merchant ship and wanted Equiano to become his personal servant. By this time Equiano had been given such "Christian" names as Michael and Jacob. Pascal renamed him *Gustavus Vassa* (after the king of Sweden), which name Equiano kept for the rest of his life.

Pascal and Equiano traveled extensively and served together during the French and Indian War in North America. As a result, both of them were with General James Wolfe at Quebec in 1759 where the British won the decisive battle of the war. Equiano also lived in England where he received the schooling that allowed him to work as "a shipping clerk and amateur navigator on the ship of his second [third] master, the Quaker Robert King of Philadelphia, trading chiefly between [North] America and the West Indies."

Growing antislavery sentiment among Quakers during the eighteenth century led King to allow Equiano to purchase his freedom for forty pounds sterling in 1766, when Equiano was about twenty-one years old. This was a considerable amount of money, amounting to more than most eighteenth-century British laborers earned in a year. Thereafter Equiano toured the Mediterranean, sailed to the Arctic and Central America, converted to Calvinism, and joined the British antislavery movement.

It was as an opponent of slavery that Equiano helped organize a colony for emancipated British slaves at Sierra Leone in West Africa in 1787. Just before embarking for that country, however, his opposition to corruption in the enterprise cost him his position as Commissary for Stores for the Black Poor. Shortly thereafter he wrote his autobiography and supported himself for the rest of his life by selling copies of it in conjunction with the antislavery movement.

Although Equiano desired to return to his native land, in April 1792 he married "a Miss Susan or Susanna Cullen" at Cambridge, England. The marriage notice recognized him "as the champion and advocate for procuring the suppression of the slave trade." Whether Equiano and his wife had children is in dispute. He probably died on April 31, 1797. At that time British abolitionist Granville Sharp wrote a brief eulogy for Equiano, noting that he "was a sober, honest man—and I went to see him when he lay on his death bed, and had lost his voice so that he could only whisper."

Equiano is significant because of his testimony about the Atlantic slave trade and his service in the antislavery cause. But his extraordinary life also reveals how baseless was the assumption among Europeans and persons of European descent that black people were naturally suited for slavery.

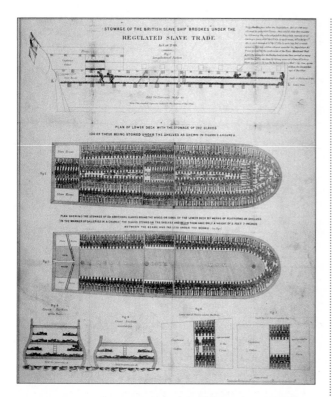

The Plan of the *Brookes,* 1788. This plan, which may even undercount the human cargo the *Brookes* carried, shows how tightly Africans were packed aboard slave ships.

captors took him to the coast and sold him to European slave traders whose ships sailed to the West Indies.

Equiano's experience at the coastal slave factory convinced him that he had entered a sort of hell, peopled by evil spirits. The stench caused by forcing many people to live in close confinement made him sick to his stomach and emotionally agitated. His African and European captors tried to calm him with liquor. But because he was not accustomed to alcohol, he became disoriented and more convinced of his impending doom. When the sailors lodged him with others below deck on the ship, he was so sick that he lost his appetite and hoped to die. Instead, because he refused to eat, the sailors took him on deck and whipped him. Later Equiano witnessed the flogging of one of the crew. The man died, and the sailors threw his body into the sea just as they disposed of dead Africans.

During the time the ship was in port awaiting a full cargo of slaves, Equiano spent much time on its deck. After putting to sea, however, he remained mostly below deck with the other slaves where "each had scarcely room to turn himself." There, the smells of unwashed bodies and of the toilet tubs, "into which the children often fell and were almost suffocated," created a loath-

some atmosphere. The darkness, the chafing of chains on human flesh, the shrieks and groans of the sick and disoriented created "a scene of horror almost inconceivable."

When slaves were allowed to get some fresh air and exercise on deck, the crew strung nets to prevent them from jumping overboard. Even so, Equiano observed two Africans, who were chained together, evade the nets and jump into the ocean, preferring drowning to staying on board. Equiano shared their desperation. He recalled that as the ship left the sight of land, "I now saw myself deprived of all chance of returning to my native country, or even the least glimpse of hope of [re]gaining the shore." Equiano insisted that "many more" would have jumped overboard "if they had not been prevented by the ship's crew."

Attempts to keep the slaves entertained and in good humor seldom succeeded. Crews sometimes forced the slaves to dance and sing, but their songs, as slave-ship surgeon Alexander Falconbridge testified, were "melancholy lamentations, of their exile from their native country." Depression among the Africans led to a catatonia that contemporary observers called melancholy or extreme nostalgia. Falconbridge noted that the slaves had "a strong attachment to their native country" and a "just sense of the value of liberty."

Although the traders, seeking to lessen the possibility of shipboard conspiracy and rebellion, separated individuals who spoke the same language, Equiano managed to find comfort in hearing others speak Ibo. They explained to him the purpose of the voyage, which he came to understand was to go to the white people's country to labor for them rather than to be eaten by them. He did not realize that work on a West Indian island could be a death sentence.

A Captain's Story

Another perspective on the middle passage is provided by white slave ship captain John Newton, who was born in London in 1725. In 1745 Newton, as an indentured servant, joined the crew of a slaver bound for Sierra Leone. Indentured servants sold their freedom or lost it as punishment for debt or crimes for a specified number of years. In 1748, on the return voyage to England, Newton survived a fierce Atlantic storm and, thanking God, became an evangelical Christian. Like most people of his era, Newton saw no contradiction between his newfound faith and his participation in the enslavement and ill treatment of men, women, and children. When he became a slaver captain in 1750, he read Bible passages to his crew twice each Sunday and forbade

VOICES

THE JOURNAL OF A DUTCH SLAVER

The following account of slavetrading on the West African coast is from a journal kept on the Dutch slaver St. Jan *between March and November 1659. Although it is written from a European point of view, it clearly indicates the sort of conditions Africans faced on board such ships.*

We weighed anchor, by the order of the Hon'ble Director, Johan Valckenborch, and the Hon'ble Director, Jasper van Heussen to proceed on our voyage to Rio Reael [on the Guinea Coast] to trade for slaves for the hon'ble company.

March 8. Saturday. Arrived with our ship before Ardra, to take on board the surgeon's mate and a supply of tamarinds for refreshment for the slaves; sailed again next day on our voyage to Rio Reael.

17. Arrived at Rio Reael in front of a village called Bany, where we found the company's yacht, named the *Vrede*, which was sent out to assist us to trade for slaves.

In April. Nothing was done except to trade for slaves.

May 6. One of our seamen died. . . .

22. Again weighted anchor and ran out of Rio Reael accompanied by the yacht *Vrede*; purchased there two hundred and nineteen head of slaves, men, women, boys and girls, and set our course for the high land of Ambosius, for the purpose of procuring food there for the slaves, as nothing was to be had at Rio Reael.

June 29. Sunday. Again resolved to proceed on our voyage, as there also but little food was to be had for the slaves in consequence of the great rains which fell every day, and because many of the slaves were suffering from the bloody flux in consequence of the bad provisions we were supplied with at El Mina. . . .

July 27. Our surgeon, named Martyn de Lanoy, died of the bloody flux.

Aug. 11. Again resolved to pursue our voyage towards the island of Annebo, in order to purchase there some refreshments for the slaves. . . .

Aug. 15. Arrived at the island Annebo, where we purchase for the slaves one hundred half tierces of beans, twelve hogs, five thousand coconuts, five thousand sweet oranges, besides some other stores.

Sept. 21. The skipper called the ships officers aft, and resolved to run for the island of Tobago and to procure water there; otherwise we should have perished for want of water, as many of our water casks had leaked dry.

24. Friday. Arrived at the island of Tobago and hauled water there, also purchased some bread, as our hands had had no ration for three weeks.

Nov. 1. Lost our ship on the Reef of Rocus [north of Caracas], and all hands immediately took to the boat, as there was no prospect of saving the slaves, for we must abandon the ship in consequence of the heavy surf.

4. Arrived with the boat at the island of Curaco; the Hon'ble Governor Beck ordered two sloops to take the slaves off the wreck, one of which sloops with eighty four slaves on board, was captured by a privateer [pirate vessel].

QUESTIONS:

1. What dangers do the slaves and crew on board the *St. Jan* face?

2. What is the attitude of the author of the journal toward slaves?

Source: Elizabeth Donnan, ed., *Documents Illustrative of the History of the Slave Trade to America,* 4 vols. (Washington, DC: Carnegie Institute, 1930–35), 1:141–45.

swearing on board his vessel. But he treated his slave cargoes as harshly as any other slaver captain.

Newton was twenty-five years old when he became captain of the *Duke of Argyle*, an old 140-ton vessel that he converted into a slaver after it sailed from Liverpool on August 11, 1750. Near the Cape Verde Islands, off the coast of Senegambia, carpenters began making the

alterations required for packing many African bodies below deck. Newton also put the ship's guns and ammunition in order to protect against pirates or African resistance. On October 23 the *Duke of Argyle* reached Frenchman's Bay, Sierra Leone, where Newton observed other ships from England, France, and New England anchored off shore. Two days later Newport

PROFILE

AYUBA SULIEMAN DIALLO OF BONDU

Ayuba Sulieman Diallo, known to Europeans as Job ben Solomon, was one of the many West Africans caught up in the Atlantic Slave Trade. But his experience was far from typical. Because he had family connections, was literate in Arabic, and used his aristocratic personality to gain favor among Europeans, Diallo was able to escape enslavement and return to his native land. His story reveals a great deal about the bonds of wealth and class in the Atlantic World during the early eighteenth century.

Diallo was born in about 1701 at the village of Marsa located in the eastern Senegambian region of Bondu. His father, the imam of the local mosque and village head, taught him Arabic and the Koran when he was a child and prepared him to become a merchant. That Samba Geladio Jegi, the future king of the nearby kingdom of Futa Toro, was a fellow student suggests the standing of Diallo's family. Diallo, following Moslem and West African custom, had two wives. He married the first of them when he was fifteen and she was eleven; he married the second when he was twenty-eight.

In February 1730 Diallo was on his way to the Gambia River to sell two slaves to an English trader when he was himself captured by Mandingo warriors and sold as well. Although the English slaver captain was willing to ransom Diallo, his ship sailed before Diallo's father was able to send the money. As a result Diallo was shipped with other Africans to Annapolis, Maryland, and delivered to Vachell Denton, factor for William Hunt, a London merchant. Shortly thereafter he was sold to a Mr. Tolsey who operated a tobacco plantation on Maryland's Eastern Shore.

Although Diallo was "about five feet ten inches high . . . and naturally of a good constitution" his "religious abstinence" and the difficulties he had experienced during the middle passage, unsuited him for field work. Therefore Tolsey assigned him to tending cattle. In June 1731, however, after a young white boy repeatedly interrupted his prayers, Diallo escaped to Dover, Delaware, where he was apprehended and jailed. There, Thomas Bluett, who published an account of Diallo's adventures in 1734, discovered that Diallo was literate in Arabic, pious in his religious devotions, and—according to Bluett's stereotypical notions—"no common slave." Bluett provided this information to Tolsey, who on Diallo's return allowed him a quiet place to pray and permitted him to write a letter in Arabic to his father.

The letter reached James Oglethorpe, the director of England's slavetrading Royal African Company, who arranged to purchase Diallo from Tolsoy and transport him by ship to England in March 1733. Accompanied by Bluett, Diallo learned, during the long voyage, to speak, read, and write English. In London Bluett contacted several well-to-do gentlemen who raised sixty pounds to secure Diallo's freedom and, with the aid of the Royal African Company, return him to Senegambia. Before he departed England in July 1734, Diallo had an audience with the British monarch, met with the entire royal family, dined with members of the nobility, and received many expensive gifts.

Diallo's wives and children greeted him upon his return to his village, but otherwise much had changed during his absence. Futa Toro had conquered Bondu, Diallo's family had suffered economically as a result, the slave trade in Senegambia had intensified, and Morocco had begun to interfere militarily in the region. Grateful to his English friends, Diallo used his influence in these difficult circumstances to help the Royal African Company hold its share of the trade in slaves and gold until the company disbanded in 1752. Quite able to differentiate between his fortunes and those of others, he retained commercial ties to the British until his death in 1773.

"The Fortunate Slave, An Illustration of African Slavery in the early eighteenth century by Douglas Grant (1968). From "Some Memoirs of the Life of Job," by Thomas Bluett 1734. Photo by Precision Chromes Inc., NYPL.

purchased two men and a woman from traders at the port, but he had to sail to several other ports to accumulate a full cargo. Leaving West Africa on May 23, 1751, for the open sea, the ship reached Antiqua in the West Indies on July 3 to deliver its slaves.

Poor health forced Newton to retire from the slave trade in 1754. Ten years later he gained ordination as an Anglican priest. In 1779 he became rector of St. Mary Woolnoth in London and served there until his death in 1807. By the late 1770s, Newton had repented his involvement in the slave trade and had become one of its leading opponents. Together with William Cowper—a renowned poet—Newton published the *Olney Hymns* in 1779. Among the selections included in this volume was "Amazing Grace," which Newton wrote as a reflection upon divine forgiveness for his sins. For several reasons, Newton and other religious Britons had begun to perceive an evil in the slave trade that, despite their piety, they had failed to see earlier.

Provisions for the Middle Passage

Slave ships left Liverpool and other European ports provisioned with food supplies for their crews. These included beans, cheese, beef, flour, and grog—a mixture of rum and water. When the ships reached the Guinea Coast in West Africa, their captains began purchasing pepper, palm oil, lemons, limes, yams, plantains, and coconuts. Because slaves were not accustomed to European foods, the ships needed these staples of the African diet. Meat and fish were rare luxuries on board, and crews did not share them with slaves. Equiano recalled that at one point during the passage crew members caught far more fish than they could eat, but threw what was left overboard instead of giving it to the Africans who were exercising on deck. "We begged and prayed for some as well as we could," Equiano noted, "but in vain." The sailors actually whipped those Africans who filched a few fish for themselves.

The crew usually fed the slaves twice per day in shifts. Cooks prepared vegetable pulps, porridge, and stews for the crew to distribute in buckets as the slaves assembled on deck during good weather or below deck during storms. At the beginning of the voyage, each slave received a wooden spoon for dipping into the buckets, which were shared by about ten individuals. But in the confined confusion below deck, slaves often lost their spoons. In such cases they had to eat from the buckets with their unwashed hands, a practice that spread disease.

While slaver captains realized it was in their interest to feed their human cargoes well, they often skimped on supplies to make room for more slaves. Some captains calculated how the eventual profits from an increased human cargo would offset the losses from inevitable deaths during a voyage. Therefore the food on a slave ship was often too poor and insufficient to prevent malnutrition and weakened immune systems among people already traumatized by separation from their families and homelands. As a result, many Africans died during the middle passage from diseases amid the horrid conditions that were normal aboard the slave ships. Others died from depression: they refused to eat despite the crews' efforts to force food down their throats.

Sanitation, Disease, and Death

Diseases such as malaria, yellow fever, measles, smallpox, hookworm, scurvy, and dysentery constantly threatened African cargoes and European crews during the middle passage. Death rates were astronomical on board the slave ships before 1750. Mortality dropped after that date because ships became faster and ships' surgeons knew more about hygiene and diet. There were also early forms of vaccinations against smallpox, which may have been the worst killer of slaves on ships. But even after 1750, poor sanitation led to many deaths. It is important to remember that before the early twentieth century no civilization had developed a germ theory of disease. Physicians blamed human illnesses on poisonous atmospheres and imbalances among bodily fluids.

Usually slavers provided only three or four toilet tubs below deck for enslaved Africans to use during the middle passage. They had to struggle among themselves to get to the tubs, and children had a particularly difficult time. Those who were too ill to reach the tubs excreted where they lay and diseases spread by human waste, such as dysentery, thrived. Dysentery, known by contemporaries as the *bloody flux*, vied with smallpox to kill the most slaves aboard ships. Alexander Falconbridge reported that during a dysentery epidemic, "The deck, that is, the floor of [the slaves'] rooms, was so covered with blood and mucus which had proceeded from them in consequence of the flux, that it resembled a slaughter-house. It is not in the power of human imagination, to picture to itself a situation more dreadful or disgusting."

John Newton's stark, unimpassioned records of slave deaths aboard the *Duke of Argyle* indicate even more about how the Atlantic slave trade devalued human life. Newton recorded deaths at sea only by number. He wrote in his journal, "Bury'd a man slave No. 84 . . . bury'd a woman slave, No. 47." Yet Newton probably was more conscientious than other slave ship captains in seeking to avoid disease. During his 1750 voyage, he noted only eleven deaths. These included ten slaves—five men, one woman, three boys, and one girl—and one crewman. Compared to the usual high mortality rates, this was an achievement.

What role ships' surgeons—general practitioners in modern terminology—played in preventing or inadvertently encouraging deaths aboard slave ships is difficult to determine. Some of them were outright frauds. Even the best were limited by the primitive medical knowledge that existed between the fifteenth and nineteenth centuries. While captains rewarded the surgeons with "head money" for the number of healthy slaves who arrived in the Americas, the surgeons could also be blamed for deaths at sea that reduced the value of the human cargo.

Many surgeons recognized that African remedies were more likely than European medications to alleviate the slaves' illnesses. The surgeons collected herbs and foods along the Guinea Coast. They also learned African nursing techniques, which they found more effective in treating on-board diseases than European procedures. What the surgeons did not understand, and regarded as superstition, was the holistic nature of African medicine. African healers maintained that body, mind, and spirit were interconnected elements of the totality of a person's well-being.

The enslaved Africans, of course, were often just as dumbfounded by the beliefs and actions of their captors. Equiano and others thought they had entered a world of bad spirits when they boarded a slave ship and attempted to counteract the spirits with rituals from their homeland. John Newton noted that during one voyage he feared slaves had tried to poison the ship's drinking water. He was relieved to discover that they were only putting what he called "charms" in the water supply. In fact such fetishes, representing the power of spirits, were important in West African religions. What the slaves hoped to accomplish is not clear. But Newton, as a Christian, certainly held their beliefs in contempt. "If it please God [that] they make no worse attempts than to charm us to death, they will not harm us," he wrote.

Resistance and Revolt at Sea

While Newton's remark shows contempt for African religion, it also expresses his relief that the slaves were not planning to poison the crew or organizing a mutiny. Because many enslaved Africans refused to accept their fate, slaver captains had to be vigilant. Uprisings were common, and Newton himself had to put down a potentially serious one aboard the *Duke of Argyle*. Twenty

men had broken their chains below deck but were apprehended before they could assault the crew.

Most such rebellions took place while the ship prepared to set sail when the African coast was in sight and the slaves could still hope to return home. But some revolts occurred on the open sea where it was unlikely that the Africans, even if their revolt succeeded, would be able to return to their homes or regain their freedom. Both sorts of revolt indicated that not even capture, forced march to the coast, imprisonment, branding, and sale could break the spirit of many captives. These Africans preferred to face death rather than accept bondage.

John Atkins, an English slave-ship surgeon who made many voyages between Africa and the Americas during the 1720s, noted that while the threat of revolt diminished on the high seas, it never disappeared:

> When we are slaved and out at sea, it is commonly imagined that the *Negroes*['] Ignorance of Navigation, will always be a Safeguard [against revolt]; yet, as many of them think themselves bought to eat, and more, that Death will send them into their own Country, there has not been wanting Examples of rising and killing a Ship's Company, distant from Land, though not so often as on the Coast: But once or twice is enough to shew, a Master's Care and Diligence should never be over till the Delivery of them.

Later in the eighteenth century, a historian used the prevalence of revolt to justify the harsh treatment of Africans on slave ships. Edward Long wrote that "the many acts of violence they [the slaves] have committed by murdering whole crews and destroying ships when they had it left in their power to do so, have made this rigour wholly chargeable on their own bloody and malicious disposition, which calls for the same confinement as if they were wolves or wild boars."

Failed slave mutineers could expect harsh punishment, although profit margins influenced sentences. Atkins chronicled how the captain of the *Robert*, which sailed from Bristol, England, punished the ringleaders, who were worth more, less harshly than their followers who were not as valuable. Atkins related that

> Captain *Harding*, weighing the Stoutness and Worth of the two [ringleaders], did, as in other Countries they do by Rogues of Dignity, whip and scarify them only; while three others, Abettors, but not Actors, nor of Strength for it, he sentenced to cruel Deaths; making them first eat the Heart and Liver of one of them killed. The Woman [who had helped in the revolt] he hoisted up by the Thumbs, whipp'd and slashed her with Knives, before the other Slaves, till she died.

Other slaves resisted their captors by drowning or starving themselves. Thomas Phillips, captain of the slaver *Hannibal* during the 1690s, commented, "We had about 12 negroes did wilfully drown themselves and others starved themselves to death; for 'tis their belief that when they die they return home to their own country and friends again." As we previously indicated, captains used nets to prevent deliberate drowning. To deal with starvation, they used hot coals or a metal device called a *speculum oris* to force individuals to open their mouths for feeding.

Cruelty

The Atlantic slave trade required more capital than any other maritime commerce during the seventeenth and eighteenth centuries. The investments for the ships, the exceptionally large crews they employed, the navigational equipment, the armaments, the purchase of slaves in Africa, and the supplies of food and water to feed hundreds of passengers were phenomenal. The aim was to carry as many Africans in healthy condition to the Americas as possible to make the large profits that justified such capital expenditures. Yet, as we have indicated, conditions aboard the vessels were abysmal.

Scholars have debated how much deliberate cruelty the enslaved Africans suffered from ships' crews. The West Indian historian Eric Williams asserts that the horrors of the middle passage have been exaggerated. Many writers, Williams contends, are led astray by those who, during the late eighteenth and early nineteenth centuries, sought to abolish the slave trade. In Williams's view—and that of other historians as well—the difficulties of the middle passage were similar to those experienced by European indentured servants who suffered high mortality rates on the voyage to America to serve out their work contracts.

From this perspective the primary cause of death at sea on all ships carrying passengers across the Atlantic Ocean to the Americas was epidemic disease, against which medical practitioners had few tools before the twentieth century. Contributing factors included inadequate means of preserving food from spoilage and keeping fresh water from becoming contaminated during the long ocean crossing. According to Williams, overcrowding by slavers was only a secondary cause for the high mortality rates.

Such observations help place conditions aboard the slave ships in a broader perspective. Cruelty and suffering are, to some degree, historically relative in that practices that were acceptable in the past are now considered inhumane. Yet cruelty aboard slavers must also be placed in a cultural context. Cultures distinguish between what constitutes acceptable behavior to their own people, on the one hand, and to strangers, on the other. For Europeans, Africans were indeed cultural strangers, and what became normal in the Atlantic slave trade was in fact exceptionally cruel in comparison to how Europeans treated each other. Slaves below deck, for example, received only one half the space allocated on board to European soldiers, free emigrants, indentured servants, and convicts. Europeans regarded slavery itself as a condition suitable only for non-Christians. And as strangers, Africans were subject to brutalization by European crew members who often cared little about the physical and emotional damage they inflicted.

African Women on Slave Ships

For similar reasons, African women did not enjoy the same protection against unwanted sexual attention from European men that European women received. Consequently, sailors during long voyages attempted to sate their sexual appetites with enslaved women. African women caught in the Atlantic slave trade were worth half the price of African men in Caribbean markets, and as a result, captains took fewer of them on board their vessels. Perhaps because the women were less valuable commodities, crew members felt they had license to abuse them sexually. The separate below-deck compartments for women on slave ships also made them easier targets than they otherwise might have been.

Historian Barbara Bush speculates that the horrid experience of the middle passage may have influenced black women's attitudes toward sexuality and procreation. This in turn may help explain why slave populations in the Caribbean and Latin America failed to reproduce themselves: exhaustion, terror, and disgust can depress sex drives.

LANDING AND SALE IN THE WEST INDIES

As slave ships neared their West Indian destinations, the crew prepared the human cargo for landing and sale. They allowed the slaves to shave, wash with fresh water, and take more vigorous exercise. Those bound for the larger Caribbean islands or for the British colonies of southern North America were often given some weeks to rest in the easternmost islands of the West Indies. French slave traders typically rested their slave passengers on Martinique. The English preferred Barbados. Sale to white plantation owners followed and then began a period of what the planters called "seasoning." This amounted to up to two years of acculturating slaves and breaking them in to plantation routines.

The process of landing and sale that ended the middle passage was often as protracted as the events that began it in Africa. After anchoring at one of the Lesser Antilles Islands—Barbados, St. Kitts, or Antigua—English slaver captains haggled with the agents of local planters over numbers and prices. They then determined whether to sell all their slaves at their first port of call, sell some of them, or sail to another island or to such North American ports as Charleston, Williamsport, or Baltimore. If the market looked good in the first port, the captain might still take a week or more to sell his cargo. The captain of the *James*, who landed at Barbados in 1676 just as the cultivation of cane sugar there was becoming extremely profitable, sold most of his slaves in just three days. "May Thursday 25th . . . sold 163 slaves. May Friday 26th. We sold 70 slaves. May Saturday 27th. Sold 110 slaves," he recorded in his journal.

Often captains and crew had to do more to prepare slaves for sale than allow them to clean themselves and exercise. The ravages of cruelty, confinement, and disease could not be easily remedied. According to legend, young African men and women arrived in the Americas with grey hair, and captains used dye to hide such indications of age before the slaves went to market. Slaves were also required to oil their bodies to conceal blemishes, rashes, and bruises. Ships' surgeons used hemp to plug the anuses of those suffering from dysentery to block the bloody discharge the disease caused.

The humiliation continued as the slaves went to market. Once again they suffered close physical inspection from potential buyers, which—according to Equiano—caused "much dread and trembling among us" and "bitter cries." Unless a single purchaser agreed to buy an entire cargo of slaves, auctions took place either on deck or in sale yards on shore. However, some captains employed "the scramble." In these barbaric spectacles, the captain established standard prices for men, women, and children, herded the Africans together in a corral, and then allowed buyers to rush pell-mell among them to grab and rope together the slaves they desired.

Equiano described such a "scramble" on Barbados. "We were conducted immediately to the merchant's yard, where we were all pent up together like so many sheep in a fold without regard to sex or age," he recalled, adding that "we were sold after their usual manner, which is this: On a signal given, (as the beat of a drum) the buyers rush at once into the yard where the slaves are confined, and make choice of that parcel they like best. The noise and clamor with which this is attended and the eagerness visible in the countenances of the buyers serve not a little to increase the apprehensions of the terrified Africans."

This engraving suggests the humiliation Africans endured as they were subjected to physical inspections before being sold.

SEASONING

Seasoning followed sale. On Jamaica and other Caribbean islands, planters divided slaves into three categories: creoles—slaves born in the Americas; old Africans—those who had lived in the Americas for some time; and new Africans, who had just survived the middle passage. For resale, creole slaves were worth three times the value of unseasoned new Africans, whom planters and creole slaves called "salt-water Negroes" or "Guinea-birds." Seasoning was the beginning of the process of making new Africans more like creoles.

In the West Indies, this process was not only an apprenticeship in the work routines of the sugar plantations on the islands. It was also a means of preparing many slaves for resale to North American planters, who preferred "seasoned" slaves to "unbroken" ones who came directly from Africa. In fact, most of the Africans who ended up in the British colonies of North America before 1720 had gone first to the West Indies. After that date the demand for slave labor in the islands had become so great that they could spare fewer slaves for resale to the North American market. Thereafter, as a result, slave imports into the tobacco, rice, and later cotton-growing regions of the American South came directly from Africa and had to be seasoned by their American masters. But many slaves still came to North America from the Caribbean to which they had been brought from Africa or where they had been born.

In either case seasoning was a disciplinary process intended to modify the behavior and attitude of slaves and make them effective laborers. As part of this process, the slaves' new masters gave them new names: Christian names, generic African names, or names from Classical Greece and Rome—Jupiter, Achilles, Plato—were common.

The seasoning process also involved slaves' learning European languages. This was especially true on the Spanish islands of the Caribbean. The Spanish of African slaves and their descendants, although retaining

Buddy.Qua

Courtesy of National Library of Jamaica

Courtesy of National Library of Jamaica

These sketches show Jamaican slaves going about their daily tasks.

TIMELINE

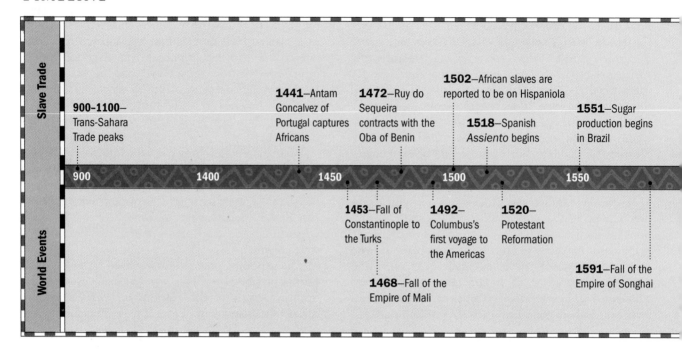

some African words, was easily understood by any Spanish-speaking person. In the French and English Caribbean islands and in parts of North America, however, slave society produced creole dialects that in grammar, vocabulary, and intonation had distinctive African linguistic features. These Africanized versions of French and English—including the Gullah dialect still prevalent on South Carolina's sea islands—were difficult for those who spoke more standardized dialects to understand.

Seasoning varied in length from place to place. Masters or overseers broke slaves into plantation work by assigning them to one of several work gangs. The strongest men joined the first or "great gang," which did the heavy field work of planting and harvesting. The second gang, including women and older males, did lighter field work, such as weeding. The third gang, composed of children, worked shorter hours and did such tasks as bringing food and water to the field gangs. Other slaves became domestic servants. New Africans served apprenticeships with old Africans from their same ethnic group or with creoles.

Some planters looked for cargoes of young people anticipating that they might be more easily acculturated than older Africans. One West Indian master in 1792 recorded his hopes for a group of children: "From the late Guinea sales, I have purchased altogether twenty boys and girls, from ten to thirteen years old." He emphasized that "it is the practice, on bringing them to the estate, to distribute them in the huts of Creole blacks, under their direction and care, who are to feed them, train them to work, and teach them their new language."

Planters had to rely on old Africans and creoles to train new recruits because white people were a minority in the Caribbean. Later, a similar demographic pattern developed in parts of the cotton-producing American South. As a result, in both regions African custom shaped the cooperative labor of slaves in gangs. But the use of old Africans and creoles as instructors and the appropriation of African styles of labor should not suggest leniency. Although the plantation overseers, who ran day-to-day operations, could be white, mixed race, or black, they invariably imposed strict discipline. Drivers, who directed the work gangs, were almost always black, but they carried whips and frequently punished those who worked too slowly or showed disrespect. Planters assigned recalcitrant new Africans to the strictest overseers and drivers.

Planters housed slaves undergoing seasoning with the old Africans and creoles who were instructing them. The instructors regarded such additions to their

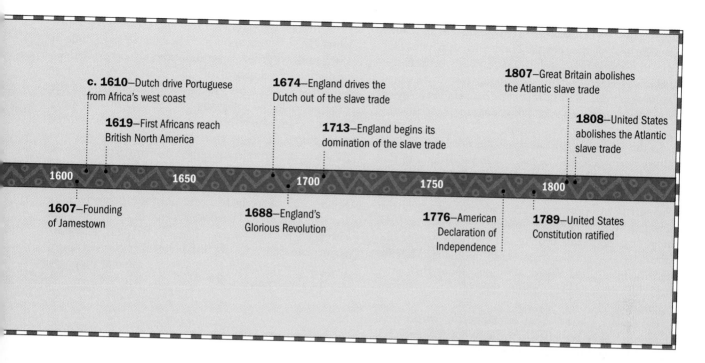

c. 1610—Dutch drive Portuguese from Africa's west coast

1619—First Africans reach British North America

1674—England drives the Dutch out of the slave trade

1713—England begins its domination of the slave trade

1807—Great Britain abolishes the Atlantic slave trade

1808—United States abolishes the Atlantic slave trade

1600   1650   1700   1750   1800

1607—Founding of Jamestown

1688—England's Glorious Revolution

1776—American Declaration of Independence

1789—United States Constitution ratified

households as economic opportunities because the new Africans provided extra labor on the small plots of land that West Indian planters often allocated to slaves. Slaves could sell surplus root vegetables, peas, and fruit from their gardens and save to purchase freedom for themselves or others. Additional workers helped produce larger surpluses to sell at local markets, thereby cutting the amount of time required to accumulate a purchase price.

New Africans also benefited from this arrangement. They learned how to build houses in their new land and to cultivate vegetables to supplement the food the planter provided. Even though many Africans brought building skills and agricultural knowledge with them to the Americas, old Africans and creoles helped teach them how to adapt what they knew to a new climate, topography, building materials, and social organization.

THE END OF THE JOURNEY: MASTERS AND SLAVES IN THE AMERICAS

By what criteria did planters assess the successful seasoning of new Africans? The first criterion was survival. Already weakened and traumatized by the middle passage, many Africans did not survive seasoning. Histo-

rian James Walvin estimates that one-third died during their first three years in the West Indies. African men died at a greater rate than African women, perhaps because they did the more arduous field work.

A second criterion was that the Africans had to adapt to new foods and a new climate. The foods included salted codfish traded to the West Indies by New England merchants, Indian corn (maize), and varieties of squash not available in West Africa. While the Caribbean islands like West Africa were tropical, North America was much cooler. Even within the West Indies, an African was unlikely to find a climate exactly like the one he or she had left behind.

A third criterion was learning a new language. Planters did not require slaves to speak the local language, which could be English, French, Spanish, Danish, or Dutch, perfectly. But slaves had to speak a creole dialect well enough to obey commands. A final criterion was psychological. When new Africans ceased to be suicidal, planters assumed that they had accepted their status and their separation from their homeland.

It would have suited the planters if their slaves had met all these criteria. Yet that would have required the Africans to have been thoroughly desocialized by the middle passage, and they were not. As traumatic as that voyage was—for all the shock of capture, separation from loved ones, and efforts to dehumanize them—most of the Africans who entered plantation society in the Americas had not been stripped of their memories or their culture. When their ties to their villages and families were broken, they created bonds with shipmates that simulated blood relationships. Such bonds became the basis of new extended families. So similar were these new synthetic families to those that had existed in West Africa that slaves considered sexual relations among shipmates and former shipmates incestuous.

As this suggests, African slaves did not lose all their culture during the middle passage and seasoning in the Americas. Their value system never totally replicated that of the plantation. Despite their ordeal, the Africans who survived the Atlantic slave trade and slavery in the Americas were resilient. Seasoning did modify behavior, yet the claim that it obliterated African Americans' cultural roots is incorrect. Anthropologist Melville Herskovits in 1941 raised questions about this issue that still shape debate about the African-American experience.

Herskovits asked, "What discussions of world view might not have taken place in the long hours when [creole] teacher and [new African] pupil were together, reversing their roles when matters only dimly sensed by the American-born slave were explained [by his pupil] in terms of African conventions he had never analyzed?" How many African beliefs and methods of coping with life and the supernatural were retained and transmitted by such private discussions? How much did African cultural elements, such as dance, song, folklore, moral values, and etiquette offset the impulse to accept European values?

THE ENDING OF THE ATLANTIC SLAVE TRADE

The cruelties associated with the Atlantic slave trade contributed to its abolition in the early nineteenth century. During the late 1700s, English abolitionists led by Thomas Clarkson, William Wilberforce, and Granville Sharp began a religiously oriented moral crusade against both slavery and the slave trade. Because the English had dominated the Atlantic trade since 1713, Britain's growing antipathy became crucial to its destruction. But it is debatable whether moral outrage alone prompted this humanitarian effort. By the late 1700s, England's economy was less dependent on the slave trade and the entire plantation system than before. To maintain its prosperity England needed raw materials and markets for its manufactured goods. Slowly but surely its industrialists realized that it was more prof-

itable to invest in industry and other forms of trade and to leave Africans in Africa.

So morals and economic self-interest were combined when Great Britain abolished the Atlantic slave trade in 1807 and enforced that abolition on other nations through a naval patrol off the coast of Africa. The United States Congress joined Britain in outlawing the Atlantic trade the following year. Although American, Brazilian, and Spanish slavers continued to defy these prohibitions for many years, the forced migration from Africa to the Americas dropped to a tiny percentage of what it had been at its peak. Ironically it was the coastal kingdoms of Guinea and western Central Africa that fought most fiercely to keep the trade going because their economies had become dependent on it. This persistence gave the English, French, Belgians, and Portuguese an excuse to establish colonial empires in Africa during the nineteenth century in the name of suppressing the slave trade.

CONCLUSION

Over more than three centuries, the Atlantic slave trade brought between nine and eleven million Africans to the Americas. Several millions more died from the trade. Of those who survived, most came between 1701 and 1810 when more Africans than Europeans were reaching the New World. Most Africans went to the sugar plantations of the Caribbean and Brazil. Only six hundred thousand reached the British colonies of North America, either directly or after seasoning in the West Indies. From them have come the more than thirty million African Americans alive today.

This chapter has described the great forced migration across the Atlantic that brought Africans into slavery in the Americas. We still have much to learn about the origins of the trade, its relationship to the earlier trans-Sahara trade, and its involvement with state formation in West and Western Central Africa. Historians continue to debate just how cruel the trade was, the ability of transplanted Africans to preserve their cultural heritage, and why Britain abolished the trade in the early nineteenth century.

We are fortunate that a few Africans, such as Olaudah Equiano, who experienced the middle passage recorded their testimony. Otherwise we would find its horror even more difficult to comprehend. But, just as important, Equiano, in overcoming his fears, in surviving the slave trade and ten years of enslavement, and in finally regaining his freedom, testifies to the human spirit that is at the center of the African-American experience.

REVIEW QUESTIONS

1. How did the Atlantic slave trade reflect the times during which it existed?

2. Think about Olaudah Equiano's experience as a young boy captured by traders and brought to a slave ship. What new and strange things did he encounter? How did he explain these things to himself? What kept him from descending into utter despair?

3. How could John Newton reconcile his Christian faith with his career as a slave ship captain?

4. What human and natural variables could prolong the middle passage across the Atlantic Ocean? How could delay make the voyage more dangerous for slaves and crew?

5. How could Africans resist the dehumanizing forces of the middle passage and seasoning and use their African cultures to build black cultures in the New World?

RECOMMENDED READING

Barbara Bush. *Slave Women in Caribbean Society, 1650–1838*. Bloomington: University of Indiana Press, 1990. The book contains an insightful discussion of African women, their introduction to slavery in the Americas, and their experience on sugar plantations.

Philip C. Curtin. *The Atlantic Slave Trade, a Census*. Madison: University of Wisconsin Press, 1969. This book provides the basis for most of the statistics used in understanding the magnitude of the trade.

Basil Davidson. *The African Slave Trade: Revised and Expanded Edition*. Boston: Little, Brown, 1980. Originally published in 1961, this readable book has been superseded in some respects by more recent studies. But it places the trade in both African and European contexts.

James A. Rawley. *The Transatlantic Slave Trade: A History*. New York: Norton, 1981. This thorough scholarly account of the Atlantic slave trade portrays it as a major "phenomenon of modern history."

Edward Reynolds. *Stand the Storm: A History of the Atlantic Slave Trade*. London: Allison and Busby, 1985. Reynolds concentrates on African societies and the responses of those subjected to the Atlantic slave trade.

ADDITIONAL BIBLIOGRAPHY

The Slave Trade in Africa

Bernard Lewis. *Race and Slavery in the Middle East: An Historical Enquiry*. New York: Oxford University Press, 1990.

Suzanne Miers and Igor Kopytoff, eds. *Slavery in Africa*. Madison: University of Wisconsin Press, 1977.

Suzanne Miers and Richard Roberts. *The End of Slavery in Africa*. Madison: University of Wisconsin Press, 1988.

Claire C. Robertson and Martin A. Klein, eds. *Slavery in Africa*. Madison: University of Wisconsin Press, 1983.

John K. Thornton. *The Kingdom of Kongo: Civil War and Transition, 1641–1718*. Madison: University of Wisconsin Press, 1983.

The Atlantic Slave Trade

Jay Coughtry. *The Notorious Triangle: Rhode Island and the African Slave Trade, 1799–1807*. Philadelphia: Temple University Press, 1981.

Paul Edwards, ed. *Equiano's Travels*. London: Heinemann, 1967.

Herbert S. Klein. *The Middle Passage: Comparative Studies in the Atlantic Slave Trade*. Princeton, NJ: Princeton University Press, 1978.

Paul E. Lovejoy. *Africans in Bondage: Studies in Slavery and the Slave Trade*. Madison: University of Wisconsin Press, 1986.

Rosemarie Robotham, ed. *Spirits of the Passage: The Transatlantic Slave Trade in the Seventeenth Century*. New York: Simon & Schuster, 1997.

Vincent Bakpetu Thompson. *The Making of the African Diaspora in the Americas, 1441–1900*. New York: Longman, 1987.

Eric Williams. *Capitalism and Slavery*. London: Andre Deutsch, 1964.

John Vogt. *Portuguese Rule on the Gold Coast, 1469–1682*. Athens: University of Georgia Press, 1979.

The West Indies

Edward Brathwaite. *The Development of Creole Society in Jamaica, 1770–1820*. New York: Oxford University Press, 1971.

William Claypole and John Robottom. *Caribbean Story: Foundations*. Kingston: Longman, 1980.

Melville J. Herskovits. *The Myth of the Negro Past*. Boston: Beacon, 1941.

Jan Rogozinski. *A Brief History of the Caribbean: From the Arawak and the Carib to the Present*. New York: Facts on File, 1992.

BLACK PEOPLE IN BRITISH NORTH AMERICA, 1619–1763

London Coffee House.

The London Coffee House was used for slave sales in colonial eighteenth-century Philadelphia.

WHEREAS, the plantations and estates of this Province [of South Carolina] cannot be well and sufficiently managed and brought into use, without the labor and service of negroes and other slaves; and forasmuch as the said negroes and other slaves brought unto the People of the Province for that purpose, are of barbarous, wild, savage natures, and such as renders them wholly unqualified to be governed by the laws, customs, and practices of this Province; . . . it is absolutely necessary, that such other constitutions, laws and orders, should in this Province be made and enacted, for the good regulating and ordering of them, as may restrain the disorderly rapines and inhumanity, to which they are naturally prone and induced; and may also tend to the safety and security of the people of this Province and their estates.

From the introduction to the original South Carolina Slave Code of 1696

African Americans were living in the British North American colonies—the region that would become the first thirteen United States—for almost a century and a half before Olaudah Equiano was briefly a slave in Virginia in the 1750s. But the black Americans of the seventeenth and early eighteenth centuries left scant written testimony about their lives. Their history, therefore, must be learned mainly through the writings of the white settlers who enslaved and oppressed them.

The passage that begins this chapter is an excellent example of what we can learn about African-American history by reading between the lines in the official publications of the colonial governments. As historian Winthrop D. Jordan points out, the founders of South Carolina in 1696 borrowed much of this section of the colony's law code from Barbados.

The code indicates that the British Carolinians believed they needed the labor of enslaved Africans for their colony to prosper. It also shows that the colonial British feared Africans and their African-American descendants. This ambivalence among white Americans concerning African Americans shaped life in colonial South Carolina and in other British colonies in North America. The same ambivalence persisted in the minds of white southerners into the twentieth century. The dichotomy of white economic dependence on black people and fear of black revolt was a central fact of American history and provided a rational for racial oppression.

The opening passage also reveals the willingness of British and other European settlers in North America to brand Africans and their American descendants as "barbarous, wild, [and] savage." Although real cultural differences underlay such negative perceptions, white people used them to justify oppressing black people. Unlike white people, black people by the 1640s could be enslaved for life. Black people did not enjoy the same legal protection as white people and were punished more harshly.

This chapter describes the history of African-American life in colonial British North America during the colonies' first century and a half, from the first permanent British mainland colony in 1607 to the end of the French and Indian War in 1763. During these years the southern plantation system that became a central part of black life in America for nearly two centuries took shape in the Chesapeake tobacco country and in the low country of South Carolina and Georgia. Unfree labor, which in the Chesapeake had originally involved white people as well as black people, solidified into a system of slavery based on race that spread to the northern British colonies. While interacting with the other peoples of early America, African Americans responded to these conditions by preserving parts of their African culture, seeking strength through religion, and finding ways to resist and rebel against enslavement.

THE PEOPLES OF EASTERN NORTH AMERICA

In the British North American colonies during the seventeenth and eighteenth centuries, African immigrants gave birth to a new African-American people. Born in North America and forever separated from their ancestral homeland, they preserved a surprisingly large core of their African cultural heritage. Meanwhile a new natural environment and contacts with people of American Indian and European descent helped African Americans shape a way of life within the circumstances that slavery forced on them. To understand the early history of African Americans, we must first briefly discuss the other peoples of colonial North America.

Eastern Woodlands Indians

Historians and anthropologists group the original inhabitants of eastern North America together as eastern woodlands Indians. But when the British began to colonize the coastal portion of this huge region during the early seventeenth century, the indigenous peoples who lived there had no such all-inclusive name. They spoke a variety of languages, lived in diverse environments, and considered themselves distinct from one another. Like other Indian peoples of the western hemisphere, they descended from Asians who had migrated eastward across a land bridge connecting Siberia and Alaska at least twelve thousand years ago. Europeans called them Indians as a result of Christopher Columbus's mistaken assumption in 1492 that he had landed on islands near India.

In Mexico, Central America, and Peru, Indian peoples developed complex, densely populated civilizations with hereditary monarchies, formal religions, armies, and social classes. They built stone temples and great cities, kept official records, and studied astronomy and mathematics. The peoples of the eastern woodlands were influenced by cultural developments in Mexico and by the northerly spread of the cultivation of maize. As early as 1000 BCE, the Adena culture, which flourished in the Ohio River Valley, had attained the social organization required for the construction of large burial mounds. Between the tenth and fourteenth centuries CE, what is known as the Mississippian culture established a sophisticated civilization, marked by extensive trade routes, division of labor, and urban centers. The largest such center was Cahokia—located near modern St. Louis—which at its peak had a population of about 30,000.

Climatic change and warfare destroyed the Mississippian culture during the fourteenth century and only remnants of it existed when Europeans and Africans arrived in North America. By that time there were a diverse variety of eastern woodland cultures in what is today the eastern portion of the United States. Indians resided in towns and villages, supplementing their agricultural economies with fishing and hunting. They held land communally, generally allowed women a voice in ruling councils, and—though warlike—regarded battle as an opportunity for young men to prove their bravery rather than as a means of conquest. Gravely weakened by disease, the woodlands Indians of North America's coastal regions were ineffective in resisting British settlers during the seventeenth century.

But because the Indians were experts at living harmoniously with the natural resources of the east coast of North America, they influenced the way people of African and European descent came to live there as well. Indian crops, such as corn (maize), potatoes, pumpkins, and squash, became staples of the newcomers' diets. British cultivation of tobacco, an Indian crop, secured the survival of the Chesapeake colonies and led directly to the enslavement of Africans in them. The Indian canoe became a means of river transportation for black and white people, and Indian moccasins became common footwear for everyone. Sexual contacts between Indians and black people were common in early America, and many African Americans have Indian ancestors.

The British and Jamestown

The British, like the eastern woodlands Indians, were also not a single nation. The British Isles—consisting principally of Britain and Ireland—are located off the northwest coast of Europe. Their native populations include the English, Welsh, Scots, and Irish. The English by the seventeenth century were dominant over the islands' other ethnic groups. But at that time, the kingdom of England was—compared to Spain, France, and the Netherlands—a poor country notable mainly for producing wool.

England's claim to the east coast of North America rested on the voyage of John Cabot, who sailed in 1497, just five years after Columbus's first westward voyage. But, unlike the Spanish who rapidly created an empire in the Americas, the English were slow to establish themselves in the region Cabot had discovered. This was partly because of the harsher North American climate, with winters much colder than in England, but also because the English monarchy was too poor to finance colonizing expeditions and because the turmoil associated with the Protestant Reformation absorbed the nation's energies.

Escaping slaves in the Carolinas during the early eighteenth century sometimes found shelter with the Tuscaroras and other Indian tribes. This map, drawn during a colonial expedition against the Tuscaroras in 1713, shows a Tuscarora fort that escaped slaves probably helped design and build.

Attempts failed in the 1580s to colonize Newfoundland and Roanoke Island, off the coast of what is today North Carolina. It took the English naval victory over the Spanish Armada in 1588 and money raised by joint-stock companies to produce in 1607 at Jamestown the first permanent British colony in North America. This settlement, established by the Virginia Company of London, was located in the Chesapeake region the British called Virginia—after Queen Elizabeth I (r. 1558–1603), the so-called Virgin Queen of England. The investors hoped to make a profit at Jamestown by finding gold, trading with the Indians, cutting lumber, or raising crops—such as rice, sugar, or silk—that could not be produced in Britain.

None of these schemes was economically viable. There was no gold, and the climate was unsuitable for rice, sugar, and silk. Because of disease, hostility with the Indians, and especially economic failure, the settlement barely survived into the 1620s. By then, however, the experiments begun in 1612 by the English settler John Rolfe to cultivate a mild strain of tobacco that could be grown on the North American mainland began to pay off. Tobacco was in great demand in Europe where smoking was becoming popular. Soon growing tobacco became the economic mainstay in Virginia and the neighboring colony of Maryland.

The sowing, cultivating, harvesting, and curing of tobacco were labor intensive. Yet colonists in the Chesapeake could not follow the Spanish example and enslave the Indians to produce the crop. Rampant disease had reduced the local Indian population, and those who survived eluded British conquest by retreating westward.

Unlike the West Indian sugar planters, however, the North American tobacco planters did not immediately turn to Africa for laborers. British advocates of colonizing North America had always promoted it as a solution to unemployment, poverty, and crime in England. The idea was to send England's undesirables to America, where they could provide the cheap labor tobacco planters needed. Consequently until 1700, white labor produced most of the tobacco in the Chesapeake colonies.

Africans Arrive in the Chesapeake

Nevertheless, Africans came early to North America. Some arrived before the British. In 1526 Luis Vasquez de Ayllon brought one hundred African slaves with him from Hispaniola (modern Haiti and the Dominican Republic) in an attempt to establish a Spanish colony near what is now Georgetown, South Carolina. A decade later, slaves, who were either African or of African descent, accompanied Hernando de Soto on a Spanish expedition from Florida to the Mississippi River. In 1565 Africans helped construct the Spanish settlement of St. Augustine in Florida, which is now the oldest city in the United States.

According to seventeenth-century accounts, the first Africans arrived at Jamestown in August 1619 aboard a Dutch warship. Although there is some evidence that thirty-two Africans lived at or near the settlement before then, those who arrived in 1619 are generally considered the first Africans in British North America. The accounts indicate that a ship sailing from Virginia joined with a Dutch warship to attack a Spanish slaver. Afterward, the Dutch ship, carrying seventeen African men and three African women, moored at Hampton Roads at the mouth of the James River. The Dutch captain then traded the Africans to local officials for provisions. The Africans became servants to the officials and favored planters.

Jamestown's inhabitants, for two reasons, regarded these twenty Africans as *unfree* but not slaves. First, unlike the Portuguese and Spanish, the English had no law providing for slavery. Second, the Africans, who bore such names as Pedro, Isabella, Antoney, and Angelo, had been converted by the Spanish to Christianity. According to English law and morality in 1619, Christians could not be enslaved. So, once the Africans had worked off their purchase price, they could regain their freedom. In 1623 Antoney and Isabella married. The next year they became parents of William, whom their master had baptized in the local Church of England. William may have been the first black person born in English America. He was almost certainly born free.

During the following years, a few other persons of African descent arrived in the expanding Virginia colony. By 1625 twenty-three black people lived in the colony, compared to a combined total of 1,275 white people and Indians. By 1649, the total Virginia population of about 18,500 included only three hundred black people. They remained, therefore, a small and distinct minority, whom the British—following the Spanish example—called "negroes." In neighboring Maryland, which was established as a haven in 1632 by persecuted English Catholics, the black population also remained small. In 1658 only 3 percent of Maryland's population was of African descent.

BLACK SERVITUDE IN THE CHESAPEAKE

As these statistics suggest, during the early years of the Chesapeake colonies, people of African descent represented a small part of a labor force comprising mainly white indentured servants. From the 1620s to the 1670s, black and white people worked in the tobacco fields together, lived together, and slept together (and also did these things with American Indians). As members of an oppressed working class, they were all *unfree* indentured servants. A clear distinction had not yet been made between white freedom and black slavery.

Indentured servitude had existed in Europe for centuries. In England parents indentured—or in other words, apprenticed—their children to "masters," who controlled their lives and had the right to their labor for a set number of years. In return, the masters supported the children and taught them a trade or profession. Unrestrained by modern notions of human equality and democracy, such masters could exercise brutal authority over those bound to them.

As the demand for labor to produce tobacco in the Chesapeake exploded, indentured servitude came to include adults who sold their freedom for two to seven years in return for the cost of their voyage to North America. Instead of training in a profession, the servants could improve their economic standing by remaining as free persons in America after completing their period of servitude.

When Africans first arrived in Virginia and Maryland, they entered into similar contracts, agreeing to work for their masters until the proceeds of their labor recouped the cost of their purchase. Such indentured servitude could be harsh in the tobacco colonies because masters sought to get as much labor as they could from their servants before the indenture ended. Most indentured servants died from overwork or disease before regaining their freedom. But those who survived, black people as well as white people, could expect eventually to leave their masters and seek their fortunes as free persons.

The foremost example in early Virginia of a black man who emerged from servitude to become a tobacco planter himself is Anthony Johnson. He had arrived in the colony in 1621, and a 1625 census listed him as a servant. By 1651 he had an estate of 250 acres and was himself the master of several servants, some of them white. Johnson was not the only person of African descent who emerged from servitude to become a free property owner in the first half of the seventeenth century. Here and there, black men seemed to enjoy a status similar to their white counterparts. During the seventeenth century, free black men living in the Chesapeake participated fully in the commercial and legal life of the colony. They owned land, farmed, lent money, sued in the courts, served as jurors and as minor officials, and even voted at times.

This eighteenth-century woodcut shows enslaved black men, women, and children engaged in the steps involved in the curing of tobacco.

The ruling elite soon began to treat black servants differently from white servants, however. Over the decades the region's British population came to assume that persons of African descent were inalterably alien. This sentiment did not become universal among the white poor during the colonial period. But it was a foundation for what historian Winthrop D. Jordan calls the "unthinking decision" among the British in the Chesapeake to establish chattel slavery—in which slaves were legally private property on a level with livestock—as the proper condition for Africans and those of African descent.

Race and the Origins of Black Slavery

Between 1640 and 1700, the British tobacco-producing colonies stretching from Delaware to northern Carolina underwent a social and demographic revolution. An economy based primarily on the labor of white indentured servants became an economy based on the labor of black slaves. In Virginia, for example, the slave population in 1671 was less than 5 percent of the colony's total non-Indian population. White indentured servants outnumbered black slaves by three to one. By 1700, however, slaves constituted at least 20 percent of Virginia's population. Probably most agricultural laborers were now slaves.

Although historians still debate how this extraordinary change occurred, several interrelated factors brought it about. Some of these factors are easily understood. Others are more complicated and profound because they involve basic assumptions about the American nation.

Among the economic and demographic developments that led to the enslavement of people of African descent in the tobacco colonies was the precedent for enslaving Africans set in the British Caribbean sugar colonies during the second quarter of the seventeenth century. Also, Britain was gaining more control over the Atlantic slave trade at a time when fewer English men and women were willing to indenture themselves in return for passage to the Chesapeake. On the one hand,

PROFILE

ANTHONY JOHNSON

Little is known of the individual Africans and African Americans who lived in British North America during the seventeenth and eighteenth centuries. A lack of contemporary accounts prevents us from truly understanding their personalities. This is also true for poorer Americans of British descent, but it is especially true of black servants or slaves. In rare instances, however, black people emerge from the bits and pieces of information preserved in court records. This is the case for Anthony Johnson and his family. Their accomplishments cast some light on African-American life in the seventeenth-century Chesapeake.

Anthony Johnson arrived at Jamestown in 1621 from England, but his original home may have been Angola. He was fortunate the following year to escape death in an Indian attack on Jamestown. He was one of four out of fifty-six inhabitants on the Bennett plantation—where he labored—to survive. He was also lucky to wed "Mary a Negro Woman," who in 1625 was the *only* woman residing at Bennett's.

In 1635 Johnson's master, Nathaniel Littleton, released him from further service. Johnson, like other free men of this time and place, then scrambled to acquire wealth in the form of land, livestock, and human beings. He received his own 250-acre plantation in 1651 under the "headright system" by which the colonial government encouraged population growth by awarding fifty acres of land for every new servant a settler brought to Virginia.

This meant that Johnson had become the master of five servants. His estate was on a neck of land between two creeks that flowed into the Pungoteague River in Northampton County. A few years later, his relatives, John and Richard Johnson, also acquired land in this area. John brought eleven servants to the colony and received 550 acres, and Richard brought two and received one hundred acres.

The Johnson estates existed among white-owned properties in the same area. Like their white neighbors, the Johnsons were not part of the planting elite. But they owned their own land, farmed, and had social, economic, and legal relations with other colonists. Anthony Johnson in particular engaged in litigation that tells us much about black life in early Virginia.

In 1654 his lawsuit against his black servant John Casor and a white neighbor set a precedent in favor of black slavery but also revealed Johnson's legal rights. Casor claimed that Johnson "had kept him his serv[an]t seaven years longer than hee should or ought." Johnson—whom court records described as an "old Negro"—responded that he was entitled to "ye Negro [Casor] for his life." Johnson momentarily relented when he realized that Casor could win damages against him if Johnson persisted in his suit. Shortly thereafter, however, Johnson brought suit against his white neighbor Robert Parker, whom Johnson charged had detained Casor "under pretense [that] the s[ai]d Jno. Casor is a freeman." This time the court ruled in Johnson's favor. It returned Casor to him and required Parker to pay court costs.

During the 1660s the extended Johnson family moved to Somerset, Maryland, where they had acquired additional land. They were still prospering as planters during the early eighteenth century when they disappeared from local records. Historian John H. Russell exaggerated when he claimed in 1913 that black people in the seventeenth century had roughly the same opportunities as free white servants. But industrious and lucky black people at that time could achieve a social and economic standing that became nearly impossible for their descendants.

FROM SERVITUDE TO SLAVERY

1619	Twenty Africans arrive at Jamestown
1621	Anthony Johnson arrives at Jamestown
1624	First documented birth of a black child occurs at Jamestown
1640	John Punch is sentenced to servitude for life
1651	Anthony Johnson receives estate of 250 acres
1661	House of Burgesses (the Virginia colonial legislature) recognizes that black servants would retain that status throughout their life
1662	House of Burgesses affirms that a child's status—slave or free—follows the status of her or his mother

poor white people found better opportunities for themselves in other regions of British North America, driving up the price of European indentured servants in the tobacco colonies. On the other, British control of the slave trade made African laborers cheaper in those colonies.

These changing circumstances provide the context for the beginnings of black slavery in British North America. But race and class played a more crucial role in shaping the *character* of slavery on this continent. From the first arrival of Africans in the Chesapeake, those English who exercised authority made distinctions that qualified the apparent social mobility the Africans enjoyed. The English had historically made distinctions between how they treated each other and how they treated those who were physically and culturally different from them. Such discrimination had been the basis of their colonial policies toward both the Irish, whom the English had been trying to conquer for centuries, and the American Indians. Because they considered Africans even more different from themselves than either the Irish or the Indians, the English assumed from the beginning that Africans were generally inferior to themselves.

Therefore, although black and white servants residing in the Chesapeake during the early seventeenth century had much in common, their masters immediately made distinctions between them based on race. The few women of African descent who arrived in the Chesapeake during those years worked in the tobacco fields with the male servants, while most white women were assigned domestic duties. Also, unlike white servants, black servants usually did not have surnames, and early

census reports listed them separately from whites. By the 1640s black people could not bear arms, and during the same decade, local Anglican priests (though not those in England itself) maintained that persons of African descent could not become Christians. Although sexual contacts among blacks, whites, and Indians were common, colonial authorities soon discouraged them. In 1662 Virginia's House of Burgesses (the colony's legislature) declared that "any christian [white person]" who committed "Fornication with a negro man or woman, he or shee soe offending" would pay double the fine set for committing the same offense with a white person.

These distinctions suggest that the status of black servants had never been the same as that of white servants. But only starting in the 1640s do records indicate a predilection toward making blacks slaves rather than servants. During that decade courts in Virginia and Maryland began to reflect an assumption that it was permissible for persons of African descent to serve their master for life rather than for a set term.

One court case, which was heard in 1640, involved the escape of three servants from Virginia to Maryland. One of the escapees was Dutch, another was a Scot, and the third—named John Punch—was of African descent. Following their capture and return to Virginia, a court ruled that all three should be whipped, that the Scot and Dutchman should have their terms of service extended for four years, and that Punch "being a negro . . . serve his said master or his assigns for the time of his natural life." By mid-decade black men, women, and children were often sold for higher prices than their white counterparts on the explicit provision that the black people would serve "for their Life tyme" or "for ever."

The Emergence of Chattel Slavery

During the 1660s, other characteristic aspects of chattel slavery emerged in legal documents and colonial statute books. Bills of sale began to stipulate that the children of black female servants would also be servants for life. In 1662 the House of Burgesses decreed that a child's condition—free or unfree—followed that of the mother. This ran counter to English common law, which assumed that a child's status derived from the father. The change permitted masters to sexually exploit their black female servants without having to acknowledge the children who might result from such contacts. Just as significant, by the mid-1660s statutes in the Chesapeake colonies assumed servitude to be the natural condition of black people.

With these laws, slavery in North America emerged in the form that it retained until the American Civil War: a racially defined system of perpetual involuntary servitude that compelled almost all black people to work as agricultural laborers. Slave codes enacted between 1660 and 1710 further defined American slavery as a system that sought as much to control persons of African descent as to exploit their labor. Slaves could not testify against white people in court, own property, leave their master's estate without a pass, congregate in groups larger than three or four, enter into contracts, marry, or—of course—bear arms. Profession of Christianity no longer protected a black person from enslavement nor was conversion a cause for manumission. In 1669 the House of Burgesses exempted from felony charges masters who killed a slave while administering punishment.

By 1700, just as the slave system began to expand in the southern colonies, enslaved Africans and African Americans had been reduced legally to the status of domestic animals except that—unlike animals (or masters when it came to abusing slaves)—the law held slaves to be strictly accountable for their transgressions.

Bacon's Rebellion and American Slavery

The series of events that led to the enslavement of black people in the Chesapeake tobacco colonies preceded their emergence as the great majority of laborers in those colonies. The dwindling supply of white indentured servants and the growing availability of Africans affected this transformation. But the key event in bringing it about was the rebellion led by Nathaniel Bacon in 1676.

Bacon was an English aristocrat who had recently migrated to Virginia. The immediate cause of his rebellion was a disagreement between him and the colony's royal governor William Berkeley over Indian policy. But Bacon's followers were white indentured servants and former indentured servants who resented the control exercised by the tobacco-planting elite over the colony's resources and government. That Bacon appealed to black slaves to join his rebellion indicates that poor white and black people still had a chance to unite against the master class.

Before such a class-based, biracial alliance could be realized, Bacon died of dysentery and his rebellion collapsed. But the uprising convinced the colony's elite that continuing to rely on white agricultural laborers, who could become free and get guns, was dangerous. By switching from indentured white servants to an enslaved black labor force that would never become free

or control firearms, the planters hoped to avoid class conflict among white people. Increasingly thereafter, white Americans perceived that both their freedom from class conflict and their prosperity rested on denying freedom to black Americans.

PLANTATION SLAVERY, 1700–1750

The increasing reliance of Chesapeake planters on slavery to meet their labor needs was thus the result of racial prejudice, the declining availability of white indentured servants, the increasing availability of Africans, and fear of class conflict. When, following this shift, the demand for tobacco in Europe increased sharply during the eighteenth century, the newly dominant slave labor system expanded rapidly.

Between 1700 and 1770, some eighty thousand Africans arrived in the tobacco colonies, and even more African Americans were born into slavery there (see Figure 3–1). Tobacco planting spread from Virginia and Maryland to Delaware and North Carolina and from the coastal plain to the foothills of the Appalachian Mountains. In the process, American slavery began to assume the form it kept for the next 165 years.

By 1750, 144,872 slaves lived in Virginia and Maryland, accounting for 61 percent of all the slaves in British North America. Another forty thousand slaves lived in the rice-producing regions of South Carolina and Georgia, accounting for 17 percent. Unlike the sugar colonies of the Caribbean, where whites had become a tiny minority, whites remained a majority in the tobacco colonies and a large minority in the rice colonies. Nor did most southern whites own slaves. Nevertheless, the economic development of the region depended on enslaved black laborers.

The conditions under which those laborers lived varied. Most slaveholders farmed small tracts of land and owned fewer than five slaves. These masters and slaves worked together and developed close personal relationships. Other masters owned thousands of acres of land and rarely saw most of their slaves. But during the early eighteenth century, even the great planters divided their slaves among several small holdings. They did this to avoid concentrating potentially rebellious Africans in one area. As the proportion of newly arrived Africans in the slave population declined later in the century, larger concentrations of slaves became more common.

Before the mid-eighteenth century, nearly all slaves—both men and women—worked in the fields.

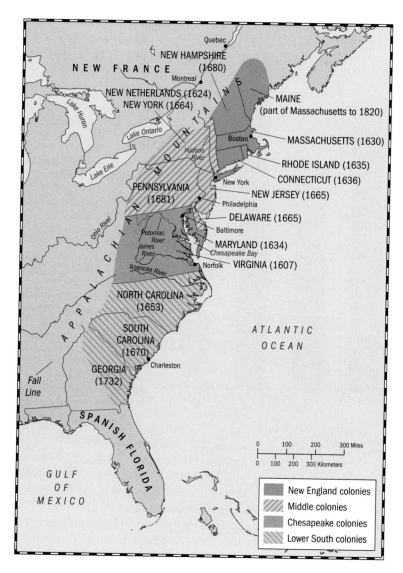

Map 3–1 The Regions of British Colonial North America in the Eighteenth Century.

On the smaller farms, they worked closely with their master. On larger estates, they worked for an overseer, who was usually white. Like other agricultural workers, enslaved African Americans normally worked from sunup to sundown with breaks for food and rest. Even during colonial times, they usually had Sunday off.

From the beginnings of slavery in North America, masters tried to make slaves work harder and faster, while the slaves sought to conserve their energy, take breaks, and socialize with each other. African men regarded field labor as women's work and tried to avoid it if possible. But, especially if they had incentives, enslaved Africans could be efficient workers. One incentive to which both slaves and masters looked forward was the annual harvest festival. These festivals were held in both Africa and Europe and became common throughout the British colonies early in the eighteenth century.

Not until after 1750 did some black men begin to hold such skilled occupations on plantations as carpenter, smith, carter, cooper, miller, sawyer, tanner, and shoemaker. By 1768 one South Carolina planter noted that "in established Plantations, the Planter has Tradesmen of all kinds in his Gang of Slaves, and 'tis a Rule with them, never to pay Money for what can be made upon their Estates, not a Lock, a Hinge, or a Nail if they can avoid it." Black women had less access to such occupations. When they did not work in the fields, they were domestic servants in the homes of their masters, cooking, washing, cleaning, and caring for children. Such duties could be extremely taxing because, unlike field work, they did not end when the sun went down.

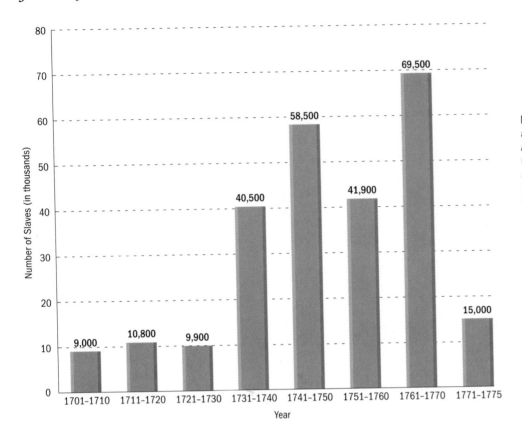

Figure 3-1 Africans Brought as Slaves to British North America, 1701–1775. The rise in the number of captive Africans shipped to British North America during the early eighteenth century reflects the increasing dependence of British planters on African slave labor. The declines in slave imports during 1751–1760 and 1771–1775 resulted from disruptions to commerce associated with the French and Indian War (or Seven Years War) and the struggle between the colonies and Great Britain that preceded the American War for Independence. Source: R.C. Simmons, *The American Colonies: From Settlement to Independence* (New York: David McKay, 1976)

Low-Country Slavery

South of the tobacco colonies, on the coastal plain—or low country—of Carolina and Georgia a distinctive slave society developed. The influence of the West Indian plantation system was much stronger here than in the Chesapeake, and rice, not tobacco, became the staple crop.

The first British settlers who arrived in 1670 at Charleston (in what would later become *South* Carolina) were mainly immigrants from Barbados rather than England. Many of them had been slaveholders on that island and brought slaves with them. Therefore, in the low country, black people were never indentured servants. They were chattel from the start. The region's subtropical climate discouraged white settlement and encouraged dependence on black labor the way it did in the sugar islands. During the early years of settlement, nearly one-third of the immigrants were African—most of them males. By the early eighteenth century, more Africans were arriving than white people. White Carolinians also enslaved more Indians than other British colonists did and during the early 1700s, approximately one-quarter of the colony's slave population was Indian.

By 1740 the Carolina low country had forty thousand slaves, who constituted 90 percent of the population in the region around Charleston. In all, 94,000 Africans arrived at Charleston between 1706 and 1776. A Swiss immigrant commented in 1737 that the region "looks more like a negro country than like a country settled by white people."

During its first three decades, Carolina supplied Barbados with beef and lumber. Since West Africans from the Gambia River region were skilled herders, white settlers sought them out as slaves. Starting around 1700, however, the low country planters concentrated on growing rice, in part because many West African slaves had experience cultivating the crop in their homelands. Economies of scale, in which an industry becomes more efficient as it grows larger, were more important in the production of rice than tobacco. While tobacco could be profitably produced on small farms, rice required large acreages. Therefore, large plantations on a scale similar to those on the sugar islands of the West Indies became the rule in the low country.

In 1732, King George II of England chartered the colony of Georgia to serve as a buffer between South Carolina and Spanish Florida. James Oglethorpe, who received the royal charter, wanted to establish a refuge

VOICES

A DESCRIPTION OF AN EIGHTEENTH-CENTURY VIRGINIA PLANTATION

The following eyewitness account of a large Virginia plantation in Fairfax County indicates the sorts of skilled labor slaves performed by the mid-eighteenth century. George Mason, one of Virginia's leading statesmen during the Revolutionary War era, owned this plantation, which he named Gunston Hall in 1758. The account is by one of Mason's sons.

My father had among his slaves carpenters, coopers, sawyers, blacksmiths, tanners, curriers, shoemakers, spinners, weavers and knitters, and even a distiller. His woods furnished timber and plank for the carpenters and coopers, and charcoal for the blacksmith, his cattle killed for his own consumption and for sale supplied skins for tanners, curriers, and shoemakers, and his sheep gave wool and his fields produced cotton and flax for the weavers and spinners, and his orchards fruit for the distiller. His carpenters and sawyers built and kept in repair all the dwelling-houses, barns, stables, ploughs, harrows, gates, &c., on the plantations and the out-houses at the home house. His coopers made the hogsheads the tobacco was prized in and the tight casks to hold the cider and other liquors. The tanners and curriers with the proper vats &c., tanned and dressed the skins as well for upper as for lower leather to the full amount of the consumption of the estate, and shoemakers made them into shoes for the negroes. . . . The blacksmith did all the iron work required by the establishment, as making and repairing ploughs, harrows, teeth chains, bolts, &c., &c. The spinners, weavers and knitters made all the coarse cloths and stockings used by the negroes, and some of finer texture worn by the white family, nearly all worn by the children of it. The distiller made every fall a good deal of apple, peach and persimmon brandy. . . . Moreover, all the beeves and hogs for consumption or sale were driven up and slaughtered there at the proper seasons, and whatever was to be preserved was salted and packed away for after distribution.

QUESTIONS

1. What does this passage indicate about plantation life in mid-eighteenth-century Virginia?

2. How does the description of black people presented here compare to the passage from the South Carolina statute book that begins this chapter?

Source: Edmond S. Morgan, *Virginians at Home: Family Life in the Eighteenth Century* (Williamsburg, VA: Colonial Williamsburg, 1952), 53–54.

---

for England's poor, who were expected to become virtuous through their *own* labor. Consequently, in 1734, he and the colony's other trustees banned slavery in Georgia. But economic difficulties combined with land hunger among white South Carolinians soon led to the ban's repeal. During the 1750s, rice cultivation and slavery spread into Georgia's coastal plain. By 1773, Georgia had as many black people—fifteen thousand—as white people.

As on Barbados, absentee plantation owners became the rule in South Carolina and Georgia because planters preferred to live in Charleston or Savannah where sea breezes provided relief from the heat. Low country plantations like those on Barbados and other sugar islands also had a high rate of mortality among enslaved Africans. Unlike the slave population in the Chesapeake colonies, the slave population in the low country did not begin to grow by reproducing itself—rather than through continued arrivals from Africa—until shortly before the American Revolution.

This low country slave society produced striking paradoxes in race relations during the eighteenth century. As the region's black population grew, white people became increasingly fearful of revolt, and by 1698, Carolina had the strictest slave code in North America. In 1721 Charleston organized a "Negro watch" to enforce a curfew on its black population, and watchmen could shoot recalcitrant Africans and African Americans on sight. Yet, as the passage that begins this chapter indicates, black people in Carolina faced the quandary of being both feared and needed by whites. Even as persons of European descent grew fearful of black

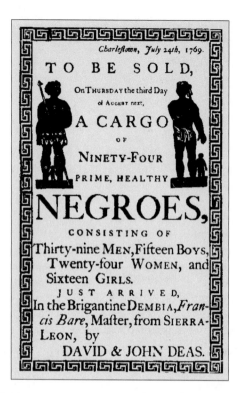

Charlestown, July 24th, 1769.

TO BE SOLD,

On Thursday the third Day of August next,

A CARGO

OF

NINETY-FOUR

PRIME, HEALTHY

NEGROES,

CONSISTING OF

Thirty-nine MEN, Fifteen Boys, Twenty-four WOMEN, and Sixteen GIRLS.

JUST ARRIVED,

In the Brigantine DEMBIA, *Francis Bare*, Master, from SIERRA-LEON, by

DAVID & JOHN DEAS.

Sales like the one announced in this 1769 broadside were common since slavery had been established in the low country ninety years earlier. South Carolina and Georgia remained dependent on imported slaves for much longer than did the Chesapeake and the North.

revolt, the colony in 1704 authorized the arming of male slaves when needed for defense against Indian and Spanish raids.

Of equal significance was the appearance in Carolina and to some extent in Georgia of distinct classes among people of color. Like the low country society itself, such classes were more similar to those in the Caribbean sugar islands than in the mainland colonies to the north. A creole population that had absorbed European values lived in close proximity to white people in Charleston and Savannah. Members of this creole population were frequently mixed-race relatives of their masters and enjoyed social and economic privileges denied to slaves who labored on the nearby rice plantations. Yet this urban mixed-race class was under constant white supervision.

In contrast slaves who lived in the country retained considerable autonomy in their daily routines. The intense cultivation required to produce rice encouraged the evolution of a "task system" of labor on the low country plantations. Rather than working in gangs as in the tobacco colonies, slaves on rice plantations had daily tasks. When they completed these tasks, they could work on plots of land assigned to them or do what they

pleased without white supervision. Because black people were the great majority in the low country plantations, they also preserved more of their African heritage than did black people who lived in the region's cities or in the more northerly British mainland colonies.

SLAVE LIFE IN EARLY AMERICA

Little evidence survives of the everyday lives of enslaved Africans and African Americans in colonial North America. This is because they, along with Indians and most white people of that era, were poor. They had few possessions, lived in flimsy housing, and kept no records. Yet recent studies provide a glimpse of their material culture.

Eighteenth-century housing for slaves was minimal and often temporary. In the Chesapeake, small log cabins with dirt floors, brick fireplaces, wooden chimneys, and few if any windows were typical. African styles of architecture were more common in coastal South Carolina and Georgia. In these regions slaves built the walls of their houses with tabby—a mixture of lime, oyster shells, and sand—or, occasionally, mud. In either case the houses had thatched roofs. Early in the eighteenth century, when single African males made up the mass of the slave population, these structures were used as dormitories. Later they housed generations of black families.

The amount of furniture and cooking utensils the cabins contained varied from place to place and according to how long the cabins were occupied. In some cabins the only furniture consisted of wooden boxes—for both storage and seating—and planks for beds. But a 1697 inventory of items contained in a slave cabin in Virginia includes chairs, a bed, a large iron kettle, a brass kettle, an iron pot, a frying pan, and a "beer barrel." Enslaved black people, like contemporary Indians and white people, used hollowed-out gourds for cups and carted water in wooden buckets for drinking, cooking, and washing. As the eighteenth century progressed, slave housing on large plantations became more substantial, and slaves acquired tables, linens, chamber pots, and oil lamps. Yet primitive, poorly furnished log cabins persisted in many regions even after the abolition of slavery in 1865.

At first, slave dress was minimal during summer. Men wore breechcloths, women wore skirts leaving their upper bodies bare, and children went naked until puberty. Later men wore shirts, trousers, and hats while working in the fields. Women wore shifts (loose, simple dresses) and covered their heads with handkerchiefs.

Thomas Coram, "View of Mulberry Street," (House and Street), oil on paper, 10 × 17.6 cm, Gibbes Museum of Art, Carolina Art Association.

About 1770, Thomas Coram painted the slave quarters and the master's house at Mulberry Plantation, located near Charleston, South Carolina. The slave cabins with their high-pitched roofs were influenced by West-African architecture.

In winter, masters provided more substantial cotton and woolen clothing and cheap leather shoes. In the early years, much of the clothing, or at least the cloth used to make it, came from England. Later, as the account of George Mason's Gunston Hall plantation indicates, homespun made by slaves replaced English cloth. From the seventeenth century onward, slave women brightened clothing with dyes made from bark, decorated clothing with ornaments, and created African-style headwraps, hats, and hairstyles. In this manner, African Americans retained a sense of personal style compatible with West-African culture.

Food consisted of corn, yams, salt pork, and occasionally salt beef and salt fish. Slaves also caught fish and raised chickens and rabbits. When farmers in the Chesapeake began planting wheat during the eighteenth century, slaves baked biscuits. In the South Carolina low country, rice became an important part of African-American diets, but even there corn was the staple. During colonial times slaves occasionally supplemented this limited diet with vegetables, such as cabbage, cauliflower, black-eyed peas, turnips, collard greens, and rutabagas, that they raised in their own gardens.

MISCEGENATION AND CREOLIZATION

When Africans first arrived in the Chesapeake during the early seventeenth century, they interacted culturally and physically with white indentured servants and with American Indians. This mixing of peoples changed all three groups. Interracial sexual contacts—miscegenation—produced people of mixed race. Meanwhile cultural exchanges became an essential part of the process of creolization that led African parents to produce African-American children. When, as often happened, miscegenation and creolization occurred together, the change was both physical and cultural. However, the dominant British minority in North America during the colonial period defined persons of mixed race as black. While enslaved mulattoes—those of mixed African and European ancestry—enjoyed some advantages over slaves who had a purely African ancestry, mulattoes as a group did not receive enhanced legal status.

Miscegenation between blacks and whites and blacks and Indians was extensive throughout British North America during the seventeenth and eighteenth centuries. But it was less extensive and accepted than it was in the European sugar colonies in the Caribbean, in Latin America, or in French Canada where many French men married Indian women. British North America was exceptional because many more white women migrated there than to Canada or the Caribbean, so that white men did not have to take black or Indian wives and concubines. Sexual relations between Africans and Indians were also more limited than they were elsewhere because the coastal Indian population had drastically declined before large numbers of Africans arrived.

Yet miscegenation between blacks and the remaining Indians was extensive, and striking examples of black-white marriage also occurred in seventeenth-century Virginia. For example, in 1656 in Northumberland County, a mulatto woman named Elizabeth Kay successfully sued for her freedom and immediately thereafter married her white lawyer. In Norfolk County in 1671, Francis Skiper had to pay a tax on his wife Anne because she was black. In Westmoreland County in 1691, Hester Tate, a white indentured servant, and her husband James Tate, a black slave, had four children; one was apprenticed to her master, and the other three to his.

Colonial assemblies banned such interracial marriages mainly to keep white women from bearing mulatto children. The assemblies feared that having free white mothers might allow persons of mixed race to sue and gain their freedom, thereby creating a legally recognized mixed-race class. Such a class, wealthy white people feared, would blur the distinction between the dominant and subordinate races and weaken white supremacy. The assemblies did little to prevent white male masters from sexually exploiting their black female slaves—although they considered such exploitation immoral—because the children of such liaisons would be slaves.

THE ORIGINS OF AFRICAN-AMERICAN CULTURE

Creolization and miscegenation transformed the descendants of the Africans who arrived in North America into African Americans. Historians long believed that in this process the creoles lost their African heritage. But since Melville J. Herskovits published *The Myth of the Negro Past* in 1941, scholars have found many African legacies not only in African-American culture but in American culture in general.

The second generation of people of African descent in North America did lose their parents' native languages and their ethnic identity as Ibos, Angolas, or Senegambians. But they retained a generalized West African heritage and passed it on to their descendants. Among the major elements of that heritage were family structure and notions of kinship, religious concepts and practices, African words and modes of expression, musical style and instruments, cooking methods and foods, folk literature, and folk arts.

The preservation of the West African extended family was the basis of African-American culture. Because most Africans imported into the British colonies during the late seventeenth and early eighteenth centuries were males, most black men of that era could not have wives and children. It was not until the Atlantic slave trade declined briefly during the 1750s that sex ratios became more balanced, and African-American family life began to flourish. Without that family life, black people could not have maintained as much of Africa as they did.

Even during the middle passage, enslaved Africans created "fictive kin relationships" for mutual support, and in dire circumstances, African Americans continued to improvise family structures. By the mid-eighteenth century, however, extended black families based on biological relationships were prevalent. Black people retained knowledge of their kinship ties to second and third cousins over several generations and wide stretches of territory. These extended families were rooted in Africa but were also a result of—and a reaction to—slavery. West African incest taboos encouraged slaves to pick mates who lived on different plantations from their own. The sale of slaves away from their immediate families also tended to extend families over wide areas. Once established, such far-flung kinship relationships made it easier for others who were forced to leave home to adapt to new conditions under a new master. Kinfolk also sheltered escapees.

Extended families influenced African-American naming practices, which reinforced family ties. Africans named male children after close relatives. This custom survived in America because boys were more likely to be separated from their parents by being sold than girls were. Having one's father or grandfather's name preserved one's family identity. When early in the eighteenth century, more African Americans began to use surnames, they clung to the name of their *original* master. This reflected a West African predisposition to link a family name with a certain location. It also helped maintain family relationships despite repeated scatterings.

The result was that African Americans preserved given and family names over many generations. Black men continued to bear such African names as Cudjo, Quash, Cuffee, and Sambo, and black women such names as Quasheba and Juba. Even when masters imposed demeaning classical names, such as Caesar, Pompey, Venus, and Juno, black Americans passed them on from generation to generation.

Bible names did not become common among African Americans until the mid-eighteenth century. This was because masters often refused to allow their slaves to be converted to Christianity. As a result, African religions—both indigenous and Islamic—persisted in parts of America well into the nineteenth century. The indigenous religions in particular maintained a premodern perception of the unity of the natural and the supernatural, the secular and the sacred, the living and the dead. Black Americans continued to perform an African circle dance known as the "ring shout" at funerals, and they decorated graves with shells and pottery in the West African manner. They looked to recently arrived Africans for religious guidance, held bodies of water to be sacred, remained in daily contact with their ancestors through spirit possession, and practiced divination and magic. When they became ill, they turned to "herb doctors" and "root workers." Even when many African Americans began to convert to Christianity during the mid-eighteenth century, West African religious thought and practice shaped their lives.

The Great Awakening

The major turning point in African-American religion came in conjunction with the religious revival known as the Great Awakening. This extensive social movement of the mid- to late-eighteenth century grew out of growing dissatisfaction among white Americans with a deterministic and increasingly formalistic style of Protestantism that seemed to deny most people a chance for salvation. During the early 1730s in western Massachusetts, a Congregationalist minister named Jonathan Edwards began an emotional and participatory ministry aimed at bringing more people into the church. Later that decade, George Whitefield, an Englishman who with John Wesley founded the Methodist Church, carried a similarly evangelical style of Christianity to the mainland colonies. In his sermons, Whitefield appealed to emotions, offered salvation to all who believed in Christ, and—while he did not advocate emancipation—preached to black people as well as white people.

Some people of African descent had converted to Christianity before Whitefield's arrival in North America. But two factors had prevented widespread black conversion. First, most masters feared that converted slaves would interpret their new religious status as a step toward freedom and equality. A South Carolina minister lamented in 1713 that "the Masters of Slaves are generally of Opinion that a Slave grows worse by being a Christian; and therefore instead of instructing them in the principles of Christianity . . . malign and traduce those that attempt it." Second, many slaves—as we note above—continued to derive spiritual satisfaction from their ancestral religions and were not attracted to Christianity.

With the Great Awakening, however, a process of conversion began. African Americans now not only became Christians but influenced white religion. This was because the religious movement unwittingly emphasized points of convergence between Christianity and indigenous West African religions. The African belief in ancestral gods, nature gods, and an almighty creator, for example, resembled the Christian trinity of Father, Son, and Holy Ghost. Even more important, the style of preaching Whitefield and other evan-

gelicals adopted had much in common with West African "spirit possession." Like their African counterparts, eighteenth-century revivalists in North America emphasized personal rebirth, singing, movement, and emotion. The practice of total body immersion during baptism in rivers, ponds, and lakes that gave the Baptist church its name paralleled West African water rites.

Because it drew African Americans into an evangelical movement that helped shape American society, the Great Awakening increased black acculturation. Revivalists appealed to the poor of all races and emphasized spiritual equality. Evangelical Anglican, Baptist, Methodist, and Presbyterian churches welcomed blacks. Members of these biracial churches addressed each other as *brother* and *sister*. Black members took communion with white members, served as church officers, and were subject to the same church discipline. By the late eighteenth century, black men were being ordained as priests and ministers and—often while still enslaved—preached to white congregations and thereby influenced the white people's perception of how services should be conducted.

Black worshipers also influenced white preachers. In 1756 a white minister in Virginia noted that African Americans spent nights in his kitchen. He recorded in his diary that "sometimes, when I have awakened about two or three a-clock in the morning, a torrent of sacred harmony poured into my chamber, and carried my mind away to Heaven."

Other factors favored the development of a distinct African-American church. From the start, white churches seated black people apart from white people, belying claims to spiritual equality. Black members took communion *after* white members. Masters also tried to use religion to instill such self-serving Christian virtues as meekness, humility, and obedience in their chattels. Consequently African Americans established their own churches when they could. Dancing, shouting, clapping, and singing became especially characteristic of their religious meetings. Black spirituals probably date from the eighteenth century and like African-American Christianity itself, blended West African and European elements.

African Americans also retained the West African assumption that the souls of the dead returned to their homeland and rejoined their ancestors. Reflecting this family-oriented view of death, African-American funerals were often loud and joyous occasions with dancing, laughing, and drinking. Perhaps most important, the emerging black church reinforced black people's collective identity and helped them persevere in slavery.

V O I C E S

A POEM BY JUPITER HAMMON

Jupiter Hammon (1711–1806?) was a favored slave living on Long Island, New York, when he composed "An Evening Thought. Salvation by Christ, with Penitential Cries" on Christmas day 1760, an excerpt of which appears here. A Calvinist preacher and America's first published black poet, Hammon was deeply influenced by the Great Awakening's emphasis on repentance and Christ's spiritual sovereignty.

Salvation comes by Jesus Christ alone,
   The only Son of God;
Redemption now to every one,
   That love his holy Word.
Dear Jesus we would fly to Thee,
   And leave off every Sin,
Thy tender Mercy well agree;
   Salvation from our King.

Salvation comes from God we know,
   The true and only One;
It's well agreed and certain true,
   He gave his only Son.

Lord hear our penitential Cry:
   Salvation from above
It is the Lord that doth supply,
   With his Redeeming Love.

Dear Jesus let the Nations cry,
   And all the People say,
Salvation comes from Christ on high,
   Haste on Tribunal Day.
We cry as Sinners to the Lord,
   Salvation to obtain;
It is firmly fixt his holy Word,
   Ye shall not cry in vain.

QUESTIONS

1. What elements in Hammon's poem might appeal to African Americans of his time?

2. Does Hammond suggest a relationship between Christ and social justice?

Source: Dorothy Porter, ed., *Early Negro Writing, 1760–1837* (1971; reprint Baltimore: Black Classic Press, 1995).

Language, Music, and Folk Literature

Although African Americans did not retain their ancestral languages, those languages contributed to the pidgins and creolized languages that became Black English by the nineteenth century. It was in the low country, with its large and isolated black populations, that African-English creoles lasted the longest. The Gullah and Geechee dialects of the sea islands of South Carolina and Georgia, which combine African words and some African grammatical elements with a basically English structure, are still spoken today. In other regions, where black people were less numerous, the creoles were less enduring. Nevertheless, they contributed many words to American—particularly southern—English. Among them are *yam, banjo* (from mbanza), *tote, goober* (peanut), *buckra* (white man), *cooter* (tortoise), *gumbo* (okra), *nanse* (spider), *samba* (dance), *tabby* (a form of concrete), and *voodoo.*

Music was another essential part of West African life, and it remained so among African Americans, who preserved an antiphonal, call-and-response style of singing with an emphasis on improvisation, complex rhythms, and strong beat. They sang while working and during religious ceremonies. Early on, masters banned drums and horns because of their potential for long-distance communication among slaves. But the African banjo survived in America, and African Americans quickly adopted the violin and guitar. At night in their cabins or around communal fires, slaves accompanied these instruments with bones and spoons. Music may have been the most important aspect of African culture in the lives of American slaves. Eventually African-American music was to influence all forms of American popular music.

West-African folk literature also survived in North America. African tales, proverbs, and riddles—with accretions from American-Indian and European stories—

This photograph depicts two versions of the African *mbanza*. They feature leather stretched across a gourd, a wooden neck, and strings made of animal gut. In America such instruments became known as banjos.

entertained, instructed, and united African Americans. Just as the black people on the sea islands of South Carolina and Georgia were most able to retain elements of African language, so did their folk literature remain closest to its African counterpart. Africans used tales of how weak animals like rabbits outsmarted stronger animals like hyenas and lions to symbolize the power of the common people over unjust rulers. African Americans used similar tales to portray the ability of slaves to outsmart and ridicule their masters.

The African-American Impact on Colonial Culture

African Americans also influenced the development of white culture. As early as the seventeenth century, black musicians performed English ballads for white audiences in a distinctively African-American style. They began to shape American music. The African-American imprint on southern diction and phraseology is particularly clear. Generations of slaveholders' children, who were often raised by black women, were influenced by African-American speech patterns and intonations. Black people also influenced white notions about portents, spirits, and folk remedies. Seventeenth- and eighteenth-century English lore about such things was not that different from West African lore, and American whites consulted black conjurors and "herb doctors." Black cooks in early America influenced both southern white and African-American eating habits. Preferences for barbecued pork, fried chicken, black-eyed peas, and collard and mustard greens owed much to West African culinary traditions.

African Americans also used West African culture and skills to shape the way work was done in the American South during and after colonial times. Africans accustomed to collective agricultural labor imposed the "gang system" on most American plantations. Masters learned that their slaves would work harder and longer in groups. Their work songs were also an African legacy as was the slow, deliberate pace of their labor. By the mid-eighteenth century, masters often employed slaves as builders. As a result, African styles and decorative techniques influenced southern colonial architecture. Black builders introduced African-style high-peaked roofs, front porches, wood carvings, and elaborate iron work.

SLAVERY IN THE NORTHERN COLONIES

The British mainland colonies north of the Chesapeake had histories, cultures, demographics, and economies that differed considerably from those of the southern colonies. Organized religion was much more important in the foundation of most of the northern colonies than those of the South (except for Maryland). In New England, where the Pilgrims settled in 1620 and the Puritans in 1630, religious utopianism shaped colonial life. The same was true in the West Jersey portion of New Jersey, where members of the English pietist Society of Friends—or Quakers—began to settle during the 1670s, and Pennsylvania, which William Penn founded in 1682 as a Quaker colony. Quakers, like other pietists, emphasized nonviolence and a divine spirit within all humans, both of which beliefs disposed some of them to become early opponents of slavery.

Even more important than religion in shaping life in northern British North America were a cooler climate, sufficient numbers of white laborers, lack of a staple crop, and a diversified economy. All these circumstances made black slavery in the colonial North less extensive than and different from its southern counterparts.

By the end of the colonial period during the 1770s, only 50,000 African Americans lived in the northern colonies in comparison to 400,000 in the southern colonies. In the North, black people were 4.5 percent of the total population, compared to 40 percent in the South. But, as in the South, the northern black population varied in size from place to place. By 1770, enslaved African Americans constituted 10 percent of the population of Rhode Island, New Jersey, New York, and Pennsylvania. New York City had a particularly large black population, 20 percent of its total by 1750 (Figure 3–2).

Like all Americans during the colonial era, most northern slaves were agricultural laborers. But, in contrast to those in the South, slaves in the North typically lived in their master's house and worked with the master, his family, and one or two other slaves on a small farm. In northern cities, which were often home ports for slavetraders, enslaved people of African descent

This woodcut shows the sentencing of two of the individuals charged in a New York City revolt of 1741. Of the 150 black people and 25 white people charged with arson, 31 black people and four white people were executed.

worked as artisans, shopkeepers, messengers, domestic servants, and general laborers.

Consequently, most northern African Americans led different lives from those in the South. Mainly because New England had so few slaves—but also because of Puritan religious principles—slavery there was least oppressive. White people had no reason to suspect that the small and dispersed black population posed a threat of rebellion. The local slave codes were milder and—except for the ban on miscegenation—not rigidly enforced. New England slaves, for example, could legally own, transfer, and inherit property. From the early seventeenth century onward, Puritans converted to Christianity the Africans and African Americans who came among them, recognizing their spiritual equality before God.

In the middle colonies of New York, New Jersey, and Pennsylvania, where black populations were larger and hence perceived by white people to be more threatening, the slave codes were stricter and penalties harsher. But even in these colonies, the curfews imposed on Africans and African Americans and restrictions on their ability to gather together were less well enforced than they were farther south.

These conditions encouraged rapid assimilation. Because of their small numbers, frequent isolation from others of African descent, and close association with their masters, northern slaves had fewer opportunities to preserve an African heritage. There was an increase in

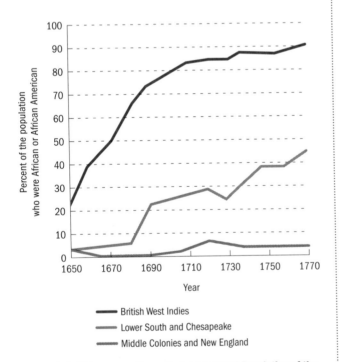

Figure 3–2 Africans as a Percentage of the Total Population of the British American Colonies, 1650–1770. From *Time on the Cross: The Economics of American Negro Slavery* by Robert W. Fogel and Stanley L. Engerman. Copyright © 1974 by Robert W. Fogel and Stanley L. Engerman. Reprinted by permission of W. W. Norton & Company, Inc.

African customs among black northerners between 1740 and 1770. Before that time most northern slaves had been born or "seasoned" in the South or West Indies. During the middle decades of the eighteenth century direct imports of African slaves into the North temporarily increased. With them came knowledge of African life. But overall, the less harsh and more peripheral nature of slavery in this region limited the retention of African perspectives, just as it allowed the slaves more freedom than most of their southern counterparts enjoyed.

BLACK WOMEN IN COLONIAL AMERICA

The differences between slavery in the New England and southern colonies are particularly clear in the lives of black women. In New England, where religion and demographics made the boundary between slavery and freedom permeable, black women distinguished themselves in a variety of ways. The thoroughly acculturated Lucy Terry Prince of Deerfield, Massachusetts, published poetry during the 1740s and had gained her freedom by 1756. Other black women succeeded as bakers and weavers. But in the South, where most black women lived, they had few opportunities for work beyond the tobacco and rice fields and domestic labor in the homes of their masters.

Although black women were more expensive than white indentured servants—because their children would be slaves and thus their master's property—slave traders and slaveholders never valued them as highly as they did black men. Until 1660 the British mainland colonies imported twice as many African men as women. Thereafter the ratio dropped to three African men for every two women, and by the mid-eighteenth century, natural population growth among African Americans had corrected the sexual imbalance.

During the late seventeenth and the eighteenth centuries, approximately 90 percent of southern black women worked in the fields, as was customary for women in West Africa. White women sometimes did field work as well, but masters considered black women tougher than white women and therefore able to do more hard physical labor. Black women also mothered their children and cooked for their families, chores that involved lugging firewood and water and tending fires, as well as preparing meals. Like other women of their time, colonial black women suffered from inadequate medical attention while giving birth. But because black women worked until the moment they delivered, they were more likely than white women to experience complications in giving birth and to bear low-weight babies.

As the eighteenth century passed, more black women became house servants. Yet most jobs as maids, cooks, and body servants went to the young, the old, or the infirm. Black women also wet-nursed their master's children. None of this was easy work; those who did it were under constant white supervision and were particularly subject to the sexual exploitation that characterized chattel slavery.

European captains and crews molested and raped black women during the middle passage. Masters and overseers similarly used their power to force themselves on female slaves. The results were evident in the large mixed-race populations in the colonies and in the psychological damage it inflicted on African-American women and their mates. In particular, the sexual abuse of black women by white men disrupted the emerging black families in North America because black men usually could not protect their wives from it.

BLACK RESISTANCE AND REBELLION

That masters regularly used their authority to sexually abuse black women and thereby humiliate black men dramatizes the oppressiveness of a slave system based on race and physical force. Masters often rewarded black women who became their mistresses, just as masters and overseers used incentives to get more labor from field hands. But slaves who did not comply in either case faced a beating. Slavery in America was always a system that relied ultimately on physical force to deny freedom to African Americans. From its start, black men and women responded by resisting their masters as well as they could.

Such resistance ranged from sullen "gold-bricking" to sabotage, escape, and rebellion. Before the late eighteenth century, however, resistance and rebellion were not part of a coherent antislavery effort. Before the spread of ideas about natural human rights and universal liberty associated with the American and French revolutions, slave resistance and revolt did not aim to destroy slavery as a social system. Africans and African Americans resisted, escaped, and rebelled not as part of an effort to free all slaves. Instead—in the case of resistance—they aimed to force masters to make concessions within the framework of slavery and—in the case of escape and rebellion—to relieve themselves, their friends, and their families from intolerable disgrace and suffering.

TIMELINE

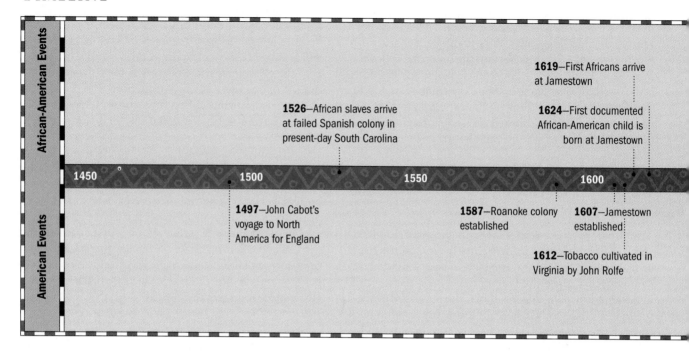

African-American Events

1526—African slaves arrive at failed Spanish colony in present-day South Carolina

1619—First Africans arrive at Jamestown

1624—First documented African-American child is born at Jamestown

1450   1500   1550   1600

American Events

1497—John Cabot's voyage to North America for England

1587—Roanoke colony established

1607—Jamestown established

1612—Tobacco cultivated in Virginia by John Rolfe

African men and women newly arrived in North America were most open in defying their masters. They frequently refused to work and often could not be persuaded by punishment to change their behavior. "You would really be surpris'd at their Perseverance," one frustrated master commented. "They often die before they can be conquered." Africans tended to escape in groups of individuals who shared a common homeland and language. When they succeeded, they usually became "outliers," living near and stealing from their master's estate. In 1672, Virginia's colonial government began paying bounties to anyone who killed such outlaws, and six decades later, the governor of South Carolina offered similar rewards. In some instances escaped slaves known as *maroons*—a term derived from the Spanish word *cimarron*, meaning wild—established their own settlements in inaccessible regions.

The most durable of such maroon communities in North America was established in the Spanish colony of Florida. In 1733 the Spanish king officially made this colony a refuge for slaves escaping from the British colonies, although he did not free slaves who were already there. Many such escapees joined the Seminole Indian nation and thereby gained protection during the period between 1763 and 1783 when the British ruled Florida and after 1821 when the United States took control. It was in part to destroy this refuge for escaped slaves that the United States fought the Seminole War from 1835 to 1842. Other maroon settlements existed in the South Carolina and Georgia backcountry and the Great Dismal Swamp of southern Virginia.

As slaves became acculturated, forms of slave resistance changed. To avoid punishment, African Americans replaced open defiance with more subtle day-to-day obstructionism. They malingered, broke tools, mistreated domestic animals, destroyed crops, poisoned their masters, and stole. Not every slave who acted this way, of course, was consciously resisting enslavement. But masters assumed that they were. In 1770 Benjamin Franklin—who owned slaves—complained to a European friend, "Perhaps you may imagine the Negroes to be mild-tempered, tractable Kind of People. Some of them indeed are so. But the Majority are of plotting Disposition, dark, sullen, malicious, revengeful and cruel in the highest Degree." Acculturation also brought different escape patterns. Increasingly it was the more assimilated slaves who escaped. They were predominantly young men who left on their own and relied on their knowledge of American society to pass as free. Although some continued to head for maroon settlements, most sought safety among relatives, in towns, or in the North Carolina piedmont where there were few slaves.

Rebellions were far rarer in colonial North America than resistance or escape. There were more and larger rebellions during the early eighteenth century in Jamaica and Brazil. This discrepancy was mainly the

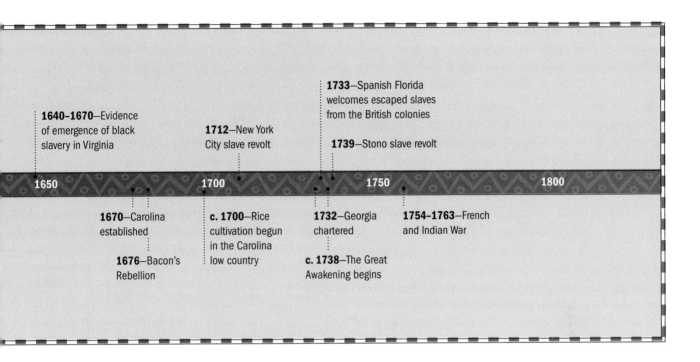

1640-1670—Evidence of emergence of black slavery in Virginia

1712—New York City slave revolt

1733—Spanish Florida welcomes escaped slaves from the British colonies

1739—Stono slave revolt

1650   1700   1750   1800

1670—Carolina established

1676—Bacon's Rebellion

c. 1700—Rice cultivation begun in the Carolina low country

1732—Georgia chartered

c. 1738—The Great Awakening begins

1754-1763—French and Indian War

result of demographics: in the sugar-producing colonies, black people outnumbered white people by six or eight to one, while in British North America, black people were a majority only in the low country. The more slaves outnumbered white people, the more likely they were to rebel. Also by the mid-eighteenth century most male slaves on the mainland colonies were creoles with families, who had more to lose from a failed rebellion than did the single African men who made up the bulk of the slave population farther south.

Nevertheless, there were waves of rebellion in British North America during the years from 1710 to 1722 and 1730 to 1740. Africans took the lead in these revolts, and the two most notable ones occurred in New York City in 1712 and near Charleston, South Carolina, in 1739. In New York twenty-seven Africans, taking revenge for "hard usage," set fire to an outbuilding. When white men arrived to put out the blaze, the rebels attacked them with muskets, hatchets, and swords. They killed nine of the white men and wounded six. Shortly thereafter local militia units captured the rebels, six of whom killed themselves. The other twenty-one were executed—some brutally.

Even more frightening for white people was the rebellion that began at Stono Bridge within twenty miles of Charleston in September 1739. Under the leadership of a man named Jemmy or Tommy, twenty slaves, who had recently arrived from Angola, broke into a "weare-house, & then plundered it of guns & ammunition." They killed the warehousemen, left their severed heads on the building's steps, and fled toward Florida. Other slaves joined the Angolans until their numbers reached one hundred. They sacked plantations and killed approximately thirty more white people. But when they stopped to celebrate their victories and beat drums to attract other slaves, planters on horseback aided by Indians routed them, killing forty-four and dispersing the rest. Many of the rebels—including their leader—remained at large for up to three years as did the spirit of insurrection. In 1740 Charleston authorities arrested 150 slaves and hanged ten daily to quell that spirit.

In South Carolina and the deep South, white people never entirely lost their fear of slave revolt. Whenever slaves rebelled or were rumored to rebel, the fear became intense. As the quotation that begins this chapter indicates, the unwillingness of many Africans and African Americans to submit to enslavement pushed white southerners into a siege mentality that became a determining factor in American history.

Conclusion

Studying the history of black people in early America is both painful and exhilarating. It is painful to learn of their enslavement, the emergence of racism in its modern form, and the loss of so much of the African heritage. But it is exhilarating to learn how much of that heritage Africans and African Americans were able to preserve, how they rebelled against and resisted their oppression and forged strong family bonds, and how an emerging African-American culture began to leave its mark on all aspects of American society.

The varieties of African-American life during the colonial period also help us understand the complexity of African-American society later in American history. Although they had much in common, black people in the Chesapeake, in the low country, and in the northern colonies had different experiences, relationships with white people and Indians, and prospects. Those who lived in the fledgling colonial towns and cities differed from those who were agricultural laborers. The lives of those who worked on small farms were quite different from the lives of those who served on large plantations.

Finally, African-American history during the colonial era raises fundamental issues about contingency and determinism in human events. Did economic necessity, racism, and class interest make the development of chattel slavery in the Chesapeake inevitable? Or had things gone otherwise—had, for example, Bacon's Rebellion not occurred or turned out differently—might African Americans in that region have retained more rights and more access to freedom? What then would have been the impact on the colonies to the north and south of the Chesapeake?

REVIEW QUESTIONS

1. Based on your reading of this chapter, do you believe that racial prejudice among British settlers in the Chesapeake led them to enslave Africans? Or did the unfree condition of the first Africans to arrive at Jamestown lead to racial prejudice among the settlers?

2. Why did vestiges of African culture survive in British North America? Did these vestiges help or hinder African Americans to deal with enslavement?

3. Compare and contrast eighteenth-century slavery as it existed in the Chesapeake, in the low country of South Carolina and Georgia, and in the northern colonies.

4. What were the strengths and weaknesses of the black family in the eighteenth century?

5. How did enslaved Africans and African Americans preserve a sense of their own humanity?

RECOMMENDED READING

Ira Berlin. *Many Thousands Gone: The First Two Centuries of Slavery in North America*. Cambridge, MA: Belknap Press, 1998. Berlin presents an impressive synthesis of black life in slavery during the seventeenth and eighteenth centuries that emphasizes the ability of black people to shape their lives in conflict with the will of masters.

John B. Boles. *Black Southerners, 1619–1869*. Lexington: University Press of Kentucky, 1983. The first two chapters deal with black life in colonial America. Boles is informative about culture and religion.

Winthrop D. Jordan. *White over Black: American Attitudes toward the Negro, 1550–1812*. Chapel Hill: University of North Carolina Press, 1968. This classic study provides a probing and detailed analysis of the cultural and psychological forces that led white people to enslave black people in early America.

Peter Kolchin. *American Slavery, 1619–1877*. New York: Hill and Wang, 1993. This is the most up-to-date and arguably the best study of the development of slavery in America. It is particularly useful on African-American community and culture.

Oscar Reiss. *Blacks in Colonial America*. Jefferson, NC: McFarland, 1997. Although short on synthesis and eccentric in interpretation, this book is packed with information about black life in early America.

Peter H. Wood. *Black Majority: Negroes in Colonial South Carolina from 1670 through the Stono Rebellion*. New York: Norton, 1974. This is the best account available of slavery and the origins of African-American culture in the colonial low country.

Donald R. Wright. *African Americans in the Colonial Era: From African Origins through the American Revolution*. Arlington Heights, IL: Harlan Davidson, 1990. Wright provides a brief but well-informed survey of black history during the colonial period.

ADDITIONAL BIBLIOGRAPHY

Colonial Society

Wesley Frank Craven. *The Southern Colonies in the Seventeenth Century, 1607–1689*. Baton Rouge: Louisiana State University Press, 1949.

John J. McCusker and Russell R. Menard. *The Economy of British America, 1607–1789*. Chapel Hill: University of North Carolina Press, 1985.

Gary B. Nash. *Red, White, and Black: The Peoples of Early America*. 3d edition. Englewood Cliffs, NJ: Prentice Hall, 1992.

Origins of Slavery and Racism in the Western Hemisphere

David Brion Davis. *The Problem of Slavery in Western Culture*. Ithaca, NY: Cornell University Press, 1966.

Ronald Sanders. *Lost Tribes and Promised Lands: The Origins of American Racism*. Boston: Little, Brown, 1978.

Frank Tannenbaum. *Slave and Citizen: The Negro in the Americas*. New York: Knopf, 1946.

The Chesapeake

Allan Kulikoff. *Tobacco and Slaves: The Development of Southern Cultures in the Chesapeake, 1680–1800*. Chapel Hill: University of North Carolina Press, 1986.

Gloria L. Main. *Tobacco Colony: Life in Early Maryland, 1650–1720*. Princeton, NJ: Princeton University Press, 1982.

Edmund S. Morgan. *American Slavery, American Freedom: The Ordeal of Colonial Virginia*. New York: Norton, 1975.

Mechal Sobel. *The World They Made Together: Black and White Values in Eighteenth-Century Virginia*. Princeton, NJ: Princeton University Press, 1987.

The Carolina and Georgia Low Country

Daniel C. Littlefield. *Rice and Slaves: Ethnicity and the Slave Trade in Colonial South Carolina*. Baton Rouge: Louisiana State University Press, 1985.

Julia Floyd Smith. *Slavery and Rice Culture in Low Country Georgia, 1750–1860*. Knoxville: University of Tennessee Press, 1985.

Betty Wood. *Slavery in Colonial Georgia, 1730–1775*. Athens: University of Georgia Press, 1984.

The Northern Colonies

Lorenzo J. Greene. *The Negro in Colonial New England, 1620–1776*, 1942; reprint, New York: Atheneum, 1968.

Edgar J. McManus. *Black Bondage in the North*. Syracuse, NY: Syracuse University Press, 1973.

William D. Piersen. *Black Yankees: The Development of an Afro-American Subculture in Eighteenth-Century New England*. Amherst: University of Massachusetts Press, 1988.

African-American Culture

Margaret W. Creel. *A Peculiar People: Slave Religion and Community Culture among the Gullahs*. New York: New York University Press, 1988.

Herbert Gutman. *The Black Family in Slavery and Freedom*. New York: Pantheon, 1976.

Melville J. Herskovits. *The Myth of the Negro Past*. 1941; reprint, Boston: Beacon, 1990.

Joseph E. Holloway, ed. *Africanisms in American Culture*. Bloomington: Indiana University Press, 1990.

Henry Mitchell. *Black Belief: Folk Beliefs of Blacks in America and West Africa*. New York: Harper & Row, 1975.

Philip D. Morgan. *Slave Counterpoint: Black Culture in the Eighteenth-Century Chesapeake and Lowcountry*. Chapel Hill: University of North Carolina Press, 1998.

Joel Williamson. *New People: Miscegenation and Mulattoes in the United States*. New York: Free Press, 1980.

Black Women in Colonial America

Joan Rezner Gunderson, "The Double Bonds of Race and Sex: Black and White Women in a Colonial Virginia Parish," in Darlene Clarke Hine, Wilma King, and Linda Reed, eds., *We Specialize in the Wholly Impossible: A Reader in Black Women's History*. Brooklyn: Carlson, 1995.

Darlene Clark Hine and Kathleen Thompson. *A Shining Thread of Hope: The History of Black Women in America*. New York: Broadway, 1998, chap. 1.

Jane Kamensky. *The Colonial Mosaic: American Women, 1600–1760: Rising Expectations from the Colonial Period to the American Revolution*. New York: Oxford University Press, 1995.

Resistance and Revolt

Herbert Aptheker. *American Negro Slave Revolts*. 1943; reprint, New York: International Publishers, 1974.

Merton L. Dillon. *Slavery Attacked: Southern Slaves and Their Allies, 1619–1865*. Baton Rouge: Louisiana State University Press, 1990.

Eugene D. Genovese. *From Rebellion to Revolution: Afro-American Slave Revolts in the Making of the Modern World*. Baton Rouge: Louisiana State University Press, 1979.

Gerald W. Mullin. *Flight and Rebellion: Slave Resistance in Eighteenth-Century Virginia*. New York: Oxford University Press, 1972.

Rising Expectations: African Americans and the Struggle for Independence, 1763–1783

According to legend, black patriot Salem Poor fired the shot that killed British Major John Pitcairn at the Battle of Bunker Hill in June 1775.

CHAPTER OUTLINE

To the Honorable Legislature of the State of Massachusetts Bay, January 13, 1777:

The petition of a great number of blacks detained in a state of slavery in the bowels of a free & Christian country humbly sheweth that your petitioners apprehend we have in common with all other men a natural and unalienable right to that freedom which the Great Parent of the Universe hath bestowed equally on all mankind, and which they have never forfeited by any compact or agreement whatever.

Lancaster Hill, *et al.*

As this quotation indicates, African Americans of the 1770s understood the revolutionary thought of their time. When a large minority of America's white population demanded independence from Britain on the basis of a natural human right to freedom, many black Americans asserted their right to be liberated from slavery. It took a momentous change in outlook from that of earlier ages for either group to perceive freedom as a right. Just as momentous was the dawning awareness among white people of the contradiction of claiming freedom for themselves and denying it to others.

The Great Awakening had nurtured humanitarian opposition to slavery, but secular thought, rooted in the European Enlightenment, was the impetus that shaped a revolutionary ethos in America. According to the precepts of the Enlightenment, all humans had natural, God-given, rights that could not be taken from them without their consent. It was to these precepts that the African-American petitioners alluded in 1777.

If the Enlightenment shaped the revolutionary discourse of the late eighteenth century, the French and Indian War, fought between 1754 and 1763, made the American struggle for independence possible. The outcome of that war, which pitted the British, Americans, and their Indian allies against the French and their Indian allies, created a volatile situation in the thirteen British colonies. That situation in turn produced the American War for Independence and efforts by many enslaved African Americans to gain their freedom.

In this chapter we explore the African-American quest for liberty during the twenty years between 1763, when the French and Indian War ended, and 1783, when Britain recognized the independence of the United States. During this period African Americans exercised an intellectual and political leadership that had far-ranging implications. A few black writers and scientists emerged; black soldiers fought in battle; black artisans proliferated, and—particularly in the North—black activists publicly argued against enslavement. Most important, many African Americans used the War for Independence to gain their freedom. Some were Patriots fighting for American independence. Others were Loyalists fighting for the British. Still others simply used the dislocations war caused to escape their masters.

THE CRISIS OF THE BRITISH EMPIRE

The great struggle for empire between Great Britain and France created the circumstances within which an independence movement and rising black hopes for freedom developed in America. Starting in 1689, the British and French fought a series of world wars in Europe, India, North America, Africa, and the Caribbean Sea. This great conflict climaxed during the French and Indian War that began in North America in 1754 and spread to Europe (and around the world) where it became known as the Seven Years War.

The war sprang from competing British and French efforts to control the Ohio River valley and its lucrative fur trade. In 1754 and 1755, the French and their Indian allies defeated Virginian and British troops in this region and then attacked the western frontier of the British colonies. Not until 1758 did Britain undertake a vigorous and expensive military effort that by 1763 had forced France to withdraw from North America. Britain took Canada from France and Florida from France's ally Spain. In compensation, Spain received New Orleans and the huge French province of Louisiana in central North America (Map 4-1).

These changes had momentous consequences. Deprived of their ability to play off Britain against France and Spain, the Eastern Woodlands Indians could no longer resist white encroachment. Although the Florida swamps remained a refuge for escaping slaves, fugitives lost their Spanish protectors. Americans no longer had to face French and Spanish threats on their frontiers. The bonds between Britain and the thirteen colonies rapidly weakened.

These last two consequences were closely linked. The colonial assemblies had not always supported the war effort against the French, and American merchants had traded with the enemy. Therefore, after the war ended, British officials determined that Americans be taxed to pay their share of the cost of the war and that their commerce be more closely regulated. In England it seemed entirely reasonable that the government should proceed in this manner. But white Americans had become accustomed to governing themselves, trading with whom they pleased, and paying only local taxes. They were well aware that with the French and Spanish gone, they no longer needed British protection. Therefore many of them resisted when the British Parliament asserted its power to tax and govern them.

During the 1760s Parliament repeatedly passed laws that Americans considered oppressive. The Proclamation Line of 1763 aimed to curtail westward expansion in order to placate Britain's Indian allies by forbidding Americans to cross the crest of the Appalachian Mountains. The Sugar Act of 1764 levied import duties designed, for the first time in colonial history, not to regulate American trade but to raise revenue for Britain. In 1765 the Stamp Act, also passed to raise revenue, heavily taxed printed materials, such as deeds, newspapers, and playing cards.

In response, Americans took their first step toward united resistance at the Stamp Act Congress held in New York City in October 1765. By agreeing not to import British goods, the congress forced Parliament to repeal the Stamp Act in 1766. But the Sugar Act and Proclamation Line remained in force, and Parliament soon indicated that it remained determined to exercise greater control in America.

In 1767 it forced the New York assembly to provide quarters for British troops and enacted the Townshend Acts, named after the British finance minister, which taxed such things as glass, lead, paint, paper, and tea imported into the colonies from Britain. Resistance to these taxes in Boston led the British government to station two regiments of troops there in 1768. The volatile

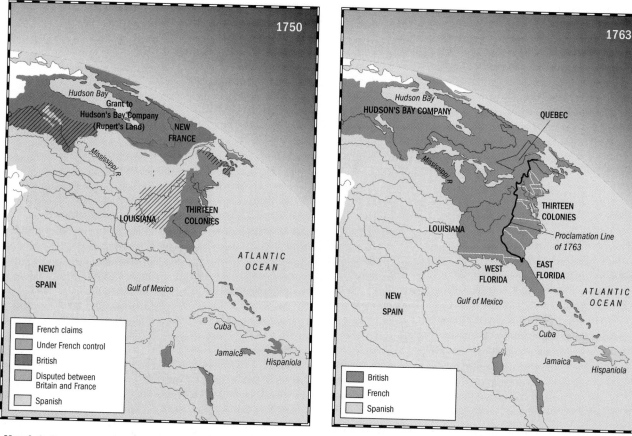

Map 4–1 European Claims in North America, 1750 and 1763. This map illustrates the dramatic change in the political geography of North America that resulted from the British victory in the French and Indian War. The war lasted from 1754 to 1763.

situation this created led in 1770 to the Boston Massacre when a small detachment of British troops fired into an angry crowd, killing five Bostonians. Among the dead was a black sailor named Crispus Attucks, who had taken the lead in accosting the soldiers.

As it turned out, Parliament had repealed the Townshend duties, except the one on tea, before the massacre. A reaction against the bloodshed in Boston, combined with Parliament's retreat, reduced the tension between the colonies and Britain. That calm lasted until May 1773 when Parliament passed the Tea Act.

The Tea Act gave the British East India Company a monopoly over all tea sold in the American colonies. A huge but debt-ridden entity, the East India Company governed India for the British Empire. At the time, Americans drank a great deal of tea and Parliament hoped that the tea monopoly would save the company from bankruptcy. But American merchants assumed that the act was the first step in a plot to bankrupt them. Because it had huge reserves, the East India Company could sell its tea much more cheaply than colonial mer-

chants could. Other Americans believed that the Tea Act was a trick to get them to pay the tax on tea by lowering its price. They feared that once Americans paid the tax on tea, British leaders would use it as a precedent to raise additional taxes.

To prevent this from happening, in December 1773, Boston's radical Sons of Liberty dumped a shipload of tea into the harbor. Britain then sent more troops to Boston in early 1774 and punished the city economically. This action sparked resistance throughout the colonies and led eventually to American independence. In September 1774 the Continental Congress met in Philadelphia and demanded the repeal of all "oppressive" legislation. By November, Massachusetts Minutemen—members of an irregular militia—had begun to stockpile arms in the villages surrounding Boston.

In April 1775 Minutemen clashed with British troops at Lexington and Concord near Boston. This was the first battle in what became a war for independence. Shortly thereafter Congress appointed George Washington commander-in-chief of the Continental Army.

PROFILE

CRISPUS ATTUCKS

Crispus Attucks was a fugitive slave who escaped in 1750 at age twenty-seven from his Farmingham, Massachusetts master. Attucks's father was black, his mother Indian. His master described him as "a mulatto fellow, about 27 years old, named Crispus, 6 feet 2 inches height, short, curl'd hair, his knees nearer together than common." During his twenty years as a fugitive, Attucks worked as a sailor, with Boston as his home port.

The death of Crispus Attucks in the Boston Massacre.

Attucks shared the anti-British sentiment that developed after the French and Indian War. This is not surprising since the tightening restrictions Parliament placed upon American trade affected his livelihood as a seaman. In Boston British soldiers were the most obvious target of such resentment. Bostonians had insulted and thrown rocks at them for some time before Attucks joined a motley crowd that, with clubs and sticks, accosted a small detachment of troops on the chilly evening of March 5, 1770. Attucks was not the only African American in the mob. One pro-British witness described those who gathered as "saucy boys, Negroes and mulattoes, Irish Teagues and outlandish Jack Tars [sailors]."

Although eyewitness accounts differ, Attucks, who brandished "a large cordwood stick" probably took the lead in confronting Captain Thomas Preston and the nine soldiers under his command. A black witness maintained that Attucks "a stout man with a long cord wood stick" hit a soldier, which led the troops to fire on the mob. John Adams, who defended the soldiers in court, credited this account, and Attucks was almost certainly the first to die when the soldiers, with their backs to a wall, fired.

Samuel Adams, John's cousin, and other Patriots in Boston declared the forty-seven-year-old Attucks the first martyr to British oppression. They carried his coffin, along with those of three of the other four men who were killed, to Faneuil Hall—called the "Cradle of Liberty" because of its association with revolutionary rhetoric. There Attucks lay in state for three days with the other victims of what Americans immediately called the Boston Massacre. From this hall ten thousand mourners accompanied four hearses to Boston's Middle Burying Ground. The inscription on the monument raised to commemorate the martyrs reads:

Long as in freedom's cause the wise contend,
Dear to your country shall your fame extend;
While to the world the lettered stone shall tell
Where Caldwell, Attucks, Gray, and Maverick fell.

Bostonians celebrated the anniversary of the massacre annually until the 1840s. They revived the practice in 1858 to protest the Supreme Court's decision in *Dred Scott v. Sanford* that African Americans were not citizens of the United States. At about the same time African Americans in Cincinnati formed the "Attucks Guards" to resist enforcement of the Fugitive Slave Law. After the Civil War, black abolitionist William C. Nell linked the service of black men in defense of the Union to Attuck's sacrifice "in defense of this nation's freedom."

Attucks has remained a symbol of African-American patriotism. In 1967, at the height of the Vietnam war, the Newark, New Jersey, board of education at the expressed desire of the city's large black community made March 5 an annual holiday in honor of Attucks. This was the first holiday to recognize an African American.

Before he took command, however, the American and British forces at Boston fought a bloody battle at Bunker Hill. After a year during which other armed clashes occurred and the British rejected a compromise, Congress in July 1776 declared the colonies to be independent states and the war became a revolution.

THE DECLARATION OF INDEPENDENCE AND AFRICAN AMERICANS

The Declaration of Independence that the Continental Congress adopted on July 4, 1776, was drafted by a slaveholder in a slaveholding country. When Thomas Jefferson wrote "that all men are created equal; that they are endowed by their Creator with certain unalienable rights; that among these are life, liberty, and the pursuit of happiness," he was not supporting black claims for freedom. Men like Jefferson and John Adams, who served on the drafting committee with Jefferson, frequently distinguished between the rights of white men of British descent and a lack of rights for people of color. In 1765 Adams had written, that God had "never intended the American colonists 'for Negroes . . . and therefore never intended us for slaves.'" So convinced were Jefferson and his colleagues that black people could not claim the same rights as white people that they felt no need to qualify their words proclaiming universal liberty.

The draft that Jefferson, Adams, and Benjamin Franklin submitted to Congress for approval did denounce the Atlantic slave trade as a "cruel war against human nature itself, violating its most sacred rights of life and liberty in the persons of a distant [African] people." But Congress deleted this passage because delegates from the Deep South objected to it. The final version of the Declaration referred to slavery only to accuse the British of arousing African Americans to revolt against their masters.

Yet, although Jefferson and the other delegates did not mean to encourage African Americans to hope that the American War for Independence could become a war against slavery, that is what African Americans believed. Black people were in attendance when Patriot speakers made unqualified claims for human equality and natural rights; they read accounts of such speeches and heard white people discuss them. Therefore African Americans began to assert that such principles logically applied as much to them as to the white population. They forced white people to confront the contradiction between the new nation's professed ideals and its reality.

Most white people would not deny that black individuals were human beings. White citizens therefore had to choose between accepting the literal meaning of the Declaration, which meant changing American society, or rejecting the revolutionary ideology that supported their claims for independence.

The Impact of the Enlightenment

At the center of that ideology was the European Enlightenment. The roots of this essentially intellectual movement—also known as the Age of Reason—lay in Renaissance secularism and humanism dating back to the fifteenth century. But it was Isaac Newton's *Principia Mathematica*, published in England in 1687, that shaped this new way of perceiving human beings and their universe.

Newton used mathematics to portray an orderly, balanced universe that ran according to natural laws that humans could discover through reason. Newton's insights supported the rationalized means of production and commerce associated with the Industrial Revolution that began in England during the early eighteenth century. An emerging market economy required the same sort of rational use of resources that Newton discovered in the universe. But what made the Enlightenment of particular relevance to the Age of Revolution was John Locke's application of Newton's ideas to politics.

Locke, in his *Essay Concerning Human Understanding*, published in 1690, maintained that human society—like the physical universe—ran according to natural laws. He contended that at the base of human laws were natural rights that all people shared. Human beings, according to Locke, created governments to protect their natural individual rights to life, liberty, and private property. If a government failed to perform this basic duty and became oppressive, he insisted, the people had the right to overthrow it. Although he wrote nearly a century before the 1777 Massachusetts petition with which this chapter begins, Locke's ideas underlie this appeal on behalf of black liberty. Locke also maintained that the human mind at birth was a *tabula rasa*—that knowledge and wisdom were not inherited but were acquired through experience. Locke saw no contradiction between these principles and human slavery. But during the eighteenth century, that contradiction became increasingly clear.

Most Americans became acquainted with Locke's ideas through pamphlets that a radical English political minority produced during the early eighteenth century. This literature portrayed the British government of the day as a conspiracy aimed at depriving British subjects of their natural rights, reducing them to slaves, and establishing tyranny. After the French and Indian War, in the 1760s, Americans, both black and white, interpreted British policies and actions from this same perspective.

The influence of such pamphlets is clear between 1763 and 1776 when white American leaders charged that the British government sought to enslave them by depriving them of their rights as Englishmen. When they made these charges, they had difficulty denying depriving African Americans of their natural rights. George Washington, for example, declared in 1774 that "the crisis is arrived when we must assert our rights, or submit to every imposition, that can be heaped upon us, till custom and use shall make us tame and abject, as the blacks we rule over with such arbitrary sway."

African Americans in the Revolutionary Debate

When during the 1760s and 1770s powerful slaveholders, such as Washington, talked of liberty, natural rights, and hatred of enslavement, African Americans listened. Most of them had been born in America; they had absorbed English culture; they were united as a people; and they knew their way in colonial society. Those who lived in or near towns and cities had access to public meetings and newspapers. They were aware of the disputes with Great Britain and the contradictions between demanding liberty for oneself and denying it to others. They understood that the ferment of the 1760s had shaken traditional assumptions about government, and many of them hoped for more changes.

The greatest source of optimism for African Americans was the expectation that white leaders would realize that their revolutionary principles were incompatible with slavery. Those in England who believed that white Americans must submit to British authority pointed out the contradiction. The most famous writer in London, Samuel Johnson, asked, "How is it that we hear the loudest *yelps* for liberty among the drivers of negroes?" But white Americans made similar comments. As early as 1763, James Otis of Massachusetts warned that "those who every day barter away other mens ['] liberty, will soon care little for their own." Thomas Paine, whose pamphlet *Common Sense* rallied Americans to endorse independence in 1776, asked them to contemplate "with what consistency, or decency they complain so loudly of attempts to enslave them, while they hold so many hundred thousands in slavery; and annually enslave many thousands more."

Such principled misgivings among white people about slavery helped improve the situation for black people in the North and upper South during the war. But African Americans acting on their own behalf was key. In January 1766 slaves marched through Charleston, South Carolina, shouting "Liberty!" In the South Carolina and Georgia low country and in the Chesapeake, slaves escaped in massive numbers throughout the revolutionary era. So many slaves fled in the South that between 1770 and 1790 the percentage of black people in South Carolina's population dropped from 60.5 percent to 43.8 percent, and in Georgia from 45.2 to 36.9. Throughout the southern colonies, rumors of slave uprisings were rife.

However, it was in New England—the heartland of anti-British radicalism—that African Americans formally made their case for freedom. As early as 1701, a Massachusetts slave won his liberty in court, and there were eleven similar suits before 1750. As the revolutionary era began, such cases multiplied. In addition, while slaves during the seventeenth and early eighteenth centuries based their suits on contractual technicalities, during the revolutionary period, they increasingly sued on the basis of principles of universal liberty. They did not always win their cases—John Adams, a future president, was the lawyer who defeated one such case in Boston in 1768—but they set precedents.

African Americans in Massachusetts, New Hampshire, and Connecticut also petitioned their colonial or state legislatures for gradual emancipation. These petitions were worded like the one at the start of this chapter, indicating that the black men who signed them were familiar with revolutionary rhetoric. African Americans learned this language as they joined white radicals to confront British authority.

In 1765 black men demonstrated against the Stamp Act in Boston. They rioted against British troops there in 1768 and joined Crispus Attucks in 1770. Black Minutemen stood with their white comrades at Lexington and Concord. In 1773 black petitioners from Boston told a delegate to the colonial assembly, "We expect great things from men who have made such a noble stand against the designs of their *fellow-men* to enslave them. . . . The divine spirit of *freedom*, seems to fire every human breast."

BLACK ENLIGHTENMENT

Besides influencing radical political discourse during the revolutionary era, the Enlightenment also shaped the careers of America's first black intellectuals. Because

VOICES

BOSTON'S SLAVES LINK THEIR FREEDOM TO AMERICAN LIBERTY

This petition was submitted in April 1773 by a committee of slaves from Boston to the delegate to the Massachusetts General Court from the town of Thompson. The petition, which overflows with sarcasm, demonstrates African-American familiarity with the principles of the Enlightenment and the irony of white Americans' contention that Britain aimed to enslave them. Its authors are of two minds about their society. They see both the potential for black freedom and the entrenched prejudice of whites. Note that the authors propose to go to Africa if they gain their freedom.

Boston, April 20th, 1773

Sir, The efforts made by the legislative of this province in their last sessions to free themselves from slavery, gave us, who are in that deplorable state, a high degree of satisfaction. We expect great things from men who have made such a noble stand against the designs of their *fellow-men* to enslave them. We cannot but wish and hope Sir, that you will have the same grand object, we mean civil and religious liberty, in view in your next session. The divine spirit of *freedom*, seems to fire every humane breast on this continent, except such as are bribed to assist in executing the execrable plan.

We are very sensible that it would be highly detrimental to our present masters, if we were allowed to demand all that of *right* belongs to us for past services; this we disclaim. Even the *Spaniards*, who have not those sublime ideas of freedom that English men have, are conscious that they have no right to all the services of their fellow-men, we mean the *Africans*, whom they have purchased with their money; therefore they allow them one day in a week to work for themselves, to enable them to earn money to purchase the residue of their time. . . . We do not pretend to dictate to you Sir, or to the Honorable Assembly, of which you are a member. We acknowledge our obligations to you for

what you have already done, but as the people of this province seem to be actuated by the principles of equity and justice, we cannot but expect your house will again take our deplorable case into serious consideration, and give us that ample relief which, *as men*, we have a natural right to.

But since the wise and righteous governor of the universe, has permitted our fellow men to make us slaves, we bow in submission to him, and determine to behave in such a manner as that we can have reason to expect the divine approbation of, and assistance in, our peaceable and lawful attempts to gain our freedom.

We are willing to submit to such regulations and laws, as may be made relative to us, until we leave the province, which we determine to do as soon as we can, from our joynt labours procure money to transport ourselves to some part of the Coast of *Africa*, where we propose settlement. We are very desirous that you should have instructions relative to us, from your town, therefore we pray you to communicate this letter to them, and ask this favor for us.

In behalf of our fellow slaves in this province, and by order of their Committee.
Peter Bestes,
Sambo Freeman,
Felix Holbrook,
Chester Joie.
For the Representative of the town of Thompson.

QUESTIONS

1. What is the object of this petition?

2. What Enlightenment principles does the petition invoke?

3. What is the significance of the slaves' vow to go to Africa if freed?

Source: Gary B. Nash, *Race and Revolution* (Madison, WI: Madison House, 1990), 173–74.

it emphasized human reason, the Enlightenment led to the establishment of colleges and libraries in Europe and America. These institutions usually served a tiny elite, but newspapers and pamphlets made science and literature available to the masses. The eighteenth cen-

tury was also an era in which amateurs could make serious contributions to human knowledge. Some of these, such as Thomas Jefferson and Benjamin Franklin, were rich and well educated. They made discoveries in botany and electricity while pursuing political careers.

What is striking is that some African Americans, whose advantages were far more limited, also became scientists and authors.

Because they had easier access to evangelical Protestantism than to secular learning, most African Americans who gained intellectual distinction during the late eighteenth century owed more to the Great Awakening than to the Enlightenment. The best known of these is Jupiter Hammon, a Long Island slave who published religious poetry in the 1760s. There were also Josiah Bishop and Lemuel Haynes, black ministers to white church congregations in Virginia and New England. But Phillis Wheatley and Benjamin Banneker, who were directly influenced by the Enlightenment, became the most famous black intellectuals of their time.

Phillis Wheatley

Wheatley came to Boston from Africa—possibly near the Gambia River—in 1761 aboard a slaver. She was seven or eight years old, small, frail, and nearly naked. John Wheatley, a wealthy merchant, purchased her as a servant for his wife. Although Phillis spoke no English when her ship docked, she was soon reading and writing in that language and studying Latin. She pored over the Bible and became a fervent Christian. She also read the fashionable poetry of British author Alexander Pope and become a poet herself by the age of thirteen.

For the rest of her short life, Wheatley wrote poems to celebrate important events. Like Pope's, Wheatley's

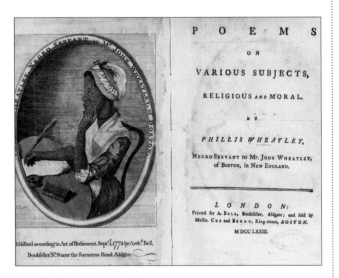

A frontispiece portrait of Phillis Wheatley precedes the title page of her first book of poetry, which was published in 1773. The portrait suggests Wheatley's small physique and studious manner.

poetry reflected the aesthetic values of the Enlightenment. She aimed to blend thought, image, sound, and rhythm to provide a perfectly balanced composition. In 1773 the Wheatleys sent her to London where her first book of poems—the first book ever by an African-American woman and the second by any American woman—was published under the title *Poems on Various Subjects, Religious, and Moral.* The Wheatleys freed Phillis after her return to Boston, although she continued to live in their house until both of them died. In 1778 she married John Peters, a black grocer, but was soon mired in illness and poverty. Two of her children died in infancy, and she herself died in December 1784 giving birth to her third child, who died with her.

Wheatley was an advocate and symbol of the adoption of white culture by black people. Before her marriage she lived almost exclusively among white people and absorbed their values. For example, while she lamented the sorrow her capture had caused her parents, she was grateful to have been brought to America:

> *'Twas mercy brought me from my Pagan land,*
> *Taught my benighted soul to understand*
> *That there's a God, that there's a Saviour too:*
> *Once I redemption neither sought nor knew.*

But Wheatley did not simply copy her masters' views. Although the Wheatleys were loyal to Britain, she became a fervent Patriot. She attended Boston's Old North Church, a hotbed of anti-British sentiment, and wrote poems supporting the Patriot cause. In early 1776, for example, she lavishly praised George Washington, "fam'd for thy valour, for thy virtues more," and received effusive thanks from the general.

Wheatley also became an advocate and symbol of John Locke's ideas concerning the influence of environment on human beings. White leaders of the Revolution and intellectuals debated whether black people were inherently inferior in intellect to white people or whether this perceived black inferiority was the result of enslavement. Some slaveholders, such as Thomas Jefferson, who held racist assumptions about innate black inferiority, dismissed Wheatley's work as "below the dignity of criticism." But those who favored an environmental perspective considered Wheatley an example of what people of African descent could achieve if freed from oppression, and she made her own views clear:

> *Some view our sable race with scornful eye,*
> *"Their colour is a diabolic dye."*
> *Remember, Christians, Negroes, black as Cain,*
> *May be refin'd, and join th' angelic train.*

VOICES

PHILLIS WHEATLEY ON LIBERTY AND NATURAL RIGHTS

Phillis Wheatley wrote the following letter to Samson Occom, an American-Indian minister in 1774 after her return from England and as tensions between that country and its American colonies intensified. In it she links divine order, natural rights, and an inner desire for personal liberty. She expresses optimism that Christianity and the emergence of order in Africa will lead to the end of the Atlantic slave trade. And she hopes that God will ultimately overcome the avarice of American slaveholders ("our modern Egyptians") and let them see the contradiction between their words and deeds.

February 11, 1774

Rev'd and honor'd Sir,

I have this Day received your obliging kind Epistle, and am greatly satisfied with your Reasons respecting the Negroes, and think highly reasonable what you offer in Vindication of their natural Rights. Those that invade them cannot be insensible that the divine Light is chasing away the thick Darkness which broods over the Land of Africa; and the Chaos which has reign'd so long, is converting into beautiful Order, and reveals more and more clearly, the glorious Dispensation of civil and religious Liberty, which are so inseparably united, that there is little or no Enjoyment of one without the other. Otherwise, perhaps, the Israelites had been less solicitous for their Freedom from Egyptian Slavery; I don't say they would have been contented without it. By no Means, for in every human Breast, God has implanted a Principle, which we call Love of Freedom; it is impatient of Oppression, and pants for Deliverance. And by the leave of our modern Egyptians, I will assert that the same principle lives in us. God grant Deliverance in his own Way and Time, and get him honor upon all those whose Avarice impels them to countenance and help forward the Calamities of their fellow Creatures. This I desire not for their Hurt, but to convince them of the strange Absurdity of their Conduct whose Words and Actions are so diametrically opposite. How well the cry for Liberty, and the reverse Disposition for the exercise of oppressive Power over others agree, I humbly think it does not require the Penetration of a Philosopher to determine.

Phillis Wheatley

QUESTIONS

1. How does this letter reflect principles associated with the Enlightenment?

2. What insights does this letter provide into Wheatley's views on slavery and its abolition?

Source: Roy Finkenbine, ed., *Sources of the African-American Past: Primary Sources in American History* (New York: Longman, 1997), 22–23.

Benjamin Banneker

In the breadth of his achievement, Benjamin Banneker is even more representative of the Enlightenment than Phillis Wheatley. Like hers, his life epitomizes a flexibility concerning race that the revolutionary era briefly promised to expand.

Banneker was born free in Maryland in 1731 and died in 1806. The son of a mixed-race mother and an African father, he inherited a farm near Baltimore from his white grandmother. As a child, Banneker, whose appearance was described by a contemporary to be "decidedly Negro," attended a racially integrated school. His farm gave him a steady income and the leisure to study literature and science.

With access to the library of his white neighbor George Ellicott, Banneker "mastered Latin and Greek and had a good working knowledge of German and French." By the 1770s he had a reputation as a man "of uncommonly soft and gentlemanly manners and of pleasing colloquial powers." Like Jefferson, Franklin, and others of his time, Banneker was fascinated with mechanics and in 1770 constructed his own clock. However, he gained international fame as a mathematician and astronomer. Because of his knowledge in these disciplines, he became a member of the survey commission for Washington, D.C. This made him the first black civilian employee of the United States government. Between 1791 and 1796, he published an almanac based on his observations and mathematical calculations.

Like Wheatley, Banneker had thoroughly assimilated white culture and was keenly aware of the fundamental issues of human equality associated with the American Revolution. In 1791 he sent United States Secretary of State Thomas Jefferson a copy of his almanac in order to counteract Jefferson's claim in *Notes on the State of Virginia* that black people were inherently inferior intellectually to white people. Noting Jefferson's commitment to the biblical statement that God had created "us all of one flesh, " and Jefferson's words in the Declaration of Independence, Banneker called the great man to account.

Referring to the Declaration, Banneker wrote, "You were then impressed with proper ideas of the great valuation of liberty, and the free possession of those blessings, to which you were entitled by nature; but, Sir, how

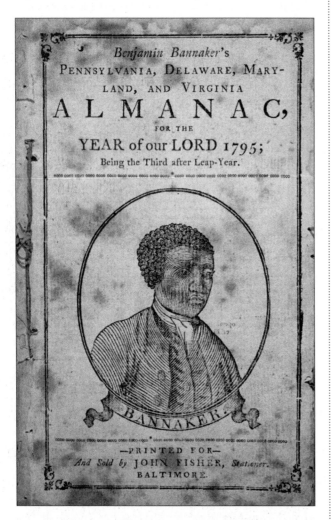

The title page of the 1795 edition of Benjamin Banneker's *Pennsylvania, Delaware, Maryland, and Virginia Almanac.* Banneker was widely known during the late eighteenth century as a mathematician and astronomer.

pitiable is it to reflect, that altho you were so fully convinced of the benevolence of the Father of Mankind, and of his equal and impartial distribution of these rights and privileges . . . that you should at the Same time counteract his mercies, in detaining by fraud and violence so numerous a part of my brethren, under groaning captivity and cruel oppression."

AFRICAN AMERICANS IN THE WAR FOR INDEPENDENCE

In the words of historian Benjamin Quarles, "The Negro's role in the Revolution can best be understood by realizing that his major loyalty was not to a place nor to a people, but to a principle." When it came to fighting between Patriots on one side and the British and their Loyalist American allies on the other, African Americans joined the side that offered freedom. In the North, where white Patriots were more consistently committed to human liberty than in the South, black men eagerly fought on the Patriot side from the beginning. In the South, where the British held out the promise of freedom in exchange for military service, black men just as eagerly fought on the British side as Loyalists.

The war began in earnest in August 1776 when the British landed a large army at Brooklyn, New York, and drove Washington's Continental Army across New Jersey into Pennsylvania. The military and diplomatic turning point in the war came the following year at Saratoga, New York, when a poorly executed British strategy to take control of the Hudson River led British General John Burgoyne to surrender his entire army to Patriot forces. This victory led France and other European powers to enter the war against Britain. Significant fighting ended in October 1781 when Washington forced Lord Cornwallis to surrender another British army at Yorktown, Virginia.

When Washington organized the Continental Army in July 1775, he forbade the enlistment of new black troops and the reenlistment of black men who had served at Lexington and Concord, Bunker Hill, and other early battles. Shortly thereafter all thirteen states followed Washington's example. There were several reasons for Washington's decision and its ratification by the Continental Congress. Although several black men had served during the French and Indian War, the colonies had traditionally excluded African Americans from militia service. Like others before them, Patriot leaders feared that if they enlisted African-American soldiers they would encourage slaves to leave their masters without permission. White people—especially in the South—also feared that armed black men would endanger the social order. Paradoxically white people simultaneously believed that black men were too cowardly to be effective soldiers. Though apparently contradictory, these last two beliefs persisted into the twentieth century.

Black Loyalists

Because so many Patriot leaders resisted employing black troops, by mid-1775 the British had taken the initiative in recruiting African Americans. From Maryland southward during the spring of that year, there were rumors that the British would instigate slave revolt. In North Carolina, for example, the white populace believed that British agents promised to reward black individuals who murdered their masters. However, no such uprisings occurred.

Instead, many slaves escaped and sought British protection as Loyalists. Thomas Jefferson later claimed that thirty thousand slaves escaped in Virginia alone. The British employed most black men who escaped to their lines as laborers and foragers. During the siege at Yorktown in 1781, the British even used the bodies of black laborers, who had died of smallpox, in a primitive form of biological warfare to try to infect the American camps. Even so, many black refugees fought for British or Loyalist units.

Black Loyalists were most numerous in the low country of South Carolina and Georgia. At the end of the war, approximately ten thousand African Americans left Savannah and Charleston when the British forces evacuated these cities in 1783. A few who remained became known as "the plunderers of Georgia." They carried out guerrilla warfare there until 1786.

The most famous British appeal to African Americans to fight for the empire in return for freedom came in Virginia. On November 7, 1775, Lord Dunmore, the last royal governor of the Old Dominion, issued a proclamation offering to liberate slaves who joined "His Majesty's Troops . . . for the more speedily reducing this Colony to a proper sense of their duty to His Majesty's crown and dignity."

Among those who responded to Dunmore's offer was Ralph Henry, a twenty-six-year-old slave of Patrick Henry. Perhaps Ralph Henry recalled his famous master's "Give me liberty or give me death" speech. Another who joined Dunmore's troops was James Reid, who later became a leader of Britain's colony for freed blacks in Sierra Leone on Africa's west coast. Reid's sixteen-year-old wife came with him, and they *both*

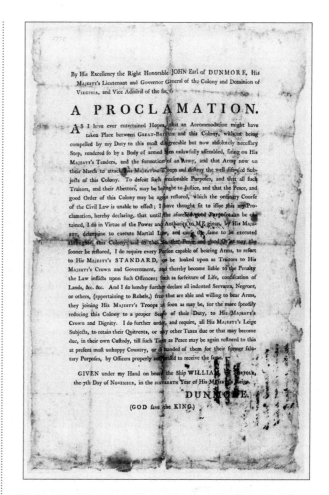

This is a broadside version of Lord Dunmore's November 7, 1775, proclamation calling on black men in Virginia to fight on the British side in the American War for Independence in return for their freedom.

served with the Royal Artillery. In 1780, at least twenty of Thomas Jefferson's slaves joined Lord Cornwallis's army when it invaded Virginia.

Dunmore recruited black soldiers out of desperation, although he became the strongest advocate—on either the British or American side—of their fighting ability. When he issued his appeal, Dunmore had only three hundred British troops and had been driven from Williamsburg, the colonial capital. Mainly because Dunmore had to seek refuge on British warships, only about eight hundred African Americans managed to reach his forces. Defeat by the Patriots at the Battle of Great Bridge in December 1775 curtailed his efforts.

But Dunmore's proclamation and the black response to it struck a tremendous psychological blow against his enemies. Of Dunmore's six hundred troops at Great Bridge, three hundred were African Americans whose uniforms bore the motto "Liberty to Slaves." As more

AFRICAN AMERICANS AND THE WAR FOR INDEPENDENCE

April 18, 1775	Black Minutemen participate in Battle of Lexington and Concord.
May 10, 1775	The Second Continental Congress convenes in Philadelphia.
June 15, 1775	Congress appoints George Washington commander-in-chief of the new Continental Army.
June 17, 1775	Black men fight with the Patriots at Bunker Hill.
November 7, 1775	Lord Dunmore, the royal governor of Virginia, offers freedom to slaves who will fight for the British.
November 12, 1775	George Washington bans African Americans from serving in the Continental Army.
December 30, 1775	Washington allows black reenlistments in the Continental Army.

and more Virginia slaves escaped, masters blamed Dunmore. Throughout the war other British and Loyalist commanders followed his example, recruiting thousands of black men who worked and sometimes fought in exchange for their freedom. In all, more African Americans became active Loyalists than Patriots during the war.

Five hundred of Dunmore's black troops died of typhus or smallpox. The remainder sailed with his fleet to New York City (which had become British headquarters in America) when he had to abandon Virginia. One of them, the notorious Colonel Tye, conducted guerrilla raids in Monmouth County, New Jersey, for several years. Tye and his interracial band of about twenty-five Loyalists plundered villages, spiked cannons, and kidnapped Patriot officers until he was killed in 1780.

Black Patriots

Washington's July 1775 policy to the contrary, black men fought on the Patriot side from the very beginning of the Revolutionary War to its conclusion (Map 4–2). Prior to Washington's arrival in Massachusetts, there were black Minutemen at Lexington and Concord; and some of the same men distinguished themselves at the bloody battle of Bunker Hill in June 1775. Among them were Peter Salem—who gained freedom in return for his military service at Lexington and Concord—Caesar

Dickerson, Pomp Fisk, Prince Hall, Cuff Hayes, Barzilli Lew, Salem Poor, Caesar Weatherbee, and Cuff Whittemore. Lew was a veteran of the French and Indian War; Hall became a prominent black leader; and Poor, who wintered with Washington's Army at Valley Forge in 1777–78, received a commendation for bravery at Bunker Hill.

It was Dunmore's use of African-American soldiers that prompted Washington to reconsider his ban on black enlistment. "If that man, Dunmore," he wrote in late 1775, "is not crushed before the Spring he will become the most dangerous man in America. His strength will increase like a snowball running down hill. Success will depend on which side can arm the Negro faster." After having received added encouragement from black veterans, Washington, on December 30, 1775, allowed African-American reenlistment in the Continental Army. Congress, fearful of alienating slaveholders,

The black soldier in this detail from John Trumbull's contemporary oil painting *The Battle of Bunker Hill* is presumed to be Salem Poor. Poor received a commendation for his bravery during the battle, which was fought in June 1775.

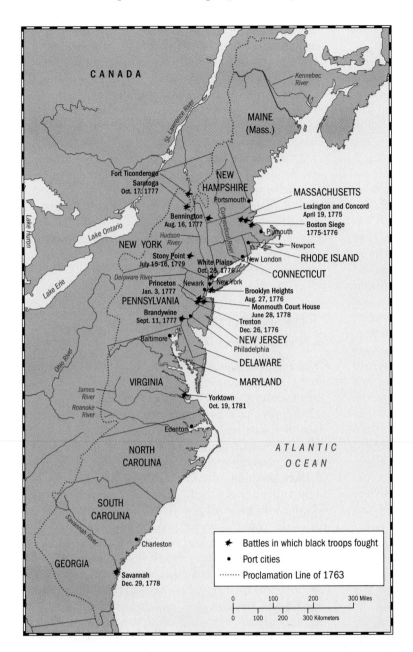

Map 4–2 Major Battles of the American War for Independence, Indicating Those in Which Black Troops Participated. Black troops fought on both sides during the American war for independence and participated in most of the major battles. Adapted from *The Atlas of African-American History and Politics*, 1/e, by A. Smallwood and J. Elliot, © 1998, The McGraw-Hill Companies. Reproduced with permission of The McGraw-Hill Companies.

initially would not allow him to go further. By the end of 1776, however, troop shortages forced Congress and the state governments to recruit black soldiers in earnest for the Continental Army and state militias. Even then, South Carolina and Georgia refused to permit black men to serve in regiments raised within their boundaries, although black men from these states joined other Patriot units.

The Patriot recruitment policy changed most quickly in New England. In early 1777, Massachusetts opened its militia to black men, and Rhode Island formed a black regiment. Connecticut enabled masters to free their slaves to serve as substitutes for the masters or their sons in the militia or Continental Army. New York and New Jersey adopted similar statutes.

Also in 1777, when Congress set state enlistment quotas for the Continental Army, state recruitment officers began to fill those quotas with black men so that white men might serve closer to home in the militia. With considerable reluctance, the southern states of Delaware, Maryland, Virginia, and North Carolina began enlisting free black men. Of these states, only Maryland allowed slaves to serve in return for freedom, but the others sometimes allowed slaves to enlist as substitutes for their masters, and this usually led to freedom.

Black men asserted that if they were to fight in a war for liberty, *their* liberty had to be ensured. When one master informed his slave that both of them would be fighting for liberty, the slave replied "that it would be a great satisfaction to know that he was indeed going to fight for *his* liberty." Once an agreement to serve the Patriot cause in return for freedom had been reached, some black soldiers took new surnames. Among the newly free soldiers in a Connecticut regiment were Jeffery, Pomp, and Sharp *Liberty*, and Ned, Cuff, and Peter *Freedom*.

Except for Rhode Island's black regiment and some companies in Massachusetts, black Patriots served in integrated military units. Enrollment officers often did not specify a man's race when he enlisted so it is difficult to know how many black men actually served in Patriot armies. Five thousand black soldiers out of a total of 300,000 is the figure usually given. A few black men, such as Salem Poor, became junior officers. Others were drummers and fifers, sailors on privateers (merchant vessels armed and authorized by a government to raid enemy shipping) commissioned by the Continental Congress, and informants and spies. Like others who gathered intelligence behind enemy lines, African Americans who informed and spied risked being hanged if they were captured.

Black men fought on the Patriot side in nearly every major battle of the war. Prince Whipple and Oliver Cromwell crossed the Delaware River with Washington

A young French officer named Jean-Baptiste-Antoine Deverger painted this watercolor of American foot soldiers who served during the York-town Campaign of 1781. The black soldier is a light infantryman from Rhode Island's black regiment.

on Christmas night 1776 to surprise Hessian mercenaries (German troops hired to fight on the British side) at Trenton, New Jersey. Others fought at Monmouth, Saratoga, Savannah, Princeton, and Yorktown. In 1777 a Hessian officer reported, "No [Patriot] regiment is to be seen in which there are not Negroes in abundance, and among them are able bodied, strong and brave fellows."

At least one black woman also fought for American independence. Deborah Gannett served as a private under the name Robert Shurtliff in the Fourth Massachusetts Regiment of the Continental Army. Gannett was in the regiment from May 1782 to October 1783. Even though this was after the decisive battle of Yorktown, in 1792 Massachusetts recognized her contribution as "an extraordinary instance of female heroism."

THE REVOLUTION AND EMANCIPATION

The willingness of African Americans to risk their lives in the Patriot cause encouraged northern legislatures to emancipate slaves within their borders. By the late 1770s, most of these legislatures were debating abolition. Petitions and lawsuits initiated by black people in Massachusetts, Connecticut, New Hampshire, and elsewhere encouraged such consideration. But an emerging market economy, the Great Awakening, and the Enlightenment established the cultural context in which people who believed deeply in the sanctity of private property could consider such a momentous change. Economic, religious, and intellectual change had convinced many that slavery should be abolished.

Enlightenment rationalism was a powerful antislavery force. In the light of reason, slavery appeared to be inefficient, barbaric, and oppressive. But rationalism alone could not convince white Americans that black people should be released from slavery. White people also had to believe that general emancipation was in their self-interest and that it was their Christian duty.

In the North, where all these forces operated and the economic stake in slave labor was relatively small, emancipation made steady progress. In the Chesapeake, where some of these forces operated, emancipationist sentiment grew, many masters manumitted their slaves, but there was no serious threat to the slave system. In the low country of South Carolina and Georgia, where economic interest and white solidarity against large black populations outweighed intellectual and religious considerations, white commitment to black bondage remained absolute.

The movement among white people to abolish slavery began within the Society of Friends, or Quakers. Quakers had always emphasized conscience, human brotherhood, and nonviolence. Moreover, many leading Quaker families were engaged in international business ventures that required educated, efficient, moral workers. This predisposed them against a system that forced workers to be uneducated, recalcitrant, and often ignorant of Christian religion. Growing numbers of Quakers, therefore, concluded that slaveholding was sinful, although members of the Society of Friends had owned and traded slaves for generations.

During the 1730s, Benjamin Lay, a former slaveholder who had moved to the Quaker-dominated colony of Pennsylvania from Barbados, began to exhort his fellow Friends to disassociate themselves from owning and buying slaves. By the 1740s and 1750s, John Woolman, from southern New Jersey, was urging northeastern and Chesapeake Quakers to emancipate their slaves. With assistance from British Quakers, Woolman and Anthony Benezet, a Philadelphia teacher, convinced the society's 1758 annual meeting to condemn slavery and the slave trade.

When the conflict with Great Britain made human rights a political as well as a religious issue, Woolman and Benezet carried their abolitionist message beyond the Society of Friends. They thereby merged their sectarian crusade with the rationalist efforts of such northern white revolutionary leaders as former slaveholder Benjamin Franklin of Philadelphia and John Jay and Alexander Hamilton of New York. Under Quaker leadership, antislavery societies came into existence in both the North and the Chesapeake. By 1774 such societies had joined African Americans in petitioning northern legislatures and—in one instance—the Continental Congress to act against slavery or the slave trade.

The antislavery societies emphasized black service in the war against British rule and the religious and economic progress of northern African Americans. They also contended that emancipation would prevent black rebellions. As a result, by 1784 all the northern states except New Jersey and New York had legislated either immediate or gradual abolition of slavery. Delaware, Maryland, and Virginia made manumission easier. Even the Deep South saw efforts to mitigate the most brutal excesses that slavery encouraged among masters. Many observers believed that the Revolution had profoundly changed the prospects for African Americans.

The Revolutionary Impact

The War for Independence dealt a heavy, though not mortal, blow to slavery (Figure 4–1). While northern states prepared to abolish involuntary servitude, an estimated 100,000 slaves escaped from their masters in the South. In South Carolina alone, approximately 25,000 escaped—about 30 percent of the state's black population.

Twenty thousand black people left with the British at the end of the war. Some, at least temporarily, joined the Loyalist expatriate community in Canada. Others went to England or Sierra Leone, and a few were reenslaved in the British West Indies (Map 4–3). Meanwhile numerous escapees found their way to southern cities or to the North where they became part of a rapidly expanding free black class.

In the Chesapeake as well as the North, individual slaves gained freedom either in return for service in the war or because their masters had embraced Enlightenment principles. Philip Graham of Maryland, for example, freed his slaves, commenting that holding one's "fellow men in bondage and slavery is repugnant to the gold law of God and the unalienable right of mankind as well as to every principle of the late glorious revolution which has taken place in America." The Virginia legislature ordered masters to free slaves who had fought for American independence.

Those Chesapeake slaves who did not become free also made gains during the Revolution because the war hastened the decline of tobacco raising. As planters switched to wheat and corn, they required fewer year-round, full-time workers. This encouraged them to free their excess labor force or to negotiate contracts that let slaves serve for a term of years rather than for life.

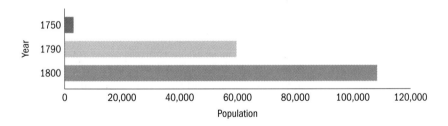

Figure 4–1 The Free Black Population of the British North American Colonies in 1750, and of the United States in 1790 and 1800. The impact of revolutionary ideology and a changing economy led to a great increase in the free black population during the 1780s and 1790s. Source: *A Century of Population Growth in the United States. 1790-1900,* (1909) p. 80. Data for 1750 estimated.

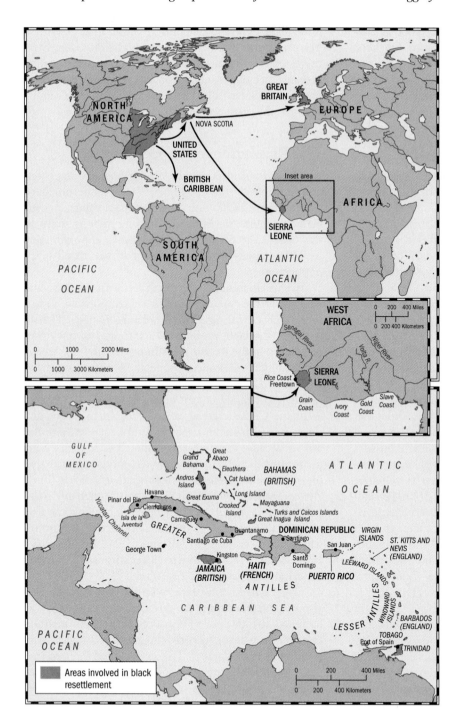

Map 4–3 The Resettlement of Black Loyalists after the American War for Independence. Like their white Loyalist counterparts, many black Loyalists left with the British following the Patriot victory. Most of those who settled in Nova Scotia soon moved on to Great Britain or the British free black colony of Sierra Leone. Some black migrants to the British Caribbean were reenslaved. Adapted from *The Atlas of African-American History and Politics*, 1/e, by A. Small-wood and J. Elliot, © 1998, The McGraw-Hill Companies. Reproduced with permission of The McGraw-Hill Companies.

Another alternative was for masters to allow slaves—primarily males—to practice skilled trades instead of doing field work. Such slaves were often hired out or "hired their own time" in return for giving their masters a large percentage of their wages.

Even those slaves who remained agricultural workers had more time to garden, hunt, and fish to supply themselves and their families with food and income. They gained more freedom to visit relatives who lived on other plantations, attend religious meetings, and interact with white people. Masters tended to refrain from the barbaric punishments used in the past, to improve slave housing, and to allow slaves more access to religion.

In South Carolina and Georgia, greater autonomy for slaves during the revolutionary era took a different form. The war increased absenteeism among masters and reduced contacts between the black and white populations. The black majorities in these regions grew larger, more isolated, and more African in culture as both South Carolina and Georgia imported more slaves from Africa. The constant arrival of Africans helped the region's African-American population retain a distinctive culture and the Gullah dialect. The increase in master absenteeism also permitted the task system of labor to expand. As historian Peter Kolchin notes, while African Americans in the North and the Chesapeake lived in close proximity to whites and interacted with them, "in the coastal region of the lower South, most blacks lived in a world of their own, largely isolated from whites, and developed their own culture and way of life."

The Revolutionary Promise

Even though the northern states were moving toward general emancipation during the revolutionary era, most newly free African Americans lived in the Chesa-

peake. They gained their freedom by serving in the war or escaping, or because of economic and ideological change. As a result, a substantial free black population emerged in the Chesapeake after the war. Free African Americans had, of course, always lived there—Anthony Johnson is a prominent example—but before the Revolution they were few. In 1782 Virginia had only 1,800 free black people out of a total black population of 220,582. By 1790 the state had 12,766 free black people and 30,570 by 1810. The free black population also grew in Delaware and Maryland.

But in South Carolina and Georgia, the free black class remained tiny. Most low country free black people were the children of white slave owners. They tended to be less independent of their former masters than their Chesapeake counterparts and lighter complexioned because their freedom was often a result of a family relationship to their masters.

In the North and the Chesapeake, free African Americans often moved to cities. Boston, New York,

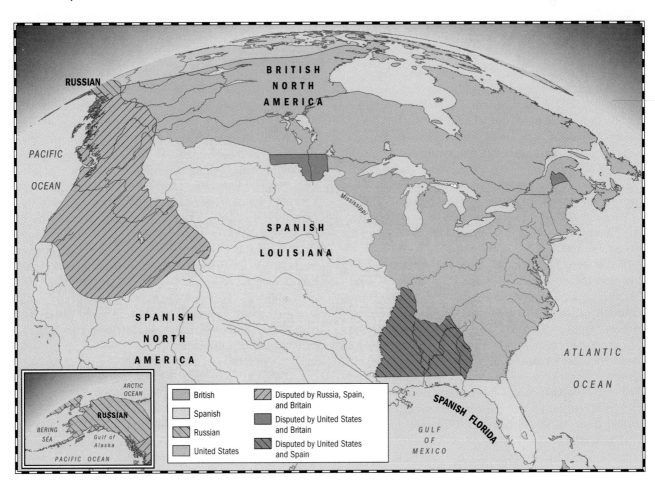

Map 4-4 North America 1783. This map shows the political geography of North America following British recognition of the independence of the United States in 1781.

TIMELINE

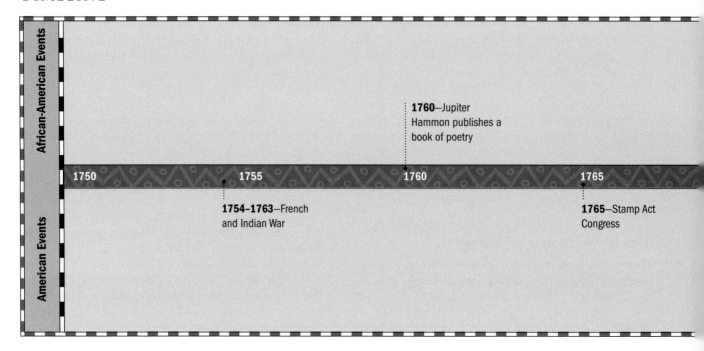

African-American Events

1760—Jupiter Hammon publishes a book of poetry

1750   1755   1760   1765

American Events

1754–1763—French and Indian War

1765—Stamp Act Congress

Philadelphia, Baltimore, Richmond, and Norfolk gained substantial free black populations after the Revolution. Black women predominated in this migration because they could more easily find jobs as domestics in the cities than in rural areas. Cities also offered free black people opportunities for community development that did not exist in thinly settled farm country. Although African Americans often used their new mobility to reunite families disrupted by slavery, relocating to a city could also disrupt families that had survived enslavement. It took about a generation for stable, urban, two-parent households to emerge.

Newly freed black people also faced economic difficulty, and their occupational status often declined. Frequently they emerged from slavery without the economic resources needed to become independent farmers, shopkeepers, or tradespeople. In the North such economic restraints sometimes forced them to remain with their former masters long after formal emancipation. To make matters worse, white artisans used legal and extralegal means to protect themselves from black competition so that African Americans who had learned trades as slaves had difficulty employing their skills in freedom.

Yet in both the North and the Chesapeake, most African Americans refused to work for their old masters and left the site of their enslavement. Those who had escaped had to leave; but for others, leaving indicated a desire to put the stigma of servitude behind them and embrace the opportunities freedom offered despite their risks. Many white people did not understand this desire and criticized their former chattels for not staying on as hired hands. One white Virginian complained, "I cannot help thinking it is too generally the case with all those of colour to be ungrateful."

Many African Americans also took new names to signify their freedom. They adopted surnames, such as *Freedom*, *Liberty*, or *Justice* and dropped such classical given names as *Pompey* and *Caesar*. Some paid homage to their African ancestry and complexion by taking surnames such as *Africa* and *Guinea*, *Brown*, and *Coal*. Others, however, expressed their aspirations in a racially stratified society by replacing African given names like *Cuffee* and *Quash* with Anglicized Bible names and the surnames of famous white people.

CONCLUSION

In the Peace of Paris signed in September 1783, Britain recognized the independence of the United States, acquiesced in American control of the territory between the Appalachian Mountains and the Mississippi River, and returned Florida to Spain (Map 4–4). Both sides

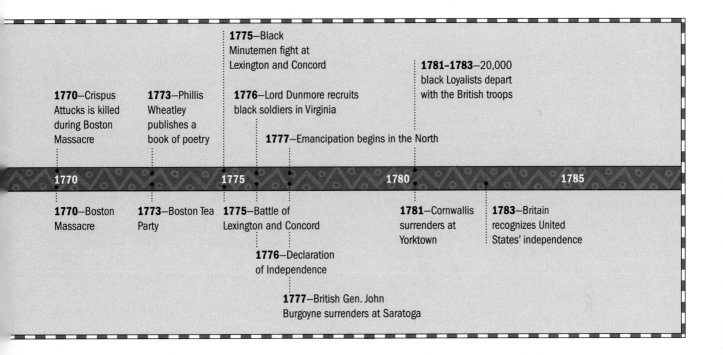

1775—Black Minutemen fight at Lexington and Concord

1781-1783—20,000 black Loyalists depart with the British troops

1770—Crispus Attucks is killed during Boston Massacre

1773—Phillis Wheatley publishes a book of poetry

1776—Lord Dunmore recruits black soldiers in Virginia

1777—Emancipation begins in the North

1770   1775   1780   1785

1770—Boston Massacre

1773—Boston Tea Party

1775—Battle of Lexington and Concord

1781—Cornwallis surrenders at Yorktown

1783—Britain recognizes United States' independence

1776—Declaration of Independence

1777—British Gen. John Burgoyne surrenders at Saratoga

promised to return confiscated property—including slaves—to their owners, but neither side complied. As the United States gained recognition of its independence, African Americans could claim that they had helped secure it. As soldiers in the Continental Army and the state militias, black men had fought and died for the revolutionary cause. Yet—like white Americans—they had been divided in their loyalties, although freedom was a common denominator for both those who chose the Patriot side and those who supported the Loyalists.

In this chapter we have sought to place the African-American experience during the struggle for independence in the broad context of revolutionary ideology derived from the Enlightenment. Black men and women, such as Benjamin Banneker and Phillis Wheatley, exemplified the intellectually liberating impact of eighteenth-century rationalism and recognized its application to black freedom.

Within the context of the war and with the assistance of white opponents of slavery, African Americans combined arguments for natural rights with action to gain freedom. Although most of their brothers and sisters remained in slavery, although the slave system began to expand again during the 1790s, and although free black people achieved *at best* second-class citizenship, they had made undeniable progress. The American Revolution seemed about to fulfill its promise of freedom to a

minority of African Americans and they were ready to embrace the opportunities it offered. By the end of the War for Independence in 1783, slavery in the North was dying and seemed to be on the wane in the Chesapeake. The first steps toward forming free black communities were under way. Black leaders and intellectuals had begun to emerge. Yet African Americans were also learning how difficult freedom could be despite the new republic's embrace of revolutionary ideals.

REVIEW QUESTIONS

1. How did the Enlightenment affect African Americans during the revolutionary era?

2. What was the relationship between the American Revolution and black freedom?

3. What was the role of African Americans in the War for Independence? How did their choices in this conflict affect how the war was fought?

4. How did the American Revolution encourage assimilation among African Americans? How did it discourage assimilation?

5. Why did a substantial class of free African Americans emerge from the revolutionary era?

RECOMMENDED READING

Ira Berlin and Ronald Hoffman, eds. *Slavery and Freedom in the Age of the American Revolution.* Charlottesville: University Press of Virginia, 1983. The essays in this collection focus on black life in America during the Revolutionary Era.

David Brion Davis. *The Problem of Slavery in the Age of Revolution, 1770–1823.* Ithaca, NY: Cornell University Press, 1975. This magisterial study discusses the influence of the Enlightenment and the industrial revolution on slavery and opposition to it in the Atlantic world.

Sylvia R. Frey. *Water from the Rock: Black Resistance in a Revolutionary Age.* Princeton, NJ: Princeton University Press, 1991. This book portrays the War for Independence in the South as a three-way struggle among Patriots, British, and African Americans. It emphasizes the role of religion and community in black resistance to slavery.

Benjamin Quarles. *The Negro in the American Revolution.* 1961; reprint, New York: Norton, 1973. This classic study remains the most comprehensive account of black participation in the War for Independence. It also demonstrates the impact of the war on black life.

Ellen Gibson Wilson. *The Loyal Blacks.* New York: G.P. Putnam's Sons, 1976. This book discusses why many African Americans chose the British side in the War for Independence. It also focuses on the fate of those loyal blacks who departed Nova Scotia in Canada for Sierra Leone.

Arthur Zilversmit. *The First Emancipation: The Abolition of Slavery in the North.* Chicago: University of Chicago Press, 1967. Zilversmit discusses the rise of an antislavery movement in the North and the process of emancipation there during the Revolutionary Era.

ADDITIONAL BIBLIOGRAPHY

The Crisis of the British Empire

Edward Countryman. *The American Revolution.* New York: Hill and Wang, 1975.

Douglas E. Leach. *Roots of Conflict: British Armed Forces and Colonial Americans, 1677–1763.* Chapel Hill: University of North Carolina Press, 1986.

Pauline Maier. *From Resistance to Revolution: Colonial Radicals and the Development of American Opposition to Britain, 1765–1776.* New York: Knopf, 1972.

Peter David Garner Thomas. *Revolution in America: Britain and the Colonies, 1765–1776.* Cardiff: University of Wales, 1992.

The Impact of the Enlightenment

Bernard Bailyn. *The Ideological Origins of the American Revolution.* Cambridge, MA: Harvard University Press, 1967.

Henry Steele Commager. *The Empire of Reason: How Europe Imagined and America Realized the Enlightenment.* Garden City, NY: Anchor, 1977.

Paul Finkelman. *Slavery and the Founders: Race and Liberty in the Age of Jefferson.* London: M.E. Sharpe, 1996.

J.G.A. Pocock. *The Machiavellian Moment: Florentine Political Thought and the Atlantic Republican Tradition.* Princeton, NJ: Princeton University Press, 1975.

Frank Shuffelton, ed. *The American Enlightenment.* Rochester, NY: University of Rochester Press, 1993.

African Americans and the American Revolution

Lerone Bennett Jr. *Before the Mayflower: A History of Black America.* 6th edition; Chicago: Johnson, 1987. Chapter 3.

Ira Berlin. "The Revolution in Black Life," in Alfred F. Young, ed. *The American Revolution: Explorations in the History of American Radicalism.* DeKalb: Northern Illinois University Press, 1976. 349–82.

Jeffrey J. Crow. *The Black Experience in Revolutionary North Carolina.* Raleigh: North Carolina Department of Cultural Resources, 1977.

Merton L. Dillon. *Slavery Attacked: Southern Slaves and their Allies, 1619–1865.* Baton Rouge: Louisiana State University Press, 1990. Chapter 2.

Sylvia R. Frey. "Between Slavery and Freedom: Virginia Blacks in the American Revolution," *Journal of Southern History* 69 (August 1983): 375–98.

Jack P. Greene. *All Men Are Created Equal: Some Reflections on the Character of the American Revolution.* Oxford: Clarendon, 1976.

Sidney Kaplan and Emma Nogrady Kaplan. *The Black Presence in the Era of the American Revolution.* Amherst: University of Massachusetts Press, 1989.

Peter Kolchin. *American Slavery, 1619–1877.* New York: Hill and Wang, 1993. Chapter 3.

Duncan McLeod. *Slavery, Race, and the American Revolution.* New York: Cambridge University Press, 1974.

Gary B. Nash. *Forging Freedom: The Formation of Philadelphia's Black Community, 1720–1840.* Cambridge, MA: Harvard University Press, 1988.

Peter H. Wood. "'The Dream Deferred': Black Freedom Struggles on the Eve of White Independence," in Gary Y. Okihiro, ed. *In Resistance: Studies in African, Caribbean, and Afro-American History.* Amherst: University of Massachusetts Press, 1986. 166–87.

Antislavery and Emancipation in the North

Robin Blackburn. *The Overthrow of Colonial Slavery, 1776–1848.* New York: Verso, 1988. Chapter 3.

Merton L. Dillon. *The Abolitionists: The Growth of a Dissenting Minority.* New York: Norton, 1974. Chapter 1.

Dwight L. Dumond. *Antislavery: The Crusade for Freedom in America.* 1961; reprint, New York: Norton, 1966.

Gary B. Nash. *Race and Revolution.* Madison, WI: Madison House, 1990.

James Brewer Stewart. *Holy Warriors: The Abolitionists and American Slavery.* Revised ed.; New York: Hill and Wang, 1997. Chapter 1.

Biography

Silvio A. Bedini. *The Life of Benjamin Banneker.* New York: Scribner, 1972.

William Henry Robinson. *Phillis Wheatley and Her Writings.* New York: Garland, 1984.

CHAPTER 5

African Americans in the New Nation, 1783–1820

BETHEL AFRICAN METHODIST EPISCOPAL CHURCH, PHILAD.ᵃ

Founded in 1784 by the Revᵈ Richard Allen, Bishop of the First African Methodist Episcopal Church in the United States. —— Rebuilt in 1805.

Drawn on Stone by W.L. Breton, Philadᵃ July 1829   Kennedy & Lucas Lithography

Philadelphia's Bethel African Methodist Episcopal Church, the mother church of the A.M.E. denomination, as it appeared in 1829.

Anytime, anytime while I was a slave, if one minute's freedom had been offered to me, and I had been told I must die at the end of that minute, I would have taken it—just to stand one minute on God's earth a free woman—I would.

Elizabeth Freeman

This, my dear brethren, is by no means the greatest thing we have to be concerned about. Getting our liberty in this world is nothing to our having the liberty of the children of God. . . . What is forty, fifty, or sixty years, when compared to eternity?

Jupiter Hammon

Death or Liberty.

proposed inscription for a flag to be used in Gabriel's planned rebellion of 1800.

Except that they were all born slaves in eighteenth-century America, Elizabeth Freeman, Jupiter Hammon, and Gabriel had little in common. Freeman was an illiterate domestic servant when in 1781, she sued for her freedom in Massachusetts. Hammon, who lived on Long Island, New York, was a poet and orthodox Calvinist preacher who enjoyed the support of his master and never sought his freedom. Gabriel was a literate, skilled slave who in 1800 masterminded a conspiracy to overthrow slavery in Virginia.

In this chapter we explore how African Americans as diverse as Freeman, Hammon, and Gabriel helped shape the lives of black people during America's early years as an independent republic. We also examine how the forces for black liberty vied with the forces of slavery and inequality between 1783 and 1820. The end of the War for Independence created great expectations among

African Americans. But by 1820, when the Missouri Compromise confirmed the power of slaveholders in national affairs, black people in the North and the South had long known that the struggle for freedom was far from over.

That struggle took place at the state and local as well as the regional and national levels. The forces involved in it were often impersonal. They included the emergence of a market economy based on wage labor in the North and an economy based on the production of cotton by slave labor in the South. A revolutionary ideology encouraged African Americans to seek freedom, by force if necessary. Meanwhile economic self-interest encouraged white northerners to limit black freedom, and fear of race war caused white southerners to strengthen the slave system.

Yet individuals and groups also shaped African-American life in the new nation. As urban, church-centered black communities arose, men and women—both slave and free—influenced culture, politics, economics, and perceptions of race. This was particularly true in the North and the Chesapeake, but also to a lesser degree in the Deep South. These were years of considerable progress for African Americans, although they ended with free black people facing deteriorating conditions in the North and with slavery spreading westward across the South.

FORCES FOR FREEDOM

During the decades after the War for Independence ended in 1783, a strong trend in the North and the Chesapeake favored emancipation. It had roots in economic change, evangelical Christianity, and a revolutionary ethos based on the natural rights doctrines of the Enlightenment. African Americans took advantage of these forces to escape from slavery, purchase the freedom of their families and themselves, sue for freedom in the courts, and petition state legislatures to grant them equal rights.

In the post-revolutionary North, slavery, though widespread, was not economically essential. Farmers could more efficiently hire hands during the labor-intensive seasons of planting and harvesting than they could maintain a year-round slave labor force. There-

THE ABOLITION OF SLAVERY IN THE NORTH

1777	Vermont constitutional convention prohibits slavery within what becomes the fourteenth state
1780	Pennsylvania begins gradually abolishing slavery within its borders
1783	Massachusetts's supreme court abolishes slavery there
1784	Connecticut and Rhode Island adopt gradual abolition plans
1785	New Jersey and New York legislatures defeat gradual abolition plans
1799	The New York legislature provides for gradual abolition within its jurisdiction
1804	New Jersey becomes the last northern state to initiate gradual abolition

fore northern slaveholders were a tiny class with limited political power. Moreover, trans-Atlantic immigration brought to the North plenty of white laborers, who worked cheaply and resented slave competition. As the Great Awakening initiated a new religious morality, as natural rights doctrines flourished, and as a market economy based on wage labor emerged, northern slaveholders had difficulty defending perpetual black slavery.

In Chapter 4 we saw that emancipation in the North was a direct result of the War for Independence. But the *process* of doing away with slavery unfolded in these states only after the war. Meanwhile antislavery societies proliferated in the upper South, and the national Congress set an important precedent in discouraging the expansion of slavery.

Northern Emancipation

There were similarities and differences in the handling of emancipation between the New England states of Massachusetts, Connecticut, Rhode Island, New Hampshire, and Vermont and the Mid-Atlantic states of Pennsylvania, New York, and New Jersey (Map 5–1). Slavery collapsed in the New England states because African Americans who lived there refused to remain in servitude and because most white residents acquiesced. The struggle against slavery in the Middle States was longer and harder because more white people there had a vested interest in maintaining it.

Two states—Vermont and Massachusetts (and possibly New Hampshire)—abolished slavery immediately

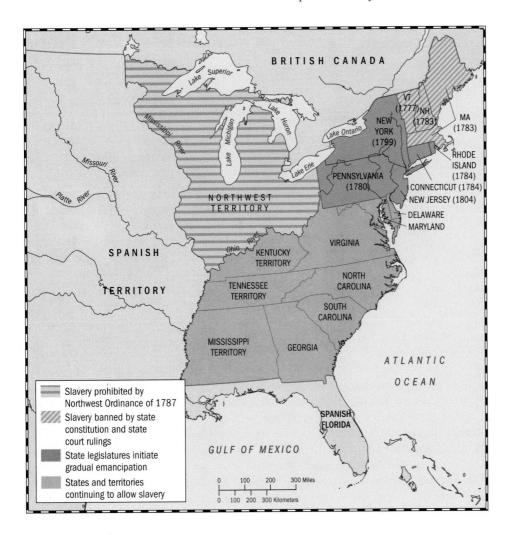

Map 5-1 Emancipation and Slavery in the Early Republic. This map indicates the abolition policies adopted by the states of the Northeast between 1777 and 1804, the antislavery impact of the Northwest Ordinance of 1787, and extent of slavery in the South during the early republic.

during the 1770s and 1780s. Vermont, where there had never been more than a few slaves, prohibited slavery in the constitution it adopted in 1777. Massachusetts, in its constitution of 1780, declared "that all men are born free and equal; and that every subject is entitled to liberty." Although this constitution did not specifically ban slavery, within a year Elizabeth Freeman and other slaves in Massachusetts sued for their freedom. Freeman, while serving as a waitress at her master's home in Sheffield, Massachusetts, overheard "gentlemen" discussing the "free and equal" clause of the new constitution. Shortly thereafter she contacted a prominent local white lawyer Theodore Sedgwick Sr., who agreed to represent her in court.

Meanwhile, another slave, Quok Walker, left his master and began living as a free person. In response, Walker's master sought a court order to force Walker to return to slavery. This case led in 1783 to a Massachusetts supreme court ruling that "slavery is . . . as effectively abolished as it can be by the granting of rights and privileges wholly incompatible and repugnant to its existence." At the same time, another judge used similar logic to grant Freeman her liberty. These decisions encouraged other Massachusetts slaves to sue for their freedom or—like Walker—to leave their masters, since the courts had ruled that the law did not recognize the right of slaveholders to their human chattel.

As a result, the first United States census in 1790 found no slaves in Massachusetts. Even before then, black men in the state had gained the right to vote. In 1780 Paul and John Cuffe, free black brothers, who lived in the town of Dartmouth, protested with five other free black men to the state legislature that they were being taxed without representation. After several setbacks, the courts finally decided in 1783 that African-American men who paid taxes in Massachusetts could vote there. This was a notable and rare victory. Before the Civil War, only several New England states and—by the mid-1840s—New York permitted black men to vote.

PROFILE

ELIZABETH FREEMAN

Known as Mum Bett, Elizabeth Freeman showed a strength of character that impressed everyone she met. Although records are contradictory, she was probably born in 1744 in Claverack, New York. As her parents were African slaves, she was also a slave. On the death of her first master in 1758, Freeman and her sister became the property of Colonel John Ashley, a court of common pleas judge, in Sheffield, Massachusetts. She married while quite young, gave birth to her only child—a daughter—and became a widow when her husband was killed fighting on the Patriot side in the War for Independence.

Freeman, who was illiterate, may have first learned of natural rights when in 1773 a group of men met at Ashley's home to draft a protest against British policies in the American colonies. "Mankind . . . have a right to the undisturbed Enjoyment of their lives, their Liberty and Property," the document declared. She took these words to heart, and when she learned while serving as a waitress in 1780 that the state of Massachusetts had adopted a bill of rights asserting that all people were born free and equal, she was ready to apply the doctrine.

In 1781 Freeman received "a severe wound" to her arm when she attempted to protect her sister from Ashley's wife, who "in a fit of passion" was threatening her with a hot kitchen shovel. Outraged at this attack, Freeman left the Ashley home and refused to return. Instead she engaged the legal assistance of Theodore Sedgwick Sr. in a suit for her freedom on the basis of Massachusetts's new bill of rights. The jury found in Freeman's favor and required Ashley to pay her thirty shillings in damages. It was at this point that Mum Bett changed her name legally to Elizabeth Freeman. Shortly thereafter the Massachusetts supreme court declared slavery unconstitutional throughout the state.

This portrait of Elizabeth Freeman was painted in watercolor on ivory by Elizabeth Sedgwick in 1811, thirty years after Freeman initiated her famous lawsuit.

For the remainder of her active life, Freeman worked as a paid domestic servant in the Sedgwick household and moved with the Sedgwicks to Stockbridge in 1785. Because Theodore Sedgwick Sr.'s wife was emotionally unstable, Freeman became a surrogate mother to the Sedgwick children, who later testified to her "superior instincts," abilities as a nurse, efficiency, and bravery.

During the 1830s, Theodore Sedgwick Jr. told British writer Harriet Martineau that in 1786 some participants in Shays's Rebellion entered the Sedgwick home while Theodore Sr. was away. Acting quickly to hide the family's silver set, Freeman confronted the men with a kitchen shovel similar to the one her former mistress had used against her. While advising the men "that they 'dare not strike a woman,'" she threatened to use the shovel against any one of them who disturbed the family possessions and she managed to usher them out with only minor damage to the Sedgwicks' property.

Freeman earned enough while employed by the Sedgwicks to purchase her own home and retire. When she died she left a small estate to her daughter, grandchildren, and great grandchildren. She left another legacy with the Sedgwick children. When Theodore Jr. became an abolitionist during the 1830s he credited Freeman as the source of his conviction that black people were not inferior to white people. Earlier Theodore's brother Charles had the following lines inscribed on Freeman's gravestone: "She never violated a trust, nor failed to perform a duty. In every situation of domestic trial, she was the most efficient helper, and the tenderest friend. Good mother fare well."

New Hampshire's record on emancipation is less clear than that of Vermont and Massachusetts. In 1779 black residents petitioned the New Hampshire legislature for freedom. There is also evidence that court rulings based on New Hampshire's 1783 constitution, which was similar to Massachusetts' constitution, refused to recognize human property. Nevertheless, New Hampshire still had about 150 slaves in 1792, and slavery may have simply withered away there rather than having been abolished by the courts.

In Connecticut and Rhode Island, the state legislatures, rather than individual African Americans, took the initiative against slavery. In 1784 these states adopted gradual abolition plans, which left adult slaves in bondage but proposed to free their children over a period of years. In Connecticut all children born to enslaved mothers after March 1, 1774, were to become free at age twenty-five. Rhode Island's plan was less gradual. Beginning that same March 1, it freed the children of enslaved women at birth. By 1790 only 3,763 slaves remained in New England out of a total black population there of 16,882. By 1800 only 1,339 slaves remained in the region, and by 1810 only 418 were left—108 in Rhode Island and 310 in Connecticut.

In New Jersey, New York, and Pennsylvania, the investment in slaves was much greater than in New England. After considerable debate, the Pennsylvania legislature in 1780 voted that the children of enslaved mothers would become free at age twenty-eight. Under this scheme, Pennsylvania still had 403 slaves in 1830 (Table 5–1). But many African Americans in the state gained their freedom much earlier by lawsuits or by simply leaving their masters.

Emancipation came even more slowly in New York and New Jersey. In 1785 their legislatures *defeated* proposals for gradual abolition. White Revolutionary leaders, such as Alexander Hamilton and John Jay, worked for abolition in New York, and Quakers had long advocated it in New Jersey. But these states had relatively large slave populations, powerful slaveholders, and white workforces fearful of free black competition.

In 1799 the New York legislature finally agreed that male slaves born after July 4 of that year were to become free at age twenty-eight and females at age twenty-five. In 1804 New Jersey adopted a similar law that freed male slaves born after July 4 of that year when they reached age twenty-five and females when they reached age twenty-one. Under this plan, New Jersey still had eighteen slaves in 1860.

The Northwest Ordinance of 1787

During the 1780s the United States Congress drew its authority from a constitution known as the Articles of Confederation. The Articles created a weak central government that lacked power either to tax or regulate commerce. Despite its weaknesses, this government acquired jurisdiction over the region west of the Appalachian Mountains and east of the Mississippi River, where several states had previously had conflicting land claims.

During the War for Independence, increasing numbers of Americans had migrated across the Appalachians into this huge region. The migrants invariably provoked hostilities with Indian nations, faced British opposition in the Northwest, and contested with Spanish forces in the Southwest. In response to these circumstances, Congress formulated policies to protect the migrants and provide for their effective government. The new nation's leaders were also concerned with the expansion of slavery into this vast region. Thomas Jefferson proposed to deal with both issues. First, he suggested that the region be divided into separate territories and prepared for statehood. Second, he proposed that after 1800 slavery be banned from the entire region stretching from the Appalachians to the Mississippi River and from Spanish Florida (Spain had regained Florida in 1783) to British Canada.

Jefferson's proposal failed to pass Congress in 1784 by a single vote. Instead in 1787, Congress adopted the Northwest Ordinance. It applied the essence of Jefferson's plan to the region north of the Ohio River—what historians call the Old Northwest. The ordinance

Table 5-1 Slave Populations in the Mid-Atlantic States, 1790–1860								
	1790	**1800**	**1810**	**1820**	**1830**	**1840**	**1850**	**1860**
New York	21,324	20,343	15,017	10,888	75	4		
New Jersey	11,432	12,343	19,851	7,557	2,243	674	236	18
Pennsylvania	3,737	1,706	795	211	403	64		

Source: Philip S. Foner, *History of Black Americans, from Africa to the Emergence of the Cotton Kingdom*, vol. 1, (Westport, CT: Greenwood, 1975), 374.

provided for the orderly sale of land, support for public education, territorial government, and the eventual formation of new states. Unlike Jefferson's plan, the ordinance banned slavery immediately. But, because it applied only to the Northwest Territory, the ordinance left the huge region south of the Ohio River open to slavery expansion.

By preventing slaveholders from taking slaves legally into areas north of the Ohio River, the ordinance set a precedent for excluding slavery from United States territories. Whether Congress had the power to do this became a contentious issue after President Jefferson annexed the huge Louisiana Territory in 1803. The issue continued to divide northern and southern politicians until the Civil War. Yet, despite the importance of the ordinance for black freedom, African Americans remained slaves in parts of the Old Northwest even after 1787. The first governor of the territory forced those who had been slaves before the adoption of the ordinance to remain slaves. In 1803 when Ohio became a state, the remainder of the Northwest Territory legalized indentured servitude. Therefore, in the southern parts of what became Illinois and Indiana, a few African Americans remained in involuntary servitude well into the nineteenth century.

Antislavery Societies in the North and the Upper South

In 1775 Quaker abolitionist Anthony Benezet organized the first antislavery society in the world. In 1787 it became the Pennsylvania Society for Promoting the Abolition of Slavery, and Benjamin Franklin became its president. Similar societies were founded in Delaware in 1788 and Maryland in 1789. By the end of the eighteenth century, there were societies in New Jersey, Connecticut, and Virginia. Organized antislavery sentiment also quickly rose in the new slave states of Kentucky and Tennessee. However, such societies never appeared in the Deep South.

From 1794 to 1832, antislavery societies cooperated within the loose framework of the American Convention for Promoting the Abolition of Slavery and Improving the Condition of the African Race. Only white people participated in these Quaker-dominated organizations, although members often cooperated with black leaders. As the northern states adopted abolition plans, the societies focused their attention on Delaware, Maryland, and Virginia. They aimed at gradual, compensated emancipation; encouraged masters to free their slaves; attempted to protect free black people from

reenslavement; and frequently advocated sending freed black people out of the country.

Experience with emancipation in the northern states encouraged the emphasis on gradual abolition. So did the reluctance of white abolitionists to challenge the property rights of masters. Abolitionists also feared that immediate emancipation might lead masters to abandon elderly slaves and assumed that African Americans would require long training before gaining freedom. Yet gradualism played into the hands of slaveholders who, like Thomas Jefferson, opposed slavery in the abstract but had no intention of freeing their own slaves.

The antislavery societies of the upper South tended to be small and short lived. A Wilmington, Delaware, society established in 1788, peaked at fifty members and ceased to exist in 1800. The Maryland society organized in 1781 with six members grew to 250 in 1797 but disbanded in 1798. African Americans and their white friends, nevertheless, hoped that antislavery sentiment was advancing southward.

Manumission and Self-Purchase

Another hopeful sign for African Americans was that most southern states liberalized their manumission laws after the Revolution. In general, masters could free individual slaves by deed or will. They no longer had to go to court or petition a state legislature to prove that an individual whom they desired to manumit had performed a "meritorious service." Virginia led the way in 1782 by repealing its long-standing ban on private manumissions. Delaware in 1787, Maryland in 1790, Kentucky in 1792, and the slaveholding territory of Missouri in 1804 followed.

As a result, hundreds of slaveholders in the upper South began freeing slaves. Religious sentiment and natural rights principles motivated many of these masters. Even though most of them opposed general emancipation, they considered the slave system immoral. Yet noble motives were not always the most important. Masters often negotiated self-purchase agreements with slaves that, while ending in manumission, gave masters a profit. Usually slaves raised money by marketing farm produce or through outside employment to purchase their freedom or that of loved ones in installments over a number of years. This allowed masters to enjoy income in addition to the slave's labor over the period of time the slave needed to raise the entire purchase price.

Masters also sometimes manumitted slaves who were no longer profitable investments. The master might be switching from tobacco to wheat or corn—crops that did not need a year-round workforce. Or a master might manumit older slaves whose best years as workers were behind them. Frequently, however, slaves—usually young men—presented masters with the alternative of manumitting them after a term of years or seeing them escape immediately.

Self-purchase often left African Americans in precarious financial condition. Sometimes they used up their savings to buy their freedom. In other instances they went into debt to their former masters, to white lawyers who acted as their agents, or to other white people who had loaned them money to cover their purchase price. On occasion masters reneged on their agreement to manumit after receiving money from a slave. Many of the freedom suits that became common in the upper South during this period resulted from such unethical behavior.

The Emergence of a Free Black Class in the South

As a result of manumission, self-purchase, and freedom suits, the free black population of the upper South blossomed between 1790 and 1810. Maryland and Virginia had the largest such populations. Between 1790 and 1810, the number of free African Americans in Maryland climbed from 8,043 to 33,927 and in Virginia from 12,766 to 30,570. By 1810 the upper South (Delaware, Maryland, Virginia, District of Columbia, Kentucky, Missouri, North Carolina, and Tennessee) had a free black population of 94,085, compared with a northern free black population of 78,181. However, most of the upper South's black population remained in slavery while the North's was on the way to general emancipation. In the North, 74 percent of African Americans were free in 1810, compared to only 10.4 percent of those in the upper South.

In the deep South, both the percentage and the absolute numbers of free black people remained even smaller. During the eighteenth century, neither South Carolina nor Georgia restricted the right of masters to manumit their slaves, but far fewer masters in these states exercised this right after the Revolution than was the case in the Chesapeake. Masters in the deep South freed only their illegitimate slave children, other favorites, or those unable to work. Only 14,180 free black people lived in the deep South in 1810. In North Carolina, a transitional area between the upper and deep South, the state legislature made manumission more difficult after 1777. But many masters—especially those who were Quakers—freed their slaves anyway or let them live in quasi-freedom.

FORCES FOR SLAVERY

The forces for black freedom in the new republic rested on widespread African-American dissatisfaction with slavery, economic change, Christian morality, and revolutionary precepts. Most black northerners had achieved freedom by 1800; three-quarters were free by 1810; and by 1840, only .7 percent remained in slavery.

Yet for the nation as a whole and for the mass of African Americans, the forces favoring slavery proved to be stronger. Abolition took place in the North where slavery was weak. In the South where it was strong, slavery thrived and expanded. For example, Virginia had 293,427 slaves in 1790. Despite manumissions and escapes, the state had 425,153 slaves in 1820. Although Virginia continued to have the largest population of enslaved African Americans in the country, the rate of growth of the slave population was greater in North Carolina, South Carolina, and Georgia. Meanwhile slavery expanded westward. For example, when Tennessee was still a territory in 1790, it had 3,417 slaves. By 1820 the state of Tennessee had 80,107.

The United States Constitution

The United States Constitution was a major force in favor of the continued enslavement of African Americans. The Continental Congress had become the central government of the United States when it declared independence from Great Britain in 1776, but the thirteen new states retained sovereignty over their internal affairs. The Articles of Confederation, in effect from 1781 to 1789, formally divided political authority between the states and the central government.

However, wealthy and powerful men soon perceived that the Confederation Congress was too weak to protect their interests. Democratic movements in the states threatened property rights. The inability of Congress to regulate commerce led to trade disputes among the states; its inability to tax left it unable to maintain an army and navy. Congress could not control the western territories, and, most frightening to the wealthy, it could not help states put down popular uprisings, such as that led by Daniel Shays in western Massachusetts in 1786.

The fears Shays's Rebellion caused led directly to a decision to hold the Constitutional Convention in Philadelphia, which in 1787 produced the constitution under which the United States is still governed. But the convention could not create a more powerful central government without first making important concessions to southern slaveholders.

The delegates to the convention omitted the words *slave* and *slavery* from the Constitution. But they included several clauses designed to secure the enslavement of African Americans in the southern states. These clauses provided for continuing the Atlantic slave trade for twenty years and returning slaves who escaped to other states to their masters. The Constitution also enhanced representation for slaveholders in Congress and the electoral college that elected the president.

Humanitarian opposition to the Atlantic slave trade had mounted during the revolutionary era. Under pressure from black activists—such as Prince Hall of Boston—and Quakers, northern state legislatures during the 1780s forbade their citizens to engage in the slave trade. Rhode Island led the way in 1787. Massachusetts, Connecticut, and Pennsylvania followed in 1788. Economic change in the upper South also prompted opposition to the trade. Virginia, for example, banned the importation of slaves from abroad nearly a decade before Rhode Island.

Yet delegates to the convention from South Carolina and Georgia maintained that they had an acute labor shortage. The delegates threatened that their citizens would not tolerate a central government that could stop them from importing slaves—at least not in the near future. The convention compromised by including a provision in the Constitution that prohibited Congress from abolishing the trade until 1808. During the twenty years between 1787 and 1808, when Congress banned the trade, thousands of Africans were brought into the southern states. Between 1804 and 1808, for example, forty thousand entered through Charleston. More slaves entered the United States during these two decades than during any other twenty years in American history. Such huge numbers helped fuel the westward expansion of the slave system.

Another proslavery clause of the United States Constitution provided that persons "held in service or labour in one State, escaping into another . . . shall be delivered up on claim of the party to whom such service or labour may be due." This clause was the basis for the Fugitive Slave Act of 1793, which allowed masters or their agents to pursue slaves across state lines, capture them, and take them before a magistrate. There, on presentation of satisfactory evidence, masters could regain legal custody of the person they claimed. This act did not stop slaves from escaping from Virginia and Maryland to Pennsylvania. But it did extend the power

of masters into the North, force the federal and northern state governments to uphold slavery, create personal tragedies for those who were recaptured, and encourage the kidnapping of free black northerners falsely claimed as escapees.

Finally the Constitution strengthened the political power of slaveholders through the Three-Fifths Clause. This clause was also a compromise between northern and southern delegates at the Convention. Southern delegates desired slaves to be counted toward representation in the national government but not counted for purposes of taxation. Northern delegates desired just the opposite. The Three-Fifths Clause provided that slaves be counted as three-fifths of a free person in determining a state's representation in the House of Representatives and in the electoral college. Slaves would be counted similarly when and if Congress instituted a per capita tax.

This gave southern slaveholders increased representation on the basis of the number of slaves they owned—slaves who, of course, had no vote or representation. The South gained enormous political advantage from it. If not for the three-fifths clause, for example, northern nonslaveholder John Adams would have been reelected president in 1800 instead of losing the presidency to southern slaveholder Thomas Jefferson. For many years this clause contributed to the domination of the United States government by slaveholding southerners, although the South's population steadily fell behind the North's. That Congress never instituted a per capita tax made this victory for slaveholders all the more remarkable.

Cotton

Three other factors were more important than constitutional provisions in fostering the continued enslavement of African Americans in the new republic:

1. Increased cultivation of cotton
2. Declining revolutionary fervor
3. Intensified white racism

The most obvious of these three developments was the increase in cotton production. By the late eighteenth century, Britain was the world's leading textile producer. As mechanization made the spinning of cotton cloth more economical, its demand for raw cotton increased dramatically. The United States took the lead in filling that demand as a result of Eli Whitney's invention of the cotton gin in 1793. This simple machine provided an easy and quick way to remove the seeds from the cotton most commonly grown in the South.

British demand combined with the cotton gin encouraged cotton production in the United States to rise from 3,000 to 178,000 bales between 1790 and 1810. Cotton became by far the United States' most lucrative export. Southern cotton production also encouraged the development of textile mills in New England, thereby creating a proslavery alliance between the "lords of the lash and the lords of the loom."

Cotton reinvigorated the slave-labor system, which spread rapidly across Georgia into the new slave states of Alabama, Mississippi, Louisiana, and Texas. Cotton was also cultivated in South Carolina, North Carolina, and parts of Virginia and Tennessee. To make matters worse for African Americans, the westward expansion of cotton production encouraged an internal slave trade. Masters in the old tobacco-growing regions of Maryland, Virginia, and other states began to support themselves by selling their slaves to the new cotton-growing regions (see Figure 5–1).

Conservatism and Racism

The waning of revolutionary humanitarianism and the rise of a more intense racism among white people are less tangible forces than the Constitution and cotton production, but they were just as important in strengthening slavery in these years. They also made life more difficult for free African Americans.

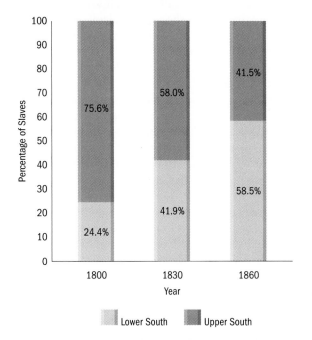

Figure 5–1 Distribution of the Southern Slave Population, 1800–1860. The demand for slaves in the cotton-growing lower South produced a major shift in the distribution of the slave population.

By the 1790s white Americans had begun a long retreat from the egalitarianism of the revolutionary era. In the North and Chesapeake, white people became less willing to challenge the prerogatives of slaveholders and more willing to accept slavery as suitable for African Americans. Most Marylanders and Virginians came to think of emancipation as best left to the distant future. This outlook strengthened the slaveholders and their nonslaveholding white supporters in the Deep South who had never embraced the humanitarian precepts of the Enlightenment and Great Awakening.

In part, increasing proslavery sentiment among white Americans stemmed from revulsion against the radicalism of the French Revolution that began in 1789. Most Americans came to value property rights—including rights to human property—and social order above liberty. Also, as cotton production spread westward and the value of slaves soared, rationalist and evangelical criticism of human bondage withered. Antislavery sentiment in the upper South that had flourished among slaveholders, nonslaveholders, Deists, Methodists, and Baptists became increasingly confined to African Americans and Quakers. By the early 1800s, manumissions began a long decline.

Using race to justify slavery was an important component of this conservative trend. Unlike white people, the argument went, black people were unsuited for freedom or citizenship. The doctrines embodied in the Declaration of Independence were, therefore, not applicable to them.

A new scientific racism supported this outlook. As early as the 1770s, some people challenged the Enlightenment's explanation that perceived racial differences were the results of different environments in which Africans and Europeans lived and were not essential or inherent. Scholars began to propose that, on the basis of a great chain of being from lesser creatures to higher creatures, black people constituted a separate species that was as close to the great apes as it was to white people. In the 1780s Thomas Jefferson reflected this view when he argued that "scientific observation" supported the conclusion that black people were inherently "inferior to whites in the endowments of both body and mind."

Such views were common among both white northerners and white southerners and had practical results. During the 1790s, Congress expressed its determination to exclude African Americans from the benefits of citizenship in "a white man's country." A 1790 law limited the granting of naturalized citizenship to "any alien, being a white person." Two years later, Congress limited enrollment in state militias to "each and every free, able-bodied white male citizen." These laws implied that African Americans had no place in the United States except as slaves. In other words, the free black class was an anomaly and, in the opinion of most white people, a dangerous anomaly.

THE EMERGENCE OF FREE BLACK COMMUNITIES

The competing forces of slavery and racism, on the one hand, and freedom and opportunity, on the other, shaped the growth of African-American communities in the early American republic. A distinctive black culture had existed since the early colonial period. But enslavement had limited black community life. The advent of large free black populations in the North and upper South after the Revolution allowed African Americans to establish autonomous and dynamic communities. They ap-

John Lewis Krimmel, "Negroes in front of the Bank of Pennsylvania" 1821. Watercolor on paper. H. 9-⅜s, W. 6-⅕₆ in. The Metropolitan Museum of Art, Rogers Fund, 1942. (42.95.16)

This watercolor depiction of industrious free black workers was painted in Philadelphia between 1811 and 1813 by a Russian diplomat. A woman, carrying a white child, greets men who are sawing wood. Often domestic work and physical labor were the only sorts of work open to black people.

peared in Philadelphia, Baltimore, Newport (Rhode Island), Richmond, Norfolk, New York, and Boston. As free black people in these cities acquired a modicum of wealth and education, they established institutions that have shaped African-American life ever since.

A combination of factors encouraged African Americans to form these distinctive institutions. First, as they emerged from slavery, they realized that they would have inferior status in white-dominated organizations or not be allowed to participate in them at all. Second, black people valued the African heritage they had preserved over generations in slavery. They wanted institutions that would perpetuate their heritage.

The earliest black community institutions were mutual aid societies. Patterned on white societies, these organizations were like modern insurance companies and benevolent organizations. They provided for their members' burial and medical expenses and helped support widows and children. African Americans in Newport, Rhode Island, organized the first such black mutual aid society in 1780. Seven years later, Richard Allen and Absalom Jones established the more famous Free African Society in Philadelphia.

Most early free-black societies admitted only men, but similar organizations for women appeared during the 1790s. For example, in 1793, Philadelphia's Female Benevolent Society of St. Thomas took over the welfare functions of the city's Free African Society. Other black women's organizations in Philadelphia during the early republic included the Benevolent Daughters—established in 1796 by Richard Allen's wife Sarah—Daughters of Africa established in 1812, the American Female Bond Benevolent Society formed in 1817, and the Female Benezet begun in 1818.

These ostensibly secular societies maintained a decidedly Christian moral character. They insisted that their members meet standards of middle-class propriety and, in effect, became self-improvement as well as mutual aid societies. Members had to pledge to refrain from fornication, adultery, drunkenness, and other "disreputable behavior." By the early 1800s, such societies also organized resistance to kidnappers who sought to recapture fugitive slaves or enslave free African Americans.

Because such societies provided real benefits and reflected black middle-class aspirations, they spread to every black urban community. More than one hundred such organizations existed in Philadelphia alone by 1830. Although they were more common in the North than in the South, Baltimore had about thirty of them by that same year, and even Charleston, South Carolina, had at least two. One of them was the Brown Fellowship, founded in 1790, which admitted only black men with light complexions. The other was open to all free black men in Charleston.

Of particular importance were the black freemasons because, unlike other free black organizations, the masons united black men from several northern cities. Combining rationalism with secrecy and obscure ritual, freemasonry was a major movement among European and American men during the late eighteenth and early nineteenth centuries. Opportunities for male bonding, wearing fancy regalia, and achieving prestige in a supposedly ancient hierarchy attracted both black and white men. As historians James Oliver Horton and Lois E. Horton suggest, black people drew special satisfaction from the European-based order's claims to have originated in ancient Egypt, which black people associated with their own African heritage.

The most famous black mason of his time was Prince Hall, the Revolutionary War veteran and abolitionist. During the 1770s he founded what became known as the African Grand Lodge of North America or—more colloquially—the Prince Hall Masons. In several respects Hall's relationship to masonry epitomizes the free black predicament in America.

In 1775 the local white masonic lodge in Boston rejected Hall's application for membership because of his black ancestry. Instead, Hall, who was a Patriot, got a limited license—for what was called African Lodge No. 1—from a British lodge associated with the British army that then occupied Boston. The irony of this situation was compounded when, after the War for Independence, American masonry refused to grant the African Lodge a full charter. Hall again had to turn to the British masons who approved his application in 1787. It was under this British charter that Hall in 1791 became Provincial Grand Master of North America and began authorizing black lodges in other cities, notably Philadelphia and Providence, Rhode Island.

The Origins of Independent Black Churches

Although black churches emerged at least a decade later than black benevolent associations, the churches quickly became the core of African-American communities. Not only did these churches attend to the spiritual needs of free black people and—in the border South—slaves, too, their pastors also became the primary African-American leaders. Black church buildings housed schools, social organizations, and antislavery meetings.

During the late eighteenth century, as the egalitarian spirit of the Great Awakening waned among white Baptists, Methodists, and Episcopalians, separate—but not

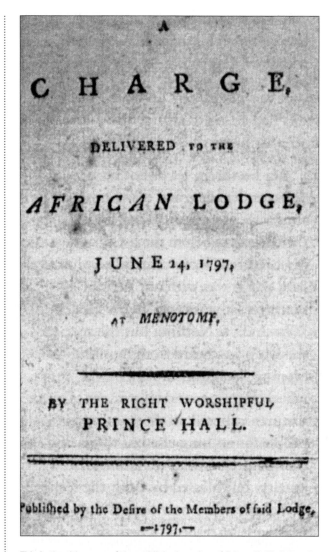

This is the title page of the published version of Prince Hall's last public speech. He delivered it in June 1797 before the Boston African Lodge that he had established. On this occasion Hall condemned assaults on black people by white mobs and noted revolutionary changes in Haiti.

independent—black churches appeared in the South. The biracial churches spawned by the Awakening had never embraced African Americans on an equal basis with white people. Although there had initially been promising tendencies within biracial churches, as time passed white people denied black people significant influence in church governance and imposed segregated seating, communion services, Sunday schools, and cemeteries on them. Separate black congregations, usually headed by black ministers but subordinate to white church hierarchies, were the ultimate result of these policies. The first such congregations appeared during the 1770s in South Carolina and Georgia.

In contrast to these subordinate churches, a truly independent black church emerged gradually in Philadelphia between the 1780s and the early 1800s. The movement for such a church began within the city's white-controlled St. George's Methodist Church. The movement's leaders were Richard Allen and Absalom Jones, who could rely on the Free African Society they had established to help them.

Both these men had been slaves. Allen purchased his freedom in 1780 and Jones bought his in 1783. A fervent Methodist since the 1770s, Allen received permission from St. George's white leadership to preach to black people in the evenings in what was then a simple church building. By the mid-1780s, Jones had joined Allen's congregation, and soon Allen, Jones, and other

black members of St. George's chafed under policies they considered unchristian and insulting. But their own faith that Methodist egalitarianism would finally prevail undermined their efforts during the 1780s to create a separate black Methodist church.

The break finally came in 1792 when St. George's white leaders grievously insulted the church's black members. An attempt by white trustees to prevent Jones from praying in what the trustees considered the white section of the church led black members to walk out. "We all went out of the church in a body," recalled Allen, "and they were no more plagued by us in the church."

St. George's white leaders fought hard and long to control the expanding and economically valuable black

VOICES

RICHARD ALLEN ON THE BREAK WITH ST. GEORGE'S CHURCH

It took an emotionally wrenching experience to convince Richard Allen, Absalom Jones, and other black Methodists that they must break their association with St. George's Church. Allen published the following account in 1833 as part of his autobiography, The Life Experiences and Gospel Labors of the Rt. Rev. Richard Allen. *Although many years had passed since the incident, Allen's account retains a strong emotional immediacy.*

A number of us usually attended St. George's church in Fourth street; and when the colored people began to get numerous in attending the church, they moved us from the seats we usually sat on, and placed us around the wall, and on Sabbath morning, we went to the church and the sexton stood at the door, and told us to go in the gallery. He told us to go, and we would see where to sit. We expected to take the seats over the ones we formerly occupied below, not knowing any better. We took those seats. Meeting had begun and they were nearly done singing, and just as we got to the seats, the elder said, "Let us pray." We had not been long upon our knees before I heard considerable scuffling and low talking. I raised my head up and saw one of the trustees, H_____ M_____, having hold of the Rev. Absalom

Jones, pulling him up off his knees, and saying, "You must get up—you must not kneel here." Mr. Jones replied, "Wait until prayer is over." Mr. H_____ M_____ said, "No, you must get up now, or I will call for aid and force you away." Mr. Jones said, "Wait until prayer is over, and I will get up and trouble you no more." With that he [H_____ M_____] beckoned to one of the other trustees, Mr. L_____ S_____ to come to his assistance. He came, and went to William White to pull him up. By this time prayer was over, and we all went out of the church in a body, and they were no more plagued with us in the church. . . . We then hired a store-room, and held worship by ourselves. Here we were pursued with threats of being disowned, and read publicly out of meeting if we did continue worship in the place we had hired; but we believed the Lord would be our friend. We got subscription papers out to raise money to build the house of the Lord.

QUESTIONS

1. What appears to have sparked the confrontation Allen describes?

2. How did white church leaders respond to the withdrawal of the church's black members?

congregation. Yet other white Philadelphians, led by abolitionist Benjamin Rush, applauded the concept of an independent "African church." Rush and other sympathetic white people contributed to the building fund. When construction began in 1793, Rush and at least one hundred other white people joined with African Americans at a banquet to celebrate the occasion.

However, the black congregation soon split. When the majority determined that the new church would be Episcopalian rather than Methodist, Allen and a few others refused to join. The result was *two* black churches in Philadelphia. St. Thomas's Episcopal Church, with Jones as priest, opened in July 1794 as an African-American congregation within the white-led national Episcopal Church. Then Allen's Mother Bethel congregation got under way as the first truly independent black church. The white leaders of St. George's tried to control Mother Bethel until 1816. But that year it became the birthplace of the African Methodist Episcopal (AME) Church. Allen became the

first bishop of this organization, which quickly spread to cities in both the North and the South.

Most significant among these other AME congregations were Daniel Coker's in Baltimore, the AME Zion in New York, and those in Wilmington, Delaware, Salem, New Jersey, and Attleboro, Pennsylvania. Other independent black churches that formed at this time out of similar conflicts with white-led congregations included the Abyssinian Baptist Church, organized in New York City in 1808 by Thomas Paul, and the African Presbyterian Church, established in Philadelphia by Samuel E. Cornish in 1811.

The First Black Schools

Schools for African-American children, slave and free, date to the early 1700s. In both North and South, white clergy, including Cotton Mather, ran the schools. So did Quakers, early abolition societies, and missionaries acting for the Anglican Society for the Propagation of the Gospel in Foreign Parts. But the first schools established by African Americans to instruct African-American children arose after the Revolution. The new black mutual aid societies and churches created and sustained them.

Schools for black people organized or taught by white people continued to flourish. But in other instances, black people founded their own schools because local white authorities regularly refused either to admit black children to public schools or to maintain adequate separate schools for them. For example, in 1796, when he failed to convince Boston's city council to provide a school for black students, Prince Hall had the children taught in his own home and that of his son Primus. By 1806 the school was meeting in the basement of the new African Meeting House, which housed Thomas Paul's African Baptist Church.

Hall was not the first to take such action. As early as 1790, Charleston's Brown Fellowship operated a school for its members' children. Free black people in Baltimore supported schools during the same decade, and during the early 1800s, similar schools opened in Washington, D.C. Such schools frequently employed white teachers. Not until Philadelphia's Mother Bethel church established the Augustine School in 1818 did a school entirely administered and taught by African Americans for black children exist.

These schools faced great difficulties. Many black families could not afford the fees, but rather than turn children away, the schools strained their meager resources by taking charity cases. Some black parents also

This pastel portrait of Richard Allen by an unknown artist was done in 1824, when Allen was only twenty-four years old and just beginning his preaching career.

believed that education was pointless when African Americans often could not get skilled jobs. White people feared competition from skilled black workers, believed that black schools attracted undesirable populations, and—particularly in the South—feared that educated free African Americans would encourage slaves to revolt.

Threats of violence against such schools and efforts to suppress them were common. The case of Christopher McPherson exemplifies these dangers. McPherson, a free African American, established a night school for black men at Richmond, Virginia, in 1811 and hired a white teacher. All went well until McPherson advertised the school in a local newspaper. In response, white residents forced the teacher to leave the city, and local authorities had McPherson committed to the state lunatic asylum. Nevertheless, similar schools continued to operate in both the North and upper South, producing a growing class of literate African Americans.

BLACK LEADERS AND CHOICES

By the 1790s, an educated black elite that was well able to provide leadership for other African Americans in religion, economic advancement, and racial politics had come into existence in the North and Chesapeake. Experience had driven this elite to a contradictory perception of themselves and of America. They were acculturated, patriotic Americans who had achieved some personal well-being and security. But they were also well aware that American society had not lived up to its revolutionary principles; they lamented the continued enslavement of the mass of African Americans; and they had misgivings about the future.

Prominent among these leaders were members of the clergy. Two of the most important of them were Richard Allen and Absalom Jones. Besides organizing his church, Allen opened a school in Philadelphia for black children, wrote against slavery and racial prejudice, and made his home a refuge for fugitive slaves. A year before his death in 1831, Allen presided over the first national black convention.

Jones, too, was an early abolitionist. In 1797 his concern for fugitives facing reenslavement led him to become the first African American to petition Congress. His petition anticipated later abolitionists in suggesting that slavery violated the spirit of the United States Constitution and that Congress could abolish it.

Other influential black ministers of the late eighteenth and early nineteenth centuries were Jupiter Hammon, Daniel Coker of Baltimore, John Chavis of Virginia, and Lemuel Haynes of New England. Hammon, who is quoted at the beginning of this chapter, became a well-known poet. Coker, who was of mixed race, conducted a school, cofounded the AME Church, and advocated black migration to Africa. Chavis also combined preaching and teaching. Born free, he served on the Patriot side in the War for Independence and entered the College of New Jersey (Princeton) in 1792. Thereafter he became a Presbyterian missionary among African Americans in Virginia, Maryland, and North Carolina and gained a wide reputation as a biblical scholar. Haynes was perhaps even better known for his intellectual accomplishments. The son of a white mother and black father, Haynes served with the Minutemen and Continental Army, spoke against slavery, and in 1780, became the first ordained black Congregationalist minister, serving as pastor to several white congregations.

Vying with clergy for influence were African-American entrepreneurs. Prince Hall, for example, owned successful leather dressing and catering businesses in Boston, and Peter Williams, principal founder of New York's AME Zion church, was a prosperous tobacco merchant. Another prominent black entrepreneur was James Forten of Philadelphia, described as "probably the most noteworthy free African-American entrepreneur in the early nineteenth century." Born to free parents in 1766, Forten was a Patriot during the War for Independence, learned the craft of sail making, and became the owner of his own business in 1798. For the rest of his life, he advocated equal rights and abolition.

American patriotism, religious conviction, organizational skill, intellectual inquisitiveness, and antislavery activism delineate the lives of most free black leaders in this era. Yet these leaders often were torn in their perceptions of what was best for African Americans. Hammon and Chavis were accommodationist about slavery and racial oppression. They both condemned slavery and lauded human liberty, but they were not activists. They maintained that God would eventually end injustice. As late as 1836, Chavis—who lived in the South—wrote "that Slavery is a national evil no one doubts, but what is to be done? . . . All that can be done, is to make the best of a bad bargain. For I am clearly of the opinion that immediate emancipation would be to entail the greatest earthly curse upon my brethren according to the flesh."

Allen, Jones, Hall, and Forten were more optimistic than Hammon and Chavis about the ability of African Americans to mold their own destiny in the United States. Although they each expressed misgivings, they

ABSALOM JONES PETITIONS CONGRESS ON BEHALF OF FUGITIVES FACING REENSLAVEMENT

Absalom Jones wrote his petition to Congress on behalf of four black men who had been manumitted in North Carolina. Because they were in danger of being reenslaved, they had taken refuge in Philadelphia. The men, over whose names the petition appears in the Annals of Congress, *were Jupiter Nicholson, Jacob Nicholson, Joe Albert, and Thomas Pritchet. Jones provided brief accounts of their troubles. Here we include only the important general principles that Jones invoked. Southern representatives argued that accepting a petition from alleged slaves would set a dangerous precedent, and Congress refused to accept the petition.*

To the President, Senate, and House of Representatives,

The Petition and Representation of the under-named Freemen, respectfully showeth:

That, being of African descent, the late inhabitants and natives of North Carolina, to you only, under God, can we apply with any hope of effect, for redress of our grievances, having been compelled to leave the State wherein we had a right of residence, as freemen liberated under the hand and seal of humane and conscientious masters, the validity of which act of justice in restoring us to our native right of freedom, was confirmed by judgment of the Superior Court of North Carolina. . . . yet, not long after this decision, a law of that State was enacted, under which men of cruel disposition, and void of just principle, received countenance and authority in violently seizing, imprisoning, and selling into slavery, such as had been so emancipated; whereby we were reduced to the necessity of separating from some of our nearest and most tender connections, and seeking refuge in such parts of the Union where more regard is paid to the public declaration in favor of liberty and the common right of man, several hundreds, under our circumstances, having, in consequence of the said law, been hunted day and night, like beasts of the forest, by armed men with dogs, and made a prey of as free and lawful plunder. . . .

We beseech your impartial attention to our hard condition, not only with respect to our personal sufferings, as freemen, but as a class of that people who, distinguished by color, are therefore with a degrading partiality, considered by many, even of those in eminent stations, as unentitled to that public justice and protection which is the great object of Government. . . .

If, notwithstanding all that has been publicly avowed as essential principles respecting the extent of human right to freedom; notwithstanding we have had that right restored to us, so far as was in the power of those by whom we were held as slaves, we cannot claim the privilege of representation in your councils, yet we trust we may address you as fellow-men, who, under God, the sovereign Ruler of the Universe, are intrusted with the distribution of justice, for the terror of evil-doers, the encouragement of protection of the innocent, not doubting that you are men of liberal minds, susceptible of benevolent feelings and clear conception of rectitude to a catholic extent, who can admit that black people . . . have natural affections, social and domestic attachments and sensibilities; and that, therefore, we may hope for a share in your sympathetic attention while we represent that the unconstitutional bondage in which multitudes of our fellows in complexion are held, is to us a subject sorrowfully affecting; for we cannot conceive their condition (more especially those who have been emancipated and tasted the sweets of liberty, and again reduced to slavery by kidnappers and man-stealers) to be less afflicting or deplorable than the situation of citizens of the United States, captured and enslaved through the unrighteous policy prevalent in Algiers . . . . May we not be allowed to consider this stretch of power, morally and politically, a Governmental defect, if not a direct violation of the declared fundamental principles of the Constitution; and finally, is not some remedy for an evil of such magnitude highly worthy of the deep inquiry and unfeigned zeal of the supreme Legislative body of a free and enlightened people?

QUESTIONS

1. On what principles does Jones believe the United States government is bound to act?

2. What does Jones's petition indicate concerning the status of African Americans before the law?

Source: *Annals of Congress,* 4 Cong., 2 sess. (January 23, 1797), 2015–18.

JAMES FORTEN

James Forten was one of the few black leaders of the early American republic to live well beyond that era. His long career as a determined opponent of slavery linked the time of Prince Hall and Richard Allen to that of the militant abolitionists William Lloyd Garrison and Frederick Douglass (see Chapters 8 and 9). From the 1790s until his death in 1842, Forten used his wealth and organizational talents to build a cohesive black community in Philadelphia. But he also struggled to create a broader American community based on merit rather than on racial privilege.

James Forten, by an unknown artist.

Forten was born in Philadelphia in 1766. Family tradition held that one of his great grandfathers was an African who had been brought to Delaware in the late 1600s. His paternal grandfather was one of the first Pennsylvania slaves to purchase his freedom.

As a child, Forten learned to read and write at a school run by Quaker abolitionist Anthony Benezet and acquired Benezet's broad humanistic philosophy. In 1781 Forten volunteered to serve as a powder boy with a cannon crew on board the American privateer *Royal Louis*. He proved himself a brave sailor in battle. He was also deeply patriotic. When taken prisoner and offered special treatment by the son of a British officer, Forten declared, "No, NO! I am here a prisoner for the liberties of my country; I *never, NEVER, shall prove a traitor to her interests.*" As a result of his defiance, Forten spent seven months on a rotting prison ship in New York harbor.

After his release Forten walked back to Philadelphia and became an apprentice sail maker. He became foreman in 1786 and bought the business in 1798. By 1807 he employed an interracial work force of thirty, and by 1832 had acquired a fortune of about $100,000—a large sum at the time.

Throughout the 1780s and most of the 1790s, Forten stood aloof from Philadelphia's developing black community. He did not join the Free African Society or help establish separate black churches. Not until 1797 did he emerge as an active black leader. At that time he joined Richard Allen and Absalom Jones in establishing the African Masonic Lodge of Pennsylvania, which Prince Hall came to Philadelphia to install. Forten then joined eighty other Philadelphia African Americans to petition Congress to repeal the Fugitive Slave Law of 1793.

By 1817 Forten had become a major opponent of black migration to Africa. Although he had previously endorsed some colonization schemes, he had come to believe such efforts were racist because they assumed that black people were not suited for American citizenship. Rather than commit resources to sending African Americans to other parts of the world, he was determined to improve their standing in the United States. In 1809 he joined Allen and Jones in creating a self-improvement organization, the Society for the Suppression of Vice and Immorality. By 1830 he hoped to use the newly organized Black National Convention movement to train young black men for skilled trades.

At about the same time, Forten became an important influence on the white abolitionist leader William Lloyd Garrison. Forten welcomed Garrison to his home, introduced him to other black leaders, and helped finance his antislavery newspaper, the *Liberator*. In 1833 Forten joined Garrison, Arthur Tappan, Lewis Tappan, and other white and black abolitionists in organizing the American Antislavery Society, pledged to the peaceful immediate abolition of slavery without colonization of the former slaves and without compensation to slaveholders. Increasingly radical during his remaining years, Forten advocated an end to war, favored equal rights for women, and resisted the enforcement of the Fugitive Slave Law. He also helped establish the American Moral Reform Society. He demonstrated his commitment to women's rights in the way he raised his daughters, Sarah, Margaretta, and Harriet, who carried on his activism.

believed that—despite setbacks—the egalitarian principles of the American Revolution would prevail if black people insisted on liberty. Forten never despaired that African Americans would be integrated into the larger American society on the basis of their individual talent and enterprise. While he was often frustrated, Hall for four decades pursued a strategy based on the assumption that white authority would reward black protest and patriotism. In 1786, when Daniel Shays led his revolt of white farmers in western Massachusetts, Hall offered to raise seven hundred black volunteers to help defeat the insurgency. Allen and Jones put more emphasis on separate black institutions than did Forten or Hall. Yet they were just as willing to organize, protest, and petition to establish the rights of black people as American citizens.

Migration

African Americans, however, had another alternative: migration from the United States to establish their own society free from white prejudices. There were great practical obstacles to mass black migration to West Africa, the Caribbean, or western North America. It was extremely expensive, difficult to organize, and involved long—often fruitless—negotiations with foreign governments. But no black leader during the early national period was immune to the appeal of such proposals.

As early as 1787, Hall petitioned the Massachusetts legislature to support efforts by black Bostonians to establish a colony in Africa. Although he recognized black progress in Massachusetts, Hall maintained that he and others found themselves "in many respects, in very disagreeable and disadvantageous circumstances; most of which must attend us so long as we and our children live in America." By 1820 Coker had become so convinced that this view was correct that he led the first party of eighty-six African Americans to the new colony of Liberia on the West African coast.

The major black advocate of migration to Africa during this period, however, was Paul Cuffe, the son of an Ashanti (in modern Ghana) father and Wampanoag Indian mother. He became a prosperous New England sea captain and, by the early 1800s, cooperated with British humanitarians and entrepreneurs to promote migration. He saw African-American colonization in West Africa as a way to end the Atlantic slave trade, spread Christianity, create a refuge for free black people, and make profits. Before his death in 1817, Cuffe had influenced not only Coker but also—at least temporarily—Forten, Allen, and Jones to consider colonization as a viable alternative for African Americans.

Slave Uprisings

While black northerners became increasingly aware of the limits of their freedom after the Revolution, black southerners saw the perpetuation of their enslavement. As cotton production expanded westward and new slave states entered the Union, as masters in such border slave states as Maryland and Virginia turned away from the revolutionary commitment to gradual emancipation, slaves faced several choices.

Some lowered their expectations and loyally served their masters. Most continued patterns of day-to-day resistance, and mounting numbers of men and women escaped. A few risked their lives to join revolutionary movements to destroy slavery violently. When just several hundred out of hundreds of thousands of slaves rallied behind Gabriel in 1800 near Richmond or Charles Deslandes in 1811 near New Orleans, they frightened white southerners and raised hopes for freedom among countless African Americans.

The egalitarian principles of the American and French revolutions influenced Gabriel and Deslandes. Unlike earlier slave rebels, they acted not to revenge personal grievances or to establish maroon communities but to destroy slavery because it denied natural human rights to its victims. The American Declaration of Independence and the legend of Haiti's Toussaint L'Ouverture provided the intellectual foundations for their efforts.

L'Ouverture, against great odds, had led the enslaved black people of the French sugar colony of Saint Domingue—modern Haiti—to freedom and independence. This bitter and bloody struggle lasted from 1791 to 1804. Many white planters fled the island with their slaves to take refuge in Cuba, Jamaica, South Carolina, Virginia, and—somewhat later—Louisiana. The Haitian slaves carried the spirit of revolution with them to their new homes.

During the early 1790s, black unrest and rumors of pending revolt mounted in Virginia. The state militia arrested suspected plotters, but they got off with whippings. In this revolutionary atmosphere, Gabriel, the human property of Thomas Prosser Sr., prepared to lead a massive slave insurrection. Gabriel was an acculturated and literate blacksmith who was well aware of the rationalist and revolutionary currents of his time. He was also a large and powerful man with a violent temper. In the fall of 1799, for example, a local court convicted him of "'biting off a considerable part of [the] left Ear' of a white neighbor."

The ideology of the American Revolution shaped Gabriel's actions. He was also aware that white people

This drawing of Haitian liberation Toussaint L'Ouverture suggests his stature as a military leader. His successful revolution inspired black rebels in the American South.

were politically divided and distracted by an undeclared naval war with France. He enjoyed some secret white support and hoped that poor people generally would rally to his cause as he and his associates planned to kill those who supported slavery and take control of central Virginia.

But on August 30, 1800—the day the uprising was to occur—two slaves revealed the plan to white authorities while a tremendous thunderstorm prevented Gabriel's followers from assaulting Richmond. Then governor—and future United States president—James Monroe quickly had suspects arrested. Gabriel, who relied on white allies to get to Norfolk, was among the last captured. In October he and twenty-six others, convicted of "conspiracy and insurrection," were hanged. But by demonstrating that slaves could organize for large-scale rebellion, they left a legacy of fear among slaveholders and hope for liberation among southern African Americans.

The far less famous Louisiana Rebellion took place under similar circumstances. By the early 1800s, refu-

gees from Haiti had settled with their slaves in what was then known as Orleans Territory. As they arrived, rumors of slave insurrection spread across the territory. The rumors became reality on January 8, 1811, when Deslandes, a Haitian native and slave driver on a plantation north of New Orleans, initiated a massive revolt in cooperation with maroons.

Although no record of Deslandes's rhetoric survives and his goals may have been less ideologically coherent than Gabriel's, he organized a force of at least 180 men and women. They marched south along the Mississippi River toward New Orleans, with leaders on horseback, and with flags and drums, but few guns. The revolutionaries plundered and burned plantations but killed only two white people and one recalcitrant slave. They were overwhelmed on January 10 by a force of about 700 territorial militia, slaveholding vigilantes, and United States troops. The "battle" was a massacre. The well-armed white men slaughtered sixty-six of the rebels and captured twenty-one, including Deslandes. These captives were tried without benefit of counsel, found guilty of rebellion, and shot. The white authorities cut off each executed rebel's head and displayed it on a pike to warn other African Americans of the consequences of revolt.

The White Southern Reaction

Although Deslandes's uprising was one of the few major slave revolts in American history, Gabriel's conspiracy and events in Haiti left the more significant legacy. For generations enslaved African Americans regarded L'Ouverture as a black George Washington and recalled Gabriel's revolutionary message. The networks among slaves that Gabriel established continued to exist after his death, and as the external slave trade carried black Virginians southwestward, they took his promise of liberation with them.

The fears that the Haitian revolution and Gabriel's conspiracy raised among white southerners deepened their reaction against the egalitarian values of the Enlightenment. Because they feared race war and believed that emancipation would encourage African Americans to begin such a war, most white people in Virginia and throughout the South determined to make black bondage stronger, not weaker.

Beginning with South Carolina in December 1800, southern states outlawed assemblies of slaves, placed curfews on slaves and free black people, and made manumissions more difficult. The old colonial practice of white men patrolling slave quarters on horseback revived. Assuming that revolutionaries like Gabriel received encouragement from white abolitionists as well as free African Americans, white southerners became suspicious of such outsiders as Yankee peddlers, evangelicals, and foreigners. Forcing free black people out of southern states became more attractive to white southerners and brought about an odd alliance between them and black advocates of emigration to Africa.

THE WAR OF 1812

Many of the themes developed in this chapter—the patriotism of African Americans, their opportunities for freedom, migration sentiment among them, and influences pushing slaves toward revolutionary action—appear in the United States' war with Great Britain that began in 1812. The roots of this conflict lay in a massive military and economic struggle between Britain and France for mastery over the Atlantic world. The struggle lasted from 1793, during the French Revolution, to the defeat of Napoleon Bonaparte by a British-led coalition in 1815.

Long-standing disputes, the desire to annex Canada, and especially Britain's interference with the United States' vital trade links to Europe drew this country into the war of 1812, which lasted until late 1814. Although the United States won some important victories, it failed to achieve its major objective—the conquest of Canada—and the war ended in a draw. Yet many Americans regarded the war as a second struggle for independence, and once again, black military service and white fear of slave revolt played important roles.

When the war began, white prejudice and fear of black revolt had nearly nullified memories of the service of black Patriot soldiers during the Revolution. The Militia Act of 1792 had eliminated armed black participation in all state militias except that of North Carolina. The secretary of the Navy ended black service on American warships in 1798. Because of the news from Haiti and because of Gabriel's conspiracy, white southerners joined John Randoph of Virginia in regarding African Americans as "an internal foe." Therefore, when the war with Great Britain began, the southern states refused to enlist black men for fear they would use their guns to aid slave revolts. Meanwhile, the lack of enthusiasm for the war among many northerners, combined with the absence of a British threat to their part of the country, kept northern states from mobilizing black troops during 1812 and 1813.

Southern fears of slave revolt mounted in the spring of 1813 when the British invaded the Chesapeake. As they had during the Revolution, British generals offered slaves freedom in Canada or the British West Indies in return for help. In response, African Americans joined the British army that burned Washington, D.C., in 1814 and attacked Baltimore.

The threat this British army posed to Philadelphia and New York led to the first active black involvement in the war on the American side. The New York state legislature authorized two black regiments, offered freedom to slaves who enlisted, and promised compensation to their masters. Meanwhile, African Americans in Philadelphia and New York City volunteered to help build fortifications. In Philadelphia, James Forten, Richard Allen, and Absalom Jones patriotically raised a "Black Brigade," which never saw action because the British halted when they failed to capture Baltimore.

African-American men did fight, however, at two of the war's most important battles. During the naval engagement on Lake Erie in September 1813 that secured control of the Great Lakes for the United States, one-quarter of Captain Oliver Hazard Perry's four hundred sailors were black. Although Perry had been staunchly prejudiced against using these men, after the battle he praised their valor.

At the Battle of New Orleans—fought in January 1815, about a month after the war was officially over (news of peace had not yet reached the area)—African Americans also fought bravely. Yet white memories of Deslandes's recent uprising almost prevented them from being allowed to fight on the American side. Many white people feared that, if mobilized, the local free black militia—which dated back to the Spanish occupation of Louisiana from 1763 to 1801—would make common cause with slaves and the British rather than take the American side.

In defiance of such fears, General Andrew Jackson included the black troops in his force defending New Orleans and offered them equal pay and benefits. At least six hundred free black men fought on the American side at the Battle of New Orleans, and Jackson lived up to his promise of equal treatment. It was a choice, he later informed President James Monroe, between having the free African Americans "in our ranks or . . . in the ranks of the enemy."

The Missouri Compromise

During the years following 1815 as the United States emerged from a difficult war, sectional issues between the North and South, which had been pushed into the background by constitutional compromises and the political climate, revived. The nation's first political parties—the Federalists and the Republicans—had failed to confront slavery as a national issue. The northern wing of the modernizing Federalist party had abolitionist tendencies. But during the 1790s when they controlled the national government, the Federalists did not raise the slavery issue. Then the victory of the state-rights oriented Republican party in the election of 1800 fatally weakened the Federalists as a national organization and brought a series of implicitly proslavery administrations to power in Washington.

It took innovations in transportation and production that began during the 1810s—as well as the continuing disappearance of slavery in the northern states—to transform the North into a region consciously at odds with the South's traditional culture and slave-labor economy. The first major expression of intensifying sectional differences over slavery and its expansion came in 1819 when the slaveholding Missouri Territory, which had been carved out of the old Louisiana Territory, applied for admission to the Union as a slave state. The negative northern reaction was—as Jefferson said—a "fire bell in the night," awakening slaveholders to an era in which slavery could no longer be avoided as an issue in national politics.

Northerners expressed deep reservations about the expansion of slavery and the creation of new slaveholding states, which threatened to destroy the political balance between the sections. It took all the skill of the slaveholding speaker of the House of Representatives, Henry Clay of Kentucky, to put together in 1820 a compromise that temporarily quieted discord. This Missouri Compromise (Map 5–2) permitted Missouri to become a slave state, maintained political balance by admitting Maine as a free state, and banned slavery north of the 36° 30′ line of latitude in the old Louisiana Territory. Yet sectional relations would never be the same, and a new era of black and white antislavery militancy soon confronted the South.

CONCLUSION

The period between the War for Independence and the Missouri Compromise was a time of transition for African Americans. On the one hand, the legacy of the American Revolution brought emancipation in the North and a promise of equal opportunity with white Americans. On the other, slavery and racism had begun to grow stronger by the 1790s. Through a combination of anti-black prejudice among white people and African-Americans' desire to preserve their own cultural traditions, black urban communities arose in the North, upper South, and occasionally—in Charleston and Savannah for example—in the deep South.

Spreading freedom in the North and the emergence of black communities in both the North and South were heartening developments. There were new opportunities for education, spiritual growth, and economic development. But the mass of African Americans remained in slavery. The forces for human bondage were growing stronger. Freedom for those who had gained it in the upper South and North was marginal and precarious.

Gabriel's conspiracy in Virginia and Deslandes's rebellion in Louisiana indicated that revolutionary principles persisted among black southerners. But these rebellions and British recruitment of slaves during the War of 1812 convinced most white southerners that black bondage had to be permanent. Therefore, African Americans looked to the future with mixed emotions. A few determined that the only hope for real freedom lay in migration from the United States.

REVIEW QUESTIONS

1. Which were stronger in the era of the early American republic, the forces in favor of black freedom or those in favor of continued enslavement?

2. How were African Americans able to achieve emancipation in the North?

3. How was the United States Constitution, as it was drafted in 1787, proslavery? How was it antislavery?

4. How important were separate institutions in shaping the lives of free black people during the late eighteenth and early nineteenth centuries?

5. What led Gabriel to believe that he and his followers could abolish slavery in Virginia through armed uprising?

RECOMMENDED READING

Ira Berlin. *Slaves without Masters: The Free Negro in the Antebellum South.* New York: New Press, 1974. The early chapters of this classic study indicate the special difficulties the first large generation of free black southerners faced.

Douglas R. Egerton. *Gabriel's Rebellion: The Virginia Slave Conspiracies of 1800 and 1802.* Chapel Hill: University of North Carolina Press, 1993. This most recent account of Gabriel's conspiracy emphasizes both the revolutionary context within which he acted and his legacy.

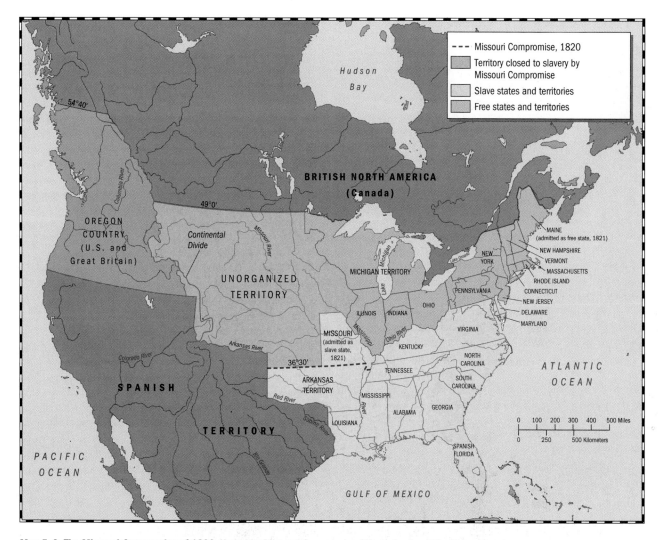

Map 5–2 The Missouri Compromise of 1820. Under the Missouri Compromise, Missouri entered the Union as a slave state, Maine entered as a free state, and Congress banned slavery in the huge unorganized portion of the old Louisiana Territory north of the 36° 30′ line of latitude.

Philip S. Foner. *History of Black Americans, from Africa to the Emergence of the Cotton Kingdom.* Westport, CT: Greenwood, 1975. This is the first volume of a comprehensive three-volume history of African Americans. It is detailed and informative about black life between 1783 and 1820.

James Oliver Horton and Lois E. Horton. *In Hope of Liberty: Culture, Community, and Protest among Northern Free Blacks, 1700–1860.* New York: Oxford University Press, 1997. This is a well-written interpretation of the northern free black community and its origins.

Sidney Kaplan and Emma Nogrady Kaplan. *The Black Presence in the Era of the American Revolution.* Rev. ed.

Amherst: University of Massachusetts Press, 1989. This delightfully written book provides informative accounts of black leaders who lived during the early American republic.

Gary B. Nash. *Forging Freedom: The Formation of Philadelphia's Black Community, 1720–1840.* Cambridge: Harvard University Press, 1988. This pathbreaking study of a black community analyzes the origins of separate black institutions.

Donald R. Wright. *African Americans in the Early Republic, 1789–1831.* Arlington Heights, IL: Harlan Davidson, 1993. This is a brief but comprehensive account that reflects recent interpretations.

TIMELINE

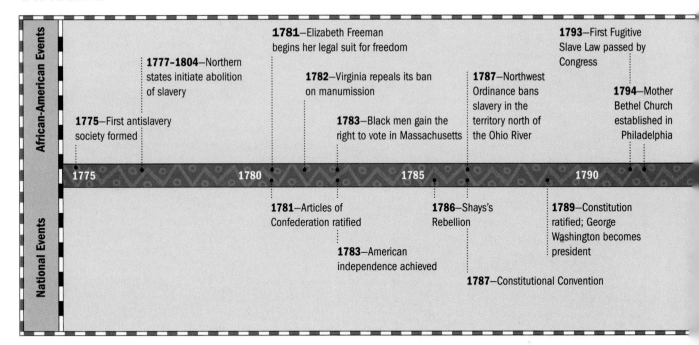

African-American Events

1775—First antislavery society formed

1777-1804—Northern states initiate abolition of slavery

1781—Elizabeth Freeman begins her legal suit for freedom

1782—Virginia repeals its ban on manumission

1783—Black men gain the right to vote in Massachusetts

1787—Northwest Ordinance bans slavery in the territory north of the Ohio River

1793—First Fugitive Slave Law passed by Congress

1794—Mother Bethel Church established in Philadelphia

1775   1780   1785   1790

National Events

1781—Articles of Confederation ratified

1783—American independence achieved

1786—Shays's Rebellion

1787—Constitutional Convention

1789—Constitution ratified; George Washington becomes president

ADDITIONAL BIBLIOGRAPHY

Emancipation in the North

James D. Essig. *The Bonds of Wickedness: American Evangelicals against Slavery, 1770–1808.* Philadelphia: Temple University Press, 1982.

Gary B. Nash and Jean R. Soderlund. *Freedom by Degrees: Emancipation in Pennsylvania and Its Aftermath.* New York: Oxford University Press, 1991.

Shane White. *Somewhat More Independent: The End of Slavery in New York City, 1770–1810.* Athens: University of Georgia Press, 1991.

Arthur Zilversmit. *The First Emancipation: The Abolition of Slavery in the North.* Chicago: University of Chicago Press, 1967.

Proslavery Forces

Paul Finkelman. *Slavery and the Founders: Race and Liberty in the Age of Jefferson.* Armonk, NY: M. E. Sharpe, 1996.

Duncan J. MacLeod. *Slavery, Race, and the American Revolution.* New York: Cambridge University Press, 1974.

Donald G. Nieman. *Promises to Keep: African Americans and the Constitutional Order, 1776 to the Present.* New York: Oxford University Press, 1991.

Donald L. Robinson. *Slavery in the Structure of the American Republic, 1765–1820.* New York: Harcourt Brace Jovanovich, 1971.

Larry E. Tise. *Proslavery: A History of the Defense of Slavery in America, 1701–1840.* Athens: University of Georgia Press, 1987.

Free Black Institutions and Migration Movements

Carol V. R. George. *Segregated Sabbaths: Richard Allen and the Emergence of Independent Black Churches, 1760–1840.* New York: Oxford University Press, 1973.

Sheldon H. Harris. *Paul Cuffe: Black America and the Africa Return.* New York: Simon & Schuster, 1972.

Leon Litwack. *North of Slavery: The Negro in the Free States.* Chicago: University of Chicago Press, 1961.

William A Muraskin. *Middle-Class Blacks in a White Society: Prince Hall Freemasonry in America.* Berkeley: University of California Press, 1975.

Julie Winch. *Philadelphia's Black Elite: Activism, Accommodation, and the Struggle for Autonomy, 1787–1848.* Philadelphia: Temple University Press, 1988.

Carter G. Woodson. *The Education of the Negro Prior to 1861.* 1915; reprint, Brooklyn, NY: A&B Books, 1998.

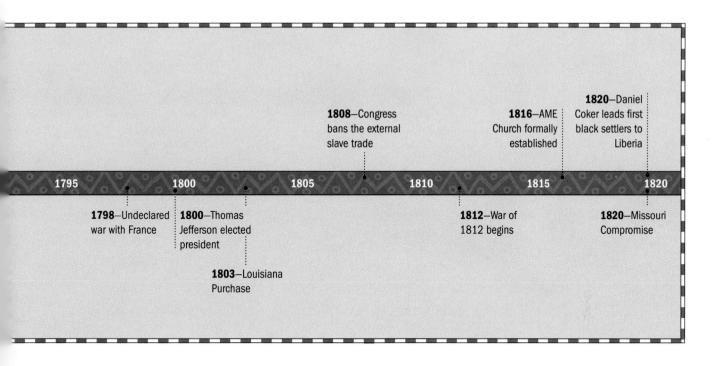

Timeline:

1795 — 1798—Undeclared war with France

1800 — 1800—Thomas Jefferson elected president

1803—Louisiana Purchase

1805

1808—Congress bans the external slave trade

1810 — 1812—War of 1812 begins

1815 — 1816—AME Church formally established

1820 — 1820—Daniel Coker leads first black settlers to Liberia

1820—Missouri Compromise

The South

John Hope Franklin. *The Free Negro in North Carolina, 1790–1860.* 1943; reprint, New York: Russell and Russell, 1969.

Peter Kolchin. *American Slavery, 1619–1877.* New York: Hill and Wang, 1993.

John Chester Miller. *The Wolf by the Ears: Thomas Jefferson and Slavery.* 1977; reprint, Charlottesville: University Press of Virginia, 1991.

T. Stephen Whitman. *The Price of Freedom: Slavery and Manumission in Baltimore and Early National Maryland.* Lexington: University of Kentucky Press, 1997.

Slave Revolts, Resistance, and Escapes

Herbert Aptheker. *American Negro Slave Revolts.* 1943; reprint, New York: International, 1983.

Merton L. Dillon. *Slavery Attacked: Southern Slaves and Their Allies, 1619–1865.* Baton Rouge: Louisiana State University Press, 1990.

Eugene D. Genovese. *From Rebellion to Revolution: Afro-American Slave Revolts in the Making of the Modern World.* Baton Rouge: Louisiana State University Press, 1979.

John R. McKivigan and Stanley Harrold, eds. *Antislavery Violence: Sectional, Racial, and Cultural Conflict in Antebellum America.* Knoxville: University of Tennessee Press, 1999.

Gerald W. Mullin. *Flight and Rebellion: Slave Resistance in Eighteenth-Century Virginia.* New York: Oxford University Press, 1972.

James Sidbury. *Ploughshares into Swords: Race, Rebellion, and Identity in Gabriel's Virginia, 1730–1810.* New York: Cambridge University Press, 1998.

PART II

SLAVERY, ABOLITION, AND THE QUEST FOR FREEDOM

THE COMING OF THE CIVIL WAR, 1793–1861

LIFE IN THE COTTON KINGDOM

This is an 1862 photograph of a black family held in slavery on a plantation in Beaufort, South Carolina. It provides an indication of slave dress and living conditions as well as of the nature of extended, multigenerational slave families.

There may be humane masters, as there certainly are inhumane ones; there may be slaves well-clothed, well-fed, and happy, as there surely are those half-clad, half-starved and miserable; nevertheless, the institution that tolerates such wrong and inhumanity . . . is a cruel, unjust, and barbarous one.

Solomon Northup, "Twelve Years a Slave: Narrative of Solomon Northup"

Solomon Northup, a free black man, had been kidnapped into slavery during the 1840s. After twelve years in bondage he finally escaped. In this passage he identifies the central cruelty of slavery. It was not that some masters failed to provide slaves with adequate food, clothing, and shelter while others did. Nor was it that some masters treated their slaves brutally while others did not. The central cruelty of slavery was that it gave masters nearly absolute power over their slaves. The sufferings of African Americans in slavery were not caused by abuses in an otherwise benevolent institution. They were caused by the institution itself.

In this chapter we describe the life of black people in the slave South from the rise of the Cotton Kingdom to the eve of the Civil War. As we have indicated in previous chapters, African Americans suffered brutal oppression on southern plantations. But they also developed means of coping with that oppression, resisting it, and escaping. Between 1820 and 1861, slavery in the South was at its peak as a productive system and a means of white control of black southerners. We seek to explain the extent of that slave system, how it varied across the South, and how it operated. We also investigate the slave communities that African-American men, women, and children built.

SOLOMON NORTHUP

Solomon Northup's aspirations as a musician led in 1841 to his kidnapping and sale into slavery. For twelve years he labored in the cotton and sugar regions of Louisiana, interacted with slaves and masters, and experienced firsthand what it was like to be caught up in a brutal labor system.

Northup was born free at Minerva, New York, in about 1808. His parents were prosperous farmers and he became a farmer as well, although he also worked occasionally as a violinist. He lived in Saratoga Springs with his wife and three children until March 1841 when two white men suggested that he become a musician in their circus, which was performing in Washington, D.C.

Enticed by the prospect of good wages and a chance to perform, Northup left with the two men without informing his wife or anyone else. Within two days of arriving in Washington, he was drugged, robbed of his money and free papers, chained, and sold to slave traders. After experiencing a terrible beating with a wooden paddle and a rope, Northup was shipped to New Orleans and sold to William Ford, who owned a cotton planation and sawmill in Louisiana's Red River region.

As Ford's slave, Northup worked at the mill "piling lumber and chopping logs." Northup liked Ford and regarded him to be a "model master," who treated his slaves well and read scripture to them each Sunday. But when Ford became insolvent and sold his slaves, Northup had to deal with a series of brutal masters. They employed him as a carpenter, as a field hand on cotton and sugar plantations, and finally as a slave driver.

At one point when he was cutting lumber and building cabins, Northup was surprised to have several "large and stout" black women join in the forestry work. Later he observed women engaged in other demanding physical labor. "There are lumberwomen as well as lumbermen in the forests of the South," he reported. "In fact . . . they perform their share of all the labor required by the planters. They plough, dray, drive team, clear wild lands, work on the highway and so forth."

Subsequently Northup spent ten years as a slave of Edwin Epps, a cotton planter, who when drunk enjoyed forcing his slaves to dance. Northup noted that Epps's slaves received a meager diet of corn and bacon. They slept in crude, crowded cabins on planks of wood. During harvest season "it was rarely that a day passed by without one or more whippings" as slaves failed to pick their quota. For three years Epps hired Northup out to "sugar plantations during the season of cane-cutting and sugar making" for $1.00 per day.

Northup had become Epps's slave driver by 1852 when he was finally able to set in motion the events that led to his rescue. Deeply disturbed by being forced to whip other slaves, he conspired with a Canadian carpenter to smuggle a letter to two white businessmen in Saratoga Springs. The letter led the governor of New York to send Henry B. Northup—a member of the family that had once owned Solomon Northup's father—to Louisiana to present evidence that Solomon Northup was a free man. By January 1853 he had been reunited with his family in New York. In July of that year he published *Twelve Years a Slave*, which sold over 30,000 copies and earned him enough money to purchase a home for his family in Glens Falls, New York, where he died in 1863.

THE EXPANSION OF SLAVERY

Eli Whitney's invention of the cotton gin in 1793 made the cultivation of cotton profitable on the North American mainland. It was the key to the rapid and extensive expansion of slavery from the Atlantic coast to Texas. By 1811 cotton cultivation had spread across South Carolina, Georgia, and parts of North Carolina and Virginia. By 1821 it had crossed Alabama and reached Mississippi, Louisiana, and parts of Tennessee. It then expanded again into Arkansas, Florida, and eastern Texas (Map 6–1). Enslaved black labor cleared forests and drained swamps to make these lands fit for cultivation.

The expansion of the cotton culture led to the forceful removal of the American Indians—some of them slaveholders—who inhabited this vast region. In the 1830s the United States Army forced the Cherokee, Chickasaw, Choctaw, Creek, and most Seminole to leave their ancestral lands for Indian Territory in what is now Oklahoma. The Cherokee remember this forced migration as "The Trail of Tears."

Slave Population Growth

With this enormous territorial expansion came an equally vast increase in the number of African Americans in bondage. The slave population of the United States increased sevenfold between 1790 and 1860, from 697,897 to 3,953,760 (Table 6–1). Seventy-five percent of the South's slave population were agricultural laborers. But these slaves were not equally distributed across the region. Slave populations blossomed in cotton-growing regions, but western North Carolina, eastern Tennessee, western Virginia, and most of Missouri never had many slaves. The slave population grew fastest in the newer cotton-producing states like Alabama and Mississippi (Map 6–2).

Virginia had the largest slave population throughout the period. But between 1820 and 1860, that population increased by only 15 percent, from 425,153 to 490,865. During the same forty years, the slave population of Louisiana increased by 209 percent, from 149,654 to 462,198, and that of Mississippi by 1,331 percent, from 32,814 to 436,631. By 1860 Mississippi had joined South Carolina as the only states that had more slave than free inhabitants.

Ownership of Slaves in the Old South

The ownership of slaves was as unevenly distributed as the slave population. In 1860, only 383,673 white southerners out of nine million owned slaves. Even

Table 6-1 United States Slave Population, 1820 and 1860		
	1820	1860
United States	1,538,125	3,953,760
North	19,108	64
South	1,519,017	3,953,696
Upper South	965,514	1,530,229
Delaware	4,509	1,798
Kentucky	127,732	225,483
Maryland	107,397	87,189
Missouri	10,222	114,931
North Carolina	205,017	331,059
Tennessee	80,107	275,719
Virginia	425,153	490,865
Washington, D.C.	6,377	3,185
Lower South	553,503	2,423,467
Alabama	41,879	435,080
Arkansas	1,617	111,115
Florida	*	61,745
Georgia	149,654	462,198
Louisiana	69,064	331,726
Mississippi	32,8114	436,631
South Carolina	258,475	402,406
Texas	*	182,566

*Florida and Texas were not states in 1820

Source: Ira Berlin, *Slaves without Masters: The Free Negro in the Antebellum South* (New York: New Press, 1974), 396-7.

when the immediate families of slaveholders are added, only 1.9 million—or less than 25 percent of the South's white population—belonged to a slave-owning family. In 1830, 36 percent of white southerners had owned slaves.

Almost half of the South's slaveholders owned fewer than five slaves, only 12 percent owned more than twenty slaves, and just 1 percent owned more than fifty slaves. Yet more than half the slaves belonged to masters who had twenty or more slaves. So, while the typical slaveholder owned few slaves, the typical slave lived on a sizable plantation.

Since the time of Anthony Johnson in the mid-1600s, a few black people had been slaveholders, and this class continued to exist. In 1830, only 2 percent or 3,775 free African Americans owned slaves. Many of them became slaveholders to protect their families from sale and disruption. As the nineteenth century progressed, southern states made it more difficult for masters to manumit slaves and for slaves to purchase their freedom. The states also threatened to expel former slaves from their territory. In response to these

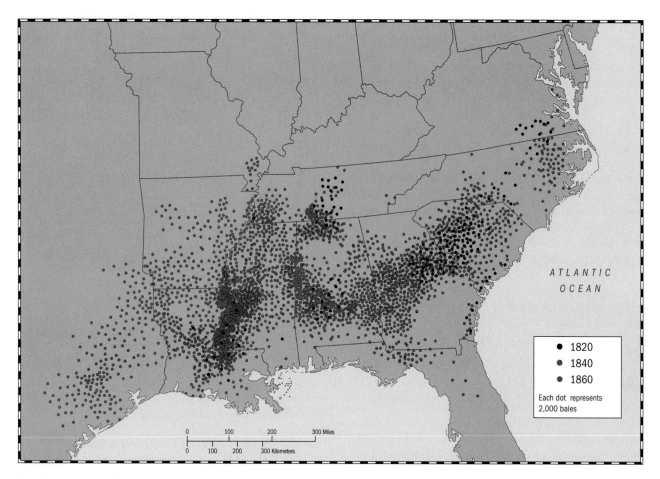

Map 6-1 Cotton Production in the South, 1820–1860. Cotton production expanded westward between 1820 and 1860. Source: Sam Bowers Hilliard, *Atlas of Antebellum Southern Agriculture* (Louisiana State University Press, 1984) pp 67–71.

circumstances black men and women sometimes purchased relatives who were in danger of sale to traders and who—if legally free—might be forced by white authorities to leave a state.

Some African Americans, however, purchased slaves for financial reasons and passed those slaves on to their heirs. Most black people who became masters for financial reasons owned five or fewer slaves. But William Johnson, a wealthy free black barber of Natchez, Louisiana, owned many slaves whom he employed on a plantation he purchased. Some black women, such as Margaret Mitchell Harris of South Carolina and Betsy Somayrac of Natchitoches, Louisiana, also became slaveholders for economic reasons. Harris was a successful rice planter who inherited twenty-one slaves from her white father. She prospered by carefully managing her resources in land and slaves. By 1849, when she sold out, she had more than forty slaves and nearly one thousand acres, which produced 240,000 pounds of rice per year.

Somayrac's case shows that economic considerations could override emotional ties between black women and their bondpeople. In her will, which a parish judge recorded in January 1845, Somayrac wrote that she intended to pass her human property on to her children. She required that "my negro woman named Jane" labor to pay off family debts. She stipulated that one of her sons own any children that Jane might produce. She even provided that a "negro boy named Solomon," who was her godson, not be manumitted until he had reached the relatively old age of thirty-five.

SLAVE LABOR IN AGRICULTURE

About 55 percent of the slaves in the South cultivated cotton; 10 percent grew tobacco; and 10 percent produced sugar, rice, or hemp. About 15 percent were domestic servants, and the remaining 10 percent worked in trades and industries.

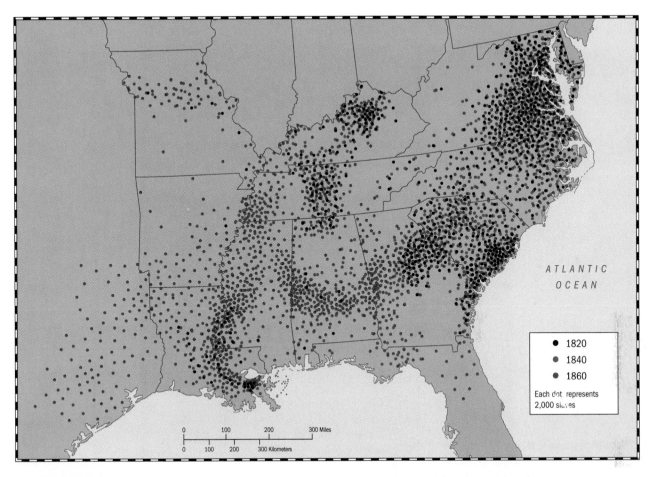

Map 6-2 Slave Population, 1820–1860. Slavery spread southwestward from the upper South and the eastern seaboard following the spread of cotton cultivation. Source: Sam Bowers Hilliard, *Atlas of Antebellum Southern Agriculture* (Louisiana State University Press, 1984), pp. 29–34.

Tobacco

Tobacco remained important in Virginia, Maryland, Kentucky, and parts of North Carolina and Missouri during the 1800s (Map 6–3). A difficult crop to produce, tobacco required a long growing season and careful cultivation. In the spring slaves had to transfer seedlings from sterilized seed beds to well-worked and manured soil. Then they had to hoe weeds, pick off insects, and prune lower leaves so that the topmost leaves grew to their full extent. Slaves also built scaffolds used to cure the tobacco leaves and made the barrels in which the tobacco was shipped to market.

Robert Ellett, a former slave, recalled that when he was just eight years old he worked in Virginia "a-worming tobacco." He "examined tobacco leaves, pull[ed] off the worms, if there were any, and killed them." He claimed that if an overseer discovered that slaves had overlooked worms on the tobacco plants, the slaves were whipped or forced to eat the worms. Nancy Williams, another Virginia slave, recalled that sometimes as a punishment slaves had to inhale burning tobacco until they became nauseated.

Rice

Unlike the cultivation of tobacco, which spread westward and southward from Maryland and Virginia, rice production remained confined to the coastal waterways of South Carolina and Georgia. As they had since colonial times, slaves in these regions worked according to task systems that allowed them considerable autonomy. Because rice fields needed to be flooded for the seeds to germinate, slaves maintained elaborate systems of dikes and ditches. Influenced by West African methods, they sowed, weeded, and harvested the rice crop.

Rice cultivation was labor intensive and rice plantations needed large labor forces to grow and harvest the crop and maintain the fields. By 1860 twenty

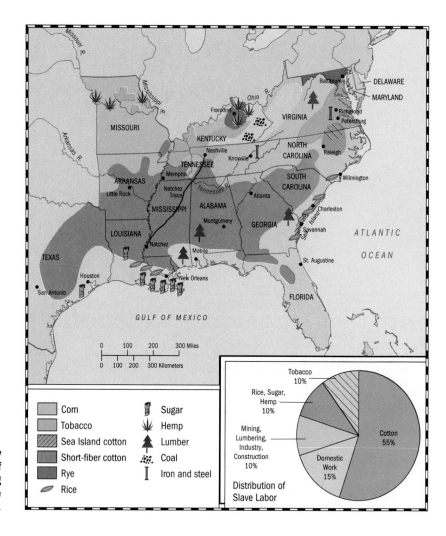

Map 6-3 Agriculture, Industry, and Slavery in the Old South, 1850. The experience of African Americans in slavery varied according to their occupation and the region of the South in which they lived.

rice plantations had three hundred to five hundred slaves, and eight others had between five hundred and one thousand. The only American plantation employing more than one thousand slaves was in the rice-producing region. These vast plantations represented sizable capital investments, and masters or overseers carefully monitored slave productivity. While slaves enjoyed considerable leeway in how they performed their assigned duties, those who missed a day's work risked forfeiting their weekly allowance "of either bacon, sugar, molasses, or tobacco."

Sugar

Another important crop that grew in a restricted region was sugar, which slaves cultivated in southern Louisiana on plantations along the Mississippi River. Commercial production of sugarcane did not begin in Louisiana until the 1790s. It required a consistently warm climate,

a long growing season, and at least sixty inches of rain per year.

Raising sugarcane and refining sugar also required constant labor. Together with the great profitability of the sugar crop, these demands encouraged masters to work their slaves hard. Slave life on sugar plantations was extremely harsh, and African Americans across the South feared being sent to labor on them. Historian Paul W. Gates details the work of slaves on sugar plantations:

> Fresh land was constantly being cleared, and the wood was used for fuel in the sugarhouses or was sold to steamboats. Levees had to be raised; ditching and draining was never completed. Planting, numerous hoeings, cutting, loading and unloading the cane, putting it through the mill, feeding the boilers, moving the huge hogsheads of sugar and molasses and drawing them to the boat landing, setting aside the seed cane, hauling the bagasse to the fields—all this took much labor.

This drawing of slaves at work in a low country rice field provides an impression of the physical size of the fields under cultivation and of the techniques employed in cultivating the rice plants.

Slaves did this work in hot and humid conditions, adding to the toll it took on their strength and health. Because cane could not be allowed to stand too long in the fields, harvest time was hectic. As one former slave recalled, "On cane plantations in sugar time, there is no distinction as to the days of the week. They [the slaves] worked on the Sabbath as if it were Monday or Thursday."

Cotton

While these other crops were economically significant, cotton was by far the South's and the country's most important staple crop. By 1860 cotton exports amounted to more than 50 percent annually of the dollar value of all United States exports (Figure 6–1). This was almost ten times the value of its nearest export competitors—wheat and wheat flour.

Cotton as a crop did not require cultivation as intensive as that needed for tobacco, rice, or sugar. But the cotton culture was so extensive that cotton planters as a group employed the most slave labor. By 1860, out of the 2,500,000 slaves employed in agriculture in the United States, 1,815,000 were producing cotton. Cotton drove the South's economy and its westward expansion. Even in rice-producing South Carolina and sugar-producing Louisiana, cotton was dominant, and cotton plantations employed the bulk of the slave populations.

Although long-staple cotton continued to be grown on the sea islands of South Carolina and Georgia, most American cotton was the more hardy short-staple variety that flourished over much of the South. Demand for cotton fiber in the textile mills of Britain and New England stimulated the westward spread of cotton cultivation. This demand increased by at least 5 percent per year between 1830 and 1860. In response—and with the essential aid of Whitney's cotton gin—American production of cotton rose from ten thousand bales in 1793 to 500,000 annually during the 1820s to 4,491,000 bales in 1860. The new states of Alabama, Louisiana, and Mississippi led this mounting production.

Picturesque scenes of ripening cotton fields are part of the romantic image of the Old South that popular novels, songs, and motion pictures have perpetuated for so long. Even a former slave could recall that "few sights are more pleasant to the eye than a wide cotton field when it is in full bloom. It presents an appearance of purity, like an immaculate expanse of light, new-fallen snow." Yet such scenes mask the backbreaking labor enslaved African Americans performed, and the anxiety and fear they experienced.

Potential profits drew white farmers to the rich Black Belt lands of Mississippi and Alabama during the early nineteenth century. Rapid population growth allowed Mississippi to gain statehood in 1817 and Alabama in 1819. White men with few slaves led the

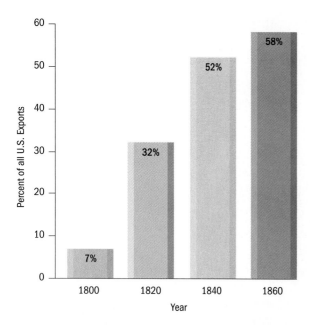

Figure 6-1 Cotton Exports as a Percentage of All United States Exports, 1800–1860. Cotton rapidly emerged as the country's most important export crop after 1800 and key to its prosperity. Because slave labor produced the cotton, increasing exports strengthened the slave system itself.

way into this southwestern cotton belt, and its frontier social structure allowed them to become plantation owners. Although their success was not certain, and many of them failed, those who did succeed created large agricultural units because profits were directly related to the amount of cotton harvested. As a result, Mississippi and Alabama—the leading producers of cotton—had by 1860 the greatest concentration of plantations with one hundred or more slaves. Twenty-four of Mississippi's slaveholders owned between 308 and 899 slaves.

As these large agricultural units drew in labor, the price of slaves increased over time. During the 1830s, for example, a prime male field hand sold for $1,250 (about $21,000 in current dollars) in the New Orleans slave market. Prices dipped during hard times in the early 1840s. But by the 1850s, such slaves cost $1,800 (about $33,000 in current dollars). Young women usually sold for up to five hundred dollars less than young men. Prices for elderly slaves dropped off sharply unless they were highly skilled.

The enslaved men and women who worked in the cotton fields rose before dawn when the master or overseer sounded the plantation bell or horn. They ate breakfast and then assembled in work gangs of twenty or twenty-five under the control of black slave drivers. They plowed and planted in the spring. They weeded with heavy hoes in the summer and harvested in the late fall. During harvest season adult slaves picked about two hundred pounds of cotton per day. Regardless of the season, the work was hard, and white overseers frequently whipped those who seemed to be lagging. Slaves usually got a two-hour break at midday in the summer and an hour to an hour and a half in the winter. Then they returned to the fields until sunset, when they went back to their cabins for dinner and an early bedtime enforced by the master or overseer.

Frederick Law Olmsted, a northern traveler, described a large gang of Mississippi slaves he saw in 1854 marching home early because of rain:

> First came, led by an old driver carrying a whip, forty of the largest and strongest women I ever saw together; they were all in a single uniform dress of a bluish check stuff, the skirts reaching little below the knee; their legs and feet were bare; they carried themselves loftily, each having a hoe over the shoulder, and walking with a free, powerful swing. Behind them came the [plowhands and their mules], thirty strong, mostly men, but a few of them women. . . . A lean and vigilant white overseer, on a brisk pony, brought up the rear. The men wore small blue Scotch bonnets; many of the women handkerchiefs, turban fashion. . . . They were evidently a picked lot. I thought every one could pass for a "prime" cotton hand.

Other Crops

Besides cotton, sugar, tobacco, and rice, slaves in the Old South produced other crops, including hemp, corn, wheat, oats, rye, white potatoes, and sweet potatoes. They also raised cattle, hogs, sheep, and horses. The hogs, and corn and other grains were mainly for consumption on the plantations themselves. But all the hemp and much of the livestock and wheat were raised for the market. In fact, wheat replaced tobacco as the main cash crop in much of Maryland and Virginia. The transition to wheat encouraged many planters to substitute free labor for slave labor, but slaves grew wheat in the South until the Civil War.

Kentucky was the center of the hemp industry. Before the Civil War, Americans used hemp, which is closely related to marijuana, to make rope and bagging for cotton bales. As a result, hemp production tied Kentucky economically to the Deep South. Hemp also led to a distinctive system of slavery in Kentucky because it required much less labor than rice, sugar, or

Slaves harvest cotton under white supervision on a southern plantation in this engraving of about 1860. Note the division of labor between men and women.

cotton. Because three slaves could tend fifty acres of hemp, slave labor forces in Kentucky were much smaller than elsewhere. Robert Wickliffe, who was the largest slaveholder in the state during the 1840s, owned just two hundred slaves—a large number, but far fewer than his counterparts in the Cotton Belt.

HOUSE SERVANTS AND SKILLED SLAVES

About 75 percent of the slave workforce in the nineteenth century consisted of field hands. But because masters wanted to make their plantations as self-sufficient as possible, they employed some slaves as house servants and skilled craftsmen. Slaves who did not have to do field labor were an elite. Those who performed domestic duties, drove carriages, or learned a craft considered themselves privileged. However, they were also suspended between two different worlds.

House slaves worked as cooks, maids, butlers, nurses, and gardeners. Their work was generally less physically demanding than field work and they often received better food and clothing. Nevertheless, nineteenth-century kitchen work could be grueling, and maids and butlers were on call at all hours. House servants' jobs were also more stressful than field hands' jobs because the servants were under closer white supervision.

In addition, house servants were by necessity cut off from the slave community centered in the slave quarters. Nevertheless, as Olmsted pointed out during the 1850s, house servants rarely sought to become field

hands. Conversely field hands had little desire to be exposed to the constant surveillance house servants had to tolerate. As Olmsted put it:

> Slaves brought up to house work dread to be employed at field-labor; and those accustomed to the comparatively unconstrained life of the Negro-settlement detest the close control and careful movements required of the house-servants. It is a punishment of a lazy field-hand to employ him in menial duties at the house . . . and it is equally a punishment to a neglectful house-servant, to banish him to the field-gangs.

Skilled slaves tended to be even more of a slave elite than house slaves. As had been true earlier, black men had a decided advantage over black women—apart from those who became seamstresses—in becoming skilled. Slave carpenters, blacksmiths, and millwrights built and maintained plantation houses, slave quarters, and machinery. Because they might need to travel to get tools or spare parts, such skilled slaves gained a more cosmopolitan outlook than field hands or house servants. They got a taste of freedom, which from the masters' point of view was dangerous.

As plantation slavery declined in the Chesapeake, skilled slaves were able to leave their master's estate to "hire their time." Either they or their masters negotiated labor contracts with employers who needed their expertise. In effect these slaves worked for money. Although masters often kept all or most of what they made, some of these skilled slaves merely paid their master a set rate and lived as independent contractors.

APRIL ELLISON

The life of April Ellison, who was born a slave in the Fairfield district of South Carolina in 1790, exemplifies several of the themes of this chapter. He was a skilled slave, used that skill to accumulate enough savings to purchase his freedom, and subsequently became a slaveholder himself. His story came to light in Georgia in 1935 when three white children discovered his personal papers.

The son of a slave mother and an unknown white father, Ellison received special treatment from his owner, who apprenticed him at age twelve to a broadly skilled white craftsman named William McCreight. Together with several white apprentices, Ellison learned carpentry, blacksmithing, and how to repair cotton gins. He also learned how to conduct a business. He did so well that in 1816, when he was twenty-six, he purchased himself and became a free man.

Once free, Ellison petitioned a court to change his name from his slave name *April* to William, in honor of his mentor—or perhaps his father. With freedom, skills, and a new name, Ellison opened a gin-making and gin-repair shop in Statesburg, South Carolina. Like the Natchez, Mississippi, barber William Johnson, Ellison achieved a respectable reputation among his white clients and neighbors as a churchgoing businessman. On the surface at least, his ties to his slave past diminished as he prospered. Because his income depended on white slaveholders, he did nothing to antagonize them.

April Ellison's house near Columbia, South Carolina.

As a result, Ellison became one of the wealthiest owners of real and personal property in the South. He owned hundreds of acres of farmland and woodland worth at least $8,250 (about $148,000 in current dollars). As early as 1820, he owned two slaves. In 1830 he owned four and in 1840, twenty-six. By 1860 he owned sixty-three and was worth in personal property alone $53,000 (about $954,000 in current dollars).

Ellison assigned tasks to his slaves according to their gender and age. The field hands—mostly women and children—produced eighty bales of cotton each in 1850. They also raised thousands of bushels of corn, sweet potatoes, and other vegetables each year. The gin shop workers—men and adolescent boys—worked as blacksmiths, carpenters, and mechanics.

When South Carolina seceded from the Union in December 1860 and the Civil War began a few months later, Ellison and his family were caught between two contradictory forces. During the war, South Carolina's state government considered free African Americans potential traitors and curtailed their liberty. Meanwhile, the Union moved relentlessly toward immediate, uncompensated emancipation. Ellison, who died on December 5, 1861, did not live to see the emancipation of his slaves in 1865. But his children did. They also saw the destruction of his business when its newly emancipated workers refused to continue to work for the Ellisons as free men and women.

URBAN AND INDUSTRIAL SLAVERY

Most skilled slaves, who hired their time, lived in the South's towns and cities where they interacted with free black communities. Many of them resided in Baltimore and New Orleans, which were major ports and the Old South's largest cities. But there were others in such smaller southern urban centers as Richmond and Norfolk, Virginia; Atlanta and Augusta, Georgia; Washington, D.C.; Charleston, South Carolina; Louisville, Kentucky; and Memphis, Tennessee.

Slave populations in southern cities were often large, although they tended to decline between 1800 and 1860.

In 1840, slaves were a majority of Charleston's population of 29,000. They nearly equaled white residents in Memphis and Augusta, which had total populations of 14,700 and 6,000, respectively. Slaves were almost one-quarter of New Orleans' population of 145,000.

As the young Frederick Douglass found when his master sent him from rural Maryland to Baltimore in the late 1830s, life in a city could be much more complicated for a slave than life on a plantation. When urban slaves were not working for their masters, they could earn money for themselves, and as a result, masters had a harder time controlling their lives. Those who contracted to provide their masters with a certain amount of money per year could live on their own, buying their own food and clothing. "You couldn't pay me," observed one slave woman, "to live at home if I could help myself."

Urban slaves served as domestics, washwomen, waiters, artisans, stevedores, drayers, hack drivers, and general laborers. (Douglass was an apprentice caulker in a shipyard.) In general they did the urban work that foreign immigrants undertook in northern cities. If these slaves purchased their freedom, they usually continued in the same line of work they had done as slaves. Particularly in border cities like Baltimore, Louisville, and Washington, however, urban slaves increasingly relied on their free black neighbors—and sympathetic whites—to escape north. Urban masters often let slaves purchase their freedom over a term of years to keep them from leaving. In Baltimore during the early nineteenth century, this sort of "term slavery" was gradually replacing slavery for life.

Industrial slavery overlapped with urban slavery, but southern industries that employed slaves were often in rural areas. By 1860 about 5 percent of southern slaves—approximately 200,000 people—worked in industry. Enslaved men, women, and children worked in textile mills in South Carolina and Georgia, sometimes beside white people. In Richmond and Petersburg, Virginia, during the 1850s, about six thousand, mostly male, slaves worked in factories producing chewing tobacco. Richmond's famous Tredegar ironworks also employed a large slave work force. So did earlier southern ironworks in Virginia, Maryland, northern Tennessee, and southern Kentucky.

The bulk of the 16,000 people who worked in the South's lumber industry in 1860 were slaves. Under the supervision of black drivers, they felled trees, operated sawmills, and delivered lumber. Slaves also did most of the work in the naval stores industry of North Carolina and Georgia, manufacturing tar, turpentine, and related products. In western Virginia, they labored in the salt-

This undated photograph shows the Tredegar Iron Works of Richmond, Virginia, as it appeared during the Civil War. Tredegar was the largest industrial complex in the Old South. It employed a slave workforce to produce a variety of weapons, tools, and locomotives.

works of the Great Kanawha River Valley, producing the salt used to preserve meat—especially the southern mainstay salt pork. During the 1820s, the Maryland Chemical Works in Baltimore, which manufactured industrial chemicals, pigments, and medicines, included many slaves among its workers.

Most southern industrialists hired slaves from their masters rather than buy them themselves, and the work slaves performed for them was often dangerous as well as physically tiring. But as historian John B. Boles points out, slaves came to prefer industrial jobs to plantation labor. Like urban slaves, industrial slaves had more opportunities to advance themselves, enjoyed more autonomy, and were often paid cash incentives. Industrial labor, like urban labor, was a path to freedom for some.

PUNISHMENT

Those who used slave labor, whether on plantations, small farms, in urban areas, or industry, frequently offered incentives to induce slaves to perform well. Yet slave labor by definition is forced labor based on the threat of physical punishment. Masters denied that this brutal aspect detracted from what they claimed was the essentially benign and paternalistic character of the South's "peculiar institution." After all, Christian masters found support in the Bible for using corporal punishment to chastise servants.

Southern whites also believed that African Americans would not work unless they were threatened with beatings. Olmsted reported that in Mississippi he had observed a young girl subjected to "the severest corporal punishment" he had ever seen. The white overseer, who had administered the flogging with a raw-hide whip "across her naked loins and thighs," told Olmsted that the girl had been shirking her duties. He claimed that "if I hadn't [punished her so hard] she would have done the same thing again to-morrow, and half the people on the plantation would have followed her example. Oh, you've no idea how lazy these niggers are. . . . They'd never do any work at all if they were not afraid of being whipped."

Fear of the lash drove slaves to do their work and to cooperate among themselves for mutual protection. Black parents and other older relatives taught slave children how to avoid punishment and still resist masters and overseers. They worked slowly—but not *too* slowly—and feigned illness to maintain their strength.

They broke tools, and injured mules, oxen, and horses to tacitly protest their condition. This pattern of covert resistance and physical punishment caused anxiety for both masters and slaves. Resistance often forced masters to reduce work hours and improve conditions. Yet few slaves escaped being whipped at least once during their lives in bondage.

THE DOMESTIC SLAVE TRADE

The expansion of the Cotton Kingdom south and west combined with the decline of slavery in the Chesapeake to stimulate the domestic slave trade. As masters in Delaware, Maryland, Virginia, North Carolina, and Kentucky trimmed excess slaves from their workforces—or switched entirely from slave to wage labor—they sold men, women, and children to slave traders. The traders in turn shipped these unfortunate people to the slave markets of New Orleans and other

VOICES

FREDERICK DOUGLASS ON THE READINESS OF MASTERS TO USE THE WHIP

This passage from the Narrative of the Life of Frederick Douglass, An American Slave, *published in 1845, suggests the volatile relationship between slaves and masters that could quickly result in violence. As Douglass makes clear, masters and overseers used the whip not just as a means of forcing slaves to work but also to enforce a distinction between what was proper and even laudable for white men and what was forbidden behavior on the part of slaves.*

It would astonish one, unaccustomed to a slave-holding life, to see with what wonderful ease a slaveholder can find things of which to make occasion to whip a slave. A mere look, word, or motion—a mistake, accident, or want of power—are all matters for which a slave may be whipped at any time. Does a slave look dissatisfied? It is said, he has the devil in him, and it must be whipped out. Does he speak loudly when spoken to by his masters? Then he is getting high-minded, and should be taken down a button-hole lower. Does he forget to pull off his hat at the approach of a white

person? Then he is wanting in reverence, and should be whipped for it. Does he ever venture to vindicate his conduct, when censured for it? Then he is guilty of impudence—one of the greatest crimes of which a slave can be guilty. Does he ever venture to suggest a different mode of doing things from that pointed out by his master? He is indeed presumptuous, and getting above himself; and nothing less than a flogging will do for him. Does he, while plowing, break a plough—or, while hoeing, break a hoe? It is owing to his carelessness, and for it a slave must always be whipped.

QUESTIONS

1. What does Douglass imply are some of the motives that led masters and overseers to whip slaves?

2. Given the sort of behavior on the part of masters that Douglass describes, how were slaves likely to conduct themselves in the presence of white people?

Source: Roy Finkenbine, ed., *Sources of the African-American Past* (New York: Longman, 1997), 43–44.

cities for resale. Masters also sold slaves as punishment, and fear of being "sold down river" led many slaves in the Chesapeake to escape. A vicious circle resulted: masters sold slaves south to prevent their escape and slaves escaped to avoid being sold south.

Some slave songs record the anxiety of those facing separation from loved ones as a result of the domestic trade. One song laments the sale of a man away from his wife and family:

> *William Rino sold Henry Silvers;*
> *Hilo! Hilo!*
> *Sold him to de Gorgy [Georgia] trader;*
> *Hilo! Hilo!*
> *His wife she cried, and children bawled*
> *Hilo! Hilo!*
> *Sold him to de Gorgy trader;*
> *Hilo! Hilo!*
>
> . . .
>
> *See wives and husbands sold apart,*
> *Their children's screams will break my heart;—*
> *There's a better day coming,*
> *Will you go along with me?*
> *There's a better day a coming,*
> *Go sound the jubilee!*

The number of people traded was huge and, considering that many of them were ripped away from their families, tragic. Starting in the 1820s, about 150,000 slaves per decade moved toward the southwest either with their masters or traders. Between 1820 and 1860, an estimated 50 percent of the slaves of the upper South moved involuntarily into the Southwest.

Traders operated compounds called *slave prisons* or *slave pens* in Baltimore, Washington, Alexandria and Richmond, Virginia, Charleston, South Carolina, and in smaller cities as well. Most of the victims of the trade moved on foot in groups called "coffles," chained or roped together. From the 1810s onward, northern and European visitors to Washington noted the coffles passing before the United States Capitol. There was also a considerable coastal trade in slaves from Chesapeake ports to New Orleans and, by the 1840s, some slave traders were carrying their human cargoes in railroad cars.

The domestic slave trade demonstrated the falseness of slaveholders' claims that slavery was a benign institution. Driven by economic necessity, by profit, or to frustrate escape plans, masters in the upper South irrevocably separated husbands and wives, mothers and children, brothers and sisters. Babies were sometimes torn from their mothers' arms. The journey from the Chesapeake to Mississippi, Alabama, or Louisiana could be

This photograph, taken during the Civil War in Alexandria, Virginia, shows the building that housed the slave-trading firm of Price, Birch, and Co. Slave traders were an essential part of the domestic slave trade that forced African Americans to leave the upper South for the cotton fields of the Old Southwest.

long and hard, and some died along the way. A few managed to keep in touch with those they had left behind through letters and travelers. But most could not, and after the abolition of slavery in 1865, many African Americans used their new freedom to travel across the South looking for relatives from whom they had been separated long before.

SLAVE FAMILIES

The families enslaved African Americans sought to preserve had been developing in America since the seventeenth century. However, such families had no legal standing. Most enslaved men and women could choose their own mates, though masters sometimes arranged such things. Masters encouraged pairings among female and male slaves because they assumed correctly that black husbands and fathers would be less rebellious. Masters were also aware that they would benefit if their human chattel reproduced. As Thomas Jefferson put it, "I consider a [slave] woman who brings [gives birth to] a child every two years as more profitable than the best man on the farm. What she produces is an addition to the capital, while his labors disappear in mere consumption."

Families were also the core of the African-American community in slavery. Even though no legal sanctions supported slave marriages and the domestic slave trade

A SLAVEOWNER DESCRIBES A NEW PURCHASE

In this letter to her mother, a white Louisiana woman, Tryphena Blanche Holder Fox, describes her husband's purchase of a slave woman and her children. Several things are apparent in the letter: that investing in slaves was expensive, that the white woman's only concern for the slave woman and her children was their economic value, that it was up to the white woman to supervise the new slaves, and that the slave woman showed her displeasure with her situation.

Hygiene [Jesuit Bend, Louisiana]
Sunday, Dec. 27th 1857

Dear Mother,

We are obliged to save every dollar he can "rake & scrape" to pay for a negro woman. . . . She has two likely children . . . and is soon to have another, and he only pays fourteen hundred for the three. She is considered an excellent bargain . . . he would not sell her and the children for less than $2,000. She came & worked two days, so we could see what she was capable of. . . . She was sold by a Frenchman. . . . He has a family of ten & she had all the work to do besides getting her own wood & water from the river. She was not used to do this, and gave them a great deal of trouble. . . . How much trouble she will give me, I don't know, but I think I can get along with her, passable well any how. Of course it increased my cares, for having invested so much in one purchase, it will be to my interest to see that the children are well taken care of & clothed and fed. All of them give more or less trouble. . . .

QUESTIONS

1. What does Tryphena reveal about the management of slaves?

2. What does she indicate about the ability of slaves to force concessions from their masters?

Source: Tryphena Blanche Holder Fox to Anna Rose Holder, December 27, 1857, Mississippi Department of Archives and History, Jackson, Mississippi.

could sunder them, many such marriages endured. Before they wed, some couples engaged in courting rituals while others rejected "such foolishness." Similarly, slave weddings ranged from simply "taking up" to religious ceremonies replete with food and frolics.

"Jumping the broom" was often part of these ceremonies, although this custom was not African but European. During the 1930s, former slave Tempie Herndon recalled her wedding ceremony conducted by "de nigger preacher dat preached at de plantation church." In particular she remembered that after the religious ceremony, "Marse George got to have his little fun" by having the newlyweds jump backwards over a broomstick. "You got to do dat to see which one gwine be boss of your household," she commented. "If both of dem jump over without touchin' it, dey won't gwine be no bossin', dey just gwine be congenial." In fact, there was more equality between husbands and wives in slave marriages than in those of the masters. Southern white concepts of patriarchy required male dominance. But because black men lacked power, their wives were more like partners than servants.

Usually slave couples lived together in cabins on their master's property. They had little privacy because even nineteenth-century slave cabins were rude, small one-room dwellings that two families might have to share. But couples who shared cabins were generally better off than husbands and wives who were the property of different masters and lived on different plantations. In these cases children lived with their mother, and their father visited when he could in the evenings. Work patterns that changed with the seasons or with the mood of a master could interfere with such visits. So could the requirement that slaves have passes to leave home.

Children

Despite these difficulties, slave parents were able to instruct their children in family history, in religion, and the skills required to survive in slavery. They sang to their children and told them stories full of folk wisdom. In particular they impressed on them the importance of extended family relationships. The ability to rely on grandparents, aunts and uncles, cousins, and honorary relatives was a hedge against the family disruption that the domestic slave trade might inflict. In this manner, too, the extended black family became in slavery the core of the black community that provided slaves with the independent resources they needed to avoid complete physical, intellectual, cultural, and moral subjugation to their masters.

During an age when infant mortality rates were much higher than they are today, those for black southerners were even higher than they were for white people. There were several reasons for this. Enslaved black women usually had to do field labor up to the time they delivered a child and their diets lacked necessary nutrients. Consequently they tended to have babies whose weight at birth was less than normal. In addition black infants were more likely to be subject to such postpartum maladies as rickets, tetany, tetanus, high fevers, intestinal worms, and influenza than were other children. More than 50 percent of slave children died before the age of five.

Slaveholders contributed to high infant mortality rates probably more from ignorance than malevolence. It was, after all, in the master's economic self-interest to have slave mothers produce healthy children. Masters often allowed mothers a month to recuperate after giving birth and time off from field work to nurse their babies for several months thereafter. Although this reduced the mother's productivity, the losses would be made up by the children's labor when they entered the plantation workforce. Unfortunately, many infants needed more than a few months of breast feeding to survive.

The care of slave children varied with the size of a slaveholder's estate, the region it was in, and the mother's work. House servants could carry their babies with them while they did their work. On small farms, slave women strapped their babies to their backs or left them at the edge of fields, so they could nurse them periodically, although the latter practice risked exposing an infant to ants, flies, or mosquitoes. On larger plantations, mothers could leave a child with an elderly or infirm adult. This encouraged a sense of community and a shared responsibility among the slaves for all black children on a plantation.

As children grew older, they spent much time in unsupervised play, often with white children. Boys played marbles and ball games; girls skipped rope and tended to their dolls. A game of hiding and whipping, like the more recent cops and robbers, was a childish commentary on a violent system.

Slave childhood was short. Early on, parents and other elders taught children about the realities of plantation life. By witnessing whippings—sometimes of their parents—and through admonitions from their elders, slave children learned that they had to be extremely careful about what they said to white people. Deceit and guile became survival skills. Slave childhood was also short because children as young as six had to do "light" chores. Such work became physically more taxing as a child grew older, until the child began doing adult field work between the ages of eight and twelve. That slave children were subject to sale away from their families, particularly in the upper South, also accelerated their progress to adulthood.

Sexual Exploitation

As with forced separations, masters' sexual exploitation of black women disrupted enslaved families. This abuse of black women began during the middle passage and continued after the abolition of slavery in the United States in 1865. Long-term relationships between masters and enslaved women were common in the nineteenth-century South. Such continuing relationships were based not on overt coercion but on masters' implicit power and authority. But even more common were masters, overseers, and their sons who, by one means or another, forced slave women to have sex against their will. This routine conduct caused great distress. Former slave Harriet Jacobs wrote in her autobiography, "I cannot tell how much I suffered in the presence of these wrongs, nor how I am still pained by the retrospect."

One of the more famous antebellum (pre–Civil War) cases of sexual exploitation occurred in Missouri during the 1850s. It involved sixty-year-old Robert Newsom and Celia, a fourteen-year-old girl he had purchased in 1850. Newsom repeatedly raped Celia until she killed him in 1855. Celia's attorneys put up a spirited defense at her trial. They argued that an 1845 Missouri law that made it a crime to "take any woman unlawfully against her will and by force, menace or duress, compel her to be defiled" gave Celia a right to defend her virtue. But the white male jury convicted her of murder anyway, and she was executed.

White southerners justified sexual abuse of black women in several ways. They maintained that black women were naturally promiscuous and seduced white men. Some proslavery apologists even argued that the sexual exploitation of black women by white men reduced prostitution and promoted purity among white women. These apologists ignored the devastating emotional impact of sexual exploitation on black women. And they failed to note that white male rape of black women emphasized in the most degrading manner the inability of black men to protect their wives and daughters.

Diet

The slaves' diet hardly raised the moral issues associated with the sexual exploitation of black women by white men. The typical plantation's weekly ration of one peck of cornmeal and three to four pounds of salt pork or bacon was enough to maintain an adult's body weight and, therefore, appeared to be adequate. But even when black men and women added vegetables and poultry that they raised or fish and small game that they caught, this diet was deficient in calcium, vitamin C, riboflavin, protein, and iron. Because these vitamins and nutrients were essential to the health of people who performed hard labor in a hot climate, slaves frequently suffered from chronic illnesses.

They often complained about being hungry and about the poor quality of their food. As one song went:

> *We raise de wheat,*
> *Dey gib us de corn;*
> *We bake de bread,*
> *Dey giv us de crust;*
> *We sif' de meal,*
> *Dey gib us de huss;*
> *We peel de meat,*
> *Dey gib us de skin*

Yet masters and white southerners generally consumed the same sort of food that slaves ate and, in comparison to people in other parts of the Atlantic world, enslaved African Americans were not undernourished. Although adult slaves were on average an inch shorter than white northerners, they were three inches taller than new arrivals from Africa, two inches taller than slaves who lived in the West Indies, and one inch taller than British Royal Marines.

African-American cooks, primarily women, developed a distinctive cuisine based on African culinary traditions. They seasoned foods with salt, onions, pepper, and other spices and herbs. They fried meat and fish, served sauce over rice, and flavored vegetables with bits of smoked meat. The availability in the South of such African foods as okra, yams, benne seeds, and peanuts strengthened their culinary ties to that continent. Cooking also gave black women the ability to control part of their lives and to demonstrate their creativity.

Clothing

Enslaved men and women had less control over what they and their children wore than how they cooked. Although skilled slaves often produced the shoes and clothing plantation workers wore, slaves in general rarely had the time or skill to make their own clothes. They went barefoot during the warm months and wore cheap shoes, usually made by local cobblers, in the winter. Slaveholding women, with the help of trained female house servants, sewed the clothes slaves wore.

This clothing was usually made of homespun cotton or wool. Some slaves also received hand-me-downs from masters and overseers. Although the distribution of clothing varied widely over time and space, and according to the generosity of masters, slaves usually received clothing allotments twice a year. At the fall distribution, slave men received two outfits for the cold weather along with a jacket and a wool cap. At the spring distribution, they received two cotton outfits. Slave drivers wore garments of finer cloth and greatcoats during the winter. Butlers and carriage drivers wore liveries appropriate to their public duties. Slave women received at each distribution two simply cut dresses of calico or homespun. In the winter they wore capes or cloaks and covered their heads with kerchiefs or bonnets.

Because masters gave priority to clothing adult workers, small children often went naked during the warm months. Depending upon their ages and the season, children received garments called *shirts* if worn by boys and *shifts* if worn by girls. "I ain' neber had no pants 'till de year befo' de [Civil] war. All de li'l boys wo' shu't-tail shu'ts, jes' a slip to de knees," recalled former Louisiana slave Jacob Branch. This androgynous garb lasted until children reached "about twelve or fourteen," when they began doing the work of adults.

Although they received standard-issue clothing, black women particularly sought to individualize what they wore. They changed the colors of clothes with dyes they extracted from roots, berries, walnut shells, oak leaves, and indigo. They wove threads of different color into their clothes to make "checkedy" and other patterns. Former slave Morris Sheppard remembered that with his mother "everything was stripedy."

To further adorn themselves, young women wore hoops under their skirts fashioned from grape vines, stiffly starched petticoats, intricately arranged turbans, and colorful kerchiefs. On special occasions they braided or twisted their hair, used rouge made from berries, eye shadow made from soot, and perfume derived from honeysuckle. Urban slaves, of course, had access to commercial products, and even plantation slaves often bought clothes, shoes, ribbons, and kerchiefs at local stores or from peddlers.

Health

Low birth weight, diet, and clothing all affected the health of slaves. Before the 1830s various diseases were endemic among bondspeople, and death could come quickly. Much of this ill health resulted from overwork in the South's hot, humid summers, from exposure to cold during the winter, and from poor hygiene. Slave quarters, for example, rarely had privies; drinking water could become contaminated; and food was prepared under less than healthy conditions. Dysentery, typhus, food poisoning, diarrhea, hepatitis, typhoid fever, salmonella, and intestinal worms were common and sometimes fatal maladies.

The South's warm climate encouraged mosquito-borne diseases, the growth of bacteria, and the spread of viruses. Some diseases were passed from one race to another. Smallpox, measles, and gonorrhea were European diseases; malaria, hookworm, and yellow fever came from Africa. The sickle-cell blood trait protected people of African descent from malaria but could cause sickle-cell anemia, a painful, debilitating, and fatal disease. African Americans were also more susceptible to other afflictions than were persons of European descent.

They suffered from lactose intolerance, which greatly limited the amount of calcium they could absorb from dairy products, and from a limited ability to acquire enough vitamin D from the sunlight in temperate regions. Because many slaves also lost calcium through perspiration while working, these characteristics led to a high incidence of debilitating diseases. These included, according to historian Donald R. Wright, "blindness or inflamed and watery eyes; lameness or crooked limbs; loose, missing or rotten teeth; and skin sores. Also, they made African Americans much more apt than whites to suffer from a number of often fatal diseases—tetanus, intestinal worms, diphtheria, whooping cough, pica (or dirt eating), pneumonia, tuberculosis, and dysentery."

However, black southerners constituted the only New World slave population that grew by natural reproduction. Although the death rate among slaves was higher than among white southerners, it was similar to that of Europeans. Slave health also improved after 1830 when their rising economic value persuaded masters to improve slave quarters, provide warmer winter clothing, reduce overwork, and hire physicians to care for bondspeople. During the 1840s and 1850s, slaves were more likely than white southerners to be cared for by a physician.

Enslaved African Americans also used traditional remedies—derived from Africa and passed down by generations of women—to treat their sick. Wild cherry bark, and herbs like pennyroyal or horehound went into teas to treat colds. Slaves used jimsonweed tea for rheumatism and chestnut leaf tea to relieve asthma. One former slave recalled that her grandmother dispensed syrup to treat colic and teas to cure fevers and stomachaches. Nineteenth-century medical knowledge was so limited that some of these folk remedies were more effective than those prescribed by white physicians. This was especially true of kaolin, a white clay also used in ceramics, which black women used to treat dysentery.

THE SOCIALIZATION OF SLAVES

African Americans had to acquire the skills needed to protect themselves and their loved ones from an often brutal slave system. Folktales, often derived from Africa but on occasion from American Indians, helped pass such skills from generation to generation. Parents, other relatives, and elderly slaves generally told such tales to teach survival, mental agility, and self-confidence.

The heroes of the tales are animal tricksters with human personalities. Most famous is Brer Rabbit who in his weakness and cleverness represents African Americans in slavery. Although the tales portray Brer Rabbit as far from perfect, he uses his wits to overcome threats from strong and vicious antagonists, principally Brer Fox, who represents slaveholders. By hearing these stories and rooting for Brer Rabbit, slave children learned how to conduct themselves in a difficult environment.

They learned to watch what they said to white people, not to talk back, to withhold information about other African Americans, to dissemble. In particular they refrained from making antislavery statements and camouflaged their awareness of how masters exploited them. As Henry Bibb, who escaped from slavery, put it, "The only weapon of self defense that I could use successfully was that of deception." Another former slave, Charshee Charlotte Lawrence-McIntyre, summed up the slave strategy in rhyme: "Got one mind for the boss to see; got another for what I know is me."

Masters tended to miss the subtlety of the divided consciousness of their bondpeople. When slaves refused to do simple tasks correctly, masters saw it as black stupidity rather than resistance. Sometimes outsiders, such as white northern missionary Charles C. Jones, understood more clearly what was going on. In 1842 Jones observed,

> Persons live and die in the midst of Negroes and know comparatively little of their real character. The Negroes form a distinct class in the community, and keep themselves very much to themselves. They are one thing before the whites and another before their own color. Deception towards the former is characteristic of them, whether bond or free. . . It is habit—long established custom, which descends from generation to generation.

RELIGION

Along with family and socialization, religion helped African Americans cope with slavery. Some masters denied their slaves access to Christianity, and some slaves ignored the religion. But by the mid-nineteenth century, most slaves practiced a Protestantism similar to but different from that of white southerners.

Biracial Baptist and Methodist congregations persisted in the South longer than they did in northern cities. The southern congregations usually had racially segregated seating. But blacks and whites joined in communion and church discipline, and they shared cemeteries. Many masters during the nineteenth century sponsored plantation churches for slaves, and white missionary organizations also supported such churches.

In the plantation churches, white ministers told their black congregations that Christian slaves must obey their earthly masters as they did God. This was not what slaves wanted to hear. Cornelius Garner, a former slave, recalled that "dat ole white preacher jest was telling us slaves to be good to our marsters. We ain't keer'd a bit 'bout dat stuff he was telling us 'cause we wanted to sing, pray, and serve God in our own way." At times slaves walked out on ministers who preached obedience.

Instead of services sponsored by masters, slaves preferred a semisecret black church they conducted themselves. This was a church characterized by self-called, often illiterate black preachers. It emphasized Moses and deliverance from bondage rather than a consistent theology or Christian meekness. Services were quite emotional and involved singing, dancing, shouting, moaning, and clapping. Mixed in with this black Christianity were, according to historian Peter Kolchin, African "potions, concoctions, charms, and rituals [used] to ward off evil, cure sickness, harm enemies, and produce amorous behavior." European settlers in America during the previous century had also melded Christian and non-Christian beliefs and practices. So it is not surprising that white as well as black people continued to seek the help of African-American conjurers.

THE CHARACTER OF SLAVERY AND SLAVES

For over a century, historians have debated the character of the slave system and the people it held in bondage. During the 1910s, southern historian Ulrich B. Phillips portrayed slavery as a benign, paternalistic institution in which Christian slaveholders cared for largely content slaves. Slavery, Phillips argued—as had

British artist John Antrobus completed this painting in about 1860. It is named *Plantation Burial* and suggests the importance of religion among enslaved African Americans.

the slaveholders themselves—rescued members of an inferior race from African barbarism and permitted them to rise as far as they possibly could toward civilization. With a much different emphasis, Marxist historian Eugene D. Genovese has, since the 1960s, seen paternalism at the heart of southern plantation slavery.

Other historians, however, have denied that paternalism had much to do with a system that rested on force. Since the 1950s, historians have contended that slaveholders exploited their bondpeople in a selfish quest for profits. Although some slaveholders were certainly concerned about the welfare of their slaves, this brutal portrait of slavery is persuasive at the dawn of the twenty-first century. Many masters never met their slaves face to face. Most slaves had experienced whipping at some point, and over half the slaves caught up in the domestic slave trade had been separated from their families.

The character of enslaved African Americans has also been debated. Historians like Phillips, who were persuaded by the slaveholders' justifications of the "peculiar institution," argued that African Americans were genetically predisposed to being slaves and were therefore content in their status. In 1959 Stanley M. Elkins changed the debate by arguing that black people were not inherently inferior or submissive, but that the concentration-camp conditions on plantations made them into childlike "Sambos" as dependent on their masters as inmates in Nazi extermination camps were on their guards.

Elkins's study stimulated the scholarship that shapes current understandings of the character of African Americans in slavery. Since the 1960s, historians have argued that rather than dehumanize blacks, slavery led African Americans to create institutions that allowed them some control over their lives. According to these historians, African-American resistance forced masters to accept the slaves' own work patterns and their autonomy in the slave quarters. Slaves built families, churches, and communities. Although these studies may over-idealize the strength of slave communities within the brutal context of plantation slavery, they have enriched our understanding of slave life.

Conclusion

African-American life in slavery during the time of the Cotton Kingdom is a vast subject. As slavery expanded westward before 1860, it varied from region to region and according to the crops slaves cultivated. Although cotton became the South's most important product,

many African-American slaves continued to produce tobacco, rice, sugar, and hemp. In the Chesapeake, slaves worked on wheat farms. Others tended livestock or worked in cities and industry. Meanwhile, enslaved African Americans continued to build the community institutions that allowed them to maintain their cultural autonomy and persevere within a brutal system.

The story of African Americans in southern slavery is one of labor, perseverance, and resistance. Black labor was responsible for the growth of a southern economy that helped produce prosperity throughout the United States. Black men and women preserved and expanded an African-American cultural heritage that included African, European, and American Indian roots. They resisted determined efforts to dehumanize them. They developed family relationships, communities, churches, and traditions that helped them preserve their character as a people.

Review Questions

1. How did the domestic slave trade and the exploitation of black women by white males affect slave families?

2. Were black slaveholders significant in the history of slavery?

3. How did urban and industrial slavery differ from plantation slavery in the Old South?

4. What impact did housing, nutrition, and disease have on the lives of slaves between 1820 and 1860?

5. How did black Christianity differ from white Christianity in the Old South? How did black Christianity in the South differ from black Christianity in the North?

Recommended Reading

Charles B. Dew. *Bonds of Iron: Masters and Slaves at Buffalo Forge.* New York: Norton, 1994. Dew offers an excellent account of one type of industrial slavery in the Old South.

Michael P. Johnson and James L. Roark. *Black Masters: A Free Family of Color in the Old South.* New York: Norton, 1984. This book provides a full account of April [William] Ellison and his slaveholding black family.

Norrece T. Jones Jr. *Born a Child of Freedom, Yet a Slave: Mechanisms of Control and Strategies of Resistance in Antebellum South Carolina.* Middleton, CT: Wesleyan University Press, 1990. This book explores

TIMELINE

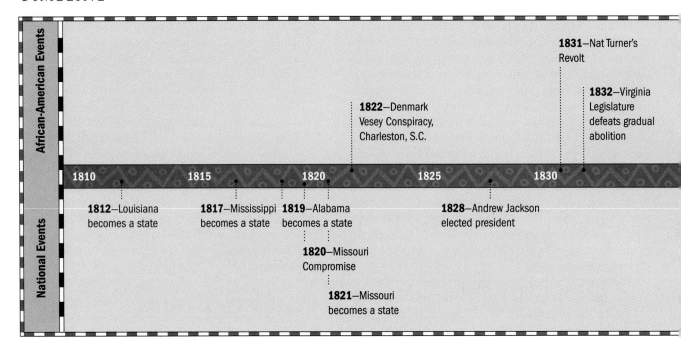

how masters controlled slaves and how slaves resisted them.

Wilma King. *Stolen Childhood: Slave Youth in Nineteenth-Century America*. Bloomington: Indiana University Press, 1995. This is the most up-to-date account of enslaved black children. It is especially useful about the work in which these children engaged.

Peter Kolchin. *American Slavery, 1619–1877*. New York: Hill and Wang, 1993. The bulk of this book deals with slavery during the antebellum period. It provides a brief but comprehensive introduction to the subject.

Melton A. McLaurin. *Celia, a Slave*. Athens: University of Georgia Press, 1991. This is the most complete study of an enslaved woman's response to sexual exploitation. MacLaurin established both the social and political context for this famous case.

ADDITIONAL BIBLIOGRAPHY

Slavery and Its Expansion

Stanley M. Elkins. *Slavery: A Problem in American Institutional and Intellectual Life*. 3d ed. Chicago: University of Chicago Press, 1976.

Eugene D. Genovese. *The Political Economy of Slavery: Studies in the Economy and Society of the Slave South*. 1961; reprint, New York: Random House, 1967.

Lewis C. Gray. *History of Agriculture in the Southern United States to 1860*. 1933; reprint, Clifton, NJ: A. M. Kelley, 1973.

Larry Koger. *Black Slaveowners: Free Black Slave Masters in South Carolina, 1790–1860*. 1985; reprint, Columbia: University of South Carolina Press, 1994.

Kenneth M. Stampp. *The Peculiar Institution: Slavery in the Antebellum South*. 1956; reprint, New York: Vintage Books, 1989.

Urban and Industrial Slavery

Ronald L. Lewis. *Coal, Iron, and Slaves: Industrial Slavery in Maryland and Virginia, 1715–1865*. Westport, CT: Greenwood, 1979.

Robert S. Starobin. *Industrial Slavery in the Old South*. New York: Oxford University Press, 1970.

Richard C. Wade. *Slavery in the Cities: The South 1820–1860*. 1964; reprint, New York: Oxford University Press, 1967.

The Domestic Slave Trade

Frederic Bancroft. *Slave Trading in the Old South*. 1931; reprint, Columbia: University of South Carolina Press, 1996.

Michael Tadman. *Speculators and Slaves: Masters, Traders, and Slaves in the Old South*. 1989; reprint, Madison: University of Wisconsin Press, 1996.

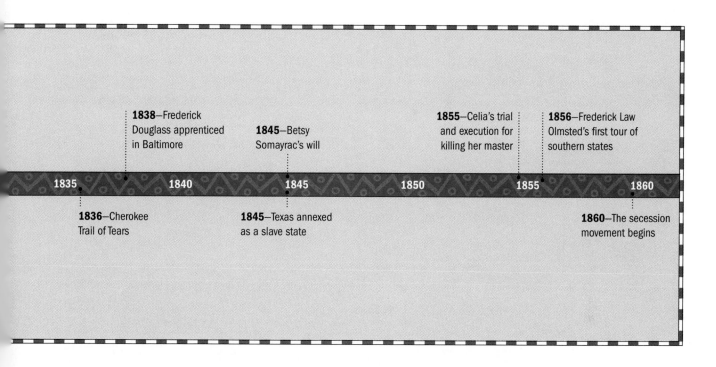

1838—Frederick Douglass apprenticed in Baltimore

1845—Betsy Somayrac's will

1855—Celia's trial and execution for killing her master

1856—Frederick Law Olmsted's first tour of southern states

1835   1840   1845   1850   1855   1860

1836—Cherokee Trail of Tears

1845—Texas annexed as a slave state

1860—The secession movement begins

The Slave Community

John W. Blassingame. *The Slave Community: Plantation Life in the Antebellum South.* 2d ed. New York: Oxford University Press, 1979.

John B. Boles. *Black Southerners, 1619–1869.* Lexington: University Press of Kentucky, 1983.

Eugene D. Genovese. *Roll, Jordan, Roll: The World the Slave Made.* 1974; reprint, Vintage Books, 1976.

Herbert Gutman. *The Black Family in Slavery and Freedom.* 1976; reprint, Vintage Books, 1977.

Charles Joyner. *Down by the Riverside: A South Carolina Community.* Urbana: University of Illinois Press, 1984.

Leslie Howard Owens. *This Species of Property: Slave Life and Culture in the Old South.* 1976; reprint, New York: Oxford University Press, 1977.

Todd L. Savitt. *Medicine and Slavery: The Diseases and Health Care of Blacks in Antebellum Virginia.* Urbana: University of Illinois Press, 1978.

Enslaved Women

David Barry Gaspar and Darlene Clark Hine, eds. *More than Chattel: Black Women and Slavery in the Americas.* Bloomington: University of Indiana Press, 1996.

Darlene Clark Hine, Wilma King, and Linda Reed, eds. *"We Specialize in the Wholly Impossible": A Reader in Black Women's History.* Brooklyn, NY: Carlson, 1996.

Patricia Morton, ed. *Discovering the Women in Slavery: Emancipating Perspectives on the American Past.* Athens: University of Georgia Press, 1996.

Deborah Gray White. *Ar'n't I a Woman? Female Slaves in the Plantation South.* New York: Norton, 1985.

Slave Culture and Religion

John B. Boles, ed. *Masters and Slaves in the House of the Lord: Race and Religion in the American South, 1740–1870.* Lexington: University Press of Kentucky, 1988.

Janet Duitsman Cornelius. *When I Can Read My Title Clear: Literacy, Slavery, and Religion in the Antebellum South.* Columbia: University of South Carolina Press, 1991.

Lawrence W. Levine. *Black Culture and Black Consciousness: Afro-American Folk Thought from Slavery to Freedom.* New York: Oxford University Press, 1977.

Albert J. Raboteau. *Slave Religion: The "Invisible Institution" in the Antebellum South.* New York: Oxford University Press, 1978.

CHAPTER 7

FREE BLACK PEOPLE
IN ANTEBELLUM AMERICA

William Matthew Prior, "Three Sisters of the Coplan Family" 1854. Oil on canvas. 26⅞ × 36⅝ in. (68.3 × 92.7 cm). Bequest of Martha C. Karolik for the M. and M. Karolik Collection of American Paintings, 1815–1865. Courtesy, Museum of Fine Arts, Boston.

Eliza, Nellie, and Margaret Coplan in an 1854 portrait by W. M. Prior. The Coplan family was
one of the few African-American families in antebellum America affluent enough to
commission such a portrait. Note the girls' fine clothing.

Our vices and our degradation are ever arrayed against us, but our virtues are passed by unnoticed. And what is still more lamentable, our [white] friends, to whom we concede all the principles of humanity and religion, from these very causes seem to have fallen into the current of popular feeling and are imperceptibly floating on the stream—actually living in the practice of prejudice, while they abjure it in theory, and feel it not in their hearts.

Freedom's Journal, March 16, 1827.

Journalist Samuel Cornish wrote this passage in 1827 when he introduced himself to his readers as the coeditor of the first African-American newspaper. He knew that pervasive white prejudice limited the lives of black people. During the 40 years before the Civil War, such prejudice was nearly as common in the North as in the South. The northern states had, of course, abolished slavery, and free black people there enjoyed more rights than they did in the South. But that made many white northerners even more hostile toward African Americans than white southerners generally were.

While southern legislatures considered expelling free black people from their states, northern legislatures—particularly in the Old Northwest—restricted black people's ability to move into their states. White workers in both the North and South, fearing competition for jobs, sponsored legislation that limited most free African Americans to the most menial employment. White people also required most black people to live in segregated areas of cities. Yet such ghettoized African-American communities cultivated a dynamic cultural legacy and built enduring institutions.

In this chapter we pick up the story of free black communities begun in Chapter 5 to provide a portrait of free African Americans between 1820 and the start of the Civil War. As in the revolutionary era, the antebellum period was one of both hope and fear. The numbers of free African Americans steadily increased. But, as we saw in Chapter 6, the number of slaves increased much faster. Here we begin by reviewing the demographic data. We then discuss black life in the North and free black life in the South.

DEMOGRAPHICS OF FREEDOM

In 1820 there were 233,504 free African Americans living in the United States. In comparison there were 1,538,125 slaves and 7,861,931 white people. Of the free African Americans, 99,281 lived in the North, 114,070 in the upper South, and just 20,153 in the deep South. Free people of color made up 2.4 percent of the American population and 3 percent of the southern population. More black women than black men were free, and—particularly in urban areas—this remained true throughout the period.

By 1860 the free African-American population had reached 488,070. Of these, 226,152 lived in the North, 224,963 in the upper South, and 36,955 in the deep South (Figures 7–1 and 7–2). Yet slaves had increased to just under four million, and massive immigration had tripled the white population to 26,957,471. The proportion of free African Americans had actually dropped to just 1.6 percent of the total American population and to 2.1 percent of the southern population when the Civil War in 1861 began the process of making all black people free.

However, 47.3 percent of the free black population lived in cities in 1860 compared with only 32.9 percent of white people—and of those urban African Americans, 62.5 percent lived in cities with populations over 100,000. As a result, black urban communities made up a significantly larger percentage of the population of large cities than they did of the total American population. In the upper South city of Baltimore, for example, free black people represented 12 percent of the city's 212,418 residents. The largest black urban population in the North was in Philadelphia, where 22,185 African Americans made up 4.2 percent of approximately 533,000 residents.

The black populations of such important northern cities as New York, Boston, Providence, New Haven, and Cincinnati were considerably smaller than Philadelphia's. But they were still large enough to develop dynamic communities. In Baltimore, Richmond, Norfolk, and other cities of the upper South, free

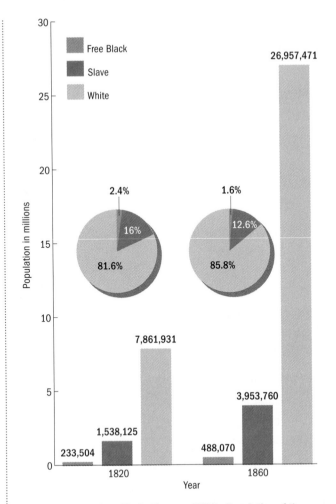

Figure 7–1 The Free Black, Slave, and White Population of the United States in 1820 and 1860. The bar graph shows the relationship among free African-American, slave, and white populations in the United States in the years 1820 and 1860. The superimposed pie charts illustrate the percentages of these groups in the population in the same years.

African Americans interacted with enslaved populations to create black communities embracing both groups.

THE JACKSONIAN ERA

After the War of 1812, free African Americans—like other Americans of the time—witnessed rapid economic, social, and political change. Between 1800 and 1860, a market revolution began to transform the North into a modern industrial society. An economy based on self-sufficient farms, goods produced by skilled artisans, and local markets grew into one marked by commercial farming, factory production, and national markets. The industrial revolution that had begun in Britain a century earlier set the stage for

Figure 7–2 **The Free Black, Slave, and White Population by Region, 1860.** These pie charts compare the free black, slave, and white populations of the North, upper South, and lower South in 1860. Note the near balance of the races in the lower South.

these changes. But transportation had to improve enormously to allow for such a revolution in America. After Robert Fulton demonstrated the practicality of steam-powered river vessels in 1807, steamboats speeded travel on the country's inland waterways. By the 1820s a system of turnpikes and canals began to unite the North and parts of the South. Of particular importance were the National Road extending westward from Baltimore and the Erie Canal that in 1825 opened a water route from New York City to the Old Northwest. By the 1830s railroads began to link urban and agricultural regions.

As faster transportation revolutionized trade, as a factory system began to replace small shops run by artisans, and as cities expanded, northern society changed in profound ways. A large urban working class arose. Artisans and small farmers feared for their future. Entrepreneurs began to replace the traditional social elite. The North also became increasingly different from a still largely premodern South. By the 1820s the northern states were bristling with reform movements designed to deal with the social dislocations the market revolution had caused.

The market revolution also helped create mass political parties. By 1810, states across the country began dropping the traditional property qualifications that had limited citizens' right to vote. One by one, they moved toward universal white manhood suffrage. This trend doomed the openly elitist Federalist party and disrupted its foe, the Republican party. As the market revolution picked up during the 1820s, unleashing hopes and fears among Americans, politicians realized the need for more broadly based political parties.

A turning point came in 1825 when Congress chose Secretary of State John Quincy Adams of Massachusetts to become president over the war hero Andrew Jackson of Tennessee after no candidate received a majority of the electoral votes. As president, Adams paradoxically represented both the old elitist style of politics *and* the entrepreneurial spirit of emerging northern capitalism. Adams—along with his secretary of state, Henry Clay—hoped to promote industrialization through a national program of federal government aid.

Jackson's supporters, led by Martin Van Buren of New York, organized a new Democratic party to counter Adams and Clay's program by making Jackson president. By appealing to slaveholders, who feared that economic nationalism would favor the North over the South, and to "the common man" throughout the country, the Democrats elected Jackson in 1828.

Jackson was a strong but controversial president. During the Nullification Crisis of 1832–1833 he acted as a nationalist in facing down the attempt of South Carolina to nullify—to block—the collection of the United States tariff (tax) on imports within the state. Otherwise, Jackson, who owned many slaves, promoted states' rights, economic localism, and the territorial expansion of slavery. In opposition to Jackson, Henry Clay—a Kentucky slaveholder—and others formed the Whig party in the early 1830s.

A national organization that fought the Democrats for power from 1834 to 1852, the Whig party mixed traditional and modern politics. It was a mass political party, but many of its leaders questioned the legitimacy of mass parties. It favored a nationalist approach to economic policy—which made it more successful in the North than in the South—opposed territorial expansion, worried about the growing number of immigrants, and endorsed the moral values of evangelical Protestantism. While Democratic politicians increasingly made racist appeals to anti-black prejudices among white voters, Whigs generally adopted a more conciliatory tone regarding race. By the late 1830s, a few northern Whigs believed that their party actually opposed slavery and racial oppression. They were, however, exaggerating. The Whigs constantly nominated slaveholders for the presidency, and few Whig politicians defended the rights of African Americans.

LIMITED FREEDOM IN THE NORTH

Addressing an interracial audience in Boston, white abolitionist Joseph C. Lovejoy in 1846 described the North as a land "partially free." Lovejoy was especially concerned that the Fugitive Slave Law of 1793 extended into the northern states the power of southern slaveholders to enslave African Americans. But white northerners also limited black freedom by enacting *Black Laws*; by rarely allowing black men to vote; by advocating segregated housing, schools, and transportation; and by limiting African Americans' employment opportunities.

The Fugitive Slave Law endangered the freedom of northern black men, women, and children. Those who had escaped from slavery, of course, lived in fear that as long as they stayed in the United States they might be seized and returned to their erstwhile masters. In fact, any black northerner could be kidnapped, taken to a southern state, and enslaved under the aegis of this law. Even such black leaders as Richard Allen and

David Ruggles faced this threat. Ruggles, a prominent northern-born abolitionist, author, and lecturer during the 1830s and 1840s, barely escaped an attempt to hail him before a judge so that he could be transported to the South. Others were less lucky, and vigilance against kidnapping became important in African-American community life in the North throughout the antebellum period.

Black Laws

As we saw in previous chapters, the racially egalitarian impulse of the revolutionary era had begun to wane among white Americans by the 1790s. Meanwhile, the dawning Romantic Age—which was characterized by a sentimental fascination with uniqueness—encouraged a general belief that each ethnic and racial group had its own inherent spirit, which set it apart from others. As white Americans began to perceive self-reliance, intellectual curiosity, the capacity for self-government, military valor, and an energetic work ethic as inherently "Anglo-Saxon" characteristics, they began to believe

This lithograph, published in 1818 by antislavery author Jesse Torrey Jun, depicts a free black man still in handcuffs and leg irons after an attempt to kidnap him into slavery. He is relating details of his experience to a sympathetic white man. The sparsely furnished attic room reflects the living conditions of many free African Americans of the time.

that other racial groups lacked these virtues. As Samuel Cornish suggested, even those white people who befriended black people considered them outsiders in a "white man's country."

Most white northerners, in fact, wanted nothing to do with African Americans. Like white southerners, they considered black people inferior in every way. They paradoxically dismissed black people as incapable of honest work *and* feared black competition for jobs. Contact with African Americans, they believed, had degraded white southerners and would also corrupt white northerners if they permitted it. Therefore, as historian Leon Litwack puts it, "Nearly every northern state considered, and many adopted, measures to prohibit or restrict the further immigration of Negroes" into their jurisdictions.

Such measures were adopted more often in the Old Northwest than in the Northeast. In 1821 a bill to restrict black people from entering Massachusetts failed to reach a vote in the state legislature on the grounds that it was inconsistent with "love of humanity." In Pennsylvania, which had a much larger influx of southern African Americans than did Massachusetts, the legislature defeated attempts to limit their entry to the state. But Ohio, Illinois, Indiana, Michigan, Iowa, and Wisconsin all limited or banned black immigration and discriminated against black residents.

Between 1804 and 1849, Ohio's "black laws" required that African Americans entering the state produce legal evidence that they were free, register with a county clerk, and post a five hundred dollar bond "to pay for their support in case of want." State and local authorities rarely enforced these provisions, and when the Ohio Free Soil party brought about their repeal in 1849, Ohio had about 25,000 African Americans. But these rules certainly made black people insecure. In 1829, for example, Cincinnati used them to force between 1,100 and 2,200 black residents to depart. Moreover, other provisions of Ohio's black laws *were* rigorously enforced, including those that prohibited black testimony against white people, black service on juries, and black enlistment in the state militia.

In 1813 the Illinois Territory threatened African Americans who tried to settle within its borders with repeated whippings until they left. In 1847, long after it had become a state, Illinois updated this provision by mandating that African Americans who sought to become permanent residents could be fined. Those who could not pay the fine could be sold at public auction into indentured servitude. Indiana citizens ratified a state constitution in 1851 that explicitly banned all African Americans from the state, and Michigan, Iowa,

	1800	1810	1820	1830	1840
Table 7-1 Black Population in the States of the Old Northwest, 1800–1840					
Ohio	337	1,899	4,723	9,574	17,345
Michigan		144	174	293	707
Illinois		781	1,374	2,384	3,929
Indiana	298	630	1,420	3,632	7,168
Iowa					188

Source: Horton and Horton, *In Hope of Liberty*, 104.

and Wisconsin followed Indiana's example. These laws testify to white prejudice and fear. They suggest how uncomfortable African Americans felt in the Old Northwest. Yet, as in Ohio, these states rarely enforced such restrictive laws. As long as they did not feel threatened, white people were usually willing to tolerate a few black people (see Table 7-1).

Disfranchisement

The disfranchisement of black voters was, excepting most of New England, common throughout the North during the antebellum decades. The movement to deny the right to vote to black men—no women could vote anywhere in the United States during most of the nineteenth century—was based on the same white antipathy to African Americans that led to exclusionary legislation. Because this sentiment was strongest in the Old Northwest, black men were never allowed to vote before the Civil War in Ohio, Indiana, Illinois, Michigan, Wisconsin, and Iowa. But the older northern states had allowed black male suffrage, and efforts to curtail it were by-products of Jacksonian Democracy.

During the eighteenth and early nineteenth centuries, the dominant elite in the northeastern states had used property qualifications to prevent *both* poor black and poor white men from voting. Since black people were generally poorer than white people, these property qualifications gave most white men the vote but denied it to most black men. Under such circumstances white people saw no danger in letting a few relatively well-to-do black men exercise the franchise. It was the egalitarian movement to remove property qualifications that led to the outright disfranchisement of most black voters in the Northeast.

Both advocates and opponents of universal white male suffrage argued that it would be dangerous to extend the same privilege to black men. They alleged that in certain places black men would be elected to office, that morally suspect African Americans would corrupt the political process, that justifiably angry white people would react violently, and that black people would be encouraged to try to mix socially with white people. Therefore, the movement for universal white manhood suffrage transformed a class issue into a racial one, and although a few white politicians opposed disfranchisement of black voters, the outcome was predictable.

New Jersey stopped allowing black men to vote in 1807 and in 1844 adopted a *white only* suffrage provision in its state constitution. In 1818 Connecticut determined that, although black men who had voted before that date could continue to vote, no new black voters would be allowed. At the other extreme, Maine, New Hampshire, Vermont, and Massachusetts—none of which had a significant African-American minority—made no effort to deprive black men of the vote. In the middle were Rhode Island, New York, and Pennsylvania, which had protracted struggles over the issue.

In 1822 Rhode Island denied that black men were eligible to vote in its elections. But a popular uprising against the state's conservative government extended the franchise to all men, black as well as white, in 1842. In New York an 1821 state constitutional convention defeated an attempt to disfranchise black men. Instead it retained a property qualification for black voters while eliminating it for white voters. To vote in New York, black men had to have property worth $250 (approximately $3,000 in current dollars) and pay taxes, whereas white men simply had to pay taxes or serve in the state militia. African Americans nevertheless remained active in New York politics. As supporters of the Whig party in 1846 and of the Free Soil party in 1848, they fought unsuccessfully to regain equal access to the polls.

A similar protracted struggle in Pennsylvania resulted in a more resounding defeat for black suffrage. From 1780 to 1837, black men who met property qualifications could vote in some counties but not in others. Then in 1838, a convention to draft a new state constitution enfranchised all white males and disfranchised all black males. The vote to disfranchise black men was seventy-seven to forty-five. Although such African-American leaders as Robert Purvis, Peter Gardner, and Frederick Hinton organized to prevent the new constitution from being adopted, Pennsylvanians narrowly ratified it by a vote of 113,971 to 112,759. As late as 1855, black Pennsylvanians, arguing that without the right to vote they faced mounting repression, petitioned Congress to help them gain equal access to the polls. But their efforts failed, and in the years before the Civil War, 93 percent of northern black people lived in states where their right to vote was either denied or severely limited.

Segregation

Exclusionary legislation was confined to the Old Northwest, and not all northern states disfranchised black men. But no black northerner could avoid being victimized by a pervasive determination among white people to segregate society.

Northern hotels, taverns, and resorts turned black people away unless they were the servants of white guests. African Americans were either banned from public lecture halls, art exhibits, and religious revivals or could attend only at certain times. When they were allowed in churches and theaters, they had to sit in segregated sections. Ohio excluded African Americans from state-supported poorhouses and insane asylums. In relatively enlightened Massachusetts, prominent black abolitionist and orator Frederick Douglass was "within the space of a few days. . . turned away from a menagerie on Boston Common, a lyceum and revival meeting in New Bedford, [and] an eating house."

African Americans faced special difficulty trying to use public transportation. They could ride in stagecoaches only if there were no white passengers. As rail travel became more common during the late 1830s, companies set aside special cars for African Americans. In Massachusetts in 1841 a railroad first used the term *Jim Crow*, which derived from a black-face minstrel act, to describe these cars. Later the term came to define other forms of racial segregation as well. In cities, many omnibus and streetcar companies barred African Americans entirely even though urban black people had little choice but to try to use them anyway. Steamboats accepted black passengers but refused to rent them cabins. African Americans had to remain on deck at night and during storms.

All African Americans regardless of their wealth or social standing were treated this way. Frederick Douglass, who made a point of challenging segregation, refused to ride in Jim Crow train cars unless physically forced to do so. He once clung so tightly to the arms of his seat when several white men attempted to move him that the seat ripped away from its supports. In 1854 in New York City, a black public school teacher named Elizabeth Jenkins was beaten by a white streetcar conductor who tried to expel her from his vehicle. All black people, regardless of their class, were also frequently insulted in public by white adults and children.

In this atmosphere African Americans learned to distrust white people. A correspondent of Douglass's newspaper, the *North Star*, wrote in 1849 that there seemed "to be a fixed determination on the part of our oppressors in this country to destroy every vestige of self-respect, self-possession, and manly independence left in the colored people." Even when African Americans interacted with white people on an ostensibly equal basis, there were underlying tensions. James Forten's wealthy granddaughter Charlotte Forten, who attended an integrated school in Boston, wrote in her diary, "It is hard to go through life meeting contempt with contempt, hatred with hatred, fearing with too good reason, to love and trust hardly any one whose skin is white—however lovable, attractive, and congenial."

African Americans moving to northern cities, therefore, were not surprised to find segregated black neighborhoods. A few wealthy northern black people lived in white urban neighborhoods, and a few northern cities, such as Cleveland and Detroit, had no patterns of residential segregation. But in most northern cities, the white belief that black neighbors led to lowered property values produced such patterns. There were "Nigger Hill" in Boston, "Little Africa" in Cincinnati, "Hayti" in Pittsburgh, and Philadelphia's Southside. Conditions in these ghettoes were often dreadful. But they provided a refuge from constant insult and places where black institutions could develop.

Because African Americans representing all social and economic classes lived in these segregated neighborhoods, the quality of housing in them varied. But at its worst, housing was bleak and dangerous. One visitor called the black section of New York City's Five Points "the worst hell of America," and other black urban neighborhoods were just as bad. People lived in unheated shacks and shanties, in dirt-floored basements, in houses without doors and windows. These conditions nurtured disease, infant mortality, alcoholism, and crime. Southern visitors to northern cities blamed the victims, insisting that the plight of many urban black northerners proved that African Americans were better off in slavery.

BLACK COMMUNITIES IN THE URBAN NORTH

Northern African Americans lived in both rural and urban areas during the antebellum decades. But it was urban neighborhoods, with their more concentrated black populations, that nurtured black community life (Table 7–2). African-American urban communities of the antebellum period developed from the free black communities that had emerged from slavery in the North during

Table 7-2 Free Black Population of Selected Cities, 1800–1850		
City	1800	1850
Baltimore	2,771	5,442
Boston	1,174	1,999
Charleston	951	3,441
New Orleans	800 (estimated)	9,905
New York	3,499	13,815
Philadelphia	4,210	10,736
Washington	123	8,158

Source: Leonard P. Curry, *The Free Black in Urban America, 1800–1850: The Shadow of the Dream* (Chicago: University of Chicago Press, 1981), 250.

the late eighteenth century. The communities varied from city to city and from region to region, yet they had much in common and interacted with each other. They were characterized by resilient families, poverty, class divisions, active church congregations, the continued development of voluntary organizations, and concern for education.

The Black Family

As they became free, northern African Americans left their masters and established their own households. Some left more quickly than others, and in states like New York and New Jersey, where gradual emancipation extended into the nineteenth century, the process continued into the 1820s. By then the average black family in northern cities had two parents and between two and four children. However, in both the Northeast and Northwest, single-parent black families, usually headed by women, became increasingly common during the antebellum period. In Cincinnati, for example, black families headed by women increased from 11 percent in 1830 to more than 22 percent in 1850. This trend may have been influenced by the difficulty black men had gaining employment. It certainly was a function of a high mortality rate among black men, which made many black women widows during their forties.

Both financial need and African-American culture encouraged black northerners to take in boarders and create extended families. By 1850 approximately one-third of black adults in such cities as Boston, Buffalo, Chicago, Detroit, and Cincinnati boarded. Economic considerations were implicit in such arrangements, but friendship and family relationships also played a part.

Sometimes entire nuclear families boarded, but most boarders were young, single, and male. As historians James Oliver Horton and Lois E. Horton put it, "The opportunity to rely on friends and family for shelter enhanced the mobility of poor people who were often forced to move to find employment. It provided financial assistance when people were unemployed; it provided social supports for people who faced discrimination; and it saved those who had left home or run away from slavery from social isolation."

The Struggle for Employment

The rising tide of immigration from Europe hurt northern African Americans economically. Before 1820, black craftsmen had been in demand, but given the choice, white people preferred to employ other white people, and black people suffered. To make matters worse for African Americans, white workers excluded young black men from apprenticeships, refused to work with black people, and used violence to prevent employers from hiring black workers when white workers were unemployed. By the 1830s these practices had driven African Americans from the skilled trades. For the rest of the antebellum period, most northern black men performed menial day labor, while a few worked as coach-

men, teamsters, waiters, barbers, carpenters, masons, and plasterers. By the 1850s black men were losing to Irish immigrants such unskilled jobs as longshoremen, drayers, railroad workers, hod-carriers, porters, and shoe-shiners as well as jobs in such skilled trades as barbering.

By 1847 in Philadelphia, for example, 80 percent of employed black men did unskilled labor. Barbers and shoemakers predominated among those black workers with skills. Only one-half of one percent held factory jobs. Among employed black women, 80 percent either washed clothes or worked as domestic servants. Three quarters of the remaining 20 percent were seamstresses. By the 1850s black women, too, were losing work to Irish immigrants. A few became prostitutes. About 5 percent of black men and women were self-employed, selling food or secondhand clothing.

Unskilled black men were often unable to find work. When they did work, they received low wages. To escape such conditions in Philadelphia and other port cities, they became sailors. By 1850 about 50 percent of

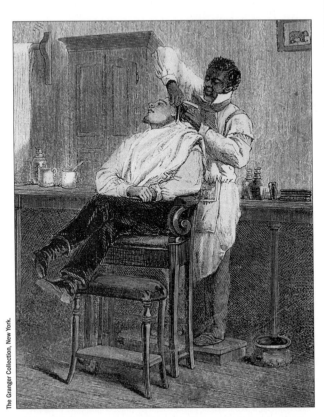

The Granger Collection, New York.

Barbering was one of the skilled trades open to black men during the antebellum years. Several wealthy African Americans began their careers as barbers.

Black sailors were rarely allowed the command of ships. But Captain Absalom Boston was the master of the *Industry,* a whaling ship that sailed out of Nantucket, in 1832.

the crewmen on American merchant and whaling vessels were black. Not only did these sailors have to leave their families for months at a time and endure brutal conditions at sea, but they also risked imprisonment if their ship anchored at southern ports.

The Northern Black Elite

Despite the poor prospects of most northern African Americans, a northern black elite emerged in the first six decades of the nineteenth century. Membership in

---

VOICES

MARIA W. STEWART ON THE CONDITION OF BLACK WORKERS

Maria W. Stewart (1803–1879) was the first black woman public speaker in the United States. She was strong-willed and spoke without qualification what she believed to be the truth. At times she angered both black and white people. In the following speech, which she delivered in Boston in September 1831, Stewart criticized the treatment accorded to black workers—especially black female workers—in the North.

Tell us no more of southern slavery; for with few exceptions, although I may be very erroneous in my opinion, yet I consider our condition but little better than that. . . . After all, methinks there are no chains so galling as those that bind the soul, and exclude it from the vast field of useful and scientific knowledge. . . .

I have asked several [white] individuals of my sex, who transact business for themselves, if providing our girls were to give them the most satisfactory references, they would not be willing to grant them an equal opportunity with others? Their reply has been—for their own part, they had no objection; but as it was not the custom, were they to take them into their employ, they would be in danger of losing the public patronage.

And such is the powerful force of prejudice. Let our girls possess whatever amiable qualities of soul they may; let their characters be fair and spotless as innocence itself; let their natural taste and ingenuity be what they may; it is impossible for scarce an individual of them to rise above the condition of servants. . . .

I observed a piece . . . respecting us, asserting that we were lazy and idle. I confute them on that point. Take us generally as a people, we are neither lazy nor idle: and considering how little we have to excite or stimulate us, I am almost astonished that there are so many industrious and ambitious ones to be found. . . .

Again it was asserted that we were "a ragged set, crying for liberty." I reply to it, the whites have so long and so loudly proclaimed the theme of equal rights and privileges, that our souls have caught the flame also, ragged as we are. As far as our merit deserves, we feel a common desire to rise above the condition of servants and drudges. I have learnt, by bitter experience, that the continual hard labor deadens the energies of the soul, and benumbs the faculties of the mind; the ideas become confined, the mind barren, and, like the scorching sands of Arabia, produces nothing: or like the uncultivated soil, brings forth thorns and thistles. . . .

Most of our color have dragged out a miserable existence of servitude from the cradle to the grave. . . . Do you [women] ask, why are you wretched and miserable? I reply, look at many of the most worthy and most interesting of us doomed to spend our lives in gentlemen's kitchens. Look at our young men, smart, active, and energetic, with souls filled with ambitious fire; if they look forward, alas! What are their prospects? They can be nothing but the humblest laborers, on account of their dark complexions; hence many of them lose their ambition, and become worthless. . . .

QUESTIONS

1. Is Stewart correct in assuming that conditions for black northerners were little better than those for slaves?

2. According to Stewart, what was the impact of northern white prejudice on black workers?

Source: Maria W. Stewart, "Lecture Delivered at the Franklin Hall, Boston, September 21, 1831," as quoted in Roy Finkenbine, *Sources of the African-American Past: Primary Sources in American History* (New York: Longman, 1997), 30–32.

this elite could be achieved through talent, wealth, occupation, family connections, complexion, and education. The elite led in the development of black institutions and culture, in the antislavery movement, and in the struggle for racial justice. It was also the bridge between the black community and sympathetic white people.

Although few African Americans achieved financial security during the antebellum decades, black people could become rich in many ways. Segregated neighborhoods gave rise to a black professional class of physicians, lawyers, ministers, and undertakers who served an exclusively black clientele. Black merchants could also gain wealth selling to black communities. Other relatively well-off African Americans included skilled tradesmen, such as carpenters, barbers, waiters, and coachmen, who generally found employment among white people.

Although less so than among African Americans in the South, complexion influenced social standing among African Americans in the North, especially in cities like Cincinnati that were close to the South. White people often preferred to hire people of mixed race; successful black men often chose light-complexioned brides; and African Americans generally accepted white notions of human beauty.

By the 1820s the black elite was becoming better educated and more socially polished than its less wealthy black neighbors, yet it could never disassociate itself from them. Segregation and discriminatory legislation in the North applied to all African Americans regardless of class and complexion, and all African Americans shared a common culture and history.

Conspicuous among the black elite were entrepreneurs who, against considerable odds, gained wealth and influence in the antebellum North. As we saw in Chapter 5, James Forten was one of the first of them. But several other examples indicate the character of such men. John Remond of Salem, Massachusetts, became a prosperous grocer, whose fortune subsidized the abolitionist career of his son Charles Lenox Remond. Louis Hayden, who escaped from slavery in Kentucky in 1845, had become a successful haberdasher and an abolitionist in Boston by 1849. Henry Boyd, like Hayden a native of Kentucky, built and operated a steam-powered furniture factory in Cincinnati during the 1840s and 1850s.

Perhaps most successful was Stephen Smith, who owned a lumber and coal business in Lancaster County, Pennsylvania, and speculated in real estate. In 1849 Smith and his partner William Whipper owned, in addition to a huge inventory of coal and lumber, twenty-two railroad cars and bank stock worth $9,000 (about $175,000 in current dollars). They grossed $100,000 (nearly $2,000,000 in current dollars) per year, and by 1860, Smith owned real estate in Lancaster and Philadelphia worth $23,000 (about $420,000 in current dollars).

Black Professionals

The northern black elite also included physicians and lawyers. Among the physicians, some, such as James McCune Smith and John S. Rock, received medical degrees. Smith, the first African American to earn a medical degree, graduated from the University of Glasgow in Scotland in 1837 and practiced in New York City until his death in 1874. Rock, who had been a dentist in Philadelphia, graduated from the American Medical College in 1852 and practiced medicine in Boston until 1860 when he undertook the study of law. In 1865 he became the first African American to argue a case before the United States Supreme Court.

Either because they had been forced out of medical school or they chose not to go, other prominent black physicians practiced medicine without having earned a degree. (This was legal in the nineteenth century.) James Still of Medford, New Jersey, had meager formal education but used natural remedies to develop a successful practice among both black and white people. The multitalented Martin R. Delany, who had been born free in Charleston, Virginia, in 1812, practiced medicine in Pittsburgh after having been expelled from Harvard Medical School at the insistence of two white classmates.

Prominent black attorneys included Macon B. Allen, who was admitted to the Maine bar in 1844, and Robert Morris, who qualified to practice law in Massachusetts in 1847. Both Allen and Morris apprenticed with white attorneys, and Morris had a particularly successful and lucrative practice. Yet white residents thwarted his attempt to purchase a mansion in a Boston suburb.

Artists and Musicians

Although they rarely achieved great wealth and have not become famous, black artists and musicians were also part of the northern African-American elite. Among the best-known artists were Robert S. Duncanson, Robert Douglass, Patrick Reason, and Edmonia Lewis. Several of them supported the antislavery movement through their artistic work.

Douglass, a painter who studied in England before establishing himself in Philadelphia, and Reason, an engraver, created portraits of abolitionists during the 1830s. Reason also etched illustrations of the sufferings of slaves. Duncanson, who was born in Cincinnati and worked in Europe between 1843 and 1854, painted landscapes and portraits. Lewis, the daughter of a black man and a Chippewa woman, was admitted to Oberlin College in Ohio with abolitionist help and studied sculpture in Rome. Her works, which emphasized African-American themes, came into wide demand after the Civil War.

The reputations of black professional musicians of the antebellum period have suffered in comparison with

PROFILE

OKAH TUBBEE

The life of James Warner, who became known as Okah Tubbee, illustrates in an eccentric manner several of the themes of this chapter. Warner, who was born in slavery in Natchez, Mississippi, became a successful musician, wrote an autobiography, faced reenslavement, and attempted to obscure his black ancestry.

He was born in 1810 or 1811 to a woman named Franky or Frances. She was owned by James McKray, a cabinetmaker from Pennsylvania who lived in Natchez. Unlike his older half siblings Robert and Kitty, whom McKray probably fathered, Warner was clearly not of mixed race. When McKray died in 1813, his will manumitted Franky, Robert, and Kitty, but left Warner the slave of his half-siblings. McKray meant this condition to be permanent. He stipulated that Warner "and his progeny were 'to be held as slaves during all and each of their lives.'"

When he became old enough to be aware of the difference between his status and that of Robert and Kitty, Warner determined to seek his freedom. He distanced himself from African Americans both free and enslaved by claiming to be the kidnapped son of a Choctaw chief named Moshulatubbe, by escaping from his family, and by becoming a riverboat musician on the Mississippi.

Warner, or Okka Tubbee as he began calling himself, was a talented musician. One person who had watched him perform recalled that "Out of his fife, he can get more music, and get it longer and stronger, and more of it, and put more twists in it, and play lower, and go up higher, and give more octaves, and crochets, ketches and sky-rockets, change the keys, and gingle them with better grace, imitate more partridges and young chickens, and come the high notes shriller and low notes softer, and take off his hat more gracefully while he is doing it, and look at the people while it is going on, on his fife, better than any other man living."

By the 1840s Warner had married Laah Ceil, an American Indian of Delaware and Mohawk parentage. She helped the illiterate Warner write *A Thrilling Sketch of the Life of a Distinguished Chief Okah Tubbee,* which the couple published in 1848. Later Laah Ceil published an embellished version under the title *A Sketch of the Life of OKAH TUBBEE (called) William Chubbee, Son of the Head Chief, Mosholeh Tubbee, of the Choctaw Nation of Indians.* These books aimed to verify Warner's claim to an Indian—and therefore free—identity. They fit the romantic spirit of the age and were part of a specific genre of long-lost-son stories.

Warner's *Sketch* differs from other slave narratives. He makes no pretense of having loved his mother, and he hated his half-siblings. Although he makes many factual errors, he provides an entertaining study of class and race relations in the antebellum South, where he—for a while at least—succeeded in establishing an Indian identity for himself.

As a free person, Warner traveled widely and continued to transform himself. In 1849 he claimed to possess the "remarkable power of ventriloquism," to have lived in France, to speak fourteen languages, and to play over fifty musical instruments. At about the same time, he moved to Missouri, bought a two-dollar license, and began a medical practice. But in 1850—the year Congress passed a new fugitive slave law—his past caught up with him when a drunken gambler recognized him as a Mississippi slave. To avoid the risk of enslavement, Warner, like hundreds of other African Americans that year, fled to Canada where he passed into obscurity.

Elizabeth Taylor Greenfield, known as the "Black Swan," was one of the more renowned vocalists of antebellum America. She made her debut in 1853 at Metropolitan Hall in New York City before an exclusively white audience.

Educated at Oberlin College, Edmonia Lewis studied sculpture in Rome and emerged as one of the more prolific American artists of the late nineteenth century.

the great tradition of black folk music epitomized by spirituals. But in Philadelphia a circle of black musicians wrote and performed a wide variety of music for orchestra, voice, and solo instruments. Similar circles existed in New Orleans, Boston, Cleveland, New York, Baltimore, and St. Louis. The best known professional black singer of the period was Elizabeth Taylor Greenfield, who was born a slave in Mississippi and raised by Quakers in Philadelphia. Known as the "Black Swan," Taylor gained renown for her vocal range.

Black Authors

In some respects the antebellum era was a golden age of African-American literature. Driven by suffering in slavery and limited freedom in the North, black authors portrayed an America that had not lived up to its revolutionary ideals. Black autobiography recounted life in bondage and dramatic escapes. Although the antislavery movement promoted the publication of scores of such narratives, the best known is Frederick Douglass's classic *Narrative of the Life of Frederick Douglass, an American Slave* published in 1845.

African Americans also published history, novels, and poetry. William C. Nell published *The Colored Patriots of the American Revolution* in 1855, which reminded its readers that black men had fought for freedom. William Wells Brown, who had escaped from slavery in Kentucky, became the first African-American novelist. His *Clotel; or the President's Daughter*, published in 1853, used the affair between Thomas Jefferson and Sally Hemings to explore in fiction the moral ramifications of slaveholders who fathered children with their bondwomen. Another black novelist of the antebellum years was Martin R. Delany. His *Blake, or the Huts of America*, a story of emerging revolutionary consciousness among southern slaves, ran as a serial in the *Weekly Anglo-African* during 1859. Black poets included George M. Horton—a slave living in North Carolina—who published *The Hope of Liberty* in 1829, and James W. Whitfield of Buffalo who in 1853 lampooned the song "My Country 'tis of Thee" when he wrote:

America, it is to thee
Thou boasted land of liberty,—
Thou land of blood, and crime, and wrong.

African-American women who published fiction during the period included Frances Ellen Watkins Harper and Harriet E. Wilson. Harper was born free in Baltimore in 1825. Associated with the antislavery cause in Pennsylvania and Maine, she published poems that depicted the sufferings of slaves. Her first collection, *Poems on Various Subjects*, appeared in 1854. Wilson published *Our Nig: Or, Sketches from the Life of a Free Black, in a Two-Story White House, North* in 1859. This was the first novel published by a black woman in the United States. It was autobiographical fiction and compared the lives of black domestic workers in the North with those of southern slaves. Wilson's book, however, received little attention during her lifetime, and until the 1980s, critics believed that a white author had written it.

AFRICAN-AMERICAN INSTITUTIONS

In the antebellum decades, the black institutions that had appeared during the revolutionary era in urban areas of the North, upper South, and—to a lesser extent—the deep South became stronger, more numerous, and more varied. This was the result of growing black populations, the exertions of the African-American elite, and the persistence of racial exclusion and segregation. Black institutions of the time included schools, mutual aid organizations, benevolent and fraternal societies, self-improvement and temperance associations, literary groups, newspapers and journals, and theaters. But, aside from families, the most important black community institution remained the church.

Black Churches

Black church buildings were community centers. They housed schools and were meeting places for a variety of organizations. Antislavery societies often met in churches, and the churches harbored fugitive slaves. This went hand-in-hand with the community leadership black ministers provided. They began schools and various voluntary associations. They spoke against slavery, racial oppression, and what they considered weaknesses among African Americans. However, black ministers never spoke with one voice. Throughout the antebellum decades, many followed Jupiter Hammon in admonishing their congregations that preparing one's soul for heaven was more important than gaining equal rights on earth.

By 1846 the independent AME (African Methodist Episcopal) Church had 296 congregations in the United States and Canada with 17,375 members. In 1848 Frederick Douglass maintained that the AME Mother Bethel Church in Philadelphia was "the largest church in this Union," with between two and three thousand worshippers each Sunday. The AME Zion Church of New York City was probably the second largest black congregation with about two thousand members.

Most black Baptist, Presbyterian, Congregationalist, Episcopal, and Roman Catholic congregations remained affiliated with white denominations, although they were rarely represented in regional and national church councils. For example, the Episcopal Diocese of New York in 1819 excluded black ministers from its annual conventions, maintaining that African Americans "*are* socially degraded, and are not regarded as proper associates for the class of persons who attend our convention." Finally in 1853, white abolitionist William Jay convinced the New York Episcopalians to admit black representatives.

Many northern African Americans continued to attend white churches. To do so, they had to submit to the same second-class status that had driven Richard Allen and Absalom Jones to establish separate black churches in Philadelphia during the 1790s. Throughout the antebellum years, northern white churches required their black members to sit in special sections during services, provided separate Sunday schools for black children, and insisted that black people take communion after white people. Even Quakers, who spearheaded white opposition to slavery in the North and South, often provided separate seating for black people at their meetings.

By the 1830s and 1840s, some black leaders had begun to criticize the existence of separate black congregations and denominations. Frederick Douglass called them "negro pews, on a higher and larger scale." Such churches, Douglass and others maintained, were part and parcel of a segregationist spirit that divided America according to complexion. Douglass also denounced what he considered the illiteracy and anti-intellectual bias of most black ministers. Growing numbers of African Americans, nevertheless, regarded such churches as sources of spiritual integrity and legitimate alternatives to second-class status among white Christians.

Schools

Education was also racially segregated in the North between 1820 and 1860. Tax-supported compulsory public education for children in the United States began in Massachusetts in 1827 and spread throughout the Northeast and Old Northwest during the 1830s. Some

This lithograph depicts the bishops of the AME church and suggests both the church's humble origins and its remarkable growth during the antebellum years. Founder Richard Allen is portrayed at the center.

public schools, such as those in Cleveland, Ohio, during the 1850s, were racially integrated. But usually, as soon as twenty or more African-American children appeared in a school district, white parents demanded that black children attend separate schools. White people claimed that black children lacked mental capacity and lowered the quality of education. White people also feared that opening schools to black children would encourage more black people to live in the school district.

How to educate African-American children who were not allowed to attend school with white children became a persistent issue in the North. Until 1848, Ohio and the other states of the Old Northwest simply excluded black children from public schools and refused to allocate tax revenues to support separate facilities. The northeastern states were more willing to undertake

such expenditures. But across the North, white people were reluctant to use tax dollars to fund education for African Americans. As a result appropriations for black public schools lagged far behind those for public schools white children attended.

This tendency extended to cities where African-American leaders and white abolitionists had created private schools for black children. In 1812 the African School established by Prince Hall in 1798 became part of Boston's public school system. As a result, like newly created black public schools in the city, it began to suffer from inadequate funding and a limited curriculum. The African Free Schools begun in New York City in 1787 by the New York Society for Promoting the Manumission of Slaves had a similar fate. In 1834, when these schools became part of New York's public

1839.]   *Anti-Slavery Almanac.*   15

SCHOOL FOR COLORED GIRLS

COLORED SCHOOLS BROKEN UP, IN THE FREE STATES.

In 1834 a white mob in Canterbury, Connecticut, attacked a school for "colored girls" that had been established by a white woman named Prudence Crandall. This drawing, published in 1839 by abolitionists, dramatizes the incident.

school system, funding and attendance declined. By the 1850s public support for the city's black schools had become negligible.

Woefully inadequate public funding resulted in poor education or none at all for most black children across the North. The few black schools were dilapidated and overcrowded. White teachers who taught in them received lower pay than those who taught in white schools. Black teachers received even less. So teaching was generally poor. Black parents, however, were often unaware that their children received an inadequate education. Even black and white abolitionists tended to expect less from black students than from white students.

Some black leaders defended segregated schools as better for black children than integrated ones. They probably feared that the real choice was between separate black schools or none at all. But by the 1830s, most northern African Americans favored racially integrated public education, and during the 1840s, Frederick Douglass became a leading advocate for such a policy. Douglass, other black leaders, and their white abolitionist allies made the most progress in Massachusetts, where by 1845, all public schools, except for those in Boston,

had been integrated. After a ten-year struggle, the Massachusetts legislature finally ended segregated schools in that city too. This victory encouraged the opponents of segregated public schools across the North. By 1860 integration had advanced among the region's smaller school districts. But, except for those in Boston, urban schools remained segregated on the eve of the Civil War.

In fact, the black elite had more success gaining admission to northern colleges during the antebellum period than most African-American children had in gaining an adequate primary education. Some colleges were exclusively for African Americans. Ashmum Institute in Oxford, Pennsylvania, was founded in 1854 to prepare black missionaries who would go to Africa. Ashmum, later renamed Lincoln University, was the first black institution of higher learning in the United States. Another exclusively black college was Wilberforce University, founded in 1855 near Columbus, Ohio, by the AME church. Earlier some northern colleges had begun to admit a few black students. They included Bowdoin in Maine, Dartmouth in New Hampshire, Harvard and Mount Pleasant in

V O I C E S

THE CONSTITUTION OF THE PITTSBURGH EDUCATION SOCIETY

Compared to black southerners, black northerners were fortunate to have access to education, and education societies were prominent among black self-improvement organizations. In January 1832 a group headed by John B. Vashon, a local black barber and philanthropist, met at Pittsburgh's African Church to establish such a society and a school. The group's motives and plans are indicated in the following extracts from its constitution.

WHEREAS, ignorance in all ages has been found to debase the human mind, and to subject its votaries to the lowest vices, and most abject depravity—and it must be admitted, that ignorance is the sole cause of the present degradation and bondage of the people of color in these United States—that the intellectual capacity of the black man is equal to that of the white, and that he is equally susceptible of improvement, all ancient history makes manifest; and even modern examples put beyond a single doubt.

WE, THEREFORE, the people of color, of the city and vicinity of Pittsburgh, and State of Pennsylvania, for the purpose of dispersing the moral gloom that has so long hung around us, have, under Almighty God, associated ourselves together, which association shall be known by the name of the *Pittsburgh African Education Society*. . . .

It shall be the duty of the Board of Managers . . . to purchase such books and periodicals as the Society may deem it expedient, they shall have power to raise money by subscription or otherwise, to purchase ground, and erect thereon a suitable building or buildings for the accommodation and education of youth, and a hall for the use of the Society. . . .

QUESTIONS

1. Why would this group claim that black ignorance was the "sole cause" of black degradation and enslavement?

2. Why was the Pittsburgh African Education Society necessary?

Source: Dorothy Porten, ed., *Early Negro Writing, 1760–1837* (1971; reprint, Baltimore: Black Classics, 1995), 120-22.

Massachusetts, Oneida Institute in New York, and Western Reserve in Ohio. Because of its association with the antislavery movement, Oberlin College in Ohio was the most famous biracial institution of higher learning during the era. By 1860 many northern colleges, law schools, medical schools, and seminaries admitted black applicants, although not on an equal basis with white applicants.

Voluntary Associations

The African-American mutual aid, benevolent, self-improvement, and fraternal organizations that originated during the late eighteenth century proliferated during the antebellum decades. So did black literary and temperance associations. Mutual aid societies became especially attractive to black women. For example, in 1830 black women in Philadelphia had twenty-seven such organizations compared to sixteen for black men. By 1855 Philadelphia had 108 black mutual aid

societies, enrolling 9,762 members, with a combined annual income of $29,600 (approximately $550,000 in current dollars).

Among black benevolent societies, African Dorcas Associations were especially prevalent. Originally organized in 1828 in New York City by black women, these societies distributed used clothing to the poor, especially poor school children. During the early 1830s, black women also began New York City's Association for the Benefit of Colored Orphans, which operated an orphanage that had helped 524 children by 1851. Other black benevolent organizations in New York maintained the Colored Seaman's Home and a home for the elderly.

Meanwhile, the Prince Hall Masons created new lodges in the cities of the Northeast and the Chesapeake. Black Odd Fellows lodges also became common from the 1840s on. But more prevalent were self-improvement, library, literary, and temperance organizations. These were manifestations of the reform spirit that swept the North and much of the upper South during the antebellum decades. Closely linked to evangelical Protestantism, reformers maintained that the moral reform of individuals was essential to regenerate society. African Americans shared this belief and formed myriad organizations to put it into practice.

Among the more prestigious of the societies for black men were the Phoenix Literary Society established in New York City in 1837, the Philadelphia Library Company of Colored Persons begun in 1833, Pittsburgh's Theban Literary Society founded in 1831, and Boston's Adelphi Union for the Promotion of Literature and Science established in 1836. Black women had the Female and Literary Society of Philadelphia begun in 1832, New York City's Ladies Literary Society founded in 1834, the Ladies Literary Society of Buffalo, which emerged in the mid-1830s, and Boston's Afric-American Female Intelligence Society begun in 1832.

Black temperance societies were even more widespread than literary and benevolent organizations, although they also tended to be more short-lived. Like their white counterparts, black temperance advocates were members of the middle class who sought to stop the abuse of alcoholic beverages by those lower on the social ladder. The temperance societies organized lecture series and handed out literature that portrayed the negative physical, economic, and moral consequences of liquor. Whether such societies were effective is debatable. But they helped unite black communities.

EARLY BLACK LITERARY SOCIETIES, 1828–1834

1828	Reading Room Society (Philadelphia)
1829	New York African Clarkson Society
1830	New York Philomathean Society
1831	Female Literary Society (Philadelphia)
	Theban Literary Society (Pittsburgh)
1832	Afric-American Female Intelligence Society (Boston)
	Female and Literary Society of Philadelphia
	Tyro and Literary Association (Newark, NJ)
1833	Library Company of Colored Persons (Philadelphia)
	Phoenix Society (New York)
1834	Minerva Literary Association (Philadelphia)
	Ladies Literary Society (New York)
	New York Garrison Literary Association
	Literary and Religious Institution (Hartford, CT)
	Washington Conventional Society (Washington, DC)

FREE AFRICAN AMERICANS IN THE UPPER SOUTH

Life for free black people in the South during the antebellum period was different from that in the North. The free black experience in the upper South was also different from what it was in the deep South. In general free African Americans in the North, despite the limits on their liberty, had opportunities their southern counterparts did not enjoy. Each of the southern regions, nevertheless, offered advantages to free black residents.

Although more free African Americans lived in the South as a whole than in the North throughout this period, few lived in the deep South. If the three regions are taken separately, slightly more free black people lived in the North than in the upper South, and the deep South had the fewest (Map 7–1). As the southern states made freedom suits and manumission more difficult, the northern free black population increased more rapidly than the free black populations in either the upper or deep South.

The free black people of the upper South had much in common with their northern counterparts. In particular, African Americans in the Chesapeake cities of Baltimore, Washington, Richmond, and Norfolk had many ties to black northerners, ranging from family and church affiliations to business connections and membership in fraternal organizations. But significant differences, which resulted from the South's agricultural economy and slavery, set free people of color in the upper South apart from those in the North. While nearly half of the free black population in the North lived in cities, only one-third did so in the upper South, hampering the development of black communities there.

More important was the impact of slavery. Unlike black northerners, free black people in the upper South lived alongside slaves. Many had family ties to slaves and were more directly involved than black northerners in the suffering of the enslaved. Free black people of the upper South often tried to prevent the sale south of relatives or friends. They paid for manumissions and freedom suits and earned a reputation among white southerners as inveterate harborers of escaped slaves. Southern white politicians and journalists used this close connection between free black southerners and slaves to justify limiting the freedom of the former group.

Free black people of the upper South were also more at risk of being enslaved than were black northerners. Except for Louisiana, with its French and Spanish heritage, all southern states assumed that African Americans were slaves unless they could prove otherwise. Free black people had to carry *free papers*, which had to be

Map 7-1 The Slave, Free Black, and White Population of the United States in 1830. This map does not break out the slave from the free black population of the free states, although the process of gradual emancipation in several northeastern states was still underway and some black northerners remained enslaved. Source: For slave states, Ira Berlin. *Slaves without Masters: The Free Negro in the Antebellum South.* (New York: New Press, 1971); for free states, *Historical Statistics of the United States* (Washington: GPO, 1960). Note: Figures for free states are rounded to the nearest thousand.

renewed periodically. They could be enslaved if their papers were lost or stolen, and sheriffs in the upper South routinely arrested free black people on the grounds that they might be fugitive slaves. Even when those arrested proved that they were free, they were sometimes sold as slaves to pay the cost of imprisoning them. Free African Americans who got into debt in the South risked being sold into slavery to pay off their creditors.

As the antebellum period progressed, the distinction between free and enslaved African Americans narrowed in the upper South. Although a few northern states allowed black men to vote, no southern state did after 1835 when North Carolina followed Tennessee—the only other southern state to allow black suffrage—in re-

voking the franchise of property-holding black men. Free black people of the upper South also had more problems in traveling, owning firearms, congregating in groups, and being out after dark than did black northerners. Although residential segregation was less pronounced in southern cities than in the North, African Americans of the upper South were more thoroughly excluded from hotels, taverns, trains and coaches, parks, theaters, and hospitals.

As slavery declined in Maryland and northern Virginia during the nineteenth century, the employment of free black people expanded. Free persons of color in rural areas were generally tenant farmers, although some owned land, and a few owned slaves. Others were miners, lumberjacks, and teamsters. Rural free black people often had to sign labor contracts that reduced them to semislavery.

In urban areas before the 1850s, free black people in the upper South faced less competition for jobs from European immigrants than those who lived in northern cities did. So, although the upper South had fewer factories than the North, more free black men were employed in them. Nevertheless, most free black men in the upper South were unskilled day laborers, waiters, whitewashers, and stevedores, while free black women washed clothes and were domestic servants. As in the North, the most successful were barbers, butchers, tailors, caterers, merchants, and those teamsters and hack drivers who owned their own horses and vehicles. But by the 1850s, free black people in the upper South faced the same competition for all types of employment from Irish and German immigrants that northern free black people did. As was the case in the North, immigrants often used violence to drive African Americans out of skilled trades.

These circumstances made it more difficult for free black people in the upper South to maintain community institutions. In addition, the measures white people adopted out of fear of slave revolt greatly limited free black autonomy, and such measures grew more pervasive after the revolt Nat Turner led in southern Virginia in 1831. Throughout the South, white authorities forced black churches and schools to close. The Baltimore Conference of the AME Church, which had been expanding during the 1820s, declined during the early 1830s. Some states required that black churches have white ministers, and some black ministers left for the North.

Yet free black southerners persevered. During the late 1830s, black churches organized in Louisville and Lexington, Kentucky, and in St. Louis, Missouri. Between 1836 and 1856, the Baltimore AME Conference rebounded and more than doubled its membership. By 1860 Baltimore had fifteen black churches. Louisville had nine, and Nashville, St. Louis, and Norfolk had four each. Most of these churches ministered to both enslaved and free members.

Black schools and voluntary associations also survived white efforts to suppress them, although the schools faced great difficulties. Racially integrated schools and public funding for segregated black schools were out of the question in the South. Most black children received no formal education. Black churches, a few white churches, and a scattering of black and white individuals maintained what educational facilities the upper South had for black children. The schools met—often sporadically—in rooms furnished by churches or in private homes and generally lacked books, chalkboards, and student desks. John F. Cook, a black minister, maintained one of the better such schools in Washington, D.C., from the late 1830s until his death in 1854, but even he never had adequate supplies. Virginia law discouraged even this level of education, and in 1847 Missouri banned entirely the instruction of free black people.

Black voluntary associations, particularly in urban areas of the upper South, fared better. By 1838, Baltimore, for example, had at least forty such organizations, including chapters of the Prince Hall Masons, Black Odd Fellows, literary societies, and religious and temperance groups. In Norfolk the Masons enrolled slaves as well as freemen. As in the North, black women also organized voluntary organizations. Washington's Colored Female Roman Catholic Beneficial Society, for example, provided death benefits for its members. Black benevolent organizations in the upper South also established schools; sought to apprentice orphans to black tradesmen; sponsored fairs, picnics, and parades; and lent protection against kidnappers.

FREE AFRICAN AMERICANS IN THE DEEP SOUTH

More than half the South's free black population lived in Maryland, Delaware, and Virginia. To the west and south of these states, the number of free people of color declined sharply. The smaller free black populations in Kentucky, Tennessee, Missouri, and North Carolina had much in common with that in the Chesapeake states. But free African Americans who lived in the deep South were different in several respects from their counterparts in other southern regions.

Neither the natural rights ideology of the revolutionary era nor changing economic circumstances led to many manumissions in the deep South. Free black people there were not only far fewer than in either the upper South or the North, they were also "largely the product of illicit sexual relations between black slave women and white men." Slaveholder fathers either manumitted their mixed-race children or let them buy their freedom. However, some free black people of the deep South traced their ancestry to free mixed-race refugees from Haiti, who sought during the 1790s to avoid that island nation's bloody revolutionary struggle, by fleeing to such deep South cities as Charleston, Savannah, and New Orleans.

A three-caste system similar to that in Latin America developed in the deep South during the antebellum period. It was composed of whites, free blacks, and slaves.

TIMELINE

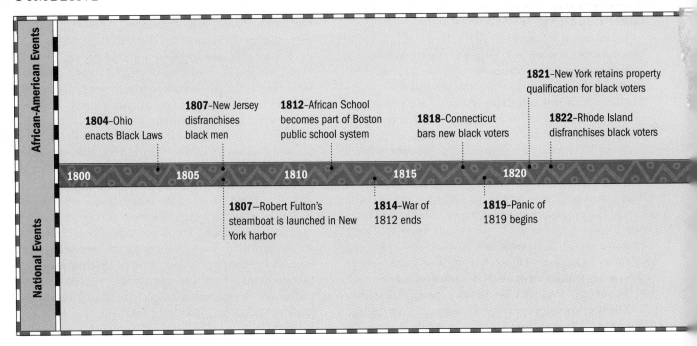

Most free African Americans in the region identified more closely with their former masters than with slaves. To ensure the loyalty of such free people of color, powerful white people provided them with employment, loans, protection, and such special privileges as the ability to vote and to testify against white people. Some states and municipalities formalized this relationship by requiring free African Americans to have white guardians—often their blood relatives. Some people of mixed descent were able to cross the racial boundary and pass as white.

The relationship between free African Americans of the deep South and their former masters was also evident in religion. An AME church existed in Charleston until 1818, when the city authorities suppressed it, fearing that it would become a center of sedition. African Baptist churches existed in Savannah in the 1850s. But free black people in the region were more likely than those farther north to remain in white churches largely because they identified with the white elite.

In the deep South, free African Americans—over half of whom lived in cities—were also more concentrated in urban areas than in either the North or the upper South. Although deep South cities restricted their employment opportunities, free black people in Charleston, Savannah, Mobile, and New Orleans maintained stronger positions in the skilled trades than free black people in the upper South or the North. By 1860 in

Charleston three-quarters of the free black men were employed in skilled trades.

Free African Americans made up only 15 percent of Charleston's male population. Yet they were 25 percent of its carpenters, 40 percent of its tailors, and 75 percent of its millwrights. In New Orleans, free black men predominated as carpenters, masons, bricklayers, barbers, tailors, cigarmakers, and shoemakers. In both cities, free African Americans compared favorably to white people in their ratio of skilled to unskilled workers. The close ties between free black people and upper-class white people who did business with them explain much of this success.

Despite such ties, free black communities comparable to those in the upper South and North arose in the cities of the deep South. Although they usually lacked separate black churches as community centers, free African Americans in the region created other institutions. In Charleston, for example, the Brown Fellowship Society survived throughout the antebellum period. Charleston also had a chapter of the Prince Hall Masons and other fraternal and benevolent associations maintained by free black men and women. In addition to these sorts of organizations, the free black elite in New Orleans published literary journals and supported an opera house. Savannah—where black churches did exist—during the 1850s also had at least three black

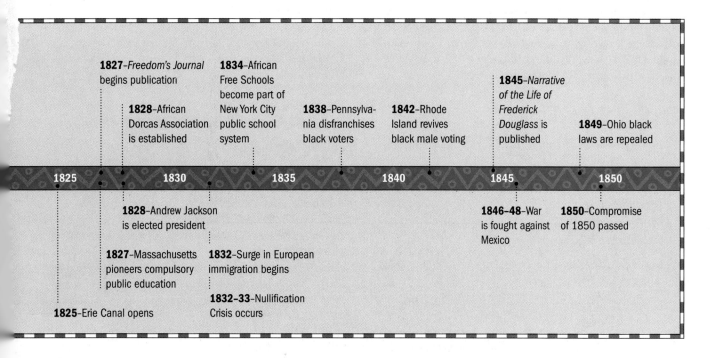

1827-*Freedom's Journal* begins publication

1828-African Dorcas Association is established

1834-African Free Schools become part of New York City public school system

1838-Pennsylvania disfranchises black voters

1842-Rhode Island revives black male voting

1845-*Narrative of the Life of Frederick Douglass* is published

1849-Ohio black laws are repealed

1825 1830 1835 1840 1845 1850

1827-Massachusetts pioneers compulsory public education

1828-Andrew Jackson is elected president

1832-Surge in European immigration begins

1832-33-Nullification Crisis occurs

1825-Erie Canal opens

1846-48-War is fought against Mexico

1850-Compromise of 1850 passed

volunteer fire companies, a porters' association, and several benevolent societies.

Because black churches were rare, wealthy African-Americans and fraternal organizations organized private schools for black children in the cities of the deep South. In Charleston the Brown Fellowship Society organized an academy. New Orleans had several schools, most of which were conducted in French—the first or second language for many free black people in the city. Some of the more wealthy free black families in these cities sent their children abroad for an education, and the literacy rate among free black people in both Charleston and New Orleans was markedly high for the antebellum period.

In all, free people of color in the deep South differed substantially from those in the upper South and the North. Their ties to the white slaveholding class gave them tangible advantages. However, they were not without sympathy for those who remained in slavery, and white authorities were never certain of their loyalty to the slave regime. In particular, white people feared contact between free African Americans in the port cities of the deep South and black northerners—especially black sailors. As a new round of slave unrest began in the South and a more militant antislavery movement got under way during the 1820s, as sectional tensions heightened between the North and South, free black people in the deep South faced difficult circumstances.

CONCLUSION

During the antebellum period, free African-American communities that had emerged during the revolutionary era grew and fostered black institutions. Particularly in the urban North, life in these segregated communities foreshadowed the pattern of black life from the end of the Civil War into the twentieth century. Although the black elite could gain education, professional expertise, and wealth despite white prejudices, most northern people of color were poor. Extended families, churches, segregation, political marginality, and limited educational opportunities still influence African-American life today.

Life for the free black populations of the upper South and deep South was even more difficult than in the North. Presumed to be slaves if they could not prove otherwise, free black people in the South were in greater danger of enslavement and were subjected to more restrictive legislation than in the North. But energetic black communities existed in the upper South throughout the antebellum period. In the deep South the small free black population was better off economically than were free black people in other regions, but it was dependent on the region's white slaveholders, who were unreliable allies as sectional controversy mounted. The antislavery movement, secession, and the Civil War would have a more profound impact on the free black communities in the South than in the North.

REVIEW QUESTIONS

1. How was black freedom in the North limited in the antebellum decades?

2. How did northern African Americans deal with these limits?

3. What was the relationship of the African-American elite to urban black communities?

4. How did African-American institutions fare between 1820 and 1861?

5. Compare black life in the North to free black life in the upper South and deep South.

RECOMMENDED READING

Ira Berlin. *Slaves without Masters: The Free Negro in the Antebellum South.* New York: New Press, 1971. This classic study is still the most comprehensive treatment of free African Americans in the antebellum South.

W. Jeffrey Bolster. *Black Jacks: African American Seamen in the Age of Sail.* Cambridge, MA: Harvard University Press, 1997. *Black Jacks* explores the lives of black seamen between 1740 and 1865.

Leonard Curry. *The Free Black in Urban America, 1800–1850: The Shadow of the Dream.* Chicago: University of Chicago Press, 1981. Curry provides a comprehensive account of urban African-American life in the antebellum period.

Philip S. Foner. *History of Black America: From the Emergence of the Cotton Kingdom to the Eve of the Compromise of 1850.* Westport, CT: Greenwood Press, 1983. This second volume of Foner's three-volume series presents a wealth of information about African-American life between 1820 and 1861, especially about the northern black community.

James Oliver Horton and Lois E. Horton. *In Hope of Liberty: Culture, Community, and Protest among Northern Free Blacks, 1700–1860.* New York: Oxford University Press, 1997. The authors focus on how the black community responded to difficult circumstances, especially during the antebellum decades.

Leon F. Litwack. *North of Slavery: The Negro in the Free States, 1790–1860.* Chicago: University of Chicago Press, 1961. This book emphasizes how northern white people treated African Americans. It is an essential guide to the status of African Americans in the antebellum North.

ADDITIONAL BIBLIOGRAPHY

Community Studies

Tommy L. Bogger. *Free Blacks in Norfolk, Virginia, 1790–1860: The Darker Side of Freedom.* Charlottesville: University Press of Virginia, 1997.

Letitia Woods Brown. *Free Negroes in the District of Columbia, 1790–1846.* New York: Oxford University Press, 1972.

Graham Russell Hodges. *Slavery and Freedom in the Rural North: African Americans in Monmouth County, New Jersey, 1665–1865.* Madison, WI: Madison House, 1995.

James Oliver Horton. *Free People of Color: Inside the African-American Community.* Washington: Smithsonian Institution Press, 1993.

James Oliver Horton and Lois E. Horton. *Black Bostonians: Family Life and Community Struggle in the Antebellum North.* New York: Holmes and Meier, 1979.

Gary B. Nash. *Forging Freedom: The Formation of Philadelphia's Black Community, 1720–1840.* Cambridge, MA: Harvard University Press, 1988.

Bernard E. Powers, Jr. *Black Charlestonians: A Social History, 1822–1885.* Fayetteville: University of Arkansas Press, 1994.

Harry Reed. *Platform for Change: The Foundations of the Northern Free Black Community, 1775–1865.* East Lansing: Michigan State University Press, 1994.

Julie Winch. *Philadelphia's Black Elite: Activism, Accommodation, and the Struggle for Autonomy, 1787–1848.* Philadelphia: Temple University Press, 1988.

State-Level Studies

Barbara Jeanne Fields. *Slavery and Freedom on the Middle Ground: Maryland during the Nineteenth Century.* New Haven: Yale University Press, 1985.

John Hope Franklin. *The Free Negro in North Carolina, 1790–1860.* Chapel Hill: University of North Carolina Press, 1943.

John H. Russell. *The Free Negro in Virginia, 1619–1865.* 1913; reprint, New York: Negro Universities Press, 1969.

H. E. Sterkx. *The Free Negro in Antebellum Louisiana.* Rutherford, N.J.: Fairleigh Dickinson University Press, 1972.

Marina Wilkramangrake. *A World in Shadow—The Free Black in Antebellum South Carolina.* Columbia: University of South Carolina Press, 1973.

Race Relations

Eugene H. Berwanger. *The Frontier against Slavery: Western Anti-Negro Prejudice and the Slavery Expansion Controversy.* Urbana: University of Illinois Press, 1967.

Phyllis F. Field. *The Politics of Race in New York: The Struggle for Black Suffrage in the Civil War Era.* Ithaca: Cornell University Press, 1982.

Noel Ignatiev. *How the Irish Became White.* New York: Routledge, 1995.

David Roediger. *The Wages of Whiteness: Race and the Making of the American Working Class.* New York: Verso, 1991.

Joel Williamson. *New People: Miscegenation and Mulattoes in the United States.* New York: Free Press, 1980.

Carol Wilson. *Freedom at Risk: The Kidnapping of Free Blacks in America, 1780–1865.* Lexington: University Press of Kentucky, 1994.

Women and Family

Herbert G. Gutman. *The Black Family in Slavery and Freedom, 1750–1925.* New York: Pantheon Books, 1977.

Jacqueline Jones. *Labor of Love, Labor of Sorrow: Black Women, Work and the Family from Slavery to the Present.* New York: Basic Books, 1985.

Suzanne Lebsock. *The Free Women of Petersburg: Status and Culture in a Southern Town, 1784–1860.* New York: Norton, 1984.

Bert James Loewenberg and Ruth Bogin, eds. *Black Women in Nineteenth-Century American Life.* University Park: Pennsylvania State University Press, 1976.

T.O. Madden Jr. with Ann L. Miller. *We Were Always Free: The Maddens of Culpeper County, Virginia, a 200 Year Family History.* New York: Norton, 1992.

Dorothy Sterling, ed. *We Are Your Sisters: Black Women in the Nineteenth Century.* New York: Norton, 1984.

Institutions and the Black Elite

Vincent P. Franklin. *The Education of Black Philadelphia.* Philadelphia: University of Pennsylvania Press, 1979.

Carlton Mabee. *Black Education in New York State.* Syracuse: Syracuse University Press, 1979.

Eileen Southern. *The Music of Black America.* 2d ed. New York: Norton, 1983.

Loretta J. Williams. *Black Freemasonry and Middle-Class Realities.* Columbia: University of Missouri Press, 1980.

CHAPTER 8

OPPOSITION TO SLAVERY, 1800–1833

WALKER'S

APPEAL,

With a Brief Sketch of his Life.

BY

HENRY HIGHLAND GARNET.

AND ALSO

GARNET'S ADDRESS

TO THE SLAVES OF THE UNITED STATES OF AMERICA.

NEW-YORK:
Printed by J. H. Tobitt, 9 Spruce-st.
1848.

David Walker's *Appeal . . . to the Colored Citizens of the World* caused fear and outrage
among white southerners when it appeared in 1829. It also helped to shape the direction
of the northern antislavery movement. Henry Highland Garnet's edition of the *Appeal*
with Garnet's *Address to the Slaves* indicates Walker's continued influence on the
antislavery movement.

Beloved brethren—here let me tell you, and believe it, that the Lord our God, as true as he sits on his throne in heaven, and as true as our Savior died to redeem the world, will give you a Hannibal [an ancient Carthaginian general], and when the Lord shall have raised him up, and given him to you for your possession, O my suffering brethren! . . . Read the history particularly of Hayti, and see how they were butchered by the whites, and do you take warning. The person whom God Shall give you, give him your support and let him go his length, and behold in him the salvation of your God. God will indeed, deliver you through him from your deplorable and wretched condition under the Christians of America.

David Walker's *Appeal*

Black abolitionist David Walker wrote these words in Boston in 1829. They suggest both the sense early nineteenth-century Americans had of the nearness of God and the anguish a free black man felt about his brothers and sisters in bondage.

In his harsh language and demands for action, Walker was a precursor of the militant black and white abolitionists of the 1830s, 1840s, and 1850s. He bluntly portrayed the oppression suffered by African Americans. He urged black men to redeem themselves by defending their loved ones from abuse. If that led to violence and death, he asked, "Had you not rather be killed than be a slave to a tyrant, who takes the life of your mother, wife and dear little children?" Through his provocative language and his efforts to have his *Appeal to the Colored Citizens of the World* distributed in the South, Walker became a prophet of violent revolution against slaveholders.

Walker's *Appeal* was not just a reaction to slavery; it was also a response to a particular *style* of antislavery reform. This chapter explores the emergence of an antislavery movement in the United States between Gabriel's conspiracy in 1800 and the organization of the American Anti-Slavery Society in 1833. We first discuss the social turmoil of the period, the Second Great Awakening, the related social reform efforts, the two strains within the abolition movement, and the black response to African colonization. We then describe how Walker, Denmark Vesey, Nat Turner, other black leaders, and white abolitionist William Lloyd Garrison radicalized the abolition movement during the 1820s and early 1830s. Chapter 9 will trace the development of abolitionism from 1833 into the 1850s.

A COUNTRY IN TURMOIL

During the late 1820s, when Walker wrote his *Appeal*, the United States was in economic, political, and social turmoil. As we have seen in earlier chapters, the invention of the cotton gin in 1793 led to a vast westward expansion of cotton cultivation. Where cotton went, so did slavery, and by the late 1820s, southern slaveholders and their slaves had pushed into what was then the Mexican province of Texas.

Meanwhile the states of the Old Northwest were passing from frontier conditions to commercial farming. The region was increasingly tied to the Northeast economically, first by the Erie Canal in 1825 and later by railroads that carried its products to East Coast cities. An enormous amount of trade also passed down the Ohio and Mississippi Rivers encouraging the growth of such cities as Pittsburgh, Cincinnati, Louisville, St. Louis, Memphis, and New Orleans.

Particularly in the North, the transportation and market revolutions changed how people lived and worked. As steamboats became common and as networks of macadam turnpikes (paved with crushed stone and tar), canals, and railroads spread, travel time diminished and Americans became increasingly mobile. As people moved from one region to another, families became more scattered, and ties to local communities became less permanent. For African Americans, sub-

ject to the domestic slave trade, mobility came with a high price.

Life in America changed further when the factory system arose in urban areas of the Northeast and spread to parts of the Old Northwest and upper South. Industrialization encouraged immigration from Europe, and native black and white people had to compete with growing numbers of foreign-born workers for urban employment. While most northerners remained farmers, they became dependent on urban markets for their crops. A money economy grew more pervasive; the banking industry became essential; and vast private fortunes began to influence public policy. Many Americans felt that forces beyond their control were threatening their way of life and the nation's republican values. They began to distrust change and wanted someone to blame for the uncertainties they faced. This outlook encouraged American politics to become paranoid—dominated by an irrational fear of hostile conspiracies.

Political Paranoia

The Jacksonian Era began with charges leveled by Andrew Jackson's supporters that John Quincy Adams and Henry Clay had conspired to cheat Jackson out of the presidency in 1824. Jackson had won a plurality of the popular vote but failed to get a majority in the electoral college, and Congress chose Adams to be president. These charges and the belief that Adams and his political allies represented the interests of rich businessmen and intellectuals rather than those of the common people led to the organization of the Democratic party to contest the national election of 1828. The Democrats claimed to stand for the natural rights and economic well-being of American workers and farmers against what they called the "money power," a conspiratorial alliance of bankers and businessmen.

Yet, from its start, the Democratic party also represented the interests of the South's slaveholding elite. Democratic politicians from both the North and South favored a states' rights doctrine that protected slavery from interference by the national government. They sought through legislation, judicial decisions, and diplomacy to make the right to hold human property inviolate. They became the most ardent supporters of expanding slavery into new regions, leading their opponents to claim that they were part of a "slave power" conspiracy. Most Democratic politicians also openly advocated white supremacy. Although their rhetoric demanded equal rights for all and special privileges for none, they were really concerned only with the rights of white males.

This was clear in their outlook toward American Indians, women, and African Americans. Democratic politicians were in the forefront of those who demanded the removal of Indians to the area west of the Mississippi River, which culminated in the Cherokee "Trail of Tears" in 1838. Generally, Democrats were also traditionalists concerning the role of women in society. They firmly supported patriarchy and a subservient role for women in both the family and the church. Finally, almost all Democratic leaders in both the North and the South believed that God and nature had designed African Americans to be slaves. Yet, during the 1820s and early 1830s, only a few radicals like Walker saw the hypocrisy of the Democrats' outlook and contended that real democracy would embrace all males regardless of race. Reformers did not even begin to propose equal rights for women until the late 1830s.

By the mid-1830s those Americans who favored a more enlightened social policy than the Democrats offered turned—often reluctantly—to the Whig Party, which opposed Jackson and the Democrats. The Whigs also attracted those who had supported the Anti-Masonic party during the early 1830s. This small party epitomized political paranoia by contending that the Freemasons were a vast conspiracy to subvert republican government.

From the late 1820s onward, politicians such as Henry Clay, Daniel Webster, William H. Seward, and John Quincy Adams who identified with the Whig party, placed much more emphasis on Christian morality and an active national government than the Democrats did. They regarded themselves as conservatives, did not seek to end slavery in the southern states, and included many of the most wealthy slaveholders within their ranks. But in the North, the party's moral orientation and its opposition to territorial expansion by the United States made it attractive to slavery's opponents.

The Whig party also served as the channel through which evangelical Christianity influenced politics. In the North, Whig politicians appealed to evangelical voters. Distrustful of slaveholders and expansionism, some northern Whig politicians and journalists defended the human rights of African Americans and American Indians. They criticized the inhumanity of slaveholders and tried to limit the federal government's support for the peculiar institution. When and where they could, black men voted for Whig candidates.

The Second Great Awakening

Evangelicals were motivated to carry their Christian morality into politics by a new era of revivalism in America. Like David Walker, they saw the hand of God everywhere. Religion, of course, had always been important in America. During the 1730s and 1740s, the widespread religious revival known as the Great Awakening had used emotional preaching and hymn singing to bring men and women to embrace God and reform their lives. African Americans helped shape this emphasis on emotion, and American churches had first made a concerted effort to convert black people at that time. Then a new wave of emotional revivalism began at the end of the eighteenth century. Known as the Second Great Awakening, it lasted into the 1830s. The new evangelicalism led ordinary black and white Americans to try to take control of religion from the established clergy and to impose moral order on an increasingly turbulent American society.

The Second Great Awakening influenced Richard Allen and Absalom Jones's efforts to establish separate black churches in Philadelphia during the 1790s. It helped shape the character of other black churches that emerged during the 1800s and 1810s. These black churches became an essential part of the antislavery

The Granger Collection, New York.

This 1844 lithograph by Peter S. Duval, derived from a painting by Alfred Hoffy, portrays Juliann Jane Tillman. Tillman was an A.M.E. preacher and one of the few women of her time to be employed in such a capacity.

movement. However, the Second Great Awakening did not reach its peak until the 1820s. With particular force in the North and Northwest, Charles G. Finney, a white Presbyterian, and other revivalists helped democratize religion in America. At camp meetings that lasted for days, Finney and other revivalists preached that all men and women—not just a few—could become faithful Christians and save their souls. Just as Jacksonian democracy revolutionized politics in America, the Second Great Awakening revolutionized the nation's spiritual life and led many Americans to join reform movements.

The Benevolent Empire

Evangelicals—both black and white—emphasized "practical Christianity." Those who were saved, they maintained, would not be content with their own salvation. Instead, they would help save others. Black evangelicals in particular called for "a *liberating* faith" that would advance both material and spiritual well-being. This emphasis on action led to what became known during the 1810s and 1820s as the Benevolent Empire, a network of church-related, voluntary organizations designed to fight sin and save souls. The Benevolent Empire launched what is now known as antebellum or Jacksonian reform.

This social movement flourished from the 1810s through the 1850s. It consisted of voluntary associations dedicated to a host of causes: public education, self-improvement, limiting or abolishing alcohol consumption (the temperance movement), prison reform, and aid to the mentally and physically handicapped. Members of the movement were also involved in distributing Bibles and religious tracts, funding missionary activities, discouraging prostitution, seeking health through diet and fads, improving conditions for seamen, and—by the 1840s—seeking rights for women. The self-improvement, temperance, and missionary associations that free black people—and sometimes slaves—formed in conjunction with their churches in urban areas were part of this movement.

The most important of these societies, however, were those dedicated to the problem of African-American bondage in the United States. At first called societies for promoting the abolition of slavery, they later became known as antislavery societies. Whatever they called themselves, their members were *abolitionists*, people who favored doing away with or abolishing slavery in their respective states and throughout the country. To understand American abolitionism in the 1820s, we must return to the first abolitionist organizations that arose during the revolutionary era.

ABOLITIONISM BEGINS IN AMERICA

The revolutionary era forged *two* antislavery movements that continued to exist until the end of the Civil War. Although different, the two movements constantly influenced each other. The first of these movements existed in the South among slaves with the help of free African Americans and a few sympathetic white people. As we mentioned in earlier chapters, from the seventeenth century onward, enslaved African Americans individually and in groups sought their freedom through both violent and nonviolent means. Before the revolutionary era, however, these slaves probably only wanted to free themselves and did not seek to destroy slavery as a social system.

The second antislavery movement consisted of black and white abolitionists in the North, with outposts in the upper South. Far more white people were in this movement than in the one southern slaves conducted. In the North, white people controlled the larger antislavery organizations, although African Americans led in direct action against slavery and its influences in the North. In the upper South, African Americans could not participate in antislavery organizations but cooperated covertly and informally with white abolitionists.

This essentially northern movement took root in the 1730s when white Quakers in New Jersey and Pennsylvania became convinced that slaveholding contradicted their belief in spiritual equality. For the rest of the eighteenth century, they advocated the abolition of slavery—at least among their fellow Quakers—in their home states and in the Chesapeake. Quakers always remained prominent in the northern antislavery movement. As members of a denomination that emphasized nonviolence, they generally expected slavery to be abolished peacefully and gradually.

The American Revolution, together with the French Revolution that began in 1789 and the Haitian struggle for independence between 1791 and 1804, revitalized *both* antislavery movements and changed their nature. The revolutionary doctrine that all men had a natural right to life, liberty, and property led other northerners besides Quakers and African Americans to endorse the antislavery cause.

Philadelphia Quakers in 1775 organized what became the first antislavery society. But when it was reorganized in 1784 as the Society for the Promotion of the Abolition of Slavery, it attracted non-Quakers. Among the first of these were Benjamin Rush and Benjamin Franklin, both of whom were influenced by natural rights doctrines. Revolutionary principles also influenced Alexander Hamilton and John Jay, who helped organize New York's first antislavery society. Prince Hall, probably the most prominent black abolitionist of his time, also based his effort to abolish slavery in Massachusetts on universal natural rights. He contended that African Americans "have in common with all other men a natural right to our freedom."

The efforts of northern black and white abolitionists were instrumental in abolishing slavery in the North. However, the early northern antislavery movement had several limiting features. First, black and white abolitionists had similar goals but worked in separate organizations. Even white Quaker abolitionists were reluctant to mix socially with African Americans or welcome them to their meetings. Second, except in parts of New England, abolition in the North proceeded *gradually* to protect the economic interests of slaveholders. Third, white abolitionists did not advocate equal rights for black people. In most northern states laws kept black people from enjoying full freedom after their emancipation. Fourth, early northern abolitionists did little to bring about abolition in the South where most slaves lived.

All this indicates that neither Quaker piety nor natural rights principles created a truly egalitarian or sectionally aggressive northern abolitionism. It took the moralistic emotionalism of the Second Great Awakening combined with the activism of the Benevolent Empire to establish the framework for a more biracial and wide-ranging antislavery movement. Even more important in providing a prod were southern slaves and their free black allies who had their own plans for emancipation.

FROM GABRIEL TO DENMARK VESEY

Gabriel's abortive slave revolt of 1800 owed as much to revolutionary ideology as did the northern antislavery movement. The arrival of Haitian refugees in Virginia had led to slave unrest throughout the 1790s. Gabriel himself hoped to attract French Revolutionary support. His conspiracy, though, was betrayed, and he and twenty-six of his followers were executed. But the revolutionary spirit and insurrectionary network Gabriel established lived on (Map 8–1). Virginia authorities had to suppress another slave conspiracy in 1802, and sporadic minor revolts erupted for years.

Map 8–1 Slave Conspiracies and Uprisings, 1800–1831. Major slave conspiracies and revolts were rare between 1800 and 1860. This was in part because those that took place frightened masters and led them to adopt policies aimed at preventing recurrences.

Gabriel's conspiracy had two unintended consequences. First, the Quaker-led antislavery societies of the Chesapeake declined rapidly. They had always been small and weak compared to antislavery societies in the North. They were more effective helping free black people who were illegally held as slaves than promoting emancipation. Nevertheless, after Gabriel's conspiracy, these organizations either became dormant, were suppressed, or withered under pressure from public opinion. The chance that Maryland, Virginia, and North Carolina would follow the northern example and gradually abolish slavery all but vanished.

Second, white southerners and many white northerners became convinced that, as long as black people lived among them, a race war like the one in Haiti could erupt in the United States. Slaveholders and their defenders argued that this threat did not result from the oppressiveness of slavery. On the contrary, they maintained, the slaves were naturally suited for and content in bondage. It was the growing class of free black people who instigated otherwise passive bondspeople to revolt.

Free African Americans were, slavery's defenders contended, a dangerous, criminal, potentially revolutionary class that had to be regulated, subdued, and ultimately expelled from the country. No system of emancipation that would increase the number of free black people in the United States could be tolerated. Slaveholders who had never shown a willingness to free their slaves began to claim that they would favor emancipation if it were not for fear of enlarging such a dangerous group. As an elderly Thomas Jefferson put it, white southerners had a wolf by the ears: Once they had enslaved black people it was impossible to free them safely. Unless African Americans were restrained by slavery, southern politicians and journalists argued, they would become an economic threat to white workers, a perpetual criminal class, and a revolutionary enemy of white rule.

Events in and about Charleston, South Carolina, in 1822 appeared to confirm the threat. In that year black informants revealed a conspiracy for a massive slave revolt. A free black man named Denmark Vesey had carefully organized it. Like Gabriel before him, Vesey could read and was well aware of the revolutions that had shaken the Atlantic world. A carpenter by trade and a former sailor who had been to Haiti, he hoped for Haitian aid for an antislavery revolution in the South Carolina low country. He understood the significance of the storming of the Bastille on July 14, 1789, that marked the start of the French Revolution and planned to start his revolution on July 14, 1822. Vesey was also

familiar with the antislavery speeches of northern members of Congress during the debates over the admission of Missouri to the Union in 1820 and may have hoped for northern aid.

But, as befitted an evangelical and romantic era, religious influence was more prominent in Vesey's plot than in Gabriel's. Vesey was a Bible-quoting Methodist who conducted religious classes. Like other free black people and slaves in Charleston, he deeply resented attempts by the white authorities to suppress the city's AME Church in 1818. He believed that passages in the Bible about the enslavement and deliverance of the Hebrews in Egypt promised freedom for African Americans as well.

Vesey also used vestiges of African religion that had survived among low country slaves to promote his revolutionary efforts. To reach slaves whose Christian convictions were blended with West African spiritualism, he relied on his closest collaborator, Jack Pritchard, who was known as Gullah Jack. A native of Angola and a "conjure-man," Pritchard distributed charms and cast spells that he claimed would make revolutionaries invincible.

Vesey and his associates planned to capture arms and ammunition and seize control of Charleston. But Gullah Jack's charms were ineffective against white vigilance and black informers. About a month before the revolt was to begin, the arrest of one of Vesey's lieutenants put local authorities on guard. Vesey moved the date of the uprising to June 16. But on June 14, a house servant revealed the conspiracy to his master; the local government called in the state militia; and arrests ensued. Over several weeks the authorities rounded up 131 suspects. The accused received public trials, and juries convicted 71. Thirty-five, including Vesey and Gullah Jack, were hanged, and thirty-seven were banished. Four white men—three of them foreigners—were convicted of inciting slaves to revolt and were imprisoned and fined.

After the executions, Charleston's city government destroyed what remained of the local AME Church, and white churches assumed responsibility for supervising other black congregations. Meanwhile, white South Carolinians sought to make slave patrols more efficient. The state legislature also outlawed assemblages of slaves, and banned teaching slaves to read. Black seamen whose ships docked in Charleston were to be jailed until the ships were ready to leave port. Assuming that free black and white abolitionists had inspired slave unrest, white South Carolinians became increasingly suspicious of all free African Americans and northerners in the state.

THE AMERICAN COLONIZATION SOCIETY

Fear of free African Americans as a subversive class shaped the program of the most significant white anti-slavery organization of the 1810s and 1820s—but whether its aim was actually abolition is debatable. In late 1816 concerned white leaders met in Washington, D.C., to form the American Society for Colonizing Free People of Colour of the United States, usually known as the American Colonization Society (ACS). Among its founders were such prominent slave-holders as Bushrod Washington—a nephew of George Washington—and Henry Clay. In 1821 the ACS, with the support of the United States government, established the colony of Liberia in West Africa as a prospective home for African Americans.

The ACS had a twofold program. First, it proposed to abolish slavery gradually in the United States, perhaps giving slaveholders financial compensation for their human property. Second, it proposed to send emancipated slaves and free black people to Liberia. The founders of the ACS believed that masters would never emancipate their slaves if they thought emancipation would increase the free black population in the United States. Moral and practical objections to this program were not immediately clear to either black or white abolitionists. In fact, the ACS became an integral part of the Benevolent Empire and commanded widespread support among many who regarded themselves friends of humanity.

Although the ACS was always strongest in the upper South and enjoyed the support of slaveholders, including Francis Scott Key, Andrew Jackson, John Tyler, and John Randoph, by the 1820s it had branches in every northern state. Such northern white abolitionists as Arthur and Lewis Tappan, Gerrit Smith, and William Lloyd Garrison initially supported colonization. They tended to emphasize the abolitionist aspects of the ACS and clung to a belief that free and soon-to-be-emancipated African Americans could choose whether to stay in the United States or go to Liberia. In either case, they hoped, black people would be free.

Black Nationalism and Colonization

Prominent black abolitionists initially shared this positive assessment of the ACS. They were part of a black nationalist tradition dating back at least to Prince Hall that—disappointed with repeated rebuffs from white people—endorsed black American migration to Africa. During the early 1800s, the most prominent advocate of this point of view was Paul Cuffe of Massachusetts. In 1811, six years before the ACS organized, Cuffe, a Quaker of African and American Indian ancestry, addressed Congress on the subject of African-American Christian colonies in Africa.

The ACS argument that appealed to Cuffe and many other African Americans was that white prejudice would never allow black people to enjoy full citizenship, equal protection under the law, and economic success in the United States. Black people born in America, went the argument for African colonization, could enjoy equal rights only in the continent of their ancestors. In the spirit of American evangelicalism, African Americans were also attracted by the prospect of bringing Christianity to African nations. Like white people, many African Americans considered Africa a pagan, barbaric place that could benefit from their knowledge of Christianity and republican government. Other black leaders who favored colonization objected to this view of Africa. They considered African cultures superior to those of America and Europe. They were often Africans themselves, the children of African parents, or individuals who had been influenced by Africans.

In 1815, Cuffe, who was the captain of his own ship, took thirty-four African-American settlers to the British free black colony of Sierra Leone, located just to the north of present-day Liberia (Map 8–2). Cuffe himself would probably have later settled in Liberia if his American Indian wife had not refused to leave her native land. So it was the AME Church bishop Daniel Coker who led the first eighty-six African-American colonists to Liberia in 1820–1821. Pro-ACS sentiment

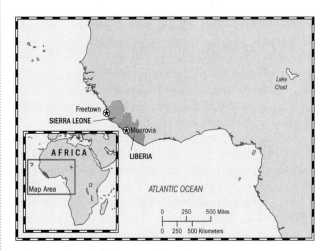

Map 8–2 The Founding of Liberia. This map shows the location of Sierra Leone and Liberia in West Africa. British abolitionists established Sierra Leone as a colony for former slaves in 1800. The American Colonization Society established Liberia for the same purpose in 1821.

was especially strong among African Americans in Coker's home city of Baltimore and other Chesapeake urban areas. By 1838 approximately 2,500 colonists had made the journey and were living less than harmoniously with Liberia's 28,000 indigenous inhabitants.

In 1847 Liberia became an independent republic. But despite the efforts of such black nationalist advocates as Henry Highland Garnet and Alexander Crummel, only about ten thousand African-American immigrants had gone there by 1860. This amounted to just .3 percent of the *increase* of the black population in the United States since 1816. Well before 1860, it was clear that African colonization would never fulfill the dreams of its black or white advocates.

Other African Americans saw Haiti as a potential refuge from the oppression they suffered in the United States. Haiti was especially attractive to those whose ancestors had lived in the Caribbean and to those who admired its revolutionary history. In 1824 about two hundred men, women, and children from Philadelphia, New York City, and Baltimore went to Haiti. By the end of the 1820s, between eight and thirteen thousand African Americans had arrived there. But African Americans found Haitian culture to be more alien than they had anticipated. They had difficulty learning French and distrusted the Roman Catholic church. By 1826 about one-third of the emigrants had returned to the United States.

Black Opposition to Colonization

Some African Americans had always opposed overseas colonization. As early as 1817, such influential black leaders as James Forten were wavering in their support of the ACS. Although Forten continued to support colonization in private, he led a meeting that year of three thousand black Philadelphians to denounce it. By the mid-1820s, many black abolitionists in East Coast cities from Richmond to Boston were criticizing colonization in general and the ACS in particular.

Among them was Samuel Cornish, who with John Russwurm began publication of *Freedom's Journal* in New York City in 1827 as the first African-American newspaper. Cornish, a young Presbyterian minister and a fierce opponent of the ACS, called for independent black action against slavery. The *Journal*—reflecting the values of antebellum reform—encouraged self-improvement, education, black civil rights in the North, and sympathy among black northerners for slaves in the South. Russwurm, however, was less opposed to the ACS than was Cornish. This disagreement helped lead

to the suspension of the newspaper in 1829. That same year Russwurm, who was one of the first African Americans to earn a college degree, moved to Liberia.

People like Cornish regarded themselves as Americans, not Africans, and wanted to improve their condition in this country. They considered Liberia foreign and unhealthy, and had no desire either to go there themselves or send other African Americans there. They feared that ACS talk about *voluntary* colonization was misleading. They knew that nearly every southern state required slaves individually freed by their masters to leave the state. They were also aware of efforts in the Maryland and Virginia legislatures to require *all* free black people to leave or be enslaved. These efforts had little practical impact, but they made African Americans fear that if they did not accept colonization under ACS auspices, it would be forced on them. In 1858, Arkansas actually required the reenslavement of free black people who did not leave that state. But, rather than migrate to Africa, most of its small free black population fled to the North, Canada, Louisiana, or the Indian territory.

By the mid-1820s most black abolitionists had concluded that the ACS was part of a proslavery effort to drive free African Americans from the United States. The ACS, they maintained in public meetings, was not an abolitionist organization at all but a proslavery scheme to force free black people to choose between reenslavement or banishment. America, they argued, was their native land. They knew nothing of Africa. Any effort to force them to go there was based on the racist assumption that they were not entitled to and were incapable of living in freedom in the land of their birth. "Do they think to drive us from our country and homes, after having enriched it with our blood and tears?" asked David Walker.

BLACK WOMEN ABOLITIONISTS

Black women, of course, joined black men in opposing slavery. When considering their role, we need to remember that the United States in the early nineteenth century was a society with a rigid gender hierarchy. Law and custom proscribed women from all political, professional, and most business activities. Those women deemed by black and white Americans to be respectable—the women of wealthy families—were expected to devote themselves exclusively to domestic concerns and to remain socially aloof. Church and benevolent activities were one of their few opportunities for public action. Even in this arena, custom relegated them to work as auxiliaries of male organizations.

This was certainly true of the first *formal* abolitionist groups for black women. Among the leaders were Charlotte Forten, the wife of James Forten, and Maria W. Stewart, the widow of a well-to-do Boston ship outfitter. Charlotte and her daughters Sarah, Margaretta, and Harriet joined with other black and white women to found the Philadelphia Female Anti-Slavery Society in 1833. A year earlier, in 1832, other black women had established in Salem, Massachusetts, the first female anti-slavery society. Women of the black elite were also active in the education of black children, which they hoped would overcome the white prejudices that supported slavery.

Stewart's brief career as an antislavery orator was far more striking and controversial than those of the Fortens or other early black female abolitionists. Influenced by *Walker's Appeal* and encouraged by William Lloyd Garrison, Stewart in 1831 and 1832 became the

---

PROFILE

MARIA W. STEWART

Maria W. Stewart had a brief but striking career as an abolitionist, feminist, and advocate of racial justice. She was born Maria Miller in Hartford, Connecticut, in 1803 to free parents, and she was orphaned at age five. Raised in the home of a minister, she had little formal education until she began attending "sabbath schools" when she was fifteen. In 1826 she married James W. Stewart, a successful Boston businessman nearly twice her age, in a ceremony conducted by Thomas Paul at his Boston church. When James W. Stewart died in 1829 he left her with limited means.

In 1830, caught up in the Second Great Awakening, Maria W. Stewart determined to dedicate herself to Christian benevolence. When William Lloyd Garrison began publishing the *Liberator* in 1831, she visited him at his office. Later that year Garrison published her pamphlet *Religion and Pure Principles of Morality, the Sure Foundation on Which We Must Build,* in which she advocated abolition and black autonomy. The following year Garrison published her second and last pamphlet, which dealt more narrowly with religion.

Meanwhile Stewart began speaking to black organizations. In early 1832 she addressed Boston's Afric-American Female Intelligence Society. Using prophetic rhetoric, she noted that the world had entered a revolutionary age and she called on African-American women to influence their husbands and children in behalf of the cause of black freedom, equality, education, and economic advancement in America. In regard to African colonization, she said, "before I go, the bayonet shall press me through."

When in February 1833 she addressed Boston's African Masonic Lodge, Stewart overplayed her role as a prophet. She invoked the glories of ancient Africa as well as black service in the American Revolution in order to chastise black men of her time for not being more active in behalf of the liberty of their people. By claiming that black men lacked "ambition and requisite courage," she provoked her audience to respond with hoots, jeers, and a barrage of rotten tomatoes.

Daunted by this stunning rejection, Stewart determined to leave Boston for New York City. In her farewell address of September 1833, which she delivered at a schoolroom in Paul's church, she asserted that her advice had been rejected because she was a woman. Nevertheless, while acknowledging that black men must lead, she called on black women to promote themselves, their families, and their race.

During the rest of her life, Stewart sought to fulfill that role in a less flamboyant manner. In New York she joined the Female Literary Society and became for many years a public school teacher. She moved to the slaveholding city of Baltimore in 1852 to start a school for black children. During the Civil War, with the assistance of black seamstress Elizabeth Keckley, she organized a black school in Washington. Later she worked as a matron at that city's Freedmen's Hospital and organized a Sunday school for poor black children. She died at Freedman's Hospital in December 1879.

VOICES

A BLACK WOMAN SPEAKS OUT ON THE RIGHT TO EDUCATION

Historians generally believe that the antebellum women's rights movement emerged from the antislavery movement during the late 1830s. But as the following letter, published in Freedom's Journal *on August 10, 1827, indicates, some black women advocated equal rights for women much earlier.*

Messrs. Editors,

Will you allow a female to offer a few remarks upon a subject that you must allow to be all important? I don't know that in any of your papers, you have said sufficient upon the education of females. I hope you are not to be classed with those, who think that our mathematical knowledge should be limited to "fathoming the dish-kettle," and that we have acquired enough of history, if we know that our grandfather's father lived and died. . . . The diffusion of knowledge has destroyed those degraded opinions, and men of the present age, allow, that we have minds that are capable and deserving of culture. There are difficulties . . . in the way of our advancement; but that should only stir us to greater efforts. We possess not the advantages with those of our sex, whose skins are not coloured like our own, but we can improve what little we have, and make our one talent produce two-fold. . . . Ignorant ourselves, how can we be expected to form the minds of our youth, and conduct them in the paths of knowledge? I would address myself to all mothers. . . . It is their bounden duty to store their daughters' minds with useful learning. They should be made to devote their leisure time to reading books, whence they would derive valuable information, which could never be taken from them. . . .

MATILDA

QUESTIONS

1. How does MATILDA use sarcasm to make her point?
2. What special difficulties did black women like MATILDA face in asserting their rights?

Source: Herbert Aptheker, ed., *A Documentary History of the Negro People in the United States*, 7 vols. (1951; reprint, New York: Citadel, 1990), 1:89.

first American woman to address male audiences in public. Although she directed some of her remarks to "Afric's daughters" and to "ye fairer sisters," she—as had Walker before her—pointedly called on black men to actively oppose slavery. "It is true," she told a group assembled at the African Masonic Hall in Boston in 1833, "our fathers bled and died in the revolutionary war, and others fought bravely under the command of [General Andrew] Jackson [at New Orleans in 1815], in defense of liberty. But where is the man that has distinguished himself in these modern days by acting wholly in the defense of African rights and liberty?" Such remarks from a woman cut deeply, and Stewart met such hostility from the black community that in September 1833 she retired as a public speaker. Henceforth, she labored in more conventionally and respectably female ways for the antislavery cause.

Many African-American women (as well as many white women), however, did not fit the early nineteenth-century criteria for respectability that applied to the Fortens, Stewart, and others in the African-American elite. Most black women were poor. They lacked education. They had to work outside their homes. Particularly in the upper South, these women were *practical* abolitionists.

From the revolutionary era onward, countless anonymous black women, both slave and free, living in such southern border cities as Baltimore, Louisville, and Washington risked everything to harbor fugitive slaves. Other heroic women saved their meager earnings to purchase freedom for themselves and their loved ones. Among them was Alethia Tanner of Washington, who purchased her own freedom in 1810 for $1,400 (about $16,000 in current dollars). In the 1820s she also purchased the freedom of her sister, her sister's ten children, and her sister's five grandchildren. In the 1830s, Tanner purchased the freedom of seven more slaves. Meanwhile, according to an account written in the 1860s, "Mrs. Tanner was alive to every wise scheme for the education and elevation of her race."

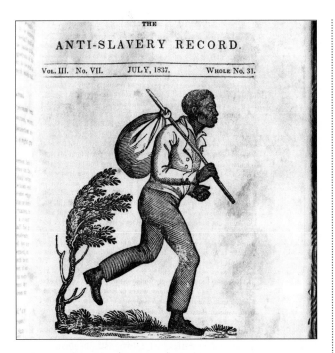

Well before this illustration of a man escaping from slavery appeared on the cover of the *Anti-Slavery Record* in 1837, fugitive slaves helped shape the development of the sectional controversy over slavery. Some of them became abolitionists, many aroused sympathy for the enslaved among black and white northerners, and all of them contributed to a southern white belief that the slave system required a vigilant defense.

THE BALTIMORE ALLIANCE

Among the stronger black abolitionist opponents of the ACS were William Watkins, Jacob Greener, and Hezekiah Grice who were associates in Baltimore of Benjamin Lundy, a white Quaker abolitionist who published an antislavery newspaper named the *Genius of Universal Emancipation*. By the mid-1820s, Watkins, a schoolteacher, had emerged, in a series of letters he published in *Freedom's Journal* and in Lundy's paper, as one of the more articulate opponents of colonization. Greener, a whitewasher and schoolteacher, helped Lundy publish the *Genius* and promoted its circulation. Grice, who later changed his mind and supported colonization, became the principal founder of the National Black Convention Movement, which during the 1830s, 1840s, and 1850s became a forum for black abolitionists.

In 1829 in Baltimore, Watkins, Greener, and Grice profoundly influenced a young white abolitionist and temperance advocate named William Lloyd Garrison, who later became the most influential of all the American antislavery leaders. Lundy had convinced Garrison to leave his native Massachusetts to come to Baltimore as the associate editor of the *Genius*. Garrison, a deeply

Despite their knowledge of slave resistance and revolt, white abolitionists in particular tended to portray slaves as peacefully begging for deliverance. The drawing of the man in chains illustrated Quaker poet John Greenleaf Whittier's "Our Countrymen in Chains," published in 1833. By 1835, as abolitionists became more receptive to feminist perspectives, similar images of chained women began to appear.

religious product of the Second Great Awakening and a well-schooled journalist, had already decided before he came to Baltimore that *gradual* abolition was neither practical nor moral. Gradualism was impractical, he said, because it continually put off the date of general emancipation. It was immoral because it encouraged slaveholders to go on sinfully and criminally oppressing African Americans.

Garrison, however, tolerated the ACS until he came under the influence of Watkins, Greener, and Grice. They set Garrison on a course that transformed the abolitionist movement in the United States during the early 1830s. They also initiated a bond between African Americans and Garrison that—although strained at times—shaped the rest of his antislavery career. That bond intensified in 1830 when Garrison was imprisoned in Baltimore jail for forty-nine days on charges that he had libeled a slavetrader. While in jail, Garrison met imprisoned fugitive slaves and denounced—to their faces—masters who came to retrieve them.

In 1831 when he began publishing his own abolitionist newspaper, *The Liberator*, in Boston, Garrison led the antislavery movement in a new, more radical direction. Although Garrison had called for the *immediate* rather than the *gradual* abolition of slavery before he arrived in Baltimore, he was not the first to make that demand or to oppose compensating masters who liberated their slaves. What made Garrison's brand of abolitionism revolution-

ary was the insight he gained from his association with African Americans in Baltimore: that immediate emancipation must be combined with a commitment to racial justice in the United States. Watkins and Greener were especially responsible for convincing Garrison that African Americans must have equal rights in America and not be sent to Africa after their emancipation. Immediate emancipation without compensation to slaveholders and without expatriation of African Americans became the core of Garrison's program for the rest of his long antislavery career.

DAVID WALKER'S APPEAL

Two other black abolitionists also influenced Garrison's brand of abolitionism. They were David Walker and Nat Turner. This chapter begins with a quote from *David Walker's Appeal . . . to the Coloured Citizens of the World*, which Walker published in 1829. As historian Clement Eaton commented in 1936, this *Appeal* was "a dangerous pamphlet in the Old South." In aggressive language, Walker furiously attacked slavery and white racism. He suggested that slaves use violence to secure

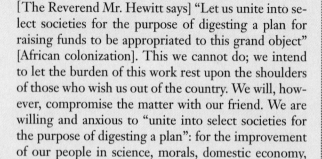

VOICES

WILLIAM WATKINS OPPOSES COLONIZATION

In response to a white clergyman who argued that migration to Africa would help improve African Americans, William Watkins stressed black unity, education, and self-improvement in this country:

[The Reverend Mr. Hewitt says] "Let us unite into select societies for the purpose of digesting a plan for raising funds to be appropriated to this grand object" [African colonization]. This we cannot do; we intend to let the burden of this work rest upon the shoulders of those who wish us out of the country. We will, however, compromise the matter with our friend. We are willing and anxious to "unite into select societies for the purpose of digesting a plan": for the improvement of our people in science, morals, domestic economy, &c. We are willing and anxious to form union societies . . . that shall discountenance and destroy, as far

as possible, those unhappy schisms which have too long divided us, though we are brethren. We are willing to unite . . . in the formation of temperance societies . . . that will enable us to exhibit to the world an amount of moral power that would give new impetus to our friends and "strike alarm" into the breasts of our enemies, if not wholly disarm them of the weapons they are hurling against us.

QUESTIONS

1. According to Watkins, how will black self-improvement societies help counter colonization?

2. What difficulties does Watkins believe African Americans must overcome to make themselves stronger in the United States?

Source: "A Colored American [Watkins] to Editors," n.d., in *Genius of Universal Emancipation*, December 18, 1829.

their liberty. "I do declare," he wrote, "that one good black can put to death six white men." This especially frightened white southerners because Walker's *Appeal* circulated among slaves in southern ports.

The *Appeal* shaped the struggle over slavery in three ways. First, although Garrison was committed to peaceful means, Walker's aggressive writing style influenced the tone of Garrison and other advocates of immediate abolition. Second, Walker's desperate effort to instill hope and pride in an oppressed people inspired an increasingly militant black abolitionism. Third, Walker's pamphlet and its circulation in the South made white southerners fearful of encirclement from without and subversion from within. This fear encouraged southern

---

PROFILE

DAVID WALKER

David Walker was born free in Wilmington, North Carolina, in 1796 or 1797. Although he learned to read and write, we know nothing of his early life. He may have attended a biracial Methodist church in Wilmington. As a young man, he traveled widely and, according to his *Appeal*, spent time in Charleston, South Carolina, where he attended a religious camp meeting in 1821. This has led historians to conjecture that Walker knew something about Denmark Vesey's conspiracy or if he was still in Charleston in 1822 that he may even have participated in it.

By 1825 Walker was in Boston dealing in secondhand clothes. He had his own shop, lived in the city's black neighborhood, was married, and had a daughter and a son. At a time when many occupations were closed to African Americans, Walker was doing relatively well. He associated with well-established local black people, including Thomas Paul, an abolitionist minister, and William C. Nell, a foe of Boston's segregated public schools. During the late 1820s, Walker was a circulation agent in Boston for John Russwurm and Samuel Cornish's *Freedom's Journal*.

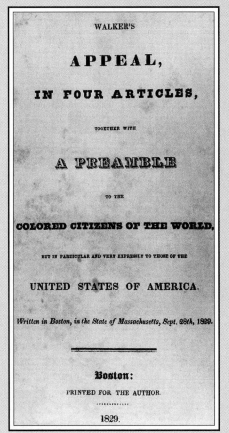

WALKER'S

APPEAL,

IN FOUR ARTICLES,

TOGETHER WITH

A PREAMBLE

TO THE

COLORED CITIZENS OF THE WORLD,

BUT IN PARTICULAR AND VERY EXPRESSLY TO THOSE OF THE

UNITED STATES OF AMERICA.

Written in Boston, in the State of Massachusetts, Sept. 28th, 1829.

Boston:
PRINTED FOR THE AUTHOR.
....
1829.

Walker, who also wrote for the *Journal*, was as conscious of the legal disabilities African Americans faced in Boston as he was of the oppressiveness of slavery. In December 1828 he addressed the Massachusetts General Colored Association on the topic of black cooperation with white abolitionists to improve the conditions of free black people and to liberate the slaves.

Not long after this, Walker became more radical. He wrote his *Appeal* and in September 1829 implemented a clandestine method to circulate it among slaves. He had black and white sailors, to whom he sold used clothes in Boston, give the pamphlet to African Americans when they visited southern ports.

When white people discovered that slaves had copies of the pamphlet, southern officials demanded that the mayor of Boston stop Walker from publishing. When the mayor refused, rumors circulated that a group of white southerners had offered a reward for Walker, dead or alive. It was not surprising, therefore, that when Walker's daughter and then Walker himself died during the summer of 1830, many assumed they had been poisoned. The most recent biography of Walker, however, indicates that they both died of tuberculosis.

TIMELINE

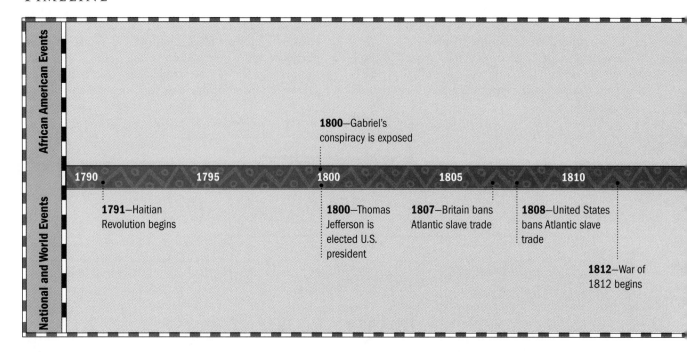

African American Events

1800—Gabriel's conspiracy is exposed

| 1790 | 1795 | 1800 | 1805 | 1810 |

National and World Events

1791—Haitian Revolution begins

1800—Thomas Jefferson is elected U.S. president

1807—Britain bans Atlantic slave trade

1808—United States bans Atlantic slave trade

1812—War of 1812 begins

leaders to make demands on the North that helped bring on the Civil War.

NAT TURNER

In this last respect, Nat Turner's contribution was even more important than Walker's. Slave conspiracies had not ended with Denmark Vesey's execution in 1822. But in 1831, Turner, a privileged slave from eastern Virginia, became the first African American actually to initiate a large-scale slave uprising since Charles Deslandes had done so in Louisiana in 1811. As a result Turner inspired far greater fear among white southerners than Walker had.

During the late 1820s and early 1830s, unrest among slaves in Virginia had increased. Walker's *Appeal*, which was circulating among some southern free black people by late 1829, may have contributed to this increase. Meanwhile, divisions among white Virginians encouraged slaves to seek advantages for themselves. In anticipation of a state constitutional convention in 1829, white people in western Virginia, where there were few slaveholders, called for emancipation. Poorer white men demanded an end to the property qualifications that denied them the vote. As the convention approached, a "spirit of dissatisfaction and insubordination" became manifest among slaves. Some armed

themselves and escaped northward. As proslavery white Virginians grew fearful, they demanded further restrictions on the ability of local free black people and northern abolitionists to influence slaves.

This contemporary drawing depicts the capture of Nat Turner in October 1831. Turner had avoided apprehension for nearly two months following the suppression of his revolt. The artist indicates Turner's personal dignity.

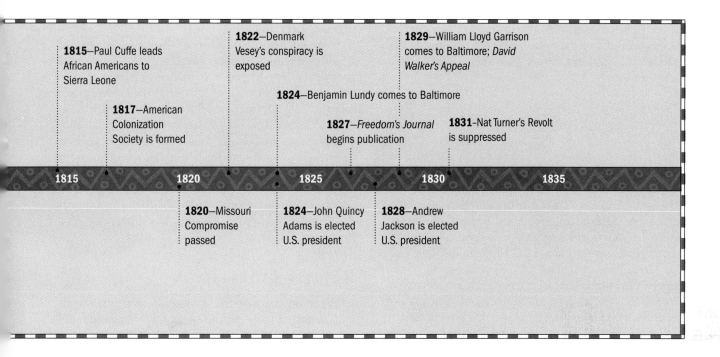

1815—Paul Cuffe leads African Americans to Sierra Leone

1822—Denmark Vesey's conspiracy is exposed

1829—William Lloyd Garrison comes to Baltimore; *David Walker's Appeal*

1817—American Colonization Society is formed

1824—Benjamin Lundy comes to Baltimore

1827—*Freedom's Journal* begins publication

1831-Nat Turner's Revolt is suppressed

1815 1820 1825 1830 1835

1820—Missouri Compromise passed

1824—John Quincy Adams is elected U.S. president

1828—Andrew Jackson is elected U.S. president

Yet there is no evidence that Nat Turner or any of his associates had read Walker's *Appeal*, had contact with northern abolitionists, or were aware of divisions among white Virginians. Although Turner knew about the successful slave revolt in Haiti, he was more of a religious visionary than a political revolutionary. Born in 1800, he learned to read as a child, and as a young man, spent much of his time studying and memorizing the Bible. He became a lay preacher and a leader among local slaves. By the late 1820s, he had begun to have visions that convinced him that God intended him to lead his people to freedom through violence.

After considerable planning, Turner began his uprising on the evening of August 21, 1831. His band, which numbered between sixty and seventy, killed fifty-seven white men, women, and children—the largest number of white Americans ever killed by slave rebels—before militia put down the revolt the following morning. In November, Turner and seventeen others were found guilty of insurrection and treason and were hanged. Meanwhile, panicky white people in nearby parts of Virginia and North Carolina killed more than one hundred African Americans whom they—almost always wrongly—suspected of being in league with the rebels.

Turner, like Walker and Garrison, shaped a new era in American abolitionism. The bloodshed in Virginia inspired general revulsion. White southerners—

and some northerners—accused Garrison and other abolitionists of inspiring the revolt. In response, northern abolitionists of both races asserted their commitment to a peaceful struggle against slavery. Yet both black and white abolitionists respected Turner. Black abolitionists accorded him the same heroic stature they gave Toussaint L'Ouverture and Gabriel. Garrison and

---

THE RADICAL TURN IN THE ABOLITION MOVEMENT

July 1829	William Lloyd Garrison joins Benjamin Lundy in Baltimore as associate editor of the *Genius of Universal Emancipation*.
September 1829	*David Walker's Appeal* is published in Boston and then circulated in the South.
November 1829	William Watkins's anticolonization letters first appear in the *Genius*.
June 1830	Garrison is sentenced to jail in Baltimore for libeling a slavetrader.
August 1830	Walker dies of tuberculosis in Boston.
January 1831	Garrison begins publication of the *Liberator* in Boston.
August 1831	Nat Turner's Revolt occurs.

other white abolitionists compared Turner to George Washington and other leaders of national liberation movements. This tension between lip service to peaceful means and admiration for violence against slavery characterized the antislavery movement for the next thirty years.

CONCLUSION

This chapter has focused on the two principal antislavery movements in the United States before the 1830s. One movement existed in the South among slaves. The other was centered in the North and the Chesapeake among free African Americans and white abolitionists. Both movements had roots in the age of revolution and gained vitality from evangelical Christianity. The Second Great Awakening and the reforming spirit of the Benevolent Empire shaped the northern antislavery effort. The black church, the Bible, and elements of African religion helped inspire slave revolutionaries.

Gabriel, Denmark Vesey, and Nat Turner had to rely on violence to fight slavery; northern abolitionists used newspapers, books, petitions, and speeches to spread their views. But the two movements had similarities and influenced each other. David Walker's life in Charleston at the time of Denmark Vesey's conspiracy influenced his beliefs. In turn, his *Appeal* may have influenced the enslaved. Turner's revolt helped determine the course of northern abolitionism after 1831. During the following decades the efforts of slaves to resist their masters, to rebel, and to escape influenced radical black and white abolitionists in the North.

In fact the antislavery movement that existed in the North and portions of the upper South was always biracial. During the 1810s and for much of the 1820s, most black abolitionists embraced a form of nationalism that encouraged them to cooperate with the conservative white people who led the ACS. As the racist and proslavery nature of that organization became clear, northern black and white abolitionists called for immediate, uncompensated general emancipation that would not force former slaves to leave the United States.

Slavery, the explicit legal disabilities imposed on free African Americans, and the widespread religious revivalism of the early nineteenth century created conditions that are hugely different from those that exist today. But some similarities between then and now are striking. As it was in the 1810s and 1820s, the United States today is in turmoil. Technological innovation and corporate restructuring have created a volatile job market, which has helped to increase interracial tension.

Also, as they did in the early nineteenth century, African American leaders today advocate various strategies to improve black life.

Samuel Cornish, William Watkins, and others who opposed the ACS sought through peaceful means to abolish slavery and gain recognition of African Americans as American citizens. David Walker advocated a more forceful strategy to achieve the same ends. Cornish, Watkins, and Walker all cooperated with white abolitionists. Paul Cuffe and others took a position closer to black nationalism by linking the abolition of slavery to an independent black destiny in Africa.

As is true today, African Americans of the early nineteenth century, who sought to deal with the problems of their time, faced difficult choices. Any strategy they followed had virtues, weaknesses, and dangers.

REVIEW QUESTIONS

1. What did the program of the ACS mean for African Americans? How did they respond to this program?

2. Analyze the role in abolitionism played (1) by Christianity and (2) by the revolutionary tradition in the Atlantic world. Which was most important in shaping the views of black and white abolitionists?

3. Evaluate the interaction of black and white abolitionists during the early nineteenth century. How did their motives for becoming abolitionists differ?

4. Discuss how Gabriel, Denmark Vesey, and Nat Turner influenced the northern abolitionist movement.

5. What risks did Maria W. Stewart take when she spoke publicly for antislavery action?

RECOMMENDED READING

Merton L. Dillon. *Slavery Attacked: Southern Slaves and Their Allies, 1619–1865.* Baton Rouge: Louisiana State University Press, 1990. Integrates slave resistance and revolt with the northern abolitionist movement.

Eugene D. Genovese. *From Rebellion to Revolution: Afro-American Slave Revolts in the Making of the Modern World.* Baton Rouge: Louisiana State University Press, 1979. Places the major American slave revolts and conspiracies in an Atlantic context.

Peter P. Hinks. *To Awaken My Afflicted Brethren: David Walker and the Problem of Antebellum Slave Resistance.* University Park: Pennsylvania State University Press, 1997. The most recent biography of Walker, which places him within the black abolitionist movement and attempts to clarify what little we know about his life.

Benjamin Quarles. *Black Abolitionists*. New York: Oxford University Press, 1969. A classic study that emphasizes cooperation between black and white abolitionists.

Harry Reed. *Platform for Change: The Foundations of the Northern Free Black Community, 1775–1865*. East Lansing: Michigan State University Press, 1994. An excellent study of the relationship between free black culture in the North and antislavery action.

P. J. Staudenraus. *The American Colonization Movement, 1816–1865* (New York: Columbia University Press, 1961). Although published in the 1960s, the most recent account of the American Colonization Society.

Shirley J. Yee. *Black Women Abolitionists: A Study in Activism, 1828–1860*. Knoxville: University of Tennessee Press, 1992. Concentrates on the period after 1833, but it is the best place to start reading about black abolitionist women.

ADDITIONAL BIBLIOGRAPHY

The Relationship among Evangelicalism, Reform, and Abolitionism

Robert H. Abzug. *Cosmos Crumbling: American Reform and the Religious Imagination*. New York: Oxford University Press, 1994.

Gilbert H. Barnes. *The Antislavery Impulse, 1830–1844*. 1933; reprint, Gloucester, MA: Peter Smith, 1973.

Ronald G. Walters. *American Reformers, 1815–1860*. Baltimore: Johns Hopkins University Press, 1978.

American Abolitionism before 1831

David Brion Davis. *The Problem of Slavery in Western Culture*. Ithaca, NY: Cornell University Press, 1966.

———. *The Problem of Slavery in the Age of Revolution*. Ithaca, NY: Cornell University Press, 1975.

———. *Slavery and Human Progress*. Ithaca, NY: Cornell University Press, 1987.

Merton L. Dillon. *The Abolitionists: The Growth of a Dissenting Minority*. New York: Norton, 1974.

———. *Benjamin Lundy and the Struggle for Negro Freedom*. Urbana: University of Illinois Press, 1966.

David Walker's Appeal, Sean Wilentz, ed. 1829; reprint, New York: Hill and Wang, 1995.

Slave Revolts and Conspiracies

Herbert Aptheker. *American Negro Slave Revolts*. 1943; new ed. New York: International Publishers, 1974.

Douglas R. Egerton. *Gabriel's Rebellion: The Virginia Slave Conspiracies of 1800 & 1802*. Chapel Hill: University of North Carolina Press, 1993.

———. *He Shall Go Out Free: The Lives of Denmark Vesey*. Madison, Wisconsin: Madison House, 1999.

Alfred N. Hunt. *Haiti's Influence on Antebellum America: Slumbering Volcano in the Caribbean*. Baton Rouge: Louisiana State University Press, 1988.

John Lofton. *Denmark Vesey's Revolt: The Slave Plot that Lit a Fuse to Fort Sumter*. Kent, OH: Kent State University Press, 1983.

Stephen B. Oates. *The Fires of the Jubilee: Nat Turner's Fierce Rebellion*. New York: Harper & Row, 1975.

Black Abolitionism and Black Nationalism

Leroy Graham. *Baltimore: Nineteenth-Century Black Capital*. Washington: University Press of America, 1982.

Vincent Harding. *There Is a River: The Black Struggle for Freedom in America*. New York: Harcourt, Brace, Jovanovich, 1981.

Floyd J. Miller. *The Search for Black Nationality: Black Colonization and Emigration, 1787–1863*. Urbana: University of Illinois Press, 1975.

Marilyn Richardson. *Maria W. Stewart: America's First Black Woman Political Writer*. Bloomington: Indiana University Press, 1987.

Sterling Stuckey. *Slave Culture: Nationalist Theory and the Foundations of Black America*. New York: Oxford University Press, 1987.

Lamont D. Thomas. *Rise to Be a People: A Biography of Paul Cuffe*. Urbana: University of Illinois Press, 1986.

Julie Winch. *Philadelphia's Black Elite: Activism, Accommodation, and Struggle for Autonomy, 1787–1840*. Philadelphia: Temple University Press, 1988.

LET YOUR MOTTO BE RESISTANCE, 1833–1850

An increase in slave escapes helped inspire the more aggressive abolitionist tactics of the 1840s and 1850s. This drawing depicts a group of twenty-eight leaving Maryland's eastern shore.

It is in your power to torment the God-cursed slaveholders, that they would be glad to let you go free. . . . But you are a patient people. You act as though you were made for the special use of these devils. You act as though your daughters were born to pamper the lusts of your masters and overseers. And worse than all, you tamely submit, while your lords tear your wives from your embraces, and defile them before your eyes. In the name of God we ask, are you men? . . . Heaven, as with a voice of thunder, calls on you to arise from the dust. Let your motto be RESISTANCE! RESISTANCE! RESISTANCE! No oppressed people have ever secured their Liberty without resistance.

Henry Highland Garnet, "Address to the Slaves of the United States of America"

When black abolitionist Henry Highland Garnet spoke these words at the National Convention of Colored Citizens, held in Buffalo, New York, on August 16, 1843, he caused a tremendous stir among the delegates. Garnet had escaped with his family from slavery in Maryland in 1824 when he was a boy. He had received an excellent education while growing up in New York and was a powerful speaker. But some of the delegates pointed out that he was far away from the slaves he claimed to address. Others believed that he had called for a potentially disastrous slave revolt, and, by a narrow margin, the convention refused to endorse his speech.

Yet, in the speech, Garnet had also advised slaves, "We do not advise you to attempt a revolution with the sword, because it would be INEXPEDIENT. Your numbers are too small, and moreover the rising spirit of the age, and the spirit of the gospel, are opposed to war and bloodshed." Rather than a bloody revolt like Nat Turner's, Garnet advocated a general strike among slaves. This, he contended, would put the onus of initiating violence on the masters. Nevertheless, Garnet's speech reflected a growing militancy among black and white abolitionists that shaped the antislavery movement during the two decades before the Civil War.

In this chapter we investigate the causes of that militancy and explore the role of African Americans in the antislavery movement from the establishment of the American Anti-Slavery Society in 1833 to the Compromise of 1850. Largely in response to changes in American culture, unrest among slaves, and sectional conflict between North and South, the biracial northern antislavery movement during this period became splintered and diverse.

A RISING TIDE OF RACISM AND VIOLENCE

The growing militancy among abolitionists occurred within the context of increasing racism and violence in the United States from the 1830s through the Civil War. While Garnet was correct about the spirit of the gospel, he was wrong about the spirit of his times. By the 1840s white Americans had embraced an exuberant nationalism called "manifest destiny" that defined political and economic progress in racial terms and legitimized war to expand the boundaries of the United States.

During this same period, American ethnologists—scientists who studied racial diversity—rejected the eighteenth-century idea that the physical and mental characteristics of the world's peoples are the product of environment. Instead, they argued that what they perceived to be racial differences were intrinsic and permanent. White people—particularly white Americans—they maintained, were a superior race culturally, physically, economically, politically, and intellectually.

These theories provided white Americans with an apparently scientific justification for the continued enslavement of African Americans and extermination of American Indians, as both these groups were deemed inferior. Prejudice against European immigrants to the United States also increased. By the late 1840s, a move-

ment known as "nativism" pitted native-born Protestants against foreign-born Roman Catholics, whom the natives saw as competitors for jobs and as culturally subversive.

Accompanying these broad intellectual and cultural developments was a wave of racially motivated violence committed by the federal and state governments as well as by white vigilantes. Starting in the 1790s, the United States Army waged a systematic campaign to remove American Indians from the states and relocate them west of the Mississippi. This campaign culminated in 1838 in the Trail of Tears, when the army forced 16,000 Cherokees from Georgia to what is now Oklahoma. Many Cherokees died along the way. During the same decade, antiblack riots became common in urban America. From 1829 until the Civil War, white mobs led by "gentlemen of property and standing" attacked abolitionist newspaper presses and wreaked havoc in African-American neighborhoods.

Antiblack and Anti-abolitionist Riots

Antiblack urban riots predated the start of immediate abolitionism in the late 1820s. But such riots became more common as abolitionism gained strength during the 1830s and 1840s (Map 9–1, Figure 9–1). Although few northern cities escaped racist mob attacks on African Americans and their property, riots in Cincinnati, Providence, New York City, and Philadelphia were especially infamous.

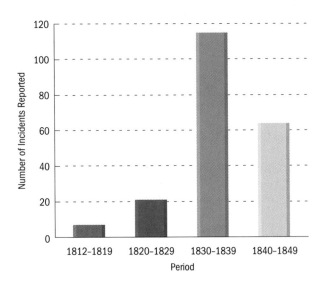

Figure 9–1 Mob Violence in the United States, 1812–1849. This graph illustrates the rise of mob violence in the North in reaction to abolitionist activity. Attacks on abolitionists peaked during the 1830s and then declined as antislavery sentiment spread in the North.

PROFILE

HENRY HIGHLAND GARNET

Henry Highland Garnet rivaled Frederick Douglass as a black leader during the antebellum decades. While Douglass emphasized assimilation, Garnet emerged as an advocate of black nationalism. The two men had much in common, however, and by the time of the Civil War were almost indistinguishable in their views.

In 1824 when Garnet was nine, his family struck out from a Maryland plantation for freedom in the North. His father led the family to New York City, where Garnet enrolled in the Free African School. Influenced by his father's pride in African heritage, by vigilance against slavecatchers, and by a youthful lameness that led to the amputation of one of his legs in 1840, Garnet brought a profound determination to all that he undertook.

In 1835 Garnet was among twelve black students admitted to Noyes Academy at Canaan, New Hampshire. When shortly thereafter local farmers reacted by tearing down the school buildings, Garnet defended his black classmates with a shotgun. The following year he enrolled at Oneida Theological Institute located near Utica, New York. There, guided by white abolitionist Beriah Green, Garnet prepared for the Presbyterian ministry. In 1842 he became pastor of the black Presbyterian church in Troy, New York.

By that time he had been an active abolitionist for several years. He worked closely with Gerrit Smith's radical New York wing of the Liberty party. He also became a strong advocate of independent antislavery action among African Americans. Referring to white abolitionists, he said, "They are our allies—*Ours* is the battle." But it was within the context of the New York Liberty party's determination to challenge slavery on its own ground that Garnet delivered his famous "Address to the Slaves" at the 1843 National Convention of Colored Citizens. By demanding what amounted to a general strike by slaves and acknowledging that violence could result, Garnet highlighted his differences with Frederick Douglass and other African Americans who remained dedicated to nonviolence.

It was Garnet's conviction that African Americans ultimately must free themselves that led him to promote migration to Africa. He always maintained that the ACS was proslavery and racist, but by 1848 he had come to believe that African colonization could become a powerful adjunct to the struggle for emancipation in the United States.

Garnet's years abroad during the early 1850s strengthened him in this outlook. He served as a delegate to the World Peace Conference in Frankfort, Germany, in 1850, spent 1851 in Great Britain, and lived in Jamaica from 1853 to 1856 as a Presbyterian missionary. Garnet returned to the United States in 1856 and in 1858 organized the African Civilization Society designed to build a strong, independent Africa through black emigration from America and the cultivation of cotton. But Garnet's views remained very much in the minority among African-American leaders and the Civil War effectively ended his nationalist efforts.

During the war Garnet was an early advocate of enlisting black troops in the Union armies. In 1863 he became pastor of the 15th Avenue Presbyterian Church in Washington, D.C., and in 1865 became the first African American to deliver a sermon in Congress. Like Douglass a staunch Republican during the postwar years, Garnet in January 1882 became the United States ambassador to Liberia and died there a month later.

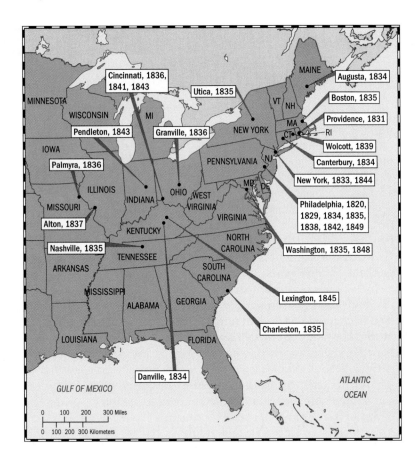

Map 9-1 Anti-Abolitionist and Antiblack Riots during the Antebellum Period. African Americans faced violent conditions in both the North and South during the antebellum years. Fear among whites of growing free black communities and white antipathy toward spreading abolitionism sparked numerous antiblack and anti-abolitionist riots.

In 1829, a three-day riot instigated by local politicians led many black people in Cincinnati to flee to Canada. In 1836 and 1841, mob attacks on the *Philanthropist*, Cincinnati's white-run abolitionist newspaper, expanded into attacks on African-American homes and businesses. Both times, black residents defended their property with guns.

In 1831 white sailors led a mob in Providence that literally tore that city's black neighborhood to pieces. With spectators cheering them on, rioters first pulled down the chimneys of black residences and then "with a firehook and plenty of axes and iron bars" tore down the buildings themselves and dragged them into the streets. The Rhode Island militia finally had to stop the mayhem.

In New York City in 1834, a mob destroyed twelve houses owned by black residents, a black church, a black school, and the home of white abolitionist Lewis Tappan. But no city had worse race riots than Philadelphia—the City of Brotherly Love. In 1820, 1829, 1834, 1835, 1838, 1842, and 1849 antiblack riots broke out there. The ugliest was in 1842 when Irish immigrants led a white mob that assaulted members of a black temper-

ance society, who were commemorating the abolition of slavery in the British colony of Jamaica. When African Americans defended themselves with muskets, the mob looted and burned Philadelphia's principal black neighborhood. Among those who successfully defended their homes was Robert Purvis, the abolitionist son-in-law of James Forten.

Texas and the War against Mexico

Violence was not confined to northern cities. Under President James K. Polk, the United States adopted a belligerent foreign policy that culminated in a war against Mexico that lasted from 1846 to 1848. Until 1836 what is now the southwest quarter of the United States—a region stretching from Texas to California—was part of the Republic of Mexico. In that year slaveholding Americans in Texas won independence from Mexico, which had abolished slavery within its boundaries in 1828. Once Texas had become an independent slaveholding republic, its leaders immediately applied for annexation to the United States. They were rebuffed for nine years because both the Democratic

Pennsylvania Hall was built in Philadelphia during the winter of 1837-1838. A distinguished group of abolitionists dedicated it to free speech when it opened on May 14, 1838. Three days later an antiabolitionist mob burned it.

and Whig parties recognized that adding a huge new slave state to the Union would divide the country along North-South sectional lines.

But the desire for new territory encouraged by Manifest Destiny and an expanding slave-labor economy could not be denied indefinitely. In 1844 Polk, the Democratic presidential candidate, called for the annexation of both Texas and Oregon, a huge territory in the Pacific Northwest that the United States and Great Britain had been jointly administering. When Polk defeated the Whig candidate Henry Clay, who favored delaying annexation, Congress in early 1845 annexed Texas by joint resolution. This vastly expanded the area within the United States that was open to slavery.

In early 1846 Polk backed away from a confrontation with Great Britain over Oregon. A few months later, however, he provoked a war with Mexico that by 1848 had forced that country to recognize American sovereignty over Texas and to cede New Mexico and California as well (Map 9–2). The states of New Mexico, Arizona, Colorado, Nevada, Utah, and California were eventually carved from these vast provinces. Immediately, the question of whether slavery would expand into the Southwest became a burning issue. Many white northerners feared that slaveholders, by adding new slave states to the Union, would dominate the federal government and enact policies detrimental to white workers and farmers.

As such sentiments spread across the North, slaveholders became fearful that they would be excluded from the western lands they had helped to wrest from Mexico. The resulting Compromise of 1850 (see Chapter 10) attempted to satisfy both sections. But it sub-

jected African Americans to additional violence because part of the Compromise met slaveholders' demands for a stronger fugitive slave law. Not only did this law make it easier for masters to recapture bondspeople who had escaped to the North, but it also caused an increase in attempts to kidnap free black northerners into slavery.

THE RESPONSE OF THE ANTISLAVERY MOVEMENT

This rising tide of race-related violence caused difficulties for an antislavery movement that suffered internal racial strife and was officially committed to using only peaceful means against slavery. African Americans found their most loyal white allies within the antislavery movement. But interracial understanding was rarely easy. White abolitionists had always assumed that they should set policy for their black collaborators, who became increasingly resentful of this presumption as the 1840s progressed. Meanwhile the abolitionist commitment to nonviolence weakened. It had arisen as both a principled rejection of the violence that pervaded America and as a shrewd response to proslavery charges that abolitionists were responsible for unrest among slaves. But from the start, nonviolence seemed to limit abolitionist options in an increasingly violent environment. By the 1840s, whether to adopt violent means and greater autonomy for black abolitionists had become contentious issues within the antislavery movement.

Map 9–2 U.S. Territorial Gains, 1846–1853. This map illustrates the territories gained by the United States as a result of the war against Mexico that ended in 1848. The question of whether slavery would be allowed to expand into all or part of this vast region caused a sectional crisis in 1849 and 1850.

The American Anti-Slavery Society

Well before the era of manifest destiny, the American Anti-Slavery Society (AASS)—the most significant abolitionist organization—emerged from a major turning point in the abolitionist cause. This was William Lloyd Garrison's decision in 1831 to create a movement dedicated to immediate, uncompensated emancipation and to equal rights for African Americans in the United States. To reach these goals, abolitionists led by Garrison organized the AASS in December 1833 at Philadelphia's Adelphi Hall. Well aware of the fears raised by Nat Turner's revolt, those assembled declared, "The society will never in any way, countenance the oppressed in vindicating their rights by resorting to physical force."

No white American worked harder than Garrison to bridge racial differences. He spoke to black groups, stayed in the homes of African Americans when he traveled, and welcomed them to his home. Black abolitionists responded with affection and loyalty. They provided financial support for his newspaper, *The Liberator*, worked as subscription agents, paid for his speaking tour in England in 1833, and served as his bodyguard.

But Garrison, like most other white abolitionists, remained stiff and condescending in conversation with his black colleagues, and the black experience in the AASS reflected this.

On the one hand, it is remarkable that the AASS allowed black men to participate in its meetings without formal restrictions. At the time, no other American organization did so. On the other hand, that black participation was paltry. Three African Americans—James McCrummell, Robert Purvis, and James G. Barbadoes—helped found the AASS and McCrummell presided at its first meeting. But, among sixty white people attending that meeting, they were the only African Americans. Although three white women participated in the meeting, no black women did so. Throughout the history of the AASS, black people rarely held positions of authority.

As state and local auxiliaries of the AASS organized across the North during the early 1830s, this pattern repeated itself. Black men participated but did not lead, although a few held prominent offices. In 1834 Barbadoes and Joshua Easton joined the board of directors of the Massachusetts Anti-Slavery Society. In 1837 seven black men, including James Forten, helped organize the Pennsylvania Anti-Slavery Society. With some exceptions, black and white women could observe but not participate in the proceedings of these organizations. It took a three-year struggle between 1837 and 1840 over "the woman question" before an AASS annual meeting elected a woman to a leadership position, and that victory helped split the organization.

Black and Women's Antislavery Societies

In these circumstances black male, black female, and white female abolitionists formed their own auxiliaries to the AASS. Some African Americans joined predominantly white organizations; others formed their own separate societies. Often African Americans belonged to both all-black and to integrated groups. Black male auxiliaries to the AASS were formed across the North during the mid-1830s. As we saw in Chapter 8, the earliest black women's abolitionist organization was organized in Salem, Massachusetts, in 1832, a year before the AASS came into being.

The black organizations arose both because of racial discord in the predominantly white organizations and because of a black desire for racial solidarity. But historian Benjamin Quarles makes an essential point when he writes that during the 1830s "the founders of Negro societies did not envision their efforts as distinctive or

Wealthy black abolitionist Robert Purvis is at the very center of this undated photograph of the Philadelphia Anti-Slavery Society. The famous Quaker abolitionist Lucretia Mott and her husband James Mott are seated to Purvis's left. As significant as Purvis's central location in the photograph is that he is the *only* African American pictured.

self-contained; rather they viewed their role as that of a true auxiliary—supportive, supplemental, and subsidiary." Despite their differences black and white abolitionists were still members of a single movement.

Although racially integrated female antislavery societies did not entirely overcome the racism of their time, they elevated more African Americans to prominent positions than their male counterparts did. Black abolitionist Susan Paul became a member of the board of the Boston Female Anti-Slavery Society when it was established in 1833. Later that year, Margaretta Forten became recording secretary of the Female Anti-Slavery Society of Philadelphia, founded by white Quaker abolitionist Lucretia Mott. Black Quaker Sarah M. Douglass of Philadelphia and Sarah Forten—Margaretta's sister—were delegates to the First Anti-Slavery Convention of American Women in New York City in May 1837. At the second convention, Susan Paul became a vice president, and Douglass became treasurer.

The main task of all the female antislavery societies was fund-raising. They held bake sales, organized antislavery fairs and bazaars, and sold antislavery memorabilia with the proceeds going to the AASS or to antislavery newspapers. But the membership of black and white women in female antislavery societies also inspired the birth of feminism by creating an awareness that women had rights and interests that a male-dominated society had to recognize. By writing essays and poems on political subjects and making public speeches, black and white female abolitionists challenged a culture that relegated *respectable* women to domestic duties. By the 1850s the famous African-American speaker Sojourner Truth was emphasizing that *all* black women through their physical labor and the pain they suffered in slavery had earned equal standing with both men and their more favored sisters.

Black men and women also formed auxiliaries during the early 1830s to the Quaker-initiated Free Produce

SOJOURNER TRUTH

Sojourner Truth does not fit easily into the history of the antislavery movement. She did not identify with a particular group of abolitionists. Instead, as her biographer Nell Irvin Painter points out, Truth served the cause by transforming herself into a symbol of the strength of all black women.

Originally named Isabella, Truth was born a slave—probably in 1797—in a Dutch-speaking area north of New York City. She had several masters, one of whom beat her brutally. Always a hard worker, she grew into a tall, muscular woman. Her voice was deep and throughout her career, enemies charged that she was really a man—despite the five children she gave birth to after her marriage in 1815.

In 1827 Truth escaped to an antislavery family who purchased her freedom. Two years later, she became a powerful revivalist preacher in New York City. Later, she joined a communal religious cult, became an ardent millenarian—predicting that Judgment Day was rapidly approaching—and in 1843 took the name Sojourner Truth. A few years later, while working at a commune in Northampton, Massachusetts, she met abolitionists Frederick Douglass and David Ruggles. This meeting led to her career as a champion of abolition and women's rights.

She lectured across the North and as far west as Kansas during the late 1840s and the 1850s. She was blunt but eloquent and used common sense to argue that African Americans and women deserved the same rights as white men. They did so, she insisted, because they could work as hard as white men. Truth almost always addressed white audiences and made a strong impression on them. During the Civil War, she volunteered to work among black Union troops, and President Lincoln invited her to the White House in 1864. She continued to advocate black and women's rights until her death in 1883.

Ironically, as Painter and others note, Truth probably never used the phrase "Ar'n't I a Woman?" for which she is most widely remembered. A white female journalist first attributed it to Truth years after the 1851 women's rights meeting in Akron, Ohio, at which Truth was supposed to have said it. Contemporary accounts indicate that she did not. Truth did, however, tell those assembled in Akron, "I have as much muscle as any man, and I can do as much work as any man. I have plowed and reaped and husked and chopped and mowed, and can any man do more than that?"

Association, which tried to put economic pressure on slaveholders by boycotting agricultural products produced by slaves. James Cornish led the Colored Free Produce Society of Pennsylvania, which marketed meat, vegetables, cotton, and sugar produced by free labor. Judith James and Laetitia Rowley organized the Colored Female Free Produce Society of Pennsylvania with a similar aim. Other black affiliates to the Free Produce Association existed in New York and Ohio, and black abolitionist William Whipper operated a free produce store in Philadelphia in 1834. During the 1850s, Frances Ellen Watkins, one of the few prominent black female speakers of the time, always included the free produce movement in her abolitionist lectures and wrote newspaper articles on its behalf.

The Black Convention Movement

The dozens of local, state, and national black conventions held in the North between 1830 and 1864 were further removed from the AASS. They were a black manifestation of the antebellum American reform impulse, and the antislavery cause was not their only agenda. They did, nevertheless, provide an independent forum for the more prominent black male abolitionists, such as Henry Highland Garnet, Frederick Douglass, and later, Martin R. Delany. They also provided a setting in which abolitionism could grow and change its tactics to meet the demands of the sectionally polarized and violent 1840s.

Hezekiah Grice, a young black man who had worked with Benjamin Lundy and William Lloyd Garrison in Baltimore during the 1820s, organized the first Black National Convention. It met on September 24, 1830, at the Bethel Church in Philadelphia with the venerable churchman Richard Allen presiding. The national convention became an annual event for the next five years and then met irregularly in Philadelphia, New York, Buffalo, Rochester, Syracuse, and Cleveland into the Civil War years. Meanwhile, many state and local black conventions also met across the North.

By twentieth-century standards, these conventions were informal, particularly those at the local level, and had no strict guidelines for choosing delegates. This informality, however, did not prevent the conventions from becoming effective forums for black concerns. They invariably called for the abolition of slavery and for improving the conditions of northern African Americans. Among other reforms, the conventions called for integrated public schools and the right of black men to vote, serve on juries, and testify against white people in court.

During the 1830s the conventions also stressed black self-help through temperance, sexual morality, education, and thrift. These causes remained important parts of the conventions' agenda throughout the antebellum years. But by the early 1840s, politics and the active resistance to oppression that Garnet called for in the speech quoted at the start of this chapter were receiving more emphasis. By the late 1840s, assertions of black nationalism and endorsements of black migration to Africa or Latin America had become common.

BLACK COMMUNITY INSTITUTIONS

Although the persistence of slavery and oppression helped shape the agenda of the Black Convention Movement, the movement itself was a product of a maturing African-American community. Free black people in the United States grew from 59,000 in 1790 to 319,000 in 1830. Gradual emancipation in the northern states, acts of individual manumission in the upper South, and escapes accounted for this fivefold increase. The growing free black population was concentrated in such large cities as New York, Philadelphia, Baltimore, Boston, and Cincinnati. These cities had enough free African Americans to provide the resources that built the churches, schools, benevolent organizations, and printing presses that created a self-conscious black community. Between 1790 and 1830 this community provided the foundations for the black antislavery institutions of the decades that followed.

Black Churches in the Antislavery Cause

Black churches were especially significant for the antislavery movement. With a few major exceptions, the leading black abolitionists were ministers. Among them were Garnet, Jehiel C. Beman, Samuel E. Cornish, Theodore S. Wright, Charles B. Ray, James W. C. Pennington, Nathaniel Paul, Alexander Crummell, Daniel A. Payne, and Samuel Ringgold Ward. Some of these men led congregations affiliated with separate African-American churches, such as the African Baptist Church or the African Methodist Episcopal Church (AME). Others preached to black congregations affiliated with predominantly white churches. A few black ministers, such as Amos N. Freeman of Brooklyn, New York, served white antislavery congregations.

These clergy used their pulpits to attack slavery, racial discrimination, proslavery white churches, and the American Colonization Society (ACS). Having covered most of these topics in a sermon to a white congregation in 1839, Daniel Payne, who had grown up free in South Carolina, declared, "Awake! AWAKE! to the battle, and hurl the hottest thunders of divine truth at the head of this cruel monster, until he shall fall to rise no more; and the groans of the enslaved are converted into the songs of the free!" Black churches also provided forums for abolitionist speakers, such as Frederick Douglass and Garrison, and meeting places for predominantly white antislavery organizations, which were frequently denied space in white churches.

Black Newspapers

Less influential than black churches in the antislavery movement, black newspapers still played an important role, particularly by the 1840s. Abolitionist newspapers, whether owned by black or white people, almost always faced financial difficulties. Few survived for more than a few years because *reform*, as opposed to *commercial*, newspapers were a luxury that many subscribers both black and white could not afford. Black newspapers faced added difficulties finding readers because most African Americans were poor, and many were illiterate. Moreover, white abolitionist newspapers, such as the *Liberator*, served a black clientele. They published speeches by black abolitionists and reported black convention proceedings. Some black abolitionists argued, therefore, that a separate black press was unnecessary. An additional, self-imposed, burden was that publishers eager to get their message out almost never required subscribers to pay in advance, thereby compounding their papers' financial instability.

Nevertheless, there were several influential black abolitionist newspapers between the establishment of the AASS in 1833 and the Civil War in 1861. The first black newspaper, *Freedom's Journal*, owned and edited by Samuel Cornish and John B. Russwurm, was published only from 1827 to 1829, but it showed that African Americans could produce interesting and competent journalism and could attract black and white subscribers. The *Journal* also established the framework for black journalism during the antebellum period by emphasizing antislavery, racial justice, and Christian and democratic values.

The most ubiquitous black journalist of the period was Philip A. Bell. Bell was either publisher or copublisher of the *New York Weekly Advocate* in 1837, the *Colored American* from 1837 to 1842, and two San Francisco newspapers—the *Pacific Appeal* and the *Elevator*—during the 1860s. But the black clergyman Charles B. Ray of New York City was the real spirit behind the *Colored American*. Well aware of the need for financial success, Ray declared in 1838, "If among the few hundred thousand free colored people in the country—to say nothing of the white population from whom it ought to receive a strong support, a living patronage for the paper cannot be obtained, it will be greatly to their reproach."

Among other prominent, if short-lived, black newspapers of the 1840s and 1850s were Garnet's *United States Clarion*, published in his home city of Troy, New York; Stephen Myers's *Northern Star and Freeman's Advocate*, which was published in Albany, New York, and had many white as well as black subscribers; Samuel Ringgold Ward's *True American*, of Cortland, New York, which in 1850 became the *Impartial Citizen;* Martin Delany's *Mystery*, published in Pittsburgh during the 1840s; and Thomas Van Rensselaer's *Ram's Horn*, which appeared in New York City during the 1850s.

However, Frederick Douglass's *North Star* and its successor *Frederick Douglass' Paper* were the most influential black antislavery newspapers of the late 1840s and the 1850s. Heavily subsidized by Gerrit Smith, a wealthy white abolitionist, and attracting more white than black subscribers, Douglass's weeklies were supported by many black abolitionist organizations. The papers were extremely well edited and attractively printed. They also employed able assistant editors, including Martin R. Delany during the late 1840s, and insightful correspondents, such as William J. Wilson of Brooklyn and James McCune Smith of New York City.

MORAL SUASION

During the 1830s, the AASS adopted a reform strategy based on moral suasion—what we would call moral *persuasion* today. This was an appeal to Americans to support abolition and racial justice on the basis of their Christian consciences and concern for their immortal souls. Slaveholding, the AASS argued, was a sin and a crime that deprived African Americans of the freedom of conscience they needed to save their souls. Simultaneously it led white masters to eternal damnation through indolence, sexual exploitation of black women, and unrestrained brutality. Abolitionists also argued that slavery was an inefficient labor system that enriched a few masters but impoverished most black and white southerners and hurt the economy of the United States as a whole.

Abolitionists, however, did not restrict themselves to criticizing white southerners. They noted that northern industries thrived by manufacturing cloth from cotton produced by slave labor. The United States government protected the interests of slaveholders in the District of Columbia, in the territories, in the interstate slave trade, and through the Fugitive Slave Act of 1793. Therefore, northerners who profited from slave labor and supported the national government with their votes and taxes bore their share of guilt for slavery and faced divine punishment.

The AASS sought to use these arguments to convince masters to free their slaves and to persuade northerners and nonslaveholding white southerners to put moral pressure on slaveholders. To reach a southern audience, the AASS in 1835 launched the Great Postal Campaign, designed to send antislavery literature to southern post offices and individual slaveholders. At about the same time, the AASS organized a massive petitioning campaign aimed to introduce the slavery issue into Congress. Antislavery women led in circulating and signing the petitions. In 1836 over 30,000 of these petitions reached Washington.

In the North, AASS agents gave public lectures against slavery and distributed antislavery literature. Often a pair of agents—one black and one white—traveled together on speaking tours. Ideally, the black agent would be a former slave, so that he could attack the brutality and immorality of slavery from personal experience. During the early 1840s, the AASS paired

ART AND CULTURE GALLERY I

Continuities between the culture of West Africa and the emerging culture of African Americans appear clearly in this eighteenth-century painting of slaves on a South Carolina plantation. The religious dance, the instruments (including drums and a banjo), and elements of the participants' clothing are all West African in origin.

Together these two woodcarvings testify to the persistence of African artistic traditions in America. The form of the work on the left, produced about 1850 by a black man living in Fayetteville, New York, closely resembles that of Yoruba ceremonial offering bowls, an example of which appears on the right.

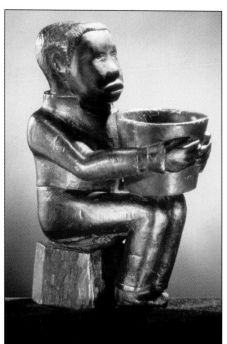

For at least 500 years, West Africans from Senegal to Sierra Leone and their descendants to this day in the Carolina low country have created baskets of countless sizes and shapes, from simple to intricate.

African Americans in South Carolina and Georgia created many ceramic face jugs like these during the period from the 1850s through the 1870s. They are similar in style to wood carvings produced by artisans living in the Kingdom of Kongo. The glazing on the jugs is distinctively African American.

Thomas Gross, "Chest-on-Chest" 1805–1810, mahogany, poplar, pine. 82 × 43⅜ × 22⅛ inches. Philadelphia Museum of Art: Gift of Mrs. Leslie Legum. 1983-167-1a,b.

This elegant chest-on-chest bears the signature of Thomas Gross Jr., a black Philadelphia cabinetmaker active between 1805 and 1839.

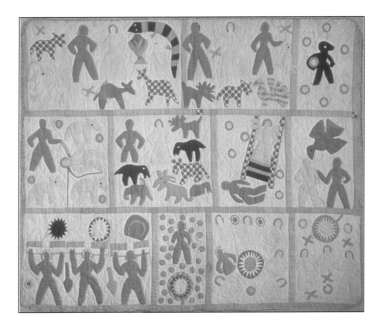

Harriet Powers was born a slave in 1837. Although she never learned to read or write, she expressed herself eloquently in her quilts. The eleven panels in this Bible Quilt, finished in 1886, illustrate stories from the Old and New Testaments that Powers absorbed from church sermons. Included are Adam and Eve, Cain and Abel, Jacob, the Birth of Christ, Betrayal of Judas, the Last Supper, and the Crucifixion.

Although early in his career black artist Robert Scott Duncanson (1821–1872) painted portraits of abolitionists, he gained fame for his landscapes. The placid scene in this 1851 painting, *Blue Hole, Flood Waters, Little Miami River,* would have been familiar to fugitive slaves escaping into Ohio from Kentucky.

Julien Hudson of New Orleans painted this self-portrait in 1839. Hudson shows himself to be of mixed racial ancestry and a well-to-do member of New Orleans's well-established free black community.

Edward Mitchell Bannister (1828–1901) began painting portraits in Boston during the 1850s and later established himself as a landscape painter in Providence, Rhode Island. This portrait of his wife, Christiana Carteaux Bannister, hangs in the Bannister Nursing Care Center in Providence, which she established in 1890.

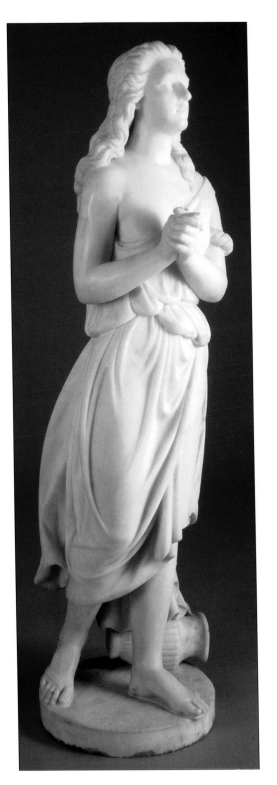

Henry Ossawa Tanner, the son of a bishop of the AME church, was raised in Philadelphia and studied there with the artist Thomas Eakins. In *The Banjo Lesson* (1893), one of his best known paintings, as well as other paintings of African-American subjects, he sought to counter the prevalent racism of his times with evocations of the humanity, decency, and quiet dignity of black people and the bonds that linked older to younger generations.

Edmonia Lewis, the daughter of a Chippewa mother and an African-American father, was a leading black sculptor of the late nineteenth century. She attended Oberlin College, began her career as an artist in Boston, and spent many years studying and working in Italy. She produced this sculpture, *Hagar in the Wilderness,* in Rome in 1869. Hagar was the Egyptian servant of the biblical patriarch Abraham, whom he expelled with their son after the birth of Isaac. Many nineteenth-century American artists saw her as a symbol of slavery.

fugitive slave Frederick Douglass with William A. White, a young white Harvard graduate, in a tour through Ohio and Indiana. In 1843 the Eastern New York Anti-Slavery Society paired white Baptist preacher Abel Brown with "the noble colored man," Lewis Washington. At first, all the agents were male. Later, the abolitionist organizations also employed female agents.

The reaction to these efforts in both the North and the South was not what the leaders of the AASS anticipated. As the story in the Voices box relates, by speaking of racial justice and exemplifying interracial cooperation, the abolitionists were treading new ground. In doing so, they created awkward situations that are—in retrospect—humorous. But their audiences often reacted violently. Southern postmasters burned antislavery literature when it arrived at their offices, and southern states censored the mail. Vigilantes drove off white southerners who openly advocated abolition. Black abolitionists, of course, did not even attempt openly to denounce slavery while in the South.

In Congress, southern representatives and their northern allies passed the Gag Rule in 1836. It required that no petition related to slavery could be introduced in the House of Representatives. In response the AASS sent 415,000 petitions in 1838 and Congressman John Quincy Adams, a former president, launched his long struggle against the Gag. Technically not an abolitionist but a defender of the First Amendment rights of white northerners to petition Congress, Adams succeeded in having the Gag Rule repealed in 1844.

Meanwhile in the North, mobs attacked abolitionist agents, disrupted their meetings, destroyed their newspaper presses, and burned black neighborhoods. In 1836 a proslavery mob killed Elijah P. Lovejoy, a white abolitionist newspaper editor, when he tried to defend his printing office at Alton, Illinois. On another occasion Douglass, White, and an older white abolitionist named George Bradburn were conducting antislavery meetings in the small town of Pendleton, Indiana, when an enraged mob attempted to kill Douglass. They shouted, "Kill the nigger, kill the damn nigger." Douglass's hand was broken by a club. White was hit in the head by a rock. Finally they escaped on foot. Years later, Douglass told White, "I shall never forget how like very brothers we were ready to dare, do, and even

VOICES

FREDERICK DOUGLASS DESCRIBES AN AWKWARD SITUATION

Frederick Douglass wrote this passage during the mid-1850s. It is from My Bondage and My Freedom, *the second of his three autobiographies. It relates with humor not only the racial barriers that black and white abolitionists had to break but the primitive conditions they took for granted.*

In the summer of 1843, I was traveling and lecturing in company with William A. White, Esq., through the state of Indiana. Anti-slavery friends were not very abundant in Indiana . . . and beds were not more plentiful than friends. . . . At the close of one of our meetings, we were invited home with a kindly-disposed old farmer, who, in the generous enthusiasm of the moment, seemed to have forgotten that he had but one spare bed, and that his guests were an ill-matched pair. . . . White is remarkably fine looking, and very evidently a born gentleman; the idea of putting us in the same bed was hardly to be tolerated; and yet there we were, and but the one bed for us, and that, by the way, was in the same room occupied by the other members of the family. . . . After witnessing the confusion as long as I liked, I relieved the kindly-disposed family by playfully saying, "Friend White, having got entirely rid of my prejudice against color, I think, as proof of it, I must allow you to sleep with me to-night." White kept up the joke, by seeming to esteem himself the favored party, and thus the difficulty was removed.

QUESTIONS

1. What does this passage reveal about American life during the 1840s?

2. What does Douglass reveal about his own character?

Source: Michael Meyer, ed., *Frederick Douglass: The Narrative and Selected Writings* (New York: Modern Library, 1984), 170–71.

die for each other. . . . How I looked running you can best describe but how you looked bleeding I shall always remember."

THE AMERICAN AND FOREIGN ANTI-SLAVERY SOCIETY AND THE LIBERTY PARTY

In 1840, the AASS splintered. Most of its members left to establish the American and Foreign Anti-Slavery Society (AFASS) and the Liberty party, the first antislavery political party. On the surface, the AASS broke apart over long-standing disagreements about the role of women in abolitionism and William Lloyd Garrison's broadening radicalism. By denouncing most organized religion, by becoming a feminist, and by embracing a form of Christian anarchy that precluded formal involvement in politics, Garrison seemed to many to be losing sight of the AASS's main concern. But the failure of moral suasion to make progress against slavery—particularly in the South—and the question of how abolitionists should respond to the increasing signs of slave unrest also helped fracture the AASS.

Garrison and a minority of abolitionists, who agreed with his radical critique of American society and were centered in New England, retained control of what became known as the "Old Organization." By 1842 they had deemphasized moral suasion and had begun calling for disunion—the separation of the North from the South—as the only means of ending northern support for slavery. The United States Constitution, Garrison declared, was a thoroughly proslavery document that had to be destroyed before African Americans could gain their freedom.

Those who withdrew from the AASS took a more traditional stand on the role of women, believed that the country's churches could be converted to abolitionism, and asserted that the Constitution could be used in behalf of abolitionism. Under the leadership of Lewis Tappan, a wealthy white New York City abolitionist, some of them formed the church-oriented AFASS. Others created the Liberty party and nominated James G. Birney, a slaveholder-turned-abolitionist, as their candidate in the 1840 presidential election. Birney received only 7,069 votes out of a total cast of 2,411,187, and William Henry Harrison, the Whig candidate, became president. But the Liberty party constituted the beginning of an increasingly powerful political crusade against slavery.

Black abolitionists joined in the disruption of the AASS. Only in New England did most black abolitionists remain loyal to the AASS. Frederick Douglass, William Wells Brown, Robert Purvis, Charles L. Remond, Susan Paul, and Sarah Douglass were notable Garrison loyalists. As might have been expected, most black clerical abolitionists joined the AFASS. Eight, including Jehiel C. Beman and his son Amos G. Beman, Christopher Rush, Samuel E. Cornish, Theodore S. Wright, Stephen H. Gloucester, Henry Highland Garnet, and Andrew Harris, were among the new organization's founders. After 1840 African Americans were always more prominent as leaders in the AFASS than the AASS.

The Liberty party also attracted black support, although few black men could vote. Particularly appealing to black abolitionists was the platform of the radical New York wing of the party led by Gerrit Smith. Philip Bell, Charles B. Ray, Samuel E. Cornish, Henry Highland Garnet, and Jermain Wesley Loguen endorsed the New York Liberty party because, of all the antislavery organizations, it advocated the most aggressive action against slavery in the South and was most directly involved in helping slaves escape.

A MORE AGGRESSIVE ABOLITIONISM

The New York Liberty party maintained that the United States Constitution, interpreted in the light of the Bible and natural law, outlawed slavery throughout the country—not only in the District of Columbia and in the territories, which were governed by the federal government, but in the states as well. This, the party's leaders asserted, meant that Congress could abolish slavery in the southern states. More practically it meant that for slaves to escape and for others to help them escape were perfectly legal actions. Some argued that neither northern state militia nor the United States Army should help suppress slave revolts.

This body of thought, which dated to the late 1830s, supported growing northern abolitionist empathy with the slaves as they struggled for freedom against their masters. During the period that the AASS was disintegrating, escapes and minor rebellions had proliferated in the border slave states of Maryland, Virginia, Kentucky, and Missouri as enslaved black people reacted to worsening conditions. Throughout this region black families were being torn apart by the domestic slave trade, which was funneling black workers into the newly opened cotton producing areas of the Southwest. In response, the radical wing of the Liberty party cited the Constitution in support of slave resistance to this brutal traffic. It also encouraged black and white northerners to go south to help slaves escape.

The *Amistad* and the *Creole*

Two maritime slave revolts were crucial in encouraging rising militancy among northern abolitionists. The first of these revolts, however, did not involve enslaved Americans. In June 1839 fifty-four African captives aboard the Spanish schooner *Amistad*—meaning "friendship"—successfully rebelled under the leadership of Joseph Cinque and attempted to sail to Africa. When a United States warship recaptured the *Amistad* off the coast of Long Island, New York, the Africans attracted the support of Lewis Tappan and other abolitionists. As a result of the abolitionists' efforts, the United States Supreme Court ruled in November 1841 that Cinque and the others were free.

Later that same month, Madison Washington led a revolt aboard the brig *Creole*, which was transporting 135 American slaves from Richmond, Virginia, to the slave markets of New Orleans. Washington had earlier escaped to Canada from slavery in Virginia. He was captured, reenslaved, and shipped aboard the *Creole* when he returned to rescue his wife. Once at sea, Washington and about a dozen other black men seized control of the vessel and sailed it to the British Bahamas. There local black fishermen surrounded the *Creole* with their boats to protect it and most of the people on board immediately gained their freedom under British law. A few days later so did Washington and the other rebels. Although Washington soon vanished, the *Creole* revolt made him a hero among abolitionists and a symbol of black bravery.

Cinque and Washington inspired others to risk their lives and freedom to help African Americans escape bondage. The New York Liberty party reinforced this commitment by maintaining that what they did was both divinely ordained and strictly legal.

The Underground Railroad

The famous underground railroad must be placed within the context of increasing southern white violence against black families, slave resistance, and aggressive northern abolitionism. Because the underground railroad had to be secret, few details of how it operated are known. We do not even know the origin of the term *underground railroad*. Slaves had always escaped from their masters, and free black people and some white people had always assisted them. But the organized escape of slaves from the Chesapeake, Kentucky, and Missouri along prede-

termined routes to Canada almost surely began during the early 1840s, and even then most slaves escaped on their own. There never was a united national underground railroad with a president or unified command. Instead there were different organizations separated in both time and space from one another (Map 9–3).

More information exists concerning the underground railroad in the East than elsewhere. Charles T. Torrey, a white Liberty party abolitionist from Massachusetts, and Thomas Smallwood, a free black resident of Washington, D.C., organized it in 1842. Between March and November of that year, they sent at least 150 enslaved men, women, and children north from Washington to Philadelphia. From there a local black vigilance committee provided the fugitives with transportation to Albany, New York, where a local, predominantly white, vigilance group smuggled them to Canada.

The escapees, however, were by no means passive "passengers" in the underground railroad network. They raised money to pay for their transportation northward, recruited and helped other escapees, and sometimes became underground railroad agents themselves. For example, during the mid-1850s, Arrah Weems of Rockville, Maryland, whose freedom black and white abolitionists had recently purchased and whose daughter Ann Maria had been rescued by underground railroad agents, became an agent herself. She brought an enslaved infant from Washington, D.C., through Philadelphia to Rochester, New York, where she met Frederick Douglass.

This was not an easy journey, and the underground railroad was always a risky business. In 1843 Smallwood had to flee to Canada as Washington police closed in on his home. In 1846 Torrey died of tuberculosis in a Maryland prison while serving a six-year sentence for helping slaves escape. Nevertheless, the underground railroad continued in the Chesapeake until the Civil War.

By the early 1850s, Harriet Tubman, a fugitive slave herself, had become the most active worker in the underground railroad. She was born in 1820 on a Maryland plantation. Her master abused her, but she did not escape until he threatened to sell her and her family south. What made Tubman extraordinary was that after her escape in 1849 she returned at least fifteen times to Maryland to help others flee. She had the help of Thomas Garrett, a white Quaker abolitionist who lived in Wilmington, Delaware, and William Still, the black leader of the Philadelphia Vigilance Association. Still, who as a child had been a fugitive slave himself, for years coordinated the work of many black and white underground agents between Washington and Canada.

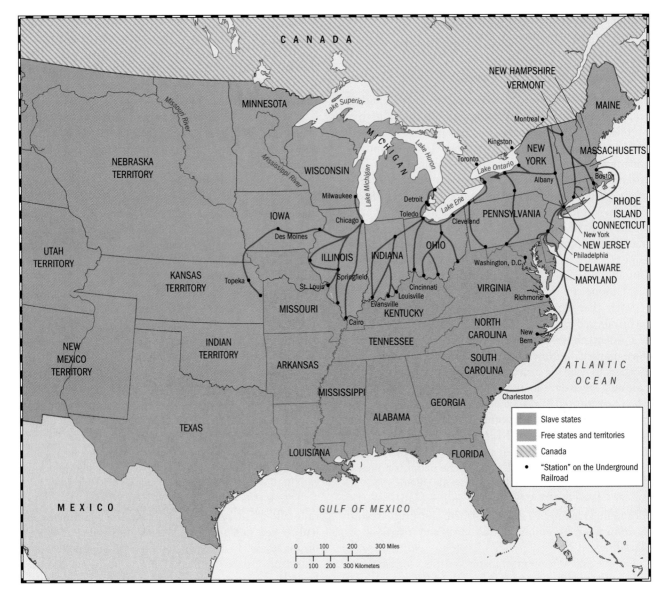

Map 9-3 The Underground Railroad. This map illustrates *approximate* routes traveled by escaping slaves through the North to Canada. Although some slaves escaped from the deep South, most who utilized the underground railroad network came from the border slave states.

Canada West

The ultimate destination for many African Americans on the underground railroad was Canada West—present-day Ontario—between Buffalo and Detroit on the northern shore of Lake Erie. Black Americans had begun to settle in Canada West as early as the 1820s and, because slavery was illegal in the British Empire after 1833, fugitive slaves were safe there. The stronger fugitive slave law that Congress passed as part of the Compromise of 1850 (see Chapter 10) made Canada an even more important refuge for African Americans. Between 1851 and 1860, the number of black Americans in Canada rose from approximately eight thousand to about sixty thousand.

There were several communal black settlements in Canada West, including the Refuge Home Society, the Buxton Community at Elgin, and the Dawn Settlement. But most black immigrants lived and worked in Toronto and Chatham. Most of them found work as craftsmen and laborers, although a few became entrepreneurs or professionals.

THE ANTISLAVERY STRUGGLE INTENSIFIES

June 1839	Joseph Cinque leads a successful revolt of enslaved Africans aboard the Spanish schooner *Amistad*.
April 1840	The Liberty party nominates James G. Birney for United States president.
November 1841	Madison Washington leads a successful revolt of American slaves aboard the *Creole*.
March 1842	Charles T. Torrey and Thomas Smallwood organize an underground railroad network to help slaves escape from Washington, D.C., and its vicinity.
August 1843	Henry Highland Garnet in Buffalo, New York, delivers his "Address to the Slaves."
December 1843	Smallwood flees to Canada to avoid arrest.
June 1844	Torrey is arrested in Baltimore on multiple charges of having helped slaves escape.
May 1846	Torrey dies in the Maryland penitentiary.

The chief advocate of black migration to Canada West—and the only advocate of migration who also supported racial integration—was Mary Ann Shadd. Shadd edited the *Provincial Freeman*, an abolitionist paper in Toronto, between 1854 and 1858 and lectured in northern cities promoting emigration to Canada. Yet, while African Americans enjoyed security in Canada, by the 1850s they also faced the same sort of segregation and discrimination there that existed in the northern United States.

BLACK MILITANCY

During the 1840s growing numbers of black abolitionists were willing to consider forceful action against slavery. This resolve accompanied a trend among black abolitionists to create their own antislavery organizations. The black convention movement revived during the 1840s and there were well attended meetings in Buffalo in 1843, in Troy, New York, in 1844, and in Cleveland in 1848. More newspapers owned and edited by black abolitionists appeared.

The rise in black militancy had several causes. The break-up of the AASS had weakened abolitionist loyalty to the national antislavery organizations. All abolitionists, black and white, were exploring new types of antislavery action. Many black abolitionists had become convinced that most white abolitionists enjoyed debate and theory more than action against slavery.

Influenced by the examples of Cinque, Madison Washington, and other rebellious slaves, many black abolitionists in the 1840s and 1850s wanted to do more to encourage slaves to resist and escape. This militancy inspired Garnet's "Address to the Slaves." A willingness to act rather than just talk helped make the Liberty party—especially its radical New York wing—attractive to African Americans. However, black abolitionists like white abolitionists approached violence and slave rebellion with caution. As late as 1857, Garnet and Frederick Douglass described slave revolt as "inexpedient."

The black abolitionist desire to go beyond rhetoric found its best outlet in the local vigilance organizations. The most famous of these is William Still's Philadelphia Vigilance Association, which was active during the late 1840s and 1850s. But such associations were first organized during the late 1830s and often had white as well

Harriet Tubman, standing at the left, is shown in this undated photograph with a group of people she helped escape from slavery. Because she worked in secret during the 1850s, she was known only to others engaged in the underground railroad, the people she helped, and a few other abolitionists.

as black members. As the 1840s progressed, African Americans formed more such associations and began to lead those that already existed. In this they were reacting to another facet of the growing violence in the United States—the use of force by "slavecatchers" in northern cities to recapture fugitive slaves.

Another aspect of black militancy during the 1840s was a willingness to charge publicly that white abolitionists were not living up to their own advocacy of racial justice. Economic slights rankled African Americans the most. At the annual meeting of the AFASS in 1852, a black delegate demanded to know why Lewis Tappan did not employ a black clerk in his business. In 1855 Samuel Ringgold Ward denounced Garrison and his associates for failing to have an African American "as clerk in an anti-slavery office, or editor, or lecturer to the same extent . . . as white men of the same calibre." These charges reflected factional struggles between the AASS and the AFASS. But they also represented real grievances among black abolitionists and real inconsistencies among their white counterparts.

FREDERICK DOUGLASS

The career of Frederick Douglass illustrates the impact of the failure of white abolitionists to live up to their egalitarian ideals. Douglass was born a slave in Maryland in 1818. Intelligent, ambitious, and charming, he resisted brutalization, learned to read, and acquired a trade before escaping to New England in 1838. By 1841 he had, with Garrison's encouragement, become an antislavery lecturer, which led to the travels with William White discussed earlier.

But as time passed, Douglass, who had remained loyal to Garrison during the 1840s when most other black abolitionists had left the AASS, suspected that his white colleagues wanted him to continue in the role of a fugitive slave when, in fact, he was becoming one of the premier American orators of his time. "People won't believe you ever was a slave, Frederick, if you keep on this way," a white colleague advised him.

Finally, Douglass decided that he had to free himself from the AASS. In 1847 he asserted his independence by leaving Massachusetts for Rochester, New York, where he began publishing the *North Star*. This decision angered Garrison and his associates, but permitted Douglass to chart his own course as a black leader. While Douglass continued to work closely with white abolitionists, especially Gerrit Smith, he could now do it on his own terms and could be more active in the black convention movement, which he now considered

Engraved by J.C.Buttre

Frederick Douglass

This engraving of Frederick Douglass was published in 1854. Douglass escaped from slavery in 1838. By the mid-1840s he had emerged as one of the more powerful speakers of his time. He began publishing his influential newspaper, the *North Star,* in 1847.

essential to winning abolition and racial justice. In 1851 he completed his break with the AASS by endorsing the constitutional arguments and tactics of the New York Liberty party as better designed to achieve emancipation than Garrison's disunionism.

BLACK NATIONALISM

Douglass always believed that black people were part of a larger American nation and that their best prospects for political and economic success lay in the United States. He was, despite his differences with some white abolitionists, an ardent integrationist. He opposed separate black churches and predicted that African Americans would eventually disappear into a greater American identity. Most black abolitionists did not go that far, but they agreed that racial oppression in all its forms could be defeated in the United States.

During the 1840s and 1850s, however, an influential minority of black leaders disagreed with this point of view. Prominent among them were Garnet and Douglass's sometime colleague on the *North Star*

VOICES

MARTIN R. DELANY DESCRIBES HIS VISION OF A BLACK NATION

The following excerpt comes from the appendix of Martin R. Delany's The Condition, Elevation, Emigration and Destiny of the Colored People of the United States, Politically Considered, *which he published in 1852. It embodies Delany's black nationalist vision.*

Every people should be the originators of their own designs, the projectors of their own schemes, and creators of the events that lead to their destiny—the consummation of their desires.

Situated as we are in the United States, many, and almost insurmountable obstacles present themselves. We are four-and-a-half millions in numbers, free and bond; six hundred thousand free, and three-and-a-half millions bond.

We have native hearts and virtues, just as other nations; which in their pristine purity are noble, potent, and worthy of example. We are a nation within a nation. . . .

But we have been, by our oppressors, despoiled of our purity, and corrupted in our native characteristics, so that we have inherited their vices, and but few of their virtues, leaving us in character, really a *broken people.*

Being distinguished by complexion, we are still singled out—although having merged in the habits and customs of our oppressors—as a distinct nation of people. . . . The claims of no people, according to established policy and usage, are respected by any nation, until they are presented in a national capacity.

To accomplish so great and desirable an end, there should be held, a great representative gathering of the colored people of the United States; not what is termed a National Convention, representing en masse, such as have been, for the last few years, held at various times and places; but a true representation of the intelligence and wisdom of the colored freemen. . . . A Confidential Council. . . .

By this Council to be appointed, a Board of Commissioners . . . to go on an expedition to the EASTERN COAST OF AFRICA, to make researches for a suitable location on that section of the coast, for the settlement of colored adventurers from the United States, and elsewhere.

The whole continent is rich in minerals, and the most precious metals, as but a superficial notice of the topographical and geological reports from that country, plainly show. . . . The land is ours—there it lies with inexhaustible resources; let us go and possess it. In Eastern Africa must rise up a nation, to whom all the world must pay commercial tribute.

QUESTIONS

1. What elements of black nationalism appear in this document?

2. How does Delany perceive Africa?

Source: Herbert Aptheker, ed., *A Documentary History of the Negro People in the United States,* 5th ed. (New York: Citadel, 1968), 1:327–28.

Martin R. Delany. Although they differed between themselves over important details, Delany and Garnet both endorsed African-American migration and nationalism as the best means to realize black aspirations.

Since the post-revolutionary days of Prince Hall, some black leaders had believed that African Americans could thrive only as a separate nation. They suggested sites in Africa, Latin America, and the American West as possible places to pursue this goal. But it took the rising tide of racism and violence emphasized in this chapter to induce a respectable minority of black abolitionists to consider migration. Almost all of them

staunchly opposed the African migration scheme of the ACS, which they continued to characterize as proslavery and racist. Nevertheless, Garnet conceded in 1849 that he would "rather see a man free in Liberia [the ACS colony], than a slave in the United States."

Douglass and most black abolitionists rejected this outlook, insisting that the aim must be freedom in the United States. Nevertheless, emigration plans developed by Garnet and Delany during the 1850s were a significant part of African-American reform culture. Delany, a physician and novelist, was born free in western Virginia in 1812. He grew up in Pennsylvania and

TIMELINE

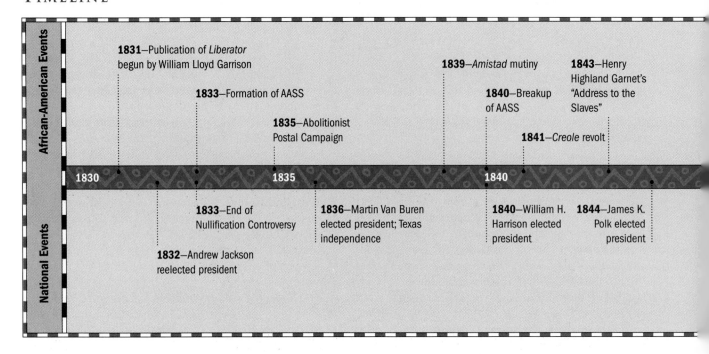

African-American Events

1831—Publication of *Liberator* begun by William Lloyd Garrison

1833—Formation of AASS

1835—Abolitionist Postal Campaign

1839—*Amistad* mutiny

1840—Breakup of AASS

1841—*Creole* revolt

1843—Henry Highland Garnet's "Address to the Slaves"

1830   1835   1840

National Events

1832—Andrew Jackson reelected president

1833—End of Nullification Controversy

1836—Martin Van Buren elected president; Texas independence

1840—William H. Harrison elected president

1844—James K. Polk elected president

by the late 1840s was a champion of black self-reliance. To further this cause, he promoted mass black migration to Latin America or Africa. "We must MAKE an ISSUE, CREATE an EVENT, and ESTABLISH a NATIONAL POSITION for OURSELVES," he declared in 1852.

In contrast, Garnet welcomed white assistance for his plan to foster Christianity and economic development in Africa by encouraging *some*—not all—African Americans to migrate there under the patronage of his African Civilization Society. In 1858 he wrote, "Let those who wished to stay, stay here—and those who had enterprise and wished to go, go and found a nation, if possible, of which the colored Americans could be proud."

Little came of these nationalist visions, largely because of the successes of the antislavery movement. Black and white abolitionists, though not perfect allies, awoke many in the North to the brutalities of slavery. They helped convince most white northerners that the slave labor system and slaveholder control of the national government threatened their economic and political interests. At the same time, abolitionist aid to escaping slaves and their defense of fugitive slaves from recapture pushed southern leaders to adopt policies that led to secession and the Civil War. The northern vic-

tory in the war, general emancipation, and constitutional protection for black rights made most African Americans—for a time—optimistic about their future in the United States.

CONCLUSION

In this chapter we have focused on the radical movement for the immediate abolition of slavery. The movement flourished in the United States from 1831, when William Lloyd Garrison began publishing the *Liberator*, through the Civil War. Garrison hoped that slavery could be abolished peacefully. But during the 1840s abolitionists had to adjust their antislavery tactics to deal with increasing racism and antiblack violence, both of which were related to the existence of slavery. Many black and white abolitionists concluded that the tactic of moral suasion, which they had emphasized during the 1830s, would not by itself achieve their goals or prevent violence against free and enslaved black people. Slave resistance also inspired a more confrontational brand of abolitionism.

Most black abolitionists came to believe that a combination of moral suasion, political involvement, and direct action against slavery was required to end

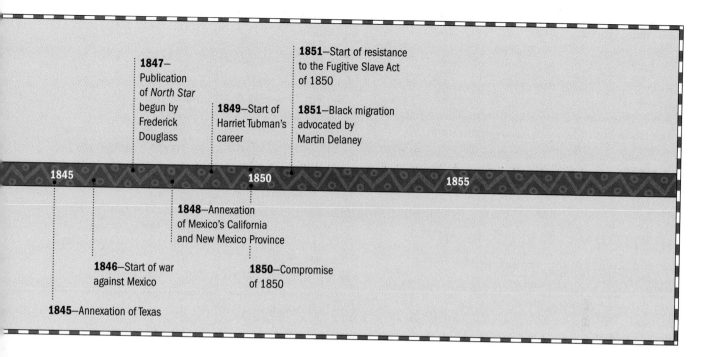

1847— Publication of *North Star* begun by Frederick Douglass

1849—Start of Harriet Tubman's career

1851—Start of resistance to the Fugitive Slave Act of 1850

1851—Black migration advocated by Martin Delaney

1845   1850   1855

1848—Annexation of Mexico's California and New Mexico Province

1846—Start of war against Mexico

1850—Compromise of 1850

1845—Annexation of Texas

slavery and improve the lives of African Americans in the United States. By the late 1840s, however, a minority of black abolitionists contended that they had to establish an independent nation beyond the borders of the United States to promote their rights, interests, and identity.

Although much has changed since the abolitionist era, these two perspectives remain characteristic of the African-American community today. Most African Americans prefer integration with a larger American nation. But black nationalism still has a powerful appeal. Individuals often embrace parts of both views just as Frederick Douglass embraced some black nationalism and Henry Highland Garnet some integrationism. Similarly, reformers are still debating whether peaceful persuasion is more effective than confrontation.

REVIEW QUESTIONS

1. What was the historical significance of Henry Highland Garnet's "Address to the Slaves?" How did Garnet's attitude toward slavery differ from that of William Lloyd Garrison?

2. Evaluate Frederick Douglass's career as an abolitionist. How was he consistent? How was he inconsistent?

3. Discuss the contribution of black women to the anti-slavery movement. How did participation in this movement alter their lives?

4. Compare and contrast the integrationist views of Frederick Douglass with the nationalist views of Martin Delany and Henry Highland Garnet.

5. Discuss the motives of the black abolitionists who left the AASS in 1840.

RECOMMENDED READING

Stanley Harrold. *The Abolitionists and the South, 1831–1861.* Lexington: University Press of Kentucky, 1995. Emphasizes the formative impact of slave resistance on northern abolitionism and the aggressiveness of that movement toward the South.

Jane H. Pease and William H. Pease. *They Who Would Be Free: Blacks' Search for Freedom, 1830–1861.* New York: Athenaeum, 1974. Deals with cooperation and conflict between black and white abolitionists. The book emphasizes conflict.

Benjamin Quarles. *Black Abolitionists.* New York: Oxford University Press, 1969. A classic study that emphasizes cooperation between black and white abolitionists.

Harry Reed. *Platforms for Change: The Foundations of the Northern Free Black Community, 1776–1865.* East Lansing: Michigan State University Press, 1994. Places black abolitionism and black nationalism within the context of community development.

Shirley J. Yee. *Black Women Abolitionists: A Study of Activism.* Knoxville: University of Tennessee Press, 1992. Discusses the activities of black women abolitionists in both white and black organizations.

R. J. Young. *Antebellum Black Activists: Race, Gender, Self.* New York: Garland, 1996. A sophisticated study of the motivation of black abolitionists.

Additional Bibliography

General Studies of the Antislavery Movement

Herbert Aptheker. *Abolitionism: A Revolutionary Movement.* Boston: Twayne, 1989.

Merton L. Dillon. *The Abolitionists: The Growth of a Dissenting Minority.* New York: Norton, 1974.

Lawrence J. Friedman. *Gregarious Saints: Self and Community in American Abolitionism, 1830–1870.* New York: Cambridge University Press, 1982.

James Brewer Stewart. *Holy Warriors: The Abolitionists and American Slavery.* 2d ed. New York: Hill and Wang, 1997.

The Black Community

John Brown Childs. *The Political Black Minister: A Study in Afro-American Politics and Religion.* Boston: G.K. Hall, 1980.

Leonard P. Curry. *The Free Black in Urban America, 1800–1850: The Shadow of a Dream.* Chicago: University of Chicago Press, 1981.

Martin E. Dann. *The Black Press, 1827–1890.* New York: Capricorn, 1971.

James Oliver Horton and Lois E. Horton. *In Hope of Liberty: Culture, Community, and Protest among Northern Free Blacks, 1700–1860.* New York: Oxford University Press, 1997.

David E. Swift. *Black Prophets of Justice: Activist Clergy before the Civil War.* Baton Rouge: Louisiana State University Press, 1989.

Black Abolitionists

Howard Holman Bell. *A Survey of the Negro Convention Movement, 1830–1861.* New York: Arno, 1969.

_____, ed. *Minutes of the Proceedings of the National Negro Conventions, 1830–1864.* New York: Arno, 1969.

R. J. M. Blackett. *Building an Antislavery Wall: Blacks in the Atlantic Abolitionist Movement, 1830–1860.* Baton Rouge: Louisiana State University Press, 1983.

Women

Blanch Glassman-Hersh. *Slavery of Sex: Feminist-Abolitionists in Nineteenth-Century America.* Urbana: University of Illinois Press, 1978.

Darlene Clark Hine, ed. *Black Women in American History: From Colonial Times through the Nineteenth Century.* 4 vols. New York: Carlson, 1990.

Jean Fagan Yellin. *Women and Sisters: Antislavery Feminists in American Culture.* New Haven: Yale University Press, 1990.

Biography

William S. McFeely. *Frederick Douglass.* New York: Simon & Schuster, 1991.

Nell Irvin Painter. *Sojourner Truth: A Life, A Symbol.* New York: Norton, 1996.

Joel Schor. *Henry Highland Garnet: A Voice of Black Radicalism in the Nineteenth Century.* Westport, CT: Greenwood, 1977.

Dorothy Sterling. *Freedom Train: The Story of Harriet Tubman.* Garden City, NY: Doubleday, 1954.

James Brewer Stewart. *William Lloyd Garrison and the Challenge of Emancipation.* Arlington Heights, IL: Harlan Davidson, 1992.

Victor Ullman. *Martin R. Delany: The Beginnings of Black Nationalism.* Boston: Beacon, 1971.

Underground Railroad

Larry Gara. *The Liberty Line: The Legend of the Underground Railroad.* Lexington: University of Kentucky Press, 1961.

Wilbur H. Siebert. *The Underground Railroad from Slavery to Freedom.* 1898. Reprint, New York: Arno, 1968.

William Still. *The Underground Railroad.* 1871. Reprint, Chicago: Johnson Publishing, 1970.

Black Nationalism

Rodney Carlisle. *The Roots of Black Nationalism.* Port Washington, NY: Kennikat, 1975.

Floyd J. Miller. *The Search for Black Nationality: Black Emigration and Colonization, 1787–1863.* Urbana: University of Illinois Press, 1975.

CHAPTER 10

"AND BLACK PEOPLE WERE AT THE HEART OF IT": THE UNITED STATES DISUNITES OVER SLAVERY

Leaflets like this reflect the outrage many Northerners felt in response to the capture and reenslavement of African Americans that resulted from the passage of a tougher Fugitive Slave Law as part of the Compromise of 1850.

A house divided against itself cannot stand. I believe this government cannot endure permanently half slave and half free. I do not expect the Union to be dissolved; I do not expect the house to fall; but I do expect it will cease to be divided. It will become all one thing, or all the other.

—Abraham Lincoln to the Republican State Convention in Springfield, Illinois, June 17, 1858.

By the end of the 1840s in the United States, no issue was as controversial as slavery. Slavery—or more accurately its expansion—deeply divided the American people and led to the bloodiest war in American history. Try as they might from 1845 to 1860, political leaders could not solve, evade, or escape slavery and whether to allow it to expand into the nation's western territories.

Caught in this monumental dispute were the South's nearly four million enslaved men, women, and children. Their future as well as the fate of the country were at stake. More than 620,000 Americans—northern and southern, black and white—would die before a divided nation would be reunified and slavery would be abolished.

Whether slavery should be permitted in the western territories was not a new issue. As early as 1787, Congress had prohibited slavery in the Northwest territory, the area north of the Ohio River that became the states of Ohio, Indiana, Illinois, Michigan, and Wisconsin. Then in 1819 a major political controversy erupted when Missouri applied for admission to the Union as a slave state. Henry Clay's Missouri Compromise—which admitted Maine as a free state, Missouri as a slave state, and outlawed slavery north of the 36° 30′ line of latitude (see Chapter 6)—settled that controversy but only postponed for twenty-five years further conflict over the expansion of slavery.

The country's desire to acquire western lands intensified in the 1830s and 1840s. Most white Americans and many free black Americans assumed that the American people should occupy the North American continent from the Atlantic Ocean to the Pacific Ocean. It was their future, their "Manifest Destiny" (see Chapter 9). In 1846 U.S. troops fought an eighteen-month conflict that resulted in the acquisition of more than half of Mexico and a major step toward the fulfillment of Manifest Destiny.

FREE LABOR VERSUS SLAVE LABOR

But westward expansion revived the issue of slavery's future in the territories. Should slavery be legal in western lands or should it be outlawed? Most white Americans held thoroughly ingrained racist beliefs that people of African descent were not and could never be their intellectual, political, or social equals. Yet those same white Americans disagreed vehemently on where those unfree African-Americans should be permitted to labor and reside.

Most northern white people adamantly opposed allowing southern slaveholders to take their slaves into the former Mexican territories. Most white Northerners detested the prospect of slavery spreading westward and limiting their opportunities to settle and farm those lands. Except for the increasing number of militant abolitionists, white Northerners detested both slavery as a labor system and the black people who were enslaved.

By the mid-nineteenth century, northern black and white people embraced the system of free labor—that is, free men and women working to earn a living and improve their lives. If southern slave owners managed to gain a foothold for their unfree labor on the western plains, in the Rocky Mountains, or on the Pacific coast, then the future for free white laborers would be severely restricted, if not destroyed.

The Wilmot Proviso

In 1846 during the Mexican War, a Democratic congressman from Pennsylvania, David Wilmot, introduced a measure in Congress to prohibit slavery in any lands acquired from Mexico. Wilmot later explained that he wanted neither slavery nor black people to taint territory that should be reserved exclusively for whites: "The negro race already occupy enough of this fair continent. . . . I would preserve for free white labor a fair country . . . where the sons of toil, of my own race and own color, can live without the disgrace which association with negro slavery brings upon free labor."

Wilmot's Proviso failed to become law, but white Southerners, who saw the measure as a blatant attempt to prevent them from moving west and enjoying the prosperity and way of life that an expanding slave labor system would create, were enraged. They considered any attempt to limit the growth of slavery to be the first step toward eliminating it. And the possibility that slavery might be abolished, as remote as that may have seemed in the 1840s, was too awful for them to contemplate.

White Southerners had convinced themselves that black people were a childlike and irresponsible race wholly incapable of surviving as a free people if they were emancipated and compelled to compete with white Americans. Most white people believed that the black race would decline and disappear if it were freed. Thus southern white people considered slavery "a positive good"—in the words of Senator John C. Calhoun of South Carolina—that benefited both races and resulted in a society vastly superior to that of the North.

To prevent slavery's expansion, the Free Soil party was formed in 1848. It was composed mainly of white people who vigorously opposed slavery's expansion and the supposed desecration that the presence of black men and women might bring to the new western lands. But some black and white abolitionists also supported the Free Soilers as a way to oppose slavery. They reasoned that even though many Free Soil supporters were hostile to black people, the party still represented a serious challenge to slavery and its expansion. Frederick Douglass felt comfortable enough with the Free Soil party to attend its convention in 1848. The Free Soil candidate for president that year was the former Democratic president Martin Van Buren. He came in a distant third behind the Whig victor and hero of the Mexican War, Zachary Taylor, who won, and the Democrat Lewis Cass. Nevertheless, ten Free Soil congressmen were elected, and the party provided a growing forum to oppose slavery's advance.

California and the Compromise of 1850

The discovery of gold in California in 1848 sent thousands of Americans hurrying west in search of wealth in 1849. The "Forty-Niners" were almost exclusively male and mostly white Americans, but they included some black Americans, Mexicans, and Europeans. By 1850 California's population had soared to more than

Though white miners resented their presence, black men too sought riches in California in the great gold rush of 1849.

100,000, and its new residents applied for admission to the Union as a free state. Southern whites were aghast at the prospect of California prohibiting slavery, and they refused to consider its admission unless slavery was lawful there. Most Northerners would not accept this.

Into the dispute stepped Whig senator Henry Clay, the same leader who had fashioned the Missouri Compromise thirty years earlier. In 1850 the aging Clay put together an elaborate compromise designed not only to settle the controversy over California but also to resolve the issue of slavery's expansion once and for all. Clay attempted to satisfy both sides. To placate Northerners, he proposed admitting California as a free state and eliminating the slave trade (but not slavery) in the District of Columbia. To satisfy white Southerners, he offered a stronger fugitive slave law to make it easier for slave owners to apprehend runaway slaves and return them to slavery. New Mexico and Utah would also be organized as territories with no mention of slavery (Map 10–1).

Clay's measures were hammered into a single bill and produced one of the most remarkable debates in the history of the Senate, but it did not pass. Southern opponents like John C. Calhoun could not tolerate the ad-

mission of California without slavery. Northern opponents like Senator William Seward of New York could not tolerate a tougher fugitive slave law. And President Zachary Taylor, shocking his fellow Southerners, insisted that California should be admitted as a free state and that Clay's compromise was unnecessary. Taylor promised to veto the compromise if the House and Senate passed it.

Clay's effort had failed—or so it seemed. But in the summer of 1850 Taylor died unexpectedly and was succeeded by Millard Fillmore, who was willing to accept the compromise. Senator Stephen Douglas, an ambitious Democrat from Illinois, guided Clay's compromise through Congress by breaking it into separate bills. California entered the Union as a free state, and a stronger fugitive slave law entered the federal legal code.

Fugitive Slave Laws

Those who may have hoped that the compromise would resolve the dispute over slavery forever were mistaken. The Fugitive Slave Law of 1850 created bitter resentment among black and white abolitionists and made slavery a more emotional and personal issue for many white people who had previously considered slavery a remote southern institution.

Had runaway slaves not been an increasingly frustrating problem for slave owners—particularly those in the upper South states of Maryland, Virginia, and Kentucky—the federal fugitive slave law would not have needed to be strengthened in 1850. The U.S. Constitution and the fugitive slave law passed in 1793 would seem to have provided ample authority for slave owners to recover runaway slaves.

The Constitution in Article IV, Section 2, stipulates that "any person held in service or labor in one state" who ran away to another state "shall be delivered up on claim of the party to whom such service or labor shall be due." The fugitive slave law of 1793 permitted slave owners to recover slaves who escaped to other states. The escaped slave had no rights—no right to a trial, no right to testify, and no guarantee of habeas corpus (the legal requirement that a person be brought before a court and not imprisoned illegally).

But by the 1830s and 1840s, as hundreds if not thousands of slaves escaped to freedom by way of the underground railroad, white Southerners increasingly found the 1793 law too weak to overcome the resistance of northern communities to the return of escapees. For example, in January 1847, four Kentuckians and a local law officer attempted to capture Adam Crosswhite, his wife, and four children after the family had escaped

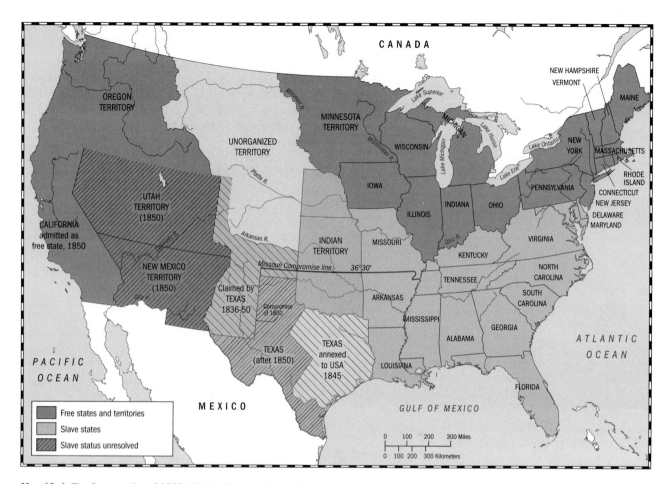

Map 10–1 The Compromise of 1850. With the Compromise, California entered the Union as a free state. The status of slavery in the New Mexico and Utah territories was left unresolved, but it was expected that they too would enter the Union as free states.

from slavery in Kentucky and settled on a farm near Marshall, Michigan. When the would-be abductors arrived, an old black man mounted a horse and galloped through town ringing a bell warning that the Crosswhites were in danger. Having been aroused by this "Black Paul Revere," about 100 people helped rescue the family and put them on a railroad train to Canada. The local citizens who had aided the Crosswhites were later sued successfully by the slave owner and fined an amount equal to the estimated value of the Crosswhites had the family been sold as slaves.

Several northern states had enacted personal liberty laws that made it illegal for state law enforcement officials to help capture runaways. (Michigan passed such a law in 1855 after the Crosswhites escaped to Canada.) Not only did many Northerners refuse to cooperate in returning fugitives to slavery under the 1793 law but they also encouraged and assisted the escaped slaves.

The local black vigilance committees that were created in many northern communities and discussed in Chapter 9—among them the League of Freedom in Boston and the Liberty Association in Chicago—were especially effective in these efforts. These actions infuriated white Southerners and prompted their demand for a stricter fugitive slave law.

The Fugitive Slave Law of 1850 was one of the toughest and harshest measures the U.S. Congress ever passed. Anyone apprehended under the law was almost certain to be sent back to slavery. The law required U.S. marshals, their deputies, and even ordinary citizens to help seize suspected runaways. Those who refused to help apprehend fugitives or who helped the runaway could be fined or imprisoned. The law made it nearly impossible for black people to prove that they were free. Slave owners and their agents only had to provide legal documentation from their home state or the testimony

V O I C E S

AFRICAN AMERICANS RESPOND TO THE FUGITIVE SLAVE LAW

These two passages reflect the outrage the Fugitive Slave Law of 1850 provoked among black Americans. In the first, John Jacobs, a fugitive slave from South Carolina, urges black people to take up arms to oppose the law. In the second, from a speech he delivered a few days after the passage of the law, Martin Delany defies authorities to search his home for runaway slaves.

My colored brethren, if you have not swords, I say to you, sell your garments and buy one. . . . They said that they cannot take us back to the South; but I say, under the present law they can; and now they say unto you; let them take only dead bodies. . . . I would, my friends, advise you to show a front to our tyrants and arm yourselves . . . and I would advise the women to have their knives too.

Source: William F. Cheek, *Black Resistance before the Civil War* (Beverly Hills: Glencoe Press, 1970), pp. 148–9.

Sir, my house is my castle; in that castle are none but my wife and my children, as free as the angels of heaven, and whose liberty is as sacred as the pillars of God. If any man approaches that house in search of a slave—I care not who he may be, whether the constable, or sheriff, magistrate or even judge of the Supreme Court—nay, let it be he who sanctioned this act to become law [President Millard Fillmore] surrounded by his cabinet as his bodyguard, with the Declaration of Independence waving above his head as his banner, and the constitution of this country upon his breast as his shield—if he crosses the threshold of my door, and I do not lay him a lifeless corpse at my feet, I hope the grave may refuse my body a resting place, and righteous Heaven my spirit a home. O, no! He cannot enter that house and we both live.

Source: Victor Ullman, *Martin R. Delany: The Beginnings of Black Nationalism* (Boston: Beacon Press, 1971), p. 112.

QUESTIONS

1. How and why did these two black men justify the use of violence against those who were enforcing a law passed by Congress?

2. Under what circumstances is it permissible to violate the law? Under what circumstances is it permissible to threaten to kill another human being?

---

of white witnesses before a federal commissioner that the captive was a runaway slave. The federal commissioners were paid $10 for captives returned to bondage, but only $5 for those declared free. Supporters of the law claimed that the extra paperwork involved in returning a fugitive to slavery necessitated the $10 fee. Opponents of the law saw the $10 as a bribe to encourage federal authorities to return men and women to bondage. During the time the law was in effect, 332 captives were returned to the South and slavery, and only eleven were released as free people.

The new fugitive slave law outraged many black and white Northerners. An angry Frederick Douglass insisted in October 1850 that "the only way to make the Fugitive Slave Law a dead letter is to make a half dozen or more dead kidnappers." White abolitionist Wendell Phillips exhorted his listeners to disobey the law. "We must trample this law under our feet."

FUGITIVE SLAVES

The fugitive slave law did more than anger black and white Northerners. It exposed them to cruel and heart-wrenching scenes as southern slave owners and slave catchers took advantage of the new law and—with the vigorous assistance of federal authorities—relentlessly pursued runaway slaves. Many white people and virtually all black people felt genuine revulsion over this crackdown on those who had fled from slavery to freedom.

In September 1850 in New York City, federal authorities captured a black porter and returned him to slavery in Baltimore, even though he insisted that because his mother was a free woman he had not been a slave. (In each of the slave states, the law stipulated that the status of the mother determined a child's legal status—free or slave.) In Poughkeepsie, New York, slave catchers captured a well-to-do black tailor

The "trial" and subsequent return of Anthony Burns to slavery resulted in the publication of a popular pamphlet in Boston. Documents like this generated increased support—and funds—for the abolitionist cause.

and returned him to slavery in South Carolina. In Indiana, a black man was apprehended while his wife and children looked on, and he was sent to Kentucky where his owner claimed he had escaped nineteen years earlier.

Not all fugitives were forced back into bondage. A Maryland slave owner attempted to recover a black woman in Philadelphia who, he asserted, had escaped twenty-two years earlier. Since then, she had had six children, and the slave owner insisted that they were also his property. In this instance, the federal commissioner ruled that the woman and her children were free.

William and Ellen Craft

Black and white abolitionists organized vigilance committees to resist the fugitive slave law and to prevent—by force if necessary—the return of fugitives to slavery. In October 1850, slave catchers arrived in Boston fully prepared to return William and Ellen Craft to slavery in Georgia. In 1848 the Crafts had devised an ingenious escape. Ellen's fair complexion enabled her to disguise herself as a sickly young white man who, accompanied by "his" slave, was traveling north for medical treatment. They journeyed to Boston by railroad and ship, and thus escaped from slavery—or so they thought.

Slave catchers vowed to return the Crafts to servitude no matter how long it took: "If [we] have to stay here to all eternity, and if there are not enough men in Massachusetts to take them, [we] will bring some from the South." While white abolitionists protected Ellen and black abolitionists hid William, the vigilance committee plastered posters around Boston describing the slave catchers, calling them "man-stealers," and threatening their safety. Within days (which must have seemed slightly less than eternity), the Southerners left without the Crafts. Soon thereafter, the Crafts sailed to security in England.

Shadrach

Black and white abolitionists were fully prepared to use force against the U.S. government and the slave owners and their agents. Sometimes the abolitionists succeeded; sometimes they did not. In early 1851 a few months after the Crafts left Boston, federal marshals apprehended a black waiter there who had escaped from slavery and given himself the name Shadrach. But a well-organized band of black men led by Lewis Hayden invaded the courthouse and escaped with Shadrach. They spirited him to safety in Canada on the underground railroad. (Shadrach later became the owner of a restaurant in Montreal.) Federal authorities brought charges against four black men and four white men who were then indicted by a grand jury for helping Shadrach. But local juries refused to convict them.

The Battle at Christiana

In September 1851, a battle erupted in the little town of Christiana, in southern Pennsylvania, when a Maryland slave owner, Edward Gorsuch, arrived to recover two runaway slaves. Accompanied by several family members and three deputy U.S. marshals, they confronted a hostile and well-armed crowd of at least twenty-five black men and several white men. Black leader William Parker bluntly told Gorsuch to give up any plans to take

THOMAS SIMS, A FUGITIVE SLAVE

By stowing away on a ship in Savannah, Georgia, in 1851, a seventeen-year-old slave named Thomas Sims escaped to Boston, where he worked as a waiter. His owner tracked him down there and had him arrested and confined in chains on the third floor of the federal courthouse in Boston. Black leader Lewis Hayden tried to free Sims, but failed. Hayden had difficulty attracting support because many of the men whom he would ordinarily have depended on had fled when authorities began to search for those who had freed Shadrach a few weeks earlier.

One plan involved piling mattresses under Sims's window and having him jump about thirty feet to freedom. It was abandoned when bars were installed in the window. Neither Sims's lawyers' attempts to win a writ of habeas corpus nor public protests succeeded in gaining his freedom.

On April 11, 1851, a federal commissioner ordered Sims returned to slavery. He was marched from the

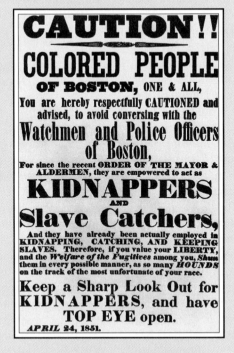

Posters went up in many Northern communities after the passage of the Fugitive Slave Law as slave catchers pursued runaways. This poster appeared after Thomas Sims was sent back to slavery from Boston in 1851.

courthouse, "protected" by three hundred armed men, and taken to a ship in the harbor. A desperate plan to free him by twenty armed men aboard another vessel failed because Sims's ship sailed for Savannah before the other ship could get under way.

Later that summer, Sims was sent to Charleston, and then to New Orleans where he was auctioned off to a brick mason from Vicksburg, Mississippi. Sims spent the next twelve years enslaved as a mason in Mississippi. In 1863, during the Civil War, when Union forces laid siege to Vicksburg, Sims again fled to freedom. He went back to Boston where he saw the return in 1865 of the all-black 54th Massachusetts Regiment from combat in South Carolina, Georgia, and Florida.

By 1877 Sims was in Washington, D.C. He obtained a job as a messenger in the Department of Justice through the intervention of U.S. Attorney General Charles Devens—the federal marshal who had arrested him in Boston in 1851.

---

the runaway slaves. Gorsuch refused, and a battle ensued. Gorsuch was killed, one of his sons was wounded, and several black and white men were hurt. The runaway slaves escaped to Canada.

Again the federal government made a determined effort to prosecute those who violated the fugitive slave law. President Fillmore sent U.S. Marines to Pennsylvania, and they helped round up the alleged perpetrators of the violence. Thirty-six black men and five white men were arrested and indicted for treason by a federal grand jury. But the government's case was weak, and after the first trial ended in acquittal, the remaining cases were dropped.

Anthony Burns

Of all the fugitive slave cases, none elicited more support or sorrow than that of Anthony Burns. In 1854 Burns escaped from slavery in Virginia by stowing away on a ship to Boston. After gaining work in a clothing store, he unwisely sent a letter to his brother who was still a slave. The letter was confiscated, and Burns's former owner set out to capture him. Burns was arrested by a deputy marshal who, recalling Shadrach's escape, placed him under guard in chains in the federal courthouse. Efforts by black and white abolitionists to break into the courthouse with axes, guns, and a battering ram failed, though a deputy U.S. marshal was killed during the assault.

President Franklin Pierce, a northern Democrat who had been elected with southern support in 1852, sent U.S. troops to Boston—including Marines, cavalry, and artillery—to uphold the law and return Burns to Virginia. The vigilance committee tried to purchase Burns's freedom, but the U.S. Attorney refused. In June 1854, with church bells tolling and buildings draped in black, thousands of Bostonians watched silently—many in tears—as Anthony Burns was marched through the streets to a ship in the harbor that would take him to Virginia.

People who had shown no particular interest in nor sympathy for fugitives or slaves were moved by the spectacle of a lone black man, escorted by hundreds of armed troops, trudging from freedom to slavery. One staunchly conservative white man remarked: "When it was all over, and I was left alone in my office, I put my face in my hands and I wept. I could do nothing less." William Lloyd Garrison burned a copy of the Constitution on the Fourth of July as thousands looked on with approval.

Yet the government was unrelenting. A federal grand jury indicted seven black men and white men for riot and inciting a riot in their attempt to free Burns. One indictment was set aside on a technicality, and the other charges were then dropped because no Boston jury would convict the accused.

Margaret Garner

If the Burns case was the most moving, then Margaret Garner's was one of the most tragic examples of the lengths to which slaves might go to gain freedom for themselves and their children. In the winter of 1856, Margaret Garner and seven other slaves escaped from Kentucky across the Ohio River to freedom in Cincinnati. But their owner, Archibald Grimes, pursued them. Grimes, accompanied by a U.S. deputy marshal and several other people, attempted to arrest the eight fugitives at a small house where they had hidden. Refusing to surrender, the slaves fought back but were finally overpowered and subdued.

Before they were captured Garner slit the throat of her daughter with a butcher knife rather than see the child returned to slavery. Before she could kill her two sons, she was disarmed. Ohio authorities charged her with murder. But by that time, she had been returned to Kentucky and then sent with her surviving three children to Arkansas to be sold. On the trip down the river, her youngest child and twenty-four other people drowned in a shipwreck, thereby cruelly fulfilling her

wish that the child not grow up to be a slave. Margaret Garner was later sold at a slave market in New Orleans. (Her story was the basis of Toni Morrison's novel *Beloved*, which won the 1988 Pulitzer Prize for fiction, and was transformed into a film by Oprah Winfrey in 1998.)

THE ROCHESTER CONVENTION, 1853

In 1853, while northern communities grappled with the consequences of the fugitive slave law, African-American leaders gathered for a national convention in Rochester, New York. The convention warned that black Americans were not prepared to submit quietly to a government more concerned about the interests of slave owners than people seeking to free themselves from bondage. The delegates looked past the grim conditions of the times to call for greater unity among black people and to find ways to improve their economic prospects. They asserted their claims to the rights of citizenship and equal protection before the law. And they worried that the wave of European immigrants entering the country would deprive poor black Northerners of the menial and unskilled jobs on which they depended. Frederick Douglass spoke of the need for a school to provide training in skilled trades and manual arts. There was even talk of establishing a Negro museum and library.

NATIVISM AND THE KNOW-NOTHINGS

The concern expressed by delegates to the Rochester convention about competition from immigrant labor echoed rising anti-immigrant feeling among many white Americans. Religious and ethnic animosities, like racism, were endemic in the 1850s. The mostly Roman Catholic Irish and German immigrants who began arriving by the thousands beginning in the 1820s alarmed native-born white Protestants. Ugly anti-Catholic propaganda raised fears that the influence of Rome and the papacy would weaken American institutions. Some even charged that there was a Catholic conspiracy to take over the United States. There were vicious attacks on Catholic churches and convents.

This nativist—or anti-immigrant—sentiment added to the political turmoil created by growing sectional differences over slavery. It even formed the ideological basis of a short-lived new political party, the

Know-Nothings, that organized in 1854 to protect traditional American values from the presumed dangers of immigration. (The name of the party derives from the reply members were supposed to give—"I know nothing"—when asked about it.) By the mid 1850s, there were more than one million Know-Nothings. Most were in New England, but the party was also strong in Kentucky, Texas, and elsewhere. It even briefly gained political control of Massachusetts. But as differences over slavery overwhelmed the bonds of ethnic bigotry that held the northern and southern branches of the party together, the Know-Nothing movement collapsed.

UNCLE TOM'S CABIN

No one contributed more to the growing opposition to slavery among white Northerners than Harriet Beecher Stowe. Raised in a deeply religious environment—her father, brothers, and husband were ministers—Stowe developed a hatred of slavery that she converted into a melodramatic but moving novel about slaves and their lives.

Uncle Tom's Cabin, or Life among the Lowly was first published in installments in the antislavery newspaper, *The National Era*. When it appeared as a book in 1852, it sold an astonishing 300,000 copies in a year. In the novel, Stowe depicted slavery's cruelty, inhumanity, and destructive impact on families through characters and a plot that appealed to the sentimentality of nineteenth-century readers. There was Little Eliza, with a babe in arms, barely escaping across the icy Ohio River from a slave owner in hot pursuit. There was Uncle Tom, the noble and devout Christian. Financial necessity forces Tom's decent master to sell the kindly slave to Simon Legree, a vicious brute and a Northerner who has embraced slavery. Legree takes perverse delight in beating Tom until the gentle old man dies.

Uncle Tom's Cabin moved Northerners to tears and made slavery more personal to readers who had previously considered it only a distant system of labor that exploited black people. In stage versions of the book that were produced across the North, Uncle Tom was transformed from a dignified man into a pitiful and fawning figure eager to please white people—hence the derogatory term "Uncle Tom."

Uncle Tom's Cabin infuriated white Southerners. They condemned it as a grossly false depiction of slavery and their way of life. They pointed out correctly that Stowe had little firsthand knowledge of slavery and had never even visited the deep South. But she had lived in Cincin-

Harriet Beecher Stowe's *Uncle Tom's Cabin* was enormously popular in the North—and despised in the South. The book generated dozens of dramatic presentations for years after its publication. The Webb family toured the North offering dramatic readings based on the novel.

nati for eighteen years and witnessed with anguish the desperate attempts of slaves to escape across the Ohio River. In response to her southern critics, Stowe wrote *A Key to Uncle Tom's Cabin*, citing the sources for her novel. Many of those sources were southern newspapers.

THE KANSAS-NEBRASKA ACT

In the wake of the Compromise of 1850, the disagreement over slavery's expansion intensified and became violent. In 1854 Stephen Douglas introduced a bill in Congress to organize the Kansas and Nebraska territories that soon provoked white settlers in Kansas to kill each other over slavery. Douglas's primary concern was to secure the Kansas and Nebraska region—which until 1853 had been part of the Indian Territory that the federal government had promised to protect from white settlement—for the construction of a transcontinental railroad. To win the support of southern Democrats, who wanted slavery in at least one of the two new territories, he included a provision in the bill permitting residents of the Kansas territory to decide for themselves whether to allow slavery (Map 10–2).

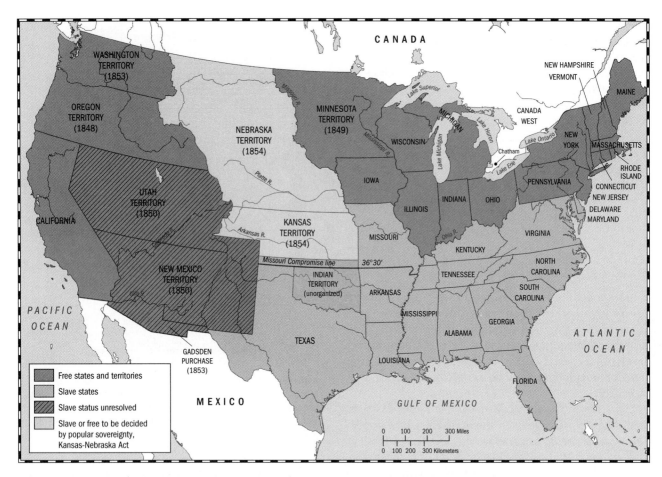

Map 10-2 The Kansas-Nebraska Act. This measure guided through Congress by Democratic Senator Steven A. Douglas opened up the Great Plains to settlement and to railroad development. It also deeply divided the nation by repealing the 1820 Missouri Compromise Line of 36° 30′ and permitting—through popular sovereignty—the people in Kansas to determine slavery's fate in that territory. Eastern Kansas became a bloody battleground between proslavery and antislavery forces.

This proposal—known as "popular sovereignty"—angered many Northerners because it created the possibility that slavery might expand to areas where it had been prohibited. The Missouri Compromise banned slavery north of the 36° 30′ N latitude. Douglas's Kansas-Nebraska Act would repeal that limitation and allow settlers in Kansas, which was north of that line, to vote on slavery there. Thus, if enough proslavery people moved to Kansas and voted for slavery, then slaves and their slave owners would be legally permitted to dwell on land that had been closed to them for more than thirty years.

Douglas managed to muster enough Democratic votes in Congress to pass the bill. But its enactment destroyed an already divided Whig party and drove a wedge between the North and South. The Whig party disintegrated. Northern Whigs joined supporters of the Free Soil party to form the Republican party, which was organized expressly to oppose the expansion of slavery. Southern Whigs drifted, often without much enthusiasm, to the Democrats.

Violence soon erupted in Kansas between proslavery and antislavery forces. "Border Ruffians" from Missouri invaded Kansas to attack antislavery settlers and vote illegally in Kansas elections. The New England Emigrant Aid Society dispatched people to the territory and the Rev. Henry Ward Beecher encouraged them to pack "Beecher's Bibles"—which were firearms and not the word of the lord. By 1856 two territorial governments existed in Kansas, and a virtual civil war—causing the press to label the territory "Bleeding Kansas"—was under way among its 8,500 settlers, including 245 slaves.

More than two hundred people died in the escalating violence. Some five hundred "Border Ruffians" attacked the antislavery town of Lawrence, damaging businesses and killing one person. Abolitionist John Brown and six of his sons sought revenge by hacking six proslavery men (none of whom actually owned slaves) to death with swords in Pottowattamie. A proslavery firing squad executed nine Free Soilers. John Brown reappeared in Missouri, killed a slave owner, and freed eleven slaves. Then he fled to begin planning an even larger and more dramatic attack on slavery.

PRESTON BROOKS ATTACKS CHARLES SUMNER

In 1856 the violence in Kansas spread to Congress. In May of that year, Massachusetts Senator Charles Sumner delivered a tirade in the Senate denouncing the proslavery settlers in Kansas and the Southerners who supported them. Speaking of "The Crime against Kansas," Sumner accused South Carolina Senator Andrew P. Butler of keeping slavery as his lover. Butler "had chosen a mistress to whom he has made his vows, and who . . . though polluted in the sight of the world, is chaste in his sight—I mean the harlot slavery." Butler was not present for the speech, but his nephew, South Carolina Congressman Preston Brooks, was in the chamber, and Brooks did not take kindly to Sumner's attack.

Two days later, Brooks exacted his revenge. Waiting until the Senate adjourned, Brooks strode to the desk where Sumner was seated and attacked him with a rattan cane. The blows rained down until the cane shattered and Sumner tumbled to the floor, bloody and semiconscious. Brooks proudly recalled: "I gave him about thirty first rate stripes." Sumner suffered lingering physical and emotional effects from the beating and did not return to the Senate for four years. Brooks resigned from the House of Representatives, paid a $300 fine, and went home to South Carolina a hero. He was easily reelected to his seat.

In the 1856 presidential election, the Democrats—though divided over the debacle in Kansas—nominated James Buchanan of Pennsylvania, another northern Democrat who was acceptable to the South. The Republicans supported a handsome military officer, John C. Fremont. Their slogan was "Free Soil, Free Speech, Free Men, and Fremont." But the Republicans were exclusively a northern party, and with the demise of the Whigs the South had become a one-party region. No white Southerner would support the Republicans, a party whose very existence was based on its opposition to slavery's expansion. Buchanan won the presidency with solid southern support and enough northern votes to

carry him to victory. But the Republicans gained enough support and confidence to give them hope for the 1860 election. Before then, however, the United States Supreme Court intervened in the controversy over slavery.

THE DRED SCOTT DECISION

Like most slaves, Dred Scott did not know his exact age. But when the U.S. Supreme Court accepted his case in 1856, Scott was in his fifties and had been entangled in the judicial system for more than a decade. Scott was born in Virginia but by the 1830s, he belonged to John Emerson, an Army doctor in Missouri. Emerson took Scott to military posts in Illinois and Fort Snelling in what is now Minnesota. While at Fort Snelling, Scott married Harriet, a slave woman, and they had a daughter Eliza before Emerson returned with the three of

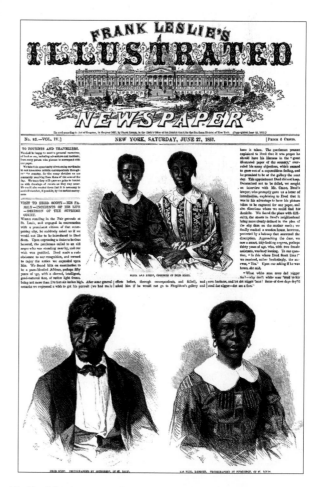

The Dred Scott case was front page news in *Frank Leslie's Illustrated Newspaper,* which featured these sympathetic portraits of Harriet and Dred Scott and their daughters. The Supreme Court decision served to intensify the crisis over slavery rather than resolving it.

them to St. Louis. (Another daughter, Lizzie, was born later.) In 1846 after Emerson's death, and with the support of white friends, Scott sued for his freedom. Scott and his lawyers contended that because Scott had been taken to territory where slavery was illegal, he had become a free man.

Scott lost his first suit, won his second, but lost again on appeal to the Missouri Supreme Court. Scott's lawyers then appealed to the U.S. Circuit Court where they lost again. The final appeal in *Dred Scott v. Sandford* was to the United States Supreme Court. Although seventy-nine-year-old Chief Justice Roger Taney of Maryland had freed his own slaves, he was an unabashed advocate of the southern way of life. Moreover, Taney, a majority of the other justices, and President Buchanan were convinced that the prestige of the Court would enable it to render a decision about slavery that might be controversial but would still be accepted as the law of the land.

Questions for the Court

Taney framed two questions for the Court to decide in the Scott case. One, could Scott—a black man—sue in a federal court? Two, was Scott free because he had been taken to a state and a territory where slavery was prohibited? In response to the first question, the Court, led by Taney, ruled that Scott—and every other black American—could not sue in a federal court because black people were not citizens. Speaking for the majority (two of the nine justices dissented) Taney emphatically stated that black people had no rights: "They had for more than a century before been regarded as beings of an inferior order; and altogether unfit to associate

with the white race, either in social or political relations; and so far inferior that they had no rights which the white man was bound to respect; and that the negro might justly and lawfully be reduced to slavery for his benefit."

Taney was wrong. Though not treated as equals, free black people in many states had enjoyed rights associated with citizenship since the ratification of the Constitution in 1788. Black men had entered into contracts, held title to property, sued in the courts, and voted at one time in five of the original thirteen states.

A majority of the Court also answered no to the second question. Scott was not a free man although he had lived in places where slavery was illegal. Scott, Taney maintained, again speaking for the Court, was slave property—and the slave owner's property rights took precedence. To the astonishment of those who opposed slavery's expansion, the Court also ruled that Congress could not pass measures—including the Missouri Compromise or the Kansas Nebraska Act—that might prevent slave owners from taking their property into any territory. To do so, Taney implied, would violate the Fifth Amendment of the Constitution, which protected people from the loss of their life, liberty, or property without due process of law.

Following the decision, a new owner freed Dred and Harriet Scott. They settled in St. Louis, where both died shortly before the Civil War.

Reaction to the Dred Scott Decision

The Court had spoken. Would the nation listen? White Southerners were delighted with Taney's decision. Republicans were horrified. But instead of earning the acceptance—let alone the approval—of most Americans, the case further inflamed the controversy over slavery. But if white Americans were divided in their reaction to the Dred Scott decision, black Americans were discouraged, disgusted, and defiant. Taney's decision delivered another setback to a people—already held in forced labor—who believed that their toil, sweat, and contributions over the previous two and a half centuries to what had become the United States gave them a legitimate role in American society. Now the Supreme Court said that they had no rights. They knew better.

At meetings and rallies across the North, black people condemned the decision. Black writer, abolitionist, and women's rights advocate Frances Ellen Watkins Harper heaped scorn on the U.S. government as "the arch traitor to liberty, as shown by the Fugitive Slave Law and the Dred Scott decision."

THE DEEPENING CRISIS OVER SLAVERY	
1846	The Wilmot Proviso
1850	The Compromise of 1850
1854	The Kansas Nebraska Act
1855–1856	Bleeding Kansas
1857	The Dred Scott Decision
1859	John Brown's Raid
1860	The Election of Lincoln as President
1860	South Carolina Secedes from the Union
1861	Formation of the Confederacy, Fort Sumter, Beginning of the Civil War

Young black leader H. Ford Douglas (no relation to Frederick Douglass) vented his rage at an American government and a constitution that could produce such a decision. "To persist," he declared,

> in supporting a government which holds and exercises the power . . . to trample a class under foot as an inferior and degraded race is on the part of the colored man at once the height of folly and the depth of pusillanimity. . . . The only duty the colored man owes to a constitution under which he is declared to be an inferior and degraded being . . . is to denounce and repudiate it, and to do what he can by all proper means to bring it into contempt.

Only Frederick Douglass could find a glimmer of hope. He believed—and events were to prove him right—that the decision was so wrong that it would help destroy slavery.

> The Supreme Court . . . [was] not the only power in the world. We, the abolitionists and the colored people, should meet this decision, unlooked for and monstrous as it appears, in a cheerful spirit. The very attempts to blot out forever the hopes of an enslaved people may be one necessary link in the chain of events preparatory to the complete overthrow of the whole slave system.

WHITE NORTHERNERS AND BLACK AMERICANS

Unquestionably, many white Northerners were genuinely concerned by the struggles of fugitive slaves, moved by *Uncle Tom's Cabin*, and disturbed by the Dred Scott decision. Yet as sensitive and sympathetic as some of them were to the plight of black people, most white Americans—including Northerners—remained decidedly indifferent to, fearful of, or bitterly hostile to people of color. By the 1850s, 200,000 black people lived in the northern states, and many white people there were not pleased with their presence. Many white Northerners—especially those living in southern Ohio, Indiana, and Illinois—supported the fugitive slave law and were eager to help return runaway slaves to bondage.

The same white Northerners who opposed the expansion of slavery to California or to Kansas also opposed the migration of free black people to northern states and communities. In 1851 Indiana and Iowa outlawed the emigration to their territory of black people, slave or free. Illinois did likewise in 1853. White male voters in Michigan in 1850 voted overwhelmingly—32,000 to 12,000—against permitting black men to vote.

Only Ohio was an exception. In 1849 it repealed legislation excluding black people from the state.

These restrictive measures were not new. Most northern states had begun to restrict or deny the rights of black Americans in the early 1800s (see Chapter 6). Although only loosely enforced, the laws reflected the prevailing racial sentiments among many white Northerners, as did the widespread antiblack rioting of the 1830s and 1840s. During the debate over excluding black people from Indiana, a state senator explained that the Bible revealed that God had condemned black people to inferiority. "The same power that has given him a black skin, with less weight or volume of brain, has given us a white skin, with greater volume of brain and intellect; and that we can never live together upon an equality is as certain as that no two antagonistic principles can exist together at the same time."

Foreign observers were struck by the depth of racism in the North. Alexis de Tocqueville, a French aristocrat, toured America in 1831 and wrote a perceptive analysis of American society. He considered Northerners more antagonistic toward black people than Southerners. "The prejudice of race appears to be stronger in the states that have abolished slavery than in those where it still exists; and nowhere is it so intolerant as in those states where servitude has never been known."

THE LINCOLN-DOUGLAS DEBATES

In 1858 Senator Stephen Douglas of Illinois, a Democrat, ran for reelection to the Senate against Republican Abraham Lincoln. The main issues in the campaign were slavery and race, which the two candidates addressed in a series of debates around the state. In carefully reasoned speeches and responses, these experienced and articulate lawyers focused almost exclusively on slavery's expansion and its future in the Union. Lincoln, a former Whig congressman, attempted to trap Douglas, the incumbent, by asking him if slavery could expand now that the Dred Scott decision had ruled that slaves were property whom their owners could take into any federal territory. In reply, Douglas, who wanted to be president and had no wish to offend either northern or southern voters, cleverly defended "popular sovereignty" and the Dred Scott decision. He insisted that slave owners could indeed take their slaves where they pleased. But, he contended, if the people of a territory failed to enact laws to protect slave property, then a slave owner was not likely to settle there.

MARTIN DELANY

"I thank God for making me a man, but Delany thanks Him for making him a *black* man."

—Frederick Douglass on Martin Delany

Martin Delany (1812–1885) was one of the first individuals to insist persistently that people of African descent in the United States should control their own destiny. In speeches, articles, and books, he evoked pride in his African heritage and stressed the need for black people to rely on themselves, and not on the white majority.

Delany was a medical doctor, a journalist, an explorer, an anthropologist, a military officer, and a political leader. He was born free in Charlestown, Virginia (now West Virginia), but the family moved to Chambersburg, Pennsylvania, in 1822. In 1831 Martin went west to Pittsburgh where he spent most of the next twenty-five years. His education was strongly influenced by Lewis Woodson, a young African Methodist Episcopal minister. He also studied medicine as an apprentice under two white physicians.

Delany was active in the Pittsburgh Anti-Slavery Society and helped slaves escape on the underground railroad. In 1843 he married Catherine Richards, the daughter of a well-to-do black butcher, and by 1860, they had had seven children, each named for a well-known black figure: Toussaint L'Ouverture, Alexander Dumas, Saint Cyprian, Faustin Soulouque, Charles L. Redmond, and their only daughter, Ethiopia Halle.

In 1843 Delany began publishing *The Mystery*, a four-page weekly newspaper devoted to abolition. It did not thrive, and in 1847 he joined Frederick Douglass briefly as the coeditor of *The North Star* (see Chapter 9). In 1850 Delany was admitted to the Harvard Medical School with two other black students for formal training, but they were forced to leave after one term because of the protests of white students.

In 1852 he wrote and published *The Condition, Elevation, Emigration and Destiny of the Colored People of the United States*—the first major statement of black nationalism. Delany observed, "We are a nation within a nation." He recommended that people of African descent abandon the United States and migrate to Cen-

Martin R. Delany played a key role in the emergence of black nationalism in the nineteenth century. An abolitionist, medical doctor, and journalist, he also was one of the few black men to be commissioned an officer in the Civil War. Here he is depicted in his uniform: he was a major. He also served with the Freedmen's Bureau during Reconstruction.

tral America, South America, or Hawaii. Delany was the key figure in organizing the National Emigration Convention in Cleveland in 1854.

He and his family left the United States for Canada and lived in Canada West (currently the Province of Ontario), where he organized a meeting of black people and John Brown in 1858. He also managed to find time to write a novel, *Blake*, the fictional account of a West Indian slave who promotes revolution in the United States and leads a black rebellion in Cuba. In 1859–1860, Delany visited Liberia and explored what is today Nigeria.

Once the United States began to enlist black troops in the Civil War, Delany helped recruit black men. His son Toussaint joined the famed 54th Massachusetts Regiment. Delany himself became one of the few black men to be commissioned an officer. Major Delany went to Charleston, South Carolina, where he helped recruit two regiments of former slaves. After the war, he remained in South Carolina, where he entered politics. But he quickly grew disillusioned with the Republicans—both black and white—who dominated southern governments during Reconstruction. He did run for lieutenant governor on a reform party ticket, but he was not elected. In 1876 he astounded many black people when he supported white Democrats who favored the restoration of white political control over South Carolina. When Democrats won the election, the new governor, Wade Hampton, rewarded Delany by naming him to a minor political office. In 1878 a group of black South Carolinians and Georgians proposed migrating to Liberia. Delany supported them and became their treasurer but did not join them. The venture soon failed.

After he failed to win an appointment to a federal position in Washington, D.C., Delany went to Xenia, Ohio, and Wilberforce University, where his family had lived since the late 1860s. He died there in 1885.

ABRAHAM LINCOLN AND BLACK PEOPLE

But the Lincoln-Douglas debates did not always turn on the fine points of constitutional law or on the fate of slavery in the territories. Thanks mainly to Douglas, who accused Lincoln and the Republicans of promoting the interests of black people over those of white people, the debates sometimes degenerated into crude and savage exchanges about which candidate favored white people more and black people less. Douglas proudly advocated white supremacy. "The signers of the Declaration [of Independence] had no reference to the negro . . . or any other inferior or degraded race when they spoke of the equality of men." He later charged that Lincoln and the Republicans wanted black and white equality. "If you, Black Republicans, think the negro ought to be on social equality with your wives and daughters, . . . you have a perfect right to do so. . . . Those of you who believe the negro is your equal . . . of course will vote for Mr. Lincoln."

Lincoln did not believe in racial equality, and he made that plain. In exasperation, he explained that merely because he opposed slavery did not mean he believed in equality. "I do not understand that because I do not want a negro woman for a slave I must necessarily have her for a wife." He bluntly added,

> I am not, nor ever have been in favor of bringing about in any way the social and political equality of the white and black races—that I am not nor ever have been in favor of making voters or jurors of negroes, nor of qualifying them to hold office, nor to intermarry with white people; and I will say in addition to this that there is a physical difference between the races which I believe will forever forbid the two races living together on terms of social and political equality.

But without repudiating these views, Lincoln later tried to transcend this blatant racism. "Let us discard all this quibbling about this man and the other man—this race and that race and the other race being inferior." Instead, he added, let us "unite as one people throughout this land, until we shall once more stand up declaring that all men are created equal." Lincoln stated unequivocally that race had nothing to do with whether a man had the right to be paid for his labor. He pointed out that the black man, "in the right to eat the bread, without leave of anybody else, which his own hand earns, he is my equal and the equal of Judge Douglas, and the equal of every living man."

Lincoln may have won the debate in the minds of many, but Douglas won the Senate election. Lincoln, however, made a name for himself that would work to his political advantage in the near future, and Douglas, despite his best efforts, had offended those Southerners who would accept no limitation on slavery in the territories. In two years, this would contribute to the breakup of the Democratic party.

JOHN BROWN AND THE RAID ON HARPERS FERRY

While Lincoln and Douglas were debating, John Brown was plotting. Following his attack on Pottowattamie in Kansas, Brown began to plan the violent overthrow of slavery in the South itself. In May 1858, accompanied by eleven white followers, he met thirty-four black people led by Martin Delany at Chatham in Canada West (now the Province of Ontario) and appealed for their support. Though Brown's plan changed over the next months, he was determined to invade the South and end slavery. He hoped to attract legions of slaves as he and his "army" moved down the Appalachian Mountains into the heart of the plantation system.

Planning the Raid

Brown suggested to the Chatham group the establishment of a semiautonomous state or nation within the United States for both black and white citizens. Black leaders were dubious. They asked, for example, how such a state could function within the United States after the Dred Scott case. Brown replied that it would be similar to the Cherokee nation or the self-governing Mormon settlement that had been founded in Utah in 1847.

Only one man at the Chatham gathering agreed to join Brown on his proposed raid. Nevertheless, the Chatham group did elect Brown the commander in chief of the army of the proposed new nation. Brown returned to the United States and got financial support from prosperous white abolitionists. Contributing money rather than risking their lives seemed more realistic to these men, who preferred to keep their identities confidential and thus came to be known as the Secret Six: Gerrit Smith, Thomas Wentworth Higginson, Samuel Gridley Howe, George L. Sterns, Theodore Parker, and Franklin Sanborn.

Brown also asked Frederick Douglass and Harriet Tubman to join him. They declined. By the summer of 1859, at a farm in rural Maryland, Brown had assembled an "army" consisting of seventeen white men (including three of his sons) and five black men. The black men who enlisted were Osborne Anderson, one of the

Chatham participants; Sheridan Leary, an escaped slave who had become a saddle and harness maker in Oberlin, Ohio; Leary's nephew John A. Copeland, an Oberlin College student; and two escaped slaves, Shields Green and Dangerfield Newby.

Newby was determined to rescue his wife, Harriet, and their seven children who were about to be sold from Virginia down the river to Louisiana. Harriet sent her husband a plaintive letter begging for him. "Oh Dear Dangerfield, com this fall . . . without fail . . . I want to see you so much that is one bright hope I have before me."

The Raid

Brown's invasion began on Sunday night October 16, 1859, with a raid on Harpers Ferry, Virginia, and the federal arsenal there. Brown hoped to secure weapons and then advance south, but the operation went awry from the start. The dedication and devotion of Brown and his men were not matched by their strategy or his leadership. The first man Brown's band killed was ironically a free black man, Heyward Shepard, who was a baggage handler at the train station. The alarm then went out, and opposition gathered.

Even though they had lost the initiative, Brown and his men neither advanced nor retreated, but instead re-

JOHN BROWN AT HARPER'S FERRY.

John Brown was captured in the Engine House at Harpers Ferry on October 18, 1859. He was tried for treason, convicted, and executed on December 2, 1859. Though his raid failed to free a single slave, it helped catapult the nation toward civil war.

mained in Harpers Ferry while Virginia and Maryland militia converged on them. Fighting began, and two townspeople, the mayor, and eight of Brown's men, including Sheridan Leary, Dangerfield Newby, and two of Brown's sons, were killed. Newby died carrying his wife's letter. But Brown managed to seize several hostages, among them Lewis W. Washington, the great grandnephew of George Washington.

By Tuesday morning, Brown, with his hostages and what remained of his "army," was holed up in an engine house. A detachment of U.S. Marines under the command of Robert E. Lee arrived, surrounded the building, and demanded Brown's surrender. He refused. The Marines broke in. Brown was wounded and captured.

The raid was an utter failure. No slaves were freed. Shields Green and John A. Copeland fled but were caught. Osborne Anderson eluded capture and later fought in the Civil War. Virginia quickly tried Brown, Green, and Copeland for treason. They were found guilty and sentenced to hang.

The Reaction

The raid failed but Brown and his men succeeded brilliantly in intensifying the deeply felt emotions of those who supported and those who opposed slavery. At first regarded as crazed zealots and insane fanatics, they showed that they were willing—even eager—to die for the antislavery cause. The dignity and assurance that Brown, Green, and Copeland displayed as they awaited the gallows impressed many black and white northerners.

Black teacher and abolitionist Frances Ellen Watkins Harper wrote to John Brown's wife two weeks before Brown was executed to express compassion and admiration for both husband and wife.

> Belonging to the race your dear husband reached forth his hand to assist, I need not tell you that my sympathies are with you. I thank you for the brave words you have spoken. A republic that produces such a wife and mother may hope for better days. Our heart may grow more hopeful for humanity when it sees the sublime sacrifice it is about to receive from his hands. Not in vain had your dear husband periled all, if the martyrdom of one hero is worth more than the life of a million cowards.

James A. Copeland wrote home to his family that he was proud to die.

> I am not terrified by the gallows, which I see staring me in the face, and upon which I am soon to stand and suffer death for doing what George Washington

was made a hero for doing. . . . Could I die in a manner and for a cause which would induce true and honest men more to honor me, and the angels more ready to receive me to their happy home of everlasting joy above? . . . I imagine that I hear you, and all of you, mother, father, sisters and brothers, say— "No, there is not a cause for which we, with less sorrow, could see you die."

Brown also eloquently and calmly announced his willingness to die as so many had died before him. "Now, if it is deemed necessary that I should forfeit my life for the furtherance of the ends of justice, and mingle my blood further with the blood of my children and with the blood of millions in this slave country whose rights are disregarded by wicked, cruel, and unjust enactments, I say, let it be done."

For many Northerners, the day Brown was executed, December 2, 1859, was a day of mourning. Church bells tolled and people bowed their heads in prayer. One unnamed black man later solemnly declared: "The memory of John Brown shall be indelibly written upon the tablets of our hearts, and when tyrants cease to oppress the enslaved, we will teach our children to revive his name, and transmit it to the latest posterity, as being the greatest man in the 19th century."

White Southerners felt differently. They were terrified and traumatized by the raid, and outraged that Northerners made Brown a hero and a martyr. A wave of hysteria and paranoia swept the South as incredulous white people wondered how Northerners could admire a man who sought to kill slave owners and free their slaves. Jane Caroline Pettigrew of Abbeville, South Carolina, wrote in a letter, "I suppose . . . you thought I would be frightened nearly out of my life. I only feel, God have mercy on us. Such revelations make us wonder how insecure is our situation & fear for the Future."

Brown's raid and the reaction to it further divided a nation already badly split over slavery. Although neither he nor anyone else realized it at the time, Brown and his "army" had propelled the South toward secession from the Union—and thereby moved the nation closer to his goal of destroying slavery.

THE ELECTION OF ABRAHAM LINCOLN

With the country fracturing over slavery, four candidates ran for president in the election of 1860. The Democrats split into a northern faction, which nominated Stephen Douglas, and a southern faction, which nominated John C. Breckenridge of Kentucky. The

Constitutional Union party, a new party formed by former Whigs, nominated John Bell of Tennessee. The breakup of the Democratic party assured victory for the Republican candidate, Abraham Lincoln (Map 10–3).

Lincoln's name was not even on the ballot in most southern states because his candidacy was based on the Republican party's adamant opposition to the expansion of slavery into any western territory. And although Lincoln took pains to reassure white Southerners that slavery would continue in states where it already existed, they were not in the least persuaded. A South Carolina newspaper was convinced that Lincoln would abolish slavery. "[Lincoln] has openly proclaimed a war of extermination against the leading institutions of the Southern States. He says that there can be no peace so long as slavery has a foot hold in America."

A Georgia newspaper preferred a bloody civil war to a Lincoln Presidency. "Let the consequences be what they may—whether the Potomac is crimsoned in human gore, and Pennsylvania Avenue is paved ten fathoms deep with mangled bodies . . . the South will never submit to such humiliation and degradation as the inauguration of Abraham Lincoln."

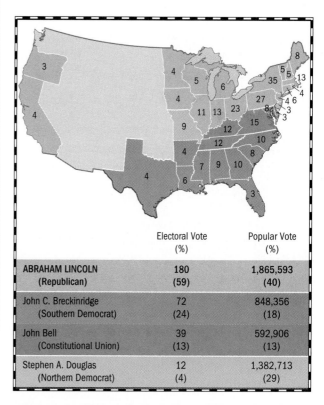

	Electoral Vote (%)	Popular Vote (%)
ABRAHAM LINCOLN (Republican)	180 (59)	1,865,593 (40)
John C. Breckinridge (Southern Democrat)	72 (24)	848,356 (18)
John Bell (Constitutional Union)	39 (13)	592,906 (13)
Stephen A. Douglas (Northern Democrat)	12 (4)	1,382,713 (29)

Map 10–3 The Election of 1860. The results reflect the sectional schism over slavery. Lincoln carried the election although he won only in northern states. His name did not even appear on the ballot in most southern states.

Black People Respond to Lincoln's Election

Although they were less opposed to Lincoln than white Southerners, black Northerners and white abolitionists were not eager to see Abraham Lincoln become president. Dismayed by his contradictions and racism—he opposed slavery, but he tolerated it; he was against slavery's expansion, but he condemned black Americans as inferiors—many black people refused to support him or did so reluctantly. The New York *Anglo-African* opposed both Republicans and Democrats in the 1860 election, telling its readers to depend on each other. "We have no hope from either [of the] political parties. We must rely on ourselves, the righteousness of our cause, and the advance of just sentiments among the great masses of the . . . people."

Abolitionists like William Lloyd Garrison and Wendell Phillips believed that Lincoln was too willing to tolerate slave-holding interests. But Frederick Douglass wrote that "Lincoln's election will indicate growth in

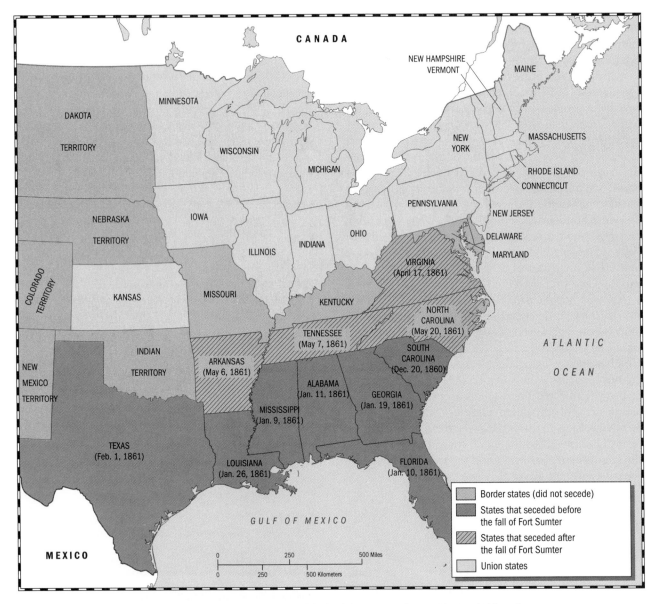

Map 10-4 The Secession of the Southern States. Following Lincoln's election, seven southern states seceded from the Union and formed the Confederate States of America. After Lincoln's inauguration and the firing on Fort Sumter, four more states joined the Confederacy. Four slave states—Missouri, Kentucky, Maryland, and Delaware—remained in the Union.

the right direction," and that his presidency "must and will be hailed as an anti-slavery triumph."

After Lincoln's election, black leaders almost welcomed the secession of southern states. H. Ford Douglas urged the southern states to leave the Union. "Stand not upon the order of your going, but go at once. . . . There is no union of ideas and interests in this country, and there can be no union between freedom and slavery." Frederick Douglass was convinced that there were men prepared to follow in the footsteps of John Brown's "army" to destroy slavery. "I am for dissolution of the Union—decidedly for a dissolution of the Union! . . . In case of such a dissolution, I believe that men could be found . . . who would venture into those states and raise the standard of liberty there."

Disunion

When South Carolina seceded on December 20, 1860, it began a procession of Southern states out of the Union. By February 1861, seven states—South Carolina, Mississippi, Alabama, Florida, Louisiana, Georgia, and Texas—had seceded and formed the Confederate States of America in Montgomery, Alabama (Map 10–4). Before there could be the kind of undertaking against slavery that Douglass had proposed, Abraham Lincoln tried to persuade the seceding states to reconsider. In his inaugural address of March 4, 1861, Lincoln attempted to calm the fears of white Southerners, sternly warning them that he would not tolerate their withdrawal from the Union. Lincoln repeated his assurance that he would not tamper with slavery in the states where it was already legal. "I have no purpose, directly or indirectly, to interfere with the institution of slavery in the States where it exists. I believe I have no lawful right to do so, and I have no inclination to do so."

Lincoln added that the "only" dispute between the North and South was over the expansion of slavery. He emphatically warned, however, that he would enforce the Constitution and not permit secession. "Plainly, the central idea of secession is the essence of anarchy." He pleaded with white Southerners to contemplate their actions patiently and thoughtfully, actions that might provoke a civil conflict. "In your hands, my dissatisfied fellow-countrymen, and not in mine, is the monumental issue of civil war."

Southern whites did not heed him. Slavery was too essential to give up merely to preserve the Union. Arthur P. Hayne of South Carolina had succinctly summed up its importance in an 1860 letter to President James Buchanan. "Slavery with us is no

abstraction—but a *great* and *vital fact*. Without it our every comfort would be taken from us. Our wives, our children, made unhappy—education, the light of knowledge—all *all* lost and our *people ruined for ever. Nothing short of separation from the Union can save us.*"

Barely a month after Lincoln's inauguration, Confederate leaders demanded that U.S. Army Major Robert Anderson surrender Fort Sumter in the harbor of Charleston, South Carolina. Anderson refused, and on April 12, 1861, Confederate artillery fired on the fort. In the aftermath, four additional states—Virginia, North Carolina, Tennessee, and Arkansas—joined the Confederacy. The Civil War had begun.

CONCLUSION

Virtually every event and episode of major or minor consequence in the United States between 1849 and 1861 involved black people and the expansion of slavery. From the Wilmot Proviso and the Compromise of 1850 to the Dred Scott decision and John Brown's raid, white Americans were increasingly perplexed about how the nation could remain half slave and half free. They were unable to resolve the problem of slavery's expansion.

Without the presence of black people in America, neither secession nor civil war would have occurred. Yet, the Civil War began because white Americans had developed contradictory visions of the future. White Southerners contemplated a future that inextricably linked their security and prosperity to slavery. The South, they believed, could neither advance nor endure without slavery.

Northern white people believed that their future rested on the opportunities for white men and their families to flourish as independent, self-sufficient farmers, shopkeepers, and skilled artisans. For their future to prevail, they insisted that the new lands in the American West should exclude the slave system that white Southerners considered so vital. Neither northern nor southern white people—except for some abolitionists—ever believed that people of color should fully participate as free people in American society or in the future of the American nation.

REVIEW QUESTIONS

1. How and why did southern and northern white people differ over slavery? On what did white people of both regions agree and disagree about race and slavery?

TIMELINE

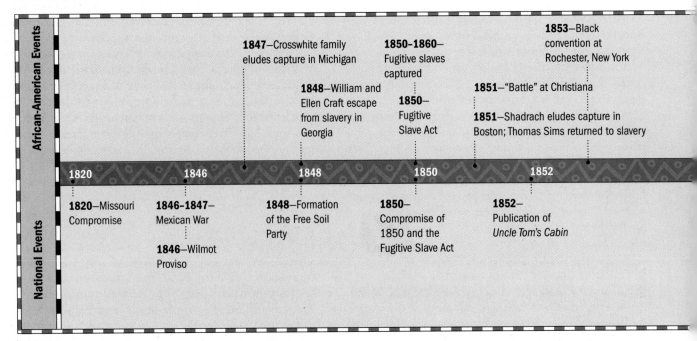

African-American Events

1847—Crosswhite family eludes capture in Michigan

1848—William and Ellen Craft escape from slavery in Georgia

1850-1860—Fugitive slaves captured

1850—Fugitive Slave Act

1853—Black convention at Rochester, New York

1851—"Battle" at Christiana

1851—Shadrach eludes capture in Boston; Thomas Sims returned to slavery

1820   1846   1848   1850   1852

National Events

1820—Missouri Compromise

1846-1847—Mexican War

1846—Wilmot Proviso

1848—Formation of the Free Soil Party

1850—Compromise of 1850 and the Fugitive Slave Act

1852—Publication of *Uncle Tom's Cabin*

---

2. If you were an African American living in the North in the 1850s, would you have been discouraged by the policies of the United States government?

3. If you were a white Southerner in the 1850s, would you have been encouraged by those policies?

4. Why did seven southern states secede from the Union within three months after Abraham Lincoln was elected president in 1860? What was their purpose?

5. If you were a black person—either a slave or free—would you have welcomed the secession of the southern states? How might secession affect the future of your people?

RECOMMENDED READING

Eric Foner. *Free Soil, Free Labor and Free Men: The Ideology of the Republican Party before the Civil War.* New York: Oxford University Press, 1970. An excellent overview of attitudes on free soil, slavery, and race.

Vincent Harding. *There Is a River: The Black Struggle for Freedom in America.* New York: Harcourt, Brace, Jovanovich, 1981. Both a tribute to and a masterful narrative about the black men and women who challenged the white majority in nineteenth-century America.

Leon Litwack. *North of Slavery: The Negro in the Free States, 1790–1860.* Chicago: University of Chicago Press, 1961. An examination of the lives of black residents of the North and the discrimination that they encountered.

James McPherson. *Battle Cry of Freedom: The Civil War Era.* New York: Oxford University Press, 1988. A superb account of the people and events involved in the crisis leading up to the Civil War and of the war itself.

David Potter. *The Impending Crisis, 1848–1861.* New York: Harper & Row, 1976. Another fine account of the events leading up to the Civil War.

ADDITIONAL BIBLIOGRAPHY

California and the Compromise of 1850

Eugene H. Berwanger. *The Frontier against Slavery: Western Anti-Negro Prejudice and the Slave Extension Controversy.* Urbana: University of Illinois Press, 1967.

Holman Hamilton. *Prologue to Conflict: The Crisis and Compromise of 1850.* Lexington: University of Kentucky Press, 1964.

Rudolph M. Lapp. *Blacks in the Gold Rush California.* New Haven: Yale University Press, 1977.

The Fugitive Slave Law and Its Victims

Stanley W. Campbell. *The Slave Catchers: Enforcement of the Fugitive Slave Law, 1850–1860.* Chapel Hill: University of North Carolina Press, 1968.

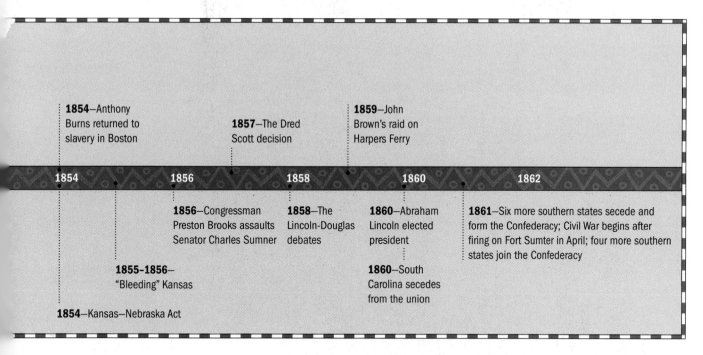

1854—Anthony Burns returned to slavery in Boston

1857—The Dred Scott decision

1859—John Brown's raid on Harpers Ferry

1854 1856 1858 1860 1862

1856—Congressman Preston Brooks assaults Senator Charles Sumner

1858—The Lincoln-Douglas debates

1860—Abraham Lincoln elected president

1861—Six more southern states secede and form the Confederacy; Civil War begins after firing on Fort Sumter in April; four more southern states join the Confederacy

1855–1856—"Bleeding" Kansas

1860—South Carolina secedes from the union

1854—Kansas–Nebraska Act

Gary Collison. *Shadrach Minkins.* Cambridge: Harvard University Press, 1998.

Albert J. Von Frank. *The Trials of Anthony Burns.* Cambridge: Harvard University Press, 1998.

Jonathan Katz. *Resistance at Christiana: The Fugitive Slave Rebellion at Christiana, Pennsylvania, September 11, 1851: A Documentary Account.* New York: Crowell, 1974.

The Late 1850s

Don E. Fehrenbacher. *The Dred Scott Case: Its Significance in American Law and Politics.* New York: Oxford University Press, 1978.

Harry V. Jaffa. *Crisis of the House Divided: An Interpretation of the Lincoln-Douglas Debates.* Garden City, NY: Doubleday, 1959.

Robert W. Johannsen. *Stephen A. Douglas.* New York: Oxford University Press, 1973.

Kenneth M. Stampp. *America in 1857: A Nation on the Brink.* New York: Oxford University Press, 1990.

John Brown and the Raid on Harpers Ferry

Paul Finkelman. *And His Soul Goes Marching On: Responses to John Brown and the Harpers Ferry Raid.* Charlottesville: University of Virginia Press, 1995.

James C. Marlin. *John Brown and Legend of Fifty-Six.* Philadelphia: The American Philosophical Society, 1942.

Truman Nelson. *The Old Man John Brown at Harpers Ferry.* New York: Holt, Rhinehart, and Winston, 1973.

Stephen Oates. *To Purge This Land with Blood: A Biography of John Brown.* New York: Harper & Row, 1970.

Secession

William L. Barney. *The Road to Secession.* New York: Prager, 1972.

Steven A. Channing. *Crisis of Fear: Secession in South Carolina.* New York: Simon & Schuster, 1970.

Kenneth M. Stampp. *And the War Came: The North and the Secession Crisis, 1860–1861.* Baton Rouge: Louisiana State University Press, 1950.

Abraham Lincoln

David Herbert Donald. *Lincoln.* New York: Simon & Schuster, 1995.

Stephen B. Oates. *With Malice toward None: A Life of Abraham Lincoln.* New York: Harper & Row, 1977.

Benjamin Thomas. *Abraham Lincoln: A Biography.* New York: Alfred A. Knopf, 1952.

Novels

Martin R. Delany. *Blake or the Huts of America.* Boston: Beacon Press, 1970.

Harriet Beecher Stowe. *Uncle Tom's Cabin, or Life among the Lowly.* New York: Modern Library, 1985.

PART III

THE CIVIL WAR, EMANCIPATION, AND BLACK RECONSTRUCTION

THE
SECOND
AMERICAN
REVOLUTION

CHAPTER 11

LIBERATION: AFRICAN AMERICANS AND THE CIVIL WAR

On February 21, 1865, the 55th Massachusetts Regiment occupied and liberated the devastated city of Charleston, South Carolina. Black residents—many of them former slaves—eagerly greeted the black troops. Defeated and discouraged white Charlestonians remained secluded indoors.

If the muse were mine to tempt it
    And my feeble voice were strong,
If my tongue were trained to measures,
    I would sing a stirring song.
I would sing a song heroic
    Of those noble sons of Ham,
Of the gallant colored soldiers
    Who fought for Uncle Sam! . . .

Ah, they rallied to the standard
    To uphold it by their might;
None were stronger in the labors,
    None were braver in the fight.
From the blazing breach of Wagner
    To the plains of Olustee,
They were foremost in the fight
    Of the battles of the free. . . .

And their deeds shall find a record
    In the registry of Fame;
For their blood has cleansed completely
    Every blot of Slavery's shame.
So all honor and all glory
    To those noble sons of Ham—
The gallant colored soldiers
    Who fought for Uncle Sam!

From "The Colored Soldiers," 1895, by Paul Laurence Dunbar, whose father, Joshua, served with the all-black 55th Massachusetts regiment.

Slavery caused the Civil War. Yet when the war began in 1861, neither the Union nor the Confederacy entered the conflict with any intention or desire to change the status of black Americans. It was supposed to be a white man's war. White Southerners would wage war to make the Confederacy a separate and independent nation free to promote slavery. White Northerners took up arms to maintain the Union, but not to free a single slave. African Americans who wanted to enlist in 1861 were emphatically rejected. The Union might be disrupted, but slavery was not going to be disturbed.

Both North and South expected a quick victory. No one anticipated that forty-eight months of brutal war would rip the nation apart. When the Civil War ended in April 1865, almost 620,000 Americans were dead—including nearly 40,000 black men. The Union was preserved, and four million people had been freed. Nothing in American history compares to it.

LINCOLN'S AIMS

When the war began, as it was fought, and when it ended, President Abraham Lincoln's unwavering objective was to preserve the Union. Any policies that helped or hindered black people were subordinate to that goal. Following the attack on Fort Sumter in April 1861 and Lincoln's call for state militias to help suppress the rebellion, four more slave states—North Carolina, Virginia, Tennessee, and Arkansas—seceded from the Union and joined the Confederacy. For most of 1861, Lincoln was determined to do nothing that would drive the four remaining slave states—Delaware, Maryland, Kentucky, and Missouri—into the Confederacy. Lincoln feared that if he did or said anything that could be interpreted as interfering with slavery, those four border states would leave the Union too.

Meanwhile, Lincoln issued a call for 75,000 men to enlist in the military for ninety days of service to the national government. Thousands of black and white men, far more than 75,000, responded to the call. White men were accepted; black men were rejected. Spurned by federal and state authorities, black men remained determined to aid the cause.

BLACK MEN VOLUNTEER AND ARE REJECTED

Black people recognized long before most white Northerners that the fate of the Union was inextricably tied to the issue of slavery, and that the future of slavery was tied to the outcome of the war. "Talk as we may," insisted the *Anglo-African*, a black New York newspaper,

> We are concerned in this fight and our fate hangs upon its issues. The South must be subjugated, or we shall be enslaved. In aiding the Federal government in whatever way we can, we are aiding to secure our own liberty; for this war can end only in the subjugation of the North or the South.

Black men in New York formed their own military companies and began to drill. In Boston, they drew up a resolution modeled on the Declaration of Independence and appealed for permission to go to war.

> Our feelings urge us to say to our countrymen that we are ready to stand by and defend our Government as equals of its white defenders; to do so with "our lives, our fortunes, and our sacred honor," for the sake of freedom, and as good citizens; and we ask you to modify your laws, that we may enlist,—that full scope may be given to patriotic feelings burning in the colored man's breast.

Black men in Philadelphia volunteered to infiltrate the South to incite slave revolts, but were turned down. In Washington, Jacob Dodson, a black employee of the U.S. Senate, wrote a letter to Secretary of War Simon Cameron shortly after the fall of Fort Sumter volunteering the services of local black men. "I desire to inform you that I know of some 300 reliable colored free citizens of this city who desire to enter the service for the defense of the city." Cameron curtly replied: "This Department has no intention at the present to call into the service of the government any colored soldiers."

UNION POLICIES TOWARD CONFEDERATE SLAVES

Slaves started to liberate themselves as soon as the war began, but Union political and military leaders had no coherent policy for dealing with them. To the deep disappointment of black Northerners and white abolitionists, Union military commanders showed more concern for the interests of Confederate slave owners than for the people in bondage. In May 1861 General George B. McClellan reassured Virginia slave owners: "Not only will we abstain from all interferences with your slaves, but we will, with an iron hand, crush any attempt at insurrection on their part."

General Henry Halleck ordered slaves who escaped in the Ohio Valley returned to their owners, and General Winfield Scott, the Army's chief of staff, asked that Confederate slave owners be permitted to recover slaves who crossed the Potomac River to what they believed was the freedom of Union lines. In Tennessee in early 1862, General Ulysses S. Grant returned runaway slaves to their owners if the owners supported the Union cause. But Grant put black people to work on fortifications if their owners favored secession.

"Contraband"

Not all Union commanders were as callous as these generals. A month after the war began, three bondsmen working on Confederate fortifications in Virginia escaped to the Union's Fortress Monroe on the coast. Their owner, a Confederate colonel, appeared at the fortress the next day under a flag of truce and demanded the return of his slaves under the 1850 Fugitive Slave Act. The incredulous Union commander, General Benjamin Butler, informed him that since Virginia had seceded from the Union, the fugitive slave law was no longer in force. Butler did not free the three slaves, but he did not reenslave them either. He declared them "contraband"—enemy property—and put them to work for the Union. Soon, over a thousand slaves fled to Fortress Monroe. The white authorities may have thought of them as contraband, but it's not likely that that's how they viewed themselves. Crossing Union lines, it's doubtful any declared, "We are contraband." Rather, they were more apt to proclaim enthusiastically, "We are free!"

On August 6, 1861, Congress clarified the status of runaway slaves when it passed the First Confiscation Act. Any property that belonged to Confederates that was used in the war effort could be seized by federal forces. Any slaves who were used by their masters to benefit the Confederacy—and only those slaves—would be freed. Almost immediately, Union General John C. Fremont (the 1856 Republican presidential candidate) exceeded the strict limits of the act by freeing all the slaves belonging to Confederates in Missouri. President Lincoln quickly countermanded the order and told Fremont that only slaves actively used to aid the Confederate war effort were to be freed. Lincoln worried that Fremont would drive Missouri or Kentucky into the Confederacy.

Black leaders were—to put it mildly—displeased with Lincoln and with federal policies that both prohibited the enlistment of black troops and ignored the plight of the enslaved. To fight a war against the South without fighting against slavery, the institution on which the South was so thoroughly dependent, seemed absurd. Frederick Douglass stated the argument cogently: "To fight against slaveholders, without fighting against slavery, is but a half-hearted business, and paralyzes the hands engaged in it. . . . fire must be met with water. . . . War for the destruction of liberty must be met with war for the destruction of slavery."

Others were less charitable. Joseph R. Hawley, a white Connecticut Republican, thought that Lincoln was foolish to worry about whether the border states might leave the Union. "Permit me to say *damn* the border states. . . . A thousand Lincolns cannot stop the people from fighting slavery." In the New York *Anglo-African*, a letter writer who identified himself as "Ivanhoe" urged Northern black men to decline any request to serve in Union military forces until the slaves were freed and black northerners received treatment equal to that of white people. "And suppose we were invited," he asked, "what duty would we then owe to ourselves and our posterity? . . . Our enslaved brethren must be made freedmen. . . . We of the North must have all of the rights which white men enjoy; until then we are in no condition to fight under the flag [which] gives us no protection."

Lincoln did not budge. Union military forces occupied an enclave on South Carolina's southern coast and the Sea Islands in late 1861, and on May 9, 1862, General David Hunter ordered slavery abolished in South Carolina, Georgia, and Florida. Lincoln quickly revoked Hunter's order and reprimanded him. Nevertheless, thousands of slaves along the South Carolina and Georgia coast threw off their shackles and welcomed Union troops as plantation owners fled to the interior.

Lincoln's Initial Position

For more than a year, Lincoln remained reluctant to strike decisively against slavery. He believed that the long-term solution to slavery and the race problem in the United States was the compensated emancipation of slaves followed by their colonization outside the country. That is, slave owners would be paid for their slaves; the slaves would be freed but forced to settle in the Caribbean, Latin America, or West Africa.

These black Virginians are freeing themselves. Regarded by Northern white authorities as contraband, they are crossing the Rappahannock River in August 1862 shortly before the battle of Antietam and Abraham Lincoln's decision to issue the Preliminary Emancipation Proclamation.

As a Whig congressman in 1849, Lincoln voted for a bill that would have emancipated slaves and compensated their owners in the District of Columbia if it had passed. In 1861, he tried—and failed—to persuade the Delaware legislature to support compensated emancipation. Then in April 1862, at Lincoln's urging, Republicans in Congress (against almost unanimous Democratic opposition) voted to provide funds to "any state which may adopt gradual abolishment of slavery." Lincoln wanted to eliminate slavery from the border states with the approval of slave owners there, and thus diminish the likelihood that those states would join the Confederacy.

But leaders in the border states rejected the proposal. Lincoln brought it up again in July. This time he warned congressmen and senators from the border states that if their states opposed compensated emancipation they might have to accept *uncompensated* emancipation. They ignored his advice and denounced compensated emancipation as a "radical change in our

social system" and an intrusion by the federal government into a state issue.

To many white Americans, Lincoln's support for compensated emancipation and colonization was a misguided attempt to link the war to the issue of slavery. But to black Americans, abolitionists, and an increasing number of Republicans, Lincoln's refusal to abolish slavery immediately was tragic. Antislavery advocates regarded Lincoln's willingness to purchase the freedom of slaves as an admission that he considered those human beings to be property. They deplored his seeming inability to realize that the Union would not win the war unless slaves were liberated.

Lincoln Moves toward Emancipation

However, by the summer of 1862, after the border states rejected compensated emancipation, Lincoln concluded that victory and the future of the Union were tied directly to the issue of slavery. Slavery became the instrument Lincoln would use to hasten the end of the war and restore the Union. He told Secretary of the Navy Gideon Welles: "We must free the slaves or be ourselves subdued. The slaves were undeniably an element of strength to those who had their service, and we must decide whether that element should be with us or against us." Emancipation, Lincoln stressed, would "strike at the heart of the rebellion."

In cabinet meetings on July 21 and 22, 1862, Lincoln discussed abolishing slavery. Except for the Postmaster General Montgomery Blair, the cabinet supported emancipation. Blair feared that eliminating slavery would cost the Republicans control of Congress in the fall elections. Secretary of State William H. Seward supported abolition but advised Lincoln not to issue a proclamation until the Union won a major victory. Otherwise emancipation might look like the desperate gesture of the leader of a losing cause. Lincoln accepted Seward's advice and postponed emancipation.

Lincoln Delays Emancipation

Nevertheless, word circulated that Lincoln intended to abolish slavery. But weeks passed, and slavery did not end. Frustrated abolitionists and Republicans attacked Lincoln. Frederick Douglass was exasperated with a president who had shown inexcusable deference to white Southerners who had rebelled against the Union.

> Abraham Lincoln is no more fit for the place he holds than was [previous president] James Buchanan. . . . The country is destined to become sick of both [General George B.] McClellan and Lincoln, and the sooner the better. The one plays lawyer for the benefit of the rebels, and the other handles the army for the benefit of traitors. We should not be surprised if both should be hurled from their places before the rebellion is ended.

In his "Prayer of Twenty Millions," Horace Greeley, editor of the New York *Tribune*, expressed his disappointment that the president had not moved promptly

Before, during, and after the Civil War black men worked on railroads in the South, mainly in construction and maintenance. Before slavery began to collapse during the war, slave labor in transportation, manufacturing, and agriculture permitted the Confederacy to put more white men in uniform.

Courtesy, Georgia Department of Archives and History.

against slavery, the issue that had led the southern states to leave the Union and go to war: "We ask you to consider that Slavery [is the] inciting cause and sustaining base of treason. . . . We think timid counsels in such a crisis [are] calculated to prove perilous, probably disastrous." Greeley insisted that Lincoln should have long ago warned white Southerners that their support of secession would endanger slavery.

On August 22, 1862, Lincoln replied to Greeley and offered a masterful explanation of his priorities. Placing the preservation of the Union before freedom for the enslaved, Lincoln declared: "My paramount object in this struggle *is* to save the Union, and is *not* either to save or destroy slavery. If I could save the Union without freeing *any* slave I would do it; and if I could save it by freeing *all* the slaves, I would do it; and if I could do it by freeing some and leaving others alone, I would also do that." Lincoln concluded, "I have here stated my purpose according to my view of *official* duty, and I intend no modification of my oft-expressed *personal* wish that all men, everywhere, could be free."

Black People Reject Colonization

Lincoln's policy on emancipation had shifted dramatically, but he remained committed to colonization. On August 14, 1862, Lincoln invited black leaders to the White House and appealed for their support for colonization. After condemning slavery as "the greatest wrong inflicted on any people," he explained that white racism made it unwise for black people to remain in the United States. "Your race suffer very greatly, many of them, by living among us, while ours suffer from your presence. There is an unwillingness on the part of our people, harsh as it may be, for you free colored people to remain among us. . . . I do not mean to discuss this, but to propose it as a fact with which we have to deal. I cannot alter it if I would." Lincoln asked the black leaders to begin enlisting volunteers for a colonization project in Central America.

Most black people were unimpressed by Lincoln's words and unmoved by his advice. A black leader from Philadelphia condemned the president. "This is our country as much as it is yours, and we will not leave it." Frederick Douglass accused Lincoln of hypocrisy and claimed that support for colonization would lead white men "to commit all kinds of violence and outrage upon the colored people."

Lincoln would not retreat from his support for colonization. Attempts were already under way to put compensated emancipation and colonization into effect. In April 1862, Congress enacted a bill to pay District of Columbia slave owners up to $300 for each slave they freed and to provide $100,000 to support the *voluntary* colonization of the freed people in Haiti or Liberia. In 1863 the government tried to settle 453 black American colonists at Île à Vache on an island near Haiti. The settlers suffered greatly from disease and starvation. This sorry attempt at government-sponsored colonization ended in 1864 when the U.S. navy returned 368 survivors to the United States.

THE PRELIMINARY EMANCIPATION PROCLAMATION

Finally on September 22, 1862—more than two months after Lincoln first seriously considered freedom for the enslaved—the president issued the Preliminary Emancipation Proclamation. It came five days after General George B. McClellan's Army of the Potomac turned back an invasion of Maryland at Antietam by General Robert E. Lee's Army of Northern Virginia. This bloody but less-than-conclusive victory allowed Lincoln to justify emancipation. But this first proclamation freed no people that September—or during the rest of 1862. Instead, it stipulated that anyone in bondage in states or parts of states still in rebellion on January 1, 1863, would be "thenceforward, and forever free." Lincoln's announcement gave the Confederate states one hundred days to return to the Union. If any or all of those states did rejoin the Union, the slaves there would remain in bondage. The Union would be preserved, and slavery would be maintained.

What were Lincoln's intentions? It might seem that he expected the Confederate leaders to give his offer serious consideration and perhaps return to the Union, and that he was thus willing to free the slaves only as a last resort. But Lincoln knew there was virtually no chance that white Southerners would return to the Union just because he had threatened to free their slaves. Most Confederates expected to win the war, thereby confirming secession and safeguarding slavery. White Southerners ridiculed the preliminary proclamation.

Northern Reaction to Emancipation

In the Union, the Preliminary Emancipation Proclamation was greeted with little enthusiasm. Most black people and abolitionists, of course, were gratified that Lincoln, after weeks of procrastination, had finally issued the proclamation. Frederick Douglass was ecstatic. "We shout for joy that we live to record this righteous decree." In *The Liberator*, William Lloyd Garrison wrote that it was "an act of immense historical consequence." But they also worried that—however remote the possibility might be—some slave states would return to the Union by January 1, denying freedom to those enslaved.

Many white Northerners resented emancipation. One New York soldier, more concerned with defeating the South than freeing the slaves, bluntly reflected these views, "We must first conquer & then its time enough to talk about the *dam'd niggers*." A northern newspaper editor vilified Lincoln as a "half-witted usurper" and the Proclamation as "monstrous, impudent, and heinous . . . insulting to God as to man, for it declares those 'equal' whom God created unequal."

Even before the announcement of emancipation, antiblack riots flared in the North. In Cincinnati in the summer of 1862, Irish dock workers invaded black neighborhoods after black men had replaced the striking wharf hands along the city's river front. In Brooklyn, New York, Irish-Americans set fire to a tobacco factory that employed black women and children.

Political Opposition to Emancipation

Northern Democrats almost unanimously opposed emancipation. They accused Lincoln and the Republicans of "fanaticism" and regretted that emancipation would liberate "two or three million semi savages" who would "overrun the North" and compete with white working people. The Democratic-controlled lower houses of the legislatures in Indiana and Illinois condemned the Proclamation as "wicked, inhuman and unholy." Republicans recognized the intense hostility among many white Northerners to black people. Senator Lyman Trumball of Illinois conceded that "there is a very great aversion in the West—I know it to be so in my state—against having free negroes come among us. Our people want nothing to do with the negro."

And as some Republicans had predicted and feared, the Democrats capitalized on dissatisfaction with the war's progress and with Republican support for emancipation to make significant gains in the fall elections. Democratic governors were elected in New York and New Jersey, and Democrats won thirty-four more seats in the U.S. House of Representatives, although the Republicans retained a majority. Overjoyed Democrats proclaimed, "Abolition Slaughtered." Republicans took solace that their losses were not greater.

THE EMANCIPATION PROCLAMATION

On January 1, 1863, Abraham Lincoln issued the Emancipation Proclamation. It was not the first step toward freedom. Since 1861 several thousand slaves had already freed themselves. But it was the first significant effort by Union authorities to assure freedom to nearly four million people of African descent who—with their ancestors—had been enslaved for two hundred fifty years in North America. The Civil War was now a war to make people free.

Black communities and many white people across the North celebrated. Church bells pealed. Poems were written, and prayers of thanksgiving offered. Many considered it the most momentous day in American history since July 4, 1776. Frederick Douglass had difficulty describing the emotions of people in Boston when word reached the city late on the night of December 31 that Lincoln would issue the Proclamation the next day. "The effect of this announcement was startling beyond description, and the scene was wild and grand. Joy and gladness exhausted all forms of expression, from shouts of praise to sobs and tears. . . . a Negro preacher, a man of wonderful vocal power, expressed the heartfelt emotion of the hour, when he led all voices in the anthem, 'Sound the loud timbrel o'er Egypt's dark sea, Jehovah hath triumphed, his people were free.'" Well into the twentieth century, New Year's Day was commemorated as Emancipation Day, a holiday zealously observed by black Americans in churches and with parades and celebrations.

Limits of the Proclamation

Despite this excitement, the language of the Emancipation Proclamation was uninspired and unmoving. It lacked the eloquence of the Declaration of Independence or the address Lincoln would deliver after the Union victory at Gettysburg in July 1863. Lincoln dryly wrote that "as a fit and necessary measure for suppressing said rebellion . . . I do order and declare that all persons held as slaves within said designated States, and parts of States, are, and henceforth shall be free."

Moreover, by limiting emancipation to those states and areas still in rebellion, Lincoln did *not* include enslaved people in the four border states still in the Union or in areas of Confederate states that Union forces had already occupied. This included forty-eight counties in western Virginia (that would soon become the state of

THE STEPS TO EMANCIPATION

April 1861	Fort Sumter is attacked; Civil War begins
May 1861	General Butler refuses to return escaped "contrabands" to slavery
August 1861	General Fremont orders emancipation of slaves in Missouri; Lincoln countermands him
August 1861	First Confiscation Act frees captured slaves used by Confederate Army
April 1862	Congress provides funds for compensated emancipation; border states spurn the proposal
May 1862	General Hunter's order abolishing slavery in South Carolina, Georgia, and Florida is revoked by Lincoln
Summer 1862	Lincoln concludes that Union victory requires emancipation
September 22, 1862	Lincoln issues Preliminary Emancipation Proclamation after Battle of Antietam
January 1, 1863	Emancipation Proclamation takes effect

West Virginia), parts of Tennessee, and thirteen parishes (counties) in Louisiana—including New Orleans (Map 11–1). Thus hundreds of thousands of people would remain in bondage despite the proclamation. The immediate practical effect of the Proclamation was negligible in the areas it was intended to affect. After all, slave owners in the Confederacy did not recognize Lincoln's authority, and they certainly did not free their slaves on January 1 or anytime soon thereafter. Yet the Emancipation Proclamation remains one of the most important documents in American history. It made the Civil War a war to free people as well as to preserve the Union and gave moral authority to the Union cause and as many black people freed themselves before the proclamation, many more would liberate themselves after.

Effects of the Proclamation on the South

The Emancipation Proclamation destroyed any chance that Great Britain or France would offer diplomatic recognition to the Confederate government. Diplomatic recognition would have meant accepting the Confederacy as a legitimate state equal in international law to the Union, and would almost surely have led to financial and military assistance for the South. British

Map 11-1 Effects of the Emancipation Proclamation. When Abraham Lincoln issued the Emancipation Proclamation on January 1, 1863, it applied only to slaves in those portions of the Confederacy *not* under Union authority. No Southern slave owners freed their slaves at Lincoln's command. But many black people already had freed themselves, and many more would liberate themselves as well as family and friends in the aftermath of Lincoln's order. The Emancipation Proclamation was of extreme importance. It helped the Union to win the war. It meant that at long last the United States government had joined the abolitionist movement.

leaders, who had considered recognizing the Confederacy, now declined to support a "nation" that relied on slavery while its opponent moved to abolish it. In this sense the Proclamation weakened the Confederacy's ability to prosecute the war.

Even more important, it undermined slavery in the South and contributed directly to the Confederacy's defeat. While the Proclamation may not have freed any of those in bondage on January 1, 1863, word of freedom spread rapidly across the South. Black people—aware that a Union victory in the war meant freedom—were far less likely to labor for their owners or for the Confederacy. More slaves ran away, especially as Union troops approached. Slave revolts became more likely,

PROFILE

ELIZABETH KECKLEY

Born a slave in 1818, Elizabeth Keckley became a skilled dressmaker for First Lady Mary Todd Lincoln. After President Lincoln's assassination in 1865, Keckley wrote one of the first personal accounts of life inside the Lincoln White House.

Elizabeth Keckley had experienced the exploitation and degradation common to thousands of slave women. She was born in Dinwiddie Court House, Virginia, and spent her childhood as a slave of the Burwell family. She saw slaves beaten and slave sales divide families. She watched as a young boy was sold away from his mother, so that his owner could buy pigs.

She was sold during adolescence to a North Carolina slave owner and beaten and eventually raped. She reluctantly described what happened: "I was regarded as fair-looking for one of my race, and for four years a white man—I spare the world his name—had base designs upon me. I do not care to dwell upon this subject, for it is one that is fraught with pain. Suffice it to say, that he persecuted me for four years, and I—I became a mother. The child of which he was the father was the only child I ever brought into the world."

She was later purchased back by one of the Burwell daughters, who took Elizabeth and her son George to St. Louis. There she learned how to sew and make dresses. She also married a slave, James Keckley, but they soon separated.

As a proficient seamstress, Keckley was able to purchase herself and her son for $1,200. She learned to read and write. In 1860 she moved to Washington and attracted a prosperous clientele that included the wives of prominent politicians, such as Varina Davis, the wife of Mississippi Senator Jefferson Davis, soon to be president of the Confederacy.

Shortly after the Lincolns arrived in Washington, Keckley began making dresses for the First Lady and became Mrs. Lincoln's confidante and traveling companion. Keckley helped convert Mrs. Lincoln, whose family owned slaves in Kentucky, to strong antislavery views. Both women lost sons. Elizabeth Keckley's son, George, was killed early in the Civil War in Missouri fighting for the Union. Eleven-year-old Willie Lincoln died of a fever in 1862 in the White House.

With Mrs. Lincoln's assistance, Elizabeth Keckley founded the Contraband Relief Association to provide aid to former slaves in Washington.

In 1868, she published *Behind the Scenes: Or Thirty Years a Slave and Four Years in the White House*. Although it was a favorable account of life in the Lincoln White House, the book upset the Lincoln family. Keckley denied that she had violated Mrs. Lincoln's privacy. "If I have betrayed confidence in anything I have published, it has been to place Mrs. Lincoln in better light before the world. My own character, as well as the character of Mrs. Lincoln, is at stake, since I have been intimately associated with the lady in the most eventful periods of her life."

Elizabeth Keckley spent the rest of her life living off the pension from her son's service as a Union soldier. She died in Washington in 1907 at the Home for Destitute Women and Children, which she had helped found years earlier.

though Lincoln cautioned against such violence in the Proclamation: "And I hereby enjoin upon the people so declared to be free to abstain from all violence, unless in necessary self-defence." The institution of slavery cracked, crumbled, and collapsed after January 1, 1863.

Without emancipation, the United States would not have survived as a unified nation. Abraham Lincoln, after first failing to make the connection between eliminating slavery and preserving the Union, came to understand it fully, and also grasped what freedom meant to both black and white people. In his annual message to Congress in December 1862, one month before the Proclamation, Lincoln described the importance of emancipation with a passion and feelings that were absent in the Proclamation itself. "We know how to save the Union. The world knows we do know how to save it. We—even *we here*—hold the power, and bear the responsibility. In *giving* freedom to the *slave*, we assure freedom to the *free*—honorable alike in what we give, and what we preserve."

BLACK MEN FIGHT FOR THE UNION

The Emancipation Proclamation not only marked the beginning of the end of slavery; it also authorized the enlistment of black troops in the Union Army. Just as white leaders in the North came to realize that the preservation of the Union necessitated the abolition of slavery, they also began to understand that black men were needed for the military effort if the Union was to triumph in the Civil War.

By early 1863, the war had not gone well for the all-white Union army. While they had won significant battlefield victories in Kentucky and Tennessee and had captured New Orleans, the war in the east was a much different matter (Map 11–2). The Union's Army of the Potomac faced a smaller but highly effective Confederate army—the Army of Northern Virginia—led by the remarkable General Robert E. Lee. Confederate troops forced a Union retreat from Richmond during the 1862 Peninsular campaign. Union forces lost at the first and second battles of Bull Run. Their only victory over Lee at Antietam provided Lincoln with the opportunity to issue the Preliminary Emancipation Proclamation. But that was followed by a crushing Union loss at Fredericksburg.

Much like the decision to free the slaves, the decision to employ black troops proceeded neither smoothly nor logically. The commitment to the Civil War as a white man's war was deeply entrenched, and the initial at-

tempts to raise black troops were strongly opposed by many white Northerners. As with emancipation, Lincoln moved slowly from outright opposition to cautious acceptance to enthusiastic support for enlisting black men in the Union Army.

Though black men had fought well in the War for Independence and the War of 1812, they were legally prohibited from joining the regular U.S. Army, and the Militia Act of 1792 also barred them from the state militias. In 1861 a few black men were able to join Union units and go off to war. H. Ford Douglas, a black leader of the 1850s who had a fair complexion, enlisted in the all-white 95th Illinois Infantry, a volunteer regiment.

The First South Carolina Volunteers

Some Union officers recruited black men long before emancipation was proclaimed and before most white Northerners were prepared to accept, much less welcome, black troops. In May 1862 General David Hunter began recruiting former slaves along the South Carolina coast and the Sea Islands, an area Union forces had captured in late 1861. But some black men did not want to enlist, and Hunter used white troops to force black men to "volunteer" for military service. He managed to organize a five-hundred-man regiment—the First South Carolina Volunteers.

The former slaves were outfitted in bright red pants, with blue coats and broad-brimmed hats. Through the summer of 1862, Hunter trained and drilled the regiment while awaiting official authorization and funds to pay them. When Congress balked, Hunter reluctantly disbanded all but one company of the regiment that August. The troops were dispersed, unpaid and disappointed. The surviving company was sent to St. Simon's Island off the Georgia coast to protect a community of former slaves.

Though Congress failed to support Hunter, it did pass the Second Confiscation Act and the Militia Act of 1862, which authorized President Lincoln to enlist black men. In Louisiana that fall, two regiments of free black men, the Native Guards, were accepted for federal service, and General Benjamin Butler organized them into the Corps d'Afrique. General Rufus Saxton gained the approval of Secretary of War Edwin Stanton to revive Hunter's dispersed regiment and to recall the company that had been sent to St. Simon's Island.

As commander, Saxton appointed Thomas Wentworth Higginson. Higginson was an ardent white abolitionist, one of the Secret Six who had provided financial support for John Brown's raid on Harpers Ferry. Higginson was determined not merely to end slavery but to

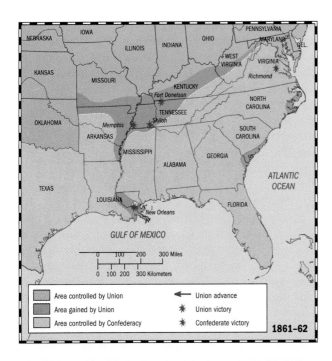

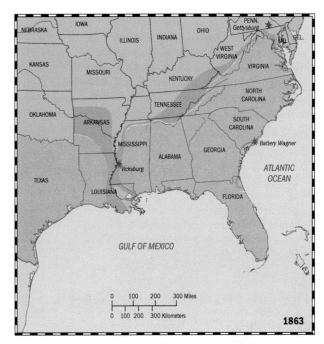

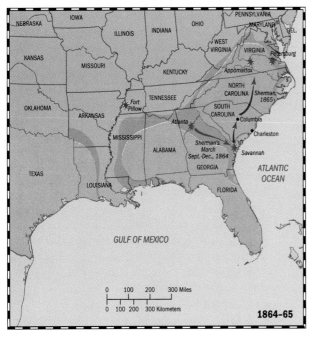

Map 11–2 The Course of the Civil War. Though the outcome of the Civil War remained in doubt until the autumn of 1864, Union armies as well as a Union naval blockade applied increasing pressure on the eleven Confederate states beginning in 1862. Black people freed themselves as Union forces carved out an enclave on the South Carolina coast, captured New Orleans, and pushed through Kentucky and Tennessee into Mississippi and Arkansas. Following the successful Union siege of Vicksburg in 1863, the Confederacy was divided along the Mississippi River. In 1864, General Ulysses S. Grant's Army of the Potomac drove General Robert E. Lee's Army of Northern Virginia into entrenchments around Richmond and Petersburg. General William Tecumseh Sherman marched from Atlanta to Savannah and then into the Carolinas. Several thousand more black people liberated themselves. The war ended in April 1865 with Lee's surrender to Grant at Appomattox Court House and Joseph E. Johnston's capitulation to Sherman near Durham, North Carolina.

prove that black people were equal to white people, a proposition that most white people regarded as preposterous. Disposing of the unit's gaudy red trousers, Higginson set out to mold this regiment of mostly former slaves into an effective fighting force. On Emancipation Day, January 1, 1863, near Beaufort, South Carolina, the First South Carolina Volunteer Regiment was inducted into the United States Army.

The Second South Carolina Volunteers

A month later, the Second South Carolina Volunteers began enrolling ex-slaves, many from Georgia and Florida. James Montgomery, another former financial supporter of John Brown, commanded them. Montgomery was determined that the regiment would wipe out all vestiges of slavery, especially the homes, plantations, and personal possessions of families who owned slaves. But like Hunter, Montgomery found that many former slaves were reluctant to volunteer for military service, so he also used force to recruit them. He concluded that black men responded to the call to arms much the way white men did, except that black men were less likely to desert once they joined the army.

> Finding it somewhat difficult to induce Negroes to enlist, we resolved to the draft. The negroes reindicate their claim to humanity by shirking the draft in every possible way; acting exactly like *white* men under similar circumstances. . . . The only difference that I notice is, the negro, after being drafted does not desert; but once dressed in the uniform with arms in his hands he feels himself a man; and acts like one.

The 54th Massachusetts Regiment

While ex-slaves joined the Union ranks in South Carolina, free black men in the North enlisted in what would become the most famous black unit, the 54th Massachusetts Regiment. In January 1863, governor of Massachusetts John A. Andrew received permission from Secretary of War Stanton to raise a black regiment. But because few black men lived in Massachusetts, Andrew asked prominent black men across the North for help. The Black Committee—as it became known—included Frederick Douglass, Martin Delany, Charles Remond, and Henry Highland Garnet.

These black leaders were convinced that by serving in the military, black men would prove that they deserved to be treated as equals, and had earned the right to be citizens. Frederick Douglass put it succinctly: "Once let the black man get upon his person the brass letters, U.S.; let him get an eagle on his button, and a musket on his shoulder and bullets in his pocket, and there is no power on earth which can deny that he has earned the right to citizenship." Two of Douglass's sons, Charles and Lewis, joined the 54th.

Lincoln, who had opposed emancipation and resisted enlisting black troops, became an enthusiastic supporter of black men in the Union Army. Writing to Andrew Johnson, who was the Union military governor of Tennessee, Lincoln perhaps over-optimistically predicted: "The bare sight of fifty thousand armed, and drilled black soldiers on the banks of the Mississippi, would end the rebellion at once. And who doubts that we can present that sight, if we but take hold in earnest."

Governor Andrew selected twenty-five-year-old Robert Gould Shaw to command the 54th Massachu-

setts Regiment. Shaw was a Harvard graduate from a prominent Massachusetts family, and he had already been wounded at the battle at Antietam. Though not an active abolitionist, he opposed slavery and was determined to prove that black men would fight well. The men the Black Committee recruited came from most of the northern states. Their average age was around twenty-five and virtually all of them were literate. They were farmers, seamen, butchers, blacksmiths, and teamsters. Only one of them had grown up in a slave state. As the ranks of the 54th filled, the 55th Massachusetts Regiment and the all-Black 5th Massachusetts Cavalry Regiment were also formed.

After training from March to May 1863, on May 28, 1863, the 54th paraded through Boston to the wharf to board a ship for the trip to South Carolina and the war. Thousands of people turned out to see the black men in blue uniforms. As they passed the home of William Lloyd Garrison, he stood erect with a bust of John Brown. As they passed the custom house where Crispus Attucks and four others had been killed in the Boston Massacre in 1770 the regiment sang "John Brown's Body." The departure of the 54th from the city was perhaps the most emotional event Boston had witnessed since Anthony Burns had been returned to slavery in 1854.

Black Soldiers Confront Discrimination

But the enthusiastic departure could not disguise the discrimination and hostility that black troops faced during the war. Many white Northerners were willing to accept neither the presence of black troops nor the idea that black men could endure combat. Many white people tolerated black troops only because they preferred that a black man die rather than a white man. A crude bit of verse in an Irish dialect that reflected this racism circulated during the war.

Sambo's Right to be Kilt
Some tell us 'tis a burnin' shame
　To Make the naygers fight;
And that the thrade of bein' kilt
　Belongs but to the white;
But as for me, upon my sowl!
　So liberal are we here,
I'll let Sambo be murthered instead of myself,
　On every day of the Year.

In the same vein, a white Union soldier wrote that a "Negro can fall from a rebel shot as well as me or my friends, and better them than us."

That black troops would serve in separate, all-black units was accepted as a matter of course. No one seriously proposed to integrate black men into previously all-white regiments. In 1863 the War Department created the Bureau of Colored Troops, and the Union Army remained segregated throughout the war. The only exception was the officers of the black regiments.

Almost all black troops had white officers. Yet many white officers, convinced that their military record would be tainted by such service, refused to command black troops. Others believed that black men simply could not be trained for combat. Even those white officers who were willing to command black troops sometimes regarded their men as "niggers" suited only for work or fatigue duty. When the 110th U.S. Colored Infantry joined General William Tecumseh Sherman's army on its march through Georgia and South Carolina in 1864 and 1865, Sherman kept the black men out of combat. Some were armed with picks and axes while others served as hospital guards and teamsters.

COME AND JOIN US BROTHERS.

PUBLISHED BY THE SUPERVISORY COMMITTEE FOR RECRUITING COLORED REGIMENTS

1210 CHESTNUT ST. PHILADELPHIA.

Lithograph: IChi-22051: "Come and join us brothers" Civil War; Philadelphia, PA; ca1863. Creator P. S. Duval & Son.

Posters and placards were widely used during the Civil War to recruit men to serve in the military. This poster depicts black troops with their weapons, winter uniforms, and white commander. Also note the drummer boy. Children served as drummers in many military units.

Black soldiers were paid less than white soldiers. Based on the assumption that black troops would be used almost exclusively for construction, transportation, cooking, and burial details, and not for fighting, the War Department authorized a lower pay scale for them. A white private earned $13 per month; a black private earned $10 per month. This demoralized black soldiers, particularly after they had shown that they were more than capable of fighting.

The 54th Massachusetts Regiment refused to accept their pay until they received equal pay. To take no compensation was an enormous sacrifice for men who had wives, children, and families to support. For some it was more than a monetary loss. Sergeant William Walker insisted—despite orders—that the men in his company take no pay until they received equal pay. He was charged with mutiny, convicted, and shot. In Texas a soldier in a black artillery unit from Rhode Island threatened a white officer in the dispute over pay. The white lieutenant shot and killed the black man, and the regiment's commander declined to charge the officer.

The pay issue festered in Congress for nearly two years. Finally near the end of the war, Congress enacted a compromise, but many black soldiers remained dissatisfied. The law equalized pay between black and white troops, but made it retroactive only to January 1, 1864—except for black men who had never been slaves. But the thousands of black men who had been slaves and had joined the military before January 1, 1864, would not be entitled to equal pay for the entire period of their service. The War Department compounded the problem with bureaucratic delays.

Black Men in Combat

Once black men put on the Union uniform, they took part in almost every battle that was fought during the rest of the Civil War. Black troops not only faced an enemy dedicated to the belief that the proper place of black people was in slavery, but they also confronted doubts about their fighting abilities among white Northerners. Yet by war's end, black units had suffered disproportionately more casualties than white units.

In October 1862, the first black unit went into combat in Missouri. James H. Lane, a white Free Soiler, recruited five hundred black men in Kansas. Most were runaway slaves from Missouri and Arkansas. After some hasty training, they advanced against a Confederate position at Island Mountain. The black troops held off an attack until reinforcements arrived, and the Confederates were repulsed. Soon thereafter, the black unit became the First Kansas Colored Infantry.

In January 1863, Thomas Wentworth Higginson led the First South Carolina Volunteers on raids on the Georgia and Florida coasts. At one point, they were surrounded at night by Confederate cavalry but managed to fight their way out and escape.

On June 3, 1863, the 54th Massachusetts Regiment arrived in South Carolina and joined the raids in Georgia. Other raids in the Carolina low country devastated rice plantations and liberated hundreds of slaves.

The Assault on Battery Wagner

Since 1861 and the Confederate capture of Fort Sumter in Charleston harbor that began the Civil War, Union leaders had been determined to retake the fort and occupy nearby Charleston—the heart of secession. In 1863 Union commanders began a combined land and sea offensive to seize the fort. But Battery Wagner, a heavily fortified installation on the northern tip of Morris Island, guarded the entrance to the harbor.

Frustrated in their initial efforts to enter the harbor, Major General Quincy A. Gilmore and Rear Admiral John Dahlgren decided on a full-scale assault on Wagner. After an unsuccessful attack by white troops, Colonel Shaw volunteered to lead the 54th in a second attack on the battery.

To improve the Union's chances, artillery fired more than 9,000 shells on Wagner on July 18, 1863. Everyone but the fort's Confederate defenders was convinced that no one could survive the bombardment. In fact only eight of the 1,620 defenders had been killed.

At sunset, 650 men of the first brigade of the 54th prepared to lead more than 5,000 Union troops in storming the battery. The regiment was tired and hungry but eager for the assault. Colonel Shaw offered brief words of encouragement to his troops. "Now I want you to prove yourselves men."

At 7:45 P.M. the 54th charged and was met by heavy rifle and artillery fire. Within minutes, the sand was littered with injured and dying men. Sergeant Major Lewis Douglass (the son of Frederick Douglass) was among those who took part. The 54th reached the walls—only to be thrown back in hand-to-hand combat. Shaw was killed.

Sergeant Major William H. Carney, though wounded four times, saved the regiment's flags. Thirty-seven years later, in May 1900, he was the first African American awarded the Congressional Medal of Honor for his gallantry that night.

Though white troops fought to support the 54th, the attack could not be sustained, and the battle was over by 1:00 A.M. But within days, the courage of the 54th was

On the evening of July 18, 1863, more than 600 black men led by their white commander, Colonel Robert Gould Shaw, attacked heavily fortified Battery Wagner on Morris Island near the southern approach to Charleston harbor. They made a frontal assault through withering fire and managed to breach the battery before Confederate forces threw them back. Shaw was killed and the 54th suffered heavy losses. It was a defining moment of the Civil War, demonstrating to skeptical white people the valor and determination of black troops.

known across the North, putting to rest—for a time—the myth that black men lacked the nerve to fight.

The day after the attack, Shaw and twenty of his men were buried in a trench outside Wagner. Several wounded men had drowned when the tide came in. Altogether 246 black and white men were killed, 890 were wounded, and 391 were taken prisoner. Forty-two percent of the men of the 54th were killed or injured, and eighty were taken prisoner.

Union forces never took Wagner. The Confederates abandoned Charleston as the war was ending in February 1865. Black Union troops—the 21st U.S. Colored Infantry and the 55th Massachusetts regiment occupied the city. Years later Charles Crowley recalled the scene. "Never, while memory holds power to retain anything, shall I forget the thrilling strain of music of the Union, as sung by our sable soldiers when marching up Meet-

ing Street with the battle stained banners flapping in the breeze."

THE CONFEDERATE REACTION TO BLACK SOLDIERS

On June 7, 1863, Confederate forces attempting to relieve the Union siege of Vicksburg attacked a Union garrison defended by black troops at Milliken's Bend on the Mississippi River. Though armed with outdated muskets and not fully trained, the defenders fought off the Confederate attack. Assistant Secretary of War Charles A. Dana claimed that their valor would change the attitudes of white people toward the use of black troops. "The bravery of the blacks completely revolutionized the sentiment of the army with regard to the

VOICES

LEWIS DOUGLASS DESCRIBES THE FIGHTING AT BATTERY WAGNER

After the failed assault on Battery Wagner, Lewis Douglass wrote this letter home to his wife Amelia.

Lewis Douglass
July 20 [1863]

My Dear Amelia:

I have been in two fights, and am unhurt. I am about to go in another I believe tonight. Our men fought well on both occasions. The last one was desperate. We charged that terrible battery on . . . Fort Wagner and were repulsed. . . . I escaped unhurt from amidst that perfect hail of shot and shell. It was terrible. . . . This regiment has established its reputation as a fighting regiment. Not a man flinched, though it was a trying time. Men fell all around me. . . . Our men would close up again, but it was no use. . . . How I got out of that fight alive I cannot tell, but I am here. My dear girl, I hope again to see you. I must bid you farewell should I be killed. Remember if I die, I die in a good cause. I wish we had a hundred thousand colored troops. We would put an end to this war.
Your own loving
Lewis

QUESTIONS

1. How graphic is this description of combat?

2. Does Douglass explain what motivated him as well as his fellow troops?

3. Does this account of combat differ in any way from the way a white soldier might describe it?

Source: Carter G. Woodson, ed., *The Mind of the Negro as Reflected in Letters Written during the Crisis 1800–1860* (1926).

---

employment of negro troops. I heard prominent officers who formerly in private sneered at the idea of negroes fighting express themselves after that as heartily in favor of it."

The southern soldiers who lost at Milliken's Bend, however, felt differently. Enraged by having to fight black troops, they executed several black men captured during the engagement and sold others into slavery.

The Abuse and Murder of Black Troops

Confederate leaders and troops refused to recognize black men as legitimate soldiers. Captured black soldiers were persistently abused and even murdered rather than treated as prisoners of war. Confederate Secretary of War James A. Seddon ordered that captured black soldiers be executed. "We ought never to be inconvenienced with such prisoners . . . summary execution must therefore be inflicted on those taken."

Protests erupted across the North after Confederate authorities decided to treat 80 men of the 54th Massachusetts Regiment who had been captured in the attack on Battery Wagner not as prisoners of war, but as rebellious slaves. Frederick Douglass refused to recruit any more black men and held Abraham Lincoln personally responsible for tolerating the mistreatment of black prisoners. "How many 54ths must be cut to pieces, its mutilated prisoners killed, and its living sold into slavery, to be tortured to death by inches, before Mr. Lincoln shall say, 'Hold, enough!'"

Lincoln issued General Order 11, threatening to execute southern troops or confine them to hard labor. "For every soldier of the United States killed in violation of the laws of war a rebel soldier shall be executed, and for every one enslaved by the enemy or sold into slavery a rebel soldier shall be placed at hard labor on the public works, and continued at such labor until the other shall be released and receive the treatment due to a prisoner of war."

Lincoln's order did not prevent the Confederates from sending the men of the 54th to trial by the state of South Carolina. The state regarded the black soldiers as either rebellious slaves or free black men inciting rebellion. Four black soldiers went on trial in Charleston police court, but the court declared that it lacked jurisdiction. The black prisoners were eventually sent to prisoner of war camps.

VOICES

A Black Nurse on the Horrors of War and the Sacrifice of Black Soldiers

Susie King Taylor was born a slave on the Georgia Sea Islands and learned to read and write in Savannah. She escaped to Union forces in 1862 and served as a nurse and laundress with the First South Carolina Volunteers. In these passages, written years later, she describes her service with black men who went into combat and pays them tribute.

It seems strange how our aversion to seeing suffering is overcome in war,—how we are able to see the most sickening sights, such as men with their limbs blown off and mangled by the deadly shells, without a shudder; and instead of turning away, how we hurry to assist in alleviating their pain, bind up their wounds, and press the cool water to their parched lips, with feelings only of sympathy and pity. . . .

I look around now and see the comforts that our younger generation enjoy, and think of the blood that was shed to make these comforts possible for them, and see how little some of them appreciate the old soldiers. My heart burns within me at this want of appreciation. There are only a few of them left now, so let us all, as the ranks close, take a deeper interest in them. Let the younger generation take an interest also, and remember that it was through the efforts of these veterans that we older ones enjoy our liberty to-day.

QUESTIONS

1. How does Taylor describe what men in combat endure?

2. Who is the object of Taylor's criticism and why does she offer the criticism?

Source: Susie King Taylor, *Reminiscences of My Life in Camp*, pp. 31–32, 51–52.

The Fort Pillow Massacre

The Civil War's worst atrocity against black troops occurred at Fort Pillow in Tennessee on April 12, 1864. Confederates under the command of Nathan Bedford Forrest slaughtered black troops and their white commander, William F. Bradford, after they had surrendered. (After the Civil War, Forrest gained notoriety as a founder of the Ku Klux Klan.) The Fort Pillow massacre became the subject of an intense debate in Lincoln's cabinet. But rather than retaliate indiscriminately—as required by General Order 11—the cabinet decided only to punish those responsible for the killings, if and when they were apprehended. But no one was punished during or after the war. Instead, black troops exacted revenge themselves. In fighting around Petersburg, Virginia, later that year, black soldiers shouting, "Remember Fort Pillow!" reportedly murdered several Confederate prisoners. Captain Charles Francis Adams Jr. reported, "The darkies fought ferociously. . . . If they murdered prisoners, as I hear they did . . . they can hardly be blamed."

On their own, Union commanders in the field also retaliated for the Confederate treatment of captured black troops. When captured black men were virtually enslaved and forced to work at Richmond and Charleston on Confederate fortifications that were under Union attack, Union officers put Confederate prisoners to work on Union installations that were under fire. Aware that they were not likely to be treated as well as white soldiers if they were captured, black men often fought desperately.

The Crater

But as impressive as black troops often were in battle, northern commanders sometimes hesitated to commit black men to combat. In 1864 after Union troops laid siege to Petersburg, Virginia, white soldiers of the 48th Pennsylvania, who had been coal miners before the war, offered to dig a tunnel and set off an explosion under Confederate lines. General Ambrose Burnside agreed to the plan, and assigned black troops to be prepared to lead the attack after the blast.

Four tons of powder were placed in the tunnel. But only hours before the blast was set to go off, Burnside's superior, General George Meade replaced the black troops with inadequately trained white soldiers

THE FORT PILLOW MASSACRE.

In April 1864, 1,500 Confederate forces under General Nathan Bedford Forrest attacked and captured Fort Pillow, a Union installation on the Mississippi River 40 miles north of Memphis, Tennessee that was defended by 550 black and white troops. After the Union forces surrendered, Confederate troops executed some of the black soldiers. Forrest and his men denied the atrocity, but there is little doubt that it occurred.

commanded by an alcoholic. Meade either lacked confidence in the black unit or was worried that he would be blamed for using black men as shields for white soldiers if the attack failed.

On July 30, 1864, at 4:45 A.M., what was perhaps the largest man-made explosion in history up to that time buried a Confederate regiment and an artillery battery and created a crater 170 feet long, 60 feet wide, and 30 feet deep. But the white Union troops rushed down into the crater instead of fanning out around it in pursuit of the stunned enemy. While the Union soldiers marveled at the destruction, the Confederates launched a counterattack that threw back the Union troops, including the black troops who were finally brought forward. Some of the black men were murdered after they surrendered. More than 4,000 Union troops, many of them black, were killed or wounded.

BLACK MEN IN THE UNION NAVY

Black men had a tradition of serving at sea and had been in the U.S. Navy almost continuously since its creation in the 1790s. In the early nineteenth century, there were so many black sailors that some white people tried to ban black men from the navy. Nor did black sailors serve in segregated units. Naval crews were integrated.

Nonetheless, black sailors encountered rampant discrimination and exploitation during the Civil War. They were paid less than white sailors. They were assigned the hardest and filthiest tasks, such as loading coal and tending the boilers, on the navy's new steam-powered vessels. Many were stewards who waited on white officers. White officers and sailors often treated black sailors with contempt. On the USS *Constellation* in 1863, the three white crew members regularly referred to the thirty-three black sailors as "God-damned nigger," "black dog," "black bitches," and kicked and swore at them.

But some white men respected and admired the black sailors. One observed: "We never were betrayed when we trusted one of them, they were always our friends and were ready, if necessary, to lay down their lives for us." (He did not say whether white men were willing to lay down their lives for black men.) About 30,000 of the 120,000 men who served in the Union Navy were black sailors.

LIBERATORS, SPIES, AND GUIDES

Besides serving as soldiers and sailors, black men and women aided themselves and the Union cause as liberators, spies, guides, and messengers. At about 3 A.M. on May 13, 1862, Robert Smalls, a twenty-three-year-old slave, fired the boiler on *The Planter*, a Confederate supply ship moored in Charleston harbor. With the aid of seven black crewmen, Smalls sailed *The Planter* past Confederate fortifications—including Fort Sumter—to the Union fleet outside the harbor and to freedom. Smalls liberated himself and fifteen other slaves including the families of several crewmen and his own wife, daughter, and son.

Smalls managed the daring escape because he knew the South Carolina coast and was familiar with Confederate navigation signals and regulations. He became an overnight hero in the North, a slave who wanted freedom and had possessed the leadership, knowledge, and tenacity to liberate sixteen people.

In 1863 Harriet Tubman organized a spy ring in the South Carolina low country, and in cooperation with the all-black Second South Carolina Volunteer Regiment, helped organize an expedition that destroyed plantations and freed nearly eight hundred slaves, many of whom joined the Union Army.

In Richmond in 1864, slaves helped more than one hundred escaped Union prisoners of war. Other slaves drew sketches and maps of Confederate fortifications and warned Union forces about troop movements. A black couple near Fredericksburg, Virginia, cleverly transmitted military intelligence to Union General Joseph Hooker. The woman washed laundry for a Confederate officer and hung shirts and blankets in patterns that conveyed information to her husband, who was a cook and groom for Union troops and relayed the information to Union officers.

Mary Elizabeth Bowser worked at the Confederate White House in Richmond. She reported conversations

ROBERT SMALLS, CAPTAIN OF THE GUN-BOAT "PLANTER."

Robert Smalls was born a slave in Beaufort, South Carolina in 1839. In 1862 while working as a pilot on a 150 foot Confederate gunboat in Charleston harbor, the young man—still in bondage—devised an audacious plan to flee with family, friends, and the vessel to the Union navy while the ship's white officers enjoyed a night on the town. Small's exploits created a sensation in the North. He went on to become a successful politician in South Carolina in the decades following the war.

by President Jefferson Davis and his subordinates to Union agents until the Confederates became suspicious. Bowser and slave Jim Pemberton managed to flee, after trying to burn down the mansion to distract their pursuers.

In Virginia's Shenandoah Valley slave John Henry Woodson was a guide for Union General Philip H. Sheridan's cavalry in 1864 and 1865. Woodson was the father of Carter G. Woodson who would become the "father" of black history in the twentieth century.

VIOLENT OPPOSITION TO BLACK PEOPLE

No matter how well black men fought, no matter how much individual black women contributed, and no matter how many people—black and white—died "to make men free," many white Northerners, both civilian and military, remained bitter and often violently hostile to black people. They used intimidation, threats, and terror to injure and kill people of color.

HARRIET TUBMAN

Long before her death in 1913, Harriet Tubman had achieved legendary status. Though she never led a slave revolt like Nat Turner or Joseph Cinque, she was personally responsible for freeing more slaves than any other individual in American history.

Thomas Wentworth Higginson, an abolitionist and commander of the First South Carolina Volunteers, called her "the greatest heroine of the age." He added, "Her tales of adventure are beyond anything in fiction and her ingenuity and generalship are extraordinary. I have known her for some time—the slaves call her Moses."

Harriet Tubman was born in 1821 on Maryland's Eastern Shore, one of eleven slave children of Harriet Greene and Benjamin Ross. When a teenager, she was struck in the head by a rock or chunk of metal hurled by an overseer at a fleeing slave. The incident left her plagued by seizures and with an ugly scar that she sometimes covered with a turban.

In 1849 she married John Tubman, a free black man. Fearing that she would be sold following the death of her owner, she escaped to Pennsylvania, but her husband refused to go with her. He later married another woman and died shortly after the Civil War.

Tubman—like Sojourner Truth—never learned to read or write. She had, however, a deep reservoir of religious faith that sustained her and helped inspire her to return to slave states again and again to free people held in bondage. She made at least fifteen trips South in ten years as a conductor on the Underground Railroad.

Working with the support of William Still and the General Vigilance Committee in Philadelphia and Quaker abolitionist Thomas Garrett in Wilmington, Delaware, she freed more than 200 people. Among them were her sister, her sister's two children, and her parents. She never lost a passenger.

Aware that she had a hefty reward on her head, Tubman devised detailed plans and elaborate disguises to elude capture. She feigned insanity, she pretended to be feeble, she forged passes, and she acquired real railroad tickets. She also packed a gun, as much to goad any of her charges whose courage might waver as to protect herself.

In 1862 during the Civil War, Tubman journeyed to the South Carolina low country where Union military forces had established a base. She worked as a nurse, cook, scout, and liberator. She made her way up the Combahee River and helped several hundred slaves free themselves. She was on Morris Island in 1863 when the 54th Massachusetts Regiment attacked Battery Wagner.

After the war, she married Nelson Davis, a Union veteran. He died in 1888. She and several of her supporters spent years in a determined effort to gain her a federal pension before they finally succeeded in securing an award of $20 a month.

Tubman was active in the women's rights movement of the late nineteenth century. She attended several women's rights conventions and she was friendly with Susan B. Anthony. She also worked to help elderly ex-slaves who faced insecurity and uncertainty after emancipation. She bought a home in Auburn, New York, and eventually died there.

Many Americans talk about freedom, but not many have done as much to make it a reality for as many people as did Harriet Tubman.

The New York City Draft Riot

Irish Catholic Americans, themselves held in contempt by prosperous white Protestants, indulged in an orgy of violence in New York City in July 1863. The New York draft riot arose from racial, religious, and class antago-nisms. Poor, unskilled Irish workers and other white Northerners were convinced by leading Democrats, including New York Governor Horatio Seymour, that the war had become a crusade to benefit black people.

The violence began when federal officials prepared to select the first men to be drafted by the Union for

During the draft riot in New York City in July 1863, black people were attacked, beaten, and lynched by white mobs.

military service. An enraged mob made up mostly of Irish men attacked the draft offices and any unfortunate black people who were in the vicinity. Many of the Irish men were angry because black men had replaced striking Irish stevedores on the city's wharves the month before and because rich white Northerners could purchase an exemption from the draft.

The riot went on for four days. The poorly trained city police could not control it. Black people were beaten and lynched. The Colored Orphan Asylum was burned to the ground, though the children had already fled. The mob attacked businesses that employed black people. Protestant churches were burned. Rioters set fire to Horace Greeley's *New York Tribune*. The houses of Republicans and abolitionists were attacked and destroyed. The violence and destruction did not end until the U.S. Army arrived. Soldiers who had been fighting Confederates at Gettysburg two weeks earlier found themselves firing on New York rioters.

Union Troops and Slaves

White Union troops who brutalized southern freedmen sometimes exceeded the savagery of northern civilians. In November 1861 men from the 47th New York Regiment raped an eight-year-old black girl. Later in Virginia, a Connecticut soldier told what men in his regiment did to a pair of black women. They took "two niger wenches . . . turned them on their heads, & put

tobacco, chips, sticks, lighted cigars & sand into their behinds." On Sherman's march through Georgia in 1864, a drunk Irish soldier from an Ohio regiment shot into a crowd of black children, badly wounding one youngster. He was tried and convicted, but released on a technicality and returned to the army.

However, not all white troops behaved despicably. Others sympathized with slaves. Some Union soldiers wanted to fight for the liberation of black people. One Wisconsin private wrote, "I have no heart in this war if the slaves cannot be free." Many were visibly moved by the desire of slaves for freedom. A Union officer noted that those who believed that slaves were satisfied with slavery were wrong. "It is claimed the negroes are so well contented with their slavery; if it ever was so, that day has ceased." Several Union soldiers wept when they witnessed a daughter reunited with her mother ten years after they had been separated in a slave sale.

REFUGEES

Throughout the war, black people took advantage of the hostilities to free themselves. It was not easy. Confederate authorities did not hesitate to reenslave or even execute black people who sought freedom. Six black people were hanged near Georgetown, South Carolina, in 1862 when they were captured as they attempted to reach Union forces.

As Union armies plunged deep into the Confederacy in 1863 and 1864, thousands of black people liberated themselves and became refugees. When General William Tecumseh Sherman's army of 60,000 troops laid waste to Georgia in 1864 an estimated 10,000 former slaves followed his troops to Savannah, though they lacked adequate food, clothing, and housing. Sherman did not like black people, and his troops tried with little success to discourage the refugees. As one elderly black couple prepared to leave a plantation, Union soldiers as well as their master urged them to remain. They declined in no uncertain terms. "We must go, freedom is as sweet to us as it is to you."

BLACK PEOPLE AND THE CONFEDERACY

The Confederacy was based on the defense of slavery, and it benefited from the usually coerced but sometimes willing labor of black people. Slaves toiled in southern fields and factories during the Civil War. The greater the burden of work the slaves took on, the more white men there were who could become soldiers. When the war began, southern whites believed that their disadvantage in manpower—the twenty-two northern states had 22,339,989 people; the eleven Confederate states had 9,103,332 (5,449,462 white people, 3,521,110 slaves, and 132,760 free black people)—would be partly offset by the slaves whose presence would free a disproportionately large number of white Southerners to go to war. While slaves would tend cotton, corn, and cattle, white southern men would fight.

The Impressment of Black People

As the war went on, the demand for more troops and laborers in the Confederacy increased. Slave owners were first asked and then compelled to contribute their slave laborers to the war effort. In July 1861, the Confederate Congress required the registration and enrollment of free black people for military labor. In the summer of 1862, the Virginia legislature authorized the impressment of 10,000 slaves between the ages of eighteen and forty-five for up to sixty days. The owners would receive $16 per month per slave.

But many slave owners who enjoyed the benefits of forced labor did not themselves want to be forced to turn their slaves over to state authorities. In October 1862 President Davis asked Virginia to draft 4,500 black people to build fortifications around Richmond, so that "whites could fight more and dig less."

The most important factory in the South was the Tredegar Iron Works in Richmond. During the war, more than 1,200 slaves and free black men worked there in every capacity—from unskilled laborers to engineers—manufacturing artillery, locomotives, nails, and much more. Other black men across the South loaded and unloaded ships, worked for railroads, and labored in salt works.

In South Carolina in 1863, Confederate officials appealed to slave owners to provide 2,500 slaves to help fortify Charleston. The owners offered fewer than 1,000. During the Union bombardment of Fort Sumter, five hundred slaves were employed in the difficult, dirty, and dangerous work of building and rebuilding the fort. Slaves were even forced into combat. Two Virginia slaves who were compelled to load and fire Confederate cannons near Yorktown were shot and killed.

While many slave owners resisted the impressment of their bondsmen, many white Southerners who did not own slaves were infuriated when the Confederate conscription law in 1862 exempted men who owned twenty or more slaves from military service. This "twenty nigger law" meant that poor white men were drafted while wealthier planters remained home, presumably to supervise and discipline their slaves. One Mississippi soldier deserted the Confederate Army, claiming that he "did not propose to fight for the rich men while they were home having a good time." Though the law was widely criticized, planters—always a small percentage of the white southern population—dominated the Confederate government and would not permit the repeal of the exemption.

Confederates Enslave Free Black People

After Lincoln's Emancipation Proclamation, Confederate President Jefferson Davis issued a counter proclamation in February 1863 declaring that free people would be enslaved, "all free negroes within the limits of the Southern Confederacy shall be placed on the slave status, and be deemed to be chattels. . . . forever." This directive was not widely enforced. Davis, however, went on to order Confederate armies that invaded Union states to capture free black people in the North and enslave them. "All negroes who shall be taken in any of the States in which slavery does not now exist, in the progress of our arms, shall be adjudged, immediately after their capture, to occupy slave status."

This was done. Several hundred Northern black people were taken South after Confederate forces invaded Pennsylvania in 1863 and fought at Gettysburg. At least

50 black people were captured by Robert E. Lee's Army of Northern Virginia at Greensburg, Pennsylvania.

Black Confederates

Most of the labor black people did for the Confederacy was involuntary. But there were a few free black men and women who offered their services to the southern cause.

In Lynchburg, Virginia, in the spring of 1861, seventy free black people volunteered "to act in whatever capacity may be assigned them." In Memphis in the fall, several hundred black residents cheered for Jefferson Davis and sang patriotic songs. These demonstrations of black support were made early in the conflict when the outcome was still much in doubt and long before the war became a crusade against slavery.

The status of many free black Southerners remained precarious. In Virginia in 1861 impressment laws, like those applying to slaves, compelled free black men to work on Confederate defenses around Richmond and Petersburg. Months before the war, South Carolina considered forcing its free black population to choose between enslavement and exile. The legislature rejected the proposal, but it terrified the state's free black people. Many people of color there had been free for generations. Fair in complexion, they had education, skills, homes, and businesses. Some even owned slaves. When the war came, many were willing to demonstrate their devotion to the South in a desperate attempt to gain white acceptance before they lost their freedom and property.

In early 1861 before the formation of the Confederacy but after the secession of South Carolina, eighty-two free black men in Charleston petitioned Governor Francis W. Pickens "to be assigned any service where we can be useful." To distinguish themselves from slaves and to show their solidarity with white Southerners, they proclaimed, "We are by birth citizens of South Carolina, in our veins is the blood of the white race in some half, in others much more, our attachments are with you, our hopes of safety and protection is in South Carolina, our allegiance is due alone to her, in her defence we are willing to offer up our lives and all that is dear to us." Pickens rejected the petition, but white South Carolinians were pleased at this show of loyalty.

White southern leaders generally ignored offers of free black support unless it was for menial labor. But in Charleston, when the city was under siege between 1863 and 1865, black and white residents were grateful that volunteer fire brigades composed of free black men turned out repeatedly to fight fires caused by Union artillery.

Personal Servants

Other black men contributed in different ways to the Confederate military effort. Black musicians in Virginia played for Confederate regiments and received the same pay as white musicians. Well-to-do white men often took their slaves—personal servants—with them when they went off to war. The servants cooked, cleaned uniforms, cared for weapons, maintained horses, and even provided entertainment. Some were loyal and devoted. They cared for owners who were wounded or fell sick. They accompanied the bodies of dead masters home.

Being the personal servant for a soldier was hard and sometimes dangerous work. Those close to combat could be killed or injured. One father warned his son not to take Sam, a valuable slave, into battle. "I hear you are likely to have a big battle soon, and I write to tell you not to let Sam go into the fight with you. Keep him in the rear, for that nigger is worth a thousand dollars." The father evidently placed a higher value on the slave than on his son.

Black Men Fighting for the South

Though it was not legal, some black men did fight for the Confederacy. White New York troops claimed to have encountered about seven hundred armed black men in late 1861 near Newport News, Virginia. In 1862 a black Confederate sharpshooter positioned himself in a chimney and shot several Union soldiers before he was finally killed. Fifty black men served as pickets for the Confederates along the Rappahannock River in Virginia in 1863.

John Wilson Buckner, a free black man with a light complexion, enlisted in the First South Carolina Artillery. As a member of the well-regarded free black Ellison family of Stateburg, South Carolina, Buckner was considered an "honorary white man." He fought for the Confederacy in the defense of Charleston at Battery Wagner in July 1863 and was wounded just before the 54th Massachusetts Regiment assaulted the fort.

Some black civilians supported the war effort and stood to profit if the South won. Buckner's uncles grew corn, sweet potatoes, peas, sorghum, and beans to feed Confederate troops on the Ellison family plantation near Stateburg, South Carolina. By hiring out horses, mules, and slaves they owned, the Ellisons had earned nearly $1,000 by 1863. By 1865, they had paid almost $5,000 in taxes to the Confederacy, nearly one-fifth of their total income. They also patriotically invested almost $7,000 in Confederate bonds and notes. Like prosperous white families, the Ellisons lost most of this investment with the defeat of the Confederacy. At war's end, the bonds were as worthless as Confederate cash, and the eighty slaves the Ellisons owned—worth approximately $100,000—were free people (see Chapter 6).

Other black Southerners also suffered economically from the Confederate defeat. Richard Mack, a South Carolina slave, went off to war as a personal servant. After his master died, he became an orderly for another Confederate officer. He worked hard and accumulated a large sum in Confederate currency. He later joked, "If we had won, I would be rich."

In Virginia, free black people and slaves also contributed to the Confederate cause. Pompey Scott of Amelia County gave $20 to the war effort. William, a slave who had amassed $150, invested in Confederate State Loan Bonds. Lewis, a Mecklenburg County slave, was not permitted to join a Confederate cavalry unit as a bugler so he donated his bugle and $20 to the Confederacy.

White Southerners effusively praised the few black people who actively supported the South. Several states awarded pensions to black men who served in the war and survived. Henry Clay Lightfoot was a slave in Culpeper, Virginia, who went to war as a body servant of Captain William Holcomb. After the war, he bought a house, raised a family, and was elected to the Culpeper town council. He collected a pension from Virginia, and when he died in 1931, the United Daughters of the Confederacy draped his coffin in a Confederate flag.

Black Opposition to the Confederacy

Though many white Southerners and some Northerners believed that most slaves would support their masters, in fact most did not. When a slave named Tom was asked if slaves would fight for their masters, he replied: "I know they say dese tings, but dey lies. Our masters may talk now all dey choose; but one ting's sartin,—*dey don't dare to try us.* Jess put de guns in our hans, and you'll soon see dat we not only knows *how* to shoot, but *who,* to shoot. *My* master wouldn't be wuff much ef I was a soldier."

The Confederate Debate on Black Troops

By late 1863 and 1864, prospects for the Confederacy had become grim. The Union naval blockade of Southern ports had become increasingly effective and the likelihood of British aid had all but vanished. Confederate armies suffered crushing defeats at Vicksburg and Gettysburg in 1863 and absorbed terrible losses in Tennessee, Georgia, and Virginia in 1864.

As defeat loomed, some white Southerners began to discuss the possibility of arming black men. Several southern newspapers advocated it. In September 1863 the Montgomery (Alabama) *Weekly Mail* admitted that it would have been preposterous to contemplate the need for black troops earlier in the war, but it had now become necessary to save the white South.

> We are forced by the necessity of our condition—by the insolence and barbarity of the enemy, by his revengeful and demoniacal spirit—to take a step which is revolting to every sentiment of pride, and to every principle that governed our institutions before the war. But the war has made great changes, and we must meet those changes, for the sake of preserving our very existence. It is a matter of necessity, therefore, that we should use every means within our reach to defeat the enemy. One of these, and the only one which will checkmate him, is the employment of negroes in the military service of the Confederacy.

In early 1864 Confederate General Patrick Cleburne recommended enlisting slaves and promising them their freedom if they remained loyal to the Confederacy. Cleburne argued that this policy would gain recognition and aid from Great Britain and that it would disrupt Union military efforts to recruit black Southerners. Yet most white Southerners considered arming slaves and free black men an appalling prospect. Jefferson Davis ordered military officers including Cleburne to cease discussing the issue.

Most white Southerners were convinced that to arm slaves and put black men in gray uniforms defied the assumptions on which southern society was based. Black people were inferior, and their proper status was to be slaves. The Richmond *Whig* declared in 1864 that "servitude is a divinely appointed condition for the highest good of the slave." It was absurd to contemplate black people as soldiers and as free people. Georgia politician Howell Cobb explained that slaves could not be armed. "If slaves will make good soldiers our whole theory of slavery is wrong."

The Civil War for white Southerners was a war to prevent the abolition of slavery. Now white southern voices were proposing abolition to preserve the southern nation. North Carolina Senator Robert M. T. Hunter opposed any attempt to enlist slaves and free them. "If we are right in passing this measure we were wrong in denying to the old government the right to interfere with the institution of slavery and to emancipate slaves. Besides, if we offer slaves their freedom . . . we confess that we were insincere, were hypocritical, in asserting that slavery was the best state for the negroes themselves."

Nevertheless, as the military situation deteriorated, the South moved toward employing black troops. In November 1864 Virginia Governor William Smith enthusiastically supported the idea. "There is not a man that would not cheerfully put the negro in the Army rather than become a slave himself. . . . Standing before God and my country, I do not hesitate to say that I would arm such portion of our able-bodied slaves population as may be necessary." In February 1865 Jefferson Davis and the Confederate cabinet conceded, "We are reduced to choosing whether the negroes shall fight for us or against us."

The opinion of General Robert E. Lee was critical to determining whether the Confederacy would decide to arm black men. No Southerner was more revered and respected. Lee had freed nearly two hundred slaves in keeping with the instructions of his father-in-law, George Washington Parke Custis's will in 1862. That will provided that the slaves be emancipated within five years of Custis's death in 1857.

With his army struggling to survive a desperate winter around Petersburg and Richmond, Lee announced in February 1865 that he favored both enrolling and emancipating black troops. "My own opinion is that we should employ them without delay." He believed that their service as slaves would make them capable soldiers. "They possess the physical qualities in an eminent degree. Long habits of obedience and subordination, coupled with moral influence which in our country the white man possesses over the black, furnish an excellent foundation for that discipline which is the best guarantee of military efficiency."

Less than a month later in March 1865, though many white Southerners still opposed it, the Confederate Congress voted to enlist 300,000 black men between the ages of eighteen and forty-five. They would receive the same pay, equipment, and supplies as white soldiers. But those who were slaves would *not* be freed *unless* their owner consented and the state where they served agreed to their emancipation.

It was a desperate measure by a nearly defeated government and did not affect the outcome of the conflict. Before the war ended in April, authorities in Virginia managed to recruit some black men and send a few into combat. By the end of March, one company of thirty-five black men—twelve free black men and twenty-three slaves—was organized. On April 4, 1865, Union troops attacked Confederate supply wagons that the black troops were guarding in Amelia County. Less than a week later, Lee surrendered to Grant at Appomattox Court House and the Civil War ended.

CONCLUSION

The Civil War ended with the decisive defeat of the Confederacy. The Union was preserved. The long ordeal of slavery for millions of people of African descent was over. Slavery—having thrived in America for nearly two hundred fifty years—was finally abolished by an amendment to the U.S. Constitution. Congress passed the Thirteenth Amendment on January 31, 1865. It was ratified by twenty-seven states and declared in effect on December 18, 1865.

Were it not for the presence and labors of more than four million black people, there would have been no Civil War. Had it not been for the presence and contributions of more than 185,000 black soldiers and sailors, the Union would not have won. Almost 40,000 of those black men died in combat and of disease during the war.

No one better represents the dramatic shift in attitudes and policies toward African Americans during the Civil War than Abraham Lincoln. When the war began, Lincoln insisted that it was a white man's conflict to suppress an insurrection of rebellious white Southerners. Black people, Lincoln remained convinced, would be better off outside the United States. But the war went on, and thousands of white men died. Lincoln issued the Emancipation Proclamation and welcomed the enlistment of black troops. The president came to appreciate the achievements and devotion of black troops and condemned the mean-spiritedness of white Northerners who opposed the war. Lincoln wrote in 1863: "And then there will be some black men who can remember that, with silent tongue, and clenched teeth, and steady eye, and well-poised bayonet, they have helped mankind on to this great consummation; while, I fear, there will be some white ones, unable to forget that, with malignant heart, and deceitful speech, they have strove to hinder it."

REVIEW QUESTIONS

1. How did the Union's purposes in the Civil War change between 1861 and 1865? What accounts for those changes?

2. How did policies of the Confederate government toward slaves change during the Civil War? What were those changes and when and why did they occur?

3. When the Civil War began, why did northern black men volunteer to serve in the Union army if the war had not yet become a war to end slavery?

TIMELINE

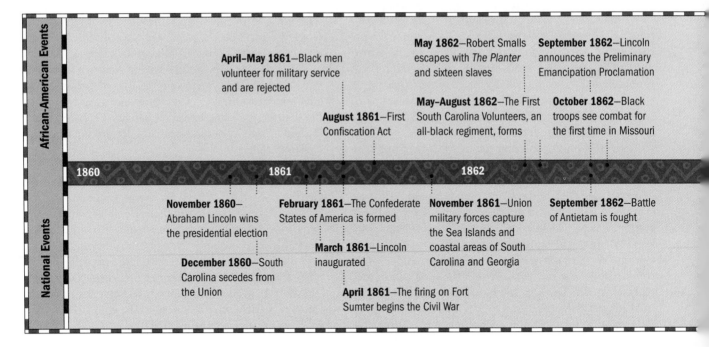

African-American Events

April–May 1861—Black men volunteer for military service and are rejected

August 1861—First Confiscation Act

May 1862—Robert Smalls escapes with *The Planter* and sixteen slaves

May–August 1862—The First South Carolina Volunteers, an all-black regiment, forms

September 1862—Lincoln announces the Preliminary Emancipation Proclamation

October 1862—Black troops see combat for the first time in Missouri

1860   1861   1862

National Events

November 1860—Abraham Lincoln wins the presidential election

December 1860—South Carolina secedes from the Union

February 1861—The Confederate States of America is formed

March 1861—Lincoln inaugurated

April 1861—The firing on Fort Sumter begins the Civil War

November 1861—Union military forces capture the Sea Islands and coastal areas of South Carolina and Georgia

September 1862—Battle of Antietam is fought

4. To what extent did Abraham Lincoln's policies and attitudes toward black people change during the Civil War? Does Lincoln deserve credit as "the Great Emancipator"? Why or why not?

5. What was the purpose of the Emancipation Proclamation? Why was it issued? Exactly what did it accomplish?

6. What did black men and women contribute to the Union war effort? Was it in their interests to participate in the Civil War? Why or why not?

7. Why did at least some black people support the southern states and the Confederacy during the Civil War?

8. Was the result of the Civil War worth the loss of 620,000 lives?

RECOMMENDED READING

Dudley Taylor Cornish. *The Sable Arm: Negro Troops in the Union Army, 1861–1865.* New York: Norton, 1956. The best single study of black men in the military during the war.

John Hope Franklin. *The Emancipation Proclamation.* Garden City, NY: Doubleday, 1963. A work written to commemorate the centennial of the Proclamation.

Michael P. Johnson and James L. Roark. *Black Masters: A Free Family of Color in the Old South.* New York: Nor-ton, 1984. A depiction of life among prosperous free black people before and during the Civil War.

Ervin Jordon. *Black Confederates and Afro Yankees in Civil War Virginia.* Charlottesville: University of Virginia Press, 1995. A rich study of life and society among African Americans in Virginia during the war.

James McPherson. *Battle Cry of Freedom: The Civil War Era.* New York: Oxford University Press, 1988. A superb one-volume account of the Civil War.

George W. Williams. *History of the Negro Troops in the War of the Rebellion.* New York: Harper & Row, 1888. An account of black soldiers in the war by America's first African-American historian.

ADDITIONAL BIBLIOGRAPHY

Military

Herman Hattaway and Archer Jones. *How the North Won: A Military History of the Civil War.* Urbana: University of Illinois Press, 1983.

Joseph T. Glatthaar. *Forged in Battle: The Civil War Alliance of Black Soldiers and White Officers.* New York: The Free Press, 1990.

Joseph T. Glatthaar. *The March to the Sea and Beyond: Sherman's Troops in the Savannah and Carolina Campaign.* New York: New York University Press, 1985.

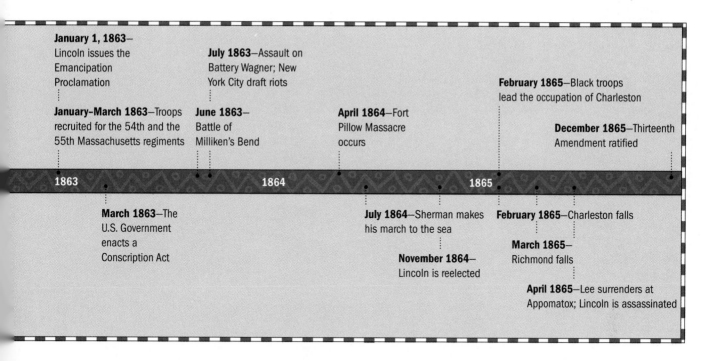

January 1, 1863— Lincoln issues the Emancipation Proclamation

July 1863—Assault on Battery Wagner; New York City draft riots

February 1865—Black troops lead the occupation of Charleston

January-March 1863—Troops recruited for the 54th and the 55th Massachusetts regiments

June 1863— Battle of Milliken's Bend

April 1864—Fort Pillow Massacre occurs

December 1865—Thirteenth Amendment ratified

1863 1864 1865

March 1863—The U.S. Government enacts a Conscription Act

July 1864—Sherman makes his march to the sea

February 1865—Charleston falls

November 1864— Lincoln is reelected

March 1865— Richmond falls

April 1865—Lee surrenders at Appomatox; Lincoln is assassinated

Geoffrey Ward and Ken Burns. *The Civil War.* New York: Alfred A. Knopf, 1990.

Stephen R. Wise. *Gate of Hell: Campaign for Charleston Harbor, 1863.* Columbia: University of South Carolina Press, 1994.

African Americans and the War

Leon Litwack. *Been in the Storm So Long: The Aftermath of Slavery.* New York: Alfred A. Knopf, 1979.

Edward A. Miller. *Gullah Statesman: Robert Smalls from Slavery to Congress, 1839–1915.* Columbia: University of South Carolina Press, 1995.

Benjamin Quarles. *The Negro in the Civil War.* Boston: Little, Brown, 1953.

Willie Lee Rose, *Rehearsal for Reconstruction: The Port Royal Experiment.* Indianapolis: Bobbs Merrill, 1964.

Bell I. Wiley. *Southern Negroes, 1861–1865.* New Haven: Yale University Press, 1938.

Documents, Letters, and Other Sources

Virginia M. Adams, ed. *On the Altar of Freedom: A Black Soldier's Civil War Letters from the Front.* [Corporal James Henry Gooding]. Amherst: University of Massachusetts, 1991.

Ira Berlin, et al., eds. *Freedom: A Documentary History of Emancipation, 1861–1867,* Series 1, Volume I, *The De-struction of Slavery.* New York: Cambridge University Press, 1985.

_____. *Freedom: A Documentary History of Emancipation, 1861–1867,* Series 1, Volume III, *The Wartime Genesis of Free Labor: The Lower South.* New York: Cambridge University Press, 1990.

Robert F. Durden. *The Gray and the Black: The Confederate Debate on Emancipation.* Baton Rouge: Louisiana State University Press, 1972.

Michael P. Johnson and James L. Roark, eds. *No Chariot Letdown: Charleston's Free People of Color on the Eve of the Civil War.* Chapel Hill: University of North Carolina Press, 1984.

James McPherson. *The Negro's Civil War: How American Negroes Felt and Acted during the War for the Union.* New York: Pantheon, 1965.

Edwin S. Redkey, ed. *A Grand Army of Black Men: Letters from African American Soldiers in the Union Army, 1861–1865.* New York: Cambridge University Press, 1992.

Reminiscences

Thomas Wentworth Higginson. *Army Life in a Black Regiment.* Boston: Beacon Press, 1962.

Elizabeth Keckley. *Behind the Scenes: or Thirty Years a Slave and Four Years in the White House.* New York: Oxford University Press, 1968.

Susie King Taylor. *Reminiscences of My Life in Camp.* Boston: Taylor, 1902.

CHAPTER 12

THE MEANING OF FREEDOM: THE PROMISE OF RECONSTRUCTION, 1865–1868

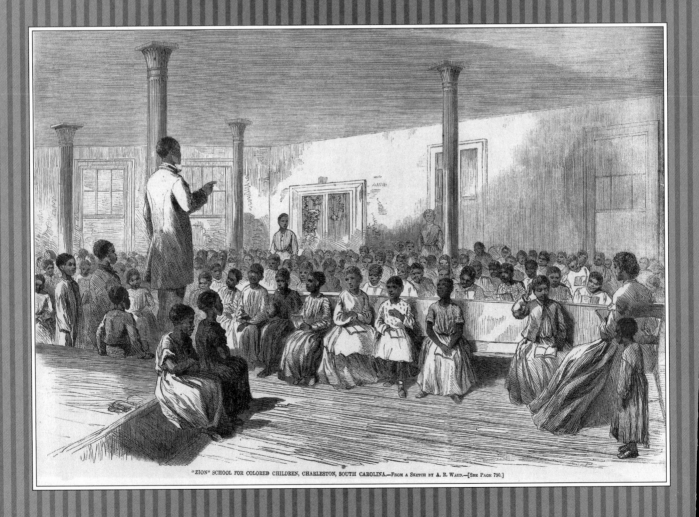

"ZION" SCHOOL FOR COLORED CHILDREN, CHARLESTON, SOUTH CAROLINA.—FROM A SKETCH BY A. R. WAUD.—[SEE PAGE 790.]

The Reverend Jonathan C. Gibbs established this school at Zion Presbyterian Church in Charleston, South Carolina, in 1865. Except for freedom itself and the reuniting of families divided during slavery, nothing was more important for most freed people than acquiring an education.

As the great day grew nearer, there was more singing in the slave quarters than usual. It was bolder, had more ring, and lasted later into the night. Most of the verses of the plantation songs had some reference to freedom. True, they had sung those same verses before, but they had been careful to explain that the "freedom" in these songs referred to the next world, and had no connection with life in this world. Now they gradually threw off the mask, and were not afraid to let it be known that the "freedom" in their songs meant freedom of the body in this world.

—Booker T. Washington, *Up from Slavery*

What did freedom mean to a people who had endured and survived two hundred fifty years of enslavement in America? What did the future hold for nearly four million African Americans in 1865?

Freedom meant many things to many people. But to most former slaves, it meant that families would stay together. Freedom meant that women would no longer be sexually exploited. Freedom meant learning to read and write. Freedom meant organizing churches. Freedom meant moving around without having to obtain permission. Freedom meant that labor would produce income for the laborer and not the master. Freedom meant working without the whip. Freedom meant land to own, cultivate, and live on. Freedom meant a trial before a jury if charged with a crime. Freedom meant voting. Freedom meant citizenship and having the same rights as white people.

Years after slavery ended, a former Texas slave, Margrett Nillin, was asked if she preferred slavery or freedom. She answered unequivocally: "Well, it's dis way, in slavery I owns nothin' and never owns nothin'. In freedom I's own de home and raise de family. All dat causes me worryment and in slavery I has no worryment, but I takes freedom."

THE END OF SLAVERY

With the collapse of slavery, many black people were quick to inform white people that whatever loyalty, devotion, and cooperation they might have shown as slaves had never been a reflection of their inner feelings and attitudes. Near Opelousas, Louisiana, a Union officer asked a young black man why he did not love his master, and the youth responded sharply. "When my master begins to lub me, den it'll be time enough for me to lub him. What I wants is to get away. I want to take me off from dis plantation, where I can be free."

In North Carolina, planter Robert P. Howell, was deeply disappointed that a loyal slave named Lovet fled at the first opportunity. "He was about my age and I had always treated him more as a companion than a slave. When I left I put everything in his charge, told him that he was free, but to remain on the place and take care of things. He promised me faithfully that he would, but he was the first one to leave . . . and I did not see him for several years."

Emancipation was a traumatic experience for many former masters. A Virginia freedman remembered that "Miss Polly died right after the surrender, she was so hurt that all the negroes was going to be free." Another former slave, Robert Falls, recalled that his master assembled the slaves to inform them that they were free. "I hates to do it, but I must. You all ain't my niggers no more. You is free. Just as free as I am. Here I have raised you all to work for me, and now you are going to leave me. I am an old man, and I can't get along without you. I don't know what I am going to do." In less than a year he was dead.

Differing Reactions of Former Slaves

Other slaves bluntly displayed their reaction to years of bondage. Aunt Delia, a cook with a North Carolina family, revealed that for a long time she had secretly gained retribution for the indignity of servitude. "How many times I spit in the biscuits and peed in the coffee just to get back at them mean white folks." In Goodman, Mississippi, a slave named Caddy learned she was free and rushed from the field to find her owner. "Caddy threw down that hoe, she marched herself up to the big house, then, she looked around and found the mistress. She went over to the mistress, she flipped up her dress and told the white woman to do something. She said it mean and ugly. This is what she said: *Kiss my ass!*"

On the other hand, some slaves, especially elderly ones, were fearful and unprepared for freedom. On a South Carolina plantation, an older black woman refused to accept emancipation. "I ain' no free nigger! I *is* got a marster and mistiss! Dee right dar in de great house. Ef you don' b'lieve me, you go dar an' see."

Reuniting Black Families

As slavery ended, the most urgent need for many freed people was finding family members who had been sold away from them. Slavery had not destroyed the black family. Husbands, wives, and children went to great lengths to reassemble their families after the Civil War. For years and even decades after the end of slavery, advertisements appeared in black newspapers appealing for information about missing kinfolk. The following notice was published in the *Colored Tennessean* on August 5, 1865:

> Saml. Dove wishes to know of the whereabouts of his mother, Areno, his sisters Maria, Neziah and Peggy, and his brother Edmond, who were owned by Geo. Dove of Rockingham county, Shenandoah Valley, Va. Sold in Richmond, after which Saml. and Edmond were taken to Nashville, Tenn., by Joe Mick; Areno was left at the Eagle Tavern, Richmond. Respectfully yours, Saml. Dove, Utica, New York.

In North Carolina a Northern journalist met a middle-age black man "plodding along, staff in hand, and apparently very footsore and tired." The nearly exhausted freedman explained that he had walked almost six hundred miles looking for his wife and children who had been sold four years earlier.

There were emotional reunions as family members found each other after years of separation. Ben and Betty Dodson had been apart for twenty years when Ben found her in a refugee camp after the war. "Glory! glory! hallelujah," he shouted as he hugged his wife. "Dis is my Betty, shuah. I foun' you at las'. I's hunted and hunted till I track you up here. I's boun' to hunt till I fin' you if you's alive."

Other searches had more heart-wrenching results. Husbands and wives sometimes learned that their spouses had remarried during the separation. Believing that his wife had died, the husband of Laura Spicer remarried—only to learn after the war that Laura was still alive. Sadly, he wrote to her but refused to meet with her. "I would come and see you but I know I could not bear it. I want to see you and I don't want to see you. I love you just as well as I did the last day I saw you, and it will not do for you and I to meet." Tormented, he wrote again pledging his love. "Laura I do not think that I have change any at all since I saw you last—I thinks of you and my children every day of my life. Laura I do love you the same. My love to you *never* have failed. Laura, truly, I have got another wife, and I am very sorry that I am. You feels and seems to me as much like my dear loving wife, as you ever did Laura."

One freedman testified to the close ties that bound many slave families when he replied bitterly to the claim that he had had a kind master who had fed him and never used the whip. "Kind! yes, he gib men corn enough, and he gib me pork enough, and he neber gib me one lick wid de whip, but whar's my wife?—whar's my chill'en? Take away de pork, I say; take away de corn, I can work and raise dese for myself, but gib me back de wife of my bosom, and gib me back my poor chill'en as was sold away."

LAND

As freed people embraced freedom and left their masters, they wanted land. Nineteenth-century Americans of virtually every background associated economic security with owning land. Families wanted to work land and prosper as self-sufficient yeoman. Former slaves believed that their future as a free people was tied to the possession of land. But just as it had been impossible to abolish slavery without the intervention of the U.S. government, it would not be possible to procure land without federal assistance. At first, federal authorities seemed determined to make land available to freedmen.

Special Field Order #15

Shortly after his army arrived in Savannah—after having devastated Georgia—Union General William T. Sherman announced that freedmen would receive land. On January 16, 1865, he issued Special Field Order #15. This military directive set aside a thirty-mile-wide tract of land along the Atlantic coast from Charleston, South Carolina, 245 miles south to Jacksonville, Florida.

Former slaves assembled in a village near Washington D.C. Black people welcomed emancipation, but without land, education, or employment, they faced an uncertain future.

White owners had abandoned the land, and Sherman reserved it for black families. The head of each family would receive "possessory title" to forty acres of land. Sherman also gave the freed men the use of army mules, thus giving rise to the slogan, "Forty acres and a mule."

Within six months, 40,000 freed people were working 400,000 acres in the South Carolina and Georgia low country and on the Sea Islands. Former slaves generally avoided the slave crops of cotton and rice and instead planted sweet potatoes and corn. They also worked together as families and kinfolk. They avoided the gang labor associated with slavery. Most husbands and fathers preferred that their wives and daughters not work in the fields as slave women had had to do.

The Port Royal Experiment

Meanwhile, hundreds of former slaves had been cultivating land for three years. In late 1861, Union military forces carved out an enclave around Beaufort and Port Royal, South Carolina, that remained under federal authority for the rest of the war. White planters fled to the interior, leaving their slaves behind. Under the supervision of U.S. Treasury officials and northern reformers and missionaries who hurried south in 1862, ex-slaves began to work the land in what came to be known as the "Port Royal Experiment." When Treasury agents auctioned off portions of the land for nonpayment of taxes, freedmen purchased some of it. But northern businessmen bought most of the real estate and then hired black people to raise cotton.

White owners sometimes returned to their former lands only to find that black families had taken charge. A group of black farmers told one former owner, "We own this land now, put it out of your head that it will ever be yours again." And on one South Carolina Sea Island, white men were turned back by armed black men.

THE FREEDMEN'S BUREAU

As the war ended in early 1865, Congress created the Bureau of Refugees, Freedmen, and Abandoned Lands—commonly called the Freedmen's Bureau. Created as a temporary agency to assist freedmen to make the transition to freedom, the bureau was placed under the control of the U.S. Army and General Oliver O. Howard was put in command. Howard, a devout Christian who had lost an arm in the war, was eager to aid the freedmen.

The bureau was given enormous responsibilities. It was to help freedmen obtain land; gain an education;

negotiate labor contracts with white planters; settle legal and criminal disputes involving black and white people; and provide food, medical care, and transportation for black and white people left destitute by the war. However, Congress never provided sufficient funds or personnel to carry out these tasks.

The Freedmen's Bureau never had more than nine hundred agents spread across the South from Virginia to Texas. Mississippi, for example, had twelve agents in 1866. One agent often served a county with a population of 10,000 to 20,000 freedmen. Few of the agents were black because few military officers were black. John Mercer Langston of Virginia was an inspector of schools assigned to the bureau's main office in Washington, D.C., while Colonel Martin R. Delany worked with freedmen on the South Carolina Sea Islands.

The need for assistance was desperate as thousands of black and white Southerners endured extreme privation in the months after the war ended. The bureau established camps for the homeless, fed the hungry, and cared for orphans and the sick as best it could. It distributed more than 13 million rations—consisting of flour, corn meal, and sugar—by 1866. The bureau provided medical care to one-half million freedmen and thousands of white people who were suffering from smallpox, yellow fever, cholera, and pneumonia. Many more remained untreated.

In July 1865, the bureau took a first step toward distributing land when General Howard issued Circular 13 ordering agents to "set aside" 40-acre plots for freedmen. But the allocation had hardly begun when the order was revoked, and it was announced that land already distributed under General Sherman's Special Field Order #15 was to be returned to its previous white owners.

The reason for this reversal in policy was that President Andrew Johnson, who had become president after Lincoln's assassination in April 1865, began to pardon hundreds and then thousands of former Confederates and restore their lands to them. General Howard was forced to tell black people that they had to relinquish the land they thought they had acquired. In a speech before some 2,000 freedmen on South Carolina's Edisto Island in October 1865, Howard pleaded with his audience to "lay aside their bitter feelings, and to become reconciled to their old masters." A black man shouted a response, "Why, General Howard, why do you take away our lands? You take them from us who are true, always true to the Government! You give them to our all-time enemies. This is not right!"

A committee rejected Howard's appeal for reconciliation and forgiveness and they insisted that the government provide land.

A Freedmen's Bureau Office. Scenes like this repeated themselves throughout the South in 1865 and 1866 as freed people (and many white people) sought the assistance of the Bureau.

You ask us to forgive the land owners of our island. *You* only lost your right arm in war and might forgive them. The man who tied me to a tree and gave me 39 lashes and who stripped and flogged my mother and my sister and who will not let me stay in his empty hut except I will do his planting and be satisfied with his price and who combines with others to keep away land from me well knowing I would not have anything to do with him if I had land of my own—that man I cannot well forgive.

Howard was moved by these appeals. He returned to Washington and attempted to persuade Congress to make land available. Congress refused, and President Johnson was determined that white people would get their lands back. It seemed so sensible to most white peo-

ple. Property that had belonged to white families for generations simply could not be given to freedmen. Freedmen saw matters differently. They deserved land that they and their families had worked without compensation for generations. Freedmen believed it was the only way to make freedom meaningful and to gain independence from white people. As it turned out, most freedmen were forced off land they thought should belong to them.

SHARECROPPING

To make matters worse, by 1866 bureau officials tried to force freedmen to sign labor contracts with white landowners—putting black people once again under

VOICES

A FREEDMAN'S BUREAU COMMISSIONER TELLS FREED PEOPLE WHAT FREEDOM MEANS

In June 1865, Charles Soule, the commissioner of contracts for the Freedmen's Bureau told a gathering of freedmen in Orangeburg, South Carolina, what to expect and how to behave in the coming year.

You are now free, but you must know that the only difference you can feel yet, between slavery and freedom, is that neither you nor your children can be bought or sold. You may have a harder time this year than you have ever had before; it will be the price you pay for your freedom. You will have to work hard, and get very little to eat, and very few clothes to wear. If you get through this year alive and well, you should be thankful. . . . You cannot be paid in money, for there is no good money in the District, nothing but Confederate paper. Then, what can you be paid with? Why, with food, with clothes, with the free use of your little houses and plots. You do not own a cent's worth except yourselves.

You do not understand why some of the white people who used to own you, do not have to work in the field. It is because they are rich. If every man were poor, and worked in his own field, there would be no big farms, and very little cotton or corn raised to sell; there would be no money, and nothing to buy. Some people must be rich, to pay the others, and they

have the right to do no work except to look out after their property.

Remember that all of your working time belongs to the man who hires you: therefore you must not leave work without his leave not even to nurse a child, or to go and visit a wife or husband. When you wish to go off the place, get a pass as you used to, and then you will run no danger of being taken up by our soldiers.

In short, do just about as the good men among you have always done. Remember that even if you are badly off, no one can buy and sell you: remember that if you help yourselves, GOD will help you, and trust hopefully that next year and the year after will bring some new blessing to you.

QUESTIONS

1. According to Soule, what is the difference between slavery and freedom?

2. Does freedom mean that freedpeople will have economic opportunities equal to those of white people?

3. How should freed people have responded to Soule's advice?

Source: Ira Berlin, Steven Hahn, Steven F. Miller, Joseph P. Reidy, and Leslie S. Rowland, "The Terrain of Freedom: The Struggle over the Meaning of Free Labor in the U.S. South," *History Workshop*, No. 22 (Autumn 1986): 108–130.

---

white authority. Black men who refused to sign contracts could be arrested. Theoretically, these contracts were legal agreements between two equals: landowner and laborer. But they were seldom freely concluded. Bureau agents usually sided with the landowner and pressured freedmen to accept unequal terms.

Occasionally the landowner would pay wages to the laborer. But most owners agreed to provide the laborer with part of the crop. The laborer usually agreed to work under the supervision of the landowner. The contracts required labor for a full year; the laborer could neither quit nor strike. Landowners demanded that the laborers work the fields in gangs. Freedmen resisted this system. They sometimes in-

sisted on making decisions involving planting, fertilizing, and harvesting as they sought to exercise independence (Map 12–1).

Thus it took time for a new form of agricultural labor to develop. But by the 1870s, the system of sharecropping had emerged and dominated most of the South. There were no wages. Freedmen worked land as families—not in gangs—and not under direct white supervision. When the landowner provided seed, tools, fertilizer, and work animals (mules, horses, oxen), the black family received one-third of the crop. There were many variations on these arrangements, and frequently black families were cheated out of their fair share of the crop.

This somewhat idealized illustration by white artist William Aiken Walker shows a fairly prosperous, nicely clothed, and contented black farm family living in a rather large dwelling. They are surrounded by plump chickens, drying laundry, amiable dogs, and gourds that served as bird houses for purple martins. As unimpressive as it may now appear, it depicts a standard of living that many freed people failed to attain.

THE BLACK CHURCH

In the years after slavery, the church again became the most important institution among African Americans other than the family. Not only did it fill deep spiritual and inspirational needs, it offered enriching music, provided charity and compassion to those in need, developed community and political leaders, and was free of white supervision. Before slavery's demise, free black people and slaves often attended white churches where they were encouraged to participate in religious services conducted by white clergymen and where they were treated as second-class Christians.

Once liberated, black men and women organized their own churches with their own ministers. Most black people considered white ministers incapable of delivering a meaningful message. Nancy Williams recalled, "Ole white preachers used to talk wid dey tongues widdout sayin' nothin', but Jesus told us slaves to talk wid our hearts."

Northern white missionaries were sometimes appalled by the unlettered and ungrammatical black preachers who nevertheless communicated effectively and emotionally with their parishioners. A visiting white clergyman was genuinely impressed and humbled on hearing a black preacher who lacked education but more than made up for it with devout faith. "He talked about Christ and his salvation as one who understood what he said. . . . Here was an unlearned man, one who could not read, telling of the love of Christ, of Christian faith and duty in a way which I have not learned."

Other black and white religious leaders anguished over what they considered moral laxity and displaced values among the freed people. They preached about honesty, thrift, temperance, and elimination of sexual promiscuity. They demanded an end to "rum-suckers, bar-room loafers, whiskey dealers and card players among the men, and to those women who dressed finely on *ill gotten* gain."

Church members struggled, scrimped, and saved to buy land and to build churches. Most former slaves founded Baptist and Methodist churches. These denominations tended to be more autonomous and less subject to outside control. Their doctrine was usually simple and direct without complex theology. Of the Methodist churches, the African Methodist Episcopal (AME) church made giant strides in the South after the Civil War.

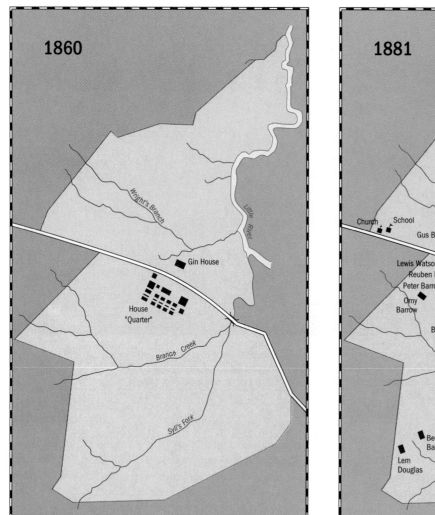

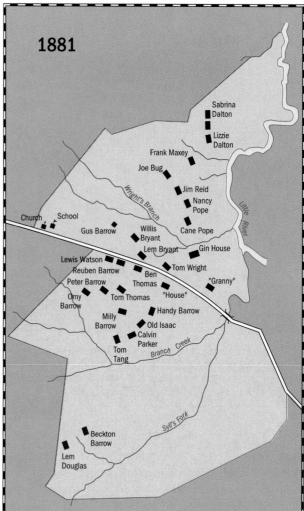

Map 12-1 The Effect of Sharecropping on the Southern Plantation: The Barrow Plantation, Oglethorpe County, Georgia. With the end of slavery and the advent of sharecropping, black people would no longer agree to work in fields as gangs. They preferred to have each family cultivate separate plots of land, thereby distancing themselves as much as possible from slavery and white supervision.

In Charleston, South Carolina, the AME church was resurrected after an absence of more than forty years. In 1822 during the turmoil over the Denmark Vesey plot, the AME church was forced to disband and its leader had to flee (see Chapter 8). But by the 1870s, three AME congregations were thriving in Charleston. In Wilmington, North Carolina, the 1,600 members of the Front Street Methodist Church decided to join the AME church soon after the Civil War ended. They replaced the longtime white minister, the Reverend L. S. Burkhead, with a black man.

White Methodists initially encouraged cooperation with black Methodists and helped establish the Colored (now Christian) Methodist Episcopal church (CME).

But the white Methodists lost some of their fervor after they tried but failed to persuade the black Methodists to keep political issues out of the CME church, and to dwell solely on spiritual concerns.

The Presbyterian, Congregational, and Episcopal churches appealed to the more prosperous members of the black community. Their services tended to be more formal and solemn. Black people who had been free before the Civil War were usually affiliated with these congregations and remained so after the conflict. Well-to-do free black people in Charleston organized St. Mark's Protestant Episcopal Church when they separated from the white Episcopal church. But they retained their white minister Joseph Seabrook as rector.

Hundreds of black churches were founded across the South following the Civil War, and they grew spectacularly in the decades that followed. This illustration shows a congregation crowded into Richmond's First African Baptist Church in 1874.

Poorer black people of darker complexion found churches like St. Mark's decidedly unappealing. Ed Barber visited, but only one time.

> When I was trampin' 'round Charleston, dere was a church dere called St. Mark, dat all de society folks of my color went to. No black nigger welcome dere, they told me. Thinkin' as how I was bright 'nough to git in, I up and goes dere one Sunday, Ah, how they did carry on, bow and scrape and ape de white folks. . . . I was uncomfortable all de time though, 'cause they were too "hifalootin" in de ways, in de singin', and all sorts of carryin' ons.

Religious differences among black people notwithstanding, the black churches, their parishioners, and clergymen would play a vital role in Reconstruction politics. More than one hundred black ministers were elected to political office after the Civil War.

EDUCATION

Freedom and education were inseparable. To remain illiterate after emancipation was to remain enslaved. One ex-slave master bluntly told his former slave, Charles Whiteside: "Charles, you is a free man they say, but Ah tells you now, you is still a slave and if you lives to be a hundred, you'll STILL be a slave, cause you got no education, and education is what makes a man free!"

Almost every freed black person—young or old—desperately wanted to learn. Elderly people were especially eager to read the Bible. Even before slavery ended, black people began to establish schools. In 1861, Mary Peake, a free black woman, opened a school in Hampton, Virginia. On South Carolina's Sea Islands, a black cabinetmaker began teaching openly after having covertly operated a school for years. In 1862 northern missionaries arrived on the Sea Islands to begin teaching. Laura Towne, a white woman, and Charlotte Forten, a black woman, opened a school on St. Helena's

Island as part of the Port Royal experiment. They enrolled 138 children and fifty-eight adults. By 1863, there were 1,700 students and forty-five teachers at thirty schools in the South Carolina low country.

With the end of the Civil War, northern religious organizations in cooperation with the Freedmen's Bureau organized hundreds of day and night schools. Classes were held in stables, homes, former slave cabins, taverns, churches, and even—in Savannah and New Orleans—in the old slave markets. Former slaves spent hours in the fields and then trudged to a makeshift school to learn the alphabet and arithmetic. In 1865 black ministers created the Savannah Educational Association, raised $1,000, employed fifteen black teachers, and enrolled six hundred students.

In 1866 the Freedmen's Bureau set aside one-half million dollars for education. The bureau furnished the buildings while former slaves hired, housed, and fed the teachers. By 1869 the Freedmen's Bureau was involved with 3,000 schools and 150,000 students. Even more impressive, by 1870 black people had contributed one million dollars to educate their people.

Black Teachers

While freedmen appreciated the dedication and devotion of the white teachers affiliated with the missionary societies, they usually preferred black teachers. The Reverend Richard H. Cain, an AME minister who came south from Brooklyn, New York, said that black people needed to learn to control their own futures. "We must take into our own hands the education of our race. . . . Honest, dignified whites may teach ever so well, it has not the effect to exalt the black man's opinion of his own race, because they have always been in the habit of seeing white men in honored positions, and respected."

V O I C E S

A NORTHERN BLACK WOMAN ON TEACHING FREEDMEN

Blanche Virginia Harris was born in 1842 in Monroe, Michigan. She graduated from Oberlin College in 1860. She became the principal of a black school in Norfolk, Virginia, attended by 230 students. She organized night classes for adults and a sewing society to provide clothing for impoverished students. Later, she taught in Mississippi, North Carolina, and Tennessee. In this letter she describes her experiences in Mississippi.

23 January 1866
Natchez, Miss.

I have been in this city now nearly five months. . . . The colored teachers three in number, sent out by the [American Missionary] Association to this city, have been brought down here it is true. And then left to the mercy of the colored people or themselves. The distinction between the two classes of teachers (white and colored) is so marked that it is the topic of conversation among the better class of colored people.

My school is very large, some of them pay and some do not. And from the proceeds I pay the board of my sister and myself, and also for the rent of two rooms; rent as well as board is very high so I have to work quite hard to meet my expenses. I also furnish lights, wood and coal. I do not write this as fault-finding, far from it. I shall be thankful if I can in any way help. I sometimes get discouraged. . . .

I have become very much attached to my school; the interest they manifest in their studies pleases me. I will now tell you how I employ my time. From 8 A.M. until 2 P.M. I teach the children. At 3 P.M. I have a class of adults and at night I have night school.

One afternoon we have prayer meeting, another sewing school. And another singing school. I hope my next letter may be more interesting to you.

Very Respectfully,
Blanche Harris

QUESTIONS

1. Why was the race of the teacher of such concern?

2. What did Harris find difficult about teaching?

3. What did she find rewarding about teaching?

Source: Ellen NicKenzie Lawson, ed., *The Three Sarahs: Documents of Antebellum Black College Women*. New York: Edward Mellon Press, 1984.

Twenty-five-year-old Charlotte Forten ventured South to teach freed people during the Civil War. A member of a prominent Philadelphia family of color, she joined white teachers Laura M. Towne and Ellen Murray on South Carolina's St. Helena Island in 1862 and helped to establish Penn School.

Black men and women responded to the call to teach. Virginia C. Green, a northern black woman felt compelled to go to Mississippi. "Though I have never known servitude they are . . . my people. Born as far north as the lakes I have felt no freer because so many were less fortunate. . . . I look forward with impatience to the time when my people shall be strong, blest with education, purified and made prosperous by virtue and industry." Hezekiah Hunter, a black teacher from Brooklyn, New York, commented in 1865 on the need for black teachers. "I believe we best can instruct our own people, knowing our own peculiarities—needs—necessities. Further—I believe we that are competent owe it to our people to teach them our speciality." And

in Malden, West Virginia, when black residents found that a recently arrived eighteen-year-old black man could read and write, they promptly hired him to teach.

In some areas of the South, the sole person available to teach was a poorly educated former slave equipped primarily with a willingness to teach his or her fellow freedmen. One such teacher explained, "I never had the chance of goen to school for I was a slave until freedom. . . . I am the only teacher because we can not doe better now."

Many northern teachers, black and white, provided more than the basics of elementary education. Black life and history were occasionally read about and discussed. Abolitionist Lydia Maria Child wrote *The*

Freedmen's Book, which offered short biographies of Benjamin Banneker, Frederick Douglass, and Toussaint L'Ouverture. More often northern teachers, dismayed at the backwardness of the freedmen, struggled to modify behavior and to impart cultural values by teaching piety, thrift, cleanliness, temperance, and timeliness.

Many former slaves came to resent some of these teachers as condescending, self-righteous, and paternalistic. Sometimes the teachers, especially those who were white, became frustrated with recalcitrant students who did not readily absorb middle-class values. Others, however, derived enormous satisfaction from teaching freedmen. A Virginia teacher commented, "I think I shall stay here as long as I live and teach this people. I have no love or taste for any other work, and I am happy only here with them."

Black Colleges

Northern churches and religious societies established dozens of colleges, universities, academies, and institutes across the South in the late 1860s and the 1870s (Map 12–2). Most of these institutions provided elementary and secondary education. Few black students were prepared for actual college or university work. The American Missionary Association—an abolitionist and Congregationalist organization—worked with the Freedmen's Bureau to establish Berea in Kentucky, Fisk in Tennessee, Hampton in Virginia, Tougaloo in Alabama, and Avery in South Carolina. The primary pur-

pose of these schools was to educate black students to become teachers.

In Missouri the black enlisted men and the white officers of the 62nd and 65th Colored Volunteers raised $6,000 to establish Lincoln Institute in 1866, which would become Lincoln University. The American Baptist Home Mission Society founded Virginia Union, Shaw in North Carolina, Benedict in South Carolina, and Morehouse in Georgia. Northern Methodists helped establish Claflin in South Carolina, Rust in Mississippi, and Bennett in North Carolina. The Episcopalians were responsible for St. Augustine in North Carolina and St. Paul in Virginia. These and many other similar institutions formed the foundation for the historically black colleges and universities.

Response of White Southerners

White Southerners considered efforts by black people to learn absurd. For generations, white Americans had looked on people of African descent as abjectly inferior. When significant efforts were made to educate former slaves, white Southerners reacted with suspicion, contempt, and hostility. One white woman told a teacher: "I do assure you, you might as well try to teach your horse or mule to read, as to teach these niggers. They *can't* learn."

Most white people were well aware that black people could learn. Otherwise, the slave codes that prohibited educating slaves would have been unnecessary. After

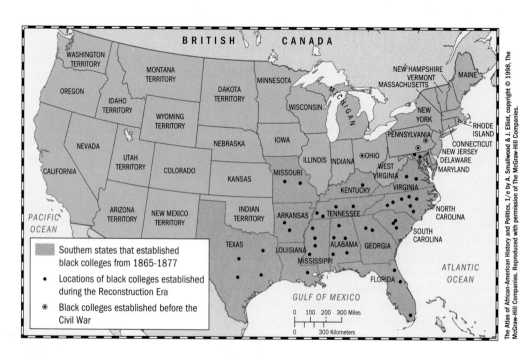

Map 12–2 The Location of Black Colleges Founded before and during Reconstruction. Three black colleges were founded before the Civil War. In Pennsylvania, Cheyney University opened in 1837, and it was followed by the establishment of Lincoln University in 1854. In 1856, Wilberforce University was founded in Ohio. After the Civil War, Northern black and white missionary groups fanned out across the South and—frequently with the assistance of Freedmen's Bureau officials—founded colleges, institutes, and normal schools in the former slave states.

Southern states that established black colleges from 1865-1877

• Locations of black colleges established during the Reconstruction Era

⊙ Black colleges established before the Civil War

PROFILE

CHARLOTTE E. RAY

Charlotte E. Ray became the first African American woman to earn a law degree and the first woman admitted to the practice of law in Washington, D.C. She was born on January 13, 1850, in New York City. One of seven children, her parents were the Reverend Charles B. Ray and his second wife, Charlotte Augusta Burroughs Ray. They were firm believers in the rights of African Americans and in their potential for success.

Charlotte attended Myrtilla Miner's Institution for the Education of Colored Youth in Washington, D.C. Myrtilla Miner, a white educator from upstate New York, was determined to demonstrate that black women were as capable of high moral and mental development as white women.

Charlotte completed high school at Miner's in 1869, and she then taught at the Normal and Preparatory Department of recently established Howard University. She also enrolled in law classes at Howard and wrote a thesis analyzing corporations. She graduated from the law school in 1872, and a month later was admitted to the bar in Washington, D.C. She opened an office and planned to practice real estate law. As a real estate lawyer, she could avoid court appearances and the discrimination that women attorneys encountered. She often used her initials, C. E. Ray, so that her clients would not suffer because their legal counsel could be identified as a woman.

Because of the Panic of 1873 and the ensuing economic depression and the difficulties of being a black woman in a white male profession, Ray gave up the practice of law. She supported women's rights, and in 1876 attended the annual meeting of the National American Woman Suffrage Association in New York City. By 1879, she had returned to New York and taught school in Brooklyn. Sometime before 1886 she had married, but little is known of her husband. Charlotte Ray died of acute bronchitis on January 11, 1911.

---

slavery's end, some white people went out of their way to prevent black people from learning. Countless schools were burned, mostly in rural areas. In Canton, Mississippi, black people collected money to open a school—only to have white residents inform them that the school would be burned and the prospective teacher lynched if it opened. The female teacher at a freedmen's school in Donaldsonville, Louisiana, was shot and killed.

Other white Southerners grudgingly tolerated the desire of black people to acquire an education. One planter bitterly conceded in 1870, "Every little negro in the county is now going to school and the public pays for it. This is one hell of [a] fix but we can't help it, and the best policy is to conform as far as possible to circumstances."

Most white people adamantly refused to attend school with black people. No integrated schools were established in the immediate aftermath of emancipation. Most black people were more interested in gaining an education than in caring whether white students attended school with them. When black youngsters tried to attend a white school in Raleigh, North Carolina, the white students stopped going to it. For a brief time in Charleston, South Carolina, black and white children attended the same school, but they were taught in separate classrooms.

VIOLENCE

In the days, weeks, and months after the end of the Civil War, an orgy of brutality and violence swept across the South. White Southerners—embittered by their crushing defeat and unable to adjust to the end of slave labor and the loss of millions of dollars worth of slave property—lashed out at black people. There were beatings, murders, rapes, and riots—often with little or no provocation.

Black people who demanded respect, wore better clothing, refused to step aside for white people, or asked to be addressed as "mister" or "misses" were attacked. In South Carolina a white clergyman shot and killed a black man who protested when another black man was removed from a church service. In Texas one black man was killed because he failed to remove his hat in the presence of a white man and another for refusing to relinquish a bottle of whiskey. A black woman was beaten for "using insolent language," while a black worker in

Alabama was killed for speaking sharply to a white overseer. In Virginia a black veteran was beaten after announcing that he had been proud to serve in the Union Army.

In South Carolina a white man asked a passing black man whom he belonged to. The black man replied that he no longer belonged to anybody. "I am free now." With that, the white man roared, "Sas me? You black devil!" He then slashed the freedman with a knife, seriously injuring him. A Freedmen's Bureau agent in North Carolina explained the intense white hostility. "The fact is, it's the first notion with a great many of these people, if a Negro says anything or does anything that they don't like, to take a gun and put a bullet into him, or a charge of shot."

There was also large-scale violence. In 1865 University of North Carolina students twice attacked peaceful meetings of black people. Near Pine Bluff, Arkansas, in 1866 a white mob burned a black settlement and lynched 24 men, women, and children. An estimated 2,000 black people were murdered around Shreveport, Louisiana. In Texas white people killed 1,000 black people between 1865 and 1868.

In May 1866 in Memphis, white residents went on a brutal rampage after black veterans forced local police to release a black prisoner. The city was already beset with economic difficulties and racial tensions caused in part by an influx of rural refugees. White people, led by Irish policemen, invaded the black section of Memphis and destroyed hundreds of homes, cabins, and shacks as well as churches and schools. Forty-six black people and two white men died.

On July 30, 1866, in New Orleans, white people—angered that black men were demanding political rights—assaulted black people on the street and in a convention hall. City policemen, who were mostly Confederate veterans, shot down the black delegates as they fled in panic waving white flags in a futile attempt to surrender. Thirty-four black people and three of their white allies died. Federal troops eventually arrived and stopped the bloodshed. General Philip H. Sheridan characterized the riot as "an absolute massacre."

Little was done to stem the violence. Most Union troops had been withdrawn from the South and demobilized after the war. The Freedmen's Bureau was usually unwilling and unable to protect the black population. Black people left to defend themselves were usually in no position to retaliate. Instead, they sometimes attempted to bring the perpetrators to justice. In Orangeburg, South Carolina, armed black men brought three white men to the local jail who had been wreaking violence in the community. In Holly Springs, Mississippi, a posse of armed black men apprehended a white man who had murdered a freedwoman.

But for black people the justice system was thoroughly unjust. Though black people could now testify against white people in a court of law, southern juries remained all-white and refused to convict white people charged with harming black people. In Texas in 1865 and 1866, five hundred white men were indicted for murdering black people. Not one was convicted.

THE CRUSADE FOR POLITICAL AND CIVIL RIGHTS

In October 1864 in Syracuse, New York, 145 black leaders gathered in a national convention. Some of the century's most prominent black men and women attended, including Henry Highland Garnet, Frances W. Harper, William Wells Brown, Francis L. Cardozo, Richard H. Cain, Jonathan J. Wright, and Jonathan C. Gibbs. They embraced the basic tenets of the American political tradition and proclaimed that they expected to participate fully in it.

Anticipating a future free of slavery, Frederick Douglass optimistically declared "that we hereby assert our full confidence in the fundamental principles of this government . . . the great heart of this nation will ultimately concede us our just claims, accord us our rights, and grant us our full measure of citizenship under the broad shield of the Constitution."

Even before the Syracuse gathering, northern Republicans met in Union-controlled territory around Beaufort, South Carolina, and nominated the state's delegates to the 1864 Republican national convention. Among those selected were Robert Smalls and Prince Rivers, former slaves who had exemplary records with the Union Army. The probability of black participation in post-war politics seemed promising indeed.

But northern and southern white leaders who already held power would largely determine whether black Americans would gain any political power or acquire the same rights as white people. As the Civil War ended, President Lincoln was more concerned with restoring the seceded states to the Union than in opening political doors for black people. Yet Lincoln suggested that at least some black men deserved the right to vote. On April 11, 1865, he wrote, "I would myself prefer that [the vote] were now conferred on the very intelligent, and on those who serve our cause as soldiers." Three days later Lincoln was assassinated.

AARON A. BRADLEY

At a time when many white people considered even the most reserved, refined, and well-educated black man holding political office an anathema, Aaron Bradley's presence in politics was intolerable. White Southerners regarded him as a dangerous revolutionary. White Republicans, who normally would have been his allies, considered him belligerent and uncooperative. But most freedmen admired and supported him. Like him or not, he was a major figure in Georgia politics during Reconstruction.

Bradley was born a slave in about 1815 in South Carolina. His father was probably white. He belonged to Francis W. Pickens, who was South Carolina's governor when the state seceded (see Chapter 10). For a time, Bradley worked as a shoemaker in nearby Augusta, Georgia. At about age twenty, he escaped and went to Boston where he studied law and met black and white abolitionists.

In 1865 after the war, Bradley moved to Savannah where he took up the cause of the freedmen and opened a school. He worked closely with the city's black longshoremen and the low country and Sea Island rice field workers.

Bradley demanded that black families keep the land they had occupied under Sherman's Special Field Order #15. He believed that black people had to have land to prosper. He criticized the Freedmen's Bureau for attempting to force black people off the land and argued that President Johnson should be impeached for supporting Confederate land owners rather than black and white people who were loyal to the union.

Bradley also insisted that black people deserved the rights to vote, testify in court, and have jury trials. After he urged black farmers to defend their land by force, Federal authorities charged him with advocating insurrection. He was sentenced to a year's confinement but was soon paroled. Almost immediately, another fiery speech got him in trouble again and he had to leave Georgia.

He returned to Boston and renewed his pleas for land for the freedmen. He wrote the head of the Freedmen's Bureau, General Oliver O. Howard: "My great object is, to give you Back-bone, and as the Chief Justice of 4 millions of Colored people, and Refugees; You can not, and must not, be a Military Tool, in the hands of Andrew Johnson."

In 1867, Bradley returned to Savannah and attacked the system of sharecropping. He complained that freedmen were compelled to work involuntarily and asked that black men be permitted to arm themselves. He also argued that justice would be fairer if the courts included black men. Although the Freedmen's Bureau considered Bradley a troublemaker, he never backed down.

In 1867 black farmers and workers elected Bradley to the state constitutional convention, but he was soon expelled. Then he was elected to the state senate—only to be expelled again along with all the black members of the Georgia legislature.

Meanwhile, Bradley carried on a running battle with Savannah's mayor, a former Confederate colonel, and with the Ku Klux Klan. He threatened the "KKK and all Bad Men, . . . if you strike a blow the man or men will be followed, and the house in which he or they shall take shelter, will be burned to the ground."

In 1868, Bradley organized black workers to arm themselves to retain the lands that they believed belonged to them. For a month, black men controlled parts of Chatham County outside Savannah. Eventually, federal authorities jailed one hundred of them. Bradley again fled north.

He returned to Georgia in 1870 and reclaimed his senate seat after Congress forced the legislature to seat its black members. He supported measures to remove Savannah's mayor, reduce taxes on workers, and institute an eight-hour workday.

Democrats regained control of Georgia politics in 1872, and Bradley and the Republicans were swept from power. He ran for Congress in South Carolina in 1874 but lost. He supported black migration to Liberia and Florida, but he moved to St. Louis and died there in 1881.

Aaron Bradley was certainly not a typical Reconstruction leader. He maintained few close ties to black or white politicians. He was constantly embroiled in factional disputes. He did not cooperate with middle-class black leaders and had no ties with local churches and their clergymen—a rarity among black politicians.

He dressed in expensive and flashy clothes. He could be pompous, abrasive, and intemperate. White people universally detested him. Yet Bradley remained exceedingly popular among freedmen.

PRESIDENTIAL RECONSTRUCTION UNDER ANDREW JOHNSON

Vice President Andrew Johnson then became president and initially seemed inclined to impose stern policies on the white South while befriending the freedmen. He announced that "treason must be made odious, and traitors must be punished and impoverished." In 1864 he had told black people, "I will be your Moses, and lead you through the Red Sea of War and Bondage to a fairer future of Liberty and Peace." Nothing proved to be further from the truth. Andrew Johnson was no friend of black Americans.

Born poor in eastern Tennessee and never part of the southern aristocracy, Johnson strongly opposed secession and was the only senator from the seceded states to remain loyal to the Union. He had nonetheless acquired five slaves and the conviction that black people were so thoroughly inferior that white men must forever govern them. In 1867 Johnson argued that black people could not exercise political power and that they had "less capacity for government than any other race of people. No independent government of any form has ever been successful in their hands. On the contrary, wherever they have been left to their own devices they have shown a constant tendency to relapse into barbarism."

Johnson quickly lost his enthusiasm for punishing traitors. Indeed, he began to placate white Southerners. In May 1865, Johnson granted blanket amnesty and pardons to former Confederates willing to swear allegiance to the United States. The main exceptions were high former Confederate officials and those who owned property in excess of $20,000, a large sum at the time. Yet even these leaders could appeal for individual pardons. And appeal they did. By 1866 Johnson had pardoned more than 7,000 high-ranking former Confederates and wealthier Southerners. Moreover, he had restored land to those white people who had lost it to freedmen.

Johnson's actions blatantly encouraged those who had supported secession, owned slaves, and opposed the Union. He permitted long-time southern leaders to regain political influence and authority only months after the end of America's bloodiest conflict. As black people and radical Republicans watched in disbelief, Johnson appointed provisional governors in the former Confederate states. Leaders in those states then called constitutional conventions, held elections, and prepared to regain their place in the Union. Johnson merely insisted that each Confederate state formally accept the Thirteenth Amendment (ratified in December 1865, it outlawed slavery) and repudiate Confederate war debts.

The southern constitutional conventions gave no consideration to the inclusion of black people in the political system or to guaranteeing them equal rights. As one Mississippi delegate explained, "'Tis nature's law that the superior race must rule and rule they will."

BLACK CODES

After the election of state and local officials, white legislators gathered in state capitals across the South to determine the status and future of the freedmen. With little debate the legislatures drafted the so-called black codes. Southern politicians gave no thought to providing black people with the political and legal rights associated with citizenship.

The black codes sought to ensure the availability of a subservient agricultural labor supply controlled by white people. They imposed severe restrictions on freedmen. Freedmen had to sign annual labor contracts with white landowners. South Carolina required black people who wanted to establish a business to purchase licenses costing from $10 to $100. The codes permitted black children ages two to twenty-one to be apprenticed to white people and spelled out their duties and obligations in detail. Corporal punishment was legal. Employers were designated "masters" and employees "servants."

The black codes also restricted black people from loitering or vagrancy, using alcohol or firearms, hunting, fishing, and grazing livestock. The codes did guarantee rights that slaves had not possessed. Freedmen could marry legally, engage in contracts, purchase property, sue or be sued, and testify in court. But black people could not vote or serve on juries. The black codes conceded—just barely—freedom to black people.

BLACK CONVENTIONS

Alarmed by these threats to their freedom, black people met in conventions across the South in 1865 and 1866 to protest, appeal for justice, and chart their future. Men who had been free before the war dominated the conventions. Many were ministers, teachers, and artisans. Few had been slaves. Women and children also attended—as spectators not delegates—but women often offered comments, suggestions, and criticism. These

Bearing a remarkable resemblance to a slave auction, this scene in Monticello, Florida, shows a black man auctioned off to the highest bidder shortly after the Civil War. Under the terms of most southern Black Codes, black people arrested and fined for vagrancy or loitering could be "sold" if they could not pay the fine. Such spectacles infuriated many Northerners and led to demands for more rigid Reconstruction policies.

meetings were hardly militant or radical affairs. Delegates respectfully insisted that white people live up to the principles and rights embodied in the Declaration of Independence and the Constitution.

At the AME church in Raleigh, North Carolina, delegates asked for equal rights and the right to vote. At Georgia's convention they protested against white violence and appealed for leaders who would enforce the law without regard to color. "We ask not for a Black Man's Governor, nor a White Man's Governor, but for a People's Governor, who shall impartially protect the rights of all, and faithfully sustain the Union."

Delegates at the Norfolk meeting reminded white Virginians that black people were patriotic. "We are Americans. We know no other country. We love the land of our birth." But they protested that Virginia's black code caused "invidious political or legal distinctions, on account of color merely." They requested the right to vote and added that they might boycott the businesses of "those who deny to us our equal rights."

Two conventions were held in Charleston, South Carolina—one before and one after the black code was enacted. At the first, delegates stressed the "respect and affection" they felt toward white Charlestonians. They even proposed that only literate men be granted the right to vote if it were genuinely applied to both races. The second convention denounced the black code and insisted on its repeal. Delegates again asked for the right to vote and the right to testify in court. "These two things we deem necessary to our welfare and elevation." They also appealed for public schools and for "homesteads for ourselves and our children." White authorities ignored these and other black conventions and their petitions. Instead they were confident that they had effectively relegated the freedmen to a subordinate role in society.

By late 1865, President Johnson's reconstruction policies had aroused black people. One black Union veteran summed up the situation. "If you call this Freedom, what do you call Slavery?" Republicans in Congress also opposed Johnson's policies toward the freedmen and the former Confederate states.

THE RADICAL REPUBLICANS

Radical Republicans, as more militant Republicans were called, were especially disturbed that Johnson seemed to have abandoned the ex-slaves to their former masters. They considered white Southerners disloyal and unrepentant, despite their military defeat. Moreover, radical Republicans—unlike moderate Republicans and Democrats—were determined to transform the racial fabric of American society by including black people in the political and economic system.

Among the most influential radical Republicans were Charles Sumner, Benjamin Wade, and Henry Wilson in the Senate and Thaddeus Stevens, George W. Julian, and James M. Ashley in the House. Few white Americans have been as dedicated to the rights of black people as these men. They had fought for the abolition of slavery. They were reluctant to compromise. They were honest, tough, and articulate, but also abrasive, difficult, self-righteous, and vain. Black people appreciated them; many white people excoriated them. One black veteran wrote Charles Sumner in 1869, "Your name shall live in our hearts forever." A white Philadelphia businessman commented on Thaddeus Stevens. "He seems to oppose any measure that will not benefit the *nigger.*"

Radical Proposals

Stevens, determined to provide freedmen with land, introduced a bill in Congress in late 1865 to confiscate 400 million acres from the wealthiest 10 percent of Southerners and distribute it free to freedmen. The remaining land would be auctioned off in plots no larger than five hundred acres. Few legislators supported the proposal. Even those who wanted fundamental change considered confiscation a gross violation of property rights.

Instead, radical Republicans supported voting rights for black men. They were convinced that black men—to protect themselves and to secure the South for the Republican party—had to have the right to vote. Moderate Republicans, however, found the prospect of black voting almost as objectionable as the confiscation of land. They preferred to build the Republican party in the South by cooperating with President Johnson and attracting loyal white Southerners.

The thought of black suffrage appalled northern and southern Democrats. Most white Northerners—Republicans and Democrats—favored denying black men the right to vote in their states. After the war, proposals to give the vote to black men were defeated in New York, Ohio, Kansas, and the Nebraska Territory. In the District of Columbia, a vote to permit black suffrage lost 6,951 to 35. However, five New England states as well as Iowa, Minnesota, and Wisconsin did allow black men to vote.

As much as they objected to black suffrage, most white Northerners objected even more strongly to defiant white Southerners. Journalist Charles A. Dana described the attitude of many Northerners. "As for negro suffrage, the mass of Union men in the Northwest do not care a great deal. What scares them is the idea that the rebels are all to be let back . . . and made a power in government again, just as though there had been no rebellion."

In December 1865, Congress created the Joint Committee on Reconstruction to determine whether the southern states should be readmitted to the Union. The committee investigated southern affairs and confirmed reports of widespread mistreatment of black people and white arrogance.

The Freedmen's Bureau Bill and the Civil Rights Bill

In early 1866 Senator Lyman Trumball, a moderate Republican from Illinois, introduced two major bills. The first was to provide more financial support for the

FEDERAL RECONSTRUCTION LEGISLATION, 1865–1867

1865	Freedmen's Bureau established
1865	Thirteenth Amendment passed and ratified
1866	Freedmen's Bureau Bill and the Civil Rights Act of 1866 passed over Johnson's veto
1866	Fourteenth Amendment passed (ratified 1868)
1867	Reconstruction Acts passed over Johnson's veto

Freedmen's Bureau and extend its authority to defend the rights of black people.

The second proposal was the first civil rights bill in American history. It made any person born in the United States a citizen (except Indians) and entitled them to rights protected by the U.S. government. Black people would possess the same legal rights as white people. The bill was clearly intended to invalidate the black codes.

Johnson's Vetoes

Both measures passed in Congress with nearly unanimous Republican support. President Johnson vetoed them. He claimed that the bill to continue the Freedmen's Bureau would greatly expand the federal bureaucracy and permit too "vast a number of agents" to exercise arbitrary power over the white population. He insisted that the civil rights bill benefited black people at the expense of white people. "In fact, the distinction of race and color is by the bill made to operate in favor of the colored and against the white race."

The Johnson vetoes stunned Republicans. Though he had not meant to, Johnson drove moderate Republicans into the radical camp and strengthened the Republican party. The president did not believe that Republicans would oppose him to support the freedmen. He was wrong. Congress overrode both vetoes. The Republicans broke with Johnson in 1866, defied him in 1867, and impeached him in 1868 (failing to remove him from office by only one vote in the Senate).

THE FOURTEENTH AMENDMENT

To secure the legal rights of freedmen, Republicans passed the Fourteenth Amendment. This amendment fundamentally changed the Constitution by compelling states to accept their residents as citizens and to guarantee that their rights as citizens would be safeguarded.

Its first section guaranteed citizenship to every person born in the United States. This included virtually every black person. It made each person a citizen of the state in which he or she resided. It defined the specific rights of citizens and then protected those rights against the power of state governments. Citizens had the right to due process (usually a trial) before they could lose their life, liberty, or property.

> All persons born or naturalized in the United States, and subject to the jurisdiction thereof, are citizens of the United States and of the State wherein they reside. No State shall make or enforce any law which shall abridge the privileges or immunities of citizens of the United States; nor shall any State deprive any person of life, liberty, or property, without due process of law; nor deny to any person within its jurisdiction the equal protection of the laws.

Eleven years after Chief Justice Roger Taney declared in the Dred Scott decision that black people were "a subordinate and inferior class of beings" who had "no rights that white people were bound to respect," the Fourteenth Amendment vested them with the same rights of citizenship other Americans possessed.

The amendment also threatened to deprive states of representation in Congress if they denied black men the vote. The end of slavery had also made obsolete the three-fifths clause in the Constitution, which had counted slaves as only three-fifths (or 60 percent) of a white person in calculating a state's population and determining the number of representatives each state was entitled to in the House of Representatives. Republicans feared that southern states would count black people in their populations without permitting them to vote, thereby gaining more representatives than those states had had before the Civil War. The amendment mandated that the number of representatives each state would be entitled to in Congress (including northern states) would be reduced *if* that state did not allow adult males to vote.

Democrats almost unanimously opposed the Fourteenth Amendment. Andrew Johnson denounced it though he had no power to prevent its adoption. Southern states refused to ratify it except for Tennessee. Women's suffragists felt badly betrayed because the amendment limited suffrage to males. Despite this opposition, the amendment was ratified in 1868.

RADICAL RECONSTRUCTION

By 1867 radical Republicans in Congress had wrested control over Reconstruction from Johnson, and they then imposed policies that brought black men into the political system as voters and office holders. It was a dramatic development, second in importance only to emancipation and the end of slavery.

Republicans swept the 1866 congressional elections despite the belligerent opposition of Johnson and the Democrats. With two-thirds majorities in the House and Senate, Republicans easily overrode presidential vetoes. Two years after the Civil War ended, Republicans dismantled the state governments established in the South under President Johnson's authority. They instituted a new Reconstruction policy.

Republicans passed the First Reconstruction Act over Johnson's veto in March 1867. It divided the South into five military districts, each under the command of a general (Map 12–3). Military personnel would protect lives and property while new civilian governments were formed. Elected delegates in each state would draft a new constitution and submit it to the voters.

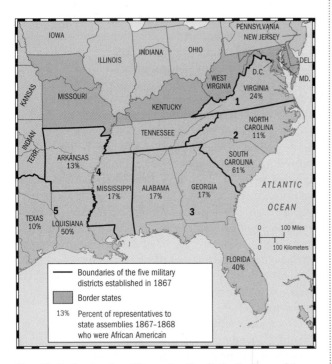

Map 12-3 Congressional Reconstruction. Under the terms of the First Reconstruction Act of 1867, the former Confederate states (except Tennessee) were divided into five military districts and placed under the authority of military officers. Commanders in each of the five districts were responsible for supervising the reestablishment of civilian governments in each state.

Universal Manhood Suffrage

The Reconstruction Act stipulated that all adult males in the states of the former Confederacy were eligible to vote—except for those who had actively supported the Confederacy or were convicted felons. Once each state had formed a new government and approved the Fourteenth Amendment, it would be readmitted to the Union with representation in Congress.

The advent of radical Reconstruction was the culmination of black people's struggle to gain legal and political rights. Since the 1864 black national convention in Syracuse and the meetings and conventions in the South in 1865 and 1866, black leaders had argued that one of the consequences of the Civil War should be the inclusion of black men in the body politic. The achievement of that goal was due to their persistent and persuasive efforts, the determination of radical Republicans, and, ironically, the obstructionism of Andrew Johnson who had played into their hands.

Black Politics

Full of energy and enthusiasm, black men and women rushed into the political arena in the spring and summer of 1867. Though women could not vote, they joined men at the meetings, rallies, parades, and picnics that accompanied political organizing in the South. For many former slaves, politics became as important as the church and religious activities. Black people flocked to the Republican party and the new Union Leagues.

The Union Leagues had been established in the North during the Civil War, but they expanded across the South as quasi-political organizations in the late 1860s. The Leagues were social, fraternal, and patriotic groups in which black people often, but not always, outnumbered white people. League meetings featured ceremonies, rituals, initiation rites, and oaths. They gave people an opportunity to sharpen leadership skills and gain an informal political education by discussing issues from taxes to schools.

Sit-Ins and Strikes

Political progress did not induce apathy and a sense of satisfaction and contentment among black people. Gaining citizenship, legal rights, and the vote generated more expectations and demands for advancement. For example, black people insisted on equal access to public transportation. After a Republican rally in Charleston, South Carolina, in April 1867, several black men staged a "sit-in" on a nearby horse-drawn streetcar before they

With the adoption of Radical Republican policies, most black men eagerly took part in political activities. Political meetings, conventions, speeches, barbecues and other gatherings also attracted women and children.

were arrested. In Charleston, black people were permitted to ride only on the outside running boards of the cars. They wanted to sit on the seats inside. Within a month—due to the intervention of military authorities—the streetcar company gave in. Similar protests occurred in Richmond and New Orleans.

Black workers also struck across the South in 1867. Black longshoremen in New Orleans, Mobile, Savannah, Charleston, and Richmond walked off the job. Black laborers were usually paid less than white men for the same work, and this led to labor unrest during the 1860s and 1870s. Sometimes the strikers won, sometimes they lost. In 1869, a black Baltimore longshoreman, Isaac Myers, organized the Colored National Labor Union.

THE REACTION OF WHITE SOUTHERNERS

White Southerners grimly opposed radical Reconstruction. They were outraged that black people could claim the same legal and political rights that they possessed. Such a possibility seemed preposterous to people who had an abiding belief in the absolute inferiority of black people. A statement by Benjamin F. Perry, whom Johnson had appointed provisional governor of South Carolina in 1865, captures the depth of this racist conviction. "The African," Perry declared, "has been in all ages, a savage or a slave. God created him inferior to the white man in form, color and intellect, and no legislation or culture can make him his equal. . . . His hair,

TIMELINE

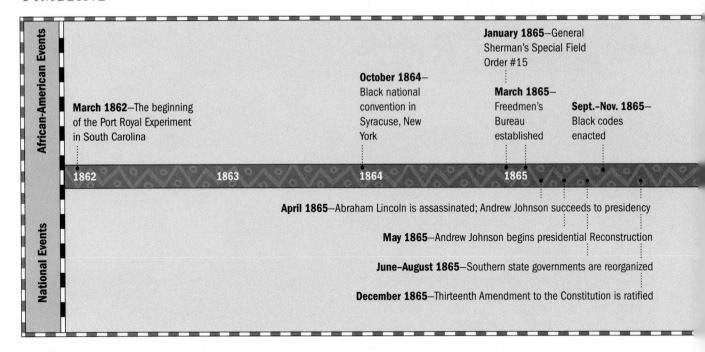

African-American Events

March 1862—The beginning of the Port Royal Experiment in South Carolina

October 1864—Black national convention in Syracuse, New York

January 1865—General Sherman's Special Field Order #15

March 1865—Freedmen's Bureau established

Sept.–Nov. 1865—Black codes enacted

1862   1863   1864   1865

National Events

April 1865—Abraham Lincoln is assassinated; Andrew Johnson succeeds to presidency

May 1865—Andrew Johnson begins presidential Reconstruction

June–August 1865—Southern state governments are reorganized

December 1865—Thirteenth Amendment to the Constitution is ratified

his form and features will not compete with the caucasian race, and it is in vain to think of elevating him to the dignity of the white man. God created differences between the two races, and nothing can make him equal."

Some white people, taking solace in their belief in the innate inferiority of black people, concluded they could turn black suffrage to their advantage. White people, they assumed, should easily be able to control and manipulate black voters just as they had controlled black people during slavery. White Southerners who believed this, however, were destined to be disappointed, and their disappointment would turn to fury.

CONCLUSION

Why were black Southerners able to gain citizenship and access to the political system by 1868? Most white Americans did not suddenly abandon two hundred fifty years of deeply ingrained beliefs that people of African descent were their inferiors. The advances that African Americans achieved fit into a series of complex political developments after the Civil War. Black people themselves had fought and died to preserve the Union, and they had earned the grudging respect of many white people and the open admiration of others. Black leaders in meetings and petitions insisted that their rights be recognized.

White Northerners—led by the radical Republicans—were convinced that President Andrew Johnson had made a serious error in supporting policies that permitted white Southerners to retain pre–Civil War leaders while the black codes virtually made freedmen slaves again. Republicans were determined that white Southerners realize their defeat had doomed the prewar status quo. Republicans established a Reconstruction program to disfranchise key southern leaders while providing legal rights to freedmen. The right to vote, they reasoned, would give black people the means to deal more effectively with white Southerners while simultaneously strengthening the Republican party in the South.

The result was to make the mid to late 1860s one of the few high points in African-American history. During this period, not only was slavery abolished but black Southerners were able to organize schools and churches, and black people throughout the south acquired legal and political rights that would have been incomprehensible before the war. Yet black people did not stand on the brink of utopia. Most freedmen still lacked land and had no realistic hope of obtaining much if any of it. White violence and cruelty continued almost unabated across much of the South. Still, for

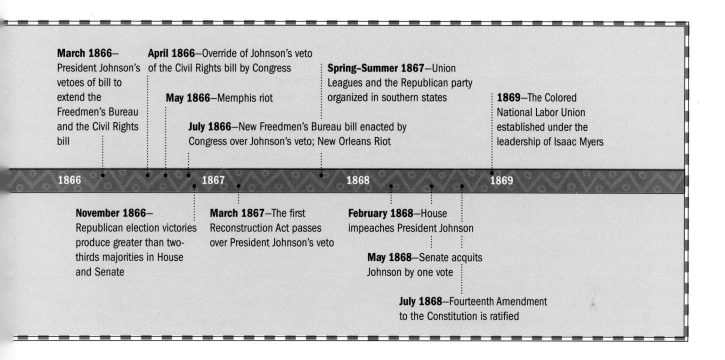

March 1866—President Johnson's vetoes of bill to extend the Freedmen's Bureau and the Civil Rights bill

April 1866—Override of Johnson's veto of the Civil Rights bill by Congress

May 1866—Memphis riot

July 1866—New Freedmen's Bureau bill enacted by Congress over Johnson's veto; New Orleans Riot

Spring–Summer 1867—Union Leagues and the Republican party organized in southern states

1869—The Colored National Labor Union established under the leadership of Isaac Myers

1866   1867   1868   1869

November 1866—Republican election victories produce greater than two-thirds majorities in House and Senate

March 1867—The first Reconstruction Act passes over President Johnson's veto

February 1868—House impeaches President Johnson

May 1868—Senate acquits Johnson by one vote

July 1868—Fourteenth Amendment to the Constitution is ratified

millions of African Americans, the future looked more promising than it had ever before in American history.

REVIEW QUESTIONS

1. How did freedmen define their freedom? What did freedom mean to ex-slaves? How did their priorities differ from those of African Americans who had been free before the Civil War?

2. What did the former slaves and the former slaveholders want after emancipation? Were these desires realistic? How did former slaves and former slaveholders disagree after the end of slavery?

3. Explain why African Americans formed separate churches, schools, and social organizations after the Civil War. What role did the black church play in the black community?

4. Evaluate the effectiveness of the Freedmen's Bureau. How successful was it in assisting ex-slaves to live in freedom?

5. Why did southern states enact black codes?

6. Why did radical Republicans object to President Andrew Johnson's Reconstruction policies? Why did Congress impose its own Reconstruction policies?

7. What factors contributed to passage of laws that enabled black men to vote?

8. Why did black men gain the right to vote but not possession of land?

9. Did congressional Reconstruction secure full legal and political equality for African Americans as American citizens?

RECOMMENDED READING

Ira Berlin and Leslie Rowland, eds. *Families and Freedom: A Documentary History of African-American Kinship in the Civil War Era* (New York: Cambridge University Press, 1997). A collection of documents that conveys the aspirations and frustrations of freedmen.

W. E. B. Du Bois. *Black Reconstruction in America: An Essay toward a History of the Part Which Black Folk Played in the Attempt to Reconstruct Democracy in America, 1860–1880* (New York: Russell & Russell, 1935). A classic account of Reconstruction challenging the traditional interpretation that it was a tragic era marked by corrupt and inept black rule of the South.

Eric Foner. *Reconstruction: America's Unfinished Revolution, 1863–1877* (New York: Harper & Row, 1988).

The best and most comprehensive account of Reconstruction.

Herbert G. Gutman. *The Black Family in Slavery and Freedom, 1750–1925* (New York: Oxford University Press, 1976). An illustration of how African-American family values and kinship ties forged in slavery endured after emancipation.

Tera W. Hunter. *To 'Joy My Freedom: Southern Black Women's Lives and Labors after the Civil War* (Cambridge: Harvard University Press, 1997). An examination of the interior lives of black women, their work, social welfare, and leisure.

Gerald D. Jaynes. *Branches without Roots: Genesis of the Black Working Class in the American South, 1862–1882* (New York: Pantheon, 1986). The changes in work and labor in the aftermath of slavery.

Leon F. Litwack. *Been in the Storm Too Long: The Aftermath of Slavery* (New York: Alfred A. Knopf, 1979). A rich and detailed account of the transition to freedom largely based on recollections of former slaves.

ADDITIONAL BIBLIOGRAPHY

Education

James D. Anderson. *The Education of Blacks in the South, 1860–1935* (Chapel Hill: University of North Carolina Press, 1988).

Ronald E. Butchart. *Northern Schools, Southern Blacks, and Reconstruction: Freedmen's Education, 1862–1875* (Westport, CT.: Greenwood Press, 1981).

Edmund L. Drago. *Initiative, Paternalism, and Race Relations: Charleston's Avery Normal Institute* (Athens: University of Georgia Press, 1990).

Robert C. Morris. *Reading, 'Riting, and Reconstruction: The Education of the Freedmen in the South, 1861–1890* (Chicago: University of Chicago Press, 1981).

Joe M. Richardson. *Christian Reconstruction: The American Missionary Association and Southern Blacks, 1861–1890* (Athens: University of Georgia Press, 1986).

Willie Lee Rose. *Rehearsal for Reconstruction: The Port Royal Experiment* (Indianapolis: Bobbs Merrill, 1964).

Land and Labor

Barbara J. Fields. *Slavery and Freedom on the Middle Ground: Maryland during the Nineteenth Century* (New Haven: Yale University Press, 1985).

Jacqueline Jones. *Labor of Love, Labor of Sorrow: Black Women, Work and Family, from Slavery to the Present* (New York: Basic Books, 1985).

Edward Magdol. *A Right to the Land: Essays on the Freedmen's Community* (Westport, CT.: Greenwood Press, 1977).

Claude F. Oubre. *Forty Acres and a Mule: The Freedmen's Bureau and Black Landownership* (Baton Rouge: Louisiana State University Press, 1978).

Roger L. Ransom and Richard Sutch. *One Kind of Freedom: The Economic Consequences of Emancipation* (New York: Cambridge University Press, 1977).

Julie Saville. *The Work of Reconstruction: From Slave to Wage Labor in South Carolina, 1860–1870* (New York: Cambridge University Press, 1994).

Black Communities

John W. Blassingame. *Black New Orleans, 1860–1880* (Chicago: University of Chicago Press, 1973).

Robert F. Engs. *Freedom's First Generation: Black Hampton, Virginia, 1861–1890* (Philadelphia: University of Pennsylvania Press, 1979).

William E. Montgomery. *Under Their Own Vine and Fig Tree, The African American Church in the South 1865–1900* (Baton Rouge: Louisiana State University Press, 1993).

Bernard E. Powers, Jr. *Black Charlestonians: A Social History, 1822–1885* (Fayetteville: University of Arkansas Press, 1994).

Clarence E. Walker. *A Rock in a Weary Land: The African Methodist Episcopal Church during the Civil War and Reconstruction* (Baton Rouge: Louisiana State University Press, 1982).

James M. Washington. *Frustrated Fellowship: The Black Baptist Quest for Social Power* (Macon, GA.: Mercer University Press, 1986).

CHAPTER 13

THE MEANING OF FREEDOM: THE FAILURE OF RECONSTRUCTION

Entered, according to act of Congress in the year 1872 by Currier & Ives, in the Office of the Librarian of Congress at Washington.

ROBERT C. DE LARGE, M.C. of S.Carolina.   JEFFERSON H. LONG, M.C. of Georgia.

U.S. Senator H.R.REVELS, of Mississippi   BENJ. S. TURNER,M.C. of Alabama.   JOSIAH T. WALLS, M.C. of Florida.   JOSEPH H. RAINY, M.C. of S.Carolina.   R. BROWN ELLIOT, M.C. of S.Carolina.

THE FIRST COLORED SENATOR AND REPRESENTATIVES.
In the 41ˢᵗ and 42ⁿᵈ Congress of the United States.

NEW YORK, PUBLISHED BY CURRIER & IVES, 125 NASSAU STREET.

The first seven African Americans to serve in the U.S. Senate and the U.S. House of Representatives. Three of them—Benjamin S. Turner, Josiah T. Walls, and Jefferson H. Long— were former slaves.

Let us with a fixed, firm, hearty, earnest, and unswerving determination move steadily on and on, fanning the flame of true liberty until the last vestige of oppression shall be destroyed, and when that eventful period shall arrive, when, in the selection of rulers, both State and Federal, we shall know no North, no East, no South, no West, no white nor colored, no Democrat nor Republican, but shall choose men because of their moral and intrinsic value, their honesty and integrity, their love of unmixed liberty, and their ability to perform well the duties to be committed to their charge.

From a speech delivered in 1872, by Jonathan J. Wright, Associate Justice of the South Carolina Supreme Court

In 1868 for the first time in American history, thousands of black men would elect hundreds of black and white leaders to state and local offices across the South. Would this newly acquired political influence enable freedmen to complete the transition from slavery to freedom? Would political power propel black people into the mainstream of American society? Equally important, would white Southerners and Northerners accept black people as fellow citizens?

Events in the decade from 1867 to 1877 generated hope that black and white Americans might learn to live together on a compatible and equitable basis. But these developments also raised the possibility that black people's new access to political power would fail to resolve the racial animosity and intolerance that persisted in American life after the Civil War.

CONSTITUTIONAL CONVENTIONS

Black men as a group first entered politics as delegates to constitutional conventions in the southern states in 1867 and 1868. Each of the former Confederate states, except Tennessee, which had already been restored to the Union, elected delegates to these conventions. Most southern white men were Democrats. They boycotted these elections to protest both Congress's assumption of authority over Reconstruction and the extension of voting privileges to black men. Thus the delegates to the conventions that met to frame new state constitutions to replace those drawn up in 1865 under President Johnson's authority were mostly Republicans joined by a few conservative southern Democrats. The Republicans represented three constituencies. One consisted of white northern migrants who moved to the South in the wake of the war. They were known as carpetbaggers because they were said to have arrived in the South with all their possessions in a single carpet bag. A second group consisted of native white Southerners, mostly small farmers in devastated upland regions of the South who hoped for economic relief from Republican governments. This group was known derogatorily as scalawags, or scoundrels, by other southern white people. African Americans made up the third and largest Republican constituency.

Of the 1,000 men elected as delegates to the ten state conventions, 265 were black. Black delegates were a majority only in the South Carolina and Louisiana conventions. In most states, including Alabama, Georgia, Mississippi, Virginia, North Carolina, Arkansas, and Texas, black men made up 10 percent to 20 percent of

Southern black men cast ballots for the first time in 1867 in the election of delegates to state constitutional conventions. The ballots were provided by the candidates or political parties, and not by state or municipal officials. Most nineteenth-century elections were not by secret ballot.

the delegates. At least 107 of the 265 had been born slaves; about forty had served in the Union Army. Several were well-educated teachers and ministers; others were tailors, blacksmiths, barbers, and farmers. Most went on to hold other political offices in the years that followed.

These delegates produced impressive constitutions. Unlike previous state constitutions in the South, the new constitutions ensured that all adult males could vote, and except in Mississippi and Virginia, they did *not* disfranchise large numbers of former Confederates. They conferred broad guarantees of civil rights. In several states they provided the first statewide systems of public education. These constitutions were progressive, not radical. Black and white Republicans hoped to attract support from white Southerners for the new state governments these documents created by encouraging state support for private businesses, especially railroad construction.

ELECTIONS

Elections were held in 1868 to ratify the new constitutions and elect officials. The white Democratic response varied. In some states, Democrats boycotted the elections. In others, they participated but voted against ratification, and in still other states they supported ratification and attempted to elect as many Democrats as possible to office. Congress required only a majority of those voting—not a majority of all registered voters—to ratify the constitutions. And in each state a majority of those voting eventually did vote to ratify. And in each state, black men were elected to political offices.

BLACK POLITICAL LEADERS

Over the next decade, 1,465 black men held political office in the South. Though black leaders individually and collectively enjoyed significant political leverage, white Republicans dominated politics during Reconstruction. In general the number of black officials in a state reflected the size of that state's African-American population. Black people were a majority of the population only in Mississippi and South Carolina, and most of the black office holders came from those two states and Louisiana, where black people were a bare majority. In most states, such as Arkansas, North Carolina, Tennessee, and Texas where black people made up between 25 percent and 40 percent of the population, far fewer black men were elected to office (Table 13–1).

Initially, black men chose not to run for the most important political offices because they feared their election would further alienate already angry white Southerners. But as white Republicans swept into office in 1868, black leaders reversed their strategy, and by 1870 black men had been elected to many key political positions. No black man was elected governor, but Lieutenant Governor P. B. S. Pinchback served one month (from December 1872 to January 1873) as governor in Louisiana after the white governor was removed from office. Blanche K. Bruce and Hiram Revels represented Mississippi in the U.S. Senate. Beginning with Joseph Rainey in 1870 in South Carolina, fourteen black men served in the U.S. House of Representatives during Reconstruction. Six men served as lieutenant governors. In Mississippi and South Carolina, a majority of the representatives in state houses were black

Table 13–1 African-American Population and Officeholding during Reconstruction in the States Subject to Congressional Reconstruction			
	African-American Population in 1870	African Americans as a Percentage of Total Population	Number of African-American Officeholders during Reconstruction
South Carolina	415,814	58.9	314
Mississippi	444,201	53.6	226
Louisiana	364,210	50.1	210
North Carolina	391,650	36.5	180
Alabama	475,510	47.6	167
Georgia	545,142	46.0	108
Virginia	512,841	41.8	85
Florida	91,689	48.7	58
Arkansas	122,169	25.2	46
Texas	253,475	30.9	46
Tennessee	322,331	25.6	20

Source: Eric Foner, *Freedom's Lawmakers: A Directory of Black Officeholders during Reconstruction* (1993), xiv; *The Statistics of the Population of the United States, Ninth Census* (1873), xvii.

Hiram R. Revels represented Mississippi in the U.S. Senate from February 1870 until March 1871, completing an unexpired term. He went on to serve as Mississippi's Secretary of State. He was born free in Fayetteville, North Carolina in 1822. He attended Knox College in Illinois before the Civil War. In 1874 he abandoned the Republican party and became a Democrat. By the 1890s he had acquired a sizable plantation near Natchez.

sional school. In fact, fourteen of the leaders had been students at Oberlin College in Ohio, which began admitting both black and female students before the Civil War.

Black farmers and artisans—tailors, carpenters, and barbers—were well represented among those who held political office. There were also 237 ministers and 172 teachers. At least 129 had served in the Union Army, and 46 had worked for the Freedmen's Bureau.

Several black politicians were wealthy, and a few were former slave owners. Antoine Dubuclet, who became Louisiana's treasurer, had owned more than one hundred slaves and land valued at more than $100,000 before the Civil War. Former slave Ferdinand Havis became a member of the Arkansas House of Representatives. He owned a saloon, a whiskey business, and two thousand acres near Pine Bluff, where he became known as "the Colored Millionaire."

Although black men did not dominate any state politically, a few did dominate districts with sizable black populations. Before he was elected to the U.S. Senate, Blanche K. Bruce all but controlled Bolivar County, Mississippi, where he served as sheriff, tax collector, and superintendent of education. Former slave and Civil War hero Robert Smalls was the political "kingpin" in Beaufort, South Carolina. He served successively in the South Carolina house and senate, and in the U.S. House of Representatives. He was also a member of the South Carolina constitutional conventions in 1868 and 1895. He was a major figure in the Republican party, and served as customs collector in Beaufort from 1889 to 1913.

men, and each of these states had two black speakers of the house in the 1870s. Jonathan J. Wright, quoted at the beginning of this chapter, served seven years as a state supreme court justice in South Carolina. Four black men served as state superintendents of education, and Francis L. Cardozo served as South Carolina's secretary of state and then treasurer. One hundred twelve black state senators and 683 black representatives were elected during Reconstruction. There were also forty-one black sheriffs, five black mayors, and thirty-one black coroners. Tallahassee, Florida, and Little Rock, Arkansas, had black police chiefs.

Many of these men—by background, experience, and education—were well qualified. Others were not. Of the 1,465 black office holders at least 378 had been free before the Civil War; 933 were literate, and 195 were illiterate (we lack information about the remaining 337). Sixty-four had attended college or professional school.

THE ISSUES

Many but not all black and white Republican leaders favored increasing the authority of state governments to promote the welfare of all the state's citizens. Before the Civil War, most southern states did not provide schools, medical care, assistance for the mentally impaired, or prisons. Such concerns—if attended to at all—were left to local communities or families.

Education and Social Welfare

Black leaders were eager to increase literacy and promote education among black people. Republican politicians created statewide systems of public education throughout the South. It was a difficult and expensive task, and the results were only a limited success. Schools had to be built, teachers employed, and textbooks

PROFILE

THE GIBBS BROTHERS

Among the many black leaders who emerged during Reconstruction were the Gibbs brothers, who had political careers in two different states, Arkansas and Florida. Mifflin W. Gibbs and Jonathan C. Gibbs grew up in a well-to-do free black family in Philadelphia where their father was a respected Methodist minister. But their paths diverged, and they spent little time together as adults.

Mifflin was born in 1823 and became a building contractor. By the 1840s he was an active abolitionist. With the discovery of gold in California in 1849, he went west and eventually established California's first black newspaper, *The Mirror of the Times*. He led a protest in 1851 against a provision in the California constitution that denied black men the right to vote. In 1858 he left California for Canada, again because gold had been discovered. He spent more than ten years in Canada and was elected to the Victoria City Council in British Columbia before returning to the United States in 1869. In 1870 he graduated from the law program at Oberlin College.

Mifflin moved to Arkansas in 1871 and was elected Little Rock Municipal Judge in 1873. Although defeated for reelection, he remained deeply involved in Republican party politics and was a delegate to every Republican national convention from 1876 to 1904. In 1897, Republican president William McKinley appointed him U.S. consul to Madagascar, a French colony of East Africa, where he served until 1901. He died in 1915. A black high school in Little Rock was named in his honor.

Mifflin Gibbs was probably the only African American in the nineteenth century elected to political office in two nations. He served as a city councilman in Victoria, British Columbia, in Canada in the late 1860s, and he was elected a judge in Little Rock, Arkansas, in 1873.

Jonathan, born in 1827 or 1828, also joined the abolitionist movement. Rejected by eighteen colleges because of his color, he finally graduated from Dartmouth in 1852. He then went to Princeton Theological Seminary and became a Presbyterian minister in Troy, New York.

Jonathan attended the 1864 National Black Convention in Syracuse, New York, taught briefly at a freedmen's school in North Carolina, and then spent two years in Charleston, South Carolina. There he joined those black leaders who favored limiting the right to vote to literate men *if* that restriction was applied both to black and white people.

In 1867, Jonathan moved to Florida, where he became a key Republican leader and the state's highest-ranking black official. He was elected to the 1868 Florida constitutional convention and was appointed secretary of state by the Republican governor. Although defeated for a seat in Congress in 1868, he remained one of Florida's most visible black leaders and was constantly threatened by the Ku Klux Klan. In 1873, another Republican governor appointed him state superintendent of education. Jonathan Gibbs died in 1874, but his son Thomas went on to serve in the Florida House of Representatives where he was instrumental in the establishment of Florida A&M University.

provided. To pay for it, taxes were increased in states still reeling from the war.

In some communities and in many rural areas, schools were not built. In other places teachers were not paid. Some people—black and white—opposed compulsory education laws, preferring to let parents determine whether their children should attend school or

work to help the family. Some black leaders favored a poll tax on voting if the funds it brought in were spent on the schools. Thus while Reconstruction leaders established a strong commitment to public education, the results they achieved were uneven.

Furthermore, white parents refused to send their children to integrated schools. Though no laws required it, public schools during and after Reconstruction were segregated. Black parents were usually more concerned that their children should have schools to attend than whether the schools were integrated. New Orleans, however, was an exception; it provided integrated schools.

Reconstruction leaders also supported higher education. In 1872, Mississippi legislators took advantage of the 1862 Federal Morrill Land-Grant Act—which provided states with funds for agricultural and mechanical colleges—to found the first historically black state university: Alcorn A&M College. Although it was named after a white Republican governor, James L. Alcorn, former U.S. Senator Hiram Revels was its first president. The South Carolina legislature created a similar college and attached it to the Methodist-sponsored Claflin University.

Black leaders in the state legislature compelled the University of South Carolina, which had been all white, to admit black students and hire black faculty. Many but not all of the white students and faculty left. Several black politicians enrolled in the law and medical programs at the university. Richard Greener, a black Harvard graduate, served on the university's faculty and was its librarian.

Despite the costs, Reconstruction leaders also created the first state-supported institutions for the insane, the blind, and the deaf in the South. Some southern states during Reconstruction began to offer medical care and public health programs. Orphanages were established. State prisons were built. Black leaders also supported revising state criminal codes, eliminating corporal punishment for many crimes, and reducing the number of capital crimes.

Civil Rights

Black politicians were often the victims of racial discrimination when they tried to use public transportation and accommodations like hotels and restaurants. Rather than provide separate arrangements for black customers, white-owned businesses simply excluded black patrons. This was true in the North as well as the South. Robert Smalls, for example, the Civil War hero who had commandeered a Confederate supply ship to escape from Charleston in 1862 (see Chapter 11), was unceremoniously ejected from a Philadelphia streetcar in 1864. After protests, the company agreed to accept black riders. In Arkansas Mifflin Gibbs (see Profile: The Gibbs Brothers) and W. Hines Furbish successfully sued a local saloon after they had been denied service. In South Carolina Jonathan J. Wright won $1,200 in a

lawsuit against a railroad after he had purchased a first-class ticket but had been forced to ride in the second-class coach.

Black leaders were determined to open public facilities to all people, in the process revealing deep divisions between themselves and white Republicans. In several southern states they introduced bills to prevent proprietors from excluding black people from restaurants, barrooms, hotels, concert halls, and auditoriums as well as railroad coaches, streetcars, and steamboats. Many white Republicans and virtually every Democrat attacked such proposals as efforts to promote social equality and gain access for black people to places where they were not welcome. The white politicians blocked these laws in most states. Only South Carolina—with a black majority in the house and many black members in the senate—enacted such a law, but it was not effectively enforced. In Mississippi, the Republican governor James L. Alcorn vetoed a bill to outlaw racial discrimination by railroads. In Alabama and North Carolina, civil rights bills were defeated, while Georgia and Arkansas enacted measures that encouraged segregation.

ECONOMIC ISSUES

Black politicians sought to promote economic development in general and for black people in particular. For example, white landowners sometimes arbitrarily fired black agricultural laborers near the end of the growing season and then did not pay them. Some of these landowners were dishonest, but others were in debt and could not pay their workers. To prevent such situations, black politicians secured laws that required laborers to be paid before the crop was sold or at the time when it was sold. Some black leaders who had been slaves also wanted to regulate the wages of laborers, but these proposals invariably failed because most Republicans did not believe that states had the right to regulate wages and prices.

Legislators also enacted measures that protected the land and property of small farmers against seizure for nonpayment of debts. Black and white farmers who lost land, tools, animals, and other property because they could not pay their debts were unlikely ever to recover financially. "Stay laws" prohibited or "stayed" authorities from taking property. Besides affording financial protection to hard-pressed poor farmers, Republicans hoped these laws would attract political support from white yeoman and draw them away from their attachment to the Democratic party.

Land

Black leaders were unable to initiate programs that would provide land to landless black and white farmers. Many black and white political leaders believed that the state had no right to distribute land. Again, South Carolina was the exception. Its legislature created a state land commission in 1869.

The commission could purchase and distribute land to freedmen. It also gave the freedmen loans on generous terms to pay for the land. Unfortunately, the commission was corrupt, was inefficiently managed, and had little fertile land to distribute. However, despite its many difficulties, the commission enabled more than 14,000 black families and a few white families to acquire land in South Carolina. Their descendants still possess some of this land today.

Though some black leaders were reluctant to use the states' power to distribute land, others had no qualms about raising property taxes so high that large landowners would be forced to sell some of their property to pay their taxes. Abraham Galloway of North Carolina explained: "I want to see the man who owns one or two thousand acres of land, taxed a dollar on the acre, and if they can't pay the taxes, sell their property to the highest bidder . . . and then we negroes shall become the land holders."

Business and Industry

Black and white leaders had an easier time enacting legislation to support business and industry. Like most Americans after the Civil War, Republicans believed that expanding the railroad network would stimulate employment, improve transportation, and generate prosperity. State governments approved the sale of bonds supported by the authority of the state to finance railroad construction. In Georgia, Alabama, Texas, and Arkansas, the railroad network did expand. But the bonded debt of these states soared and taxes increased to pay for it. Moreover, railroad financing was often corrupt. Most of the illegal money wound up in the pockets of white businessmen and politicians. Black politicians rarely had access to truly large financial transactions.

So attractive were business profits that some black political leaders formed corporations. They invested modest sums and believed—like so many capitalists—that the rewards outweighed the risks. In Charleston, twenty-eight black leaders (and two white politicians) formed a horse-drawn streetcar line they called the Enterprise Railroad to carry freight between the city wharves and the railroad terminal. Black leaders in

South Carolina also created a company to extract the phosphate used for fertilizer from riverbeds and riverbanks in the low country. Neither business lasted long. Black men found it far more difficult than white entrepreneurs to finance their corporations.

BLACK POLITICIANS: AN EVALUATION

Southern black political leaders on the state level did create the foundation for public education; for providing state assistance for the blind, deaf, and insane; and for reforming the criminal justice system. They tried but mostly failed to outlaw racial discrimination in public facilities. They encouraged state support for economic revival and expansion.

But black leaders could not create programs that significantly improved the lives of their constituents. Because white Republicans almost always outnumbered them, they could not enact an agenda of their own. Moreover, black leaders often disagreed among themselves about specific issues and programs. Class and prewar status frequently divided them. Those leaders who had not been slaves and had not been raised in rural isolation were less likely to be concerned with land and agricultural labor. More prosperous black leaders showed more interest in civil rights and encouraging business. Even when they agreed about the need for public education, black leaders often disagreed about how to finance it and whether or not it should be compulsory.

REPUBLICAN FACTIONALISM

Disagreements among black leaders paled compared to the internal conflicts that divided the Republican party during Reconstruction. Black and white Republicans often disagreed on political issues and strategy. But the lack of party cohesion and discipline was even more harmful. The Republican party in the South constantly split into factions as groups fought with each other. Most disagreements were over who should run for and hold political office.

During Reconstruction, hundreds of would-be Republican leaders—black and white—sought public offices. If they lost the Republican nomination in county or state conventions, they often formed a competing slate of candidates. Then Republicans ran against each other and against the Democrats in the general election. It was not a recipe for political success.

THE ROLLIN SISTERS

Few women, black or white, were as influential in Reconstruction politics as the Rollin sisters of South Carolina. Although they could not vote or hold political office, the five sisters, and especially Frances and Katherine, were closely associated with the black and white Republican leadership in South Carolina. With their education, knowledge, and charm, these black women affected political decisions and policies.

The sisters were born and raised in the elite antebellum free black community in Charleston. Their father, William Rollin, a prosperous lumber dealer, traced his ancestors back to French Catholic families in Haiti. He insisted that his daughters obtain a first-rate education. Frances, who was born in 1844, was sent to Philadelphia to take the "ladies course" at the Quaker's Institute for Colored Youth. At least two of the other sisters attended school in Boston. After the war, Frances wrote the biography of the black abolitionist leader Martin Delaney. This was the first major nonfiction work published in America by a black woman.

In 1867 and 1868, as black men were entering the political arena, the Rollin sisters also gravitated to politics. Against her father's wishes, Frances married one of Reconstruction South Carolina's most controversial figures, William Whipper, a black attorney from Philadelphia who settled in Beaufort, South Carolina, after the war. He was elected to the state constitutional convention and then the South Carolina House of Representatives. Whipper was a tough, able, shrewd, and not altogether honest politician. He enjoyed an expensive lifestyle. Most white people detested him.

While the legislature was in session, the Whippers and the Rollin sisters took up residence in Columbia, the state capital. There, the sisters were enormously popular. They were well educated, intelligent, refined, and sophisticated. One observer described them as "ravishingly beautiful." Katherine Rollin was frequently seen with white state Senator George W. McIntyre.

Frances Rollin Whipper was an author, teacher, political activist, wife, and mother. With her sisters, she was deeply involved in Reconstruction politics in South Carolina. She had five children and three survived to adulthood.

The Rollin sisters were well aware of their social status. They rarely associated with freedmen and poor white people and denied any connection with corrupt politicians. Katherine even criticized William Whipper for his reputation.

The Rollin sisters were enthusiastic proponents of women's rights and women's suffrage. They enlisted the wives of prominent black and white Republican politicians in their cause. Charlotte and Katherine organized a women's rights convention in Columbia in 1870, and formed the South Carolina Branch of the American Women's Suffrage Association.

Charlotte Rollin pleaded for the right to vote.

> We ask suffrage not as a favor, not as a privilege, but as a right based on the grounds that we are human beings and as such entitled to human rights. While we concede that woman's ennobling influence should be confined chiefly to the home and society, we claim that public opinion has had a tendency to limit a woman's sphere to too small a circle and until woman has the right of representation this will last, and other rights will be held by insecure tenure.

Their black and white male allies tried to amend South Carolina's constitution to enable women to vote. After a bitter debate, the legislature rejected women's suffrage.

After the Democrats regained political power in 1877, the Rollin sisters left for the North. Charlotte and Louise settled with their mother in Brooklyn, New York. William and Frances Whipper and their five children moved to Washington, D.C., in 1882, where he practiced law and she was a clerk in the General Land Office. In 1885, William Whipper returned to Beaufort where he entered local politics. In the 1890s, Frances rejoined him there. She died in 1901 in Beaufort.

These bitter and angry contests were based less on race and issues than on the desperate desire to gain an office that would pay even a modest salary. Most black and white Republicans were not well off; public office assured them a modicum of economic security.

Ironically, these factional disputes led to a high turnover in political leadership and the loss of that very economic security. It was difficult for black leaders (and white leaders too) to be renominated and reelected to more than two terms. Few office holders served three or four consecutive terms in the same office during Reconstruction. This made for inexperienced leadership and added to Republican woes.

OPPOSITION

Even if black and Republican leaders had been less prone to internecine conflict and more effective in adopting a political platform, they might still have failed to sustain themselves for long. Most white Southerners led by conservative Democracts remained absolutely opposed to letting black men vote or hold office. As a white Floridian put it, "The damned Republican party has put niggers to rule us and we will not suffer it." Of course, because black people voted did not mean that they ruled during Reconstruction, but many white people failed to grasp that. Instead, for most white Southerners the only acceptable political system was one that excluded black men and the Republican party.

As far as most white people were concerned, the end of slavery and the enfranchisement of black men did not make black people their equals. They did not accept the Fourteenth Amendment. They attacked Republican governments and their leaders unrelentingly. White Southerners blamed the Republicans for an epidemic of waste and corruption in state government. But most of all, they considered it preposterous that former slaves could vote and hold political office.

James S. Pike spoke for many white people when he ridiculed black leaders in the South Carolina House of Representatives in 1873.

> The body is almost literally a Black Parliment. . . . The Speaker is black, the Clerk is black, the doorkeepers are black, the little pages are black, the chairman of the Ways and Means is black, and the chaplain is coal-black. At some of the desks sit colored men whose types it would be hard to find outside of Congo; whose costume, visages, attitudes, and expression, only befit the forecastle of a buccaneer. It must be remembered, also, that these men, with not more than a half a dozen exceptions, have been themselves slaves, and that their ancestors were slaves for generations.

Pike's observations circulated widely in both North and South.

White Southerners were determined to rid themselves of Republicans and the disgrace of having to live with black men who possessed political rights. White Southerners would "redeem" their states by restoring white Democrats to power. This did not simply mean defeating black and white Republicans in elections; it meant removing them from *any* role in politics. White Southerners believed that any means—fair or foul—were justified in exorcising this evil.

THE KU KLUX KLAN

If the black role in politics was illegitimate—in the eyes of white Southerners—then it was acceptable to use violence to remove it. This thinking gave rise to militant terrorist organizations, such as the Ku Klux Klan, the Knights of the White Camellia, the White Brotherhood, and the Whitecaps. Threats, intimidation, beatings, rapes, and murder would restore conservative white Democratic rule and force black people back into subordination.

The Ku Klux Klan was founded in Pulaski, Tennessee, in 1866. It was originally a social club for Confederate veterans who adopted secret oaths and rituals—similar to the Union Leagues, but with far more deadly results. One of the key figures in the Klan's rapid growth was former Confederate General Nathan Bedford Forrest who became its Grand Wizard. The Klan drew its members from all classes of white society, not merely from among the poor. Businessmen, lawyers, physicians, and politicians were active in the Klan as well as farmers and planters.

The Klan and other terrorist organizations functioned mainly where black people were a large minority and where their votes could affect the outcome of elections. Klansmen virtually took over areas of western Alabama, northern Georgia, and Florida's panhandle. The Klan controlled the up country of South Carolina and the area around Mecklenburg County, North Carolina. However, in the Carolina and Georgia low country where there were huge black majorities, the Klan never appeared.

Though the Klan and similar societies were neither well organized nor unified, they did reduce support for the Republican party and helped eliminate its leaders. Often wearing hoods and masks to hide their faces,

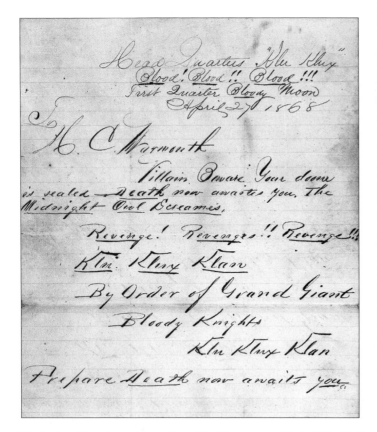

The flowing white robes and cone-shaped headdresses associated with the Ku Klux Klan today are mostly a twentieth-century phenomenon. The Klansmen of the Reconstruction era, like these two men in Alabama in 1868, were well armed, disguised, and prepared to intimidate black and white Republicans. The note is a Klan death threat directed at Louisiana's first Republican governor, Henry C. Warmoth.

white terrorists embarked on a campaign of violence rarely matched and never exceeded in American history.

Mobs of marauding terrorists beat and killed hundreds of black people—and many white people. Black churches and schools were burned. Republican leaders were routinely threatened and often killed. The black chairman of the Republican party in South Carolina, Benjamin F. Randolph, was murdered as he stepped off a train in 1868. Black legislator Lee Nance and white legislator Solomon G. W. Dill were murdered in 1868 in South Carolina. In 1870 black lawmaker Richard Burke was killed in Sumter County, Alabama, because he was considered too influential among "people of his color."

As his wife looked on, Jack Dupree—a local Republican leader—had his throat cut and was eviscerated in Monroe County, Mississippi. In 1870, North Carolina Senator John W. Stephens, a white Republican, was murdered. After Alabama freedman George Moore voted for the Republicans in 1869, Klansmen beat him, raped a girl who was visiting his wife, and attacked a neighbor. An Irish-American teacher and four black men were lynched in Cross Plains, Alabama, in 1870.

White men attacked a Republican campaign rally in Eutaw, Alabama, in 1870 and killed four black men and wounded fifty-four other people. After three black leaders were arrested in 1871 in Meridian, Mississippi, for delivering what many white people considered inflammatory speeches, shooting broke out in the courtroom. The Republican judge and two of the defendants were killed, and in a wave of violence, thirty black people were murdered including every black leader in the small community. In the same year, a mob of five hundred men broke into the jail in Union County, South Carolina, and lynched eight black prisoners who had been accused of killing a Confederate veteran.

Nowhere was the Klan more active and violent than in York County, South Carolina. Almost the entire adult white male population joined in threatening, attacking, and murdering the black population. Hundreds were beaten and at least eleven killed. Terrified families fled from their homes into the woods. Appeals for help were sent to Governor Robert K. Scott (see Voices: An Appeal for Help against the Klan).

But Scott did not send aid. He had already sent the South Carolina militia into areas of Klan activity, and even more violence had resulted. The militia was made up mostly of black men, and white terrorists retaliated by killing militia officers. Scott could not send white men to York County because most of them sympathized with the Klan. Thus Republican governors like Scott responded ineffectually. Republican-controlled legislatures passed anti-Klan measures that made it illegal to appear in public in disguises and masks, and they strengthened laws against assault, murder, and conspiracy. But enforcement was weak.

VOICES

AN APPEAL FOR HELP AGAINST THE KLAN

H. K. Roberts, a black lieutenant in the South Carolina State Militia, described Klan terror in York County in late 1870 to Governor Robert K. Scott. Roberts desperately appealed for aid to protect Republicans and defend the black community.

Antioch P.O.
York County
S.C.
Dec. the 6th 1870. To Your Excelency R. K. Scott

Sir I will tell you that on last friday night the 2nd day of this [month] 8 miles from here thier was one of the worst outrages Commited that is on record in the state from 50 to 75 armed men went to the house of Thomas Blacks a colored man fired shots into the house and cald for him he clibed up in the loft of the house they fired up their and he came down jumped out at a window ran about 30 steps was shot down then they shot him after he fell they then draged him about 10 steps and cut his throat from ear to ear their was about 30 bullet holes in his body some 50 to one hundred shots in the house. . . . [They] abused his wife and enquired for one or two more colored men some of the colored people are leaving and a great many lying out in the woods and they reports comes to me evry day that they Ku Kluxs intend to kill us all out and I heard yesterday that they had 30 stands of arms. . . . I wish you would give me 20 or 25 men or let me enroll that many and I will stop it or catch some of them or send some U S Soldiers on for I tell you their must be something don and that quick to for I do believe that they intend to beat and kill out the Radical party in the upper Counties of the state where the vote is close if we was to have the ellection now the Radicals would turn [out] to vote their ticket I leave the matter with you I hope you will wright back to me by return mail and let me heare what you think you can do for us up here I cant tell whether I can hold my own or not I know some men that stay with us at night for safety but if they come as strong as they were the other night they may kill me and all of my men I remain yours truly as ever
H.K. Roberts, Lieut.
Commanding Post
of State Guards Kings Mountain

QUESTIONS

1. What motivated Roberts to write this letter?

2. Would Roberts have had any reason to exaggerate the violence in York County?

3. Does Roberts explain why these murderous assaults occurred?

Source: H. K. Roberts to Governor Robert K. Scott, South Carolina Department of Archives and History.

A few Republican leaders did deal harshly and effectively with terrorism. Governors in Tennessee, Texas, and Arkansas declared martial law and sent in hundreds of well-armed white and black men to quell the violence. Hundreds of Klansmen were arrested, many fled, and three were executed in Arkansas. But when Governor William W. Holden of North Carolina sent the state militia after the Klan, he succeeded only in provoking an angry reaction. Subsequent Klan violence in ten counties helped Democrats carry the 1870 legislative elections, and the North Carolina legislature then removed Holden from office.

Outnumbered and outgunned, black people in most areas did not retaliate against the Klan, and the Klan was rarely active where black people were in a majority

and prepared to defend themselves. In the cause of white supremacy, the Klan usually attacked those who could not defend themselves.

THE FIFTEENTH AMENDMENT

The federal government under Republican domination tried to protect black voting rights and defend Republican state governments in the South. In 1869 Congress passed the Fifteenth Amendment, which was ratified in 1870. It stipulated that a person could not be deprived of the right to vote because of race. "The right of citizens of the United States to vote shall not be denied or abridged by the United States or by any State on account of race,

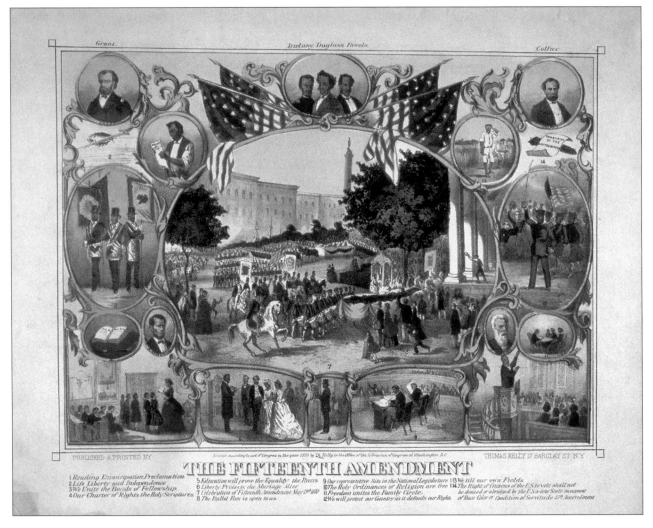

This optimistic 1870 illustration exemplifies the hopes and aspirations generated during Reconstruction as black people gained access to the political system. Invoking the legacy of Abraham Lincoln and John Brown, it suggests that African Americans would soon assume their rightful and equitable role in American society.

FEDERAL RECONSTRUCTION LEGISLATION, 1868–1877

1869	Fifteenth Amendment passed (ratified 1870)
1870	Enforcement Act passed
1871	Ku Klux Klan Act passed
1875	Civil Rights Act of 1875 passed

color, or previous condition of servitude." Black people, abolitionists, and reformers hailed the amendment as the culmination of the crusade to end slavery and give black people the same rights as white people.

Northern black men were the amendment's immediate beneficiaries because before its adoption, black men could vote in only eight northern states. Yet to the disappointment of many, the amendment said nothing about women voting and did not outlaw poll taxes, literacy tests, and property qualifications that could disfranchise citizens.

THE ENFORCEMENT ACTS

In direct response to the terrorism in the South, Congress passed the Enforcement Acts in 1870 and 1871, and the federal government expanded its authority over the states. The 1870 act outlawed disguises and masks and protected the civil rights of citizens. The 1871 act—known as the Ku Klux Klan Act—made it a federal offense to interfere with an individual's right to vote, hold office, serve on a jury, or enjoy equal protection of the law. Those accused of violating the act would be tried in federal court. For extreme violence, the act authorized the president to send in federal troops and suspend the writ of habeas corpus. (Habeas corpus is the right to be brought before a judge and not be arrested and jailed without cause.)

Black congressmen who had long advocated federal action against the Klan, endorsed the Enforcement acts. Representative Joseph Rainey of South Carolina wanted to suspend the constitution to protect citizens. "I desire that so broad and liberal a construction be placed on its provisions, as will insure protection to the humblest citizen. Tell me nothing of a constitution which fails to shelter beneath its rightful power the people of a country."

Armed with this new legislation, the Justice Department and Attorney General Amos T. Ackerman moved vigorously against the Klan. Hundreds of Klansmen were arrested—seven hundred in Mississippi alone. Faced with a full-scale rebellion in late 1871 in South Carolina's up country, President Ulysses S. Grant declared martial law in nine counties, suspended the writ of habeas corpus, and sent in the U.S. Army. Mass arrests and trials followed. But federal authorities permitted many Klansmen to confess and thereby escape prosecution. The government lacked the human and financial resources to bring hundreds of men to court for lengthy trials. Some white men were tried, mostly before black juries, and were imprisoned or fined. But comparatively few Klansmen were punished severely, especially considering the enormity of their crimes.

THE NORTH LOSES INTEREST

While the federal government did reduce Klan violence for a time, white Southerners remained convinced that white supremacy must be restored and Republican governments overturned. Klan violence did not overthrow any state governments, but it gravely undermined freedmen's confidence in the ability of these governments to protect them. Meanwhile, radical Republicans in Congress grew frustrated that the South and especially black people continued to demand so much of their time and attention year after year. There was less and less sentiment in the North to continue support for the freedmen and involvement in southern affairs.

Many Republicans in the North lost interest in issues and principles and became more concerned with elections and economic issues. By the mid 1870s, there was more discussion in Congress of patronage, veterans' pensions, railroads, taxes, tariffs, the economy, and monetary policy than civil rights or the future of the South. Republicans began to question the necessity for more support for African Americans. Others, swayed by white Southerners' views of black people, began to doubt the wisdom of universal manhood suffrage. Many white people who had nominally supported black suffrage began to believe the exaggerated complaints about corruption among black leaders and the unrelenting claims that freedmen were incapable of self-government. Some white Northerners began to conclude that reconstruction had been a mistake.

Economic conditions contributed to changing attitudes. A financial crisis—the Panic of 1873—sent the economy into a slump for several years. Businesses and financial institutions failed, unemployment soared, and prices fell sharply. In 1874, the Democrats recaptured a majority in the House of Representatives for the first time since 1860 and also took political control of several northern states.

THE FREEDMEN'S BANK

One of the casualties of the financial crisis was the Freedmen's Savings Bank, which failed in 1874. Founded in 1865 when hope flourished, the Freedmen's Savings and Trust Company had been chartered by Congress but was not connected to the Freedmen's Bureau. However, the bank's advertising featured pictures of Abraham Lincoln, and many black people assumed that it was a federal agency. Freedmen, black veterans, black churches, fraternal organizations, and benevolent societies opened thousands of accounts in the bank. Most of the deposits totaled under $50, and some amounted to only a few cents.

Though it had many black employees, the bank's board of directors consisted of white men. They unwisely invested the bank's funds in risky ventures including Washington, D.C., real estate. With the Panic of 1873, the bank lost large sums in unsecured railroad loans. To restore confidence, its directors asked Frederick Douglass to serve as president and persuaded him to invest $10,000 of his own money to help shore up the bank. Douglass lost his money, and African Americans from across the South lost more than one million dollars when the bank closed in June 1874. Eventually about half the depositors received three-fifths of the value of their accounts; but many African Americans believed that the U.S. government owed them a debt, and well into the twentieth century, they wrote to Congress and the president to get back their hard-earned money.

THE CIVIL RIGHTS ACT OF 1875

Before Reconstruction finally expired, Congress made one final—some said futile—gesture to protect black people from racial discrimination when it passed the Civil Rights Act of 1875. Strongly championed by Senator Charles Sumner of Massachusetts, it was originally intended to open public accommodations including schools, churches, cemeteries, hotels, and transportation to all people regardless of race. It passed in the Republican-controlled Senate in 1874 shortly before Sumner died. But House Democrats held up passage until 1875 and deleted bans on discrimination in churches, cemeteries, and schools.

The act stipulated "That all persons . . . shall be entitled to the full and equal enjoyment of the accommodations, advantages, facilities, and privileges of inns, public conveyances on land or water, theaters, and other places of public amusement." After its passage, no attempt was made to enforce these provisions, and in 1883, the U.S. Supreme Court declared it unconstitutional. Justice Joseph Bradley wrote that the Fourteenth Amendment protected black people from discrimination by states but not by private businesses. Black newspapers likened the decision to the Dred Scott case a quarter century earlier.

THE END OF RECONSTRUCTION

Reconstruction ended as it began—in violence and controversy. By 1875, conservative white Democrats had regained control of all the former Confederate states except Mississippi, Florida, Louisiana, and South Carolina (Map 13-1). Democrats had redeemed Tennessee

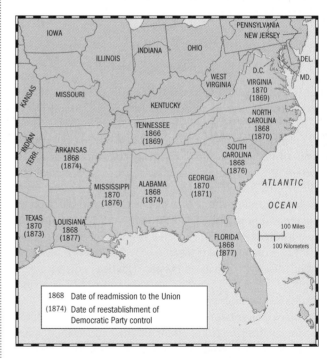

Map 13-1 Dates of Readmission of Southern States to the Union and Reestablishment of Democratic Party Control. Once conservative, white Democrats regained political control of a state government from black and white Republicans, they considered that state "redeemed." The first states the Democrats "redeemed" were Georgia, Virginia, and North Carolina. Louisiana, Florida, and South Carolina were the last. (Tennessee was not included in the Reconstruction process under the terms of the 1867 Reconstruction Act).

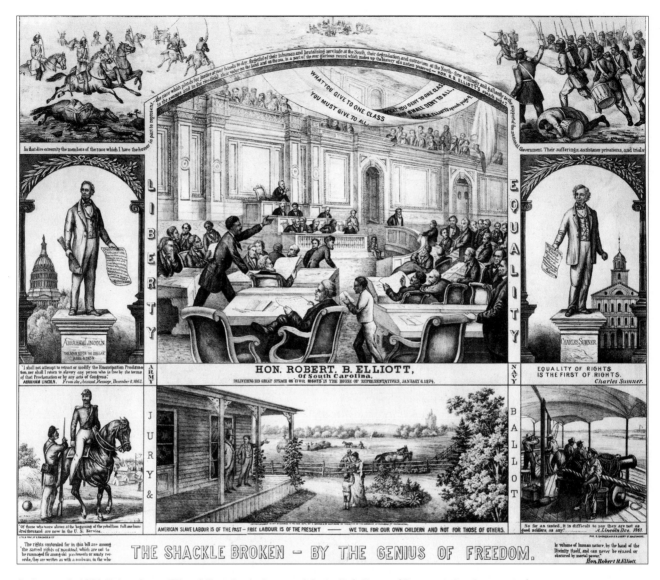

On January 6, 1874, Robert Brown Elliott delivered a ringing speech in the U. S. House of Representatives in support of the Sumner Civil Rights bill. Elliott was responding in part to words spoken the day before by Virginia congressman John T. Harris: ". . . I say there is not a gentlemen on this floor who can honestly say he really believes that the colored man is created his equal."

in 1870 and Georgia in 1871. Democrats had learned two valuable lessons. First, few black men could be persuaded to vote for the Democratic party—no matter how much white leaders wanted to believe that former slaves were easy to manipulate. Second, intimidation and violence would win elections in areas where the number of black and white voters was nearly equal. The federal government had stymied Klan violence in 1871, but by the mid 1870s the government had become reluctant to send troops to the South to protect black citizens.

Violent Redemption

In Alabama in 1874, black and white Republican leaders were murdered, and white mobs destroyed crops and homes. On election day in Eufaula, white men killed seven and injured nearly seventy unarmed black voters. Black voters were also driven from the polls in Mobile. Democrats won the election and redeemed Alabama.

White violence accompanied every election in Louisiana from 1868 to 1876. After Republicans and

V O I C E S

BLACK LEADERS SUPPORT THE PASSAGE OF A CIVIL RIGHTS ACT

Black Congressmen Robert Brown Elliott of South Carolina and James T. Rapier of Alabama both spoke passionately in favor of the Sumner Civil Rights bill in 1874. Both men had been free before the war. Both were lawyers, and though they each accumulated considerable wealth, both died in poverty in the 1880s.

[James T. Rapier]

I must confess it is somewhat embarrassing for a colored man to urge the passage of this bill, because if he exhibit an earnestness in the matter and expresses a desire for its immediate passage, straightaway he is charged with a desire for social equality, as explained by the demagogue and understood by the ignorant white man. But then it is just as embarrassing for him not to do so, for, if he remains silent while the struggle is being carried on around, and for him, he is liable to be charged with a want of interest in a matter that concerns him more than anyone else, which is enough to make his friends desert his cause. So in steering away from Scylla I may run upon Charybdis. But the anomalous, and I may add the supremely ridiculous, position of the Negro at this time, in this country, compel me to say something. Here his condition is without comparison, parallel alone to itself. Just that the law recognizes my right upon this floor as a law-maker, but that there is no law to secure to me any accommodations whatever while traveling here to discharge my duties as a Representative of a large and wealthy constituency. Here I am the peer of the proudest, but on a steamboat or car I am not equal to the most degraded. Is not this most anomalous and ridiculous?

[Robert Brown Elliott]

The results of the war, as seen in Reconstruction, have settled forever the political status of my race. The passage of this bill will determine the civil status, not only of the Negro but of any other class of citizens who may feel themselves discriminated against. It will form the capstone of that temple of liberty begun on this continent under discouraging circumstances, carried on in spite of the sneers of monarchists and the cavils of pretended friends of freedom, until at last it stands in all its beautiful symmetry and proportions, a building the grandest which the world has ever seen, realizing the most sanguine expectations and the highest hopes of those who in the name of equal, impartial and universal liberty, laid the foundation stone.

QUESTIONS

1. According to James T. Rapier, why will he be criticized for his support of a civil rights measure?

2. Exactly who would benefit most from the passage of this bill?

3. What specific argument in opposition to this bill do Rapier and Elliott attempt to counter?

Sources: *Congressional Record*, vol. II, part 1, 43d Congress, 1st session, pp. 565–567; Peggy Lamson, *The Glorious Failure*, p. 181.

Democrats each claimed victory in the 1872 elections, black people seized the small town of Colfax to protect themselves against a Democratic takeover. They held out for three weeks, and then on Easter Sunday, a well-armed white mob attacked and slaughtered 280 black people indiscriminantly. In 1874 the White League almost redeemed Louisiana in an astonishing wave of violence. Black people were murdered, courts attacked, and white people refused to pay taxes to the Republican state government. Six Republicans were murdered in Red River Parish. In September, President Grant finally sent federal troops to New Orleans after 3,500 White Leaguers attacked and nearly wiped out the black militia and the Metropolitan Police. But the stage had been set for the 1876 campaign.

The Shotgun Policy

In 1875 white Mississippians, no longer fearful that the national government would intervene in force, declared open warfare on the black majority. The masks and hoods of the Klan were discarded. One newspaper publicly proclaimed that Democrats would carry the election, "peaceably if we can, forcibly if we must." Another paper carried a bold banner: "Mississippi is a white man's country, and by the eternal God we'll rule it."

White Mississippi unleashed a campaign of violence known as the "Shotgun Policy" that was extreme even for Reconstruction. Many Republicans fled and others were murdered. In late 1874, an estimated three hundred black people were hunted down outside Vicksburg after black men armed with inferior weapons had lost a "battle" with white men. In 1875 thirty teachers, church leaders, and Republican officials were killed in Clinton. The white sheriff of Yazoo county, who had married a black woman and supported the education of black children, had to flee the state.

Mississippi Governor Adelbert Ames appealed for federal help, but President Grant refused: "The whole public are tired out with these annual autumnal outbreaks in the South . . . . [and] are ready now to condemn any interference on the part of the Government." No federal help arrived. The terrorism intensified, and many black voters went into hiding on election day, afraid for their lives and the lives of their families. Democrats redeemed Mississippi and prided themselves that they—a superior race representing the most civilized of all people—were back in control.

In Florida in 1876, white Republicans noted that support for black people in the South was fading. They nominated an all-white Republican slate, and even refused to renominate black Congressman Josiah Walls.

The Hamburg Massacre

South Carolina Democrats were divided between moderate and extreme factions, but they united to nominate former Confederate General Wade Hampton for governor after the Hamburg Massacre. The prelude to this event occurred on July 4, 1876—the nation's centennial—when two white men in a buggy confronted the black militia that was drilling on a town street in Hamburg, a small mostly black town. Hot words were exchanged, and days later, Democrats demanded that the militia be disarmed. White rifle club members from around the state arrived in Hamburg and attacked the armory, where forty black members of the militia defended themselves. The rifle companies brought up a cannon and reinforcements from Georgia. After the militia ran low on ammunition, white men captured the armory. One white man was killed, twenty-nine black men were taken prisoner, and the other eleven fled. Five of the black men identified as leaders were shot down in cold blood. The rifle companies invaded and wrecked Hamburg. Seven white men were indicted for murder. All were acquitted.

The Hamburg Massacre incited South Carolina Democrats to imitate Mississippi's "Shotgun Policy." It also forced a reluctant President Grant to send federal troops to South Carolina. In the 1876 election campaign, hundreds of white men in red shirts turned out on mules and horses to support Wade Hampton in his contest against incumbent Republican Governor Daniel Chamberlain and his black and white allies. When Chamberlain and fellow Republicans tried to speak in Edgefield, they were ridiculed, threatened, and shouted down by six hundred Redshirts, many of them armed.

Democrats attacked, beat, and killed black people to prevent them from voting. Democratic leaders instructed their followers to treat black voters with contempt. "In speeches to negroes you must remember that argument has no effect on them. They can only be influenced by their *fears*, superstition, and cupidity. . . . Treat them so as to show them you are a superior race and that their natural position is that of subordination to the white man."

As the election approached, black people in the up country of South Carolina knew that it would be exceedingly dangerous if they tried to vote. But in the low country, black people went on the offensive, and attacked Democrats. In Charleston, a white man was killed in a racial melee. At a campaign rally at Cainhoy, a few miles outside Charleston, armed black men killed five white men.

A few black men supported Wade Hampton and the Red Shirts. Hampton had a paternalistic view of black people and, although he considered them inferior to white people, promised to respect their rights. Martin Delany believed that Hampton and the Democrats were more trustworthy than unreliable Republicans; Delany campaigned for Hampton and was later rewarded with a minor political post. A few genuinely conservative black men during Reconstruction also supported the Democrats and curried their favor and patronage. Most black people despised them. When one black man threw his support to the Democrats, his wife threw him and his clothes out, declaring that she would prefer to "beg her bread" than live with a "Democratic nigger."

The Compromise of 1877

Threats, violence, and bloodshed accompanied the elections of 1876, but the results were confusing and contradictory. Both Democrats and Republicans claimed to have won in Florida, Louisiana, and South Carolina, the last three southern states that had not been redeemed. This created a stand-off between the

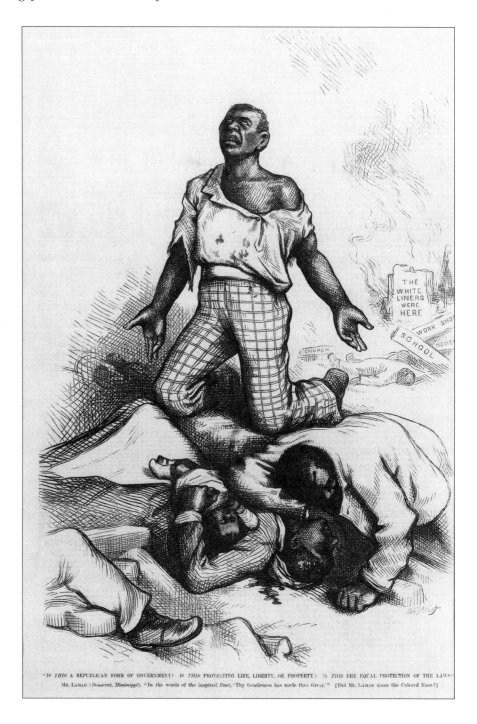

"IS *THIS* A REPUBLICAN FORM OF GOVERNMENT? IS *THIS* PROTECTING LIFE, LIBERTY, OR PROPERTY? IS *THIS* THE EQUAL PROTECTION OF THE LAWS?

Mr. LAMAR (*Democrat, Mississippi*). "In the words of the inspired Poet, 'Thy Gentleness has made thee Great.'" [Did Mr. LAMAR mean the Colored Race?]

Editorial cartoonist Thomas Nast chronicled the travails of freedmen during the twelve years of Reconstruction in the pages of *Harper's Weekly.* Here Nast deplores the violence and intimidation that accompanied the 1876 election campaign and questions the willingness of white Americans to respect the rights of black Americans.

two presidential candidates, the Republican Rutherford B. Hayes and the Democrat Samuel J. Tilden. Hayes had won 167 electoral votes. Tilden had 185. Whoever took the nineteen electoral votes of the three contested states would be the next president (Map 13–2).

The controversy precipitated a constitutional crisis in 1877. Eventually a compromise was arranged. Democrats accepted a Hayes victory, but Hayes promised southern Democrats that he would not support Republican governments in Florida, Louisiana, and South Carolina. Hayes withdrew the last federal troops from the South, and the Republican administration in those states collapsed. Democrats immediately took control.

Redemption was now complete. Each of the former Confederate states was under the authority of white

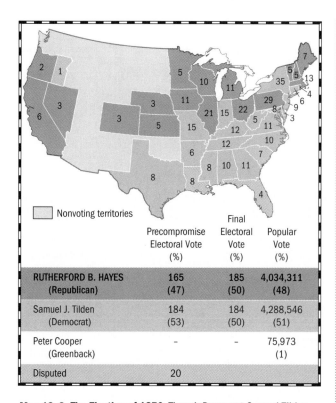

	Precompromise Electoral Vote (%)	Final Electoral Vote (%)	Popular Vote (%)
RUTHERFORD B. HAYES (Republican)	**165** **(47)**	**185** **(50)**	**4,034,311** **(48)**
Samuel J. Tilden (Democrat)	184 (53)	184 (50)	4,288,546 (51)
Peter Cooper (Greenback)	–	–	75,973 (1)
Disputed	20		

Nonvoting territories

Map 13–2 The Election of 1876. Though Democrat Samuel Tilden appeared to have won the election of 1876, Rutherford B. Hayes and the Republicans were able to claim victory after a prolonged political and constitutional controversy involving the disputed electoral college votes from Louisiana, Florida, and South Carolina (and one from Oregon). In a complex compromise in 1877, Democrats agreed to accept electoral votes for Hayes from those states, and Republicans agreed to permit those states to be "redeemed" by the Democrats. The result was to leave the entire South under the political control of conservative white Democrats. For the first time since 1867, black and white Republicans no longer effectively controlled any former Confederate state.

Democrats. Henry Adams, a black leader from Louisiana, explained what had happened. "The whole South—every state in the South had got into the hands of the very men that held us as slaves."

CONCLUSION

The glorious hopes that emancipation and the Union victory in the Civil War had aroused among African Americans in 1865 appeared forlorn by 1877. To be sure, black people were no longer slave laborers or property. They lived in tightly knit families that white people no longer controlled. They had established hundreds of schools, churches, and benevolent societies. The Constitution now endowed them with freedom,

citizenship, and the right to vote. Some black people had even acquired land.

But no one can characterize Reconstruction as a success. The epidemic of terror and violence made it one of the bloodiest eras in American history. Thousands of black people had been beaten, raped, and murdered since 1865, simply because they had acted as free people. Too many white people were determined that black people could not and would not have the same rights that white people enjoyed. White Southerners would not tolerate either the presence of black men in politics or white Republicans who accepted black political involvement. Gradually most white Northerners and even radical Republicans grew weary of intervening in southern affairs and became convinced again that black men and women were their inferiors and were not prepared to participate in government. Reconstruction, they concluded, had been a mistake.

Furthermore, black and white Republicans hurt themselves by indulging in fraud and corruption, and by engaging in angry and divisive factionalism. But even if Republicans had been honest and united, white southern Democrats would never have accepted black people as worthy to participate in the political system.

Southern Democrats would accept black people in politics only if Democrats could control black voters. But black voters understood this, rejected control by former slave owners, and were loyal to the Republican party—as flawed as it was.

But as grim a turn as life may have taken for black people by 1877, it would get even worse in the decades that followed.

REVIEW QUESTIONS

1. What issues most concerned black political leaders during Reconstruction?

2. What did black political leaders accomplish and fail to accomplish during Reconstruction? What contributed to their successes and failures?

3. How would you respond to those who argued that black political leaders were unqualified to hold office so soon after the end of slavery?

4. To what extent did African Americans dominate southern politics during Reconstruction? Should we refer to this era as "Black Reconstruction?"

5. Why was it so difficult for the Republican party to maintain control of southern state governments during Reconstruction?

TIMELINE

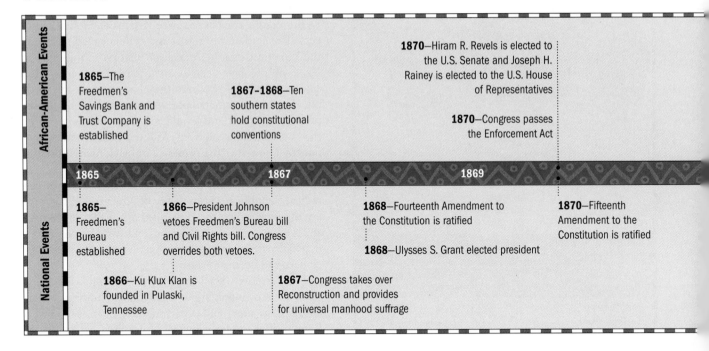

African-American Events

1865—The Freedmen's Savings Bank and Trust Company is established

1867–1868—Ten southern states hold constitutional conventions

1870—Hiram R. Revels is elected to the U.S. Senate and Joseph H. Rainey is elected to the U.S. House of Representatives

1870—Congress passes the Enforcement Act

1865   1867   1869

National Events

1865—Freedmen's Bureau established

1866—President Johnson vetoes Freedmen's Bureau bill and Civil Rights bill. Congress overrides both vetoes.

1866—Ku Klux Klan is founded in Pulaski, Tennessee

1867—Congress takes over Reconstruction and provides for universal manhood suffrage

1868—Fourteenth Amendment to the Constitution is ratified

1868—Ulysses S. Grant elected president

1870—Fifteenth Amendment to the Constitution is ratified

6. What was "redemption?" What happened when redemption occurred? What factors contributed to redemption?

7. How did Reconstruction end? What events marked its conclusion?

8. How would you evaluate Reconstruction? How effective was it in assisting black people to make the transition from slavery to freedom? How effective was it in restoring the southern states to the Union?

RECOMMENDED READING

Eric Foner. *Freedom's Lawmakers: A Directory of Black Officeholders During Reconstruction* (New York: Oxford University Press, 1993). Biographical sketches of every known Southern black leader during the era.

John Hope Franklin. *Reconstruction after the Civil War* (Chicago: University of Chicago Press, 1961). An excellent summary and interpretation of the postwar years.

William Gillette. *Retreat from Reconstruction, 1869–1879* (Baton Rouge: Louisiana State University Press, 1979). An analysis of how and why the North lost interest in the South.

Thomas Holt. *Black Over White: Negro Political Leadership in South Carolina* (Urbana: University of Illinois Press, 1979). A masterful and sophisticated study of black leaders in the state with the most black politicians.

Michael L. Perman. *Emancipation and Reconstruction, 1862–1879* (Arlington Heights, IL.: Harlan Davidson, Inc., 1987). Another excellent survey of the period.

Howard N. Rabinowitz, ed. *Southern Black Leaders of the Reconstruction Era* (Urbana: University of Illinois Press, 1982). A series of biographical essays on black politicians.

ADDITIONAL BIBLIOGRAPHY

Reconstruction in Specific States

Edmund L. Drago. *Black Politicians and Reconstruction in Georgia* (Athens: University of Georgia Press, 1982).

Edmund L. Drago. *Hurrah for Hampton: Black Red Shirts in South Carolina during Reconstruction* (Fayetteville: University of Arkansas Press, 1998).

Luther P. Jackson. *Negro Officeholders in Virginia, 1865–1895* (Norfolk: Guide Quality Press, 1945).

Peter Kolchin. *First Freedom: The Responses of Alabama's Blacks to Emancipation and Reconstruction* (Westport, CT.: Greenwood Publishing, 1972).

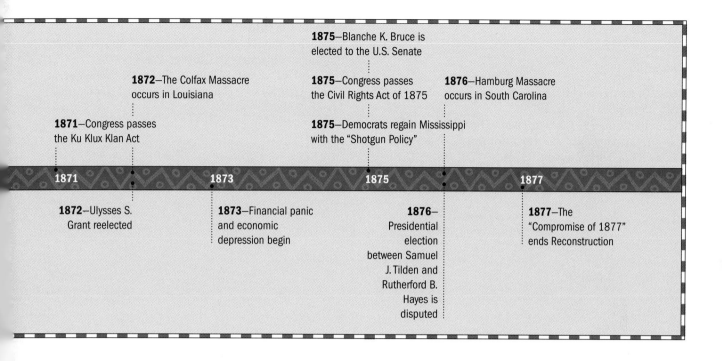

- **1871**—Congress passes the Ku Klux Klan Act
- **1872**—The Colfax Massacre occurs in Louisiana
- **1875**—Blanche K. Bruce is elected to the U.S. Senate
- **1875**—Congress passes the Civil Rights Act of 1875
- **1875**—Democrats regain Mississippi with the "Shotgun Policy"
- **1876**—Hamburg Massacre occurs in South Carolina

1871 | 1873 | 1875 | 1877

- **1872**—Ulysses S. Grant reelected
- **1873**—Financial panic and economic depression begin
- **1876**—Presidential election between Samuel J. Tilden and Rutherford B. Hayes is disputed
- **1877**—The "Compromise of 1877" ends Reconstruction

Merline Pitre. *Through Many Dangers, Toils, and Snares: The Black Leadership of Texas, 1868–1900* (Austin: Eakin Press, 1985).

Joe M. Richardson. *The Negro in the Reconstruction of Florida, 1865–1877* (Tallahassee: Florida State University Press, 1965).

Buford Stacher. *Blacks in Mississippi Politics, 1865–1900* (Washington, DC: University Press of America, 1978).

Charles Vincent. *Black Legislators in Louisiana During Reconstruction* (Baton Rouge: Louisiana State University Press, 1976).

Joel Williamson. *After Slavery: The Negro in South Carolina: 1861–1877* (Chapel Hill: University of North Carolina Press, 1965).

National Politics: Andrew Johnson and the Radical Republicans

Michael Les Benedict. *A Compromise of Principle: Congressional Republicans and Reconstruction* (New York: Norton, 1974).

Eric L. McKitrick. *Andrew Johnson and Reconstruction, 1865–1867* (Chicago: University of Chicago Press, 1960).

James M. McPherson. *The Struggle for Equality: Abolitionists and the Negro in the Civil War and Reconstruction* (Princeton: Princeton University Press, 1964).

Hans L. Trefousse. *The Radical Republicans: Lincoln's Vanguard for Racial Justice* (Baton Rouge: Louisiana State University Press, 1969).

Economic Issues: Land, Labor, and the Freedmen's Bank

Elizabeth Bethel. *Promiseland: A Century of Life in a Negro Community* (Philadelphia: Temple University Press, 1981).

Carol R. Bleser. *The Promised Land: The History of the South Carolina Land Commission, 1869–1890* (Columbia: University of South Carolina Press, 1969).

Donald G. Nieman. *To Set the Law in Motion: The Freedmen's Bureau and Legal Rights for Blacks, 1865–1869* (Millwood, NY: KTO, 1979).

Carl R. Osthaus. *Freedmen, Philanthropy and Fraud: A History of the Freedman's Savings Bank* (Urbana: University of Illinois Press, 1976).

Violence and the Ku Klux Klan

George C. Rable. *But There Was No Peace: The Role of Violence in the Politics of Reconstruction* (Athens: University of Georgia Press, 1984).

Allen W. Trelease. *White Terror: The Ku Klux Klan Conspiracy and Southern Reconstruction* (New York: Harper & Row, 1973).

Lou Falkner Williams. *The Great South Carolina Ku Klux Klan Trials, 1871–1872* (Athens: University of Georgia Press, 1996).

Biography

Peter D. Klingman. *Josiah Walls* (Gainesville: University Presses of Florida, 1976).

Peggy Lamson, *The Glorious Failure: Black Congressman Robert Brown Elliott and Reconstruction in South Carolina* (New York: Norton, 1973).

Edward A. Miller. *Gullah Statesman: Robert Smalls: From Slavery to Congress, 1839–1915* (Columbia: University of South Carolina Press, 1995).

Loren Schweninger. *James T. Rapier and Reconstruction* (Chicago: University of Chicago Press, 1978).

Okon E. Uya. *From Slavery to Public Service: Robert Smalls, 1839–1915* (New York: Oxford University Press, 1971).

PART IV

SEARCHING

FOR

SAFE

SPACES

CHAPTER 14

White Supremacy Triumphant: African Americans in the South in the Late Nineteenth Century

For more than a century—from the early 1800s until the 1920s—cotton was *the* crop across much of the deep South. First as slaves, then as sharecroppers, renters, and land owners, generations of black people toiled in the cotton fields.

The supremacy of the white race of the South must be maintained forever, and the domination of the negro race resisted at all points and at all hazards—because the white race is the superior race. This is the declaration of no new truth. It has abided forever in the marrow of our bones, and shall run forever with the blood that feeds Anglo-Saxon hearts.

Henry Grady, Editor of the *Atlanta Constitution*, 1887.

I remember a crowd of white men who rode up on horseback with rifles on their shoulders. I was with my father when they rode up, and I remember starting to cry. They cursed my father, drew their guns and made him salute, made him take off his hat and bow down to them several times. Then they rode away. I was not yet five years old, but I have never forgotten them.

Benjamin E. Mays on his childhood in Epworth, South Carolina, in 1898

Black people struggled against a rising tide of white supremacy in the late nineteenth century. White Southerners—and most white Northerners, for that matter—had long been convinced that as a race they were superior to black people intellectually and culturally. They were certain that black people—because of their inferiority—must play only a subservient role in society. During slavery, white Southerners had taken that subservience for granted. With the Civil War and with slavery's end, black people allied themselves with radical Republicans during Reconstruction, and they effectively challenged white supremacy as they became citizens and participated in the political system. The federal government established and enforced—though unevenly—the rights of all citizens to enjoy equal protection of the law and due process of law. But the commitment of the Republicans and the federal government wavered, waned, and then largely collapsed by the mid 1870s.

As memories of the Civil War dimmed and antagonism between white Northerners and Southerners faded, many northern white people who had expressed at least some sympathy for former slaves and hostility toward southern rebels immediately after the war became less concerned with the South. They were increasingly preoccupied with the frontier West or with opportunities presented by the industrial revolution that was so dramatically transforming American society.

Congress, the president, and especially the Supreme Court abandoned the commitment to protect civil and legal rights of African Americans. Political and judicial leaders embraced a laissez-faire approach to social and economic issues. The government would keep hands off the rapidly expanding railroad, steel, and petroleum industries. Neither would government intervene to safeguard the rights of black citizens. The Supreme Court interpreted the Fourteenth Amendment to protect corporations from government regulation but failed to protect the basic rights of black people.

As a result, the conservative white Democrats who had regained political power in the South were no more than mildly fearful that the U.S. government or Republicans would intrude as white authority expanded over virtually every aspect of the lives of southern African Americans in the last quarter of the nineteenth century. Between 1875 and 1900, black people in the South were gradually excluded from politics. They were segregated in public life and denied equal, even basic, rights. They were forced to behave in a demeaning and deferential manner to white people. Most of them were limited to doing menial agricultural and domestic jobs that left them poor and dependent on white landowners and merchants. They were often raped, lynched, and beaten. The southern system of justice was systematically unjust.

Unwilling and unable to tolerate such conditions, some African Americans left the South for Africa or the American West. However, most black people remained in the South where many acquired a semblance of education, some managed to purchase land, and a few even prospered.

POLITICS

In the late nineteenth century, black people remained important in southern politics. Black men served in Congress, state legislatures, and local governments. They received federal patronage appointments to post offices and custom houses. But as southern Democrats steadily disfranchised black voters in the 1880s and 1890s, the number of black politicians declined until the political system was virtually all white by 1900 (Figure 14–1).

When Reconstruction ended in 1877 and the last Republican state governments collapsed, black men who held major state offices were forced out. In South Carolina, Lieutenant Governor Richard H. Gleaves resigned in 1877, but not without a protest. "I desire to place on record, in the most public and unqualified manner, my sense of the great wrong which thus forces me practically to abandon rights conferred on me, as I fully believe by a majority of my fellow citizens of this State."

For a time, some conservative white Democrats accepted limited black participation in politics as long as no black leader had power over white people and black participation did not challenge white domination. South Carolina's governor Wade Hampton even assured black people that he respected their rights and would appoint qualified black men to minor political offices. Hampton condescendingly told black people in 1878: "We propose to protect you and give you all your rights; but while we do this you cannot expect that we should discriminate in your favor, and say because you *are* a colored man, you have the right to rule the State. We say to you that we intend to take the best men we can find to represent the State, and you must qualify yourselves to do so before you can expect to be chosen."

Paternalistic Democrats like Hampton did appoint black men to lower-level positions. Hampton, for example, appointed Richard Gleaves and Martin Delany trial justices. In turn, some black men supported the Democrats. A few black Democrats were elected to state legislatures in the 1880s. Some had been Democrats throughout Reconstruction; others had abandoned the Republican party.

Most black voters, however, remained loyal Republicans even though the party had become a hollow shell of what it had been during Reconstruction. Its few white supporters usually shunned black Republicans.

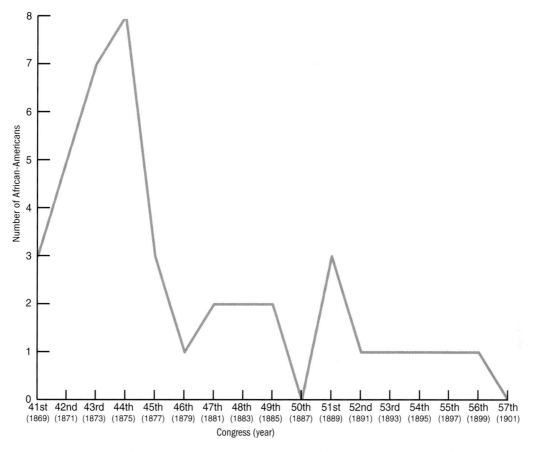

Figure 14-1 African-American Representation in Congress, 1867–1900. Black men served in the U.S. Congress from Joseph Rainey's election in 1870 until George White's term concluded in 1900. All were Republicans.

Black Congressmen

Democrats skillfully created oddly shaped congressional districts to confine much of the black population of a state to one district, such as Mississippi's third district, South Carolina's seventh, Virginia's fourth, and North Carolina's second. A black Republican usually represented these districts while the rest of the state elected white Democrats to Congress. This diluted black voting strength, and it reduced the number of white people represented by a black congressman. Thus Henry Cheatham of North Carolina, John Mercer Langston of Virginia, Thomas E. Miller of South Carolina, and George H. White of North Carolina were elected to the House of Representatives long after Reconstruction had ended (Table 14–1).

The party rarely fielded candidates for statewide elections, limiting itself to local races in regions where Republicans remained strong.

But like their predecessors during Reconstruction, these black men wielded only limited power in Washington. They could not persuade their white colleagues to enact significant legislation to benefit their black constituents. They did, however, get Republican presidents to appoint black men and women to federal positions in their districts—including post offices and custom houses—and they spoke out about the plight of African Americans. North Carolina's George H. White, for example, rebuked white leaders for their readiness to label black people as inferior while denying them the means to prove otherwise. "It is easy . . . to taunt us with our inferiority, at the same time not mentioning the causes of this inferiority. It is rather hard to be accused of shiftlessness and idleness when the accuser . . . closes the avenues for labor and industrial pursuits to us. It is hardly fair to accuse us of ignorance when it was made a crime under the former order of things to learn enough about letters to even read the Word of God."

Table 14-1 Black Members of the U.S. Congress, 1870-1901

	Dates	Name	State	Occupation	Prewar Status
1.	1870-1879	Joseph H. Rainey	South Carolina	Barber	Slave, then freed
2.	1870-1873	Jefferson Long	Georgia	Tailor, storekeeper	Slave
3.	1870-1873	Hiram Revels*	Mississippi	Barber, minister, teacher, college president	Free
4.	1871-1877	Josiah T. Walls	Florida	Editor, planter, teacher, lawyer	Slave
5.	1871-1873	Benjamin Turner	Alabama	Businessman, farmer, merchant	Slave
6.	1871-1873	Robert C. DeLarge	South Carolina	Tailor	Free
7.	1871-1875	Robert B. Elliott	South Carolina	Lawyer	Free
8.	1873-1879	Richard H. Cain	South Carolina	AME minister	Free
9.	1873-1875	Alonzo J. Ransier	South Carolina	Shipping clerk, editor	Free
10.	1873-1875	James T. Rapier	Alabama	Planter, editor, lawyer, teacher	Free
11.	1873-1877, 1882-1883	John R. Lynch	Mississippi	Planter, lawyer, photographer	Slave
12.	1875-1881	Blanche K. Bruce*	Mississippi	Planter, teacher, editor	Slave
13.	1875-1877	Jeremiah Haralson	Alabama	Minister	Slave
14.	1875-1877	John A. Hyman	North Carolina	Storekeeper, farmer	Slave
15.	1875-1877	Charles E. Nash	Louisiana	Mason, cigar maker	Free
16.	1875-1887	Robert Smalls	South Carolina	Ship pilot, editor	Slave
17.	1883-1887	James E. O'Hara	North Carolina	Lawyer	Free
18.	1889-1893	Henry P. Cheatham	North Carolina	Lawyer, teacher	Slave
19.	1889-1891	Thomas E. Miller	South Carolina	Lawyer, college president	Free
20.	1889-1891	John M. Langston	Virginia	Lawyer	Free
21.	1893-1897	George W. Murray	South Carolina	Teacher	Slave
22.	1897-1901	George H. White	North Carolina	Lawyer	Slave

*Revels and Bruce served in the Senate and the twenty remaining black legislators served in the House of Representatives.

Democrats and Farmer Discontent

Black involvement in politics survived Reconstruction, but it did not survive the nineteenth century. Divisions within the Democratic party and the rise of a new political party—the Populists—accompanied successful efforts to remove black people entirely from southern politics.

Militant Democrats stridently opposed the more moderate and paternalistic conservatives who took charge after Reconstruction. In the eyes of the militants, these redeemers seemed too willing to tolerate even limited black participation in politics while showing little interest in the needs of white yeoman farmers. Dissatisfied independents, "readjusters," and other disaffected white people resented the domination of the Democratic party by former planters, wealthy businessmen, and lawyers who often favored limited government and reduced state support for schools, asylums, orphanages, and prisons while encouraging industry and railroads. Nor did the redeemer and paternalistic Democrats always agree among themselves. Some did favor agricultural education, the establishment of boards of health, and even separate colleges for black youngsters. This lack of redeemer unity permitted insurgent Democrats and even Republicans sometimes to exploit economic and racial issues to undermine Democratic solidarity.

Many farmers felt betrayed as the industrial revolution transformed American society. They fed and clothed America, but large corporations, banks, and railroads increasingly dominated economic life. Wealth was concentrated in the hands of big industrialists and financiers. Farmers were no longer self-sufficient, admired for their hard work and self-reliance. They now depended on banks for loans, were exploited when they bought and sold goods, and found themselves at the mercy of railroads when they shipped their agricultural commodities. As businessmen got richer, farmers got poorer.

Small independent (yeoman) farmers in the South suffered from a sharp decline in the price of cotton between 1865 and 1890. Overwhelmed by debt, many lost their land and were forced into tenant farming and sharecropping. By 1890 most farmers, both black and white—between 58 percent and 62 percent in each state in the deep South—worked land they did not own.

In response to their economic woes and political weakness, farmers organized. In the 1870s they formed the Patrons of Husbandry, or Grange. Initially a social and fraternal organization, the Grange promoted the formation of cooperatives and involvement in politics.

Grangers especially favored government regulation of the rates railroads charged to transport crops. By the early 1880s, many hard-pressed small farmers turned to farmers' alliances. The first of these was the Southern Farmers' Alliance, which formed in Texas. Alliances soon spread throughout the South and northward into the states of the Great Plains and westward to the Pacific coast. These organizations further encouraged farmers to buy and sell products cooperatively and to unite politically. They favored railroad regulation, currency inflation (to increase crop prices and ease debt burdens), and support for agricultural education. By 1888 many of them joined in the National Farmers' Alliance.

The Colored Farmers' Alliance

Although the alliances were radical on economic issues, they were conservative on racial issues and did not challenge the racial status quo. The Southern Alliance did not include black farmers, who instead formed their own Colored Farmers' Alliance. It spread from Texas across the South in 1888 and 1889 and claimed over one million members. Even if it did not have that many supporters, the Colored Farmers' Alliance was one of the largest black organizations in American history. When the white alliances met in St. Louis in 1889, so did the black alliance—in a separate convention. The alliances maintained strict racial distinctions but promised to cooperate to resolve their economic woes.

However, black and white alliance members did not always see their economic difficulties from the same perspective. Some of the white farmers owned the land that the black farmers lived on and worked. Black men saw their alliance as a way of getting a political education. In 1891, sixteen black men organized a branch of the Colored Farmers' Alliance in St. Landry Parish in Louisiana. Their purpose was to help their race and their families and to acquire enough information to vote effectively. "This organization is for the purpose of trying to elevate our race, to make us better citizens, better husbands, better fathers and sons, to educate ourselves so that we may be able to vote more intelligently on questions that are of vital importance to our people."

But white people were less certain that they wanted black men to vote at all—intelligently or otherwise. Many white alliance members harbored serious doubts about the right of black men to vote, and they opposed electing black men to office. Paradoxically, they also encouraged black men to vote as long as the black voters supported candidates the alliances backed, and by the late 1880s alliance-backed candidates in the South were elected to state legislatures, to Congress, and to four governorships.

The Populist Party

By 1892, many alliance farmers threw their political support to a new political party—the People's party, generally known as the Populist party—that mounted a serious challenge to the Democrats and Republicans. Convinced that neither of the traditional parties cared about the plight of American farmers and industrial workers, the Populists hoped to wrestle political control of the nation's economy from bankers and industrialists and their allies in the Republican and Democratic parties and to let the "people" shape the country's economic destiny. The Populists favored no less than the government takeover of railroads, telegraph, and telephone companies. The Populists ran candidates for local and state offices and for Congress. In 1892 they nominated James B. Weaver of Iowa for president. The Populists urged southern white men to abandon the Democratic party and southern black men to reject the Republican party and to unite politically to support the Populists.

The foremost proponent of black and white political unity was Thomas Watson of Georgia. He and other populist leaders believed that economic and political cooperation could transcend racial differences. During the 1892 campaign, Watson explained that black and white farmers faced the same economic exploitation but that they failed to cooperate with each other because of race. "The white tenant," he said,

> lives adjoining the colored tenant. Their homes are almost equally destitute of comforts. Their living is confined to bare necessities. They are equally burdened with heavy taxes. They pay the same high rent for gullied and impoverished land. . . .
>
> Now the Peoples' Party says to these two men, You are kept apart that you may be separately fleeced of your earnings. You are made to hate each other because upon that hatred is rested the keystone of the arch of financial despotism which enslaves you both. You are deceived and blinded that you may not see how this race antagonism perpetuates a monetary system which beggars both.

Despite such remarks, Watson was not calling for improved race relations. He opposed economic exploitation that was disguised by race, but when Democrats accused him of promoting racial reconciliation, he denied it and bluntly supported segregation to a black audience.

> They say I am an advocate of social equality between the whites and the blacks. THAT IS AN ABSOLUTE FALSEHOOD, and the man who utter[s] it knows it, I have done no such thing, and you colored men know it as well as the men who formulated the slander. It is best for your race and my race that we dwell apart in our private affairs. It is best for you to go to your churches, and I will go to mine; it is best that you send your children to the colored school, and I'll send my children to mine; you invite your colored friends to your home, and I'll invite my friends to mine.

Years after the failure of the Populists, Watson became a racial demagogue who warmly and thoroughly supported white supremacy. But in 1892, Watson and the Populists desperately wanted black and white voters to support Populist candidates. The Populists lost the national election that year and again in 1896, although they did win several congressional and governor's races. Southern Democrats, furious and outraged at the Populist appeal for black votes, resorted again to fraud, violence, and terror to prevail. It is not a coincidence that in 1892, when the Democrats carried every southern state, 235 people were lynched in the United States, more than in any other year in U.S. history.

The Populist challenge heightened the fears of southern Democrats that black voters could tip the balance of elections if the white vote split. But years before the alliances and the Populists emerged, southern Democrats had begun to eliminate the black vote.

DISFRANCHISEMENT

As early as the late 1870s, southern Democrats had found ways to undermine black political power. Violence and intimidation, so effective during Reconstruction, continued in the 1880s and 1890s. Frightened, discouraged, or apathetic, many black men stopped voting. Black sharecroppers and renters could sometimes be intimidated or bribed by their white landlords not to vote, or to vote for candidates the landlord favored.

There was also simple injustice. In 1890, black congressman Thomas E. Miller ran for reelection and won—or so he thought. But he was charged with using illegal ballots and declared the loser. He appealed to the South Carolina Supreme Court, which ruled that while his ballots were printed on the required white paper, it was "white paper of a distinctly yellow tinge." He did not return to Congress.

Evading the Fifteenth Amendment

More militant and determined Democrats in the South were not content to rely on an assortment of unreliable methods to curtail the black vote. Some "legal" means had to be found to prevent black men from voting. However, the Fifteenth Amendment to the Constitution was a serious obstacle to this goal. It explicitly stated that the right to vote could not be denied on "account of race, color, or previous condition of servitude."

White leaders worried that if they imposed what were then legally acceptable barriers to voting—literacy tests, poll taxes, and property qualifications—they would disfranchise many white voters as well as black voters. But resourceful Democrats committed to white supremacy found ways around this problem. In 1882, for example, South Carolina passed the Eight Box Law, a primitive literacy test that required voters to deposit separate ballots for separate election races in the proper ballot box. Illiterate voters could not identify the boxes unless white election officials assisted them.

Mississippi

Mississippi made the most concerted and successful effort to eliminate black voters without openly violating the Fifteenth Amendment. Black men had continued to vote in Mississippi despite hostility and intimidation. In 1889 black leaders from forty Mississippi counties protested the "violent and criminal suppression of the black vote." In response white men called a constitutional convention to do away with the black vote.

With one black delegate and 134 white delegates, the convention adopted complex voting requirements that—without mentioning race—disfranchised black voters. Voting required proof of residency and payment of all taxes, including a two-dollar poll tax. A person who had been convicted of arson, bigamy, or petty theft—crimes the delegates associated with black people—could not vote. People convicted of so-called white crimes—murder, rape, and grand larceny—could vote.

Above all, the new Mississippi constitution required voters to be literate, but with a notable exception. Illiterate men could still qualify to vote by demonstrating that they understood the constitution if the document was read to them. It was taken for granted that white voting registrars would accept almost all white applicants and fail most black applicants seeking to register under this provision.

South Carolina

Black voting had been declining in South Carolina since the end of Reconstruction. In the 1876 election, 91,870 black men voted; in the 1888 election, only 13,740 did. Unhappy that even so few voters might decide an election, U.S. senator Benjamin R. Tillman won approval for a constitutional convention in 1895. The convention followed Mississippi's lead and created an "understanding clause," but not without a vigorous protest from black leaders.

Six black men and 154 white men were elected to the South Carolina convention. Two of the black men—Robert Smalls and William Whipper (see Chapter 13)—had been delegates to the 1868 constitutional convention. The six black men protested black disenfranchisement. Thomas E. Miller explained that it was not just a matter of black power but that the basic rights of citizens were at stake. "The Negroes do not want to dominate. They do not and would not have social equality, but they do want to cast a ballot for the men who make their laws and administer the laws. I stand here pleading for justice to a people whose rights are about to be taken away with one fell swoop."

It was all for naught. Black voters were disfranchised in South Carolina. White delegates did not even pretend that elections should be fair. William Henderson of Berkeley County admitted:

> We don't propose to have fair elections. We will get left at that every time. . . . I tell you, gentlemen, if we have fair elections in Berkeley we can't carry it. There's no use to talk about it. The black man is learning to read faster than the white man. And if he comes up and can read you have got to let him vote. Now are you going to throw it out. . . . We are perfectly disgusted with hearing so much about fair elections. Talk all around, but make it fair and you'll see what'll happen.

The Grandfather Clause

In 1898, Louisiana added a new twist to disfranchisement. Its grandfather clause stipulated that only men who had been eligible to vote before 1867—or whose father or grandfather had been eligible before that year—would be qualified to vote. Since virtually no black men had been eligible to vote before 1867—most had just emerged from slavery—the law immediately

THE SPREAD OF DISFRANCHISEMENT

	STATE	STRATEGIES
1889	Florida	Poll tax
	Tennessee	Poll tax
1890	Mississippi	Poll tax, literacy test, understanding clause
1891	Arkansas	Poll tax
1893, 1901	Alabama	Poll tax, literacy test, grandfather clause
1894, 1895	South Carolina	Poll tax, literacy test, understanding clause
1894, 1902	Virginia	Poll tax, literacy test, understanding clause
1897, 1898	Louisiana	Poll tax, literacy test, grandfather clause
1899, 1900	North Carolina	Poll tax, literacy test, grandfather clause
1902	Texas	Poll tax
1908	Georgia	Poll tax, literacy test, understanding clause, grandfather clause

Source: Goldfield et al., *The American Journey* (1991, Prentice Hall)

disfranchised almost all black voters. In Louisiana in 1896, 130,000 black men voted; in 1904, 1,342 voted.

Except for Kentucky and West Virginia, each southern state had enacted elaborate restrictions on voting by the 1890s. As a result, few black men continued to vote, and no black men were elected to office.

The federal government demonstrated a fleeting willingness to protect black voting rights. Republican Senator Henry Cabot Lodge of Massachusetts introduced a bill in 1890 to send federal supervisors to states and congressional districts where election fraud was alleged. But southern Democrats blocked it.

SEGREGATION

When black attorney T. McCants Stewart visited Columbia, South Carolina, in 1885, he told readers of the New York *Age* that he had been pleasantly received and had encountered little discrimination. "I can ride in first class cars on the railroads and in the streets. I can go into saloons and get refreshments even as in New York.

I can stop in and drink a glass of soda and be more politely waited upon than in some parts of New England." Stewart's visit occurred before most segregation laws requiring separation of the races in public places had been enacted. In fact, the word *segregation* was almost never used before the twentieth century.

Not that black and white people mingled freely in the 1880s and the 1890s. They did not. Since Reconstruction, schools, hospitals, asylums, and cemeteries had been segregated. Many restaurants and hotels did not admit black people, and many black people did not venture where they felt unwelcome or where they were likely to meet hostility. But what came to be known as "Jim Crow" had not yet become legally embedded in the southern way of life.

Jim Crow

The term *Jim Crow* originated with a minstrel show routine called "Jump Jim Crow" that a white performer, Thomas "Daddy" Rice, created in the 1830s and 1840s. Rice blackened his face with charcoal and ridiculed black people. How Rice's character came to be synonymous with segregation and discrimination is not clear. What is clear is that by the end of the nineteenth century Jim Crow and segregation were rapidly expanding in the South, greatly restricting the lives of African Americans.

In the decades following slavery's demise, segregation evolved gradually as an arrangement to enforce white control and domination. Many white Southerners resented the presence of black people in public facilities, places of entertainment, and business establishments. If black people were—as white Southerners believed—a subordinate race, then their proximity in shops, parks, and on passenger trains suggested an unacceptable equality in public life.

There were, moreover, many black people who acquiesced in some facets of racial separation. During Reconstruction, people of color formed their own churches and social organizations. Black people were invariably more comfortable around people of their own race than they were among white people. Furthermore, black Southerners often accepted separate seating in theaters, concert halls, and other facilities that previously had been closed to them. Segregation represented an improvement over exclusion.

Segregation on the Railroads

Many white people particularly objected to the presence of black people in the first-class coaches of trains. Before segregation laws, white passengers and railroad conductors sometimes forced black people who had purchased first-class tickets into second-class coaches. In 1889 black Baptists from Savannah bought first-class tickets to travel to a convention in Indianapolis. News was telegraphed ahead, and they were confronted by a white mob at a railroad stop in Georgia where they were threatened and beaten. A white man shoved a pistol into the breast of a black woman who had screamed in fear. He demanded, "You G-d d-d heffer, if you don't hush your mouth and get out of here, I will blow your G-d d-d brains out."

In another instance, a young black woman, Mary Church (later Mary Church Terrell), was traveling alone in a first-class coach when the conductor attempted to move her to the second-class car. She managed to remain, but only after informing the conductor that she would send a telegram to her father telling him that "you are forcing me to ride all night in a Jim Crow car. He will sue the railroad for compelling his daughter who has a first class ticket to ride in a second class car."

The first segregation laws involved passenger trains. Despite the spirited opposition of black politicians, the Tennessee legislature mandated segregation on railroad coaches in 1881. Florida passed a similar law in 1887. The railroads opposed these laws, but not because they wanted to protect the civil rights of black people. Rather, they were concerned about the expense of maintaining separate cars or sections within cars for black and white people. Whether they could pay for a first-class ticket or not, most black passengers found themselves confined to grimy second-class cars crowded with smoking and tobacco chewing black and white men. Hitched at the head of the train just behind the smoke-belching locomotive, these cars were filthy with soot and cinders.

Plessy v. Ferguson

In 1891 the Louisiana legislature required segregated trains within the state, despite opposition from a black organization, the American Citizens' Equal Rights Association of Louisiana, the state's eighteen black legislators, and the railroads.

In a test case, black people challenged the Louisiana law. In 1892 Homer A. Plessy bought a first-class ticket and attempted to ride on the coach designated for white people. He was arrested for violating the new segregation law.

The case—*Plessy v. Ferguson*—wound its way through the judicial system. Plessy's lawyers argued that segregation deprived their client of equal protection of the law guaranteed by the Fourteenth Amendment. But in 1896 the U.S. Supreme Court in an 8 to 1 decision upheld Louisiana's segregation statute. Speaking for the majority, Justice Henry Brown ruled that the law, merely because it required separation of the races, did not deny Plessy his rights, nor did it imply that he was inferior. The lone dissenter from this "separate but equal" doctrine, Justice John Marshall Harlan, whose father had owned slaves, likened the majority opinion to the Dred Scott decision thirty-nine years earlier.

Thus with the complicity of the Supreme Court, the Fourteenth Amendment was emasculated. It no longer afforded black Americans equal treatment under the law. After the Plessy decision, southern states and cities passed hundreds of laws that created an American apartheid—an elaborate system of racial separation.

Streetcar Segregation

In the late nineteenth century, before the automobile, the electric streetcar was the primary form of public transportation in American cities and towns. Beginning with Georgia in 1891, states and cities across the South segregated these vehicles. In some communities, the streetcar companies had to operate separate cars for black and white passengers; in other towns they designated separate sections within individual cars. The companies often resisted segregation, citing the expense of duplicating equipment and hiring more employees.

But black people were even more bitterly opposed to Jim Crow streetcars. During Reconstruction, they had fended off streetcar discrimination with boycotts and sit-ins. Thirty years later they tried the same techniques. There were streetcar boycotts in at least twenty-five southern cities between 1891 and 1910. Black people refused to ride segregated cars in Atlanta, Augusta, Jacksonville, Montgomery, Mobile, Little Rock, and Columbia. They walked or took horse-drawn hacks. Initially, the boycotts succeeded in Atlanta and Augusta, where segregation was briefly abandoned. The boycotts seriously hurt the streetcar companies.

Black people also attempted to form alternative transportation companies in Portsmouth and Norfolk, Virginia, and in Chattanooga and Nashville, Tennessee. In 1905 the black community in Nashville organized a black-owned bus company and committed $25,000 to it. They purchased five buses, but they could not raise enough capital to keep the company going and it failed after a few months.

VOICES

MAJORITY AND DISSENTING OPINIONS ON PLESSY V. FERGUSON

The Supreme Court's 8 to 1 decision in Plessy v. Ferguson *sanctioned legal segregation and opened the way for a host of segregation laws throughout the South. The majority opinion ruled that segregation was constitutional so long as both races were provided equal facilities. In practice, of course, the facilities for African Americans were invariably inferior to those for white people.*

From Justice Henry Brown of Michigan's majority opinion:

The object of the [Fourteenth] amendment was undoubtedly to enforce the absolute equality of the two races before the law, but in the nature of things it could not have been intended to abolish distinctions based upon color, or to enforce social, as distinguished from political, equality, or a commingling of the two races upon terms unsatisfactory to either.

We consider the underlying fallacy of the plaintiff's argument to consist in the assumption that the enforced separation of the two races stamps the colored race with a badge of inferiority. If this be so, it is not by the reason of anything found in the act, but solely because the colored race chooses to put that construction upon it. . . . If the two races are to meet on terms of social equality, it must be the result of natural affinities, a mutual appreciation of each other's merits and a voluntary consent of individuals. . . . Legislation is powerless to eradicate racial instincts or to abolish distinctions based upon physical differences. . . . If one race be inferior to the other socially, the Constitution of the United States cannot put them upon the same plane.

From Justice John Marshall Harlan of Kentucky, the lone dissent:

In my opinion, the judgement this day rendered will, in time, prove to be quite as pernicious as the decision made by this tribunal in the Dred Scott Case. . . . But it seems that we have yet, in some of the states, a dominant race, a superior class of citizens, which assumes to regulate the enjoyment of civil rights, common to all citizens, upon the basis of race. The present decision, it may well be apprehended, will not only stimulate aggressions, more or less brutal and irritating, upon the admitted rights of colored citizens, but it will encourage the belief that it is possible, by means of state enactments, to defeat the beneficent purposes which the people of the United States had in view when they adopted the recent amendments of the Constitution, by one which the blacks of this country were made citizens of the United States and of the states in which they respectively reside and whose privileges and immunities, as citizens, the states are forbidden to abridge. . . . What can more certainly arouse race hate, what more certainly create and perpetuate a feeling of distrust between these races, than state enactments which in fact proceed on the ground that the colored citizens are so inferior and degraded that they cannot be allowed to sit in public coaches occupied by white citizens? . . . But in view of the Constitution, in the eyes of the law, there is in this country no superior, dominant, ruling class of citizens. There is no caste here. Our Constitution is color-blind, and neither knows nor tolerates classes among citizens. In respect of civil rights, all citizens are equal before the law.

QUESTIONS

1. How does Justice Brown reconcile the constitutional guarantee of "equality before the law" with a law mandating segregation?

2. What does Justice Brown mean when he distinguishes between political and social equality?

3. With what arguments does Justice Harlan counter the majority opinion?

Source: 163 U.S. 537 *United States Reports: Cases Adjudged in the Supreme Court* (New York: Banks and Brothers, 1896).

Segregation Proliferates

Jim Crow proceeded inexorably. "White" and "colored" signs appeared in railroad stations, theaters, auditoriums, and restrooms and over drinking fountains. Southern white people were willing to go to any length to keep black and white people apart. Courtrooms maintained separate Bibles for black and white witnesses "to swear to tell the truth." New Orleans segregated black and white prostitutes.

Although *Plessy v. Ferguson* required "separate but equal" facilities for black and white people, when facilities were made available to black people, they were inferior to those afforded white people. Often, no facilities at all were provided for people of color. They were simply excluded. Few hotels, restaurants, libraries, bowling alleys, public parks, amusement parks, swimming pools, golf courses, or tennis courts would admit black people. The only exceptions would be black people who accompanied or assisted white people. For example, a black woman caring for a white child could visit a "white only" public park with the child, but she dare not visit it with her own child.

RACIAL ETIQUETTE

Since slavery, white people had insisted that black people act in an obedient and subservient manner. Such behavior made white dominance clear. After emancipation, white Southerners sought to maintain that dominance through a complex pattern of racial etiquette that determined how black and white people dealt with each other in their day-to-day affairs.

Black and white people did not shake hands. Black people did not look directly into the eyes of white people. They were supposed to stare at the ground when addressing white men and women. Black men removed their hats in the presence of white people. White men did not remove their hats in a black home or in the presence of a black woman. Black people went to the back door, not the front door, of a white house. A black man or boy was never to look at a white woman. A black man in Mississippi observed, "You couldn't smile at a white woman. If you did you'd be hung from a limb." It was a serious offense if a black male touched a white woman, even inadvertently.

White customers were always served first in a store, even if a black customer had been the first to arrive. Black women could not try on clothing in white businesses. White people did not use titles of respect—mister, Mrs., miss—when addressing black adults. They used first names, or "boy" or "girl," or sometimes even

The Pullman Company manufactured and operated passenger, sleeping, and dining cars for the nation's railroads. The company employed black men to serve and wait on passengers who were usually white people. Black porters and attendents were expected to be properly deferential as they dealt with passengers.

"nigger." Older black people were sometimes called "auntie" or "uncle." But black people were expected to use mister, Mrs., and miss when addressing white people, including adolescents. "Boss" or "cap'n" might do for a white man.

VIOLENCE

In the late nineteenth century, the South was a violent place. Political and mob violence, so prevalent during Reconstruction, continued unabated into the 1880s and

1890s as Democrats often used armed force to drive the dwindling number of black and white Republicans out of politics.

Washington County, Texas

In 1886 in Washington County in eastern Texas, Democrats were determined to keep the political control that they had only won in 1884 through fraud. Masked Democrats tried to seize ballot boxes in a Republican precinct. But armed black men resisted and, with a shotgun blast, killed one of the white men. Eight black men were arrested. A mob of white men in disguise broke into the jail, kidnapped three of the black men, and lynched them. Three white Republicans fled for their lives but convinced federal authorities to investigate. The U.S. Attorney twice tried to secure convictions for election fraud. The first trial ended in a hung jury, the second in acquittal. The white Democratic sheriff did not investigate the lynching. But the black man charged with firing the shotgun was sentenced to twenty-five years in prison.

The Phoenix Riot

In the tiny South Carolina community of Phoenix in 1898, a white Republican candidate for Congress urged black men to fill out an affidavit if they were not permitted to vote. This produced a confrontation with Democrats. Words were exchanged, shots were fired, and the Republican candidate was wounded. White men then went on a rampage through rural Greenwood County. Black men were killed—how many is unknown. Others—including Benjamin Mays's father, as related in one of the quotes that opens this chapter—had to humiliate themselves by bowing down and saluting white men.

The Wilmington Riot

While white men roamed Greenwood County in search of black victims, an even bloodier riot erupted in Wilmington, North Carolina. Black men still held political offices in 1898 in Wilmington, including seats on the city council. White Democrats were determined to drive them from power. During the tense campaign, the young editor of a local black newspaper, Alex Manly, published an editorial condemning white men for the sexual exploitation of black women. Manly also suggested that black men had sexual liaisons with rural white women, which infuriated the white community. "Poor white men are careless in the matter of protecting their women, es-

pecially on the farms. . . . Tell your men that it is no worse for a black man to be intimate with a white woman than for a white woman to be intimate with a colored man. . . . Don't think ever that your women will remain pure while you are debauching ours."

A white mob that included some of Wilmington's business and professional leaders destroyed the newspaper office. Black officials resigned in a vain attempt to prevent further violence. But at least a dozen black men were murdered. Some 1,500 black residents of Wilmington fled. White people then bought up black homes and property at bargain rates. Black congressman George H. White, who represented Wilmington and North Carolina's second district, served out the remainder of his term and then moved north. He ruefully remarked, "I can no longer live in North Carolina and be a man." White was the last black man to serve in Congress from the South until the election of Andrew Young in Atlanta in 1972.

Lynching

Lynching had become common in the South by the 1890s. Between 1889 and 1932, 3,745 people were lynched in the United States (Figure 14–2). An average of two to three people were lynched every week for thirty years. Most lynchings happened in the South, and black men were usually the victims. Sometimes white people were lynched. In 1891 in New Orleans eleven Italians were lynched for alleged involvement with the Mafia and for the murder of the city's police chief. For black Southerners, violence was an ever-present possibility. Rarely did a sheriff or police officer protect a potential victim, and even if one did, that protection was often not enough.

The people who carried out the lynchings were never apprehended, tried, or convicted. Prominent community members frequently encouraged and even participated in lynch mobs. White political leaders, journalists, and clergymen rarely denounced lynching in public. The *Atlanta Constitution* dismissed lynching as relatively inconsequential. "There are places and occasions when the natural fury of men cannot be restrained by all the laws in Christendom."

There was no such thing as a civilized lynching. Lynchings were barbaric, savage, and hideous. Such mob brutality was another manifestation of white supremacy. Black people were murdered, beaten, burned, and mutilated for trivial reasons—or for no reason. Most white Southerners justified lynching as a response to the raping of white women by black men. But many

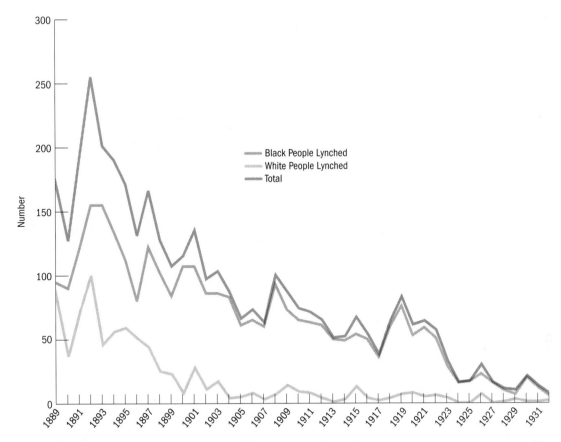

Figure 14-2 Lynching in the United States, 1889–1932. Depending on the source, statistics on lynching vary. It was difficult to assemble information on lynching, particularly in the nineteenth century. Not every lynching was recorded. Source: *The Negro Year Book, 1931–32*, p. 293.

lynchings involved no alleged rape, and even when they did, the victims often had no connection to the alleged offense.

After a white family was murdered in Statesboro, Georgia, in 1904, Paul Reed and Will Cato were convicted of murder and then seized by a mob that invaded the courtroom. They were burned alive in front of a large crowd. Then the violence spread. Albert Roger and his son were lynched "for being Negroes." A black man named McBride attempted to protect his wife who had had a baby three days earlier. He "was beaten, killed, and shot to death."

Mobs often attacked black people who had achieved economic success. In Memphis, Thomas Moss with two friends opened the People's Grocery Company in a black neighborhood. The store flourished, but it competed with a white-owned grocery. "[T]hey were succeeding too well," one of Moss's friends observed. After the white grocer had had the three black men indicted for conspiracy, black people organized a protest and vi-

olence followed. The three black men were jailed. A white mob attacked the jail, lynched them, and then looted their store. Ida B. Wells, a newspaper editor and a friend of Moss, was heartbroken. "A finer, cleaner man than he never walked the streets of Memphis." She considered his lynching an "excuse to get rid of Negroes who were acquiring wealth and property and thus keep the race terrorized and keep the nigger down." Responding to the incident in her paper, Wells began a lifelong crusade against lynching. (See Profile: Ida Wells Barnett.)

Though less often than men, black women were also lynched. In 1914 in Wagoner County, Oklahoma, seventeen-year-old Marie Scott was lynched because her brother had killed a white man who had raped her. In Valdosta, Georgia, in 1918 after Mary Turner's husband was lynched, she publicly vowed to bring those responsible to justice. Though she was eight months pregnant, a mob considered her determination a threat. They seized her, tied her ankles together, and hanged

Lynchings were common and public events in the South at the turn-of-the-century. Often hundreds of people took part in and witnessed these gruesome spectacles.

VOICES

AN ACCOUNT OF A LYNCHING

Sam Hose, a literate black farm laborer, was accused of murdering his employer in a quarrel over wages. He escaped, and days later, while he was being hunted, he was also charged with raping his employer's wife. When apprehended a few days later he confessed to the murder, but refused, even under duress, to confess to rape. A huge mob seized him from prison and lynched him. A later investigation revealed that Hose had indeed been involved in a dispute over pay with his employer, Alfred Cranford. As Cranford reached for his pistol, Hose killed him in self-defense with an ax. Hose never attacked Mrs. Cranford. No indictments were ever brought against any of the lynchers. The following account of the lynching is taken from the New York Tribune *for April 24, 1899.*

Georgia, 1899

In the presence of nearly 2,000 people, who sent aloft yells of defiance and shouts of joy, Sam Hose (a Negro who committed two of the basest acts known to crime) was burned at the stake in a public road, one and a half miles from here. Before the torch was applied to the pyre, the Negro was deprived of his ears, fingers and other portions of his body with surprising fortitude. Before the body was cool, it was cut to pieces, the bones were crushed into small bits and even the tree upon which the wretch met his fate was torn up and disposed of as souvenirs.

The Negro's heart was cut in several pieces, as was also his liver. Those unable to obtain the ghastly relics directly, paid more fortunate possessors extravagant sums for them. Small pieces of bone went for 25 cents and a bit of the liver, crisply cooked, for 10 cents.

Source: *New York Tribune*, April 14, 1899, as quoted in *Thirty Years of Lynching in the United States, 1889–1918*, pp. 12–13.

her upside down from a tree. A member of the mob slit her abdomen, and her nearly full-term child fell to the ground. The mob stomped the infant to death. They then set her clothes on fire and shot her.

Rape

Although white people often justified lynching as a response to the presumed threat black men posed to the virtue of white women, white men routinely harassed and abused black women. There are no statistics on such abuse, but it surely was more common than lynching. Like lynching, rape inflicted pain and suffering, and demonstrated the power of white men over black men and women.

Black men tried to keep their wives and daughters away from white men. They refused to permit black women to work as maids and domestics in homes where white men were present. One black man commented in 1912, "I believe nearly all white men take, and expect to take, undue liberties with their colored female servants, not only the fathers, but in many cases the sons also." A black man could not easily protect a black woman. He might be killed trying to do it, as an Alabama clergyman pointed out. "[W]hite men on the high ways and in their stores and on the trains will insult our women and we are powerless to resent it as it would only be an invitation for our lives to be taken."

Many white people believed that black women "invited" white males to take advantage of them. Black women were considered inferior, immoral, and lascivious. White people reasoned that it was impossible to defend the virtue of black women because they had none. Governor Coleman Blease of South Carolina pardoned black and white men found guilty of raping black women. "I am of the opinion," he said in 1913, "as I have always been, and have very serious doubts as to whether the crime of rape can be committed upon a negro."

MIGRATION

In 1900, AME minister Henry M. Turner despaired for black people in America. "Every man that has the sense of an animal must see that there is no future in this country for the Negro. [W]e are taken out and burned, shot, hanged, unjointed and murdered in every way. Our civil rights are taken from us by force, our political rights are a farce."

It is, therefore, not surprising that thousands of African Americans fled poverty, powerlessness, and brutality in the South. What is surprising is that more did not leave. In the 1910s, 90 percent of black Americans still lived in the southern states. And of those who left the South, most did not head north along the old Underground Railroad. The Great Migration to the northern industrial states did not begin until about 1915. Emigrants of the 1870s, 1880s, and 1890s were more likely to strike out for Africa, or move west to Kansas, Oklahoma, and Arkansas, or move from farms to southern towns or cities.

The Liberian Exodus

When white Democrats redeemed Mississippi in 1875 with the "shotgun policy," a group of black people from Winona, Mississippi, wrote to Governor Adelbert Ames "to inquire about the possibility of moving to Africa. [W]e the colored people of Montgomery County are in a bad fix for we have no rights in the county and we want to know of you if there is any way for us to get out of the county and go to some place where we can get homes . . . so will you please let us know if we can go to Africa?"

They did not go to Africa, but some black Georgians and South Carolinians did. In 1877, black leaders in South Carolina, including AME minister and congressman Richard H. Cain, Probate Judge Harrison N. Bouey, and Martin Delany urged black people to migrate to Liberia. Many black communities and churches caught "Liberia Fever" while black people in upper South Carolina still felt the trauma of the political terror that had ended Reconstruction.

A white journalist described the situation in Chester County: "At some places in this county the desire to shake off the dust of their feet against this Democratic State is so great, that they are talking of selling out their crops and their personal effects, save what they would need in their new home." They were given promising though sometimes inaccurate information about Liberia: One potato in Liberia, they were told, could feed an entire family.

Several black men organized the Liberian Exodus Joint Stock Steamship Company. They raised $6,000 and hired a ship, the *Azor*, for the trip to Africa. The ship left Charleston in April 1878 with 206 migrants aboard and 175 left behind because there was not enough room for them. With inadequate food and fresh water and no competent medical care, twenty-three migrants died at sea. The ship arrived in Liberia on June 3.

Once settled in Liberia, several of the migrants prospered. Sam Hill established a 700-acre coffee plantation, and C. L. Parsons became the chief justice of the Liberian Supreme Court. But others did less well, and

IDA WELLS BARNETT

Ida Wells Barnett began life as a slave in 1862 and grew up during Reconstruction. As a young woman, she saw the worst indignities and cruelties that the Jim Crow South could inflict. But she fought back as a journalist, agitator, and reformer who was determined to improve the lives of black men and women.

Ida Wells was one of eight children born to Jim and Lizzie Wells in Holly Springs, Mississippi. After the Civil War, she attended a school for freed people with her mother, and they learned to read and write. Her parents and one of her brothers died in the yellow fever epidemic of 1878. Sixteen-year-old Ida became mother and father to her five surviving brothers and sisters. She attended Shaw University in Holly Springs (now Rust College) and taught school in Mississippi and Tennessee.

In 1884, a railroad conductor removed Wells from a first-class car. She sued the railroad and won a $500 settlement. "Dusky Damsel Gets Damages," a Memphis newspaper reported. But a higher court reversed the decision.

Wells then took up journalism and wrote a weekly column for *The Living Way*. In 1889, she bought a one-third interest in the Memphis *Free Speech and Headlight*. She wrote about racial issues and criticized black educators for the quality of black schools. In 1892 her friend Thomas Moss was lynched with two other men for the crime of running a successful grocery store. Wells expressed her rage and horror in a fiery editorial, thus beginning a lifelong crusade against lynching.

Wells blamed the white people of Memphis for her friend's murder and pointed out that more black men were lynched for challenging the myth of white superiority than for allegedly raping a white woman. She angered white people even more by writing that white women could be attracted to black men.

While Wells was out of town, a mob destroyed the offices of the *Free Speech*. Her life in danger, she did not return to Memphis. For a time, she wrote for the New York *Age* and continued to condemn the horrors of lynching. She blamed white clergymen and their parishioners for tolerating lynching. "[O]ur American

Ida Wells Barnett was born in Mississippi and lived in Memphis until she published an outraged exposé of the lynching of one of her friends, Thomas Moss. Forced to leave Tennessee, she settled in Chicago but remained an antilynching crusader. She also supported women's suffrage and women's rights. She was a key figure in the National Association of Colored Women after its founding in 1896.

Christians are too busy saving the souls of white Christians from burning in hell-fire to save the lives of black ones from present burning in fires kindled by white Christians." She urged black people to fight back. "The more the Afro-American yields and cringes and begs, the more he has to do so, the more he is insulted, outraged, and lynched."

Wells moved to Chicago and wrote a pamphlet criticizing the racism at the 1893 World's Fair: *The Reason Why the Colored American is Not in the Columbian Exposition*. In 1895 she married Ferdinand Barnett, the owner of the *Chicago Conservator*.

After a white journalist from Missouri wrote that black women were immoral—"having no sense of virtue and altogether without character"—black women including Wells Barnett founded the National Association of Colored Women in 1896.

In 1909, Wells Barnett was one of two black women who supported the founding of the National Association for the Advancement of Colored People (NAACP) although she later broke with the group because of its mostly white board of directors and what she considered its cautious stands. She also helped organize the Negro Fellowship League in 1910.

Wells Barnett became an ardent supporter of black voting rights. She believed that if enough black men and women could vote, their political power would end lynching. In 1913 she helped found the Alpha Suffrage Club, the first black women's suffrage organization in Illinois, and was a delegate to the National American Woman's Suffrage Association meeting in Washington, D.C. In 1915 she helped elect Oscar DePriest, Chicago's first black alderman.

She continued to write, campaign, speak out, and organize. Only death from kidney failure in 1931 ended her efforts to secure justice for black Americans.

some returned to the United States. The Liberian Exodus Company experienced financial difficulties and could not pay for further voyages.

The Exodusters

In May 1879, black delegates from 14 states met in a convention in Nashville presided over by Congressman John R. Lynch of Mississippi. The convention resolved to support migration. The delegates declared that "the colored people should emigrate to those States and Territories where they can enjoy all the rights which are guaranteed by the laws and Constitution of the United States." They also asked Congress—in vain—to appropriate $500,000 for this venture.

Nevertheless, black people headed west. Between 1865 and 1880, 40,000 black people moved to Kansas. These "Exodusters" as they came to be known established all-black towns including Nicodemus. In 1879, 6,000 people left South Carolina, Mississippi, Tennessee, Louisiana, and Texas for Kansas.

In late December 1881, more than 5,000 black residents of violent and bloody Edgefield, South Carolina, taking only the belongings they could carry, left for Augusta, Georgia, where they boarded a train to Arkansas and what they hoped would be a better life. One Edgefield migrant explained: "For ten years we have tried to make money and have not been able to do so. We are poorer now than when we began, we have less, in fact we have nothing. . . . There is no help for us here, there's no use in trying to get along under the old conditions any longer, and so we have just determined to go somewhere else and take a new start."

Railroads encouraged migration by offering reduced fares. Some western farmers and agents were eager to sell land, but some of it was of little value. Some of the white residents of Mississippi and South Carolina, which had large black majorities in their population, were glad to see the black people go. Others were alarmed at the loss of cheap black labor.

Some black leaders opposed migration and urged black people to stay put. In 1879, Frederick Douglass insisted that more opportunities existed for black people in the South than elsewhere. "Not only is the South the best locality for the Negro on the ground of his political powers and possibilities, but it is best for him as a field of labor. He is there, as he is nowhere else, an absolute necessity." Robert Smalls urged black people to come to his home county of Beaufort, South Carolina, "where I hardly think it probable that any prisoner will ever be taken from jail by a mob and lynched."

Migration within the South

Many black people left the poverty and isolation of farms and moved to nearby villages and towns in the South. Others went to larger southern cities including

Though most black people remained in the Southern states in the 1870s and 1880s, several thousand migrated to Kansas as well as Arkansas, Oklahoma, and Nebraska. Some obtained land under the 1862 Homestead act, which entitled them to 160 acres on the Great Plains.

Atlanta, Richmond, and Nashville where they settled in growing black neighborhoods. Urban areas offered more economic opportunities than rural areas. Though black people were usually confined to menial labor—from painting and shining shoes to domestic service—city work paid cash on a fairly regular basis whereas rural residents received no money until their crops were sold. Towns and cities also afforded more entertainment and religious and educational activities. Black youngsters in towns spent more time in school than rural children, who had to help work the farms.

Black women had a better chance than black men of finding regular work in a town, though it was usually as a domestic or cleaning woman. This economic situation adversely affected the black family. Before the increase in migration, husband and wife headed 90 percent of black families. But with migration, many black men remained in rural areas where they could get farm work while women went to urban communities. Often these women became single heads of households.

BLACK FARM FAMILIES

Most black people did not leave the South or move to towns. They remained poverty-stricken sharecroppers and renters on impoverished land white people owned. They were poorly educated. They lacked political power. They were always in debt. Many rural black families remained precariously close to involuntary servitude in the decades after Reconstruction.

Many black and white people were little better off than medieval serfs. They lived in drafty, leaky cabins without electricity or running water. Outdoor toilets created health and hygiene problems. Medical care was often unavailable. Diets were dreary and unbalanced—mostly pork and cornbread—and deficient in vitamins and protein.

Sharecroppers

Most black farm families (and many white families as well) were sharecroppers. Sharecropping had emerged during Reconstruction as landowners allowed the use of their land for a share of the crop. The landlord also usually provided housing, horses or mules, tools, seed, and fertilizer as well as food and clothing. Depending on the agreement or contract, the landowner received from one-half to three-quarters of the crop.

Sharecropping lent itself to cheating and exploitation. By law, verbal agreements were considered con-

tracts. In any case, many sharecroppers were illiterate and could not have read written contracts. The landowner informed the sharecropper of the value of the product raised—typically cotton—as well as the value of the goods provided to the sharecropping family. Black farmers who disputed white landowners put themselves in peril. Though many sharecroppers were aware that the proprietor's calculations were wrong, they could do nothing about it. Also, cotton brokers and gin owners routinely paid black farmers less than white farmers per pound for cotton. A forlorn ditty circulating among black people in the South in the late nineteenth century captured this inequity:

> A naught's a naught, and a figger's a figger—
> All fer de white man—none fer de nigger!

Black men were forced to accept the white man's word. One Mississippi sharecropper explained, "I have been living in this Delta thirty years, and I know that I have been robbed every year; but there is no use jumping out of the frying pan into the fire. If we ask any questions we are cussed, and if we raise up we are shot, and that ends it."

Renters

When they could, black farmers preferred renting to sharecropping. As tenants, they paid a flat charge to rent a given number of acres. Payment would be made in either cash—perhaps $5 per acre—or more typically in a specified amount of the crop—two bales of cotton per twenty acres. Tenants usually owned their own animals and tools. As Bessie Jones explained, "You see, a sharecropper don't ever have nothing. Before you know it, the man done took it all. But the renter always have something, and then he go to work when he want to go to work. He ain't got to go to work on the man's time. If he didn't make it, he didn't get it."

Crop Liens

In addition to the landowner, many sharecroppers and renters were also indebted to a local merchant for food, clothing, tools, and farm supplies. The merchant advanced the merchandise but took out a lien on the crop. If the sharecropper or renter failed to repay the merchant, the merchant was legally entitled to all or part of the crop once the landowner had received his payment. Merchants tended to charge high prices and high interest rates. They usually insisted that farmers plant cotton before they would agree to a lien. Cotton could be sold quickly for cash.

Peonage

Many farmers fell deeply into debt to landowners and merchants. They were cheated. Bad weather destroyed crops. Crop prices declined. Farmers who were in debt could not leave the land until the debt was paid. If they tried to depart, the sheriff pursued them. This was called peonage, and it amounted to enslavement, holding thousands of black people across the South in a state of perpetual bondage. Peonage violated federal law, but the law was rarely enforced. When landowners and merchants were prosecuted for keeping black people in peonage, white juries acquitted them.

Black Landowners

Considering the incredible obstacles against them, black farm families acquired land at an astonishing rate after the Civil War. Many white people refused to sell land to black buyers, preferring to keep them dependent. Black people also found it difficult to save enough money to purchase land even when they could find a

---

VOICES

CASH AND DEBT FOR THE BLACK COTTON FARMER

Benjamin E. Mays was born in 1895 in Epworth, South Carolina. He was the youngest and eighth child of parents who had been slaves and whose lives revolved around agriculture. Mays went on to South Carolina State College, to Bates College, and the University of Chicago. He became the president of Morehouse College where he served as a mentor to Martin Luther King Jr. Mays delivered the eulogy at King's funeral in 1968.

As I recall, Father usually rented forty acres of land for a two-mule farm, or sixty acres if we had three mules. The rent was two bales of cotton weighing 500 pounds each, for every twenty acres rented. So the owner of the land got his two, four, or six bales of cotton out of the first cotton picked and ginned.

To make sixteen bales of cotton on a two-mule farm was considered excellent farming. After four bales were used to pay rent, we would have twelve bales left. The price of cotton fluctuated. If we received ten cents a pound, we would have somewhere between five and six hundred dollars, depending on whether the bales of cotton weighed an average of 450, 475, or 500 pounds. When all of us children were at home we, with our father and mother, were ten. We lived in a four-room house, with no indoor plumbing—no toilet facilities, no running water.

We were never able to clear enough from the crop to carry us from one September to the next. We could usually go on our own from September through February; but every March a lien had to be placed on the crop so that we could get money to buy food and other necessities from March through August, when we would get some relief by selling cotton. Strange as it may seem, neither we nor our neighbors ever raised enough hogs to have meat year round, enough corn and wheat to insure having our daily bread, or cows in sufficient numbers to have enough milk. The curse was cotton. It was difficult to make farmers see that more corn, grain, hogs, and cows meant less cash but more profit in the end. Cotton sold instantly, and that was *cash* money. Negro farmers wanted to *feel* the cash—at least for that brief moment as it passed through their hands into the white man's hands!

QUESTIONS:

1. In what specific ways did the Mays family depend on white people?

2. What might have led to greater independence for people like the Mays family?

3. Why were southern black and white families so large?

Source: Mays, *Born to Rebel*, pp. 5–6.

willing seller. Still, they steadily managed to accumulate land.

Some black families had kept land that had been distributed in the Carolina and Georgia low country under the Port Royal Experiment and Sherman's Special Field Order #15 (see Chapter 11). In 1880, black people on South Carolina's Sen Islands held 10,000 acres of land worth $300,000.

By 1900, more than 100,000 black families owned their own land in the eight states of the deep South (Figure 14–3). Black land ownership increased more than 500 percent between 1870 and 1900. Most black people possessed small farms of about twenty acres. In many cases these small plots of land were subsequently subdivided among sons and grandsons making it more difficult for their families to prosper. But some black farmers owned impressive estates. Prince Johnson had 360 acres of excellent Mississippi Delta land. Freedman Leon Winter was the richest black man in Tennessee with real estate worth $70,000 in 1889. Florida farmer J. D. McDuffy had an 800-acre farm near Ocala and raised cantaloupes, watermelons, cabbages, and tomatoes. Texas freedman Daniel Webster Wallace had a 10,000-acre cattle ranch.

White Resentment of Black Success

Many white Southerners found it difficult to tolerate black economic success. They resented black progress and lashed out at those who had achieved it. When one rural black man built an attractive new house, local white people told him not to paint it—lest it look better than theirs. He accepted the advice and left the dwelling bare.

When automobiles arrived in the early twentieth century, Henry Watson—a well-to-do black farmer in Georgia—drove a new car to town. Enraged white people surrounded the car, forced Watson and his daughter

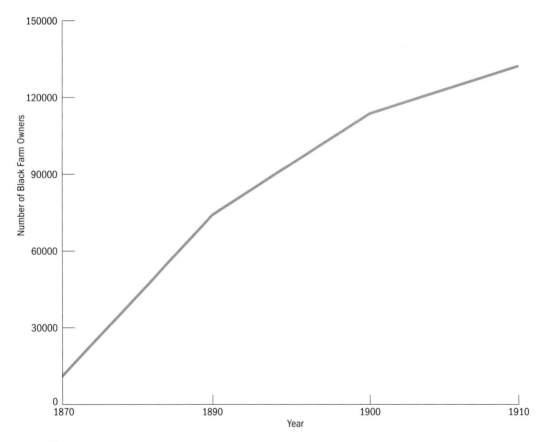

Figure 14–3   Black Farm Owners in Alabama, Arkansas, Florida, Georgia, Louisiana, Mississippi, South Carolina, and Texas, 1870–1910. It was very difficult for black families to acquire land. Many former slaves had barely enough money to survive, and saving money to buy land was almost impossible. Moreover, many white people would not sell land to black people. Thus, it is remarkable that so many black families purchased land in the decades after emancipation. Source: Loren Schweninger, *Black Property Owners in the South, 1790–1915*, p. 164.

JOHNSON C. WHITTAKER

Shortly after 6 A.M. on April 6, 1880, West Point's lone black cadet, Johnson C. Whittaker, was found lying unconscious on the floor of his room in the barracks. He was splattered with blood. His hands were tied together, and his feet were tied to the bed. In the months that followed, Whittaker's case attracted nationwide attention.

Whittaker was born a slave in 1858 on Mulberry Plantation near Camden, South Carolina, the son of house slave and a free man. In 1876 white Republican congressman Solomon L. Hoge nominated Whittaker to West Point.

During his first year at the Academy, Whittaker roomed with the only other black cadet, Henry O. Flipper. But Flipper graduated in 1877—the first black man to graduate from the Academy—and Whittaker spent the next four years completely ostracized as the only remaining black cadet. White cadets refused to associate or room with him. Quiet and studious, he established a creditable academic record, but when he failed an exam in 1878, he was required to repeat a year.

When he was found bloody and bound, Whittaker claimed he had been assaulted by three masked men after receiving a warning note the day before. A Court of Inquiry, however, declared that he had mutilated himself. Whittaker then insisted on a court martial to prove his innocence. In February 1881, that court martial convened in New York City. Whittaker was represented by Daniel H. Chamberlain, who had served as South Carolina's last Republican governor during Reconstruction and by Whittaker's close friend Richard Greener, the former dean of the Howard University Law School.

Whittaker was charged with conduct unbecoming an officer and with lying. After four months of testimony, the court found him guilty. The court determined that Whittaker was "shamming"—making it all up to avoid failing an exam. Major Asa Bird Gardiner

Johnson C. Whittaker was the sole black cadet at West Point in 1880. Ostracized and shunned by white cadets, he was court martialed and convicted of conduct unbecoming an officer. Though the conviction was overturned by President Chester Arthur, Whittaker was dismissed from the Military Academy in 1882.

told the court: "Negroes are noted for their ability to sham and feign." Gardiner maintained that Whittaker was unfit. "By his own story the accused has shown himself a coward without one redeeming quality. . . . his mental attitude [was] inferior to the average Anglo-Saxon."

The court ordered Whittaker dishonorably discharged, fined one dollar, and sentenced to a year's hard labor. But the controversy did not end. In March 1882, President Chester Arthur overturned the verdict. But on the same day, the secretary of war, Robert Lincoln (Abraham's son), ordered Whittaker discharged from West Point.

Whittaker spent most of the rest of his life working with young black people at South Carolina State College and at Douglass High School in Oklahoma City. He died in South Carolina in 1931 at age 72. Whittaker had two sons. Both were commissioned officers and served in all-black units in World War I.

Whittaker summed up the meaning of his experience at West Point in a speech after the court martial found him guilty.

> West Point has tried to take from me honor and good name, but West Point has failed. I have honor and manhood still left me. I have an education which none can take from me. That education has come to me at fearful cost. The government may not wish me to use it in her service, but I shall use it for the good of my fellow men and for the good of those around me. . . . Poverty and sneers can never crush manhood. With God as my guide, duty will be my watchword, I can, I must, I will win a place in life!

In July 1995, President Bill Clinton posthumously awarded Johnson C. Whittaker his commission in the United States Army.

out at gunpoint, and burned the vehicle. Watson was told, "From now on, you niggers walk into town, or use that ole mule if you want to stay in this city."

In 1916, Anthony Crawford—the owner of 427 acres of prime cotton land in Abbeville, South Carolina, secretary of the Chapel AME Church, a married man with sixteen children—was arrested and then released after he quarreled with a local white merchant over the price of cotton seed. But a mob, infuriated that Crawford spoke so bluntly to a white man, went after him. "When a nigger gets impudent we stretch him out and paddle him a bit," exclaimed one white man. But Crawford resisted and crushed the skull of a white attacker. The mob then stabbed and beat Crawford before the sheriff rescued him and put him in jail. Several hours later, a second mob broke into the jail and beat him to death. His body was left hanging at the fairgrounds. After his first beating, Crawford had told a friend, "I thought I was a good citizen." The coroner's jury ruled that his death had occurred at the hands of persons unknown.

AFRICAN AMERICANS AND SOUTHERN COURTS

The southern criminal justice systems yielded nothing but injustice to black people who ran afoul of it. Southern lawmakers worried incessantly about what they considered the growing black crime problem, and they worked diligently to control the black population. They enacted laws and ordinances to regulate black people's behavior. Vagrancy laws made it easy to arrest any idle black man or one who was passing through a community. Contract evasion laws ensnared black people who attempted to escape peonage and perpetual servitude.

Segregated Justice

The legal system also became increasingly white after Reconstruction. Black police officers were gradually eliminated, and white policemen acquired a deserved reputation for brutality. Fewer and fewer black men served on juries, which were all white by 1900. (No women served on southern juries.) When black men were accidentally called for jury duty, they were rejected. In Alabama, a black man called for a local grand jury insisted on serving until he was beaten and forced to step down. Judges were white men. Most attorneys were white. The few black lawyers faced daunting hur-

dles. Some black defendants believed—correctly—that they would be found guilty and sentenced to a longer term if they retained a black attorney rather than a white one. Court personnel treated black plaintiffs, defendants, and witnesses with contempt—referring to them as "niggers," "boy," and "gal." Black people were rarely "mister" or "misses" in court proceedings.

A black defendant could not get justice. Black men and women were more often charged with crimes than white people. They were almost always convicted regardless of the strength of the evidence or the credibility of witnesses. In one of the few instances when a black man was found not guilty of killing a white man, the defendant's attorney advised him to leave town because local white people were unlikely to accept the verdict. He fled, but returned twenty years later—and was castrated by two white men.

Race was always the priority with jurors. Even when black people were the victims of crime, they were punished. In 1897, in Hinds County, Mississippi, a white man beat a black woman with an ax handle. She took him to court only to have the justice of the peace rule that he knew of "no law to punish a white man for beating a negro woman."

Juries rarely found white people guilty of crimes against black people. In a Georgia case in 1911, the evidence against several white people for holding black families in peonage was so overwhelming that the judge virtually ordered the jury to return a guilty verdict. Nonetheless, after five minutes of deliberation, the jury found the defendants not guilty. Many black and white people were, therefore, astonished in 1898 in Shreveport, Louisiana, when a jury actually found a white man guilty of murdering a black man. He was sentenced to five years in prison.

Black people could receive leniency from the judicial system, but it was not justice. They were much less likely to be charged with a crime against another black person, like raping a black woman, than against a white person. Black people often were not charged with crimes like adultery and bigamy because white people considered such offenses typical of black behavior.

Black defendants who had some personal or economic connection to a prominent white person were less likely to be treated or punished the same way as black people who had no such relationship. In Vicksburg, Mississippi, a black woman watched as the black man who had murdered her husband was acquitted because a white man intervened. Those black people known as "a white man's nigger" had a decided advantage in court.

Black people received longer sentences and larger fines than white people. In Georgia, black convicts served much longer sentences than white convicts for the same offense—five times as long for larceny, for example. An eighty-year-old black preacher went to prison "for what a white man was fined five dollars." In New Orleans, a black man was sentenced to ninety days in jail for petty theft. According to a local black newspaper, it was "three days for stealing and eighty-seven days for being colored."

The Convict Lease System

Conditions in southern prisons were indescribably wretched. Black prisoners—many incarcerated for vagrancy, theft, disorderly conduct, and other misdemeanors—spent months and years in oppressive conditions and were subjected to the unrelenting abuse of white authorities. But conditions could and did get worse.

Southern politicians devised the convict lease system in the late nineteenth century. Businesses and planters leased convicts from the state to build railroads, clear swamps, cut timber, tend cotton, and work mines. The company or planter had to feed, clothe, and house the prisoners. Of course, the convicts were not paid. The state and local community was not only freed of the burden of maintaining prisons and jails; it also received revenue. For example, South Carolina was paid three dollars per month per prisoner. Some states and counties found this so remunerative that law enforcement officials were encouraged to charge even more black men with assorted crimes so they could contribute to this lucrative enterprise.

Leased convicts endured appalling treatment and conditions. They were shackled and beaten. They were overworked and underfed; they slept on vermin-infested straw mattresses and received little or no medical care. They sustained terrible injuries on the job and at the hands of guards; diseases proliferated in the camps. Hundreds died, meaning that they had, in effect, been sentenced to death for their petty crimes.

Businessmen and planters found such cheap labor almost irresistible, and black prisoners found it "nine kinds of hell." It was worse than slavery because these black lives had no value to either the government or the businesses involved in this sordid system. As one employer explained in 1883, "But these convicts; we don't own em. One dies, get another." The inhumanity of convict leasing became such a scandal that states outlawed it by the early twentieth century. Convicts were returned to state-operated penitentiaries.

The state of Florida leased these black prisoners to Bradford Farms, a large, private agricultural enterprise.

CONCLUSION

With the end of the Civil War and slavery in 1865, more than four million Americans of African descent had looked with hope and anticipation to the future. Four decades later, there were more than nine million African Americans, and more than eight million of them lived in the South. The crushing burden of white supremacy increasingly limited their hopes and aspirations. The U.S. government abandoned black people to white Southerners and their state and local governments. The federal government that had assured their rights as citizens during Reconstruction ignored the legal, political, and economic situation that entrapped most black Southerners.

Although the Thirteenth Amendment abolished slavery, thousands of black people were hopelessly trapped in peonage; thousands of others labored as sharecroppers and renters, indebted to white landowners and merchants. Yet, more than 100,000 black families managed to acquire farms of their own by 1900. Many black farmers had also organized and participated in the Colored Farmers' Alliance and the Populist Party, though it brought few tangible benefits.

The Fourteenth Amendment had guaranteed the rights of citizenship that included due process of law—no state could deprive a person of life, liberty, or property without a court proceeding. The amendment also ensured each citizen equal protection of the law. But the Supreme Court had ruled that racial segregation in public places did not infringe on the right to equal protection of the law. And as for the right to life, hundreds

TIMELINE

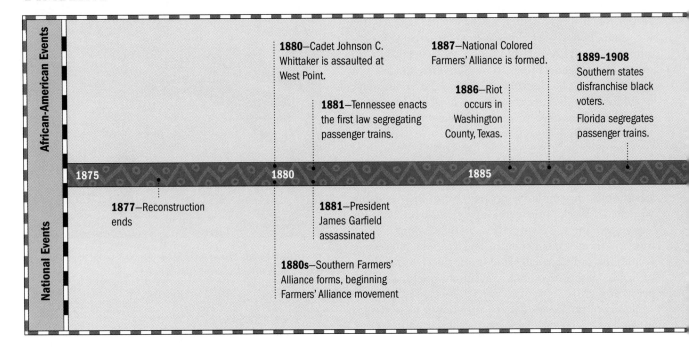

of black people had lost their lives at the hands of lynch mobs by the early 1900s.

The Fifteenth Amendment stipulated that race could not be used to deprive a man of the right to vote. Nevertheless, southern states circumvented the amendment with poll taxes, literacy tests, and the grandfather clause. Thus, by 1900, after black men had held political offices across the South for the previous thirty years, no black person served in any elected political position in any southern state.

White people clearly regarded black Americans as an inferior race not entitled to those rights that the Constitution so emphatically set forth. What could black people do about the intolerance, discrimination, violence, and powerlessness that they had to endure? What strategies, ideas, and leadership could they use to overcome the burdens that they were forced to bear? What realistic chances did they have of overcoming white supremacy? How could black people organize to gain fundamental rights that were guaranteed to them?

REVIEW QUESTIONS

1. How were black people prevented from voting in spite of the provisions of the Fifteenth amendment?

2. What were the legal and ethical arguments used by white Americans to justify segregation?

3. What accounts for the epidemic of violence and lynching in the South in the late nineteenth century?

4. Why didn't more black people migrate from the South in this period?

RECOMMENDED READING

Edward L. Ayers, *The Promise of the New South: Life after Reconstruction*. New York: Oxford University Press, 1992. An excellent overview of how people lived in the late nineteenth-century South.

Leon Litwack, *Trouble in Mind: Black Southerners in the Age of Jim Crow*. New York: Alfred A. Knopf, 1998. In moving words and testimony, black people describe what life was like in a white supremacist society.

Rayford Logan, *The Negro in American Life and Thought: The Nadir, 1877–1901*. New York: Dial Press, 1954. Explorations of the contours and oppressiveness of racism.

Benjamin E. Mays, *Born to Rebel: An Autobiography*. New York: Charles Scribner, 1971. Eloquent and graphic recollection of what it was like to grow up black in the rural South at the turn of the century.

C. Vann Woodward, *The Strange Career of Jim Crow*. New York: Oxford University Press, 1955. The evolution of legal segregation in the South.

1891—Georgia segregates streetcars.

1892—255 people are lynched in the United States, 155 of them African American, the most in American history.

1896—In *Plessy v. Ferguson*, the U.S. Supreme Court upholds legal segregation.

1898—The Phoenix Riot occurs in South Carolina.

The Wilmington Riot occurs in North Carolina.

1899-1901—Term of George H. White of North Carolina ends—the South's last black congressman until 1972.

1890 — 1895 — 1900

1892—The Populist Party challenges the Democrats and Republicans in national elections.

1893—Panic of 1893 begins a serious economic depression

1896—Republican William McKinley is elected president; Populist Party holds last national campaign

ADDITIONAL BIBLIOGRAPHY

State Studies

Eric Anderson, *Race and Politics in North Carolina, 1872–1901: The Black Second*. Baton Rouge: Louisiana State University Press, 1981.

Helen G. Edmonds, *The Negro and Fusion Politics in North Carolina, 1894–1901*. Chapel Hill: University of North Carolina Press, 1951.

Neil R. McMillen, *Dark Journey: Black Mississippians in the Age of Jim Crow*. Urbana: University of Illinois Press, 1989.

George B. Tindall, *South Carolina Negroes, 1877–1900*. Columbia: University of South Carolina Press, 1952.

Vernon Wharton, *The Negro in Mississippi, 1865–1890*. Chapel Hill: University of North Carolina Press, 1947.

Biographies and Autobiographies

Alfreda Duster, ed., *Crusade for Justice: The Autobiography of Ida B. Wells*. Chicago: University of Chicago Press, 1972.

Henry O. Flipper, *The Colored Cadet at West Point*. New York: Arno Press, 1969.

John F. Marszalek, Jr. *Court Martial: The Army vs. Johnson Whittaker*. New York: Scribner, 1972.

Politics and Segregation

J. Morgan Kousser, *The Shaping of Southern Politics: Suffrage Restriction and the Establishment of the One-Party South, 1880–1910*. New Haven: Yale University Press, 1974.

Lynching

W. Fitzhugh Brundage, ed., *Under Sentence of Death: Lynching in the South*. Chapel Hill: University of North Carolina Press, 1997.

W. Fitzhugh Brundage, *Lynching in the New South: Georgia and Virginia, 1880–1930*. Urbana: University of Illinois Press, 1993.

NAACP, *Thirty Years of Lynching in the United States, 1889–1918*. New York: NAACP, 1919.

Migration, Mobility, and Land Ownership

William Cohen, *At Freedom's Edge: Black Mobility and the Southern White Quest for Racial Control, 1861–1915*. Baton Rouge: Louisiana State University Press, 1991.

Pete Daniel, *The Shadow of Slavery: Peonage in the South, 1901–1969*. Urbana: University of Illinois Press, 1972.

Nell Painter, *Exodusters: Black Migration to Kansas after Reconstruction*. New York: Alfred A. Knopf, 1977.

Loren Schweninger, *Black Property Owners in the South, 1790–1915*. Urbana: University of Illinois Press, 1990.

Black Southerners Challenge White Supremacy

Black and white land-grant colleges stressed training in agriculture and industry. Here Hampton Institute students learn milk production. Note that the men are in military uniforms, which was typical for males at both black and white agricultural and mechanical schools. Military training was a required part of the curriculum.

CHAPTER OUTLINE

The Anglo-Saxon said to the negro, in most haughty tones: "in this great 'battle for bread,' you must supply the brute force while I will supply the brain." . . . He will contribute the public funds to educate the negro and then exert every possible influence to keep the negro from earning a livelihood by means of that education.

They pay our teachers poorer salaries than they do their own; they give us fewer and inferior school buildings and they make us crawl in the dust before the very eyes of our children in order to secure the slightest concessions. . . .

In school, they are taught to bow down and worship at the shrine of men who died for the sake of liberty, and day by day they grow to disrespect us, their parents[,] who have made no blow for freedom. But it will not always be thus!—

Black novelist Sutton E. Griggs in *Imperium in Imperio*, 1899.

Industrialization and the rise of large, powerful corporations transformed the American economy in the late nineteenth century. As millions of European immigrants crowded into the cities of the North and Midwest to find jobs in the nation's new factories, agriculture production increased and prices declined, impoverishing many rural Southerners. Most black people—nearly eight million—remained in the Southern states where they struggled to confront the malignant effects of white supremacy. Living in a society that largely sought to disregard their rights and to exclude them from its institutions and culture, black Americans increasingly relied on their own resources and depended on their own communities to adjust to the forces of white supremacy and to forge a path into the future.

Some African Americans turned to education to elevate themselves and their people, but they disagreed about the most appropriate approach to take to education. Some African-American men sought to advance themselves and prove their worth to American society through military service. By the late nineteenth century, however, black Americans mostly relied on each other and the resources of their community to sustain themselves. As they had during Reconstruction, they continued to organize and support churches, schools, and colleges. They established businesses and sometimes formed labor unions and went on strike. They founded their own hospitals. They expressed themselves in music by creating ragtime, jazz, and blues. At times they were allowed to participate with white people in organized sports like professional boxing, baseball, and college football. More often, they formed their own athletic teams. African Americans refused to allow white supremacy to prevent them from creating a meaningful place for themselves in American Society.

SOCIAL DARWINISM

Pseudo-scientific evidence and academic scholarship bolstered the conviction of many Americans that white people, especially those of English and Germanic descent—Anglo-Saxons—were culturally and racially superior to nonwhites and even other Europeans. Sociologists Herbert Spencer and William Graham Sumner drew on Charles Darwin's theory of evolution and concluded that life in modern industrial societies mirrored life in the animal kingdom. This theory, called Social Darwinism, held that through a process of natural selection, the strong would thrive, prosper, and reproduce while the weak would falter, fail, and die. Life was a struggle; only the fittest survived.

Social Darwinism applied to both individuals and "races." It conveniently justified great disparities in wealth, suggesting that such men as John D. Rockefeller and Andrew Carnegie were rich because they were "fit" whereas many European immigrants and most African Americans were poor and unlikely to succeed because they were "unfit." The same logic explained the strength and prosperity of the United States, Great Britain, and Germany compared to countries like Spain and Italy and conveniently explained why African, Asian, and Latin American societies seemed so backward and primitive. In absorbing this ideology of class and race, many Americans and Europeans came to believe that they had a responsibility—a duty—to introduce the political, economic, and religious benefits and values of Western cultures to the "less advanced" and usually darker peoples of the globe. This presumed responsibility was summed up in the words of the English poet Rudyard Kipling as "the white man's burden."

Social Darwinism increasingly influenced the way most Protestant white Americans perceived their society, leading them to believe that people could be ranked from superior to inferior based on their race, nationality, and ethnicity. Black people were invariably ranked at the bottom of this hierarchy, and the eastern and southern European immigrants who were flooding the country only slightly above them. Black people were capable, so the reasoning went, of no more than a subordinate role in a complex and advanced society as it rushed into the twentieth century. And if their position was biologically ordained, why should society devote substantial resources to their education?

EDUCATION AND SCHOOLS

A black youngster who wanted an education in the late nineteenth century faced formidable obstacles. Most black people were poor farmers who had few opportunities for an education and even fewer prospects for a career in business or one of the professions. It is remarkable—and a testimony to black perseverance—that so many black people did manage to acquire some education and to free themselves from illiteracy (Figure 15–1).

Gaining even a rudimentary education was not easy. Rural schools for black children rarely operated for more than thirty weeks a year. Because of the demands of field work, most black youngsters could not attend school on a regular basis. Brothers and sisters sometimes alternated work and school with each other on a daily basis. Benjamin Mays was nineteen years old before he went to school for more than four months a year—and even then he had to defy his father's demand that he leave school in February to work on the farm.

Schools were often dilapidated shacks. They lacked plumbing, electricity, books, and teaching materials.

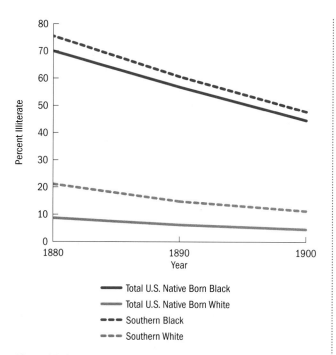

Figure 15-1 Black and White Illiteracy in the United States and the Southern States, 1880–1900. Although more than half of adult black Southerners were still illiterate in 1900, black people had made substantial progress in education during the last two decades of the nineteenth century. This progress is especially remarkable considering the difficulties black youngsters and adults faced in acquiring even an elementary education.

Some schools were in churches and homes. Teachers were poorly paid and often poorly prepared. Septima Clark remembered her first teaching experience on Johns Island on the South Carolina coast in the early twentieth century.

> Here I was, a high-school graduate, eighteen years old, principal in a two-teacher school with 132 pupils ranging from beginners to eighth graders, with no teaching experience, a schoolhouse constructed of boards running up and down, with no slats on the cracks, and a fireplace at one end of the room that cooked the pupils immediately in front of it but allowed those in the rear to shiver and freeze on their uncomfortable, hard, back-breaking benches.

Segregated Schools

Though southern states could not afford to support even one first-rate public school system, each of them operated separate schools for black and white children (see Table 15–1). The South had almost no public black high schools. In 1915 in twenty-three southern

cities with populations of more than 20,000—including Tampa, New Orleans, Charleston, and Charlotte—there was not one black public high school. But these twenty-three cities had thirty-six high schools for white youngsters. In 1897 over the vehement protests of the black community and after a prolonged court fight, white school officials in Augusta, Georgia, closed Ware High School, the black secondary school, and transferred its annual budget of $845 to black primary schools.

Young black people who sought more than a primary education often had to travel to a black college or university that offered a high school program. For example, in 1911, at the age of sixteen, Benjamin Mays boarded a train and traveled one hundred miles to South Carolina State College and enrolled in the seventh grade. He graduated from high school there in 1916 at the age of twenty-two, and then graduated from Maine's Bates College four years later.

In many communities, black people, with the assistance of churches and Northern philanthropists, operated private academies and high schools—like Georgia's Fort Valley High and Industrial School and Camden,

Table 15-1 South Carolina's Black and White Public Schools, 1908–1909		
Black Schools		**White Schools**
2,354	Public Schools	2,712
894	Men Teachers	933
1,802	Women Teachers	3,247
181,095	Total Pupils	153,807
123,481	Average Attendance	107,368
77	Pupils per School	55
63	Pupils per Teacher	35
14.7	Average Number of Weeks of School	25.2
$118.17	Average Yearly Salary for Men Teachers	$479.79
$91.45	Average Yearly Salary for Women Teachers	$249.13
$308,153.16	Total Expenditures	$1,590,732.51

School for most southern black students and teachers was a part-time activity. Because of the demands of agriculture, few rural students, black or white, attended school more than six months a year. Very few teachers were graduates of four-year college programs. The situation was better in urban communities and upper South schools, where the school year lasted longer and education was better financed. But all public schools were segregated in the South.

Source: Department of Education Annual Report, South Carolina, 1908–09, pp. 935, 961.

South Carolina's, Mather Academy—to fill the void created by the lack of public schools. Typically students were charged a modest tuition, and those who attended came from the more prosperous families of the black community. In 1890, the number of black youngsters between the ages of fifteen and nineteen attending black public or private high schools in the South was 3,106. By 1910, that number had risen to 26,553.

The Hampton Model

Some black people and many white people regarded education for black youngsters a pointless exercise. Benjamin Mays's father put little value in education. "My greatest opposition to going away to school was my father. When I knew that I had learned everything that I could in the one-room Brickhouse School and realized how little that was, my father felt that this was sufficient—that it was all I needed. . . . He was convinced that education went to one's head and made him a fool and dishonest." In 1911, South Carolina's governor Coleman Blease was even more blunt: "Instead of making an educated negro, you are ruining a good plow hand and making a half-trained fool."

Many of those who did value schooling were convinced that the most appropriate education for a black child was industrial or domestic training. Black youngsters, these people maintained, should learn skills they could teach others and use to make themselves productive members of the community.

Hampton Normal and Agricultural Institute was founded in 1868 in Virginia and was dominated for decades by Samuel Chapman Armstrong, a white missionary with strong paternalistic inclinations. Hampton trained legions of African Americans and Native Americans to teach skills and to embrace the importance of hard work, diligence, and Christian morality. Armstrong stressed learning trades, such as shoemaking, carpentry, tailoring, and sewing. Hampton placed little emphasis on critical or independent thinking. Students were taught to conform to middle-class values. Armstrong cautioned against black involvement in politics, and he acquiesced in Jim Crow racial practices. The chapel walls at Hampton featured pictures of Robert E. Lee and Andrew Johnson.

Washington and the Tuskegee Model

Armstrong's prize student and Hampton's foremost graduate was Booker T. Washington, who became the nation's leading apostle of industrial training and one of the preeminent leaders and most remarkable men—black or white—in American history. Washington was born a slave in western Virginia (now West Virginia) in 1856. His father was a white man whose identity is unknown. He was raised by his mother, Jane, in an unimpressive but tidy cabin of split logs on a small farm. As a child, he was employed at a salt works and in coal mines. He was also a houseboy for a prominent white family. He attended a local school where he learned to read and write.

Intensely ambitious, Washington set off for Hampton Institute in 1872. While there he was much affected by Armstrong and his curriculum and method of instruction. He worked his way through school and taught for two years at Hampton after graduating. In 1881 he accepted an invitation to found a black college in Alabama—Tuskegee Institute. The result was an institution, which he forged almost single-handedly, that reflected his experience at Hampton and the influence of Armstrong.

From the day he arrived at Tuskegee until his death in 1915, Washington worked tirelessly to persuade black and white people that the surest way for black people to advance was by learning skills and demonstrating a willingness to do manual labor. In a famous speech at the Cotton States Exposition in Atlanta in 1895 (the impact of which is discussed in Chapter 16), Washington told his segregated audience: "No race can prosper till it learns that there is as much dignity in tilling a field as in writing a poem. It is at the bottom of life we must begin, and not at the top." Washington believed that if black people acquired skills and became prosperous small farmers, artisans, and shopkeepers, they would in time earn the respect and acceptance of white Americans and eventually eradicate the race problem—all without unseemly protest and agitation.

Washington's message earned accolades from white political leaders and philanthropists, who were more inclined to support the promotion of trades and skills among black people than an academic and liberal education. Steel magnate Andrew Carnegie—impressed by Washington—financed the construction of twenty-nine buildings on the campuses of black schools and colleges. White railroad executive Roger Baldwin provided millions of dollars for black industrial education, and the John F. Slater Fund poured large sums of money into vocational education. Disciples of Washington and graduates of Tuskegee fanned out across the South as industrial and agricultural educational training for black youngsters proliferated.

Booker T. Washington, looking almost imperial in this portrait, was the most influential black leader in America by 1900. White business and political leaders were reassured by his message that black people themselves were responsible for their economic progress and that people of color should avoid a direct challenge to white supremacy. Although W. E. B. Du Bois appreciated Washington's commitment to the advancement of black people, he believed that more emphasis should be placed on developing an educated elite who would take the lead in solving the race problem. Washington was a Southerner who looked for practical solutions to the problems of everyday life while Du Bois was a Northerner who stressed the need for intellectual advancement.

The Morrill Act, which Congress passed in 1862, entitled each state to the proceeds from the sale of federal land (most of it in the West) for establishing land-grant colleges to provide agricultural and mechanical training. However, southern states did not admit black students to their A&M (Agricultural and Mechanical) schools. A second Morrill Act, however, passed in 1890 that permitted states to establish and fund separate black land-grant colleges. The 1890 act accelerated the development of practical education through the appropriation of federal money to such institutions as Alcorn A&M in Mississippi, Florida A&M, Southern University in Louisiana, South Carolina State University, and Tuskegee Institute. By 1915, there were sixteen black land-grant colleges.

Most of the institutions were not actually colleges. Few of their students graduated with bachelor's degrees, and many of them—like Benjamin Mays—were enrolled in primary and secondary programs. Virtually all the students at the black land-grant schools had to take courses in trades, agriculture, and domestic sciences. Most of the schools required students to do manual labor for which they were paid small sums. Students built and maintained the campuses, and they raised the food served in the school cafeteria. Some of the students were in the "normal" curriculum, which prepared them to teach at a time when most states did not require a college degree for a teaching certificate. Students enrolled in "normal" schools or programs earned a licentiate of instruction that certified them to teach.

Critics of the Tuskegee Model

Not everyone shared Washington's stress on industrial and agricultural training for young black men and women to the near exclusion of the liberal arts, including literature, history, philosophy, and languages. Washington's program, some critics charged, seemed to be designed to train black people for a subordinate role in American society. Black people, they worried, would continue to labor much as they had in slavery, and not far removed from it.

W. E. B. Du Bois, a Fisk- and Harvard-trained scholar, and AME Bishop Henry M. Turner believed that education went beyond mere training and the acquisition of skills. It involved intellectual growth and development. It would confront racial problems. It would create wise men. According to Du Bois, "The function of the Negro college, then, is clear, it must maintain standards of popular education, it must seek the social regeneration of the Negro, and it must help in the solution of problems of race contact and cooperation. And finally, beyond all this, it must develop men."

Many of the private black colleges resisted the emphasis on agricultural and mechanical training. American Missionary Association schools like Fisk, Talladega, and Tougaloo, AME schools like Allen, Paul Quinn, and Morris Brown, and Methodist institutions like Claflin, Bennett, and Rust still promoted the liberal arts and taught Latin, Greek, mathematics, and natural sciences. Henry L. Morehouse of the American Baptist Home Missionary Society explained that the purpose of

VOICES

THOMAS E. MILLER AND THE MISSION OF THE BLACK LAND-GRANT COLLEGE

In 1896 the South Carolina General Assembly established the Colored Normal, Industrial, Agricultural and Mechanical College of South Carolina. It derived funds from the Second Morrill Act of 1890 and from the state itself. Its first president was former black congressman and lawyer, Thomas E. Miller. In an address to the Bamberg County Colored Fair in 1897, Miller embraced the Hampton and Tuskegee models as he described the mission of his institution.

The work of our college is along the industrial line. We are making educated and worthy school teachers, educated and reliable mechanics, educated, reliable and frugal farmers. We teach your sons and daughters how to care for and milk the cows, how to make gilt-edged butter, how to make cheese, what kind of fertilizer each crop needs, the natural strength and productive qualities of the various soils, and last to make a compost heap and how to take care of it. We teach them how to make a wagon, plow and hoe, how to shoe a horse and nurse him when sick. We teach your children how to keep books and typewrite, we teach your girls how to make a dress or undergarment, how to cook, wash and iron. We teach your boys how to make and run an engine, how to make and control electricity, we teach them mechanical and artistic drawing, house and sign painting.

QUESTIONS

1. Given the racial climate of the 1890s, wasn't agricultural and mechanical training the most suitable education for most black youngsters?

2. If a young black person did learn the skills mentioned by Miller, was he or she educated for an inferior place in society?

3. How well prepared for life in the early twentieth century were students trained in these skills?

Source: I. A. Newby, *Black Carolinians, A History of Blacks in South Carolina from 1895 to 1968* (Columbia, 1973), p. 263.

---

education was to develop strong minds. He believed that gifted intellectuals—a "talented tenth" as he characterized them in 1896—could lead people forward. Du Bois likewise stressed the need for the best educated 10 percent of the black population to promote progress and to advance the race.

In fairness to Washington, he did not deny the importance of a liberal arts education, but he also believed that industry was the foundation to progress.

> On such a foundation as this will grow habits of thrift, a love of work, economy, ownership of property, bank accounts. Out of it in the future will grow practical education, professional education, and positions of public responsibility. Out of it will grow moral and religious strength. Out of it will grow wealth from which alone can come leisure and the opportunity for the enjoyment of literature and the fine arts.

Ultimately, however, Washington was wrong to believe that education for black people that focused on economic progress would earn the respect of most white Americans. As Du Bois explained, most white people preferred ignorant and unsuccessful black people to educated and prosperous ones.

> If my own city of Atlanta had offered it to-day the choice between 500 Negro college graduates—forceful, busy, ambitious men of property and self-respect, and 500 black cringing vagrants and criminals, the popular vote in favor of the criminals would be simply overwhelming. Why? Because they want Negro crime? No, not that they fear Negro crime less, but that they fear Negro ambition and success more. They can deal with crime by chain-gang and lynch law, or at least they think they can, but the South can conceive neither machinery nor place for the educated, self-reliant, self-assertive black man.

As the next chapter will discuss, the conflict among black leaders over the most suitable form of education would expand by the early twentieth century into a larger controversy. What began as a disagreement over the value of practical education would become a passionate debate among Washington, Du Bois, and others over the most effective strategy—accommodation or confrontation—for overcoming Jim Crow and white supremacy.

CHURCH AND RELIGION

In a world in which white people otherwise so thoroughly dominated the lives and limited the possibilities of black people, the church had long been the most important institution—after the family—that African Americans controlled for themselves. After the Civil War, black people organized their own churches and religious denominations, which grew and thrived as sources of spiritual comfort and centers of social activity. Black clergymen were often the most influential members of the black community.

In 1890 the South had more black Baptists than all other denominations combined. Baptist congregations were more independent and under less supervision by church hierarchy than other denominations. Bishops, for example, in the African Methodist Episcopal Zion church and the African Methodist Episcopal (AME) church exercised considerable authority over congregations as did Methodist and Presbyterian leaders. Many black people (and many Southern white people as well) preferred the autonomy of the Baptist churches (Figure 15–2).

But whatever the denomination, the church was integral to the lives of most black people. It fulfilled spiritual needs through sermons and music. It gave black people the opportunity, free from white interference, to plan, organize, and lead. It was especially a sanctuary for black women, who immersed themselves in church activities. Though church members usually had little money to spare, they helped the sick, the bereaved, and people displaced by fires and natural disasters. Black congregations also helped thousands of youngsters attend school and college.

The church service itself was the most important aspect of religious life for most black congregations. Parishioners were expected to participate in the service and not merely listen quietly to the minister's sermon. Black people had long considered white church services too sedate. One black school principal believed that black people gave added meaning to Christianity: While "the white man gives it system logic and abstraction, the Negro is necessary to impart feeling, sanctioned emotions, heart throes and ecstasy." In most black churches, members punctuated the minister's call with many an "Amen." They testified, shouted, laughed and cried, and sometimes fainted. Choirs provided joyful music and solemn songs.

Most congregations did not want scholarly sermons or theologically sound addresses. When Frederick Jones, a well-dressed new black minister in North Carolina, offered a deliberate message brimming with rationality, he was met with silence and rebuked by a senior member of the congregation. "Dese fellers comes out heah wid dere starched shirts, and dey' beaver hats, and dere kid gloves, but dey don't know nuffin b[o]ut 'ligion." The next time Jones preached, he had changed his clothes and delivered a passionate sermon.

Many black ministers had little or no education. Benjamin E. Mays's father told him that the clergy did not need an education. "God called men to preach; and when He called them, He would tell them what to say!" Poorly prepared and unqualified clergymen who relied on ungrammatical and rhetorical appeals disturbed some black leaders. In 1890 Booker T. Washington claimed that "three-fourths of the Baptist ministers and two-thirds of the Methodists are unfit, either mentally

Church Affiliation among Southern Black People, 1890

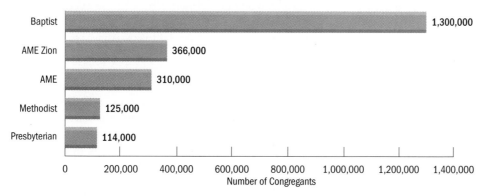

Baptist	1,300,000
AME Zion	366,000
AME	310,000
Methodist	125,000
Presbyterian	114,000

0   200,000   400,000   600,000   800,000   1,000,000   1,200,000   1,400,000
Number of Congregants

Figure 15–2 **Church Affiliation among Southern Black People, 1890.** The vast majority of black Southerners belonged to Baptist, Methodist, and Presbyterian congregations in the late nineteenth century, though there were also very small numbers of black Episcopalians and Roman Catholics.
Source: Edward L. Ayers, *The Promise of the New South*, pp. 160–161.

or morally, or both, to preach the Gospel to any one or to attempt to lead any one." W. E. B. Du Bois wanted black churches free of "the noisy and unclean leaders of the thoughtless mob" and the clergy replaced by thoughtful "apostles of service and sacrifice." But a black Alabama farmer observed that solemn and erudite preachers would not survive. "You let a man preach de true Gospel and he won't git many nickels in his pocket; but if he hollers and jumps he gits all the nickels he can hold and chickens besides."

Though infrequently, black women sometimes led congregations. Nannie Helen Burroughs established Women's Day in Baptist churches. Women delivered sermons and guided the parishioners. But Burroughs complained that Women's Day quickly became more an occasion to raise money than to raise women.

The Church as Solace and Escape

For many black people, the emotional involvement and enthusiastic participation in church services was an escape from their dreary and oppressive daily lives. Growing up in rural Greenwood County, South Carolina, Benjamin E. Mays admitted that his Baptist preacher, James F. Marshall, who barely had a fifth-grade education, "emphasized the joys of heaven and the damnation of hell" and that the "trials and tribulations of the world would all be over when one got to heaven." But Mays understood the need for such messages to assuage the impact of white supremacy. "Beaten down at every turn by the white man, as they were, Negroes could perhaps not have survived without this kind of religion."

Black clergymen like Marshall refused to challenge white supremacy. Even veiled comments might invite retaliation or even lynching. When a visiting minister began to criticize white people to Marshall's congregation, Marshall immediately stopped him. Despite the reluctance of many black clergymen to advocate improvement in race relations, many white people still viewed black religious gatherings as a threat. Black churches were burned and black ministers assaulted and killed with tragic regularity in the late-nineteenth-century South.

Black clergymen, like their white counterparts, often stressed middle-class values to their congregations while suggesting that many black people found themselves in shameful situations because of their sinful ways. They urged them to improve their behavior. The black clergyman at Mount Ever Rest Colored Church in rural Mississippi warned his congregation to quit their "cussin; lyin; stealin; crap shootin; whisky drinkin, and backbiting one another to de white folks." Black

people who had acquired sinful reputations sometimes received funeral sermons that consigned them to eternal damnation in a fiery hell. As Benjamin Mays recalled, "The church was usually full at funerals, especially if the deceased had been well known; and when a man of bad reputation died the church was jammed."

Not all black religious leaders avoided discussing white supremacy. Some clergymen insisted that black people demand their rights. AME Bishop Henry M. Turner persistently spoke out on racial matters. In 1883 after the U.S. Supreme Court declared the 1875 Civil Rights Act unconstitutional, Turner called the Constitution "a dirty rag, a cheat, a libel and ought to be spit upon by every Negro in the land."

The Holiness Movement and the Pentecostal Church

Not all black people belonged to mainline denominations. The Holiness movement and the emergence of Pentecostal churches affected Methodist and Baptist congregations. Partly in reaction to the elite domination and stiff authority of white Methodism, the Holiness movement gained a foothold among white people and then spilled over among black Southerners. Holiness churches ordained women such as Neely Terry to lead them. Holiness clergy preached that sanctification allowed a Christian to receive a "second blessing" and to feel the "perfect love of Christ." Believers thus achieved an emotional reaffirmation and a new state of grace.

The Church of God in Christ became the leading black Holiness church, and it went beyond other Holiness denominations by offering a "third blessing" and complete sanctification. It was led by two former black Baptists—Charles Henry Mason and C. P. Jones—who held a series of successful revival meetings in Memphis and Mississippi. They had the church legally chartered and even ordained several white ministers. They also had a women's department led by Lizzie Woods Roberson. Some of the appeal of the church lay in the music—including ragtime, blues, and jazz—that was often part of its services.

First organized by a dynamic white minister, Charles Fox Parham, the Pentecostal church evolved in the early twentieth century in the Houston-Galveston area of Texas. William J. Seymour, who was born a slave in Louisiana, played a key role in the development of the church. After hearing black people speak in tongues in Houston, he went to Los Angeles where he and others also began to speak in tongues. There he founded the

HENRY MCNEAL TURNER

Henry McNeal Turner began as a supporter of racial harmony and a U.S. patriot. As he aged, however, he became steadily more disenchanted with the way white Americans contradicted their professed dedication to the principles of fairness and justice by their treatment of black Americans.

Turner was born to free black parents in Newberry, South Carolina, in 1834. After his father's death, he worked in cotton fields and learned to be a blacksmith and a carriage maker. He also learned to read and write while working for a white lawyer. Drawn to religion, he was licensed to preach by the Methodist Episcopal church, a white denomination. In 1859 he moved to Baltimore and was ordained in the AME church. He then became pastor of Union Bethel Church, the largest black congregation in Washington, D.C. During the Civil War, he served as a chaplain with the First Regiment of U.S. Colored Troops.

After the war, he briefly worked for the Freedmen's Bureau in Georgia. In an Emancipation Day address in Savannah in 1866 he praised the American flag and predicted that white people would soon accept black people.

Turner became active in Republican politics and was elected to the 1867–68 Georgia constitutional convention where he was the only black delegate to favor a literacy requirement for voting. He also supported a measure to help white planters who had not paid their taxes to keep their land. He conceded that "no man in Georgia has been more conservative than I. Anything to please white folks has been my motto."

In 1868 Turner was elected to the Georgia House of Representatives. When white legislators voted to remove the thirty-two black representatives, he objected: "I shall neither fawn nor cringe before any party, nor stoop to *beg* for my rights. . . . I am here to demand my rights, and to hurl thunderbolts at the men who dare to cross the threshold of my manhood." The black lawmakers were reinstated.

In 1880 he was elected one of the twelve bishops in the AME church and became president of Morris Brown College in Atlanta, where he served until 1900.

He also became an advocate of emigration to Africa and supported the Liberian Exodus of 1877. Turner supported women's suffrage and ordained a woman as a deacon in the AME church in 1888, but the AME Council of Bishops withdrew the appointment.

Turner had little tolerance for those who considered Christianity a white man's religion. He asserted that "God is a Negro" and attacked those who "believe God is a white-skinned, blue-eyed, projecting-nosed, compressed-lipped, and finely-robed *white* gentleman.

He helped establish and edited a monthly AME newspaper, the *Voice of Missions.* In its pages he took a progressively black nationalist stance and criticized white supremacy and lynching. Growing older and angrier, he told black readers of the *Voice of Missions* to get guns and attack white predators. "Let every Negro in this country who has a spark of manhood in him supply his house with one, two, or three guns . . . and when your domicile is invaded . . . turn loose your missiles of death and blow the fiendish wretches into a thousand giblets."

He denounced black soldiers who fought to suppress the Philippine Insurrection. "I boil over with disgust when I remember that colored men from this country . . . are there fighting to subjugate a people of their own color. . . . I can scarcely keep from saying that I hope the Filipinos will wipe such soldiers from the face of the earth. . . . To go down there and shoot innocent men and take the country away from them, is too much for me to think about.

Embittered and tired, Turner lost faith in the intentions of white people and no longer praised the flag. "I used to love what I thought was the grand old flag, and sing with ecstasy about the Stars and Stripes, but to the Negro in this country the American flag is a dirty and contemptible rag. . . . Without multiplying words, I wish to say that hell is an improvement on the United States where the Negro is concerned."

Bishop Henry McNeal Turner died of a heart attack in 1915. He was married four times, outliving three wives and all but two of his children.

highly evangelistic church that became the Pentecostal church. It attracted enormous interest and grew quickly. Charles Henry Mason and C. P. Jones joined the Pentecostal movement, thereby making the Church of God in Christ the leading Pentecostal denomination. It soon spread across the South among both black and white people. Though there were tensions between black and white believers, the Pentecostal church was the only movement of any significance that crossed the racial divide in early twentieth-century America.

RED VERSUS BLACK: THE BUFFALO SOLDIERS

After the Civil War, the U.S. Army was reduced to fewer than 30,000 troops. Congressional Democrats tried to eliminate black soldiers and their regiments from this reduced force. But radical Republicans, led by Massachusetts Senator Henry Wilson, prevailed to keep the military open to black men. The Army Reorganization Act of 1869 maintained four all-black regiments:

the Ninth and Tenth Cavalry Regiments and the Twenty-fourth and Twenty-fifth Infantry Regiments. These four regiments spent most of the next three decades on the western frontier fighting the Plains Indians. Nearly 12,500 black men served during the late nineteenth century in these segregated units commanded—as black troops had been during the Civil War—by white officers.

Military service in the West was wretched for white troops and invariably worse for black soldiers. Many white officers considered black troops lazy, undisciplined, and cowardly. Black regiments were assigned mainly to the New Mexico and Arizona territories and to Texas because the Army thought that black people tolerated heat better than white people. The ancestors of the slaves were "from the tropics," claimed Army Quartermaster General Montgomery C. Meigs, and "not from the Northern or Southern extremities of Africa but from the Torrid Zone almost entirely." Most black soldiers were thus compelled to endure the hot, dry, and dusty Southwest desert. Still some black troops were sent to Kansas, Colorado, and the Dakotas where

Men of the 25th Infantry—one of the four black regiments formed after the Civil War—pose for a photograph at Fort Snelling, Minnesota. Though life on the frontier was anything but glamorous, many black men found service in the U.S. Army offered a better opportunity to demonstrate their pride and manhood than civilian society.

they confronted instead howling blizzards, subzero temperatures, and frostbite.

Discrimination in the Army

Black troops faced more than adverse weather. The Army routinely provided them inferior food and inadequate housing. While white soldiers received dried apples and peaches, canned tomatoes, onions, and potatoes, black troops were given foul beef, bad bread, and canned peas unfit for human consumption. In 1867 white troops at Fort Leavenworth in Kansas lived in barracks while black troops were forced to sleep in tents on wet ground. Black regiments were allotted used weapons and equipment. The Army sent its worst horses—often old and lame—to the black cavalry.

Long stretches of boredom, tedious duty, and loneliness marked army life for black and white men in the West. Weeks and months might pass without combat. Commanders constantly had to deal with desertion and alcoholism. Black soldiers were much less likely to desert or turn to drink than were white troops. For example, in 1877, eighteen men deserted from the all-black Tenth Regiment while 184 white soldiers deserted from the all-white Fourth Regiment. Black troops realized that while army life could be harsh and dangerous, it compared favorably to the civilian world, which held few genuine opportunities for them. Army food was poor, but the private's pay of $13 per month was regular. Moreover, black troops developed immense pride in themselves as professional soldiers.

The Plains Indians who fiercely resisted U.S. forces were so impressed with the performance of their black adversaries that they called them "buffalo soldiers." Indians associated the hair of black men with the shaggy coat of the buffalo—a sacred animal. Black troops considered it a term of respect and began to use it themselves. The Tenth Cavalry displayed a buffalo in their unit emblem.

The Buffalo Soldiers in Combat

It was ironic that white military authorities would employ black men to subdue red people. Most black soldiers, however, had no qualms about fighting Indians, protecting white settlers, or apprehending bandits and cattle rustlers. From the late 1860s to the early 1890s, the four black regiments repeatedly engaged hostile Indians.

In September 1867, 700 Cheyenne attacked fifty U.S. Army scouts along a dry riverbed in eastern Col-orado. The scouts held out for over a week until the Tenth Cavalry rescued them. For more than twelve months in 1879 and 1880, the Ninth and Tenth Cavalry fought the Apaches under Chief Victorio in New Mexico and Texas in a campaign of raid and counterraid. The Apaches slipped across the Mexican border and then returned to southwest Texas. In clashes at Rattlesnake Springs and near Fresno Spring, the Tenth killed more than thirty Apaches before Victorio fled again to Mexico where he was killed by the Mexican army. But the Ninth and Tenth Cavalry deserve most of the credit for Victorio's defeat with their dogged pursuit of the Apaches for months over hundreds of miles of rugged terrain.

In late 1890, military units including the Ninth Cavalry were sent to the Pine Ridge Reservation in South Dakota where Sioux Indians were holding an intense religious ceremony known as the Ghost Dance. Confined to reservations, some Indians—out of desperation and yearning for the past—believed that their fervent participation in the Ghost Dance would bring both their ancestors and the almost extinct buffalo back to the Great Plains. Then white people would vanish, and Indian life would be restored to what it had been decades earlier. But white authorities considered the Ghost Dance a dangerous symbol of defiance.

On December 29, the Seventh Cavalry attempted to disarm a band of Sioux at Wounded Knee on the Pine Ridge Reservation. Shooting erupted, and 146 Indian men, women, and children, and twenty-six soldiers were killed. The Ninth Cavalry, 108 miles away in the Badlands, rode the next day through a blizzard and arrived tired and freezing to come to the aid of elements of the Seventh Cavalry.

Civilian Hostility to Black Soldiers

Despite the gallant performance of the buffalo soldiers, civilians frequently treated them with hostility. In southern Texas in 1875, Mexicans ambushed five black soldiers, killed two of them, and mutilated their bodies. The next day the infuriated white commander of the Ninth Cavalry, Colonel Edward Hatch, rode out with sixty soldiers and apprehended the Mexicans. A local grand jury indicted nine of them for murder, but the only one tried was acquitted, and the other eight were released without a trial. Hatch, another white officer, and three buffalo soldiers were then indicted for breaking into and burglarizing the shack where the Mexicans had sought refuge. The charges were eventually dropped, but the five men had to hire their own lawyers.

A black cowboy in Idaho. Cowboys were skilled agricultural laborers who spent days and nights tending and driving thousands of head of cattle to market. It was mostly boring work in a hot, dry, and lonely environment. But many black, white, and Mexican men found the independent and outdoor life appealing. As many as 5000 of the several thousand men who rode herd on cattle in the 1870s and 1880s were black men who had been slaves or served in the cavalry with the U.S. Army.

Brownsville

One of the worst examples of hostility to black troops, the so-called Brownsville Affair, also occurred in Texas. In 1906 the First Battalion of the Twenty-fifth Infantry was transferred from Fort Niobrara, Nebraska, to Fort Brown in Brownsville, Texas, along the Rio Grande. The black soldiers immediately encountered discrimination from both white people and Mexicans in this border community. They were not permitted in public parks, and white businesses refused to serve them. Several times civilians provoked and attacked individual black soldiers.

Shortly after midnight on August 14, shooting erupted in Brownsville. About 150 shots were fired, and a policeman and a resident were injured. Black troops were blamed for the violence when clips and cartridges from the Army's Springfield rifles were found in the street. Two military investigations concluded that black soldiers did the shooting. The Army could not identify the specific soldiers responsible because no one would confess or name the alleged perpetrators.

With no hearing or trial, President Theodore Roosevelt dismissed three companies of black men—167 soldiers—from the Army. They were barred from rejoining the military and from government employment, and were denied veterans' pensions or benefits. The black community, which had supported Roosevelt, reacted angrily. Booker T. Washington, a Roosevelt supporter, privately wrote, "There is no law, human or divine, which justifies the punishment of an innocent man." Washington added, "I have the strongest faith in the President's honesty of intention, high mindedness of purpose, sincere unselfishness and courage, but I regret for all these reasons all the more that this thing has occurred."

Republican Senator James B. Foraker of Ohio later led a Senate investigation that upheld Roosevelt's dismissals. But Foraker, a strong opponent of Roosevelt, questioned the guilt of the black men. The clips and cartridges that served as evidence were apparently planted. After Roosevelt left office in 1909, the War Department reinstated fourteen of the soldiers. In 1972, the Justice Department determined that an injustice had occurred. The black soldiers were posthumously awarded honorable discharges. The only survivor of the Brownsville affair—Dorsie Willis—received $25,000 from Congress and the right to treatment at veteran's facilities.

AFRICAN AMERICANS IN THE NAVY

Naval service was even more unappealing than life in the Army. In the late nineteenth century, as the Navy made the transition from timber and sail to steam and steel, approximately one sailor in ten was a black man. Although the Navy's ships were "integrated," in that black and white sailors served on them together, white sailors were hostile to black sailors. They would not eat or bunk with them or take orders from them. Increasingly, and to enforce a de facto shipboard segregation, black sailors were restricted to stoking boilers in the bowels of naval vessels and to cooking and serving food to white sailors.

Although several black men enrolled as midshipmen at the Naval Academy in the 1870s, they faced social ostracism and none of them graduated. Not until 1949 did a black man graduate from the academy.

THE SPANISH-AMERICAN WAR

With the western frontier subdued by 1890, many Americans concluded that the United States should expand overseas. European nations had already carved out extensive colonies in Africa and Asia. Many—but by no means all—Americans favored the extension of U.S. political, economic, and military authority to Latin America and the Pacific. In 1893 the U.S. Navy and American businessmen toppled the monarchy in Hawaii, and the United States annexed that chain of islands in 1898.

The same year, the United States went to war to liberate Cuba from Spanish control. As in the Civil War, black men enlisted, fought, and died. Twenty-two black sailors were among the 266 men who died when the battleship U.S.S. *Maine* blew up in Havana harbor, the event that helped trigger the war. Many black Americans were convinced—as they had been in previous wars—that the willingness of black people to support the war against Spain would impress white Americans sufficiently to reduce or even eliminate white hostility. E. E. Cooper, editor of the Washington *Colored American*, declared that the war would bring black people and white people together in "an era of good feeling the country over and cement the races into a more compact brotherhood through perfect unity of purpose and patriotic affinity." The war, he asserted, would help white Americans "unloose themselves from the bondage of race prejudice."

Many black and white Americans, however, questioned the American cause. Some black people saw the war as an effort to extend American influence and racial practices—including Jim Crow— beyond U.S. borders. The Reverend George W. Prioleau, chaplain of the Ninth Cavalry, wondered why black Americans supported what he considered a hypocritical war.

> Talk about fighting and freeing poor Cuba and of Spain's brutality. . . . Is America any better than Spain? Has she not subjects in her very midst who are murdered daily without a trial of judge or jury? Has she not subjects in her own borders whose children are half-fed and half-clothed, because their father's skin is black. . . . Yet the Negro is loyal to his country's flag.

Whether they harbored doubts or not, black men by the thousands served in the Spanish-American War and in the Philippine Insurrection that followed it. Shortly before war was declared, the Army ordered its four black regiments of regular troops transferred from their western posts to Florida to prepare for combat in Cuba. President William McKinley also appealed for volunteers. The War Department designated four of the black volunteer units "immune regiments" because it believed that black men would tolerate the heat and humidity of Cuba better than white troops and that black people were immune or at least less susceptible to yellow fever, which was endemic to Cuba. (Yellow fever was carried by mosquitoes, but this was unknown in 1898. Most people believed that the disease was caused by the tropical Caribbean climate.)

State militia (national guard) units were also called into federal service, and several states including Alabama, Ohio, Massachusetts, Illinois, Kansas, Virginia, Indiana, and North Carolina sent all-black militias as well as white units. But Georgia's governor refused to permit that state's black militia to serve, and New York would not permit black men to enlist in its militia. The states typically followed the federal example and kept black men confined to all-black units commanded by white officers, but there were exceptions.

Black Officers

The buffalo soldiers of the Ninth and Tenth Cavalry and the Twenty-fourth and Twenty-fifth Infantry remained under the leadership of white officers. But the men of several volunteer units insisted that they be led by black officers: "No officers, no fight." So for the first time in American military history, black men commanded all-black units: the Eighth Illinois, the Twenty-third Kansas, and the Third North Carolina. Mindful that many people doubted the ability of black men to lead, the colonel of the Eighth Illinois cautioned his men, "If we fail, the whole race will have to shoulder the burden." The War Department also permitted black men to serve as lieutenants with other black volunteer units, but all higher ranking officers were white men. Charles Young, a black graduate of West Point who was serving as a military science instructor at Wilberforce University in Ohio, was given command of Ohio's Ninth Battalion, and he served with distinction and was promoted from captain to colonel.

As black and white troops assembled in Georgia and Florida before departing for Cuba, black men soon realized that a U.S. uniform did not lessen white racial prejudice. White civilians in Georgia killed four black men of the Third North Carolina. All-white juries acquitted those who were charged with the murders. After the white proprietor of a drug store in Lakeland, Florida, refused to serve a black soldier at the soda fountain, a mob of black troops gathered. The proprietor was pistol whipped, and another white man was killed by a stray bullet before the troops were disarmed. In Tampa, where the troops were embarking for Cuba, a bloody all-night riot broke out after drunken white soldiers from Ohio decided to shoot at a black child for target practice. Twenty-seven black soldiers and three white soldiers were seriously injured. It is not surprising that when the men of the all-black Third Alabama adopted an injured crow as the unit mascot, they named it Jim.

Most of the black units never saw combat. White military authorities considered black men unreliable and inadequately trained for combat. Black volunteer units stayed behind in Florida when white units embarked for Cuba. However, the four regiments of regular black troops, the buffalo soldiers, did go to Cuba where they performed well despite the doubts and persistent criticism of some white men. The Spanish troops were impressed enough to give the black men the nickname "smoked yankees."

A Splendid Little War

In the summer of 1898, U.S. troops arrived in Cuba. Black men of the Tenth Cavalry fought alongside Cuban rebels, many of whom were themselves black. Four black American privates earned the Congressional Medal of Honor for their part in an engagement in southwestern Cuba. Black and white troops were best

remembered for their role in the assault on San Juan and Kettle Hills overlooking the key Cuban port of Santiago in eastern Cuba. Santiago was the main Spanish naval base in Cuba and its capture would break Spain's hold over the island.

In this assault, black soldiers from the Twenty-fourth Infantry and the Ninth and the Tenth Cavalry regiments fought alongside white troops including Theodore Roosevelt's volunteer unit, the Rough Riders. In the fiercest fighting of the war and amid considerable confusion, black and white men were thrown together as they encountered withering Spanish fire. Though for a time the outcome was in doubt, they took the high ground overlooking Santiago harbor. White soldiers praised the performance of the black troops. One commented: "I am not a negro lover. My father fought with Mosby's Rangers [in the Confederate Army] and I was born in the South, but the negroes saved that fight." In his campaign for vice president in 1900, Theodore Roosevelt stated that black men saved his life during the battle. Later, however, Roosevelt reversed himself and accused several black men of cowardice.

After the War

As hostilities concluded, men of the Twenty-fourth Infantry agreed to work in yellow fever hospitals after white regiments refused the duty. About half the black soldiers—some 471 men—contracted yellow fever. Other black troops arrived in Cuba after the war to serve garrison duty. The Eighth Illinois and the Twenty-Third Kansas built roads, bridges, schools, and hospitals. The black men were especially pleased at the lack of discrimination and absence of Jim Crow in Cuba. Some black soldiers discussed the possibility of organizing emigration to Cuba, but nothing came of it. Still other black troops from the Sixth Massachusetts joined in the invasion of Puerto Rico as the United States took that island from Spain.

THE PHILIPPINE INSURRECTION

With the resounding victory in the Spanish-American War, many Americans decided that their nation had an obligation to uplift those less fortunate peoples who had been part of the Spanish Empire. Thus President William McKinley and American diplomats insisted that the United States acquire Guam, Puerto Rico, and the Philippines from Spain in the Treaty of Paris that ended the war in December 1898. The Filipinos—like the Cubans—had long opposed Spanish rule and fully

V O I C E S

BLACK MEN IN BATTLE IN CUBA

On October 1, 1898, a letter appeared in the Illinois Record, *a black newspaper, from one of the men in the Tenth Cavalry. The author was probably John E. Lewis, and he wrote the letter from Montauk Point on the eastern tip of Long Island in New York where black and white troops were sent after the war. Lewis described the enthusiastic reaction of the Rough Riders to the Ninth and Tenth Cavalry, but complained that the contributions of the black soldiers were too often overlooked and ignored.*

The Rough Riders were mustered out on the 12th and 13th [of September], and when Colonel Roosevelt bade the regiment good-bye he paid a glowing tribute to the 9th and 10th Cavalry, especially in saving them from ambush.

Mr. Editor, if your readers could have heard the Rough Riders yell when the 10th Cav. was mentioned as the 'Smoked Yankees' and that they were of a good breed, they would have been doubly proud of the members of their race who rendered such signal service on the battle field. . . .

When a troop of the 10th made their famous charge of 3,000 yards under the command of Capt. [William J.] Beck, the non-commissioned officers, all colored, distinguished themselves in a manner that will redound to the glory of the race. Among those who distinguished themselves are Carter Smith, acting 1st Sergeant, Sgts. Geo. Taylor, James F. Cole, James H. Williams, Smith Johnson and Corpl. Joseph G. Mitchell who was wounded at San Juan.

All are soldiers whose names should go down in history. They never faltered in the thickest of the battle; they encouraged on in a rain of shot and shell and showed by their actions that they were the leaders. They did not hesitate to take the lead, and when that charge was made it was "save your cartridges, don't waste a shot."

The half will never be told of their deeds upon the battlefield. All deserve praise from the private up, but the praise has been given those who should have been in the lead instead of laying in the rear under cover. And yet they say that the black is not fit to lead.

If our war reports would only give credit where credit is due there would be no need writing these poorly composed lines that your readers might know of the deeds and hardships their dear ones have passed through.

You will read that colored troops, or companies did so and so, but the white papers never mention a name and the world only knows one who has done an act of bravery as a Negro soldier, nameless and friendless. It was never mentioned how, at that famous charge of the 10th Cav. And the rescue of the Rough Riders at San Juan Hill, the yell was started by a single trooper of C Troop, 10th Cav. and was carried down the line.

Brave 1st Sgt. Adam Huston at the head of his troop commanded "forward" which seemed into almost certain death. In him the troop found an able leader; Lieut. [E.D.] Anderson who was in command and fell to the rear and when the command "Forward March," was given, the brave Major [Theodore J.] Wint only smiled, for he admired bravery and did not change the command although he knew that the troops was in a desperate position. The troops were carried safely through. . . .

Will it ever be known how Sgt. Thomas Griffith of Troop C cut the wire fence along the line so that the 10th Cav. and Rough Riders could go through?

Never once did these brave men give thought to danger. . . .

The Spaniard would have sent our army home in disgrace had it not been for the daring and almost reckless charge of the Negro regiments. God was with them in that charge and no man who has ever seen the place will say that it was possible to make the charge without being slaughtered. . . .

[Unsigned]

QUESTIONS

1. What is the source of the bitterness revealed in this letter?

2. What motivated black men to risk their lives in combat in the Spanish-American War?

3. Do any portions of this account seem strained, exaggerated, or unreliable? Why or why not?

Source: Willard B. Gatewood, Jr., *Smoked Yankees and the Struggle for Empire: Letters from Negro Soldiers, 1898–1902,* pp. 76–78.

expected the American government to support their independence. Instead, they were infuriated to learn that the United States intended to annex the Philippines. The Filipinos, under Emilio Aguinaldo, switched from fighting the Spanish to fighting the occupying U.S. forces.

Would Black Men Fight Brown Men?

Many black and white Americans denounced the U.S. effort to take the Philippines. They were unconvinced that the Filipinos would benefit from American benevolence. AME Bishop Henry Turner termed it an "unholy war of conquest," and Booker T. Washington believed that the Filipinos "should be given an opportunity to govern themselves." In a grim but humorous attempt to taunt those who proclaimed the superiority of white civilization, a group of black men formed the "Black Man's Burden Association."

Opposition to U.S. involvement in the Philippines notwithstanding, black men in the military served throughout the campaign in the Pacific islands. The black troops included the regular Twenty-fifth Infantry and Twenty-fourth Infantry, the Ninth Cavalry, and the Forty-eighth and Forty-ninth volunteer regiments. Through propaganda, the Filipino rebels attempted to convince black troops to abandon the cause. Posters reminded "The Colored American Soldier" of injustice and lynching in the United States. White troops did not help by calling Filipinos "niggers." Though many black soldiers had reservations about the fighting, they remained loyal. By the time the conflict ended with an American victory in 1902, only five black men had deserted. David Fagen of the Twenty-fourth Infantry joined Filipino forces and became an officer, fighting American troops for two years before he was killed. Two black men from the Ninth Cavalry were executed for desertion while fifteen white soldiers who deserted had their death sentences commuted.

Though black men had served with distinction as professional soldiers for forty years after the Civil War—on the frontier, in Cuba, and in the Philippines—the Army little valued their achievements and sacrifice, as the Brownsville Affair showed. White military and political leaders persistently relied on passions and prejudices over evidence of achievement. Time and again, these circumstances dashed the hopes of those black civilians and soldiers who believed that the performance of black troops would challenge white supremacy and demonstrate that black citizens had earned the same rights and opportunities as other Americans.

BLACK BUSINESSPEOPLE AND ENTREPRENEURS

Well-educated black men and women stood no chance of gaining employment with any major business or industrial corporation at the turn of the century. White males not only monopolized management and supervisory positions; they also occupied nearly every job that did not involve manual labor. In 1899 black novelist Sutton E. Griggs described the frustrations that an educated black man encountered.

> He possessed a first class college education, but that was all. He knew no trade nor was he equipped to enter any of the professions. . . . He would have made an excellent drummer, salesman, clerk, cashier, government official (county, city, state, or national), telegraph operator, conductor, or anything of such a nature. But the color of his skin shut the doors so tight that he could not even peep in. . . . It is true that such positions as street laborer, hod carrier, cart driver, factory hand, railroad hand were open to him; but such menial tasks were uncongenial to a man of his education and polish.

While white supremacy and the proliferation of Jim Crow severely restricted opportunities for educated black people, those same limitations enabled enterprising black men and women to open and operate businesses that served black clientele. By the early twentieth century, black Americans not only had their own churches and schools but they had also established banks, newspapers, insurance companies, retail businesses, barbershops, beauty salons, and funeral parlors. Virtually every black community had its own small businesses, markets, street vendors, and other entrepreneurs.

Some black men and women established thriving and substantial businesses. In Atlanta, Union Army veteran Alexander Hamilton was a successful building contractor. He supervised construction of the Good Samaritan Building, oversaw the erection of buildings on the Morris Brown College campus, and built many of the impressive houses on Peachtree Street. Hamilton employed both black and white workmen on his projects.

Alonzo Herndon was a former slave who also achieved financial success in Atlanta. He operated a fashionable barbershop on Peachtree Street that served well-to-do white men. The shop had crystal chandeliers and polished brass spittoons. Herndon expanded and opened two other shops, eventually employing seventy-five men. He also founded the Atlanta Life Insurance Company, the largest black stock company in the world.

In Montgomery, Alabama, H. A. Loveless, a former slave, became a butcher and then diversified his business

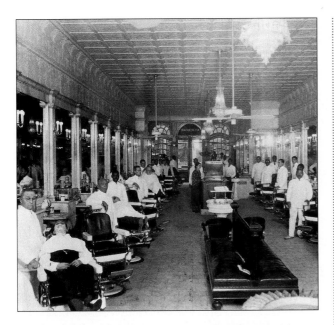

Alonzo Herndon's palatial barbershop on Peachtree Street in Atlanta was unlike most black owned businesses in that its customers were exclusively white men. The shop served as many as twenty-five clients with its ceiling fans, crystal chandeliers, marble floors, and leather benches.

operations by opening an undertaking establishment and operating a hack and dray company. By 1900, Loveless also ran a coal and wood yard and sold real estate. In Richmond, Virginia, Maggie Lena Walker—the secretary-treasurer of the Independent Order of St. Luke, a mutual benefit society, and a founder of the St. Luke's Penny Savings Bank—became the wealthiest black woman in America. Also in Richmond, former slave John Dabney owned an exclusive catering business that served wealthy white Virginians. He catered two state dinners for President Grover Cleveland. He used his earnings to purchase several houses and to invest in real estate.

Madam C. J. Walker may have been the most successful black entrepreneur of them all. Born Sarah Breedlove in 1867 on a Louisiana cotton plantation, she married at age fourteen and was a widowed single parent by age twenty. She spent the next two decades struggling to make ends meet. In 1905 with $1.50, she developed a formula to nourish and enrich the hair of black women. She insisted that it was not a process to straighten hair.

She sold the product door-to-door in Denver but could not keep up with the demand. The business rapidly expanded and became a thriving enterprise that employed hundreds of black women. She established the company's headquarters in Indianapolis. In the meantime, she married Charles Joseph Walker and took his name and the title Madam. As she accumulated wealth, she shared it generously with Bethune Cookman College, Tuskegee Institute, and the NAACP. She was a major contributor to the NAACP's antilynching campaign. When she died of a stroke at age fifty-one in 1915 she was reportedly a millionaire.

Despite such successes, most black people who went into business had difficulty surviving, and many failed. Too often they depended on black customers who were themselves poor. White-owned banks were unlikely to provide credit to aspiring black businesspeople. And even the wealthiest black entrepreneurs did not come close to possessing the wealth the richest white Americans accumulated.

AFRICAN AMERICANS AND LABOR

Thousands of black Southerners worked in factories, mills, and mines. Though most textile mills refused to hire black people except for janitorial duties, many black laborers toiled in tobacco and cigar-making facilities, flour mills, coal mines, sawmills, turpentine camps, and on railroads. Black women worked for white families as cooks, maids, and laundresses. Black workers usually were paid less than white men employed in the same capacity. Conversely, white working people frequently complained that they were not hired because employers retained black workers who worked for less pay. In 1904 in Georgia white railroad firemen went on strike in an unsuccessful attempt to compel railroad operators to dismiss black firemen. Invariably, there was persistent antagonism between black and white laborers.

Unions

When white workers formed labor unions in the late nineteenth century, they usually excluded black workers. The Knights of Labor, however, founded in 1869, was open to all workers (except whiskey salesmen, lawyers, and bankers), and by the mid-1880s counted 50,000 women and 70,000 black workers among its nearly 750,000 members. But by the 1890s, after unsuccessful strikes and a deadly riot in Chicago, the Knights had lost influence to a new organization, the American Federation of Labor (AFL). Founded in 1886, the AFL was ostensibly open to all skilled workers, but most of its local craft unions barred women and black tradesmen. In contrast, the United Mine Workers (UMW),

MAGGIE LENA WALKER

By the early twentieth century, Maggie Lena Walker was a successful businesswoman, community leader, and one of the wealthiest black women in America. She was also an ardent advocate for her race and her gender. She was born Maggie Mitchell in Richmond, Virginia, on July 15, 1867 to Elizabeth Draper, a laundress. Her mother married William Mitchell in 1870. Young Maggie was much influenced by the determination, fortitude, and hard work of her mother. Throughout her childhood, she helped her mother wash, iron, and carry laundry.

Maggie Mitchell graduated from a normal school in 1883 and taught primary school. She was active in the First African Baptist Church and remained a committed member for life. In 1886 she married Armstead Walker. Her views on marriage were progressive. Explaining the responsibilities that she shared with her husband, she wrote: "Since marriage is an equal partnership, I believe that the woman and the man are equal in power and should by consultation and agreement, mutually decide as to the conduct of the home and the government of the children."

The Independent Order of St. Luke was one of many black mutual aid societies that flourished in the nineteenth century. Black people contributed small sums of money and, in the event of sickness or death, the society paid benefits to members or their survivors. But the Order was also a fraternal and social organization that stressed racial pride as well as compassion, generosity, and charity.

Maggie Lena Walker became active in the order at the age of fourteen in 1881. She was elected Grand Matron and became the Right Worthy Grand Secretary in 1899. When she assumed her duties, the Order had $31.61 in funds and 1,080 members. She proved to be a dynamic leader and an inspirational speaker. She traveled extensively and spoke regularly to members. She stressed racial concerns and attacked discrimination and lynching. She appealed to audiences to patronize black enterprises. By the early twentieth century under Walker's guidance, the order operated in twenty-two states. Its membership had increased, and its financial standing had improved. In 1924 the Independent Order of St. Luke had funds totaling $3,480,540.

The Order ran a newspaper, the *St. Luke Herald*, and a bank with Maggie Lena Walker as president. She was the first black woman to serve as the chief executive of a bank in the United States. The bank subsequently merged with two other banks and became the Consolidated Bank and Trust Company with Walker as president. She was especially pleased that the bank enabled black customers to purchase homes. By 1920, 645 black families had acquired their houses with the financial assistance of the bank.

Walker was deeply concerned with the plight of black women, and she made certain that the Order employed black women in significant positions. In 1909 she paid homage to women of color.

> And the great all absorbing interest, this thing which has driven sleep from my eyes and fatigue from my body, is the love I bear women, our Negro women, hemmed, circumscribed, with every imaginable obstacle in our way, blocked and held down by the fears and prejudices of the whites, ridiculed and sneered at by the intelligent blacks.

Maggie Lena Walker became a wealthy woman and lived in a twenty-two-room house. She was deeply involved in community affairs and organizations. She supported Virginia Union University, which later awarded her an honorary degree, and the Industrial School for Colored Girls. She worked with the Piedmont Tuberculosis Sanitarium for Negroes. She served on Richmond's Council for Colored Women and with the Virginia Federation of Colored Women's Clubs, and she was among the prominent women who helped organize the Council of Women of the Darker Races. She joined the National Association of Colored Women in 1912 and was active in the NAACP. She was also a committed Republican and ran unsuccessfully for state superintendent of public instruction. She died on December 15, 1934.

formed in 1890, encouraged black coal miners to join the union rather than serve as strikebreakers. By 1900 approximately 20,000 of the 91,000 members of the UMW were black men. The Industrial Workers of the World (IWW), a revolutionary labor organization founded in 1905, brought black and white laborers together in, among other places, the Brotherhood of Timber Workers in the Piney Woods of east Texas.

In 1869 a Baltimore ship caulker, Isaac Myers, organized the National Colored Labor Union, which lasted for seven years. It discouraged strikes and encouraged its members to work hard and be thrifty. It lost whatever effectiveness it had when it was largely taken over by Republican leaders during Reconstruction.

Strikes

During the late nineteenth and early twentieth centuries, although some strikes by unions won concessions from business owners, most failed because owners could rely on strikebreakers and the police or national guard to intervene and bring the strikes to an often violent end. For a time, black shipyard workers in Southern ports did achieve some success. Black stevedores who loaded and unloaded ships endured oppressive conditions and long hours for low pay. They periodically went on strike in Charleston, Savannah, and New Orleans. The Longshoremen's Protective Union in Charleston won several strikes in the 1870s. In Nashville in 1871 black dockyard workers went on strike, demanding twenty cents an hour. Steamboat owners broke the strike by hiring state convicts for fifteen cents an hour.

Black and white laborers who toiled in the Louisiana sugarcane fields earned an average of $13 a week in the 1880s. They were paid in scrip—not cash—that was redeemable only in stores the planters owned where prices were exorbitant. Workers lived in 12 × 15 cabins that they rented from the planters. In some ways, it was worse than slave labor.

Though most Southern black people worked long hours in cotton fields, there were thousands who toiled in factories, mills, and mines. Here black women stem tobacco in a Virginia factory under the supervision of a white man.

Though the state militia had broken previous strikes, 9,000 black and 1,000 white workers responded to a call for a new strike in 1887 by organizers from the Knights of Labor. They quit the sugar fields in four parishes (as Louisiana counties are called) to demand more pay. The strike was peaceful, but planters convinced the governor to send in the militia. The troops fired into a crowd at Pattersonville and killed four people. The next day local officials killed several strikers who had been taken prisoner. In the town of Thibodaux, "prominent citizens" organized and armed themselves and had martial law declared. More than thirty-five unarmed black people, including women and children, were killed in their homes and churches. Two black strike leaders were lynched. The strike was broken.

Black washerwomen went on strike in Atlanta in 1881. The women, who did laundry for white families, refused to do any more until they were guaranteed $1 per twelve pounds of laundry. The strike was well organized through black churches and it spread to cooks and domestics. A strike committee used persuasion and intimidation to ensure support. Some 3,000 black people joined the strike. White families went two weeks without clean clothes. However, Atlanta's white community broke the strike. Police arrested strike leaders for disorderly conduct. Several black women were fined from $5 to $20. The city council threatened to require each member of the Washer Women's Association of Atlanta to purchase a city business license for $25. Though the strike gradually ended without having achieved its goal, it did demonstrate that poor black women could organize effectively.

BLACK PROFESSIONALS

Like business and labor, the medical and legal professions were strictly segregated. Most black physicians, nurses, and lawyers attended all-black professional schools in the late nineteenth century. Black people in need of medical care were either excluded from white hospitals or confined to all-black wards. Black physicians were denied staff privileges at white hospitals. Thus black people in many communities formed their own hospitals. Most were small facilities with fifty or fewer beds.

Medicine

In 1891 Dr. Daniel Hale Williams established Provident Hospital and Training Institute in Chicago, the first black hospital operated solely by African Americans. In 1894 the Freedmen's Hospital was organized in Washington, D.C., and it later affiliated with Howard University. Frederick Douglass Memorial Hospital and Training School was founded in Philadelphia in 1895. Dr. Alonzo McClennan in cooperation with several other black physicians established the Hospital and Training School for Nurses in Charleston, South Carolina, in 1897.

In 1900 Williams, explaining why black medical institutions were necessary, wrote:

> In view of this cruel ostracism, affecting so vitally the race, our duty seems plain. Institute Hospitals and Training Schools. Let us no longer sit idly and inanely deploring existing conditions. Let us not waste time trying to effect changes or modifications in the institutions unfriendly to us, but rather let us seek to promote the doctrine of helping and stimulating our race.

By 1890 there were 909 black (mostly male) physicians practicing in the United States. They served a black population of seven and a half million people. Barred from membership in the American Medical Association, black doctors organized the National Medical Association in Atlanta in 1895. Most black doctors had been educated at seven black medical schools that included Leonard Medical School at Shaw University in Raleigh, North Carolina; Flint-Goodridge Medical College in New Orleans; Meharry Medical School in Nashville; and the Howard University School of Medicine in Washington.

In 1910 in a report issued by the Carnegie Foundation for the Advancement of Teaching, Abraham Flexner recommended improving medical education in the United States by eliminating weaker medical schools. He suggested raising admission standards and expanding laboratory and clinical training in the stronger schools. As a result of the implementation of these recommendations, sixty of 155 white medical schools closed, and among black medical schools, only Howard and Meharry survived. By 1920 there were 3,885 black physicians, of whom fewer than seventy were women. Many had completed medical school before the Flexner report was compiled.

Nursing was another matter. By 1920 there were thirty-six black nurse training schools and 2,150 white nursing schools. White nurses resented the competition from black nurses for positions as private duty nurses. And the black physicians who ran nurse training schools exploited their students by hiring them out, as part of their training, for private duty work but requiring them to relinquish their pay to the schools. Moreover, many people—black and white—regarded black nurses more as domestics than as trained professionals. Unlike white nurses, for example, black nurses were usually addressed by their first names. To confront such obstacles, fifty-two black nurses met in New York City in 1908 and formed the National Association of Colored Graduate Nurses (NACGU). By 1920, the NACGU had five hundred members.

Black physicians and nurses struggled to provide medical care to people who were often desperately ill and sought treatment only as a last resort. Disease and sickness flourished among people who were ill-nourished, poorly clad, and inadequately housed. Tuberculosis, pneumonia, pellagra, hookworm, and syphilis afflicted many poor black people—as they also did poor white people. Bessie Hawes, a 1918 graduate of Tuskegee Institute's Nurse Training program, described the kind of situation she faced in rural Alabama.

> A colored family of ten were in bed and dying for the want of attention. No one would come near. I was glad of the opportunity. As I entered the little country cabin, I found the mother in bed. Three children were buried the week before. The father and the remainder of the family were running a temperature of 102–104. Some had influenza, others had pneumonia. No relatives or friends would come near. I saw at a glance I had work to do. I rolled up my sleeves and killed chickens and began to cook. . . . I milked the cow, gave medicine, and did everything I could to help conditions. I worked day and night trying to save them for seven days. I had no place to sleep. In the meantime the oldest daughter had a miscarriage and I delivered her without the aid of any physicians. . . . I only wished that I could have reached them earlier and been able to have done something for the poor mother.

The Law

Unlike black physicians and nurses, who were excluded from white hospitals, black lawyers were permitted to practice in what was essentially a white male court system. But white judges and attorneys did not welcome them. Rather than create additional problems for themselves, black defendants and plaintiffs often retained white lawyers in the hope that white legal counsel might improve their chances of receiving justice. As a result, many black attorneys had a hard time making a living from the practice of law.

The American Bar Association (ABA) would not admit black attorneys to membership. Attorney William H. Lewis, a graduate of Amherst College and the Harvard Law School who was appointed an assistant U.S.

attorney general by President William Howard Taft in 1911, was expelled by the ABA in 1912 when its leaders discovered he was black. The leaders defended his expulsion by claiming that the association was mainly a social organization. In 1925, black lawyers—led by Howard Law School graduate George H. Woodson—organized the National Bar Association.

In 1910 the United States had about 800 black lawyers. Some, like Lewis, had attended white law schools, such as Harvard or the University of South Carolina during Reconstruction in the 1870s. Others attended black law schools like Howard or Allen University's law school in South Carolina. Still other black men (and white men) learned the law by reading and working in the law offices of practicing attorneys.

MUSIC

In the half century after the Civil War, music created and performed by black people evolved into the uniquely American art forms of ragtime, jazz, and blues. The roots of these extraordinary musical innovations are obscure and uncertain. Some late-nineteenth-century music can be traced to African musical forms and rhythms. One source is slave work songs; another is the spirituals of the slavery era.

Traveling groups of black men, some of them ex-slaves, put on minstrel shows that featured "coon songs" after the Civil War. Many black Americans resented these popular shows as caricatures and exaggerations of black behavior. At least 600 "coon songs" that attracted a predominantly white audience were published by 1900 including "All Coons Look Alike to Me," "Mammy's Little Pickaninny," and "My Coal Black Lady."

Most black people did not perform in or enjoy the demeaning minstrel shows. They had other forms of musical entertainment. "The Civil Rights Juba" published in 1874, was a precursor to ragtime. In 1871 the Fisk University Jubilee Singers began the first of many fund-raising concert tours that entertained black and white audiences in the United States and Europe for years thereafter with slave songs and spirituals. Other black colleges and universities also sent choirs and singers on similar trips.

Ragtime

Ragtime, which emerged in the 1890s, was composed music, written down for performance on the piano. Ragtime pieces were not accompanied by lyrics and were not meant to be sung. The creative genius of the form, Scott Joplin, was born in Texarkana, Texas, in 1868. He learned to play on a piano his mother bought from her earnings as a maid, and he may have had some training in classical music. Joplin subsequently learned to transfer complex banjo syncopations to the piano as he fused European harmonies and African rhythms. He traveled to Chicago in 1893 and played at the Columbian Exposition. He soon began to write ragtime sheet music that sold well. In 1899 he composed his best-known tune, the "Maple Leaf Rag," named after a social club (brothel) in Sedalia, Missouri. It sold an astonishing one million copies.

Jazz

Jazz gradually replaced ragtime in popularity in the early twentieth century. Unlike ragtime, jazz was mostly improvised, not composed, and it was not confined to the piano. Jazz incorporated African and European musical elements drawn from such diverse sources as plantation bands, minstrel shows, river boat ensembles, and Irish and Scottish folk tunes. The first jazz bands emerged in and around New Orleans where they played at parades, funerals, clubs, and outdoor concerts. Instead of the banjos, pipes, fifes, and violins of earlier black musical groups, these bands relied more on brass, reeds, and drums.

Ferdinand Pechet, regarded as the first prominent jazz musician, grew up in a French-speaking family in New Orleans. Young Pechet played several musical instruments before settling on the piano. He was also a superb composer and arranger. Later he changed his name to Morton and came to be known as Jelly Roll Morton. He played in the "red light" district of New Orleans known as Storeyville and moved to Los Angeles in 1917 where he subsequently led and recorded with "Morton's Red Hot Peppers."

The Blues

In rural, isolated areas of the South, poor black people composed and sang songs about their lives and experiences. W. C. Handy, the father of the blues, later recalled: "Southern Negroes sang about everything.

An early jazz band arrives in a small Texas town in about 1915 for a performance at a black fair.

Trains, steamboats, steam whistles, sledge hammers, fast women, mean bosses, stubborn mules." They accompanied themselves on anything from a guitar, to a harmonica, to a washboard. They played in juke joints (rural nightclubs), at picnics, lumber camps, and urban night clubs.

Handy, who was born in Florence, Alabama, in 1873, took up music despite the opposition of his devoutly Christian parents. He learned to play the guitar though his mother and father regarded it as the "devil's plaything." He later led his own nine-man band. In the Mississippi Delta in 1903, Handy encountered "primitive" or "boogie" music unlike anything he had heard before. Handy was not initially impressed by the mostly unskilled and itinerant musicians whose lives swirled around cheap whiskey, gambling, prostitution, and violence. "Then I saw the beauty of primitive music. They had the stuff people wanted. It touched the spot. Their music wanted polishing, but it contained the essence. People would pay money for it." Handy went on to compose many tunes including "Memphis Blues" and "St. Louis Blues."

Handy was not the only musician to "discover" the blues. Gertrude Pridget sang in Southern minstrel shows. In 1902 she heard a young black woman in a small Missouri town sing forlornly about a lover who had left her. Pridget took the song and included it in her shows. In 1904 she married William "Pa" Rainey, and became "Ma" Rainey. Rainey proceeded to create other "blues" songs based on ballads, hymns, and the experiences of black people. As "Mother of the Blues," she recorded extensively and continuously in the 1920s and 1930s.

By 1920, two forms of American music were well along in their evolution—jazz and the blues. Both drew on African and American musical elements as well as on European styles. But most of all, jazz and the blues represented the experiences of African Americans and the creativity of the exceptional musicians who developed and performed the music.

SPORTS

While talented black men and women were making dramatic musical innovations, black athletes found that white athletes and sports entrepreneurs were increasingly opposed to the presence of black men in the boxing ring and on the playing field. In boxing, black men regularly fought white men through the end of the nineteenth century. But many white people, especially Southerners, were offended by the practice. In 1892, George Dixon, a black boxer, won the world feather-weight title, and some white men cheered his victory, distressing a Chicago journalist. "It was not pleasant," he complained, "to see white men applaud a negro for knocking another white man out. It was not pleasant to see them crowding around 'Mr.' Dixon to congratulate him on his victory, to seek an introduction with 'the distinguished colored gentleman' while he puffed his cigar and lay back like a prince receiving his subjects." Despite such opinions, there was never any official prohibition of interracial bouts.

Jack Johnson

The success of another black boxer, heavyweight Jack Johnson, angered many white Americans. Johnson was born in Galveston, Texas, in 1878 and became a professional boxer in 1897. Between 1902 and 1907 he won fifty-seven bouts against black and white fighters. In 1908 he badly beat the white heavyweight champion, Tommy Burns, in Australia. Many white boxing fans were unwilling to accept Johnson as the champion and looked desperately for "a great white hope" who could defeat him. Jim Jeffries, a former champion, came out of retirement to take on Johnson. In a brutal fight under a scorching sun in Reno, Nevada, in 1910, Johnson knocked Jeffries out in the fifteenth round.

Johnson's personal life as well as his prowess in the ring provoked white animosity. Having divorced his black wife, he married a white woman in 1911. Several months later, overwhelmed by social ostracism, she committed suicide. After Johnson married a second white woman, he was convicted of violating the Mann Act, which made it illegal to transport a woman across state lines for immoral purposes. In Johnson's case the "immorality" was his marriage to white women. Sentenced to a year in prison and fined $1,000, Johnson fled to Canada and then to France to avoid punishment. He lost his title to Jesse Willard in 1915 in Havana in the twenty-sixth round in a fight many people believe that Johnson threw. He returned to the United States in 1920 and served ten months in Leavenworth Prison.

Baseball

Baseball was a relatively new sport that became popular after the Civil War. As professional baseball developed in the 1870s and 1880s, both black and white men competed to earn money playing the game. It was not easy. They were the nation's first professional athletes, but professional baseball was unstable. Teams were formed and dissolved with depressing regularity. Players moved from team to team. Some thirty black men played

TIMELINE

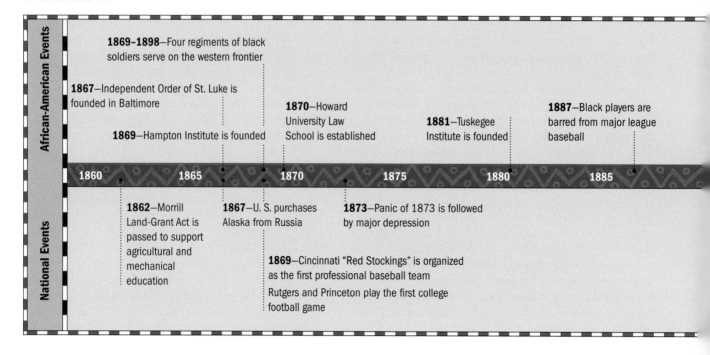

African-American Events

1869–1898—Four regiments of black soldiers serve on the western frontier

1867—Independent Order of St. Luke is founded in Baltimore

1869—Hampton Institute is founded

1870—Howard University Law School is established

1881—Tuskegee Institute is founded

1887—Black players are barred from major league baseball

1860   1865   1870   1875   1880   1885

National Events

1862—Morrill Land-Grant Act is passed to support agricultural and mechanical education

1867—U. S. purchases Alaska from Russia

1873—Panic of 1873 is followed by major depression

1869—Cincinnati "Red Stockings" is organized as the first professional baseball team

Rutgers and Princeton play the first college football game

professional baseball in the quarter century after the Civil War.

White players led by Adrian Constantine "Cap" Anson of the Chicago White Stockings tried to get baseball club owners to stop signing black men to contracts. Anson, who was from Iowa, bitterly resented having to play against black men. In 1887, International League officials rescinded a rule that had permitted them to sign black baseball players. One black player, Weldy Wilberforce Walker, protested the exclusion in a letter to *Sporting Life*. He insisted that black men be judged by their skills, not by their color. "There should be some broader cause—such as lack of ability, behavior, and intelligence—for barring a player, rather than his color. It is for these reasons and because I think ability and intelligence should be recognized first and last—at all times and by everyone—I ask the question again, 'Why was the law permitting colored men to sign repealed, etc.?'" There was no intelligent answer to Walker's question. But Jim Crow was now on the baseball diamond. Moses Fleetwood Walker—Weldy's brother—was the last black man to play major league baseball in the nineteenth century as a catcher with Toledo of the American Association. No black men would be allowed to play with white men in major league baseball until Jackie Robinson joined the Brooklyn Dodgers in 1947.

In reaction to their exclusion, black men formed their own teams. By 1900, there were five black profes-

sional teams including the Norfolk Red Stockings, the Chicago Unions, and the Cuban X Giants of New York. The Negro Leagues would be an integral (but not integrated) part of sports for the next half century.

Basketball and Other Sports

James Naismith invented basketball in 1891 in Springfield, Massachusetts. Black youngsters were playing organized basketball by 1906 in YMCAs and later YWCAs in New York City, Philadelphia, and Washington, D.C. By 1910–11, Howard University and Hampton Institute had basketball teams. In horse racing, black jockeys regularly won major races. Willie Simms won the Kentucky Derby in 1894, 1895, 1896, and 1898. Bicycling and bicycle racing were enormously popular by the 1890s, and in 1900 a black rider, Marshall W. "Major" Taylor, won the U.S. sprint championship.

College Athletics

Generally, white colleges and universities in the North that admitted black students would not let them participate in intercollegiate sports. (Southern colleges and universities did not admit black students.) There were, however, exceptions. In 1889, W. T. S. Jackson and William Henry Lewis played football for Amherst College. Lewis was the captain of the team in 1890. As a law

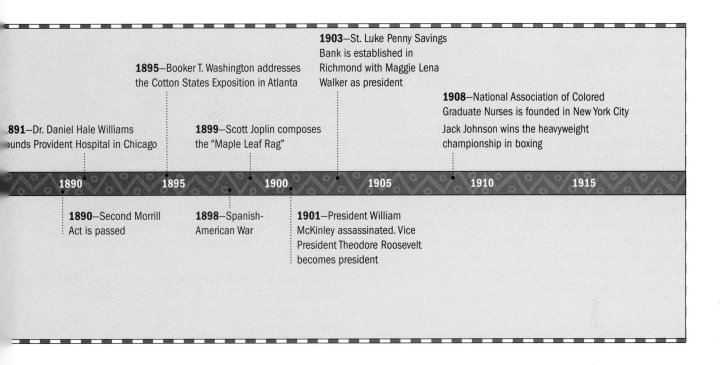

1903—St. Luke Penny Savings Bank is established in Richmond with Maggie Lena Walker as president

1895—Booker T. Washington addresses the Cotton States Exposition in Atlanta

1908—National Association of Colored Graduate Nurses is founded in New York City

Jack Johnson wins the heavyweight championship in boxing

1891—Dr. Daniel Hale Williams founds Provident Hospital in Chicago

1899—Scott Joplin composes the "Maple Leaf Rag"

| 1890 | 1895 | 1900 | 1905 | 1910 | 1915 |

1890—Second Morrill Act is passed

1898—Spanish-American War

1901—President William McKinley assassinated. Vice President Theodore Roosevelt becomes president

school student, Lewis played for Harvard and was named to the Walter Camp All-American team in 1892. (Lewis became a distinguished attorney who was forced out of the American Bar Association because of his color. See the section "The Law" in this chapter.) White institutions with black players often encountered the racism so rampant during the era. In 1907, the University of Alabama baseball team canceled a game with the University of Vermont after learning that the Vermont squad had two black infielders. Moreover, black players were frequently subjected to abuse from opposing teams and their fans.

Intercollegiate athletics emerged at black colleges and universities in the late nineteenth century. White schools occasionally played black institutions. The Yale Law School baseball team, for example, played Howard in 1898. But black college teams were far more likely to play each other. The first football game between two black colleges took place on December 27, 1892, when Biddle University (today Johnson C. Smith University) defeated Livingston College in Salisbury, North Carolina.

Eventually black athletic conferences were formed. The Central Intercollegiate Athletic Association (CIAA) was organized in 1912 with Hampton, Howard, Virginia Union, and Shaw College in Raleigh, North Carolina, among its early members. The Southeastern Conference was established in 1913 and consisted of Morehouse, Fisk, Florida A&M, and Tuskegee among others. In Texas in 1920, five black colleges founded the Southwestern Athletic Conference: Prairie View A&M, Bishop College, Paul Quinn College, Wiley College, and Sam Houston College.

CONCLUSION

White supremacy was debilitating, discouraging, and dangerous, but black Americans were sometimes able to turn Jim Crow to their advantage. To lessen the effects of white racism and to improve the economic status of black people, educators like Samuel Chapman Armstrong and Booker T. Washington recommended agricultural and mechanical training for most black Americans. But critics such as W. E. B. Du Bois stressed the need to cultivate the minds as well as the hands of black people to develop leaders.

Black men served with distinction in all-black military units in the Indian wars, the Spanish-American War, and the Philippine Insurrection. But no matter how loyal or how committed black men in uniform were, the white majority never fully trusted nor displayed confidence in them. African Americans could only react with dismay and outrage when President Theodore Roosevelt dismissed 167 black soldiers in 1906 in the Brownsville affair.

As they tried to shape their own destinies in the late nineteenth century, black Americans organized a variety of institutions. Mostly barred from white schools, churches, hospitals, labor unions, and places of entertainment, they developed businesses and facilities to serve their communities. Black businesses, organizations, and institutions functioned in an environment mostly free from white control and interference. Black people relied on their own experiences and imaginations to create new forms of music. They participated in sports with white athletes but more often played separately from them as segregation and white hostility spread.

While black people recognized that their churches, hospitals, schools, and businesses were often inadequately financed and usually less imposing than those of white people, they also knew that at a black school or church, in a black store, or in the care of a black physician or nurse, they would not be abused, mistreated, or ridiculed because of their color.

REVIEW QUESTIONS

1. How and why did the agricultural and mechanical training offered by Hampton Institute and Tuskegee Institute gain so much support among black people and white people? Why did black colleges and universities emphasize learning trades and acquiring skills?

2. How compatible was the educational philosophy of the late nineteenth century with the racial ideology of that era?

3. Of what value was an education for a black person in the 1890s or early 1900s? To what use could a black person put an education? What exactly was the benefit of an education?

4. What purpose did the black church serve? What were the strengths and weaknesses of the black church? How would you assess the role of black clergymen in late-nineteenth-century America?

5. How could a black man in the U.S. Army justify participating in wars against Native Americans, the Spanish, and the Filipinos? What motivated black soldiers to serve? How well did they serve?

6. What, if any, benefits did black people derive from the growth and expansion of segregation and Jim Crow?

7. How do you explain the emergence of ragtime, jazz, and the blues in American music? How do you account for their development and popularity?

8. How did segregation affect the development of amateur and professional athletics in the United States?

RECOMMENDED READING

James D. Anderson. *The Education of Blacks in the South, 1860–1931.* Chapel Hill: University of North Carolina Press, 1988. Anderson is highly critical of the education and philosophy promoted and provided by Hampton Institute and Tuskegee Institute.

Edward L. Ayers. *The Promise of the New South: Life after Reconstruction.* New York: Oxford University Press, 1992. This wide-ranging study encompasses almost every aspect of life in the late-nineteenth-century South, including religion, education, sports, and music.

Sutton E. Griggs. *Imperium in Imperio.* New York: Arno Press reprint, 1899. This novel describes the formation of a separate black nation in Texas at the end of the nineteenth century.

Leon Litwack. *Trouble in Mind: Black Southerners in the Age of Jim Crow.* New York: Alfred A. Knopf, 1998. The author lets the words of black people of the time—including lawyers, physicians, and musicians—explain what life was like in an age of intense white supremacy.

Leon Litwack and August Meier, eds. *Black Leaders in the Nineteenth Century.* Urbana: University of Illinois Press, 1988. This volume contains eighteen brief but valuable biographical essays.

Benjamin E. Mays. *Born to Rebel.* New York: Scribner, 1971. May's autobiography includes penetrating insights into religion and education among rural black Southerners.

Howard N. Rabinowitz. *Race Relations in the Urban South, 1865–1890.* New York: Oxford University Press, 1978. The author examines black life in Atlanta, Montgomery, Nashville, Raleigh, and Richmond.

ADDITIONAL BIBLIOGRAPHY

Education

James D. Anderson and V. P. Franklin, eds. *New Perspectives on Black Education.* Boston: G. K. Hall, 1978.

Henry A. Bullock. *A History of Negro Education in the South from 1619 to the Present.* Cambridge: Harvard University Press, 1967.

Religion

Iain MacRobert. *The Black Roots and White Racism of Early Pentecostalism in the USA*. Basingstoke: Macmillan, 1988.

Edwin S. Redkey, ed. *The Writings and Speeches of Henry McNeal Turner*. New York: Arno Press, 1971.

Clarence E. Walker. *A Rock in a Weary Land: The African Methodist Episcopal Church during the Civil War and Reconstruction*. Baton Rouge: Louisiana State University Press, 1982.

The Military

John M. Carroll, ed. *The Black Military Experience in the American West*. New York: Liveright, 1973.

Willard B. Gatewood, ed. *Smoked Yankees and the Struggle for Empire: Letters from Negro Soldiers, 1898–1902*. Urbana: University of Illinois Press, 1971.

William H. Leckie. *The Buffalo Soldiers: A Narrative of the Negro Cavalry in the West*. Norman: University of Oklahoma Press, 1967.

John D. Weaver. *The Brownsville Raid*. New York: Norton, 1971.

Labor

Tera W. Hunter. *To 'Joy My Freedom: Southern Black Women's Lives and Labors after the Civil War*. Cambridge: Harvard University Press, 1997.

Gerald D. Jaynes. *Branches without Roots: Genesis of the Black Working Class in the American South, 1862–1882*. New York: Oxford University Press, 1986.

The Professions

V. N. Gamble. *The Black Community Hospital: Contemporary Dilemmas in Historical Perspective*. New York: Garland, 1989.

Darlene Clark Hine. *Speak Truth to Power: Black Professional Class in United States History*. Brooklyn, NY: Carlson Publishing Co., 1996.

J. Clay Smith, Jr., ed. *Rebels in Law: Voices in History of Black Women Lawyers*. Ann Arbor: University of Michigan Press, 1998.

Music

W. C. Handy. *Father of the Blues: An Autobiography*. New York: Macmillan, 1941.

John Edward Hasse, ed. *Ragtime, Its History, Composers, and Music*. London: Macmillan, 1985.

Alan Lomax. *Mr. Jelly Roll: The Fortunes of Jelly Roll Morton, New Orleans Creole and "Inventor of Jazz."* New York: Grove Press, 1950.

Gunther Schuller. *Early Jazz: Its Roots and Musical Development*. New York: Oxford University Press, 1968.

Sports

Ocania Chalk. *Black College Sport*. New York: Dodd, Mead and Co., 1976.

Robert W. Peterson. *Only the Ball Was White: Negro Baseball: A History of Legendary Black Players and All-Black Professional Teams before Black Men Played in the Major Leagues*. New York: Prentice-Hall, 1970.

CHAPTER 16

CONCILIATION, AGITATION, AND MIGRATION

AFRICAN AMERICANS IN THE EARLY TWENTIETH CENTURY

On July 28, 1917, the NAACP organized a silent march in New York City to protest the East St. Louis, Illinois, race riot in which thirty-five black people died as well as to denounce the ongoing epidemic of lynchings. The marchers were accompanied by the beat of muffled drums.

The wisest of my race understand that the agitation of questions of social equality is of the extremest folly, and that progress in the enjoyment of all privileges that will come to us must be the result of severe and constant struggle rather than of artificial forcing. No race that has anything to contribute to the markets of the world is long in any degree ostracized. It is important and right all privileges of the law be ours, but it is vastly more important that we be prepared for the exercises of these privileges.

Booker T. Washington, Atlanta Cotton States and International Exposition, September 18, 1895

Mr. Washington distinctly asks that black people give up, at least for the present three things,—
First, political power,
Second, insistence on civil rights,
Third, higher education of Negro youth,—
and concentrate all their energies on industrial education, the accumulation of wealth, and the conciliation of the South.

W. E. B. Du Bois, *The Souls of Black Folk*, 1903

As the twentieth century dawned, black and white Americans had profoundly different views on the future of black people in America. Most white people believed that black Americans were an inferior race capable of little more than manual labor and entitled to only the most basic legal rights. Black Americans rejected that assertion and worked for a more equitable place in society. Black scholar W. E. B. Du Bois announced in 1903 that race would be the century's most critical issue. "The problem of the twentieth century is the problem of the color-line,—the relation of the darker to the lighter races of men in Asia and Africa, in America and the islands of the sea."

Black people refused to accept the inferiority to which they had been consigned. They devised strategies and organized institutions to enable them to prosper in a hostile society. However, African Americans and their leaders disagreed about how to secure the constitutional rights and the material comforts that so many white Americans took for granted. Some, following W. E. B. Du Bois, a founder of the Niagara Movement and the National Association for the Advancement of Colored People (NAACP), favored a frontal assault on discrimination, disfranchisement, and Jim Crow in the quest for racial progress. Others, following Booker T. Washington of the Tuskegee Institute, cautioned against the vigorous pursuit of civil rights and political power and insisted that agricultural and industrial training would generate prosperity and self-sufficiency among people of color.

The emergence of the club movement among black women and other self-help organizations (see Chapter 15) enabled more prosperous black people to aid those suffering acutely from poverty and prejudice. The black elite—often reviled for ostentatious social displays—came to be designated the Talented Tenth, and many of them took seriously their responsibilities to aid their brethren.

When the United States entered World War I in 1917, black men responded patriotically, as they had in previous conflicts. They joined a Jim Crow military that was fighting to make the world safe for democracy. But black people in America were not safe, and democracy did not prevail. Riots and racial violence erupted before, during, and after the war.

In the meantime one of the most important episodes in American history—a vast and prolonged migration of hundreds of thousands of rural black Southerners to northern cities—began in earnest after 1910. Drawn mainly by economic opportunities, black people moved to New York, Philadelphia, Cleveland, Chicago, and other urban centers.

RACE AND THE PROGRESSIVE MOVEMENT

By the first decade of the twentieth century, many Americans were concerned and even alarmed about the rapid economic and social changes that confronted the United States including industrialization, the rise of powerful corporations, the explosive growth of cities, and the influx of millions of immigrants. Their apprehensions spawned a disparate collection of efforts at reform known as the progressive movement. In general, progressives believed that America needed a new social awareness to deal with the new social and economic problems. But most of the middle- and upper-class white people who formed the core of the movement showed little interest in white racism and its impact. Indeed, many were racists themselves. They were primarily concerned with the concentration of wealth in monopolies like Standard Oil, with pervasive political corruption in state and local governments, and with the plight of working-class immigrants in American cities. They cared deeply about the debilitating effects of alcohol, tainted food, and prostitution but little about the grim impact of white supremacy. When Upton Sinclair wrote his muckraking novel, *The Jungle*, to expose the exploitation of European immigrants in Chicago meatpacking houses, he depicted black people as brute laborers and strikebreakers.

The reforms of the progressive movement nonetheless offered at least a glimmer of hope that racial advancement was possible. If efforts were made to improve America, was it not possible that there be some advances achieved in policies and conditions affecting black Americans? But how much militancy or forbearance was necessary to achieve significant racial progress? Did it even make sense for black people to demand a meaningful role in a nation that despised them? Perhaps it was wiser to turn inward and rely on each other rather than plead for white recognition and respect.

BOOKER T. WASHINGTON'S APPROACH

Booker T. Washington's commitment to agricultural and industrial education served as the basis for his approach to "the problem of the color line." By the beginning of the twentieth century, Washington was convinced that black men and women who had mastered skills acquired at institutions like Tuskegee and Hampton would be recognized, if not welcomed, as productive contributors to the southern economy. Washington believed that economic acceptance would lead in due course to political and social acceptance.

The Tuskegee leader eloquently outlined his philosophy in the speech he delivered at the opening ceremonies of the Cotton States Exposition in Atlanta in 1895 (see Chapter 15). Black people, he told his segregated audience, would find genuine opportunities in the South. "[W]hen it comes to business, pure and simple, it is in the South that the Negro is given a man's chance in the commercial world." Washington added that black people should not expect too much but should welcome menial labor as a first step in the struggle for progress. Ever optimistic, he looked for opportunities while deprecating those who complained. "Nor should we permit our grievances to overshadow our opportunities." He told white listeners that the lives of black and white Southerners were historically linked and that black people were far more loyal and steadfast than newly arrived immigrants. "[I]n our humble way, we shall stand by you with a devotion that no foreigner can approach, ready to lay down our lives, if need be, in defence of yours, interlacing our industrial, commercial, civil, and religious life with yours in a way that shall make the interests of both races one."

Then in a striking metaphor, Washington reassured white people that cooperation between the races in the interest of prosperity did not endanger segregation. "In all things that are purely social we can be as separate as the fingers, yet one as the hand in all things essential to mutual progress." Finally, Washington implied that black people need not protest because they were denied rights white men possessed. Instead, he urged his black listeners to struggle steadily rather than make defiant demands. "The wisest among my race understand that the agitation of questions of social equality is the extremest folly, and that progress in the enjoyment of all the privileges that will come to us must be the result of severe and constant struggle rather than of artificial forcing." Washington was convinced that as African Americans became productive and made economic progress, white people would concede them their rights.

The speech was warmly received by both white and black listeners and by those who read it when it was widely reprinted. T. Thomas Fortune, the black editor of the *New York Age*, told Washington that he had re-

placed Frederick Douglass (who died in 1895) as a leader. "It looks as if you are our Douglass, the best equipped of the lot of us to be the single figure ahead of the procession."

But not everyone was complimentary. The black editor of the *Washington Bee*, W. Calvin Chase, complained: "He said something that was death to the Afro-American and elevating to white people." Bishop Henry M. Turner of the AME church added that Washington "will have to live a long time to undo the harm he has done our race."

White people regarded Washington's speech as moderate, sensible, and altogether praiseworthy. Almost overnight he was designated the spokesman for African Americans. Washington accepted the recognition and took full advantage of it.

Washington's Influence

Booker T. Washington was a complex man. Many people found him unassertive, dignified, and patient. Yet he was ambitious, aggressive, and opportunistic as well as shrewd, calculating, and devious. He had an uncanny ability to determine what he might say to other people that would elicit a positive response from them. He became extraordinarily powerful. In the words of his assistant, Emmett J. Scott, Washington was "the Wizard of Tuskegee."

After the Atlanta speech, Washington's influence soared. He received extensive and mostly positive coverage in black newspapers. Some of that popularity stemmed from admiration for his leadership and agreement with his ideas. But Washington also cultivated and flattered editors, paid for advertisements for Tuskegee, and subsidized struggling journalists.

He was especially effective in dealing with prominent white businessmen and philanthropists. William H. Baldwin, vice president of the Southern Railroad, was so impressed with Washington's management of Tuskegee that Baldwin agreed to serve as the chairman of Tuskegee's board. Washington developed support among the nation's industrial elite including steel magnate Andrew Carnegie and Julius Rosenwald, the head of Sears, Roebuck, and Company. They trusted Washington's judgment and invariably consulted him before contributing to black colleges and universities. Washington assured them of the wisdom of investing in the training of black men and women in agricultural and mechanical skills. These students, he repeatedly reminded donors, would be self-sufficient and productive members of southern society.

The Tuskegee Machine

Washington advised black people to avoid politics, but he ignored his own advice. Though he never ran for office nor was appointed to a political position, Washington was a political figure to be reckoned with. His connections to white businesspeople and politicians gave him enormous influence. Critics and admirers alike referred to him as "the Wizard of Tuskegee," and the way he wielded his influence as "the Tuskegee Machine." In 1896 he supported winning Republican presidential candidate William McKinley over the Democratic and Populist William Jennings Bryan. Washington got along superbly with McKinley's successor, Theodore Roosevelt. Though Roosevelt subscribed to social Darwinism (see Chapter 15) and regarded black Americans as inferiors, he liked and respected Washington.

In 1901 Roosevelt invited Washington to dinner at the White House, where Roosevelt's wife, daughter, three sons, and a Colorado businessman joined them. Black people applauded, but the white South, alarmed by such a flagrant breach of racial etiquette (black people did not dine with white people), recoiled. "The most damnable outrage which has ever been perpetrated by any citizen of the United States," a Memphis newspaper fumed, "was committed yesterday by the President when he invited a nigger to dine with him at the White House." Roosevelt was unmoved, and a few days later the two men dined again together at Yale University. Still, Roosevelt never invited Washington for another meal at the Executive Mansion.

Washington and Roosevelt regularly consulted each other on political appointments. In the most notable case, Washington urged Roosevelt to appoint William D. Crum, a black medical doctor, as the collector of customs for the port of Charleston, South Carolina. White Southerners, led by Senator Benjamin R. Tillman, a South Carolina Democrat, opposed Crum's appointment and delayed final confirmation by the Senate for nearly three years. With Washington's assent, Roosevelt appointed black attorney and former all-American football player William Lewis to be U.S. District Attorney in Boston. Several years later, President William Howard Taft appointed Lewis Assistant Attorney General of the United States. (For more details on Lewis, see Chapter 15.)

Most of Washington's political activities were not public. He secretly helped finance an unsuccessful court case against the Louisiana grandfather clause. (The statute disfranchised those voters—black men—whose grandfathers had not possessed the right to vote; see Chapter 14.) Washington provided funds to carry two

Booker T. Washington had access to and influence among the most powerful political and business leaders in the United States. Here he shares the podium with President Theodore Roosevelt. Washington persuaded Republican leaders like Roosevelt to appoint black men to an assortment of federal offices and convinced businessmen to contribute sizable sums to black colleges and universities. Nevertheless, some African Americans criticized the Tuskegee leader for not speaking out more candidly in opposition to white supremacy and Jim Crow.

cases challenging Alabama's grandfather clause to the U.S. Supreme Court, which ultimately rejected both on a technicality. He tried to persuade railroad executives to improve the conditions on segregated coaches and in station waiting rooms. He worked covertly with white attorneys to free a black farm laborer imprisoned under Alabama's peonage law. In many of these secret activities, Washington used code names in correspondence to hide his involvement. In the Louisiana case he was identified only as X.Y.Z.

Washington was a conservative leader who did not directly or publicly challenge white supremacy. He was willing to accept literacy and property qualifications for voting *if they were equitably enforced regardless of race*. He also opposed women's suffrage. He attacked lynching only occasionally. But he did write an annual letter to white newspapers filled with data on lynchings that had been compiled at Tuskegee. Washington let the grim statistics speak for themselves rather than denounce the injustice himself.

Washington founded the National Negro Business League in 1900 and served as its president until he died in 1915. The League brought together merchants, retailers, bankers, funeral directors, and other owners and operators of small enterprises. It helped to promote black businesses in the black community and brought businessmen together to exchange information. Moreover, the League's annual meetings allowed Washington to develop support for the Tuskegee Machine from black businessmen who were community leaders from across the nation. Similarly, he worked closely with leaders in black fraternal orders such as the Odd Fellows and Pythians.

Opposition to Washington

Years before Washington rose to prominence, there were black leaders who favored a direct challenge to racial oppression. In 1889, delegates representing twenty-three states met to form the Afro-American League in Chicago. The League's main purpose was to press for civil and political rights guaranteed by the U.S. Constitution. "The objects of the League are to encourage State and local leagues in their efforts to break down color bars, and in obtaining for the Afro-American an equal chance with others in the avocations of life . . . in securing the full privileges of citizenship." But the League did not flourish, and it was eventually displaced by the Niagara Movement.

Opposition to Washington's conciliatory stance on racial matters steadily intensified. William Monroe Trotter became the most vociferous critic of Booker T. Washington and the Tuskegee Machine. Trotter was the Harvard-educated editor of the Boston *Guardian*, and he savagely attacked Washington as "the Great Traitor," "the Benedict Arnold of the Negro Race," and "Pope Washington." At a 1903 meeting of the National Negro Business League in Boston, Trotter stood on a chair and interrupted a speech by Washington, defiantly asking, "Are the rope and the torch all the race is to get under your leadership?" Washington ignored him, and the police arrested the editor for disorderly conduct. He spent thirty days in jail for what newspapers labeled "the Boston Riot."

W. E. B. DU BOIS

William Edward Burghardt Du Bois, who was twelve years younger than Booker T. Washington, would eventually eclipse the influence and authority of the Wizard of Tuskegee. Du Bois emerged as the most significant black leader in America during the first half of the twentieth century. While Washington's life had been shaped by slavery, poverty, and the industrial work ethic fostered at Hampton Institute, Du Bois was born and raised in the largely white New England town of Great Barrington, Massachusetts. It was a small community where he encountered little overt racism and developed a passion for knowledge.

Du Bois possessed—as he put it—"a flood of Negro blood, a strain of French, a bit of Dutch, but, thank God! no Anglo-Saxon." He graduated from Great Barrington High School at a time when few white and still fewer black youngsters attended more than primary school. He went South to Fisk University in Nashville and graduated at age twenty. He was the first black man to earn a Ph.D. (in history) at Harvard in 1895, and he pursued additional graduate study in Germany.

Du Bois was perhaps the greatest scholar-activist in American history. He was an intellectual at ease with words and ideas. He wrote sixteen nonfiction books, five novels, and two autobiographies. He was a fearless activist determined to confront disfranchisement, Jim Crow, and lynching. While Washington solicited the goodwill of powerful white leaders and was comfortable with a gradual approach to the eradication of white supremacy, Du Bois was impatient with white people who accepted or ignored white domination. Moreover, he had little tolerance for black people who were unwilling to demand their civil and political rights.

Du Bois was well aware that he and Washington came from dissimilar backgrounds.

> I was born free. Washington was born a slave. He felt the lash of an overseer across his back. I was born in Massachusetts, he on a slave plantation in the South. My great-grandfather fought with the Colonial Army in New England in the American Revolution. I had a happy childhood and acceptance in the community. Washington's childhood was hard. I had many more advantages: Fisk University, Harvard, graduate years in Europe. Washington had little formal schooling.

Du Bois was not always critical of Washington. Following Washington's speech at the Cotton States Exposition in 1895, Du Bois, then a young Harvard Ph.D. teaching at Ohio's Wilberforce University, wrote to praise him. "Let me heartily congratulate you upon your phenomenal success at Atlanta—it was a word fitly spoken." But in 1903, the same year as the Boston Riot, Du Bois—by then an Atlanta University professor—published *The Souls of Black Folk*. One of the major literary works of the twentieth century, it contained the first formal attack on Washington and his leadership. In "Of Booker T. Washington and Others," Du Bois conceded that it was painful to challenge Washington, a man so highly praised and admired. "One hesitates, therefore, to criticise a life which, beginning with so little, has done so much. And yet the time is come when one may speak in all sincerity and utter courtesy of the mistakes and shortcomings of Mr. Washington's career, as well as the triumphs." Du Bois attacked Washington for failing to stand up for political and civil rights and higher education for black Americans. Du Bois found even more infuriating Washington's willingness to compromise with the white South and Washington's apparent agreement with white Southerners that black people were not their equals. "Mr. Washington represents in Negro thought the old attitude of adjustment and submission . . . and Mr. Washington's programme practically accepts the alleged inferiority of the Negro races."

In concluding, Du Bois stressed that he agreed with Washington on some issues, but disagreed even more about significant ones, and that on these issues it was vital to oppose Washington.

> So far as Mr. Washington preaches Thrift, Patience, and Industrial Training for the masses, we must hold up his hands and strive with him. . . . But so far as Mr. Washington apologizes for injustice, North or South, does not rightly value the privilege and duty of voting, belittles the emasculating effects of caste distinctions, and opposes higher training and ambition of our brighter minds,—so far as he, the South, or the Nation, does this,—we must unceasingly and firmly oppose them.

Washington worried that the opposition of Trotter, Du Bois, and others would jeopardize the flow of funds

VOICES

W. E. B. DU BOIS ON BEING BLACK IN AMERICA

W. E. B. Du Bois's The Souls of Black Folk *(1903) contained perhaps the most eloquent statement ever written on being black in white America. The difficulties of their circumstances, Du Bois believed, create a double consciousness among Americans of African descent.*

After the Egyptian and Indian, the Greek and Roman, the Teuton and Mongolian, the Negro is a sort of seventh son, born with a veil, and gifted with second-sight in this American world,—a world which yields him no true self-consciousness, but only lets him see himself through the revelation of the other world. It is a peculiar sensation, this double-consciousness, this sense of always looking at one's self through the eyes of others, of measuring one's soul by the tape of a world that looks on in an amused contempt and pity. One ever feels his two-ness,—an American, a Negro; two souls, two thoughts, two unreconciled strivings; two warring ideals in one dark body, whose dogged strength alone keeps it from being torn asunder.

The history of the American Negro is the history of this strife,—this longing to attain self-conscious manhood, to merge his double self into a better and truer self. In this merging he wishes neither of the older selves to be lost. He would not Africanize America, for America has too much to teach the world and Africa. He would not bleach his Negro soul in a flood of white Americanism, for he knows that Negro blood has a message for the world. He simply wishes to make it possible for a man to be both a Negro and an American, without being cursed and spit upon by his fellows, without having the doors of Opportunity closed roughly in his face.

QUESTIONS

1. Why, in the judgment of W. E. B. Du Bois, is it impossible for a black person to be simply an American?

2. Why did people of color have to look at themselves "through the eyes of others"?

3. Would Du Bois agree, based on his concept of double consciousness, that African Americans have a separate identity and separate culture from other Americans?

Source: Du Bois, *The Souls of Black Folk*, pp. 8–9.

from white philanthropists to black colleges and universities. In an effort to reconcile with his opponents, he organized a meeting with them, funded by white philanthropists, at Carnegie Hall in New York City in 1904. But Du Bois and other opponents of Washington came to the gathering determined to adopt a radical agenda. When Washington loyalists monopolized the proceedings, Du Bois quit in disgust.

Du Bois—joined by a small cadre of black intellectuals—then set out to organize an aggressive effort to secure the rights of black citizens. He was convinced that the advancement of black people was the responsibility of the black elite, those he called the Talented Tenth, meaning the upper 10 percent of black Americans. Education, he believed, was the key.

> Work alone will not do it unless inspired by the right ideals and guided by intelligence. Education must not simply teach work—it must teach Life. The Talented Tenth of the Negro race must be made leaders of thought and missionaries of culture among people. No others can do this work, and Negro colleges must train men for it. The Negro race, like all other races, is going to be saved by its exceptional men.

THE NIAGARA MOVEMENT

In 1905 Du Bois carried the anti-Washington crusade a step further and invited a select group to meet at Niagara Falls, in Canada. The twenty-nine delegates to this meeting insisted that black people no longer quietly accept the loss of the right to vote. "We believe that [Negro] American citizens should protest emphatically and continually against the curtailment of their political rights." They also demanded an end to segregation, declaring, "All American citizens have the right to equal treatment in places of public entertainment." They appealed for better schools, health care, and housing; protested the discrimination endured by black soldiers; and criticized the racial prejudice of most churches as "wrong, unchristian and disgraceful to the twentieth century civilization." Perhaps most important, the Niagara gathering insisted that white people did not know what was best for black people. "We repudiate the monstrous doctrine that the oppressor should be the sole authority as to the rights of the oppressed."

The Niagara Movement that emerged from this meeting attracted four hundred members and remained active for several years. Du Bois composed annual addresses to the nation designed to arouse black and white support. But the Niagara Movement was no match for the powerful, efficient, and well-financed Tuskegee Ma-

The founders of the Niagara movement posed in front of a photograph of the falls when they met at Niagara Falls, Ontario, Canada, in 1905. W. E. B. Du Bois is second from the right in the middle row.

chine. Washington used every means at his disposal to undermine the movement. Black newspaper editors like the *Washington Bee*'s W. Calvin Chase—who had earlier attacked Washington's Atlanta Compromise address—were paid to attack Du Bois and to praise Washington. Washington dispatched spies to Niagara meetings to report on the organization's activities.

Washington sent a telegram requesting that black lawyer Clifford Plummer infiltrate the first Niagara meeting. "See Plummer at once. Give him fifty dollars. Tell him to go to Buffalo tonight or tomorrow morning ostensibly to attend Elks convention but to report fully what goes on at meeting. . . . Get into meeting, if possible but be sure [to get] name of all who attend and what they do." Washington let it be known that black federal workers might lose their positions if they joined in the Niagara Movement.

There were also internal problems among Niagara members. Du Bois was an inexperienced leader, and difficulties developed between Du Bois and Trotter. In 1908, the Niagara Movement virtually collapsed. Most

THE EMERGENCE OF NATIONAL AFRICAN-AMERICAN ORGANIZATIONS

1889	Afro-American League organized in Chicago
1892	Colored Women's League of Washington formed
1893	New Era Club founded in Boston
1895	National Federation of Afro-American Women organized in Boston
1896	National Association of Colored Women (NACW) formed in Washington
1897	First Phillis Wheatley home established in Detroit
1900	National Negro Business League established in Boston
1905	Niagara Movement organized in Niagara Falls, Ontario, Canada
1909	National Association for the Advancement of Colored People (NAACP) founded in New York City
1910	National League on Urban Conditions among Negroes (Urban League) formed in New York City

black and white Americans were not prepared to support an organization that seemed so uncompromising in its demands.

THE NAACP

As the Niagara Movement expired, the National Association for the Advancement of Colored People (NAACP) came to life. There was no direct link between the demise of the Niagara Movement and the rise of the NAACP. But the relatively small numbers of people—black and white—who felt comfortable with the Niagara Movement's assertive stance on race were inclined to support the NAACP. In its early years the NAACP was a militant organization dedicated to racial justice. White leaders dominated it and white contributors largely financed it.

A few white progressives were deeply concerned about the rampant racial prejudice manifested so graphically in lynchings, Jim Crow, black disfranchisement, and a vicious riot in 1908 in Springfield, Illinois—Abraham Lincoln's hometown. After a gathering of leaders in January 1909 in New York City, Oswald Garrison Villard issued a call on February 12—Lincoln's Birthday—to "all believers in democracy to join a national conference to discuss present evils, the voicing of

protests, and the renewal of the struggle for civil and political liberty."

Villard was the president and editor of the New York *Evening Post* and the grandson of abolitionist William Lloyd Garrison. Prominent progressives endorsed the call, including social workers Lillian Wald and Jane Addams, literary scholar Joel E. Spingarn, and respected attorneys Clarence Darrow and Moorfield Storey. W. E. B. Du Bois, Ida Wells-Barnett, and Mary Church Terrell were the black leaders most involved in the formation of the NAACP.

Using the System

The NAACP was determined that black citizens should fully enjoy the civil and political rights the Constitution guaranteed to all citizens. It relied on the judicial and legislative systems in what would be a persistent and decades-long effort to secure those rights. The NAACP won its first major legal victory in 1915 when the Supreme Court overturned Oklahoma's grandfather clause in *Guinn v. United States.* But poll taxes and literacy tests continued to disfranchise black citizens.

In 1917 in a case brought by the Louisville NAACP branch and argued before the Supreme Court by Moorfield Storey, the court struck down a local law that enforced residential segregation by prohibiting black people and white people from selling real estate to people of the other race. The NAACP also tried in 1918 to secure a federal law prohibiting lynching. With the assistance of Congressman Leonidas Dyer, a white St. Louis Republican, the antilynching measure—the Dyer bill—passed in the House of Representatives in 1922 over vigorous Democratic opposition. But the Senate blocked it, and it never became law.

Du Bois and *The Crisis*

W. E. B. Du Bois was easily the most prominent black figure associated with the NAACP during its first quarter century. He became director of publicity and research and edited the NAACP publication, *The Crisis,* while largely leaving leadership and administrative tasks to others.

With *The Crisis,* Du Bois the scholar became Du Bois the propagandist. In the pages of *The Crisis,* he denounced white racism and atrocities and demanded that black people stand up for their rights. "Agitate, then, brother; protest, reveal the truth and refuse to be silenced. . . . A moment's let up, a moment's acquiescence, means a chance for the wolves of prejudice to get at our necks." He would not provoke violence, but he would not tolerate mistreatment either. "I am resolved to be quiet and law abiding, but to refuse to cringe in body or in soul, to resent deliberate insult, and to assert my just rights in the face of wanton aggression." These were not the even-tempered, cautious words of Booker T. Washington to which so many Americans had grown accustomed. *The Crisis* became required reading in many black homes. By 1913 it had 30,000 subscribers when the membership of the NAACP was only 3,000.

Washington versus the NAACP

In 1909 with the founding of the NAACP, Oswald Garrison Villard tried to reassure Washington that the organization posed no threat and to gain his support for the new association. "It is not to be a Washington movement, or a Du Bois movement. The idea is that there shall grow out of it, first, an annual conference . . . for the discussion by men of both races of the con-

ditions of the colored people, politically, socially, industrially and educationally."

Many black leaders and members of the NAACP, however, despised Washington and his ideology, and Washington returned the sentiment. With the assistance of his followers, he worked to subvert the new organization. Washington looked on Du Bois as little more than the puppet of white people, who dominated the leadership of the NAACP, and the Tuskegee leader declined to debate Du Bois. One of Washington's aides commented that "it would be entirely out of place for Dr. Washington to enter into any discussion with a man occupying the place that Dr. Du Bois does, for the reason that Dr. Washington is at the head of a large institution. . . . Dr. Du Bois, on the other hand, is a mere hired man, as it were, in an institution completely controlled by white people."

Charles Anderson, a Tuskegee loyalist in New York City, wrote to Washington in 1909 that the NAACP was meeting secretly and that he would attempt to disrupt its efforts. "I will find out as much about them as

W. E. B. Du Bois, the editor of *The Crisis,* assumes a reflective pose as he sits at work at his paper-strewn desk in his office. Befitting his leadership in the NAACP and his status in the Talented Tenth, Du Bois was invariably nattily attired.

possible and let you know the facts. I am doing all I can to discredit this affair." Washington relied again on allies who were editors of black newspapers to criticize the NAACP.

He also wrote Clark Howell, the white editor of the Atlanta *Constitution*, to attack Du Bois. "I think that it is too bad that an institution like Atlanta University has permitted Dr. Du Bois to go on from year to year stirring up racial strife in the South." Washington later told an alumnus of Tuskegee that the main aim of the NAACP was to destroy Washington and Tuskegee. "As a matter of straight fact, this organization is for the purpose of tearing down our work wherever possible and I think none of our friends should give it comfort."

Washington became so obsessed with the NAACP that he was not above manipulating white supremacists to damage those connected with the Association. When he learned that a group of black and white progressives associated with the NAACP were going to gather at the Café Boulevard in New York City in 1911, he allowed Charles Anderson to alert the hostile white press, which gleefullly described the multiracial dinner in the most inflammatory terms. "Fashionable White Women Sit at Board with Negroes, Japs and Chinamen to Promote 'Cause' of Miscegenation" proclaimed one headline. The New York *Press* added: "White women, evidently of the cultured and wealthier classes, fashionably attired in low-cut gowns, leaned over the tables to chat confidentially with negro men of the true African type."

Ultimately, Washington's efforts to ruin the NAACP and to reduce the influence of its supporters failed. By the time of his death in 1915, the NAACP had grown steadily to over 6,000 members and fifty local branches. Its aggressive campaign for civil and political rights replaced Washington's strategy of progress through conciliation and accommodation.

THE URBAN LEAGUE

In 1910 the National League on Urban Conditions among Negroes was founded in New York City. The goal of this social welfare organization, soon known simply as the Urban League, was to alleviate conditions black people encountered as they moved into large cities in ever increasing numbers in the early twentieth century. Like the NAACP, the Urban League was created by black and white progressives. It worked to improve housing, medical care, and recreational facilities among black residents who lived in segregated neighborhoods in New York, Philadelphia, Atlanta,

Nashville, Norfolk, and other cities. The league also assisted youngsters who ran afoul of the law, and it helped establish the Big Brother and Big Sister movements.

BLACK WOMEN AND THE CLUB MOVEMENT

Years before the Urban League and the NAACP were founded, black women began creating clubs and organizations. The local groups that began forming in the 1870s and 1880s, like the Bethel Literary and Historical Association in Washington, D.C., were mainly concerned with cultural, religious, and social matters. But many of the mostly middle-class women active in these clubs eventually became less interested in tea and gossip and more involved with community problems. In 1893 black women in Boston founded the New Era Club. They published a monthly magazine, *Woman's Era*, that featured articles on fashion, health, and family life.

In 1895 a New Era Club member, Josephine St. Pierre Ruffin, enraged by white journalist James W. Jack's vilification of black women as "prostitutes, thieves, and liars" who were "altogether without character," issued a call to "Let Us Confer Together" that drew 104 black women to a meeting in Boston. The result was the formation of the National Federation of Afro-American Women, which soon included thirty-six clubs in twelve states. In the meantime, the Colored Women's League of Washington, D.C., which had been founded in 1892, published an appeal in *Woman's Era* for black women to organize a national association at the 1895 meeting of the National Council of Women. At that gathering, representatives from several local black women's clubs organized the National Colored Woman's League.

The NACW: "Lifting as We Climb"

The two groups—The National Federation of Afro-American Women and the National Colored Woman's League—merged in 1896 to form the National Association of Colored Women (NACW) with Mary Church Terrell elected the first president. The NACW adopted the self-help motto "Lifting as We Climb," and in the reforming spirit of the progressive age, they stressed moral, mental, and material advancement. By 1914 there were 50,000 members of the NACW in 1,000 clubs nationwide.

The organization worked to eradicate poverty, end racial discrimination, and promote education, including the formation of kindergartens and day nurseries. Members cared for older people, especially former slaves. They aided orphans; assisted working mothers by providing nurseries, health care, and information on child rearing; and established homes for delinqent and abandoned girls. But there were also disagreements and conflicts among the club women. Mary Church Terrell considered Ida Wells-Barnett too abrasive and contentious. There were also regional rivalries and ideological conflicts and sensitivity over the light complexion of some leaders, including Terrell.

Phillis Wheatley Clubs

Black women also formed Phillis Wheatley clubs and homes across the nation (named in honor of the eighteenth-century African-American poet). The residences offered living accommodations for single, black working women in many cities where they were refused admittance to YWCA facilities. Some Phillis Wheatley clubs also provided nurseries and classes in domestic skills. In Cleveland, nurse Jane Edna Hunter organized a residence for single, black working women who could not find comfortable and affordable housing. In 1911 she formed the Working Girls' Home Association for cleaning women, laundresses, and private duty nurses. With association members contributing five cents a week, Hunter opened a twenty-three-room residence in 1913 that expanded to a seventy-two-room building in 1917.

Women's Suffrage

Historically, many black women had supported women's suffrage. Before the Civil War, many abolitionists, including Mary Ann Shadd Cary, Sojourner Truth, and Frederick Douglass, had also backed women's suffrage. Cary and Truth tried unsuccessfully to vote after the war. Black women, such as Caroline Remond Putnam of Massachusetts, Lottie Rollin of South Carolina, and Frances Ellen Watkins Harper of Pennsylvania attended conventions of the mostly white American Woman's Suffrage Association in the 1870s.

Black women were also involved in the long struggle for women's suffrage on the state level. Ida Wells-Barnett was a leader in the Illinois suffrage effort. By 1900 Wyoming, Utah, Colorado, and Idaho permitted women to vote, and by 1918 women in seventeen northern and western states had gained the vote. But as more women won voting rights, women's suffrage became more controversial. The proposed Nineteenth Amendment to the U.S. Constitution drove a wedge between black and white advocates of women's political rights. Many opponents of women's suffrage, especially white Southerners, warned that granting

women the right to vote would increase the number of black voters. Some white women advocated strict literacy and educational requirements for voting in an effort to limit the number of black voters, both women and men.

As it turned out, only two southern states—Kentucky and Tennessee—ratified the Nineteenth Amendment before its adoption in 1920. Black suffragists understood that the right to vote meant political power, and political power could be exercised to acquire civil rights, improve education, and gain respect. White Southerners also grasped the importance of voting rights. Thus despite the Nineteenth Amendment, large numbers of black people in the South—both men and women—remained unable to vote.

THE BLACK ELITE

Many of the black leaders described by W. E. B. Du Bois as the Talented Tenth formed protest organizations, joined reform efforts, and organized self-help groups. The leaders were middle- and upper-class black people who were better educated than most Americans—black or white.

The Upper Class

By the early twentieth century, there were several hundred wealthy African Americans. These black aristocrats were as sophisticated, refined, and conscious of their status as any group in American society. They distanced themselves from less affluent black and white people, and lived in expensive houses. Many of them possessed fair complexions. They were medical doctors, lawyers, and businessmen. While they possessed vastly more wealth than most Americans, that wealth paled in comparison to the huge fortunes of the richest American families like the Rockefellers, Carnegies, and Vanderbilts.

The black elite formed exclusive organizations that jealously limited membership to the small black upper class. In the 1860s the Ugly Fishing Club was transformed into an organization made up of New York City's wealthiest black men. It soon came to be known simply as the Ugly Club, and its membership spread to Newport, Rhode Island, Baltimore, and Philadelphia. In 1904 two wealthy Philadelphia physicians, a dentist, and a pharmacist formed Sigma Pi Beta, better known as Boulé. It was restricted to male college graduates, and it aimed to provide "inspiration, relaxation, intellectual stimulation, and brotherhood." Boulé expanded

MARY CHURCH TERRELL

Mary Church Terrell lived from the year of the Emancipation Proclamation (1863) to the year that the U.S. Supreme Court declared segregated schools unconstitutional (1954). During those nine decades, she exemplified the African-American leaders whom W. E. B. Du Bois called the Talented Tenth. The daughter of slaves, she acquired a superb education and became prominent in Washington's black elite. She was ever conscious of her social status, education, and fair complexion. She was also absolutely dedicated to the elimination of Jim Crow and the cause of African-American women.

Mary Church was born in Civil War Memphis and raised during Reconstruction. She led a sheltered life and went on to Oberlin College where she studied classics, became proficient in languages, and earned an M.A. In 1891 she married Robert H. Terrell, a Harvard graduate who had earned a law degree at Howard. He was an auditor in the U.S. Treasury Department and later became a District of Columbia municipal judge.

Mary Church Terrell immersed herself in literary, social, and political activities. She spearheaded the creation of the Colored Women's League and became the first president of the NACW in 1896. Terrell believed that well-to-do black women had a responsibility to assist struggling and poorer women of color.

Terrell was an inspirational speaker. She spoke in 1904 at the International Congress of Women in Berlin—in German, French, and English. Mamie Garvin Fields recalled a speech Terrell delivered in Charleston, South Carolina, in 1916:

Oh, my, when I saw her walk onto that podium in her pink evening dress and long white gloves, with her beautifully done hair, she *was* the Modern Woman. . . . Regal, intelligent, powerful, reaching out from time to time with that long glove, she looked and sounded like the Modern Woman that she talked about.

Terrell was active in the NAACP, which was not easy in light of her close relationship with Booker T. Washington and his wife, Margaret Murray Washington. She could not afford to alienate Washington because he possessed enough influence to prevent her husband's reappointment as judge. Terrell managed to convince Washington that she supported him, but in fact, she was devoted to the NAACP and its program. She served on its board, and spoke forcefully on civil rights. She risked the wrath of President Theodore Roosevelt after she criticized his dismissal of three companies of black soldiers following the Brownsville incident (see Chapter 15). She presented President William Howard Taft with NAACP petitions against lynching. She wrote articles attacking chain gangs, peonage, disfranchisement, and lynching. She worked with progressive organizations, such as the Women's International League for Peace and Freedom, and supported women's suffrage and the Nineteenth Amendment.

The Terrells were active in Washington's black elite—the Four Hundred. They attended balls, concerts, and parties, traveled extensively, and belonged to Washington's most exclusive black congregation, the Lincoln Temple Congregational Church, and she was active in Delta Sigma Theta sorority.

Mary Church Terrell consistently opposed racial discrimination and protested to Oberlin College officials when her daughters encountered more prejudice as students than she had. A lifelong Republican, she opposed President Franklin Roosevelt's inaction on civil rights. At the age of eighty-seven she demonstrated against Thompson's Restaurant, an all-white establishment in Washington. Her death in 1954 ended her campaign against Jim Crow and for women's rights.

Mary Church Terrell summed up her legacy in her 1940 autobiography, *A Colored Woman in a White World*. "This is the story of a colored woman living in a white world. It cannot possibly be like a story written by a white woman. A white woman has only one handicap to overcome—that of sex. I have two—both sex and race. I belong to the only group in this country which has two such huge obstacles to surmount. Colored men have only one—that of race."

to seven chapters in cities that included Chicago and Memphis, but its membership totaled a mere 177.

Organizations like the Diamondback Club and the Cosmos Club in Washington, the Loendi Club in Pittsburgh, and the Bachelor-Benedict Club in New York sponsored luxurious banquets, dances, and debutante balls. Several of these groups owned ornate clubhouses. These elite societies and cliques typically competed to demonstrate social exclusivity and preeminence.

Fraternities and Sororities

Among the black elite were also the African Americans who established the Greek letter black fraternities and sororities. In 1906, seven students at Cornell University formed Alpha Phi Alpha, the first college fraternity for black men. Within a few years, it had chapters at the University of Michigan, Yale, Columbia, and Ohio State. The first black sorority, Alpha Kappa Alpha, was founded in 1908 at Howard University.

Several other Greek letter organizations were subsequently launched at Howard: Omega Psi Phi fraternity in 1911, Delta Sigma Theta sorority in 1913, Phi Beta Sigma in 1914, and Zeta Phi Beta sorority in 1920. In addition, in 1911 Kappa Alpha Psi fraternity was founded at Indiana University, and Sigma Gamma Rho sorority was formed in Indianapolis in 1922.

Besides providing college students with an opportunity to enjoy each other's company, the black fraternities and sororities stressed scholarship, social graces, and

---

PROFILE

LEWIS LATIMER, BLACK INVENTOR

Lewis H. Latimer (1848–1928) was a draftsman, inventor, and pioneer in the electrical industry. During his lifetime, Latimer was awarded eight patents for his inventions. He was born in Chelsea, Massachusetts, in 1848. His parents had fled from slavery and settled in Boston where abolitionists including William Lloyd Garrison and Frederick Douglass raised funds to purchase their freedom.

After a year in the Union Navy during the Civil War, Latimer worked as an office boy for the patent solicitor firm of Crosby and Gould. There he taught himself drafting. As a draftsman, Latimer worked closely with inventors and began to tinker with ideas for inventions. In 1874, he received his first patent for improving the toilet on passenger railroad cars. He developed a flushing mechanism that prevented the upflow of sewage and cinders. He also executed drawings for Alexander Graham Bell's patent application for the telephone. Latimer later worked on electric lights, and in 1882 he

Lewis H. Latimer published *Incandescent Lighting: A Practical Description of the Edison System*—one of the first books on electric lighting—in 1896.

received a patent for producing carbon filaments that made electric lighting more practical.

Latimer became superintendent of the incandescent lamp department of the United States Electric Lighting Company and supervised the installation of lights for buildings in the United States and Canada. In 1883, Thomas A. Edison hired Latimer as an engineer, chief draftsman, and expert witness in patent infringement cases. In 1890, Latimer published a book, *Incandescent Lighting: A Practical Description of the Edison System*. He served as chief draftsman for General Electric/Westinghouse Board of Patent Control when it was established in 1896.

Men who had worked with Thomas A. Edison joined together in 1918 as the Edison Pioneers to preserve memories of their early days working together and to honor Edison's genius and achievements. Latimer was a founding member and the only African-American Edison Pioneer. He died in Flushing, New York, on December 11, 1928.

PROFILE

GEORGE WASHINGTON CARVER AND ERNEST EVERETT JUST

George Washington Carver and Ernest Everett Just each rose from humble beginnings in the nineteenth century to become highly regarded biologists. Carver was born in 1864 or 1865 to slave parents in Diamond Grove, Missouri. Eager to learn, he spent much of his youth engaged in menial labor around Missouri, Iowa, and Kansas as he acquired an uneven education. He spent a year at Simpson College and then enrolled at Iowa State University in 1891 at age 25 as its sole black student. He compiled a superb academic record, participated in an array of student activities, and took charge of the campus greenhouse. He became fascinated with botany and focused on mycology (the study of fungi) and cross-fertilization.

Just was born in Charleston, South Carolina, in 1883 and grew up on nearby James Island where his mother toiled in phosphate mines following the death of his father. He attended local schools and earned a teacher training certificate in 1899 from what is now South Carolina State University. Just went on to Kimball Union Academy in New Hampshire, and he graduated with honors from Dartmouth College in 1907 with a major in biology and minors in Greek and history.

Just was hired by Howard University in Washington, D.C., and spent the rest of his teaching career there. In 1911 he helped establish Omega Psi Phi, which emerged as a major black fraternity. Although hired to teach English and rhetoric, he soon changed to zoology and biology, the subjects in which he had developed an abiding interest. He spent several summers at the Marine Biology Laboratory at Woods Hole, Massachusetts, and earned a Ph.D. in zoology from the University of Chicago in 1916.

While Just felt more at home engaged in research in a laboratory, Carver felt more comfortable experimenting with crops in a field. At the invitation of Booker T. Washington, Carver left a promising career at Iowa State in 1896 to take charge of the agriculture program at Tuskegee Institute. Having studied with two men at Iowa State—James Wilson and Henry C. Wallace—who became U.S. secretaries of agriculture, Carver established political ties to Washington that greatly benefitted Tuskegee. He became the director of the nation's only black agricultural experiment station.

Carver was a superb teacher in and out of the classroom, but he was a less than efficient administrator who sometimes clashed with Booker T. Washington. Carver committed himself to working with impoverished black farmers, seeking to make them more productive and less dependent on cotton. He sponsored outreach programs and farmers' institutes. He discovered hundreds of uses for the protein-rich peanut. And he experimented extensively with sweet potatoes.

Carver became a folk hero by the 1930s with his gregarious personality and self-effacing demeanor. He never married and lived in a student dormitory at Tuskegee. He wore a tattered coat with a fresh flower in the lapel. Though he never earned more than $1,200 a year, he gave more than $60,000 to Tuskegee before he died in 1943.

Just, confronted with the lack of opportunities available to a dedicated black scientist at white universities, pursued his research in the fertilization of marine animals at Woods Hole. But even there some scientists shunned him and others patronized him. Nevertheless, by 1928 he had published 35 articles, mostly on fertilization. Awarded a sizable grant from the Julius Rosenwald Foundation, he spent much of the 1930s engaged in research in Italy, Germany, and France. In 1939 he published *Biology of the Cell Surface*.

Just married Ethel Highwarden, a Howard faculty member, in 1912. They had three children, but later divorced. In 1939 he married Maid Hedwig Schnetzler, a German scientist. Just died of cancer in 1941.

Both George Washington Carver and Ernest Everett Just were awarded the NAACP's Spingarn Medal—Just in 1915 and Carver in 1923.

community involvement. Alpha Phi Alpha created the "Go to High School, Go to College" campaign in 1919. Kappa Alpha Psi adopted the "Guide Right" program to assist black youngsters in 1922. In 1923 Alpha Kappa Alpha opened a mobile health clinic in Mississippi.

PRESIDENTIAL POLITICS

Since Reconstruction, black voters had loyally supported the Republican party and its presidential candidates. "The Party of Lincoln" welcomed that support and periodically rewarded black men with federal jobs. Republican presidents Theodore Roosevelt (1901–1909) and William Howard Taft (1909–1913) continued that policy.

Frustrated by the Republicans

But other presidential actions more than offset whatever goodwill these appointments generated. Roosevelt discharged three companies of black soldiers after the Brownsville incident in 1906, and Taft tolerated restrictions on black voters in the South and encouraged the development of a "lily white" Republican party, removing black people from federal jobs in the region.

In 1912 the Republican party split in a bitter feud between President Taft and Theodore Roosevelt, and a third political party—the Progressive party—emerged. The Progressives nominated Roosevelt to run against Taft and the Democratic candidate, Woodrow Wilson. But as the delegates at the Progressive convention in Chicago sang the "Battle Hymn of the Republic," southern black men who had come to the gathering stood outside the hall, denied admission by white Progressives.

Woodrow Wilson

It was not a complete shock that militant black leaders like William Monroe Trotter and W. E. B. Du Bois urged black voters to support Woodrow Wilson, the Democrat, in the 1912 presidential election. Wilson was the reform governor of New Jersey, and he had been president of Princeton University. Trotter and Du Bois were impressed with Wilson's academic background and his promise to pursue a progressive policy toward black Americans. Du Bois wrote:

> Wilson is a cultivated scholar and he has brains. We have, therefore, a conviction that Mr. Wilson will treat black men and their interests with foresighted fairness. He will not advance the cause of

an oligarchy in the South, he will not seek further means of 'jim crow' insult, he will not dismiss black men wholesale from office, and he will remember that the Negro has a right to be heard and considered.

But as president, Wilson proved to be no friend of black people. Born in Virginia and raised in South Carolina, Wilson had thoroughly absorbed white southern racial views. Federal agencies and buildings were fully segregated early during Wilson's tenure. In 1914 Trotter and a black delegation met with Wilson to protest segregation in the treasury department and the post office. Wilson defended separation of the races as a means to avoid friction. Trotter vehemently disagreed, and Wilson became visibly irritated. The president warned that he would no longer meet with the group if Trotter remained their spokesman.

BLACK MEN AND THE MILITARY IN WORLD WAR I

In 1915–1916, Wilson faced more than problems with dissatisfied black people. U.S.-Mexican relations had steadily deteriorated after a revolution and civil war in Mexico. War in Europe threatened to draw the United States into conflict with Germany.

The Punitive Expedition to Mexico

In 1914, war almost broke out between the United States and Mexico when U.S. marines landed at Vera Cruz after an attack on American sailors. Then in March 1916, Francisco "Pancho" Villa, one of the participants in Mexico's civil war, led a force of Mexican rebels across the border into New Mexico in an effort to provoke war between Mexico and the United States. Fifteen Americans were killed, including seven U.S. soldiers. In response, Wilson dispatched a "punitive expedition" that eventually numbered 15,000 U.S. troops under the command of General John J. "Black Jack" Pershing. Pershing acquired the nickname "Black Jack" after commanding black troops in Cuba during the Spanish-American War.

U.S. forces, including the black Tenth Cavalry (see Chapter 15), spent ten months in Mexico in a futile effort to capture Villa. The Tenth Cavalry was—as had been the case with black troops since the Civil War—commanded by white men. But Lieutenant Colonel Charles Young, an 1889 black graduate of the U.S. Military Academy at West Point, helped lead the regiment.

Young led the black troops against a contingent of Villa's rebels who had ambushed an element of the Thirteenth Cavalry, a white unit, at Santa Cruz de Villegas. Major Frank Tompkins of the Thirteenth was so relieved to be rescued that he reportedly exclaimed to Young: "By God, Young, I could kiss every black face out there." Young supposedly replied, "If you want to, you may start with me." U.S. troops were withdrawn from Mexico in 1917 as the probability increased that the United States would enter World War I against Germany.

World War I

Wilson initially sought to stay out of the war in Europe, which had been raging since 1914, but repeated German submarine attacks on civilian vessels and the loss of large numbers of American lives infuriated the president and much of the nation. So when the United States declared war on Germany on April 6, 1917, most African Americans supported the war effort. As in previous conflicts, black people sought to demonstrate their loyalty and devotion to the country through military service. "If this is *our* country," declared W. E. B. Du Bois, "then this is *our* war. We must fight it with every ounce of blood and treasure."

Some white leaders were less enthusiastic about the participation of black men. One southern governor wondered about the wisdom of having the military train and arm thousands of black men at southern camps and posts. General Pershing argued for the use of black troops, but insisted on white leadership. "Under capable white officers and with sufficient training, negro soldiers have always acquitted themselves creditably."

Black Troops and Officers

There were about 10,000 black regulars in the U.S. Army in 1917: The Ninth and Tenth Cavalry regiments and the Twenty-Fourth and Twenty-Fifth Infantry regiments. There were more than 5,000 black men in the Navy, but virtually all of them were waiters, kitchen attendants, and stokers for the ships' boilers. The Marine Corps did not admit black men. During World War I, the newly formed Selective Service system drafted more than 370,000 black men—13 percent of all draftees—though none of the local draft boards had black members. Several all-black state national guard units were also incorporated into federal service.

Though the military remained rigidly segregated, there was political pressure from black newspapers and the NAACP to commission black officers to lead black troops. The War Department created an officer training

school at Fort Des Moines, Iowa. Nearly 1,250 black men enrolled—1,000 were civilians and 250 were enlisted men from the regular regiments—and over 1,000 received commissions. Black officers, however, were confined to the lower ranks. None of these new black officers were promoted above captain, and the overall command of black units remained in white hands.

Lieutenant Colonel Charles Young was eligible to lead black and white troops in World War I. He had already served in Cuba, the Philippines, Haiti, and Mexico. Several white soldiers complained, however, that they did not want to take orders from a black man, and over Young's protests, military authorities forced him to retire by claiming that he had high blood pressure. Young insisted that he was in good health, and he rode a horse from his home in Xenia, Ohio, to Washington, D.C., to prove it. But Young remained on the retired list until he was given command of a training unit in Illinois five days before the war ended.

Discrimination and Its Effects

Most white military leaders, politicians, and journalists embraced racial stereotypes and expected little from black soldiers. As in earlier American wars, black troops were discriminated against, abused, and neglected. Some were compelled to drill with picks and shovels rather than rifles. At Camp Hill, Virginia, black men lived in tents with no floors, no blankets, and no bathing facilities through a cold winter. White men failed to salute black officers, and black officers were denied admission to officers' clubs. Morale among black troops was low, and their performance sometimes reflected it.

Military authorities did not expect to use black troops in combat. The Army preferred to employ black troops in labor battalions, as stevedores, in road construction, and as cooks and bakers. Of more than 380,000 black men who served in World War I, only 42,000 went into combat. Black troops represented 3 percent of U.S. combat strength. The Army did not prepare black soldiers adequately for combat, but military leaders complained when black soldiers who did face combat performed poorly in battle.

The 368th Infantry Regiment of the 92nd Division came in for especially harsh criticism. Fighting alongside the French in September 1918, the second and third battalions fell back in disorder. Some black officers and enlisted men ran. The white regimental commander blamed black officers, and thirty of them were relieved of command. Five officers were court-martialed for cowardice; four were sentenced to death and one to life in prison. All were later freed. But black Lieutenant

Lieutenant Colonel Charles D. Young, an 1889 graduate of the U.S. Military Academy at West Point who served in Cuba, the Philippines, Haiti, and Mexico, was not permitted to command troops during World War I. He returned to military service at the end of the war, and was sent to Liberia to help train that country's army. He died while on furlough in Nigeria in 1922.

Howard H. Long agreed that the perceptions of white officers caused the poor performance. "Many of the [white] field officers seemed far more concerned with reminding their Negro subordinates that they were Negroes than they were in having an effective unit that would perform well in combat."

Even the white commander of the 92nd Division, General Charles C. Ballou, identified white officers as the main problem. "It was my misfortune to be handicapped by many white officers who were rabidly hostile to the idea of a colored officer, and who continually conveyed misinformation to the staff of the superior units, and generally created much trouble and discon-

tent. Such men will never give the Negro the square deal that is his just due."

While white officials stressed the weaknesses of the 368th Infantry Regiment, they mostly ignored the commendable records of the 369th, 370th, 371st, and 372nd regiments. The 369th compiled an exemplary combat record. Sent to the front for ninety-one consecutive days, these "Men of Bronze"—as they came to be known—consisted mainly of soldiers from the Fifteenth New York National Guard. They fought alongside the French and were given French weapons, uniforms, helmets, and food (but not the wine that French soldiers received). They had an outstanding military band led by Jim Europe, one of the finest musical leaders of the early twentieth century. The 369th lived up to their motto, "Let's Go," as they took part in some of the war's heaviest fighting. They never lost a trench nor gave up a prisoner. By June 1918, French commanders were asking for all the black troops the Americans could send.

Most French civilians and troops, unfazed by racist warnings from white American officials about the presumed danger black men posed to white women, praised the conduct of black soldiers and accepted them as equals. Following the triumph of the Allies in World War I, French authorities awarded the Croix de Guerre, one of France's highest military medals, to the men of the 369th, the 371st, and the 372nd Regiments.

Black troops returned to America on segregated ships. The Fifteenth New York National Guard Unit from the 369th Regiment and its famed band were not permitted to join the farewell parade in New York City. Even when white Americans offered praise, it was riddled with racist stereotypes. The Milwaukee *Sentinel* offered a typical compliment. "Those two colored regiments fought well, and it calls for special recognition. Is there no way of getting a cargo of watermelons over there?"

Du Bois's Disappointment

Black leaders who had supported American entry in the war were embittered at the treatment of black soldiers. During the war in 1918, Du Bois appealed to black people in *The Crisis* to "close ranks" and support the war.

> We of the colored race have no ordinary interest in the outcome. That which the German power represents today spells death to the aspirations of Negroes and all darker races for equality, freedom and democracy. Let us not hesitate. Let us, while this war lasts, forget our special grievances and close ranks with our own white fellow citizens and the allied nations that are fighting for democracy.

Du Bois's unequivocal support may well have been connected to his effort to secure an officer's commission in military intelligence through the intervention of Joel E. Spingarn, chairman of the NAACP Board of Directors. Du Bois did not get his commission. What he did get was criticism for his "close ranks" editorial. His former ally, William Monroe Trotter, said that Du Bois had "finally weakened, compromised, deserted the fight, [and] betrayed the cause of his race." To Trotter, Du Bois was "a rank quitter in the cause for equal rights."

In 1930 Du Bois confessed that he should not have supported U.S. intervention in the war.

> I was swept off my feet during the world war by the emotional response of America to what seemed to be a great call to duty. The thing that I did not understand is how easy and inevitable it is for an appeal to blood and force to smash to utter negation any ideal for which it is used. Instead of a war to end war, or a war to save democracy, we found ourselves during and after the war descending to the meanest and most sordid of selfish actions.

By the end of World War I, Du Bois—who had visited black troops in France—could see that black loyalty and sacrifice had not eroded white racism. He wrote defiantly in *The Crisis* that black people were determined to make America yield to its democratic ideals.

> But by the God of heaven, we are cowards and jackasses if now that the war is over, we do not marshal every ounce of our brain and brawn to fight a sterner, longer, more unbending battle against the forces of hell in our own land.
>
> *We return.*
> *We return from fighting.*
> *We return fighting.*
>
> Make way for Democracy! We saved it in France, and by the Great Jehovah, we will save it in the United States of America, or know the reason why.

RACE RIOTS

Despite the reformist impulse of the progressive era and the democratic ideals trumpeted as the United States went to war against Germany, most white Americans clung to social Darwinism and white supremacy. White people reacted with contempt and violence to demands by black people for fairer treatment and equal opportunities in American society. The campaigns of the NAACP, the efforts of the black club women, and the services and sacrifices of black men in the war not only failed to alter white racial perceptions but were sometimes accompanied by a backlash against African Americans. Ten black men still in uniform were lynched in 1919.

Many white Americans concurred with Mississippi senator James K. Vardaman when he declared in 1914 that white people would not accept black claims for a meaningful political and legal role in America.

> God Almighty never intended that the negro should share with the white man in the government of this

country. . . . Do not forget that. It matters not what I may say or others may think; it matters not what constitutions may contain or statutes provide, wherever the negro is in sufficient numbers to imperil the white man's civilization or question the white man's supremacy the white man is going to find some way around the difficulty. And that is just as true in the North as it is in the South. You need not deceive yourselves about that. The feeling against the negro in Illinois when he gets in the white man's way is quite as strong, more bitter, less regardful of the negro's feelings and conditions than it is in Mississippi.

The racial violence that had permeated southern life in the late nineteenth century expanded into northern communities as many white Americans responded with hostility to the arrival of black migrants from the South. Black people defended themselves, and casualties among both races escalated (Map 16–1).

Atlanta 1906

In 1906—eleven years after Booker T. Washington delivered his Cotton States Exposition address there—white mobs attacked black residents in Atlanta. Several factors aggravated white racial apprehensions in the city. In 1902 four black and four white people had been killed in a riot there. Many rural black people, attracted by economic opportunities, had moved to Atlanta. But white residents considered the newcomers more lawless and immoral than the long-time black residents. The Atlanta newspapers—*The Constitution*, *The Journal*, and *The Georgian*—ran inflammatory accounts about black crime and black men who brutalized white women. Many of these stories were false or exaggerated. Two white Democrats, Hoke Smith and Clark Howell, were engaged in a divisive campaign for a U.S. Senate seat in 1906, and both candidates stirred up racial animosity. There were also determined and ultimately successful efforts underway to disfranchise black voters in Georgia.

On a warm Saturday night, September 22, 1906, a white man jumped on a box on Decatur Street, one of Atlanta's main thoroughfares, and waved an Atlanta newspaper emblazoned with the headline: "THIRD ASSAULT." He hollered, "Are white men going to stand for this?" The crowd roared, "No! Save our women!" "Kill the niggers." A five-day orgy of violence followed.

The mayor, police, and fire departments vainly tried to stop the mob. Thousands of white people roamed the

Map 16–1 Major Race Riots, 1900–1921. In the fifteen years between 1906 and 1921, race conflicts and riots occurred in dozens of American communities as black people migrated in increasing numbers to urban areas. The violence reached a peak in the immediate aftermath of World War I during the Red Summer of 1919. White Americans—North and South—were determined to keep black people confined to a subordinate role as menial laborers and restricted to well defined all-black neighborhoods. African Americans who had made significant economic and military contributions to the war effort and who had congregated in large numbers in American cities insisted on participating on a more equitable basis in American society.

streets in search of black victims. Black people were indiscriminately tortured, beaten, and killed. White men pulled black passengers off streetcars. They destroyed black businesses. As white men armed themselves, the police disarmed black men. Black men and women who surrendered to marauding white mobs in hopes of mercy were not spared. Black men who fought back only further infuriated the crazed white crowd. Twenty-five black people and one white person died, and hundreds were injured in the riot.

Du Bois hurried home to Atlanta from a trip to Alabama to defend his wife and child. He waited on his porch with a shotgun for a mob that never came. He later explained, "I would without hesitation have sprayed their guts over the grass." In New York, black editor T. Thomas Fortune called for a violent black response: "It makes my blood boil. I would like to be there with a good force of armed men to make Rome howl." Fortune demanded retribution. "I cannot believe that the policy of non-resistance in a situation like that of Atlanta can result in anything but contempt and massacre of the race."

Booker T. Washington looked for a silver lining in the awful affair by noting that "while there is disorder in one community there is peace and harmony in thousands of others." He said that black resistance would merely result in more black fatalities. Washington went to Atlanta and appealed for racial reconciliation.

A Committee of Safety of ten black and ten white leaders was formed. Charles T. Hopkins, an influential white Atlantan, warned in strong paternalist terms, "If we let this dependent race be butchered before our eyes, we cannot face God in the judgement day." But little real racial cooperation resulted. No members of the white mob were brought to justice. Black Georgia voters were disfranchised. Atlanta's streetcars were segregated. The city had no public high school for black youngsters. The Carnegie Library did not admit black people, and the Atlanta police force had no black officers.

Springfield 1908

Two years later in August 1908, white citizens of Springfield, Illinois, attacked black residents in an episode that led to the creation of the NAACP in 1909. George Richardson, a black man, was falsely accused of raping a white woman. The sheriff managed to save Richardson by getting him out of town. But an angry mob tore into Springfield's small black population. Six black people were shot and killed, two were lynched, dozens were injured, and damage in the thousands of dollars was inflicted on black homes and businesses. About 2,000 black people were driven out of the community.

There was even more violence in the second decade of the twentieth century as major racial conflicts occurred between 1917 and 1921 in East St. Louis, Illinois; Houston, Texas; Chicago; Elaine, Arkansas; and Tulsa, Oklahoma. Smaller violent confrontations occurred at Washington, D.C.; Charleston, S.C.; Knoxville, Tennessee; Omaha, Nebraska; and Waco and Longview, Texas. While different incidents sparked each riot, the underlying causes tended to be similar. White residents were concerned that recently arrived black migrants would compete for jobs and housing.

East St. Louis 1917

East St. Louis, Illinois, was a gritty industrial town of nearly 60,000 across the Mississippi River from St. Louis, Missouri. About 10 percent of the inhabitants were black. The town's schools, public facilities, and neighborhoods were segregated. Racial tensions increased in February 1917 after 470 black workers were hired to replace white members of the American Federation of Labor who had gone on strike against the Aluminum Ore Company. On July 1, several white people drove through a black neighborhood firing guns. Shortly after, two white plainclothes police officers drove into the same neighborhood and were shot and killed by residents who may have believed that the drive-by shooters had returned.

Angry white mobs then sought revenge. Black people were mutilated and killed, and their bodies were thrown into the river. Black homes, many of them little more than cabins and shacks, were burned. Hundreds of black people were left homeless. The police joined the rioters. Thirty-five black people and eight white people died in the violence.

The NAACP sent W. E. B. Du Bois and Martha Gruening to East St. Louis. They compiled a twenty-four-page report, "Massacre at East St. Louis," that documented instance after instance of brutality. "Negroes were 'flushed' from the burning houses, and ran for their lives, screaming and begging for mercy. A Negro crawled into a shed and fired on the white men. Guardsmen started after him, but when they saw he was armed, turned to the mob and said: 'He's armed boys. You can have him. A white man's life is worth the lives of a thousand Negroes.'"

To protest the riot, the NAACP organized a silent march in New York City and thousands of well-dressed black people marched to muffled drums down Fifth Avenue.

Houston 1917

A month after the East St. Louis riot, black soldiers in Houston attacked police officers and civilians. The Third Battalion of the 24th Infantry recently had been transferred from Wyoming and California to Camp Logan near Houston where the black troops came face-to-face with Jim Crow. Streetcars and public facilities were segregated. Local white and Hispanic people regularly called the black troops "niggers."

On August 23 a black soldier tried to prevent a police officer, Lee Sparks, from beating a black woman. Sparks clubbed the soldier and hauled him off to jail. Corporal Charles W. Baltimore later attempted to determine what had happened, and he was also beaten and incarcerated. Both soldiers were later released. But black troops were infuriated as word of the abuse spread.

About one hundred armed black soldiers mounted a two-hour assault on the police station. Sixteen white and Hispanic residents, including five policemen, and four black soldiers and two black civilians were killed. The Army charged the sixty-three black soldiers with mutiny. The NAACP retained the son of Texas legend Sam Houston to help defend them, but nineteen black troops were hanged (including Corporal Baltimore), and sixty-seven others sentenced to prison. Officer Lee Sparks remained on the police force and killed two black people later that year.

Chicago 1919

Between 1916 and 1919, the black population of Chicago doubled as migrants from the South moved north in search of jobs, political rights, and humane treatment. Many encountered a violent reception. A severe housing shortage strained the boundaries between crowded, segregated black neighborhoods and white residential areas. In the months after World War I ended in November 1918, racial tensions increased as black men were hired to replace striking white workers in several industries in Chicago.

The Chicago riot began on Sunday, July 27, 1919—one day after black troops were welcomed home with a parade down the city's Michigan Avenue. Eugene Williams, a young black man, was swimming in Lake Michigan and inadvertently crossed the invisible boundary that separated the black and white beaches and bathing areas. He was stoned by white people and drowned. Instead of arresting the alleged perpetrators, the police arrested a black man who complained about police inaction.

Williams's death set off a week of violence that left twenty-three black people and fifteen white people dead. More than five hundred were injured and nearly 1,000 were left homeless after fire raged though a Lithuanian neighborhood. Not only did police fail to stem the violence; they often also joined roaming white mobs as they attacked black pedestrians and streetcar passengers. Black men formed a barrier along State Street to stop the advance of white gangs from the stockyard district. Three regiments of the Illinois National Guard were sent into the streets, but the violence ended only on Saturday, August 1, as heavy rains kept people indoors.

During the riot, the Chicago *Defender,* the city's black newspaper, reported many violent incidents. "In the early [Tuesday] morning a thirteen-year-old lad standing on his porch at 51st and Wabash Avenue was shot to death by a white man who, in an attempt to get away, encountered a mob and his existence became history. A mounted policeman, unknown, fatally wounded a small boy in the block of Dearborn Street and was shot to death by some unknown rioter."

Elaine 1919

In the fall of 1919, black sharecroppers in and around Elaine, Arkansas, attempted to organize a union and withhold their cotton from the market until they received a higher price. Deputy sheriffs tried to break up a union meeting in a black church, and one of the deputies was killed. In retaliation, white people killed dozens of black people. No white people were prosecuted, but twelve black men were convicted of the deputy's murder. They were sentenced to death, and sixty-seven other black men received prison terms of up to twenty years. Many were tortured and beaten while they were held in jail. Ida Wells-Barnett and the Equal Rights League generated enormous publicity about the case. The NAACP appealed the convictions and in 1923 the Supreme Court overturned them. The court agreed with NAACP attorney Moorfield Storey that the defendants had not received a fair trial.

Tulsa 1921

Violence erupted in Tulsa, Oklahoma, on May 31, 1921, after still another black man was accused of rape. Dick Rowland allegedly assaulted a white woman elevator operator, and rumors circulated that white men intended to lynch him. To protect Rowland, who was later found innocent, black men assembled at the courthouse jail where white men also gathered. Angry words were exchanged, and shooting erupted. Several black and white men died in the chaos that ensued.

Black men retreated to their neighborhood, known as Greenwood, to guard their families and homes. The governor dispatched the national guard, and the sheriff removed Rowland from the jail to an unknown location. By the morning of June 1, some five hundred white men confronted about 1,000 black men across a set of railroad tracks. White men in sixty to seventy automobiles were also cruising around the black residential area. Approximately fifty armed black people defended themselves in a black church near the edge of their neighborhood as white men advanced on them. The attackers set fire to the church. As black people fled the burning building, they were shot. More fires were set. About 2,000 black residents managed to escape to a convention hall as most of Greenwood's homes, churches, and businesses went up in flames. As many as three hundred black people and twenty white people may have perished in perhaps the single bloodiest episode of racial violence in American history.

THE GREAT MIGRATION

The great migration of African Americans from the rural South to the urban North began as a trickle of people after the Civil War and became a flood of human beings by the second decade of the twentieth century

(Table 16–1). Between 1910 and 1940, 1,750,000 black people left the South. As a result, the black population outside the South doubled by 1940. Most of the initial wave of migrants were younger people born in the 1880s and 1890s who had no recollection of slavery, but who anticipated a better future for themselves and their families in the North.

Why Migrate?

People moved for many reasons. Often they were both pushed from their rural circumstances and pulled toward urban areas. The push resulted from disasters in southern agriculture in the 1910s. The boll weevil destroyed cotton crops across the South from Mexico to the Carolinas, and floods devastated Mississippi and Alabama in 1915. The pull resulted from labor shortages created by World War I in northern industry and manufacturing. The war all but ended European immigration to the United States, eliminating a main source of cheap labor. At the same time, European governments and the United States placed huge orders for war material with northern factories. Thousands of jobs became available in steel mills, railroads, meatpacking plants, and the automobile industry. Northern businessmen sent labor agents to recruit southern workers.

Table 16-1 Black Population Growth in Selected Northern Cities, 1910–1920

	1910		1920		
	Number	Percent	Number	Percent	Percent Increase
New York	91,709	1.9%	152,467	2.7%	66.3%
Chicago	44,103	2.0	109,458	4.1	148.2
Philadelphia	84,459	5.5	134,229	7.4	58.9
Detroit	5,741	1.2	40,838	4.1	611.3
St. Louis	43,960	6.4	69,854	9.0	58.9
Cleveland	8,448	1.5	34,451	4.3	307.8
Pittsburgh	25,623	4.8	37,725	6.4	47.2
Cincinnati	19,739	5.4	30,079	7.5	53.2
Indianapolis	21,816	9.3	34,678	11.0	59.0
Newark	9,475	2.7	16,977	4.1	79.2
Kansas City	23,566	9.5	30,719	9.5	30.4
Columbus	12,739	7.0	22,181	9.4	74.1
Gary	383	2.3	5,299	9.6	1,283.6
Youngstown	1,936	2.4	6,662	5.0	244.1
Buffalo	1,773	.4	4,511	.9	154.4
Toledo	1,877	1.1	5,691	2.3	203.2
Akron	657	1.0	5,580	2.7	749.3

Source: U.S. Department of Commerce.

Many southern white people reacted ambivalently to the loss of black residents. They welcomed the departure of people whom they held in such low regard, but they also worried about the loss of tenants and sharecroppers. Southern states and municipalities required labor agents to obtain licenses to recruit workers. Angry white landowners and businessmen threatened some of these agents and forced them to leave southern towns.

Black newspapers, such as the Pittsburgh *Courier* and especially the Chicago *Defender*, encouraged black Southerners to move north. Black railroad porters and dining car employees distributed thousands of copies of the *Defender* throughout the South. One unnamed black man wrote in the *Defender* that sensible men would leave the poverty, injustice, and violence of the South for the cold weather of the North. "To die from the bite of frost is far more glorious than that of the mob. I beg of you, my brothers, to leave that benighted land. You are free men."

A black resident of one of South Carolina's Sea Islands explained in 1917 that he left to earn more money. "I could work and dig all year on the Island and best I could do would be to make $100 and take a chance of making nothin'. Well, I figured I could make 'roun' thirty or thirty-five dollars every week and at that rate save possibly $100 every two months." Like many migrants, he moved more than once. He first went to Savannah, and then to Philadelphia, before finally settling in Brooklyn, New York.

Black people who departed the South escaped the most blatant forms of Jim Crow and the injustice in the judicial system. Black women fled the sexual exploitation of white and black men. Black people in the North could vote. The North offered better public schools. In the early twentieth century the South had almost no public high schools for black youngsters, and the longer school year in the urban North was not tied to the demands of planting and harvesting crops.

Some black people migrated to escape the dull, bleak, impoverished life and culture of the rural South. One young woman left South Carolina's St. Helena Island in 1919. "[I] got tired of the Island. Too lonesome. Go to bed at six o'clock. Everything dead. No dances, no moving picture show, no nothing. 'Coz every once in a while they would have a dance, but here you could go to 'em every Saturday night. That's why people move more than anything else."

The decision to migrate could take years of pondering and planning. To depart was to leave family, friends, and familiar surroundings behind for the uncertainty, confusion, and rapid pace of urban communities. Migrants often first moved to southern towns or cities, and

then headed for a larger city. Poet and writer Langston Hughes was born in Joplin, Missouri, in 1902 and moved to Lincoln, Illinois. "I had no sooner graduated from grammar school in Lincoln than we moved from Illinois to Cleveland. My stepfather sent for us. He was working in a steel mill during the war, and making lots of money. But it was hard work, and he never looked the same afterwards."

Some people made the decision to move impulsively. After she was fired from her nursing position at Hampton Institute in Virginia in 1905, Jane Edna Hunter decided to go to Florida, but changed her mind:

> En route, I stopped at Richmond, Virginia, to visit with Mr. and Mrs. William Coleman, friends of Uncle Parris. They were at church when I arrived; so I sat on the doorstep to await their return. After these good friends had greeted me, Mrs. Coleman said, 'Our bags are packed to go to Cleveland, Jane. We are going to take you with us.' I was swept off my feet by the cheerful determination of the Colemans. My trunk, not yet removed from the station, was rechecked to Cleveland.

Most migrants maintained a genuine fondness for their southern homes and kinfolk. They returned regularly for holidays, weddings, and funerals. Kelly Miller, who had grown up in South Carolina, spent years as a scholar and teacher at Howard University in Washington, D.C., but he still had "an attachment for the old state that time and distance cannot destroy. After all, we love to be known as a South Carolinian." Thousands of black migrants routinely sent money home to the South. Over the years, several million dollars earned in the North flowed into southern communities.

Destinations

Though many black Southerners went to Florida, most migrants from the Carolinas and Virginia settled in Washington, Philadelphia, and New York (Map 16–2). Black people who left Georgia, Alabama, and Mississippi tended to move to Pittsburgh, Cleveland, and Detroit. Migrants from Louisiana, Mississippi, and Arkansas often rode the Illinois Central Railroad to Chicago. Once they experienced a metropolis, many black people then resettled in smaller communities. Migrants to Philadelphia, for example, moved on to Harrisburg or Altoona, Pennsylvania, or to Wilmington, Delaware.

Few black Southerners moved west to California, Oregon, or Washington. There were only 22,000 black residents of California in 1910. Substantial black

VOICES

A MIGRANT TO THE NORTH WRITES HOME

People who migrated to northern communities often wrote home to describe their new surroundings and experiences, and to confess that they missed their old homes. One unidentified black man who had moved to Philadelphia made his feelings known to a medical doctor.

Philadelphia, Pa., Oct. 7, 1919

Dear Sir:

I take this method of thanking you for yours early responding and the glorious effect of the treatment. Oh. I do feel so fine. Dr. the treatment reach me almost ready to move I am now housekeeping again I like it so much better than rooming. Well Dr. with the aid of God I am making very good I make $75 per month. I am carrying enough insurance to pay me $20 per week if I am not able to be on duty. I don't have to work hard. dont have to mister every little white boy comes along I havent heard a white man call a colored nigger you no now—since I been in the state of Pa. I can ride in the electric street and steam cars any where I get a seat. I dont care to mix with white what I mean I am not crazy about being with white folks, but if I have to pay the same fare I have learn to want the same accomidation. and if you are the first in a place here

shoping you dont have to wait until the white folks get thro tradeing yet amid all this I shall ever love the good old South and I am praying that God may give every well wisher a chance to be a man regardless of his color, and if my going to the front [World War I] would bring about such conditions I am ready any day—well Dr. I dont want to worry you but read between the lines; and maybe you can see a little sense in my weak statement the kids are in school every day I have only two and I guess that all. Dr. when you find time I would be delighted to have word from the good old home state. Wife join me in sending love you and yours.

QUESTIONS

1. What is the letter writer's main reason for having migrated?

2. How does this black man respond to the absence of Jim Crow in Philadelphia?

3. What is the author of the letter suggesting when he advised the doctor to "read between the lines"?

Source: Emmett J. Scott, ed., "Letters of Negro Migrants of 1916–1918," *Journal of Negro History*, 4 (1 July 1919) in Fishel and Quarles, *The Negro American: A Documentary History*, pp. 398–399.

---

migration west did not occur until the 1930s and 1940s. But in 1920 Mallie Robinson made the long trek west. Deserted by her husband Jerry, she set out with her five children (including one-year-old Jackie who would become a baseball legend) and eight other relatives. They boarded a train in Cairo, Georgia, traveled to Los Angeles, and settled in nearby Pasadena. Mallie's half-brother, who had already moved west, assured her that she would be closer to heaven in California.

However, most black migrants found that their destination was neither near heaven nor the Promised Land. Black people congregated in all-black neighborhoods—Harlem in New York City, Chicago's South Side, Paradise Valley in Detroit, Cleveland's East Side, and the Hill District of Pittsburgh—that later would be called ghettoes. White property owners resisted selling or

renting real estate to black people outside the confines of these neighborhoods. And many southern black migrants themselves, wary of white hostility, preferred to live among black people, often friends and family who had preceded them north.

NORTHERN COMMUNITIES

Even before the Civil War, most northern cities had small free black populations. By the late nineteenth century, southern migrants began to gravitate to these urban areas and make their presence felt. Black residents established churches, social organizations, businesses, and medical facilities. They gained representation in community and political affairs.

Map 16–2 **The Great Migration and the Distribution of the African-American Population in 1920.** Though several hundred thousand black Southerners migrated north in the second and third decades of the twentieth century, most African Americans remained in the Southern states.

There was less overt segregation in the North. Most northern states as well as California had enacted laws in the late nineteenth century that prohibited racial discrimination in public transportation, hotels, restaurants, theaters, and barbershops. Most of these states also forbade segregated schools. However, passage of such laws and their enforcement were two different matters. Many white businesses and communities ignored the statutes and embraced Jim Crow, especially in areas along the Ohio River in southern Ohio, Indiana, and Illinois.

Chicago

As early as 1872, Chicago had a black policeman, and in 1876 John W. E. Thomas became the first black man elected to the Illinois Senate. Black physician Daniel Hale Williams established African-American-staffed Provident Hospital on Chicago's South Side in 1891. By

1900, black Chicagoans were the twelfth largest ethnic group in the city, behind such European immigrant groups as the Irish, Poles, and Germans.

Chicago's black population surged during the first three decades of the twentieth century as migrants poured into the city. Black institutions flourished. In 1912 an NAACP branch was established. By 1920 black Chicago had eighty Baptist and thirty-six Methodist churches. The Olivet Baptist Church grew from 3,500 members in 1916 to 9,000 by 1922. Because the downtown YMCA barred black men, black people raised $50,000 and Julius Rosenwald of Sears, Roebuck, and Company contributed $25,000 to build the Wabash YMCA for the black community in 1913. However, many black Chicagoans considered this a surrender to segregation and insisted that black men should be admitted to the white YMCA.

The Chicago *Defender* was the city's leading black newspaper. Its founder, Robert S. Abbott, the son of

Black Southerners like these traveled by the thousands from Mississippi, Louisiana, and Arkansas on the Illinois Central Railroad to Chicago during the World War I era. Drawn mainly by economic opportunities, the migrants often arrived carrying all their worldly possessions.

slaves, began publishing the *Defender* in 1905, and by 1920 it had a nationwide circulation of 230,000. Chicago's first black bank, Jesse Binga's State Bank, was established in 1908, and in 1919 Frank L. Gillespie organized the Liberty Insurance Company.

In 1915 black Chicago's political influence expanded when Oscar DePriest was elected second ward alderman. Two other black men were elected to the city council by 1918. DePriest was then elected to the U.S. House of Representatives as a Republican in 1928, becoming the first black congressman since North Carolina's George White left the house in 1901.

As the number of black people in Chicago swelled, racial tensions increased and exploded in the 1919 race riot. Competition for jobs was a critical issue. White employers, such as the meatpacking companies, regularly replaced white strikers with black workers. Black men usually did not hesitate to take such jobs because most labor unions would not admit them. But a few weeks before the riot in 1919, the Amalgamated Meatcutters Union tried to sponsor a unity parade of black and white stockyard workers. The police prohibited it because, some observers believed, the meatpacking companies feared that black and white workingmen might unite.

Housing was an even more divisive issue than employment. Chicago's black population was almost entirely confined to an eight-square-mile area on the South Side east of State Street. Prosperous black people who could afford more expensive housing outside the area could not purchase it because of their race. As the black population grew, housing became more congested, and crime and vice increased.

Langston Hughes described the similar housing situation his family experienced in Cleveland.

> Rents were very high for colored people in Cleveland, and the Negro district was extremely crowded, because of the great migration. It was difficult to find a place to live. We always lived, during my high school years, either in an attic or a basement, and paid quite a lot for such inconvenient quarters. White people on the east side of the city were moving out of their frame houses and renting them to Negroes at double and triple the rents they could receive from others. An eight room house with one bath would be cut up into apartments and five or six families crowded into it, each two-room kitchenette apartment renting for what the whole house had rented for before.

Harlem

Harlem was a white community in upper Manhattan that had declined by the latter 1800s. It then enjoyed an incredible building boom that occurred in anticipation of the construction of the subway that would link upper Manhattan to downtown New York City by the early twentieth century. But real estate speculators overbuilt and were left with empty houses and apartments. Facing foreclosure, many white property owners sold or rented to black people in Harlem. In 1904 Philip A. Payton formed the Afro American Realty company that sold homes and rented apartments to black clients before it failed in 1908.

Harlem's white residents opposed the influx of black people. Some of them formed the Harlem Property Owners' Improvement Corporation in 1910 to block black settlement. Its founder, John G. Taylor, warned in 1913: "We are approaching a crisis, it is a question of whether the white man will rule Harlem or the Negro." However, many white property owners—eager for a profit—preferred to sell to black people than to maintain white unity.

As thousands of black people moved to Harlem, many left the "Tenderloin" and "San Juan Hill" areas of Manhattan's West Side where New York's black residents had lived in the nineteenth century. The construction of Pennsylvania Station forced many to vacate the "Tenderloin." Black churches took the lead in the "On to Harlem" movement as they occupied churches formerly used by white denominations. Some of the black churches were among the largest property owners in Harlem.

St. Philip's Protestant Episcopal Church, the wealthiest black church in the United States and noted for its solemn services and elite parishioners, moved from West 25th Street in the "Tenderloin" in 1910 to Harlem. In 1911, St. Philip's purchased ten apartment houses on West 135th Street between Lenox and Seventh Avenues for $640,000. The Reverend Adam Clayton Powell Sr. and the Abyssinian Baptist Church, St. Mark's Episcopal Church, and the African Methodist Episcopal Zion Church ("Mother Zion") also moved to Harlem and acquired extensive real estate holdings there. The black churches helped make Harlem a black community.

As the black population increased in Harlem, large houses and apartments were often subdivided among working families who could not rent or buy in other areas of New York. They paid higher prices for real estate than white people did. The average Harlem family paid $9.50 a room per month while white working families paid $6.50 for similar accommodations elsewhere in New York.

By 1920, 75,000 black people lived in Harlem (Map 16–3). Harlem became the "Negro Capital of the World." Black businesses and institutions including the Odd Fellows, Masons, Elks, Pythians, the NAACP, the

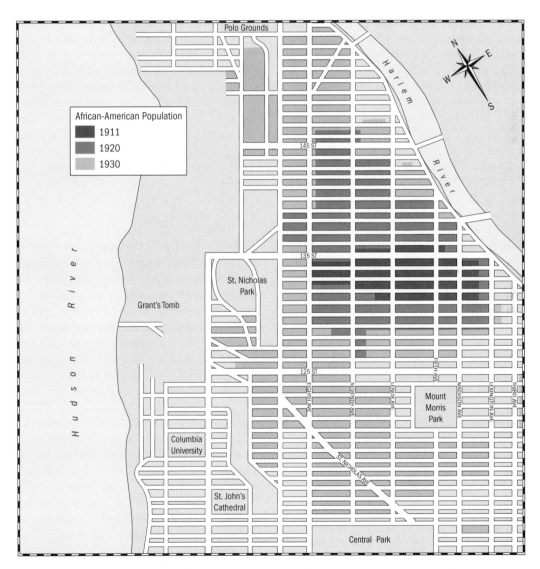

Map 16–3 The Expansion of Black Harlem, 1911–1930. Before the American Revolution, Harlem was a small Dutch village located at the northern end of Manhattan Island. In the early twentieth century, African Americans transformed it into a thriving black metropolis. Migrants who arrived either after a short trip of just a few miles from the "Tenderloin" or "San Juan Hill" sections of midtown Manhattan or after much longer journeys from the Carolinas or Georgia took over block after block of Harlem homes and apartments. Adapted from: Steven Watson, *The Harlem Renaissance*, New York: Pantheon Books. 1996.

Urban League, and the YMCA and YWCA moved to Harlem. Black newspapers—the New York *News* and *Amsterdam News*—opened in Harlem to compete with the older New York *Age*. One resident observed, "If my race can make Harlem, good lord, what can't it do?"

FAMILIES

Migration placed black families under enormous strains. Relatives frequently moved north separately. Fathers or mothers would leave a spouse and children behind as they sought employment and housing. Children might be left with grandparents for extended periods. In other instances, extended family members—cousins, in-laws, brothers and sisters—crowded into limited living space.

Men generally found more opportunities for work in northern industries than did women. There was a huge demand for unskilled labor during and after World War I. In 1915, Henry Ford astounded industrial America when he began to pay employees of the Ford Motor Company in Detroit the unprecedented sum of $5 per day, and that included black men and occasionally black women. Rarely, however, would a black man be promoted beyond menial labor. Except for some opportunities in manufacturing during the war, black women were confined to domestic and janitorial work. Mary Ellen Washington recalled the experience in her family. "In the 1920s my mother and five aunts migrated to Cleveland, Ohio from Indianapolis and, in spite of their many talents, they found every door except the kitchen door closed to them."

Black women employed as domestics lived with white families, worked long hours, and saw more of their white employer's children than they did their own. One maid explained her dreary and unhappy situation.

> I am now past forty years of age and am the mother of three children. My husband died nearly fifteen years ago. . . . For more than thirty years—or since I was ten years old—I have been a servant in one capacity or another in white families.
>
> I frequently work from fourteen to sixteen hours a day. I am compelled . . . to sleep in the house. I am allowed to go home to my own children, the oldest of whom is a girl of 18 years, only once in two weeks, every other Sunday afternoon—even then I'm not permitted to stay all night. . . . I don't know what it is to go to church; I don't know what it is to go to a lecture or entertainment of any kind; I live a treadmill life. . . . You might as well say that I'm on duty all

the time—from sunrise to sunrise, every day in the week. I am the slave, body and soul, of this family.

Some vulnerable younger women were lured into prostitution in the intimidating urban environment. Black women's organizations worked to prevent newly arrived migrants from falling prey to sexual exploitation. They did not always succeed. Some women made a calculated decision to turn sex to their economic advantage. Sara Brooks caustically commented, "Some women woulda had a man to come and live in the house and had an outside boyfriend too, in order to get the house paid for and the bills. They meet a man and if he promises 'em four or five dollars to go to bed, they's grab it. That's called sellin' your own body, and I wasn't raised like that."

Despite the stresses and pressures, most black families survived intact. Most northern black families, though hardly well-to-do, were two-parent households. Women headed comparatively few families. Fathers were present in seven of ten black families in New York City in 1925. But the great migration transformed southern peasants into an urban proletariat.

CONCLUSION

In 1900, Booker T. Washington was the nation's most influential black leader. He soothed white people and reassured black Americans as he counseled conciliation, patience, and agricultural and mechanical training as the most effective means to bridge the racial divide. His 1895 speech at the Cotton States Exposition in Atlanta elicited support and praise from both white and black listeners.

The Wizard of Tuskegee, as Washington was known, had little appreciation for criticism and did not hesitate to attack his opponents, including William Monroe Trotter and W. E. B. Du Bois. He worked to subvert the Niagara Movement and the NAACP. But support for Washington and his conservative strategy gradually diminished as the NAACP openly confronted racial discrimination. By 1920—after Washington's death—the NAACP assumed the lead in the struggle for civil rights as it fought in the courts and legislatures.

The "Talented Tenth" of black Americans, distinguished by their educational and economic resources, promoted "self-help" through a variety of organizations—from women's groups to fraternities and sororities—to enhance their own status and to help less affluent black people.

As black men served in World War I and as thousands of black Southerners migrated north, many white Americans became alarmed that African Americans were not as content with their subordinate and isolated status as Booker T. Washington had suggested they were. Some white Americans responded with violence in race riots as they attempted to prevent black Americans from assuming a more equitable role in American society. By 1920, despite white opposition, black Americans had demonstrated that they would not accept economic subservience and the denial of their rights.

REVIEW QUESTIONS

1. Compare and evaluate the strategies promoted by Booker T. Washington with those of W. E. B. Du Bois and the NAACP.

2. On which specific issues did Booker T. Washington and W. E. B. Du Bois agree? On which did they disagree?

3. Assess Booker T. Washington's contributions to the advancement of black people.

4. To what extent did middle class and prosperous black people contribute to progress for their race? Were their efforts effective?

5. Why did most African Americans support U.S. participation in World War I? Was that support justified?

6. What factors contributed to race riots and violence in the World War I era?

7. Why did many black people leave the South in the 1920s? Why didn't this migration begin earlier or later?

8. What factors affected the decision to migrate or stay?

RECOMMENDED READING

W. E. B. Du Bois. *The Souls of Black Folk*. New York: Library of America, 1903. An essential collection of essays.

John Hope Franklin and August Meier. *Black Leaders of the Twentieth Century*. Urbana: University of Illinois Press, 1982. A series of "mini biographies" of fifteen people including Washington, Du Bois, T. Thomas Fortune, and Ida Wells-Barnett.

Willard Gatewood. *Aristocrats of Color: The Black Elite, 1880–1920*. Bloomington: Indiana University Press,

1990. An examination of the lives and activities of well-to-do black people.

Louis R. Harlan. *Booker T. Washington: The Making of a Black Leader, 1856–1901*. New York: Oxford University Press, 1972 and *Booker T. Washington: The Wizard of Tuskegee, 1901–1915*. New York: Oxford University Press, 1983. The definitive two-volume biography of Washington.

David Levering Lewis. *W. E. B. Du Bois: Biography of a Race, 1868–1919*. New York: Henry Holt and Co., 1993. A magisterial account with a second volume forthcoming.

Deborah Gray White. *Too Heavy a Load: Black Women in Defense of Themselves*. New York: Norton, 1999. An exploration of the contours of black women's history in the twentieth century.

ADDITIONAL BIBLIOGRAPHY

Leadership Conflicts and the Emergence of African-American Organizations

Charles F. Kellogg. *NAACP: A History of the National Association for the Advancement of Colored People*. Baltimore: Johns Hopkins University Press, 1967.

August Meier. *Negro Thought in America, 1880–1915*. Ann Arbor: University of Michigan Press, 1967.

B. Joyce Ross. *J. E. Spingarn and the Rise of the N.A.A.C.P.* New York: Atheneum, 1972.

Elliott Rudwick. *W. E. B. Du Bois*. New York: Atheneum, 1968.

Nancy Weiss. *The National Urban League, 1910–1940*. New York: Oxford University Press, 1974.

Shamoon Zamir. *Dark Voices: W. E. B. Du Bois and American Thought, 1888–1903*. Chicago: University of Chicago Press, 1995.

African-American Women in the Early Twentieth Century

Elizabeth Clark-Lewis. *Living In, Living Out: African American Domestics in Washington, D.C., 1910–1940*. Washington: Smithsonian Institution Press, 1994.

Cynthia Neverdon-Morton. *Afro-American Women of the South and the Advancement of the Race, 1895–1925*. Knoxville: University of Tennessee Press, 1998.

Jacqueline A. Rouse. *Lugina Burns Hope: A Black Southern Reformer*. Athens: University of Georgia Press, 1989.

Stephanie J. Shaw. *What a Woman Ought to Be and to Do: Black Professional Women Workers during the Jim Crow Era*. Chicago: University of Chicago Press, 1996.

TIMELINE

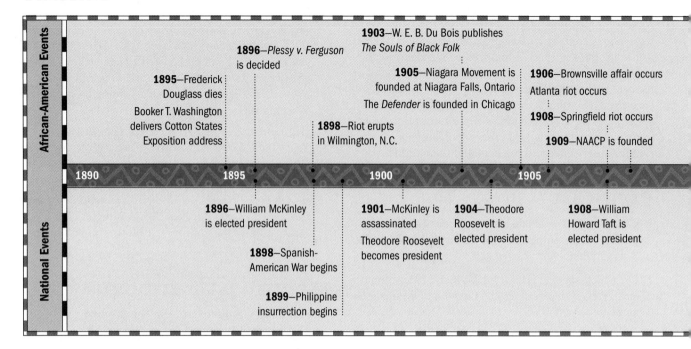

Rosalyn Terborg-Penn. *African American Women in the Struggle for the Vote, 1850–1920.* Bloomington: Indiana University Press, 1998.

African Americans in the Military in the World War I Era

Arthur E. Barbeau and Florette Henri. *Black American Troops in World War I.* Philadelphia: Temple University Press, 1974.

Edward M. Coffman. *The War to End All Wars: The American Military Experience in World War I.* Madison: University of Wisconsin Press, 1986.

Arthur W. Little. *From Harlem to the Rhine: The Story of New York's Colored Volunteers.* New York: Covici, Friede, 1936.

Bernard C. Nalty. *Strength for the Fight: A History of Black Americans in the Military.* New York: The Free Press, 1986.

Cities and Racial Conflict

St. Clair Drake and Horace R. Clayton. *Black Metropolis: A Study of Negro Life in a Northern City.* [Chicago], 2 vols. Chicago: Harcourt, Brace and Co., 1945.

Scott Ellsworth. *Death in a Promised Land: The Tulsa Race Riot of 1921.* Baton Rouge: Louisiana State University Press, 1982.

Robert V. Haynes. *A Night of Violence: The Houston Riot of 1917.* Baton Rouge: Louisiana State University Press, 1976.

David M. Katzman. *Before the Ghetto: Black Detroit in the Nineteenth Century.* Urbana: University of Illinois Press, 1973.

Kenneth L. Kusmer. *A Ghetto Takes Shape: Black Cleveland, 1870–1930.* Urbana: University of Illinois Press, 1976.

Gilbert Osofsky. *Harlem: The Making of a Ghetto, 1890–1930.* New York: Harper & Row, 1966.

Christopher Reed. *The Chicago NAACP and the Rise of Black Professional Leadership, 1910–1966.* Bloomington: Indiana University Press, 1997.

Elliott M. Rudwick. *Race Riot at East St. Louis, July 2, 1917.* Cleveland: World Publishing, 1966.

Roberta Senechal. *The Sociogenesis of a Race Riot: Springfield, Illinois, in 1908.* Urbana: University of Illinois Press, 1990.

Allan H. Spear. *Black Chicago: The Making of a Negro Ghetto, 1890–1920.* Chicago: University of Chicago Press, 1967.

Joe William Trotter, Jr. *Black Milwaukee: The Making of an Industrial Proletariat. 1915–1945.* Urbana: University of Illinois Press, 1985.

William Tuttle. *Chicago in the Red Summer of 1919.* New York: Atheneum, 1970.

Lee E. Williams. *Anatomy of Four Race Riots: Racial Conflict in Knoxville, Elaine (Arkansas), Tulsa, and Chicago,*

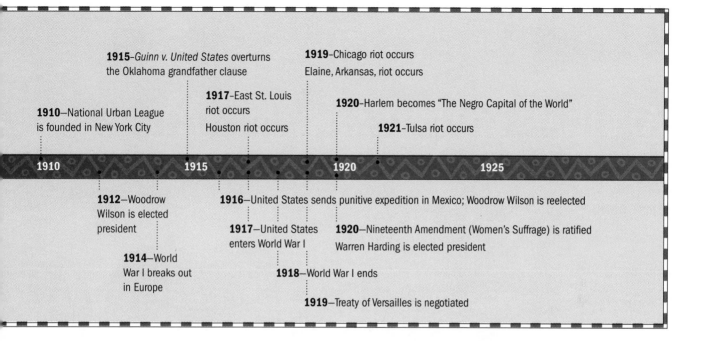

1915-*Guinn v. United States* overturns the Oklahoma grandfather clause

1919-Chicago riot occurs
Elaine, Arkansas, riot occurs

1917-East St. Louis riot occurs
Houston riot occurs

1920-Harlem becomes "The Negro Capital of the World"

1910-National Urban League is founded in New York City

1921-Tulsa riot occurs

1910   1915   1920   1925

1912-Woodrow Wilson is elected president

1916-United States sends punitive expedition in Mexico; Woodrow Wilson is reelected

1917-United States enters World War I

1920-Nineteenth Amendment (Women's Suffrage) is ratified
Warren Harding is elected president

1914-World War I breaks out in Europe

1918-World War I ends

1919-Treaty of Versailles is negotiated

1919–1921. Hattiesburg: University and College Press of Mississippi, 1972.

The Great Migration

Peter Gottlieb. *Making Their Own Way: Southern Blacks' Migration to Pittsburgh. 1916–1930.* Urbana: University of Illinois Press, 1987.

James R. Grossman. *Land of Hope: Chicago, Black Southerners, and the Great Migration.* Chicago: University of Chicago Press, 1989.

Florette Henri. *Black Migration, 1900–1920.* Garden City, NY: Anchor Press, 1975.

Carole Marks. *Farewell—We're Good and Gone: The Great Black Migration.* Bloomington: Indiana University Press, 1989.

Milton C. Sernett. *Bound for the Promised Land: African American Religion and the Great Migration.* Durham: Duke University Press, 1997.

Joe William Trotter, Jr., ed. *The Great Migration in Historical Perspective.* Bloomington: Indiana University Press, 1991.

Autobiography and Biography

W. E. B. Du Bois. *Dusk of Dawn.* New York: Harcourt, Brace & Co., 1940.

W. E. B. Du Bois. *The Autobiography: A Soliloquy on Viewing My Life from the Last Decade of Its First Century.* New York: International Publishers, 1968.

Stephen R. Fox. *The Guardian of Boston: William Monroe Trotter.* New York: Atheneum, 1970.

Kenneth R. Manning. *Black Apollo of Science: The Life of Ernest Everett Just.* New York: Oxford University Press, 1983.

Linda O. McMurry. *George Washington Carver: Scientist and Symbol.* New York: Oxford University Press, 1981.

Arnold Rampersad. *The Art and Imagination of W. E. B. Du Bois.* Cambridge: Harvard University Press, 1976.

Mary Church Terrell. *A Colored Woman in a White World.* New York: Arno Press reprint, 1940.

Emma Lou Thornbrough. *T. Thomas Fortune.* Chicago: University of Chicago Press, 1970.

Booker T. Washington. *Up from Slavery.* New York: Doubleday, 1901.

CHAPTER 17

AFRICAN AMERICANS AND THE 1920S

The Universal Negro Improvement Association led by Marcus Garvey sponsored many parades and rallies in Harlem during the 1920s. This 1924 photograph was taken by James Van Der Zee, Harlem's preeminent photographer.

CHAPTER OUTLINE

I, TOO

I, too, sing America.

I am the darker brother.
They send me to eat in the kitchen
When company comes.
But I laugh,
And eat well,
And grow strong.

To-morrow
I'll sit at the table
When company comes
Nobody'll dare
Say to me,
"Eat in the kitchen"
Then.

Besides, they'll see how beautiful I am
And be ashamed,—

I, too, am America.

—Langston Hughes, 1926

Many Americans had difficulty adjusting to life following World War I. The Allied victory brought little long-term satisfaction or security, and the U.S. Senate's rejection of the Treaty of Versailles and membership in the League of Nations in 1920 left many Americans disillusioned.

The Bolshevik Revolution in Russia in 1917 and labor agitation at home heightened fears and increased anxiety. Racial and ethnic intolerance escalated as thousands of rural black Southerners continued to stream into northern cities, and more than 800,000 immigrants arrived in America in 1920 and 1921.

Americans shunned Europe and its problems and closed their eyes to the imperfections of American society. Enthusiasm for progressive reforms faded as many Americans concluded that governmental efforts to mitigate poverty, control vice, improve working conditions, and regulate big business had been excessive. Middle-class Americans became preoccupied with making money and with acquiring—usually on credit and for the first time—automobiles, radios, and home appliances.

Many native white Americans, convinced that black people and immigrants—especially Jewish and Catholic immigrants—posed a threat to their Anglo-Saxon ethnic purity, ever more fervently embraced social Darwinism. Many sought reassurance in organizations that stressed religious, racial, and national pride. Millions of white Americans joined the revived Ku Klux Klan in the 1920s as it promoted white supremacy, American patriotism, and Protestant values.

Led by the NAACP, African Americans denounced injustice and pressed for inclusion in society, for the enforcement of civil rights, and for economic opportunities. Black workers—notably the members of Brotherhood of Sleeping Car Porters—organized and demanded recognition and improved working conditions, hours, and wages. But the 1920s also saw hundreds of thousands of African Americans enthusiastically support Marcus Garvey and the Universal Negro Improvement Association. Garvey celebrated black nationalism and urged his followers to forsake white America, take pride in themselves, and look to Africa. And the 1920s also saw black culture blossom and flourish as the artists, writers, musicians, and entertainers of the Harlem Renaissance celebrated black life and society.

STRIKES AND THE RED SCARE

In 1919 and 1920, Americans were bewildered and angered by labor unrest and afraid that the communists (or "Reds") in the new Soviet Union would try to incite a revolution in America. There were 3,600 strikes in 1919 as workers who had deferred demands during the war for pay raises and improved working conditions walked off their jobs. More than 300,000 steel workers in Pittsburgh and Gary, Indiana, struck, including 7,000 unskilled black steel workers in Pittsburgh. In a demonstration of solidarity with striking shipyard workers, most of Seattle's working people shut the city down in a general strike. Americans were even more alarmed when police officers in Boston went on strike. Many worried that labor agitation was a prelude to revolution.

Political leaders exacerbated these feelings by warning that communists and foreign agents were plotting to overthrow the government. Attorney General A. Mitchell Palmer grimly warned Americans of the Red menace and the threat aliens posed. He ordered more than two hundred aliens deported, a gross violation of their rights but an action that many Americans warmly approved. Palmer went too far, however, when he predicted that the Red revolution would begin in the United States on May 1, 1920. There was no revolution, and confidence in Palmer waned. There were, however, several terrorist bombings, including one on Wall Street in September 1920 that killed thirty-three people.

Prompted in part by the Red Scare, xenophobia (fear of foreigners) swept the nation in the 1920s. Two Sicilian immigrants, Nicola Sacco and Bartolomeo Vanzetti, who were anarchists, were charged in 1920 with a murder that had occurred during a payroll robbery near Boston. They were found guilty, and after a prolonged controversy they were executed in 1927. But their supporters believed that the guilty verdict was due more to their foreign origins and radical beliefs than to conclusive proof that they had committed the murder.

VARIETIES OF RACISM

The entrenched racism of American society found continued expression in more than one form in the twenties. There was the sophisticated racism associated with supposedly scholarly studies that reflected the ideology of social Darwinism. There was also the raw bigotry that manifested itself in various aspects of popular culture and in the ideology of the increasingly popular Ku Klux Klan.

Scientific Racism

Many white Americans believed that the United States was under siege as European immigrants and black migrants flooded American cities. Pseudo-scholars gravely warned about the peril these "inferior" peoples posed. In 1916 Madison Grant published *The Passing of the Great Race*. Grant warned that America was committing "race suicide" because northern Europeans and their descendants—the Great Race—were being diluted by inferior people from eastern and southern Europe. Lothrop Stoddard's *The Rising Tide of Color* in 1920 argued that people of color would never be equal to white Americans. Stoddard stated his case unequivocally in 1927.

> Even a general knowledge of historical and scientific facts suffices to show the need for a racial basis to our national life,—as it has been, and as we intend that it shall be. We know that *our* America is a *White* America. "America," in the traditional sense of the word, was founded by White men, who evolved institutions, ideals, and cultural manifestations which were spontaneous expressions of their racial temperament and tendencies. And the overwhelming weight of both historical and scientific evidence shows that only so long as the American people remains White will its institutions, ideals, and culture continue to fit the temperament of its inhabitants,—and hence continue to endure.

These racist claims were cloaked in the trappings of legitimate scholarship, and they strengthened the cause of white supremacy in the 1920s and helped "protect" America from the "threat" of immigration. In 1921 and in 1924, Congress imposed quotas that severely restricted immigration from southern and eastern Europe and prohibited it entirely from Asia.

The Birth of a Nation

In 1915 D. W. Griffith released *The Birth of a Nation*, a cinematic masterpiece and historical travesty based on Thomas Dixon's 1905 novel, *The Clansman*. Both the book and the film purported to depict Reconstruction in South Carolina authentically. In this account, immoral and ignorant Negroes joined by shady mulattoes and greedy white Republicans ruthlessly seize control of state government until the heroic and honorable Ku Klux Klan save the state and rescue its white womanhood. The film was enormously popular. President Woodrow Wilson had it screened in the White House. It grossed $18 million dollars ($252 million in 1998 dollars) and helped to assure a future for Metro Goldwyn Mayer (MGM), which produced it. It also distorted public perceptions about Reconstruction and black Americans.

The NAACP was enraged by *The Birth of a Nation* and fought to halt its presentation. W. E. B. Du Bois complained in *The Crisis* that in the film "the Negro [was] represented either as an ignorant fool, a vicious rapist, a venal or unscrupulous politician or a faithful but doddering idiot." The motion picture unleashed racist violence. After seeing the film in Lafayette, Indiana, an infuriated white man killed a young black man. In Houston, white theatergoers shouted, "Lynch him!" during a scene in which a white actor in blackface pursued the film's star, Lillian Gish. In front of a St. Louis theater, white real estate agents passed out circulars calling for residential segregation.

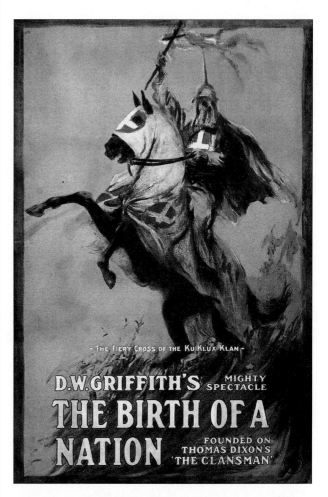

The glorification of the Ku Klux Klan in D. W. Griffith's *Birth of a Nation,* reflected in this publicity poster, outraged African Americans. The NAACP protested when the silent film was first distributed in 1915 and again when a sound version was released in 1930. The demonstrations attracted publicity to both the film and the NAACP.

V O I C E S

THE NEGRO NATIONAL ANTHEM: "LIFT EVERY VOICE AND SING"

In 1900 to celebrate Abraham Lincoln's birthday, James Weldon Johnson wrote "Lift Every Voice and Sing." His younger brother John Rosamond Johnson composed music to accompany the words. It was published in 1921 and soon thereafter—with the encouragement of the NAACP—the song was embraced as the Negro National Anthem. (In 1998, the New Yorker magazine suggested that it replace the "Star Spangled Banner" as the U.S. National Anthem.)

-1-

Lift every voice and sing, 'til earth and heaven ring,
Ring with the harmonies of liberty
Let our rejoicing rise, high as the list'ning skies,
Let it resound loud as the rolling sea.

Sing a song full of the faith that the dark past has
*   taught us,*
Sing a song full of the hope that the present has
*   brought us;*
Facing the rising sun of our new day begun
Let us march on till victory is won.

-2-

Stony the road we trod, bitter the chast'ning rod
Felt in the days when hope unborn had died
Yet with a steady beat, have not our weary feet
Come to the place for which our fathers sighed?

We have come over a way that with tears has been
*   watered,*
We have come, treading our path thro' the blood of
*   the slaughtered*
Out from the gloomy past, 'til now we stand at last
Where the white gleam of our bright star is cast.

-3-

God of our weary years, God of our silent tears
Thou who has brought us thus far on the way
Thou who hast by Thy might, led us into the light
Keep us forever in the path, we pray.

Lest our feet stray from the places, our God, where
*   We met Thee*
Lest our hearts, drunk with the wine of the world, we
*   forget Thee*
Shadowed beneath Thy hand, may we forever stand
True to our God, true to our native land.

QUESTIONS

1. Are these words hopeful and positive? Or is this mainly a lament and dirge that recites the horrors that African Americans have experienced?

2. What does James Weldon Johnson mean in the last line: "True to our God, true to our native land"? To what native land does he refer?

3. Do the words of the song apply to all Americans or only to African Americans? Would the song be appropriate as the American national anthem?

Thanks largely to NAACP opposition, the film was banned in Pasadena, California, Wilmington, Delaware, and Boston. With an election looming in Chicago, Republican Mayor "Big Bill" Thompson appointed AME bishop Archibald Carey to the board of censors, which temporarily banned the film there. When the sound version of *The Birth of a Nation* was released in 1930, the NAACP renewed its opposition. Ironically, the NAACP campaign may have provided publicity that attracted more viewers to the film. By the same token, however, the campaign also helped increase NAACP membership.

The Ku Klux Klan

The Ku Klux Klan, which disappeared after Reconstruction, was resurrected a few months after *The Birth of a Nation* was released. On Thanksgiving night in 1915, William J. Simmons and thirty-four other men gathered at Stone Mountain near Atlanta, and in the flickering shadows of a fiery cross, they brought the Klan back to life.

The Ku Klux Klan that rose to prominence and power in the 1920s stood for white supremacy—and more. Klansmen styled themselves as "100 percent Americans" who opposed perceived threats from immigrants as well as black Americans. The Klan claimed to represent white, Anglo-Saxon, Protestant America. With European immigrants flocking to America, William Simmons announced that the United States was no melting pot. "It is a garbage can! . . . When the hordes of aliens walk to the ballot box and their votes outnumber yours, then that alien horde has got you by the throat."

The Klan found enormous support among apprehensive white middle-class Americans in the North and West. Many of these people believed that the liberal, immoral, and loose lifestyles that they associated with urban life, immigrants, and African Americans threatened their religious beliefs and conservative cultural values. The Klan attacked the theory of evolution, fought for the prohibition of alcoholic beverages, and claimed to uphold the "sanctity" of white womanhood. The KKK opposed Jews, Roman Catholics, and black people. Klansmen often used violent intimidation to convey their patriotic, religious, and racial convictions. They burned synagogues and Catholic churches. They beat, branded, and lynched their opponents.

By 1925 the Klan had an estimated five million members, and 40,000 of them marched in Washington, D.C., that year. The Klan attracted small businessmen, shopkeepers, clerks, Protestant clergymen, farmers, and professional people. It was open only to native-born white men, but it also had a Women's Order, a Junior Order for boys, and a Tri K Klub for girls. The Klan was active in Oregon, Colorado, Illinois, and Maine, and it became a potent political force in Indiana, Oklahoma, and Texas. In those three states in particular, candidates for public office who refused to support or join the Klan stood little chance of election.

The Klan was also a highly effective money-making machine. Its leaders collected millions of dollars in initiation fees, membership dues, and income from selling Klan paraphernalia. But the Klan declined rapidly in the late 1920s when its leaders fought among themselves. Its claim to uphold the purity of white womanhood was damaged when one of its leaders, D. C. Stephenson, was arrested in Indiana and charged with raping a young woman who subsequently committed suicide. Stephenson was sentenced to life in prison, and the Klan never fully recovered.

PROTEST, PRIDE, AND PAN-AFRICANISM: BLACK ORGANIZATIONS IN THE TWENTIES

African Americans responded to racism and to larger cultural and economic developments in the 1920s in several ways. The NAACP forged ahead with its efforts to secure constitutional rights and guarantees by advocacy in the political and judicial systems. Many working-class black people who had migrated to northern cities were attracted to the racial pride promoted by Marcus Garvey and the Universal Negro Improvement Association. There were also ongoing attempts to foster racial cooperation among peoples of African descent and to exert diplomatic influence through the work of several Pan-African congresses that were held during the first three decades of the twentieth century.

The NAACP

During its second decade, the NAACP expanded its influence and increased its membership. In 1916 James Weldon Johnson (who wrote "Lift Every Voice and Sing") joined the NAACP as field secretary. He played a pivotal role in the organization's development and in its growth from 9,000 members in 1916 to 90,000 in 1920. Johnson traveled tirelessly, recruiting members and establishing branches. He journeyed to rural southern communities, to northern cities, and to the West Coast.

Johnson impressed both black and white people. He got along well with W. E. B. Du Bois—not always an easy task considering Du Bois's sometimes haughty and acerbic demeanor. Johnson was an excellent diplomat who could negotiate and compromise, but he could also be blunt when necessary. He methodically reported the gruesome details of lynchings, and when some NAACP directors complained in 1921 that these graphic descriptions offended people, Johnson stood his ground. "What we need to do is to root out the thing which makes possible these horrible details. I am of the opinion that this can be done only through the fullest publicity."

In 1918 Johnson hired Walter White to assist him. White was from Atlanta and, like Johnson, a graduate of Atlanta University. White's fair complexion permitted him to move easily among white people to investigate racial discrimination and violence. Though his domineering personality offended some NAACP officials and supporters, White devoted his life to the organization and to racial justice.

JAMES WELDON JOHNSON

James Weldon Johnson was a man of immense talents. At various times he was a lawyer, diplomat, journalist, teacher, and gifted writer of prose and poetry. Most important, he was an effective and dynamic civil rights leader.

Johnson was born in 1871 in Jacksonville, Florida, to parents who had not been slaves. His father was a waiter in a fashionable hotel, and his mother was a schoolteacher. He received his secondary and collegiate education at Atlanta University where he also earned a master's degree. He read law in the office of a white Jacksonville attorney and was admitted to the Florida bar. In 1902 he moved to New York City.

With his brother John Rosamond and black entertainer Robert Cole, he became part of a successful song-writing team. They contributed two musical numbers to Theodore Roosevelt's 1904 presidential campaign: "You're All Right Teddy" and "The Old Flag Never Touched the Ground." Johnson's connection to the Republican party and his support for Booker T. Washington helped secure diplomatic appointments for him. Johnson spent seven years as a consul in Venezuela and Nicaragua. In 1910 he married Grace Neal, the sister of a prominent New York real estate broker.

With the election in 1912 of Woodrow Wilson, a Democrat, Johnson's diplomatic career ended. He became an editorial writer for the New York *Age*. He also published anonymously *The Autobiography of an Ex-Colored Man*. In 1916 Joel Spingarn, the president of the NAACP, asked Johnson to take a leadership role with that organization, and Johnson—who had not openly supported the NAACP before Booker T. Washington's death in 1915—became its field secretary.

Johnson spent the next fourteen years with the NAACP. In 1920 he became chief executive, responsible for the association's day-to-day operations. He had organized the silent march on Fifth Avenue on July 28, 1917, to protest the East St. Louis riot (see Chapter 16). He publicized lynchings. He recruited members and established new branches. In 1920 in *The Nation*,

James Weldon Johnson in a portrait by Winold Reiss.

he documented the mistreatment of Haitians by U.S. troops who had occupied that Caribbean nation. He supported black workers and A. Philip Randolph and the Brotherhood of Sleeping Car Porters. He arranged legal counsel for Ossian Sweet in Detroit in 1925 after Sweet and several of his supporters were charged with murder.

Johnson also managed to write prolifically and imaginatively. In 1920, he wrote "The Creation: A Negro Sermon." He wrote "God's Trombones: Seven Negro Sermons in Verse" in 1927 and many other works of prose and poetry. In 1930 he finished *Black Manhattan*, which traced the cultural contributions of black people in music, poetry, and theater to New York City from the seventeenth to the twentieth centuries.

Like so many civil rights leaders, Johnson could be inconsistent in his stands on racial issues. Though dedicated to the proposition that black and white people should enjoy equal access to public facilities, he supported an all-black YMCA in Harlem and the separate training of black military officers during World War I. He opposed moving NAACP headquarters from Fifth Avenue to Harlem. He supported building an all-black veteran's hospital at Tuskegee, Alabama, as long as it would be staffed by black physicians and nurses. He appreciated Marcus Garvey's emphasis on black pride, but he considered the back-to-Africa movement as an attempt to escape from America's racial problems rather than a solution to them.

In 1930 Johnson left the NAACP to become a professor of creative writing at Fisk University in Nashville. He left the NAACP a far more visible and stronger organization than he had found it in 1916. At Fisk, he worked with some of the twentieth century's leading black scholars, including Horace Mann Bond, Alrutheus Taylor, and E. Franklin Frazier. Historian John Hope Franklin was one of his students. Johnson's autobiography, *Along the Way*, was published in 1933. He died in an automobile accident in 1938.

Johnson and the NAACP fought hard in Congress to secure passage of the Dyer Anti-Lynching bill in 1921 and 1922 (see Chapter 16). The legislation ultimately failed, but the NAACP succeeded in publicizing the persistence of barbaric behavior by mobs in a nation supposedly devoted to fairness and the rule of law. It was the first campaign by a civil rights organization to lobby Congress, and—like the attempt to block *The Birth of a Nation*—it won favorable publicity and goodwill for the NAACP.

Johnson blamed the Dyer bill's failure on Republican senators. He charged that the Republican party took black support for granted because southern Democrats remained openly committed to white supremacy and, therefore, black people had little choice but to vote Republican: "The Republican Party will hold the Negro and do as little for him as possible, and the Democratic Party will have none of him at all." He warned, however, that black voters in the North would abandon the Republicans.

> The Negro can serve notice that he is no longer a part of the agreement by voting in the coming elections in each State against Republicans who have betrayed him, who are in league with the Ku Klux Klan, who are found to be hypocrites and liars on the question of the Negro's essential rights, and by letting them know he has done it. I am in favor of doing the job at once.

Johnson pointed out that black voters in Harlem had elected a black Democrat to the state legislature.

The NAACP continued to rely on the judicial system to protect black Americans and enforce their civil rights. By the 1920s, the Democratic party in virtually every southern state barred black people from membership, which excluded them from voting in Democratic primary elections. The result was what were known as "white primaries." Because the Republican party had almost ceased to exist in most of the South, victory in the Democratic primary elections led invariably to victory in the general election. In 1924 the NAACP, in cooperation with its branch in El Paso, filed suit over the exclusion of black voters from the Democratic primary in Texas. In 1927 the Supreme Court ruled in *Nixon vs. Herndon* that the Democratic primary was unconstitutional—the first victory in what would become a twenty-year legal struggle to permit black men and women to vote in primary elections across the South.

In Detroit in 1925, black physician Ossian Sweet and his family moved into an all-white neighborhood. For several nights a mob threatened the Sweet family and other people who joined in their defense. One eve-

ning, shots were fired from the Sweet home that killed a white man. Twelve occupants of the house were charged with murder. The NAACP retained Clarence Darrow and Arthur Garfield Hayes, two of the nation's finest criminal attorneys, to defend the Sweets. The Sweets pleaded self-defense, and after two trials, they were acquitted.

"Up You Mighty Race": Marcus Garvey and the UNIA

With several million loyal and enthusiastic followers, Marcus Garvey's Universal Negro Improvement Association (UNIA) became the largest mass movement of black people in American history. The UNIA enabled people—often dismissed by the white majority for having no genuine history or culture—to celebrate one another and their heritage and to anticipate a glorious future. Garvey was an energetic, charismatic, and flamboyant leader who wove racial pride, Christian faith, and economic cooperation into a black nationalist organization that had spread throughout the United States by the early 1920s.

Garvey was born in 1887 in the British colony of Jamaica, the eleventh child in a rural family. He quit school at age fourteen and became a printer in Kingston, the island's capital; he was promoted to foreman before he was fired in 1907 for pro-labor activities during a strike. He traveled to Costa Rica, Panama, Ecuador, and Nicaragua and became increasingly disturbed over the conditions black workers endured in fields, factories, and mines. He returned to Jamaica and with a growing appreciation of the power of the written and spoken word, he set out to educate himself. He spent two years in London where he sharpened his oratorical and debating skills discussing the plight of black people with Africans and people from the Caribbean.

He returned to Jamaica and founded the UNIA in 1914. With the slogan: "One God! One Aim! One Destiny!" he stressed the need for black people to organize for their own advancement. Garvey had read Booker T. Washington's *Up from Slavery* and was much impressed with Washington's emphasis on self-help and on progress through education and the acquisition of skills. Garvey also—like Washington—could criticize black people for their lack of progress: "The bulk of our people are in darkness and are really unfit for good society." They had no right to aspire to equality because they had "done nothing to establish the right to equality."

Garvey came to the United States in 1916 just as thousands of African Americans were migrating to cities. A dynamic speaker whose message resonated among the disaffected urban working class, Garvey quickly built the UNIA into a major movement. He urged his listeners to take pride in themselves as they restored their race to its previous greatness. "We must canonize our own saints, create our own martyrs, and elevate to positions of fame and honor black men and women who have made their distinct contributions to our racial history." He reminded people that Africa had a remarkable past. "Africa was peopled with a race of cultured black men, who were masters in art, science and literature; men who were cultured and refined; men, who, it was said, were like the gods. . . . Black men, you were once great; you shall be great again." He insisted that his followers change their thinking. "We have outgrown slavery, but our minds are still enslaved to the thinking of the Master Race. Now take these kinks out of your mind, instead of out of your hair."

With the formation of the New York division of the UNIA in Harlem in 1917, Garvey exhorted, "Up you mighty race!" as he commanded black people to

V O I C E S

MARCUS GARVEY APPEALS FOR A NEW AFRICAN NATION

Marcus Garvey and the UNIA offered hope to African Americans in the 1920s. In the following words, Garvey passionately calls for African Americans and West Indians to support the creation of a new African nation.

For five years the Universal Negro Improvement Association has been advocating the cause of Africa for the Africans—that is, that the Negro peoples of the world should concentrate upon the object of building up for themselves a great nation in Africa. . . .

It is only a question of a few more years when Africa will be completely colonized by Negroes, as Europe is by the white race. What we want is an independent African nationality, and if America is to help the Negro peoples of the world establish such a nationality, then we welcome the assistance.

It is hoped that when the time comes for American and West Indian Negroes to settle in Africa, they will realize their responsibilities and duty. It will not be to go to Africa for the purpose of exercising an overlordship over the natives, . . .

It will be useless, as stated before, for bombastic Negroes to leave America and the West Indies to go to Africa, thinking that they will have privileged positions to inflict upon the race that bastard aristocracy that they have tried to maintain in this Western world at the expense of the masses. Africa shall develop an aristocracy of its own, but it shall be based upon service and loyalty to race. Let all Negroes work toward that end. . . .

The time has really come for the Asiatics to govern themselves in Asia, as the Europeans are in Europe and the Western world, so also is it wise for the Africans to govern themselves at home, and thereby bring peace and satisfaction to the entire human family.

So Negroes, I say, through the Universal Negro Improvement Association, that there is much to live for. I have a vision of the future, and I see before me a picture of redeemed Africa, with her dotted cities, with her beautiful civilization, with her millions of happy children going to and fro. Why should I lose hope, why should I give up and take a back place in this age of progress? . . .

Africa shall reflect a splendid demonstration of the worth of the Negro, of the determination of the Negro, to set himself free and to establish a government of his own.

QUESTIONS

1. On what logical basis does Garvey rest his call for a black homeland in Africa? How realistic was this call in the 1920s for nationhood in Africa?

2. Who does Garvey believe should lead (or should not lead) the new African nation? What are the qualifications for such leadership?

3. What vision does Garvey offer for what the globe will look like in the future? Does he suggest how peoples of various colors will coexist?

Source: David Levering Lewis, ed., *The Portable Harlem Renaissance Reader* (Viking Penguin, 1994), pp. 17, 19, 20, 21, 25.

take control of their destiny. Still, he blamed them for their predicament. "That the Negro race became a race of slaves was not the fault of God Almighty . . . it was the fault of the race." Their salvation would result from their own exertion and not from concessions by white people.

Garvey's message and the UNIA spread to black communities large and small. He regularly couched his rhetoric in religious terms, and he came to be known as the Black Moses, a messiah. Garvey dwelled on Christ's betrayal as he identified himself with Jesus. "If Garvey dies, Garvey lives." "Christ died to make men free, I shall die to give courage and inspiration to my race."

Garvey's followers enjoyed the pageantry, ceremonies, and titles that were a part of the UNIA. The African Legionnaires and the Black Cross Nurses, resplendent in their uniforms, assembled in New York's Liberty Hall, and they paraded through Harlem. They prayed from *The Universal Negro Catechism* and reflected on their connection to Africa. "O Blessed Lord

Jamaican-born Marcus Garvey arrived in the United States in 1916 and quickly rose to prominence as the head of the Universal Negro Improvement Association. Thousands of urban and rural black people rallied to his call for people of African descent to take pride in their racial heritage and to assume control of their destiny.

Jesus, redeem Africa from the hands of those who exploit and ravish her."

Garvey and the UNIA also established businesses that employed nearly 1,000 black people. The weekly newspaper, *Negro World*, promoted Garvey's ideology. In New York City, the Negro Factories Corporation operated three grocery stores, two restaurants, a printing plant, a steam laundry, and a factory that turned out uniforms, hats, and shirts for UNIA members. The association also owned buildings, vehicles, and facilities in other cities. Garvey proudly declared to white Americans that the UNIA "employs thousands of black girls and black boys. Girls who could only be washer women in your homes, we made clerks, stenographers. . . . You will see from the start we tried to dignify our race."

Garvey may be best remembered for his proposal to return black people to Africa by way of the Black Star Line, a steamship company he founded in 1919. Garvey sold stock in the company for five dollars a share, and he hoped to establish a fleet with black officers and crew members. In 1920 the company purchased the *Yarmouth*, a dilapidated vessel that became the first ship in the fleet. Garvey raised enough capital to buy two additional ships, the *Kanawha* and the *Booker T. Washington*, but lacked the financial resources to maintain them or to transport anyone to Africa.

Moreover, he knew that it was unrealistic to expect several million black residents of the Western Hemisphere to join the back-to-Africa enterprise, but he genuinely believed that the UNIA could liberate Africa from European colonial rule. "Wake up Ethiopia! Wake up Africa! Let us work towards the one glorious end of a free, redeemed and mighty nation." The UNIA adopted a red, green, and black flag for the proposed African republic that represented the blood, land, and race of the people of the continent.

The UNIA attempted to establish a settlement on the Cavalla River in southern Liberia. Garvey also petitioned the League of Nations to permit the UNIA to take possession of the former German colony of Tangaruyka (today's Tanzania) in East Africa. But the major colonial powers in Africa—Britain and France—and the United States thwarted Garvey's plans, and the UNIA never gained a foothold on the continent.

The United States government and several black American leaders also undermined the UNIA and Garvey. J. Edgar Hoover and the Bureau of Investigation (the predecessor of the FBI) considered Garvey a serious threat to the racial status quo. Hoover employed black agents to infiltrate the UNIA and compile information that could be used to deport Garvey, who had never become an American citizen.

Garvey had few friends or admirers among African-American leaders because he and they differed fundamentally on strategy and goals. Garvey deplored efforts to gain legal and political rights within the American system. By appealing to the black masses, he rejected Du Bois's notion that the Talented Tenth would lead the race to liberation. He mocked the NAACP as the National Association for the Advancement of Certain People. Not long after he arrived in the United States, Garvey visited the NAACP office in New York, and he commented sourly that it was essentially a white organization. "There was no representation of the race there that any one could recognize. . . . you had to be as near white as possible, otherwise there was no place for you as stenographer, clerk or attendant in the office of the National Association for the Advancement of 'Colored' People."

Garvey called W. E. B. Du Bois a "lazy, dependent mulatto." In return, Du Bois described Garvey as "a little, fat black man, ugly but with intelligent eyes and big head," who was "the most dangerous enemy of the Negro race in America and the world . . . either a lunatic or a traitor." A. Philip Randolph, the black labor leader, was no less critical, calling Garvey "the supreme Negro Jamaican Jackass," an "unquestioned fool and ignoramus."

Unlike African-American leaders, Garvey believed that black and white people had separate destinies, and he regarded interracial cooperation as absurd. Thus Garvey considered a meeting he had with Ku Klux Klan leaders in Atlanta in 1922 consistent with his racial views. He praised the white supremacist organization. "They are better friends to my race, for telling us what they are, and what they mean, thereby giving us a chance to stir for ourselves." He added that "every whiteman is a Klansman . . . and there is no use lying about it."

In 1922 Garvey and three other UNIA leaders were arrested and indicted on twelve counts of fraudulent use of the U.S. mail to sell stock in the Black Star Line. Eight African-American leaders wrote to the U.S. Attorney General to condemn Garvey and insist on his prosecution. Though Garvey was guilty of no more than mismanagement and incompetence, he was eventually found guilty and sent to the federal penitentiary in Atlanta in 1925. President Calvin Coolidge commuted his sentence in 1927, and he was deported.

The UNIA barely survived the loss of its inspirational leader, and it declined steadily in the late 1920s and the 1930s. The various UNIA businesses closed, and its property—including the *Yarmouth*—was sold. Garvey was never permitted to return to the United States, and he died in London in 1940. However, his

legacy persisted. The Reverend Earl Little, a Baptist minister and the father of Malcolm X, belonged to the UNIA and much admired Garvey. Malcolm X recalled his father's association with Garvey. "I remember hearing that he had black followers not only in the United States but all around the world, and I remember how the meetings always closed with my father saying, several times, and the people chanting after him, 'Up, you mighty race, you can accomplish what you will!'"

Pan-Africanism

As diametrically opposed as Garvey and Du Bois were on most matters, they shared an abiding interest in Africa. Garvey, Du Bois, and other black leaders believed that people of African descent from around the world should come together to share their heritage, discuss their ties to the continent, and to explore ways to moderate—if not eliminate—colonial rule in Africa.

By 1914, Britain, France, Germany, Portugal, Belgium, Spain, and Italy had established colonies across almost all of Africa. Only Liberia and Ethiopia (then called Abyssinia) remained independent. The Europeans assumed the "white man's burden" in their imperialist "scramble" for Africa. Christian missionaries sought to convert Africans, and European companies exploited Africa's human and natural resources. As they gained control over the continent, the European powers confirmed their conviction that they represented a superior race and culture.

The first Pan-African Congress had convened in London in 1900 and was organized principally by Henry Sylvester Williams, a lawyer from Trinidad who had resided in Canada and then London. Du Bois attended and chaired the Committee on the Address to the Nations of the World. He called for the creation of "a great central Negro state of the world." But Du Bois did not insist on the immediate withdrawal of the European powers from Africa. Instead he offered a modest recommendation that would provide "as soon as practicable the rights of responsible self-government to the black colonies of Africa and the West Indies."

The second Pan-African Congress met in Paris for three days in February 1919, near Versailles, where the peace conference ending World War I was assembled. There were fifty-eight delegates from sixteen nations. Du Bois was among the sixteen African Americans in attendance. (None of them had been to Africa.) Marcus Garvey did not attend. The delegates took seriously the Fourteen Points that U.S. President Woodrow Wilson had proposed to fashion the postwar world. They were especially interested in the fifth point, which called for the interests of colonial peoples to be given "equal weight" in the adjustment of colonial claims after the war. The congress recommended that the League of Nations assume authority over the former German colonies in East Africa. The League later established mandates over those colonies, but delegated authority to administer those mandates to Britain, France, and Belgium. Two more Pan-African Congresses in the 1920s met in Brussels and London, but also failed to influence the policies of the colonial powers.

LABOR

The arrival of thousands of black migrants in American cities during and after World War I changed the composition of the industrial workforce and intensified pressure on labor unions to admit black members. By 1916, 12,000 of the nearly 50,000 workers in the Chicago stockyards were black people. In Detroit, black laborers made up nearly 14 percent of the workforce in the automobile industry. The Ford Motor Company employed fifty black people in 1916 and 2,500 by 1920.

Yet even with the industrial revolution and the great migration, more than two-thirds of black workers in 1920 were employed in agriculture and domestic service (Figure 17–1). Less than 20 percent were engaged in manufacturing. Those who were part of industrial America disproportionately worked in the dreary, dirty, and sometimes dangerous unskilled jobs that paid the least. Still work in the factories, mills, and mines paid more than agricultural labor.

Most of the major labor unions would not admit black workers. Since its founding in 1886, the American Federation of Labor (AFL) officially prohibited racial discrimination, but most of its local unions were all white and all male. The AFL was made up of skilled laborers and less than 20 percent of black workers were skilled (Figure 17–2). But even those with skills were usually not admitted to the local craft unions that made up the AFL. More than fifty trade unions within the AFL had no black members. Unions that did admit black workers included those representing cigar makers, coal miners, garment workers, and longshoremen.

By the World War I years, the NAACP and the Urban League regularly appealed to employers and unions

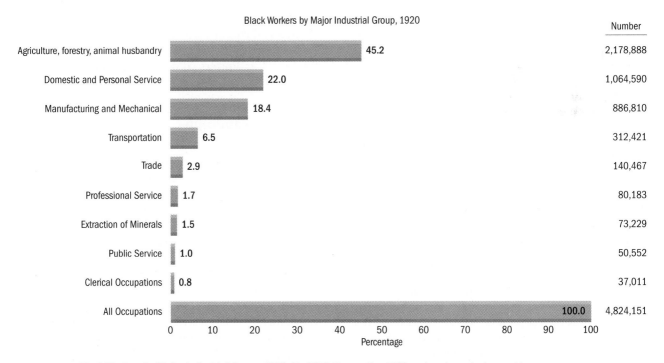

Black Workers by Major Industrial Group, 1920

Industrial Group	Percentage	Number
Agriculture, forestry, animal husbandry	45.2	2,178,888
Domestic and Personal Service	22.0	1,064,590
Manufacturing and Mechanical	18.4	886,810
Transportation	6.5	312,421
Trade	2.9	140,467
Professional Service	1.7	80,183
Extraction of Minerals	1.5	73,229
Public Service	1.0	50,552
Clerical Occupations	0.8	37,011
All Occupations	100.0	4,824,151

Figure 17–1 Black Workers by Major Industrial Group, 1920. By 1920 thousands of African Americans had moved to northern cities and were employed in a variety of mostly unskilled and low paying industrial jobs that nonetheless paid more than farm labor. Still, agriculture remained the largest single source of employment among black people, and agriculture and domestic service together employed more than two-thirds of African-American men and women. About five percent were employed in "white collar" jobs. Source: Sterling D. Spero and Abram L. Harris, *The Black Worker: The Negro and the Labor Movement* (1928), 81.

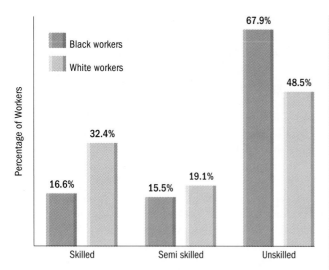

Figure 17-2　Black and White Workers by Skill Level, 1920. Only one third of black workers, compared to slightly more than one half of white workers, found employment in skilled or semiskilled jobs in 1920. Source: Sterling D. Spero and Abram L. Harris, *The Black Worker: The Negro and the Labor Movement* (1928), 85.

to accept black laborers. The Urban League attempted to convince business owners that black employees would be efficient and reliable. But many employers preferred to divide black and white workers by hiring black men and women as strikebreakers, thereby enraging striking white workers. In 1918 Urban League officials met with Samuel Gompers, the long-time president of the AFL, and he agreed to bring more black people into the federation, but there were few tangible results. The Urban League did succeed in persuading the U.S. Department of Labor to establish a Division of Negro Economics to advise the secretary of labor on issues involving black workers.

The Brotherhood of Sleeping Car Porters

By the 1920s, the Pullman company, which owned and operated passenger railroad coaches, was the single largest employer of black people in the United States. More than 12,000 black men worked as porters on Pullman railroad cars. After founding the Pullman Palace Car Company in 1867, George Pullman decided to employ only black men as porters—on the assumption that prosperous white people were accustomed to being waited on by black servants. Furthermore, black employees could be and were paid less than white workers.

Pullman porters toiled for upwards of four hundred hours each month to maintain the coaches and serve the passengers. Porters had to prepare the cars before the train's departure and service them after the train arrived

at its destination, though they were paid only for the duration of the trip. They assisted passengers, shined shoes (they had to purchase the polish themselves), and arranged sleeping compartments. Considered mere servants by most passengers, porters had little time for rest. To add to the indignity, white travelers invariably referred to these black men as "George," no matter what their actual name was. Porters were paid an average of $67.50 per month—about $810 per year. But with tips, they earned more, occasionally as much as $300 a month, but usually far less. They were required to buy their own uniforms during their first ten years of employment.

Though strenuous and time-consuming, Pullman employment was the most satisfactory work many black men could hope to achieve. Barred from business and industry, black men with college degrees worked as sleeping car porters. As poorly paid as they were compared to many white workers, they still earned more than most black schoolteachers. Most of these Pullman employees regarded themselves as solid, respectable members of the middle class.

It seemed unlikely that men as subservient and unobtrusive as the Pullman porters would form a labor union to challenge one of America's most powerful corporations. But they did. The key figure in this effort was A. Philip Randolph. In 1925 a gathering of Pullman porters in Harlem invited Randolph to become their "general organizer" as they formed the Brotherhood of Sleeping Car Porters (BSCP). Randolph accepted the invitation.

A. Philip Randolph

Randolph was a socialist with superb oratorical skills who had earned a reputation as a radical on the streets of Harlem. He was born in 1889 in Crescent City, Florida. He attended high school at Cookman Institute (later Bethune Cookman College) and migrated to New York City in 1911 where he attended City College and joined the Socialist party. With Chandler Owen, he founded *The Messenger,* a monthly socialist journal that drew the attention of federal agents. Randolph vigorously opposed American involvement in World War I. In 1919 Department of Justice officials arrested Randolph and Owen for their radical activities and held them briefly.

Randolph was an improbable militant. He was handsome, dignified, impeccably dressed, and aloof. Save for his color, he could have been mistaken for the sort of Wall Street broker or powerful corporate attorney he detested. But blessed with a rich baritone voice, he "damned the claasses and exalted the maasses" and maintained an unwavering commitment to economic

Chicago Historical Society, R. D. Jones, ICHi-22642

A. Philip Randolph (fifth from left) with officers of the Brotherhood of Sleeping Car Porters. Randolph, the longtime leader of the BSCP was a socialist and regarded as a left-wing radical by many people. His patient but determined leadership of the porters eventually won them recognition from the Pullman company and the American Federation of Labor.

and racial change. He became one of the nation's foremost protest leaders and remained so for more than five decades.

Randolph faced the daunting task of recruiting support for the brotherhood, winning recognition from the Pullman company, and gaining the union's acceptance by the AFL. There was considerable opposition, much of it from within the black community. Many porters were too frightened to join the brotherhood. Black clergymen counseled against union activities. Black newspapers, including the Chicago *Defender*, editorially opposed the BSCP.

But Randolph persevered with the assistance of Milton Webster, who became vice president of the Brotherhood after Randolph assumed the presidency. With the slogan "Service not servitude," the two men recruited members, organized the brotherhood, and attempted to negotiate with the Pullman company. Pullman executives ignored Randolph's overtures. They fired porters who joined the union, infiltrated union meetings with company agents, and organized the Employees' Representation Plan, an alternative company union that they claimed actually represented the black employees.

Though the NAACP and the Urban League strongly supported the BSCP, progress was painfully slow. In 1928 Randolph threatened to call a strike against the Pullman company but called it off after AFL President William Green promised modest assistance to the as-yet unrecognized union. Green's offer simply saved face for Randolph. It is unlikely that a strike would have succeeded or that most porters would have followed Randolph's leadership and left the trains. The Great Depression of the 1930s brought layoffs and mass resignations from the brotherhood. The AFL barely responded to repeated charges of discrimination by Randolph, the NAACP, and Urban League. The BSCP nearly collapsed. Not until the passage of legislation during President Franklin D. Roosevelt's New Deal in the mid-1930s did the BSCP make substantial gains.

THE HARLEM RENAISSANCE

For most of American history, most black and white Americans have shown little interest in serious literature or intellectual developments. The 1920s were no exception. People were far more fascinated by sports, automobiles, the radio, and popular music than they were by poetry, plays, museums, or novels. Still the twenties witnessed a proliferation of creative works by a remarkable group of gifted writers and artists. Among white writers T. S. Eliot, Ezra Pound, Edith Wharton, Ernest Hemingway, Sinclair Lewis, Eugene O'Neill, Willa Cather, and F. Scott Fitzgerald produced literary works that explored a range of themes but were mostly critical of American life and society. Eliot, Pound, Wharton, Fitzgerald, and Hemingway found American culture so unappealing that they exiled themselves in Europe.

Black intellectuals congregated in Manhattan and gave rise to the creative movement known as the Harlem Renaissance. Poets, novelists, and painters probed racial themes and grappled with what it meant to be black in America. There was no precise beginning to this renaissance. As early as 1920, W. E. B. Du Bois wrote in *The Crisis* that the nation was on the verge of a "renaissance of American Negro literature." In 1925 the New York *Herald Tribune* declared that America was "on the edge, if not already in the midst of, what might not improperly be called a Negro renaissance." No matter when it began, the Harlem Renaissance produced a stunning collection of artistic works, especially in creative writing, that continued into the 1930s.

Before Harlem

There had certainly been serious cultural developments among African Americans before the 1920s. At the turn of the century, novelist Charles W. Chestnutt depicted a young black woman's attempt to pass for white in *The House behind the Cedars,* and he wrote about racist violence in the post–Reconstruction South in *The Marrow of Tradition.* Ohio poet Paul Lawrence Dunbar wrote evocatively of black life, frequently relying on black dialect, before he died at age thirty-four in 1906. Henry Ossawa Tanner attended the Pennsylvania Academy of Fine Arts and had an illustrious career as a painter. Shortly after he produced "The Banjo Lesson" in 1893, Tanner left for Paris and spent most of the rest of his life in Europe. He died there in 1937.

Carter G. Woodson, the son of Virginia slaves, earned a Ph.D. at Harvard in history and founded the Association for the Study of Negro Life and History in 1915. He stressed the need for the scholarly examination of Negro history and established the *Journal of Negro History* and the *Negro History Bulletin.* He also founded Associated Publishers to publish books on black history. Woodson wrote several major works, including *The Negro in Our History.* In 1926 he established Negro History Week during February. Not surprisingly, Woodson became known as the "father of Negro history."

During the bloody Red Summer of 1919 when racial violence erupted in Chicago and elsewhere, Claude McKay, a Jamaican who settled—like Marcus Garvey—in New York City wrote a powerful poem, "If We Must Die," in response to the brutal attacks by white people in Chicago on black residents:

> *If we must die, let it not be like hogs*
> *Hunted and penned in an inglorious spot,*
> *While round us bark the mad and hungry dogs,*
> *Making their mock at our accursèd lot.*
> *If we must die, O let us nobly die,*
> *So that our precious blood may not be shed*
> *In vain; then even the monsters we defy*
> *Shall be constrained to honor us though dead!*
> *O kinsmen! We must meet the common foe!*
> *Though far outnumbered let us show us brave,*
> *And for their thousand blows deal one deathblow!*
> *What though before us lies the open grave?*
> *Like men we'll face the murderous, cowardly pack,*
> *Pressed to the wall, dying, but fighting back!*

McKay left the United States for the Soviet Union in 1922, and spent the next twelve years in Europe. In 1928 while in France, he wrote *Home to Harlem,* a novel that depicted life among pimps, prostitutes, loan sharks, and petty criminals. McKay was not on cordial terms with the African-American intellectuals who formed the core of the Harlem Renaissance, and he did not consider himself part of the Talented Tenth. He later commented, "I was an older man and not regarded as a member of the renaissance, but more as a forerunner."

Writers and Artists

Few white Americans and still fewer black Americans had access to a college education in the early twentieth century. Only slightly more than 2,000 African Americans were pursuing college degrees by 1920. Yet the writers and artists who came to be associated with the Harlem Renaissance were the products of some of the nation's finest schools, and with the exception of Zora Neale Hurston, they did not come from isolated, rural southern communities. Hurston was born in Notasulga, Alabama, and raised in the all-black town of Eatonville, Florida, near Orlando. She attended Morgan State University and Howard University, and graduated from Barnard College. Alain Locke was a native of Philadelphia and Phi Beta Kappa graduate of Harvard. He was the first African American to win a Rhodes scholarship to Oxford University, and he also earned a Ph.D. in philosophy from Harvard. Aaron Douglas (one of whose works graces the cover of this book) was born in Kansas and was an art major at the University of Nebraska.

Langston Hughes was born in Joplin, Missouri, graduated from high school in Cleveland, and attended Columbia University before he graduated from Pennsylvania's Lincoln University. Jessie Fauset came from a prominent Philadelphia family of color. She was a graduate of Cornell University and a member of Phi Beta Kappa; she earned an M.A. from the University of Pennsylvania in romance languages. Jean Toomer was born in Washington, D.C., and was raised largely by his grandparents in a fashionable white neighborhood. Toomer went to the University of Wisconsin and then the Massachusetts College of Agriculture. Wallace Thurman was born in Salt Lake City and attended both the University of Utah and the University of Southern California. Countee Cullen was a native of Lexington, Kentucky, and a Phi Beta Kappa graduate of New York University.

The Renaissance gradually emerged in the early 1920s and then expanded dramatically later in the decade as more creative figures were drawn to Harlem. In 1923 Jean Toomer published *Cane*, a collection of stories and poetry about southern black life. It sold a mere five hundred copies, but it had a major impact on Jessie Fauset and Walter White. Fauset was the literary editor of *The Crisis*, and in 1924 she finished *There Is Confusion*, the first novel published during the Renaissance. Her novels explored the manners and color consciousness among well-to-do Negroes. Walter White, who was James Weldon Johnson's assistant at the NAACP, published *The Fire in the Flint* in 1924, a novel that dealt with a black physician who confronted white brutality in Georgia.

In the meantime, *The Crisis* as well as *Opportunity*, a new publication of the Urban League, published the poetry and short stories of black authors, including Langston Hughes, Countee Cullen, and Zora Neale Hurston. White publishers were also attracted to black literary efforts. In 1925 *Survey Graphic* published a special edition devoted to black life and culture called "Harlem: Mecca of the New Negro." Howard University Professor Alain Locke then edited *The New Negro*, which drew much of its material from *Survey Graphic* as well as *Opportunity* and included silhouette drawings with Egyptian motifs by Aaron Douglas. In his opening essay, Locke explained Harlem's literary significance: "Harlem has the same role to play for the new Negro as Dublin has had for the New Ireland or Prague for the New Czechoslovakia."

Sharp disagreements erupted during the Harlem Renaissance over the definition and purpose of black literature. Some, such as Alain Locke, W. E. B. Du Bois, Jessie Fauset, and Benjamin Brawley, wanted black writ-

During the summer of 1927, three of the major figures associated with the Harlem Renaissance visited the Booker T. Washington Memorial on the Tuskegee Institute campus in Alabama. One can only wonder what pointed comments about the "Wizard of Tuskegee" were exchanged as (from left to right) Jessie Fauset, Langston Hughes, and Zora Neale Hurston posed to have their photograph taken.

ers to promote positive images of black people in their works. They hoped that inspirational literature could help resolve racial conflict in America, and they believed that black writers should be included in the larger (and mostly white) American literary tradition. Claude McKay, Langston Hughes, and Zora Neale Hurston disagreed. They portrayed the streets and shadows of Harlem and the lives of poor black people in their poetry and stories. In *The Ways of White Folks*, Hughes ridiculed the notion that writers could promote racial reconciliation. One of his characters derisively declares, "Art would break down color lines, art would save the race and prevent lynchings! Bunk!"

W. E. B. Du Bois commented caustically after he read Claude McKay's bawdy *Home to Harlem*: "I feel distinctly like taking a bath." Du Bois was less than impressed with Jake, the novel's protagonist, who is intimately involved with the reality of life in Harlem that included opium, alcohol, and sex. Alain Locke dismissed McKay as a mere propagandist, and McKay in turn called Locke "a dyed-in-the-wool pussy-footing professor." Black critic George Schuyler's "The Negro Art Hokum" in *The Nation* ridiculed black writers who contended that black people even had their own expressive culture that was separate from that of white people. "As for the literature, painting, and sculpture of Afroamericans—such as there is—it is identical in kind with the literature, painting, and sculpture of white Americans."

Langston Hughes meanwhile defended the authenticity of black art and literature but insisted that the approval or disapproval of white people and black people was of little consequence.

> We younger Negro artists who create now intend to express our individual dark-skinned selves without fear or shame. If white people are pleased, we are glad. If they are not, it doesn't matter. We know we are beautiful. And ugly too. The tom-tom cries and the tom-tom laughs. If colored people are pleased we are glad. If they are not, their displeasure doesn't matter either. We build our temples for tomorrow, strong as we know how, and we stand on top of the mountain, free within ourselves.

Hughes pursued racial themes in *Fine Clothes to the Jew* (1927), which contained "Red Silk Stockings," a poem that depicted young black women who were tempted by liaisons with white men, a subject that offended some readers.

Red Silk Stockings

Put on yo' red silk stockings,
Black gal.
Go out an' let de white boys
Look at yo' legs.

Ain't nothin' to do for you, nohow.
Round this town.—
You's too pretty.
Put on yo' red silk stockings, gal,
An' tomorrow's chile'll
Be a high yaller.

Go out an' let de white boys
Look at yo' legs.

Even more upsetting to those who wanted to safeguard the reputation of black people was Wallace Thurman, who arrived in New York in 1925. Thurman worked briefly at *The Messenger*, the socialist publication that had been absorbed by A. Philip Randolph's Brotherhood of Sleeping Car Porters. He was a voracious

---

THE HARLEM RENAISSANCE

1919 Claude McKay publishes "If We Must Die"

1920 Eugene O'Neill's *The Emperor Jones* opens featuring Charles Gilpin
Langston Hughes publishes "The Negro Speaks of Rivers"

1922 *Shuffle Along* by Noble Sissle and Eubie Blake opens on Broadway with Florence Mills and Josephine Baker
Claude McKay publishes *Harlem Shadows*

1923 Jean Toomer publishes *Cane*
The Cotton Club opens
Opportunity: A Journal of Negro Life edited by Charles S. Johnson and supported by the National Urban League begins publication

1924 Jessie R. Fauset publishes *There Is Confusion*
Walter White publishes *The Fire in the Flint*
Paul Robeson stars in Eugene O'Neill's drama *All God's Chillun Got Wings*

1925 Countee Cullen publishes his book of poetry, *Color*
James Weldon Johnson publishes *The Book of American Negro Spirituals*
The New Negro edited by Alain Locke is published

1926 Langston Hughes publishes *The Weary Blues*
George Schuyler's "The Negro Art Hokum" appears in *The Nation*
The Savoy Ballroom opens
Wallace Thurman publishes one issue of *Fire*
Florence Mills dies

1927 Langston Hughes publishes *Fine Clothes to the Jew*
James Weldon Johnson publishes *God's Trombones: Seven Negro Sermons in Verse*

1928 Claude McKay publishes *Home to Harlem*
Duke Ellington's band appears at the Cotton Club

1929 Jessie R. Fauset publishes *Plum Bun*
Wallace Thurman publishes *The Blacker the Berry . . .*
Claude McKay publishes *Banjo*
Countee Cullen publishes *The Black Christ*
Fats Waller's *Ain't Misbehavin'* opens on Broadway

1930 James Weldon Johnson publishes *Black Manhattan*

1931 Jessie R. Fauset publishes *The Chinaberry Tree*

1933 Jessie R. Fauset publishes her last novel, *Comedy American Style*
James Weldon Johnson publishes his autobiography, *Along the Way*

1934 Wallace Thurman dies

1935 Zora Neale Hurston publishes *Mules and Men*

1937 Zora Neale Hurston publishes *Their Eyes Were Watching God*

reader with a brilliant mind and an eccentric personality who attracted many loyal admirers. He once wrote, "I cannot bear to associate with the ordinary run of people. I have to surround myself with individuals who for the most part are more than a trifle insane."

In 1926 Thurman published *Fire*, a journal that lasted only one issue but managed to incite enormous controversy and leave Thurman deeply in debt. *Fire* included Thurman's short story, "Cordelia the Crude," about a prostitute, and a one-act play by Zora Neale Hurston, "Color Struck." Hurston effectively replicated the speech of rural black Southerners while depicting the jealousy a darker woman feels when a light-skinned rival tries to take her man. Black critic Benjamin Brawley complained that with *Fire* "vulgarity had been mistaken for art."

Thurman, who was a dark black man, antagonized still more people when *The Blacker the Berry . . .* was published in 1929. In it he described the tribulations and sorrows of Emma Lou, a young woman who did not mind being black, "but she did mind being too black." The book made it plain that many black people had absorbed a color prejudice that they did not hesitate to inflict on darker members of their own race.

White People and the Harlem Renaissance

Like many of the writers associated with the Harlem Renaissance, Zora Neale Hurston had a pen that sliced like a scalpel. She called the white people who took an interest in Harlem "Negrotarians," and she labeled her black literary colleagues the "Niggerati." But no matter how they were described, black and white people developed pleasant but often uneasy relationships during the Renaissance.

No white man was more attracted to the cultural developments in Harlem than photographer and writer Carl Van Vechten. In 1926 he caused a furor with his novel, *Nigger Heaven*. Many people were offended by the title—which referred to the balcony where black patrons had to sit in segregated theaters and auditoriums. The novel dealt with the coarser aspects of life in Harlem, which irritated Du Bois, Fauset, and Countee Cullen. But Van Vechten's purpose was in part a call for a more honest depiction of the black experience, and James Weldon Johnson, Walter White, and Langston Hughes approved of the novel.

Most black writers and artists welcomed the encouragement, support, and financial backing they received from white authors, critics, and publishers. White writers, including Eugene O'Neill, Sherwood Anderson, Sinclair Lewis, and Van Wyck Brooks, were fascinated by black people and interested in the works of black authors. Major publishers, such as Alfred A. Knopf, brought out the works of Harlem writers. Black and white literary figures sometimes gathered for cocktails, small talk, and music at Carl Van Vechten's spacious apartment on West 55th Street.

The attention and support of white people were sometimes accompanied by condescension and disdain. Too many "Negrotarians" considered Harlem and its inhabitants exotic, curious, and uncivilized. They found life in Harlem—its clubs, music, and entertainers as well as its poetry, prose, and painting—energetic, lively, and sensual compared to white life and culture. Black culture was also—many white people believed—unsophisticated and primitive, which is what made it so fascinating. Black writers like Langston Hughes, Claude McKay, and Countee Cullen wanted to depict black life realistically—from its gangsters to its gamblers. But they and other black artists resented the notion that black culture was inherently crude and unrefined.

White patrons like Amy Spingarn, whose husband Joel was president of the NAACP Board of Directors, and Charlotte Osgood Mason—"Godmother"—supported black writers and artists. Spingarn helped finance Langston Hughes's education at Lincoln University. "Godmother" Mason was a wealthy widow who offered substantial amounts of money to black artists. She worked closely with Alain Locke who helped identify Langston Hughes, Zora Neale Hurston, and Aaron Douglas among others who became her "godchildren."

Mason wanted no publicity for herself, but the acceptance of her money had its costs. Mason gave Hughes $150 a month and Hurston $200 a month as well as an automobile. She also gave Hughes expensive clothing and writing supplies. In return, Mason demanded that the black writers keep her fully informed about their activities, and she did not hesitate to tell them when they were not productive enough. She also tried to influence what they wrote. She preferred that black writers confine themselves to exotic themes. As helpful as Mason's financial assistance and personal encouragement were, she created a system of dependency, and Hughes and Hurston finally broke free from the arrangement. Hughes later fondly recalled, "I can only say that those months when I lived by and through her were the most fascinating and fantastic I have ever known."

Harlem's cultural icons sometimes congregated away from the curiosity and paternalism of white admirers. The plush twin town houses of A'Lelia Walker at

108–110 West 136 Street also attracted Harlem's literary figures as well as entertainers. Walker was the daughter of black cosmetics millionairess Madam C. J. Walker. Though she read little herself, A'Lelia Walker enjoyed hosting musicians, writers, and artists at "The Dark Tower," as she called it. Her home was named for Countee Cullen's column, "The Dark Tower," that appeared regularly in *Opportunity*. But Harlem artists also gathered in the much less luxurious surroundings of "Niggerati Manor" on 267 West 136 Street. This was a rooming house where Thurman, Hurston, and Hughes resided in the late 1920s.

The profusion of literary works associated with the Harlem Renaissance did not so much end as fade away. Black writers remained active into the 1930s. Zora Neale Hurston wrote her two most important works then—*Mules and Men* in 1935 and *Their Eyes Were Watching God* in 1937. Claude McKay and Langston Hughes continued to write and have their work published. But the Great Depression that began in 1929 devastated book and magazine sales. Subscriptions to *The Crisis* and *Opportunity* declined, and both journals published fewer works by creative writers. Many black intellectuals left Harlem. James Weldon Johnson and Aaron Douglas went to Fisk University in Nashville. W. E. B. Du Bois had a falling out with the NAACP and returned to Atlanta University. Alain Locke remained on the faculty at Howard University. Jessie Fauset married an insurance executive and took up housekeeping after her last novel was published in 1931. Wallace Thurman died an alcoholic in 1934. Countee Cullen taught French at DeWitt Clinton High School in New York City where James Baldwin was one of his students in the late 1930s.

HARLEM AND THE JAZZ AGE

As powerful and important as these black literary voices were, they were less popular than the entertainers, musicians, singers, and dancers who were also part of the Harlem Renaissance. Without Harlem, the twenties would not have been the Jazz Age. From wailing trumpets, beating drums, dancing feet, plaintive and mournful songs, Harlem's clubs, cabarets, theaters, and ballrooms echoed with the vibrant and soulful sounds of African Americans. By comparison, white American music seemed sedate and bland.

Black and white people flocked to Harlem to enjoy themselves—and to break the law. In 1919–1920, the Eighteenth Amendment and the Volstead Act prohibited the manufacture, distribution, and sale of al-

coholic beverages. But liquor flowed freely in Harlem's fancy establishments and smoky dives. Musicians and entertainers—like Harlem's working-class residents—had migrated there from elsewhere. The blues and their sorrowful tales of troubled and broken relationships arrived from the Mississippi Delta and rural South. Jazz had its origins in New Orleans, but it drew on ragtime and spirituals as it moved up the Mississippi River to Kansas City and Chicago on its way to Harlem.

The Cotton Club was Harlem's most exclusive and fashionable nightspot. Opened in 1923 by white gangster Owney Madden to peddle illegal beer, it catered to well-to-do white people who regarded a trip to Harlem as a foreign excursion. The Cotton Club's entertainers and waiters were black, but the customers were white. Black patrons were not admitted. The club featured well-choreographed and fast paced two-hour revues that included a chorus line of attractive young women—all brown skinned, all under twenty-one years old, and all over 5'6" tall. No dark women appeared. Music was provided by assorted ensembles. Cab Calloway might sing "She's Tall, She's Tan and She's Terrific," or "Cotton Colored Gal of Mine." In 1928, Edward K. "Duke" Ellington and his orchestra began a twelve-year association with the Cotton Club. Although Ellington had not yet begun to compose his own music in earnest, his band already had an elegant, sophisticated, and recognizable African-American sound.

Born in Washington, D.C., in 1899, Edward Kennedy "Duke" Ellington moved to New York City in 1923 and organized a five-piece band. He began recording in 1924, and first appeared at the Cotton Club with a ten-piece orchestra in 1928. He did not stop playing, conducting, and composing music until his death in 1974.

BESSIE SMITH

No one personified the blues more than Bessie Smith. She knew the blues. She sang the blues. She lived the blues. She was the "Empress of the Blues." During the 1920s, no singer in America was more popular than she was.

Bessie Smith was born in poverty on April 15, 1894, in Chattanooga, Tennessee. She was one of seven children of a Baptist preacher, William Smith, and his wife, Laura. Both of Bessie's parents and two brothers died while she was still a child and the surviving children were raised by an older sister, Viola.

With her brother Andrew accompanying her on the guitar, Bessie began to sing on Chattanooga street corners to earn money for the family. It was an apprenticeship that helped shape her career. In 1912 she briefly toured with a musical group that featured Gertrude "Ma" Rainey. In 1913 she worked in Atlanta for ten dollars a week plus tips. Her fame spread and soon she was touring the South. By the 1920s she was singing in Philadelphia and Atlantic City.

No one has ever sung the blues better than Bessie Smith. "The Empress of the Blues" appeared in theaters and clubs across the country before mostly all-black audiences, but thousands of white people bought her recordings in the 1920s and 1930s. Her contract with Columbia Records, which earned her only $28,575 for eight years of recordings, profited the company at her expense.

She knew of what she sang. When she sang "Money Blues," "Pickpocket Blues," or "Empty Bed Blues," she revealed the pathos but also the humor that so many northern and southern black people had experienced. Smith's blues tore at the raw feelings that sociologists and academics missed when they discussed poverty, unemployment, alcoholism, or sexual relationships. Smith's blues were firmly grounded in African-American oral and musical traditions.

Bessie Smith was not a delicate woman. She was married twice. Her first husband, Earl Love, died shortly after they married. Her second marriage, to Jack Gee, was marked by jealousy, drinking, and physical conflict that ended in separation in 1930. She had a profusion of lovers—male and female. Her warmest and most enduring relationship was with Richard Morgan, a Chicago bootlegger.

People did not trifle with Bessie Smith. She was a large lady—over 200 pounds. She ate, drank, and fought to excess. She could be mean, contentious, and violent. She physically attacked others and was herself attacked. But she also had a sweet and loyal side. She could be helpful, generous, and compassionate. However, she seemed fond of some of the sleaziest, most dangerous, and seediest nightclubs in America. She could not resist Detroit's Koppin Theater, a den of debauchery. She admitted that she wanted to go where "the funk was flying."

Initially her voice was considered too rough for the infant recording industry. But in 1923 Frank Walker signed her to a contract with Columbia Records. She recorded what were known in the 1920s as "race" records, produced for black audiences by white recording companies. Her first recordings included "Downhearted Blues" and "Gulf Coast Blues." Her second session brought "Tain't Nobody's Business If I Do." She sold an astonishing 780,000 records within months.

In 1925 she recorded "St. Louis Blues" and "Careless Love" with Louis Armstrong—their only recordings together. She toured major cities, including Pittsburgh, Cleveland, Cincinnati, St. Louis, and Chicago, in a private railroad coach and huge crowds lined up for admission to clubs and theaters to hear her. Though it could sound coarse, she had a striking and appealing voice that conveyed the depths of her emotions and experiences.

She continued to record even after record sales declined during the Depression. Her last recording session included "Nobody Knows When You're Down and Out." Bessie Smith died at age forty-three in 1937 in an automobile accident near Clarksdale, Mississippi. Perhaps Louis Armstrong summed up her musical legacy best. "She used to thrill me at all times, the way she could phrase a note with a certain something in her voice no other blues singer could get. She had music in her soul and felt everything she did."

Another club, Connie's Inn, also served a mostly white clientele. Thomas "Fats" Waller played a rambunctious piano at Connie's. Waller's father was the deacon at the Abyssinian Baptist Church in Harlem, and his mother was the organist. The songs and music their son wrote, including "Honeysuckle Rose" and "Ain't Misbehavin,'" were hardly sacred, but they were popular. Connie's also put on stunning musical revues, perhaps the best known of which was *Hot Chocolates*. Dancers who performed at Connie's included the legendary Bill "Bojangles" Robinson and Earl "Snakehips" Tucker. A young cornetist from New Orleans, Louis Armstrong, played briefly at Connie's. Armstrong amazed listeners with his virtuoso trumpet and his gravelly singing voice.

Harlem's black residents avoided the Cotton Club or Connie's Inn. They were more likely to step into one of Harlem's less pretentious and less expensive establishments like the Sugar Cane. The beer and liquor were cheap. The food was plentiful. The music was good, and there were no elaborate production numbers. Even less impressive clubs and bars remained open after the legal closing hour of 3 A.M. "Arrangements" were made with the police who looked the other way as the music and alcohol continued through the night. Musicians from "legal" clubs drifted into the after-hours joints and played until dawn.

Another popular—and sometimes necessary—form of entertainment among Harlemites was the rent party. Housing costs in Harlem were extravagant, and white people and real estate agents refused to rent or sell to black people in most other areas of New York City. To make the steep monthly rent payments, apartment dwellers would push the furniture aside, begin cooking chicken, chitterlings, rice, okra, and sweet potatoes. They would distribute a few flyers and hire a musician or two. The party was usually on a Saturday or a Thursday night. (Most domestic servants had Thursdays off.) Party-goers paid ten cents to fifty cents admission. Food and liquor were sold. With a decent crowd, the month's rent was paid.

Song, Dance, and Stage

Black women became popular as singers and dancers in Harlem and then often appeared in Broadway shows and revues. Florence Mills entranced audiences with her diminutive singing voice in several Broadway productions including *Plantation Review, Dixie to Broadway*, and *Blackbirds* before she died of appendicitis in 1927. Adelaide Hall also appeared in *Blackbirds* and later opened her own nightclubs in London and Paris. Ethel

Waters worked her way up from smoky gin joints in Harlem basements where she sang risqué and comic songs to Broadway shows, and then to films. Many years later she toured with the Billy Graham crusade.

White men wrote many of the popular Broadway productions that starred black entertainers. In 1921, however, Eubie Blake and Noble Sissle put on *Shuffle Along*, which became a major hit. Its most memorable tune was "I'm Just Wild about Harry." Sissle and Blake wrote several more shows, including *Chocolate Dandies* in 1924. It was created especially for a thin, lanky, dark, and funny young lady named Josephine Baker. But in 1925 Baker left New York and moved to Paris where she starred in the *Revue Nègre*, which created a sensation in the French capital. She remained in France for the rest of her life.

White playwright Eugene O'Neill wrote serious drama involving black people. Charles Gilpin and then Paul Robeson appeared in O'Neill's *Emperor Jones*. Robeson—who went on to an illustrious performing career—was a graduate of Rutgers University where he was an All-American football player. He earned a law degree at Columbia University, but abandoned the law for the stage. He appeared in numerous productions, including O'Neill's *All God's Chillun Got Wings*, Shakespeare's *Othello*, Gershwin's *Porgy and Bess*, and Kern and Hammerstein's *Showboat*. He often sang spirituals in his magnificent, rich voice, and later recorded many of them.

SPORTS

Sports flourished in America in the 1920s. Americans worshiped their athletic heroes. Babe Ruth and Jack Dempsey were as well known as President Calvin Coolidge. Professional athletics, especially baseball and boxing, expanded dramatically. Professional football and basketball emerged later. Black men had been banned from major league baseball in 1887 (see Chapter 15). Nevertheless, in 1901 New York Giants' manager John J. McGraw signed a black man, Charlie Grant, to play second base. McGraw claimed that Grant was "Chief Tokohoma," a full-blooded Cherokee Indian. Chicago White Sox owner Charles Comiskey knew otherwise, and Grant did not play in the major leagues.

Playing among themselves, black baseball players barely made a living as they moved from team to team in an ever-fluctuating and disorganized system that saw teams come and go with monotonous regularity. No leagues functioned effectively for the black teams and players. Black teams crisscrossed the country on trains and in automobiles as they played each other in small towns and large cities for meager amounts of money shared from gate receipts. It was an insecure and nomadic life.

Rube Foster

Andrew "Rube" Foster was the father of black baseball in twentieth-century America. He was a crafty pitcher from Texas who combined athletic skills with mental dexterity. In 1911 he founded the Chicago American Giants, and he pitched with them regularly until 1915 and then mainly managed after that. As fine an athlete as Foster was, he was an even more talented organizer and administrator.

In 1919 in the Chicago *Defender*, he argued for the establishment of a Negro baseball league. In 1920 he was the catalyst in the formation of the eight-team Negro National League and became its president and secretary. It was the first stable black league, with franchises in Kansas City, St. Louis, Indianapolis, Detroit, Dayton, and two teams in Chicago. The eighth team was the Cuban Stars.

Foster and the new league took advantage of the migration of black people to northern cities. The black ball clubs usually played late in the afternoon or in the early evening so that fans could attend after a day's work. (This was before night baseball.) Sunday doubleheaders in Chicago or Kansas City might draw 8,000 to 10,000 people. Players were paid regularly, and athletes on Foster's Giants earned at least $175 a month. The biggest obstacle black teams faced was the lack of their own fields or stadiums. They were forced to rent, often at exorbitant rates, from major league clubs, which frequently kept the profits from concessions.

Black baseball thrived in the 1920s thanks mostly to Foster's force of personality and dedication. He was a tireless worker and strict disciplinarian, but the pressure may have been too much. In 1926 he suffered a mental breakdown and died in 1930. Foster's loss—combined with the impact of the Depression—severely disrupted the league system.

College Sports

Football, baseball, basketball, and track and field were popular at the collegiate level. Amateur sports were not as rigidly segregated as professional baseball. Black men continued to play for white northern universities, although few teams had more than one black player. Paul Robeson was on the Rutgers football team in 1916 that played against Frederick Douglass "Fritz" Pollard and Brown University. Pollard was the first black man to play in the Rose Bowl where his Brown team lost to Washington State in 1916.

Black players on white teams encountered discrimination when the teams traveled. Spectators taunted and threatened them. The Big Ten had an unwritten agreement that basketball coaches would not accept black players. All-white college teams sometimes refused to play against schools with black players. In 1920, Virginia's Washington and Lee University canceled a football game against Washington and Jefferson College of Pennsylvania because Charles West, a black man, played in the Washington and Jefferson backfield.

Sports in black colleges and universities thrived in the 1920s. Baseball and football were the most popular spectator events. Traditional rivalries attracted large crowds. Several schools played baseball religiously each Easter Monday. In 1926 Livingston College defeated Biddle University (now Johnson C. Smith University) before a crowd of 6,000 in Charlotte, North Carolina. With the migration of black people to the North, black colleges began to play football in northern cities. Howard and Lincoln played to a scoreless tie before 18,000 people in Philadelphia on Thanksgiving in 1925. Hampton and Lincoln played at New York's Polo Grounds on the edge of Harlem in 1929 in a game won by Lincoln 13–7 before 10,000 spectators.

CONCLUSION

For African Americans who lived through it, the 1920s must have seemed little more than a depressing continuation of earlier decades. Little appeared to have changed. Racial violence and lynching persisted. *The Birth of a Nation* mocked black people and inflamed racial animosity. "Experts" offered "proof" that people of color were inferior and threatened America's ethnic purity. The Ku Klux Klan became a formidable organization again. Millions of white men joined the Klan, and millions of other Americans supported it.

Nevertheless, some genuinely positive developments in the twenties gave hope for a more promising future. The NAACP became an organization to be reckoned with as it fought for antilynching legislation in Congress and for civil and political rights in the courts. Its membership exceeded 100,000 during the twenties. Though many black and white Americans ridiculed Marcus Garvey for his flamboyant style and excessive rhetoric, he offered racial pride and self-respect as he enrolled hundreds of thousands of black people in the UNIA.

TIMELINE

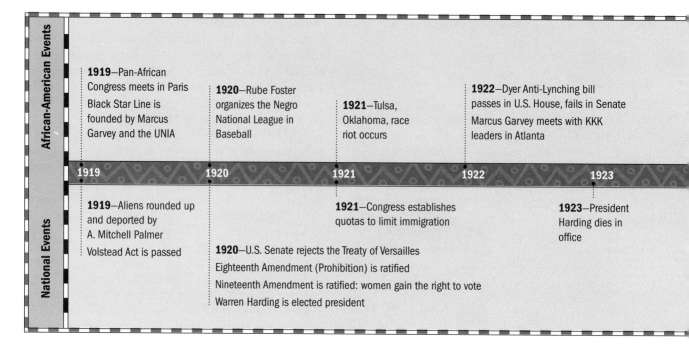

African-American Events

1919—Pan-African Congress meets in Paris
Black Star Line is founded by Marcus Garvey and the UNIA

1920—Rube Foster organizes the Negro National League in Baseball

1921—Tulsa, Oklahoma, race riot occurs

1922—Dyer Anti-Lynching bill passes in U.S. House, fails in Senate
Marcus Garvey meets with KKK leaders in Atlanta

1919   1920   1921   1922   1923

National Events

1919—Aliens rounded up and deported by A. Mitchell Palmer
Volstead Act is passed

1920—U.S. Senate rejects the Treaty of Versailles
Eighteenth Amendment (Prohibition) is ratified
Nineteenth Amendment is ratified: women gain the right to vote
Warren Harding is elected president

1921—Congress establishes quotas to limit immigration

1923—President Harding dies in office

Black workers made very little progress as they sought concessions from big business and representation within the ranks of organized labor. A. Philip Randolph founded the Brotherhood of Sleeping Car Porters and began a struggle with the Pullman company and the American Federation of Labor that would begin to pay off in the 1930s.

The Harlem Renaissance was a cultural awakening in literature and the arts that was unprecedented in African-American history. A torrent of words poured forth from novelists, essayists, and poets. Though they disagreed—sometimes vehemently—on the purposes of black art, the writers and artists who were a part of the Renaissance had an enduring impact. Black musicians, dancers, singers, entertainers, and athletes made names for themselves and contributed to popular culture in a mostly urban environment. As the nation moved into the 1930s, it remained to be seen whether the modest but real progress of the 1920s would be sustained.

REVIEW QUESTIONS

1. To what extent, if any, had the intensity of white supremacy changed by the 1920s from what it had been two to three decades earlier?

2. What specific examples of progress could leaders like W. E. B. Du Bois, James Weldon Johnson, A. Philip Randolph, and Marcus Garvey point to in the twenties?

3. How do you account for Marcus Garvey's lack of acceptance among African-American leaders?

4. Explain how the black nationalism of the Universal Negro Improvement Association differed from the white nationalism of the Ku Klux Klan.

5. What specific economic opportunities existed for African Americans who had migrated to northern cities?

6. How do you explain the emergence of literary and artistic movement known as the Harlem Renaissance?

7. How distinctive and unique were black writers, artists, and musicians? Were their creative works essentially a part of American culture or separate from it?

8. Were there any genuine reasons for optimism among African Americans by the late 1920s?

RECOMMENDED READING

William H. Harris. *Keeping the Faith: A. Philip Randolph, Milton P. Webster and the Brotherhood of Sleeping Car Porters, 1925–1937.* Urbana: University of Illinois

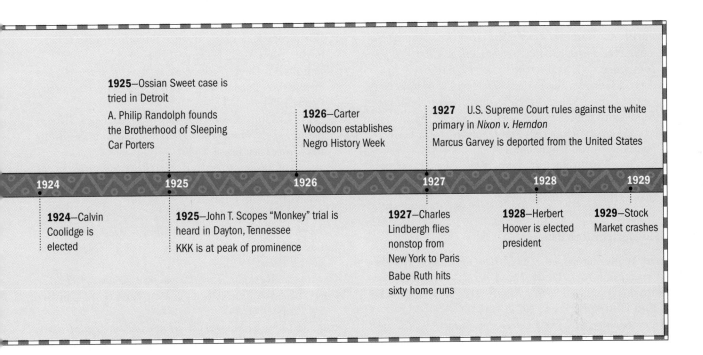

1925—Ossian Sweet case is tried in Detroit
A. Philip Randolph founds the Brotherhood of Sleeping Car Porters

1926—Carter Woodson establishes Negro History Week

1927 U.S. Supreme Court rules against the white primary in *Nixon v. Herndon*
Marcus Garvey is deported from the United States

1924 1925 1926 1927 1928 1929

1924—Calvin Coolidge is elected

1925—John T. Scopes "Monkey" trial is heard in Dayton, Tennessee
KKK is at peak of prominence

1927—Charles Lindbergh flies nonstop from New York to Paris
Babe Ruth hits sixty home runs

1928—Herbert Hoover is elected president

1929—Stock Market crashes

Press, 1977. This is an excellent account of the struggle of Randolph and the BSCP for recognition.

David Levering Lewis. *When Harlem Was in Vogue*. New York: Alfred A. Knopf, 1981. Lewis captures the life and vitality of Harlem in the twenties.

David Levering Lewis, ed. *The Portable Harlem Renaissance Reader*. New York: Penguin Books, 1994. Essays, poems, and excerpts from the works of virtually every writer associated with the Renaissance are contained in this volume.

Nancy MacLean. *Behind the Mask of Chivalry: The Making of the Second Ku Klux Klan*. New York: Oxford University Press, 1994. This is the most recent study of the revived KKK.

Arnold Rampersad. *The Life of Langston Hughes*, Vol. 1, 1902–1941, *I, Too, Sing America*. New York: Oxford University Press, 1986. Here is a rich study of a complex and extraordinary man and writer.

Judith Stein. *The World of Marcus Garvey: Race and Class in Modern Society*. Baton Rouge: Louisiana State University Press, 1991. This is an effective examination of Garvey and the Universal Negro Improvement Association.

ADDITIONAL BIBLIOGRAPHY

The Ku Klux Klan

David M. Chalmers. *Hooded Americanism: A History of the Ku Klux Klan*. New York: Franklin Watts, 1965.

Kenneth T. Jackson. *The Ku Klux Klan in the City*. New York: Oxford University Press, 1967.

The NAACP

Charles F. Kellogg. *NAACP: A History of the National Association for the Advancement of Colored People*. Baltimore: Johns Hopkins University Press, 1967.

Robert L. Zangrando. *The NAACP Campaign against Lynching, 1909–1950*. Philadelphia: Temple University Press, 1980.

A. Philip Randolph and the Brotherhood of Sleeping Car Porters

Jervis B. Anderson. *A. Philip Randolph: A Biographical Portrait*. New York: Harcourt, Brace, Jovanovich, 1973.

Jack Santino. *Miles of Smiles, Years of Struggle: Stories of Black Pullman Porters*. Urbana: University of Illinois Press, 1989.

Marcus Garvey and the Universal Negro Improvement Association

Randall K. Burkett. *Garveyism as a Religious Movement: The Institutionalization of a Black Civil Religion.* Metuchen, NJ: Scarecrow Press, 1978.

E. David Cronon. *Black Moses: The Story of Marcus Garvey and the Universal Negro Improvement Association.* Madison: University of Wisconsin Press, 1955.

Marcus Garvey. *Philosophy and Opinions of Marcus Garvey.* New York: Atheneum, 1969.

Theodore Kornweibel, Jr. *Seeing Red: Federal Campaigns against Black Militancy, 1919–1925.* Bloomington: Indiana University Press, 1998.

The Harlem Renaissance

Arna W. Bontemps, ed. *The Harlem Renaissance Remembered.* New York: Dodd, Mead, 1972.

Nathan Huggins. *Harlem Renaissance.* New York: Oxford University Press, 1971.

Bruce Kellner, ed. *The Harlem Renaissance: A Historical Dictionary of the Era.* Westport, CT: Greenwood Press, 1984.

Steven Watson. *The Harlem Renaissance: Hub of African American Culture, 1920–1930.* New York: Pantheon, 1995.

Biographies and Autobiographies

Pamela Bordelon, ed. *Go Gator and Muddy the Water: Writings by Zora Neale Hurston from the Federal Writers Project.* New York: Norton, 1999.

Thadious M. Davis. *Nella Larsen: Novelist of the Harlem Renaissance.* Baton Rouge: Louisiana State University Press, 1994.

Gloria T. Hull. *Color, Sex, and Poetry: Three Women Writers of the Harlem Renaissance.* Bloomington: Indiana University Press, 1987.

Wayne F. Cooper. *Claude McKay, Rebel Sojourner in the Harlem Renaissance: A Biography.* Baton Rouge: Louisiana State University Press, 1987.

Robert Hemenway. *Zora Neale Hurston: A Literary Biography.* Urbana: University of Illinois Press, 1977.

James Weldon Johnson. *Along the Way.* New York: Viking Press, 1933.

Cynthia E. Kerman. *The Lives of Jean Toomer: A Hunger for Wholeness.* Baton Rouge: Louisiana State University Press, 1987.

Eugene Levy. *James Weldon Johnson: Black Leader, Black Voice.* Chicago: University of Chicago Press, 1973.

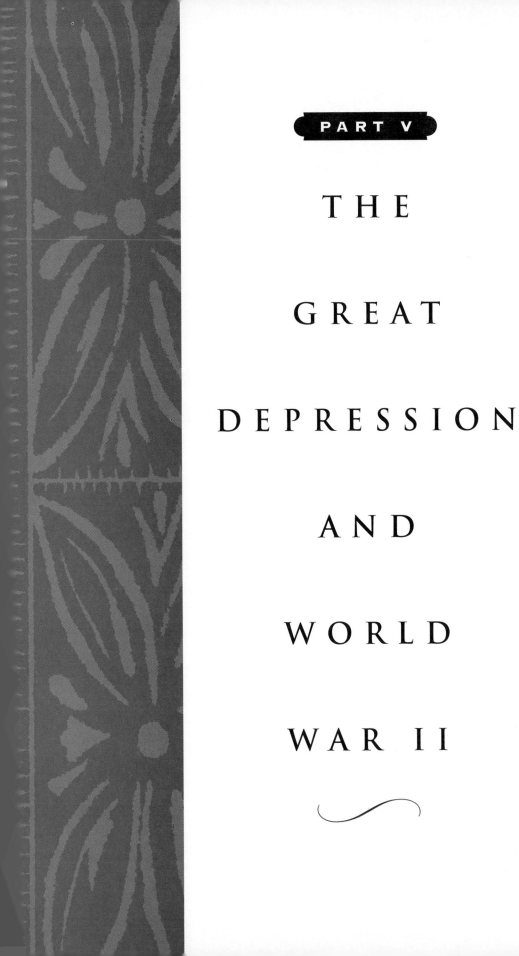

PART V

THE

GREAT

DEPRESSION

AND

WORLD

WAR II

CHAPTER 18

THE GREAT DEPRESSION AND THE NEW DEAL

This photograph by Margaret Bourke White captures the contrast between the American dream of prosperity—for white families—and the harsh realities of life for black Americans during the Depression.

The Depression brought everyone down a peg or two. And the Negro had but a few pegs to fall.

Langston Hughes

The only thing that we not only can, but must do, is voluntarily and insistently to organize our economic and social power, no matter how much segregation it involves. Learn to associate with ourselves and to train ourselves in methods of democratic control within our own group. Run and support our own institutions.

W. E. B. Du Bois

For African Americans the Great Depression was at once an era of suffering made worse by all the horrors and burdens of American racism and a time of profound political change that would lay the foundation for the progress of ensuing decades. At the beginning of the economic collapse most African Americans were either trapped in the already failing southern agricultural system or eking out a bare existence at the margins of the booming urban economy. The fall of the economy pushed many black Americans to the very edge of starvation throwing them off the land and out of the small niches they had carved out in other occupations. Coming out of the southern dominated Democratic party, President Franklin Roosevelt's New Deal program for fighting the Depression might have simply reinforced existing racism, as in fact it did to some extent. From another perspective, the emerging political power of African-American voters in the north, the continuing development of civil rights organizations, and the growth of an antiracist agenda among radicals and labor unions created the preconditions for a profound change in American politics. Amid economic despair, peonage, lynchings, and labor conflict, black men, women, and their children saw glimmers of hope in protests against racial segregation and radical critiques of capitalist exploitation. The 1930s were thus the dark dawn of a new era.

THE CATACLYSM, 1929–1933

The Great Depression was a cataclysmic event in American history. National income fell by over half, from $81 billion in 1929 to $40 billion in 1932. Americans lost faith in banks, and the resulting panic deepened the despair. Overnight millions of Americans saw their life savings swept away in bank closings and foreclosures. Individual Americans responded by limiting purchase of consumer goods and, in turn businesses reacted by cutting back production, investment, and payrolls. The result was a downward spiral of economic activity matched by increases in the number of unemployed people. According to the statistics of the American Federation of Labor (AFL), the number of unemployed people increased from 3,216,000 in January 1930 to 13,689,000 in March 1933 (Figure 18–1). Nearly everyone from farmers to small businessmen and entrepreneurs to wage laborers saw their standard of living drop to a fraction of what it had been before 1929.

In the popular imagination, the stock market crash and Republican president Herbert Hoover took the blame for the hard times, but the explanation is more complicated. Although still a hotly debated issue, more than likely the Great Depression was caused by a combination of factors including rampant speculation, corporate capitalism's drive for markets and profits unchecked by federal regulation, the failure of those in the government or private sector to understand the workings of the economy, a weak international trading system, and most important, the great inequality of wealth and income that limited the purchasing power of millions of Americans.

Harder Times for Black America

The collapse of the American economy hit African Americans particularly hard. The majority of black people remained in the rural South mired in an increasingly exploitive agricultural system. Indeed, the depression exacerbated the key problems besetting cash-crop production in the 1920s. Consumer demand for cotton and sugar fell with the economy, but as farmers grew more of these crops to make ends meet, the supply of these staples increased. The result was a catastrophe, with prices for cotton, still the mainstay of the southern economy, plunging from eighteen cents a pound in 1929 to six cents in 1933. Families of black sharecroppers and tenant farmers, nearly powerless in the rural South, found themselves pushed over the edge of starvation or thrown off the land.

The hard times also struck those one and a half million African Americans who had escaped the South for northern urban communities. Even during the height of the prosperous 1920s black Americans suffered layoffs and witnessed a steady deterioration in their living standards. After 1929 the same forces that impoverished those in the countryside swept those in urban areas further toward the economic margins as waves of refugees from the farms crowded into the cities (see Table 18–1). By 1934, when the federal government noted that 17 percent of white citizens were incapable of self-support, the figure for black Americans stood at an increase of 38 percent overall. In Chicago, the jobless rate for African-American men was 40 percent, in Pittsburgh it was 48

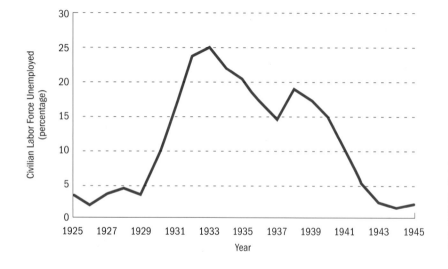

Figure 18–1 Unemployment, 1925–1945. With the collapse of the American economy, unemployment soared in the 1930s. New Deal programs alleviated some of the suffering, but full recovery did not come until the defense industries swung into action with the U.S. entry into World War II.

Table 18-1	Median Income of Black Families Compared to the Median Income of White Families for Selected Cities, 1935–1936		
City and Type of Family	Black	White	Black Income as a Percentage of White Income
Husband–Wife Families			
New York	$980	$1,930	51%
Chicago	$726	$1,687	43%
Columbus	$831	$1,622	51%
Atlanta	$632	$1,876	34%
Columbia	$576	$1,876	31%
Mobile	$481	$1,419	38%
Other Families			
Atlanta	$332	$940	35%
Columbia	$254	$1,403	18%
Mobile	$301	$784	38%

Source: Gunnar Myrdal, et al., *An American Dilemma,* New York: Harper and Brothers, 1944.

percent, in Harlem it climbed to 50 percent, in Philadelphia it reached 56 percent, and in Detroit it rose to 60 percent. The figures were even more dire for black workers in southern cities. In Atlanta, Georgia, 65 percent of black workers needed public assistance, and in Norfolk, Virginia, a stunning 80 percent were forced to apply for welfare.

African Americans lost jobs in those parts of the economy where they had gained a tenuous foothold. Before 1929, jobs in low-status or demeaning occupations such as garbage collection, foundries, or domestic service had been regarded as "Negro work" and, hence, were generally immune from white competition. As desperation set in, white Southerners not only competed for these jobs but also used the old tactics of terror and intimidation to compel employers to fire black people. Unions north and south continued their practice of excluding African Americans from membership and likewise pressured manufacturers to hire white people.

Black women workers, overwhelmingly concentrated in domestic service and laundry work, were affected to an even greater degree than black men. Jobs were fewer because many middle- and working-class families could no longer afford the cost of domestic help. With large numbers of impoverished women coming into the cities, those white people with the money to employ found that they could pay almost nothing and still get help from these desperate women. In 1935 two black women, Marvel Cooke and Ella Baker, published an exposé of the exploitation of these women laborers in *The Crisis.* They entitled the article "The Bronx Slave Market" because the buying and selling of labor reminded them of the old slave marts in the antebellum South. Cooke and Baker described how the street corner market worked: "The Simpson avenue block exudes the stench of the slave market at its worst. Not only is human labor bartered and sold for a slave wage, but human love also is a marketable commodity." Cooke and Baker reported that the women gathered on particular street corners and waited as well-to-do white women selected them for a day's labor. They received "wages as low as 15 to 25 cents an hour, some working only two or three hours a day." Some black people were hired but then deceitful white employers refused to pay them.

African Americans were no strangers to adversity and many used the survival strategies developed through centuries of hardship to eke out an existence during the first years of the Great Depression. Survival demanded that black women pool their resources and adhere to a collective spirit that found such fertile ground in segregated northern neighborhoods. In Chicago, for example, women and their families lived in crowded tenements in which they shared bathroom facilities and other items including hot plates, stoves, and sinks. They bartered and exchanged goods and services because money was so scarce. One woman might dress the hair of a neighbor in return for permission to borrow her dress or use her pots and pans. Another woman might trade bread and sugar or some other household staple for milk or beans or soap. Grandmothers watched over

Federal relief for food, shelter, and clothing helped many families, like this large extended family in Chicago, survive the Great Depression.

A market woman with burdens on her head and in her arms. Black women drew upon proven strategies of self-help, hard work, and communal sharing to survive the Great Depression.

children as their mothers went to look with rising futility for a domestic job. They helped each other in the best way they could.

Rural black women, like their urban sisters, had to rely on their individual and collective ingenuity to survive. As one observer of black women household heads in rural Georgia noted, "In their effort to maintain existence, these people are catching and selling fish, reselling vegetables, sewing in exchange for old clothes, letting out sleeping space, and doing odd jobs. They understand how to help each other. Stoves are used in common, wash boilers go their rounds, and garden crops are exchanged and shared." Nonetheless, the depth and duration of this downturn pressed these mutual aid strategies to the breaking point. By 1933 it seemed that the clock had been turned all the way back to 1865 when many African Americans could claim little more than their bodies as possessions.

Black Businesses in the Depression: Collapse and Survival

Members of the black elite experienced economic casualties that reverberated throughout various regional communities. African Americans who had built successful businesses faced the same depression-borne problems as other businesses but suffered even more because of the greater poverty of the communities on which they depended. A description of two kinds of business, banking and insurance, illustrates the way in which black enterprises stood or fell during the economic crisis.

The Binga Bank, Chicago's first black-owned-and-operated financial institution had been founded in 1908 by its president Jesse Binga (1865–1950), a Detroit-born real estate broker who had previously worked as a barber and a Pullman porter. Binga had managed the bank with such effectiveness that by 1930 its deposits had grown to more than $1.5 million dollars. Binga once boasted that he could lay claim to more footage on State Street, Chicago's principal thoroughfare, than any other man in the city. The Binga Bank was, during its early years, an important symbol of successful black capitalism and as such it represented the hopes and aspirations of Chicago's black people. But too many of the bank's assets were too heavily invested in mortgage loans to black churches and fraternal societies, many of which found it impossible to meet their payments after members suffered massive layoffs. Binga refused to seize the properties of these community institutions, but his restraint, coupled with some financial improprieties, led to the bank's failure. On July 31, 1930, Illinois state bank auditors padlocked the institution and filed a federal misuse-of-funds charge against the once proud financier. Sentenced to prison in 1932, Binga was pardoned by President Franklin Delano Roosevelt a year later. He was, however, never able to rebuild his bank or his fortune.

Some black businesses did survive the economic cataclysm, although often in a much weakened state. Among the fortunate businesses still standing when prosperity finally returned in the 1940s were the leading insurance companies such as Atlanta Life, Supreme Life, Golden State, and the North Carolina Mutual Life Insurance Company. Atlanta Life Insurance Company, for example—founded by a former Georgia slave, Alonzo Franklin Herndon in 1905—not only survived the Depression but recorded substantial profit. Between 1931 and 1936, the company's assets increased by more than $1 million. In part this was because insurance companies like Atlanta Life provided an essential service for African Americans, particularly in an era before government provided social security, and could thus depend on a continued flow of premiums. The officers of the Atlanta Life Insurance Company also avoided one practice that had spelled disaster for Binga Bank. They cut back drastically in the percentage of their investment capital that secured mortgage loans in the black community.

The North Carolina Mutual Life Insurance Company, in Durham, North Carolina, weathered the Great Depression under the astute leadership of Charles Clinton Spaulding (1874–1952), a former manager of a black cooperative grocery store. In 1899 Spaulding accepted the invitation to join with two other African Americans to transform the insurance company into the nation's largest black business. His partners were John Merrick, a former slave and leading realtor and barber (he owned six barbershops, three for whites and three for blacks), and his uncle, Dr. Aaron McDuffie Moore, Durham's only black physician. Following on the heels of the great migration to the North, Spaulding expanded the company's territory northward into Virginia, Maryland, and the District of Columbia. The company adhered to the thrift, hard work, and self-help philosophy so ardently expressed by Booker T. Washington. It remains today, one of the three largest, black-owned insurance companies in the United States.

The Failure of Relief

Before Franklin Roosevelt's New Deal, the responsibility for providing relief from economic hardship rested with private charities or, as a last resort, state and local governments. Even in good times these institutions provided too little for all those in need. Moreover, African Americans had a much harder time than white people in receiving aid and were given less when they did get it. With the onset of the Depression the nation's charitable organizations proved unable to address the needs of more than a small portion of the hungry, homeless, and unemployed millions. In turn, state and local governments were unable or unwilling to provide unemployment insurance or increased welfare benefits to ease the pain and suffering of those most vulnerable to the economic disaster. Even where there was a strong desire to remedy the problem, the magnitude of the economic collapse so lowered tax receipts as to make it nearly impossible for relief agencies to act.

Despite the great need for some kind of relief from the economic disaster, President Herbert Hoover hesitated to act. Steeped in the free market orthodoxy of his time, he believed that government should do very little to interfere with the workings of the economy. Nevertheless, he did more to counteract a depression than any previous president had done. Hoover attempted to convince businesses to retain employees and resist the temptation to cut wages, believing that companies would see that their long-term interest lay in so contributing to the health of the general economy. The president also approved loans to banks, railroads, and insurance companies by the Reconstruction Finance Corporation, a federal agency set up to rescue large corporations. He hoped that these businesses would reinvigorate production, create new jobs, and restore consumer spending. His faith was misplaced; businesses, seeking to save themselves, took the government loans even as they laid off workers.

Hoover's reluctance to use the federal government to intervene in the economy extended to the provision of relief. He suggested that local governments and charities should address the needs of the unemployed, the homeless, and the starving masses. Hoover was not a callous person but rather was someone trapped in a rigid ideology. He watched with dismay the wandering groups of men, women, and children who began settling into what they called, with grim humor, "Hoovervilles," sordid clusters of shacks made of tin, cardboard, and burlap adjacent to railroad tracks and dumps. Still, he flatly refused to allow the federal government to take a role in directly providing relief.

Hoover's inactivity was bad enough, but his political agenda proved to be as racist as that of the Democratic party. Indeed, Hoover wanted to create a white Republican party in the South and to that end cultivated white Southerners by attempting to appoint John Parker, a racist judge, to the U.S. Supreme Court and by displacing black Republican party leaders. Hoover's policy was not new; for decades the national Republican party had treated black voters with contempt and often declined to reward them with patronage appointments. This policy took on a different meaning during the early 1930s against the backdrop of black suffering. As NAACP director Walter White put it, Hoover

sat stolidly in the White House, refusing bluntly to receive Negro citizens who wished to lay before him the facts of their steadily worsening plight or to consider any remedial legislation or governmental action. His attitude toward Negroes caused me to coin a phrase which gained considerable currency, particularly in the Negro world, in which I described Hoover as "the man in the lily-White House."

AFRICAN AMERICANS AND THE NEW DEAL

In 1932, the third year of the Great Depression, voters elected New York governor Franklin Delano Roosevelt to the presidency with a total of nearly twenty-three million votes. Roosevelt's lopsided victory over Hoover, who received fewer than sixteen million votes, demonstrated the country's loss of faith in the Republican party and its economic philosophy and heralded the emergence of a new electoral coalition. The new president appealed to the Democratic party's base of support in the white South, but to this group he added a coalition of western farmers, industrial workers, urban voters from the white ethnic groups in northern cities, and reform-minded intellectuals. For the time being, however, black Americans still clung to the Republican banner. In Chicago, for example, less than 25 percent of black voters cast their ballots for Roosevelt. But this was the last election in which the party of Lincoln could take them for granted. In his first term Roosevelt inaugurated a multitude of programs to counter the Depression—collectively known as the New Deal—which would shift the allegiance of African Americans. Initially his programs continued past patterns of discrimination against African Americans, but by 1935 it had evolved in a way that provided more equal benefits and prompted profound social changes. The result was a new political order that ultimately undermined key portions of the edifice of American racism.

Roosevelt and the First New Deal, 1933–1935

During his first 100 days in office Franklin Roosevelt pressed through Congress a profusion of bold new economic initiatives that came to be known as the first New Deal. To combat the Depression, Roosevelt, unlike Hoover, followed no predetermined plan. Instead he favored experimentation—tempered by political expediency—over ideology as the guide to federal action. With little resistance Congress passed the president's sprawling and complex laws aimed at overhauling the nation's financial, agricultural, and industrial systems. Most hoped, vainly as it turned out, that these changes would eventually bring a return to prosperity. In the meantime Roosevelt moved forcefully to counter the immediate suffering of the unemployed with a massive emergency federal relief effort. Many of the first New Deal's programs benefited both white and black people, but the strength of white Southerners in the Democratic party and the nearly complete lack of African-American political power in the South caused much of this early program to be unfairly administered.

The Agricultural Adjustment Act (AAA), designed to protect farmers by giving them subsidies to limit production and thereby stabilize prices, illustrates the key benefits and problems experienced by African Americans during the first New Deal. The theory underlying the AAA was that creating scarcity would increase agricultural prices. So farmers would be paid to grow less. The program provided for sharecroppers and tenant farmers to get part of the subsidies and approved a plan that allowed newly instituted rural relief agencies to dispense supplementary income to off-season wageworkers.

This program had a positive impact on many African Americans, mainly because it pumped billions of dollars into an economic sector on which over 4,500,000 black people relied for their livelihood. Also, the AAA was designed to remedy the problems of those farmers—disproportionately African American—who were over-reliant on such cash crops as cotton. By 1929 three out of four black farmers, compared to two out of five white farmers, received at least 40 percent of their gross income from cotton. The flow of money from the AAA did, for a time, reduce the rate at which black people left farming: Fewer left the farms in the first two years of the program than in the two years before it began. Indeed, from a broader perspective the New Deal appears to have had some effect in slowing the rate at which black people left the land. During the 1930s, only 4.5 percent of African Americans abandoned farming, compared to 8.6 percent who did so during the 1920s.

But if the AAA brought some real benefits to black farmers, it was often, contrary to protections written into the law, administered unfairly and corruptly. Local control of the AAA resided in the hands of the Extension Service and County Agricultural Conservation Committees, which were supposed to represent all farmers. The county agents, however, were often the planters themselves and the committees mirrored southern politics as a whole by excluding black people. African Americans were further disadvantaged by the system of unilateral bookkeeping and oppressive credit relations between landlords and tenants. During the first two years of the AAA, black farmers complained bitterly that white landlords simply grabbed and pocketed the millions of dollars of benefit checks they were supposed to forward to tenants. To compound the injury, some planters then evicted the sharecroppers and tenants from the land.

When unscrupulous white landowners pocketed AAA payments intended to aid all farmers, thousands of evicted share-croppers congregated in refugee-like camps along the roads to protest the injustice. A sharecropper strike occurred in the bootheel of Missouri in 1935.

The experience of African Americans with the National Industrial Recovery Act (NIRA) mimicked that with the AAA. The NIRA was intended to promote the revival of manufacturing by allowing various industries to cooperate in establishing codes of conduct governing prices, wage levels, and employment practices, all of which were to be overseen by a National Recovery Administration (NRA). The NRA oversaw the drafting of the codes but faced tremendous resistance from employers and unions in eliminating racial disparities in wage rates and working conditions. Even when African-American advocates succeeded in winning wage increases for occupations in which black people predominated, the result was often a shift to white labor. These policies prompted some African-American newspapers and protest organizations to claim that "NRA" really stood for the "Negro Removal Agency" or "Negroes Robbed Again." To the relief of many African-American advocates and workers, the NIRA was declared unconstitutional by the U.S. Supreme Court in spring 1935.

The New Deal's national welfare programs included the Federal Emergency Relief Administration (FERA), the Civilian Conservation Corps (CCC), Public Works Administration (PWA), and Civil Works Administration (CWA). Although inadequate and unfairly administered on local levels, these programs often proved to be the only thing standing between black people and starvation. FERA provided funds for local and state relief operations to restart and expand their programs. Millions of people found themselves pulled back from the brink of starvation by the program. Because African

V O I C E S

A BLACK SHARECROPPER DETAILS ABUSE IN THE ADMINISTRATION OF AGRICULTURAL RELIEF

This is one of many letters black sharecroppers sent to the NAACP in search of assistance to halt the mass evictions and abuse of New Deal relief efforts.

Alabama

June 21, 1934

Dear Sir:–I am writing you these few lines ask you if it is any possible chance of you fining out just why F.E.R.A. office here in . . . refuse to gave me work when I have six in family to care for and also my wife's mother who is over 65 years old and been under the Doctor care for the past seven years of course my wife has a little job but its not with the relief work which some weeks she makes five dollars and some weeks less with four children to take care off which range in age 8–6–4–3 years old and we have $5 per month rent and also $1.74 per week Insurance which that don't enclude Food and Clothing and Fuel to burn. Now Mr. White in the past two and half months I am being going to the relief office trying to get on the relief work and it seem like it is empossible and also just before the first of April I went up to the relief office and explain my case to Mr. . . . ., the man that gave out the work cards and he gave me a food order for the amount of $2—two dollars and also I got some work to do. But as soon as I got paid for the 24 hours work he came to me to collect $2 for the food order that he gave me and I refuse to gave him $2 and I havent been able to get any more work to do and I have been going up to the office each day sence. But they tell me at the office that they cant gave me work because my wife is working. Of course if that maybe the case I can gave you the name and the address of at least a hundred families where there is two and three in one family who are working on the relief project and I know of at least twenty single men with no one but theirself to take care of and are working 24 hours every week and they got to gave their foreman one dollar each every week if they want to stay on the job.

Now Mr. White the white man who my wife work for and my wife told him that they refuse to gave me work because she was working for me and he went up to relief office to see about it But they told him that they didnt cut me out of work because my wife were working but they cut me off because I were unable to do the work. and of course I know that to be very much untrue. The trouble is I refuse to be a fool like so many of my race here and else where around here to pay for a food order that is supose to be giving to the needy free of charge but lots are paying for them and also paying for their job. Of course Mr. White I am colored and when you go up to the relief office The Colored people is treated just as if they were dogs and not human beings. I have been up in the office and I have seen with my own eyes my color kicked and beaten down a whole flight of stairs. I have seen everything done except been murder. Understand Mr. White the little job that my wife has isnt on the releif is a private and everybody that is head of any thing here in the releif office is kin to one another. Now Mr. White the lady that is head of the relief is Mrs. . . . which I saw here once since I was cut off from work and I explained my case to her and she told that she would send a investigator around to my home the next morning whose name is Miss . . . and she told me that when I gave Mr. . . . the $2 for the food order she would O.K. my work card. Mr. White if possible will you please fine out for me just what is the reason they refuse to gave me work when I have six in family and rent to pay. Insurance, Doctor bill, milk bill, buy food and clothing and with only my wife at work it is impossible Mr. White.

QUESTIONS

1. Describe the conditions that led the writer to seek help from Walter White and the NAACP.

2. What kinds of corrupt practices in relief benefits distribution are revealed in this letter?

3. What were some of the factors and reasons implied and noted that prevented even greater numbers of black people from protesting economic inequality?

Source: Herbert Aptheker, ed., *A Documentary History of the Negro People in the United States, 1933–1945* (New York: Citadel Press Book, 1990), pp. 58–60.

Americans suffered greater economic devastation, they received benefits at a higher rate than whites. In most cities north and south, 25 to 40 percent of African Americans were on relief rolls that were funded wholly or in part by FERA. Direct welfare, however, was deemed by many in the Roosevelt administration to be debilitating, so it placed an emphasis on hiring many of the unemployed for public works projects. The CWA was a temporary agency created to help people through the winter of 1933–1934. The Civilian Conservation Corps (CCC) built segregated camps to employ young men and to take them away from the poverty and hopelessness of urban areas. By the time it was abolished in 1945, more than 200,000 African-American youth had taken part in the program.

All these relief programs included substantial numbers of African Americans and helped many through the worst parts of the Depression. But they also tended to be less helpful to black people than similarly situated whites. In its early days the CCC, for example, was a tightly segregated institution, with only about 5 percent of its slots going to black youths during its first year. Likewise, although FERA tended to be administered fairly in northern cities, in the South it reached only a small proportion of those in need.

Black Officials in the New Deal

The first New Deal was not completely bleak for African Americans. In addition to the benefits, however grudgingly disbursed, they derived from New Deal relief programs, African Americans also gained hitherto unknown levels of influence and new allies within the Roosevelt administration. Their experience reflected both the growing availability of highly trained African Americans for government service and the emerging consciousness among white liberals about the problems—and potential electoral power—of black people.

Black people found a staunch ally in First Lady Eleanor Roosevelt. She was revered for her relentless commitment to racial justice. She arranged meetings at the White House for some black leaders. She cajoled her husband to consider legislation on behalf of black rights. She personally defied Jim Crow laws by refusing to sit in a "white only" section while attending a meeting in the South. Moreover, she wrote newspaper columns calling for "fair play and equal opportunity for Negro citizens." Roosevelt further endeared herself to black Americans when she resigned her membership in the Daughters of the American Revolution after that organization refused to allow a young black opera singer, Marian Anderson, to perform at its Constitution Hall in Washington in 1939. (Administration officials subsequently arranged for Anderson to perform in front of the Lincoln Memorial on Easter Sunday before a crowd of 75,000. The first song she sang was "My Country, 'Tis of Thee.")

Eleanor Roosevelt was joined by other liberals to press the cause of racial justice and to seek the appointment of African Americans throughout the government. Early in 1933 President Roosevelt acceded to their request that he appoint someone in his administration to assume responsibility for ensuring that African Americans received fair treatment. He asked Harold Ickes, a former president of the Chicago chapter of the NAACP, and a white man whom most black Americans recognized as a tried and true friend, to make this happen. Ickes invited Clark Foreman, a young white Georgian who had rejected his region's racism, to handle the assignment. Foreman recognized the irony of a white man representing black people in the government and immediately began the recruitment of highly trained African Americans. Similar efforts to bring African Americans into government positions were under way by Eleanor Roosevelt, Ickes, and other administration officials such as Daniel Roper, Secretary of Commerce, and Harry Hopkins, FDR's relief administrator. The result was that doors to the government began opening in a way never before seen. For the first time, the government employed professional black architects, lawyers, engineers, economists, statisticians, interviewers, office managers, social workers, and librarians. The Department of Commerce hired Eugene K. Jones, on leave from the National Urban League. The National Youth Administration brought in Mary McLeod Bethune and the Department of Interior employed William H. Hastie and Robert Weaver. Ira De A. Reid joined the Social Security Administration, and Lawrence W. Oxley worked for the Department of Labor, with Ambrose Caliver serving in the Office of Education.

A core of highly placed African Americans became linked in a network called the Federal Council on Negro Affairs, more loosely known as Roosevelt's "Black Cabinet." Mary McLeod Bethune was the undisputed leader of this body, which consisted primarily of "New Deal race specialists." It numbered twenty-seven men and three women working mostly in temporary emergency agencies such as the Works Progress Administration (WPA) and included such stalwarts as housing administrator Robert Weaver. This group met with Bethune every Friday in her Washington home, while a smaller and younger group met occasionally in Robert Weaver's apartment. This cadre of advisers pressured the president and the heads of different federal agencies

MARY MCLEOD BETHUNE

Mary McLeod Bethune played a powerful role in Roosevelt's black cabinet but this was only one of the many forums in which she exercised consummate leadership and diplomatic skill. Bethune's life and work are major links connecting the social reform efforts of post-reconstruction black women to the civil rights protest activities of the generation emerging after World War II. All the various strands of black women's struggle for education, political rights, racial pride, and sexual autonomy are united in Bethune's writings, speeches, and organizational work.

Mary McLeod Bethune forged a mutually sustaining friendship with First Lady Eleanor Roosevelt that gave her considerable access to the president.

Bethune, born on July 10, 1875, near Mayesville, South Carolina, graduated from Scotia Seminary in 1894 and entered Dwight Moody's Institute for Home and Foreign Missions in Chicago. After teaching in a number of mission schools, she settled in Daytona, Florida, where she founded the Daytona Educational and Industrial Institute for Training Negro Girls. Reflecting on her work years later Bethune recalled, "The school expanded fast. In less than two years I had 250 pupils. . . . I concentrated more and more on girls, as I felt that they especially were hampered by lack of educational opportunities." Eventually, however, she agreed to merge with Cookman Institute, an educational facility for black boys under the auspices of the Methodist Church. Thus, in 1923 the now coeducational institution was renamed Bethune-Cookman College.

During the 1920s Bethune became the leader of the National Association of Colored Women, a federation of women's clubs. As the NACW's president she attempted to turn the organization away from its previous focus on self-help and moral uplift and toward broader goals. Although she made progress, by 1935 she had become frustrated by the NACW's caution and founded the National Council of Negro Women (NCNW), an "organization of organizations." The women present at the creation of the NCNW were the who's who of black women's activism. They included educators Charlotte Hawkins Brown and Mary Church Terrell; executive director of the National Association of Colored Graduate Nurses Mabel K. Staupers; NAACP national field director Daisy Lampkins; and Addie W. Hunton, former president of the Empire State Federation of Women's Clubs and of the International Council of Women of the Darker Race. Eventually, the NCNW included twenty national affiliates and ninety local councils located in cities, towns, and rural communities across the country. Club engagement strengthened their resolve to struggle for black rights and provided safe space for them to develop the skills and networks that proved critical in the post–World War II civil rights movement.

The New Deal brought Bethune forth as a Democratic party activist and a government official. Bethune had a close personal relationship with First Lady Eleanor Roosevelt that gave her access to the president that few others enjoyed. She and Eleanor Roosevelt had persuaded the president that the National Youth Administration (NYA) needed a negro division to assure that benefits would be distributed fairly. When the organization started, Bethune was named the NYA's Director of Negro Affairs. She was the first African-American woman to hold a high position in the government. Bethune supported the administration during the 1936 campaign by helping to convince African Americans that their best interests lay with the Democratic rather than Republican party.

One of Bethune's many noteworthy accomplishments was the 1937 conference held by the Department of Labor on the Problems of the Negro and Negro Youth, at which Eleanor Roosevelt delivered a key speech. During the session entitled "Security of Life and Equal Protection under the Law" the conference called for a federal antilynching law, equal access to the ballot in federal elections, and elimination of segregation and discrimination on interstate carriers. This was a virtual blueprint of the agenda of the civil rights movement. No other general meeting on civil rights during the Roosevelt administration generated the interest, support, and publicity of this 1937 conference. With this Negro Youth Conference, Bethune assumed the middle ground of black politics.

Roosevelt's "Black Cabinet" in a 1938 photograph. Mary McLeod Bethune is in the center of the front row.

to adopt and support color-blind policies and lobbied to advance the status of black Americans.

Black Social Scientists and the New Deal

Many black intellectuals, scholars, and writers believed that the social sciences could be used to adjudicate race relations in the country and during the New Deal they found greater receptiveness to their work than ever before. Nearly 200 African Americans received Ph.D.s during the 1930s, more than four times the combined total from the first three decades of the century. Several of these young scholars reached the top ranks of the social sciences studying the economic, political, and sociological problems of black people with a depth of experience and theoretical sophistication lacking in earlier generations of scholars. In sociology E. Franklin Frazier and Charles S. Johnson took the lead. Frazier's pioneering studies of black families, although now quite dated, placed him at the forefront of debates on social policy. Johnson served as editor of *Opportunity*, the journal of the Urban League, throughout the 1930s; in this position he published insightful critiques of American racial practices and policies as well as the work of a number of emerging black novelists, poets, and playwrights. Meanwhile Ralph Bunche became well known within the field of political science, while Abram Harris and Robert Weaver gained renown in economics.

Historians such as Carter G. Woodson, Lorenzo Greene, Benjamin Quarles, and John Hope Franklin advanced the idea that black people had been active agents in the past and not simply the passive objects of white people's actions. Through the Association for the Study of Negro Life and History as well as the Negro History Week, Woodson and his co-workers Greene, Alrutheus Taylor, and Monroe Work deployed their scholarship to dismiss claims of black inferiority. Their scholarly emphasis on racial pride, achievement, and autonomy was an important boost to black morale.

The increasing importance of black scholars became apparent late in the 1930s when the Carnegie Corporation, a philanthropic foundation, sponsored a major study of black life. Although the study was led by Gunnar Myrdal, a Swedish social scientist, nearly half the large staff of scholars were African Americans, and several, most particularly Bunche, had a major impact on the work. Published in 1944 as *An American Dilemma*, this massive study had a profound effect on the public's understanding of the way in which racism undermined the personal and group progress of African Americans and helped to set the agenda for the civil rights movement.

African Americans and the Second New Deal

After two years marked by a slow recovery, much of the first New Deal lay in shambles. Major parts of it had been invalidated by the U.S. Supreme Court and an emerging conservative backlash was rising against the Roosevelt administration. This political situation prompted Roosevelt to press for a second burst of legislation marked by the passage of the Social Security Act (SSA), the National Labor Relations Act (NLRA), the creation of the Works Progress Administration (WPA), and other measures considerably more radical than those that had come in 1933. The NLRA, for example, aided in the formation and growth of unions. The SSA provided the rudiments of a social welfare system as well as unemployment and retirement insurance. This new set of laws, known as the second New Deal, survived legal challenges and changed the United States, particularly by strengthening the role of the federal government.

Roosevelt's leftward political shift helped him to win the 1936 presidential election in a landslide. This election cemented a new electoral coalition that yoked the southern wing of the Democratic party with more liberal farmers and working-class voters who were labor union members in the North and West. The Democratic party outside the South began to pursue successfully the votes of the large African-American populations in the great cites of the North. The great migration had effectively relocated tens of thousands of prospective black voters in northern urban centers, traditional strongholds of Democratic party machines, such as in Chicago. Institutionalized housing segregation combined with the often conscious choice to live in their own neighborhoods concentrated the black electorate and increased its political power. This power had already appeared in the 1928 election of Republican Oscar De Priest to the United States House of Representatives, the first African-American congressman from the North. In 1934, reflecting a shift in partisan allegiance, Chicago's black voters elected Democrat Arthur W. Mitchell to Congress to replace De Priest. Mitchell, a registered Republican at the outset of the Great Depression, switched to the Democratic party and by doing so became the first black Democrat ever to win a seat in the House of Representatives.

Mitchell's election was only the beginning of the change in black people's political party identification. The powerful black press fanned the shifting winds and increasingly large numbers of black urban dwellers developed an intense interest in politics. They began to connect political power with the prospect of improving their economic conditions. By the end of the decade, black urban voters garnered noteworthy influence in key states such as Illinois, Ohio, Pennsylvania, and New York. This political consciousness led to the election of black state legislators in California, Illinois, Indiana, Kansas, Kentucky, New Jersey, New York, Ohio, Pennsylvania, and West Virginia.

In another indication of change, some Democrats began supporting antilynching legislation. Congressman Mitchell wrote a strong speech printed in the *Congressional Record* in 1935 supporting President Roosevelt as an antilynching advocate. "No President," he declared, "has been more outspoken against the horrible crime of lynching than has Mr. Roosevelt. In speaking of lynching some time ago he characterized it as 'collective murder' and spoke of it as a crime which blackens the record of America." Mitchell told black audiences, "Let me say again, the attitude of the administration at the White House is absolutely fair and without prejudice, insofar as the Negro citizenry is concerned."

So the 1936 election results recorded more than a Roosevelt victory. The ballots cast revealed that Roosevelt had captured the allegiance of the vast majority of African Americans. Robert Vann, editor of the *Pittsburgh Courier* had urged black people, after casting their ballots, to go home to "turn Lincoln's picture to the wall." There are many complex reasons for this revolutionary transformation in black political allegiance. The shift to the Democratic party did not occur without anxiety. At least some black people feared that by joining the party they would open the door for even larger numbers of white southern Democrats to assume national political power and thwart black advancement. But by 1936 the majority of African-American voters were willing to take the risk.

While some African Americans feared they would help racist white southern Democrats, the increased participation of African Americans in the Democratic party sent chills of fear down the spines of the white southern elite. The tension between black Democrats and white conservative Democrats erupted at the party's 1936 convention in Philadelphia. The seating of thirty-two black Democratic party delegates provoked the wrath of southern politicians. The selection of a black Baptist minister to open one session with a prayer especially outraged South Carolina Senator Ellison D. "Cotton Ed" Smith, who, accompanied by Mayor Burnet Maybank of Charleston, South Carolina, and one or two other delegates, marched ostentatiously off the floor proclaiming that they refused to support "any political organization that looks upon the Negro and caters to him as a political and social equal." Smith declared that he was "sick of the whole damn thing." Undaunted, the black minister simply observed that "Brother Smith needs more prayer." The next day when Congressman Mitchell of Illinois took to the floor, Ed Smith repeated his walkout. The South Carolina delegation subsequently adopted a protest resolution denouncing the appearance of black men on the convention's program. The protests of southern white politicians, however, had no effect on the political decisions of black men and women. Heeding the advice of the NAACP, they voted their personal interests.

Despite the rise of black people in the Democratic party, southern congressmen succeeded in excluding many African Americans from key government programs. For example, they insisted on denying the benefits of the National Labor Relations Act and Social Security Act to agricultural laborers and domestic servants. These white Southerners could not, however, stop the tilt toward fairer administration of programs or the revival of the push for equal rights, which had lain all but dormant since the end of the Reconstruction Era.

An examination of the Works Progress Administration (WPA) illustrates the changes wrought by the Second New Deal and by the increasing shift of African

Americans to the Democratic party. The WPA, with Harry Hopkins (1890–1946) as its head, was created to employ the unemployed. Under Hopkins's direction, and sustained with an appropriation of $1.39 billion, the WPA put thousands of men and women to work building new roads in the United States, as well as new hospitals, city halls, courthouses, and schools. Under the aegis of the WPA, American citizens built bridges, ports, and a host of local water-supply systems. Larger scale projects included the Lincoln Tunnel under the Hudson River connecting New York and New Jersey, the Triborough Bridge system linking Manhattan to Long Island, and the Bonneville and Boulder Dams (Boulder Dam was later renamed the Hoover Dam by a Republican-controlled Congress in 1946).

The WPA was administered far more fairly than were the first New Deal programs. The national government explicitly rejected racial discrimination and worked to make sure local officials complied. It was by no means a perfect program, but by 1939 it provided assistance to one million black families on a far more equitable basis than ever before.

The same pattern can be seen in the WPA's four arts programs—the Federal Art Project, the Federal Music Project, the Federal Theater Project, and the Federal Writers Project—which employed thousands of musicians, intellectuals, writers, and artists. A fifth program, the Historical Records Survey, created in 1937, sent teams of writers including Zora Neale Hurston to collect folklore and study various ethnic groups. One team collected the life histories and reminiscences of some 2,000 former slaves.

Between 1935 and 1943 the WPA helped artists display their talents and made their work widely available. Among the black artists hired to adorn government buildings, post offices, and public parks were Aaron Douglas, Charles Alston, Richmond Barthe, Sargent Johnson, Archibald Motley Jr., and Augusta Savage. Savage was a sculptor who worked in clay, marble, and bronze; she established arts schools in the 1930s—the Savage School of Arts and Crafts, Savage Studios, and the Uptown Art Laboratory. She became the first director of the Harlem Community Art Center in 1937. Her students included Jacob Lawrence, William Artis, Norman Lewis, and Elton Fax.

The Federal Theater Project established sixteen black theater units. Among their most notable productions was a version of *Macbeth* set in Haiti with an all-black cast. White actor John Houseman and black actress Rose McClendon conducted the Harlem Federal Theater Project. This project—more than the others—proved to be very controversial.

In the 1930s black theater benefited greatly from the support of the WPA's Federal Theater Project. One of the most provocative and theatrically creative results was this production of Shakespeare's *Macbeth* with a cast composed entirely of black performers.

BLACK PROTEST DURING THE GREAT DEPRESSION

During the 1930s African-American men and women initiated their own agenda and determined to use every resource at their disposal to destroy the obstacles to racial justice and barriers to equal opportunity. The NAACP sponsored a legal campaign against educational discrimination and political disfranchisement led by Charles Houston and Thurgood Marshall, mobilized black communities, and sustained hope in struggle. Black people benefited from the New Deal but not to the extent that white people did. The disparity between black and white lives was a spur to action. The juxtaposition of black subordination and misery alongside the new forms of federal aid so willingly distributed to white citizens convinced black Americans to intensify their own struggle for their American rights. Many embraced radical critiques of American capitalism, but few ever considered Communism a viable alternative to American democracy. Black people would emerge from the Depression more determined than ever to make democracy work for them.

The NAACP and Civil Rights Struggles

During the 1930s the NAACP developed a new effectiveness as an advocate for African-American civil rights. The biracial organization took the lead in pressing the government to protect African-American rights and to eliminate the blatant racism in government programs. Part of the reason for this new dynamism was the astute leadership of Walter White, a man whose physical characteristics could have easily permitted him to pass for white—he had blonde hair and blue eyes—and turn away from the problems of black people. Instead he became an insistent voice of protest, personally investigating forty-two lynchings and eight race riots, and he was an ardent lobbyist for civil rights legislation and racial justice. Throughout the thirties African Americans of all hues moved into leadership positions in the NAACP and added their names to the membership roles of its many branches.

The new dynamism of the NAACP became apparent in 1930 when Walter White took a prominent role in the successful campaign to defeat Hoover's nomination of Circuit Court Judge John J. Parker of North Carolina to a seat on the United States Supreme Court. Parker had raised the ire of the organization because he openly embraced white supremacy, stating, for example, that the "participation of the Negro in politics is a source of evil and danger to both races." The NAACP formed a coalition with the American Federation of Labor to derail the Parker nomination. Although the NAACP could take only part of the credit, White trumpeted the victory and let it be known that African Americans would not be silent while "the Hoover administration proposed to conciliate southern white sentiment by sacrificing the Negro and his rights."

Du Bois Ignites a Controversy

The NAACP was not without critics, even within its own ranks. Many younger black people criticized its focus on civil liberties and deplored it for ignoring the economic misery of the great majority of African Americans. In 1934 W. E. B. Du Bois, editor of the NAACP's journal *The Crisis*, joined the chorus. Criticizing what he considered the group's overemphasis on integration, Du Bois advocated a program of self-determination he hoped would permit black people to develop "an economic nation within a nation." Du Bois acknowledged that this internal economy could only provide for a fraction of the needs of the African-American community. But he insisted it could be developed and expanded in numerous ways. It was possible, he wrote, "that this smaller part could be so important and wield so much power that its influence upon the total economy of Negroes and the total industrial organization of the United States would be decisive for the great ends towards which the Negro moves."

The black intellectual community quickly took Du Bois to task for his advocacy of this "voluntary segregation." Sociologist E. Franklin Frazier, for example, declared that the idea of black businesses succeeding within a segregated economy was a black upper-class fantasy and social myth. Nevertheless, Du Bois held fast to his position that the NAACP should continue to oppose legal segregation yet combine that opposition with vigorous support for the improvement of segregated institutions as long as discrimination remained in force. He was eventually forced from the editorship of *The Crisis*, but his resignation did not end the controversy. By the late 1930s the NAACP had developed, alongside its older activities, a much greater emphasis on economic policy and worked to develop stronger ties to the burgeoning labor movement.

Challenging Racial Discrimination in the Courts

The NAACP's effectiveness was enhanced by a dramatic expansion of its legal campaign against racial discrimination. Central to this project was the hiring of Charles Hamilton Houston, a Harvard-trained African-American lawyer and scholar, to lead it. Houston had been dean of Howard University Law School, which he had transformed into a powerful institution for training black attorneys in the intricacies of civil rights law. At the NAACP, Houston laid out a plan for a legal program to challenge inequality in education and the exclusion of black people from voting in the South. Houston used lawsuits both to force state and local governments to live up to the Constitution and as a way to inspire community organization. "This is no star performance," he said of his strategy. "My ideal of administration is to make the movement self-perpetuating. . . . Our idea should be to press upon the opposition and public that what we have is a real program, sweeping up . . . [from] popular demand."

Houston did not focus directly on eliminating segregation but rather sought to force southern states to equalize their facilities. Studies by the NAACP had revealed great disparities in per capita expenditures for white and black students, and huge differences in salaries paid to white and black teachers. In Georgia, for example, the average per pupil expenditure for white students was $36.29 compared to $4.59 for black students. White teachers' salaries averaged $97.88 per month while black teachers received only $49.41. Houston was no supporter of segregation. He hoped to use litigation to secure judgments that would so increase the cost of separate institutions that states would be forced to abandon them.

To execute his agenda, Houston convinced Walter White to hire his former student at the Howard

University Law School, Thurgood Marshall, in 1936. Marshall was born in Baltimore in 1908. His father was a dining-car waiter and club steward; his mother had been a teacher before her marriage. During the 1930s Marshall and Houston focused on bringing greater parity between black and white teachers, a project that they hoped would increase NAACP membership among teachers, their students, and parents. The two men, working with a remarkable network of African-American attorneys, also attempted to end discrimination against black men and women in professional and graduate schools. Inequalities were obvious here because many southern states offered no graduate facilities of any kind to black students. Like other campaigns, this focus on graduate education was intended to establish precedents that might be used to gain equality in other areas and as an organizing tool for developing strong local NAACP branches.

The fight against political disfranchisement also helped to mobilize local and state communities and branches. Nowhere was this more apparent than in Texas. In 1923 the Texas legislature enacted the Terrell Law, which expressly declared: "In no event shall a Negro be eligible to participate in a Democratic primary election . . . in . . . Texas." In the one-party South, the primary elections were more important than the general elections. The general election often merely rubber-stamped the choice made in the primary. Thus to be denied the right to vote in Democratic party primary elections was to be disfranchised. The NAACP developed a case to test the constitutionality of the Terrell Law and commenced a twenty-year battle through the courts. The Texas branches of the NAACP raised money and coordinated local involvement in the campaign to overthrow the Democratic white primary that kept so many black Texans from making their political will felt.

The Texas white primary fight was the most sustained and intense effort undertaken by any NAACP chapter during the interwar period. It began in the 1920s and achieved its first victory when the Supreme Court ruled in 1927 in *Nixon v. Herndon* that the Texas Democratic primary was unconstitutional (see Chapter 17). At the national headquarters, Charles H. Houston and Thurgood Marshall orchestrated the assault. Their efforts were rewarded in subsequent decisions that further chipped away at the legal basis for the white primary. Finally, in 1944 the United States Supreme Court issued a ruling in *Smith v. Allwright* that ended the white primary altogether. It was the NAACP's greatest legal victory to that time. It would soon be followed by many more.

Black Women and Community Organizing

A number of black women made exceptional contributions to the NAACP during the 1930s through their successful fund-raising efforts and membership drives. Three agitators for racial justice were Daisy Adams Lampkins (c. 1884–1965), Juanita Mitchell (1913–1992), and Ella Baker (1903–1986). These women worked closely with White and the NAACP throughout the Depression and World War II decades. Lampkin, a native of Washington, D.C., became in 1915 the president of the Negro Women's Franchise League, a group dedicated to fighting for the vote. During World War I she directed Liberty Bond sales in the black community of Pennsylvania's Allegheny County and in Pittsburgh, selling some $2 million worth of government securities. In 1930, Walter White enlisted her as regional field secretary of the NAACP, a post she held until she was made national field secretary in 1935. She continued raising funds for the NAACP and played leading roles within organized black womanhood.

The NAACP in the 1930s and 1940s depended on the formidable fund-raising talents of black women like Daisy Lampkin (shown here), Ella Baker, and Juanita Mitchell. These women played a major role in building NAACP membership.

Juanita E. Jackson was born in Hot Springs, Arkansas, and raised in Baltimore, Maryland. She earned a degree in education from the University of Pennsylvania in 1931, then returned to Baltimore, where she helped to found the City-Wide Young People's Forum. This organization encouraged young people to discuss and plan attacks on such scourges as unemployment, segregation, and lynching. The success of the group, which she headed from 1931 to 1934, attracted Walter White's attention and he subsequently offered her the leadership of the NAACP's new youth program. From 1935 to 1938 she served as NAACP national youth director. In 1938 Jackson married fellow civil rights activist Clarence Mitchell, had four sons, and directed the NAACP's voter registration campaigns. In 1950 she received a law degree from the University of Maryland. As the first black woman admitted to practice law in Maryland she embarked upon a series of cases that helped to destroy racial segregation on the state's public beaches as well as in its public schools.

Ella Baker, who became one of the most important women in the civil rights movement of the 1950s and 1960s, began her life's work during the Depression era. Born in Norfolk, Virginia, Baker moved to New York City in 1927 and worked as a waitress and as an organizer involved in radical politics. She was on the staff of two local newspapers, *The American West Indian News*, and *Negro National News*. Within two years after her arrival she had cofounded with George Schuyler the Young Negroes' Cooperative League in Harlem. The group practiced collective decision making and attempted to involve all segments of the community in the cooperatives. As she worked with the young men and women, Baker developed a strong belief in grassroots mobilization. Meanwhile, she also worked with women's and labor groups, such as the Harlem Housewives Cooperative, the Women's Day Workers and Industrial League, and the YWCA. In 1935 she served as publicity director of the Sponsoring Committee of the National Negro Congress. In 1936 she worked as a teacher with the New Deal's Works Progress Administration and eventually became an assistant project supervisor of the WPA. Walter White was impressed with her relentless organizing and management skills. After much persuasion Baker accepted, in 1941, White's offer to become an assistant field secretary of the NAACP. This position enabled her to travel across the country and throughout the South, making friendships that would serve her well in the coming decades. From 1943 to 1946 Baker worked as director of NAACP branches and measurably enhanced the membership of the organization. After resigning from the NAACP she assumed a position on the staff of the New York Urban League.

Other black women organized outside the NAACP. Black women in Detroit provide a potent illustration of this kind of activity. On June 10, 1930, a group of fifty black women responded to a call issued by Fannie B. Peck, wife of Reverend William H. Peck, pastor of the two-thousand-member Bethel African Methodist Episcopal Church and the president of the Booker T. Washington Trade Association. Out of this initial meeting emerged the Detroit Housewives' League, an organization that combined economic nationalism and black women's self-determination to help black families and businesses survive the Depression. Peck conceived the ideal of creating an organization of housewives after hearing a lecture by M. A. L. Holsey, secretary of the National Negro Business League. Holsey described the directed spending campaigns of housewives in Harlem that enabled them to consolidate their economic power to persuade businesses to hire black women and children. Peck became convinced that if such an organization worked in Harlem it would be equally as successful in Detroit. An admirer recalled that Peck effectively "focused the attention of women on the most essential, yet most unfamiliar factor in the building of homes, communities, and nations, namely, 'The Spending Power of Women.'"

The Detroit organization grew with phenomenal speed. From the original fifty members, its membership by 1934 had increased to ten thousand black women. According to Peck, the black woman had finally realized "that she has been traveling through a blind alley, making sacrifices to educate her children with no thought as to their obtaining employment after leaving school." The only requirement for membership was a pledge to support black businesses, buy black products, and patronize black professionals, thereby keeping money in the community. The League quickly spread to other cities. Housewives' leagues in Chicago, Baltimore, Washington, Durham, North Carolina, Harlem, and Cleveland relied on boycotts of merchants who refused to sell black products and employ black children as clerks or stock persons as their means of securing an estimated 75,000 new jobs for black people.

ORGANIZED LABOR AND BLACK AMERICA

The relationship of African Americans to labor unions underwent a profound change during the 1930s. Before this time most local unions affiliated with the national

AFL barred black people or restricted them to segregated locals; the railroad unions, which called themselves "brotherhoods," excluded black workers entirely. The New Deal, especially after 1935, did much to transform the labor movement. The National Labor Relations Act and the militancy of workers provided the opportunity to organize the nation's great mass production industries. Still, leaders of the AFL dragged their feet, unwilling to incorporate into their unions the masses of unskilled workers, many of whom were African American or recent European immigrants. Frustrated by this situation, in 1935 John L. Lewis (1880–1969), head of the United Mine Workers, and his followers formed the Committee for Industrial Organization (CIO) to take on the task.

Unlike the AFL, the CIO was committed to interracial and multiethnic organizing and so opened the door for more African Americans to participate in the labor movement. Its leaders had long known that it was in organized labor's best interest to admit black men and women to membership. As one black union organizer said, "We colored folks can't organize without you and you white folks can't organize without us." But it took a massive change in outlook to achieve this unity. By 1940, the CIO had enlisted approximately 210,000 black members. Unions that valued and sustained interracial cooperation included the International Mine, Mill, and Smelter Workers; the Food, Tobacco, and Agricultural Workers Union; and the United Farm Equipment and Metal Workers.

A. Philip Randolph's Brotherhood of Sleeping Car Porters (BSCP) remained with the AFL, but it also benefited from New Deal legislation. In 1934 Congress had amended the Railway Labor Act in a way that helped the BSCP to overcome the opposition of the Pullman company. The law required that corporations bargain in good faith with unions if the unions could demonstrate through elections monitored by the National Mediation Board that they genuinely represented the corporations' employees. The Pullman company resisted, but in 1937, long after an election certified the BSCP as the workers' representative, the company relented and recognized the brotherhood. Then—and only then—did the AFL grant the BSCP full membership as an international union. After more than twelve years, A. Philip Randolph and thousands of black men won their struggles against a giant corporation and a powerful labor organization. These were no small victories.

Although most black people in unions were men, some unions also represented and helped improve the lives of black working women. This was the case in the tobacco industry, one of the few areas of the economy outside agriculture or domestic service that employed many black women. Since the early nineteenth century, there had been a rigid hierarchy among tobacco workers. Jobs were assigned on the basis of race and gender, with black women receiving the most difficult and tedious job, that of "stemmer." In 1939, stemmer Louise "Mama" Harris instigated a series of walkouts at the I. N. Vaughn Company in Richmond. The strikes were supported by CIO affiliates, including the white women of the International Ladies Garment Workers Union. The strikes led to the formation of the Tobacco Workers Organizing Committee, another CIO affiliate. In 1943, a number of black women union leaders and activists, including Theodosia Simpson and Miranda Smith, were involved in a strike against the R. J. Reynolds tobacco company to force it to the negotiating table. Smith later became southern regional director of the Food, Tobacco, Agricultural, and Allied Workers of America. It was the highest position held by a black woman in the labor movement up to that time.

THE COMMUNIST PARTY AND AFRICAN AMERICANS

Throughout the 1930s the Communist party intensified its support of African Americans' efforts to address unemployment and job discrimination and to seek social justice. Some African Americans were attracted to the party because of its militant antiracism and its conscious determination to be interracial. Demonstrating its seriousness on these issues, the party expelled members who exhibited racial prejudice. The party also placed black men in key positions within the leadership. James Ford, an African-American member of the party, ran as a vice-presidential candidate with Earl Browder in 1932. While nationally few black men and women actually joined the Communist party, some became increasingly sympathetic to left-wing ideas and prescriptions as the Depression wore on.

Many black workers were drawn to the Communist party because it criticized the refusal of organized white labor to include them. The communists maintained that "the low standard of living of Negro workers is made use of by the capitalists to reduce the wages of the white workers." They chided "the mis-leaders of labor, the heads of the reformist and reactionary trade union organizations" for refusing to organize black workers. They insisted "this anti-Negro attitude of the reactionary labor leaders helps to split the ranks of labor, allows the employers to carry out their policy of 'divide and rule,' frustrates the efforts of the working class to

ANGELO HERNDON

In the South, the Communist party gravitated toward those areas where black and white laborers were grossly exploited. The party's efforts in Georgia, Alabama, and Mississippi produced black organizers such as Hosea Hudson, Nate Shaw, and Angelo Herndon, who by virtue of their activism became targets of white supremacists.

In 1932, a young organizer, Angelo Herndon was arrested, tried and convicted in Atlanta for inciting insurrection. One of thirteen children, Herndon was born May 6, 1913, in Ohio. Seeking better opportunities, Herndon, at age thirteen escaped the poverty of his home region to work in the coal mines in Alabama. At eighteen he was already a seasoned miner but deeply disillusioned and angry at the exploitation of coal miners. He attended a meeting called by the Communist party and was impressed by its commitment to equality, both racially and socially. He joined the party and poured enormous energy into organizing and recruiting members from among the mine workers and the unemployed. In 1934, Angelo Herndon explained why he joined the party:

All my life I'd been sweated and stepped on and Jim-Crowed. I lay on my belly in the mines for a few dollars a week, and saw my pay stolen and slashed, and my buddies killed. I lived in the worst section of town, and rode behind the "Colored" signs of streetcars, as though there was something disgusting about me? I heard myself called "nigger" and "darky" and I had to say "Yes, sir" to every white man. . . . I had always detested it, but I had never known that anything could be done about it. And here, all of a sudden, I had found organizations . . . that weren't scared to come out for equality for the Negro people, and for the rights of workers. The Jim-Crow system, the wage-slave system, weren't everlast-

Following his release from prison in Georgia, Angelo Herndon was met at New York City's Penn Station by a group of supporters that included Ruby Bates and Communist leader Robert Minor.

ing after all! It was like all of a sudden turning a corner on a dirty, old street and finding yourself facing a broad, shining highway. . . . I felt then, and I know now, that the Communist program is the only program that the Southern workers—whites and Negroes both—can possibly accept in the long run. It's the only program that does justice to the southern worker's ideas that everybody ought to have an equal chance, and that every man has rights that must be respected.

The party sent Herndon to Atlanta, Georgia, where he organized an interracial relief group and staged peaceful demonstrations against hunger. This was to prove his undoing. One week later, while picking up his mail at the post office, he was arrested on the charge that he had violated an old ordinance forbidding black and white people from mingling together. Herndon's trial and conviction made him the best-known African-American communist in the nation. The case underscored the fear that white Southerners had concerning the specter of social equality across racial lines. The Communist party assigned a young black attorney, Benjamin Davis Jr. of Atlanta, to represent Herndon. Davis challenged the constitutionality of the ordinance as well as Atlanta's jury system, which excluded African Americans from service. Davis's defense was unsuccessful and the judge sentenced Herndon to twenty years on a chain gang. The severity of the sentence and the judge's racist sentiments sparked a nationwide movement to free Herndon as black organizations, labor unions, and religious groups joined with the Communist party to fight for Herndon's immediate release. After four years of appeals, in 1937 the United States Supreme Court, in a five to four decision, declared Georgia's slave insurrection law unconstitutional and ordered the state to let him go.

emancipate itself from the yoke of capitalism, and dims the class-consciousness of the white workers as well as of the Negro workers." Indeed, much of the push for racial equality within the CIO emanated from those connected with the party.

The International Labor Defense and the Scottsboro "Boys"

The Scottsboro case brought the Communist party to the attention of many African Americans. The case began when nine black youths who had caught a ride on a freight train were taken from it, tried, convicted, and sentenced to death for allegedly raping two white women. Their ordeal began on the night of March 25, 1931, when they were accosted by a group of young white hobos and a fight broke out. During the fight the black youths succeeded in throwing the white youths off the train. The losers filed a compliant with the Scottsboro, Alabama, sheriff, charging that black hoodlums had viciously assaulted them. The sheriff ordered his deputies to round up every black person on the train. The sweep netted the nine young black men: Ozie Powell, Clarence Norris, Charlie Weems, Olen Montgomery, Willie Robertson, Haywood Patterson, Eugene Williams, Andy Wright, and Roy Wright. The police also discovered two young white women: nineteen-year-old Victoria Price and seventeen-year-old Ruby Bates.

Afraid of being arrested, and perhaps ashamed of being women hobos, Price and Bates concocted a story falsely claiming that the nine black youths had sexually assaulted them. On the basis of that accusation, the "boys" (ranging in ages from thirteen to twenty), were given a hasty trial. The "Scottsboro Boys," as they became known, never had a chance. Their white, court-appointed attorney came to court drunk each day. Three days after the trial started, and fifteen days after their arrest, the jurors found all of them guilty. Eight received the death sentence and the youngest, a thirteen-year-old, was sentenced to life imprisonment. This verdict ignored the fact that medical examinations of Price and Bates proved that neither had been raped.

While other organizations either dawdled or refused to intervene, the Communist Party's International Labor Defense (ILD) rushed to the aid of the "boys" by appealing the conviction and death sentence to the United States Supreme Court. The case produced two important decisions that reaffirmed black people's right to basic protections enjoyed by all other American citizens. In *Powell v. Alabama* (1932), the Court ruled that the nine Scottsboro defendants had not been given adequate legal counsel and that the trial had taken place in a hostile and volatile atmosphere. Asserting that the youths' right to due process as set forth in the Fourteenth Amendment had been violated, the Court ordered a new trial. Alabama did as instructed, but the new trial resulted in a similar verdict of guilty and sentences of death or life imprisonment. The ILD lost little time in appealing this decision. The result was that in *Norris v. Alabama* (1935), the Supreme Court decided that all Americans have the right to a trial by a jury of their peers. The systematic exclusion of African Americans from the Scottsboro juries, the Court held, denied the defendants equal protection under the law, which the Fourteenth Amendment guaranteed. Chief Justice Charles Evans Hughes pointed out that no black citizens had served on juries in the Alabama counties for decades, even though there were many qualified to serve. The Court noted that the exclusion was blatant racial discrimination. Reversing the decision of the lower court, the Justices of the Supreme Court called for yet another trial.

Despite these stunning defeats and increasing evidence that the "boys" had been falsely convicted, the state of Alabama still pursued the case. Even when Ruby Bates publicly admitted that the rape charge had been a hoax, white Alabamians ignored her, but not for long. Finally, in 1937, Alabama dropped its charges against five of the nine men, and in the 1940s the state released those still in jail. Altogether, nine innocent black men had collectively served some three-quarters of a century in prison. Clarence Willie Norris, however, escaped and fled to Michigan, returning decades later to receive a ceremonious pardon from Governor George Wallace. When a reporter asked Norris how he felt, he declared, "I'm just glad to be free." He remarked that this experience had taught him a crucial lesson, "To stand up for your rights, even if it kills you. That's all life consists of."

Debating Communist Leadership

Throughout the Scottsboro case, the NAACP tried unsuccessfully to wrest control from the Communist party. Indeed, as the case evolved, tensions and competition between the Communist party and the NAACP for leadership of black America flared into open hostility. The NAACP had responded slowly to the young men's plea for help, hesitant to rush to the defense of accused rapists. Although the leadership did not want to risk damaging the organization's reputation, it moved more decisively after the Communist party had taken the lead.

The contest between the NAACP and the communists reveals the differences between the two groups.

VOICES

HOBOING IN ALABAMA

Ralph Ellison, the noted author of the great novel Invisible Man *(1952), here vividly recalls his harrowing experience as a young black "hobo" in the aftermath of the arrest of the "Scottsboro Boys."*

During June of 1933, I found myself traveling by freight train in an effort to reach Tuskegee Institute in time to take advantage of a scholarship granted me. Having little money and no time left in which to earn the fare for a ticket, I grabbed an armful of freight car, a form of illegal travel quite common during the Great Depression. In fact, so many young men, young women, prostitutes, gamblers, and even some quite respectable but impoverished elderly and middle-aged couples were hoboing that it was quite difficult for the railroad to control such passengers. I justify this out of sheer desperation, college being my one hope of improving my condition.

But I was young and adventurous and regarded hoboing as the next best thing to floating down the Mississippi on a raft. My head was full of readings of the *Rover Boys* and *Huckleberry Finn*. I converted hoboing into a lark until I found myself in the freight yards of Decatur, Alabama, where two white railroad detectives laying about them with the barrels of long nickel-plated .45 revolvers forced some forty or fifty of us, black and white alike, off the train and ordered us to line up along the tracks. For me, this was a most frightening moment. Not only was I guilty of stealing passage on a freight train, but I realized that I had been caught in the act in the town where, at that very moment, the *Scottsboro* case was being tried. The case and the incident leading to it were widely reported in the black press, and what I had read of the atmosphere of the trial led me to believe that the young men in the case had absolutely no possibility of receiving a just decision. As I saw it, the trial was a macabre circus, a kangaroo proceeding that would be soon followed by an enactment of the gory rite of lynching, that ultimate form of racial victimage.

I had no idea of what the detectives intended to do with me, but given the atmosphere of the town, I feared that it would be most unpleasant and brutal. I, too, might well be a sacrificial scapegoat, simply because I was the same race as the accused young men then being prepared for death. Therefore, when a group of white boys broke and ran, I plunged into their midst, and running far closer to the ground than I had ever managed to do as a high school football running back, I kept running and moving until I came to a shed with a railroad loading dock, under which I scooted; and there I remained until dawn, when I grabbed the first thing that was smoking and headed south.

A few days later I reached Tuskegee, but that scrape with the law—the fear, the horror and sense of helplessness before legal injustice—was most vivid in my mind, and it has so remained.

QUESTIONS

1. How does Ralph Ellison's experience as a hobo illuminate the nature of race relations in the South?

2. How did the Scottsboro Boys case increase Ellison's sense of vulnerability? Why were so many people engaged in "hoboing"? How did the black experience of "hoboing" differ from that of white Americans?

Source: Ralph Ellison, "Perspective of Literature," in *Going to the Territory* (New York: Vintage Books, 1995), pp. 324–325.

The party organized protest marches and demonstrations and used its press to denounce more cautious middle-class organizations. In Harlem, for example, the Communists staged a 1931 protest march that attracted over three thousand black men and women and ended with an address by Scottsboro mother Ada Wright who praised the ILD for rushing to provide assistance.

The NAACP countered with a carefully orchestrated campaign that questioned the sincerity and effectiveness of the communists and worked to repair its reputation as a respectable and effective advocate for African Americans.

Black public opinion divided in its evaluation of the party. Some black men and women warmly applauded the communists. Journalist Eugene Gordon expressed a pro-Communist point of view when he wrote:

> Negro workers think of the countless times Communists have been beaten insensible for defending . . . Negro workers. . . . They see the ILD . . . supported by the Communist Party, rushing to the defense of the nine Negro youths at Scottsboro before other Negro organizations in the country condescended to glance superciliously in their direction. . . . Seeing and hearing all these things, the Negro worker in the United States would be a fool not to recognize the leadership that he has been waiting for since his freedom.

Historian Carter G. Woodson wrote appreciatively of the Communist party's contributions to the black struggle. In the *New York Age* he declared,

> I have talked with any number of Negroes who call themselves Communists, and I have never heard one express a desire to destroy anyone or anything but oppression. . . . Negroes who are charged with being Communists advocate the stoppage of peonage, equality in employment of labor. . . . If this makes a man 'Red,' the world's greatest reformers belong to this class, and we shall have to condemn our greatest statesmen, some of whom have attained the presidency of the United States.

But other African Americans relentlessly attacked and ridiculed the Communist party. George Schuyler, a columnist for the *Pittsburgh Courier*, seized every opportunity and used his razor-sharp wit to castigate the party and to persuade black people that the party was fraudulent in its claim to be a champion for African Americans. Schuyler objected to the communists' "campaign of vilification . . . against the NAACP. No Ku Kluxer," he wrote, "ever denounced the latter organization more vigorously and unfairly. The Communists know they are lying when they assert time and time again that the NAACP wants to see the boys convicted and is betraying the race" (p. 194). He continued,

> They have quite the same sort of grooved mentality as Ku Kluxers, Garveyites and other race fanatics, black and white. The course they tentatively pursue is held the only true one and whoever takes exception is denounced as an enemy of humanity, even though they may have to change that course in a few months.

Schuyler's columns proved to be so popular that by the middle of the 1930s the *Pittsburgh Courier* displaced *The Chicago Defender* as the nation's largest black newspaper.

Although the majority of African Americans applauded the antiracist work that the Communist party supported and performed, there was never a chance of mass defection from the traditional American political system. W. E. B. Du Bois enunciated one of the main reasons that many African Americans remained wary of the Communist party in spite of its good deeds and strong commitment to equal rights and social justice. In 1931 he declared,

> American Negroes do not propose to be the shock troops of the Communist Revolution, driven out in the front to death, cruelty and humiliation in order to win victories for white workers. . . . Negroes know perfectly well that whenever they try to lead revolution in America, the nation will unite as one fist to crush them and them alone.

The National Negro Congress

The infighting between the Communist party and other groups doomed a major attempt to unite all the disparate African-American protest groups into the National Negro Congress (NNC). John P. Davis, a Washington-based economist, organized the NNC, modeling it on his experience as the executive secretary of the Joint Committee on National Recovery (JCNR), a coalition of black groups that pressed for fairness in the early New Deal. The NNC was to be a federation of organizations on a grand national scale supported by a number of regional councils. Over 800 delegates representing 585 organizations attended its first meeting, held in Chicago in 1936. Several prominent black activists, leaders, and intellectuals were conspicuously absent, most noticeably those associated with the NAACP. A. Philip Randolph was elected president and Davis became the executive secretary. The group passed a resolution mandating that it not be dominated by any one political faction and that it build on the strength of all parts of the black community. Although handicapped by lack of funds, the National Negro Congress initially worked effectively at the local or community level. With branches in approximately seventy cities, the organization gained for its members increased employment opportunities, better housing, and adequate relief work.

At the NNC's second meeting in Philadelphia in 1937, Davis, who had begun as a Republican, told the delegates that he would become a member of the Communist party. This move reflected his belief that the Democratic party would never allow black people to benefit justly and fairly from the New Deal. The increasing importance of communists in the NNC alienated

TIMELINE

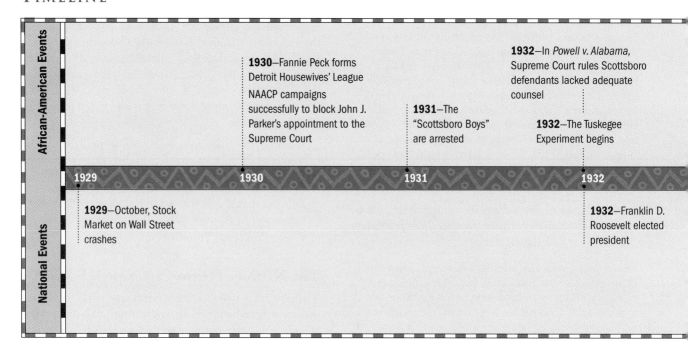

most other groups and reduced the organization's ability to speak for the majority of black people. By 1940 it was greatly reduced in strength. Randolph was voted out of office and the once-promising NNC lingered on as little more than a front group for the Communist party.

THE TUSKEGEE EXPERIMENT

The 1930s marked the rising prominence of black scholars and intellectuals, but paradoxically, the decade also witnessed the worst manifestation of racism in American science. This most shocking episode of virulent bigotry and racial mistreatment occurred in Macon County, Alabama. There, in 1932, United States Public Health Service (USPHS) officials initiated a major study of syphilis, a sexually transmitted disease that can cause paralysis, insanity, and heart failure. For the subjects of its program—entitled the Tuskegee Study of Untreated Syphilis in the Male Negro—the USPHS recruited 622 black men, all of them poor sharecroppers and the majority illiterate. Of these men, 431 had advanced cases of syphilis; the rest were free of the disease and served as controls for comparison.

The Tuskegee Study was called a treatment program, but it turned out to be an experiment, designed to chart the progression and development of a potentially fatal disease. To gain the trust of the men, the government

doctors centered their work at Tuskegee Institute and hired a black nurse, Eunice Rivers, who convinced the men that they had "bad blood" and needed special treatment. Although the drug penicillin, which could cure the disease, became available in the 1940s, the sharecroppers never received it. Instead, they were given ineffective placebos, which they were told would cure them.

Initially the Tuskegee Study was to last only six to twelve months, but it was repeatedly extended. The men received regular physical examinations, which included a painful lumbar puncture. This insertion of a needle into the spinal cord to obtain fluid for diagnosis often caused the men severe headaches, and in a few isolated cases, resulted in paralysis and even death. For almost forty years, Tuskegee Study doctors observed the men, keeping careful records of their health and performing autopsies on those who died; but never did they treat them for syphilis. So little understood was the Tuskegee Study that men not only remained in the program but believed that they were fortunate to have the physical examination, the hot lunches provided on examination days, and the burial allowance the government guaranteed their families. The medical community knew of the Tuskegee experiment, but the general public learned of it only in 1972 when an Associated Press reporter broke the story. Black attorney Fred D. Gray of Alabama sued the U.S. government on

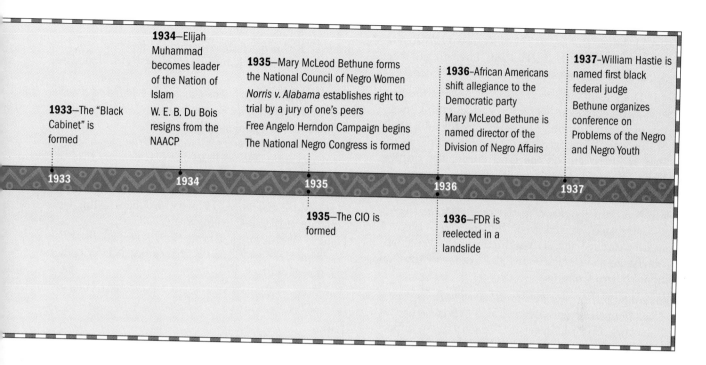

1933—The "Black Cabinet" is formed

1934—Elijah Muhammad becomes leader of the Nation of Islam

W. E. B. Du Bois resigns from the NAACP

1935—Mary McLeod Bethune forms the National Council of Negro Women

Norris v. Alabama establishes right to trial by a jury of one's peers

Free Angelo Herndon Campaign begins

The National Negro Congress is formed

1936-African Americans shift allegiance to the Democratic party

Mary McLeod Bethune is named director of the Division of Negro Affairs

1937-William Hastie is named first black federal judge

Bethune organizes conference on Problems of the Negro and Negro Youth

1933 1934 1935 1936 1937

1935—The CIO is formed

1936—FDR is reelected in a landslide

behalf of the participants and their families, but before the case went to trial, the government made a $9 million settlement to the Tuskegee survivors and the descendants of those who had died.

CONCLUSION

Notable political changes occurred during the early 1930s: the NAACP came of age, black women found their voice, white left leaders joined with black men and women in interracial alliances, organized labor bridged the race chasm, and black men and women switched from affiliation with the Republican party to allegiance with the Democratic party. The New Deal had stimulated some economic recovery, and more important, laid the basis for a strong national state and a political coalition that, beginning with World War II, would come to challenge profoundly the reigning racial system in the nation.

REVIEW QUESTIONS

1. Describe the process that led to the great political realignment of black Americans to the Democratic party. How did President Roosevelt entice black people to identify with the Democratic party and to abandon their long association with the Republican party?

2. How did black people respond to and survive the economic cataclysm of the Great Depression? How did the experiences of black women during the Depression reflect their race, class, and gender status in American society?

3. What impact did the New Deal agencies and programs have on the lives of African Americans and their communities? How did the New Deal adversely affect black sharecroppers, tenants, and farmers?

4. Discuss the political, social, and economic repercussions of the large-scale migration of African Americans out of the South during the 1930s.

5. Compare and contrast the Tuskegee Experiment with the Scottsboro "Boys" case.

6. Why were W. E. B. Du Bois's *Crisis* editorials "on segregation" so divisive and explosive? Discuss the various responses of black activists and scholars to the idea of voluntary self-segregation.

RECOMMENDED READING

John Egerton. *Speak Now against the Day: The Generation before the Civil Rights Movement in the South.* New York: Knopf, 1994. An excellent survey of the period before the southern civil rights era, with chapters on the

Depression in the South and black and white Southerners' reactions to it.

James H. Jones. *Bad Blood: The Tuskegee Syphilis Experiment.* New York: Free Press, 1981. The best and most comprehensive study of the Tuskegee experiment.

Robin D. G. Kelley. *Hammer and Hoe: Alabama Communists during the Great Depression.* Chapel Hill: University of North Carolina Press, 1990. A splendid study of the radicalizing activism of working people in the steel industry and on the farm during the thirties. Kelley does an excellent job of showing why the Communists appealed to black workers.

Mark Naison. *Communists in Harlem during the Depression.* Urbana: University of Illinois Press, 1983. A well-researched and clear-sighted study of the Communist party in Harlem and the history of the National Negro Congress.

Harvard Sitkoff. *A New Deal for Blacks: The Emergence of Civil Rights as a National Issue, Vol. I: Depression Decade.* New York: Oxford University Press, 1978. An important work that covers the New Deal era and presents it as a period when the groundwork for the civil rights movement was laid.

Patricia Sullivan. *Days of Hope: Race and Democracy in the New Deal Era.* Chapel Hill: University of North Carolina Press, 1996. An invaluable study showing how the ideas of civil rights and democracy were forged in the New Deal South.

Raymond Wolters. *Negroes and the Great Depression: The Problem of Economic Recovery.* Westport, CT: Greenwood Publisher Group Incorporated, 1974. A solid survey of African Americans in the Depression that covers the impact of the Depression on African Americans, the workings of the Black Cabinet, and the effects of the New Deal Agencies on the lives of black Americans.

ADDITIONAL BIBLIOGRAPHY

Politics

Kenneth W. Goings. *'The NAACP Comes of Age': The Defeat of Judge John J. Parker.* Bloomington: Indiana University Press, 1990.

Charles V. Hamilton. *Adam Clayton Powell, Jr., the Political Biography of an American Dilemma.* New York: Atheneum, 1991.

Darlene Clark Hine. *Black Victory: The Rise and Fall of the White Primary in Texas.* Millwood, NY: KTO Press, 1979.

Charles F. Kellogg. *NAACP: A History of the National Association for the Advancement of Colored People.* Baltimore: Johns Hopkins University Press, 1967.

John B. Kirby. *Black Americans in the Roosevelt Era: Liberalism and Race.* Knoxville: University of Tennessee Press, 1980.

Christopher R. Reed. *The Chicago NAACP and the Rise of Black Professional Leadership, 1910–1966.* Bloomington: Indiana University Press, 1997.

Bernard Sternsher, ed. *The Negro in Depression and War: Prelude to Revolution, 1930–1945.* Chicago: Quadrangle Books, 1969.

Mark V. Tushnet. *The NAACP's Legal Strategy against Segregated Education, 1925–1950.* Chapel Hill: University of North Carolina Press, 1987.

Nancy J. Weiss. *Farewell to the Party of Lincoln: Black Politics in the Age of Lincoln.* Princeton, NJ: Princeton University Press, 1983.

Labor

Lizabeth Cohen. *Making a New Deal: Industrial Workers in Chicago, 1919–1939.* New York: Cambridge University Press, 1990.

Dennis C. Dickerson. *Out of the Crucible: Black Steelworkers in Western Pennsylvania, 1875–1980.* Albany, NY: SUNY Press, 1986.

William H. Harris. *The Harder We Run: Black Workers since the Civil War.* New York: Oxford University Press, 1982.

August Meier and Elliott Rudwick. *Black Detroit and the Rise of the UAW.* New York: Oxford University Press, 1979.

Education

James D. Anderson. *The Education of Blacks in the South, 1860–1935.* Chapel Hill: University of North Carolina Press, 1988.

Horace M. Bond. *The Education of the Negro in the American Social Order.* New York: Octagon Books, 1934, rev. 1966.

Richard Kluger. *Simple Justice: The History of* Brown v. Board of Education *and Black America's Struggle for Equality.* 1976.

Mark V. Tushnet. *Making Civil Rights Law: Thurgood Marshall and the Supreme Court, 1935–1961.* 1994.

Doxey Wilkerson. *Special Problems in Negro Education.* Washington, DC: U.S. Government Printing Office, 1939.

Black Radicalism

Dan Carter. *Scottsboro: A Tragedy of the American South.* Baton Rouge: Louisiana State University Press, 1969.

Kenneth W. Goings. *Mammy and Uncle Mose: Black Collectibles and American Stereotyping.* Bloomington: Indiana University Press, 1994.

Michael K. Honey. *Southern Labor and Black Civil Rights: Organizing Memphis Workers.* Urbana: University of Illinois Press, 1993.

Jacqueline Jones. *Labor of Love, Labor of Sorrow: Black Women, Work, and the Family from Slavery to the Present.* New York: Basic Books, 1985.

Nicholas Natanson. *The Black Image in the New Deal: The Politics of FSA Photography.* Knoxville, University of Tennessee Press, 1992.

Richard H. Pells. *Radical Visions and American Dreams: Culture and Social Thought in the Depression Years.* New York: Harper & Row, 1973.

Daryl Michael Scott. *Contempt and Pity: Social Policy and the Image of the Damaged Black Psyche, 1880–1996.* Chapel Hill: University of North Carolina Press, 1997.

Mark Solomon. *The Cry Was Unity: Communists and African Americans, 1917–1936.* Jackson: University Press of Mississippi, 1998.

Richard W. Thomas. *Life for Us Is What We Make It: Building Black Community in Detroit, 1915–1945.* Bloomington: Indiana University Press, 1992.

Economics

Charles T. Banner-Haley. *To Do Good and to Do Well: Middle Class Blacks and the Depression, Philadelphia, 1929–1941.* New York: Garland, 1993.

Abram L. Harris. *The Negro as Capitalist: A Study of Banking and Business among American Negroes.* Originally published by the American Academy of Political and Social Sciences, 1936; Reprint, Chicago: Urban Research Press, 1992.

Alexa Benson Henderson. *Atlanta Life Insurance Company: Guardian of Black Economic Dignity.* Tuscaloosa: University of Alabama Press, 1990.

Robert E. Weems, Jr. *Black Business in the Black Metropolis: The Chicago Metropolitan Assurance Company, 1924–1985.* Bloomington: Indiana University Press, 1996.

Biography and Autobiography

Andrew Buni. *Robert L. Vann of the Pittsburgh Courier.* Pittsburgh: University of Pittsburgh Press, 1974.

Joanne Grant. *Ella Baker: Freedom Bound.* New York: John Wiley, 1998.

Wil Haywood. *King of the Cats: The Life and Times of Adam Clayton Powell, Jr.* Boston: Houghton Mifflin, 1993.

Spencie Love. *One Blood: The Death and Resurrection of Charles R. Drew.* Chapel Hill: University of North Carolina Press, 1996.

Genna Rae McNeil. *Groundwork: Charles Hamilton Houston and the Struggle for Civil Rights.* Philadelphia: University of Pennsylvania Press, 1983.

Nell Irvin Painter. *The Narrative of Hosea Hudson: His Life as a Negro Communist in the South.* Cambridge, MA: Harvard University Press, 1979.

Paula F. Pfeffer. *A. Philip Randolph, Pioneer of the Civil Rights Movement.* Baton Rouge: Louisiana State University Press, 1990.

George S. Schuyler. *Black and Conservative: The Autobiography of George S. Schuyler.* New Rochelle, NY: Arlington House, 1966.

Gilbert Ware. *William Hastie: Grace under Pressure.* New York: Oxford University Press, 1984.

Roy Wilkins with Tom Mathews. *Standing Fast: The Autobiography of Roy Wilkins.* New York: Da Capo Press, 1994.

CHAPTER 19

BLACK CULTURE AND SOCIETY
IN THE 1930s AND 1940S

Trumpeter Cootie Williams plays to an appreciative audience at the Savoy in New York
in the 1930s.

He would not Africanize America, for America has too much to teach the world and Africa. He would not bleach his Negro soul in a flood of white Americanism, for he knows that Negro blood has a message for the world. He simply wished to make it possible for a man to be both a Negro and an American, without being cursed and spit upon by his fellows, without having the doors of opportunity closed roughly in his face. This, then, is the end of his striving: to be a co-worker in the kingdom of culture, to escape both death and isolation, to husband and use his best powers and his latent genius.

W. E. B. Du Bois, *The Souls of Black Folk: Essay and Sketches*

W. E. B. Du Bois commented often on the gifts black people had made to America. Even before he wrote the passage that opens this chapter, Du Bois had proclaimed, "We are the first fruits of this new nation. . . . We are the people whose subtle sense of song has given America its only American music, its only American fairy tales, its only touch of pathos and humor amid its money-getting plutocracy." African-American "destiny is not a servile imitation of Anglo-Saxon culture, but a stalwart originality which shall unswervingly follow Negro ideals."

A key theme in black life during the 1930s and 1940s was the many strategies African Americans devised to protest segregation, discrimination, and disfranchisement, and to resist the negative racial stereotypes and the appropriation of black culture by white entrepreneurs. At heart this was a quest to shape the representation of black people in American society and create a viable black culture for a rapidly urbanizing people. A central issue in this chapter is the extent to which black culture during the 1930s and 1940s became a source of strength—cultural power—that helped

445

African Americans define and assert themselves within American society.

Cultural power allowed African Americans to define and create new images that replaced the distortion of the true appearance, intellect, religious practice, and family values of black people in American society. The new black cultural power had to fight the well-worn stereotypes of the dumb, lazy black man; the selfless mammy; and the promiscuous dark Venus. As we have seen throughout this book, black people were disfranchised and socially and economically marginalized. But in the arts, black people drove a small wedge into the wall of racism through which they could explode onto America's center stage. In the performing arts, talented African Americans compelled the attention of white Americans. The 1930s and 1940s—ironically also a time when most black people were suffering from the combined effects of the Depression and the entrenched Jim Crow regime—were a fertile period in the history of black expressive culture.

BLACK CULTURE IN A MIDWESTERN CITY

During the 1930s and 1940s black migrants flocked to St. Louis, swelling its population to make it the fifth largest city in the United States. Yet, because of segregation and discrimination, the black community in St. Louis developed institutions to address their own educational and cultural needs. While attention has usually focused on the contributions of St. Louis to popular culture, there was considerable interest in classical music also. Black community residents had to struggle to secure training in this genre of music and for opportunities to perform it.

> St. Louis! The town where Scott Joplin and Tom Turpin used to play ragtime. The town that W. C. Handy made famous in his great song, "The St. Louis Blues." The town where Josephine Baker started out as a $15.00 a week waitress, and end[ed] up in Paris as one of the most glamorous stars of the international theater. St. Louis, the town that gave a laugh-hungry world the joy of E. Simms Campbell and his rib-tickling cartoons of *Esquire* and King Features fame. The town where the river boats used to run from New Orleans with Louis Armstrong's horn blasting the night away.

Langston Hughes wrote these words to recall the possibilities and excitement that life in a midwestern city held for black people. St. Louis is in the heart of a region often considered remote from the nation's cultural centers. It has produced nationally known jazz musicians, and it was where Chuck Berry virtually invented rock and roll. White citizens ignored and marginalized the contributions of black artists in the city. A closer look at black support for classical music in St. Louis during the 1930s and 1940s reveals the interior diversity of black community life. Not all black musicians wanted to play ragtime and jazz and many resented being relegated solely to these forms.

Schools, churches, labor, and media within the St. Louis black community had to create opportunities for black children to study, appreciate, and perform classical music. The two largest black newspapers, the *St. Louis Argus* and the *St. Louis American*, publicized recitals and concerts. Two all-black institutions supported classical music education: Lincoln University in Jefferson City (founded in 1866 as a school created by and for black Civil War veterans and their families) and Sumner High School (founded in 1875 as the first secondary school for black people west of the Mississippi).

By the 1940s Lincoln University had become the institution for training St. Louis musicians, and its music instructors were active in the black community's cultural affairs. Sumner High School had orchestras, bands, choirs, and glee clubs. Many of its music teachers had advanced degrees from prestigious music departments. The most influential teacher was Kenneth Billups, an arranger, composer, and founding director of the Legend Singers, a black professional chorus.

The Legend Singers appeared with the St. Louis Symphony and with the Municipal Opera Company (MUNY) in many productions of *Showboat*, where they dressed in demeaning slave costumes. Billups's response to criticism of these appearances indirectly addressed the dilemma of black artists in a racially restrictive environment:

> I've seen situations where I felt inwardly . . . I might have had to do some things; for example, let's take this *Showboat* thing at MUNY Opera. There is the need of a black chorus to go there, and I had the privilege of doing that with my Legend Singers, simply because one of the first requirements was to have a black chorus.

Black churches, including Antioch Baptist, Central Baptist, and Berea Presbyterian, sponsored religious programs highlighting the works of both black and white composers. Local 197 of the American Federation of Musicians and the St. Louis Music Association, which was the local branch of the National Association of Negro Musicians, were active in promoting black performing organizations and training. These groups sponsored choirs, orchestras, and other musical organizations and devoted part of its members' dues to scholarships and summer choirs for boys and girls.

THE BLACK CULTURE INDUSTRY AND AMERICAN RACISM

Black American artists had to confront institutional racism in the culture industry. Individual black creative artists could rarely afford to produce and disseminate their work. This power often resided in the hands of record companies, publishers, and the owners of radio stations and film studios. Yet through their work, black artists in the 1930s and 1940s were shaping a new black consciousness that would erupt in the 1950s as the modern civil rights movement.

The issue of the political content of black art provoked heated debates among black artists. Many black Americans insisted that music, visual and performing arts, literature, and oratory serve both a functional and an aesthetic purpose. They expected black artists not only to generate items of beauty but also to use their art to further black freedom from white oppression. Another source of tension among black artists during these decades concerned the involvement of white people in black culture. While many white Americans had long appreciated black culture, some had also historically appropriated it for their own profit.

During the late 1930s and 1940s, corporate America recognized the money that could be made in producing and marketing black culture. But there was a problem: Black artists had to be made "acceptable" if they were to be successfully marketed to affluent white consumers. These artists had to compromise, mask, and subordinate their true feelings and expressiveness if they wanted to earn income from their work. Artists who exhibited the right combination of showmanship, charm, and talent could reap some of the financial rewards their creativity generated. Nowhere was this more apparent than in music.

THE MUSIC CULTURE FROM SWING TO BEBOP

Ironically, the very creativity that white Americans valued and often appropriated depended on the artists' ability to preserve some intellectual and emotional autonomy. Black artists had to juxtapose the require-

ments of earning a living with the need to remain true to their art. Black musicians continuously had to refine, expand, and perfect their art not only for themselves and each other but for a white-dominated marketplace. In many respects black music is virtually synonymous with black culture, and segregation or self-imposed separation often made possible the creation of new cultural expressions. Music encapsulates and reflects the core values and underlying tensions and anxieties in black communities. In black music we witness cultural producers developing strategies of resistance against white domination.

The Great Depression wrought havoc on the vibrant black culture industry of the 1920s. Record sales in 1932 were only a sixth of those in 1927. Black musicians like Louis Armstrong had enjoyed a golden age of creativity during the 1920s. The record companies had their separate black music labels and sold thousands of records to southern migrants to the big cities. New bands sprouted up from Kansas City to Chicago, Memphis to Detroit, Washington, D.C., to New York. Los Angeles, San Francisco, and Seattle had their own black music enthusiasts and performers. The territorial (traveling) bands took the music to the outposts of black America, while the big bands under Fletcher Henderson, Duke Ellington, Count Basie, and Cab Calloway played in white urban dance halls and ballrooms that admitted black people only as staff or entertainers.

New York was where black musicians felt they had to go to prove themselves. After entertaining affluent white people, or providing backup music for the Apollo Theater in Harlem, black musicians discarded their masks of docility and deference and made a different sound in their own space and on their own time in late-night jam sessions. The small clubs, such as Monroe's Uptown House and Minton's Playhouse in Harlem a few blocks from the Apollo Theater, became the most fertile sites for innovation in melody, tempo, and dexterity. In them a new kind of jazz was born.

The big band *swing* style that became popular in the 1930s transformed white American culture. Swing emerged as white bands reduced the music of the more innovative black bandleaders to a broadly appealing formula based on a swinging 4/4 beat, well-blended saxophone sections, and pleasant-sounding vocals. The big swing bands of the 1930s played written-out, completely arranged music. The popularity of swing helped to boost the careers of black and white bandleaders, but it also led to a creative slump that disheartened many of the younger black musicians. Tired of swing's predictability, they began improvising in the jazz clubs, sharpening their reflexes, ears, and minds.

In the 1940s at least seven musicians were among the men most responsible for making a revolution in jazz, ushering in a new sound and dimension that became known, scornfully at first, as bebop. These musicians were Charlie Parker, Dizzy Gillespie, Thelonious Monk, Bud Powell, Kenny Clarke, Max Roach, and Ray Brown. Bebop featured complex rhythms and harmonies and highlighted improvisation. Gillespie (1917–1993) said that Kansas City-born Charlie "Yardbird" and then just "Bird" Parker (1920–1955) was "the architect of the style." "Yard and I," Gillespie reminisced, "were so close, so wrapped up in one another, that he would think 'three,' and I would say 'four,' and I would say 'seven,' and he'd say 'eight'. . . . It wasn't difficult for us, really together, sometimes it sounded like one horn playing, and sometimes it was one horn, but sometimes it was both of us sounding like one horn."

Bebop met considerable resistance from white America. The nation was about to enter World War II and was too preoccupied to make the adjustment from the big band swing ballroom dancing music to bebop. Moreover, jazzmen had more freedom from the expectations of white society playing in small, intimate clubs than in big bands. Bebop music was of such enduring quality, however, that it shaped the contours of American popular culture and style for two generations. Before long, bebop became the principal musical language of jazz musicians around the world.

Bebop was a way of life and had its own attendant styles whose nuances depended on class status and, perhaps, age. Gillespie helped to create one side of bebop style in dress, language, and demeanor. He began to wear dark glasses on stage to cut down the glare of lights after he had cataract surgery. He grew a goatee because shaving every day irritated his bottom lip. He wore pegged pants, jackets with wide lapels, and a beret when men were still wearing hats with brims. Other bebop musicians emulated and modified this attire. For example, they wore cashmere jackets without lapels. Beboppers also created their own form of slang, or hip black English that mingled colorful and obscene language. They challenged convention in other ways too, engaging in a free-wheeling lifestyle that often included love across the color line. There was also a down side to bebop. Some musicians became drug addicts, became engaged in parasitical relationships with women, and were left impoverished from reckless spending.

Black working-class young men adopted their own style of talking and of hip dressing, reflected in their zoot suits and conked hair. Zoot suits featured high-waisted, baggy, pegged pants and long draped coats. A sixteen-year-old Malcolm Little (later to take the name Malcolm X) purchased a zoot suit when he moved to Boston and plunged into hipster culture. His first zoot suit was sky blue with a matching hat, gold watch chain, and a monogrammed belt. To savor this new identity, he recalled, "I took three of those twenty-five cent sepia-toned, while-you-wait pictures of myself, posed the way 'hipsters' wearing their zoots would 'cool it'—hat dangled, knees drawn close together, feet wide apart, both index fingers jabbed toward the floor." He then mastered the lindy hop dance style and took to the floor of the Roseland Ballroom where he shed his life as an unskilled wage worker and became someone freer and more empowered. He recalled the Ballroom's patrons' escape from their dreary urban lives: "They'd jampack that ballroom, the black girls in wayout silk and satin dresses and shoes, their hair done in all kinds of styles, the men sharp in their zoot suits and crazy conks, and everybody grinning and greased and gassed."

Bebop was the dominant black music of the war decade, but after 1945, returning veterans preferred a slower-paced music, simple love songs, and melodies. This contributed to bebop's waning and led to more transformations. All artistic innovation extracts a high price. Bebop was no exception. Many of the most talented musicians, like Billie Holiday, whom we discuss later in this chapter, paid that price in lives decimated by drugs, poverty, sickness, and broken relationships. With few exceptions, black musicians did not receive the respect, recognition, and financial rewards from white America that their creativity warranted. Ultimately, white Americans wanted the art but not the artists.

POPULAR CULTURE FOR THE MASSES: COMIC STRIPS, RADIO, AND MOVIES

The masses of African Americans participated in more accessible black popular culture outlets. Everyone needed relief from the bleakness and despair of the Depression years. Comic strips, radio programs, and movies were affordable forms of artistic creativity that permitted at least a momentary escape for even the most destitute. Newspapers were widely shared, passing from hand to hand, and whole families gathered around the radio for nightly programs of comedy and music. For black city dwellers, the movies offered momentary escape from lives of poverty and want.

ART AND CULTURE GALLERY II

Born in Topeka, Kansas, Aaron Douglas (1899–1979) was the only black student at the University of Nebraska when he graduated in 1922. He migrated to Harlem in 1925 and shortly after that visited Paris where he met the celebrated black artist, Henry Ossawa Tanner. Douglas went back to Harlem and then taught art at Fisk University in Nashville from 1937 until 1966. In *Building More Stately Mansions* (1944), Douglas returned to a favorite theme—the bond between black Americans and their African heritage.

Archibald Motley (1891–1981) was raised in Chicago where his father was a Pullman employee active in the Brotherhood of Sleeping Car Porters. Motley attended the Art Institute of Chicago and graduated in 1918. In works like *Barbecue*, painted in 1934 when he was employed by a New Deal arts program, Motley vividly captured the exuberance and vitality of nightlife in Chicago's Bronzeville.

As the child of an impoverished preacher near Jacksonville, Florida, Augusta Savage (1892–1962) learned to shape clay figures into farm animals. She eventually moved to New York City and furthered her artistic education at Cooper Union. In 1923 she was rejected for a summer school program in Paris because French officials feared her presence might offend Southern white students. During the New Deal she was an active teacher and administrator with the Works Progress Administration. Only a small number of her works survive. The model for *Gamin* (1929) was a youngster in Savage's Harlem neighborhood.

Horace Pippin (1888–1946). *Mr. Prejudice*, 1943, oil on canvas, 18" x 14". Philadelphia Museum of Art, Gift of Dr. and Mrs. Matthew T. Moore. Photo by Graydon Wood.

Horace Pippin (1888–1946), a self-taught artist, was born and raised in the rural community of West Chester, Pennsylvania. He enlisted in the Army during World War I and was badly wounded in combat in France. He patiently rehabilitated himself and learned to draw again during the 1920s. Pippin's work explores Biblical themes and African-American life and history. *Mr. Prejudice*, created in 1943 during World War II, captures the conflict many African Americans felt about fighting abroad while enduring prejudice at home.

William H. Johnson, *Lamentation or Descent from the Cross*, ca. 1944. National Museum of American Art, Washington, DC./Art Resource, NY.

William H. Johnson (1901–1970) was born and raised in Florence, North Carolina. He moved to New York at the age of seventeen and put himself through art school on his earnings as a stevedore. Gaining recognition from his teachers as a young artist of great promise, he moved to Europe in 1926 to pursue his career. Fleeing the growing Nazi menace on the eve of World War II, he returned to New York with his Danish wife in 1938. In his later paintings, including *Lamentation or Descent from the Cross*, (1944), he adopted a flat, deliberately "primitive" style and began documenting African-American life and religion.

Selma Burke, *Jim*, 1935, Plaster, 13 1/2" x 8" x 9 1/2". Photo Manu Sassoonian. Schomburg Center for Research in Black Culture, Art & Artifacts Division, The New York Public Library, Astor, Lenox and Tilden Foundations.

Every American is familiar with the work of Selma Burke (1900–1995) without knowing it. She created the profile of President Franklin D. Roosevelt that appears on the Roosevelt dime. Burke's original bronze plaque of the president—which the U.S. mint relied on when it designed the coin—was made for the Recorder of Deeds Building in Washington in 1945. Born in Mooreseville, North Carolina, Burke earned a master of fine arts degree from Columbia University. *Jim*, an undated work, captures the quiet dignity of its subject.

Though he quit high school and had little artistic training, Jacob Lawrence (born 1917) emerged as one of the most prominent artists of the twentieth century. During the Depression he attended a Works Progress Administration art program in Harlem administered by Augusta Savage. Lawrence was fascinated by black history and enamored of storytelling. *Migration of the Negro, Panel 1* (1940-1941) is the first of 60 panels documenting the migration of black Southerners to the North.

Jacob Lawrence, *The Migration of the Negro Panel No. 1*, 1940-1941. Tempera on masonite 12" x 18". (30.5 x 45.7 cm). Acquired 1942. The Philips Collection, Washington, D.C.

Charles White (1918–1979) was born in Chicago and nurtured his talent in high school art classes and weekend classes at the Art Institute of Chicago. He won scholarship competitions at two Chicago art schools but was rejected by both because he was black. In 1937 he won a scholarship to the Art Institute of Chicago. Following World War II, when American art turned to abstraction, White remained devoted to a realistic style and socially engaged subject matter. *Contribution of the Negro to American Democracy* (1943), a mural at Hampton University, depicts black heroes—Crispus Attucks, Denmark Vesey, Booker T. Washington, and George Washington Carver—as well as ordinary folk.

Romare Bearden, (1911–1988) a self-taught artist, grew up in Charlotte, North Carolina. He experimented with a variety of styles and techniques in his work. In photomontages evocative of jazz and the blues like *Watching the Trains Go By* (1964), he celebrated rural black folk traditions and rituals. "I use the train," Bearden explained, "as a symbol of the other civilization—the white civilization and its encroachment upon the lives of blacks. The train was always something that could take you away and could also bring you to where you were. And in the little towns it's the black people who live near the trains."

Romare Bearden, *Watching the Trains Go By*, 1964. Photograph by Sharon Goodman. ©Romare Bearden Foundation/Licensed by VAGA, New York, NY.

Elizabeth Catlett, *Malcolm X Speaks for Us*, 1969. Lithograph, 95 x 70 cm. ©Elizabeth Catlett./ Licensed by VAGA, New York, NY.

Elizabeth Catlett (born 1919) grew up in Washington, DC. Her father died before she was born, leaving her mother to support three children. Catlett studied art at Howard University. After a brief stint as a high school teacher she attended graduate school at the University of Iowa. *Malcolm X Speaks For Us* (1969), a linoleum block print, is part of her series on African-American heroes.

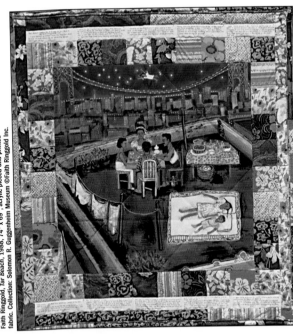

Faith Ringgold, *Tar Beach*, 1988, 74" x 69", acrylic pieced and printed fabric. Collection: Solomon R. Guggenheim Museum ©Faith Ringgold Inc.

Faith Ringgold (born 1934) grew up in Harlem. During the Black Arts Movement of the 1960s and 1970s she gained a reputation for her perceptive exploration of cultural, sexual, and racial issues. In story quilts like *Tar Beach* (1988), which are reminiscent of Harriet Powers's Bible quilts, Ringgold makes powerful use of a traditional woman's art form.

Steve Prince (born 1968) draws on themes from black history in his work. *Noble Sounds* (1995), addresses the issues of black identity and gender relations within the context of domination and resistance. "The three central characters represent dispossessed populations of the diaspora," Prince explains. "Their mental, physical, and spiritual power is unleashed as they remove the mask that grins and lies" while they dance in front of a white house, symbolic of the master's house on a plantation, with menacing white-hooded figures in the windows.

CHARLIE PARKER

Charlie Parker was one of the most innovative and influential of all American musicians. With his inspired saxophone playing; his technical mastery of his instrument; his melodic, rhythmic, and harmonic innovations, he was one of the architects of modern jazz, or "bebop." His playing challenged his contemporaries, profoundly influenced subsequent generations of jazz musicians, and helped transform jazz from entertainment to one of America's most respected art forms. But Parker was also troubled by drug addiction, mental instability, and tumultuous personal relationships.

Charlie Parker, playing the alto sax, with Miles Davis on trumpet.

Charles Parker Jr. was born on August 29, 1920, in Kansas City, Kansas. In 1927, his family moved across the state line to Kansas City, Missouri. Except what he acquired playing for his high school band, he had no formal musical instruction. But Kansas City had a rich, dynamic jazz scene. Pianist and composer Mary Lou Williams remembered the freewheeling atmosphere this way: "Now, at this time, which was still Prohibition . . . [m]ost of the night spots were run by politicians and hoodlums, and the town was wide open for drinking, gambling, and pretty much every form of vice. Naturally, work was plentiful for musicians though some of the employers were tough people." This scene appealed to young Parker and he became a fixture at many of the local clubs. It was also in this milieu that Parker began to use heroin, acquiring a drug habit that was to plague him the rest of his life.

In 1939, searching for a wider audience and hoping to learn from the great instrumentalists of the time, Parker left Kansas City for New York, then the jazz capital of the country. In New York, Parker began to sit in, or "jam," at a number of Harlem nightclubs such as Monroe's and Minton's. Two and a half years later he was back in Kansas City playing as a member of Jay McShann's band, a popular "territory band" that traveled as far north as Lincoln, Nebraska, and as far south as New Orleans, Louisiana. During this time he acquired the nickname "Bird."

Parker left the McShann Band in 1942 to join pianist Earl Hines's band in New York. In March and April of 1943, all the following musicians were in the band with Parker: "Little" Benny Harris, Bennie Green, Wardell Gray, Billy Eckstine, and vocalist Sarah Vaughan. This collection of talent reflected a musical environment conducive to innovation. New ideas spread by word of mouth from musician to musician and in late night jam sessions. It was from the close collaboration between Parker and Dizzy Gillespie in this period that bebop emerged.

Charlie Parker joined the first bebop big band, formed by Billy Eckstine in 1944. Eckstine's friend and valet, Bob Redcross, remembers a particular night when the band was at its best.

> Everybody was on. [Art] Blakey was on; John [Gillespie] was on; Bird was on; Bidd [Johnson] was on; everybody. Man, they upset this place. They had people screaming and hollering.

In the same year a recording of Parker's composition, "Red Cross," the first to be copyrighted in his name, was released on the Savoy label.

Parker and Gillespie recorded together commercially for the first time in 1945. Gillespie formed his first bebop big band and took it on a tour of the South as part of the "Hepations 1945" package tour. Also in 1945, Parker led an expanded group at the Spotlite club that included trumpeter Miles Davis, tenor saxophonist Dexter Gordon, bassist Leonard Gaskin and drummer Stan Levey. During a disastrous trip to California, Parker had a nervous breakdown and spent several months at Camarillo State Hospital.

In 1947, when Parker returned to New York, he formed what came to be known as his "classic" quintet, with trumpeter Miles Davis, drummer Max Roach, pianist Duke Jordan, and Tommy Potter on bass. The recordings produced by this quintet, four sides on the Savoy label, are the foundation on which much of Parker's reputation rests.

In 1949, in a fitting tribute to his genius by his contemporaries, a New York nightclub, "Birdland," was named for him. Charlie Parker died in New York on March 12, 1955.

The Comics

African Americans were quick to note the difference between the fun that black people made of each other, and the mockery white people made of them. These differences were reflected in tone, intent, and sympathetic versus derisive laughter. During the Depression, comic strips in newspapers and comic books featuring superheroes diverted millions of Americans. Comic strips in black newspapers entertained but also affirmed the values and ideals of black people. They portrayed humorous situations and elaborated tales of intrigue and action.

The *Philadelphia Independent*, a black paper, ran a serial in the thirties called "The Jones Family." This strip, drawn by an editorial cartoonist named Branford, was a good example of the dual function of entertaining and affirming. The strip emphasized black people's desire for achievement and respectability. The plot centered around the young Jones boy's search for the "good life" of money, success, and love with marriage as a happy ending. But at every turn he confronts the harsh reality of his environment. Unable to get a job because of the Depression, he becomes an outlaw and narrowly escapes jail. He is constantly "on the run" from oppression. His only consolations are his family and his beautiful, ever-faithful girlfriend.

"The Jones Family" illuminates the gray areas that most African Americans, regardless of their class, faced when attempting to live rational and coherent lives in the northern cities. While they espoused and cherished middle-class values, they often had to live among poverty, crime, and racial oppression. The black comic strips sought to provide entertaining, nonjudgmental prescriptions and blueprints for middle-class life, but to more cynical and alienated black people they seemed to be promoting unattainable values and lifestyles.

Radio and Race

Although there were individual exceptions, during the Depression black performers in radio and film were marginalized, exploited, or excluded. Commercial radio operated to deliver an audience of white consumers to white advertisers, and it denied black people jobs as announcers, broadcast journalists, or technicians. White entertainers schooled in blackface minstrelsy portrayed black radio characters. The major labor unions involved in the entertainment side of the radio industry restricted membership to white people. Still—with its offerings of vaudeville, big bands, drama, and comedy—radio provided relief from the miseries of the Depression to all Americans, black as well as white.

The most popular comedy radio program in the early thirties—a precursor to the soap operas and sitcoms that were to become staples of radio and television programming—was *The Amos 'n' Andy Show*. The inauguration of this program was a significant moment in radio history. The title roles were played by two white performers, Charles Correll and Freeman Gosden, who wrote and performed scripts laced with oxymorons and malapropisms. Skillful showmen, Correll and Gosden ingratiated themselves in Chicago's black community, appearing at parades and posing with black children. The *Chicago Defender* endorsed them and they received standing ovations at the Regal Theater in Chicago's black south side. Part of the amusement they generated derived from their mispronounced words, garbled grammar, and their show's minstrel ambience. Each episode highlighted an improbable situation involving the black cab driver (Amos) and his gullible overweight friend (Andy). Other characters included the scheming con artist Kingfish, his overbearing wife Sapphire, and his domineering mother-in-law, Mama. On radio, Gosden and Correll furnished voices for the members of Amos and Andy's fraternal lodge and for a whole array of other characters. The characters and their humor reinforced unflattering racial and gender stereotypes, but the show was not mean spirited. Some of the characters conducted themselves with dignity, modeling such positive values as marital fidelity, strong families, hard work, and economic independence. An Amos 'n' Andy movie, *Check and Double Check*—released in 1930 when hard times made black entertainers grateful for any employment they could get—featured musical numbers by Duke Ellington's orchestra. The movie introduced Ellington to a wider audience of affluent white people and enhanced his reputation.

Black audiences recognized the minstrel tradition stereotyping in *Amos 'n' Andy*, yet many among them still enjoyed the show. A vocal component of the ever more sophisticated and urbanized black population, however, complained that this show, and other radio programs, reinforced negative images—of black women as bossy Sapphires or Mammies and black men as childish clowns—in the nation's consciousness. Educator and activist Nannie Helen Burroughs considered the show demeaning. Robert L. Vann, editor of the *Pittsburgh Courier*, argued that it exploited African Americans for white commercial gain. Vann sponsored a petition to the Federal Communications Commission to ban the show, but his efforts were futile.

By the 1940s *The Amos 'n' Andy Show* was waning in popularity. In the early 1950s it had a brief life as a television series, this time with black actors. Alvin Childress, an experienced stage actor and director, became Amos. The part of Andy went to Spencer Williams Jr. who had written, directed, and starred in several independent all-black movies. Tim Moore assumed the role of the King-fish of the Mystic Knights of the Sea Lodge, while Johnny Lee portrayed the shyster lawyer, Algonquin J. Calhoun.

For almost two decades, *Amos 'n' Andy* was the only depiction of black people on the nation's airwaves. By stereotyping African Americans so negatively, the show buttressed white people's notions of their own superiority. The show never demonstrated the impact that the characters' race had on their lives or the psychological or economic costs of racism. It taught white America that to laugh at the striving of black men and women was all right.

The best-known and most successful African American on network radio in the late 1930s was Eddie Anderson, who played Jack Benny's sidekick Rochester in NBC's *The Jack Benny Show*. Like the characters in *Amos 'n' Andy*, Anderson's character reinforced negative racial stereotypes. Anderson, in a statement that suggests discomfort with his role, rationalized it this way:

> I don't see why certain characters are called stereotypes. The Negro characters being presented are not labeling the Negro race any more than "Luigi" is labeling the Italian people as a whole. The same goes for "Beulah," who is not playing the part of thousands of Negroes, but only the part of one person, "Beulah." They're not saying here is the portrait of the Negro, but here is "Beulah."

The *Beulah* radio show, which premiered in 1947, featured Hattie McDaniel in the role of a wise but subservient maid who provides the family that employs her with advice, guidance, and direction.

Race, Representation, and the Movies

In the 1930s and 1940s—after the introduction of sound in motion pictures—black and white producers began to make what were known as race films for African-American audiences. With the exception of these race films, white film executives, since the beginning of the film industry, had cast black men and women in roles designed to comfort, reassure, and entertain white audiences. Continuing this trend, when African Americans appeared in Hollywood movies of the 1930s, they were usually cast in servile roles and often portrayed as comic buffoons. For example, the first black actor to receive major billing in American films, Stepin Fetchit (1902–1985, born Lincoln Theodore Monroe Perry), purportedly earned two million dollars in ten years playing a cringingly servile, dim-witted, slow-moving character.

Black performers appeared as servants in many other box office successes during the Depression era. Among them were Gertrude Howard and Libby Taylor, who played servants to Mae West's character in West's *I'm No Angel* (1933) and *Belle of the Nineties* (1934). In *Imitation of Life* (1934), Louise Beavers played a black servant whose light-skinned daughter, played by Fredi Washington, seeks to pass for white. The black tap dancer and stage performer Bill "Bojangles" Robinson was featured in four popular films—*The Little Colonel* (1935), *The Littlest Rebel* (1935), *Just around the Corner* (1938), and *Rebecca of Sunnybrook Farm* (1938)—as a servant to white child star Shirley Temple.

The film that most firmly cemented the role of black Americans as servants in the American consciousness was *Gone with the Wind* (1939). Hattie McDaniel and Butterfly McQueen were the black "stars" in this epic adaptation of Margaret Mitchell's romanticized literary salute to the Old South. McDaniel had played servant or "Mammy" roles throughout the 1930s. The image of Mammy, the headscarf-wearing, obese, dutiful black woman who preferred nurturing white families to caring for her own children appealed to white America. But in *Gone with the Wind*, McDaniel gave the performance of a lifetime and in 1940 became the first African American to win an Oscar. Many in the black community criticized her for playing "female Tom" roles. Defensively, McDaniel retorted that she would rather play a maid than be one. Some black actors such as McDaniel, dismayed by their relegation to demeaning roles, formed the Fair Play Committee (FPC) to lobby the white-dominated movie industry for more substantial roles, to get rid of dialect speech, and to ban the term *nigger* from the screen.

Eventually, during and after World War II, Hollywood developed more sophisticated race-directed movies. Of particular significance was the positive, even romanticized, portrayal of black Americans in a movie financed by the War Department to gain support among African Americans for the U.S. role in WWII. *The Negro Soldier*, directed by Frank Capra in 1944, played to vast audiences of enthusiastic black people. But even before the *The Negro Soldier*, some motion pictures had displayed African Americans positively. Paul Robeson made two movies, *The Emperor Jones* (1933) and *Showboat* (1936), in which he attempted to change how black men and women were represented on screen. He proclaimed in 1934, "In my music, my plays, my films I want to carry always this central idea: to be

Louise Beavers (1908–1962) was a splendid actress whose talent was largely restricted to "mammy" roles. Here she appears with Claudette Colbert in a scene from the melodramatic film *Imitation of Life,* which deals with the theme of black people passing for white.

African. Multitudes of men have died for less worthy ideals; it is even more eminently worth living for." Robeson's films, however, were not box office successes, and he left the United States to pursue his career in Europe. There, his commitment to communism and leftist politics made him a target of the anticommunist hysteria that gripped the United States as the Cold War took hold in the late 1940s (see Chapter 20).

To succeed commercially, African-American filmmakers had to disguise their dissent or create art purely for other black people. One of the most enterprising black filmmakers, Oscar Micheaux (1884–1951), made films aimed primarily at the black public, a group that Hollywood directors and producers of race movies ignored or insulted with stereotypical representations. Unlike the dominant Hollywood stereotypes, the black men and women in Micheaux's films were often educated, cultured, and prosperous. Micheaux endowed black Americans with cinematic voice and subjectivity. In his films, middle-class or identity issues such as "passing for white" were featured.

Micheaux produced more than thirty feature films between 1919 and 1948. In 1932, he released *The Exile,* the first sound motion picture to be made by, with, and for black Americans. The following year he produced *Veiled Aristocrats,* about passing for white among Chicago's black professional class. The characters in the film are considered "aristocrats" because they are descended from the white gentry of the Old South and Europe; they are "veiled" because of their color. The plot turns on the revelation that the wealthy "white" heroine is actually "colored," which enables her to marry the talented mulatto hero.

Micheaux endeavored to transform Hollywood without changing it, much as members of the black bourgeoisie struggled to be included in American society. His films capture the dilemma of black double consciousness. As W. E. B. Du Bois put it, black people always experienced that "peculiar sensation," that "sense of always looking at one's self through the eyes of others, of measuring one's soul by the tape of a world that looks on in amused contempt and pity." Black culture existed within and was shaped by, while simultaneously transforming, American culture. To the degree that black Americans had been assimilated, white American culture was their culture as well.

The white ethnic immigrants who constructed Hollywood did so with a determination to help marginal and excluded groups like Jews and Italians assimilate into the American mainstream. Hollywood sought to create the illusion that these groups belonged to the power elite. However, these Hollywood entrepreneurs did not do the same for African Americans. Their films during the Depression represented black people as unassimilable. A small cadre of black filmmakers and actors created independent films and showed them in cinema houses exclusively for black patrons. Following the lead of pioneers like Micheaux, they continued to create an alternative cinema in which they introduced nuanced and fully human characters.

VOICES

MARGARET WALKER ON BLACK CULTURE

In 1942, poet Margaret Walker (1915–1998) published For My People, *the most important collection of poetry written by a participant in the Black Chicago Renaissance before Gwendolyn Brooks's* A Street in Bronzeville *(1945). In a 1992 collection of her essays, Walker reflected on the meaning and significance of black culture.*

Black culture has two main streams: a sociological stream . . . and an artistic stream. . . . In this artistic stream black culture has five branches. These are language, religion, art, music, and literature. . . .

Black music is perhaps the most acceptable of our black culture. The modern world is willing to accept the unique character of African rhythms and the language of the drum. White America, in general, reluctantly admits that black American music is *the* American music and most indigenous to our culture. In every category or classification of music, moreover, Black America has achieved monumentally. With a broad base of folk music—spirituals and gospel music, seculars (blues, work songs, prison hollers)—individuals have risen in notable achievement in classical, popular, and various forms of jazz. From Black Patti to Marian Anderson and Leontyne Price, the great black American singer has gained worldwide eminence. Roland Hayes, William Warfield, Todd Duncan, the late Ellabelle Davis, Dorothy Maynor, and Mattiwilda Dodds are notable black artists known the world over. Our blues singers like Bessie Smith, Ma Rainey, and B.B. King; folk singers like Leadbelly, and the greats like Louis Armstrong, Jimmie Lunceford, and Count Basie; great composers like Scott Joplin, Eubie Blake, Charlie Parker, and the incomparable Duke Ellington are significant contributors to the modern world and all represent the undeniable genius of the black American musician.

Individual achievement, while part of our general cultural picture is not all. It is in language and religion that Black Americans as a group have made a significant contribution to the national fiber of American life and to the modern world. As spiritual creatures we have shown through unmerited suffering that we have a sense of humanity that can enrich the moral fiber and contribute to a new world ethos. Our black culture is aware of human needs and human values. Handicapped as we have been by a racist system of dehumanizing slavery and segregation, our American history of nearly five hundred years reveals that our cultural and spiritual gifts brought from our African past are still intact. It is not only that we are singers and dancers, poets and prophets, great athletes and perceptive politicians—but we are also a body of charismatic and numinous people yet capable of cultic fire as seen in our black churches and still creative enough in intellect to signal the leap forward into a new and humanistic age. We are the authors of the new paradigm. . . .

How then has black culture been disseminated and kept alive? Black culture has survived in the black institutions of Black America. In the black family, the Black Church, the black school, the black press, the black nation, and the black world. This is where our black culture has survived and thrived. This is where it must continue to grow. The ground of common humanity is not yet a reality in the modern world but when it comes as it must in the twenty-first century, Black Africa, and black humanity must be as always the foundation on which it stands and from which it logically proceeds. One world of international brotherhood does not negate the nationalism of black people. It only enforces and re-enforces our common humanity.

QUESTIONS

1. According to Walker, what significant external factors influenced and sustained black culture? What are some of the central themes found in black culture?

2. What does the general acceptance by white Americans of black music suggest about this cultural form? Of the people Margaret Walker mentions above, who were the most influential in jazz?

3. What political and symbolic use have African Americans made of black culture?

Source: *On Being Female, Black, and Free: Essays by Margaret Walker, 1932–1992,* edited by Maryemma Graham (Knoxville: University of Tennessee Press, 1997).

THE BLACK CHICAGO RENAISSANCE

Like Harlem in the 1920s, Chicago during the 1930s and 1940s was an important center of black culture. In contrast to some of the artists of the "Harlem Renaissance," the leading writers in Chicago harbored no illusions that art would solve the problems caused by white supremacy and black subordination. The Chicago writers of the 1930s and 1940s emphasized the idea that black art had to combine aesthetics and function. It had to serve the cause of black freedom in some meaningful way.

Arna Bontemps (1902–1973) was to the Chicago Renaissance what Alain Locke had been to the Harlem Renaissance. "The Depression," Bontemps asserted,

> put an end to the dream world of renaissance Harlem and scattered the band of poets and painters, sculptors, scholars and singers who had in six exciting years made a generation of Americans aware of unnoticed and hitherto unregarded creative talents among Negroes. . . . What they did not dream was that a second awakening, less gaudy but closer to realities, was already in prospect. . . . One way or the other, Harlem got its renaissance in the middle twenties, centering around the *Opportunity* contests and the Fifth Avenue Awards Dinners. . . . Ten years later Chicago reenacted it on WPA [Works Projects Administration] without finger bowls but with increased power.

Louisiana-born Arna Bontemps migrated to Chicago from California in 1935, shortly thereafter met Richard Wright, and through him joined the South Side Writers Group, which Wright founded in 1936. The membership included poet Margaret Walker and playwright Theodore Ward. The group offered criticism and moral support to black writers. Bontemps' own writing was influenced by his association with the group. After 1935 his novels and short stories reflected a militant restlessness and revolutionary spirit. In 1936, he published *Black Thunder*, which depicted the nineteenth-century slave conspiracy led by Gabriel, and his *Drums at Dusk* published in 1939 was about the Haitian Revolution under the leadership of Toussaint L'Ouverture (1746–1803). Richard Wright's writings also celebrated resistance, but with more nuance. He published *Uncle Tom's Children* in 1938, and his masterpiece, *Native Son*, in 1940.

Among the artists who launched their careers on WPA funds were Margaret Walker and Willard Motley. Walker attracted widespread attention when her collected poems appeared as the book *For My People* in the Yale Series of Younger Poets. Willard Motley worked with a radio group while writing his powerful novel *Knock on Any Door* (1947), which depicted the transformation of an Italian-American altar boy into a criminal headed for the electric chair. The novel invited comparisons with Wright's *Native Son*.

Before the 1930s, several black intellectuals misjudged the potential of Chicago to become a vibrant center of black culture. In the late 1920s, black social scientists Charles S. Johnson and E. Franklin Frazier expressed disdain for black Chicago's artistic and intellectual prospects. Frazier proclaimed that "Chicago has no intelligentsia," and in 1923, Johnson asked rhetorically,

> Who can write of lilies and sunsets in the pungent shadows of the stockyards? . . . It is no dark secret why literary societies fail, where there are no Art exhibits or libraries about, why periodicals presuming upon an I.Q. above the age of 12 are not read, why so little literature comes out of the city. No, the kingdom of the second ward [the black neighborhood] has no self-sustaining intelligentsia, and a miserably poor acquaintance with that of the world surrounding it.

Johnson did, however, admit one saving grace in Chicago's cultural wasteland. "[I]t leads these colored United States in its musical aspirations with, perhaps, the best musical school in the race, as these go."

Johnson and Frazier were too harsh. Just as Chicago's industrial economy attracted working-class black men and women, it also nurtured artists who drew inspiration from and reflected this stratum of moving and striving, strolling and styling black people who wanted to transgress class and geographical lines. These working-class people aspired to enjoy the middle-class life of accomplishment and consumption. A critical pulse point on Chicago's South Side came to be known as Bronzeville. It measured and reflected the reality of the lives of ordinary working-class people. As Harlem had its 125th Street, Chicago had 35th and State Street and 47th and South Park (now Martin Luther King Jr. Drive).

Chicago was heir to the Harlem Renaissance. In 1930, Langston Hughes published *Not without Laughter*, the first major novel about the black experience in Chicago. Hughes moved to the city himself in 1941 and became a frequent contributor to the widely read *Chicago Defender*. The city epitomized urban industrial America. As the northern terminus of the Illinois Central Railroad and the home of the *Defender*, it had long attracted displaced agricultural workers from the southern cotton fields, and by 1930 it had a black population of 233,903. The migrants arrived eager to absorb Chicago's hard-driving blues and jazz culture.

LANGSTON HUGHES

Langston Hughes identified with poor and working-class black people. He used his poetry, prose, and playwriting skills to make the dignity and beauty of black people visible and known.

Hughes once referred to himself as "a literary sharecropper." Admirers called him a range of names—"Poet Laureate of the Negro People," for starters. During his career he produced fifteen volumes of poetry, two collections of short stories, one novel, two volumes of autobiography—*The Big Sea* (1940), and *I Wonder as I Wander* (1956)—and fifteen plays, along with librettos, scripts, essays, songs, translations, anthologies, children's stories, biographies and histories for the young, and two decades of weekly newspaper columns. He recorded the humor, wisdom, dialects, moods, and music of black people. One of the best examples of his social poetry was *The Negro Speaks of Rivers*:

Langston Hughes, in a painting by Winold Reiss.

I've known rivers:
I've known rivers ancient as the world and older than the
*   flow of human blood in human veins.*

My soul has grown deep like the rivers.

I bathed in the Euphrates when dawns were young.
I built my hut near the Congo and it lulled me to sleep.
I looked upon the Nile and raised the pyramids above it.
I heard the singing of the Mississippi when Abe Lincoln
*   went down to New Orleans, and I've seen its muddy*
*   bosom turn all golden in the sunset.*

I've known rivers:
Ancient, dusky rivers.

My soul has grown deep like the rivers.

Hughes was born in Joplin, Missouri, in 1902 and was raised by his maternal grandmother, Mary Langston. His father, James Hughes emigrated to Mexico, and his mother Carrie Langston remarried. Hughes became fascinated by black urban folk culture, which had been transplanted from the rural South by the great migration. He joined his mother in Cleveland in 1916, attended an integrated high school, and began to publish. Hughes had ambivalent feelings about his parents, who left him adrift, emotionally and financially. He dropped out of Columbia University in 1922, lived in Harlem, and traveled to Europe and Africa.

With the publication of *The Weary Blues* in 1926, his career took off. Hughes was enraptured by the language of the blues—its warmth, stoicism, incongruous humor, ironic laughter mixed with tears, and the "pain that was swallowed in a smile." In 1943 he introduced in his Chicago *Defender* column the character Jesse B. Semple, a racially conscious barfly philosopher—unlettered, but wise. The college-educated, somewhat uptight narrator of the series interrogates Semple about black life, from love of women and watermelon to the fortunes of rich gospel singers and the whereabouts of leaders who hide from the black people they lead. At one point Semple observed:

Not only am I half dead right now from pneumonia, but everything else *has* happened to me! I've been cut, shot, stabbed, run over, hit by a car, and tromped by a horse. I have also been robbed, fooled, deceived, two-timed, double-crossed, dealt seconds, and mightily near blackmailed—but I'm still here! . . . I have been fired, laid off, and last week given an indefinite vacation, also Jim Crowed, segregated, barred out, insulted, eliminated, called black, yellow, and red, locked in, locked out, locked up, and also left holding the bag.

In 1932 Hughes visited Moscow where he felt comfortable and appreciated. He was impressed by the absence of Jim Crow segregation and discrimination and ignored Stalin's oppression and murders. But Hughes was never a member of the Communist party and eventually become disillusioned with the Soviet Union. Hughes remains an enduring symbol of the artist who championed black folk culture as authentic American culture.

During the 1920s a discernible class structure among African Americans emerged in Chicago, fueled in part by the new migrants. These men and women expanded the consumer base and gave rise to a cadre of educated professionals and entrepreneurs who developed an appreciation for the arts. The Black Metropolis, as social scientists St. Clair Drake and Horace R. Cayton designated Chicago's South Side, became a black city within a city. Black businesses, such as banks and insurance companies, formed the financial foundation. Entrepreneur Walter L. Lee started Your Cab Company and each day put on the streets a half dozen chauffeur-uniformed drivers of vehicles. In the late 1940s, John Johnson would launch a publishing empire with such magazines as *Negro Digest*, *Jet*, and *Ebony*. These businesses depended less on white patronage than on black support. It was in their best interest to support the arts and provide venues for performances.

Revolutionary work in music occurred in Chicago. It was a pioneering center for recording as well as performing music. As black music became a commodity, influential black disk jockeys, like Al Benson, appeared on radio in Chicago. Benson proved to be as skilled a businessman as he was a cultural impresario. Music was the primary inspiration for the creativity that characterized black cultural movements in America. Avant-garde developments in black music preceded black cultural activity in the visual arts, poetry, drama, dance, literature, film, and sports. Cultural creativity was a potent force for black liberation and occurred simultaneously in different locations in America.

Jazz in Chicago

Within the confines of the South Side of Chicago, black musical giants, such as trumpeter Louis Armstrong (1898–1971) and his wife, Lillian Hardin, a noted jazz pianist, performed and nurtured a distinct jazz culture. Duke Ellington in his autobiography, *Music Is My Mistress*, remarked,

> Chicago always sounded like the most glamorous place in the world to me when I heard the guys in Frank Holliday's poolroom talking about their travels . . . . They told very romantic tales about nightlife on the South Side. By the time I got there in 1930, it glittered even more . . . the Loop, the cabarets . . . city life, suburban life, luxurious neighborhoods—and the apparently broken-down neighborhoods where there were more good times than any place in the city.

At this point Ellington was recording some of his best jazz, such as *Mood Indigo* (1930) and *Ko-Ko* (1940).

Ellington's stay in Chicago left a powerful impression on vocalist Joe Williams. Williams recalled,

> I used to arrange my classes so that I could get home in time to hear a program they [Ellington's band] had in Chicago called "Red Hot and Low Down.". . . The program's theme was Ellington's East St. Louis Toodle-oo. Later on, they changed the theme to "Sepia Panorama." Then they changed it again, to "Take the 'A' Train." But I used to come home early from high school so that I could hear Duke Ellington on the radio.

The seeds that blossomed into full-bodied jazz culture were planted across America at the turn of the century. The most famous musicians, however, all went to or passed through Chicago. As the Chicago Jazz Age came into its own, the beguiling tune "Pretty Baby" became the city's theme song. It was written by Tony Jackson, whom Jelly Roll Morton (the self-proclaimed "inventor of jazz") called "maybe the best entertainer the world has ever seen." The South Side, specifically along State Street between 31st and 35th, was the beating heart of the city's Jazz Age. Chicago did not replace New York as the major location for the aspiring jazz musician. It remained the place you went to prove you had what it took to make a name for yourself.

Gospel in Chicago

The term *gospel* designates the traditional religious music of the black church. It was nurtured and flourished in Chicago's Holiness, Sanctified, Pentecostal, Baptist, and Methodist churches, in storefronts or large edifices. Gospel music became the backbone of urban and contemporary black religion and is deeply entrenched in worship. The use of instruments—tambourines, drums, pianos, horns, guitars, and Hammond organs— characterizes gospel and distinguishes it from the earlier spiritual and black folk music. During the 1930s and 1940s, it developed its own idioms and performance techniques.

The doctrines of black "folk churches" encourage free expression, group participation, spontaneous testimonies, prayers, witnessing, and music. Singers and choirs rarely perform the same songs in the same way more than once. The performer must pay attention to the quality of the sound and to the careful manipulation of timbre, range, and shading. The style of the delivery uses the whole body in synchronized movement. The mechanics of the delivery are designed to intensify the performance, giving it added textual variation and melodic improvisation. Performers expand a melody by a variety of technical devices, including repetition, shouts, slides, slurs, moans, and grunts. The supporting piano and organ frequently engage in call-and-response interplay.

Gospel singer Pearl Williams-Jones makes clear the distinction between black church music and music of the other churches: "The traditional liturgical forms of plain chant, chorales, and anthems do not fulfill the needs of traditional Black folk religious worship and rituals."

In Chicago, Thomas Dorsey (1899–1993)—one of Chicago's leading composers of the blues since the mid-twenties—was most responsible for developing black urban gospel. Dorsey's genius lay in his ability to synthesize elements of the blues with religious hymns to create a gospel blues. His composed gospel pieces, performed with a ragtime-derived, boogie-woogie piano accompaniment, radiated an urban religious spirit. In 1930 Dorsey gained widespread attention when gospel singer Willie Mae Ford Smith (1904–1994) performed his "If You See My Savior, Tell Him That You Saw Me" at the National Baptist Convention meeting in Chicago. Two years later, in 1932, Dorsey's place in musical history was assured when Theodore Frye, with Dorsey at the piano, performed in the Ebenezer Baptist Church in Chicago his now classic gospel song, "Take My Hand, Precious Lord." The song had a profound impact on gospel performers and their audiences. Dorsey's abundant works provided a foundation for shout worship in the urban Protestant churches formed by transplanted black Southerners in the 1930s and succeeding decades.

One of the greatest gospel singers, Chicago-based Mahalia Jackson (1911–1972), sang and promoted Dorsey's songs all over the country on the church circuit and at religious conventions between 1939 and 1944. Jackson once said of the music, "Gospel songs are the songs of hope. When you sing them you are delivered of your burden." During the Depression and World War II, gospel became big business.

Chicago in Dance and Song: Katherine Dunham and Billie Holiday

The influence of the WPA in Chicago was especially reflected in dance. Dance has always been an integral part of African-American life, and the dances of black people have always been important in the American theater. The first performances by black dancers given within and taken seriously by the concert dance world occurred in the 1930s. The first "Negro Dance Recital in America" was performed in 1931 by the New Negro Art Theater Dance Company, co-founded by Edna Buy and Hemsley Winfield. In that same year, Katherine Dun-

Katherine Dunham was one of the leading forces in the development of black concert dance. A gifted choreographer and anthropologist, she founded one of the first black dance companies, appeared in several films, and wrote an insightful autobiography, *A Touch of Innocence* (1959), while championing the cause of black freedom and the overthrow of the Jim Crow regime.

ham (1909–) founded the Negro Dance Group in Chicago, which survived thanks to WPA support. As Dunham later recalled, "Black dancers were not allowed to take classes in studios in the '30s. I started a school because there was no place for blacks to study dance. I was the first to open the way for black dancers and I was the first to form a black dance company."

Dunham was unique. Trained in anthropology, she studied African-based ritual dance in the Caribbean. In 1938 her troupe stunned an audience with the sexual vitality of its performance of one of her works. When the company, now renamed the Katherine Dunham Dance Company, performed in February 1940, audiences and critics were awed. The *New York Times* declared, "With the arrival of Katherine Dunham on the scene the development of a substantial Negro dance Art begins to look decidedly bright." The reviewer continued,

Her performance with her group at the Windsor Theater may very well become a historic occasion, for certainly never before in all efforts of recent years to establish the Negro dance as a serious medium has there been so convincing and authoritative approach. . . . The potential greatness of the Negro dance lies in its discovery of its own roots and the crucial nursing of them into growth and flower. . . . It is because she has showed herself to have both the objective quality of the student and the natural instinct of the artist that she has done such a truly important job.

What kept audiences returning to Dunham dance performances, however, was the dancer's bold sensuality. A reviewer of *Tropical Revue,* for example, wrote that it was "likely to send thermometers soaring to the bursting point. . . . Tempestuous and torrid, raffish and revealing." The *New York Sun* marveled, "Shoulders, midsections and posteriors went round and round. Particularly when the cynosure was Miss Dunham, the vista was full of pulchritude."

Dunham explained her motivation:

> I felt a new dance form was needed for black people to be able to appear in any theater in the world and be accepted and exciting. One of the prerequisites of art is uniqueness. Rather than taking years to build a classical ballet company for blacks, I decided to create a dance with an authentic base for black people. Through my anthropological work, I studied primitive and folk dances and created the Dunham dance from them.

The success in New York led to film offers. The producers of the all-black musical extravaganza *Cabin in the Sky* hired the dance troupe and gave the feature role of Georgia Brown to Dunham. The role gave Dunham, as the *Times* dance critic wrote, the chance "to sizzle." But it also undermined her seriousness, allowing white audiences to view her as the stereotypical sultry black sexpot.

Nevertheless, the profits from the film funded the dancers' stage performances and Dunham's research. In 1943 Dunham moved to New York and opened the Katherine Dunham School of Arts and Research, which trained artists not only in dance, but in theater, literature, and world cultures.

Dunham was not afraid to jeopardize her career to protest racial segregation, even though it hurt her popularity. In the early 1940s, she denounced racial segregation and discrimination. In 1944 in Louisville, Kentucky, after a performance, Dunham announced, "We are glad we have made you happy. We hope you have enjoyed us. This is the last time I shall play Louisville because the management refuses to let people like us sit by people like you. Maybe after the war we shall have democracy and I can return." Dunham is important for two reasons. First, she was a gifted and talented pioneer in dance whose choreography inspired future generations. Second, she underscored the responsibility that a black artist had to the black community to fight racism.

Billie Holiday (1915–1959), another great performer whose career took shape during the Depression, also used her art to challenge the oppression of black people. Holiday, popularly known as "Lady Day," began singing at age fifteen and was discovered three years later by John Hammond, a well-known Chicago jazz producer and promoter. In 1933, Hammond arranged for Holiday's first recording session, and in 1934 she made her debut at the Apollo Theater in Harlem. An incomparable singer known for subtle and artful improvisation, she left her fans a wealth of recordings. She performed with the Count Basie Orchestra in 1938, and in a reflection of the increasing challenge to segregation in popular music, she appeared with the white Artie Shaw band. Unfortunately, despite her standing as one of jazz's all-time greats, Holiday's life

Billie Holiday was one of the greatest jazz singers of all time. Between 1935 and 1938, she released some eighty titles on the Brunswick label for marketing to the black jukebox audience.

was made miserable by racism, abusive relationships, and heroin addiction. She died in an automobile accident in 1959.

One of the most powerful songs in Holiday's repertoire was "Strange Fruit," a wrenching antilynching keen she first performed in 1939. "Every time she sang that song," recalled Barney Josephson, a New York nightclub owner,

> it was unforgettable. . . . I made her do it as her last number. . . . When she sang "Strange Fruit" she never moved. Her hands were down. She didn't even touch the mike. With the little light on her face. The tears never interfered with her voice, but the tears would come and just knock everybody in that house out.

Holiday was criticized for performing the song, but she refused to stop. Some people walked out when she sang it; others resented hearing about lynching when they had come to be entertained. But black people were still being lynched in 1939, and the NAACP had been trying unsuccessfully to get an antilynching law enacted by Congress. Determined to protest racial violence, Holiday recorded "Strange Fruit" on the Commodore label because her usual recording company, Columbia, refused. "Strange Fruit" sold well even though most radio stations banned it. The sales may have been driven by the popularity of the juke-box hit "Fine and Mellow" on the flip side.

BLACK GRAPHIC ART

Chicago artists, such as Charles White, Elizabeth Catlett, and Eldzier Cortor, and Harlem's Jacob Lawrence, celebrated both rural and urban working-class black people while implicitly criticizing the racial hierarchy of power and privilege. Their art belonged to the social realism school that flourished in the United States in the 1930s. Social realist art was intensely ideological. It strove to fuse propaganda—both left-wing and right-wing—to art to make it socially and politically relevant.

As the Depression worsened, black artists became even more determined to use their art to portray the crisis in capitalism. This involved depicting social and racial inequality. Chicago's Charles White wrote that "paint is the only weapon I have with which to fight what I resent. If I could write I would write about it. If I could talk I would talk about it. Since I paint, I must paint about it."

Defense Worker, a painting by Dox Thrash, reflects these concerns. Completed in 1942, just after the United States had entered World War II, it shows an isolated black worker looming over the horizon. The heroic proletarian imagery alludes to the dream of a racially integrated labor force, equal opportunity, and social reform in the wake of the New Deal and the sudden demand for labor triggered by the war.

VOICES

"STRANGE FRUIT"

This song, which became Billie Holiday's signature piece, was written by a white schoolteacher who went by the name of Lewis Allan (his real name was Abel Meerpol).

> Southern trees bear a strange fruit,
> Blood on the leaves and blood at the root,
> Black body swinging in the Southern breeze,
> Strange fruit hanging from the poplar trees.
>
> Pastoral scene of the gallant South,
> The bulging eyes and the twisted mouth,
> Scent of magnolia sweet and fresh,
> And the sudden smell of burning flesh!

> Here is a fruit for the crows to pluck
> For the rain to gather, for the wind to suck,
> For the sun to rot, for a tree to drop.
> Here is a strange and bitter crop.

QUESTIONS

1. How do these lyrics capture the brutality of lynching?

2. What does the term *pastoral* mean? Why is the fruit strange?

3. Discuss the historical context of this song.

Source: Lewis Allan (written in 1939, recorded by Billie Holiday).

Dox Thrash's *Defense Worker* celebrates the power and dignity of black industrial workers. The work captured the dream of a racially integrated labor force as the country was mobilizing for war.

The Harmon Foundation sponsored five juried exhibitions (1926–31, 1933) of the work of black artists. The William E. Harmon Awards for Distinguished Achievement among Negroes celebrated black artists in the hope that they would serve as role models for others. William E. Harmon, a real estate investor from Iowa, established the New York-based foundation in 1925. In the 1930s the WPA established art workshops and community art centers in black urban communities, such as Chicago (Southside Community Art Center), Cleveland (Karamu House Artist Association), Detroit (Heritage House), and Harlem (Harlem Art Workshop and the Harlem Community Art Center) to teach art to neighborhood young people and provide work for artists. Sculptor Augusta Savage, as the first director of the Harlem Community Art Center, presided over more than 1,500 students enrolled in day and evening classes in drawing, painting, sculpture, printmaking, and design. Among the teachers was Selma Burke (1900–1995) who sculpted the relief of Franklin D. Roosevelt that appears on the dime.

One of the initiatives of the Federal Arts Project, another New Deal agency, was to sponsor the creation of murals in public buildings, such as post offices and schools, that celebrated American ideals. Murals by black artists celebrated the heritage, contributions to society, and struggles of African Americans. Aaron Douglas, a leading painter of such public art, spoke about his work and that of his colleagues in a 1936 essay, "The Negro in American Culture":

> One of our chief concerns has been to establish and maintain recognition of our essential humanity, in other words, complete social and political equality. This has been a difficult fight as we have been the constant object of attack by all manner of propaganda from nursery rhymes to false scientific racial theories. . . . In this struggle the rest of the proletariat almost invariably has been arrayed against us. . . . But the Negro artist, unlike the white artist, has never known the big house. He is essentially a product of the masses and can never take a position above or beyond their level.

Douglas and other black artists pressed the WPA to appoint more African Americans to its local boards and to hire them for more projects. The Harlem Artists Guild and the Arts and Crafts Guild in Chicago provided forums where black artists could meet and plan strategies to foster the visual arts and support the social and political issues that affected black people's lives.

BLACK LITERATURE

Black literature, like black art, has been assessed in terms of what it reveals about the social, cultural, and political landscape at a given historical moment. The most distinguishing feature of black literature may be the way that black writers have attempted to create spaces of freedom in their work, to liberate place, a trait that also marks black religious culture and folk cultural practices, such as storytelling. Black literature, like all black cultural production, is valued both for aesthetic reasons on its own and for the way it represents the struggles of black people to attain freedom. In their work black writers in the 1930s and 1940s felt obliged to address questions of identity and to define and describe urban life to the dispossessed and impoverished black migrants to the cities. They tried to delineate the dimensions of a shared American heritage by portraying the specific contributions that African Americans had made to American society. Finally, and perhaps most ambitiously, black writers explored the issue of the rights African Americans were entitled to as Americans and the demands they could and should make on the state and society.

Richard Wright's *Native Son*

In 1940, Richard Wright (1908–1960) published *Native Son*, the first of many important novels by Depression-generation black authors. Reviewers hailed it as "the new American tragedy." Its tale of the downfall of the young Bigger Thomas could be read as a warning about how economic hardship combined with persistent segregation and discrimination could lead young black men to lash out in violence and rage. Setting out for an interview for a job as a chauffeur, Bigger meets with his neighborhood friends who want him to join them in robbing a grocery store. Bigger's fear of whites prevents him from going along. Instead, he picks a fight to camouflage his fear and avoid committing the crime. Bigger gets the chauffeur's job, which requires him to drive the wealthy Dalton family. On his first assignment, he is supposed to drive young Mary Dalton to a university lecture. But she talks him into picking up her boyfriend,

Jan—a communist—and taking them to a restaurant in the black neighborhood. Jan and Mary are completely oblivious to the offensively patronizing way they treat Bigger. After dinner Bigger drives them around the city while they drink and make love in the back seat.

When Jan leaves, Bigger takes an intoxicated Mary home. Because Mary is too drunk to walk, Bigger carries her to her room and is putting her to bed when blind Mrs. Dalton comes to check on her daughter. Bigger panics. He covers Mary's head with a pillow to keep her quiet. When Mrs. Dalton leaves, Bigger discovers that he has inadvertently smothered Mary. He burns her body in the basement furnace. Not fully grasping what he has done, Bigger writes a ransom note signed with a phony name to make it seem Mary has been kidnapped. When Mary's remains are discovered, Bigger flees. Fearing that she might betray him, Bigger then murders his girlfriend, Bessie. Bigger is captured, tried, and condemned. The remainder of the novel explores the hysteria and bigotry that envelops the case, the harsh criminal justice system, the insensitivity of the Communist party, which seeks to exploit Bigger's plight, and the poverty and social ills that plague Chicago's African-American communities during the Depression.

At the center of the drama is Wright's exploration of how Bigger comes to terms with his murder of Mary and Bessie. In conversations with Max, his lawyer, he realizes that his irrational fear of white people had caused him to kill the two women. Bigger realizes that he was in fact a product of his experiences in the ghetto. At the end of the novel he says, "What I killed for I am."

Wright's novel poignantly and chillingly thrust the impact of urbanization and racism on black men and women into the collective consciousness of the American people. One white critic declared, "Speaking from the black wrath of retribution, Wright insisted that history can be punishment. He told us the one thing even the most liberal whites preferred not to hear: that Negroes were far from patient or forgiving, that they were scarred by fear, that they hated every moment of their suppression even when seeming most acquiescent, and that often enough they hated *us* the decent and cultivated white men who from complicity or neglect shared in the responsibility of their plight."

In his closing arguments, Bigger's communist lawyer, Max, describes the psychological conditions that led Bigger to kill and warns of the destructive potential of suppressed black rage:

> The hate and fear which we have inspired in him, woven by our civilization into the very structure of his consciousness and into his blood and bones, into

the hourly functioning of his personality, have become the justification of his existence. . . . Kill him and swell the tide of pent up lava that will some day break loose, not in a single, blundering crime, but in a wild cataract of emotion that will brook no control.

Native Son was an immediate success. It became a Book-of-the-Month Club selection, and has sold millions of copies.

James Baldwin Challenges Wright

Wright's influence on American literature has been immense. He was the first black writer to enjoy an international reputation and showed that success and militancy were not mutually exclusive. A younger generation of black writers, however, especially James Baldwin (1924–1987), positioned themselves against Wright. African Americans, they argued, need not all be portrayed as hapless victims of American racism. In a famous short essay, "Everybody's Protest Novel" in 1949, Baldwin argued that Bigger's tragedy was not that he was black, poor, and scared, but that he had accepted "a theology that denies him life, that he admits the possibility of his being sub-human and feels constrained, therefore, to battle for his humanity according to those brutal criteria bequeathed him at his birth." Baldwin concluded, "The failure of the protest novel lies in its rejection of life, the human being, the denial of his beauty, dread, power, in its insistence that it is his categorization alone which is real and which cannot be transcended." In turn, Wright accused Baldwin of trying to destroy his reputation and of betraying all African-American writers who wrote protest literature. "What do you mean, *protest!*" Wright demanded. "*All* literature is protest. You can't name a single novel that isn't protest."

Baldwin answered Wright in a second essay in 1951 entitled, "Many Thousand Gone." "Wright's work," Baldwin declared, "is most clearly committed to the social struggle. . . . [T]hat artist is strangled who is forced to deal with human beings solely in social terms; and who has, moreover, as Wright had, the necessity thrust on him of being the representative of some thirteen million people. It is a false responsibility (since writers are not congressmen) and impossible, by its nature, of fulfillment."

The controversy ended the budding friendship between Wright and Baldwin, and Baldwin, whose work would soon include many powerful and revealing novels and insightful essays, inherited the mantle of "best-known black American male writer."

Ralph Ellison and *Invisible Man*

The most intricately diverse novel about the black experience in America written during this era was Ralph Ellison's (1914–1994) *Invisible Man*, which won the National Book Award for fiction in 1952. Partially autobiographical, it traces the life of a young black man from his early years in a southern school (a thinly disguised Tuskegee Institute) through his migration to New York City. The novel explores class tensions within American society and within the black community. It illuminates the interaction between white and black Americans with a balanced incisive perspective.

Ellison wrote numerous essays, but *Invisible Man* was to be his only completed novel. He argued that the black tradition teaches one "to deflect racial provocation and to master and control pain. . . . It is a tradition which abhors as obscene any trading on one's own anguish for gain or sympathy. . . . It takes fortitude to be a man and no less to be an artist. Perhaps it takes even more if the black man would be an artist." He concluded, "It would seem to me, therefore, that the question of how the 'sociology of his existence' presses upon the Negro writer's work depends upon how much of his life the individual writer is able to transform into art."

Echoing Du Bois's now classic characterization of the "twoness" of the African-American character, Ellison observed, "[Black people] are an American people who are geared to what *is* and who yet are driven by a sense of what it is possible for human life to be in this society."

AFRICAN AMERICANS IN SPORTS

It is in the arena of professional sports that black Americans demonstrated the possibilities of what human life could achieve when unconstrained by racism. The experiences of black men and women in American sports are a microcosm of their lives in American society. The privileges whites enjoyed in sports in this era paralleled the disadvantages and exclusions that were a constant part of black life. In the 1930s two black athletes, Jesse Owens and Joe Louis, captured the world's attention and inspired African Americans with pride, hope, and pleasure.

Jesse Owens and Joe Louis

Jesse Owens (1913–1980) was born on an Alabama sharecropping farm but grew up in Cleveland, Ohio. A talented runner, he studied at Ohio State University and

AFRICAN-AMERICAN MILESTONES IN SPORTS

1934	The Negro National League is revived.
1936	Jesse Owens wins four gold medals at Berlin Olympics.
1937	Joe Louis defeats James J. Braddock to win world heavyweight title. The Negro American League is formed.
1938	Joe Louis defeats the German Max Schmeling.
1947	Jackie Robinson signs with the Brooklyn Dodgers to become the first black major league baseball player. Dodgers win the National League Pennant.
1948	Alice Coachman wins a gold medal in the high jump to become the first black woman Olympic champion. Larry Doby joins the Cleveland Indians, becoming the first black player in the American League. Brooklyn Dodgers hire their second black player, Roy Campanella.
1949	Jackie Robinson wins the National League's Most Valuable Player Award.

prepared for the 1936 Olympics, which were to be held in Berlin, the capital of Nazi Germany. Many African-American leaders objected to participating in the games because they believed this would help legitimate the Nazi myth of the superiority of the so-called Aryan race. Owens believed otherwise. He wanted to debunk that myth and he succeeded. At the 1936 Games he became the first Olympian ever to win four gold medals. Adolf Hitler left the stadium to avoid congratulating Owens. Hitler's snub meant little to African Americans who relished Owens's victory over racism.

Joe Louis Barrow (1914–1981), like Owens, was the son of Alabama sharecroppers. His family migrated to Detroit, Michigan, when he was twelve. Although his mother wanted him to be a violinist, Joe Louis—he dropped the name Barrow—had other interests. As a youth, Louis displayed impressive boxing ability and won a string of local victories. In 1935 he faced former heavyweight champion, Primo Carnera. A record crowd of 62,000 attended the fight in New York. The fight had political overtones. Louis was fighting an Italian-American at a time when Benito Mussolini, the Fascist dictator of Italy, was about to invade Ethiopia; this was the oldest black independent nation in Africa, whose ruler, Emperor Haile Selassie, many black Americans admired. Sports writers and police were amazed to observe *everybody* cheering when Louis beat Carnera in the sixth round.

Louis won the world heavyweight title against James J. Braddock in 1937 and beat the German Max Schmeling in a symbolic victory over Nazism in 1938. Louis retained the world heavyweight title until 1949.

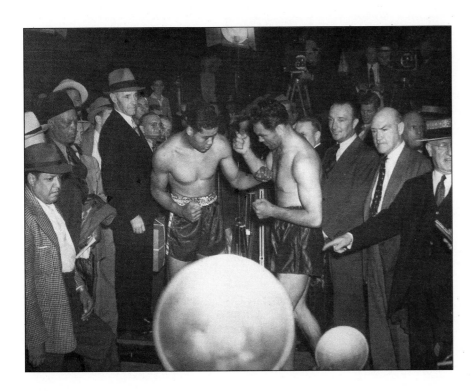

Joe Lewis and Max Schmeling square off for photographers before their 1938 bout in Madison Square Garden.

Breaking the Color Barrier in Baseball

While African Americans were integrated in track and in boxing, professional baseball remained strictly segregated until after World War II. Despite the hardships of the Depression, however, virtually every major black community tried to field its own baseball team. The Negro National League, which had folded in 1932, was revived in 1934, and a second league, the Negro American League, formed in 1937. Many of the players in the Negro leagues—including such legends as Josh Gibson, Satchel Paige, Leon Day, and Cool Papa Bell—would certainly have equaled or excelled their white counterparts in the major leagues, but, with the exception of Paige, they never had the chance.

In 1947, however, major league baseball, which had been a white man's game since the departure of Fleetwood Walker in 1887, became integrated again when Jackie Robinson (1919–1972) signed to play with the Brooklyn Dodgers. In 1945 Branch Rickey, the General Manager of the Dodgers, decided to sign a black ball player to improve the Dodgers' chances of winning the National League pennant and the World Series. After scouting the Negro Leagues, he signed twenty-six-year-old Jackie Robinson.

Robinson was the ideal choice. He was a superb athlete and a man of fortitude and immense determination. Born in Georgia and raised in southern California, he had been an All-American running back in football at UCLA and then had played baseball for the legendary Kansas City Monarchs of the Negro leagues. Robinson was also committed to black people and racial progress. Robinson played the 1946 season for the Brooklyn Dodgers minor league team in Montreal where he and his wife Rachel were warmly received by the Canadians. But spring training in segregated Florida was difficult to endure.

Robinson broke the color barrier when he opened at first base for the Dodgers in April 1947. Taunted, ridiculed, and threatened by some spectators and players, he responded by playing spectacular baseball. He won the Rookie of the Year honors in 1947, and the Dodgers won the National League pennant. Robinson retired in 1958, but remained outspoken on racial issues until his death from diabetes in 1972.

In 1948 Larry Doby became the first black player in the American League when he joined the Cleveland Indians. As other major league teams also signed black players, the once-popular Negro Leagues all but ceased to exist.

BLACK RELIGIOUS CULTURE

Just as black religion was the "invisible institution" that helped African Americans to survive slavery, the black church was the visible institution that helped hundreds

Jackie Robinson broke the color barrier in American baseball when he joined the Brooklyn Dodgers in April 1947. During his first season he withstood the vicious taunts and threats of white spectators and players with quiet dignity while playing spectacular baseball and earning Rookie of the Year honors. Robinson spoke out against racial discrimination and segregation throughout his life.

of thousands of migrants adjust to urban life while affirming an enduring set of core values consisting of freedom, justice, equality, and an African heritage. There was of course, no single "black church." The term is a shorthand way of referring to a pluralistic collection of institutions, including most prominently seven independent, historic, and black-controlled denominations: the African Methodist Episcopal Church, the African Methodist Episcopal Zion Church; the Christian Methodist Episcopal Church; The National Baptist Convention, Incorporated; the National Baptist Convention of America, Unincorporated; the Progressive National Baptist Convention; and the Church of God in Christ. Together, these denominations account for more than 80 percent of all black Christians.

The black church helped black workers make the transition from being southern peasants to being part of a northern urban proletariat. Yet the relationship between black religious tradition and the secular lives of black people was always changing. The blues and jazz performed in nightclubs were transformed into urban gospel music. Many of the nightclub musicians and singers received their training and first public performances in their churches. During the Depression, the black church helped black people survive by helping them pool their resources and by offering inspiration and spiritual consolation. Here we focus on alternative religious groups that became prominent during the 1930s and 1940s and addressed specific needs growing out of the Depression and the traumatic experience of relocating to alien and often hostile northern cities. Elijah Muhammad's Nation of Islam and Father Divine's Peace Mission Movement combined secular concerns with sacred beliefs. Both strengthened a sense of identity, affirmation, and community among their members.

The Nation of Islam

The Nation of Islam emerged in 1929, the year Timothy Drew died. Drew, who took the name Nobel Drew Ali, was founder of the Moorish Science Temple of America, which flourished in Chicago, Detroit, and other cities in the 1920s. After his death, a modified version of the Moorish Science Temple emerged in 1930 in Detroit. It was led by a mysterious door-to-door peddler of silks and other items that supposedly originated in Africa, known variously as Wallace D. Fard, Master Farad Muhammad, or Wali Farad. He wrote two manuals of instruction, *The Secret Ritual of the Nation of Islam* and *Teaching for the Lost-Found Nation of Islam in a Mathematical Way*. His teachings that black people were the true Muslims attracted many poor residents in Depression-era Detroit. In addi-

tion to the beliefs of Nobel Drew Ali, Fard's Nation of Islam also taught a mixture of Koranic principles, the Christian Bible, his own beliefs, and those of nationalist Marcus Garvey.

In 1934, after establishing a Temple of Islam, Fard disappeared, and one of his disciples, Elijah Poole (1897–1975) renamed Elijah Muhammad by Fard, became leader of the Detroit temple and then of a second temple in Chicago. The Nation attracted the attention of federal authorities during World War II when its members refused to serve in the military. Muhammad was arrested in May 1942 on charges of inciting his followers to resist the draft and was imprisoned in Milan, Michigan, until 1946. After his release he settled in Chicago and began to expand his movement.

The Nation of Islam taught that black people were the Earth's original human inhabitants who had lived, according to Elijah Muhammad, in the Nile Valley. Approximately 6,000 years ago, a magician named Yakub produced white people. These white people proved so troublesome that they were banished to Europe where they began to spread evil. Their worst crime was their enslavement of black people. Elijah Muhammad taught that white supremacy was ending and that black people would rediscover their authentic history and culture. To prepare for the coming millennium, he instructed members to adhere to a code of behavior that included abstaining from many traditionally southern black foods, especially pork. Members subscribed to a family-centered culture in which women's role was to produce and rear the next generation. The Nation also demanded part of the South for a black national state.

Father Divine and the Peace Mission Movement

Father Major Jealous Divine (1877?–1965) was born George Baker in Savannah. Like Elijah Muhammad, little is known about his early life. He captured attention in 1919 when he settled with twenty followers in Sayville, New York, and began what became known in the 1930s as the Peace Mission Movement. Divine secured domestic jobs for many of his followers on the surrounding estates and preached a gospel of hard work, honesty, sobriety, equality, and sexual abstinence. He provided free, or nearly free, meals and shelter for anyone who asked. In 1930, he changed his name to Father Divine. His Peace Movement espoused a racially neutral and economically empowering dogma that appealed to poor and needy black and white urbanites by offering them spiritual guidance and mental and physical healing. The movement embodied

TIMELINE

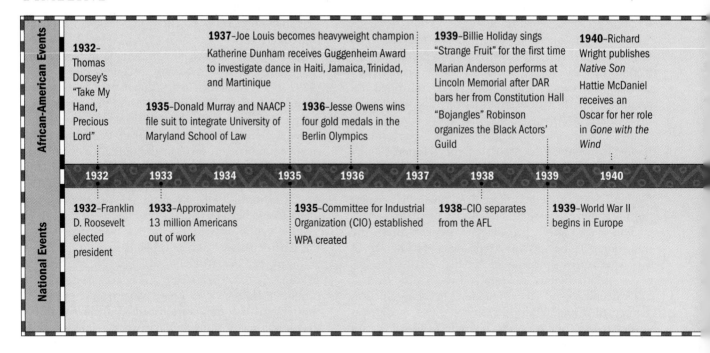

African-American Events

1932- Thomas Dorsey's "Take My Hand, Precious Lord"

1935-Donald Murray and NAACP file suit to integrate University of Maryland School of Law

1937-Joe Louis becomes heavyweight champion
Katherine Dunham receives Guggenheim Award to investigate dance in Haiti, Jamaica, Trinidad, and Martinique

1936-Jesse Owens wins four gold medals in the Berlin Olympics

1939-Billie Holiday sings "Strange Fruit" for the first time
Marian Anderson performs at Lincoln Memorial after DAR bars her from Constitution Hall
"Bojangles" Robinson organizes the Black Actors' Guild

1940-Richard Wright publishes *Native Son*
Hattie McDaniel receives an Oscar for her role in *Gone with the Wind*

| 1932 | 1933 | 1934 | 1935 | 1936 | 1937 | 1938 | 1939 | 1940 |

National Events

1932-Franklin D. Roosevelt elected president

1933-Approximately 13 million Americans out of work

1935-Committee for Industrial Organization (CIO) established
WPA created

1938-CIO separates from the AFL

1939-World War II begins in Europe

ideas from the New Thought, Holiness, Perfectionist, and Adventist religions. Hundreds of people traveled to see Father Divine on weekends, feast at his communal banquet table, and listen to his promises of heaven on earth. The feasts were symbolic of the early Christian Eucharist and became the defining practices of Divine's religion.

In 1931, the police arrested Divine and eighty followers on charges of being a "public nuisance." Three days after a judge sentenced Divine to a year in jail and a $500 fine, the judge died of a heart attack. Divine was quoted as saying, "I hated to do it." The conviction was reversed, and Divine's reputation as a master of cosmic forces soared. Some of his followers now believed that he was God. Aside from the belief in the divinity of Father Divine, members of the Peace Movement were drawn to the mission's strong emphasis on ending racial prejudice and economic inequalities.

In 1933, Divine moved his headquarters to Harlem, where his Peace Mission Movement prospered, eventually purchasing key real estate and housing projects called "heavens." These acquisitions and other businesses in the Midwest enhanced Divine's ability to provide shelter, jobs, and incomes for his followers. He launched a journal entitled *New Day* in 1937 and used it to disseminate his teachings. Divine also protested social injustice and encouraged his followers to become

politically engaged. Between 1936 and 1940, he lobbied strenuously for a federal antilynching law. At the time of Divine's death in 1965, the holdings of the Peace Mission were estimated to be worth $10 million. Father Divine's movement echoed the Protestant ethic: work hard, keep both your mind and body healthy; eat right; dress properly; keep good company; and avoid all manner of evil and vice.

CONCLUSION

The Depression ushered in a period of intense hardship, but as this chapter indicates, it was also a period in which black Americans had an unprecedented impact on American culture. Black people excelled in sports, arts, drama, and music. The Works Progress Administration (WPA) funded a wide spectrum of artists whose cultural productions were accessible, inclusive, and populist. The Chicago Black Renaissance reflected the impact of the WPA on the lives and fortunes of hundreds of artists. A new generation of black jazz musicians transformed black music into an art form that won worldwide admiration and emulation. Black musicians weaned Americans from swing to bebop, while gospel music became a dynamic genre that satisfied the needs of the black urban migrants to express their spiritual and communal feelings.

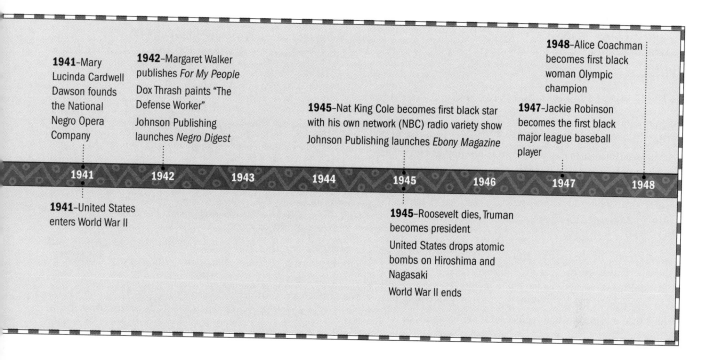

1941-Mary Lucinda Cardwell Dawson founds the National Negro Opera Company

1942-Margaret Walker publishes *For My People*

Dox Thrash paints "The Defense Worker"

Johnson Publishing launches *Negro Digest*

1945-Nat King Cole becomes first black star with his own network (NBC) radio variety show

Johnson Publishing launches *Ebony Magazine*

1948-Alice Coachman becomes first black woman Olympic champion

1947-Jackie Robinson becomes the first black major league baseball player

1941 1942 1943 1944 1945 1946 1947 1948

1941-United States enters World War II

1945-Roosevelt dies, Truman becomes president

United States drops atomic bombs on Hiroshima and Nagasaki

World War II ends

These positive changes were made against a backdrop of entrenched racism. While some African Americans found satisfying jobs in film and radio, many others were excluded or relegated to demeaning, stereotypical roles. This bias and negative typecasting motivated innovative filmmakers to develop alternative films and artistic institutions that allowed a more balanced and accurate representation of black life and culture to develop. Such creative ventures seldom produced the profits that white entrepreneurs reaped from marketing black cultural productions to white consumers. The mass appeal and unparalleled success of entertainers such as Louis Armstrong and Duke Ellington should not obscure the fate of those artists who refused to entertain white America and instead sought to oppose racism and social and economic injustice. They remained poor and unnoticed by the dominant culture.

Still, black counterculture artists had a tremendous impact on America and reflected a growing pride and a determination to resist complete assimilation into white culture. The comic strips, the Semple stories of Langston Hughes, the black press, and the black church preserved black people's dignity. Black culture prepared black people for the next level of struggle against the American Jim Crow regime and against all ideologies of white supremacy, both in the United States and abroad.

REVIEW QUESTIONS

1. How did the Great Depression affect the development of black culture? What role did the New Deal's Works Progress Administration (WPA) play in the democratization of black expressive culture? How did black religious culture change during this era?

2. How did black artists, musicians, filmmakers, and writers negotiate the dilemma of dual consciousness as articulated by W. E. B. Du Bois? Which parts of black art did white corporate executives find easiest to appropriate and shape for white consumption?

3. Discuss the transition from swing era big band music to bebop. What problems did the bebop musicians encounter? How did black music affect American culture?

4. Discuss the representations of black Americans in Hollywood films during the 1930s and 1940s. How did these images affect white Americans' attitudes and behavior toward black Americans? How did these representations contribute to the emergence of an alternative or independent black cinema?

5. How did the cultural production of the Chicago Renaissance compare with that of the Harlem Renaissance? Why did black athletes become prominent

during the 1930s and 1940s? What was their impact on American culture? To what extent did the experiences of black sports figures reflect the status of race relations in the United States?

RECOMMENDED READING

William Barlow. *Voice Over: The Making of Black Radio.* Philadelphia: Temple University Press, 1999. A lucidly written, informative cultural history of the evolution of black radio and the personalities who made it a powerful instrument for disseminating black music, culture, language, and politics, and for constructing an African-American public sphere.

Scott DeVeaux. *BeBop: A Social and Musical History.* Berkeley: University of California Press, 1997. A perceptive study of the creative artistry and lives of the pivotal black professional musicians in the jazz world during the 1930s and 1940s and how they made bebop into a commercially successful art movement.

Manthia Diawara, ed. *Black American Cinema.* New York: Routledge, 1993. A collection of provocative essays. Three examine the work of filmmaker Oscar Micheaux. Others provide fresh interpretations of the recent independent cinema movement.

Melvin Patrick Ely. *The Adventures of Amos 'N' Andy: A Social History of an American Phenomenon.* New York: Free Press, 1991. A subtle and penetrating examination of the complexities of racial stereotyping in one of the most influential and controversial radio and television programs in the history of media race relations.

Samuel A. Floyd Jr. *The Power of Black Music: Interpreting Its History from Africa to the United States.* New York: Oxford University Press, 1995. An excellent overview of the history of black music with an insightful comparison of the Harlem and Chicago flowerings.

ADDITIONAL BIBLIOGRAPHY

Art

Sharon F. Patton. *African-American Art.* New York: Oxford University Press, 1998.

Richard J. Powell. *Black Art and Culture in the 20th Century.* New York: Thames and Judson, 1997.

William E. Taylor and Harriet G. Warkel. *A Shared Heritage: Art by Four African Americans.* Bloomington: Indiana University Press, 1996.

Black Chicago Renaissance

Robert Bone. "Richard Wright and the Chicago Renaissance." *Callaloo* 9, no. 3 (1986):446–468.

Craig Werner. "Leon Forrest, the AACM and the Legacy of the Chicago Renaissance." *The Black Scholar* 23, no. 3/4 (1993): 10–23.

Culture

St. Clair Drake and Horace R. Cayton. *Black Metropolis: A Study of Negro Life in a Northern City.* New York: Harper & Row, 1962.

Gerald Early, ed. *"Ain't But a Place": An Anthology of African American Writing about St. Louis.* St. Louis: Missouri Historical Society Press, 1998.

Geneviève Fabre and Robert O'Meally, eds. *History and Memory in African-American Culture.* New York: Oxford University Press, 1994.

Kenneth W. Goings. *Mammy and Uncle Mose: Black Collectibles and American Stereotyping.* Bloomington: Indiana University Press, 1994.

Robin D. G. Kelley. *Race Rebels: Culture, Politics, and the Black Working Class.* New York: Free Press, 1994.

Lawrence Levine. *Black Culture and Black Consciousness: Afro-American Folk Thought from Slavery to Freedom.* New York: Oxford University Press, 1977.

Tommy L. Lott. *The Invention of Race: Black Culture and the Politics of Representation.* Malden, MA: Blackwell Publishers, 1999.

Daryl Scott. *Contempt and Pity: Social Policy and Image of the Damaged Black Psyche, 1880–1996.* Chapel Hill: University of North Carolina Press, 1997.

Mel Watkins. *On the Real Side: Laughing, Lying, and Signifying.* New York: Simon & Schuster, 1994.

Robert E. Weems Jr. *Desegregating the Dollar: African American Consumerism in the Twentieth Century.* New York: New York University Press, 1998.

Dance

Katherine Dunham. *A Touch of Innocence.* London: Cassell 1959.

Terry Harnan. *African Rhythm-American Dance.* New York: Knopf, 1974.

Film

Donald Bogle. *Brown Sugar: Eighty Years of America's Black Female Superstars.* New York: Crown Publishers, 1980.

Thomas Cripps. *Making Movies Black: The Hollywood Message Movie from World War II to the Civil Rights Era*. New York: Oxford University Press, 1993.

Literature

Ralph Ellison. "The World and the Jug." In Joseph F. Trimmer, ed. *A Casebook on Ralph Ellison's Invisible Man* (pp. 172–200). New York: T. Y. Crowell, 1972.

Michael Fabre. *The Unfinished Quest of Richard Wright*. Iowa City: University of Iowa Press, 1973.

Henry Louis Gates and Nellie Y. McKay, eds. *Norton Anthology of African American Literature*. New York: W. W. Norton, 1997.

Joyce Ann Joyce. *Richard Wright's Art of Tragedy*. New York: Warner Books, 1986.

Robert G. O'Meally. *The Craft of Ralph Ellison*. Cambridge, MA: Harvard University Press, 1980.

Arnold Rampersad. *The Life of Langston Hughes*. New York: Oxford University Press, 1986.

Margaret Walker. *Richard Wright, Daemonic Genius: A Portrait of the Man, a Critical Look at His Work*. New York: Morrow, 1988.

Music and Radio

William Barlow. *Looking Up at Down: The Emergence of Blues Culture*. Philadelphia: Temple University Press, 1989.

Jack Chalmers. *Milestones I: The Music and Times of Miles Davis to 1960*. Toronto: University of Toronto Press, 1983.

John Chilton. *The Song of the Hawk: The Life and Recordings of Coleman Hawkins*. Ann Arbor: University of Michigan Press, 1990.

Donald Clarke. *Wishing on the Moon: The Life and Times of Billie Holiday*. New York: Viking Penguin, 1994.

Miles Davis and Quincy Troupe. *Miles: The Autobiography*. New York: Simon & Schuster, 1989.

Duke Ellington. *Music Is My Mistress*. New York: Da Capo Press, 1973.

John Birks Gillespie and Wilmot Alfred Fraser. *To Be or Not . . . to Bop: Memoirs/Dizzy Gillespie with Al Fraser*. New York: Doubleday, 1979.

Michael Harris. *The Rise of Gospel Blues: The Music of Thomas Andrew Dorsey in the Urban Church*. New York: Oxford University Press, 1992.

Robert G. O'Meally. *Lady Day: The Many Faces of Billie Holiday*. New York: Arcade Publishers, 1991.

Thomas Owens. *Bebop: The Music and Its Players*. New York: Oxford University Press, 1955.

Barbara Dianne Savage. *Broadcasting Freedom: Radio, War, and the Politics of Race, 1938–1948*. Chapel Hill: University of North Carolina Press, 1999.

Jules Schwerin. *Got To Tell It: Mahalia Jackson, Queen of Gospel*. New York: Oxford University Press, 1992.

Alyn Shipton. *Groovin' High: The Life of Dizzy Gillespie*. New York: Oxford University Press, 1999.

Eileen Southern. *The Music of Black Americans: A History*, 2nd ed. New York: W. W. Norton, 1983.

J. C. Thomas. *Chasin' the Trane: The Music and Mystique of John Coltrane*. Garden City, New York: Doubleday, 1975.

Dempsey J. Travis. *Autobiography of Black Jazz*. Chicago: Urban Research Press, 1983.

Sports

Arthur Ashe, with the assistance of Kip Branch, Ocania Chalk, and Francis Harris. *A Hard Road to Glory: A History of the African-American Athlete*. New York: Warner Books, Inc., 1988.

Richard Bak. *Joe Louis: The Great Black Hope*. New York: Da Capo Press, 1998.

R. Peterson. *Only the Ball Was White: A History of Legendary Black Players and All-Black Professional Teams*. New York: McGraw Hill, 1984.

Arnold Rampersad. *Jackie Robinson: A Biography*. New York: Knopf, 1997.

Jackie Robinson. *I Never Had It Made*. New York: G. P. Putnam's Son, 1972.

Jeffrey T. Sammons. *Beyond the Ring: The Role of Boxing in American Society*. Urbana: University of Illinois Press, 1988.

Religion

Claude Andrew Clegg III. *An Original Man: The Life and Times of Elijah Muhammad*. New York: St. Martin's Griffin, 1997.

C. Eric Lincoln and Lawrence H. Mamiya. *The Black Church in the African American Experience*. Durham, NC: Duke University Press, 1990.

Elijah Muhammad. *The True History of Elijah Muhammad: Autobiographically Authoritative*. Atlanta: Secretrius Publications, 1997.

Jill Watts. *God, Harlem USA: The Father Divine Story*. Berkeley: University of California Press, 1992.

Robert Weisbrot. *Father Divine and the Struggle for Racial Equality*. Urbana: University of Illinois Press, 1983.

THE WORLD WAR II ERA
AND SEEDS OF A REVOLUTION

The distinguished World War II record of the "Tuskegee Airmen," pilots who trained and fought in all-black fighter squadrons, confounded the expectations of white officers who doubted that black men had the ability or nerve to pilot fighter aircraft.

The treatment that the Negro soldier has received has been resented not only by the Negro soldier but by the Negro civilian population as well. In fact, any straight-thinking person with a sense of justice and right, without any respect to color or race, must realize the dangers inherent in the evil practices that have been permitted to exist in the Army. It is not a pleasant thought for Negroes to ponder that their tax money is being spent to help maintain an army that has little regard for the real principles of democracy.

David H. Bradford, the Louisville *Courier Journal*, September 2, 1941

The years between 1939 and 1954 witnessed a fundamental transformation of the role of the United States in the world. The victory in World War II of the Allies—the USSR, Great Britain, the United States, and dozens of other countries—over the Axis powers of Germany, Italy, and Japan marked the emergence of America as the dominant global power. This international role placed new constraints on the nation's domestic policies, particularly when, after the Axis surrender in 1945, mutual suspicions between the United States and the Soviet Union quickly developed into a "Cold War." This long conflict led to a vast expansion in the size and power of the federal government, particularly its military, and cast a long shadow over domestic politics.

International events replaced the Great Depression as the defining force in the lives of African Americans. In preparing for and fighting World War II, America finally emerged from the Depression and laid the basis for an era of unprecedented prosperity. Industrial and military mobilization resulted in profound demographic changes with the movement of millions of people, many of them African American, out of agriculture and into the cities.

This population shift substantially increased black voting strength in the North and West, which, combined with a moral recoil from the savage racial policies of the Nazis, drove the issue of black equality to the forefront of national politics. Moreover, hundreds of thousands of black men and women learned new skills and ideas while serving in the armed forces and many resolved to come home and claim their rights.

The Cold War also had a tremendous impact on African Americans and their struggle for freedom. The two sides of this conflict avoided direct confrontation with each other; instead, to a great degree, they enlisted the peoples of Africa, Asia, and Latin America as proxies. U.S. leaders, seeking to convince these peoples of America's virtues as a democracy, were pressed to address the segregation and racial discrimination that remained firmly imbedded in the basic fabric of American life. The advocacy groups and black press that had come of age during the 1930s and 1940s focused attention on fighting racism and demanded the full rights and responsibilities of citizens for all people. The result was a powerful movement for civil rights that was backed by many liberal white Americans and, increasingly, key institutions in the national government.

These favorable developments, however, provoked powerful resistance. Egged on by their politicians, white Southerners used all the power at their command to defend segregation. The emerging hostilities with the Soviet Union prompted many white conservatives to charge that all those seeking to fight racial injustice were in fact agents of the communist enemy. These contrary currents—the push for a new democracy on one hand and the Cold War mentality on the other—would indelibly place their stamp on the emerging civil rights movement.

ON THE EVE OF WAR, 1936–1941

As the world economy wallowed in the Great Depression, the international order collapsed in Europe and Asia. Germany under the dictatorship of Adolf Hitler (1889–1945) and Italy under the dictatorship of Benito Mussolini (1883–1943) created an alliance, known as the Axis, aimed at taking economic and political control of Europe. These fascist dictators advocated a political program based on extreme nationalism that brutally suppressed all internal opposition, and used violence to gain their will abroad. Germany was the dominant partner in the Axis. Its Nazi or National Socialist party in part blamed communists and foreign powers for the nation's economic depression and loss of power. But more than by anticommunism, Hitler was driven by a virulent form of racism. Unlike racists in the United States, he focused his hatred on Jews, blaming them for all Germany's social and economic problems. Through the late 1930s the Germans and Italians embarked on a series of military campaigns that placed much of Central Europe under their power. In August 1939 Germany signed a nonaggression pact with the Soviet Union, a prelude to a September 1 attack on Poland by both nations. A few days later Britain and France reacted to the invasion by declaring war on the Axis, thus beginning World War II.

As Germany and Italy pursued their plans in Europe during the 1930s, the Japanese Empire attempted to gain control of Asia. Through most of the decade it extended its dominion over China and, by the end of the 1930s, was poised to push European and American forces out of the region. This threat led to a rising tide of conflict with the United States, which held the Philippines, Guam, Hawaii, and other islands in the Pacific and had extensive trade interests in Asia. Many American leaders were also concerned about the security of their nation's west coast should the Japanese achieve their goals. These tensions led to war on December 7, 1941, when the Japanese bombed American warships at Pearl Harbor, Hawaii, and launched a massive offensive against British, Dutch, and American holdings throughout the Pacific.

President Franklin D. Roosevelt watched the events in Europe and Asia with growing concern but had only a limited ability to react. Despite its large economy, America was not a preeminent military power at the time. FDR had trouble convincing Congress to enlarge the Army and Navy because a large segment of the American population, the isolationists, believed the United States had been hoodwinked into fighting World War I and should avoid again becoming entangled in a foreign war. During the late 1930s the president had managed to overcome some of this opposition and had won the authority to increase the size of the nation's armed forces. By early 1940 the United States had instituted its first peacetime draft to provide men for the U.S. Army and Navy.

African Americans and the Emerging World Crisis

Many African Americans responded to the emerging world crisis with growing activism. When Ethiopia was invaded by Italy in 1935, it was the only truly independent black-ruled nation in the world, and black communities throughout the United States organized to send it aid. Mass meetings in support of the embattled Ethiopians were held in New York and other large cities while reporters from black newspapers, such as J. A. Rogers of the Pittsburgh *Courier*, brought the horror of this war home to their readers. Although the mechanized Italian army soon won the war, the conflict alerted many African Americans to the dangers of fascism and reawakened an interest in the fate of Africa.

A war in Spain had a similar effect on leftist African Americans. In 1936 the left-leaning Spanish Republic became embroiled in a civil war against a fascist movement led by General Francisco Franco (1892–1975) and supported by Germany and Italy. About 100 African Americans traveled to Spain in 1936–1937 to serve with the Abraham Lincoln Battalion, an integrated fighting force of 3,000 American volunteers. Among the 100 were two women: Salaria Kee, who fought on the battlefield, and Chicagoan Thyra Edwards, who participated in the Medical Bureau and North American Committee to Aid Spanish Democracy. Support of the Abraham Lincoln Battalion reflected a commitment to the communists' vision of internationalism found among a small sector of African Americans. Mobilization for war, however, would soon bring the vast majority of black people and their organizations into the fight against fascism abroad and for equality and justice in the United States.

A. Philip Randolph and the March on Washington Movement

Between 1939 and 1940 the American government, along with the governments of France and Britain, spent so much on arms that the U.S. economy was finally lifted out of the Depression. But as the United States mobilized its economy for war and rebuilt its military, it did so in keeping with past practices of discrimination and exclusion. As unemployed white workers streamed into aircraft factories, shipyards, and other centers of war production, jobless African Americans most often found themselves left waiting at the gate.

The great majority of aircraft manufacturers, for example, would hire black people only in janitorial positions no matter what their skills. Many all-white AFL unions enforced closed-shop agreements that prevented their employers from hiring black workers who were not members of the labor organization. Government-funded training programs regularly rejected black applicants, often reasoning that training them would be pointless given their poor prospects of finding skilled work. The United States Employment Service (USES) filled "whites only" requests for defense workers. The military itself made it clear that although it would accept black men in their proportion to the population, about 11 percent at the time, it would put them in segregated units and assign them to service duties. The U.S. Navy limited black servicemen to menial positions while the Marine Corps and the Army Air Corps refused to accept them altogether.

When a young African American man wrote the Pittsburgh *Courier* and suggested a "Double V" campaign—victory over fascism abroad and over racism at home—his words were quickly adopted by the newspaper as the battle cry for the entire race. Fighting this struggle in a nation at war was to be no easy task, but the effort led to the further development of black organizations and transformed the worldview of many African American solders and civilians.

Embodying the spirit of the "Double V" campaign, African-American protest groups and newspapers criticized discrimination in the defense program. Two months before the 1940 presidential election, the NAACP, Urban League, and other groups pressed President Roosevelt to take action. The president listened to their protests, but aside from a few token gestures—appointing Howard University Law School dean William Hastie as a "civilian aide on Negro affairs" in the Department of War and promoting Benjamin O. Davis, the senior black officer in the army, to the rank of brigadier general—he responded with little of substance. As a result, during late 1940 the NAACP and other groups staged mass protest rallies around the nation. With the election safely won, the president, anxious not to offend white southern politicians he needed to back his war program, now refused even to meet with black leaders.

In January 1941, A. Philip Randolph, who was president of the Brotherhood of Sleeping Car Porters and who had been working with other groups to get the attention of Roosevelt, called on black people to unify their protests and direct them at the national government. He suggested that 10,000 African Americans march on Washington under the slogan "We loyal Negro-American citizens demand the right to work and fight for our country." In the coming months Randolph helped to create the March on Washington Movement (MOWM), which soon became the largest mass movement of black Americans since the activities of Marcus Garvey's Universal Negro Improvement Association of the 1920s. The MOWM's demands included a presidential order forbidding companies with government contracts from engaging in racial discrimination, eliminating race-based exclusion from defense training courses, and requiring the USES to supply workers on a nonracial basis. Randolph also wanted an order to abolish segregation in the armed forces and the president's support for a law withdrawing the benefits of the National Labor Relations Act from unions that refused to grant membership to black Americans. Departing from the leadership tactics of most other African-American protest groups of the time, Randolph prohibited white

participation and specifically encouraged the participation of the black working class.

Randolph's powerful appeal captured the support of many African Americans who had not before taken part in the activities of middle-class dominated groups like the NAACP. Soon he alarmed the president by raising the number expected to march to 50,000. FDR, fearing that the protest would undermine America's democratic rhetoric and provide grist for the German propaganda mills, dispatched First Lady Eleanor Roosevelt and New York City Mayor Fiorello La Guardia to dissuade Randolph from marching. Their pleas for patience fell on deaf ears, compelling Roosevelt and his top military officials to meet with Randolph and other black leaders. FDR offered a set of superficial changes but the African Americans stood firm in their demands and raised the stakes by increasing their estimate of the number of black marchers coming to Washington to 100,000. By the end of June 1941, the president capitulated and

WHY SHOULD WE MARCH?

What Are Our Immediate Goals?

1. To mobilize five million Negroes into one militant mass for pressure.

2. To assemble in Chicago the last week in May, 1943, for the celebration of

"WE ARE AMERICANS – TOO" WEEK

And to ponder the question of Non-Violent Civil Disobedience and Non-Cooperation, and a Mass March On Washington.

15.000 Negroes Assembled at St. Louis, Missouri
20.000 Negroes Assembled at Chicago, Illinois
23.500 Negroes Assembled at New York City
Millions of Negro Americans all Over This Great
Land Claim the Right to be Free!

FREE FROM WANT!
FREE FROM FEAR!
FREE FROM JIM CROW!

"Winning Democracy for the Negro is Winning the War for Democracy!" — A. Philip Randolph

440

Posters like this sought both to attract black support for A. Philip Randolph's March on Washington Movement and to convince political leaders of the strength of the movement.

had his aides draft Executive Order #8802, prompting Randolph to call off the march. It was a grand moment. "To this day," NAACP leader Roy Wilkins wrote in his autobiography, "I don't know if he would have been able to turn out enough marchers to make his point stick . . . but, what a bluff it was. A tall, courtly black man with Shakespearean diction and the stare of an eagle had looked the patrician Roosevelt in the eye—and made him back down."

Executive Order #8802

On the surface at least, the president's order marked a significant change in the government's stance. It stated in part:

> I do hereby affirm the policy of the United States that there shall be no discrimination in the employment of workers in the defense industry or government because of race, creed, color, or national origin.

The order instructed all agencies engaged in worker training to take appropriate special measures to ensure that such programs were administered without discrimination. To ensure full cooperation with these guidelines, Roosevelt created the Fair Employment Practices Committee (FEPC) with the power to investigate complaints of discrimination. The order said nothing about desegregation of the military, but private assurances were made that the barriers to entry in key services would be lowered.

Executive Order #8802, although the first major presidential action countering discrimination since Reconstruction, was no new Emancipation Proclamation. Black excitement with the order soon turned sour as many industries, particularly in the South, found ways to evade its clear intent and engaged in only token hirings. What the black community learned in this instance and would witness repeatedly in the decades to come was that mere articulation of antidiscrimination principles and the establishment of commissions and committees did not lead to eradication of inequalities. Moreover, the order left out mention of union discrimination. Nonetheless, the threat of the march, the issuance of the executive order, and creation of the FEPC marked the formal acknowledgment by the federal government that it bore some responsibility for protecting black and minority rights in employment. Black activists and their allies would have to continue their fight if the order was to have any meaning. Randolph sought to lead them but would find it difficult to do so because of the opposition of key government agencies—notably the military—the political power of southern congress-

men, and a belief among white people that racial issues could wait for attention until after the war.

RACE AND THE U.S. ARMED FORCES

The demands of A. Philip Randolph and other black leaders for an end to segregation in the armed forces initially met stiffer resistance than their pleas for change in the civilian sector. Black men were expected to serve their country but, at the beginning of the war, most were assigned to segregated service battalions, relegated to noncombat positions, kept out of the more prestigious branches of the service, and faced tremendous obstacles to appointment as commissioned officers. This situation was particularly galling because military segregation was a symbol of the discrimination black men and women encountered in virtually every aspect of their daily lives.

Institutional Racism in the American Military

Much of the armed forces' policy derived from negative attitudes and discriminatory practices common in American society. Reflecting this ingrained racism, a 1925 study by the American War College concluded that African Americans were physically unqualified for combat duty, were by nature subservient and mentally inferior, believed themselves to be inferior to white people, were susceptible to the influence of crowd psychology, could not control themselves in the face of danger, and did not have the initiative and resourcefulness of white people.

Based on this and later studies in 1941 the War Department laid out two key policies for the use of black soldiers. Although they would be taken into the military at the same rate as white inductees, African Americans would be segregated and would serve primarily in noncombat units. Responding with characteristic disdain for those who criticized these policies, Under Secretary of War Robert Patterson wrote:

> The Army is not a sociological laboratory; to be effective it must be organized and trained according to principles which will insure success. Experiments to meet the wishes and demands of the champions of every race and creed for the solution of their problems are a danger to efficiency, discipline and morale and would result in ultimate defeat. Out of these fundamental thoughts have been evolved broad principles relating to the employment of all persons in the military service.

"above and beyond the call of duty"

DORIE MILLER
Received the Navy Cross
at Pearl Harbor, May 27, 1942

The War Department did not hesitate to recognize the heroism of Dorie Miller at Pearl Harbor in this recruitment poster, but it neglected to mention that black sailors were routinely relegated to the kitchens and boiler rooms of navy vessels.

In creating these policies the Army and Navy ignored evidence of the fighting ability exhibited by African Americans in previous wars, and which the heroism of Dorie Miller during the attack on Pearl Harbor confirmed. Miller was the son of Texas sharecroppers who had enlisted in the Navy in 1938 and, like all black sailors in the Navy at the time, had been assigned to mess attendant duty. In other words, he was a cook and a waiter. When the Japanese air force attacked the naval base on December 7, 1941, the twenty-two-year-old Miller was below decks on the battleship *Arizona*. When his captain was seriously wounded, Miller braved bullets to help move him to a more protected area of the deck. He then took charge of a machine gun, shooting down at least two and perhaps as many as six enemy aircraft before running out of ammunition. Miller had never before fired the gun. On May 27, 1942, the navy cited him for "distinguished devotion to

duty, extraordinary courage and disregard for his own personal safety" and awarded him a Navy Cross. Not yet willing to change its policies, the Navy then sent Miller back to mess duty without a promotion.

The Costs of Military Discrimination

Although the War and Navy departments held to the fiction of "separate but equal," in their segregation program, their policies most often gave black Americans inferior resources or excluded them entirely. Segregation at Army camps most often meant that black soldiers were placed in the least desirable spots and denied the use of officers clubs, base stores, and recreational areas. Four-fifths of all training camps were located in the South, where black soldiers were subjected to harassment and discrimination off base as well as on. Even on leave black soldiers were not offered space in the many hotels leased by the government but had to make do with the limited accommodations that had been available to black people before the war. For southern African Americans, even going home in uniform could be a danger. For example, when Rieves Bell of Starkville, Mississippi, arrived for a visit with his family in 1943, three young white men cornered him on a street and attempted to strip off his uniform. Bell fought back and injured one of them with a knife. The army could not save him from the wrath of local civilian authorities who tried and sentenced Bell to three and a half years in the notorious Parchman state penitentiary for the crime of self-defense.

Perhaps most galling was to see German prisoners of war accorded better treatment than African-American soldiers. Veteran Dempsey Travis of Chicago recalled his experiences at Camp Shenango, Pennsylvania: "I saw German prisoners free to move around the camp, unlike black soldiers who were restricted. The Germans walked right into the doggone places like any white American. We were wearin' the same uniform, but we were excluded."

Due to the military's policies, most of the nearly one million African Americans who served during World War II did so in auxiliary units, most notably in the transportation and engineering corps. Soldiers in the transportation corps, almost half of whom were black, loaded supplies and drove them in trucks to the front lines. Operating in the Redball or Whiteball express, the names for the trucking operations used to supply the American Forces as they drove toward Germany in 1944 and 1945, African Americans braved enemy fire and delivered the fuel, ammunition, and other goods that made the fight possible. Black engineers built camps and ports, constructed and repaved roads, and performed a multitude of other tasks in support of frontline troops.

Black soldiers performed well in these tasks but were often subject to unfair military discipline. In Europe, black soldiers were executed in vastly greater numbers than whites even though African Americas made up only 10 percent of the total number of soldiers. One of the most glaring examples of unfair treatment was the Navy's handling of a "mutiny" at its Port Chicago base north of San Francisco. On July 17, 1944, in the worst home-front disaster of the War, an explosion at the base killed over 300 American sailors. Of the 320 men killed in the blast, 202 were black ammunition loaders. In the following month 328 of the surviving ammunition loaders were sent to fill another ship. When 258 of them refused to do so they were arrested and eventually fifty were singled out as the ringleaders. The Navy charged these men with mutiny, convicted them, and sentenced them to terms of imprisonment ranging from eight to fifteen years at Terminal Island in Southern California. The NAACP's Thurgood Marshall filed a brief on behalf of the fifty men arguing that they had been railroaded into prison because of their race, but to no avail.

Soldiers and Civilians Protest Military Discrimination

In military segregation, black American leaders—including A. Philip Randolph; Walter White of the National Association for the Advancement of Colored People (NAACP); both T. Arnold Hill and Lester Granger of the National Urban League; New York Congressman Adam Clayton Powell Jr.; Robert Vann, editor of the *Pittsburgh Courier;* and Mabel K. Staupers of the National Association of Colored Graduate Nurses, among others—identified a potent but vulnerable target. Employing a variety of strategies they successfully mobilized the black civilian workforce, black women's groups, college students, and an interracial coalition to participate in active resistance against this blatant inequality. In time, they were able to provoke an open dialogue with government and military officials at a pivotal moment when America's leaders most desired to present a united democratic front to the world.

Examples of this protest abound. In 1942 the NAACP's *Crisis*, and *Opportunity*, the organ of the National Urban League, published numerous editorials denouncing the Army's segregation policy. Walter White traveled across the country and throughout the world visiting camps and making contacts with black soldiers and their white officers. He inundated the War Department and the president with letters citing examples of improper, hostile, and humiliating treatment of black servicemen by military personnel and in the white communities in which bases were located. Frustration with continued military intransigence, however, forced William Hastie into a most dramatic protest. He tendered his resignation on January 5, 1943.

Black Women in the Struggle to Desegregate the Military

The role of black women in the struggle to desegregate the military has often been overlooked, but they were quite militant and made important contributions to the effort. The reason for this is suggested in a 1942 editorial in the *Crisis* which stated:

> [T]he colored woman has been a more potent factor in shaping Negro society than the white woman has been in shaping white society because the sexual caste system has been much more fluid and ill-defined than among whites. Colored women have worked with their men and helped build and maintain every institution we have. Without their economic aid and counsel we would have made little if any progress.

The most prominent example of black women's struggle is found in the history of the National Association of Colored Graduate Nurses (NACGN). Mabel K. Staupers, executive director of the NACGN, led a particularly aggressive fight to eliminate quotas established by the U.S. Army Nurse Corps. Although many black nurses volunteered their services during World War II, they were refused admittance into the navy, and the army allowed only a limited number to serve. In an effort to draw attention to the unfairness of quotas, Staupers requested a meeting with Eleanor Roosevelt. In November of 1944, the First Lady and Staupers met, and Staupers described black nurses' troubled relationship with the armed forces. She informed the First Lady that eighty-two black nurses were serving 150 patients at the station hospital at Fort Huachuca, Arizona, at a time when the army was complaining of a dire nursing shortage and debating the need to institute a draft of nurses. Staupers expounded on the practice of using black women to care for German prisoners of war. She asked, rhetorically, if this was to be the special role of the black nurse in the war? Staupers elaborated, "When our women hear of the great need for nurses in the

WILLIAM H. HASTIE RESIGNS IN PROTEST

In January 1943, William H. Hastie, who had been on leave from his post as dean of the Howard University Law School, resigned as civilian aide to Secretary of War Henry L. Stimson to protest official failure to outlaw discrimination in the military. He had assumed the position in 1940 and throughout his tenure he had experienced frustration and hostility toward all his efforts to secure equal treatment for black men and women in uniform. In his letter of resignation, which he published in the Chicago Defender, *he explains that the Army Air Forces' reactionary policies and discriminatory practices were the immediate catalyst to his resignation.*

The Army Air Forces are growing in importance and independence. In the post war period they may become the greatest single component of the armed services. Biased policies and harmful practices established in this branch of the army can all too easily infect other branches as well. The situation had become critical. Yet, the whole course of my dealings with the Army Air Forces convinced me that further expression of my views in the form of recommendations within the department would be futile. I, therefore, took the only course which can, I believe, bring results. Public opinion is still the strongest force in American life.

To the Negro soldier and those who influence his thinking, I say with all the force and sincerity at my command that the man in uniform must grit his teeth, square his shoulders and do his best as a soldier, confident that there are millions of Americans outside of the armed services, and more persons than he knows in high places within the military establishment, who will never cease fighting to remove every racial barrier and every humiliating practice which now confront him. But only by being, at all times a first class soldier can the man in uniform help in this battle which shall be fought and won.

When I took office, the Secretary of War directed that all questions of policy and important proposals relating to Negroes should be referred to my office for comment or approval before final action. In December, 1940, the Air Forces referred to me a plan for a segregated training center for Negro pursuit pilots at Tuskegee. I expressed my entire disagreement with the plan, giving my reasons in detail. My views were disregarded. Since then, the Air Command has never on its own initiative submitted any plan or project to me for comment or recommendation. What information I obtained, I had to seek out. Where I made proposals or recommendations, I volunteered them.

This situation reached its climax in late December, 1942, when I learned through army press releases sent out from St. Louis and from the War Department in Washington that the Air Command was about to establish a segregated officer candidate school at Jefferson Barracks, Mo., to train Negro officers for ground duty with the Army Air Forces. Here was a proposal for a radical departure from present army practice, since the officer candidate training program is the one large field where the army is eliminating racial segregation.

Moreover, I had actually written to the Air Command several weeks earlier in an attempt to find out what was brewing at Jefferson Barracks. The Air Command replied as late as December 17, 1942, giving not even the slightest hint of any plan for a segregated officer candidate school. It is inconceivable to me that consideration of such a project had not then advanced far enough for my office to have been consulted, even if I had not made specific inquiry. The conclusion is inescapable that the Air Command does not propose to inform, much less counsel with, this office about its plans for Negroes.

QUESTIONS

1. Why did Hastie publish his letter of resignation in the *Chicago Defender*? Did he resign because he objected to the creation of a segregated officer candidate school or because his office was not consulted about the plans for this initiative?

2. Why did African Americans fight so relentlessly to end segregation in the U.S. military? What did the military represent or symbolize to the nation?

3. Under what circumstances did African Americans appear to accept segregation and the establishment of separate programs such as the Tuskegee Airmen? Why then did African Americans object strenuously to the military's efforts to provide equal but separate facilities and educational programs?

Source: William H. Hastie, "Why I Resigned," *Chicago Defender*, February 6, 1943.

Army and when they enter the service it is with the high hopes that they will be used to nurse sick and wounded soldiers who are fighting our country's enemies and not primarily to take care of these enemies."

Soldiers and sailors also resisted segregation and discrimination while in the service. Their action included well-organized attempts to desegregate officers' clubs. At Freeman Field, Indiana, for example, one hundred black officers refused to back down when their commanders threatened to arrest them for seeking to use the officers' club. In other bases African-American soldiers responded with violence to violence, intimidation, and threats. Their actions, although put down with dispatch, prompted the Army brass to reevaluate their belief in the military efficiency of discrimination.

The Beginning of Military Desegregation

In response to the militancy of black officers, civil rights leaders, and the press, the War Department made changes and began to take on the challenge of reeducating soldiers, albeit in a limited fashion. The Advisory Committee on Negro Troop Policies was charged with coordinating the use of black troops and developing policy on social questions and personnel training. In 1943 the War Department also produced its own propaganda film—*The Negro Soldier*, directed by Frank Capra—to alleviate racial tensions. This patronizing film emphasized the contributions black soldiers had made in the nation's wars since the American Revolution and was designed to appeal to both black and white audiences.

The War Department also attempted to use propaganda to counter black protest groups and the claims of discrimination found in the black press. The key to this effort was fighter Joe Louis, whom the Army believed was "almost a god" to most black Americans. "The possibilities for using him," a secret internal report stated, "are almost unlimited, such as touring the army camps as special instructor on physical training; exhibition bouts, for use in radio or in movies; in a movie appearance a flashback could be shown of Louis knocking out Schmeling, the champion of the Germans." The same report also mentioned other prominent black men and women who had "great value in any propaganda programs. Other athletes like Ray Robinson, also track athletes, etc.; *name* bands like Cab Calloway, Lunceford; stage, screen and concert stars like Ethel Waters, Bill Robinson, Eddie Anderson, Paul Robeson, etc." The effect of this propaganda barrage is impossible to gauge, but it did little to counter the real incidents of prejudice and discrimination that most black people experienced in their daily lives.

Racism remained strong throughout the war, but the persistent push of protest groups and the military's need for manpower gradually loosened its grip. After the attack on Pearl Harbor, nearly all services had to relax previous restrictions on African Americans. The Navy, previously the most resistant of services, began to accept black men as sailors and noncommissioned officers. By 1943 it allowed African Americans into officer training schools. The Marine Corps, exclusively white throughout its history, began taking African Americans in 1942. Black officers were trained in integrated settings in all services except the Army's Air Corps. The War Department even acted to compel recalcitrant commanding officers to recommend black servicemen for admission to the officer training schools, and soon, over two thousand a year were graduated.

Many African Americans also saw combat, although under white officers. Several African-American artillery, tank destroyer, antiaircraft, and combat engineer battalions fought with distinction in Europe and Asia. Military prejudice seemed to be borne out by the poor showing of the all-black 92nd combat division, but investigation revealed that its failure was the result of poor training and leadership by a white officer with no confidence in his men. After the Battle of the Bulge, a massive late-1944 German counterattack, 2,500 black volunteers fought in integrated units. Although the experiment would not be repeated during the war, its success laid the groundwork for later changes. Although subject to many of the same kinds of discrimination as African-American men, African-American women also found expanded opportunities in the military. Approximately 4,000 black women served in the Women's Army Auxiliary Corps (WAACs).

Mabel Staupers's efforts also bore fruit in early 1945. When the War Department claimed that there was a shortage of nurses, Staupers mobilized nursing groups of all races to write letters and send telegrams protesting the discrimination against black nurses in the Army and Navy Nurse Corps. There was an immediate groundswell of public support for the removal of quotas. Buried beneath an avalanche of telegrams from an inflamed public, the War Department declared an end to quotas and exclusion. On January 10, 1945, the Army opened its Nurse Corps to all applicants without regard to race, and five days later the Navy followed suit. Within a few weeks, Phyllis Daley became the first black woman to break the color barrier and be inducted into the Navy's Nurse Corps. Over three hundred nurses were eventually accepted into the Army Nurse Corps.

Black women nurses, like black male servicemen, served in all-black units in the U.S. military during World War II. The War Department assigned them to care for German prisoners of war, but initially prohibited them from caring for sick and wounded white Americans. Under the leadership of Mabel Staupers, black nurses successfully fought against enlistment quotas and other discriminatory treatment.

The Tuskegee Airmen

The most visible group of black soldiers served in the Army Air Force. In January 1941, the War Department announced the formation of an all-black Pursuit Squadron and the creation of a training program at Tuskegee Army Air Field, Alabama, for black pilots. Unlike all other units in the Army, the 99th Squadron and the 332nd Group, made up of the 100th, 301st, and 302nd Squadrons, had black officers. The 99th went to North Africa in April 1943 and flew its first combat mission against the island of Pantelleria on June 2. Later the squadron participated in the air battle over Sicily, operating from its base in North Africa, and supported the invasion of Italy. The squadron regularly engaged German pilots in aerial combat. General Benjamin O. Davis Jr. commanded the 332nd Group when it was deployed to Italy in January 1944. In July, the 99th was added to the 332nd and the Group participated in campaigns in Italy, Romania, France, Germany, and the Balkans.

The Tuskegee Airmen amassed an impressive record. They flew over 15,500 sorties and completed 1,578 missions. During the 200 missions in which they escorted heavy bombers deep into Germany's Rhineland, not one of the "heavies" was lost to enemy fighter opposition. They destroyed 409 enemy aircraft, sank an enemy destroyer, and knocked out numerous ground installations with strafing runs. They were well regarded and recognized for their heroism. They accumulated 150 Distinguished Flying Crosses, one Legion

of Merit, one Silver Star, fourteen Bronze Stars, and 744 Air Medals. Tuskegee pilot Coleman Young (1919–1997, mayor of Detroit 1973–1993) recalled, "once our reputation got out as to our fighting ability, we started getting special requests for our group to escort their group, the bombers. They all wanted us because we were the only fighter group in the entire air force that did not lose a bomber to enemy action. Oh, we were much in demand."

The Transformation of Black Soldiers

A new generation of African Americans became soldiers during World War II and many would emerge from the experience with an enhanced sense of themselves and a commitment to the fight for black equality. Unlike the black soldiers in World War I, a greater percentage of those drafted at the outset of World War II had attended high school and more were either high school or college graduates. Some black soldiers brought "radical" ideas with them as they were drafted and sent to segregated installations. The urban and northern black servicemen and women and many of the southern rural recruits had a strong sense of their own self-worth and dignity. In their study of Chicago, sociologists St. Clair Drake and Horace Cayton noted:

At least half of the Negro soldiers—and Bronzeville's men fall into this class—were city people who had

VOICES

SEPARATE BUT EQUAL TRAINING FOR BLACK ARMY NURSES?

In August 1944, Maple Staupers received this reply from Under Secretary of War Robert Patterson in response to her query about a training center the Army had established at Fort Huachaca, Arizona, for black nurses.

August 7, 1944
Mrs. Mabel K. Staupers R.N.,
Executive Secretary,
National Association
    of Colored Graduate Nurses, Inc.,
1790 Broadway,
New York 19, N.Y.

Dear Mrs. Staupers:

Thank you for your letter of July 19 with reference to the establishment of the first basic training center for Army Negro nurses at Fort Huachuca.

In establishing the first basic training center for Army Negro nurses at Fort Huachuca, the War Department desired that these nurses receive the best possible training and the most valuable experience for the type of service they would be required to render as Army nurses. It is the policy of the War Department to assign Negro nurses to those hospitals where there is a substantial number of Negro troops in relation to the personnel of the entire installation. The trainee at Fort Hauchuca will therefore have the advantage of serving in a facility and under conditions parallel to those under which she will serve as an Army nurse.

You may be assured that the facilities for training afforded Negro nurses at Fort Huachuca will in no way be inferior to those of other similar establishments, and in their subsequent assignments these nurses will have full opportunity to render valuable service to the Army.

Sincerely yours,
(Signed) ROBERT P. PATTERSON
ROBERT P. PATTERSON,
Under Secretary of War

QUESTIONS

1. How does Patterson's letter reflect the U.S. military's position that "separate but equal" did not constitute discrimination against African Americans?

2. Why did Mabel Staupers and the National Association of Colored Graduate Nurses object to the establishment of separate training facilities for black women?

Source: War Department Files, File #2912, National Archives, Washington, DC.

---

lived through a Depression in America's Black Ghettoes, and who had been exposed to unions, the Communist movement, and to the moods of racial radicalism that occasionally swept American cities. Even the rural southern Negroes were different this time—for the thirty years between the First and Second World War has seen a great expansion of school facilities in the South and distribution of newspapers and radios.

Serving in the armed forces provided many African Americans with their first exposure to a world outside the segregated South. Haywood Stephney of Clarksdale, Mississippi, recalled that when he first encountered segregation in the military he simply thought it was supposed to be that way. He explained, "Because you grow up in this situation you don't see but one side of the coin. Having not tasted the freedom or the liberty of being and doing like other folks then you didn't know what it was like over across the street. So we accepted it." Like many others, the experiences he had during the war quickly removed him from "total darkness" and raised fundamental questions for him about the racial system of the nation.

Douglas Conner, another Mississippi veteran, captured the collective understanding of the social and political meaning of the war shared by the men in his unit, the 31st Quartermaster Battalion stationed in Okinawa: "The air people in Tuskegee, Dorie Miller, and the others gave the blacks a sense that they could succeed and compete in a world that had been saying that 'you're nothing.'" Conner insisted that "because of the world war, I think many people, especially blacks, got the idea that we're going back, but we're not going back to business as usual. Somehow we're going to change this nation so that there's more equality than there is now." The personal transformation that Conner and others experienced combined with a number of international, national, and regional forces to lay the foundation for a Second Reconstruction in the American South.

BLACK PEOPLE ON THE HOME FRONT

Just as they did in the military, African Americans on the home front fought a dual war against the Axis and discrimination. Black workers and volunteers helped staff the factories and farms that produced goods for the fight while also purchasing war bonds and participating in other defense activities. At the same time, the changes brought on by the war created new points of conflict

Before World War II, few white women, and still fewer black women, worked in heavy industries, but with so many men in the armed forces, women were recruited for jobs in shipyards and airplane factories. Between 1940 and 1944, the percentage of black women in the industrial workforce increased from 6.8 percent to 18 percent.

while exacerbating preexisting problems and occasionally igniting full-scale riots. Throughout the war, protest groups and the black press continued the fight against employment discrimination and political exclusion.

Black Workers: From Farm to Factory

The war accelerated the migration of African Americans from rural areas to the cities. Even though the farm economy recovered during the war, the lure of high-paying defense jobs and other urban occupations tempted many black farmers to abandon the land. By the 1940s the bitter experiences of the previous decades had made it clear that there was little future in the cotton fields. Boll weevils, competition from other parts of the world, and the rapid advance of mechanization reduced the need for black labor. Indeed, by the end of the war, only 28 percent of black men worked on farms, a decline of 13 percent since 1940. More than 300,000 black men left agricultural labor between 1940 and 1944 alone.

The wartime need for workers, backed by pressure from the government, helped break down some of the barriers to the employment of African Americans in industry. During the war the total number of black workers in nonfarm employment rose from 2,900,000 to 3,800,000. Nearly all industries relaxed their resistance to hiring African-American workers, and thousands moved into previously whites-only jobs. African Americans found employment in the aircraft industry, and likewise tens of thousands were employed in the nation's shipyards.

With so many of their brothers, sons, and fathers away at war, black women increasingly found work outside the laundry and domestic service that had previously been their lot. Nationally 600,000 black women—400,000 of them former domestic servants—shifted into industrial jobs. As one aircraft worker wryly put it, "Hitler was the one that got us out of the white folks' kitchen." Even those women who stayed in domestic work often saw their wages improve as the supply of competing workers dwindled.

The abundance of industrial jobs helped spur and direct the migration of African Americans during and after World War II. Some 1,500,000 migrants, nearly 15 percent of the population, left the South, swelling the black communities in northern and western cities with significant war industries. By 1950 the proportion of the nation's black population living in the South had fallen from 77 percent to 68 percent. The most dramatic rise in black population was in southern California. Because of its burgeoning aircraft industry and the success of civil rights groups and the federal government in limiting discrimination, Los Angeles saw its relatively small African-American community increase by more than 340,000 during the war.

During the war many unions became more open to African-American workers. As black men and women took jobs in industries, they joined unions in large numbers. Between 1940 and 1945, black union membership rose from 200,000 to 1.25 million. Those unions connected to the CIO, particularly the United Automobile Workers, were the most open to black membership, whereas AFL affiliates were the most likely to treat African Americans as second-class members or to continue to exclude them altogether. Some white unionized workers continued to oppose the hiring of black workers, even going on strike to prevent it, but their resistance was often deflected by the union leadership, the government, or employers. The growth in black membership did not mean an end of racism in unions, even in the CIO, but it did provide African Americans a stronger foundation upon which to protest continuing discrimination in employment.

The FEPC during the War

Responding to the ineffectiveness of the Fair Employment Practices Committee during the first years of the war, in May 1943 President Roosevelt issued Executive Order #9346. The order established a new Committee on Fair Employment Practice, increased its budget, and placed its operation directly under the Executive Office of the President. FDR appointed Malcolm Ross, a combative white liberal, to head the committee. Ross proved to be more effective than the committee's previous leadership. He initiated nationwide hearings of cases concerning discrimination in the shipbuilding and railroad industries. These proceedings caused embarrassment for companies and brought some compliance with the FEPC's orders. A more common result, however, was resistance. In Mobile, Alabama, for example, the white employees of the Alabama Dry Dock and Shipbuilding Company opposed the FEPC's efforts to pressure the company to promote twelve of the seven thousand African Americans it employed in menial positions to racially mixed welding crews. The white workers went on a rampage, assaulting fifty African Americans. The FEPC thereupon withdrew its plan and acquiesced to the traditional Jim Crow arrangements in all work assignments. White workers retained their more lucrative positions. As a result of this kind of intransigence, the committee failed to redress most of the grievances of black workers. A concerted effort to continue the committee after the war was soundly defeated.

Anatomy of a Race Riot: Detroit, 1943

One of the bloodiest race riots in the nation's history took place in 1943 in Detroit, Michigan, where black and white workers were competing fiercely over jobs and housing. Relations between the white and black communities in the city had been smoldering for months, with open fighting in the plants and on the streets. White racism, housing segregation, and economic discrimination were part of the problem. The brutality of white police officials was an especially potent factor. Tensions were so palpable that weeks before the riot NAACP leader Walter White had warned the city's leadership that the city could explode in violence at any moment.

The immediate trigger for the riot was a squabble on June 20 between groups of white and black bathers at the segregated city beaches on Belle Isle in the Detroit River. Within a matter of hours, two hundred white sailors from a nearby base joined the white mob that pursued and attacked individual black men and women. A rumor that white citizens had killed a black woman and thrown her baby over the bridge spread across the city. The riot was in full swing, spreading quickly along Woodward Avenue, the city's major thoroughfare, into Paradise Valley where some thirty-five thousand southern black migrants, had, in the spring of 1943, joined the city's already crowded black population. By Monday morning downtown Detroit was overrun with white men roaming in search of more victims. At first the mayor refused to acknowledge that the situation had gotten out of hand, but by Tuesday evening he could no longer deny the crisis.

Six thousand federal troops had to be dispatched to Detroit to restore order. When the violence ended, thirty-four people had been killed (twenty-five black men and women and nine white people), with more than 700 injured. Of the twenty-five black people who died, the Detroit police killed seventeen. The police did not kill any of the white men who assaulted African Americans or committed arson. Property damage exceeded two million dollars and one million man hours were lost in war production.

In the aftermath, the city created the Mayor's Interracial Committee, the first permanent municipal body designed to promote civic harmony and fairness. In spite of the efforts of labor leaders and black leaders, the majority of the white people in Detroit, including the Wayne County prosecutor William E. Dowling, blamed the black press and the NAACP as the primary instigators of the riot. Dowling and others accused the city's black citizens of pushing too hard for economic and political equality and insisted that they operated under communist influence. One of many commissioned reports concluded that black leaders were responsible for provoking the riot because of their comparing "victory over the axis . . . [with] a corresponding overthrow in the country of those forces which . . . prevent true racial equality." In contrast, black leaders, radical trade unionists, and members of other ethnic organizations, especially Jewish groups, pointed fingers towards, "the KKK, the Christian Front, the Black Dragon Society, the National Workers League, the Knights of the White Camelia, the Southern Voters League, and similar organizations based on a Policy of terror and . . . white supremacy."

Old and New Protest Groups on the Home Front

The NAACP grew tremendously during the war and by its end stood poised for even greater achievements. Under the editorial direction of Roy Wilkins, the circulation of the NAACP's *Crisis* grew spectacularly—from 7,000 to 45,000. During the war, the *Crisis* was one of the most important sources for information on the status of black men and women. The NAACP's membership increased from 50,000 in 1940 to 450,000 at the end of the war. Even more important, much of this growth occurred in the South, which had more than 150,000 members by 1945. Supreme Court victories and especially close monitoring of the "Double V" campaign undoubtedly help explain these huge increases.

With success, however, came conflict and ambivalence. Leaders split over the value of integration versus self-segregation and questioned the benefit of relying so heavily on legal cases rather than paying more attention to the concerns and needs of working-class black men and women. Wilkins acknowledged the organization's uncertainty and indecisiveness:

> The war was a great watershed for the NAACP. We had become far more powerful, and now the challenge was to keep our momentum. Everyone knew the NAACP stood against discrimination and segregation, but what was our postwar program to be? Beyond discrimination and segregation, where would we stand on veterans, housing, labor-management relations, strikes, the Fair Employment Practices Commission, organizations at state levels, education? What would we do to advance the fight for the vote in the South? . . . We had a big membership . . . but we didn't know how to use them.

In 1944, a number of southern white liberals joined with African Americans to establish the Southern Regional Council (SRC). This interracial coalition, an important example of the local initiative of private citizens, was devoted to expanding democracy in a region better known for the political and economic oppression and exploitation of its black citizens. The SRC conducted research and focused attention on the political, social, and educational inequalities endemic to black life in the region. Although its patient, gradualist program would soon be overtaken by the events of the 1950s and 1960s, the SRC challenged the facade of southern white supremacy.

In 1942 a far more strident group called the Congress of Racial Equality (CORE) had been formed. This organization would pursue different tactics from those of the NAACP, Urban League, and other existing civil rights groups. CORE began in Chicago when an interracial group of Christian pacifists gathered to find ways to make America live up to the ideals of equality and justice on which it based its war program. Activists James Farmer and Bayard Rustin were key in getting the group off the ground. Unlike the NAACP, CORE was a decentralized, intensely democratic organization. CORE dedicated itself to the principles of nonviolent direct action as expounded by Indian leader Mohandas Gandhi. Over the course of the war this pacifist organization expanded to other large urban areas and challenged segregation in northern cities with sit-ins and other protest tactics that would later be taken up by the civil rights movement.

In addition to the work of the NAACP, SRC, and CORE, African Americans found many other ways to fight discrimination. Women were central to all these efforts. Throughout the 1940s, in countless communities across the South and the Middle West, black women organized women's political councils and other groups to press for integration of public facilities—hospitals, swimming pools, theaters, restaurants—and for the right to pursue collegiate and professional studies. Others were galvanized by the war and took advantage of the limited social and political spaces afforded them to create lasting works in the arts, literature, and popular culture. Women whose names would become virtually synonymous with the modern civil rights movement in the 1950s and 1960s helped to lay its foundation in the World War II era. Ella Baker was accumulating contacts and sharpening her organizing skills as she served as the NAACP field secretary. Rosa Parks began resisting segregation laws on Montgomery buses in the 1940s.

Black college students also began protesting segregation in places of public accommodation. The spark that ignited the Howard University campus civil rights

BAYARD RUSTIN

Bayard Rustin, the preeminent strategist of nonviolent resistance, was born on March 17, 1912, in West Chester, Pennsylvania. Rustin worked behind the scenes to give shape and coherence to the modern civil rights movement. During his youth he belonged to the Young Communist League. But in the 1940s he, along with Pauli Murray and James Farmer, became staff members of the pacifist organization Fellowship of Reconciliation (FOR) and experimented with Gandhian techniques of nonviolent resistance to racial injustice. In 1942, Rustin and Farmer were active in founding the Congress of Racial Equality (CORE). A year later, Rustin refused to be drafted, rejecting even the traditional Quaker compromise of alternative service in an army hospital. Convicted of violating the Selective Service Act, he served three years in a federal penitentiary in Ashland, Kentucky.

While in prison, Rustin honed the philosophy that would guide his life, which he summed up this way:

There are three ways in which one can deal with an injustice. (a) One can accept it without protest. (b) One can seek to avoid it. (c) One can resist the injustice nonviolently. To accept it is to perpetuate it. To avoid it is impossible. To resist by intelligent means, and with an attitude of

Bayard Rustin was a close confidante of A. Philip Randolph in the 1940s and of Martin Luther King, Jr. in the 1950s and 1960s. An uncompromising advocate of nonviolence, Rustin helped organize both the 1941 March on Washington Movement and the march on Washington of 1963.

mutual responsibility and respect, is much the better course.

Upon release from prison, Rustin became race relations secretary for FOR and participated in an endless number of protest organizations. He organized a Free India Committee and directed A. Philip Randolph's Committee against Discrimination in the Armed Forces. He orchestrated CORE's 1947 Journey of Reconciliation, a precursor to the Freedom Rides of 1961, in which sixteen black and white men traveled by bus through the upper South to test new federal laws prohibiting segregated services in interstate transportation. Outside Chapel Hill, North Carolina, the group was assaulted and arrested. Rustin and three of his colleagues were sentenced to thirty days on a road gang, of which he served twenty-two days. In the late 1950s Rustin served as an important adviser to Martin Luther King Jr. and was one of the key figures in nearly all phases of the civil rights movement of the 1950s and 1960s.

Rustin, who was gay, fought oppression all his life. After the ebbtide of the civil rights movement he shifted his attention to combating homophobia. He declared shortly before his death on August 24, 1987, that "the barometer of where one is on human rights questions is no longer the black community, it's the gay community. Because it is the community which is most easily mistreated."

movement came in January 1943. Three sophomore women, Ruth Powell from Massachusetts and Marianne Musgrave and Juanita Morrow from Ohio, sat at a lunch counter near the campus and were refused service. They demanded to see the manager and vowed to wait until he came. Instead of the manager, two policemen arrived who instructed the waitress to serve them. When the check arrived the trio learned that they had

been charged 25 cents instead of the customary 10 cents. They placed a total of 35 cents on the counter, turned to leave, and were arrested. Ruth Power later reported that "the policemen who arrested us told us we were being taken in for investigation because he had no proof that we weren't *subversive agents*." Actually, no charges were lodged against the women. The purpose of their arrest had been to intimidate them, but the incident instead fanned the smoldering embers of resentment in the Howard University student body.

THE TRANSITION TO PEACE

After the German surrender in May 1945 and the Japanese surrender in August 1945, the United States began the transition to peace. Many of the gains of black men and women were wiped away as the armed forces demobilized and the factories began reinstituting the discriminatory hiring systems in place before the conflict. Nonetheless, in 1945 it was clear that segregation would face a huge challenge in the coming years and that the African American community was ready, willing, and able to fight in ways undreamed of in earlier eras.

THE COLD WAR AND INTERNATIONAL POLITICS

As the defeat of the Axis powers neared in early 1945, the United Nations began planning the peace. Within a short time, however, the opposing interests of the Soviet Union and the United States led to a long period of intense hostility that became known as the Cold War. This conflict soon led to a division of Europe into two spheres, with the Soviets dominating part of Germany and the nations to its east and a coalition of democratic capitalist regimes allied with the United States in the west. Thereafter the overriding goal of the United States and its allies was the "containment" of communism. To this end, the North Atlantic Treaty Organization (NATO) was formed in 1949 to provide a military counter-force to Soviet power in Europe while American dollars helped rebuild the western region's war shattered economy. The United States forged a similarly close relationship with Japan. Much of the rest of the world, however, became contested terrain during the Cold War.

As the nations of Asia and Africa gained independence from colonial domination over the ensuing decades, the United States struggled to keep them out of the Soviet orbit. It did so through foreign aid, direct military force, and, occasionally, through the use of clandestine operations run by the Central Intelligence Agency (CIA). These military interventions were matched by a rising diplomatic and propaganda effort aimed at convincing the emerging nations of the world that the United States was a model to be emulated and an ally to be trusted.

The Cold War had an enormous influence on American society at precisely the time when the powerful movement for African-American rights was beginning to emerge. The long conflict resulted in the rise of a permanent military establishment in the United States. Small in scope before World War II, the reorganized American military enlisted millions of men and women by the early 1950s and claimed a massive share of the national budget. The federal government also grew in power during the war and provided a check on the control that white Southerners had so long exercised over race relations in their region. At the same time, American policy makers became acutely concerned about the nation's ability to win the allegiance of Africans and other nonwhite people who formed the population of the emerging nations. The Soviet Union possessed a powerful propaganda advantage because it could discredit American sincerity by pointing to the deplorable state of race relations within the United States. Hence, during the Cold War, external pressures reinforced efforts to change American racial policy.

African Americans in World Affairs: W. E. B. Du Bois and Ralph Bunche

The Cold War gave new importance to the voices of African Americans in world affairs. Two men, W. E. B. Du Bois and Ralph Bunche, represent alternative strategies for responding to this opportunity. Du Bois took a highly critical approach to American policy. For half a century he had linked the fate of African Americans with that of Africans and by 1945 was widely hailed as the Father of Pan-Africanism. In that year he directed the Fifth Pan-African Congress, which met in Manchester, England. The conference was dominated by Africans who had been radicalized by World War II and encouraged the body to adopt militant resolutions denouncing Western imperialism. Du Bois himself identified the United States as a protector of the colonial system and thus opposed its stance in the Cold War. His implication was thus clear when, on returning from the Manchester congress, Du Bois declared,

> We American Negroes should know . . . until Africa is free, the descendants of Africa the world over cannot escape their chains . . . . The NAACP should therefore put in the forefront of its program the freedom of Africa in work and wage, education and health, and the complete abolition of the colonial system.

In contrast to Du Bois, scholar diplomat Ralph Bunche opted to work within the American system.

Bunche held a Harvard doctorate in government and international relations and had spent much of the 1930s studying the problems of African Americans. During World War II the American government found his expertise on Africa of tremendous value and Bunche became one of the key policy makers for the region. Bunche's analysis of events and changes in Africa and the Far East in the aftermath of World War II led to his appointment as adviser to the United States delegation at the San Francisco conference that drafted the United Nations (UN) Charter. In 1948 he served as Acting Mediator of the UN Special Committee on Palestine, and in the following year he negotiated an armistice agreement between Egypt and Israel. He received the Spingarn Medal of the NAACP in 1949 and the following year became the first African American to receive the Nobel Peace Prize (1950). Although Bunche worked in concert with national policy makers, he was committed to winning independence for African nations and freedom for his own people. As he wrote:

> Today, for all thinking people, the Negro is the shining symbol of the true significance of democracy. He has demonstrated what can be achieved with democratic liberties even when grudgingly and incompletely bestowed. But the most vital significance of the Negro . . . to American society . . . is the fact that democracy which is not extended to all of the nation's citizens is a democracy that is mortally wounded.

Anticommunism at Home

The rising tensions with the USSR had a profound impact on all aspects of domestic life in the United States. Conservatives used fears of communist subversion to attack anyone who advocated change in America. This included people who were, or had been, members of the Communist party, union members, liberals, and people who had fought for African-American rights. The Truman administration responded to fears of subversion by instituting government loyalty programs. Government employees were dismissed for the merest suspicion of disloyalty. Militant American anticommunism reached a feverish peak in the immediate postwar years and gave rise to an explosion of red-baiting hysteria that led to the rise of Wisconsin Republican Senator Joseph McCarthy (1909–1957) and the House Un-American Activities Committee (HUAC). The relentless pursuit of "communist sympathizers" by McCarthy and HUAC ruined many careers. HUAC in particular hounded people in the media and in the entertainment industry. Even so prominent a figure as W. E. B. Du Bois was ripe

for attack. On February 8, 1951, the House Un-American Activities Committee indicted him for allegedly serving as an "agent of a foreign principal" in his work with the Peace Information Center. In November a federal judge dismissed all charges against Du Bois. The government had been unable to prove that he was an agent of communism. Despite Du Bois's past contributions, fear and personal malice prevented most African-American leaders from coming to his defense.

Paul Robeson

Paul Robeson was one of the most tragic victims of these anticommunist witch hunts. This fine scholar and star collegiate athlete, Columbia Law School graduate, consummate performer, and star of stage and screen had always been an advocate for the rights of African Americans and workers. During the 1930s he worked closely with the Communist party (although he was never a member), becoming one of the most famous defenders of the Soviet Union. Many leftists of the time became disaffected with the USSR after its 1939 pact with Hitler and after its brutal repressiveness became clear. Robeson, however, doggedly stuck to his belief in Soviet communism through the 1940s and beyond.

In the late 1940s, Robeson's pro-Soviet views and inflammatory statements aroused the ire of the U.S. government and its red hunters. A statement he made at the World Congress of the Defenders of Peace in Paris in 1949 provoked particular outrage. "It is unthinkable," Robeson said, "that American Negroes would go to war on behalf of those [the United States] who have oppressed us for generations against a country [the Soviet Union] which in one generation has raised our people to full human dignity of mankind." Later in 1949 crowds of rock-throwing locals twice disrupted a Robeson concert in Peekskill, New York, the first time preventing the concert from being held, the second time terrorizing performers and audience members at the concert's conclusion.

Throughout the 1940s Robeson consistently linked the struggles of black America with the struggles of black Africa, brown India, yellow Asia, the black men and women of Brazil and Haiti, and oppressed workers in Mexico and throughout South America. Robeson also refused to sign an affidavit concerning past membership in the Communist party. In response, the U.S. State Department revoked his passport in 1950, explaining that "the action was taken because the Department considers that Paul Robeson's travel abroad at this time would be contrary to the best interest of the United States." The travel ban remained in effect until ruled unconstitutional by the Supreme Court in 1958.

Robeson had combined his art and his politics to launch a sustained attack against racial discrimination, segregation, and the ideology of white supremacy and black inferiority as practiced in American society. During the Cold War the state would tolerate no such dissent by even a world-acclaimed black artist.

Henry Wallace and the 1948 Presidential Election

Robeson's struggles illustrate the way in which conservative attacks choked off left-wing involvement in the struggle for black equality. The increasing importance of black votes to Democrats, however, meant that key elements of the African American liberation struggle remained at the center of national politics. Nowhere was this more apparent than in the 1948 presidential election.

President Harry S. Truman was not expected to win this election because he faced a strong challenge from Thomas Dewey, the popular and well-financed Republican governor of New York. Truman's problems were compounded by a challenge from former Secretary of Commerce Henry Wallace, Roosevelt's vice president from 1941 to 1945. Wallace ran on the ticket of the communist-backed Progressive Party, which sought to take the votes of liberals, leftists, and civil rights advocates disappointed by Truman's moderation. Wallace also supported a peaceful accommodation with the Soviet Union. In order to undercut Wallace's challenge, Truman began to press Congress to pass liberal programs.

Black votes in key northern states were central to Truman's strategy for victory. African Americans in these tightly contested areas could make the difference between victory and defeat, so Truman, to retain their allegiance, sought to demonstrate his administration's support of civil rights. In January 1948 he embraced the findings of his biracial Committee on Civil Rights and called for their enactment into law. The committee's report, *To Secure These Rights*, was a blueprint for changing the racial caste system in the United States. It recommended passage of federal antilynching legislation, ending discrimination at the ballot box, abolishing the poll tax, desegregating the military, and a whole range of other measures.

The reaction of white southern politicians was swift and threatening, causing Truman to pause; but as the election neared, fear of black abandonment at the polls grew to such an extent that the party's convention passed a strong pro–civil rights plank. Many white Southerners, led by South Carolina's Governor Strom Thurmond, bolted the convention and formed their own States' Rights, or "Dixiecrat" party. The Dixiecrats carried four states in the election; Wallace carried none. The failure of the bulwark of white supremacy to prevent the Democratic party from advocating African-American rights, and Truman's ultimate victory despite the defection of hard-line racists, represented a profound turning point in American politics.

Desegregating the Armed Forces

The importance of the black vote, the fight for the allegiance of the emerging nations, and the emerging civil rights movement hastened the desegregation of the military. In February 1948, a Communist coup in Czechoslovakia raised the possibility of war between the United States and the Soviet Union and heightened concerns among military leaders about the willingness of African Americans to serve yet again in a Jim Crow Army. When President Truman reinstated the draft in March 1948, A. Philip Randolph—who, in a replay of the March on Washington scenario, had formed the League for Non-Violent Civil Disobedience against Military Segregation in 1947—warned the nation that black men and women were fed up with segregation and Jim Crow and would not take a Jim Crow draft lying down. New York Congressman Adam Clayton Powell Jr. also supported this stance. He declared that there weren't enough jails in America to hold the black men who would refuse to bear arms in a Jim Crow army. On June 24, 1948, the Soviet Union heightened tensions even further when it imposed a blockade on West Berlin. On July 26, Truman, anticipating war between the superpowers and hoping to shore up his support among black voters for the approaching November elections, issued Executive Order 9981, officially desegregating the armed forces.

Executive Order 9981, which mandated "equality of treatment and opportunity for all persons in the armed services without regard to race, color, religion, or national origin," signaled the victorious culmination of a decades-long struggle by black civilians and soldiers to win full integration into the nation's military. After Truman signed the order, Randolph and Grant Reynolds, a former minister and co-chair of the League for Nonviolent Civil Disobedience against Military Segregation, disbanded the organization and called off marches planned for Chicago and New York.

Not until 1950 and the outbreak of the Korean War, however, was Truman's order fully implemented. The war reflected the American Cold-War policy of containment, which was intended to stop what American leaders believed to be a worldwide conspiracy orchestrated by Moscow to spread communism. In 1950, North Koreans, allied to the Soviets, attacked the American-supported government in South Korea and launched the "hot war" in the midst of the Cold War. After the North Koreans moved into South Korean territory, the United States intervened. Heavy casualties early in the war depleted many white combat units. Thus, early in 1951 the Army acted on Truman's executive order and authorized the formal integration of its units in Korea. By 1954 the Army had disbanded its last all-black units and the armed forces became one of the first sectors of American society to abandon segregation.

THE ROAD TO BROWN

In 1954, with the United States Supreme Court's decision in *Brown v. Board of Education of Topeka, Kansas*, progress in the desegregation of American society moved from the military into the civilian realm. Ultimately, the *Brown* decision would undermine state-sanctioned segregation in all aspects of American life. The NAACP's legal program of the 1920s and 1930s was largely responsible for this turn of events. In 1940 the NAACP set up the Legal Defense and Educational Fund (NAACP-LDF) as a tax-exempt agency to pursue its assault on the legal foundations of race inequality in American education. Thereafter, NAACP-LDF fought segregation and discrimination in education, housing, employment, and politics. In the first years of its existence, attorneys for the Fund won a series of stunning victories including a 1944 United States Supreme Court decision, *Smith v. Allwright*, declaring white primaries to be unconstitutional. The life and career of one of the NAACP-LDF lawyers, Constance Baker Motley, symbolizes the struggle to overcome all manner of exclusion

in American life and the coalescence of disparate forces that carried the seeds of the coming revolution. We use Motley as our guide on the road to Brown.

Constance Baker Motley and Black Lawyers in the South

Constance Baker Motley was born in 1921 to immigrant parents, Rachel Huggins and Willoughby Alva Baker, from Nevis, in the British West Indies. She grew up in a tightly knit West Indian community in New Haven, Connecticut. The members of New Haven's black community, including Baker's parents, worked as domestics or in service jobs for the Yale University community. Baker attended integrated schools and experienced episodic racism, including being refused admission to a local beach or to a roller-skating rink. During her high school years, Baker developed a strong racial consciousness. She recalled: "[M]y interest in civil rights [was] a very early interest which developed when I was in high school. The fact that I was a Black, a woman, and a member of a large, relatively poor family was also the base of this great ambition [to enter the legal profession]."

The most important event in her early life was the lecture that George Crawford, a 1903 Yale Law School graduate, who worked as an NAACP lawyer in the New Haven community, gave at the local Dixwell Community Center. The talk concerned the Supreme Court decision in *State of Missouri ex rel. Gaines v. Canada*. Young Baker listened with rapt attention as Crawford explained that the University of Missouri's law school had denied Gaines admission but had offered to pay his tuition expenses to an out-of-state school. The NAACP Legal Committee under Charles H. Houston's leadership won a victory before the U.S. Supreme Court when it ruled that the state had violated the clause in the Fourteenth Amendment mandating that state laws provide equal protection regardless of race. After *Gaines*, states were required to furnish within their borders facilities for legal education for black people equal to those offered white citizens.

Baker desperately wanted to go to law school but there was no money in her household even for college. For a year and a half following graduation from high school in 1939, Baker earned $50 a month varnishing chairs for a building restoration project under the auspices of the National Youth Administration. In 1940, however, Baker came to the attention of Clarence Blakeslee, a local white businessman and philanthropist who, after hearing her speak so eloquently at a meeting of black and white community residents, offered to finance her education. She attended Fisk University until

THE ROAD TO *BROWN*	
1938	*Missouri ex rel. Gaines v. Canada*
1948	*Sipuel v. Oklahoma State Board of Regents*
1950	*McLaurin v. Oklahoma*
	Sweatt v. Painter
1954	*Brown v. Board of Education of Topeka*

Black attorneys Arthur Shores and Constance Baker Motley endured many hardships and even assaults as they tried school desegregation cases in the South. Here they leave the Federal Court in Birmingham after an unsuccessful attempt to force the University of Alabama to accept a black student.

1942 and then transferred to New York University where she earned a bachelor's degree in economics in 1943. Afterward Columbia University Law School accepted her, making her the second black woman ever to attend the school. In 1946, shortly after she finished her legal training she married a former New York University law student Joel Motley and went to work with the NAACP's Legal Defense and Education Fund.

Constance Baker, now Constance Baker Motley, first met Thurgood Marshall in October 1945 when he hired her as a law clerk during her second year in law school. Marshall assigned her to work on the hundreds of Army court martial cases filed after World War II. Motley recalled, "From the first day I knew that this was where I wanted to be. I never bothered interviewing anywhere else." She added, "But for this fortuitous event, I do not think that I would have gotten very far as a lawyer. Women were simply not hired in those days."

In the late 1940s the NAACP-LDF's attack on inequality in graduate education intensified and provided the basis for a full-scale assault on segregation. No longer would the organization be satisfied only to push for fulfillment of the promise of "separate but equal" facilities. In 1948 Ada Lois Sipuel was denied admission to the University of Oklahoma Law School because she was black. The U.S. Supreme Court, signaling that it was willing to take a more activist stance, quickly heard the case and ordered Oklahoma, in *Sipuel v. Board of Regents of the University of Oklahoma*, to "provide [a legal education] for [Sipuel] in conformity with the equal protection clause of the Fourteenth Amendment and provide it as soon as it does for applicants of any other group." Another case, *Sweatt v. Painter*, which the Supreme Court decided in 1950, began when the University of Texas at Austin attempted to circumvent court orders to admit Herman Sweatt into its law school by creating a separate facility consisting of three basement rooms, a small library, and a few instructors who would lecture to him alone. The court ruled that the University of Texas had deprived Sweatt of intangibles such as "the essential ingredient of a legal education . . . the opportunity for students to discuss the law with their peers and others with whom they would be associated professionally in later life." On the same day the Justices ruled in *Sweatt*, they also declared illegal the University of Oklahoma's segregation of G. W. McLaurin from white students attending the graduate school of education. In these important, precedent-setting cases, the U.S. Supreme Court signaled a readiness to reconsider the "separate-but-equal" doctrine and to redefine the meaning of the "equal protection of the laws" clause.

A year after the *Sweatt* and *McLaurin* decisions, black parents and their lawyers filed suits in the states of Kansas, South Carolina, Virginia, Delaware, and the District of Columbia asking the courts to apply the qualitative test of the *Sweatt* case to elementary and secondary schools and to declare the "separate-but-equal" doctrine invalid in public education.

This black student at the University of Oklahoma was not allowed to sit in a classroom with white students. It took two Supreme Court decisions to end such segregation at the University of Oklahoma.

Brown and the Coming Revolution

It was not easy being a black lawyer in the South handling civil rights cases. Black lawyers were frequently assaulted. On February 27, 1942, for example, NAACP attorney Leon A. Ransom was attacked by a former deputy sheriff in the hall of the Davidson County Courthouse in Nashville, Tennessee. The *Crisis* reported:

> The attack came when Ransom walked out into the hall from the courtroom where he was sitting with Z. Alexander Looby, local NAACP attorney, on a case involving the exclusion of Negroes from a jury . . . . When the scuffle began, Negroes who would have aided Ransom were held back by a former constable (white) named Hill, who drew his gun and shouted: "We are going to teach these northern Negroes not to come down here raising fancy court questions."

At Ransom's death in 1954, Thurgood Marshall eulogized:

> Negro Americans, whether they know it or not, owe a great debt of gratitude to Andy Ransom and men like him who battled in the courts down a span of years to bring us to the place we now occupy in the enjoyment of our constitutional rights as citizens, in helping to build up the NAACP legal program step by step, in the skill which he gave to individual cases

and to the planning of strategy, Dr. Ransom left a legacy to the whole population.

It was no less difficult for a black woman lawyer to venture into the South in search of justice. Black attorney Derrick Bell, who also worked for the LDF, said of Motley's work,

> Nothing in the Southern lawyers' background could have prepared them for Connie. To them Negro women were either mammies, maids, or mistresses. None of them had ever dealt with a Negro woman on a peer basis, much less on a level of intellectual equality, which in this case quickly became superiority.

Motley was keenly aware of the precarious nature of her situation. "Often a southern judge would refer to men attorneys as Mister, but would make a point of calling me 'Connie,' since traditionally Black women in the South were only called by their first name." Among the other hardships of being a black lawyer in the South arguing civil rights was housing. Motley recalled that when in a southern town for a long trial, "I knew that it was going to be impossible to stay in a decent hotel." These lawyers had to depend upon the good graces and courage of local people. Motley explained, "Usually in these situations a Black family would agree to put you up. But there was so much publicity involved with civil rights cases that no Black family dared have us—they were too afraid." While in Mississippi arguing a teachers' equalization of salaries case, Motley, declared, "A Black doctor invited us to dinner, but that was about it." She privately mused, "I wonder how many lawyers have had the experience of preparing for trial in a flophouse. That was the only room I could get."

The black parents of Scott's Branch School in Clarendon County, South Carolina, had approached R.W. Elliott, the chairman of the school board, with a modest request. There were 6,531 black students and only 2,375 whites students enrolled in the county's schools. Although the county had thirty buses to convey the white students to their schools, not one bus was available to black school children. Some of the black students had to walk as much as eighteen miles round trip each day. Once they arrived they entered buildings heated by wood stoves and lit by kerosene lamps. For a drink of water or to go to the toilet they had to go outdoors.

With the encouragement of AME pastor and schoolteacher, the Reverend Joseph A. DeLaine, the parents mustered the courage and resolve to petition the school board for buses. Elliott's memorable reply was short: "We ain't got no money to buy a bus for your nigger children." In 1949 DeLaine paid a visit to the NAACP

officials in Columbia and Thurgood Marshall was there. On December 20, 1950, Harry Briggs, a navy veteran, and twenty-four other Clarendon County residents filed suit against the Summerton School District (Clarendon District 22). The case, *Briggs v. Elliott*, was the first legal challenge to elementary school segregation to originate in the South. Meanwhile, however, four other cases in different parts of the country were inexorably making their way up through the federal courts. These would be combined into one case that would decide the fate of the *Plessy* doctrine of "separate but equal."

The years of preparation and hardship paid off. Motley worked with the dream team of black lawyers, an inner circle of advisers that included Louis Redding from Wilmington, Delaware; James Nabrit from Washington, D.C.; Robert Ming from Chicago; psychologist Kenneth Clark from New York; and historian John Hope Franklin to prepare the case, *Brown v. Board of Education of Topeka*, and argue it before the United States Supreme Court. In addition, Motley, Robert Carter, Jack Greenberg, and Marshall sought assistance from Spottswood Robinson of Richmond, Virginia, and read papers prepared by historians C. Vann Woodward and Alfred Kelly about the original equalitarian intentions of the post–Civil War amendments and other legislation.

In his argument, Marshall appealed to the Court to

> meet the Plessy doctrine head on and declare that it is erroneous. It stands mirrored today as a legal aberration, the faulty conception of an era dominated by provincialism, by intense emotionalism in race relations . . . and by the preaching of a doctrine of racial superiority that contradicted the basic concept upon which our society was founded. Twentieth century America, fighting racism at home and abroad, has rejected the race views of *Plessy v. Ferguson* because we have come to the realization that such views obviously tend to preserve not the strength but the weakness of our heritage.

By the time Marshall made this argument, black intellectuals, scholars, and activists and their progressive white allies had closed ranks in support of integration. To suggest alternatives as the goal for African Americans was to find oneself swimming against the current.

During late 1953 and early 1954, the newly sworn in Chief Justice Earl Warren brought the court in support of Marshall's position. On May 17, 1954, the court ruled unanimously in favor of the NAACP lawyers and their clients that a classification based solely on race

A jubilant George E. Hayes (left), Thurgood Marshall (center), and James Nabrit (right) share a triumphant moment following the 1954 Supreme Court decision in *Brown v. Board of Education of Topeka*.

violated the Fourteenth Amendment to the U.S. Constitution. In a stirring passage Warren declared,

> We come then to the question presented: Does segregation of children in public schools solely on the basis of race, even though the physical facilities and other 'tangible' factors may be equal, deprive the children of the minority group of equal educational opportunities? We believe that it does . . . . To separate them from others of similar age and qualifications solely because of their race generates a feeling of inferiority as to the status in the community that may affect their hearts and minds in a way unlikely ever to be undone . . . . We conclude that in the field of public education the doctrine of "separate but equal" has no place. Separate educational facilities are inherently unequal.

The *Brown* decision would eventually lead to the dismantling of the entire structure of Jim Crow laws that regulated important aspects of black life in America: movement, work, marriage, education, housing, even death and burial. The *Brown* decision, more than any other case, signaled the emerging primacy of equality as a guide to constitutional decisions. This and subsequent decisions helped to advance the rights of other minorities and women. As Motley, reflecting, said, "In the *Brown* case and in the decisions that followed, we blazed a trail for others by showing the competence of Black lawyers."

CONCLUSION

The years between 1940 and 1954 constituted a dynamic period of black activism and witnessed a rising international consciousness among African Americans. The quest for racial justice in the military and on the home front became an integral part of the ongoing struggle for economic, political, and social progress. President Roosevelt's Executive Order #8802 was a significant victory for A. Philip Randolph's March on Washington Movement and for black workers who were able to appeal racial discrimination in defense industries to the Fair Employment Practices Commission. The rise of fascism in Europe alarmed black and white Americans who correctly perceived ideologies based on racial tyranny and state dominance to be inimical to individual freedom and democracy. The crisis of World War II also had far-reaching consequences. Black servicemen and servicewomen were profoundly transformed by this conflict.

Following the victory in World War II, the Cold War created a climate in America that was at once hospitable and hostile to the emerging African-American freedom movement. Radicals such as Paul Robeson and W. E. B. Du Bois found no place in the movement or American society in general. Moderate organizations, such as the NAACP-LDF, pursuing their goals within the ideological and legal constraints of the nation, would meet with some success. The coming civil rights movement would, however, soon expand this narrow field of action and pave the way for a more varied, vibrant, and successful challenge to racism.

REVIEW QUESTIONS

1. How did World War II alter the status of African Americans? What were some of the consequences of large numbers of black servicemen participating in battles on European fronts against the forces of fascism and Nazism?

2. Discuss the participation of black women in the campaign to desegregate the United States military. Discuss the participation of black women in the Abraham Lincoln Brigade. What strategies did Mabel Staupers employ to win acceptance of black women into the nurses corps of the various military branches?

3. What were the consequences of the "Double V" campaign? How did African-American civilians indicate their support of black servicemen? What institutional resources were African Americans able to marshal in their campaign for victory against racism at home?

4. What impact did World War II have on the status of black workers in America? Assess the significance of A. Philip Randolph's March on Washington Movement and President Roosevelt's response to it.

5. Discuss the origins of the Cold War and the significance it held for black activism. How did the World War II era promote the rising internationalization of African-American consciousness? How did the state department attempt to downplay black dissent in America, and why?

6. Discuss the importance of 1954 as a watershed year in the history of African Americans in the twentieth century. Why did President Harry S. Truman decide to desegregate the U.S. military? Discuss the decades of preparation by black lawyers that resulted in the victorious *Brown* decision. Describe the conditions black men and women lawyers labored under during the long years of fighting antisegregation cases in the South.

TIMELINE

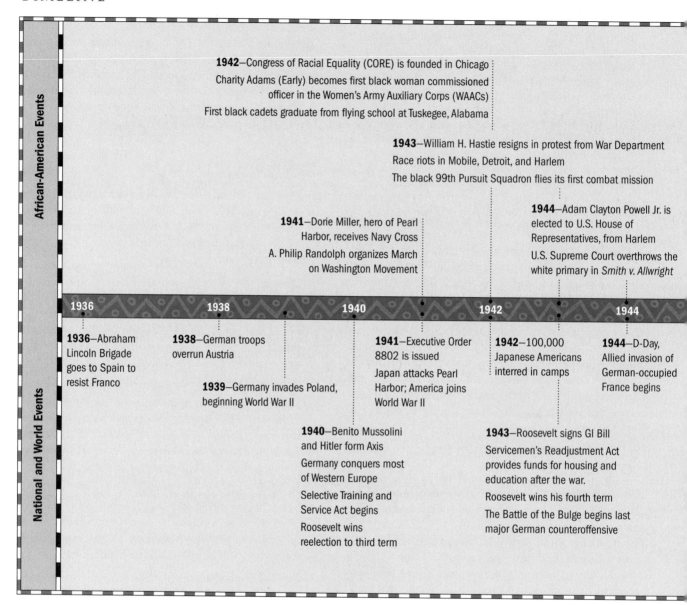

African-American Events

1942—Congress of Racial Equality (CORE) is founded in Chicago
Charity Adams (Early) becomes first black woman commissioned officer in the Women's Army Auxiliary Corps (WAACs)
First black cadets graduate from flying school at Tuskegee, Alabama

1943—William H. Hastie resigns in protest from War Department
Race riots in Mobile, Detroit, and Harlem
The black 99th Pursuit Squadron flies its first combat mission

1941—Dorie Miller, hero of Pearl Harbor, receives Navy Cross
A. Philip Randolph organizes March on Washington Movement

1944—Adam Clayton Powell Jr. is elected to U.S. House of Representatives, from Harlem
U.S. Supreme Court overthrows the white primary in *Smith v. Allwright*

1936   1938   1940   1942   1944

National and World Events

1936—Abraham Lincoln Brigade goes to Spain to resist Franco

1938—German troops overrun Austria

1939—Germany invades Poland, beginning World War II

1941—Executive Order 8802 is issued
Japan attacks Pearl Harbor; America joins World War II

1942—100,000 Japanese Americans interred in camps

1944—D-Day, Allied invasion of German-occupied France begins

1940—Benito Mussolini and Hitler form Axis
Germany conquers most of Western Europe
Selective Training and Service Act begins
Roosevelt wins reelection to third term

1943—Roosevelt signs GI Bill
Servicemen's Readjustment Act provides funds for housing and education after the war.
Roosevelt wins his fourth term
The Battle of the Bulge begins last major German counteroffensive

RECOMMENDED READING

Richard Kluger. *Simple Justice: The History of "Brown v. Board of Education" and Black America's Struggle for Equality*. New York: Knopf, 1976. An excellent treatment of the historical events leading up to the *Brown* decision and the local individuals and national leaders who played instrumental roles in the legal challenge to Jim Crow segregation in the South.

Genna Rae McNeil. *Groundwork: Charles Hamilton Houston and the Struggle for Civil Rights*. Philadelphia:

University of Pennsylvania Press, 1983. An excellent biography of the brilliant Howard University Law School Dean who, as head of the NAACP Legal Council, planned the legal strategy that resulted in the *Brown* decision and transformed American civil rights jurisprudence.

Paula F. Pfeffer. *A. Philip Randolph, Pioneer of the Civil Rights Movement*. Baton Rouge: Louisiana State University Press, 1990. A richly insightful biography of a pioneering labor leader and activist whose March on Washington Movement in 1941 was essential to

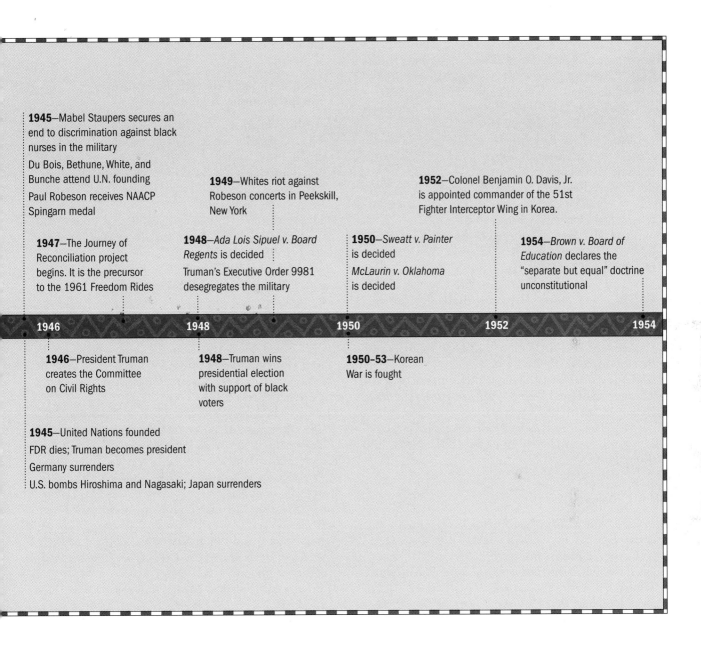

1945—Mabel Staupers secures an end to discrimination against black nurses in the military

Du Bois, Bethune, White, and Bunche attend U.N. founding

Paul Robeson receives NAACP Spingarn medal

1949—Whites riot against Robeson concerts in Peekskill, New York

1952—Colonel Benjamin O. Davis, Jr. is appointed commander of the 51st Fighter Interceptor Wing in Korea.

1947—The Journey of Reconciliation project begins. It is the precursor to the 1961 Freedom Rides

1948—*Ada Lois Sipuel v. Board Regents* is decided

Truman's Executive Order 9981 desegregates the military

1950—*Sweatt v. Painter* is decided

McLaurin v. Oklahoma is decided

1954—*Brown v. Board of Education* declares the "separate but equal" doctrine unconstitutional

| 1946 | 1948 | 1950 | 1952 | 1954 |

1946—President Truman creates the Committee on Civil Rights

1948—Truman wins presidential election with support of black voters

1950–53—Korean War is fought

1945—United Nations founded

FDR dies; Truman becomes president

Germany surrenders

U.S. bombs Hiroshima and Nagasaki; Japan surrenders

the formation of the first Fair Employment Practices Committee and the integration of the armed services.

Mark V. Tushnet. *Making Civil Rights Law: Thurgood Marshall and the Supreme Court, 1936-1961*. New York: Oxford University Press, 1994. A fine overview of Charles Houston's protege and his impressive legal campaign against Jim Crow in numerous cases argued before the United States Supreme Court.

ADDITIONAL BIBLIOGRAPHY

African Americans and the Military

Allen, Robert. *Port Chicago Mutiny: The Story of the Largest Mass Mutiny in U.S. Naval History*. New York: Warner Books–Amistad Books, 1989.

Dalfiume, Richard. *Desegregation of the U.S. Armed Forces: Fighting on Two Fronts 1939–1953*. Columbia: University of Missouri Press, 1969.

Dryden, Charles W. *A-Train: Memoirs of a Tuskegee Airman*. Tuscaloosa: University of Alabama Press, 1997.

Earley, Charity Adams. *One Woman's Army: A Black Officer Remembers the WAC.* College Station: Texas A & M University Press, 1989.

Hine, Darlene Clark. *Black Women in White: Racial Conflict and Cooperation in the Nursing Profession, 1890–1950.* Bloomington: Indiana University Press, 1989.

Lee, Ulysses. *The Employment of Negro Troops.* Washington, DC: Center of Military History, 1990.

McMillen, Neil, ed. *Remaking Dixie: The Impact of World War II on the American South.* Jackson: University Press of Mississippi, 1997.

Motley, Mary Penick. *The Invisible Soldier: The Experience of the Black Soldier, World War Two.* Detroit: Wayne State University Press, 1975.

Osur, Alan M. *Blacks in the Army Air Forces during World War II: The Problem of Race Relations.* Washington, DC: Office of Air Force History, 1977.

Potter, Lou. *Liberators: Fighting on Two Fronts in World War II.* New York: Harcourt Brace Jovanovich, 1992.

Sandler, Stanley. *Segregated Skies: All-Black Combat Squadrons of WWII.* Washington: DC: Smithsonian Institution Press, 1992.

Sitkoff, Howard. "Racial Militancy and Interracial Violence in the Second World War." *Journal of American History* 58, no. 3 (1971): 663–83.

Stillwell, Paul, ed. *The Golden Thirteen: Recollections of the First Black Naval Officers.* Annapolis, MD: Naval Institute Press, 1993.

Black Urban Studies

Broussard, Albert. *Black San Francisco: The Struggle for Racial Equality in the West, 1900-1954.* Lawrence: University of Kansas Press, 1993.

Capeci, Dominic. *The Harlem Riot of 1943.* Philadephia: Temple University Press, 1977.

Capeci, Dominic. *Race Relations in Wartime Detroit: The Sojourner Truth Housing Controversy of 1942.* Philadelphia: Temple University Press, 1984.

Capeci, Dominic, and Martha Wilkerson. *Layered Violence: The Detroit Rioters of 1943.* Jackson: University Press of Mississippi, 1991.

Drake, St. Clair, and Horace R. Cayton. *Black Metropolis: A Study of Negro Life in a Northern City.* New York: Harcourt Brace, 1945.

Meier, August, and Elliott Rudwick. *Black Detroit and the Rise of the UAW.* New York: Oxford University Press, 1979.

Shogan, Robert, and Tom Craig. *The Detroit Race Riot: A Study in Violence.* New York: Chilton Books, 1964.

Thomas, Richard W. *Life for Us Is What We Make It: Building Black Community in Detroit, 1915–1945.* Bloomington: Indiana University Press, 1992.

Black Americans, Domestic Radicalism, and International Affairs

Berman, William C. *The Politics of Civil Rights in the Truman Administration.* Columbus: Ohio State University Press, 1970.

Blum, John Morton. *V Was for Victory: Politics and American Culture during World War II.* New York: Harcourt Brace Jovanovich, 1996.

Dudziak, Mary L. "Josephine Baker, Racial Protest and the Cold War." *The Journal of American History* 81, no. 2 (1994): 543–570.

Freeland, Richard M. *The Truman Doctrine and the Origins of McCarthyism.* New York: New York University Press, 1985.

Garfinkel, Herbert. *When Negroes March: The March on Washington Movement in the Organizational Politics for FEPC.* New York: Atheneum, 1973.

Harris, Joseph. *African American Reactions to War in Ethiopia, 1936–1941.* Baton Rouge: Louisiana State University Press, 1994.

Horne, Gerald. *Black and Red: W. E. B. Du Bois and the Afro-American Response to the Cold War.* Albany: State University of New York Press, 1986.

Kapur, Sudarshan. *Raising Up a Prophet: The Afro-American Encounter with Gandhi.* Boston: Orbis, 1992.

Lipsitz, George. *Rainbow at Midnight: Labor and Culture in the 1940s.* Urbana: University of Illinois Press, 1994.

Meier, August, and Elliott Rudwick. *CORE: A Study in the Civil Rights Movement, 1942–1968.* Urbana: University of Illinois Press, 1975.

O'Brien, Gail Williams. *The Color of the Law: Race, Violence and Justice in the Post–World War II South.* Chapel Hill: University of North Carolina Press, 1999.

Plummer, Brenda Gayle. *Rising Wind: Black Americans and U.S. Foreign Affairs, 1935–1960.* Chapel Hill: University of North Carolina Press, 1996.

Reed, Linda. *Simple Decency and Common Sense: The Southern Conference Movement, 1938–1963.* Bloomington: Indiana University Press, 1991.

Scott, William R. *The Sons of Sheba's Race: African-Americans and the Italo-Ethiopian War, 1935–1941.* Bloomington: Indiana University Press, 1993.

Washburn, Patricia Scott. *A Question of Sedition: The Federal Government's Investigation of the Black Press during World War II.* New York: Oxford University Press, 1986.

Autobiography and Biography

Buni, Andrew. *Robert Vann of the Pittsburgh Courier*. Pittsburgh: University of Pittsburgh Press, 1974.

Duberman, Martin Bauml. *Paul Robeson: A Biography*. New York: Ballantine Press, 1989.

DuBois, Shirley Graham. *His Day Is Marshing On: A Memoir of W. E. B. Du Bois*. New York: Lippincott, 1971.

Janken, Kenneth R. *Rayford W. Logan and the Dilemma of the African-American Intellectual*. Amherst: University of Massachusetts Press, 1993.

Love, Spencie. *One Blood: The Death and Resurrection of Charles Drew*. Chapel Hill: University of North Carolina Press, 1996.

Marable, Manning. *W. E. B. Du Bois: Black Radical Democrat*. Boston: Twayne, 1986.

Motley, Constance Baker. *Equal Justice under Law: An Autobiography*. New York: Farrar, Straus and Giroux, 1998.

Murray, Pauli. *Song in a Weary Throat: An American Pilgrimage*. New York: Harper and Row, 1987.

Rustin, Bayard. *Troubles I've Seen*. New York: HarperCollins, 1996.

Terkel, Studs, ed. *The Good War*. New York: Pantheon, 1984.

Urquhart, Brian. *Ralph Bunche: An American Life*. New York: W. W. Norton, 1993.

Ware, Gilbert. *William Hastie: Grace under Pressure*. New York: Oxford University Press, 1984.

Wilkins, Roy, with Tom Mathews. *Standing Fast: The Autobiography of Roy Wilkins*. New York: Da Capo Press, 1994.

Williams, Juan. *Thurgood Marshall: American Revolutionary*. New York: Times Books, 1998.

PART VI

THE

BLACK

REVOLUTION

THE FREEDOM MOVEMENT,
1954-1965

Martin Luther King Jr. delivers his "I Have a Dream" speech during the March on
Washington, August 28, 1963.

When the history books are written in the future, somebody will have to say, "There lived a race of people, black people, fleecy locks and black complexion, people who had the moral courage to stand up for their rights. And thereby they injected a new meaning into the veins of history and of civilization." And we're gonna do that. God grant that we will do it before it's too late.

—Martin Luther King Jr., December 5, 1955

Between 1955 and 1965 the civil rights movement reached its peak of effectiveness and achieved so many of its goals that the era has been dubbed the "Second Reconstruction." Bold movements, beginning with the Montgomery bus boycott of 1955–1956 and culminating in a series of massive protests throughout the South in 1963 and 1964, changed the face of race relations in the United States. Despite fierce resistance, legally sanctioned segregation, racial discrimination, and disfranchisement fell before a mighty coalition of civil rights groups and their allies. Demonstrations and the pressures of the Cold War compelled high government officials to abandon their early caution and take action. Although racism remained a powerful force in American life after 1965 and African Americans continued to suffer from economic disadvantages, the changes of this Second Reconstruction far outstripped those of the first.

The heart of the story of the modern civil rights movement is the remarkable courage and tenacity people in their own communities showed in their determination to attack segregation and exclusion from the political process. Behind the charismatic leaders and the powerful spectacle of marches and demonstrations captured so dramatically on television were the ordinary citizens who initiated protests, formulated strategies and tactics, and garnered other essential resources that made collective action work. The people's actions were made effective through their families, churches, voluntary associations, political organizations, women's clubs, and college organizations and facilities. The sacrifices and experience gained in the previous one hundred years of struggle had, by the mid-1950s, accumulated sufficiently to permit an all-out attack on white supremacy. The civil rights movement would be long and bloody and it would not lead to the promised land, but it would profoundly change America.

THE 1950S: PROSPERITY AND PREJUDICE

For the majority of white Americans, the 1950s ushered in an era of unparalleled prosperity. The more affluent fled to the suburbs and by 1960, 52 percent of Americans owned their own homes. The decade is remembered nostalgically as a time of large stable nuclear families untroubled by drugs and juvenile delinquency. It was a time of backyard barbecues and hula hoops, when nightly television shows like *Ozzie and Harriet* and *I Love Lucy* projected a vision of domestic tranquillity.

For the majority of black Americans, however, the 1950s were not so blissful. American society remained rigidly segregated. Despite the gains African Americans made during the World War II era, Jim Crow was still in evidence. Although the *Smith v. Allwright* Supreme Court decision in 1944, which declared the "white primary" unconstitutional, helped reenfranchise black voters in Florida, Tennessee, and Texas, Jim Crow restrictions and the ever-present threat of white violence kept millions of African Americans from voting in the deep South.

Nor did most African Americans benefit from the economic boom of the 1950s that allowed so many white Americans to purchase homes in the suburbs. Moving into urban centers just as the number of factories and jobs there began to decline, they suffered a higher unemployment rate than any other segment of the population. White workers, fearing for their jobs, felt threatened by competition from unemployed black workers. As urban neighborhoods deteriorated, conditions ripened for a massive explosion.

Brown II

A year after the 1954 *Brown* decision, in May 1955, the Supreme Court issued a second ruling, commonly known as *Brown* II, which addressed the practical process of desegregation. The Court underscored that the states in the suits should begin prompt compliance with the 1954 ruling, but concluded that this should be done with "all deliberate speed." Many black Americans interpreted this to mean "immediately." White Southerners hoped it meant a very long time, or never. Ominously, President Eisenhower seemed displeased with the Court's rulings and steadfastly refused to put the moral authority of his office behind their enforcement.

Nevertheless, in 1955 and early 1956, desegregation proceeded without hindrance in Maryland, Kentucky, Delaware, Oklahoma, and Missouri. Alabama governor Jim Folsom declared that his state would obey the courts and, initially, many other moderate white southern politicians counseled calm and worked to head off a full-scale conflict between their region and the federal government.

White Massive Resistance

White moderates, however, soon found themselves a shrinking minority, as extremists, determined to maintain white supremacy at any cost, prepared for mass resistance to the Court's decisions. The rhetoric of these extremists bordered on hysteria but found a receptive audience among many white people. A young minister from Virginia named Jerry Falwell, for example, explained that black people were the descendants of Noah's son Ham and destined to be servants because of a curse God had put on him. Falwell also claimed the Supreme Court's decisions were inspired by Moscow. In 1955, leading businessmen, white-collar professionals, and clergy began organizing White Citizens' Councils in virtually every southern city; these were groups dedicated to preserving the southern way of life and the South's "sacred heritage of freedom." The councils used their economic and political power to intimidate black people who challenged segregation. They fired people from their jobs, evicted them from their homes, and refused them credit.

Many white politicians took up the banner of massive resistance. James O. Eastland, a senator from Mississippi, declared that the *Brown* decision was a "monstrous crime." The legislature of Virginia closed all public schools in Prince Edward County to thwart integration. Most dramatically, on March 12, 1956, ninety-six southern congressmen led by North Carolina's Senator Sam Ervin Jr. issued "The Southern Manifesto" vowing to fight to preserve segregation and the southern way of life. The Manifesto characterized the *Brown* decisions as an "unwarranted exercise of power by the court, contrary to the Constitution."

The NAACP came under siege in the wake of the *Brown* decision as southern states tried to wipe it out of existence. By 1957 nine southern states had filed suit to destroy the organization. Some states, alleging that the NAACP was a subversive organization linked to a worldwide communist conspiracy, made membership illegal. Membership plummeted from 128,716 to 79,677, and the association lost 246 branches in the South.

Under these pressures, desegregation ground to a halt. By 1958, thirteen school systems had been desegregated. By 1960, two years later, the total had risen to only seventeen. Massive resistance was challenging the possibility of achieving change through court action alone.

The Lynching of Emmett Till

The violent reaction of white Southerners to the growing assertiveness of black people found expression in the summer of 1955 in the lynching of fourteen-year-old Emmett Till of Chicago, an event that helped galvanize the emerging civil rights movement. Till was visiting relatives in the small town of Money, Mississippi. On a dare from his friends, he entered Bryant's grocery store, bought candy, and said "Bye, baby" to Carolyn Bryant, the wife of the owner, as he left. Till was unaware how far white people in the town would go to avenge this small breach of white supremacy's racial etiquette. In the middle of the night a few days after the incident, Bryant's husband and brother-in-law arrived at the small home where Till was staying and kidnaped him at gunpoint. His body was subsequently found in the Tallahatchie River tied to a heavy cotton gin fan. Till had a bullet lodged in his head and had clearly been tortured before his murder. Despite overwhelming evidence and the brave testimony of Mose Wright, Till's uncle, and other local black people, the two men who lynched Till were acquitted by an all white-jury. In early 1956, the murderers sold their confession to *Look* magazine and gloated over their escape from justice.

The Till lynching shaped the consciousness of an entire generation of young African-American activists. Partly this was due to the efforts of Till's mother, Mamie Bradley. Unwilling to let America turn away from this injustice, Till's mother had her son's mangled body displayed in an open casket in Chicago. Thousands of mourners filed by to pay their respects and many committed themselves to fighting the system that made this crime possible. Bradley also traveled around the nation speaking to groups on whom her grief had a profound impact. Myrlie Evers, who would later have a role in the movement, remembered how she felt. "I bled for Emmett Till's mother. I know when she came to Mississippi and appeared at the mass meetings how everyone poured out their hearts to her, went into their pockets when people had only two or three pennies, and gave."

After Emmett Till was lynched in Money, Mississippi, his mother, Mamie Bradley, had his body returned to Chicago for a public burial. The Till lynching had a profound impact on young African-American civil rights activists.

NEW FORMS OF PROTEST: THE MONTGOMERY BUS BOYCOTT

Strong local communities formed the core of the civil rights movement and they were often sparked to action by the deeds of brave and committed individuals. The first and one of the most important expressions of this process occurred in Alabama's small capital city of Montgomery (Map 21–1). Blessed with well-organized educational, religious, and other institutions, this city's African-American community of 45,000 was poised to make history.

The Roots of Revolution

The movement in Montgomery did not emerge out of the blue, although it must have seemed that way to many white residents in the city; it was the result of years of organization and planning by protest groups. In addition to its numerous churches, two black colleges, and other social organizations, the Alabama capital had a strong core of protest groups. One, the Women's Political Council (WPC), had been founded in 1946 by Mary Frances Fair Burks, chair of Alabama State College English Department, after the all-white League of Women Voters had refused to allow black women to participate in its activities. Although the WPC consisted of only forty members, all middle-class women, it had a courageous and competent leadership with the will to stand up to powerful white people. The WPC was joined by a chapter of the NAACP led by E. D. Nixon, a Pullman train porter and head of the Alabama chapter of the Brotherhood of Sleeping Car Porters. In 1943, Nixon had founded the Montgomery Voters League, an organization dedicated to helping African Americans navigate Alabama's tortuous process of voter registration. In the decade after 1945 these groups searched for a way of mobilizing the black community to challenge white power.

The 1954 *Brown* decision seemed to provide a means to destroy segregation and discrimination in the city. Four days after it was announced, Jo Ann Robinson, a professor at Alabama State College, wrote a letter to Montgomery's mayor on behalf of the WPC. In it she

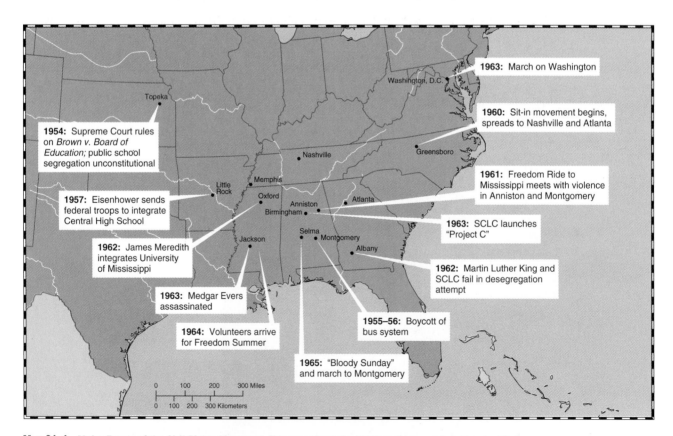

Map 21–1 Major Events of the Civil Rights Movement. This map shows the location of key events in the struggle for civil rights between 1954 and 1965.

reiterated the complaints of the black community concerning conditions on the city's buses and ended, "Please consider this plea, for even now plans are being made to ride less, or not at all, on our buses." The mayor ignored the warning and practices continued on the buses much as before. All seemed quiet on the surface but Montgomery's black lawyers and NAACP chapter began laying the groundwork for a test case challenging segregation of the city's bus lines.

On March 2, 1955, a fifteen-year-old girl, Claudette Colvin, was arrested for refusing to give up her seat on a bus to a white person. The Women's Political Council

---

VOICES

LETTER OF THE MONTGOMERY WOMEN'S POLITICAL COUNCIL TO MAYOR W. A. GAYLE

In this letter threatening a boycott of Montgomery's buses, the Women's Political Council politely asks not for the desegregation of the buses but only for practices that would prevent black riders from being forced to move to accommodate white riders.

May 21, 1954
Honorable Mayor W. A. Gayle
City Hall
Montgomery, Alabama

Dear Sir:

The Women's Political Council is very grateful to you and the City Commissioners for the hearing you allowed our representative during the month of March, 1954, when the "city-bus-fare-increase case" was being reviewed. There were several things the Council asked for:

1. A city law that would make it possible for Negroes to sit from back toward front, and whites from front toward back until all the seats were taken.

2. That Negroes would not be asked or forced to pay fare at front and go to the rear of the bus to enter.

3. That buses stop at every corner in residential sections occupied by Negroes as they do in communities where whites reside.

We are happy to report that buses have begun stopping at more corners now in some sections where Negroes live than previously. However, the same practices in seating and boarding the bus continue.

Mayor Gayle, three-fourths of the riders of these public conveyances are Negroes. If Negroes did not patronize them, they could not possibly operate.

More and more of our people are already arranging with neighbors and friends to ride to keep from being insulted and humiliated by bus drivers.

There has been talk from twenty-five or more local organizations of planning a city-wide boycott of buses. We, sir, do not feel that forceful measures are necessary in bargaining for a convenience which is right for all bus passengers. We, the Council, believe that when this matter has been put before you and the Commissioners, that agreeable terms can be met in a quiet and in a sensible manner to the satisfaction of all concerned.

Many of our Southern cities in neighboring states have practiced the policies we seek without incident whatsoever. Atlanta, Macon and Savannah in Georgia have done this for years. Even Mobile, in our own state, does this and all the passengers are satisfied.

Please consider this plea, and if possible, act favorably upon it, for even now plans are being made to ride less, or not at all, on our buses. We do not want this.

Respectfully yours,
The Women's Political Council
Jo Ann Robinson, President

QUESTIONS

1. When the Women's Political Council made their initial requests to the Mayor of Montgomery, what were these designed to accomplish?

2. What does this letter suggest about the importance of black women's political organization in the early years of the civil rights movement?

Source: Stewart Burns, *Daybreak of Freedom: The Montgomery Bus Boycott* (Chapel Hill: University of North Carolina Press, 1997), 58.

was ready to use this incident to initiate the threatened bus boycott, but Nixon dissuaded them. Nixon felt that Colvin, who was unmarried and pregnant at the time, would not be an appropriate symbol around which to organize. He and other activists resolved to wait for another chance.

Rosa Parks

On Thursday, December 1, 1955, Rosa Parks, a forty-three-year-old department store seamstress and civil rights activist boarded a city bus and moved to the back where African Americans were required to sit. All seats were taken so she sat in one toward the middle of the bus. When a white man boarded the bus, the driver ordered Parks to vacate her seat for him. There was nothing unusual in his request, but on this fateful day, Rosa Parks refused to move. She had not planned to resist on that day but, as she later said, she had "decided that I would have to know once and for all what rights I had as a human being and a citizen." Parks elaborated: "I was so involved with the attempt to bring about freedom from this kind of thing . . . I felt just resigned to give what I could to protest against the way I was being treated, and felt that all of our meetings, trying to negotiate, bring about petitions before the authorities . . . really hadn't done any good at all." At the time Parks was portrayed as someone who was simply tired, but she had in fact been training for just this kind of challenge for years. When her moment came she seized it and with this act of resistance launched the Montgomery bus boycott movement and inspired the modern civil rights struggle for freedom and equality.

The plans of the WPC and NAACP came into play after Park's arrest for violating Montgomery's transportation laws. She was ordered to appear in court on the following Monday. Meanwhile, E. D. Nixon bailed her out of city jail and began mobilizing the leadership of the black community behind her. Working in tandem with Nixon, Robinson wrote and circulated a flyer calling for a one-day boycott of the buses followed by a mass meeting of the community to discuss the matter. Robinson took the flyer to the Alabama State College campus, stayed up all night and, with the help of a colleague, mimeographed forty thousand copies of the flyer. The WPC had planned distribution routes months earlier, and the next day, Robinson and nearly two hundred volunteers distributed bundles of flyers to beauty parlors and schools, to factories and grocery stores, to taverns and barber shops throughout the black neighborhoods.

Montgomery Improvement Association

On December 5, 1955, the black community did not ride the buses and the movement had begun. Nixon and other community leaders decided to form a new organization, the Montgomery Improvement Association (MIA) to coordinate the protest; they also selected a twenty-six-year-old minister, Martin Luther King Jr., to act as its president. That evening there was an overflowing mass meeting of the black community at the large Holt Street Baptist church to decide whether to continue the boycott. King, with barely an hour to prepare, spoke to the crowd and delivered a message that would define the goals of the boycott and the civil rights movement that followed. In his dramatic voice he connected the core values of America and of the Judeo-Christian tradition to the goals of African Americans nationwide as well as in Montgomery. "We are here this evening," he began,

> for serious business. We are here in a general sense because first and foremost we are American citizens, and we are determined to apply our citizenship to the fullness of its means. . . . You know, my friends, there comes a time when people get tired of being trampled over by the iron feet of oppression. There comes a time, my friends, when people get tired of being flung across the abyss of humiliation, when they experience the bleakness of nagging despair. . . . We are not wrong in what we are doing. If we are wrong, the Supreme Court of this nation is wrong. If we are wrong, the Constitution of the United States is wrong. If we are wrong, God Almighty is wrong. If we are wrong, Jesus of Nazareth was merely a utopian dreamer that never came down to earth. If we are wrong, justice is a lie. Love has no meaning. And we are determined here in Montgomery to work and fight until justice runs down like water, and righteousness like a mighty stream.

Martin Luther King Jr.

King's speech electrified the mass meeting, which unanimously decided to stay off the city's buses until the MIA's demands were met. The speech also marked the beginning of King's role as a leader of the civil rights movement. King had been raised in a prominent ministerial family with a long history of standing up for African-American rights. King's grandfather had led a protest to force Atlanta to build its first high school for African Americans. King's father continued speaking out for African-American rights as pastor of Ebenezer Baptist Church. At age fifteen, King had entered Morehouse College but did not embrace the ministry as his profession until he came under the influence of its president, Dr. Benjamin E. Mays. By age twenty-five, King had been awarded a Ph.D. in theology from Boston College. He moved to Alabama with his wife, Coretta Scott King, to become pastor of Dexter Avenue Baptist Church in Montgomery.

In addition to his verbal artistry, King had the ability to inspire moral courage and to teach people how to maintain themselves under excruciating pressure. King merged Gandhian nonviolence with black Christian faith and church culture to create a unique ideology well suited for the civil rights struggle. King declared that the boycott would continue with or without its leaders because the conflict was not "between the white and the Negro" but "between justice and injustice." He explained to the boycotting community, "If we are arrested every day, if we are exploited every day, if we are trampled over every day, don't ever let anyone pull you so low as to hate them. . . . We must realize so many people are taught to hate us that they are not totally responsible for their hate." King's faith was severely tested. As the boycott proceeded, his home was bombed. Segregationists also bombed Nixon's home and those of two other black Montgomery clergymen and MIA leaders, Ralph Abernathy and Fred Shuttlesworth, and inflicted violence on many other boycott participants.

Walking for Freedom

Although men occupied the top leadership positions in the boycott, women were the key to its effectiveness. The boycott lasted more than a year—381 days—and over its course nearly all the black women previously dependent on the buses to get to work refused to ride them. Some walked up to twelve miles a day. Others had the support of their white women employers, who provided transportation. And many helped to organize a highly efficient car pool of two hundred vehicles that proved critical to sustaining the boycott. The community at large participated in mass meetings held nightly in local churches. Robinson edited the MIA newsletter. Other women supported the boycott in dozens of ways. Some organized bake sales and others made door-to-door solicitations to raise the $2,000 per week needed to keep the car pools going.

The boycott took 65 percent of the bus company's business, forcing it to cut schedules, lay off drivers, and raise fares. White merchants suffered as well. The bus company, however, could scarcely afford to break the laws of the city that chartered it, and in spite of the company's losses, the city government refused to capitulate. Officials would not even accede to such a modest demand as a "first come, first served" seating arrangement—like that proposed by the Montgomery

When Rosa Parks was arrested for violating a Montgomery, Alabama, segregation ordinance, it was not because she tried to sit near the front of the bus, but because she refused to relinquish her seat near the middle of the bus to a white man after the front of the bus had filled with white passengers. This photo was taken several weeks later, during the bus boycott, when she and other black leaders were charged with violating a state law that made boycotts illegal.

Women's Political Council before the boycott began—in which black riders would sit from back to front and white riders from front to back.

Impressive as it was, the boycott by itself could not end segregation on the buses. Black Montgomery needed a two-pronged strategy of mass local pressure and legal recourse through the courts. The legal backing of the federal government was necessary to end Jim Crow. Thus NAACP lawyers and MIA's lawyer Fred Gray filed a suit in the names of Claudette Colvin, Mary Louise Smith, and three other women.

Friends in the North

The Montgomery movement was not without allies outside the South. Money poured into the MIA's coffers from concerned Americans. At the same time, many northern activists who had long been hoping that black Southerners would begin just this kind of resistance swung into action to help. Two people were particularly important at this juncture: Bayard Rustin, and liberal Jewish lawyer Stanley Levinson. Two and a half months into the boycott, Montgomery officials indicted King and one hundred other leaders on charges of conspiracy to disrupt the bus system. At this juncture Bayard Rustin arrived in Montgomery and immediately encouraged the leaders to follow Gandhian practice and submit freely to arrest. In a diary entry, Rustin wrote,

Many of them did not wait for the police to come but walked to the police station and surrendered. Nixon was the first. He walked into the station and said, "You are looking for me? Here I am." This procedure had a startling effect on both the Negro and the white communities. White community leaders, politicians, and police were dumbfounded. Negroes were thrilled to see their leaders surrender without being hunted down. Soon hundreds of Negroes gathered outside the police station and applauded the leaders as they entered, one by one.

Rustin continued working behind the scenes as one of King's most trusted advisers on nonviolent principles and tactics. Levinson and Ella Baker created a group called In Friendship, which raised money for the boycott.

Levinson was a wealthy attorney committed to social justice. He had worked with the Communist party, and Rustin had a long history of association with radical groups. Their influence soon attracted the attention of the Federal Bureau of Investigation, which had long been obsessed with black leaders and organizations. King was not a communist, but FBI director J. Edgar Hoover developed an intense hatred of him and other black leaders. At one point Hoover called King, "the most dangerous man in America" and he pressed his subordinates to prove King was a communist and that the civil rights movement was a Moscow-inspired conspiracy. Hoover and his men began tapping King's telephone and hotel rooms and went so far as to threaten exposure of his extramarital affairs if he did not commit suicide. By the early 1960s the agency had stopped warning King when it uncovered threats to his life.

Victory

As the bus boycott reached the one-year mark, it was obvious that the all-white city government would not budge, no matter how long the boycott lasted. Any white politician who hoped to remain in office had to defend segregation. King and all the others who suffered through the ordeal grew discouraged and their hopes seemed to fade in November 1956 when it became clear that the state courts would soon move to declare the car pools illegal.

Salvation for the movement came from the cases local women and the NAACP had taken to the federal courts. In keeping with the *Brown* precedent, on November 13, 1956, the United States Supreme Court ordered an end to Montgomery's bus segregation. The *Gayle v. Browder* decision, unlike the one delivered in *Brown*, expressly overturned the 1896 *Plessy v. Ferguson* decision because like *Plessy* it applied to transportation. Ironically, the ruling was handed down on the same day that the city of Montgomery finally secured a state court injunction to end the MIA car pool. The bus company agreed not only to end segregation but to hire African-American drivers and to treat all passengers with equal respect.

The city's black community rejoiced. On the morning of December 21, 1956, black citizens of Montgomery boarded the buses and sat wherever they pleased.

No Easy Road to Freedom: 1957-1960

The victory at Montgomery set an example for protests to come. It was the result of a highly organized black community led by committed and capable black leaders. These local efforts were bolstered by the advice and involvement of activists outside the South, the attention of a sympathetic national press, and, crucially, intervention from the federal courts. But local victories could only go so far, particularly as white resistance intensified. In the three years following the boycott, black Southerners and their allies across the nation prepared for a broader movement. At the same time, federal officials outside the judiciary found that they could not ignore the white South's incipient rebellion without grave consequences for the nation and their own power.

Martin Luther King and the SCLC

By the end of the campaign in Montgomery, Martin Luther King Jr. had emerged as a moral leader of national stature. On the advice of Levinson, Rustin, and Ella Baker, he helped create a new organization, the Southern Christian Leadership Council (SCLC) to provide an institutional base for continuing the struggle. The SCLC was a federation of civil rights groups, community organizations, and churches that aimed at coordinating all the burgeoning local movements. King assumed leadership of the SCLC, crisscrossing the nation in the ensuing years to build support for the organization and to raise money to fund its activities. Members of the organization also began training black activists, particularly on college campuses, in the tactics of nonviolent protest. Because the ballot was deemed the critical weapon needed to complete school desegregation and secure equal employment opportunity, adequate housing, and equal access to public accommodations, the SCLC focused its efforts on securing voting rights for black people. In the three years after the Montgomery bus boycott, the SCLC also aided black communities in applying the lessons of that struggle to challenge bus segregation in Tallahassee, Florida, and in Atlanta.

The SCLC shared many of the NAACP's goals, but tensions arose between the two organizations. The NAACP's leadership doubted the effectiveness of the protest tactics favored by the SCLC. They resented having to divert resources away from work on important court cases to defend people arrested in protests and were troubled by the left-wing connections of King's advisers. The fortunes of the NAACP in the South, however, plummeted in the late 1950s as southern states persecuted its members; this left the field to the SCLC. Despite their differences, the SCLC and the NAACP worked together, but the tensions over tactics were never far from the surface.

Civil Rights Act of 1957

Despite President Eisenhower's tepid response to *Brown*, Congress proved willing to take at least a modest step toward ending racial discrimination. Buttress-

ing the Supreme Court's desegregation initiatives, it enacted the Civil Rights Act of 1957, the first such legislation since the end of Reconstruction. In a departure from the past, liberals in the Senate were able to end a filibuster by Southerners, but the bill they passed was, for all its symbolic import, quite weak. The act created a commission to monitor violations of black civil rights and to propose remedies for infringements on black voting. It upgraded the Civil Rights Section into a division within the Justice Department and provided it with the power to initiate civil proceedings against those states and municipalities that discriminated on the basis of race. Although an important step on the long road toward black enfranchisement, this act disappointed black activists because it was not strong enough to counter white reaction and because they felt the Eisenhower administration would not enforce it.

Little Rock, Arkansas

Eisenhower may have had little inclination to support the fight for black rights, but the defiance of Arkansas governor Orville Faubus would soon force him to. At the beginning of the school year in 1957, Faubus posted 270 soldiers from the Arkansas National Guard outside Little Rock Central High School in an attempt to prevent nine black youths from entering. Faubus was determined to flout the *Brown* ruling and to maintain school segregation. When a federal district court order forced the governor to allow the children into the school, he simply withdrew the state guard and left the children alone to face a hate-filled mob of local citizens.

To defend the sovereignty of the federal court and the Constitution, Eisenhower had to act. He sent in 1,100 paratroopers from the 101st Airborne to Little Rock and put the state national guard under federal authority. It was the first time since Reconstruction that troops had been sent to the South to protect the rights of African-American citizens. The troops remained in Little Rock Central High School for the rest of the school year. Governor Faubus closed the Little Rock public schools in 1958–1959, and black students did not actually attend the high school until August 1959. Eight of the nine black students valiantly withstood the abuse, harassment, and curses of segregationists both inside and outside the facility and eventually desegregated the school. Courage like theirs would soon be seen in the deeds of other young African Americans throughout the South.

Elizabeth Eckerd, one of nine black students who sought to enroll at Little Rock Central High School in September 1957, endures the taunts of an angry white crowd as she tries to make her way to the school.

BLACK YOUTH STAND UP BY SITTING DOWN

Beginning in 1960, motivated black college students developed an effective new strategy—the sit-in—and emerged as the dynamic vanguard of the civil rights movement. Their distinctive and independent contributions to the black protest movement helped significantly to accelerate the pace of social change. Before long the movement would inspire an even larger number of northern black and white students.

Sit-Ins: Greensboro, Nashville, Atlanta

Early on the morning of February 1, 1960, Ezell Blair Jr., Joseph McNeil, Francis McCain, and David Richmond, all freshmen at North Carolina Agricultural and Technical College (A & T), decided to desegregate local restaurants by sitting at the lunch counter of Greensboro North Carolina's Woolworth five-and-dime store. Although black people were welcome to spend their money in the store, they were not permitted to dine at the lunch counter, making it a particularly painful symbol of white supremacy. At 4:30 in the afternoon the students sat at the counter. They received no service

that day but sat quietly doing their school work until the store closed. The action of these four young men electrified their fellow students and the next day they were joined by many others. Soon, black women students from Bennett College and a few white students from the University of North Carolina Women's College joined the protest and by the fifth day hundreds of young, studious, neatly dressed African Americans crowded the downtown store demanding their rights.

Like the black people of Montgomery, the students in Greensboro acted with forethought and with the support of their community. They had long debated how they could best participate in the desegregation movement. All four of the black students had been members of NAACP college or youth groups and were aware of the currents of change flowing through the South. Although they began the sit-in on their own, it quickly gained the support of people throughout the black community. Many people in the North and West—both black and white—also joined the campaign by picketing local stores of the national chains that approved of segregation in the South. After facing the collective power of the black community and their allies for many months, white businessmen and politicians finally gave into the black community's demands.

Four students—from the left they are Joseph McNeil, Franklin McCain, Billy Smith, and Clarence Henderson—sit patiently at Woolworth's lunch counter on February 2, 1960, the second day of the sit-in in Greensboro, North Carolina. Although not the first sit-in protest against segregated facilities, the Greensboro action triggered a wave of sit-ins by black high school and college students across the South.

The students at Greensboro were not alone in their desire to strike out at discrimination. Indeed, at Fisk University in Nashville, Tennessee, Diane Nash, John Lewis, Marion Barry, James Bevel, Curtis Murphy, Gloria Johnson, Bernard Lafayette, and Rodney Powell had begun organizing nonviolent workshops before the Greensboro sit-in. Imbued with youthful exuberance and idealism, they determined to follow the Reverend James Lawson's courageous leadership and his teaching on nonviolence and Christian brotherhood. Even better organized than their comrades in North Carolina, they had been undergoing intensive training for a sit-in campaign. Twelve days after the first sit-ins began, the Nashville group swung into action. Hundreds were arrested and those who sat suffered insults, mob violence, beatings, arrest, and torture while in jail. Nonetheless, they prevailed, compelling major restaurants to desegregate by May 1960.

Atlanta, Martin Luther King Jr.'s home base and the site of a large African-American community, spawned an even more dramatic movement. It began after Spelman College freshman Ruby Doris Smith persuaded her friends and classmates to launch sit-ins in the city. On March 15, 1960, at Atlanta University, two students, Julian Bond and Lonnie King, executing a carefully orchestrated plan, deployed two hundred sit-in students to ten different eating places. They targeted government-owned property and public places, including bus and train stations and the state capitol, that should have been willing to serve all customers. At the Federal Building, Bond and his classmates attempted to eat in the municipal cafeteria and were arrested. After hours of incarceration they were released. In earlier years, a jail stint had been a mark of shame, but these students returned as heroes to the campus. The Atlanta sit-in students broadened their campaign demands to include desegregation of all public facilities, black voting rights, and equal access to educational and employment opportunities. On September 27, 1961, the Atlanta business and political elite gave in.

Just as in Greensboro, the students in Nashville, Atlanta, and numerous other southern cities won the support of local people who had not been involved in organized resistance before. By April 1960 more than two thousand students from black high schools and colleges had been arrested in seventy-eight southern towns and cities. Local people demonstrated their allegiance to them in numerous ways, but their most effective tactic was the economic boycott. When business began to suffer as a result of the protests, white leaders proved willing to negotiate the racial status quo. By the summer, more than thirty southern cities had set up community organizations to respond to the complaints of local black citizens.

The Student Nonviolent Coordinating Committee

Recognizing the significance of the regionwide student action and fearing that it would soon melt away, the SCLC's Ella Baker organized a conference for 150 students at her alma mater, Shaw University, in Raleigh, North Carolina. Baker, who managed operations in the SCLC's Atlanta headquarters, chafed under the rigid male leadership of the organization. In contrast, she advocated decentralized leadership and celebrated participatory democracy. Her skepticism about the SCLC struck a chord with the students.

On April 15–17, 1960, delegates representing over fifty colleges and high schools from thirty-seven communities in thirteen states arrived and began discussing what should be done to keep the movement going. Baker addressed the group in a speech entitled "More Than a Hamburger" and became the midwife of a new organization named the Student Nonviolent Coordinating Committee (SNCC). The newest addition to the roster of civil rights associations adhered to the ideology of nonviolence, but it also acknowledged the possible need for increased militancy and confrontation. More accommodating black leaders, even some of those in the SCLC, objected to the students' use of direct confrontational tactics that disrupted race relations and community peace.

Freedom Rides

The sit-in movement paved the way for the "Freedom Rides" of 1961. CORE's James Farmer and Bayard Rustin resolved that it was time for a reprise of their 1947 mission to ride interstate buses and trains in the upper South. That early effort—a planned bus trip from Washington, D.C., to Kentucky—reached only as far as Chapel Hill, North Carolina. There the group of interracial riders met violent resistance, were arrested, and were sentenced to thirty days on a road gang. This new journey tested the Justice Department's willingness to

On May 14, in Anniston, Alabama, a white mob firebombed this Freedom Rider's bus and attacked passengers as they escaped the flames.

PROFILE

ROBERT PARRIS MOSES

Bob Moses, one of the most dedicated and revered young civil rights activists, was a soft-spoken man possessed of a powerful intellect, iron courage, and a rare purity of moral conviction. Born in 1935 in Harlem, Moses was an excellent student. He attended Hamilton College and from his reading in philosophy there, including works on Buddhism and Existentialism, he developed a sophisticated understanding of nonviolent protest, a topic he continued to explore during his graduate studies in philosophy at Harvard University.

Robert "Bob" Moses instructs volunteers for the Freedom Summer campaign of 1964.

When Moses learned of the sit-ins in 1960, he immediately went south to participate. It was a fateful trip during which he met Amzie Moore, one of the World War II veterans who had returned home to make Mississippi safe for democracy. Moore was the vice president of the state conferences of the NAACP branches. The two men developed a deep-seated appreciation for each other's strengths and Moore soon convinced Moses to center his work in Mississippi. By August 1961 Moses was a SNCC organizer in the small town of McComb, Mississippi. There his group registered black voters. In early 1962 the SNCC activist became the program director of the Council of Federated Organizations (COFO) and remained in the center of the struggle in Mississippi for the next three years.

The violence of white people and the courage of local black people had a profound effect on Moses. In McComb he was arrested, jailed, beaten, and threatened with death. One of the local black people who helped his group was murdered in cold blood by a state senator who was subsequently acquitted of the crime by an all-white jury. Moses respected anyone who had the courage to take a stand after suffering a lifetime of such abuse. His goal was to give local people the tools to continue to control their lives long after movement organizers had left.

Although Moses refused to become a formal leader of the SNCC forces in Mississippi, he had a profound impact on the movement. The young civil rights worker set an example of nonviolent resistance for other members of SNCC and encouraged the entire organization to avoid developing a hierarchical leadership structure. In late 1963 Moses became the driving force behind the Freedom Summer project and played a central role in persuading SNCC to accept white volunteers from the North. He also stood for principle rather than expediency when he rejected the meager deal offered the Mississippi Freedom Democratic Party (discussed later in the chapter) at the 1964 Democratic Convention. Moses spoke for many young activists when he said in disgust, "You can't trust the political system. I will have nothing to do with the political system any longer."

In 1965 Moses began to drift away from the civil rights movement and toward active opposition to the war in Vietnam. Exhausted from his ordeal in the South and seeking to avoid the draft, he emigrated first to Canada and then to the African nation of Tanzania. Moses returned soon after President Jimmy Carter offered amnesty to draft resisters and began teaching math and science to inner-city black children. After receiving a MacArthur Foundation "genius grant" he developed the Algebra Project, which uses many of the empowerment strategies pioneered during the civil rights era to help children and their families gain the education they need in the emerging computer-oriented economy.

protect the rights of African Americans to use bus terminal facilities on a nonsegregated basis.

The Freedom Rides showed the world how far some white Southerners would go to preserve segregation. The first ride ran into trouble on May 4, 1961, when John Lewis, one of the seven black riders, tried to enter the white waiting room of the Greyhound bus terminal in Rock Hill, South Carolina, and was brutally beaten by local white people in full view of the police. The interracial group continued through Alabama toward Jackson, Mississippi, but repeated acts of white violence made escape from Alabama exceedingly difficult. At Anniston, Alabama, a mob firebombed a bus and beat the escaping riders. A group of local African Americans led by the Reverend Fred Shuttlesworth provided rescue assistance and took many of the shocked and injured riders to Birmingham.

With the police offering no protection, CORE abandoned the Freedom Rides and all but a few of the original riders left Alabama. But SNCC activists and students in Nashville refused to let the idea die. At least twenty civil rights workers went to Birmingham where they vowed on May 20 to ride on to Montgomery. John Lewis remained with the group that arrived in Montgomery. Awaiting them was another angry mob of more than 1,000 white people, and not a policeman in sight. This time Lewis was knocked unconscious and all the riders had to be hospitalized. Even a presidential aide assigned to monitor the crisis was injured.

News services flashed graphic images of the violence around the world, and the federal government resolved to end the bloodletting. Attorney General Robert Kennedy sent four hundred federal marshals to restore law and order. Martin Luther King and Ralph Abernathy joined the conflict on May 21 as 1,200 men, women, and children met at Abernathy's church. The federal marshals averted further bloodshed by surrounding the building. Only then did Governor John Patterson order the National Guard and state troopers to protect the protesters. When the group arrived in Jackson, Mississippi, white authorities promptly arrested them. By summer's end, more than three hundred Freedom Riders had served time in Mississippi's notorious prisons.

A SIGHT TO BE SEEN: THE MOVEMENT AT HIGH TIDE

Between 1960 and 1963 the civil rights movement developed the techniques and organization that would finally bring America face to face with the conflict between its democratic ideals and the racism of its politics. Day after day the movement squared off against the die-hard resistance of the white South and created a situation demanding that the president and Congress take action.

The Election of 1960

One of the persistent fears of white Southerners was that black Americans, if armed with the ballot, would possess the balance of political power. The presidential election of 1960 proved this to be the case. Initially, many African Americans favored the Republican party's nominee, Richard Nixon, who had been an advocate of strong civil rights legislation. Baseball star Jackie Robinson was a Nixon supporter as were many other well-known African Americans. It seemed as if the New Deal coalition had weakened and that black citizens would reverse their move into the Democratic party. The Democratic nominee, Massachusetts Senator John F. Kennedy, in contrast, had done little to distinguish himself to black Americans throughout the struggles of the 1950s. As the campaign progressed, however, Kennedy made more sympathetic statements in support of black protests. Meanwhile, Nixon attempted to strengthen his position with white southern voters and remained silent about civil rights issues, even though the Republican party had a strong pro-civil rights record.

Shortly before the election, Martin Luther King was sentenced to four months in prison for leading a nonviolent protest march in Atlanta. Kennedy seized the opportunity to telephone King's wife, Coretta Scott King, to offer his support while his brother Robert F. Kennedy used his influence to obtain King's release. These acts impressed African Americans and won their support. African American voters in key northern cities provided the crucial margin that elected John F. Kennedy. In Illinois, for example, with black voters casting 250,000 ballots for Kennedy, the Democrats carried the state by merely 9,000 votes.

The Kennedy Administration and the Civil Rights Movement

Early in his administration John F. Kennedy grew concerned about the mounting violence occasioned by the civil rights movement. As the Freedom Rides continued across the deep South, the activists provoked crises and confrontations and forced the federal government to intervene in their behalf. Kennedy's primary interest at this point was to prevent disorder from getting out of hand and to avoid compromising America's position with the developing nations. But Kennedy had little room to maneuver given the continued power of white Southerners in his party and in Congress.

Despite these limitations, Kennedy did take some important steps to aid the cause of civil rights. He issued Executive Order 11063, which required government agencies to discontinue discriminatory policies and practices in federally supported housing, and he named Vice President Lyndon B. Johnson to chair the newly established Committee on Equal Employment Opportunity. Kennedy pleased black Americans when he nominated Thurgood Marshall to the Second Circuit Court of Appeals on September 23, 1961 (although determined opposition in Congress blocked Marshall's senate confirmation until September 11, 1963). He named journalist Carl Rowan deputy assistant secretary of state. More than forty African Americans took positions in the new administration, including Robert Weaver, director of the Housing and Home Finance Agency; Mercer Cook, ambassador to Norway; and George L. P. Weaver, assistant secretary of labor. Moreover, Kennedy's brother Robert, who served as attorney general, put muscle into the Civil Rights Division of the Justice Department by hiring an impressive team of lawyers headed by Washington attorney Burke Marshall.

Like Eisenhower, when President Kennedy felt his authority being challenged by intractable southern governors, he acted decisively. On June 25, 1962, one year after James Meredith had filed a complaint of racial discrimination against the University of Mississippi, the U.S. Circuit Court of Appeals for the Fifth Circuit ruled that the university had to admit him. Mississippi governor Ross Barnett vowed to prevent implementation of the order but Kennedy sent three hundred federal marshals to uphold the court's decision. Thousands of students rioted at the campus; two people died, two hundred were arrested, and nearly half the marshals were injured. Kennedy did not back down but rather federalized the Mississippi National Guard to ensure Meredith's admission. Although isolated and harassed throughout his time at Ole Miss, Meredith persevered and was eventually graduated. Likewise, in June of 1963, the Kennedy administration compelled Governor George Wallace of Alabama to allow the desegregation of the University of Alabama.

Voter Registration Projects

On June 16, 1961, Robert Kennedy met with student leaders and urged them to redirect their energies to voter registration projects and to lessen their concentration on direct-action activities. He and the Justice Department aides persuaded the students that the free exercise of the ballot would result in profound and significant social change. James Foreman, SNCC's executive director, followed Kennedy's lead. By October 1961, SNCC had joined forces with the NAACP, SCLC, and CORE in the voter education project funded by major philanthropic foundations and administered by the Southern Regional Council. SNCC was responsible for Alabama and Mississippi. Drawing heavily on the expertise of Robert Moses and working closely with a cadre of local leaders like Amzie Moore, head of the NAACP in Mississippi's Cleveland county, and Fannie Lou Hamer of Ruleville, SNCC opened a series of voter registration schools. The "graduates" thereupon attempted to register to vote. These attempts unleashed a wave of white violence and murder across Mississippi.

THE ALBANY MOVEMENT

In Albany, Georgia, the burgeoning civil rights movement met sophisticated resistance and experienced its most profound defeat up to that time. The movement in Albany began in the summer of 1961 when SNCC members moved into the city to conduct a voter registration project. Soon representatives of various local groups decided to form a coalition called the Albany movement and elected osteopath William G. Anderson as its president. The movement's goal quickly expanded from securing the vote to the total desegregation of the town.

In Laurie Pritchett, Albany's police chief, the movement faced an uncommonly sophisticated opponent. Pritchett studied the past tactics of SNCC and King and resolved not to confront the federal government directly and to avoid the kind of violence that brought negative media attention. When students from a black college decided to begin demonstrations by desegregating the bus terminal, Pritchett immediately arrested them after they entered the white waiting room and attempted to eat in the bus terminal dining room. Shrewdly, he charged the students with violating a city ordinance of failing to obey the orders of a law enforcement officer. They were not arrested on a federal charge.

The Albany movement decided to invite King and the SCLC to aid them and to overwhelm the police department by filling the jails with protesters. King answered the call. On December 16, 1961, he and more than 250 demonstrators were arrested, joining the 507 people already in jail. The plan was to stay in jail in order to, as Charles Sherrod explained, "break the system down from within. Our ability to suffer was somehow going to

VOICES

BERNICE JOHNSON REAGON ON HOW TO RAISE A FREEDOM SONG

Civil rights activists created a special culture in which black music helped communicate a sense of common purpose, strengthen the resolve to endure hardship and pain, and overcome despair and fear. One of the great singers to emerge out of the Albany Movement was Bernice Johnson Reagon, who today is known internationally as founder of the a capella group, Sweet Honey in the Rock. During the 1960s, she and Cordell Reagon and others formed the SNCC Freedom Singers and traveled the country performing freedom songs. In this statement Reagon describes the significance of song to the civil rights participants.

I f you cannot sing a congregational song at full power, you cannot fight in any struggle. . . . It is something you learn.

In congregational singing you don't sing a song— you raise it. By offering the first line, the song leader just offers the possibility, and it is up to you, individually, whether you pick it up or not. . . . It is a big personal risk because you will put everything into the song. It is like stepping off into space. A mini-revolution takes place inside you. Your body gets flushed, you tremble, you're tempted to turn off the circuits. But that's when you have to turn up the burner and commit yourself to follow that song wherever it leads. This transformation in yourself that you create is exactly what happens when you join a movement. You are taking a risk—you are committing yourself and there is no turning back. . . .

Organizing is not gentle. When you organize somebody, you create great anxiety in that person because you are telling them to risk everything. Put yourself in the place of a woman getting by as a hairdresser. You spend your day curling and frying hair, curling and frying. Somebody asks you to put up some civil rights workers in your home. You have to imagine what is going to happen: there may be people shooting up your home; you have to picture the check you get, the car you drive; everything you own, going on the block. You decide to take that risk because this is important enough. . . .

When you get together at a mass meeting you sing the songs which symbolize transformation, which make that revolution of courage inside you. . . . You raise a freedom song.

QUESTIONS

1. How does Reagon compare singing a freedom song to deciding to become involved in civil rights protest activity?

2. What different personal, social, and economic risks did people run when they became part of the black freedom movement? Given the dangers, why did so many ordinary people become involved?

Source: Bernice Johnson Reagon, "We'll Never Turn Back," in *Everybody Says Freedom: A History of the Civil Rights Movement in Songs and Pictures,* edited by Pete Seeger and Bob Reiser (New York: W. W. Norton, 1989), p. 82.

overcome their ability to hurt us." King vowed to remain in jail until the city desegregated. Sheriff Pritchett, however, was prepared for the protest and made arrangements to house almost two thousand people in surrounding jail facilities and trained his deputies in the use of nonviolent techniques. Thus Pritchett was able to avoid confrontation, violence, and federal intervention.

On December 18, 1961, two days after King's arrest, the city and the Albany Movement announced a truce. King immediately returned to Atlanta and the city refused to implement the terms of the agreement. When

King and Ralph Abernathy returned to Albany in July 1962 for sentencing on their December arrests, they chose forty-five days in jail rather than admit guilt by paying a fine. The mass marches resumed, but again Pritchett thwarted King by having him released from jail to avoid negative publicity. The city's attorney then secured a federal injunction to prevent King and the other leaders from demonstrating. Given his dependence on the federal government, King felt he could not violate the injunction and abandoned the protest. For King, the Albany movement was a failure, his most glaring defeat, and one that called into question the future of the movement.

THE BIRMINGHAM CONFRONTATION

By early 1963 the movement appeared to be stalled. Black communities in many parts of the South were strong and well organized, but for all their enormous effort they had achieved only modest changes. It was impossible to overcome the power of southern state and local government without the intervention of the federal government, but national politicians, including President Kennedy, remained reluctant to act unless faced with open defiance by white people or televised violence against peaceful protesters. King and other black leaders knew that if city government throughout the South followed the model of Sheriff Pritchett in Albany, the civil rights movement might lose momentum. In order to rejuvenate the movement, the SCLC decided to launch a massive new campaign during 1963, the year of the one hundredth anniversary of the Emancipation Proclamation.

Birmingham, Alabama, a large, tightly segregated industrial city, was chosen as the site for the action. The city was ripe for such a protest, in part because the city's black community suffered from severe police brutality as well as economic, educational, and social discrimination. The Ku Klux Klan terrorized people with impunity. The black community had, however, developed a strong phalanx of protest organizations called the Alabama Christian Movement for Human Rights (ACMHR) led by the Reverend Fred Shuttlesworth. The ACMHR and SCLC planned a campaign of boycotts, pickets, and demonstrations code-named Project C for Confrontation. Their program would be far more extensive than any before, with demands for the integration of public facilities, guarantees of employment opportunities for black workers in downtown businesses, desegregation of the schools, improvement of services in black neighborhoods, and the provision of low-income housing. Organizers hoped to provide the city's public safety commissioner Eugene T. "Bull" Connor, who, unlike Albany's police chief Laurie Pritchett, had a reputation for viciousness. Civil rights leaders believed his conduct would horrify the nation and compel Kennedy to act.

Project C began on the third of April with college students conducting sit-ins. Days later, marches began and Connor, following the lead of Pritchett, arrested all who participated but avoided overt violence. When the state courts prohibited further protests, King and Abernathy among others violated the ruling. They were arrested and jailed on Good Friday, April 12, 1963.

While in jail King received a letter from eight local Christian and Jewish clergymen who objected to what they considered the "unwise and untimely" protest activities of black citizens. King had smuggled a pen into jail and on scraps of paper, including toilet paper and the margins of the *Birmingham News*, he wrote an eloquent treatise on the use of direct action. His "Letter from Birmingham Jail" was widely published in newspapers and magazines. In it, King dismissed those who called for black people to wait: "I guess it is easy for those who have never felt the stinging darts of segregation to say, 'Wait.'" But, he declared, "freedom is never voluntarily given by the oppressor; it must be demanded by the oppressed." In the letter King also explained, "Nonviolent direct action seeks to create such a crisis and foster such a tension that a community which has constantly refused to negotiate is forced to confront the issue. It seeks so to dramatize the issue that it can no longer be ignored. . . . Any law that degrades human personality is unjust. All segregation statutes are unjust because segregation distorts the soul and damages the personality. It gives the segregator a false sense of superiority and the segregated a false sense of inferiority."

King's letter had a powerful national impact but the Birmingham movement was beginning to lose momentum because many of the protesters were either in jail or could not risk new arrests. At this juncture James Bevel of the SCLC proposed using schoolchildren to continue the protests. Many observers criticized this idea, as did some of those in the movement. But King and other leaders believed that it was necessary to risk harm to children in order to ensure their freedom. Thus, on May 2 and 3, 1963, a "children's crusade" involving thousands of youths, some as young as six, marched. This tactic enraged "Bull" Connor and his officers. The police not only arrested the children, but flailed away with nightsticks and set vicious dogs on them. On Connor's order, firefighters aimed their powerful hoses at the youngsters, ripping the clothes from backs, cutting flesh, and tumbling children down the street. In the ensuing days many of the children and their parents began to fight back, hurling bottles and rocks at the uniformed tormentors. As the violence escalated, white businessmen became concerned and the city soon came to the bargaining table.

President Kennedy deployed Assistant Attorney General for Civil Rights Burke Marshall to negotiate a

In April and May, 1963, Birmingham's police broke up demonstrations by children and young people with dogs, fire hoses, and nightsticks. Images like this—taken on May 3 when more than 900 young people were jailed—appeared in newspapers and on television nationwide, creating sympathy and support for the civil rights movement.

settlement between city officials and civil rights leaders. On May 10, 1963, white businessmen agreed to integrate downtown facilities and to hire black men and women. The following night the KKK bombed the A. G. Gaston Motel, where the SCLC had its headquarters, and the house that belonged to King's brother, the Reverend A. D. King. Black citizens in turn burned cars and buildings and attacked the police. Only intervention by King and other movement leaders prevented a riot. White moderates delivered on the promises and the agreement stuck.

Although the SCLC did not win on every demand, Birmingham was a major triumph and a turning point in the movement. The summer of 1963 saw a mas-

sive upsurge in protests across the South with nearly eight hundred marches, demonstrations, and sit-ins. Ten civil rights protesters were killed and twenty thousand arrested as the white South desperately sought to stem the tide. In one of the most tragic losses for the movement, white extremist Byron de la Beckwith gunned down Medgar Evers in the driveway of his home on June 12, 1963, in Jackson, Mississippi. Evers had been the executive secretary of the NAACP's Mississippi organization and the center of a powerful movement in that city. His cold-blooded murder dramatized the depth of hatred among some white southerners and the lengths to which they would go to prevent change.

A HARD VICTORY

The sacrifices in Birmingham and the intensification of the movement throughout the South set the stage for Congress to pass legislation for a Second Reconstruction that would at last fulfil the promise of the first.

The March on Washington

The lingering image of Birmingham and the growing number of demonstrations throughout the South compelled action from President Kennedy. On June 11, 1963, he addressed the nation with his strongest statement about civil rights. He declared, "We face . . . a moral crisis as a country and a people. It cannot be met by repressive police action. It cannot be left to increased demonstrations in the streets. It cannot be quieted by token moves or talk. It is a time to act in the Congress, in your state and local legislative body, and above all, in all our daily lives." Kennedy continued, "A great change is at hand, and our task, our obligation, is to make that revolution . . . peaceful and constructive for all." Kennedy subsequently proposed the strongest civil rights bill the country had yet seen, but despite the public's heightened awareness of discrimination, he still could not muster sufficient support in Congress to counter the powerful southern bloc within his own party.

To demonstrate their support for the civil rights legislation that Kennedy proposed, a coalition of civil rights organizations—SCLC, NAACP, CORE, SNCC, and the National Urban League—and their leaders resurrected the idea initially conceived of by A. Philip Randolph in 1941, of organizing a march on Washington. In 1962 Randolph and Bayard Rustin had proposed a march to protest black unemployment. Initially their call received a tepid response, but after Birmingham many of the major civil rights organizations reconsidered. Reflecting renewed hope, Randolph christened it a march for "Jobs and Freedom."

In August 1963, nearly 250,000 marchers gathered before the Lincoln Memorial to show their support for the civil rights bill and the movement at large. Throughout the day they sang freedom songs and listened to speeches from a seemingly endless succession of civil rights leaders. Finally, late in the afternoon, Martin Luther King Jr. arose, and casting aside his prepared remarks, delivered an impassioned speech. Most powerfully, King spoke of this vision of the future:

> I say to you today, my friends, that in spite of the difficulties and frustrations of the moment I still have a dream. It is a dream deeply rooted in the American dream. I have a dream that one day this nation will rise up and live out the true meaning of its creed: "We hold these truths to be self-evident; that all men are created equal." I have a dream that one day on the red hills of Georgia the sons of former slaves and the sons of former slaveowners will be able to sit down together at the table of brotherhood. I have a dream that one day even the state of Mississippi, a desert state sweltering with the heat of injustice and oppression, will be transformed into an oasis of freedom and justice. I have a dream that my four children will one day live in a nation where they will not be judged by the color of their skin but by the content of their character. I have a dream today. I have a dream that one day the state of Alabama, whose governor's lips are presently dripping with the words of interposition and nullification, will be transformed into a situation where little black boys and black girls will be able to join hands with little white boys and white girls and walk together as sisters and brothers. I have a dream today . . .

King's words did not still the angry opposition of some white Southerners. On September 15, 1963, only days after the march on Washington, white racists bombed the 16th St. Baptist Church in Birmingham and killed four little girls attending Sunday school: Addie Mae Collins, Denise McNair, Carole Robertson, and Cynthia Wesley. Chris McNair, the father of the youngest victim, pleaded for calm out of the depth of his own pain, "We must not let this change us into something different than who we are. We must be human." In a similar vein, Martin Luther King sadly intoned, "The innocent blood of these little girls may well serve as the redemptive force that will bring new light to this dark city. . . . Indeed, this tragic event may cause the white South to come to terms with its conscience." The event did have a profound impact on the nation, and combined with the reaction to the assassination of John F. Kennedy in November 1963, set the stage for real change.

The Civil Rights Act of 1964

After Kennedy's death, his successor Lyndon B. Johnson lobbied hard to secure passage of the landmark Civil Rights Act. Many in the civil rights movement feared that Johnson, a Southerner, would back his region's defiance. Nonetheless, only four days after taking the oath of office, Johnson told the nation that he planned to support the civil rights bill as a memorial for the slain president. A master politician, Johnson proceeded to push the bill through Congress despite a marathon filibuster by its opponents.

VIOLENCE AND THE CIVIL RIGHTS MOVEMENT

May 7, 1955	The Reverend George Lee killed for leading voter registration drive, Belzoni, MS
August 13, 1955	Lamar Smith murdered for organizing black voters, Brookhaven, MS
August 28, 1955	Emmett Louis Till murdered for speaking to white woman, Money, MS
October 22, 1955	John Earl Reese slain by nightriders opposed to black school improvements, Mayflower, TX
January 23, 1957	Willie Edwards Jr. killed by Klan, Montgomery, AL
September 24, 1957	President Eisenhower orders federal troops to enforce school desegregation, Little Rock, AK
April 27, 1959	Mack Charles Parker taken from jail and lynched, Popularville, MS
May 14, 1961	Freedom Riders attacked in Alabama while testing compliance with bus desegregation laws
September 25, 1961	Voter registration worker Herbert Lee killed by a white legislator, Liberty, MS
April 1, 1962	Civil rights groups join forces to launch voter registration drive
April 9, 1962	Roman Ducksworth Jr. taken from bus and killed by police, Taylorsville, MS
September 30, 1962	Riots erupt when James Meredith, a black student, enrolls at the University of Mississippi. Paul Guihard, European reporter, killed
April 23, 1963	William Lewis Moore slain during one-man march against segregation, Attalla, AL
May 3, 1963	Birmingham police attack marching children with dogs and fire hoses
June 12, 1963	Medgar Evers, civil rights leader, assassinated, Jackson, MS
September 15, 1963	Schoolgirls Addie Mae Collins, Denise McNair, Carole Robertson, and Cynthia Wesley die in the bombing of the 16th St. Baptist Church, Birmingham, AL
September 15, 1963	Virgin Lamar Ware killed during racist violence, Birmingham, AL
January 31, 1964	Louis Allen, witness to the murder of a civil rights worker, assassinated, Liberty, MS

VIOLENCE AND THE CIVIL RIGHTS MOVEMENT—CONT'D

April 7, 1964	The Reverend Bruce Klunder killed protesting construction of segregated school, Cleveland, OH
May 2, 1964	Henry Hezekiah Dee and Charles Eddie Moore killed by Klan, Meadville, MS
June 21, 1964	Civil rights workers James Chaney, Andrew Goodman, and Michael Schwerner abducted and slain by Klan, Philadelphia, MS
July 11, 1964	Lt. Col. Lemuel Penn killed by Klan while driving north, Colbert, GA
February 26, 1965	Jimmie Lee Jackson, civil rights marcher killed by state trooper, Marion, AL
March 11, 1965	Selma to Montgomery march volunteer, the Reverend James Reeb, beaten to death, Selma, AL
March 25, 1965	Viola Gregg Liuzzo killed by Klan while transporting marchers, Selma Highway, AL
June 2, 1965	Oneal Moore, black deputy, killed by nightriders, Varnado, LA
July 18, 1965	Willie Wallace Brewster killed by nightriders, Anniston, AL
August 20, 1965	Jonathan Daniels, seminary student, killed by deputy, Hayneville, AL
January 3, 1966	Samuel Younge Jr., student civil rights activist, killed in dispute over whites only restroom, Tuskegee, AL
January 10, 1966	Vernon Dahmer, black community leader killed in Klan bombing, Hattiesburg, MS
June 10, 1966	Ben Chester White killed by Klan, Natchez, MS
July 30, 1966	Clarence Triggs slain by nightriders, Bogalusa, LA
February 2, 1967	Wharlest Jackson, civil rights leader, killed when police fired on protesters, Jackson, MS
February 8, 1968	Students Samuel Hammond Jr., Delano Middleton, and Henry Smith killed when highway patrolmen fire on protesters, Orangeburg, SC
April 4, 1968	Dr. Martin Luther King Jr. assassinated, Memphis, TN

The Civil Rights Act of 1964 was the culmination of the civil rights movement to that time. The most important provisions of the act banned discrimination in places of public accommodation, including restaurants, hotels, gas stations, and entertainment facilities, as well as schools, parks, playgrounds, libraries, and swimming pools. The desegregation of public accommodations irrevocably changed the face of American society. The issue of legally mandated racial separation was now settled. The act also banned discrimination by employers of labor unions on the basis of race, color, religion, national origin, and sex in regard to hiring, promoting, dismissing, or making job referrals. The act had strong provisions for enforcement. Most important, it allowed government agencies to withhold federal money from any program permitting or practicing discrimination. This provision had particular import for the desegregation of schools and colleges across the country. The act also gave the U.S. attorney general the power to initiate proceedings against segregated facilities and schools on behalf of people who could not do so on their own. Finally it created the Equal Employment Opportunity Commission to monitor discrimination in employment.

Mississippi Freedom Summer

While Congress considered the Civil Rights Act, movement activists renewed their focus on voter registration in the deep South. In the fall of 1963, many CORE and SNCC workers saw segregation crumbling, but they knew that without the ballot, African Americans could never drive racist politicians from office, gain a fair hearing in court, reduce police and mob violence, or get equal services from state and local governments. CORE took responsibility for running registration campaigns in Louisiana, South Carolina, and Florida while SNCC took on the two most repressive states, Alabama and Mississippi. Mississippi was widely known in the movement as the "toughest nut to crack"—the symbolic center of American racism and white violence. By the summer of 1964 national attention had shifted from Alabama to Mississippi, the site of a massive project known as "Freedom Summer."

The voter registration campaign in Mississippi began in late 1963 when Robert "Bob" Moses mobilized the Council of Federated Organizations (COFO), which had been established in 1961 to aid imprisoned freedom riders. Moses convinced the members of COFO (CORE, SNCC, SCLC, and the NAACP) to sponsor a mock Freedom Election in Mississippi. On election day 80,000 disfranchised black people cast ballots for COFO candidates. Impressed with the turnout, Moses and other COFO members believed that a massive effort to register voters during the summer of 1964 might break the white monopoly on the ballot box.

After much debate, COFO decided to invite a large number of northern white students to participate in the Mississippi project. These students, about one thousand in all, were to be drawn primarily from the nation's most prestigious universities. This move contradicted the movement's emphasis on black empowerment, but COFO leaders calculated that the presence of elite white students in the Magnolia State would attract increased media attention and pressure the federal government to provide protection.

Shortly after the project began, three volunteers, two white New Yorkers—twenty-four-year-old Michael Schwerner and twenty-one-year-old Andrew Goodman—and a black Mississippian, twenty-one-year-old James Chaney disappeared. Unknown at the time, Cecil Price, deputy sheriff of Philadelphia, Mississippi, had arrested the three on a trumped-up speeding charge. That evening the young men were delivered to a deserted road where three carloads of Klansmen waited. Schwerner and Goodman were shot to death. Chaney was beaten with chains and then shot.

These events were not publicly known until Klan informers, enticed by a $30,000 reward, led investigators to the earthen dam in which Goodman, Schwerner, and Chaney had been buried. The disappearance of the three nonetheless focused national attention on white terrorism. During the summer, approximately thirty homes and thirty-seven churches were bombed, thirty-five civil rights workers were shot at, eighty people were beaten, six were murdered, and more than 1,000 arrested. In the face of this violence, uncertainty, and fear, many SNCC activists rejected Martin Luther King's commitment to nonviolence, the inclusion of white activists in the movement, and the wisdom of integration. Divisions over these issues greatly increased tensions among the groups that made up the movement.

Despite all the problems it encountered, the Freedom Summer succeeded in organizing dozens of Freedom Schools and community centers throughout Mississippi. Its efforts mobilized the black people of Mississippi to an extent not seen since the first Reconstruction. Many communities began to develop the rudiments of a political movement, one that would grow in coming years.

The Mississippi Freedom Democratic Party

Freedom Summer intersected with national politics at the Democratic party's national convention in August 1964 in Atlantic City, New Jersey. White Mississippians routinely excluded African Americans from the political process, and Robert Moses encouraged COFO to set up the Mississippi Freedom Democratic Party (MFDP) to mount a challenge to the state's regular Democratic delegation at the convention. Under the leadership of veteran activists Fannie Lou Hamer, Victoria Gray, Annie Divine, and Aaron Henry, the MFDP held its first state convention on August 6. Approximately 80,000 citizens

PROFILE

FANNIE LOU HAMER

Fannie Lou Hamer (1917–1977) emerged from the ranks of "local people" in Mississippi to become one of the most powerful leaders and orators of the civil rights movement. Unlike many major leaders, Hamer, the youngest of twenty children, had grown up in extreme poverty and had only a few years of education. She worked and lived as a timekeeper on a plantation in Ruleville, Mississippi. When SNCC workers came to the community for a voting rights campaign, Hamer was one of the first to participate. Despite the great danger of doing so, Hamer supported the civil rights workers because, as she said,

Fannie Lou Hamer and other delegates from the Mississippi Freedom Democratic Party protest outside the convention hall in Atlantic City after being denied seats at the 1964 Democratic National Convention.

> Nobody ever came out into the country and talked to real farmers and things because this is the next thing this country has done: it divided us into classes, and if you hadn't arrived at a certain level, you wasn't treated no better by blacks than you was by the whites. And it was these kids who broke a lot of that down. They treated us like we were special and we loved 'em. . . . We didn't feel uneasy about our language might not be right or something. We just felt we could talk to 'em. We trusted 'em.

On August 1, 1962, Hamer attempted to register to vote in Indianapolis, Mississippi. The response was immediate. She was fired from her plantation job and evicted from her land. Still, she refused to capitulate to threats and instead accepted full-time employment as a field secretary for SNCC and worked on the Voter Education Project. This aroused even more police hostility. On June 9, 1963, she and eight other women on their way back from a workshop in South Carolina were arrested by the police in Winona, Mississippi. Hamer was beaten severely and never fully recovered from the injuries she suffered.

Despite her lack of education, Hamer was a spellbinding orator who had the ability to move not only her friends and neighbors but the nation as well. Her televised testimony before the 1964 Democratic convention won tremendous national support for the MFDP's challenge to the party regulars from Mississippi. The next year Hamer, who had run for the House of Representatives, challenged the seating of the Mississippi congressional delegation. Although unsuccessful, her action helped to reduce tolerance for disfranchisement and paved the way for the Voting Rights Act of 1965.

After 1965, Hamer continued to fight for her people. Although basic civil and voting rights had been won by then, most black people in the Mississippi Delta still lived in deep poverty. In 1968 Hamer sought to address this problem by setting up the nonprofit Freedom Farms Corporation as an agricultural cooperative. With help from northern supporters, the enterprise had some success, but the problems it confronted proved overwhelming. The mixed results of this last campaign, however, cannot diminish the profound changes that Fannie Lou Hamer was so instrumental in bringing about. She died in 1977.

put their names on the rolls. The convention elected sixty-four delegates who traveled to the national convention to present their credentials.

The MFDP challenge caused considerable difficulty for the Democratic party. Many liberals wanted to seat the civil rights delegation, but President Lyndon Johnson, who was running for reelection, did not want to alienate white Southerners, fearing that they would vote for Barry Goldwater, his Republican opponent. Liberal Democratic senator from Minnesota, Hubert H. Humphrey, worked out a compromise calling for Mississippi regulars to be seated if they swore loyalty to the national party and agreed to cast their forty-four votes accordingly. The compromise also provided for the creation of two "at large" seats to be filled by members of the MFDP, specifically Aaron Henry and Ed King. The rest of the Freedom Democrats could attend the convention as nonvoting guests.

Martin Luther King Jr., Bayard Rustin, and other black leaders counseled acceptance of this compromise. Johnson and the Democrats, they argued, had achieved much of the legislative program favored by the movement, and if the party were returned to power they could do much more. But most of the MFDP delegation, fed up with the violence of Mississippi and unwilling to settle for token representation, were deeply disappointed and rejected the compromise. Many members of SNCC, bitter and angry, turned their backs on liberalism and cooperation with white people of any political persuasion.

Selma and the Voting Rights Act of 1965

The Civil Rights Act of 1964 contained provisions for helping black voters to register, but white resistance in the deep South had rendered them ineffective. In Alabama, for example, at least 77 percent of black citizens were unable to vote. Their cause was taken up by businesswoman Amelia P. Boynton, owner of an employment and insurance agency in Selma, along with her husband and a high school teacher, the Reverend Frederick Reese, who also led the Dallas County Voters League. These three, with others, fought for black enfranchisement and an end to discriminatory treatment. Their struggle would help to pass the Voting Rights Act of 1965, which finally ended the systematic exclusion of African Americans from southern politics.

Selma's sheriff James G. Clark worked to block the voter registration activity sponsored by the Boyntons, Reese, and SNCC suffrage workers. By 1964 fewer than four hundred of the 15,000 eligible African Americans had registered to vote in Dallas County. President Lyn-

don Johnson refused requests to deploy federal marshals to the county to protect voter registration workers. Seeking reinforcements, the workers sent a call to Martin Luther King Jr. and the SCLC. King came and was promptly arrested. In mid-February 1965, during a night march in neighboring Perry County, twenty-six-year-old Jimmie Lee Jackson was shot in the stomach as he tried to shield his mother from a beating by a state trooper. His death and the thrashing of several reporters attracted the national media.

SCLC announced plans for a mass march from Selma to Montgomery to begin on Sunday, March 7, 1965. At the forefront of six hundred protesters were King; one of his aides, Hosea Williams; and the chairman of SNCC, John Lewis. As the marchers approached the Edmund Pettus Bridge, state troopers and Sheriff Clark's county

On March 25, 1963, more than two weeks after "Bloody Sunday," when police brutalized civil rights marchers trying to cross Selma's Edmund Pettus Bridge, a second march finally completed the 53-mile trek to Montgomery. Among the leaders are Martin Luther King Jr., Coretta Scott King, Hosea Williams, Bayard Rustin, and Ralph Bunche. The violence preceding this successful march convinced President Johnson, proclaiming "We shall overcome," to submit voting rights legislation to Congress.

police, in a shocking display of aggression, teargassed and brutally beat the retreating marchers while their horses trampled the fallen. Captured in graphic detail by television cameras, this battle became known as "Bloody Sunday." Seizing the moment, King and the activists rescheduled a pilgrimage for March 9. The SCLC leader soon found himself in a dilemma. A federal judge, who was normally supportive of civil rights, had issued an injunction against the march. Moreover, President Johnson and many other key figures in the government urged King not to go through with it. King was reluctant to violate a federal injunction and he knew that he needed Johnson's support to win strong voting rights legislation. At the same time, the people of Selma and the hundreds of young SNCC workers would probably march even if King did not.

When the day of the march came 1,500 protesters marched to the bridge singing "Ain't Gonna Let Nobody Turn Me 'Round" and other freedom songs. To their surprise, King crossed the Pettus Bridge, prayed briefly, and turned around. He had privately made a face-saving compromise with the federal authorities. SNCC workers felt betrayed and King's leadership fell into question. That evening a white Unitarian minister

from Boston, James Reeb, was clubbed to death by local white people. His martyrdom created a national outcry and prompted Johnson to action. On March 15, the president in a televised address to Congress, announced that he would submit voter registration legislation. In his address he praised civil rights activists electrifying them when he invoked the movement's slogan to declare, in his Texas drawl, "We shall overcome."

The protests at Selma and the white massive resistance spurred the United States Congress to pass the Voting Rights Act of 1965, which President Johnson signed on August 6. The major provision of the act outlawed educational requirements for voting in states or counties where less than half the voting age population had been registered on November 1, 1964, or had voted in the 1964 presidential election. A second component of the act empowered the attorney general to have the Civil Rights Commission assign federal registrars to enroll voters. The attorney general, Nicholas Katzenbach, immediately deployed federal registrars in nine southern counties. Within months, federal examiners had registered approximately 80,000 new voters. In Mississippi, black registrants soared from 28,500 in 1964 to 251,000 in 1968 (Map 21–2).

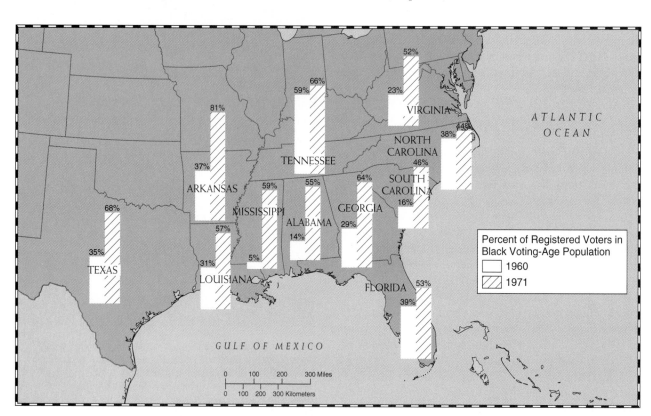

Map 21–2 The Effect of the Voting Rights Act of 1965. The Voting Rights Act enabled millions of previously disfranchised African Americans in the South to vote.

Gaining voting rights made a tremendous difference. Before passage of the act, Fannie Lou Hamer had unsuccessfully challenged the seating of the regular Mississippi representatives before the U.S. House of Representatives. In 1968 she was selected a delegate to the Democratic party convention. To be sure, southern state legislators did not accept the implementation of the act without resistance. They instituted a dazzling array of disfranchisement devices such as gerrymandering, at-large elections, more appointive offices, and higher qualifications for candidates. But the era when white supremacy lay at the core of southern politics was at an end.

CONCLUSION

The success of the civil rights movement depended on many factors. The federal government intervened at crucial moments to enact historic civil rights legislation, issue judgments on behalf of the civil rights protesters, and protect the rule of law with federal marshals and soldiers. Black leaders deliberately pursued strategies to provoke confrontations that would ensure intervention by the federal government and garner widespread media coverage. For more than a decade, the victorious freedom fighters of the civil rights movement stormed the legal barricades of segregation. The uncompromising struggle of African Americans, their organizations, and their white allies pressured federal officials in the legislative, executive, and judicial branches of government to enact major civil rights legislation, issue executive orders, and deliver significant judicial decisions that dismantled segregation in the South.

The victories of this era were far reaching, but as they were achieved, new issues arose that would fracture the movement. The civil rights movement had largely been focused on the South. Black Northerners already had many of the rights granted by the federal legislation of the era; nonetheless, they still suffered from many forms of discrimination. Addressing their problems required different techniques and new ways of thinking that would emerge over the coming decade.

REVIEW QUESTIONS

1. Discuss the role that "ordinary" or local people played in the civil rights movement. What were some of the specific contributions of children to the overall struggle for social change?

2. What were the key issues and events that provoked intervention by the federal government into the civil

rights movement? What were the major pieces of legislation enacted and how did they dismantle legalized segregation?

3. What were the ideologies, objectives, and tactics of the major civil rights organizations and their leaders?

4. What were the human costs of the civil rights movement? Who were some of the people who lost their lives in the struggle?

5. What were the major successes and failures of the freedom movement? What were some of the intergenerational tensions that plagued the movement? In what way did the movement transform American politics and society?

RECOMMENDED READING

Taylor Branch. *Parting the Waters: America in the King Years, 1954–63.* New York: Simon & Schuster, 1988. Richly researched, lively study that places King at the center of American politics during a critically transformative decade.

Clayborne Carson. *In Struggle: SNCC and the Black Awakening of the 1960s.* Cambridge, MA: Harvard University Press, 1981. One of the best historical studies of SNCC and the contributions students made to galvanize the civil rights movement.

Vickie Crawford, Jacqueline Rouse, and Barbara Woods, eds. *Women in the Civil Rights Movement: Trailblazers and Torchbearers.* Brooklyn: Carlson Publishing, 1990. An anthology of essays presented at a symposium. The meeting was designed to draw attention to the women whose contributions to the freedom struggle of the 1950s and 1960s are often overlooked or neglected.

Henry Hampton and Steve Fayer, eds. *The Voices of Freedom: An Oral History of the Civil Rights Movement from the 1950s through the 1980s.* New York: Bantam Books, 1990. A remarkable and indispensable oral history of all the participants in the civil rights movement, from the least well known to the internationally celebrated.

Steven F. Lawson. *Running for Freedom: Civil Rights and Black Politics in America since 1941.* Philadelphia: Temple University Press, 1991. A succinct analysis of the politics, legislative measures, and individuals that figured in the successes and failures of the civil rights movement.

Aldon D. Morris. *The Origins of the Modern Civil Rights Movement: Black Communities Organizing for Change.*

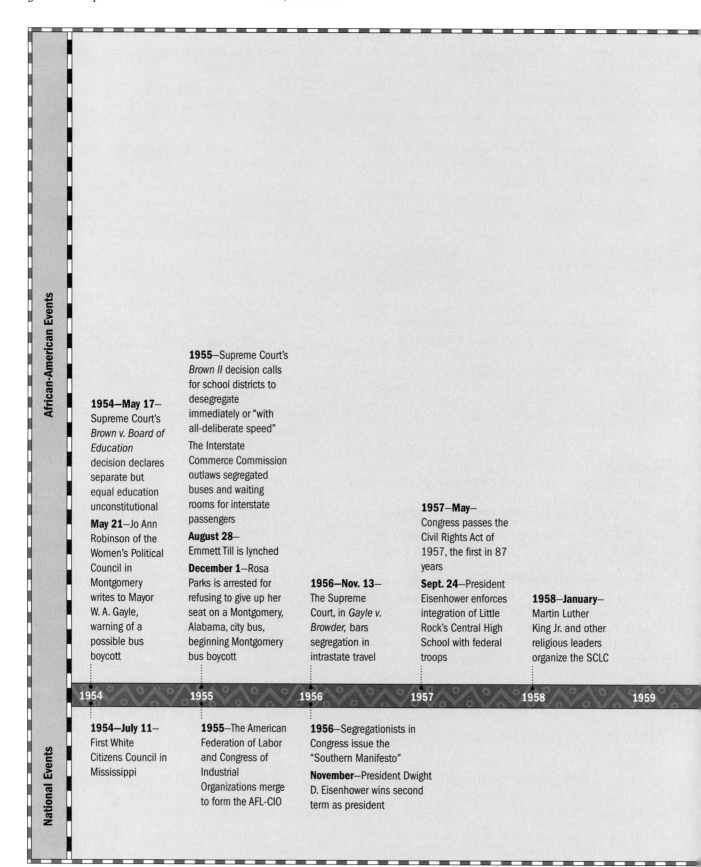

African-American Events

1954—May 17—Supreme Court's *Brown v. Board of Education* decision declares separate but equal education unconstitutional

May 21—Jo Ann Robinson of the Women's Political Council in Montgomery writes to Mayor W. A. Gayle, warning of a possible bus boycott

1955—Supreme Court's *Brown II* decision calls for school districts to desegregate immediately or "with all-deliberate speed"

The Interstate Commerce Commission outlaws segregated buses and waiting rooms for interstate passengers

August 28—Emmett Till is lynched

December 1—Rosa Parks is arrested for refusing to give up her seat on a Montgomery, Alabama, city bus, beginning Montgomery bus boycott

1956—Nov. 13—The Supreme Court, in *Gayle v. Browder,* bars segregation in intrastate travel

1957—May—Congress passes the Civil Rights Act of 1957, the first in 87 years

Sept. 24—President Eisenhower enforces integration of Little Rock's Central High School with federal troops

1958—January—Martin Luther King Jr. and other religious leaders organize the SCLC

| 1954 | 1955 | 1956 | 1957 | 1958 | 1959 |

National Events

1954—July 11—First White Citizens Council in Mississippi

1955—The American Federation of Labor and Congress of Industrial Organizations merge to form the AFL-CIO

1956—Segregationists in Congress issue the "Southern Manifesto"

November—President Dwight D. Eisenhower wins second term as president

1963—April–May— Project C highlights racial injustices in Birmingham

King writes his celebrated "Letter from Birmingham Jail"

June—Federal government compels Alabama Governor George C. Wallace to desegregate the University of Alabama

June 12—Medgar Evers is murdered

Aug. 17—W. E. B. DuBois dies in Ghana, Africa, at 95

Aug. 28—The March on Washington; Martin Luther King Jr. delivers his "I Have A Dream" speech

Sept. 15—Ku Klux Klan bombs the 16th Street Baptist Church in Birmingham, Alabama, killing four girls

December—Malcolm X breaks with Elijah Muhammad and the Nation of Islam and founds his own movement, Muslim Mosque

1964—SNCC launches the Mississippi Freedom Summer Project to promote voter registration

January—Twenty-fourth Amendment to the United States Constitution is ratified, outlawing the poll tax

June 21—James E. Chaney, Michael Schwerner, and Andrew Goodman murdered in Mississippi

July 2—Civil Rights Act of 1964 enacted

August—The Mississippi Freedom Democratic Party denied seating at the Democratic National Convention

December—Martin Luther King Jr. wins the Nobel Peace Prize

1961—May— Freedom riders attacked in Alabama and Mississippi

Sept. 23— Kennedy names Thurgood Marshall to the Second Circuit Court of Appeals

Sept. 25—Herbert Lee, a local activist, is killed in Amite County, Mississippi

1962—February— The Council of Federated Organizations (COFO) is formed.

June 25—James Meredith desegregates the University of Mississippi with federal support

July—The Albany Movement fails

August—Voter Education Project launched

1960—Feb. 1— Black students sit in at Woolworth lunch counter in Greensboro, North Carolina launching the sit-in movement

April—SNCC founded

November—Black vote critical to Kennedy's election

1965—March 21— Civil rights marchers walk from Selma to Montgomery after violent confrontation in Selma

Aug. 6—Voting Rights Act of 1965 enacted

1960	1961	1962	1963	1964	1965

1960—November— John F. Kennedy elected president

1963—Nov. 22— President Kennedy is assassinated

Lyndon Johnson succeeds to the presidency

1964—Equal Employment Opportunity Commission established

1965—Lyndon Johnson outlines the Great Society Program to attack poverty

New York: Free Press; London: Collier Macmillan, 1984. An important and insightful analysis of the mobilization and organizing strategies pursued by diverse communities for social change that paved the way for the modern civil rights movement.

ADDITIONAL BIBLIOGRAPHY

General Overviews of Civil Rights Movement and Organizations

Robert Fredrick Burk. *The Eisenhower Administration and Black Civil Rights.* Knoxville: University of Tennessee Press, 1984.

Stewart Burns. *Daybreak of Freedom: The Montgomery Bus Boycott.* Chapel Hill: University of North Carolina Press, 1997.

John Dittmer. *Local People: The Struggle for Civil Rights in Mississippi.* Urbana: University of Illinois Press, 1994.

Adam Fairclough. *To Redeem the Soul of America: The Southern Christian Leadership Conference and Martin Luther King, Jr.* Athens: University of Georgia Press, 1987.

David R. Goldfield. *Black, White and Southern: Race Relations and the Southern Culture, 1940 to the Present.* Baton Rouge: Louisiana State University Press, 1991.

Martin Luther King, Jr. *Stride Towards Freedom: The Montgomery Story.* New York: Harper, 1958.

Steven F. Lawson. *Black Ballots: Voting Rights in the South, 1944–1969.* New York: Columbia University Press, 1976.

Manning Marable. *Race, Reform, and Rebellion: The Second Reconstruction in Black America, 1945–1982.* Jackson: University Press of Mississippi, 1984.

Anne Moody. *Coming of Age in Mississippi.* New York: Dial Press, 1968.

August Meier and Elliot Rudwick. *CORE: A Study of the Civil Rights Movement, 1942–1968.* New York: Oxford University Press, 1973.

Donald G. Nieman. *Promises to Keep: African-Americans and the Constitutional Order, 1776 to the Present.* New York: Oxford University Press, 1991.

Robert J. Norrell. *Reaping the Whirlwind: The Civil Rights Movement in Tuskegee.* New York: Knopf, 1985.

Charles M. Payne. *I've Got the Light of Freedom: The Organizing Tradition and the Mississippi Freedom Struggle.* Berkeley: University of California Press, 1995.

Fred Powledge. *Free at Last? The Civil Rights Movement and the People Who Made It.* Boston: Little, Brown, 1991.

Howell Raines. *My Soul Is Rested: Movement Days in the Deep South Remembered.* New York: Putnam, 1977.

Belinda Robnett. *How Long? How Long? African-American Women in the Struggle for Civil Rights.* New York: Oxford University Press, 1997.

Juan Williams. *Eyes on the Prize: America's Civil Rights Years, 1954–1965.* New York: Viking, 1987.

Black Politics/White Resistance

Numan V. Bartley. *The Rise of Massive Resistance: Race and Politics in the South during the 1950's.* Baton Rouge: Louisiana State University Press, 1969.

Elizabeth Jacoway and David R. Colburn. *Southern Businessmen and Desegregation.* Baton Rouge: Louisiana State University Press, 1982.

Doug McAdam. *Freedom Summer.* New York: Oxford University Press, 1988.

Neil R. McMillen. *The Citizen's Council: A History of Organized Resistance to the Second Reconstruction.* Urbana: University of Illinois Press, 1971.

Frank R. Parker. *Black Votes Count: Political Empowerment in Mississippi after 1965.* Chapel Hill: University of North Carolina Press, 1990.

Autobiography and Biography

Daisy Bates. *The Long Shadow of Little Rock: Memoir.* New York: David McKay Co., 1962.

Taylor Branch. *Pillar of Fire: America in the King Years, 1963–65.* New York: Simon & Schuster, 1998.

Eric R. Burner. *And Gently He Shall Lead Them: Robert Parris Moses and Civil Rights in Mississippi.* New York, New York University Press, 1994.

Septima Clark. *Ready from Within: Septima Clark and the Civil Rights Movement.* Navarro, CA: Wild Tree Press, 1986.

Robert S. Dallek. *Flawed Giant: Lyndon Johnson and His Times, 1961–1973.* New York: Oxford University Press, 1998.

Dennis C. Dickerson. *Militant Mediator: Whitney M. Young, Jr., 1921–1971.* Lexington: University Press of Kentucky, 1998.

James Farmer. *Lay Bare the Heart: An Autobiography of the Civil Rights Movement.* New York: Arbor House, 1985.

Cynthia Griggs Fleming. *Soon We Will Not Cry: The Liberation of Ruby Doris Smith Robinson.* Lanham, MD: Rowman & Littlefield, 1998.

David J. Garrow. *Bearing the Cross: Martin Luther King, Jr., and the Southern Christian Leadership Conference.* New York: William Morrow & Company, 1986.

———. *The FBI and Martin Luther King, Jr.* New York: Penguin Books, 1981.

Chana Kai Lee. *For Freedom's Sake: The Life of Fannie Lou Hamer.* Urbana: University of Illinois Press, 1999.

David Levering Lewis. *King: A Critical Biography.* New York: Praeger, 1970.

Timothy B. Tyson. *Radio Free Dixie: Robert F. Williams and the Roots of Black Power.* Chapel Hill: University of North Carolina Press, 1999.

Jo Ann Gibson Robinson, with David Garrow. *The Montgomery Bus Boycott and the Women Who Started It.* Knoxville: University of Tennessee Press, 1987.

Reference Works

Charles Eagles, ed., *The Civil Rights Movement in America.* Jackson: University Press of Mississippi, 1986.

Charles S. Lowery and John F. Marszalek, eds. *Encyclopedia of African-American Civil Rights: From Emancipation to the Present.* New York: Greenwood Press, 1992.

CHAPTER 22

THE STRUGGLE CONTINUES,
1965–1980

The Black Panther Party advocated a radical economic, social, and educational agenda that made it the target of a determined campaign of suppression by police and the FBI.

CHAPTER OUTLINE

We must work on two levels. In every city we have a dual society. . . . In every city, we have two economies. In every city, we have two housing markets. In every city, we have two school systems. This duality has brought about a great deal of injustice. . . . Black Power in the positive sense is a psychological call to manhood . . . and a sense of dignity. . . . Black Power is pooling black political resources in order to achieve our legitimate goals. . . . Black Power in its positive sense is a pooling of black economic resources in order to achieve legitimate power. . . . What is necessary now is to see integration in political terms. . . . [T]here are times when we must see segregation as a temporary way-station to the ultimate goal which we seek . . . a truly integrated society where there is shared power.

—Martin Luther King Jr.

Black Power . . . a call for black people in this country to unite, to recognize their heritage, to build a sense of community . . . to define their own goals, to lead their own organizations . . . to reject the racist institutions and values of this society. The concept of Black Power rests on a fundamental premise: *Before a group can enter the open society, it must first close ranks.* [emphasis in the original]

—Stokely Carmichael and Charles V. Hamilton

When Lyndon Johnson became president in 1963 after John F. Kennedy's assassination, he brought to the office impressive political skills and a determination to reconcile the racial, social, and economic disparities dividing black from white Americans. Johnson's escalation of America's involvement in Vietnam, however, undermined his domestic social policies. Meanwhile, some African Americans lost faith in and patience with American society. In the face of a white backlash against the gains of the civil rights movement, many leaders and scholars—like Carmichael and Hamilton—argued for black power and black separatism. Black power, which challenged both the interracialism of the civil rights movement and Johnson's democratic liberalism, became the dominant ideology for many younger activists. King remained ambivalent about black power, preferring to define it as a temporary strategy for black solidarity in the struggle for an integrated society. A. Philip Randolph called black power a "menace to peace and prosperity" and added, "No Negro who is fighting for civil rights can support black power, which is opposed to civil rights and integration." These opposing ideologies represent a generational shift and the tensions between them frame many of the key events of the post–civil rights movement years.

THE FADING DREAM OF RACIAL INTEGRATION: WHITE BACKLASH AND BLACK NATIONALISM

Even though President Johnson easily defeated Republican senator Barry Goldwater, the 1964 election could hardly be called a mandate for civil rights. In California, for example, voters gave Johnson a decisive victory but also approved an amendment to the state constitution that not only repealed all existing legislation prohibiting discrimination in the sale or rental of housing but prevented such legislation from ever being enacted in the future. Although the amendment was later struck down by the Supreme Court, its passage suggested that white opposition to racial integration was not confined to the South. When, in 1966, Johnson asked Congress for federal legislation to ban discrimination in housing, a weakened version of his bill died in

the Senate. In elections that year, white opposition to civil rights helped elect a number of Republicans, including former movie actor Ronald Reagan as governor of California.

Meanwhile, Alabama governor George Wallace, an outspoken opponent of racial integration and civil rights legislation, was emerging as a national political figure. With limited resources, he had run surprisingly well against Johnson in the 1964 Wisconsin, Indiana, and Maryland Democratic primaries. Heartened by the favorable response he received from northern white voters, Wallace was planning a full-scale presidential race in 1968.

With many white Americans increasingly reluctant to support the goals of the civil rights movement, many black Americans began searching for new approaches to their problems. The reign of terror experienced by COFO (Council of Federated Organizations) workers in Mississippi had undermined the commitment to integration and nonviolence of the civil rights movement and would help radicalize a new, younger generation of activists. Men like Floyd McKissick of the Congress of Racial Equality (CORE) and Stokely Carmichael of the Student Nonviolent Coordinating Committee (SNCC) became disillusioned, rejecting King's moderation, nonviolence, and universalism. The differences between King's SCLC (Southern Christian Leadership Conference) and Carmichael's SNCC grew with each confrontation. Carmichael had argued after the 1964 failure of the Mississippi Freedom Democratic party that it was time to form an independent black political party. In 1965, after the Selma-to-Montgomery march, he helped found the Lowndes County (Mississippi) Freedom Organization (LCFO). It became the first political organization in the civil rights movement to adopt the symbol of the black panther.

Black residents of northern and western cities also lost patience with the slow pace of change. Growing numbers of young African Americans, dismayed by the great political and economic disparities between themselves and white Americans, emerged as the catalyst for an increasingly radical turn in the civil rights movement.

Malcolm X

After 1965, the year in which he died, no one had more influence on young black activists and the residents of America's ghettoized inner cities than Malcolm X. The son of a Baptist preacher, he was born Malcolm Little in Omaha, Nebraska, and grew up in Lansing, Michigan. His family's home was burned by Klan terrorists, and his father was murdered two years later. His mother was subsequently committed to a mental institution and welfare agencies split the children up. Malcolm was sent to a juvenile detention home, quit school after the eighth grade, and moved to Boston to live with his sister. There, he became involved in the street life of gambling, drugs, and burglary. He was arrested and sentenced to a ten-year prison term in 1942. During the six and a half years he spent in prison, he embraced the teachings of Elijah Muhammad of the Nation of Islam and renounced what he considered his "slave name" to become Malcolm X. In 1954 he became minister of Harlem's Temple Number 7. Articulate, charismatic, and forceful, Malcolm did not believe in nonviolence or advocate integration. His was the voice of the northern urban "second ghettoes." In 1961 he began publishing *Muhammad Speaks*, the official newspaper of the Nation. In *The Autobiography of Malcolm X*, published in 1965 by the writer Alex Haley of *Roots* fame, Malcolm declared:

> Few white people realize that many black people today dislike and avoid spending any more time than they must around white people. This "integration" image, as it is popularly interpreted, has millions of vain, self-exalted white people convinced that black people want to sleep in bed with them—and that's a lie! Oh you can't tell the average white man that the Negro man's prime desire isn't to have a white woman—another lie! Like a black brother recently observed to me, "Look, you ever smell one of them wet?"

Malcolm X attracted black people's attention. His dismissal of the goal of racial integration and King's message of redemption through brotherly love resonated with many younger civil rights workers disillusioned by white violence. "The day of nonviolent resistance is over," Malcolm insisted. And in 1964, he declared, "Revolutions are never based upon love-your-enemy, and pray-for-those-who-despitefully-use-you. And revolutions are never waged by singing 'We Shall Overcome.' Revolutions are based on bloodshed."

Malcolm X's New Departure

Malcolm X's popularity created tensions between himself and the leadership of the Nation of Islam. He grew disillusioned with Elijah Muhammad's aversion to political activism, and Elijah Muhammad grew jealous of Malcolm's success. When Malcolm described the Kennedy assassination as a case of "the chickens coming home to roost" (meaning Kennedy was a victim of the same kind of violence that afflicted black people), Elijah

Malcolm X frightened white Americans and captivated black Americans with his blunt assertiveness. The passions he aroused have cooled since his death. In 1999 the U.S. Postal Service issued a stamp bearing his likeness.

Muhammad reprimanded and suspended him. In 1964, Malcolm broke with the Nation of Islam and founded his own organization, the Muslim Mosque, Inc. That same year he went on a pilgrimage to Mecca that had a profound influence on him. He changed his name to El-Hajj Malik El-Shabazz, founded the Organization for Afro-American Unity (after the Organization of African Unity), repudiated the Nation of Islam doctrine that all white people are evil, and began lecturing on the connection between the civil rights struggle in the South and the struggle against colonialism in Africa. On February 14, 1965, assassins associated with the Nation of Islam killed Malcolm X as he addressed an audience in Harlem.

Malcolm's militant advocacy of self-defense, of "overturning systems" that deprive African Americans of basic human rights, helped to prod other black leaders of the civil rights movement towards more radical positions.

Stokely Carmichael and Black Power

In 1966 Stokely Carmichael, a native of Trinidad who had been raised in New York City and educated at Howard University, became chairman of SNCC. By then he had given up on the ideal of interracial collaboration and was determined to move SNCC toward black nationalism. He dismissed SNCC's few white staffers, including Bob Zellner, who had been with the organization since its inception.

About this time, James Meredith began a one-man "march against fear" from Tennessee to Jackson, Mississippi, to encourage black Southerners to register and vote. On this march, he was shot and wounded by white gunmen. In June 1966, after this incident, SNCC and Carmichael joined with other organizations to complete the march. It was at this time that Carmichael popularized the slogan "Black Power" that was to become SNCC's rallying cry. "The only way we gonna stop them white men from whippin' us," he announced to a cheering crowd, "is to take over. We been saying freedom for six years and we ain't got nothin'. What we gonna start saying is Black Power." Carmichael was specific about what black power meant to black Southerners.

> In Lowndes County [Mississippi], for example, black power will mean that if a Negro is elected sheriff, he can end police brutality. If a black man is elected tax assessor, he can collect and channel funds for the building of better roads and schools serving black people—thus advancing the move from political power into the economic arena. . . . Politically, black power means what it has always meant to SNCC: the coming-together of black people to elect representatives and to force those representatives to speak to their needs. It does not mean merely putting black faces into office.

Critics accused advocates of black power of reverse racism, but Carmichael argued on the contrary that they were promoting positive self-identity, racial pride, and the development of independent political and economic power. The slogan nonetheless splintered the civil rights movement. In 1968, CORE followed SNCC's example and ejected its white members. Both organizations began to decline, and by the end of the 1960s, SNCC had virtually disappeared.

Martin Luther King reacted with mixed emotions to the ideology of black power. On the one hand, he welcomed its promotion of black political and economic strength, psychological assertiveness, and cultural pride. But when black power degenerated into a mantra of taunts against white people, King denounced it as "a nihilistic philosophy born out of the conviction that the Negro can't win." King also objected to black power's "implicit and often explicit belief in Black separatism" and the assertion of its proponents that "there can be a separate Black road to power and fulfillment."

In May 1967 Hubert G. Brown followed Carmichael as head of SNCC. "H. Rap" Brown, as he came to be known, raised the militancy of the black power movement's rhetoric to a new level, calling white people "honkies," and the police "pigs." "Violence," he said, was "as American as apple pie." In August 1967 Brown told enthusiastic listeners in the black neighborhood of Cambridge, Maryland, that "black folks built America, and if America don't come around, we're going to burn America down." When a few hours later, a fire erupted in a dilapidated school in the heart of the city's black community, white firemen refused to fight it. Police charged Brown with inciting a riot and committing arson, but he posted bail and fled. Later he was arrested on other charges.

THE BLACK PANTHER PARTY

The most institutionalized expression of the new black militancy was the Black Panther Party for Self-Defense created by Huey P. Newton and Bobby Seale in Oakland, California, in October, 1966. Newton and Seale took the name of the party from the black panther symbol of the Lowndes County Freedom Organization (LCFO). The Black Panthers combined black nationalist ideology with Marxist-Leninist doctrines. Working with white radicals, they hoped to fashion the party into a revolutionary vanguard dedicated to overthrowing capitalist society and to ending police brutality. For a few months Stokely Carmichael, who had become estranged from SNCC, aligned himself with the Panthers and was named the party's prime minister. (Soon thereafter Carmichael shifted his interest to Africa and pan-Africanism. He moved to Africa and changed his name to Kwame Turé.) Eldridge Cleaver, the Panther's minister of education, helped formulate the party's ideology. Cleaver was a convicted rapist who had spent most of his youth in prison, where he became a follower of Malcolm X and began writing the autobiographical essays that would be published in 1968 as *Soul on Ice*. In that year the party dropped "Self-Defense" from its name. Black people, Cleaver maintained, were victims of colonization, not just disfranchised American citizens. Thus the politics of integrationism could not meet their needs. They needed, instead, like other colonized peoples, to be liberated. "To achieve these ends," he wrote, "we believe that political and military machinery that does not exist now and has never existed must be created. We need functional machinery that is able to deal with these two interrelated sets of political dynamics which, strictly speaking, make up the total political situation on the North American continent." Cleaver and other top Panther leaders were arrested after a shootout with Oakland police in 1968. Cleaver escaped and fled into exile. While abroad, he abandoned his radicalism, eventually becoming involved in Republican party politics and fundamentalist Christianity after his return to the United States in 1975.

Police Repression

The Panthers, imposing in black leather jackets, berets, and "Afro" haircuts, alarmed white Americans when they took up arms for self-defense and patrolled their neighborhoods to monitor the police. A series of bloody confrontations and shoot-outs in Oakland distracted attention from the Panthers' broader political objectives and community service projects. In Oakland and Chicago, the Panthers arranged free breakfast and health care programs, worked to instill racial pride, disseminated information about black history, and launched some of the earliest drug education programs. These activities were captured in the slogan, "Power to the People."

VOICES

THE BLACK PANTHER PARTY PLATFORM

Huey Newton and Bobby Seale's Ten Point Program reflects their determination to move from the pursuit of civil rights to a radical restructuring of American society along socialist lines, with work and rewards equally shared.

October 1966

BLACK PANTHER PARTY, PLATFORM
  AND PROGRAM
WHAT WE WANT, WHAT WE BELIEVE

1. We want freedom. We want power to determine the destiny of our Black Community . . .
2. We want full employment for our people . . .
3. We want an end to the robbery of the capitalists of our Black Community . . .
4. We want decent housing fit for shelter of human beings . . .
5. We want education for our people that exposes the true nature of this decadent American society. We want education that teaches us our true history and our role in present-day society . . .
6. We want all Black men to be exempt from military service . . .
7. We want an immediate end to POLICE BRUTALITY and MURDER of Black people . . .

8. We want freedom for all Black men held in federal, state, county and city prisons and jails . . .
9. We want all Black people when brought to trial to be tried in court by a jury of their peer group or people from their Black communities, as defined by the Constitution of the United States . . .
10. We want land, bread, housing, education, clothing, justice, and peace. And as our major political objective, a United Nations supervised plebiscite to be held throughout the Black colony in which only Black colonial subjects will be allowed to participate, for the purpose of determining the will of Black people as to their national destiny.

QUESTIONS

1. In what ways is the Panthers' Ten Point Program similar to the Bill of Rights in the United States Constitution? How do they differ?

2. How did the Panthers propose to achieve black liberation? What significance did they place on the study of history? How did the Panthers' program conflict with that of the older civil rights organizations?

Source: Clayborne Carson, *et al.*, eds., *The Eyes on the Prize Civil Rights Reader: Documents, Speeches, and Firsthand Accounts from the Black Freedom Struggle, 1954–1990* (New York: Viking Penguin, 1991) 346–347.

FBI director J. Edgar Hoover was determined to infiltrate, harass, destabilize, and destroy the Panthers, and law enforcement officials soon weakened the party. Undercover agents infiltrated the party and deliberately promoted violence and criminal acts. To be sure, the Panthers were not saints. Huey P. Newton, for example, had a long criminal record. He was imprisoned for murder in 1968, but was acquitted and released, only to be charged with murder and assault again in 1974. After fleeing to Cuba to avoid trial, he returned in 1977 and was again acquitted. He was eventually killed at age forty-two in a drug dispute in Oakland in 1989.

In their effort to destroy the party, law enforcement officials killed an estimated twenty-eight Panthers and imprisoned 750 others. In perhaps the most egregious incident, police in Chicago killed Fred Hampton and Mark Clark in their sleep in a predawn raid on the Illinois Black Panther Headquarters on December 4, 1969. The police fired hundreds of rounds but only two shots were fired from within the apartment.

Prisoners' Rights

Despite such repression, black militancy survived in many forms, including the prisoners' rights movement. One of the Black Panthers' social programs had focused on the conditions of black prisoners. By 1970, more than half the inmates in U.S. prisons were African American. In New York State, black Americans constituted approximately 70 percent of the prison population. Black activists in the prison reform movement argued that many African Americans were in jail for political reasons and suffered from unfair sentences and deplorable conditions because of racism and class exploitation.

Angela Davis became the first black woman to be listed on the FBI's Ten Most Wanted list because of her involvement in prisoners' rights. In 1969 Davis was a philosophy instructor at the University of California in Los Angeles and a member of the Communist party. During the late 1960s, she had worked on behalf of the Soledad Brothers; these were three prisoners—George Jackson, John Clutchette, and Fleeta Drumgo—accused of murdering a white guard at Soledad Prison. On August 7, 1970, George Jackson's younger brother, seventeen-year-old Jonathan Jackson, staged a one-man raid on the San Rafael courthouse in Marin County, California, to try to seize hostages to trade for the Soledad Brothers. In the ensuing shoot-out, Jonathan Jackson, two prisoners, and a judge were killed. Angela Davis, accused of supplying the weapons for the raid, was charged with murder, kidnaping, and conspiracy but was eventually acquitted. On August 21, 1971,

George Jackson was shot and killed at San Quentin Prison by guards who claimed he was trying to escape.

Across the country, prisoners at Attica, a maximum security prison in northern New York State, began a fast in memory of George Jackson that within days erupted into a full-scale rebellion. On September 9, 1971, 1,200 inmates seized control of half of Attica and took hostages. Four days later, state police and prison guards suppressed the uprising. Tom Wicker, a columnist for *The New York Times*, filed this report:

> A task force consisting of 211 state troopers and corrections officers retook Attica using tear gas, rifles, and shotguns. After the shooting was over, ten hostages and twenty-nine inmates lay dead or dying. At least 450 rounds of ammunition had been discharged. Four hostages and eighty-five inmates suffered gunshot wounds that they survived. After initial reports that several hostages had died at the hands of knife-wielding inmates, pathologists' reports revealed that hostages and inmates all died from gunshot wounds. No guns were found in the possession of inmates.

The McKay Commission, assembled in October 1971 to reconstruct the events at Attica, concluded: "With the exception of Indian massacres in the late nineteenth-century, the State Police assault which ended the four-day prison uprising was the bloodiest one-day encounter between Americans since the Civil War."

THE INNER-CITY REBELLIONS

The militant nationalism of Malcolm X and Stokely Carmichael and the radicalism of the Panthers reflected growing alienation and anger in America's impoverished inner cities. In 1965, 29.1 percent of black households, compared to only 7.8 percent of white households, lived below the poverty line. Almost 50 percent of nonwhite families lived in substandard housing compared to 18 percent of white families. Despite a drop in the number of Americans living in poverty from 38.0 million in 1959 to 32.7 million in 1965, the percentage of poor black people increased from 27.5 percent to 31 percent. In 1965 the black unemployment rate was 8.5 percent, almost twice the white unemployment rate of 4.3. For black teenagers the unemployment rate was 23 percent compared to 10.8 percent for white teenagers. As psychologist Kenneth Clark declared in 1967, "The masses of Negroes are now starkly aware of the fact that recent civil rights victories benefitted a very small percentage of middle-class Negroes while their predicament remained the same or worsened."

The passage of civil rights legislation did not resolve these disparities or diminish inner-city alienation. As jobs moved increasingly to suburbs to which inner-city residents could neither travel nor relocate, inner-city neighborhoods sank deeper into poverty. School dropout rates reached epidemic proportions, crime and drug use increased, and fragile family structures weakened. It was these conditions that led militants like the Panthers to liken their neighborhoods to exploited colonies kept in poverty by repressive white political and economic institutions. Few white Americans fully perceived the depths of the black despair that flared into violence each summer between 1965 and 1969, beginning with the Watts rebellion of 1965.

Watts

In the summer of 1965, a section of Los Angeles called Watts exploded. Watts was 98 percent black. Its residents suffered from overcrowding, high unemployment, inaccessible health care facilities, inadequate public transportation, and increasing crime and drug addiction. Almost 30 percent of the black male population was unemployed. The poverty, combined with anger at the often brutal behavior of Los Angeles's police force in Watts, proved to be an incendiary combination. On August 11, 1965, a policeman pulled over a young black man to check him for drunk driving. The man was arrested, but not before a crowd gathered. The policeman called for reinforcements, and when they arrived, the crowd pelted them with stones, bot-

The first major urban uprising of the 1960s was in the Watts neighborhood of East Los Angeles in August 1965. It lasted nearly a week and left thirty-four people dead.

tles, and other objects. Within a few hours, Watts was in a total riot.

Governor Pat Brown sent in the National Guard to restore order, but by the sixth day of the conflagration, Watts had been reduced to rubble and ashes. One reporter commented that Watts looked like Germany at the end of World War II. Thirty-four people had been killed; more than 900 injured; and 4,000 arrested. Total property damage was more than $35 million, equivalent to hundreds of millions of dollars today. The Watts rebellion was the beginning of four summers of uprisings that would engulf cities in the North and Midwest. There were riots in the summer of 1966, but even worse ones erupted in Newark and Detroit in 1967.

Newark

Newark, New Jersey, was a city of more than 400,000 inhabitants in 1967. As was true in many other urban areas, white flight to the suburbs in the 1950s and 1960s made Newark a majority black city, but one that operated on an inadequate tax base and under white political control. Inadequate revenues left the city without the means to address its inhabitants' pressing social needs. The school system deteriorated as unemployment had increased. In 1967, Newark had the highest unemployment rate among black men in the entire nation. As tensions flared and police brutality escalated, white officials paid little attention to black people's complaints. On July 12, after a black cab driver in police custody was beaten, protesters gathered at the police station near the Hayes Homes housing project. When a firebomb hit the wall of the station house, the police charged, clubbing the crowd. This triggered one of the most destructive civic rebellions of the period. During four days of rioting, the police and National Guard killed twenty-five black people—most of them innocent bystanders, including two children; a white policeman and fireman were also killed. Widespread looting and arson resulted in millions of dollars in property damage.

Detroit

When Detroit erupted a few days after Newark, it caught everyone by surprise except the residents of its inner-city neighborhoods. On the surface Detroit seemed like a model of prosperity and interracial accord. Some of the country's most dynamic popular music flowed from Detroit's Motown recording company. Owned by the astute Berry Gordy, Motown was a classic up-by-the-bootstraps success story. Gordy and his wife Raynoma and their extended family had, by 1967, produced such stars as Diana Ross and Mary Wells. "Before Motown," said Wells, "there were three careers available to a black girl in Detroit—babies, the factories or daywork."

But success like the Gordy's was rare among the black migrants and their children, who poured into Detroit during and after World War II. The parents held their disappointment in check, but the children, particularly young men between seventeen and thirty-five, sought an outlet for their anger and alienation. Some joined the Nation of Islam; others embraced the Panthers or formed even more radical organizations calling for an all-black nation.

On the night of Saturday, July 23, police raided an after-hours drinking establishment in the center of the black community where more than eighty people had gathered to celebrate the return of two veterans from Vietnam. Police efforts to clear the club triggered five days of rioting. Congressman John Conyers, the black U.S. representative for Michigan's First District, knew many of the people in the area and tried to get them to disperse, but they refused. Later, Conyers said, "People were letting feelings out that had never been let out before, that had been bottled up. It really wasn't that they were that mad about an after-hours place being raided and some people being beat up as a result of the closing down of that place. It was the whole desperate situation of being black in Detroit."

Of the fifty-nine urban rebellions that occurred in 1967, the one in Detroit was the deadliest. Forty-three black people died, most of them shot by members of the National Guard, which had been sent in by Republican governor George Romney. But even the National Guard, combined with 200 state police and 600 Detroit police, could not restore order. A reluctant President Johnson had to order 4,700 troops of the elite 82nd and 101st Airborne units to Detroit. Republicans criticized Johnson's move as designed to embarrass Romney, who was a contender for the Republican presidential nomination in 1968. Johnson vehemently denied the charge. Others blamed Johnson's social welfare policies for having subsidized the rioters, arguing that these programs had raised expectations beyond the country's ability or desire to fulfill them.

The Kerner Commission

On July 29, 1967, in the wake of the Newark and Detroit riots, Johnson established the National Advisory Commission on Civil Disorders, headed by Illinois governor Otto Kerner. The commission included two black members, Republican senator Edward W. Brooke of Massachusetts (in 1966 elected the first black senator since Reconstruction) and Roy Wilkins, executive director of the NAACP. In a speech explaining why he had set up the commission, Johnson declared:

> The only genuine, long-range solution for what has happened lies in an attack—mounted at every level—upon the conditions that breed despair and violence. All of us know what those conditions are: ignorance, discrimination, slums, poverty, disease, not enough jobs. We should attack these conditions—not because we are frightened by conflict, but because we are fired by conscience. We should attack them because there is simply no other way to achieve a decent and orderly society in America.

In its final report, released in 1968, the Kerner Commission indicted white racism as the underlying cause of the riots and warned that America was "moving towards two societies, one white, one black—separate and unequal." The commission emphasized that "Negroes firmly believe that police brutality and harassment occur repeatedly in Negro neighborhoods. This belief is unquestionably one of the major reasons for intense Negro resentment against the police." The report added, "Physical abuse is only one source of aggravation in the ghetto. In nearly every city surveyed, the Commission heard complaints of harassment of interracial couples, dispersal of social street gatherings and the stopping of Negroes on foot or in cars without objective basis." The report called for massive government aid to the cities, including funds for public housing, better and more integrated schools, two million new jobs, and funding for a "national system of income supplementation." None of its major proposals was enacted.

DIFFICULTIES IN CREATING THE GREAT SOCIETY

The urban riots of the late 1960s undercut support for the broadest attack the federal government had yet waged on the problems of poor Americans, what President Johnson in his election campaign in 1964 had called "the Great Society." Much of the legislation Johnson pushed through Congress in 1964 and 1965—the Medicare program, for example, which provided medical care for the elderly and disabled under the Social Security system, or federal aid to education from elementary through graduate schools—remained popular. But the most ambitious Great Society programs—what Johnson called "an unconditional war on poverty"—generated controversy as they tested the limits of American reform.

Lyndon Johnson was a savvy politician. He had to be to come from Stonewall, Texas, to the pinnacle of power. But he never lost a deep sympathy for the disadvantaged and the powerless. Entering the House of Representatives in 1937, he had been an enthusiastic New Dealer. Elected to the Senate in 1948, he had refused to sign the Southern Manifesto (see Chapter 21) and, as majority leader, had overcome southern filibusters to win passage of the 1957 and 1960 Civil Rights Acts. As president, he exerted even more pressure to get the 1964 Civil Rights Act and the 1965 Voting Rights Act through Congress.

Johnson's concern for the disadvantaged showed itself in the cornerstone of his War on Poverty, the Economic Opportunity Act of 1964. This act created an Office of Economic Opportunity that administered several programs: Head Start to help disadvantaged preschoolers, Upward Bound to prepare impoverished teenagers for college, and Volunteers in Service to America (or VISTA) to serve as a domestic peace corps to help the poor and undereducated across the country. These programs included community governing boards on which black men and women gained representation, learning such essential political skills as bargaining and organizing.

One of the most prominent programs of President Johnson's War on Poverty was the Job Corps, which provided occupational training for poor Americans. In this photo, Johnson speaks with James Truesville at a Job Corps center in Camp Catoctin, Maryland.

The War on Poverty was the first government-sponsored effort to involve poor African Americans directly in designing and implementing programs to serve low-income communities. For example, in the New Careers program, residents of poor neighborhoods found jobs as community organizers, day care workers, and teacher aides. The program provided meaningful work, access to education, and critical material resources to poor people, so that they would become leaders in their own communities and run for office. The Community Action Programs (CAPs) insisted on "maximum feasible participation" by the poor. On another level, the Education Act increased federal funding to colleges and universities and provided low-interest student loans. This initiative increased college enrollments and put higher education within the reach of many more Americans than before.

Johnson faced considerable opposition to CAPs and other Great Society programs. Local politicians, fearing that the federal government was subsidizing their opponents and undercutting their power, were especially threatened by programs that empowered the previously disfranchised and dispossessed. Others, reflecting persistent white stereotypes of African Americans, complained that Johnson was rewarding lawlessness and laziness with handouts to the undeserving poor. The black residents of America's inner cities, for their part, had their expectations raised by the promises of the Great Society only to be frustrated by white backlash and minimal gains. They felt as betrayed by its programs as Johnson's white critics felt robbed by them.

No one will ever know whether Lyndon Johnson could have won his war on poverty had he been given the resources to do so. As it turned out, the nation's resources were increasingly going into his other war, the war in Vietnam. Statistics tell the story. Government spending, including spending for domestic programs, increased dramatically under Johnson. But most of the money spent on domestic programs during Johnson's presidency, $44.3 billion, went to Social Security benefits, which now included Medicare. Appropriations for the War on Poverty came to only $10 billion. The war in Vietnam, in contrast, consumed $140 billion.

JOHNSON AND THE WAR IN VIETNAM

Vietnam was a French colony from the 1860s until the Japanese seized it during World War II. After the war the Vietnamese Communists, led by Ho Chi Minh, declared independence, but the French, with massive

U.S. financial aid, fought to reassert their control from 1945 until they were finally defeated in 1954. In retrospect it is easy to argue that American policy makers should have been more impressed by the failure of the French to defeat the Communists in Vietnam. But in 1954, with the French pulling out, the Americans arranged a temporary division of the country into a Communist-controlled North Vietnam and a U.S. supported South Vietnam (which, however, contained many Communist guerrillas, called by the Americans "Viet Cong"). The United States ignored the possibility that as guarantor of South Vietnam, it would replace the French as targets for those Vietnamese who were determined to end white colonial domination and unify their country.

For nine years, under Presidents Eisenhower and Kennedy, American aid and advisers propped up the corrupt and incompetent South Vietnamese government in Saigon. By the time Johnson became president, only the dramatic escalation of American involvement—the bombing of North Vietnam and the introduction of large numbers of American troops into combat in South Vietnam—could keep the South Vietnamese government in power. Johnson himself doubted the advisability of a wholesale American commitment and did not want a foreign war to distract the public's attention or take away resources from the Great Society programs about which he cared so much. "I knew from the start," Johnson claimed later,

> that I was bound to be crucified either way I moved. If I left the woman I really loved—the Great Society—in order to get involved with that bitch of a war on the other side of the world, then I would lose everything at home. All my programs. All my hopes to feed the hungry and shelter the homeless. All my dreams to provide education and medical care to the browns and the blacks and the lame and the poor. But if I left that war and let the Communists take over South Vietnam, then I would be seen as a coward and my nation would be seen as an appeaser and we would both find it impossible to accomplish anything for anybody anywhere on the entire globe.

And so, half-aware that he was entering a quagmire but determined to see his way through it, Johnson intervened in Vietnam—gradually, massively, and inexorably.

After an incident involving an alleged North Vietnamese attack on U.S. Navy destroyers in the Gulf of Tonkin in August 1964, Johnson pushed a resolution through Congress that gave him authority to escalate American involvement in Vietnam. In the spring of 1965 he authorized the bombing of selected North Vietnamese targets, but the bombing failed to stop the North Vietnamese from resupplying and reinforcing their forces in the south. The American military presence in South Vietnam then grew rapidly. By the end of 1966 there were more than 385,000 U.S. troops there, and by 1968 more than 500,000.

Black Americans and the Vietnam War

In the mid-1960s, black Americans made up 10 percent of the armed forces. This percentage increased during America's involvement in the Vietnam War. (In the Persian Gulf War in 1991, African Americans were 25 percent of the troops deployed.) Black men and women entered the military for many reasons. One was patriotism. Another was that the military offered educational and vocational opportunities that were otherwise not available to the children of the working black poor. Still another was Project 100,000.

Project 100,000

In 1966 the United States Defense Department launched Project 100,000 to reduce the high rejection rate of African Americans by the military. The project enabled recruitment officers to accept applicants whom they otherwise would have rejected because of criminal records or lack of skills. The project supplied more than 340,000 new recruits for Vietnam, 40 percent of whom were African Americans. As some have argued, this made the Vietnam War a white man's war but a black man's fight. Although the recruits were promised training and "rehabilitation," they saw more combat duty than regular recruits.

JOHNSON: VIETNAM DESTROYS THE GREAT SOCIETY

By the end of 1967, the nation seemed to be heading toward total racial polarization. In their rage against economic exploitation and police brutality, some inner-city black people had destroyed many of their own neighborhoods. Frightened white people, unable to comprehend black anger, rallied behind those who promised to restore order by any means. The two men who, only a few years before, had seemed the most effective advocates of racial reconciliation—Lyndon Johnson and Martin Luther King Jr.—were each trying to regain the initiative. Each, tragically, ended by alienating himself from the other.

THEY CALLED EACH OTHER "BLOODS"

Captain Joseph B. Anderson Jr. of Topeka, Kansas, served as a platoon leader at An Khe, June 1966–June 1967, and as company commander in Cambodia, Phouc Vinh, May 1970–April 1971, 1st Cavalry Division, U.S. Army. His unit was the subject of The Anderson Platoon, *a 1967 French documentary film.*

Shortly after I got to Vietnam, we got into a real big fight. We were outnumbered at least ten to one. But I didn't know it. I had taken over 1st Platoon of B Company of the 12th Cav. We were up against a Viet Cong battalion. There may have been 300 to 400 of them. And they had just wiped out one of our platoons. At that time in the war, summer of 1966, it was a terrible loss. A bloody massacre.

I was an absolute rarity in Vietnam. A black West Pointer commanding troops. One year after graduation, I was very aggressive about my role and responsibilities as an Army officer serving in Vietnam. I was there to defend the freedom of the South Vietnamese government, stabilize the countryside, and help contain Communism. The Domino Theory was dominant then, predominant as a matter of fact. I was gung ho. And I thought the war would last three years at the most.

There weren't many opportunities for blacks in private industry then. And as a graduate of West Point, I was an officer and a gentleman by act of Congress. Where else could a black go and get that label just like that?

Throughout the Cav, the black representation in the enlisted ranks was heavier than the population as a whole in the United States. One third of my platoon and two of my four squad leaders were black. For many black men, the service, even during a war, was the best of a number of alternatives to staying home and working in the fields or bumming around the streets of Chicago or New York.

There were only a very few incidents of sustained fighting during my tours. Mostly you walked and walked, searched and searched. If you made contact, it would be over in 30 or 40 minutes. One burst and then they're gone, because they didn't want to fight or could not stand up against the firepower we could bring with artillery and helicopter gunships.

I had a great deal of respect for the Viet Cong. They were trained and familiar with the jungle. They relied on stealth, on ambush, on their personal skills and wile, as opposed to firepower. They knew it did not pay for them to stand and fight us, so they wouldn't. . . .

. . . What was very clear to me was an awareness among our men that the support for the war was declining in the United States. The gung ho attitude that made our soldiers so effective in 1966, 67, was replaced by the will to survive. They became more security conscious. They would take more defensive measures so they wouldn't get hurt. They were more scared. They wanted to get back home.

Career officers and enlisted men like me did not go back to a hostile environment in America. We went back to bases where we were assimilated and congratulated and decorated for our performance in the conduct of the war.

Personally it was career-enhancing. A career Army officer who has not been to war during the war is dead, careerwise. I had done that. I received decorations. Two Silver Stars, five Bronze Stars, eleven Air Medals. . . . But in 1978 I decided I did not want to cool my heels for the next eight to ten years to become a general. . . . I resigned my commission, worked a year as a special assistant to the U.S. Secretary of Commerce, and joined General Motors as a plant manager.

The Anderson Platoon won both an Oscar and an Emmy. As time passes, my memory of Vietnam revolves around the film. I have a print, and I look at it from time to time. And the broadness and scope of my two-year experience narrows down to 60 minutes.

QUESTIONS

1. How do the experiences of this Vietnam veteran compare with those of black soldiers in previous wars, specifically World War II?

2. Why were African-American men attracted to military service? What benefits did they derive from the military, and what does their disproportionate representation suggest about social and economic conditions in black communities?

3. How does this soldier regard the Viet Cong? What reasons does he give for declining American morale?

Source: "Captain Joseph B. Anderson Jr.," in Wallace Terry, *Bloods: An Oral History of the Vietnam War by Black Veterans* (New York: Ballantine Books, 1984), 219–228.

Black men served in disproportionately high numbers in Vietnam. Black and white troops fought together but tended mostly to keep to themselves behind the lines.

By 1967 Johnson was in an untenable situation. He had escalated the war in Vietnam without convincing many Americans that it was worth fighting. With misleadingly optimistic claims about the progress of the war, his administration had forfeited public trust and opened what journalists called "the credibility gap." Johnson hoped that, with more bombing and more troops, the Vietnamese Communists would give up, but he knew that if Congress had to choose between spending on the war and spending on domestic programs, it would choose the war. After Johnson asked for a tax increase, his Great Society programs met increasing resistance. When, for example, he proposed a special program to exterminate the rats that infested inner-city neighborhoods, congressional opponents turned it into a joke, calling it a "civil rats bill," and proposing to enlist an army of cats.

An even more dramatic example of the ugly mood on Capitol Hill was the 1967 decision of the House of Representatives to expel the most prominent African-American politician in the United States, Adam Clayton Powell Jr. (1908–1972). Pastor of the Abyssinian Baptist Church in Harlem and a long-time civic activist, Powell had first been elected to represent his Harlem district in 1944 and became the foremost champion of civil rights in the House. Because of his seniority he became chairman of the Education and Labor Committee in 1961 and had been instrumental in passing Johnson's education and antipoverty legislation.

Powell himself was largely to blame for his downfall. He mismanaged the committee's budget, took numerous trips abroad at government expense, and was exiled from his district when threatened with arrest there because of his refusal to pay a slander judgment against him. Yet the sentiment behind his ouster owed much to the dislike he inspired as a champion of minorities and the poor and as a flamboyant black man. The Supreme Court, overruling the House action, upheld his right to his seat, and his Harlem constituents continued to maintain him in office.

Despite opposition in Congress, Johnson did not give up on the Great Society. He knew he could initiate no major programs while the war lasted, but he continued to push a variety of measures, including a law to prohibit discrimination in housing. He also named the architect of the NAACP's attack on segregation, Thurgood Marshall, to the Supreme Court in 1967.

Vietnam trapped Johnson. As the hundreds of thousands of people who demonstrated against the war reminded him, Vietnam was incontestably "Lyndon Johnson's war." It was not, he would have replied, the war he had wanted to fight—that was the war against poverty and discrimination—but he was increasingly committed to seeing it through. He believed that his and the nation's honor were at stake. Even though objective commentators considered the conflict a stalemate, there were enough optimistic reports in 1967, from military commanders and intelligence agents, to convince the president that he might yet prevail.

Then, on January 30, 1968, at the start of the Vietnamese new year (called Tet), Communist insurgents attacked thirty-six of the forty-four provincial capitals in South Vietnam as well its national capital, Saigon, where they penetrated the grounds of the American

MUHAMMAD ALI

Boxing is a brutal sport. During the 1960s and 1970s, Cassius Clay convincingly demonstrated that boxing was also an art, that it could be beautiful, and that the boxer could become a symbol of racial pride, endearing wit, and even love. Born Cassius Marcellus Clay in 1942 in Louisville, Kentucky, Clay went to Rome in 1960 where he won a gold medal as a member of the U.S. Olympic boxing team.

Clay turned the boxing world on its head with audacious declarations of his own greatness as a boxer and beauty as a black man. His defeats of Floyd Patterson and Sonny Liston confirmed the first claim. On February 25, 1964, Clay pounded Liston to become the world heavyweight champion. The next day he announced that he had joined the Nation of Islam and had taken a new name, Muhammad Ali. Explaining his timing of the announcement, he said: "When I joined the Nation in 1961, I figured I'd be pressured if I revealed it, so I kept it quiet for about three years. . . . But after beating Sonny Liston, I was getting more recognition and more power. I revealed it after that fight."

Ali was a master at "playing the dozens," a boasting style that angered his opponents and annoyed white reporters covering his bouts. In 1967, however, it was his refusal to be drafted into the military that brought down on his head the wrath of the boxing establishment and white America. Ali argued that his religion was opposed to military service just as it was against civil rights activism and integration. Muhammad Ali was the new black man who refused to accept the white man's rules about how to behave. He embodied the assertive black consciousness that invaded all forms of social and cultural life in the 1960s and 1970s.

But there were other reasons that most black people adored him, recalled basketball player Kareem Abdul-Jabbar, who in 1971 discarded the name Lew Alcindor:

> When Ali announced his refusal to accept the draft, I thought it was a very brave stand. . . . A

Muhammad Ali declared himself "The Greatest" and for many African Americans he was the epitome of the uncompromised and proud black man.

meeting to help Ali was called by black athletes back in 1967. We let black people around the country know that we supported Ali. I think by that time Black Americans understood that their presence in Vietnam was highly disproportionate to their percentage of the American population and that the front-line casualties were being absorbed by Black Americans in much greater numbers than they should have.

A federal court found Ali guilty of draft evasion but he was released on bail pending his appeal. Ali immediately became a popular anti-war speaker. In June 1970 the United States Supreme Court overturned his conviction on the grounds that the FBI had placed an illegal wiretap on his telephone.

Actor Harry Belafonte described Ali in admiring terms:

> He brought America to its most wonderful and its most naked moment. "I will not play in your game of war. I will not kill in your behalf. What you ask is immoral, unjust, and I stand here to attest to that fact. Now do with me what you will," he said. I mean he was, in many ways, as inspiring as Dr. King, as inspiring as Malcolm. Cassius was a black, young American. Out of the womb of oppression he was our phoenix, he was the spirit of our young. He was our manhood. . . . He was the vitality of what we hoped would emerge. . . . the perfect machine, the wit, the incredible athlete, the facile, articulate, sharp mind on issues, the great sense of humor, which was out of our tradition.

In 1974 Ali fought George Foreman to regain his world heavyweight boxing title. Four years later he lost the title to Leon Spinks. He regained it, retired, then attempted a comeback that ended with his October 2, 1980, loss to Larry Holmes. He was elected to the Boxing Hall of Fame in 1987. In 1996 he lit the Olympic Flame to open the summer games in Atlanta.

embassy. Although American and South Vietnamese forces quickly recaptured all the territory that was lost and inflicted massive casualties on the enemy, the Tet Offensive was a major psychological blow for the American public, deepening the suspicion that the administration had not been telling the truth about the war. Washington was forced to reconsider its strategy.

On March 31, 1968, President Johnson told the nation that he would halt the bombing of North Vietnam to encourage the start of peace negotiations, which began in Paris in May. Then, almost as an afterthought, he added that he would not seek renomination as president. Worn out by Vietnam, frustrated in his efforts to achieve the Great Society, the target of bitter criticism, Lyndon Johnson ended his public career.

KING: SEARCHING FOR A NEW STRATEGY

Like President Johnson, Martin Luther King was attacked on many fronts. Many white people considered him a dangerous radical while black militants considered him an ineffectual moderate. His first response to the urban rebellions in 1965 and 1966 had been to move his campaign to the North to demonstrate the national range of the civil rights movement. In 1966, King and the SCLC set up operation in Chicago at the invitation of the Chicago Freedom Movement. King was confident that he would receive the support of the city's white liberals and the entire black community. James Bevel, King's Chicago lieutenant, declared, "We are going to create a new city. . . . Nobody will stop us." His optimism proved unwarranted.

Chicago's powerful, wily mayor Richard Daley viewed King suspiciously from the outset but treated him with respect and cautioned the police not to use violence against King's civil rights demonstrators. Because King's movement depended on provoking confrontation, not much happened until King attempted to march into the white ethnic enclave of Marquette Park and the all-white suburb of Cicero.

The ensuing violence attracted the nation's television cameras. Chicago's white liberals joined with King and Daley in negotiating the Summit Agreement on housing, which amounted to a hasty retreat by King in the face of virulent white rage and black militancy. The Chicago strategy was a dismal failure.

But Chicago reinforced two important lessons for King. First, racial discrimination was more than a southern problem: In Chicago he witnessed a degree and intensity of hatred and hostility that surpassed even that of Birmingham. Second, racial discrimination was inextricably intertwined with the country's economic structure. And so he began to think more critically about the need not only to eradicate poverty but to end systemic economic inequality. "What good is it to be allowed to eat in a restaurant," he remarked, "if you can't afford a hamburger?" In the fall of 1967, he announced plans for his most ambitious and militant project, an integrated, nonviolent "Poor People's Campaign" the following spring. According to the plan, tens of thousands of the nation's dispossessed would descend on Washington to focus attention on the disadvantaged members of American society. Among other things, King and his aides wanted a federally supported guaranteed income policy.

King on the Vietnam War

During the planning of the Poor People's Campaign, King began to criticize the war in Vietnam strongly. King rejected what he considered the hypocrisy of the federal government's determination to send black and white men to Vietnam "to slaughter, men, women, and children," while failing to protect black American civil rights protesters in places like Albany, Birmingham, and Selma. His statements that the president was more concerned about winning in Vietnam than winning the "war against poverty" in America turned Johnson against him and further alienated King from many of Johnson's black supporters, including the more traditional civil rights leaders who supported the war in Vietnam. At the same time, the young militants in SNCC, who had already condemned the war, did not rush to embrace him. But King persisted, and by 1968 he had become one of the war's most trenchant critics.

King's Murder

His search for a new strategy led King to a closer involvement with the struggles of workers. In February 1968, attempting to gain union recognition for municipal workers in Memphis, 1,300 members of a virtually all-black sanitation workers local went on strike and together with the local black community boycotted downtown merchants. But Memphis mayor Henry Loeb refused to negotiate. On March 18, 1968, King, responding to a call from long-time civil rights activist and minister of Centenary Methodist Church in Memphis, James Lawson, went to Memphis to address the striking sanitation workers.

The occasion was marked by violence. Nevertheless, King returned to Memphis on April 3 and delivered his last and perhaps most prophetic speech:

> I would like to live a long life. Longevity has its place. But I'm not concerned about that now. I just want to do God's will. And He's allowed me to go up to the mountaintop, and I've looked over. And I've seen the promised land. I may not get there with you. But I want you to know tonight that we as a people will get to the promised land. So I'm happy tonight. I'm not worried about anything. I'm not fearing any man. "Mine eyes have seen the glory of the coming of the Lord."

The next day King was murdered by James Earl Ray as he stood on the balcony of the Lorraine Motel in Memphis. His assassination unleashed a torrent of civic rage in black communities. More than 125 cities experienced uprisings. By April 11, forty-six people were dead, 35,000 were injured, and more than 20,000 had been arrested.

In what seemed to many a belated gesture of racial reconciliation, within days of King's assassination, Congress passed the Civil Rights Act of 1968. Proposed by Johnson two years before, the act outlawed discrimination in the sale and rental of housing and gave the Justice Department authority to bring suits against such discrimination.

King's assassination also boosted support for the SCLC's faltering Poor People's Campaign. The campaign began in May when more than 2,000 demonstrators settled into a shantytown they called Resurrection City in Washington, D.C. For more than a month, they marched daily to various federal offices and took part in a mass demonstration on June 19. On June 24, police evicted them and the campaign ended, leaving an uncertain legacy.

THE RISE OF BLACK ELECTED OFFICIALS

Just as King searched for a new strategy after the victories of the early phase of the civil rights movement, other black leaders mobilized the newly enfranchised black electorate to win political office. After the adoption of the Voting Rights Act of 1965, Vernon Jordan, director of the Voter Education Project, coordinated registration drives and workshops across the South. As he explained, "Too many of these people have been alienated from the political process for too long a time

Participants in the Poor People's Campaign marched daily to various federal offices and neighborhoods in Washington, D.C.

. . . and so we have to . . . teach them what a local government is, how it operates, and try to relate their votes to the things they want."

By 1974 there were 1,593 black elected officials outside the South, and by 1980 the number had risen to 2,455. Although black people in northern cities had been able to vote for a century and had been slowly developing political muscle and winning representation in state legislatures and on municipal councils, they had not been able to command an equal voice in city governance. The rise of black power and the inspiration of the Voting Rights Act, however, signaled a new departure. People now eagerly engaged in the electoral process to achieve a political influence reflecting their numbers. In 1967 in Cleveland, where the black population had increased tremendously after World War II, Carl Stokes became the first black mayor of a major American city, winning election with the support of white business leaders and the solid backing of the black community. In the same year prosecutor Richard G. Hatcher became mayor of Gary, Indiana, where the black population had similarly increased greatly after the war. Hatcher won by a mere 1,389 votes, garnering 96 percent of the black vote and 14 percent of the white vote.

The Gary Convention and the Black Political Agenda

The victories of Stokes, Hatcher, and others made possible one of the most significant events of recent black political history, the Gary convention of 1972. The three co-chairs of the convention were Detroit Congressman Charles Diggs, Hatcher, and writer and cultural nationalist Amiri Baraka of Newark, New Jersey. Political scientist Ronald Walters, who helped plan the convention, recalled that various ideological factions had to be placated to make the convention work: "The most important thing about 1972 was the fact that it was an election year, so it provided the environment for the politics taking place. So you had two groups of people who saw this as an opportunity to make some very important statements. One of these, of course, was the black nationalist movement led by Amiri Baraka, Maulana Karenga, and others at that time." The nationalists interpreted "black power" to mean that black people should control their own communities and create separate cultural institutions distinct from those of white society. These views clashed with the ideas espoused by the black elected officials represented by Stokes and Hatcher. According to Walters, "It was this body of people who really were contending for the national leadership of the black community in the early seventies. And in the seventies this new group of black elected officials joined the civil rights leaders and became a new leadership class, but there was sort of a conflict in outlook between them and the more indigenous, social, grass roots-oriented nationalist movement."

Hatcher observed that "people had come to Gary from communities all over the United States where they were politically impotent, but . . . they went back home and rolled up their sleeves and dived into the political arena." Approximately 8,000 people gathered to develop an agenda for black empowerment. The discussions about bloc voting, the efficacy of coalitions, and the feasibility of a third party inspired scores of individual African Americans to run for local office. The convention was not homogeneous, however, and no unified black consensus emerged.

Several discussions over strategies to secure common interests revealed deep-seated internal divisions that allowed ancillary issues to provoke even more impassioned disagreement. Coleman Young and other Michigan delegates walked out to protest a proposal calling for African Americans to reject "discriminatory" unions and form their own. Others walked out over a resolution condemning Israel for its "expansionist policy" toward the Palestinians. Others opposed "forced racial integration of schools" through busing, arguing that such practices insulted black students and would cost black teachers their jobs.

The Gary convention was important because it signaled a shift in the political focus of the black community toward electoral politics and away from mass demonstrations and protest measures. Unity continued to elude subsequent conventions, however, and delegates attending the last National Black Convention at Little Rock, Arkansas, in 1974 abandoned the idea of a black political party. Deep ideological differences and institutional cleavages precluded coalitions and cooperation between black nationalists and the rising numbers of black elected officials. These same differences prevented some nationalists and elected officials from taking seriously the 1972 Democratic party presidential bid of New York congresswoman Shirley Chisholm.

Black People Gain Local Offices

Despite the demise of the National Black Convention movement, African Americans continued to register impressive gains in electoral politics. A few statistics indicate the success of black politicians. When the leaders first convened the Gary convention, there were thirteen African-American members of Congress; by 1997 there were forty. In 1972 there were 2,427 black elected officials; by 1993 there were 8,106. An amendment to the Voting Rights Act in 1975 enabled minorities to mount court challenges to at-large voting practices that diluted the impact of bloc voting; this helped increase the number of black elected officials. Districts were redrawn with race as the predominant factor in their reconfiguration. On November 5, 1985, state senator L. Douglas Wilder was elected lieutenant governor in Virginia, making him the first African-American lieutenant governor in a southern state since Reconstruction. In 1989 he was elected governor, making him the first black governor of any state since Reconstruction.

Between 1971 and 1975, the number of African-American mayors rose from eight to 135, leading to the founding of the National Conference of Black Mayors in 1974. In 1973, Coleman Young in Detroit and Thomas Bradley in Los Angeles became the first African-American mayors of cities of more than a million citizens. Bradley won in Los Angeles even though

THE NATIONAL BLACK CONVENTION MOVEMENT OF THE BLACK POWER ERA

1965	Maulena Karenga founds the US (as opposed to them) Organization in Los Angeles, California. Advocates cultural nationalism.
1966	Amiri Baraka founds Spirit House Movers and Players in Newark, New Jersey. Advocates cultural nationalism.
1966	Huey P. Newton and Bobby Seale found the Black Panther Party
1966	Stokely Carmichael coins the term "black power."
1966	Representative Adam Clayton Powell Jr. hosts the first Black Power Conference
1967	Second Black Power Conference, held in Newark, New Jersey, calls for partitioning the United States into separate black and white nations.
1968	Third Black Power Conference is held in Philadelphia, Pennsylvania.
1969	National Black Economic Development Conference held in Detroit, Michigan.
1969	Last Black Power Conference, held in Bermuda, ends in disarray.
1970	Congress of Afrikan Peoples, led by Amiri Baraka, is organized in Atlanta, Georgia. Adopts the slogan, "It's nation time."
1971	The Reverend Jesse Jackson founds People United to Save Humanity (PUSH) in Chicago, Illinois.
1972	National Black Political Convention is held in Gary, Indiana.
1973	National Black Feminist Organization is founded by Eleanor Holmes Norton and Margaret Sloan.
1974	Last National Black Political Convention is held in Little Rock, Arkansas.

black people made up only 15 percent of the city's electorate. Ten years later, in 1983, Chicago swore in its first black mayor, Harold Washington. The era of the black elected official had arrived.

THE BLACK ARTS MOVEMENT AND BLACK CONSCIOUSNESS

The years between 1967 and 1975 witnessed some of the most intense political and cultural discussions in the history of the black freedom struggle. Black power stimulated debate about both the future of black politics in the post–civil rights era and the role of black art and artists in the quest for black liberation. Creative people revisited the long-standing issue of whether black art is political or aesthetic. For a decade, discussion about black culture and identity focused on the relationship between art and the artist, and the political movement within the black community. This period became known as the black arts movement.

The formal beginning of the movement was the founding in 1965 of the Black Arts Repertory Theater by the writer LeRoi Jones, who changed his name to Imamu Amari Baraka in 1967. Jones was the bridge that linked the political and cultural aspects of black power. He had been closely associated with the white avant-garde poets in New York in the 1950s and early 1960s, but began to change in 1965 from an integrationist to a black cultural nationalist.

The guiding ethos of the black arts movement was the determination of black artists to produce black art for black people and thereby to accomplish black liberation. Baraka declared, "The Black man must seek a Black politics, an ordering of the world that is beneficial to his culture, to his interiorization and judgment of the world. The Black Artist . . . is desperately needed to change the images his people identify with, by asserting Black feeling, Black mind, Black judgment." In 1968 he co-edited with Larry Neal the anthology *Black Fire*, which revealed the extent to which black writers and thinkers had rejected the premises of integration in favor of a new black consciousness and nationalist political engagement.

Larry Neal, who was part of the revolutionary action movement, offered a succinct definition of this important dimension of the freedom struggle:

The Black Arts Movement is radically opposed to any concept of the artist that alienates him from his community. Black Art is the aesthetic and spiritual sister of the Black Power concept. As such, it envisions an art that speaks directly to the needs and aspirations of Black Americans. In order to perform this task, the Black Arts Movement proposes a radical reordering of the western cultural aesthetic. It proposes a separate symbolism, mythology, critique, and iconology. The Black Arts and the Black Power concept both relate broadly to the Afro-American's desire for self-determination and nationhood. Both concepts are nationalistic. One is concerned with the relationship between art and politics; the other with the art of politics.

While the black arts movement was criticized because of its celebration of black maleness, its racial exclusivity, and its homophobia, prominent integrationist writers agreed with some of its fundamental tenets and were converted to its principles.

The works of Langston Hughes, Lorraine Hansberry, Gwendolyn Brooks, and James Baldwin linked the black cultural renaissances of the 1930s, 1940s, and 1950s to the black arts movement. The works of Brooks, for example, stressed the commitment of artist to community and the importance of the relationship between the artist and her audience. Brooks had consistently supported community-based arts programs, and it seemed natural that she should "convert" to a black nationalist perspective during the sixties and join forces with younger artists.

But the most popular black writer of the era, especially among white audiences, was James Baldwin. Baldwin was an integrationist. In his work he had resisted the simple inversion of racial hierarchies that characterized some parts of the black power and black arts movements. He wrote: "I think all theories are suspect, that the finest principles may have to be modified, or may even be pulverized by the demands of life, and that one must find therefore, and move through the world hoping that center will guide one aright."

Yet in many ways, Baldwin was as alienated and angry as some of the artists identified with black arts. In *The Fire Next Time* (1963), he concluded with a phrase that echoed through discussions of the rebellions in Watts, Newark, and Detroit. "If we do not now dare everything, the fulfillment of that prophecy, recreated from the bible in song by a slave, is upon us: 'God gave Noah the rainbow sign, No more water, the fire next time!'"

Baldwin was also an unflinching commentator on white racism and had a major impact on public discourse. At one point he told his white readers, "There appears to be a vast amount of confusion on this point, but I do not know many Negroes who are eager to be 'accepted' by white people, still less to be loved by them; they, the blacks, simply don't wish to be beaten over the head by the whites every instant of our brief passage on this planet." And in *No Name in the Street*, Baldwin declared: "I agree with the Black Panther position concerning black prisoners: not one of them has ever had a fair trial, for not one of them has ever been tried by a jury of his peers." He explained: "White middle-class America is always the jury, and they know absolutely nothing about the lives of the people on whom they sit in judgment: and this fact is not altered, on the contrary it is rendered more implacable by the presence of one or two black faces in the jury box."

Poetry and Theater

The black arts movement had its greatest and most significant impact in poetry and theater. The movement had three geographical centers: Harlem, Chicago and Detroit, and San Francisco.

The Chicago-based *Negro Digest/Black World*, edited by Hoyt Fuller and published by John Johnson, promoted many of the works of the new generation of creative artists. Fuller, a well-connected intellectual with an exhaustive command of black literature, became editor of the monthly magazine in 1961. In 1970 he changed the name of the magazine to *Black World* to signal the rejection of "Negro" and the adoption of "black" to designate people of African descent. The name change identified African Americans with both the diaspora and Africa.

In Detroit, Naomi Long Madgett's Lotus Press and Dudley Randall's Broadside Press republished the previous generation of black poets, notably Gwendolyn Brooks, Margaret Walker, and Sterling Brown. In Chicago, poet and literary critic, Don L. Lee, who changed his name to Haki Madhabuti, launched Third World Press, which published many of the black arts poets and writers.

The Chicago-Detroit publishing nexus promoted new poets like Nikki Giovanni, Etheridge Knight, and Sonia Sanchez. These and other poets produced some of the most accomplished and experimental work of the black arts movement. It resonated with the sounds of the African-American vernacular, combining the rhythmic cadences of sermons with popular music and black "street speech" into a spirited new form of poetry that was free, conversational, and militantly cool.

Theater was another prominent genre of the black arts movement. Playwright Ed Bullin edited a special issue of the journal *Drama Review* in the summer of 1968 that featured essays and plays by most of the major activists in black arts, including Sonia Sanchez, Ron Milner, and Woodie King Jr. This volume became the textbook of black arts. In his plays Bullins, who was greatly influenced by Baraka, portrayed ordinary black life and explored the inner forces that prevented black people from realizing their own liberation and full potential. He showed how racism had deformed the black experience and consciousness. Across the country local black communities formed their own theater groups, including Val Gray Ward's Kuumba Workshop in Chicago and Baraka's Spirit House Theater in New Jersey. These groups reached out to people by hosting seminars, guest appearances, fashion shows, art exhibits, dance recitals, parades, and mass media parties.

Poet Nikki Giovanni was one of the major figures in the Black Arts Movement of the 1970s.

On the West Coast, in 1969, Robert Chrisman and Nathan Hare launched *The Black Scholar*, the first serious journal to promote black studies. Chrisman compared the black arts movement with the renaissance in Harlem during the 1920s: "More so than the Harlem Renaissance, in which Black artists were always on the leash of white patrons and publishing houses, the Black Arts movement did it for itself. Black people going out nationally, in mass, saying we are an independent Black people and this is what we produce."

Music

The cultural nationalists in the black arts movement cultivated an appreciation for modern jazz musicians, making them icons of the quest for black freedom. Baraka argued that jazz and all other black music was the language that black people developed to give uncensored accounts of their experiences. He and other cultural nationalists believed that music could promote black identity and encourage the pride that was vital for political struggle. The music of the jazzmen was often

dense and austere, but it could also be powerfully primitive and dazzlingly complex. Above all, the music appeared to challenge Western conceptions of harmony, rhythm, melody, and tone. In jazz you have to improvise, to create your own form of expression by using whatever information inspires you. The emphasis is not on the original but on individual articulation.

Cultural nationalists perceived jazz to be a self-consciously engaged, economically independent, politically useful art form. Novelist Ralph Ellison put it most succinctly:

> True jazz is an art of individual assertion within and against the group. Each true jazz moment (as distinct from the uninspired commercial performance) springs from a contest in which each artist challenges all the rest; each solo flight, or improvisation, represents (like the successive canvases of a painter) a definition of his identity: as individual, as member of the collectivity and as a link in the chain of tradition.

This outlook explains why Miles Davis's legendary album *Kind of Blue* (1959), one of the most progressive jazz albums ever produced, also became one of the most popular. Davis showed that art could be accessible without sacrificing excellence and rigor. Davis, in the words of one admirer, was able to "dance underwater and not get wet." For black cultural nationalists, Davis projected an image of uncompromising and uncompromised black identity.

Among other intensely celebrated jazzmen were Charlie Parker, Archie Shepp, Ornette Coleman, Pharoah Sanders, Eric Dophy, Thelonious Monk, and John Coltrane. Playwright Ronald Milner described Coltrane as "a man who through his saxophone before your eyes and ears completely annihilates every single western influence." Coltrane also played the deep, and deeply political, blues of "Alabama" written in response to the Birmingham church bombings.

Jazz, however, tended to appeal to intellectuals. Most black people preferred rhythm and blues, gospel, and soul. During the height of the black consciousness movement, black popular musicians gave performances and concerts to raise funds and to assert racial pride. Aretha Franklin and Ray Charles, for example, allowed SNCC workers to attend their concerts free. Just as the freedom songs had done, the soul music of the black power era helped unify black people.

No history of the era would be complete without mentioning the performances of the "Godfather of Soul," James Brown, the "Queen of Soul," Aretha Franklin's powerful rendition of the song

"R.E.S.P.E.C.T.," and the financial contributions of Berry Gordy of Motown. James Brown's "Say It Loud, I'm Black and I'm Proud" became an anthem for the era. Brown linked sound commercial marketing to social commentary, confronting American racism with racial pride and righteous indignation. He confessed, "I may not do as much as some other individuals who have made it big," but, "you can bet your life that I'm doing the best I can. . . . I owe it to the black community to help provide scholarships, to help children stay in school, to help equip playgrounds and recreation centers, and to keep kids off the streets." Brown was "totally committed to black power, the kind that is achieved not through the muzzle of a rifle but through education and economic leverage."

Berry Gordy contributed to black freedom struggles both artistically and financially. To support King's Chicago movement, Gordy arranged for Stevie Wonder to give a benefit concert at Soldier Field in Chicago. He made cash contributions to black candidates, to the NAACP and its Legal Defense and Educational Fund, and to the Urban League.

With Gordy's encouragement, his performers flirted just enough with black radicalism to gain a patina of militancy. During the late 1960s and early 1970s the musical and lyrical innovations of the Temptations, Stevie Wonder, and Marvin Gaye reflected Motown's politicization. In an address to one of the sessions launching Jesse Jackson's People United to Save Humanity (PUSH) in 1971, Gordy declared, "I have been fortunate to be able to provide opportunities for young people. . . . Opportunities are supposed to knock once in a lifetime, but too often we have to knock for an opportunity. The first obligation we (as black businessmen) have is to ourselves and our own employees, the second is to create opportunities for others." The musician Curtis Mayfield, on the other hand, simply explained, "Our purpose is to educate as well as to entertain. Painless preaching is as good a term as any for what we do."

THE SECOND PHASE OF THE BLACK STUDENT MOVEMENT

The most dramatic expression of militant assertiveness after 1968 was among black college students. The black power generation of students was committed to transforming society, although those on predominantly white campuses often, but not always, seemed to be more reformist than revolutionary. Some observers describe the period of activism between 1968 and 1975 as the "second phase" of the black students movement.

The Orangeburg Massacre

The first phase, in this view, was launched by students at southern black colleges in the early 1960s. It began with the sit-ins in Greensboro, North Carolina, and the freedom rides, and culminated in the Mississippi Freedom Summer of 1964. By 1968, however, many of the student organizations that had grown out of the civil rights movement, most notably SNCC, were in decline. The massacre of three black students at South Carolina State College in Orangeburg on February 8, 1968, marks the end of the first phase and the beginning of the second. Students attending the historically black institution had protested a local bowling alley's whites-only admission policy. When the tension and protests escalated, state officials deployed the highway patrol and National Guard. On the evening of February 8, the students assembled at the front of the campus and taunted the officers; some threw rocks, bricks, and bottles. One officer was hit by a piece of lumber. Later, without warning, nine highway patrolmen opened fire on the students with shotguns. The officers killed three young men and wounded more than thirty. All the officers involved were later acquitted, but a young black activist and SNCC leader, Cleveland Sellers, was convicted of rioting, and served a year in prison before ultimately being released. He was pardoned in 1993.

Black Studies

The second phase owed much of its inspiration to the black power and black arts movements. It began when significant numbers of black students enrolled in predominantly white institutions for the first time. The black students at the white campuses demanded courses in black history, culture, literature, and art as alternatives to the "Eurocentric" bias of the average university curriculum. Many black students also formed all-black organizations, such as the Black Allied Students' Association at New York University and the Black Organization of Students at Rutgers University.

Black students understood that education was essential to empowerment. In 1967 black students accounted for only 2 percent of the total enrollment at predominantly white colleges and universities. This meant that only 95,000 African Americans were among the approximately five million full-time undergraduates at these schools. Rutgers University in New Jersey provides a case study. Out of 24,000 baccalaureate degrees the university awarded between 1952 and 1967, only about two hundred went to African Americans. Federal legislation—especially the Civil Rights Act of 1964 and the Higher Education Act of 1965—outlawed discrimination or segregation in higher education, and by instituting an array of financial aid programs, it spurred colleges and universities to take affirmative action to recruit black students. Where there had been about one hundred black undergraduates at Rutgers in 1965, there were more than four hundred by 1968, accounting for nearly 3 percent of the undergraduate enrollment.

On the national level, the overall status of black people in education reflected the accomplishments of the classic phase of the civil rights movement, but the black power generation was determined to make its own mark on the struggle. In 1960, only 227,000 black Americans attended the nation's colleges (including those at predominantly black institutions). By the end of the 1960s, enrollments had increased by 100 percent, and in 1977, 1.1 million black students attended America's universities. This was an almost 500 percent increase over 1960. There was wide political diversity among this generation of students, but they shared the sense of being strangers in a white-controlled environment. Many found the campuses hostile, alien places and discovered little there with which they could identify. They resolved to change this situation.

At San Francisco State College, Nathan Hare, formerly a professor at Howard University, and black students demanded not only curriculum changes, but the structural transformation of the college. In the 1966–1967 academic year the Black Student Union (BSU) orchestrated a strike that involved thousands of students of diverse ethnic and racial backgrounds. The students deliberately chose to strike, rather than take over buildings, so that they could circulate freely on the campus, increasing their support, and maintaining their momentum. Among their demands were the creation of an autonomous degree-granting black studies department and the admission of more black students. The college ultimately did create the first black studies department in 1968, with Hare as its head.

Black students also took over administration buildings at a number of institutions, demanding not only that the schools offer more black studies courses and programs and hire more black faculty, but often that classrooms and facilities also be made available for use by local black communities. The upheavals that shut down Columbia University in 1968, for example, began when black student members of the Students Afro-American Society and Students for a Democratic Society at Columbia University demonstrated to block plans to construct a university gymnasium in nearby Morningside Park. The demonstrators argued that the gym would impinge on one of the few parks located in Harlem and that it was being built over strenuous objections from the Harlem community.

In 1968, Yale University's Black Student Alliance sponsored a symposium to discuss the need, status, and function of Afro-American Studies. Conference organizer Armstead Robinson saw it as the first attempt to create a viable program of Afro-American Studies. In December 1968 the faculty voted to make Yale one of the first major universities in the country to institute a degree-granting African-American Studies program. In 1969 Harvard University created an Afro-American Studies Department, and other schools soon followed. In 1969, the Institute of the Black World in Atlanta conducted a project to define the methods and purpose of black studies and then sponsored a black studies director's seminar. Ron Karenga wrote what remains a major textbook for the new field, *Introduction to Black Studies*. By 1973 some two hundred black studies programs existed in the United States. By the late 1980s, several of the programs, such as those at Cornell, Yale, and UCLA offered master's degrees in African-American studies. In 1988 Temple University, under the leadership of Molefi Kete Asante, became the first university to offer a Ph.D. in African-American studies.

Still, there was no universally accepted definition of black studies. James E. Turner, founder of Africana Studies at Cornell, viewed it as a collective, interdisciplinary scholarly approach to the experiences of people of African descent throughout the world. History, in black studies, constituted the foundation for the analysis of common patterns of life that reflected the social conditions of black people. Africana studies or black studies theoreticians have generally agreed on four goals for this new scholarly field. (1) It should develop solutions to the problems facing black people in diaspora. (2) It should provide analyses of black culture and life that challenge and replace preexisting Eurocentric models. (3) It should promote social change and educational reform throughout the academy. And (4) it should institutionalize the study of black people as a field with its own theories, methods, ideologies, symbols, language, and culture. In short, the first generation of advocates envisioned black studies as being a revolutionary, historically grounded educational reform movement that sought to make the study of African descendants—their culture, problems, worldviews, and spirituality—a serious scholarly endeavor with practical implications for improving black peoples' lives.

THE ELECTION OF 1968

In the presidential campaign of 1968, the Democrats provided the excitement but lost the election. In late 1967, Senator Eugene McCarthy of Minnesota entered the race as the antiwar alternative to Lyndon Johnson, but few politicians took him seriously, even though he won several primaries. Robert Kennedy, U.S. senator from New York, was taken seriously, even though by the time he entered the race in mid-March, most of the convention delegates were already pledged to Johnson, and, after Johnson's withdrawal, quickly transferred their allegiance to Vice President Hubert Humphrey. Whether Kennedy could have gained the nomination will never be known because—in the second traumatic assassination of 1968—he was murdered in June. Grief over his death, bitterness over the war, and personal rivalries spilled over to produce the most tumultuous convention in modern American history, with Chicago policemen clubbing and gassing antiwar demonstrators.

Republican Richard Nixon narrowly defeated Humphrey by 43.1 percent to 42.7 percent in the popular vote and 301 to 191 in the electoral vote. George Wallace, the segregationist ex-governor of Alabama, in his first serious bid for the presidency, won 13.5 percent of the popular vote and 46 electoral votes. Running as the candidate of the American Independent party, Wallace denounced civil rights legislation and court-ordered desegregation, but now he also endorsed the repression of demonstrators and rioters and promised to stamp out communism in Southeast Asia once and for all.

THE NIXON PRESIDENCY

Of all modern presidents, Richard Nixon is probably the hardest to pin down with neat ideological labels. By the standards of the late 1990s, much of his record seems progressive: He created the Environmental Protection Agency, endorsed an equal rights amendment to the Constitution that would have prohibited gender discrimination, and signed more regulatory legislation than any other president. His willingness to innovate in policy affecting African Americans can be illustrated by his naming of Daniel Patrick Moynihan, one of

Johnson's experts on social policy, to be his domestic policy adviser.

The "Moynihan Report" and FAP

Moynihan first attracted national attention as assistant secretary of labor in the Johnson administration when a confidential memorandum of his—loosely organized and full of sweeping generalizations—was leaked to the press. It would later be published as "The Negro Family: The Case for National Action" and is popularly known as the "Moynihan Report." Moynihan's guiding assumption was that civil rights legislation, necessary as it was, would not address the problems of the inner city. There, he argued, the breakdown of the "lower-class" black family had led to the "pathology" of juvenile delinquency, illegitimacy, drug addiction, and poor performance in school. He attributed the vulnerability of the black family to "three centuries of almost unimaginable treatment" by white society: exploitation under slavery, the strain of urbanization, and persistent unemployment.

These forces, he argued, weakened the role of black men and resulted in a disproportionate number of dysfunctional, female-headed families. In the most-often repeated passage in the report, Moynihan declared that the black community had been forced into "a matriarchal structure, [which] because it is so out of line with the rest of American society, seriously retards the progress of the group as a whole, and imposes a crushing burden on the Negro male. . . . Obviously, not every instance of social pathology afflicting the Negro community can be traced to the weakness of family structure . . . [but] once or twice removed, it will be found to be the principal source of most of the aberrant, inadequate, or anti-social behavior that did not establish, but now serves to perpetuate the cycle of poverty and deprivation."

Though based on the work of earlier black scholars, such as E. Franklin Frazier, Moynihan's condemnation of "matriarchy" drew fire. Black social scientists, such as Joyce Ladner, Andrew Billingsley, and Carol Stack, countered that the structure of the black family reflected a functional adaptation that black people had made to survive in a hostile and racist American society. Historians Herbert Gutman and John Blassingame argued that Moynihan underestimated the prevalence of two-parent black families in the past. While many of the criticisms of the report were deserved, they diverted attention from its positive thrust. Moynihan wanted to eliminate poverty and unemployment in the black community and he recommended vigorous enforcement of the civil rights laws to achieve equality of opportunity.

Setting himself apart from other Johnson administration policy makers, Moynihan was one of the first to appreciate how white resentment of the Community Action Program (CAPs) and the expansion of the welfare rolls would make both politically unfeasible. Intrigued with Moynihan's independence, Nixon set him to work to develop a plan to assist poor families. Under the Family Assistance Plan (FAP) that Nixon unveiled in the summer of 1969, each family of four with no wage earner would receive an annual payment of $1,600 plus $800 of food stamps. With its across-the-board guarantee of income, the plan eliminated an oppressive welfare bureaucracy and reduced the invidious comparison between "welfare recipients" and everyone else.

Had it passed, FAP would have preserved and promoted two-parent families by removing the prohibition against assistance to dependent children whose fathers were alive, well, and living at home. It would also have encouraged work by requiring able-bodied recipients to accept jobs or vocational training and by providing benefits to those accepting low-paying jobs. But although the House approved the plan, the Senate, under pressure both from conservatives who objected to any government programs for the poor and from welfare-rights advocates who complained that the payments were too low, killed it. Arguably, at least until President Clinton's failed health care plan in the 1990s, Nixon's FAP was the most significant failed initiative in the history of American social policy.

Busing

Yet however flexible he might have been on many issues, Nixon was acutely aware that he moved in a changed political environment and particularly in a far more conservative Republican party than he had when he ran against and lost to John F. Kennedy in 1960. Then, as a presidential candidate, he had had to appease Eastern, pro–civil rights liberals led by New York governor Nelson Rockefeller (1908–1979). But in 1968, thanks to the influx of southern segregationists whom Barry Goldwater had attracted to the Republican party in 1964, he found himself having to deal with South Carolina senator Strom Thurmond, a Republican who had abandoned the Democratic party in 1964. Thurmond and his allies had demanded that if elected, Nixon would slow down the process of court-ordered school desegregation in the South. Finally, Nixon could hardly

ignore George Wallace, with his racist appeals. In another three-way race in 1972, Wallace might ensure Nixon's defeat.

As a result of these pressures, the Nixon administration set itself on a collision course with civil rights organizations, such as the NAACP, which supported busing to achieve school integration. Thus, the major battle over civil rights in the early 1970s was over the federal courts' willingness to implement desegregation goals by busing students across district lines. Nixon used the busing controversy to lure Wallace voters. In 1971 he had advised federal officials to stop pressing to desegregate schools through "forced busing." He argued that such efforts were ultimately "counterproductive, and not in the interest of better race relations."

Educational segregation in the North reflected residential segregation. In Boston, site of some of the most acrimonious busing protests, schools in black neighborhoods received less funding than their white counterparts. Buildings were derelict, seriously overcrowded, and deficient in supplies and equipment, even desks. In 1974 U.S. district judge W. Arthur Garrity ruled in favor of a group of black parents who had filed a class action suit against the Boston School Committee. The ruling found the school committee guilty of violating the equal protection clause of the Fourteenth Amendment. To achieve racial balance in the Boston schools, the judge ordered the busing of several thousand students between mostly white South Boston, Hyde Park, and Dorchester, and mostly black Roxbury.

White people who opposed busing organized demonstrations and boycotts to prevent their children from being bused into black communities and black children from being bused into white schools. During the first week of busing to achieve desegregation, white students and their mothers clashed with police officers outside South Boston High School. Violence and hostilities continued for weeks despite the arrests of dozens of people and the closing of bars and liquor stores. Sporadic violence persisted for another two years in Boston.

Nixon and the War

Meanwhile, the war in Vietnam seemed to drag on endlessly, with the peace negotiations that had begun in Paris in May 1968 making no apparent progress. Nixon realized that what most Americans disliked about the war was that it was killing their sons and husbands. So in 1969, he began to phase out direct U.S. involvement in the war. This "Vietnamization," he claimed, was made possible by the growing ability of the South Vietnamese to fight for themselves. What Nixon did not say was that another reason for troop withdrawals was that the morale of American soldiers was plunging rapidly. Drug abuse among troops was widespread, some soldiers had killed their officers, and some of those incidents had racial overtones. Along with his domestic record, Nixon's promise to "wind down the war" was widely popular and assured his reelection. In 1972 he defeated South Dakota senator George McGovern in a landslide.

Few in the Nixon administration, however, took South Vietnamese military capability seriously, and Nixon, just as much as Johnson, was unwilling to "lose" Vietnam. Between 1969 and 1971, Nixon stepped up the war. Even as American soldiers were being sent home, he escalated the air war dramatically. In the bombing of Cambodia in 1969–1970, for example—which was kept secret from Congress and the public—the United States dropped more bombs than it had on all of Asia in the Second World War.

But each time Nixon escalated the war—in the spring of 1970 with a joint American-South Vietnamese invasion of Cambodia, in the spring of 1971 with American air support for an invasion of Laos, in the spring of 1972 with the bombing of North Vietnam and the mining of its harbors—opposition to it grew. Antiwar demonstrations kept Nixon off balance and may have deterred him from further escalation.

The most dramatic response to Nixon's escalation in the Vietnam war came after the invasion of Cambodia in April 1970. The invasion triggered antiwar protests on many campuses. In one such protest, on May 4, Ohio National Guardsmen shot and killed four white students at Kent State University. The response of students across the country was electric: the first nationwide student strike in American history. Ten days later in Mississippi, the shooting and killing of two black students at Jackson State University attracted much less attention from either white students or the media. Three years later, at the beginning of 1973, the United States and North Vietnam signed a peace agreement. Congress then prohibited the reintroduction of American troops and the resumption of bombing, and in 1974 began cutting off military aid to the South Vietnamese government. The result of this loss of American support was predictable: In 1975 the Communists launched their final offensive, and South Vietnam collapsed.

Nixon's Downfall

If Nixon assumed the presidency in 1969 with any popular mandate, it was to restore law and order. The disorder that irritated the American public included many things: the inner-city riots, the antiwar demonstrations and campus protests, and the rise in crime. Responding to this mood, Nixon pushed legislation through Congress that gave local law enforcement officials expanded power to use wiretaps and enter premises without advance warning.

But Nixon's personality—a combination of paranoia and ruthlessness—pushed him beyond what the public would tolerate, and even beyond the law itself. He increasingly confused ordinary criminals, principled protesters, and his political opponents, and decided to punish them all. One method was to create an extralegal ring of burglars, operating out of the White House to gather incriminating information. In June 1972 these burglars were discovered breaking into Democratic National Committee headquarters in the Watergate apartment complex in Washington. Full details emerged in a Senate investigation in 1973–1974, and on August 9, 1974, threatened with impeachment, Nixon resigned. His downfall, however, left no one of his stature or with his flexible attitude toward public policy to resist the takeover of the Republican party by more ideologically dogmatic conservatives. One early intimation of this was the difficulty Nixon's successor Gerald Ford had in securing the 1976 Republican presidential nomination against the right's new hero, former California governor Ronald Reagan.

ECONOMIC DOWNTURN

The 1970s were a decade of recessions and economic instability. Many black people experienced this economic downturn as a depression. During the 70s, as the gap between the incomes of the upper 20 percent of African Americans and their white counterparts narrowed, the gap between black men and women at the bottom of the economic ladder and their counterparts expanded. Poor black people were losing ground. In 1969, approximately 10 percent of white men and 25 percent of black men earned less than $10,000 (in 1984 constant dollars). In 1984 about 40 percent of black men between twenty-five and fifty-five earned less than $10,000 compared to 20 percent of comparable white men. Put a different way, between 1970 and 1986, the proportion of black families with incomes of less than $10,000 grew from 26.8 to 30.2 percent. Still, the period did register some improvements. The black middle class grew despite the alternating periods of growth and stagnation. In 1970, 4.7 percent of black families had incomes of more than $50,000; by 1986 the number had almost doubled to 8.8 percent. But in

BARBARA JORDAN

Barbara Jordan grew up in segregated Houston, Texas, where she was born on February 21, 1936. In 1964 and 1965 she served as an administrative assistant to Harris County judge Bill Elliott and as project coordinator of a nonprofit corporation to help the unemployed. In 1966 she became the first black person since 1883 elected to the Texas Senate.

In 1972 Jordan became the first African-American woman from the South to serve in the United States House of Representatives. She was renowned for her oratorical skills and was an adept politician, able to win the support of the good old boys who controlled Texas Democratic party politics and those of like disposition who operated in the nation's capital. While not an outspoken feminist, she approved of the 1973 *Roe v. Wade* United States Supreme Court decision permitting women the right to choose whether to have an abortion.

It was the 1974 Watergate hearings, however, that catapulted Jordan into national prominence. Her captivating voice, piercing insight, and firm conviction during the Nixon impeachment discussions resonated with the American people. As a member of the House Judiciary Committee she declared, "My faith in the Constitution is whole, it is complete, it is total." She added, "I'm not going to sit here and be an idle spec-

Barbara Jordan during her tenure in the U.S. House of Representatives.

tator to the diminution, the subversion, the destruction of the Constitution." She helped to preserve the dignity of the impeachment proceedings and prevent them from degenerating into a sordid, partisan squabble.

Being a first in anything is fraught with danger but Jordan carried it off with gentle grace. In 1975 she was instrumental in persuading Congress to renew the 1965 Voting Rights Act that had enfranchised millions of African Americans and to extend its coverage to other minorities, including Hispanic Americans, Alaskan Natives, and Asian Americans.

One of Jordan's finest speeches was her keynote address at the 1976 Democratic National Convention with its call for national reconciliation instead of racial polarization. She was the first black person and the first woman to deliver a keynote address to a major party convention.

In 1978, multiple sclerosis forced Jordan to leave the House and return to Texas. The following year she became a professor at the University of Texas at Austin. Throughout her illness she carried on with consummate skill, refusing to discuss her health problems and effectively concealing them until her death in early 1996.

general, the relative economic status of black workers did not improve.

BLACK AMERICANS AND THE CARTER PRESIDENCY

In 1976 the United States celebrated its bicentennial. Flags flew from every flagpole, and fire hydrants were painted red, white, and blue. Tall ships sailed into New York harbor from around the world, and there were more parades than anyone could count. For African Americans, it was an important year, but for another reason. For the first time since 1964, the man most of them voted for was elected president—Jimmy Carter, a former governor of Georgia. Ninety percent of African American voters favored the soft-spoken religious Georgia Democrat over incumbent president Gerald Ford. As in 1960, their votes were crucial; without them, Carter could not have even carried his native South.

Black Appointees

Carter acknowledged his debt to the black electorate by appointing African Americans to highly visible posts. He named Patricia Harris secretary of Housing and Urban Development, making her the first black woman to serve in the Cabinet. Carter appointed Andrew Young, former congressman from Georgia and a long-time political ally, ambassador to the United Nations. (Young was forced to resign in 1979.) Clifford Alexander Jr. became the secretary of the Army. Eleanor Holmes Norton became the first woman to chair the Equal Employment Opportunity Commission (EEOC). Ernest Green, who had been one of the nine students to desegregate Little Rock's Central High School, was appointed assistant secretary of the Department of Labor. Wade McCree was appointed solicitor general in the Justice Department. Drew Days III became assistant attorney general for civil rights. Historian and former

Housing and Urban Development Secretary Patricia Harris visits New York City's impoverished South Bronx neighborhood with President Jimmy Carter and New York City Mayor Abraham Beame. Harris was the first black woman to serve in the Cabinet.

University of Colorado chancellor Mary Frances Berry was appointed assistant secretary for education. Carter also named Louis Martin his special assistant, making him the first African American in a position of influence on the White House staff.

Carter's Domestic Policies

There are many ways to judge the significance of the Carter presidency to African Americans. Carter's black appointments were practically and symbolically important. Never had so many black men and women occupied positions that had direct and immediate impact on the day-to-day operations of the federal government. Carter also helped to cement some gains for civil rights. When Congress passed legislation to stop busing for school children as a means to achieve integration in the schools, Carter vetoed it. He tried to improve fair employment practices by strengthening the enforcement powers of the EEOC. His Justice Department chose cases to prosecute under the Fair Housing Act that involved widespread discrimination, to make the greatest possible impact.

Yet Carter's overall record proved unsatisfactory to most African Americans. Despite a Public Works Employment Act that directed 10 percent of public works funds to minority contractors and helped spur the creation of 585,000 jobs, Carter failed to help Democrats in Congress pass either full-employment or universal health care bills. He also cut a number of social welfare programs in an attempt to balance the budget, including school lunch programs and financial aid to black students.

Although the sluggish economy undermined Carter's popularity, the event that proved his undoing was the Iran hostage crisis that began in the fall of 1979. For many black people, however, Carter had become a disappointment long before. They believed that he had done little to help them achieve social justice and economic advancement. Still the nomination of the conservative Ronald Reagan by the Republicans left black voters no alternative to Carter. In the election of 1980, 90 percent of black voters again supported him, but this time they could not prevent his defeat. Carter pulled down scores of Democrats with him and the Republicans regained the Senate for the first time since 1954.

CONCLUSION

The civil rights movement's victories changed African-American life in particular and American culture in general. The black power and black arts movements continued the struggle for freedom in northern and western urban areas where housing segregation, rising unemployment, and persistent police brutality sparked rebellions that resulted in many deaths and widespread destruction in Watts, Newark, Detroit, and other cities. The black political convention movement was unable to create a black third party. But one of the most enduring legacies of the era was the rise of black elected officials. Black student militancy persisted despite the destruction of the Black Panther party. Throughout the late 1960s and 1970s, black students fought for the creation and institutionalization of black studies as a new academic field. The black arts and black consciousness movement opened up new avenues for the expression of black unity and positive black identity. A new generation of black poets, dramatists, and musicians found receptive audiences.

The legislative successes of the early phase of the civil rights movement illuminated how much more needed to be done to achieve a truly egalitarian society. Poor people, black and white, needed jobs, housing, medical care, and education. To varying degrees, Presidents Johnson, Nixon, and Carter attempted to address these pressing needs. Their efforts produced mixed results in the face of a disastrous war in Vietnam and a massive white backlash. In the 1980s Republicans would reap the benefit of the Democratic party's disarray, and the plight of the poor would deteriorate.

Still, some black intellectuals chose a long view in their assessment of the significance of the post–World War II decades of struggle. Historian and theologian Vincent Harding put it most eloquently:

> It may be that the greatest discovery . . . was the fact that there is no last word in the human struggle for freedom, justice, and democracy. Only the continuing word, lived out by men, women, and children who dance and rest, who wrestle with alligators and stand firm before tanks, and presidents, and drug lords and deep, deep, fears. We learn again that the continuing word remains embedded in those who determined not to be moved, who know, against all odds, that they will overcome, will continue to create a more perfect union, a more compassionate world. The world remains with those who discover, in the midst of unremitting struggle, deep amazing powers within their own lives, power from, power for, the planet.

REVIEW QUESTIONS

1. Why did African-American residents of Watts, Newark, and Detroit rebel in 1965–1966? What did these rebellions suggest about the value of civil rights movement victories?

2. How did the visions and ideals, successes and failures of Martin Luther King Jr. compare with those of Lyndon B. Johnson? Why were these men at odds with each other?

3. What role did African Americans play in the Vietnam War? How did Muhammad Ali's refusal to serve in the military affect African-American attitudes toward the War?

4. In what ways can the presidency of Richard Nixon be considered progressive? Which reforms initiated by President Lyndon B. Johnson did Nixon advance once he took office?

5. What were the major ideological concerns of the artists of the black arts movement? To what extent did Baldwin and Amiri Baraka have similar views about art, consciousness, aesthetics, and politics?

6. What factors prevented African Americans from forming a third political party? What was the significance of the rise of black elected officials?

7. Why were African Americans disappointed with the presidency of Jimmy Carter?

RECOMMENDED READING

Stokely Carmichael and Charles V. Hamilton. *Black Power: The Politics of Liberation in America*. New York: Vintage Books, 1967. One of the most important books of the era of black power, by Carmichael, who popularized the slogan, and political scientist Hamilton.

Theodore Cross. *The Black Power Imperative: Racial Inequality and the Politics of Nonviolence*. New York: Faulkner Books, 1984. Provides a useful critique of the black power movement and explores the persistence of racial inequality.

Robert Dalleck. *Flawed Giant: Lyndon B. Johnson and His Times 1961–1973*. New York: Oxford University Press, 1998. A definitive biography of President Lyndon Johnson with fresh insights, grounded in exhaustive research.

Henry Hampton and Steve Fayer, eds. *Voices of Freedom: An Oral History of the Civil Rights Movement from the 1950s through the 1980s*. New York: Bantam Books, 1990. Contains the recollections of all the key participants in the critical battles and movements of the three decades that transformed race relations in America.

Robert C. Smith, *We Have No Leaders: African Americans in the Post–Civil Rights Era*. New York: State University

TIMELINE

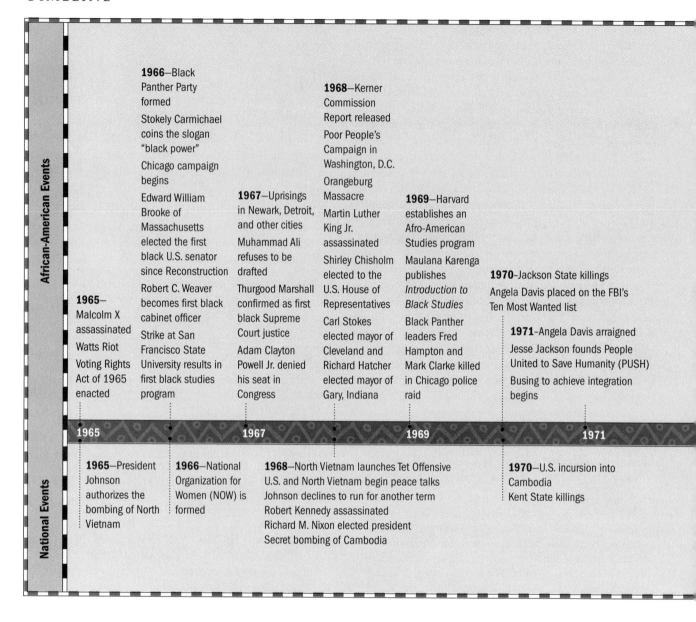

African-American Events

1965– Malcolm X assassinated
Watts Riot
Voting Rights Act of 1965 enacted

1966–Black Panther Party formed
Stokely Carmichael coins the slogan "black power"
Chicago campaign begins
Edward William Brooke of Massachusetts elected the first black U.S. senator since Reconstruction
Robert C. Weaver becomes first black cabinet officer
Strike at San Francisco State University results in first black studies program

1967–Uprisings in Newark, Detroit, and other cities
Muhammad Ali refuses to be drafted
Thurgood Marshall confirmed as first black Supreme Court justice
Adam Clayton Powell Jr. denied his seat in Congress

1968–Kerner Commission Report released
Poor People's Campaign in Washington, D.C.
Orangeburg Massacre
Martin Luther King Jr. assassinated
Shirley Chisholm elected to the U.S. House of Representatives
Carl Stokes elected mayor of Cleveland and Richard Hatcher elected mayor of Gary, Indiana

1969–Harvard establishes an Afro-American Studies program
Maulana Karenga publishes *Introduction to Black Studies*
Black Panther leaders Fred Hampton and Mark Clarke killed in Chicago police raid

1970-Jackson State killings
Angela Davis placed on the FBI's Ten Most Wanted list

1971-Angela Davis arraigned
Jesse Jackson founds People United to Save Humanity (PUSH)
Busing to achieve integration begins

1965   1967   1969   1971

National Events

1965–President Johnson authorizes the bombing of North Vietnam

1966–National Organization for Women (NOW) is formed

1968–North Vietnam launches Tet Offensive
U.S. and North Vietnam begin peace talks
Johnson declines to run for another term
Robert Kennedy assassinated
Richard M. Nixon elected president
Secret bombing of Cambodia

1970–U.S. incursion into Cambodia
Kent State killings

of New York Press, 1996. A thoughtful critique of the successes and failures of black politics beginning with the National Black Political Convention in Gary, Indiana, in 1972.

Wallace Terry. *Bloods: An Oral History of the Vietnam War by Black Veterans.* New York: Ballantine Books, 1984. One of the best sources for firsthand accounts of the Vietnam War as experienced by black soldiers.

Brian Ward, *Just My Soul Responding: Rhythm and Blues, Black Consciousness, and Race Relations.* Berkeley: Uni-

versity of California Press, 1998. An excellent study of black popular culture during the civil rights and black power movement era.

Craig Hansen Werner. *Playing the Changes: From Afro-Modernism to the Jazz Impulse.* Urbana: University of Illinois Press, 1994. An insightful study of the gospel, blues, and jazz impulse in the writings of key black writers, including James Baldwin and Leon Forrest, during the post–civil rights movement era.

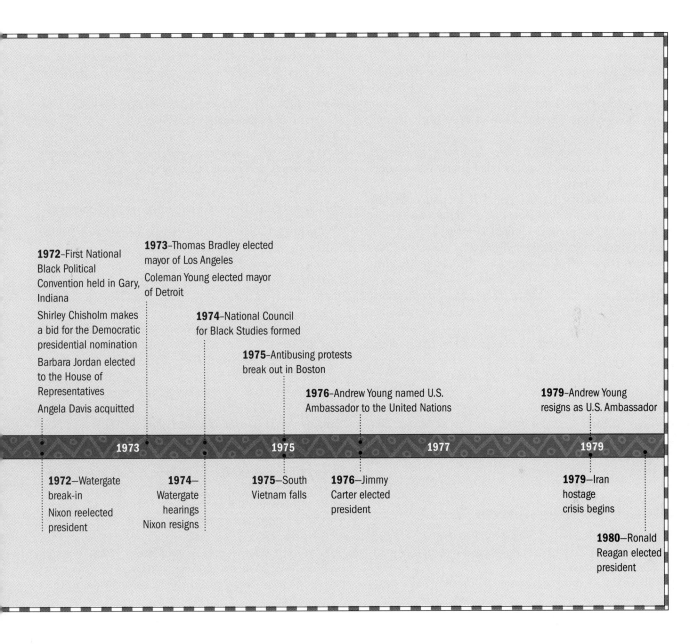

1972-First National Black Political Convention held in Gary, Indiana

Shirley Chisholm makes a bid for the Democratic presidential nomination

Barbara Jordan elected to the House of Representatives

Angela Davis acquitted

1973-Thomas Bradley elected mayor of Los Angeles

Coleman Young elected mayor of Detroit

1974-National Council for Black Studies formed

1975-Antibusing protests break out in Boston

1976-Andrew Young named U.S. Ambassador to the United Nations

1979-Andrew Young resigns as U.S. Ambassador

1973   1975   1977   1979

1972—Watergate break-in

Nixon reelected president

1974— Watergate hearings Nixon resigns

1975—South Vietnam falls

1976—Jimmy Carter elected president

1979—Iran hostage crisis begins

1980—Ronald Reagan elected president

ADDITIONAL BIBLIOGRAPHY

Black Panthers

Philip S. Foner, ed. *The Black Panther Speaks.* Philadelphia: Lippincott, 1970.

Toni Morrison, ed. *To Die for the People: The Writings of Huey P. Newton.* New York: Writers and Readers Publishing, 1995.

Kenneth O'Reilly. *Racial Matters: The FBI's Secret File on Black America, 1960–1972.* New York: Free Press, 1989.

Robert Scheer, ed. *Eldridge Cleaver: Post-Prison Writings and Speeches.* New York: Random House, 1969.

Black Power and Politics

Robert L. Allen. *Black Awakening in Capitalist America.* Trenton, NJ: Africa World Press, Inc., 1990.

Elaine Brown. *A Taste of Power: A Black Woman's Story.* New York: Pantheon, 1992.

Sidney Fine. *Violence in the Model City: The Cavanagh Administration, Race Relations and the Detroit Riot of 1967.* Ann Arbor: University of Michigan Press, 1989.

Frye Gaillard. *The Dream Long Deferred.* Chapel Hill: University of North Carolina Press, 1988.

B. I. Kaufman. *The Presidency of James E. Carter, Jr.* Lawrence: University of Kansas Press, 1993.

Steven Lawson. *In Pursuit of Power: Southern Blacks and Electoral Politics, 1965–1982.* New York: Columbia University Press, 1985.

J. Anthony Lukas. *Common Ground.* New York: Knopf, 1985.

John T. McCartney. *Black Power Ideologies: An Essay in African-American Thought.* Philadelphia, PA: Temple University Press, 1992.

William E. Nelson Jr. and Philip J. Meranto. *Electing Black Mayors: Political Action in the Black Community.* Columbus: Ohio State University Press, 1977.

Gary Orfield. *Must We Bus? Segregated Schools and National Policy.* Washington, DC: Brookings Institution, 1978.

Robert A. Pratt. *The Color of Their Skin: Education and Race in Richmond, Virginia, 1954–89.* Charlottesville: University Press of Virginia, 1992.

James R. Ralph Jr. *Northern Protest: Martin Luther King, Jr., Chicago, and the Civil Rights Movement.* Cambridge, MA: Harvard University Press, 1993.

Diane Ravitch. *The Great School Wars.* New York: Basic Books, 1974.

Wilbur C. Rich. *Coleman Young and Detroit Politics.* Detroit: Wayne State University Press, 1989.

Bobby Seale. *Seize the Time.* New York: Random House, 1970.

Black Studies and Black Students

Talmadge Anderson, ed. *Black Studies: Theory, Method, and Cultural Perspectives.* Pullman: Washington State University Press, 1990.

William H. Exum. *Paradoxes of Protest: Black Student Activism in a White University.* Philadelphia, Temple University Press, 1985.

Richard P. McCormick. *The Black Student Protest Movement at Rutgers.* New Brunswick: Rutgers University Press, 1990.

Cleveland Sellers, with Robert Terrell. *The River of No Return: The Autobiography of a Black Militant and the Life and Death of SNCC.* New York: William Morrow, 1987.

Class and Race

Jack M. Bloom. *Class, Race, and the Civil Rights Movement.* Bloomington: Indiana University Press, 1987.

Martin Gilens. *Why Americans Hate Welfare: Race, Media, and the Politics of Antipoverty Policy.* Chicago: University of Chicago Press, 1999.

Michael Katz. *The Underserving Poor: From the War on Poverty to the War on Welfare.* New York: Pantheon Books, 1989.

Bart Landry. *The New Black Middle Class.* Berkeley: University of California Press, 1987.

William Julius Wilson. *The Truly Disadvantaged: The Inner City, the Underclass, and Public Policy.* Chicago: University of Chicago Press, 1987.

Black Arts and Black Consciousness Movements

William L. Andrews, Frances Smith Foster, and Trudier Harris, eds. *The Oxford Companion to African American Literature.* New York: Oxford University Press, 1997.

James Baldwin. *Notes of a Native Son.* New York: Dial Press, 1955.

———. *Nobody Knows My Name.* New York: Dial Press, 1961.

———. *The Fire Next Time.* New York: Dial Press, 1963.

———. *No Name in the Street.* New York: Dial Press, 1972.

Imamu Amiri Baraka. *Dutchman and the Slave, Two Plays by LeRoi Jones.* New York: William Morrow, 1964.

Samuel A. Hay. *African American Theater: An Historical and Critical Analysis.* Cambridge: Cambridge University Press, 1994.

LeRoi Jones and Larry Neal, eds. *Black Fire: An Anthology of Afro-American Writing.* New York: William Morrow, 1968.

LeRoi Jones. *Blues People: Negro Music in White America.* New York: William Morrow, 1963.

———. *Home: Social Essays.* New York: William Morrow, 1966.

Frank Kofsky. *Black Nationalism and the Revolution in Music.* New York: Pathfinder Press, 1970.

Larry Neal. *Visions of a Liberated Future: Black Arts Movement Writings.* New York: Thunder's Mouth Press, 1989.

Leslie Catherine Sanders. *The Development of Black Theater in America: From Shadow to Selves.* Baton Rouge: Louisiana State University Press, 1988.

Autobiography and Biography

Imamu Amiri Baraka. *The Autobiography of LeRoi Jones.* New York: Freundlich Books, 1984.

Dennis C. Dickerson. *Militant Mediator: Whitney M. Young, Jr.* Lexington: University Press of Kentucky, 1998.

James Farmer. *Lay Bare the Heart: An Autobiography of the Civil Rights Movement.* New York: Arbor House, 1985.

Jimmie Lewis Franklin. *Back to Birmingham: Richard Arrington, Jr., and His Times.* Tuscaloosa: University of Alabama Press, 1989.

Elliott J. Gorn, ed. *Muhammad Ali: The People's Champ.* Urbana: University of Illinois Press, 1995.

Charles V. Hamilton. *Adam Clayton Powell, Jr.: The Political Biography of an American Dilemma.* New York: Atheneum, 1991.

Hil Haygood. *King of the Cats: The Life and Times of Adam Clayton Powell, Jr.* Boston: Houghton Mifflin Co., 1993.

David Remnick. *King of the World: Muhammad Ali and the Rise of an American Hero.* New York: Random House, 1998.

Mary Beth Rogers. *Barbara Jordan: American Hero.* New York: Bantam Books, 1998.

Kathleen Rout. *Eldridge Cleaver.* Boston, MA: Twayne Publishers, 1991.

Bobby Seale. *Seize the Time.* New York: Random House, 1970.

Nancy J. Weiss. *Whitney M. Young, Jr., and the Struggle for Civil Rights.* Princeton, NJ: Princeton University Press, 1989.

MODERN BLACK AMERICA, 1980–2000

Presidential candidate Jesse Jackson addresses the 1988 Democratic National Convention in Atlanta.

Many were lost in the struggle for the right to vote: Jimmie Lee Jackson, a young student, gave his life; Viola Liuzzo, a White mother from Detroit, called nigger lover, had her brains blown out at point blank range; [Michael] Schwerner, [Andrew] Goodman and [James] Chaney—two Jews and a Black—found in a common grave, bodies riddled with bullets in Mississippi; the four darling little girls in a church in Birmingham, Alabama. They died that we might have a right to live.

Dr. Martin Luther King Jr. lies only a few miles from us tonight. Tonight he must feel good as he looks down upon us. We sit here together, a rainbow, a coalition—the sons and daughters of slavemasters and the sons and daughters of slaves, sitting together around a common table, to decide the direction of our party and our country. His heart would be full tonight.

We meet tonight at the crossroads, a point of decision. Shall we expand, be inclusive, find unity and power; or suffer division and impotence?

Address by the Reverend Jesse Louis Jackson to the Democratic National Convention, July 19, 1988

The civil rights movement achieved noteworthy success in dismantling legal and political barriers to black freedom, but as the decade of the seventies ended, profound divisions within the black community emerged. For centuries slavery and racism and the relentless struggles to end them had bound black American communities together, burying many differences. Now, however, rifts expanded between the interests of the black middle class, which had grown considerably during the preceding decades, and those left to languish in impoverished inner-city neighborhoods. At the same time, heated debates erupted among advocates of different ideologies—integrationism, assimilationism, and nationalism. As in American society as a whole, the quest for gender equality resulted in increasing tensions between black men and women. For better or worse, in recent decades it has become more difficult to speak of a united African America than at any time in the past.

But the need for solidarity did not diminish with the destruction of state-sanctioned segregation. Racism remains a powerful force in American politics and society. One of the driving forces behind the conservative resurgence of the 1980s was a reaction to the gains of black Americans. Now the whole edifice of laws and court cases that was built at such cost during the 1960s has come under attack. The need to counter this assault and to solve the problems of economic deprivation and continued discrimination remain.

PROGRESS AND POVERTY

During the 1960s an increasing number of African Americans began to share in the wealth enjoyed by other Americans. Some became famous or wealthy and most, for the first time, emerged from the extreme poverty and deprivation that had been the lot of nearly every African American in the past. Many, however—a far greater proportion than among white Americans—remained in troublingly persistent poverty.

The years after 1970 witnessed the consolidation of black economic, civic, and political progress. In part this was exemplified by the rising prominence of such visible African Americans as entertainer Oprah Winfrey, Secretary of Commerce Ronald Brown, General Colin Powell, and basketball star Michael Jordan. These people, joined by many others, countered notions of white supremacy by rising to the top of their fields.

The very rich remained rare in the black community, but their numbers did grow. Oprah Winfrey, Bill Cosby, Michael Jackson, and Michael Jordan numbered among those few fortunate enough to acquire immense fortunes in the entertainment industry. Others, such as Reginald Lewis, made enormous sums in business. In the mid-1980s Lewis was, by some accounts, the wealthiest black American. Armed with a law degree

from Harvard University Law School, this prodigious businessman first purchased the $55 million dollar McCall Pattern Company in a leveraged buyout, and then in 1987 he purchased an international packaged goods company, Beatrice Foods, for $2.5 billion dollars. At that time it was the largest leveraged buyout in U.S. history. Before his untimely death in 1993 he demonstrated an understanding of the need to give back to the community by donating $3 million to Harvard Law School, $1 million to Howard University, and another $2 million to the NAACP.

The Growth of the Black Middle Class

The achievements of the most successful African Americans are impressive, but more significant is the growth of the black middle class. In 1940 only 5.2 percent of black men and 6.4 percent of black women worked in white-collar occupations. By 1990 those figures had risen to 32 percent for black men and 58.9 percent for black women. Although still on average below that of white families, black family income has also increased dramatically. In 1940 only 1 percent of black families, compared to 12 percent of white families, had income at least twice as high as the government's poverty line; by 1995 almost 49 percent of black families did, compared to 75 percent of white families. Income in relation to white families also improved. In 1960, for example, two-parent black families earned 61 percent as much as two-parent similar white families, but by 1995 they earned 87 percent as much. This figure is even more impressive when one considers that a larger proportion of black people live in the low-wage South than do white people.

The economic boom of the Clinton years has been particularly beneficial for black people. Although the median family income of black families remains substantially below that of white families, it has risen at a greater rate (Table 23–1). Black women now make 94 percent of what white women earn. In 1992, 39.1 percent of black households earned less than $15,000 annually; by 1997, the percentage had declined to 31 percent. The overall black poverty rate in 1997 was 26.5

Table 23–1 Median Income of Black and White Households, 1992 and 1997				
	1992	1997	Change	Percent Change
White	$36,846	$38,972	+$2,126	+5.8
Black	$21,455	$25,050	+$3,595	+16.8

Source: U.S. Census Bureau Study of Income Data, 1997.

P R O F I L E

OPRAH WINFREY: WORLD'S RICHEST BLACK WOMAN

"Communicating with people is how I always developed any kind of value about myself. All my life," Oprah Winfrey recounts, "I've always known I was born to greatness." She remembers being two years old and speaking in church and hearing people say to her grandmother: "Hattie Mae, that child sure can talk. That is one talking child."

Winfrey was born to a young unmarried woman, Vernita Lee, in Kosciusko, Mississippi, on January 29, 1954; she was raised by her maternal grandmother, Hattie Mae, and her father, Vernon Winfrey. Educated at Tennessee State University, she managed to overcome the barriers that confront young, poor, black women in America to become one of the most admired and revered women in the country.

In 1984 Winfrey took over the ailing talk show *A.M. Chicago*. Within one month her ratings matched those of her formidable competitor, Phil Donahue, and within three months she was trouncing him. In less than a year, *A.M. Chicago* expanded to one hour and was renamed *The Oprah Winfrey Show*. Winfrey, who always wanted to be an actress but had no professional experience, then landed a role in Steven Spielberg's 1985 cinematic adaptation of Alice Walker's *The Color Purple* as the character Sofia. For her movie performance, Winfrey scored an Oscar nomination for Best

Oprah Winfrey with Michael Jordan on her television show in 1996.

Supporting Actress. In 1986, *The Oprah Winfrey Show* was nationally syndicated. Winfrey formed her own production company, HARPO (Oprah spelled backward), and in 1989, bought her own television and movie production studio. She accumulated thirty-two Emmy Awards—seven for Outstanding Talk Show Host—and the Emmy Lifetime Achievement Award (1998). Now one of the most powerful people in show business, Winfrey is also one of the richest women in America and one of the few African Americans on the Forbes 1998 list of the Top 40 Entertainers in the American entertainment industry.

Winfrey has forged a powerful connection with the viewing public with revelations about the pains of her private life. She has told of being the victim of incest, of having a still-born child when only a child herself, of her promiscuous adolescence, and of her struggles with an eating disorder.

During her decade and a half on national television, Winfrey has developed an astonishing influence over American society and culture. She can focus attention on important problems in the black community and American society at large. She has also helped rid mass entertainment of the negative stereotypes it had imposed on black women since slavery.

---

percent, the lowest on record. In real terms, approximately 1.7 million black Americans went off the poverty rolls between 1992 and 1998. The decline in the poverty rate corresponds to increasing employment, although many of the jobs working-poor African Americans are finding are in the low-paying service industry. In 1997, with the nation's overall unemployment rate at 4.6 percent, the lowest since 1970, black unemployment dropped below 10 percent for the first time in almost twenty-five years.

The increasing affluence of many black people rested not only on the removal of racial barriers to their employment and the implementation of affirmative action programs but also on increased educational attainment. Many more black youths graduate from high school than ever before. In 1960 the number of African Americans between the ages of twenty-five and twenty-nine who had completed high school stood at just 37.7 percent, but by 1995 it had climbed to 86.5 percent, almost exactly the same proportion (87.4 percent) as for white

Americans. Black enrollment in college also climbed, rising from a mere 136,000 in 1960 to nearly 1,300,000 in 1990. Although the college completion rate for African Americans remains well below that for white Americans, statistics like these suggest that the number of African Americans trained for higher paying jobs has increased greatly since the 1960s.

The Persistence of Black Poverty

Despite the emergence of a substantial black middle class, many African Americans remain mired in poverty. The 26.5 percent of African Americans living below the poverty line in 1997 translates into more than nine million people. The black poverty rate is slightly lower than that of Hispanic Americans (27.1 percent) but more than twice that of non-Hispanic white Americans (11 percent). Most poor black people are trapped in devastated inner-city neighborhoods, plagued by gang warfare, drug addiction, and high rates of HIV infection, and cut off from meaningful participation in the social and economic life of the nation.

The high rate of poverty in the black community is particularly troubling because it disproportionately affects children. More than half of all African Americans under the age of eighteen live in families with only one parent, almost always the mother (Table 23–2). Partly for this reason, the poverty rate for black children in 1997 was much higher—39 percent—than the overall black poverty rate. Female-headed single-parent families suffer from limited earning capacity, meager public assistance, poor housing, and inferior education. These conditions can handicap children for the rest of their lives, helping to perpetuate poverty.

RONALD REAGAN AND THE CONSERVATIVE REACTION

Beginning in the late 1970s American politics took a hard turn to the right. This shift had a profound impact on African Americans, particularly the poor. With the election of Ronald Reagan to the presidency in 1980, the executive branch turned away from support for expanded civil rights. It also sought to reduce welfare programs and it staffed key agencies and the federal judiciary with opponents of affirmative action. The now overwhelmingly white Republican party became increasingly entrenched in the South, ending the Democratic party's long dominance in that region.

Ronald Reagan's defeat of Jimmy Carter in the 1980 presidential election marked the emergence of the New

Table 23–2 Black and White Children and the Conditions Contributing to Poverty

Children Living in Households Headed by Their Mothers: 1960–1990

Year	Black	White	Black Percentage as Multiple of White Percentage
1960	19.9%	6.1%	3.26
1970	29.4%	7.8%	3.78
1980	43.9%	12.9%	3.43
1990	58.1%	16.1%	3.61

Children with Unmarried Mothers, 1960–1990

Year	Black	White	Black Percentage as Multiple of White Percentage
1960	2.1%	0.11%	19.1
1970	4.6%	0.22%	20.9
1980	13.2%	0.73%	18.1
1990	33.1%	2.91%	11.4

Infant Mortality Rates (Deaths per 1,000 Births), 1960–1990

Year	Black	White	Black Percentage as Multiple of White Percentage
1960	43.9	22.9	1.92
1970	32.6	17.8	1.83
1980	21.4	11.0	1.95
1990	17.0	7.7	2.21

Location of Households Headed by Women, 1990

Location	Black	White
Central Cities	60.9%	27.7%
Suburbs	24.3%	49.5%
Nonmetropolitan Areas	14.8%	22.8%

Source: Adapted from Andrew Hacker, *Two Nations: Black and White, Separate, Hostile, Unequal* (New York: Ballantine Books, rev., 1995), p. 256.

Right as the dominant force in American politics. Reagan possessed considerable charm and a remarkable ability to communicate his vision to the American people. His election was, however, the result of more than personal charisma. Over the previous decade, many groups unhappy with the changes of the 1960s had developed powerful political organizations that subsequently found a home in the Republican party. These groups included those opposed to equal rights for women, to abortion rights, to the Supreme Court's decisions protecting the rights of the accused and banning compulsory prayer from the public schools, and a whole range of other issues. A key part of this coalition was made up of white Southerners opposed to the changes wrought by the civil rights movement and white Northerners angry at school busing, affirmative action programs, and the tax burden they associated with welfare.

Dismantling the Great Society

One of the New Right's key goals was to reverse the growth of social welfare programs created during and after the New Deal. To this end, from 1981 to 1993 Reagan and his Republican successor George Bush cut federal grants to cities in half and terminated several programs crucial to the stability of many black families. As the federal government cut funds for the redevelopment of inner cities and the construction of public housing between 1980 and 1992, the percentage of city budgets derived from the federal government declined from 14.3 percent to 5 percent. As a consequence of these policies, inner-city neighborhoods, where 56 percent of poor residents were African American, became more unstable.

Reagan advanced a "trickle-down" theory of economics. He believed that if the financial position of the wealthiest Americans improved, their increased prosperity would percolate through the middle and working classes to the poor. Unemployment statistics soon challenged this theory. By December of 1982, the unemployment rate had risen to 10.8 and the rate for African Americans was twice that of white Americans. The real income of the highest paid 1 percent of the nation, meanwhile, increased from $312,206 to $548,970 during the 1980s.

Reagan and Bush often cloaked their intent to undermine rights-oriented policies by appointing black conservatives to key administrative positions. Reagan chose William Bell, for example, to replace the effective Carter appointee Eleanor Holmes Norton as chair of the Equal Employment Opportunity Commission (EEOC). Because he was a conservative with few qualifications for the post, civil rights leaders and organizations immediately protested Bell's appointment. Reagan simply replaced Bell the following year with yet another black conservative, Clarence Thomas, who strongly opposed affirmative action. Thomas reduced the commission's staff and allowed the backlog of affirmative action cases to grow to 46,000 and processing time to increase to ten months.

Reagan similarly tried to change the direction of the U.S. Commission on Civil Rights (CCR), but in this case he met with resistance. Since its creation in 1957 the commission had served as a civil rights watchdog, with no real enforcement powers, but with considerable influence on public opinion. Soon after Reagan took office, it began to issue reports critical of his civil rights policies. Reagan responded by trying to load the commission with members sympathetic to his perspective. He fired the commission's chair, Arthur S. Flemming, who was white, and replaced him with a black Republican, Clarence Pendleton, former executive director of the San Diego Urban League. The vice chair, however, was Mary Frances Berry, a well-respected, long-time civil rights activist and historian who had been appointed by Carter and who frequently clashed with the new president. In 1984, Reagan tried to remove Berry from the Commission on Civil Rights but she resisted, suing in court to retain her position. When her suit was successful, she became known as "the woman the president could not fire." Even with Berry, however, the Commission on Civil Rights declined to virtual insignificance under Pendleton during the Reagan years.

Black Conservatives

Men like Bell, Thomas, and Pendleton were part of a vocal cadre of black, middle-class, conservative intellectuals, professionals, and politicians who gained visibility and prominence during the Reagan years. To augment their influence in the Republican party these conservatives cultivated a small, well-educated, articulate group of black men and women intellectuals in addition to black politicians. Prominent black proponents of conservative ideology include Thomas Sowell, Walter Williams, Shelby Steele, Armstrong Williams, and, until he broke with the others in the late 1990s, Glenn Loury. There was a critical difference, however, between elite black Republicans and the black politicians in the Democratic camp. Black Republican politicians rarely exercised meaningful power within the party. They were expected to embrace the existing values and goals set down by the white party leaders. In contrast, elite black Democratic politicians could and often did make their influence felt. Moreover, they represented a large and essential constituency within the party.

The Thomas/Hill Controversy

The role of black conservatives acquired its greatest visibility when, in 1991, Reagan's successor, President George Bush, nominated Clarence Thomas to the United States Supreme Court. The symbolism of Thomas, who opposed the expansion of civil rights, replacing Thurgood Marshall, the greatest civil rights lawyer of the twentieth century, could not have been more dramatic.

George Bush's nomination of Thomas also precipitated the most public exposure of gender conflict within the black community in history. Marshall had been one of the Court's great liberals and a staunch defender of civil rights. Thomas was a black conservative whose record on civil rights did not endear him to white liberals or for that matter to many individuals within the black community. In addition, his credentials for the position were open to question; he had served only fifteen months as an appellate court judge. However, he was a black man and the black community was loath publicly to contest his nomination or to challenge the cynical tokenism of the Bush administration. The anticipated easy confirmation process derailed when black law professor Anita Hill agreed to appear before the Senate Judiciary Committee, which heard testimony on Thomas's confirmation, with accusations that he had sexually harassed her when she worked for him at the Equal Employment Opportunity Commission.

Both Anita Hill and Clarence Thomas were conservative Republicans and both had earned law degrees at Yale University School of Law. Hill did not volunteer to testify about Thomas's sexual harassment of her. She had answered questions put to her in a confidential investigation. When her answers were leaked to the press, she was asked to appear before the committee and she agreed. Some senators grilled her with questions about her own character and integrity. Thomas countered her charges with charges of his own. He declared that he was a victim of a "high-tech lynching" in the media and that Hill's accusations were false. Although many in the black community supported Thomas, progressive feminists, white liberals, and some people in the black community supported Hill. Activist black women were especially incensed by the treatment that Hill received from the Senate and were determined to voice their opposition to Thomas's political views. Despite the opposition, Clarence Thomas won confirmation to the United States Supreme Court by a narrow 52–48 majority.

Debating the "Old" and the "New" Civil Rights

The Reagan and Bush administrations distinguished between what might be called the "old civil rights law," which they claimed to support, and the "new civil rights law," which they opposed. Developed in the decade between the *Brown* decision and the Voting Rights Act of 1965, the old civil rights law prohibited *intentional* discrimination, whether legal segregation in the schools, informal discrimination in the workplace, or racially biased restrictions on voting. The new civil rights law is concerned with discriminatory *outcomes*, as measured by statistical disparities, rather than with discriminatory *intent*. If, for example, black children are in disproportionately all-black schools, or if the workforce in a given firm, compared with the community in which it is located, is disproportionately white (or male), or

Anita Hill testifies before the Senate Judiciary Committee about her charge that Supreme Court nominee Clarence Thomas had sexually harassed her.

BLACK WOMEN IN DEFENSE OF THEMSELVES

Within days after Anita Hill appeared before the Senate Judiciary Committee, a group of black women led by Elsa Barkley Brown, Barbara Ransby, and Deborah King raised more than $50,000 to purchase a three-quarter-page ad in the New York Times *to print this statement, "In Defense of Ourselves." Appearing on November 17, 1991, it was accompanied by the names of 1,603 black women signers. Six black newspapers—the San Francisco* Sun Reporter, *the* Los Angeles Sentinel, *the* New York City Sun, *the* Atlanta Inquirer, *and the* Chicago Defender—*also published the statement:*

As women of African descent, we are deeply troubled by the recent nomination, confirmation and seating of Clarence Thomas as an Associate Justice of the U.S. Supreme Court. We know that the presence of Clarence Thomas on the Court will be continually used to divert attention away from the historic struggles for social justice through suggestions that the presence of a Black man on the Supreme Court constitutes an assurance that the rights of African Americans will be protected. Clarence Thomas's public record is ample evidence that this will not be true. Further, the consolidation of a conservative majority on the Supreme Court endangers the working class people and the elderly. The seating of Clarence Thomas is an affront not only to African American women and men, but to all people concerned with social justice.

We are particularly outraged by the racist and sexist treatment of Professor Anita Hill, an African American woman who was maligned and castigated for daring to speak publicly of her own experience of sexual abuse. The malicious defamation of Professor Hill insulted all women of African descent and sent a dangerous message to all women who might contemplate a sexual harassment complaint.

We speak here because we recognize that the media are now portraying the Black community as prepared to tolerate the dismantling of affirmative action and the evil of sexual harassment in order to have any Black man on the Supreme Court. We want to make clear that the media have ignored and distorted many African American voices. We will not be silenced.

Many have erroneously portrayed the allegations against Clarence Thomas as an issue of either gender or race. As women of African descent, we understand sexual harassment as both. We further understand that Clarence Thomas outrageously manipulated the legacy of lynching in order to shelter himself from Anita Hill's allegations. To deflect attention away from the reality of sexual abuse in African American women's lives, he trivialized and misrepresented this painful part of African American people's history. This country, which has a long legacy of racism and sexism, has never taken the sexual abuse of Black women seriously. Throughout U.S. history Black women have been sexually stereotyped as immoral, insatiable, perverse, the initiators in all sexual contacts—abusive or otherwise. The common assumption in legal proceedings as well as in the larger society has been that Black women cannot be raped or otherwise sexually abused. As Anita Hill's experience demonstrates, Black women who speak of these matters are not likely to be believed.

In 1991, we cannot tolerate this type of dismissal of any one Black woman's experience or this attack upon our collective character without protest, outrage, and resistance.

As women of African descent, we express our vehement opposition to the policies represented by the placement of Clarence Thomas on the Supreme Court. The Bush administration, having obstructed the passage of civil rights legislation, impeded the extension of unemployment compensation, cut student aid and dismantled social welfare programs, has continually demonstrated that it is not operating in our best interests. Nor is this appointee. We pledge ourselves to continue to speak out in defense of one another, in defense of the African American community and against those who are hostile to social justice no matter what color they are. No one will speak for us but ourselves.

QUESTIONS

1. From what did the African-American women who signed this letter feel the need to defend themselves?

2. What reasons did they give for opposing the confirmation of Clarence Thomas to the Supreme Court?

3. Why were they unsympathetic to Thomas's claim that he had been a victim of a "high-tech" lynching?

Source: The *New York Times*, November 17, 1991.

if elected officials in a multiracial state or municipality are disproportionately white, then discrimination is assumed.

The remedies for such historic discrimination, collectively labeled "affirmative action," tend to be statistical in nature. They include increasing the number of minority pupils, minority employees, or (by redrawing the districts from which they were elected) minority elected officials to correspond to the percentage of the relevant minority population. In employment (and in admissions to colleges and universities) the methods used in reaching these goals became known as affirmative action "guidelines." Sometimes guidelines were imposed by court order; more often they were the result of voluntary efforts by legislatures, government agencies, business firms, and colleges and universities to comply with civil rights laws and court rulings.

Affirmative Action

Few civil rights policies in the twentieth century have proved more persistently controversial than affirmative action. Many white Americans oppose affirmative action, arguing that it runs contrary to the concept of achievement founded on objective merit and amounts to reverse racial or sexual discrimination. Ironically, because gender discrimination in employment was made illegal in the 1964 Civil Rights Act, prompting federal agencies to scrutinize the percentage of women in a given workforce, white women have been among the major beneficiaries of affirmative action. But the major advocates of affirmative action have been African Americans, the majority of whom see it as a remedy for centuries of discrimination. The debate over affirmative action has thus, inevitably, led to racial polarization, and it even became a potent wedge issue within the black community.

The term *affirmative action* was first used by President Lyndon Johnson in a 1965 executive order that required federal contractors to "take affirmative action" to guarantee that job seekers and employees "are treated without regard to their race, color, religion, sex, or national origin." Much of the credit for affirmative action compliance belongs to conservative Republican president Richard Nixon. In 1969, Arthur A. Fletcher, a black assistant secretary of labor in the Nixon administration, developed the "Philadelphia Plan," in which firms with federal government contracts in the construction industry would have to set and meet hiring goals for African Americans or be penalized. The plan served as a model for subsequent "set-aside" programs that reserved some contracts for minority-owned busi-

---

SUPREME COURT CASES ON AFFIRMATIVE ACTION IN EMPLOYMENT

1979 *United Steelworkers v. Weber* upholds preferential treatment in hiring and training by private firms

1980 *Fullilove v. Klutznick* upholds government programs that reserve places for minorities

1984 *Memphis Firefighters v. Stotts* rejects a judicial order for retaining less-senior black employees over white employees during layoffs

1986 *Wygant v. Jackson Board of Education* rejects school board's plan for laying off white teachers while retaining less-senior black teachers, but also rejects Reagan administration position that affirmative action be limited to actual victims of discrimination, thus broadly upholding affirmative action

1986 *Local 93 of International Association of Firefighters v. City of Cleveland* upholds promotion of minorities ahead of white applicants with higher test scores and greater seniority

1986 *Local 28 of Sheet Metal Workers v. EEOC* upholds order that union meet minority quota for membership

1987 *U.S. v. Paradise* upholds judicial order imposing racial quotas in hiring and promotions of Alabama state troopers

1987 *Johnson v. Transportation Agency of Santa Clara County* upholds plan that promoted women over men

1987 *American Tobacco Co. v. Patterson* upholds seniority plans in place before 1964 unless discriminatory intent could be shown

1989 *Martin v. Wilks* rules that employees may challenge affirmative action plan after it has gone into effect. This decision is overruled by Congress in the Civil Rights Act of 1991

1989 *Richmond v. J. Croson and Co.* rules that 14th Amendment prohibits set-asides for minority contractors, thus going against spirit of *Weber* and against the letter of *Fullilove v. Klutznick* and implying that all such plans face "strict scrutiny"

1990 *Metro Broadcasting v. FCC* upholds affirmative action plan increasing minority broadcasting owners, returning to *Fullilove*

1995 *Adarand Constructors v. Pena* strikes down a congressional statute requiring 10% of federal highway money to go to minority contractors and broadly asserts that any such programs using racial classifications are constitutionally suspect

nesses or that favored the hiring of women and minorities. The process of setting goals and timetables to achieve full compliance with federal civil rights requirements appealed to large corporations and accounted for the early success of affirmative action initiatives.

The Backlash

Though it has produced more litigation, the issue of affirmative action in employment has been less controversial than that of affirmative action in college and university admissions. State higher education institutions have been at the center of the controversy both because they are narrowly bound by the Fourteenth Amendment's prohibitions on racial discrimination and because they represent, far more than do elite private institutions, the gateways to upward mobility for millions of Americans, white and black. As the 1970s progressed, in the interest both of aiding disadvantaged minorities and of increasing racial and cultural diversity on campus, admissions offices began using different criteria for white and minority admissions.

In the late 1970s reaction to affirmative action set in. The case of the *Regents of the University of California v. Bakke* was a key part of this backlash. The medical school at the University of California, as a form of affirmative action, had set aside sixteen of its one hundred places in each entering class for disadvantaged and minority students. They were considered for admission in a separate system. A white male student named Alan Bakke sued the university for discrimination after his application for admission was rejected. In 1976, the California Supreme Court ruled that he should be admitted to the university, but the university appealed the ruling to the U.S. Supreme Court, which heard the case in October 1977; in June 1978, it ruled in Bakke's favor. Of the nine justices, five agreed that Bakke's rights were violated by the university. However, there were a number of related legal issues involved, and the court split *without a majority* on nearly every one of those issues. Only one justice declared that affirmative action cases should be judged on the same strict level of scrutiny that was applied to "invidious" discrimination. All the other justices stated that race-conscious remedies could be used in some circumstances to correct past discrimination.

California remains the center of the affirmative action storm because of its multiracial population. In 1995 Governor Pete Wilson ended affirmative action in state employment. In 1996 California voters approved Proposition 209, the so-called California Civil Rights Initiative, which banned all state agencies from implementing affirmative action programs. The campaign for

Black, Asian, Hispanic, and white women protest in support of affirmative action at a meeting of the University of California's board of trustees at UCLA in 1994.

the proposition was led by Ward Connerly, a conservative black entrepreneur who had benefited from state contracts set aside for minority businesses. Connerly maintained that affirmative action exacerbated the negative stereotyping of African Americans. He and his supporters insisted moreover that affirmative action had failed to address problems of poverty, unemployment, and inadequate education that beset the truly disadvantaged. Instead, it had merely elevated to higher status those least in need of assistance, especially middle-class white women. Finally, Connerly accepted the broader argument that affirmative action assaulted the concept of individual merit and violated core American values of equality and opportunity. Fifty-four percent of California voters agreed with Connerly, and after the U.S. Supreme Court upheld the proposition, it went into effect.

The effect of Proposition 209 and similar laws or court rulings around the nation is as yet unknown. The number of African Americans and other protected minorities admitted to the whole University of California system has dropped slightly since the proposition was upheld by the U.S. Supreme Court, but the numbers at U.C. Berkeley, its most prestigious campus, have fallen far more precipitously. In both California and Texas, which abandoned affirmative action in its university system after a court challenge, administrators have attempted to assure a diverse student body by other means. Both states now offer admission to their top schools to all students in the top ranks of their high school class. It remains to be seen whether this strategy will succeed in providing access to underrepresented groups.

BLACK POLITICAL ACTIVISM IN THE AGE OF CONSERVATIVE REACTION

Presidents Reagan and Bush did not completely reverse the advancement of the civil rights agenda. The increased participation of black men and women in the upper echelons of the Democratic party reflected the extent to which they had overcome political exclusion. In 1964 there were only 103 black elected officials in the nation; by 1994 there were nearly 8,500. Forty-one African Americans served in Congress by 1996. In 1988, Representative William H. Gray of Pennsylvania became chair of the House Democratic caucus, making him the first African American to reach the top ranks of congressional leadership. In June 1989, he became majority whip of the House of Representatives. In February 1989, Ronald H. Brown became the first African American to lead a major national political party when he was elected chairman of the Democratic party. That same year, David Dinkins was elected the first black mayor of New York City. In 1990, Sharon Pratt Dixon (Kelly) was elected mayor of Washington, D.C., becoming the first woman and the first D.C. native to serve in that position. By the mid-1990s blacks held the mayor's office in four hundred towns and cities. Clearly the days of black political powerlessness have ended.

During the Reagan-Bush era, one and often both houses of Congress were in the hands of the Democratic party. Reflecting the importance of African American voters to the party, it used its power to pass many equal rights laws. Among the most important of these were the Voting Rights Act of 1982, the Civil Rights

Ron Brown, an influential Washington, D.C., attorney who supported Jesse Jackson's campaigns for president, became the chairman of the Democratic National Committee in 1989. President Clinton appointed him Secretary of Commerce in 1993. He was killed in a plane crash in Bosnia in 1995.

Restoration Act of 1988, and the Fair Housing Act of 1988. The Civil Rights Restoration Act of 1988 authorized the withholding of federal funds to an *entire* institution if *any* program within it discriminated against women or racial minorities, or the aged, or the handicapped. The Fair Housing Act of 1988 provided for enforcing fair housing laws. It stipulated that either an individual or the Department of Housing and Urban Development (HUD) could bring a complaint of housing discrimination and authorize administrative judges to investigate housing complaints, issue injunctions and fines, and award punitive damages. With both laws, Congress was responding to Supreme Court decisions that had narrowed the scope of earlier legislation. The Civil Rights Act of 1991 was likewise a response to a spate of restrictive Supreme Court decisions. In it, Democrats secured the protection of many of the defenses of civil rights the court had called into question.

The King Holiday

Many African Americans invested symbolic importance in an effort to make Martin Luther King Jr.'s birthday a national holiday, elevating him to the stature of Presidents George Washington and Abraham Lincoln, both of whom are honored with a holiday. At first Reagan resisted the effort, but he eventually gave in to pressure from African Americans and their white allies. On November 2, 1983, Reagan signed a law designating the third Monday in January to honor the great civil rights leader. On January 20, 1985, the United States officially observed Martin Luther King Jr. Day for the first time. In 1988, more than 60,000 people made the pilgrimage to Washington, D.C., to commemorate the twenty-fifth anniversary of the 1963 March on Washington and to remember Martin Luther King Jr.'s "I Have a Dream" speech.

TransAfrica and the Anti-Apartheid Movement

Black activism persisted on the international as well as the national front. Much of this effort focused on ending the oppressive conditions of apartheid—the complete, social, political, and economic isolation of black people—in South Africa. A particularly detestable aspect of apartheid was its glorification of white racial supremacy, an ideology reminiscent of Adolf Hitler's Germany and the American South in the early 20th century.

Activist Randall Robinson, a native of Richmond, Virginia, and a graduate of Harvard Law School who had worked as an assistant for Michigan congressman Charles Diggs, sought to link African-American liberation struggles with those waged by Africans in South Africa and elsewhere. In 1977 he founded TransAfrica to lobby for black political prisoners in South Africa, most notably Nelson Mandela. In 1984, Robinson was joined by Mary Francis Berry of the U.S. Commission on Civil Rights, Eleanor Holmes Norton, and others for a year-long series of sit-ins at the South African Embassy in Washington, D.C., during which hundreds were arrested.

The anti-apartheid movement became a major priority for African American activists. They were able to enlist the sympathy and help of white Americans on college campuses and to pressure many universities into divesting their investments in South Africa. Similar pressures were put on corporations, especially those vulnerable to consumer boycotts. In 1986 the Black Congressional Caucus persuaded their colleagues to enact a U.S. trade embargo against South Africa and sustain it over President Reagan's veto.

Bowing to international pressure and a souring domestic economy, in 1990 South African President F.W. deKlerk announced a removal of the ban on the African National Congress, the key opposition party, and a few days afterward ended the twenty-eight-year prison term of its leader, Nelson Mandela. Soon thereafter, South Africa was transformed into a multiracial democracy and Mandela was elected its president.

JESSE JACKSON AND THE RAINBOW COALITION

As Reagan's first term ended, Jesse Jackson made history by announcing that he would campaign for the presidency of the United States. The first African American to seek the presidential nomination of a major political party was Shirley Chisholm, in 1972. Chisholm had little money and only a small campaign organization and was never taken as a serious threat by her male competitors or by the press. Her campaign had nonetheless helped raise the visibility of African-American voters. She remained in the race until the convention and captured more than 150 votes on the first ballot at the Democratic National Convention. In the thoroughly male world of presidential politics, however, a black man was a more credible contender.

Jesse Jackson's preparation for political battle was not the traditional climb from one elective office to another. Rather, he came up through the ranks of the civil rights movement, working alongside Martin Luther King Jr., in the Southern Christian Leadership Conference (SCLC) and heading Operation Breadbasket, an organization that attempted to mobilize Chicago's black poor. After King's death, Jackson founded People United to Save (later Serve) Humanity (PUSH). This Chicago-based organization successfully pressured major corporations with large markets in the black community to adopt affirmative action programs. PUSH-EXCEL, which focused on education, was successful in raising students' test scores and was given a large grant by the Carter administration.

In 1983, angered by the effects of Reagan's social welfare and civil rights rollbacks, Jackson and PUSH began a successful drive to register black voters. Jackson's charismatic style engendered enthusiasm, especially as the Democratic party searched for a presidential candidate who could challenge Reagan's popularity.

In November 1983, Jackson declared his candidacy for the Democratic nomination and honed an already highly effective style of grassroots mobilization. He began by appealing to what he would call a "rainbow coalition" of people who felt politically marginalized and underrepresented. The Rainbow Coalition was composed of diverse groups, including black people, white workers, liberals, Latinos, feminists, students, and environmentalists. Jackson developed a comprehensive economic policy focusing on tax reform, deficit reduction, industrial policy, and employment. The centerpiece of his plan was "Rebuilding America," a plan to coordinate government, business, and labor in a national industrial policy. The Jackson platform was well within the tradition of American liberal reform, but nonetheless far more progressive than anything his competitors proposed. In January 1984, Jackson gained credentials in international affairs when he traveled to Syria to plead for the release of U.S. Air Force pilot Robert Goodman, who had been held captive there for a year after being shot down in Syrian-controlled airspace. Jackson returned to this country in triumph with the freed pilot.

Jackson eventually garnered almost one-fourth of the votes cast in the Democratic primaries and caucuses and one-eighth of the delegates to the convention. Jackson's speech to the convention cemented his position as a voice for progressive change and a spiritual heir to both Martin Luther King Jr. and Robert Kennedy. Walter Mondale, Jimmy Carter's vice president, who won the nomination, broke new ground when he made Geraldine Ferraro his running mate and the first woman on a major party's presidential ticket. But Mondale's choice disappointed many Jackson supporters.

In November 1984, black voters again overwhelmingly favored the Democratic ticket, but Reagan nonetheless won by a landslide with 59 percent of the popular vote. Mondale carried only his home state of Minnesota and the largely black District of Columbia. Clearly, most white Americans backed Reagan's conservative policies.

Undeterred by defeat, Jackson worked to build his Rainbow Coalition, reaching out to a variety of constituencies, including the unemployed, militant trade unionists, small farmers, and gay people. He criticized the Democratic party for its timid opposition to Reagan. Perhaps most important, he continued to promote voter registration and indeed inspired the registration of enough new voters to affect several races in the 1986 midterm elections. Democrats held on to control of the House and regained a majority in the Senate.

By the time Jackson announced that he would again run for president in October 1987, he had become a very serious contender. During the presidential primaries he won fifteen primaries and caucuses and garnered seven million votes, one-third of all those cast. His hopes of a "rainbow coalition," however, never materialized. His primary victories were based on mobilizing his black supporters; almost all his white support tended to come from college towns and the highly educated. Michael Dukakis, governor of Massachusetts, won the 1988 Democratic nomination.

In spite of Jesse Jackson's voter registration drive and the hopes of the black community, Reagan's vice president, George Bush, triumphed in the 1988 election. Bush's call for "a kinder, gentler America" was belied by the most memorable feature of his campaign, a polarizing ad that featured Willie Horton, a black convict who had raped a white woman while on furlough from a Massachusetts prison as part of a program approved by Dukakis. Jackson and other black leaders criticized the ad as a blatant appeal to white racism, but Bush would not renounce it.

POLICING THE BLACK COMMUNITY

In March 1991, Los Angeles police pulled Rodney King from his car after a high-speed chase and beat him with nightsticks. A bystander captured the incident on videotape, which television newscasts broadcast repeatedly, increasing long-simmering anger over police brutality among African Americans in Los Angeles. When a jury of eleven white Americans and one Hispanic American acquitted the four police officers involved in the incident of all but one of the charges brought against them, South-Central Los Angeles burst into flames of protest.

The verdict highlighted the gulf between the perceptions of white and black Americans about the police and the criminal justice system. Where the white jury had seen the police imposing justice and maintaining law and order, black Americans saw proof of injustice, police repression, and racism. The number of casualties from the outbreak that followed the verdict may have been as high as fifty-two. Arsonists and looters devastated a large part of the community. Thousands of people were injured, 4,000 were arrested, and there were estimates that up to one-half billion dollars in property had been damaged or destroyed. The four officers were later retried in federal court on charges of violating

The videotaped beating of Rodney King by Los Angeles police—shown repeatedly on national television—bolstered charges by African Americans in Los Angeles that they were frequent victims of police brutality. Despite the graphic evidence, the officers were acquitted of using excessive force.

King's civil rights. This time juries found two of them guilty and acquitted the other two.

The Rodney King episode resonated with many black men across the country. Writer Earl Ofari Hutchinson suggested why.

> Black professionals or business owners still tell harrowing tales of being spread-eagle over the hoods of their expensive BMW's or Porsches while the police ran makes on them and tore their cars apart searching for drugs. In polls taken after the Rodney King beating, blacks were virtually unanimous in saying that they believed any black person could have been on the ground that night being pulverized by the police. These were eternal reminders to the "new" black bourgeoisie that they could escape the hood, but many Americans still considered them hoods.

Several such high-profile cases focused public attention on the relation of black communities to white police authorities throughout the 1980s and 1990s. In a sense the issue of police repression, a long simmering cause of tension and hostility that had been behind many of the riots of the 1960s, remained a constant.

Human Rights in America

In October 1998, the human rights group Amnesty International, known for its condemnation of human rights abuse in countries with repressive governments, published a report on police brutality in the United States. The report covered the actions of local and state police, the Federal Bureau of Investigation, the Immigration and Naturalization Service, and the prison system. Its contents came as no surprise to most black Americans or, indeed, to anyone who lived in America's poor, urban neighborhoods. The report detailed violations of the United Nations Code of Conduct for Law Enforcement Officials and the United Nations Basic Principles on the Use of Force and Firearms. Among the violations reported were these:

- the shooting of unarmed suspects fleeing a minor crime scene
- excessive force used on mentally ill or disturbed people
- multiple shootings of a suspect, sometimes after the suspect was apprehended or disabled
- the beating of unresisting suspects
- the misuse of batons, chemical sprays, and electro-shock weapons

These violations all involve the misuse of force during arrests, traffic stops, searches, and so forth. This was by far the greatest area of concern. Other violations listed in the report included sexual abuse of prisoners and denial of food and water, among others. One of the most important points in the Amnesty International report was that the vast majority of the victims of American law enforcement abuse were members of racial and ethnic minorities, while most police officers were white.

It is far too easy to interpret these findings as showing that American police officers, as a group, are racists who purposefully use their authority to oppress people they don't like. In fact, the issue of police brutality is not nearly so simple. Police officers are under tremendous pressure and live dangerous lives, in part because of the wide availability of guns in American society. Perfect judgment with regard to the use of force cannot be expected of anyone, and the cumulative effect of years of dealing with violence can destroy a person's sense of perspective and moral equilibrium.

Neither is the problem of crime by black Americans a simple one. The level of crime in black communities is extremely high. The murder rate, for example, for African Americans in 1997 was seven times that of whites, and black victims accounted for 49 percent of all those murdered, even though African Americans make up only 12 percent of the population. The vast majority, over 90 percent, of perpetrators of murder and other similar violent crimes on black people are black people themselves. The murder rate for young black men between the ages of fourteen and seventeen tripled between 1976 and 1993. Although this rate, like the rate of violent crime in the country in general, fell in the 1990s, the security of many African Americans remains imperiled.

Crime has had a devastating effect on black neighborhoods. High crime rates raise the costs of business, driving jobs and investment dollars out of those areas most in need of them. Fear of violence leads many in the inner cities to barricade themselves inside their homes. The result has been a transformation of once vibrant neighborhoods into virtual ghost towns where the silence of the streets is punctuated only by the sound of gunfire. Filmmaker Spike Lee was shocked when he returned to the Brooklyn neighborhood in which he had grown up to shoot his film *Crooklyn*. He found that the streets had become so unsafe that the local children he used as extras had to be taught how to play the games he had played growing up in the 1970s because they had never been allowed to play outside. "Nowadays," Lee reflected after completing the film in 1994, "these kids, they'll shoot you dead in a second and not even think about it. The two big problems are crack and how accessible guns are. And also, you're talking about what Reagan did during his eight years. If I was a parent, I'd be terrified anytime my children left my sight. When I was growing up, I just had to be home by dark." Even Rosa Parks, heroine of the civil rights movement, has not been immune to the urban crime wave. In 1994 she was brutally beaten and robbed in her Detroit home by a twenty-eight-year-old unemployed black man. Her assailant recognized Parks but victimized her anyway.

Being disproportionately the victims of crime, the vast majority of African Americans have looked to the nation's police departments for aid. Because of their growing political power they have sought, not always successfully, to make the police both responsive to crime and fair in the enforcement of laws. One key device for changing the behavior of law enforcement officials has been the appointment of black police chiefs.

Police Director Hubert Williams of Newark

Black mayor Kenneth Gibson appointed Hubert Williams as the police director in Newark, New Jersey, and he served from 1974 to 1985. Williams had earned a law degree from Rutgers University Law School and a master's in public administration from the City University of New York. A native of Georgia, Williams served for twelve years on Newark's police force before his appointment as police director.

Upon assuming command, Williams demoted and transferred several entrenched deputy chiefs and captains. He implemented a 911 system to increase police response to citizens' calls for assistance, and placed police decoys on city streets to thwart muggers. Among the many innovations that the reform-minded Williams introduced were police sweeps of high-crime sections, roadblocks to deter drunken drivers, a truancy task force to discourage teenage crime, and police storefronts to foster the image of law enforcement officers as community service workers. Williams also acknowledged that he would use "color-conscious" policies in promoting and assigning officers. He argued that in a city where black people made up more than 50 percent of the population, it was good policy to assign detectives and administrators who reflected the racial composition of specific neighborhoods.

Williams received high marks for his performance and soon white mayors in other cities also began appointing black officers—like Benjamin Ward in New York City; Lee P. Brown in Houston; William H. Moore in Pittsburgh, Pennsylvania; and Reuben Greenberg in Charleston, South Carolina—to head their police departments. By 1982 there were black police chiefs in fifty American cities. A decade later the number has increased to more than 130, and six of the nation's largest cities (Baltimore, New York, Detroit, Chicago, Philadelphia, and Houston) have black police chiefs.

THE ELECTION OF 1992

During his first campaign for the presidency, the personable, saxophone-playing, Democratic party candidate, Arkansas governor Bill Clinton, was welcomed by black Americans into their churches, schools, and homes. They warmly embraced his bid for the presidency against incumbent George Bush. Bush had done little to win their loyalty, nominating conservatives to the federal courts and attacking civil rights legislation. White Americans, too, were dissatisfied with the Bush presidency. Although he enjoyed high approval ratings in early 1991 following American military success in evicting Iraq from Kuwait in the Gulf War, by early 1992 his ratings had slumped in the face of an economic downturn.

Politically Clinton was a centrist. Undeterred by charges of womanizing, draft evasion, and marijuana smoking, he sharply attacked Bush's record and promised to make government more responsive. Clinton won in November with just 43 percent of the popular vote to Bush's 38 percent and third-party candidate H. Ross Perot's 19 percent. The election did not present the Democrats with a clear mandate. While maintaining control of Congress, they gained no seats in the Senate and lost seats in the House. Republicans would use the ambiguous outcome to oppose most of Clinton's economic programs.

During his tumultuous presidency, most black people considered Clinton, in spite of some major disappointments, the best president on race issues since Lyndon Johnson. In Clinton, they had a friend. He created a cabinet that mirrored the diversity of the American population—in some cases, as with his appointment of Hazel O'Leary as secretary of the Department of Energy, appointing black people to posts that had nothing to do with race. He appointed African Americans to many judicial posts. He counted black men, like the highly successful Washington, D.C., attorney Vernon Jordan, among his friends. And he was the first American president to visit Africa.

"It's the Economy, Stupid!"

Throughout his two terms in office, Clinton focused attention on the economy, a strategy that won grudging support from moderate Republicans. His objective was to strengthen the economy and to make more opportunities available for black Americans and other previously excluded groups. Toward this end, in a significant departure from the policies of his predecessors, he supported a new tax bill that increased the taxes of higher-income

Americans. He also advocated expansion of the earned income tax credit to help improve the lives of working-poor and very poor Americans. His college student aid program made available increased federal loan benefits. The economy boomed during his presidency. Unemployment plummeted from 7.2 percent when he took office to 5.5 percent in 1992 and continued to decline in ensuing years. American businesses created 10 million new jobs, and many black people who feared they would never gain a foothold in the economy found positions, some for the first time. A combination of reduced federal spending coupled with the 1993 tax increase helped to cut the annual federal deficit in half. As interest rates fell and the stock market soared, optimistic Americans increased their consumer spending.

Clinton Signs the Welfare Reform Act

Shortly before his reelection, in August 1996, Clinton signed the Personal Responsibility and Work Opportunity Reconciliation Act, a welfare reform bill. His action was a serious disappointment to many African Americans and to political progressives in general. The legislation combined Clinton's own ideas with others espoused in the Republicans' "Contract with America" blueprint for conservative reform.

The main target of the Personal Responsibility Act was Aid to Families of Dependent Children (AFDC), a program created in 1935 as part of the Social Security Act to prevent children from suffering because of the poverty of their parents. Critics claimed that AFDC stipends discouraged poor mothers from finding work, that it was responsible for the breakdown of the family among the nation's poor, and that it did little to reduce poverty. Proponents of the welfare reform bill also insisted that the states did not have enough flexibility in administering welfare. The conservative welfare "reform" measure ended guarantees of federal aid to poor children, turning control of such programs over to the states along with allocations of block grants. It denied benefits to *legal* immigrants, called for drastic reductions in food stamp appropriations, and limited families to five years of benefits. The law also required most adult welfare recipients to find employment within two years.

There were good reasons to believe that the welfare reform bill would not accomplish its sponsors' purposes. Most of the people who would be "encouraged to find work" by having their benefits reduced or cut entirely are among the least employable people in the labor force. A study of people terminated from general assistance in Michigan, for example, revealed that as many as two-thirds remained unemployed. As for the bill's effect on families, it is true that the majority of women on welfare had their first children when they were unmarried teenagers. But there is little evidence that cutting welfare will prevent teenage pregnancies. And there is evidence that reforms targeted at improving the collection of child support payments for divorced mothers would reduce welfare costs far more effectively and humanely.

Clinton's support of the welfare act was consistent with his centrist ideology and it was politically astute. His stance on the Welfare Reform Act immunized him from Republican attacks on the issue and had little impact on his support among African Americans. The president easily defeated his Republican opponent Senator Robert Dole of Kansas in the election of 1996 to become the first Democratic president to win a second term in office since Franklin Delano Roosevelt.

AFRICAN-AMERICAN CULTURAL AND INTELLECTUAL MOVEMENTS AT THE END OF THE MILLENNIUM

The most positive developments for black Americans during the 1980s and 1990s have come in the realm of culture. Beginning in the 1980s a cultural renaissance emerged in every American community with a substantial African-American presence. Black consciousness institutions proliferated and flourished. They included black history and culture museums, festivals, expositions, publishing houses, bookstores and boutiques, concerts, theaters, and dance troupes. In 1996, *Publishers Weekly* reported that bookstores specializing in African-American books had grown in number from a dozen a few years earlier to more than two hundred. By 1994, there were seventy-five African-American publishing companies. In 1998 the National Literary Hall of Fame for Writers of African Descent opened at Chicago State University.

Black painters used outdoor murals to celebrate and cultivate positive images of the black experience. Playwrights such as August Wilson, Charles Fuller, and George C. Wolfe helped revitalize American theater, and the musician Prince's film *Purple Rain* (1984) broke new ground in African-American rock cinematography. Wilson won two Pulitzer Prizes for his plays—*Fences* in 1987 and *The Piano Lesson* in 1990. In 1987 PBS aired Henry Hampton's *Eyes on the Prize*, a six-part documentary on the civil rights movement. Spike Lee changed the status of black filmmakers in Hollywood with films such as *Do the Right Thing* and *Malcolm X*. Wynton Marsalis became a leading figure in American jazz. The

Rodney King case inspired two important works: a symphony entitled *56 Blows*, by Alvin Singleton, and a one-woman docudrama entitled *Twilight: Los Angeles, 1992*, by Anna Deavere Smith.

The new cultural renaissance differs in many ways from the black arts movement of the 1960s and 1970s. The contemporary fluorescence is more inclusive and more appreciative of women artists. It also includes the work of openly gay and lesbian artists, such as documentary filmmaker Marlon Riggs and dance choreographer Bill T. Jones. Whereas poets and dramatists dominated the earlier movement, novelists, particularly women novelists, hold sway in the new cultural renaissance. And much of the new work appeals to white audiences as much as to black audiences, providing new insights into the lives of people of African heritage in a predominantly European society.

There were signs of this new trend as early as 1977, when Toni Morrison's *Song of Solomon* became a Book-of-the-Month Club selection, the first by a black author since Richard Wright's *Native Son* in 1940. Then Barbara Chase-Riboud made waves with *Sally Hemings* (1979), a fictional treatment of a woman who was both slave to and mistress of President Thomas Jefferson. In 1980, Toni Cade Bambara won the American Book Award for *The Salt Eaters*. At least as significant as these individual books was the founding in 1981 of a new publishing house, Kitchen Table: Women of Color Press. Then, in 1982, Alice Walker won the Pulitzer Prize and the American Book Award for *The Color Purple*, which was later made into a movie by director Steven Spielberg, with Whoopi Goldberg in the starring role. In 1987, poet Rita Dove won the Pulitzer Prize for Poetry. In 1993 she became America's poet laureate, and in the same year, Toni Morrison became the first African American to win the Nobel Prize for literature, and President Bill Clinton invited Maya Angelou to read an original poem during his inauguration ceremony.

It wasn't only critics who took an interest in these works. In 1992 novels by three African-American women—Morrison, Walker, and Terry McMillan—made the New York Times best-seller list at the same time. This literary flowering reflected a new point of view that Alice Walker labeled "womanism" and others called black feminism.

Black Feminism

The women's rights movement first blossomed in the 1970s in the wake of the civil rights struggles and the antiwar protests of the 1960s. The National Organization for Women, founded in 1966, spearheaded efforts to end job discrimination against women, to legalize abortion, and to secure federal and state support for child care. One of the movement's early successes was Title IX of the Educational Amendments Act of 1972, which required colleges and universities to take affirma-

tive action to ensure equal opportunity for women. Another was the Supreme Court's decision in *Roe v. Wade* legalizing abortion.

Feminism at first held little appeal for most black women, but they were affected by it nonetheless. But

SPIKE LEE, A VOICE OF PROTEST

Shelton "Spike" Jackson Lee, the son of composer and bassist Bill Lee and schoolteacher Jacqueline Lee, was born March 20, 1957, in Atlanta, Georgia. He is the eldest of six children.

Spike Lee is the most productive and influential black filmmaker in America today. He completed undergraduate studies at Morehouse College and in 1982 earned a degree from New York University Film School. His films appeal to the hip-hop generation because they grapple with many of

the same issues that affect their lives, such as police brutality, persistent racism, and a yearning for black empowerment. Between 1986 and 1998, Spike Lee wrote, produced, directed, and starred in more than ten films. These have examined a variety of controversial subjects: interracial love in *Jungle Fever;* a black woman's sexuality in *She's Gotta Have It;* color discrimination and sexism in the black fraternities in *School Daze;* and the deep fissures of race and class in American society in *Do the Right Thing.* He made a film about Malcolm X's life and documentaries about a cross-section of men who attended the Million Man March and the death of four girls in the bombing of the 16th Street Baptist Church, in Birmingham, Alabama, in 1963.

In 1986, *She's Gotta Have It* won critical and commercial success. The film looks at black relationships in the 1980s from the perspective of one woman, Nola Darling. She juggles sexual relations with three black men: one, a narcissist; the second, a violent middle-class overachiever; and the third, a bicycling homeboy from the neighborhood, played by Lee. About this last

character, Lee confided, "For me, Mars represented black youth, hip-hop, but he doesn't take or sell drugs or rape and mug people, ya know what I'm talkin' 'bout. He's funny." The movie shatters stereotypes—like the conventional wisdom that men shun commitment while women yearn for it—with humor and insight. Shot in approximately twelve days for $175,000, the film signaled the emergence of Lee's prodigious talent. It netted $8.5 million at the box office and won the Prix de Jeunesse Award at the film festival in Cannes, France. About the film Lee said, "I think it's important young people know that there is no such animal as overnight success. I made that movie asking friends for donations."

Three years later, in 1989, Spike Lee scored another success with *Do the Right Thing,* a compelling look at racial and generational conflict in a Brooklyn neighborhood. The film probes the way some white people are simultaneously attracted to and repelled by black people, worshipping black stars and athletes, for example, while despising poor black people. The film also explores the explosiveness of racial confrontation across class lines. The movie grossed more than $27 million at the box office and earned an Oscar nomination for best screenplay.

Lee's combination of story telling, cinematographic craft, and social comment has paved the way for a new generation of black filmmakers. "African American cinema, as far as Hollywood's concerned, is in its infancy," according to Lee, and has not produced "any Michael Jordon, Duke Ellington, James Baldwin, Toni Morrison. We will, but it's gonna take time."

The works of author Toni Morrison gained national acclaim in the 1970s. She won the Nobel Prize for Literature in 1993 for her novel *Beloved.*

later in the 1970s, many black women writers and activists, disillusioned with the attitudes of their male counterparts in the civil rights, black power, and black arts movements, sought to make the struggle against sexism as important as the struggle against racism.

Black feminists founded journals such as *SAGE* and organizations such as the Association of Black Women Historians founded by Rosalyn Terborg-Penn and Eleanor Smith. Gradually, their scholarly, literary, historical, and polemical works found readers in the general public and a place in the curricula of women's studies courses. The work of visual artists like Faith Ringgold appeared in museums and community centers. As the number of black women enrolled in college climbed, courses with titles like "Black Women Writers" and "Black Women's History" became part of college and black studies curricula. By the early 1990s there were more black women in higher education, graduate, and professional degree programs than there were black men.

Within the academy, the field of black women's history has grown rapidly; scholarly monographs, reference works, anthologies, conferences, and exhibitions have been produced, all devoted to the contribution black women have made to the political struggles and artistic accomplishments of African Americans. These historians have productively explored the role of race, class, and gender in the oppression of marginalized people in American society.

Black Intellectuals

An important part of the recent black cultural renaissance has been the rise to national prominence of black public intellectuals. These individuals go beyond their roles as scholars to participate in public debate and discourse about major issues.

In the past, most public intellectuals were white males. Among the few exceptions were the formidable W. E. B. Du Bois and novelists Richard Wright, James Baldwin, and Ralph Ellison. Within the past two decades, however, many of the most prominent public intellectuals to emerge have been African American. Among them are Cornel West, Henry Louis Gates Jr., William Julius Wilson, Michele Wallace, Ishmael Reed, Stanley Crouch, Charles Johnson, Patricia Williams, John Edgar Wideman, Manning Marable, Robin D. G. Kelley, Michael Eric Dyson, Nell Irvin Painter, and bell hooks, among others. They are a diverse group ideologically, ranging from Marxist to extreme conservative. What they have in common is a desire to redefine black identity in this country and to explore how race is involved in its social and political workings. Historian Kelley put it well when he declared: "Culture and questions of identity have been at the heart of some of the most intense battles facing African Americans at the end of the century. . . . Not only has globalization continued to transform black culture, but it has also dramatically changed the nature of work, employment opportunities, class structure, public space, the cultural marketplace, the criminal justice system, political strategies, even intellectual work." The emergence of these figures and the acclaim accorded them mark the end of America's long refusal to acknowledge the intellectual accomplishments of African Americans. In 1991 Henry Louis Gates assumed the leadership of both the Afro-American Studies Department and the W. E. B. Du Bois Institute at Harvard University. He lured philosopher Cornel West from Princeton and sociologist William Julius Wilson from the University of Chicago to create one of the strongest black studies departments in the country.

Afrocentricity

In the 1980s and 1990s a philosophy of culture referred to as Afrocentricity or Afrocentrism captured widespread media and academic attention. Although the philosophy and practice of Afrocentricity had been a prominent feature of black studies courses for more than a decade, the emergence of Temple University professor Molefi Kete Asante gave it a presence and a personality. In 1980 Asante published *Afrocentricity*, in which he argued that an African-centered perspective was needed to challenge the dominance of Eurocentric values in education. Other leading Afrocentrists include Asa Hillard and John Henrik Clarke.

Many black educators enthusiastically embraced Afrocentricity as a way to celebrate and reclaim a positive African identity and to find unity with other peoples of the African diaspora. Afrocentrists rejected the idea of America as melting pot. Assimilation, they argued, meant a rejection of their African cultural heritage. At the heart of this position is a strong indictment of American ideals and institutions for their complicity in the long oppression of black people.

Afrocentrists vigorously defended their perspective. Asante explained to his critics, "Afrocentricity is a terribly maligned concept. Afrocentricity is the idea that African people and interests must be viewed as actors and agents in human history, rather than as marginal to the European historical experience—which has been institutionalized as universal." Similarly, Tsehloane Keto declared that it was the responsibility of black scholars to challenge the Eurocentric paradigm that "interpret[ed] the roles of African Americans through the invisible person model, the Ghetto model, the spook who sat by the door model, and the Sambo model." Black historians and social scientists, Afrocentrists argued, had to place Africa and her descendants at the center of their studies to foster a greater appreciation of the contributions of black people in world history.

Many black people, however, vehemently rejected Afrocentricity, insisting that it was anti-progressive and would foster self-segregation. Writer Earl Ofari Hutchinson conceded that Asante's idea merited attention while expressing skepticism about the claims of some Afrocentrist academics: "In their zeal to counter the heavy handed 'Eurocentric' imbalance of history, some have crossed the line between historic fact and fantasy. They've constructed groundless theories in which Europeans are 'Ice People,' suffer 'genetic defects,' or are obsessed with 'color phobias.' They've re-placed the shallow European 'great man' theory of history with a feel good interpretation of history." White writers, notably historian Arthur Schlesinger Jr. in *The Disuniting of America*, weighed in with blistering attacks. White and black critics alike cautioned that the Afrocentrist desire to fabricate "a glorious past" for black people did a disservice to the truth. Harvard University philosophy professor Cornel West assessed both the positive and negative value of Afrocentrism in 1993:

> Afrocentrism, a contemporary species of black nationalism, is a gallant yet misguided attempt to define an African identity in a white society perceived to be hostile. It is gallant because it puts black doings and sufferings, not white anxieties and fears, at the center of discussion. It is misguided because—out of fear of cultural hybridization and through silence on the issue of class, retrograde views on black women, gay men, and lesbians, and a reluctance to link race to the common good—it reinforces the narrow discussions about race.

Louis Farrakhan and the Nation of Islam

Beginning in the 1980s, the Nation of Islam's Minister Louis Farrakhan became a potent source of racial division in this country. Farrakhan was the younger of two sons of immigrant parents Mae Clark of Barbados and Louis Eugene Wolcott of Jamaica. Named after his father, he became known as Minister Louis X when he assumed leadership of the Boston Temple of the Nation of Islam. As a young man Farrakhan attended a black teachers' college in Winston-Salem, North Carolina, but dropped out to become a Calypso singer known as the Charmer. In 1955 while performing in Chicago, he went with some friends to hear Elijah Muhammad preach at the Nation of Islam's mosque. This marked a turning point in his life. Farrakhan joined the Nation and quickly ascended within its hierarchy in the wake of Malcolm X's rupture with Elijah Muhammad and subsequent murder in February 1965. Farrakhan became minister of the Harlem Mosque No. 7 and Muhammad's national representative. When Elijah Muhammad died in 1975, he designated his son, Wallace Deen Muhammad, or Warith, as he renamed himself, to be his successor. Warith sought to distance the Nation of Islam from the more far-fetched teachings of his father and to bring it more in line with actual Islamic teachings. He renamed the group the World Community of al-Islam in the West (WCIW) and in 1985 changed it again to the American Muslim Mission (AMM), after which it disbanded.

Farrakhan opposed Warith's decisions and within three years of Elijah Muhammad's death established himself as the leader of the Nation of Islam. In 1982 he purchased a building to publish a newspaper, *The Final Call*, and in 1985 he bought and moved into Muhammad's mansion in Chicago. Under Farrakhan's direction, and with $5 million in start-up capital from Libyan Colonel Muammar Qaddafi and subsequent federal government contracts, the Nation developed a number of economic enterprises, including media ventures, restaurants, clothing stores, and companies to provide security for apartment buildings, distribute soap and cosmetics, and manufacture pharmaceuticals. Farrakhan recruited among poor and marginalized urban African Americans and within the black prison population. The conservatism of the Reagan era complemented the reconstituted Nation's conservative social ideals, which harked back to those advanced by Booker T. Washington at the turn of the century. Farrakhan downplayed the struggle for civic and political rights. In 1985 he declared:

> God wants us to build a new world order: A new world order based on peace, justice and equality. Where do we start? . . . Physical separation is greatly feared [by whites], and it is not now desired by the masses of black people, but America is not willing to give us eight or ten states, or even one state. Let's be reasonable. . . . What we propose tonight is a solution that is in between two extremes. If we cannot go back to Africa, and America will not give us a separate territory, then what can we do here and now to redress our own grievances? . . . We propose that we use the blessings that we have received from our sojourn in America to do for ourselves what we have been asking the whites in this nation to do for us.

Until 1984 most Americans were barely aware of Farrakhan's existence. In that year, however, he broke the Nation of Islam's long-standing tradition of abstaining from politics to support Jesse Jackson's bid for the presidential nomination of the Democratic party and soon ignited a firestorm of controversy. When some Jews took offense at Jackson's off-the-record reference to New York as "Hymietown" during a conversation with two African-American reporters, Farrakhan, whose Fruit of Islam provided Jackson's campaign security, rose to his defense and made matters worse. On the February 24, 1984, CBS *Evening News*, Farrakhan warned, "I say to the Jewish people, who may not like our brother: It is not Jesse Jackson you are attacking. . . . When you attack him, you are attacking the millions who are lining up with him. You're attacking all of us. . . . Why dislike us? Why attack our champion? Why hurl stones at him? It's our champion. If you harm this brother, what do you think we should do about it?"

In 1984 as in the past, Farrakhan's verbal assaults against Jews, whom he characterized as being a principal enemy of African Americans, attracted support from ultra right-wing, anti-Semitic forces and condemnation from Jewish Americans and the Anti-Defamation League. Dredging up anti-Semitic shibboleths reminiscent to some of Hitler's Germany, Farrakhan blamed Jews for many of the ills plaguing African Americans. Jewish Americans, many of whom had been among the principal allies of African Americans during the civil rights movement, called on African-American organizations and leaders to repudiate Farrakhan and his rhetoric of "Jewish domination and control."

The Million Man March

The culminating event of Farrakhan's tenure as leader of the Nation of Islam was the Million Man March in Washington, D.C., on October 16, 1995. Farrakhan called this a "Holy Day of Atonement and Reconciliation," to "reconcile our spiritual inner beings and to redirect our focus to developing our communities, strengthening our families, working to uphold and protect our civil and human rights, and empowering ourselves through the Spirit of God, more effective use of our dollars, and through the power of the vote."

While the Million Man March had its detractors, and the actual numbers of men to attend was disputed, it was a symbolic success and generated positive coverage even in the mainstream media. It inspired many black men to become more engaged with their communities and to speak out more forcefully against oppression. On this occasion the Nation's conservative philosophy of religion, self-respect, family values, community responsibility, and "bootstrap capitalism" found a responsive audience.

Yet the goodwill dissipated when, three months after the march, Farrakhan embarked on a World Friendship Tour to some twenty countries in Africa and the Middle East. To the consternation of many, he met with the leader of the brutally repressive military regime in Nigeria, General Sani Abacha. At home, Farrakhan continued to attract attention for intemperate rhetoric. In the wake of the Million Man March he failed to forge a coherent strategy to resolve African America's continuing social problems.

Several black intellectuals have made known their objection to or displeasure with Farrakhan, none more effectively than political scientist Adolph Reed. According

Several hundred thousand black men gathered in Washington, D.C., on October 16, 1995, for the Million Man March. The event was conceived by Louis Farrakhan, the charismatic but controversial leader of the Nation of Islam.

to Reed, Farrakhan "weds a radical oppositional style to a program that proposes private and individual responses to social problems; he endorses moral repressiveness; he asserts racial essentialism; he affirms male authority; and he lauds bootstrap capitalism. . . . His focus on self-help and moral revitalization is profoundly reactionary and meshes perfectly with the victim-blaming orthodoxy of the Reagan/Bush era."

The Million Woman March

The success of the Million Man March inspired black women, and later black youths, to organize similar demonstrations. On October 25, 1997, well over half a million black women gathered in Philadelphia to listen to speeches by California congresswoman Maxine Waters and South African activist Winnie Mandela. The march was a celebration, a call to unity, and a forum for black women to speak out against domestic violence, inadequate access to quality health care and educational opportunities, and the proliferation of drugs and violence in their communities. The march did not garner nearly as much media attention as had the Million Man March, perhaps because its organizers were relatively unknown. The march nonetheless symbolized the ongoing struggle of black women to be seen and heard in American society, and to counter negative stereotypes and derogatory images of black womanhood.

Black Christianity on the Front Lines

Faced with the problems of the black community and with a changing population, African-American Christians in both traditional and nontraditional religious institutions have developed outreach programs to create supportive communities for the embattled and vulnerable. An example of a modern religious reformer is the Reverend Eugene Rivers, founder along with like-minded former students at Harvard University of the small Azusa Christian Community in a crime-plagued neighborhood in Boston. An evangelical Christian, Rivers believes that "the church is the last best hope that black people have." He turned a former crackhouse into a Christian settlement named Ella J. Baker House. Its primary goal, Rivers says, is to keep children from killing one another. He and fellow black clergy formed the 10-Point Coalition and entered into a partnership with the police. The collaboration helped eliminate juvenile murders for two-and-a-half years. Rivers advocates a pragmatic black nationalism aimed at developing a rich, viable black civil society centered on the church.

The Hip-Hop Nation

Just as black feminists used the novel, and black arts nationalists used poetry, a younger generation of African Americans, collectively known as the hip-hop nation, uses rap music to express its concerns. Rap is a form of rhythmic speaking in rhyme; hip-hop refers to the back-up music for rap, which is often composed of a collage of excerpts, or "samples," from other songs. Hip-hop also refers to the culture of rap.

The first rap hit, *Rapper's Delight* by the Sugar Hill Gang, came out in 1979; it popularized the term *hip-hop*. Rap's first superstars were Grandmaster Flash and the Furious Five. In the group's album, *The Adventures of Grandmaster Flash on the Wheels of Steel* (1981), Flash used the disk jockey technique of "scratching"—moving a record back and forth underneath a needle to produce

V O I C E S

BLACK WOMEN DEFINING THEMSELVES: MAXINE WATERS'S ADDRESS TO THE MILLION WOMAN MARCH

The more than half a million women assembled in Philadelphia on October 25, 1997, for the Million Woman March heard California congresswoman Maxine Waters deliver a passionate speech that succinctly summed up the material and political status of black women.

Thank you—thank you grassroots women for understanding your power to make today a reality!

Today, I speak for my mother and her mother and her mother's mother. I speak for the mothers long passed, the mothers born into slavery, the mothers today, and the mothers yet to be born. I speak for Black women and girls, for African American women, for colored women, for Negro women, for women who claim color, and for women who are confused about color. I speak on behalf of sisters all!

Lest someone else try to define us—let us set the record straight about who we are:

we are 7% of the population;

78% of us have completed a high school education; 12.9% have completed 4 years of college;

59.9% of us are in the work force. We are underrepresented as professionals—managers and supervisors. Far too many of us are concentrated in low paying jobs;

We are married, we are single (53% of us are heads of households);

Our median income earning is $20,000. We are middle class, we are rich, and we are disproportionately poor;

Despite the rhetoric of right-wing politicians, we are not the welfare population in America. 39% of mothers receiving welfare are African American compared to 55% of white mothers;

While white women earn 72 cents to every dollar earned by a white male, African American women earn 64 cents to every dollar earned by a white male;

28.9% of African American women live in poverty as compared to 9.8% of white women.

Our life expectancy is only 74.2 years, compared to 79.6 years for white women and 77.1 years for Hispanic women.

We die from heart attacks at twice the rate of other women. We die from strokes at 33% higher rate than white women. Yet, we are rarely included in the research of cardiovascular diseases;

Although we develop breast cancer less frequently than white women, we die at higher rates; and

AIDS is the number one killer of African American women in this country. Yet, our community receives less than our fair share of government dollars for AIDS education, prevention and treatment.

We don't need anybody to lecture us about responsibility—we are profoundly responsible. We don't need to "promise keep," atone, bemoan or scapegoat. We need to use our collective power to shape public policy, create opportunity, fight discrimination, racism, favoritism, and "old boy networkism."

QUESTIONS

1. What issues of inequality did Waters identify as most detrimental to the future prospects of African-American women?

2. How does the social, political, and economic status of black women compare to that of white women?

---

a rhythmic, jarring sound. Flash is also credited with an innovative technique that involved hooking two turntables to the same set of speakers and manipulating different records on the turntables, switching quickly from one to the other to create a third, original composition.

N.W.A., a California group, created gangsta rap with their release in 1989 of *Straight Outta Compton*. In 1991,

rapper Ice-T co-starred in a box-office smash film, *New Jack City*. This film, along with *Boyz N the Hood* and *Menace II Society*, ushered in a new genre of black urban films that depicted the violence and alienation of many inner-city youths.

Rap draws inspiration from earlier black musical forms—rhythm and blues, soul, jazz, and gospel. Its rhythmic commentary on life in America's black communities draws on earlier black poets and messages of past and present political activists such as Martin Luther King Jr., Malcolm X, and Lewis Farrakhan. Rap lyrics call attention to the dangers of drug use, AIDS, teenage pregnancy, and dropping out of school. As Grandmaster Flash and the Furious Five's lead vocalist Melle Mel rapped, "It's like a jungle sometimes, it makes me wonder, how I keep from going under."

When it first appeared, critics called rap music a fad. They were wrong. After two decades, in February 1999, *Time Magazine* signaled the coming of age of this genre of black music with an eleven-page cover story featuring the most celebrated rap performers and producers of the past twenty years. Hip-hop performer Lauryn Hill, twenty-three years old and nominated for an unprecedented ten Grammy Awards in 1999 (she won five), graced the cover of the issue.

Rap lyrics, the rap lifestyle, and rap artists have all aroused the consternation of older African Americans. The post–civil rights, black power, and black feminist elders have criticized rappers for their offensive, misogynist language, gang warfare, and violence against women. In 1995, for example, Black Women for Political Action pressured Time-Warner to sell its rap label. The white media pilloried Ice-T for his antipolice lyrics.

CONCLUSION

New forms of music, art, literature, dance, and film reflect the divisions and the strengths of contemporary black America. Without a unifying movement, various black constituencies developed their own strategies to secure the resources they needed to advance their interests. Black women organized feminist groups, welfare mothers joined welfare rights organizations, black professionals created caucuses and networked, students fought for the institutionalization of black studies programs at colleges and universities, and artists founded museums and publishing concerns and launched aesthetic movements. Meanwhile, politicians forged national caucuses and local associations. Writers produced trenchant commentaries about black life in America and memoirs and autobiographies that placed their private pains in the collective consciousness of the nation. Black gays and lesbians focused attention on their struggle to eradicate homophobia.

Jesse Jackson, whose Rainbow Coalition of the 1980s was a reflection of this creative fragmentation, a quest for unity amidst diversity, asked at the 1988 Democratic convention "Shall we expand, be inclusive, find unity and power; or suffer division and impotence?" His question remains unanswered as the black odyssey toward freedom and the transformation of American society continues into the next millennium.

REVIEW QUESTIONS

1. To what extent and in what key areas did the Reagan and Bush presidencies succeed in nullifying or dismantling much of the Great Society legislation? How did African Americans respond to the era of Republican conservative reform?

2. What was the significance of the Jesse Jackson campaigns for the presidential nomination of the Democratic party? What explains the chasm between black and white America over the controversial Minister Louis Farrakhan?

3. What factors contributed to the gulf between black middle-class Americans and poor African Americans in the inner city?

4. Why do so many Americans associate welfare with black people?

5. Why did affirmative action become one of the most hotly contested issues of the 1990s? What are the differences between the old civil rights and the new civil rights? How did affirmative action in the workplace differ from affirmative action in education?

6. How did the Rodney King case illuminate the different perceptions black and white Americans have of the police and the justice system?

7. What were some of the major issues or concerns of black women in the 1990s? What factors gave rise to black feminism? What is the black women's literary renaissance?

8. What are the reasons for the increased attention devoted to identity and culture issues by black intellectuals?

RECOMMENDED READING

Cathy J. Cohen. *The Boundaries of Blackness: AIDS and the Breakdown of Black Politics.* Chicago: University of Chicago Press, 1999. A black political scientist provides a sophisticated and provocative exploration into

TIMELINE

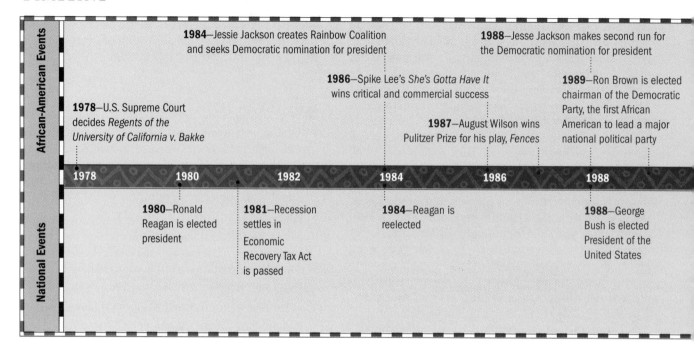

African-American Events

1978—U.S. Supreme Court decides *Regents of the University of California v. Bakke*

1984—Jessie Jackson creates Rainbow Coalition and seeks Democratic nomination for president

1986—Spike Lee's *She's Gotta Have It* wins critical and commercial success

1987—August Wilson wins Pulitzer Prize for his play, *Fences*

1988—Jesse Jackson makes second run for the Democratic nomination for president

1989—Ron Brown is elected chairman of the Democratic Party, the first African American to lead a major national political party

1978   1980   1982   1984   1986   1988

National Events

1980—Ronald Reagan is elected president

1981—Recession settles in Economic Recovery Tax Act is passed

1984—Reagan is reelected

1988—George Bush is elected President of the United States

the social, political, and cultural impact of the AIDS epidemic on the African-American community.

Patricia Hill Collins. *Black Feminist Thought: Knowledge, Consciousness, and the Politics of Empowerment.* Boston: Unwin Hyman, 1990. A classic text in the study of black feminist theory and practice at the intersection of race, class, and gender by one of black studies' foremost sociologists.

Robin D. G. Kelley. *Yo' Mama Is DysFunkshional!* Boston: Beacon Press, 1998. Insightful essays about America's culture wars, and an excellent critique of social science scholarship about black working-class culture and aesthetics by one of this generation's finest historians.

Ismael Reed. *Airing Dirty Laundry.* Reading, MA: Addison-Wesley Publishing Company, 1993. A collection of provocative, iconoclastic, and entertaining essays written by one of America's most insightful cultural critics.

Deborah Gray White. *Too Heavy a Load: Black Women in Defense of Themselves, 1894–1994.* New York: W. W. Norton, 1998. A brilliant study by a black woman historian of black women and the organizations they founded to fight for the ballot, against segregation, and against the sexism and misogny of black nationalism in the contemporary era.

ADDITIONAL BIBLIOGRAPHY

Black Culture Studies

Brian Cross. *It's Not about a Salary . . . Rap, Race and Resistance in Los Angeles.* London: Verso, 1993.

Michael Eric Dyson. *Between God and Gangsta Rap: Bearing Witness to Black Culture.* New York: Oxford University Press, 1996.

Patricia Liggins Hill, general ed. *Call and Response: The Riverside Anthology of the African American Literary Tradition.* New York: Houghton Mifflin, 1999.

bell hooks. *Outlaw Culture: Resisting Representations.* New York: Routledge, 1994.

Robin D. G. Kelley. *Race Rebels: Culture, Politics, and the Black Working Class.* New York: Free Press, 1994.

Terry McMillan. *Five for Five: The Films of Spike Lee.* New York: Stewart, Tabori & Chang, 1991.

Joan Morgan. *When Chickenheads Come Home to Roost: My Life as a Hip-Hop Feminist.* New York: Simon & Schuster, 1999.

Tricia Rose. *Black Noise: Rap Music and Black Culture in Contemporary America.* Hanover, NH: Wesleyan University Press, 1994.

Greg Tate. *Flyboy in the Buttermilk.* New York: Fireside, 1992.

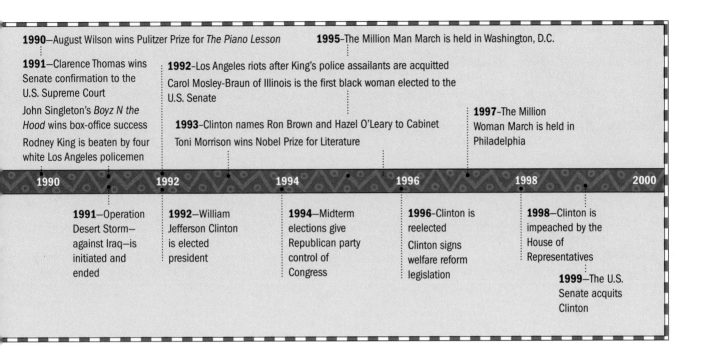

1990—August Wilson wins Pulitzer Prize for *The Piano Lesson*

1991—Clarence Thomas wins Senate confirmation to the U.S. Supreme Court

John Singleton's *Boyz N the Hood* wins box-office success

Rodney King is beaten by four white Los Angeles policemen

1995—The Million Man March is held in Washington, D.C.

1992—Los Angeles riots after King's police assailants are acquitted

Carol Mosley-Braun of Illinois is the first black woman elected to the U.S. Senate

1993—Clinton names Ron Brown and Hazel O'Leary to Cabinet

Toni Morrison wins Nobel Prize for Literature

1997—The Million Woman March is held in Philadelphia

1990　1992　1994　1996　1998　2000

1991—Operation Desert Storm—against Iraq—is initiated and ended

1992—William Jefferson Clinton is elected president

1994—Midterm elections give Republican party control of Congress

1996—Clinton is reelected

Clinton signs welfare reform legislation

1998—Clinton is impeached by the House of Representatives

1999—The U.S. Senate acquits Clinton

Black Politics and Economics

Andrew Billingsley. *Climbing Jacob's Ladder: The Enduring Legacy of African-American Families.* New York: Simon & Schuster, 1993.

Barry Bluestone and Bennett Harrison. *The Deindustrialization of America: Plant Closings, Community Abandonment, and the Dismantling of Basic Industry.* New York: Basic Books, 1982.

Martin Carnoy. *Faded Dreams: The Politics and Economics of Race in America.* Cambridge, England: Cambridge University Press, 1994.

Robert Dallek. *Ronald Reagan: The Politics of Symbolism.* Cambridge, MA: Harvard University Press, 1984.

W. Avon Drake and Robert D. Holsworth. *Affirmative Action and the Stalled Quest for Black Progress.* Urbana: University of Illinois Press, 1996.

Robert Gooding-Williams, ed. *Reading Rodney King: Reading Urban Uprising.* New York: Routledge, 1993.

Lani Guinier. *Tyranny of the Majority: Fundamental Fairness and Representative Democracy.* New York: Free Press, 1995.

Andrew Hacker. *Two Nations: Black and White, Separate, Hostile, Unequal.* New York: Ballantine Books, rev., 1995.

Charles P. Henry. *Jesse Jackson: The Search for Common Ground.* Oakland, CA: Black Scholar Press, 1991.

Anita Faye Hill and Emma Coleman Jordan, eds. *Race, Gender, and Power in America: The Legacy of the Hill-Thomas Hearings.* New York: Oxford University Press, 1995.

Douglas S. Massey and Nancy A. Denton. *American Apartheid: Segregation and the Making of the Underclass.* Cambridge: Harvard University Press, 1993.

Adolph Reed Jr. *The Jesse Jackson Phenomenon: The Crisis in Afro-American Politics.* New Haven, CT: Yale University Press, 1986.

Andrea Y. Simpson. *The Tie That Binds: Identity and Political Attitudes in the Post–Civil Rights Generation.* New York: New York University Press, 1998.

Identity Studies

Molefi Kete Asante. *The Afrocentric Idea.* Philadelphia: Temple University Press, 1987.

Martin Bernal. *Black Athena: The Afroasiatic Roots of Classical Civilization: The Fabrication of Ancient Greece, 1785–1985.* New Brunswick: Rutgers University Press, 1987.

F. James Davis. *Who Is Black? One Nation's Definition.* University Park: Pennsylvania State University Press, 1991.

Tsehloane Keto. *Vision, Identity and Time: The Afrocentric Paradigm and the Study of the Past.* Dubuque, IA: Kendall/Hunt Publishing Co., 1995.

Wilson Jeremiah Moses. *Afrotopia: The Roots of African American Popular History.* Cambridge: Cambridge University Press, 1998.

Arthur M. Schlesinger Jr. *The Disuniting of America.* New York: W. W. Norton, 1992.

Cornel West. *Race Matters.* Boston: Beacon Press, 1993.

Liberation Studies

Derrick Bell. *Faces at the Bottom of the Well: The Permanence of Racism.* New York: Basic Books, 1992.

Michael C. Dawson. *Behind the Mule: Race and Class in African-American Politics.* Princeton, NJ: Princeton University Press, 1994.

W. Marvin Dulaney. *Black Police in America.* Bloomington: Indiana University Press, 1996.

Henry Hampton and Steve Fayer. *Voices of Freedom: An Oral History of the Civil Rights Movement from the 1950s through the 1980s.* New York: Bantam Books, 1990.

Race, Gender, and Class

Michael Awkward. *Negotiating Difference: Race, Gender, and the Politics of Positionality.* Chicago: University of Chicago Press, 1995.

Paul M. Barrett. *The Good Black: A True Story of Race in America.* New York: Dutton, 1999.

Lois Benjamin. *The Black Elite: Facing the Color Line in the Twilight of the Twentieth Century.* Chicago: Nelson-Hall Publishers, 1991.

Ellis Cose. *The Rage of the Privileged Class.* New York: HarperCollins, 1993.

Douglas G. Glasgow. *The Black Underclass: Poverty, Unemployment, and Entrapment of Ghetto Youth.* New York: Random House, 1981.

Lawrence Otis Graham. *Our Kind of People: Inside America's Black Urban Class.* New York: HarperCollins, 1999.

Stanlie M. James and Abena P. A. Busia, eds. *Theorizing Black Feminisms: The Visionary Pragmatism of Black Women.* New York: Routledge, 1993.

Christopher Jencks. *Rethinking Social Policy: Race, Poverty, and the Underclass.* Cambridge, MA: Harvard University Press, 1992.

Jonathan Kozel. *Savage Inequalities: Children in America's Schools.* New York: Crown, 1991.

Haki R. Madhubuti. *Black Men—Obsolete, Single, Dangerous? Afrikan American Families in Transition: Essays in Discovery, Solution and Hope.* Chicago: Third World Press, 1990.

Leith Mullings. *On Our Own Terms: Race, Class, and Gender in the Lives of African American Women.* New York: Routledge, 1997.

Jill Nelson. *Voluntary Slavery: My Authentic Negro Experience.* Chicago, Noble Press, 1993.

Black Conservatives

Shelby Steele. *A Dream Deferred: The Second Betrayal of Black Freedom in America.* New York: HarperCollins Publishers, 1998.

———. *The Content of Our Character: A New Vision of Race in America.* New York: St. Martin's Press, 1990.

Thomas Sowell. *Preferential Policies: An International Perspective.* New York: William Morrow, 1990.

Autobiography and Biography

Amy Alexander, ed. *The Farrakhan Factor: African-American Writers on Leadership, Nationhood and Minister Louis Farrakhan.* New York: Grove Press, 1998.

Marshall Frady. *Jesse: The Life and Pilgrimage of Jesse Jackson.* New York: Random House, 1996.

Randall Robinson. *Defending the Spirit: A Black Life in America.* New York: NAL/Dutton, 1998.

"A NATION WITHIN A NATION"

Since the first Africans were brought to these shores in the seventeenth century, black people have been a constant and distinct presence in America. During the prolonged course of the Atlantic slave trade, approximately 600,000 Africans were sold into servitude in what became the United States. By the outbreak of the Civil War in 1861 there were nearly four million African Americans in this country. Today black people number over 30 million and make up slightly over 10 percent of the nation's population.

Initially regarded merely as an enslaved labor force to produce cash crops and not as a people who would or could enjoy an equal role in the political and social affairs of American society, African Americans constituted a separate ethnic, racial, and cultural group. For more than two centuries they remained outcasts.

People of African descent developed decidedly ambivalent relationships with the white majority in America. Never fully accepted and never fully rejected, black people relied on their own resources as they created their own institutions and communities. In 1852 Martin Delany declared, "We are a nation within a nation." A half century later W. E. B. Du Bois observed that the black man wanted to retain his African identity and to be an American as well. "He would not Africanize America, for America has too much to teach the world and Africa. He would not bleach his Negro soul in a flood of white Americanism, for he knows that Negro blood has a message for the world. He simply wishes to make it possible for a man to be both a Negro and an American, without being cursed and spit upon by his fellows, without having the doors of Opportunity closed roughly in his face."

Sometimes in desperation or disgust, some black people have been willing to abandon America or reject assimilation. The slaves who engaged in South Carolina's 1739 Stono rebellion attempted to reach Spanish Florida. As early as 1773, slaves in Massachusetts pledged to go to Africa after emancipation. From the 1790s to the start of the Civil War, visions of nationhood in Africa attracted a minority of African Americans. During the 1920s, Marcus Garvey and the Universal Negro Improvement Association glorified Africa while seeking black autonomy in the United States. By the 1950s, Elijah Muhammad, Malcolm X, and the Nation of Islam attracted black people by emphasizing a separate black destiny.

Yet in spite of the horrors of slavery, the indignity and cruelty of Jim Crow, and the unrelenting violence and discrimination inflicted on people of color, most African Americans have not rejected America but worked and struggled to participate fully in the American way of life. African slaves accepted elements of Christianity, and their descendants found solace in their spiritual beliefs. Black Americans have embraced American principles of brotherhood, justice, fairness, and equality before the law that are embedded in the Declaration of Independence and the Constitution. Again and again, African Americans have insisted that America be America, that the American majority live up to its professed ideals and values.

The nation within a nation has never been homogeneous. There have been persistent class, gender, and color divisions. There have been tensions and ideological conflicts among black leaders and organizations as they sought strategies to overcome racial inequities and white supremacy. Some leaders, such as Booker T. Washington, have emphasized self-reliance and economic advancement while others, including W. E. B. Du Bois and leaders of the NAACP, have advocated full inclusion in the nation's political, economic, and social fabric.

Furthermore, African Americans have been far more than victims, than an exploited labor force, than the subjects of segregation and stereotypes. They have contributed enormously to the development and character of American society and culture. As slaves, they provided billions of hours of unrequited labor to the American economy. Black people established churches, schools, and colleges that continue to thrive. Black people demonstrated a willingness to fight and die for a country that did not fully accept or appreciate their sacrifices. African Americans have made remarkable and innovative contributions to art, music, folklore, science, politics, and athletics that have shaped and enriched American society.

America is no longer what it was in 1700, 1800, or 1900. Chattel slavery ended in 1865. White supremacy is no longer fashionable or openly acceptable. Legal segregation was prohibited a generation ago. The capacity and willingness of Americans of diverse backgrounds and origins to live together in harmony has vastly improved in recent decades. But as the twenty-first century begins, the long odyssey of people of African descent has not ended nor will it end in the immediate future. Black people will continue to help mold and define this society, and they will continue to be "a nation within a nation."

THE DECLARATION OF INDEPENDENCE

When in the course of human events it becomes necessary for one people to dissolve the political bands which have connected them with another and to assume, among the powers of the earth, the separate and equal station to which the laws of nature and of nature's God entitle them, a decent respect to the opinions of mankind requires that they should declare the causes which impel them to the separation.

We hold these truths to be self-evident, that all men are created equal; that they are endowed by their Creator with certain unalienable rights; that among these are life, liberty, and the pursuit of happiness. That, to secure these rights, governments are instituted among men, deriving their just powers from the consent of the governed; that, whenever any form of government becomes destructive of these ends, it is the right of the people to alter or to abolish it, and to institute a new government, laying its foundation on such principles, and organizing its powers in such form, as to them shall seem most likely to effect their safety and happiness. Prudence, indeed, will dictate that governments long established should not be changed for light and transient causes; and, accordingly, all experience hath shown that mankind are more disposed to suffer, while evils are sufferable, than to right themselves by abolishing the forms to which they are accustomed. But when a long train of abuses and usurpations, pursuing invariably the same object, evinces a design to reduce them under absolute despotism, it is their right, it is their duty, to throw off such government and to pro-

vide new guards for their future security. Such has been the patient sufferance of these colonies, and such is now the necessity which constrains them to alter their former systems of government. The history of the present King of Great Britain is a history of repeated injuries and usurpations, all having, in direct object, the establishment of an absolute tyranny over these States. To prove this, let facts be submitted to a candid world:

He has refused his assent to laws the most wholesome and necessary for the public good.

He has forbidden his governors to pass laws of immediate and pressing importance, unless suspended in their operation till his assent should be obtained; and, when so suspended, he has utterly neglected to attend to them.

He has refused to pass other laws for the accommodation of large districts of people, unless those people would relinquish the right of representation in the legislature, a right inestimable to them and formidable to tyrants only.

He has called together legislative bodies at places unusual, uncomfortable, and distant from the depository of their public records, for the sole purpose of fatiguing them into compliance with his measures.

He has dissolved representative houses, repeatedly for opposing, with manly firmness, his invasions on the rights of the people.

He has refused, for a long time after such dissolutions, to cause others to be elected; whereby the legislative powers, incapable of annihilation, have returned to the people at large for their exercise; the state remaining, in the meantime, exposed to all the danger of invasion from without and convulsions within.

He has endeavored to prevent the population of these States; for that purpose, obstructing the laws for naturalization of foreigners, refusing to pass others to encourage their migration hither, and raising the conditions of new appropriations of lands.

He has obstructed the administration of justice by refusing his assent to laws for establishing judiciary powers.

He has made judges dependent on his will alone for the tenure of their offices and the amount and payment of their salaries.

He has erected a multitude of new offices and sent hither swarms of officers to harass our people and eat out their substance.

He has kept among us, in time of peace, standing armies, without the consent of our legislatures.

He has affected to render the military independent of, and superior to, the civil power.

He has combined with others to subject us to a jurisdiction foreign to our Constitution and unacknowledged by our laws, giving his assent to their acts of pretended legislation—

For quartering large bodies of armed troops among us;

For protecting them, by mock trial, from punishment for any murders which they should commit on the inhabitants of these States;

For cutting off our trade with all parts of the world;

For imposing taxes on us without our consent;

For depriving us, in many cases, of the benefit of trial by jury;

For transporting us beyond seas to be tried for pretended offences;

For abolishing the free system of English laws in a neighboring province, establishing therein an arbitrary government, and enlarging its boundaries, so as to render it at once an example and fit instrument for introducing the same absolute rule into these colonies;

For taking away our charters, abolishing our most valuable laws, and altering, fundamentally, the powers of our governments.

For suspending our own legislatures and declaring themselves invested with power to legislate for us in all cases whatsoever.

He has abdicated government here by declaring us out of his protection and waging war against us.

He has plundered our seas, ravaged our coasts, burnt our towns, and destroyed the lives of our people.

He is, at this time, transporting large armies of foreign mercenaries to complete the works of death, desolation, and tyranny already begun with circumstances of cruelty and perfidy scarcely paralleled in the most barbarous ages, and totally unworthy the head of a civilized nation.

He has constrained our fellow citizens, taken captive on the high seas, to bear arms against their country, to become the executioners of their friends and brethren, or to fall themselves by their hands.

He has excited domestic insurrections amongst us and has endeavored to bring on the inhabitants of our frontiers, the merciless Indian savages, whose known rule of warfare is an undistinguished destruction of all ages, sexes, and conditions.

In every stage of these oppressions, we have petitioned for redress in the most humble terms; our repeated petitions have been answered only by repeated injury. A prince whose character is thus marked by every act which may define a tyrant is unfit to be the ruler of a free people.

Nor have we been wanting in attention to our British brethren. We have warned them, from time to time, of attempts made by their legislature to extend an unwarrantable jurisdiction over us. We have reminded them of the circumstances of our emigration and settlement here. We have appealed to their native justice and magnanimity, and we have conjured them, by the ties of our common kindred, to disavow these usurpations, which would inevitably interrupt our connections and correspondence. They, too, have been deaf to the voice of justice and consanguinity. We must, therefore, acquiesce in the necessity which denounces our separation, and hold them, as we hold the rest of mankind, enemies in war, in peace, friends.

We, therefore, the representatives of the United States of America, in general Congress assembled, appealing to the Supreme Judge of the world for the rectitude of our intentions, do, in the name and by the authority of the good people of these colonies, solemnly publish and declare, that these united colonies are, and of right ought to be, free and independent states: that they are absolved from all allegiance to the British Crown, and that all political connection between them and the state of Great Britain is, and ought to be, totally dissolved; and that, as free and independent states, they have full power to levy war, conclude peace, contract alliances, establish commerce, and to do all other acts and things which independent states may of right do. And, for the support of this declaration, with a firm reliance on the protection of Divine Providence, we mutually pledge to each other our lives, our fortunes, and our sacred honor.

Proposed clause on the slave trade omitted from the final draft of the Declaration

He has waged cruel war against human nature itself, violating its most sacred rights of life and liberty in the person of a distant people who never offended him; captivating and carrying them into slavery in another hemisphere, or to incur miserable death in their transportation thither. This piratical warfare, the opprobrium of infidel powers, is the warfare of the Christian king of Great Britain. Determined to keep open a market where men should be bought and sold, he has prostituted his negative for suppressing every legislative attempt to prohibit or restrain this execrable commerce.

THE CONSTITUTION OF THE UNITED STATES OF AMERICA
(WITH CLAUSES PERTAINING TO THE STATUS OF AFRICAN AMERICANS HIGHLIGHTED)

We the people of the United States, in order to form a more perfect union, establish justice, insure domestic tranquillity, provide for the common defense, promote the general welfare, and secure the blessings of liberty to ourselves and our posterity, do ordain and establish this Constitution for the United States of America.

ARTICLE I

Section 1. All legislative powers herein granted shall be vested in a Congress of the United States, which shall consist of a Senate and House of Representatives.

Section 2. 1. The House of Representatives shall be composed of members chosen every second year by the people of the several States, and the electors in each State shall have the qualifications requisite for electors of the most numerous branch of the State legislature.

2. No person shall be a representative who shall not have attained to the age of twenty-five years, and been seven years a citizen of the United States, and who shall not, when elected, be an inhabitant of that State in which he shall be chosen.

3. Representatives and direct taxes[1] shall be apportioned among the several States which may be included within this Union, according to their respective numbers, which shall be determined by adding to the whole number of free persons, including those bound to service for a term of years, and excluding Indians not taxed, three fifths of all other persons.[2] The actual enumeration shall be made within three years after the first meeting of the Congress of the United States, and within every subsequent term of ten years, in such manner as they shall by law direct. The number of representatives shall not exceed one for every thirty thousand, but each State shall have at least one representative; and until such enumeration shall be made, the State of New Hampshire shall be entitled to

choose three, Massachusetts eight, Rhode Island and Providence Plantations one, Connecticut five, New York six, New Jersey four, Pennsylvania eight, Delaware one, Maryland six, Virginia ten, North Carolina five, South Carolina five, and Georgia three.

4. When vacancies happen in the representation from any State, the executive authority thereof shall issue writs of election to fill such vacancies.

5. The House of Representatives shall choose their speaker and other officers; and shall have the sole power of impeachment.

Section 3. 1. The Senate of the United States shall be composed of two senators from each State, chosen by the legislature thereof,[3] for six years; and each senator shall have one vote.

2. Immediately after they shall be assembled in consequence of the first election, they shall be divided as equally as may be into three classes. The seats of the senators of the first class shall be vacated at the expiration of the second year, of the second class at the expiration of the fourth year, and of the third class at the expiration of the sixth year, so that one third may be chosen every second year; and if vacancies happen by resignation, or otherwise, during the recess of the legislature of any State, the executive thereof may make temporary appointments until the next meeting of the legislature, which shall then fill such vacancies.[4]

3. No person shall be a senator who shall not have attained to the age of thirty years, and been nine years a citizen of the United States, and who shall not, when elected, be an inhabitant of that State for which he shall be chosen.

4. The Vice President of the United States shall be President of the Senate, but shall have no vote, unless they be equally divided.

5. The Senate shall choose their other officers, and also a president pro tempore, in the absence of the Vice President, or when he shall exercise the office of the President of the United States.

6. The Senate shall have the sole power to try all impeachments. When sitting for that purpose, they shall be on oath or affirmation. When the President of the United States is tried, the chief justice shall preside: and no person shall be convicted without the concurrence of two thirds of the members present.

7. Judgment in cases of impeachment shall not extend further than to removal from office, and disqualification to hold and enjoy any office of honor,

---

[1]See the Sixteenth Amendment.
[2]See the Fourteenth Amendment.

[3]See the Seventeenth Amendment.
[4]See the Seventeenth Amendment.

trust or profit under the United States: but the party convicted shall nevertheless be liable and subject to indictment, trial, judgment and punishment, according to law.

Section 4. 1. The times, places, and manner of holding elections for senators and representatives, shall be prescribed in each State by the legislature thereof; but the Congress may at any time by law make or alter such regulations, except as to the places of choosing senators.

2. The Congress shall assemble at least once in every year, and such meeting shall be on the first Monday in December, unless they shall by law appoint a different day.

Section 5. 1. Each House shall be the judge of the elections, returns and qualifications of its own members, and a majority of each shall constitute a quorum to do business; but a smaller number may adjourn from day to day, and may be authorized to compel the attendance of absent members, in such manner, and under such penalties as each House may provide.

2. Each House may determine the rules of its proceedings, punish its members for disorderly behavior, and, with the concurrence of two thirds, expel a member.

3. Each House shall keep a journal of its proceedings, and from time to time publish the same, excepting such parts as may in their judgment require secrecy; and the yeas and nays of the members of either House on any question shall, at the desire of one fifth of those present, be entered on the journal.

4. Neither House, during the session of Congress, shall, without the consent of the other, adjourn for more than three days, nor to any other place than that in which the two Houses shall be sitting.

Section 6. 1. The senators and representatives shall receive a compensation for their services, to be ascertained by law, and paid out of the Treasury of the United States. They shall in all cases, except treason, felony, and breach of the peace, be privileged from arrest during their attendance at the session of their respective Houses, and in going to and returning from the same; and for any speech or debate in either House, they shall not be questioned in any other place.

2. No senator or representative shall, during the time for which he was elected, be appointed to any civil office under the authority of the United States, which shall have been created, or the emoluments whereof shall have been increased, during such time; and no person holding any office under the United States shall be a member of either House during his continuance in office.

Section 7. 1. All bills for raising revenue shall originate in the House of Representatives; but the Senate may propose or concur with amendments as on other bills.

2. Every bill which shall have passed the House of Representatives and the Senate, shall, before it become a law, be presented to the President of the United States; If he approves he shall sign it, but if not he shall return it, with his objections, to that House in which it shall have originated, who shall enter the objections at large on their journal, and proceed to reconsider it. If after such reconsideration two thirds of that House shall agree to pass the bill, it shall be sent, together with the objections, to the other House, by which it shall likewise be reconsidered, and if approved by two thirds of that House, it shall become a law. But in all such cases the votes of both Houses shall be determined by yeas and nays, and the names of the persons voting for and against the bill shall be entered on the journal of each House respectively. If any bill shall not be returned by the President within ten days (Sundays excepted) after it shall have been presented to him, the same shall be a law, in like manner as if he had signed it, unless the Congress by their adjournment prevent its return, in which case it shall not be a law.

3. Every order, resolution, or vote to which the concurrence of the Senate and the House of Representatives may be necessary (except on a question of adjournment) shall be presented to the President of the United States; and before the same shall take effect, shall be approved by him, or being disapproved by him, shall be repassed by two thirds of the Senate and House of Representatives, according to the rules and limitations prescribed in the case of a bill.

Section 8. The Congress shall have the power

1. To lay and collect taxes, duties, imposts, and excises, to pay the debts and provide for the common defense and general welfare of the United States; but all duties, imposts, and excises shall be uniform throughout the United States.

2. To borrow money on the credit of the United States;

3. To regulate commerce with foreign nations, and among the several States, and with the Indian tribes;

4. To establish a uniform rule of naturalization, and uniform laws on the subject of bankruptcies throughout the United States;

5. To coin money, regulate the value thereof, and of foreign coin, and fix the standard of weights and measures;

6. To provide for the punishment of counterfeiting the securities and current coin of the United States;

7. To establish post offices and post roads;

8. To promote the progress of science and useful arts, by securing for limited times to authors and inventors the exclusive right to their respective writings and discoveries;

9. To constitute tribunals inferior to the Supreme Court;

10. To define and punish piracies and felonies committed on the high seas, and offenses against the law of nations;

11. To declare war, grant letters of marque and reprisal, and make rules concerning captures on land and water;

12. To raise and support armies, but no appropriation of money to that use shall be for a longer term than two years;

13. To provide and maintain a navy;

14. To make rules for the government and regulation of the land and naval forces;

15. To provide for calling forth the militia to execute the laws of the Union, suppress insurrections and repel invasions;

16. To provide for organizing, arming, and disciplining the militia, and for governing such part of them as may be employed in the service of the United States, reserving to the States respectively, the appointment of the officers, and the authority of training the militia according to the discipline prescribed by Congress;

17. To exercise exclusive legislation in all cases whatsoever, over such district (not exceeding ten miles square) as may, by cession of particular States, and the acceptance of Congress, become the seat of the government of the United States, and to exercise like authority over all places purchased by the consent of the legislature of the State in which the same shall be, for the erection of forts, magazines, arsenals, dockyards, and other needful buildings; and

18. To make all laws which shall be necessary and proper for carrying into execution the foregoing powers, and all other powers vested by this Constitution in the government of the United States, or any department or officer thereof.

Section 9. 1. The migration or importation of such persons as any of the States now existing shall think proper to admit, shall not be prohibited by the Congress prior to the year one thousand eight hundred and eight, but a tax or duty may be imposed on such importation, not exceeding ten dollars for each person.

2. The privilege of the writ of habeas corpus shall not be suspended, unless when in cases of rebellion or invasion the public safety may require it.

3. No bill of attainder or ex post facto law shall be passed.

4. No capitation, or other direct, tax shall be laid, unless in proportion to the census or enumeration herein-before directed to be taken.[5]

5. No tax or duty shall be laid on articles exported from any State.

6. No preference shall be given by any regulation of commerce or revenue to the ports of one State over those of another: nor shall vessels bound to, or from, one State be obliged to enter, clear, or pay duties in another.

7. No money shall be drawn from the treasury, but in consequence of appropriations made by law; and a regular statement and account of the receipts and expenditures of all public money shall be published from time to time.

8. No title of nobility shall be granted by the United States: and no person holding any office of profit or trust under them, shall, without the consent of the Congress, accept of any present, emolument, office, or title, of any kind whatever, from any king, price, or foreign State.

Section 10. 1. No State shall enter into any treaty, alliance, or confederation; grant letters of marque and reprisal; coin money; emit bills of credit; make any thing but gold and silver coin a tender in payment of debts; pass any bill of attainder, ex post facto law, or law impairing the obligation of contracts, or grant, any title of nobility.

2. No State shall, without the consent of the Congress, lay any imposts or duties on imports or exports, except what may be absolutely necessary for executing its inspection laws: and the net produce of all duties and imposts laid by any State on imports or exports, shall be for the use of the treasury of the United States; and all such laws shall be subject to the revision and control of the Congress.

3. No State shall, without the consent of the Congress, lay any duty of tonnage, keep troops, or ships of war in time of peace, enter into any agreement or compact with another State, or with a foreign power, or engage in war, unless actually invaded, or in such imminent danger as will not admit of delay.

---

[5]See the Sixteenth Amendment.

ARTICLE II

Section 1. 1. The executive power shall be vested in a President of the United States of America. He shall hold his office during the term of four years, and, together with the Vice President, chosen for the same term, be elected, as follows:

2. Each State shall appoint, in such manner as the legislature thereof may direct, a number of electors, equal to the whole number of senators and representatives to which the State may be entitled in the Congress: but no senator or representative, or person holding any office of trust or profit under the United States, shall be appointed an elector.

The electors shall meet in their respective States, and vote by ballot for two persons, of whom one at least shall not be an inhabitant of the same State with themselves. And they shall make a list of all the persons voted for, and of the number of votes for each; which list they shall sign and certify, and transmit sealed to the seat of the government of the United States, directed to the president of the Senate. The president of the Senate shall, in the presence of the Senate and House of Representatives, open all the certificates, and the votes shall then be counted. The person having the greatest number of votes shall be the President, if such number be a majority of the whole number of electors appointed; and if there be more than one who have such majority, and have an equal number of votes, then the House of Representatives shall immediately choose by ballot one of them for President; and if no person have a majority, then from the five highest on the list the said House shall in like manner choose the President. But in choosing the President, the votes shall be taken by States, the representation from each State having one vote; a quorum for this purpose shall consist of a member or members from two thirds of the States, and a majority of all the States shall be necessary to a choice. In every case after the choice of the President, the person having the greatest number of votes of the electors shall be the Vice President. But if there should remain two or more who have equal votes, the Senate shall choose from them by ballot the Vice President.[6]

3. The Congress may determine the time of choosing the electors, and the day on which they shall give their votes; which day shall be the same throughout the United States.

4. No person except a natural born citizen, or a citizen of the United States, at the time of the adoption of this Constitution, shall be eligible to the office of President; neither shall any person be eligible to the office who shall not have attained to the age of thirty-five years, and been fourteen years a resident within the United States.

5. In case of the removal of the President from office, or of his death, resignation, or inability to discharge the powers and duties of the said office, the same shall devolve on the Vice President, and the congress may by law provide for the case of removal, death, resignation or inability, both of the President and Vice President, declaring what officer shall then act as President, and such officer shall act accordingly until the disability be removed, or a President shall be elected.

6. The President shall, at stated times, receive for his services a compensation which shall neither be increased nor diminished during the period for which he shall have been elected, and he shall not receive within that period any other emolument from the United States, or any of them.

7. Before he enter on the execution of his office, he shall take the following oath or affirmation:—"I do solemnly swear (or affirm) that I will faithfully execute the office of President of the United States, and will to the best of my ability, preserve, protect and defend the Constitution of the United States."

Section 2. 1. The President shall be commander in chief of the army and navy of the United States, and of the militia of the several States, when called into the actual service of the United States; he may require the opinion in writing, of the principal officer in each of the executive departments, upon any subject relating to the duties of their respective offices, and he shall have power to grant reprieves and pardons for offenses against the United States, except in cases of impeachment.

2. He shall have power, by and with the advice and consent of the Senate, to make treaties, provided two thirds of the senators present concur; and he shall nominate, and by and with the advice and consent of the Senate, shall appoint ambassadors, other public ministers and consuls, judges of the Supreme Court, and all other officers of the United States, whose appointments are not herein otherwise provided for, and which shall be established by law; but the Congress may by law vest the appointment of such inferior officers, as they think proper, in the President alone, in the courts of laws, or in the heads of departments.

3. The President shall have power to fill up all vacancies that may happen during the recess of the Senate, by granting commissions which shall expire at the end of their next session.

---

[6]Superseded by the Twelfth Amendment.

Section 3. He shall from time to time give to the Congress information of the state of the Union, and recommend to their consideration such measures as he shall judge necessary and expedient; he may, on extraordinary occasions, convene both Houses, or either of them, and in case of disagreement between them with respect to the time of adjournment, he may adjourn them to such time as he shall think proper; he shall receive ambassadors and other public ministers; he shall take care that the laws be faithfully executed, and shall commission all the officers of the United States.

Section 4. The President, Vice President, and all civil officers of the United States, shall be removed from office on impeachment for, and conviction of, treason, bribery, or other high crimes and misdemeanors.

ARTICLE III

Section 1. The judicial power of the United States shall be vested in one Supreme Court, and in such inferior courts as the Congress may from time to time ordain and establish. The judges, both of the Supreme and inferior courts, shall hold their offices during good behavior, and shall, at stated times, receive for their services, a compensation, which shall not be diminished during their continuance in office.

Section 2. 1. The judicial power shall extend to all cases, in law and equity, arising under this Constitution, the laws of the United States, and treaties made, or which shall be made, under their authority;—to all cases of admiralty and maritime jurisdiction;—to controversies to which the United States shall be a party;[7]—to controversies between two or more States;—between a State and citizens of another State;—between citizens of different States;— between citizens of the same State claiming lands under grants of different States, and between a State, or the citizens thereof, and foreign States, citizens or subjects.

2. In all cases affecting ambassadors, other public ministers and consuls, and those in which a State shall be party, the Supreme Court shall have original jurisdiction. In all the other cases before mentioned, the Supreme Court shall have appellate jurisdiction, both as to law and fact, with such exceptions, and under such regulations as the Congress shall make.

3. The trial of all crimes, except in cases of impeachment, shall be by jury; and such trial shall be held in the State where the said crimes shall have been committed; but when not committed within any State, the trial shall be such place or places as the congress may by law have directed.

Section 3. 1. Treason against the United States shall consist only in levying war against them, or in adhering to their enemies, giving them aid and comfort. No person shall be convicted of treason unless on the testimony of two witnesses to the same overt act, or on confession in open court.

2. The Congress shall have power to declare the punishment of treason, but no attainder of treason shall work corruption of blood, or forfeiture except during the life of the person attained.

ARTICLE IV

Section 1. Full faith and credit shall be given in each State to the public acts, records, and judicial proceedings of every other State. And the Congress may by general laws prescribe the manner in which such acts, records and proceedings shall be proved, and the effect thereof.

Section 2. 1. The citizens of each State shall be entitled to all privileges and immunities of citizens in the several States.[8]

2. A person charged in any State with treason, felony, or other crime, who shall flee from justice, and be found in another State, shall on demand of the executive authority of the State from which he fled, be delivered up to be removed to the State having jurisdiction of the crime.

3. No person held to service or labor in one State under the laws thereof, escaping into another, shall, in consequence of any law or regulation therein, be discharged from such service or labor, but shall be delivered up on claim of the party to whom such service or labor may be due.[9]

Section 3. 1. New States may be admitted by the Congress into this Union; but no new State shall be formed or erected within the jurisdiction of any other State, nor any State be formed by the junction of two or more States, or parts of States, without the consent of the legislatures of the States concerned as well as of the Congress.

[7]See the Eleventh Amendment.

[8]See the Fourteenth Amendment, Sec. 1.
[9]See the Thirteenth Amendment.

2. The Congress shall have power to dispose of and make all needful rules and regulations respecting the territory or other property belonging to the United States; and nothing in this Constitution shall be so construed as to prejudice any claims of the United States, or of any particular State.

Section 4. The United States shall guarantee to every State in this Union a republican form of government, and shall protect each of them against invasion; and on application of the legislature, or of the executive (when the legislature cannot be convened) against domestic violence.

ARTICLE V

The Congress, whenever two thirds of both Houses shall deem it necessary, shall propose amendments to this Constitution, or, on the application of the legislatures of two thirds of the several States, shall call a convention for proposing amendments, which in either case shall be valid to all intents and purposes, as part of this Constitution, when ratified by the legislatures of three fourths of the several States, or by conventions in three fourths thereof, as the one or the other mode of ratification may be proposed by the Congress; Provided that no amendment which may be made prior to the year one thousand eight hundred and eight shall in any manner affect the first and fourth clauses in the ninth section of the first article; and that no State, without its consent, shall be deprived of its equal suffrage in the Senate.

ARTICLE VI

1. All debts contracted and engagements entered into, before the adoption of this Constitution, shall be as valid against the United States under this Constitution, as under the Confederation.[10]

2. This Constitution, and the laws of the United States which shall be made in pursuance thereof; and all treaties made, or which shall be made, under the authority of the United States, shall be the supreme law of the land; and the judges in every State shall be bound thereby, any thing in the Constitution or laws of any State to the contrary notwithstanding.

3. The senators and representatives before mentioned, and the members of the several State legislatures, and all executive and judicial officers, both of the United States and of the several States, shall be bound by oath or affirmation to support this Constitution; but no religious test shall ever be required as a qualification to any office or public trust under the United States.

ARTICLE VII

The ratification of the conventions of nine States shall be sufficient for the establishment of this Constitution between the States so ratifying the same.

Done in Convention by the unanimous consent of the States present the seventeenth day of September in the year of our Lord one thousand seven hundred and eighty-seven, and of the independence of the United States of America the twelfth. In witness whereof we have hereunto subscribed our names.

[Names omitted]

Articles in addition to, and amendment of, the Constitution of the United States of America, proposed by Congress, and ratified by the legislatures of the several States, pursuant to the fifth article of the original Constitution.

AMENDMENT I [FIRST TEN AMENDMENTS RATIFIED DECEMBER 15, 1791]

Congress shall make no law respecting an establishment of religion, or prohibiting the free exercise thereof; or abridging the freedom of speech, or of the press; or the right of the people peaceably to assemble, and to petition the government for a redress of grievances.

AMENDMENT II

A well regulated militia, being necessary to the security of a free State, the right of the people to keep and bear arms, shall not be infringed.

AMENDMENT III

No soldier shall, in time of peace be quartered in any house, without the consent of the owner, nor in time of war, but in a manner to be prescribed by law.

---

[10]See the Fourteenth Amendment, Sec. 4.

AMENDMENT IV

The right of the people to be secure in their persons, houses, papers, and effects, against unreasonable searches and seizures, shall not be violated, and no warrants shall issue, but upon probable cause, supported by oath or affirmation, and particularly describing the place to be searched, and the persons or things to be seized.

AMENDMENT V

No person shall be held to answer for a capital or otherwise infamous crime, unless on a presentment or indictment of a grand jury, except in cases arising in the land or naval forces, or in the militia, when in actual service in time of war or public danger; nor shall any person be subject for the same offense to be twice put in jeopardy of life or limb; nor shall be compelled in any criminal case to be a witness against himself, nor be deprived of life, liberty, or property, without due process of law; nor shall private property be taken for public use, without just compensation.

AMENDMENT VI

In all criminal prosecutions, the accused shall enjoy the right to a speedy and public trial, by an impartial jury of the State and district wherein the crime shall have been committed, which district shall have been previously ascertained by law, and to be informed of the nature and cause of the accusation; to be confronted with the witnesses against him; to have compulsory process for obtaining witnesses in his favor, and to have the assistance of counsel for his defense.

AMENDMENT VII

In suits at common law, where the value in controversy shall exceed twenty dollars, the right of trial by jury shall be preserved, and no fact tried by a jury shall be otherwise reexamined in any court of the United States, than according to the rules of the common law.

AMENDMENT VIII

Excessive bail shall not be required, nor excessive fines imposed, nor cruel and unusual punishments inflicted.

AMENDMENT IX

The enumeration in the Constitution of certain rights shall not be construed to deny or disparage others retained by the people.

AMENDMENT X

The powers not delegated to the United States by the Constitution, nor prohibited by it to the States, are reserved to the States respectively, or to the people.

AMENDMENT XI [JANUARY 8, 1798]

The judicial power of the United States shall not be construed to extend to any suit in law or equity, commended or prosecuted against one of the United States by citizens of another State, or by citizens or subjects of any foreign State.

AMENDMENT XII [SEPTEMBER 25, 1804]

The electors shall meet in their respective States, and vote by ballot for President and Vice President, one of whom, at least, shall not be an inhabitant of the same State with themselves; they shall name in their ballots the person voted for as President, and in distinct ballots, the person voted for as Vice President, and they shall make distinct lists of all persons voted for as President and of all persons voted for as Vice President, and of the number of votes for each, which lists they shall sign and certify, and transmit sealed to the seat of the government of the United States, directed to the President of the Senate;—The President of the Senate shall, in the presence of the Senate and House of Representatives, open all the certificates and the votes shall then be counted;—The person having the greatest number of votes for President, shall be the President, if such number be a majority of the whole number of electors appointed; and if no person have such majority, then from the persons having the highest numbers not exceeding three on the list of those voted for as President, the House of Representatives shall choose immediately, by ballot, the President. But in choosing the President, the votes shall be taken by States, the representation from each State having one vote; a quorum for this purpose shall consist of a member or members from two thirds of the States, and a majority of all the States shall be necessary to a choice. And if the House of Representatives shall not choose a President whenever the right of choice shall devolve upon them, before the fourth day of March next following, then the Vice President shall act as President, as in the case of the death or other constitutional disability of the President. The person having the greatest number of votes as Vice President shall be the Vice President, if such number be a majority of the whole number of electors appointed, and if no person have a majority, then from the two highest numbers on the list, the Senate shall choose the Vice President; a quorum for the purpose shall consist of two thirds of the whole number of Senators, and a majority of the whole number shall be necessary to a choice. But no person constitutionally ineligible to the office of President shall be eligible to that of Vice President of the United States.

AMENDMENT XIII [DECEMBER 18, 1865]

Section 1. Neither slavery nor involuntary servitude, except as a punishment for crime whereof the party shall have been duly convicted, shall exist within the United States, or any place subject to their jurisdiction.

Section 2. Congress shall have power to enforce this article by appropriate legislation.

AMENDMENT XIV [JULY 28, 1868]

Section 1. All persons born or naturalized in the United States, and subject to the jurisdiction thereof, are citizens of the United States and of the State wherein they reside. No State shall make or enforce any law which shall abridge the privileges or immunities of citizens of the United States; nor shall any State deprive any person of life, liberty, or property, without due process of law; nor deny to any person within its jurisdiction the equal protection of the laws.

Section 2. Representatives shall be apportioned among the several States according to their respective numbers, counting the whole number of persons in each State, excluding Indians not taxed. But when the right to vote at any election for the choice of electors for President and Vice President of the United States, representatives in Congress, the executive and judicial officers of a State, or the members of the legislature thereof, is denied to any of the male inhabitants of such State, being twenty-one years of age, and citizens of the United States, or in any way abridged, except for participating in rebellion, or other crime, the basis of representation there shall be reduced in the proportion which the number of such male citizens shall bear to the whole number of male citizens twenty-one years of age in such State.

Section 3. No person shall be a senator or representative in Congress, or elector of President and Vice President, or hold any office, civil or military, under the United States, or under any State, who having previously taken an oath, as a member of Congress, or as an officer of the United States, or as a member of any State legislature, or as an executive or judicial officer of any State, to support the Constitution of the United States, shall have engaged in insurrection or rebellion against the same, or given aid or comfort to the enemies thereof. But Congress may by a vote of two thirds of each House, remove such disability.

Section 4. The validity of the public debt of the United States, authorized by law, including debts incurred for payment of pensions and bounties for services in suppressing insurrection or rebellion; shall not be questioned. But neither the United States nor any State shall assume or pay any debt or obligation incurred in aid of insurrection or rebellion against the United States, or any claim for the loss or emancipation of any slave; but all such debts, obligations, and claims shall be held illegal and void.

Section 5. The Congress shall have the power to enforce, by appropriate legislation, the provisions of this article.

AMENDMENT XV [MARCH 30, 1870]

Section 1. The right of citizens of the United States to vote shall not be denied or abridged by the United States or by any State on account of race, color, or previous condition of servitude.

Section 2. The Congress shall have power to enforce this article by appropriate legislation.

AMENDMENT XVI [FEBRUARY 25, 1913]

The Congress shall have power to lay and collect taxes on incomes, from whatever source derived, without apportionment among the several States, and without regard to any census or enumeration.

AMENDMENT XVII [MAY 31, 1913]

The Senate of the United States shall be composed of two senators from each State, elected by the people thereof, for six years; and each senator shall have one vote. The electors in each State shall have the qualifications requisite for electors of the most numerous branch of the State legislature.

When vacancies happen in the representation of any State in the Senate, the executive authority of such State shall issue writs of election to fill such vacancies: *Provided,* That the legislature of any State may empower the executive thereof to make temporary appointments until the people fill the vacancies by election as the legislature may direct.

This amendment shall not be so construed as to affect the election or term of any senator chosen before it becomes valid as part of the Constitution.

AMENDMENT XVIII[11] [JANUARY 29, 1919]

After one year from the ratification of this article, the manufacture, sale, or transportation of intoxicating liquors within, the importation thereof into, or the exportation thereof from the United States and all territory subject to the jurisdiction thereof for beverage purposes is thereby prohibited.

The Congress and the several States shall have concurrent power to enforce this article by appropriate legislation.

This article shall be inoperative unless it shall have been ratified as an amendment to the Constitution by the legislatures of the several States, as provided in the constitution, within seven years from the date of the submission hereof to the States by Congress.

AMENDMENT XIX [AUGUST 26, 1920]

The right of citizens of the United States to vote shall not be denied or abridged by the United States or by any State on account of sex.

Congress shall have the power to enforce this article by appropriate legislation.

AMENDMENT XX [JANUARY 23, 1933]

Section 1. The terms of the President and Vice President shall end at noon on the 20th day of January and the terms of Senators and Representatives at noon on the 3d day of January, of the years in which such terms would have ended if this article had not

---

[11]Repealed by the Twenty-first Amendment.

been ratified; and the terms of their successors shall then begin.

Section 2. The Congress shall assemble at least once in every year, and such meeting shall begin at noon on the 3d day of January, unless they shall by law appoint a different day.

Section 3. If, at the time fixed for the beginning of the term of President, the President-elect shall have died, the Vice President-elect shall become President. If a President shall not have been chosen before the time fixed for the beginning of his term, or if the President-elect shall have failed to qualify, then the Vice President-elect shall act as President until a President shall have qualified; and the Congress may by law provide for the case wherein neither a President-elect nor a Vice President-elect shall have qualified, declaring who shall then act as President, or the manner in which one who is to act shall be selected, and such person shall act accordingly until a President or Vice President shall have qualified.

Section 4. The Congress may by law provide for the case of the death of any of the persons from whom, the House of Representatives may choose a President whenever the right of choice shall have devolved upon them, and for the case of the death of any of the persons from whom the Senate may choose a Vice President whenever the right of choice shall have devolved upon them.

Section 5. Sections 1 and 2 shall take effect on the 15th day of October following the ratification of this article.

Section 6. This article shall be inoperative unless it shall have been ratified as an amendment to the Constitution by the legislatures of three-fourths of the several States within seven years from the date of its submission.

AMENDMENT XXI [DECEMBER 5, 1933]

Section 1. The Eighteenth Article of amendment to the Constitution of the United States is hereby repealed.

Section 2. The transportation or importation into any State, Territory, or possession of the United States for delivery or use therein of intoxicating liquors in violation of the laws thereof, is hereby prohibited.

Section 3. This article shall be inoperative unless it shall have been ratified as an amendment to the Constitution by conventions in the several States, as provided in the Constitution, within seven years from the date of the submission thereof to the States by the Congress.

AMENDMENT XXII [MARCH 1, 1951]

No person shall be elected to the office of the President more than twice, and no person who has held the office of President, or acted as President, for more than two years of a term to which some other person was elected President shall be elected to the office of the President more than once.

But this article shall not apply to any person holding the office of President when this article was proposed by the Congress, and shall not prevent any person who may be holding the office of President, or acting as President, during the term within which this article becomes operative from holding the office of President or acting as President during the remainder of such term.

This article shall be inoperative unless it shall have been ratified as an amendment to the Constitution by the legislatures of three-fourths of the several States within seven years from the date of its submission to the States by the Congress.

AMENDMENT XXIII [MARCH 29, 1961]

Section 1. The District constituting the seat of Government of the United States shall appoint in such manner as the Congress may direct.

A number of electors of President and Vice President equal to the whole number of Senators and Representatives in Congress to which the District would be entitled if it were a State, but in no event more than the least populous State; they shall be in addition to those appointed by the States, but they shall be considered, for the purposes of the election of President and Vice President, to be electors appointed by a State; and they shall meet in the District and perform such duties as provided by the twelfth article of amendment.

Section 2. The Congress shall have power to enforce this article by appropriate legislation.

AMENDMENT XXIV [JANUARY 23, 1964]

Section 1. The right of citizens of the United States to vote in any primary or other election for President or Vice President, for electors for President or Vice President, or for Senator or Representative in Congress, shall not be denied or abridged by the United States or any State by reason of failure to pay any poll tax or other tax.

Section 2. The Congress shall have power to enforce this article by appropriate legislation.

AMENDMENT XXV [FEBRUARY 10, 1967]

Section 1. In case of the removal of the President from office or of his death or resignation, the Vice President shall become President.

Section 2. Whenever there is a vacancy in the office of the Vice President, the President shall nominate a Vice President who shall take office upon confirmation by a majority of both Houses of Congress.

Section 3. Whenever the President transmits to the President pro tempore of the Senate and the Speaker of the House of Representatives his written declaration that he is unable to discharge the powers and duties of his office, and until he transmits to them a written declaration to the contrary, such powers and duties shall be discharged by the Vice President as Acting President.

Section 4. Whenever the Vice president and a majority of either the principal officers of the executive departments or of such other body as Congress may by law provide, transmit to the President pro tempore of the Senate and the Speaker of the House of Representatives their written declaration that the President is unable to discharge the powers and duties of his office, the Vice President shall immediately assume the powers and duties of the office as Acting President.

Thereafter, when the President transmits to the President pro tempore of the Senate and the Speaker of the House of Representatives his written declaration that no inability exists, he shall resume the powers and duties of his office unless the Vice President and a majority of either the principal officers of the executive departments or of such other body as Congress may by law provide, transmit within four days to the President pro tempore of the Senate and the Speaker of the House of Representatives their written declaration that the President is unable to discharge the powers and duties of his office. Thereupon Congress shall decide the issue, assembling within forty-eight hours for that purpose if not in session. If the Congress, within twenty-one days after receipt of the latter written declaration, or, if Congress is not in session, within twenty-one days after Congress is required to assemble, determines by two-thirds vote of both Houses that the President is unable to discharge the powers and duties of his office, the Vice President shall continue to discharge the same as Acting President; otherwise, the President shall resume the powers and duties of his office.

AMENDMENT XXVI [JUNE 30, 1971]

Section 1. The right of citizens of the United States who are eighteen years of age or older to vote shall not be denied or abridged by the United States or by any State on account of age.

Section 2. The Congress shall have power to enforce this article by appropriate legislation.

AMENDMENT XXVII[12] [MAY 7, 1992]

No law, varying the compensation for services of the Senators and Representatives, shall take effect until an election of Representatives shall have intervened.

---

[12]James Madison proposed this amendment in 1789 together with the ten amendments that were adopted as the Bill of Rights, but it failed to win ratification at the time. Congress, however, had set no deadline for its ratification, and over the years—particularly in the 1980s and 1990s—many states voted to add it to the Constitution. With the ratification of Michigan in 1992 it passed the threshold of 3/4ths of the states required for adoption, but because the process took more than 200 years, its validity remains in doubt.

THE EMANCIPATION PROCLAMATION

By the President of the United States of America:

Whereas, on the twenty-second day of September, in the year of our Lord one thousand eight hundred and sixty-two, a proclamation was issued by the President of the United States, containing, among other things, the following, to wit:

That on the first day of January, in the year of our Lord one thousand eight hundred and sixty-three, all persons held as slaves within any State or designated part of a State, the people whereof shall then be in rebellion against the United States, shall be then, thenceforward, and forever free; and the Executive Government of the United States, including the military and naval authority thereof, will recognize and maintain the freedom of such persons, and will do no act or acts to repress such persons, or any of them, in any efforts they may make for their actual freedom.

That the Executive will, on the first day of January aforesaid, by proclamation, designate the States and parts of States, if any, in which the people thereof, respectively, shall then be in rebellion against the United States; and the fact that any State, or the people thereof, shall on that day be, in good faith, represented in the Congress of the United States by members chosen thereto at elections wherein a majority of the qualified voters of such State shall have participated, shall, in the absence of strong countervailing testimony, be deemed conclusive evidence that such State, and the people thereof, are not then in rebellion against the United States.

Now, therefore I, Abraham Lincoln, President of the United States, by virtue of the power in me vested as Commander-in-Chief, of the Army and Navy of the United States in time of actual armed rebellion against the authority and government of the United States, and as a fit and necessary war measure for suppressing said rebellion, do, on this first day of January, in the year of our Lord one thousand eight hundred and sixty-three, and in accordance with my purpose so to do publicly proclaimed for the full period of one hundred days, from the day first above mentioned, order and designate as the States and parts of States wherein the people thereof respectively, are this day in rebellion against the United States, the following, to wit:

Arkansas, Texas, Louisiana, (except the Parishes of St. Bernard, Plaquemines, Jefferson, St. John, St. Charles, St. James Ascension, Assumption, Terrebonne, Lafourche, St. Mary, St. Martin, and Orleans, including the City of New Orleans), Mississippi, Alabama, Florida, Georgia, South Carolina, North Carolina, and Virginia, (except the forty-eight counties designated as West Virginia, and also the counties of Berkley, Accomac, Northampton, Elizabeth City, York, Princess Ann, and Norfolk, including the cities of Norfolk and Portsmouth), and which excepted parts, are for the present, left precisely as if this proclamation were not issued.

And by virtue of the power, and for the purpose aforesaid, I do order and declare that all persons held as slaves within said designated States, and parts of States, are, and henceforward shall be free; and that the Executive government of the United States, including the military and naval authorities thereof, will recognize and maintain the freedom of said persons.

And I hereby enjoin upon the people so declared to be free to abstain from all violence, unless in necessary self-defense; and I recommend to them that, in all cases when allowed, they labor faithfully for reasonable wages.

And I further declare and make known, that such persons of suitable condition, will be received into the armed service of the United States to garrison forts, positions, stations, and other places, and to man vessels of all sorts in said service.

And upon this act, sincerely believed to be an act of justice, warranted by the Constitution, upon military necessity, I invoke the considerate judgment of mankind, and the gracious favor of Almighty God.

In witness whereof, I have hereunto set my hand and caused the seal of the United States to be affixed. Done at the City of Washington, this first day of January, in the year of our Lord one thousand eight hundred and sixty-three, and of the Independence of the United States of America the eighty-seventh.

By the President: Abraham Lincoln

William H. Seward, Secretary of State.

KEY PROVISIONS OF THE CIVIL RIGHTS ACT OF 1964

AN ACT

To enforce the constitutional right to vote, to confer jurisdiction upon the district courts of the United States to provide injunctive relief against discrimination in public accommodations, to authorize the Attorney General to institute suits to protect constitutional rights in public facilities and public education, to extend the Commission on Civil Rights, to prevent discrimination in federally assisted programs, to establish a Commission on Equal Employment Opportunity, and for other purposes.

Be it enacted by the Senate and House of Representatives of the United States of America in Congress assembled, that this Act may be cited as the "Civil Rights Act of 1964."

TITLE I—VOTING RIGHTS
Section 101 . . .

(2) No person acting under color of law shall—

(A) In determining whether any individual is qualified under State law or laws to vote in any Federal election, apply any standard, practice, or procedure different from the standards, practices, or procedures applied under such law or laws to other individuals within the same county, parish, or similar political subdivision who have been found by State officials to be qualified to vote;

(B) deny the right of any individual to vote in any Federal election because of an error or omission on any record or paper relating to any application, registration, or other act requisite to voting, if such error or omission is not material in determining whether such individual is qualified under State law to vote in such election;

(C) employ any literacy test as a qualification for voting in any Federal election unless (i) such test is administered to each individual and is conducted wholly in writing, and (ii) a certified copy of the test and of the answers given by the individual is furnished to him within twenty-five days of the submission of his request made within the period of time during which records and papers are required to be retained and pre-

served pursuant to title III of the Civil Rights Act of 1960 (42 U.S.C. 1974–74e; 74 Stat. 88): Provided, however, That the Attorney General may enter into agreements with appropriate State or local authorities that preparation, conduct, and maintenance of such tests in accordance with the provisions of applicable State or local law, including such special provisions as are necessary in the preparation, conduct, and maintenance of such tests for persons who are blind or otherwise physically handicapped, meet the purposes of this subparagraph and constitute compliance therewith.

TITLE II—INJUNCTIVE RELIEF AGAINST DISCRIMINATION IN PLACES OF PUBLIC ACCOMMODATION
Section 201.

(a) All persons shall be entitled to the full and equal enjoyment of the goods, services, facilities, and privileges, advantages and accommodations of any place of public accommodation, as defined in this section, without discrimination or segregation on the ground of race, color, religion, or national origin.

(b) Each of the following establishments which serves the public is a place of public accommodation within the meaning of this title if its operations effect commerce, or if discrimination or segregation by it is supported by State action:

(1) any inn, hotel, motel, or other establishment which provides lodging to transient guests, other than an establishment located within a building which contains not more than five rooms for rent or hire and which is actually occupied by the proprietor of such establishment as his residence;

(2) any restaurant, cafeteria, lunchroom, lunch counter, soda fountain, or other facility principally engaged in selling food for consumption on the premises, including, but not limited to, any such facility located on the premises of any retail establishment; or any gasoline station;

(3) any motion picture house, theater, concert hall, sports arena, stadium or other place of exhibition or entertainment;

(4) any establishment (A)(i) which is physically located within the premises of any establishment otherwise covered by this subsection, or (ii)

within the premises of which is physically located any such covered establishment, and (B) which holds itself out as serving patrons of such covered establishment. . . .

(d) Discrimination or segregation by an establishment is supported by State action within the meaning of this title if such discrimination or segregation

> (1) is carried on under color of any law, statute, ordinance, or regulation; or

> (2) is carried on under color of any custom or usage required or enforced by officials of the State or political subdivision thereof; or

> (3) is required by action of the State or political subdivision thereof. . . .

Section 202.   All persons shall be entitled to be free, at any establishment or place, from discrimination or segregation of any kind on the ground of race, color, religion, or national origin, if such discrimination or segregation is or purports to be required by any law, statute, ordinance, regulation, rule, or order of a State or any agency or political subdivision thereof.

Section 203.   No person shall (a) withhold, deny, or attempt to withhold or deny, or deprive or attempt to deprive, any person of any right or privilege secured by section 201 or 202, or (b) intimidate, threaten, or coerce, or attempt to intimidate, threaten, or coerce any person with the purpose of interfering with any right or privilege secured by section 201 or 202, or (c) punish or attempt to punish any person for exercising or attempting to exercise any right or privilege secured by section 201 or 202.

Section 204.
(a) Whenever any person has engaged or there are reasonable grounds to believe that any person is about to engage in any act or practice prohibited by section 203, a civil action for preventive relief, including an application for a permanent or temporary injunction, restraining order, or other order, may be instituted by the person aggrieved and, upon timely application, the court may, in its discretion, permit the Attorney General to intervene in such civil action if he certifies that the case is of general public importance. Upon application by the complainant and in such circumstances as the court may deem just, the court may appoint an attorney for such complainant and may authorize the commencement of the civil action without the payment of fees, costs, or security. . . .

Section 206.
(a) Whenever the Attorney General has reasonable cause to believe that any person or group of persons is engaged in a pattern or practice of resistance to the full enjoyment of any of the rights secured by this title, and that the pattern or practice is of such a nature and is intended to deny the full exercise of the rights herein described, the Attorney General may bring a civil action in the appropriate district court of the United States by filing with it a complaint

> (1) signed by him (or in his absence the Acting Attorney General),

> (2) setting forth facts pertaining to such pattern or practice, and

> (3) requesting such preventive relief, including an application for a permanent or temporary injunction, restraining order or other order against the person or persons responsible for such pattern or practice, as he deems necessary to insure the full enjoyment of the rights herein described. . . .

TITLE III—DESEGREGATION OF PUBLIC FACILITIES

Section 301.
(a) Whenever the Attorney General receives a complaint in writing signed by an individual to the effect that he is being deprived of or threatened with the loss of his right to the equal protection of the laws, on account of his race, color, religion, or national origin, by being denied equal utilization of any public facility which is owned, operated, or managed by or on behalf of any State or subdivision thereof, other than a public school or public college as defined in section 401 of title IV hereof, and the Attorney General believes the complaint is meritorious and certifies that the signer or signers of such complaint are unable, in his judgment, to initiate and maintain appropriate legal proceedings for relief and that the institution of an action will materially further the orderly progress of desegregation in public facilities, the Attorney General is authorized to institute for or in the name of the United States a civil action in any appropriate district court of the United States against such parties and for such relief as may be appropriate. And such court shall have and shall exercise jurisdiction of proceedings instituted pursuant to this section. The Attorney General may implead as defendants such additional parties as are or become necessary to the grant of effective relief hereunder. . . .

TITLE IV—DESEGREGATION OF PUBLIC EDUCATION
DEFINITIONS

Section. 401.   As used in this title—. . . .
(b) "Desegregation" means the assignment of students to public schools and within such schools without regard to their race, color, religion, or national origin, but "desegregation" shall not mean the assignment of students to public schools in order to overcome racial imbalance. . . .

SURVEY AND REPORT OF EDUCATIONAL OPPORTUNITIES

Section 402.   The Commissioner shall conduct a survey and make a report to the President and the Congress, within two years of the enactment of this title, concerning the lack of availability of equal educational opportunities for individuals by reason of race, color, religion, or national origin in public educational institutions at all levels in the United States, its territories and possessions, and the District of Columbia. . . .

TITLE V—COMMISSION ON CIVIL RIGHTS . . .
DUTIES OF THE COMMISSION

Section 104.
(a) The Commission shall—

(1) investigate allegations in writing under oath or affirmation that certain citizens of the United States are being deprived of their right to vote and have that vote counted by reason of their color, race, religion, or national origin; which writing, under oath or affirmation, shall set forth the facts upon which such belief or beliefs are based;

(2) study and collect information concerning legal developments constituting a denial of equal protection of the laws under the Constitution because of race, color, religion or national origin or in the administration of justice;

(3) appraise the laws and policies of the Federal Government with respect to denials of equal protection of the laws under the Constitution because of race, color, religion or national origin or in the administration of justice;

(4) serve as a national clearinghouse for information in respect to denials of equal protection of the laws because of race, color, religion or national origin, including but not limited to the fields of voting, education, housing, employment, the use of public facilities, and transportation, or in the administration of justice;

(5) investigate allegations, made in writing and under oath or affirmation, that citizens of the United States are unlawfully being accorded or denied the right to vote, or to have their votes properly counted, in any election of presidential electors, Members of the United States Senate, or of the House of Representatives, as a result of any patterns or practice of fraud or discrimination in the conduct of such election; . . .

TITLE VI—NONDISCRIMINATION IN FEDERALLY ASSISTED PROGRAMS

Section 601.   No person in the United States shall, on the ground of race, color, or national origin, be excluded from participation in, be denied the benefits of, or be subjected to discrimination under any program or activity receiving Federal financial assistance.

Section 602.   Each Federal department and agency which is empowered to extend Federal financial assistance to any program or activity, by way of grant, loan, or contract other than a contract of insurance or guaranty, is authorized and directed to effectuate the provisions of section 601 with respect to such program or activity by issuing rules, regulations, or orders of general applicability which shall be consistent with achievement of the objectives of the statute authorizing the financial assistance in connection with which the action is taken. No such rule, regulation, or order shall become effective unless and until approved by the President. Compliance with any requirement adopted pursuant to this section may be effected

(1) by the termination of or refusal to grant or to continue assistance under such program or activity to any recipient as to whom there has been an express finding on the record, after opportunity for hearing, of a failure to comply with such requirement, but such termination or refusal shall be limited to the particular political entity, or part thereof, or other recipient as to whom such a finding has been made and, shall be limited in its effect to the particular program, or part thereof, in which such non-compliance has been so found, or

(2) by any other means authorized by law:
Provided, however, that no such action shall be taken until the department or agency concerned has advised

the appropriate person or persons of the failure to comply with the requirement and has determined that compliance cannot be secured by voluntary means. In the case of any action terminating, or refusing to grant or continue, assistance because of failure to comply with a requirement imposed pursuant to this section, the head of the federal department or agency shall file with the committees of the House and Senate having legislative jurisdiction over the program or activity involved a full written report of the circumstances and the grounds for such action. No such action shall become effective until thirty days have elapsed after the filing of such report. . . .

TITLE VII—EQUAL EMPLOYMENT OPPORTUNITY . . .
DISCRIMINATION BECAUSE OF RACE, COLOR, RELIGION, SEX, OR NATIONAL ORIGIN
Section 703.

(a) it shall be an unlawful employment practice for an employer—

> (1) to fail or refuse to hire or to discharge any individual, or otherwise to discriminate against any individual with respect to his compensation, terms, conditions, or privileges of employment, because of such individual's race, color, religion, sex, or national origin; or

> (2) to limit, segregate, or classify his employees in any way which would deprive or tend to deprive any individual of employment opportunities or otherwise adversely affect his status as an employee, because of such individual's race, color, religion, sex, or national origin.

(b) it shall be an unlawful employment practice for an employment agency to fail or refuse to refer for employment, or otherwise to discriminate against, any individual because of his race, color, religion, sex, or national origin, or to classify or refer for employment any individual on the basis of his race, color, religion, sex, or national origin.

(c) it shall be an unlawful employment practice for a labor organization—

> (1) to exclude or to expel from its membership, or otherwise to discriminate against, any individual because of his race, color, religion, sex, or national origin;

> (2) to limit, segregate, or classify its membership, or to classify or fail or refuse to refer for employment any individual, in any way which would de-

prive or tend to deprive any individual of employment opportunities, or would limit such employment opportunities or otherwise adversely affect his status as an employee or as an applicant for employment, because of such individual's race, color, religion, sex, or national origin; or

> (3) to cause or attempt to cause an employer to discriminate against an individual in violation of this section.

(d) It shall be an unlawful employment practice for any employer, labor organization, or joint labor-management committee controlling apprenticeship or other training or retraining, including on-the-job training programs to discriminate against any individual because of his race, color, religion, sex, or national origin in admission to, or employment in, any program established to provide apprenticeship or other training. . . .

OTHER UNLAWFUL EMPLOYMENT PRACTICES
Section 704.

(a) It shall be an unlawful employment practice for an employer to discriminate against any of his employees or applicants for employment, for an employment agency to discriminate against any individual, or for a labor organization to discriminate against any member thereof or applicant for membership, because he has opposed any practice made an unlawful employment practice by this title, or because he has made a charge, testified, assisted, or participated in any manner in an investigation, proceeding, or hearing under this title.

(b) It shall be an unlawful employment practice for an employer, labor organization, or employment agency to print or publish or cause to be printed or published any notice or advertisement relating to employment by such an employer or membership in or any classification or referral for employment by such a labor organization, or relating to any classification or referral for employment by such an employment agency, indicating any preference, limitation, specification, or discrimination, based on race, color, religion, sex, or national origin, except that such a notice or advertisement may indicate a preference, limitation, specification, or discrimination based on religion, sex, or national origin when religion, sex, or national origin is a bona fide occupational qualification for employment.

EQUAL EMPLOYMENT OPPORTUNITY COMMISSION
Section 705.

(a) There is hereby created a Commission to be known as the Equal Employment Opportunity Commission, which shall be composed of five members, not more than three of whom shall be members of the same political party, who shall be appointed by the President by and with the advice and consent of the Senate. One of the original members shall be appointed for a term of one year, one for a term of two years, one for a term of three years, one for a term of four years, and one for a term of five years, beginning from the date of enactment of this title, but their successors shall be appointed for terms of five years each, except that any individual chosen to fill a vacancy shall be appointed only for the unexpired term of the member whom he shall succeed. The President shall designate one member to serve as Chairman of the Commission, and one member to serve as Vice Chairman. The Chairman shall be responsible on behalf of the Commission for the administrative operations of the Commission, and shall appoint, in accordance with the civil service laws, such officers, agents, attorneys, and employees as it deems necessary to assist it in the performance of its functions and to fix their compensation in accordance with Classification Act of 1949, as amended. . . .

TITLE VIII—REGISTRATION AND VOTING STATISTICS

Section 801.   The Secretary of Commerce shall promptly conduct a survey to compile registration and voting statistics in such geographic areas as may be recommended by the Commission on Civil Rights. Such a survey and compilation shall, to the extent recommended by the Commission on Civil Rights, only include a count of persons of voting age by race, color, and national origin, and determination of the extent to which such persons are registered to vote, and have voted in any statewide primary or general election in which the Members of the United States House of Representatives are nominated or elected, since January 1, 1960. Such information shall also be collected and compiled in connection with the Nineteenth Decennial Census, and at such other times as the Congress may prescribe. The provisions of section 9 and chapter 7 of title 13, United States Code, shall apply to any survey, collection, or compilation of registration and voting statistics carried out under this title: Provided, however, that no person shall be compelled to disclose his race, color, national origin, or questioned about his political party affiliation, how he voted, or the reasons therefore, nor shall any penalty be imposed for his failure or refusal to make such disclosure. Every person interrogated orally, by written survey or questionnaire or by any other means with respect to such information shall be fully advised with respect to his right to fail or refuse to furnish such information.

KEY PROVISIONS OF THE VOTING RIGHTS ACT OF 1965

AN ACT

To enforce the fifteenth amendment to the Constitution of the United States, and for other purposes.

Be it enacted by the Senate and House of Representatives of the United States of America in Congress assembled, That this Act shall be known as the "Voting Rights Act of 1965."

Section 2.   No voting qualification or prerequisite to voting, or standard, practice, or procedure shall be imposed or applied by any State or political subdivision to deny or abridge the right of any citizen of the United States to vote on account of race or color.

Section 3.

(a) Whenever the Attorney General institutes a proceeding under any statute to enforce the guarantees of the fifteenth amendment in any State or political subdivision the court shall authorize the appointment of Federal examiners by the United States Civil Service Commission in accordance with section 6 to serve for such period of time and for such political subdivisions as the court shall determine is appropriate to enforce the guarantees of the fifteenth amendment (1) as part of any interlocutory order if the court determines that the appointment of such examiners is necessary to enforce such guarantees or (2) as part of any final judgment if the court finds that violations of the fifteenth amendment justifying equitable relief have occurred in such State or subdivision: *Provided*, That the court need not authorize the appointment of examiners if any incidents of denial or abridgment of the right to vote on account of race or color (1) have been few in number and have been promptly and effectively corrected by State or local action, (2) the continuing effect of such incidents has been eliminated, and (3) there is no reasonable probability of their recurrence in the future.

(b) If in a proceeding instituted by the Attorney General under any statute to enforce the guarantees of the fifteenth amendment in any State or political subdivision the court finds that a test or device has been used for the purpose or with the effect of denying or abridging the right of any citizen of the United States to vote on account of race or color, it shall suspend the use of tests and devices in such State or political subdivisions as the court shall determine is appropriate and for such period as it deems necessary. . . .

Section 4

(a) To assure that the right of citizens of the United States to vote is not denied or abridged on account of race or color, no citizen shall be denied the right to vote in any Federal, State, or local election because of his failure to comply with any test or device in any State with respect to which the determinations have been made under subsection (b). . . .

(b) The provisions of subsection (a) shall apply in any State or in any political subdivision of a state which (1) the Attorney General determines maintained on November 1, 1964, any test or device, and with respect to which (2) the Director of the Census determines that less than 50 per centum of the persons of voting age residing therein were registered on November 1, 1964, or that less than 50 per centum of such persons voted in the presidential election of November 1964. . . .

(c) The phrase "test or device" shall mean any requirement that a person as a prerequisite for voting or registration of voting (1) demonstrate the ability to read, write, understand, or interpret any matter, (2) demonstrate any educational achievement or his knowledge of any particular subject, (3) possess good moral character, or (4) prove his qualifications by the voucher of registered voters or members of any other class. . . .

Section 6.   Whenever (a) a court has authorized the appointment of examiners pursuant to the provisions of section 3 (a), or (b) unless a declaratory judgment has been rendered under section 4 (a), the Attorney General certifies with respect to any political subdivision named in, or included within the scope of, determinations made under section 4 (b) that (1) he has received complaints in writing from twenty or more residents of such political subdivision alleging that they have been denied the right to vote under color of law on account of race or color, and that he believes such complaints to be meritorious, or (2) that in his judgment (considering, among other factors, whether the ratio of nonwhite persons to white persons registered to vote within such subdivision appears to him to be reasonably attributable to violations of the fifteenth amendment or whether substantial evidence exists that bona fide efforts are being made within such subdivision to comply with the fifteenth amendment), the appointment of examiners is otherwise necessary to enforce the guarantees of the fifteenth amendment, the Civil Service Commission shall appoint as many examiners for such subdivision as it may deem appropriate to prepare and maintain lists of persons eligible to vote in Federal, State, and local elections. . . . Examiners and hearing officers shall have the power to administer oaths. . . .

Section 10

(a) The Congress finds that the requirement of the payment of a poll tax as a precondition to voting (i) precludes persons of limited means from voting or imposes unreasonable financial hardship upon such persons as a precondition to their exercise of the franchise, (ii) does not bear a reasonable relationship to any legitimate State interest in the conduct of elections, and (iii) in some areas has the purpose or effect of denying persons the right to vote because of race or color. Upon the basis of these findings, Congress declares that the constitutional right of citizens to vote is denied or abridged in some areas by the requirement of the payment of a poll tax as a precondition to voting.

(b) In the exercise of the powers of Congress under section 5 of the fourteenth amendment and section 2 of the fifteenth amendment, the Attorney General is authorized and directed to institute forthwith in the name of the United States such actions, including actions against States or political subdivisions, for declaratory judgment or injunctive relief against the enforcement of any requirement of the payment of a poll tax as a precondition to voting, or substitute thereof enacted after November 1, 1964, as will be necessary to implement the declaration of subsection (a) and the purposes of this section. . . .

Section 11

(a) No person acting under color of law shall fail or refuse to permit any person to vote who is entitled to vote under any provision of this Act or is otherwise qualified to vote, or willfully fail or refuse to tabulate, count, and report such person's vote.

(b) No person, whether acting under color of law or otherwise, shall intimidate, threaten, or coerce, or attempt to intimidate, threaten, or coerce any person for voting or attempting to vote, or intimidate, threaten, or coerce, or attempt to intimidate, threaten, or coerce any person for urging or aiding any person to vote or attempt to vote, or intimidate, threaten, or coerce any person for exercising any powers or duties under section 3 (a), 6, 8, 9, 10, or 12 (e).

Institution and Location	Year Founded	Land-Grant, Public, or Church Affiliated Denomination	Institution and Location	Year Founded	Land-Grant, Public, or Church Affiliated Denomination
Alabama A&M University, Normal, Alabama	1875	Land-grant	Fisk University, Nashville, Tennessee	1866	United Church of Christ
Alabama State University, Montgomery, Alabama	1867	Public	Florida A&M University, Tallahassee, Florida	1887	Land-grant
Albany State University, Albany, Georgia	1903	Public	Florida Memorial College, Miami, Florida	1879	Baptist
Alcorn State University, Lorman, Mississippi	1871	Land-grant	Fort Valley State College, Fort Valley, Georgia	1895	Land-grant
Allen University, Columbia, South Carolina	1870	AME	Grambling State University, Grambling, Louisiana	1901	Public
Arkansas Baptist College, Little Rock, Arkansas	1884	Baptist	Hampton University, Hampton, Virginia	1868	Private
Barber-Scotia College, Concord, North Carolina	1904	Presbyterian	Harris-Stowe State College, St. Louis, Missouri	1857	Public
Benedict College, Columbia, South Carolina	1870	Baptist	Howard University, Washington, DC	1867	Public
Bennett College, Greensboro, North Carolina	1873	United Methodist	Huston-Tillotson College, Austin, Texas	1952	United Church of Christ/ United Methodist
Bethune-Cookman College, Daytona Beach, Florida	1904	United Methodist	Jackson State University, Jackson, Mississippi	1877	Public
Bluefield State College, Bluefield, West Virginia	1895	Public	Jarvis Christian College, Hawkins, Texas	1913	Disciple of Christ Christian Church
Bowie State University, Bowie, Maryland	1865	Public	Johnson C. Smith University, Charlotte, North Carolina	1867	Presbyterian
Central State University, Wilberforce, Ohio	1887	Public	Kentucky State University, Frankfort, Kentucky	1886	Land-grant
Cheyney University, Cheyney, Pennsylvania	1837	Public	Knoxville College, Knoxville, Tennessee	1875	Presbyterian
Claflin College, Orangeburg, South Carolina	1869	United Methodist	Lane College, Jackson, Tennessee	1882	Christian Methodist Episcopal
Clark Atlanta University, Atlanta, Georgia	1988	United Methodist	Langston University, Langston, Oklahoma	1897	Land-grant
Concordia College, Selma, Alabama	1922	Lutheran	LeMoyne-Owen College, Memphis, Tennessee	1870	United Church of Christ
Coppin State University, Baltimore, Maryland	1900	Public	Lincoln University, Jefferson City, Missouri	1866	Land-grant
Delaware State University, Dover, Delaware	1891	Land-grant	Lincoln University, Lincoln, Pennsylvania	1854	Public
Dillard University, New Orleans, Louisiana	1930	Congregational/ United Methodist	Livingstone College, Salisbury, North Carolina	1879	AME
Edward Waters College, Jacksonville, Florida	1866	AME	Miles College, Birmingham, Alabama	1908	Christian Methodist Episcopal
Elizabeth City State University, Elizabeth City, North Carolina	1891	Public	Mississippi Valley State University, Ita Bena, Mississippi	1946	Public
Fayetteville State University, Fayetteville, North Carolina	1867	Public			

Institution and Location	Year Founded	Land-Grant, Public, or Church Affiliated Denomination	Institution and Location	Year Founded	Land-Grant, Public, or Church Affiliated Denomination
Morehouse College, Atlanta, Georgia	1867	Baptist	Southwestern Christian College, Terrell, Texas	1949	Church of Christ
Morgan State University, Baltimore, Maryland	1867	Public	Spelman College, Atlanta, Georgia	1876	Presbyterian
Morris Brown College, Atlanta, Georgia	1881	AME	Stillman College, Tuscaloosa, Alabama	1876	Presbyterian
Morris College, Sumter, South Carolina	1908	Baptist	Talladega College, Talladega, Alabama	1867	United Church of Christ
Norfolk State University, Norfolk, Virginia	1935	Public	Tennessee State University, Nashville, Tennessee	1912	Land-grant
North Carolina A&T St. U, Greensboro, North Carolina	1892	Land-grant	Texas College, Tyler, Texas	1894	Christian Methodist Episcopal
North Carolina Central University, Durham, North Carolina	1909	Public	Texas Southern University, Houston, Texas	1947	Public
Oakwood College, Huntsville, Alabama	1896	Seventh Day Adventist	Tougaloo College, Tougaloo, Mississippi	1869	United Church of Christ/United Missionary Society
Paine College, Augusta, Georgia	1882	United Methodist	Tuskegee University, Tuskegee Institute, Alabama	1881	Land-grant
Paul Quinn College, Dallas, Texas	1872	AME	University of Arkansas at Pine Bluff, Pine Bluff, Arkansas	1873	Land-grant
Philander Smith College, Little Rock, Arkansas	1877	United Methodist	University of the District of Columbia, Washington, DC	1977	Public
Prairie View A&M University, Prairie View, Texas	1878	Land-grant	University of Maryland, Eastern Shore, Princess Anne, Maryland	1886	Land-grant
Rust College, Holly Springs, Mississippi	1866	United Methodist	University of the Virgin Islands, St. Thomas, United States Virgin Islands	1962	Public
Saint Augustine's College, Raleigh, North Carolina	1867	Episcopal	Virginia State University, Petersburg, Virginia	1882	Land-grant
Saint Paul's College, Lawrenceville, Virginia	1888	Episcopal	Virginia Union University, Richmond, Virginia	1865	Baptist
Savannah State College, Savannah, Georgia	1890	Public	Voorhees College, Denmark, South Carolina	1897	Episcopal
Selma University, Selma, Alabama	1878	Baptist	West Virginia State College, Institute, West Virginia	1891	Public
Shaw University, Raleigh, North Carolina	1865	Baptist	Wilberforce University, Wilberforce, Ohio	1856	AME
Sojourner-Douglass College, Baltimore, Maryland	1980	Private	Wiley College, Marshall, Texas	1873	United Methodist
South Carolina State University, Orangeburg, South Carolina	1896	Land-grant	Winston-Salem State University, Winston-Salem, North Carolina	1892	Public
Southern University and A&M College, Baton Rouge, Louisiana	1880	Land-grant	Xavier University of New Orleans, New Orleans, Louisiana	1925	Roman Catholic
Southern University at New Orleans, New Orleans, Louisiana	1956	Public			

1. George Washington (1789)
   John Adams (1789)

2. John Adams (1797)
   Thomas Jefferson (1797)

3. Thomas Jefferson (1801)
   Aaron Burr (1801)
   George Clinton (1805)

4. James Madison (1809)
   George Clinton (1809)
   Elbridge Gerry (1813)

5. James Monroe (1817)
   Daniel D. Thompkins (1817)

6. John Quincy Adams (1825)
   John C. Calhoun (1825)

7. Andrew Jackson (1829)
   John C. Calhoun (1829)
   Martin Van Buren (1833)

8. Martin Van Buren (1837)
   Richard M. Johnson (1837)

9. William H. Harrison (1841)
   John Tyler (1841)

10. John Tyler (1841)

11. James K. Polk (1845)
    George M. Dallas (1845)

12. Zachary Taylor (1849)
    Millard Fillmore (1849)

13. Millard Fillmore (1850)

14. Franklin Pierce (1853)
    William R. King (1853)

15. James Buchanan (1857)
    John C. Breckinridge (1857)

16. Abraham Lincoln (1861)
    Hannibal Hamlin (1861)
    Andrew Johnson (1865)

17. Andrew Johnson (1865)

18. Ulysses S. Grant (1869)
    Schuyler Colfax (1869)
    Henry Wilson (1873)

19. Rutherford B. Hayes (1877)
    William A. Wheeler (1877)

20. James A. Garfield (1881)
    Chester A. Arthur (1881)

21. Chester A. Arthur (1881)

22. Grover Cleveland (1885)
    T. A. Hendricks (1885)

23. Benjamin Harrison (1889)
    Levi P. Morgan (1889)

24. Grover Cleveland (1893)
    Adlai E. Stevenson (1893)

25. William McKinley (1897)
    Garret A. Hobart (1897)
    Theodore Roosevelt (1901)

26. Theodore Roosevelt (1901)
    Charles Fairbanks (1905)

27. William H. Taft (1909)
    James S. Sherman (1909)

28. Woodrow Wilson (1913)
    Thomas R. Marshall (1913)

29. Warren G. Harding (1921)
    Calvin Coolidge (1921)

30. Calvin Coolidge (1923)
    Charles G. Dawes (1925)

31. Herbert C. Hoover (1929)
    Charles Curtis (1929)

32. Franklin D. Roosevelt (1933)
    John Nance Garner (1933)
    Henry A. Wallace (1941)
    Harry S. Truman (1945)

33. Harry S. Truman (1945)
    Alben W. Barkley (1949)

34. Dwight D. Eisenhower (1953)
    Richard M. Nixon (1953)

35. John F. Kennedy (1961)
    Lyndon B. Johnson (1961)

36. Lyndon B. Johnson (1963)
    Hubert H. Humphrey (1965)

37. Richard M. Nixon (1969)
    Spiro T. Agnew (1969)
    Gerald R. Ford (1973)

38. Gerald R. Ford (1974)
    Nelson A. Rockefeller (1974)

39. James E. Carter Jr. (1977)
    Walter F. Mondale (1977)

40. Ronald W. Reagan (1981)
    George H. Bush (1981)

41. George H. Bush (1989)
    James D. Quayle III (1989)

42. William J. Clinton (1993)
    Albert Gore (1993)

Name*	Years on Court	Appointing President
JOHN JAY	1789–1795	Washington
James Wilson	1789–1798	Washington
John Rutledge	1790–1791	Washington
William Cushing	1790–1810	Washington
John Blair	1790–1796	Washington
James Iredell	1790–1799	Washington
Thomas Jefferson	1792–1793	Washington
William Paterson	1793–1806	Washington
JOHN RUTLEDGE†	1795	Washington
Samuel Chase	1796–1811	Washington
OLIVER ELLSWORTH	1796–1800	Washington
Bushrod Washington	1799–1829	J. Adams
Alfred Moore	1800–1804	J. Adams
JOHN MARSHALL	1801–1835	J. Adams
William Johnson	1804–1834	Jefferson
Brockholst Livingston	1807–1823	Jefferson
Thomas Todd	1807–1826	Jefferson
Gabriel Duvall	1811–1835	Madison
Joseph Story	1812–1845	Madison
Smith Thompson	1823–1843	Monroe
Robert Trimble	1826–1828	J. Q. Adams
John McLean	1830–1861	Jackson
Henry Baldwin	1830–1844	Jackson
James M. Wayne	1835–1867	Jackson
ROGER B. TANEY	1836–1864	Jackson
Philip P. Barbour	1836–1841	Jackson
John Cartron	1837–1865	Van Buren
John McKinley	1838–1852	Van Buren
Peter V. Daniel	1842–1860	Van Buren
Samuel Nelson	1845–1872	Tyler
Levi Woodbury	1845–1851	Polk
Robert C. Grier	1846–1870	Polk
Benjamin R. Curtis	1851–1857	Fillmore
John A. Campbell	1853–1861	Pierce
Nathan Clifford	1858–1881	Buchanan
Noah H. Swayne	1862–1881	Lincoln
Samuel F. Miller	1862–1890	Lincoln
David Davis	1862–1877	Lincoln
Stephen J. Field	1863–1897	Lincoln
SALMON P. CHASE	1864–1873	Lincoln
William Strong	1870–1880	Grant
Joseph P. Bradley	1870–1892	Grant
Ward Hunt	1873–1882	Grant
MORRISON R. WAITE	1874–1888	Grant
John M. Harlan	1877–1911	Hayes

*Capital letters designate Chief Justices
†Never confirmed by the Senate as Chief Justice

SUPREME COURT JUSTICES *Continued*

Name	Years on Court	Appointing President
William B. Woods	1881–1887	Hayes
Stanley Matthews	1881–1889	Garfield
Horace Gray	1882–1902	Arthur
Samuel Blatchford	1882–1893	Arthur
Lucious Q. C. Lamar	1888–1893	Cleveland
MELVILLE W. FULLER	1888–1910	Cleveland
David J. Brewer	1890–1910	B. Harrison
Henry B. Brown	1891–1906	B. Harrison
George Shiras, Jr.	1892–1903	B. Harrison
Howel E. Jackson	1893–1895	B. Harrison
Edward D. White	1894–1910	Cleveland
Rufus W. Peckman	1896–1909	Cleveland
Joseph McKenna	1898–1925	McKinley
Oliver W. Holmes	1902–1932	T. Roosevelt
William R. Day	1903–1922	T. Roosevelt
William H. Moody	1906–1910	T. Roosevelt
Horace H. Lurton	1910–1914	Taft
Charles E. Hughes	1910–1916	Taft
EDWARD D. WHITE	1910–1921	Taft
Willis Van Devanter	1911–1937	Taft
Joseph R. Lamar	1911–1916	Taft
Mahlon Pitney	1912–1922	Taft
James C. McReynolds	1914–1941	Wilson
Louis D. Brandeis	1916–1939	Wilson
John H. Clarke	1916–1922	Wilson
WILLIAM H. TAFT	1921–1930	Harding
George Sutherland	1922–1938	Harding
Pierce Butler	1923–1939	Harding
Edward T. Sanford	1923–1930	Harding
Harlan F. Stone	1925–1941	Coolidge
CHARLES E. HUGHES	1930–1941	Hoover
Owen J. Roberts	1930–1945	Hoover
Benjamin N. Cardozo	1932–1938	Hoover
Hugo L. Black	1937–1971	F. Roosevelt
Stanley F. Reed	1938–1957	F. Roosevelt
Felix Frankfurter	1939–1962	F. Roosevelt
William O. Douglas	1939–1975	F. Roosevelt
Frank Murphy	1940–1949	F. Roosevelt
HARLAN F. STONE	1941–1946	F. Roosevelt
James F. Brynes	1941–1942	F. Roosevelt
Robert H. Jackson	1941–1954	F. Roosevelt
Wiley B. Rutledge	1943–1949	F. Roosevelt
Harold H. Burton	1945–1958	Truman
FREDERICK M. VINSON	1946–1953	Truman
Tom C. Clark	1949–1967	Truman
Sherman Minton	1949–1956	Truman
EARL WARREN	1953–1969	Eisenhower

SUPREME COURT JUSTICES *Continued*

Name	Years on Court	Appointing President
John Marshall Harlan	1955–1971	Eisenhower
William J. Brennan, Jr.	1956–1990	Eisenhower
Charles E. Whittaker	1957–1962	Eisenhower
Potter Stewart	1958–1981	Eisenhower
Byron R. White	1962–1993	Kennedy
Arthur J. Goldberg	1962–1965	Kennedy
Abe Fortas	1965–1970	L. Johnson
Thurgood Marshall	1967–1991	L. Johnson
WARREN E. BURGER	1969–1986	Nixon
Harry A. Blackmun	1970–1994	Nixon
Lewis F. Powell, Jr.	1971–1987	Nixon
William H. Rehnquist	1971–1986	Nixon
John Paul Stevens	1975–	Ford
Sandra Day O'Connor	1981–	Reagan
WILLIAM H. REHNQUIST	1986–	Reagan
Antonin Scalia	1986–	Reagan
Anthony Kennedy	1988–	Reagan
David Souter	1990–	Bush
Clarence Thomas	1991–	Bush
Ruth Bader Ginsburg	1993–	Clinton
Stephen Breyer	1994–	Clinton

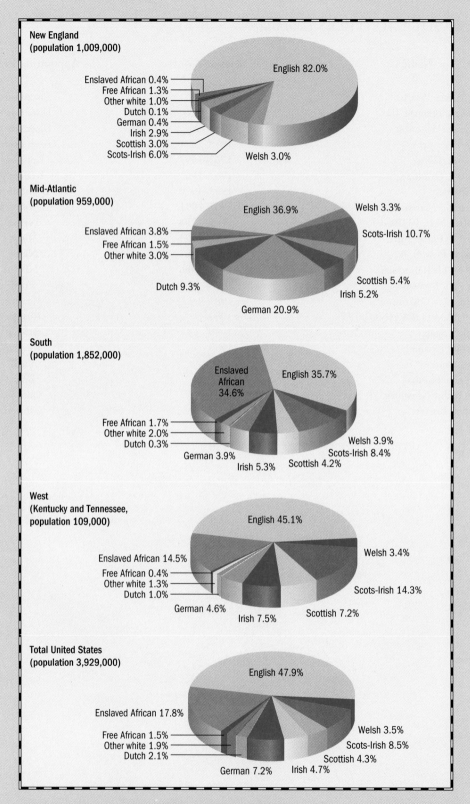

Ethnic composition of the United States in 1790, by Region

ADMISSION OF STATES INTO THE UNION

State	Slave Status (before 1860)	Date of Admission	State	Slave Status (before 1860)	Date of Admission
1. Delaware	Slave	December 7, 1787	26. Michigan	Free	January 26, 1837
2. Pennsylvania	Free	December 12, 1787	27. Florida	Slave	March 3, 1845
3. New Jersey	Free	December 18, 1787	28. Texas	Slave	December 29, 1845
4. Georgia	Slave	January 2, 1788	29. Iowa	Free	December 28, 1846
5. Connecticut	Free	January 9, 1788	30. Wisconsin	Free	May 29, 1848
6. Massachusetts	Free	February 6, 1788	31. California	Free	September 9, 1850
7. Maryland	Slave	April 28, 1788	32. Minnesota	Free	May 11, 1858
8. South Carolina	Slave	May 23, 1788	33. Oregon	Free	February 14, 1859
9. New Hampshire	Free	June 21, 1788	34. Kansas	Free	January 29, 1861
10. Virginia	Slave	June 25, 1788	35. West Virginia	NA	June 20, 1863
11. New York	Free	July 26, 1788	36. Nevada	NA	October 31, 1864
12. North Carolina	Slave	November 21, 1789	37. Nebraska	NA	March 1, 1867
13. Rhode Island	Free	May 29, 1790	38. Colorado	NA	August 1, 1876
14. Vermont	Free	March 4, 1791	39. North Dakota	NA	November 2, 1889
15. Kentucky	Slave	June 1, 1792	40. South Dakota	NA	November 2, 1889
16. Tennessee	Slave	June 1, 1796	41. Montana	NA	November 8, 1889
17. Ohio	Free	March 1, 1803	42. Washington	NA	November 11, 1889
18. Louisiana	Slave	April 30, 1812	43. Idaho	NA	July 3, 1890
19. Indiana	Free	December 11, 1816	44. Wyoming	NA	July 10, 1890
20. Mississippi	Slave	December 10, 1817	45. Utah	NA	January 4, 1896
21. Illinois	Free	December 3, 1818	46. Oklahoma	NA	November 16, 1907
22. Alabama	Slave	December 14, 1819	47. New Mexico	NA	January 6, 1912
23. Maine	Free	March 15, 1820	48. Arizona	NA	February 14, 1912
24. Missouri	Slave	August 10, 1821	49. Alaska	NA	January 3, 1959
25. Arkansas	Slave	June 15, 1836	50. Hawaii	NA	August 21, 1959

RACIAL COMPOSITION OF THE POPULATION
(IN THOUSANDS)

Year	White	African American	Indian	Hispanic	Asian	Year	White	African American	Indian	Hispanic	Asian
1790	3,172	757	(NA)	(NA)	(NA)	1930	110,287	11,891	(NA)	(NA)	(NA)
1800	4,306	1,002	(NA)	(NA)	(NA)	1940	118,215	12,866	(NA)	(NA)	(NA)
1820	7,867	1,772	(NA)	(NA)	(NA)	1950	134,942	15,042	(NA)	(NA)	(NA)
1840	14,196	2,874	(NA)	(NA)	(NA)	1960	158,832	18,872	(NA)	(NA)	(NA)
1860	26,923	4,442	(NA)	(NA)	(NA)	1970	178,098	22,581	(NA)	(NA)	(NA)
1880	43,403	6,581	(NA)	(NA)	(NA)	1980	194,713	26,683	1,420	14,609	3,729
1900	66,809	8,834	(NA)	(NA)	(NA)	1990	205,710	30,486	2,065	22,354	7,458
1910	81,732	9,828	(NA)	(NA)	(NA)	1996	219,749	30,503	2,288	28,269	9,743
1920	94,821	10,463	(NA)	(NA)	(NA)						

Source: U.S. Bureau of the Census, *U.S. Census of Population: 1940*, vol. II, part 1, and vol. IV, part 1; *1950*, vol. II, part 1; *1960*, vol. I, part 1; *1970*, vol. I, part B; and *Current Population Reports*, P25-1095 and P25-1104; *Statistical Abstract of the United States* (1997); and unpublished data.

African Americans as a Percentage of Total Population, by County, 1890. From *Historical Atlas of The United States,* National Geographic Society, 1993, p. 56.

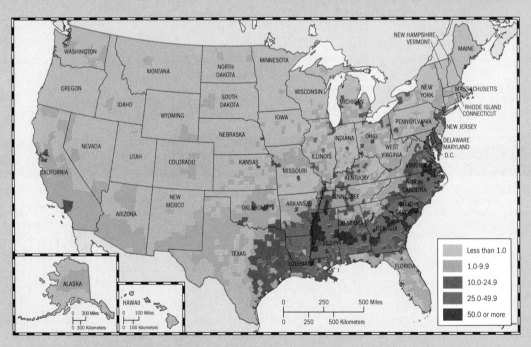

African Americans as a Percentage of Total Population, by County, 1980. From *Historical Atlas of The United States,* National Geographic Society, 1993, p. 66.

PHOTO AND TEXT CREDITS

Chapter 1: Photos: British Museum, London/Bridgeman Art Library, London/ SuperStock, Inc., 2; John Reader/Science Photo Library, Cincinnati Art Museum, Photo Researchers, Inc., 5; Timothy Kendall, 8; Courtesy of the Library of Congress, 12; Figure of woman and children. Yoruba peoples, Nigeria. Wood, pigment, 38.5 cm (15¼ in). Museum purchase, 85-1-11. Photograph by Franko Khoury. National Museum of African Art, Franko Khoury, National Museum of African Art/Smithsonian Institution, 14; "King Mounted With Attendants," Bronze, H. 19½, W. 16½ in. (49.5 cm). The Metropolitan Museum of Art, The Michael C. Rockefeller Memorial Collection, Gift of Nelson A. Rockefeller, 1978. (1978.412.309), 16; Courtesy of the Library of Congress, 17; Christie's Images, Ltd., 1999, 19. Text: Excerpt from Chapter XXVIII from *Omeros* by Derek Walcott. Copyright © by Derek Walcott. Reprinted by permission of Farrar, Strauss, and Giroux, L.L.C., 25; Figure 2-1: Adapted from *Africa and Africans in the Making of the Atlantic World, 1400–1680* by John Thornton, © 1992. Reprinted with the permission of Cambridge University Press, 27; Table 2-1: Adapted from Philip D. Curtin, *The Atlantic Slave Trade: A Census*, © 1969. Reprinted by permission of The University of Wisconsin Press, 28.

Chapter 2: Photos: The Granger Collection, New York, 24; The Granger Collection, New York, 28; Culver Pictures, Inc., 32; *Portrait of a Negro Man, Olaudah Equiano*, 1780s (previously attributed to Joshua Reynolds) by English School (18th c.), Royal Albert Museum, Exeter, Devon, UK/Bridgeman Art Library, London/New York, The Bridgeman Art Library International, 33; Courtesy of the Library of Congress, 34; "The Fortunate Slave", An Illustration of African Slavery in the early eighteenth century by Douglas Grant (1968). From "Some Memoirs of the Life of Job," by Thomas Bluett 1734. Photo by Robert D. Rubic/Precision Chromes, Inc., The New York Public Library, Research Libraries, 36; Courtesy of the Library of Congress, 40; (left) Courtesy of the National Library of Jamaica, 41; (right) Courtesy of the National Library of Jamaica, 41.

Chapter 3: Photos: The Library Company of Philadelphia, 46; The South Carolina Historical Society, 49; Courtesy of The Library of Congress, 51; American Antiquarian Society, 58; Thomas Coram, "View of Mulberry Street," (House and Street), oil on paper, 10 × 17.6 cm, Gibbes Museum of Art, Carolina Art Association, 59; Blue Ridge Institutes & Museum/Blue Ridge Heritage Archive of Ferrum College, Ferrum, Virginia, Heritage Archive, 63; Stock Montage, Inc./Historical Pictures Collection, 64.

Chapter 4: Photos: Corbis, 70; Corbis, 74; Library of Congress, 78; The Maryland Historical Society, 80; University of Virginia Library, 81; John Trumbull, "The Death of General Warren at the Battle of Bunker's Hill," June 17, 1775. Oil on canvas. Signed lower center: "Jn. Trumbull/1786." unframed: 63.5 × 86.4 cm (25 × 34 in). Yale University Art Gallery. Trumbull Collection, 82; Anne S. K. Brown Military Collection, Brown University Library, 84.

Chapter 5: Photos: The Library Company of Philadelphia, 92; Courtesy Massachusetts Historical Society, Boston, Massachusetts Historical Society, 96; John Lewis Krimmel, "Negroes in Front of the Bank of Pennsylvania" 1821. Watercolor on paper. H. 9³⁄₁₆, W. 6¹¹⁄₁₆ in. The Metropolitan Museum of Art, Rogers Fund, 1942. (42.95.16), 102; The Metropolitan Museum of Art, 102; Courtesy of the Library of Congress, 103; Moorland-Spingam Research Center, 105; The Historical Society of Pennsylvania, 108; Stock Montage, Inc./Historical Pictures Collection, 110.

Chapter 6: Photos: The Library of Congress, 118; The New York Public Library, Research Libraries, 120; Photographs and Prints Division, Schomburg Center for Research in Black Culture, The New York Public Library. Astor, Lenox, and Tilden Foundations, 125; The Granger Collection, New York, 127; The State, 128; Courtesy of the Library of Congress, 129; UPI/Corbis, 131; The Historic New Orleans Collection, 136. Text: Table 6-1: From *Slaves Without Masters*, © 1974 by Ira Berlin. Reproduced by permission of The New Press, 121; Maps 6-1 and 6-2: Reprinted by permission of Louisiana State University Press from *Atlas of Antebellum Southern Agriculture* by Sam Bowers Hilliard, © 1990 by Louisiana State University Press, 122–123.

Town of the Photographer. Bonham, Texas. nitrate negative, 1910–1915. LC.S611.790 The Erwin E. Smith Collection of the Library of Congress on deposit at the Amon Carter Museum, Fort Worth, Texas, 354.

Chapter 16: Photos: Courtesy of the Library of Congress, 360; Brown Brothers, 364; Photographs and Print Division, Schomburg Center for Research in Black Culture, The New York Public Library, Astor, Lenox and Tilden Foundations, 367; Schomburg Center for Research in Black Culture, 369; Courtesy of the Library of Congress, 372; Schomburg Center for Research in Black Culture, 373; Courtesy of the Library of Congress, 377; Stock Montage, Inc./ Historical Pictures Collection, 386. Text: Voices, page 384, "A Migrant to the North Writes Home:" Leslie H. Fishel, Jr. and Benjamin Quarles, *The Negro: A Documentary History* (Glenview, IL: Scott, Foresman Co., 1967) pp. 398–399, and Winthrop D. Jordan and Leon F. Litwack, *The United States*, 6/e. (Englewood Cliffs, NJ: Prentice Hall, 1987), p. 601. Jordon and Litwack cite Emmett J. Scott, ed., "Letters of Negro Migrants of 1916–1918," *Journal of Negro History*, IV (July 1919), pp. 290–340. Map 16–3 reprinted by permission, 387.

Chapter 17: Photos: U.N.I.A. Protest Parade, 1924 by James VanDerZee. ©Donna Mussenden VanDerZee, 392; The Granger Collection, 395; The Granger Collection, 398; New York Daily News, 401; Chicago Historical Society, R. D. Jones, ICHi-22642, 405; Yale Collection of American Literature, Beinecke Rare Book and Manuscript Library, 407; Frank Driggs Collection, 410; Frank Driggs Collection, 411. Text: Langston Hughes. "I, Too" from *Collected Poems* by Langston Hughes. Copyright © 1994 by the Estate of Langston Hughes. Reprinted by permission of Alfred A. Knopf, a Division of Random House, Inc. Electronic rights by permission of Harold Ober Associates Incorporated, 393; Langston Hughes. "Red Silk Stockings" from *Collected Poems* by Langston Hughes. Copyright © 1994 by the Estate of Langston Hughes. Reprinted by permission of Alfred A. Knopf, a Division of Random House, Inc. Electronic rights by permission of Harold Ober Associates Incorporated, 408.

Chapter 18: Photos: Margaret Bourke-White/LIFE Magazine ©TIME Inc., 418; Courtesy of the Library of Congress, 421; Doris Ulmann, Schomburg Center for Research in Black Culture, 422; UPI/Corbis, 425; Cor-

bis, 428; Scurlock Studios, 429; Federal Theatre Archive, Library of Congress, Washington, DC, 431; courtesy Mary McLeod Bethune Council House National Historic Site, Washington, DC, 433; Corbis, 436. Text: Table 18–1, Gunnar Myrdal, et al. (1944). Table from *An American Dilemma*. Reprinted by permission of HarperCollins Publishers, 421; Excerpt of letter from a sharecropper to the National Association for the Advancement of Colored People, June 21, 1934. The publishers wish to thank The National Association for the Advancement of Colored People for the use of this work., 426; Ralph Ellison. Excerpt from "Perspective of Literature," from *Collected Essays of Ralph Ellison*. Copyright © 1967 by Ralph Ellison. Reprinted by permission of Modern Library, a Division of Random House, Inc., 438.

Chapter 19: Photos: Corbis, 444; Frank Driggs Collection, 449; Archive Photos, 451; 452; Reiss, Winold. Portrait of Langston Hughes (1902–1967 Poet) ©1925. National Portrait Gallery, Washington, DC, USA, Art Resource, NY, 455; Everett Collection, Inc., 457; Archive Photos, 458; Print and Picture Collection, The Free Library of Philadelphia, 460; Archive Photos, 463; AP/Wide World Photos, 464. Text: Margaret Walker. Excerpt from "On Being Female, Black, and Free," from *On Being Female, Black, and Free: Essays by Margaret Walker, 1932–1992*, edited by Maryemma Graham, (1997). University of Tennessee Press. Used with permission., 453; Langston Hughes. "The Negro Speaks of Rivers," from *Collected Poems* by Langston Hughes. Copyright © 1994 by the Estate of Langston Hughes. Reprinted by permission of Alfred A. Knopf, a Division of Random House, Inc. Electronic rights by permission of Harold Ober Associates Incorporated., 455; Lewis Allan. "Strange Fruit." © 1939 (Renewed) by Music Sales Corporation and Carlin America, Inc. All rights outside the U.S. controlled by Edward B. Marks Music Company. All rights in the U.S. controlled by Music Sales Corporation. Used by permission. All rights reserved., 459.

Chapter 20: Photos: Courtesy of the Library of Congress, 470; Courtesy of the Library of Congress, 474; Courtesy of the Library of Congress, 476; NAACP Collection/Library of Congress, 480; National Archives, 482; Burns/New York Times Co., Archive Photos, 485; UPI/Corbis, 490; UPI/Corbis, 491; AP/Wide World Photos, 492. Text: William H. Hastie. Excerpt from "Why I Resigned," *Chicago Defender*, February 6, 1943. Reprinted by permission of the *Chicago Defender*., 478.

Chapter 21: Photos: Archive Photos, 500; UPI/Corbis, 503; AP/Wide World Photos, 507; AP/Wide World Photos, 510; John G. Moebes, Greensboro News & Record, 511; UPI/Corbis, 512; Steve Schapiro/Black Star, 513; Bill Hudson/AP/Wide World Photos, 518; George Ballis/Take Stock-Images of Change, 522; ©1976, Matt Herron/Take Stock–Images of Change, 523. Text: Martin Luther King, Jr. Excerpts of Birmingham bus boycott speech given on December 5, 1955. Reprinted by arrangement with The Heirs to the Estate of Martin Luther King, Jr., c/o Writers House, Inc. as agents for the proprietor. Copyright 1955 by Martin Luther King, Jr., copyright renewed 1983 by Coretta Scott King. Electronic permission of Intellectual Properties Management, Atlanta, GA, 501 and 506; Letter from Jo Ann Robinson, President of the Women's Political Council to the Mayor of Montgomery, Alabama, May 21, 1954. From *Daybreak of Freedom: The Montgomery Bus Boycott* by Stewart Burns. Copyright © 1997 by The University of North Carolina. Used by permission of the publisher., 505; Bernice Johnson Reagon. Excerpt from "We'll Never Turn Back," from *Everybody Says Freedom: A History of the Civil Rights Movement in Songs and Pictures*, by Pete Seeger and Bob Reiser. Copyright © 1989 by Pete Seeger and Bob Reiser. Reprinted by permission of W. W. Norton and Company, Inc. Electronic rights by permission of Bob Reiser., 516; Martin Luther King, Jr. Excerpts of "I have a dream. . ." speech given on August 28, 1963. Reprinted by arrangement with The Heirs to the Estate of Martin Luther King, Jr., c/o Writers House, Inc. as agents for the proprietor. Copyright 1963 by Martin Luther King, Jr., copyright renewed 1991 by Coretta Scott King. Licensor represents and warrants that it is the exclusive licensing agent of the Estate of Martin Luther King, Jr., Inc., and that it possesses the right and power to license the copyrights, trademarks, rights of publicity, and other intellectual property rights belonging to the Estate of Martin Luther King, Jr., Inc. Licensor grants licensee permission to use the licensed property in accordance with the terms of this Agreement, but Licensor makes no representations or warranties of any kind with respect to the licensed property and expressly disclaims any warranties of fitness for a particular purpose, any warranty or representation concerning the copyright status of the licensed property, and any other implied warranties with respect to the licensed property. Electronic rights by permission of Intellectual Properties Management, Atlanta, Georgia., 519.

Chapter 22: Photos: Leonard Freed/Magnum Photos, Inc., 530; John Launois, Black Star, 533; AP/Wide World Photos, 537; Archive Photos, 539; Chillysmith, Inc., 542; Frank Johnston/Black Star, 543; Corbis, 545; By permission of author/subject, Nikki Giovanni, 549; United States Senate, 555; AP/Wide World Photos, 556. Text: Wallace Terry. Excerpt, "Captain Joseph B. Anderson, Jr." from *Bloods* by Wallace Terry. Copyright © 1984 by Wallace Terry. Reprinted by permission of Random House, Inc., 541.

Chapter 23: Photos: Paul Conklin/PhotoEdit, 562; Steve Green/AP Wide World Photos, 565; Paul Conklin/PhotoEdit, 568; Damian Dovarganes/AP/Wide World Photos, 571; Democratic National Committee, 572; Rob Crandall/Stock Boston, 575; Chrvstvna Czajkowsky/AP/Wide World Photos, 579; Maria Mulas/Maria Mulas Photografa, 580; James Nubile/The Image Works, 583. Text: Table 23–2: Andrew Hacker. Table excerpted and adapted from *Two Nations: Black and White, Separate, Hostile, Unequal*. Copyright © 1995 by Andrew Hacker. Reprinted by permission of Andrew Hacker, 566; (1991). "African American Women In Defense of Ourselves," advertisement in *New York Times*, November 17, 1991, p. 53, 569; Maxine Waters. Speech given on October 25, 1997, at the Million Woman March in Philadelphia, PA. Reprinted by permission of the Million Woman March National Organization., 584.

Color Insert I: *The Old Plantation*, Abby Aldrich Rockefeller Folk Art Center, Williamsburg, VA; Figure Holding Vessel, Abby Aldrich Rockefeller Folk Art Center, Williamsburg, VA; Yoruba Offering Bowl from Ekiti Efon-Alaye, (BON46967) Bonhams, London, UK/Bridgeman Art Library, London/New York; Sweetgrass basket, The Charleston Museum, Charleston, South Carolina; Two Afro-Carolinian face vessels, National Museum of American History/Smithsonian Institution; Thomas Gross, "Chest-on-Chest" 1805-1810, Mahogany, poplar, pine. 82 × 43¼ × 22⅛ inches. Philadelphia Museum of Art, gift of Mrs. Leslie Legum. 1983-167-1a,b, Philadelphia Museum of Art; Bible scenes quilt, The Granger Collection; Robert S. Duncanson, 1821-1872. "Blue Hole, Little Miami River"/Cincinnati Art Museum, Gift of Norbert Heeran and Arthur Helbig; Self-portrait by Julien Hudson, from the collection of the Louisiana State Museum; Portrait of Christiana Carteaux Bannister, Bannister Health and Rehabilitation Center, Providence, RI; Edmondia Lewis, "Hagar in the Wilderness" 1875. Carved marble. 52⅝ × 15¼ × 17 inches (133.6 × 38.8 × 43.4 cm). The National

Museum of American Art, Washington DC/Art Resource, NY. Gift of Delta Sigma Theta Sorority, Inc. 1983.9.178; Henry Ossawa Tanner, "The Banjo Lesson" 1893. Oil on canvas. 49″ × 35½″. Hampton University Museum, Hampton, Virginia. Courtesy of The Charleston Museum, Charleston, South Carolina.

Color Insert II: *Building More Stately Mansions*, Aaron Douglas (1944) Oil on canvas 58″ × 42″, Carl Van Vechten Gallery of Fine Arts, Fisk University. *Barbecue*, by Archibald Motley, Jr., oil on canvas, 36¼″ × 40⅛″, 1934, The Howard University Gallery of Art, Jarvis Grant/ Howard University. August Savage, *Gamin*, 1929, plaster, 9¼″ × 6″ × 3½″. Photo Manu Sassoonian, Schomburg Center for Research in Black Culture, Art & Artifacts Division, The New York Public Library, Astor, Lenox and Tilden Foundations. Charles White, *The Contribution of the Negro to Democracy in America*. 1043.Egg tempera (fresco secc), 11′9″ × 17′3″. Hampton University Museum, Hampton, Virginia. Horace Pippin (1888–1946), *Mr. Prejudice*, 1943, oil on canvas, 18 × 14 inches. Philadelphia Museum of Art. Gift of Dr. and Mrs. Matthew T. Moore. Photo by Graydon Wood. Selma Burke, *Jim*, 1935, plaster, 13½″ × 8″ × 9½″. Photo Manu Sassoonian, Schomburg Center for Research in Black Culture, Art & Artifacts Division, The New York Public Library, Astor, Lenox and Tilden Foundations. William H. Johnson, *Lamentation or Descent from the Cross*, ca. 1944. National Museum of American Art, Washington, DC/Art Resource, NY. Jacob Lawrence, *The Migration of the Negro Panel No. 1*, 1940–1941. Tempera on masonite 12 × 18 in. (30.5 × 45.7 cm). Acquired 1942. The Phillips Collection, Washington, DC. Romare Bearden, *Watching the Trains Go By*, 1964. Photograph by Sharon Goodman. © Romare Bearden Foundation/Licensed by VAGA, New York, NY. Elizabeth Catlett, *Malcolm X Speaks for Us*, 1969. Lithograph, 95 × 70 cm. © Elizabeth Catlett/ Licensed by VAGA, New York, NY. Faith Ringgold *Tar Beach*, 1988, 74 × 69 in., acrylic pieced and printed fabric. Collection: Solomon R. Guggenheim Museum ©Faith Ringgold Inc. Steve Prince, *Noble Sounds*, Darlene Clark Hine.

INDEX

A

Abbott, Robert S., 385–386
Abdul-Jabbar, Kareem, 543
Abernathy, Ralph, 507; Albany movement, 516; Birmingham confrontation, 517–518; Freedom Rides, 514
Abolitionism; *See also* Antislavery movement (1838–1850); *Amistad* and the *Creole*, 195; defined, 168; more aggressive, 194–197; underground railroad, 195–197
Abolitionism, beginnings of: American Colonization Society (ACS), 171–172; Baltimore alliance, 175–176; Benevolent Empire, 168; Gabriel (Prosser) conspiracy, 93, 109–110, 169–170; Garrison, role of, 108, 171, 173, 175–176, 188; political paranoia, 166–167; Quakers, role of, 168–169; Second Great Awakening, 167–168; timeline, 178–179; Turner rebellion, 159, 178–180; Vesey conspiracy, 170; Walker, role of, 165–166, 172, 176–178
Abolitionists: *See also under name of* black women, 172–174, 188–189
Abraham Lincoln Battalion, 473
Abyssinian Baptist Church, 105, 387
Ackerman, Amos T., 295
Actors/actresses, 451–452
Adams, Charles Francis, Jr., 245
Adams, Henry, 301
Adams, John, 74–75, 100
Adams, John Quincy, 143, 166–167, 193
Adams, Samuel, 74
Addams, Jane, 368
Adelphi Union for the Promotion of Literature and Science, 157
Adena culture, 48
Adventures of Grandmaster Flash on the Wheels of Steel, 583–584
Affirmative action, 570–572
Affonso I (Nzinga Mbemba), 16–17
Africa: *See also* West Africa; ancient civilizations in, 6–8; climatic regions and early sites, 4; evolution, 5; Garvey's Universal Negro Improvement Association (UNIA) and the return to, 394, 399–402; geography of, 3–5; Pan-Africanism, 402–403
Afric-American Female Intelligence Society, 157, 173
African-American culture: *See also under different forms of*; impact on colonial culture, 63; origins of, 60–63
African Baptist Church, 191
African Dorcas Associations, 156
African Free Schools, 154
African Grand Lodge of North America, 103
African Methodist Episcopal (AME) Church, 105, 153, 191, 263–264, 339, 341, 465
African Methodist Episcopal Zion Church, 339, 387, 465
African Presbyterian Church, 105
African School, 154
Afro-American League (Chicago), 365, 368
Afro American Realty Co., 386
Afrocentricity, 581
Age of Reason. *See* Enlightenment

Agricultural Adjustment Act (AAA), 424–425
Agriculture: *See also under type of crop*; Carver, work of, 374; crop liens, 324–325; farmer alliances, 311–312; farmer discontent following Reconstruction, 311; forest region, 18; harvest festivals, 55; New Deal and impact on, 424–426; peonage, 325; plantation, 54–55; renters, 324; sharecropping, 261–262, 324; slave labor in, 122–127; West African, 18; World War II, effects of, 482
Aguinaldo, Emilio, 348
Aid to Families of Dependent Children (AFDC), 577
Akan states, 14, 18
Alabama: Birmingham confrontation, 517–518; bombing of 16th St. Baptist Church, 519; cotton in, 125–126; desegregation in, 502; disfranchisement in, 314; Freedom Rides in Anniston, 514; Montgomery bus boycott, 504–508; secession from the Union, 223; Tuskegee experiment in Macon County, 440–441; violence against black voters, 297; Voting Rights act of 1965 and Selma, 523–525
Alabama Christian Movement for Human Rights (ACMHR), 517
Alabama Dry Dock and Shipbuilding Co., 483
Al Bakri, 10, 16
Albany movement, 515–517
Albert, Joe, 107
Alcindor, Lew. *See* Abdul-Jabbar, Kareem
Alcorn, James L., 288
Alcorn A&M College, 288, 337
Alexander, Clifford, Jr., 556
Alfa Suffrage Club, 322
Alfred A. Knopf publishers, 409
Algebra Project, 513
Ali, Muhammad, 543
Allen, Lewis, 459, 520
Allen, Macon B., 150
Allen, Richard, 102, 104–106, 111, 144, 167
Allen, Sarah, 102
Allen University, 337, 353
All God's Chillun Got Wings, 412
Almoravids, 11
Along the Way (Johnson), 398
Alpha Kappa Alpha, 373, 375
Alpha Phi Alpha, 373, 375
Alston, Charles, 431
"Amazing Grace" (Newton), 37
America, colonial: British and Jamestown, 49–50; Chesapeake, slavery in, 50–54; eastern woodlands Indians, 48–49; slavery in northern colonies, 63–65; women in, 65
American and Foreign Anti-Slavery Society (AFASS), 194
American Anti-Slavery Society (AASS), 108, 188; breakup of, 194; moral suasion (persuasion), 192–194
American Baptist Home Mission Society, 268
American Bar Association (ABA), 353
American Citizens' Equal Rights Association of Louisiana, 315
American Colonization Society (ACS), 171–172

American Convention for Promoting the Abolition of Slavery and Improving the Condition of the African Race, 98
American Dilemma, An, 429
American Federation of Labor (AFL), 349, 403–404, 432, 435, 483
American Federation of Musicians, 446–447
American Female Bond Benevolent Society, 102
American Missionary Association, 268
American Moral Reform Society, 108
American Muslim Mission (AMM), 581
American Revolution/American War for Independence: African Americans and the debate of, 76; African Americans in, 80–84; events leading to, 72–75; impact of, 84–88; petition from Boston slaves, 77; timeline/chronology, 82, 88–89
American War College, 475
American West Indian News, 434
American Women's Suffrage Association, 290
Ames, Adelbert, 299
Amherst College, 356–357
Amistad, 195
Amnesty International, 575–576
Amos 'n' Andy Show, 450–451
Amsterdam News, 388
Anderson, Charles, 369–370
Anderson, Eddie, 451, 479
Anderson, Joseph B., Jr., 541
Anderson, Marian, 427, 453
Anderson, Osborne, 219–220
Anderson, Robert, 223
Anderson, Sherwood, 409
Anderson, William G., 515
Anderson Platoon, The, 541
Andrew, John A., 240
Angelou, Maya, 578
Anglican Society for the Propagation of the Gospel in Foreign Parts, 105
Angola, 15–16
Anniston, Alabama, 514
Anson, Adrian Constantine "Cap," 356
Antebellum years: *See also* Antislavery movement (1838–1850); black communities in the urban North, 147–153; black institutions, 153–157; demographics of free blacks, 142; free blacks in the deep South, 159–161; free blacks in the upper South, 157–159; Jacksonian era, 142–143; limited freedom in the North, 144–147; timeline, 160–161
Anthony, Susan B., 248
Anti-apartheid movement, 573
Anti-Lynching bill (1921, 1922), 368, 399; in 1935, 430
Anti-Masonic party, 167
Antioch Baptist, 446
Anti-Slavery Convention of American Women (1837), 189
Antislavery movement (1838–1850): *See also* Abolitionism; black convention movement, 190–192; black institutions involved in, 191–192; black nationalism, 185, 198–200; moral suasion (persuasion), 192–194; response of antislavery societies to violence, 187–191; rising tide of racism and violence, 184, 186–187; timeline, 200–201

I-1

LIVING WORDS

AN AUDIO CD OF AFRICAN-AMERICAN ORAL TRADITIONS

KEVIN EVEROD QUASHIE AND STUART L. TWITE

CONTENTS